Cooking Light®

ANNUAL
RECIPES 2008

Oxmoor
House®

Our Year at *Cooking Light*

Cooking Light magazine was founded in 1987 with a great idea and little fanfare. "It is our intent to publish a magazine that will represent a way of life for you and millions of Americans," the magazine promised in the first issue. "We hope to influence your eating and exercise habits, and, in general, help you achieve a healthier life." The goal: no hype, just solid information readers could trust and put into practice.

In the 20 years since then, we've run tens of thousands of recipes, photos, and stories in an effort to live up to that goal; in so doing, we've gained more than 11.5 million readers. To celebrate our anniversary, we've spent this year saluting the innovative people and ideas that have changed the face of healthy living since we began. Some of the highlights that have made 2007 special, both for *Cooking Light* and for this cookbook, are listed on the facing page.

Cooking Light photo and food stylists make sure our photography is eye-catching. From left: Leigh Ann Ross, Jan Gautro, Cindy Barr, Kathleen Kanen, and Kellie Kelley share their secrets for setting a smart table. Follow their lead (page 445) and you can have a table setting that's perfect for whatever the occasion.

• Our January/February section, "A Fresh Start," kicked off the year by examining the best, most successful ways to eat smart, be fit, and live well—the magazine's mantra. From trying new foods to cooking dinner more often, our delicious ideas and recipes make it a pleasure to stick to your resolutions (page 19).

• The magazine's popular "Cooking Class" series focused this year on the ingredients essential to light, healthful meals. From Salt in March (page 72) to Milk in May (page 125) to Oils in August (page 257), we examined the brightest, most flavorful ways for you to use these pantry staples.

• In June, our annual Summer Cookbook (page 147) offered the season's brightest ways with fresh produce. From starters and drinks to sweet desserts, these recipes feature innovative grilling, smoking, and even a few no-cook techniques for keeping cool in the kitchen.

• Since its sign-on in 1999, the magazine's website, CookingLight.com, has always been a social networking hub. This year, thousands of reader exchanges on the bulletin boards highlighted their recipe reviews, cooking tips, and *Cooking Light* Supper Club ideas. We featured a remarkable California club in September, who shared their top menus and recipes (page 290).

• We began the holiday season in the November issue with our traditional gift to our readers—*Cooking Light* magazine's Holiday Cookbook (page 339). Then, in December, we produced a special double issue with scores of tasty new recipes as well as our best holiday recipes—one for every day of the month (page 427), a memorable way to wrap up a banner year.

I hope you find this edition of *Cooking Light* Annual Recipes worthy of celebration, an essential guide to help you eat smart, be fit, and live well.

Mary Kay Culpepper
Editor in Chief

◀ Lend pizzazz to your go-to weeknight meals: tacos, pasta, and casseroles (page 92).

▲ Add innovative twists to the all-American burger at your next backyard cookout (page 218).

◀ Take advantage of the bounty of the season with our Summer Cookbook (page 147). We offer 45 recipes that make the most of the tastiest vegetables, the sweetest fruits, and the most fragrant herbs of the year.

Our Favorite Recipes

Not all recipes are created equal. At *Cooking Light*®, only those that have passed muster with our Test Kitchens staff and food editors—not an easy crowd to please—make it onto the pages of our magazine. We rigorously test each recipe, often two or three times, to ensure not only that they're healthy and reliable, but also that they taste as good as they possibly can. So which of our recipes are our favorites? They're the ones readers keep calling and writing about, the ones our staff whip up for their own families and friends. They're not always the ones that rated the highest, but they're the dishes that are definitely the most memorable.

◀ **Angel Food Cake Stuffed with Whipped Cream and Berries** (*page 126*)
This light cake yields a pleasant surprise when cut—a colorful, tasty filling of whipped cream and fresh berries. Garnish with orange rind or additional fresh berries.

Hickory Grilled Beef with Henry Bain Sauce (*page 120*)
The zesty sauce, created in 1881 by Henry Bain, headwaiter of the Louisville Pendennis Club, is also great with grilled steak, pork, or chicken.

Memphis Pork and Coleslaw Sandwiches *(page 195)*
If you've never eaten slaw *on* rather than *with* a sandwich, you're in for a treat. Season the pork and soak the wood chunks a day ahead; you can make the mustard-laced slaw a day in advance as well.

**Roasted Nectarines
with Buttermilk Custard** *(page 158)*
Roasting the nectarines concentrates their natural sugar, providing the perfect amount of sweetness for this dessert. They're delicious with the smooth custard sauce.

Shrimp and Bacon Deviled Eggs *(page 97)*
An ideal take-along dish to any picnic or potluck, this colorful appetizer can be prepared a day ahead; just cover with plastic wrap, and refrigerate.

Carrot Cake *(page 92)*
Our version of the classic cake is a sure crowd-pleaser. Top the buttercream frosting with additional grated carrot for an extra dash of color.

Our Favorite Recipes   5

Fish Chowder *(page 33)*
Bacon brings a welcome smokiness to this creamy soup. Serve with fresh, crusty bread or oyster crackers.

Our Favorite Recipes

◀ **Lemon-Scented Blueberry Cupcakes** (*page 28*) These cupcakes took the grand prize in our 2007 Reader Recipe contest in the dessert category. Blueberries or fresh, edible flowers make an easy, pretty decoration.

▼ **Sangría Ice** (*page 193*) This frozen version of the Spanish beverage made with red wine and fruit earned our Test Kitchens' highest rating. Serve as a refreshing aperitif at your next get-together.

Our Favorite Recipes

▶ **Grilled Eggplant Sandwiches with Red Onion and Aïoli** *(page 207)* Sink your teeth into this veggie delight piled high with grilled eggplant slices, red onion, fresh-from-the-vine tomatoes, and good-for-you greens. You won't leave the table hungry!

▼ **Fettuccine Alfredo** *(page 42)* This healthful remake of a classic dish maintains the traditional creamy texture while keeping the fat in check. Add a bit of freshly ground black pepper just before serving.

Santa Maria Smoked Tri-Tip (*page 198*)
Compared to other styles of barbecue, this recipe comes together quickly, making it ideal for a weeknight as well as special dinners.

Coconut Banana Bread with Lime Glaze (*page* 272)
The tangy lime glaze nicely balances the sweetness of the bread. Toast a slice for breakfast or pack some for a snack.

Our Favorite Recipes

◀ **Port-Fig Napoleons with Walnut Oil and Honey Cream** *(page 258)*
This pastry is well suited for any season since it calls for dried fruit. Walnut oil adds a distinctive nutty essence to the crisp phyllo layers and fig mixture.

▼ **Risotto with Fresh Mozzarella, Grape Tomatoes, and Basil** *(page 299)*
The sweet grape tomatoes, creamy mozzarella, and luscious risotto complement each other perfectly in this fresh side dish.

Our Favorite Recipes

▶ **Whole Wheat Cinnamon Rolls** (*page 166*)
Serve these sticky sweet rolls as a weekend breakfast treat. Brown sugar sweetens the filling, and powdered sugar dissolves into a milky glaze that's drizzled over the top.

▼ **Penne with Wild Mushrooms** (*page 325*)
Wild mushrooms are more flavorful than their cultivated counterparts. Oyster, hedgehog, or chanterelle mushrooms are best for this dish, although cultivated oyster mushrooms are also suitable.

Our Favorite Recipes

◀ **Scallop Chowder**
(page 62)
For a warming meal on a cold winter eve, serve this creamy chowder with a slice of crusty baguette and a glass of crisp rosé.

▼ **Fiery Flank Steak with Tomato Jam**
(page 150)
Need to capitalize on a bumper crop of fresh tomatoes? This tart jam brings summer's bounty to your table. For a quick appetizer, serve it with cream cheese on crackers.

▲ **Classic Mint Juleps** *(page 119)*
This lightly sweetened concoction has been enjoyed throughout the South since long before the first Kentucky Derby. This rendition won our Test Kitchens' highest rating.

▶ **Chocolate Chip Irish Cream Pound Cake** *(page 97)*
A finalist in our 2007 Reader Recipes contest, this bundt cake pairs well with coffee laced with a hint of Irish cream.

Our Favorite Recipes

◀ **Korean Barbecue Burgers** *(page 219)*
These burgers are based on bulgogi, a traditional Korean barbecue specialty of marinated sirloin. If you prefer a more authentic flavor, just top with a splash of rice vinegar and kimchi, the spicy-hot pickled vegetable condiment available at Asian markets.

▼ **Beef Daube Provençal** *(page 269)*
This French braised beef, red wine, and vegetable stew is both simple and satisfying. Add a whole-grain baguette, bagged salad greens, and bottled vinaigrette for an easy yet company-worthy meal.

Our Favorite Recipes

Yukon Gold Potatoes Sautéed in Clarified Butter *(page 44)*
Clarified butter flavors these potatoes and helps them turn an attractive golden brown as they cook. Chopped fresh flat-leaf parsley adds a dash of color to the dish.

Classic Gravlax *(page 72)*
High-quality wild salmon yields the best results in this dish. Serve the buttery-soft cured salmon as an appetizer on brown bread with Dijon mustard, thinly sliced cucumbers, and grated lemon rind. Garnish each serving with a sprig of fresh dill.

Italian Cream Cake *(page 71)*
This rich, moist cake is a go-to dessert for *Cooking Light* staffers for special occasions. The combination of pecans and coconut in the cake topped with a rich cream cheese frosting prove to be a delectable treat for any gathering.

New Orleans-Style Shrimp *(page 100)*
Serve these tasty shrimp for a fun hands-on meal. Peel them at the table alongside a slice of crusty baguette.

Chocolate Chip Cookies *(page 163)*
These cookies will keep up to one week in an airtight container, if they last that long. We suggest also keeping a dozen in the freezer for emergencies.

Lemon Pound Cake with Cherry Compote *(page 157)*
This cake received our Test Kitchens' highest rating. For a pretty presentation, cut each slice in half. Place the two halves on a plate, and top with the cherry compote. The sauce is delicious served over ice cream, as well.

Bagna Cauda Bruschetta *(page 257)*
A sublime starter (pronounced BAHN-yah KOW-dah broo-SKEH-tah), the dish is based on the popular Northern Italian appetizer of warm olive oil, anchovies, and garlic that's usually served with vegetable dippers. Here, the dip is drizzled onto bread and then topped with a colorful mix of grilled vegetables.

Herbed Basmati Rice *(page 304)*
Keep this recipe handy as a side dish for almost any meal; add some shredded rotisserie chicken or cooked shrimp for a delicious entrée. In a pinch, you can substitute dried herbs for fresh. Toss in some pine nuts for a pleasant crunch.

▼ Chocolate Shortcakes with Bananas and Caramel *(page 34)*
The richness of the chocolate shortcakes balances nicely with the simple sweetness of bananas and cream. A drizzle of caramel sauce adds a yummy finishing touch.

contents

ISBN-13: 978-0-8487-3156-4
ISBN-10: 0-8487-3156-5
ISSN: 1091-3645

Printed in the United States of America
First printing 2007

Be sure to check with your health-care provider
before making any changes in your diet.

Oxmoor House, Inc.
Editor in Chief: Nancy Fitzpatrick Wyatt
Executive Editor: Katherine M. Eakin
Art Director: Keith McPherson
Managing Editor: Allison Long Lowery

Cooking Light® Annual Recipes 2008
Editor: Heather Averett
Assistant Editor: Rachel Quinlivan, R.D.
Copy Chief: L. Amanda Owens
Copy Editor: Jacqueline Giovanelli
Editorial Assistant: Vanessa Rusch Thomas
Photography Director: Jim Bathie
Director of Production: Laura Lockhart
Senior Production Manager: Greg A. Amason
Production Assistant: Faye Porter Bonner

Contributors:
Designer: Carol Damsky
Indexer: Mary Ann Laurens
Interns: Tracey Apperson, Cory L. Bordonaro,
    Amy Edgerton

To order additional publications, call 1-800-765-6400.
For more books to enrich your life, visit **oxmoorhouse.com**

To search, savor, and share thousands of recipes, visit
myrecipes.com

Cover: *Peach-Blueberry Cobbler (page 199)*
Page 1: *Pasta Carbonara Florentine (page 104)*

Cooking Light®
Editor in Chief: Mary Kay Culpepper
Executive Editor: Billy R. Sims
Creative Director: Susan Waldrip Dendy
Managing Editor: Maelynn Cheung
Senior Food Editor: Alison Mann Ashton
Senior Editor: Phillip Rhodes
Projects Editor: Mary Simpson Creel, M.S., R.D.
Food Editor: Ann Taylor Pittman
Associate Food Editors: Timothy Q. Cebula,
    Kathy Kitchens Downie, R.D., Julianna Grimes
Associate Editor: Cindy Hatcher
Assistant Editor: Brandy Rushing
Test Kitchens Director: Vanessa Taylor Johnson
Senior Food Stylist: Kellie Gerber Kelley
Food Stylist: M. Kathleen Kanen
Test Kitchens Professionals: Mary Drennen Ankar, SaBrina Bone,
    Kathryn Conrad, Jan Moon, Tiffany Vickers, Mike Wilson
Assistant Art Director: Maya Metz Logue
Senior Designers: Fernande Bondarenko, J. Shay McNamee
Designer: Brigette Mayer
Senior Photographer: Randy Mayor
Senior Photo Stylist: Cindy Barr
Photo Stylists: Jan Gautro, Leigh Ann Ross
Studio Assistant: Hayden Patton
Copy Chief: Maria Parker Hopkins
Senior Copy Editor: Susan Roberts
Copy Editor: Johannah Gilman Paiva
Research Assistant: Michelle Gibson Daniels
Production Manager: Liz Rhoades
Production Editor: Hazel R. Eddins
Production Assistant: Lauri Short
Administrative Coordinator: Carol D. Johnson
Office Manager: Rita A. Jackson
Editorial Assistant: Jason Horn
Interns: Heather Goff, Katy McNulty, Eunice Mun,
    Krysta Parsons

CookingLight.com
Editor: Kim Cross

Eat Smart

Start the year off right—meet your health goals with great recipes.

After a serious health scare requiring surgery in 2004, Kathy Carlson of Naperville, Illinois, decided she needed to make serious changes to her lifestyle.

In addition to starting an exercise routine, Carlson zeroed in on her eating habits and made important changes to her diet—from giving up caffeine to substituting more nutritious sweet potatoes for white potatoes.

"I made a few changes at a time," says Carlson. "Once I mastered a couple, I moved on to the next bunch. It's amazing how much of your health you have control over. And small choices really do add up."

Make a fresh start with a few easily attainable nutrition resolutions of your own. Pick one, two, or all of these recipes to incorporate changes into your eating routine.

Vegetarian Supper Menu
serves 4

Prepare the turnovers in advance, and freeze them for up to two months.

Spinach and Kale Turnovers

Cream of tomato soup*

Pound cake

*Heat 2 teaspoons olive oil in a large saucepan over medium-high heat. Add 1 cup chopped onion and 3 minced garlic cloves; sauté 3 minutes or until tender. Add 1 (28-ounce) can crushed tomatoes, 1 tablespoon balsamic vinegar, ½ teaspoon salt, and ¼ teaspoon crushed red pepper. Bring to a boil. Reduce heat, and simmer 30 minutes. Place in a blender; process until smooth. Return tomato mixture to pan. Stir in ¾ cup half-and-half; cook until thoroughly heated.

MAKE AHEAD • FREEZABLE
Spinach and Kale Turnovers

Serve as a side dish with steak or roast chicken, or enjoy two turnovers as a meatless entrée. They're great made ahead and brown-bagged; reheat in a microwave or toaster oven.

  - 2   teaspoons olive oil
  - 1   cup chopped onion
  - 1   garlic clove, chopped
  - 3   cups chopped kale (about 1 small bunch)
  - 1   (6-ounce) package fresh baby spinach
  - ½   teaspoon freshly ground black pepper
  - ¼   teaspoon salt
  - ⅛   teaspoon ground nutmeg
  - ¾   cup (3 ounces) crumbled feta cheese
  - 1   (11.3-ounce) can refrigerated dinner roll dough (such as Pillsbury)
  - Cooking spray
  - 2½   tablespoons grated fresh Parmesan cheese

1. Preheat oven to 375°.
2. Heat oil in a large skillet over medium-high heat. Add onion; sauté 10 minutes or until tender and lightly browned. Add garlic; sauté 2 minutes. Add kale and spinach; sauté 8 minutes or until kale is tender. Stir in pepper, salt, and nutmeg. Remove from heat; cool slightly. Stir in feta.
3. Separate dough into 8 pieces. Roll each dough piece into a 5-inch circle. Spoon about ⅓ cup kale mixture on half of each circle, leaving ½-inch borders. Fold dough over kale mixture until edges almost meet. Bring bottom edge of dough over top edge; crimp with fingers to form a rim.
4. Place turnovers on a baking sheet coated with cooking spray. Lightly coat turnovers with cooking spray; sprinkle each turnover with about 1 teaspoon Parmesan. Bake at 375° for 18 minutes or until golden brown. Let stand at least 5 minutes before serving; serve warm or at room temperature. Yield: 8 servings (serving size: 1 turnover).

CALORIES 184 (27% from fat); FAT 5.5g (sat 2g, mono 1.6g, poly 1.2g); PROTEIN 8.1g; CARB 25.4g; FIBER 2.7g; CHOL 7mg; IRON 2.3mg; SODIUM 516mg; CALC 110mg

MAKE AHEAD
Slow-Cooker Beef Brisket with Beer

If your slow cooker includes a removable insert, brown the brisket and onion mixture a day ahead, place all ingredients in the insert, and refrigerate. The next morning, place insert in the slow cooker, and when you arrive home from work, a tasty entrée will await you. The onion and parsnips function as flavorings, so you'll want to serve a vegetable side dish. Try Spinach and Kale Turnovers (recipe at left) or mashed potatoes.

  - 1   (3-pound) beef brisket, trimmed
  - 1   teaspoon salt
  - ½   teaspoon freshly ground black pepper
  - Cooking spray
  - ¼   cup water
  - 2   cups vertically sliced onion (about 1 large)
  - 1½   cups chopped parsnip (about 2)
  - 1   tablespoon balsamic vinegar
  - 1   bay leaf
  - 1   (12-ounce) bottle light beer

Continued

1. Rub brisket with salt and pepper. Heat a large heavy skillet over medium-high heat. Coat pan with cooking spray. Add brisket to pan; cook 10 minutes, browning on all sides. Remove brisket from pan. Add ¼ cup water to pan, stirring to loosen browned bits. Add onion and parsnip; sauté 5 minutes or until vegetables are tender.

2. Place onion mixture, vinegar, bay leaf, and beer in a 6- to 8-quart electric slow cooker. Place brisket on top of onion mixture. Cover and cook on LOW 8 hours. Discard bay leaf. Cut brisket diagonally across grain into thin slices. Serve with sauce. Yield: 12 servings (serving size: about 3 ounces brisket and ⅓ cup sauce).

CALORIES 160 (28% from fat); FAT 5g (sat 1.9g, mono 2.1g, poly 0.2g); PROTEIN 20.5g; CARB 5.6g; FIBER 1.1g; CHOL 49mg; IRON 1.9mg; SODIUM 232mg; CALC 20mg

Escarole with Bacon and White Beans

Escarole, a pleasantly bitter leafy vegetable, contains more fiber than other common salad greens. It works in both raw and cooked applications; here, its earthiness complements the creamy beans and smoky bacon. It's also great in soups—toss a handful of chopped escarole into your favorite recipe during the last 10 to 15 minutes of cooking.

  2 bacon slices, chopped
  1 cup chopped onion
  1 garlic clove, thinly sliced
  6 cups chopped escarole (about 2 [8-ounce] heads)
  1 teaspoon sugar
  ¼ teaspoon salt
  ¼ teaspoon freshly ground black pepper
  1 (14-ounce) can fat-free, less-sodium chicken broth
  1 (16-ounce) can cannellini beans or other white beans, rinsed and drained

1. Cook bacon in a large saucepan over medium heat until crisp. Remove bacon from pan with a slotted spoon, reserving 2 teaspoons drippings in pan; set bacon aside. Add onion to drippings in pan; cook 12 minutes or until golden brown, stirring occasionally. Add garlic; cook 2 minutes, stirring frequently. Add escarole; cook 2 minutes or until escarole wilts, stirring frequently. Add sugar, salt, pepper, and broth; cook 15 minutes or until escarole is tender, stirring occasionally. Add beans; cook 2 minutes or until thoroughly heated. Sprinkle with bacon. Yield: 4 servings (serving size: about 1 cup).

CALORIES 123 (29% from fat); FAT 3.9g (sat 1.3g, mono 1.6g, poly 0.7g); PROTEIN 5.7g; CARB 16.3g; FIBER 5g; CHOL 6mg; IRON 1.7mg; SODIUM 525mg; CALC 62mg

Smoked Cheese Pasta Bake

Make this dish on a Sunday afternoon, and enjoy leftovers for another meal during the week. Or you can assemble the casserole, refrigerate overnight, and bake shortly before serving.

  1 pound uncooked penne (tube-shaped pasta)
  1 (26-ounce) jar fat-free marinara sauce
  ½ teaspoon salt
  ½ teaspoon freshly ground black pepper
  1 (10-ounce) package frozen chopped spinach, thawed, drained, and squeezed dry
  Cooking spray
  1½ cups reduced-fat sour cream
  1 cup (4 ounces) shredded smoked farmer or mozzarella cheese
  ¼ cup chopped fresh basil
  ½ cup (2 ounces) grated Parmigiano-Reggiano cheese

1. Preheat oven to 350°.
2. Cook pasta according to package directions, omitting salt and fat. Drain.
3. Heat marinara sauce in a large saucepan over medium heat. Add salt, pepper, and spinach, stirring until blended; cook 10 minutes, stirring occasionally. Remove from heat; stir in pasta.
4. Spoon half of pasta mixture into a 13 x 9–inch baking dish coated with cooking spray. Combine sour cream, smoked cheese, and chopped basil; spread over pasta mixture in dish. Spoon remaining pasta mixture over sour cream mixture; sprinkle evenly with Parmigiano-Reggiano. Bake at 350° for 25 minutes or until bubbly. Let stand 10 minutes before serving. Yield: 8 servings (serving size: about 1 cup).

CALORIES 395 (25% from fat); FAT 10.8g (sat 7.5g, mono 2g, poly 0.4g); PROTEIN 19.1g; CARB 54.9g; FIBER 4.4g; CHOL 19mg; IRON 2.5mg; SODIUM 419mg; CALC 310mg

Cumin-Dusted Chicken Breasts with Guacamole Sauce

This flavorful entrée calls for a simple side dish; try a green salad and yellow rice or canned black beans.

SAUCE:
  ¼ cup finely chopped green onions
  ¼ cup finely chopped parsley
  ¼ cup fat-free sour cream
  2 tablespoons fresh lime juice
  ¼ teaspoon salt
  ⅛ teaspoon ground cumin
  ⅛ teaspoon ground red pepper
  1 ripe peeled avocado, seeded and coarsely mashed

CHICKEN:
  2 tablespoons brown sugar
  1 teaspoon ground cumin
  ½ teaspoon salt
  ½ teaspoon freshly ground black pepper
  4 (6-ounce) skinless, boneless chicken breast halves
  Cooking spray

1. To prepare sauce, combine first 8 ingredients; set aside.
2. Preheat oven to 400°.
3. To prepare chicken, combine sugar and next 3 ingredients; sprinkle evenly over chicken. Heat a large ovenproof skillet over medium-high heat. Coat pan with cooking spray. Add chicken; cook 3 minutes or until browned. Turn chicken over. Place pan in oven; bake at 400° for 10 minutes or until done. Serve chicken with sauce. Yield: 4 servings

(serving size: 1 breast half and about 3 tablespoons sauce).

CALORIES 301 (27% from fat); FAT 9g (sat 1.5g, mono 4.8g, poly 1.3g); PROTEIN 41.6g; CARB 12.5g; FIBER 3.6g; CHOL 101mg; IRON 2.1mg; SODIUM 575mg; CALC 76mg

Soba Noodle Salad with Seared Tuna

Look for Japanese soba noodles in the ethnic-food section of your supermarket.

  6 ounces uncooked soba
      (buckwheat noodles)
     Cooking spray
  1 (1-pound) sushi-grade tuna steak
  ½ teaspoon salt, divided
  ¼ teaspoon freshly ground black
      pepper
  1 cup finely chopped English
      cucumber
  1 cup shredded carrot
  ½ cup julienne-cut radishes
  ⅓ cup finely chopped red bell pepper
  ¼ cup finely chopped green onions
  3 tablespoons rice vinegar
  2 tablespoons low-sodium soy sauce
  1 tablespoon peanut oil
  1½ teaspoons dark sesame oil
  1 teaspoon sugar
  ½ teaspoon crushed red pepper
  2 tablespoons sesame seeds, toasted

1. Cook noodles according to package directions; drain and rinse with cold water. Drain; set aside.
2. Heat a large nonstick skillet over medium-high heat. Coat pan with cooking spray. Sprinkle both sides of tuna with ¼ teaspoon salt and black pepper. Place tuna in pan, and cook 3 minutes on each side or until desired degree of doneness. Transfer to a platter; cool slightly. Cut tuna into 6 equal pieces.
3. Combine noodles, ¼ teaspoon salt, cucumber, and next 10 ingredients in a large bowl; toss well to combine. Arrange 1 cup noodle mixture on each of 6 plates. Top each serving with 1 teaspoon sesame seeds and 1 tuna piece. Yield: 6 servings.

CALORIES 256 (22% from fat); FAT 6.3g (sat 1g, mono 2.6g, poly 2.5g); PROTEIN 22g; CARB 28.2g; FIBER 2.9g; CHOL 34mg; IRON 1.9mg; SODIUM 570mg; CALC 62mg

Barley Risotto with Roasted Winter Vegetables

Barley makes a tasty stand-in for rice in this hearty, fiber-rich risotto. All you need to complete the meal is a salad and a glass of white wine.

  2 cups diced parsnip
  2 cups chopped cauliflower
      florets
  1½ cups chopped red bell pepper
      (about 1 large)
  2 teaspoons olive oil
  ½ teaspoon freshly ground black
      pepper
  ¼ teaspoon salt
     Cooking spray
  1 teaspoon olive oil
  ½ cup chopped onion
  4 cups fat-free, less-sodium chicken
      broth, divided
  1¼ cups uncooked pearl barley
  ⅔ cup (about 2½ ounces) grated
      Parmigiano-Reggiano cheese,
      divided
  ⅓ cup chopped pecans, toasted
  2 tablespoons chopped fresh
      parsley

1. Preheat oven to 400°.
2. Combine first 6 ingredients on a jelly-roll pan coated with cooking spray, and toss well to coat. Bake at 400° for 20 minutes or until lightly browned, stirring after 10 minutes.
3. Heat 1 teaspoon oil in a large saucepan over medium-high heat. Add onion; sauté 4 minutes or until browned. Add 3 cups broth and barley; bring to a boil. Cover, reduce heat, and simmer 30 minutes or until liquid is absorbed and barley is al dente. Add 1 cup broth, ½ cup at a time, stirring constantly until first portion of broth is absorbed before adding the next. Stir in parsnip mixture and ⅓ cup cheese. Sprinkle with cheese, pecans, and parsley. Yield: 6 servings (serving size: about ¾ cup risotto, about 1 tablespoon cheese, about 1 tablespoon nuts, and 1 teaspoon parsley).

CALORIES 325 (30% from fat); FAT 11g (sat 2.8g, mono 5.4g, poly 2.1g); PROTEIN 12.2g; CARB 47.3g; FIBER 10.3g; CHOL 8mg; IRON 2.3mg; SODIUM 566mg; CALC 197mg

Roasted Red Pepper and Cannellini Bean Dip

This Mediterranean-inspired appetizer offers a little extra protein, heart-healthy mono-unsaturated fat, and fiber.

  ¼ cup chopped fresh basil
  1 teaspoon balsamic vinegar
  1 (16-ounce) can cannellini beans,
      rinsed and drained
  1 (7-ounce) bottle roasted red bell
      peppers, rinsed and drained
  1 large garlic clove
  2 tablespoons extravirgin olive oil
  ½ teaspoon salt
  ½ teaspoon freshly ground black
      pepper

1. Place first 5 ingredients in a food processor; process until smooth. With processor on, slowly add oil through food chute. Stir in salt and black pepper. Yield: 8 servings (serving size: ¼ cup).

CALORIES 62 (51% from fat); FAT 3.5g (sat 0.5g, mono 2.5g, poly 0.5g); PROTEIN 1.5g; CARB 5.9g; FIBER 1.5g; CHOL 0mg; IRON 0.6mg; SODIUM 272mg; CALC 16mg

Quick Breakfast Tostada

  ¼ cup 1% low-fat milk
  ¼ teaspoon salt
  ⅛ teaspoon freshly ground black
      pepper
  4 large egg whites
  2 large eggs
  4 (6-inch) corn tortillas
  ½ cup (2 ounces) shredded reduced-
      fat sharp Cheddar cheese
  1 cup canned black beans, rinsed
      and drained
  ¼ cup chopped green onions
  ½ cup bottled salsa
  ¼ cup fat-free sour cream

1. Combine first 5 ingredients in a large microwave-safe dish, stirring with a whisk. Microwave at HIGH 3 minutes; stir. Microwave 1 minute or until done. Arrange 1 tortilla on each of 4 microwave-safe plates; divide egg mixture
Continued

evenly among tortillas. Layer each serving with 2 tablespoons cheese, ¼ cup beans, and 1 tablespoon green onions. Microwave each tostada at HIGH 30 seconds. Top each tostada with 2 tablespoons salsa and 1 tablespoon sour cream. Serve immediately. Yield: 4 servings (serving size: 1 tostada).

CALORIES 201 (29% from fat); FAT 6.5g (sat 3g, mono 1.8g, poly 0.7g); PROTEIN 15.9g; CARB 23.4g; FIBER 4.4g; CHOL 120mg; IRON 1.6mg; SODIUM 633mg; CALC 214mg

---

QUICK & EASY
Blueberry-Passion Fruit Smoothie

With plenty of fruit, fiber, and protein, this quick shake makes a sweet snack.

  1   cup plain fat-free yogurt
  ½   cup passion fruit nectar
  ½   cup ice cubes
 1½   teaspoons toasted wheat germ
  2   teaspoons honey
  1   (12-ounce) bag frozen blueberries
  1   ripe banana, cut into 4 pieces

1. Place all ingredients in a blender, and process until smooth. Yield: 4 servings (serving size: about 1 cup).

CALORIES 126 (5% from fat); FAT 0.7g (sat 0.1g, mono 0.1g, poly 0.3g); PROTEIN 3.5g; CARB 29.9g; FIBER 3.5g; CHOL 1mg; IRON 0.4mg; SODIUM 37mg; CALC 84mg

---

MAKE AHEAD • FREEZABLE
Sweet Corn Muffins

After baking, cool completely, place in a zip-top plastic bag, and refrigerate or freeze a batch of these simple muffins.

 1½   cups all-purpose flour (about 6¾ ounces)
  ¾   cup granulated sugar
  ½   cup yellow cornmeal
  2   teaspoons baking powder
  ¼   teaspoon salt
  ⅔   cup plain low-fat yogurt
  ¼   cup butter, melted
  3   tablespoons fat-free milk
  1   large egg, lightly beaten
  2   tablespoons turbinado sugar (optional)

1. Preheat oven to 375°.
2. Lightly spoon flour into dry measuring cups; level with a knife. Combine flour and next 4 ingredients in a medium bowl, stirring with a whisk. Make a well in center of mixture. Combine yogurt, butter, milk, and egg, stirring with a whisk; add to flour mixture, stirring just until moist.
3. Place 12 paper muffin cup liners in muffin cups. Divide batter evenly among cups. Sprinkle batter evenly with turbinado sugar, if desired. Bake at 375° for 20 minutes or until a wooden pick inserted in center comes out clean. Cool on a wire rack. Yield: 1 dozen (serving size: 1 muffin).

CALORIES 185 (22% from fat); FAT 4.5g (sat 2.6g, mono 1.2g, poly 0.3g); PROTEIN 3.5g; CARB 32.7g; FIBER 0.6g; CHOL 29mg; IRON 1mg; SODIUM 201mg; CALC 33mg

---

kitchen strategies
Homemade Convenience

Problem: A time-pressed Amarillo, Texas, family wants more dinners made from scratch. Strategy: We show them how to use fresh ingredients to create speedy suppers.

Work-at-home mom Christy Milton's electronic funds transfer business keeps her on the run. So by the end of the day, she scrambles to put dinner on the table before shuttling her three daughters to a sports practice or game.

Milton wants to fix more fresh foods for her family. But she doesn't know where to start, and time is short. A complicating factor is the family's food likes and dislikes. She and her husband aren't picky, but the three girls are finicky, particularly when it comes to vegetables.

Our goal was to provide the Miltons with ideas for how to prepare fresh foods that cook quickly or with little fuss and that would appeal to everyone. While still allowing for handy products such as bottled minced garlic and prechopped vegetables, we developed various main dishes and sides that capitalize on tasty and nutritious ingredients.

Cornmeal-Crusted Tilapia Salad

While the ingredient list is long, most of the work is simply measuring out seasonings and prepared ingredients. The dish comes together in less than 30 minutes. Substitute any firm white fish, such as red snapper or flounder, for tilapia.

  4   (6-inch) corn tortillas, cut into ¼-inch strips
 Cooking spray
  1   teaspoon chili powder, divided
  ¾   teaspoon salt, divided
  ¼   cup all-purpose flour (about 1 ounce)
  ¼   cup yellow cornmeal
  1   teaspoon onion flakes, crushed
  4   (6-ounce) tilapia fillets
  7   teaspoons canola oil, divided
  6   cups chopped romaine lettuce
 1½   cups chopped red bell pepper (about 1 large)
  1   cup halved grape tomatoes
  ¼   cup thinly sliced red onion
  2   tablespoons chopped fresh cilantro
 1½   tablespoons fresh lime juice
  ¼   teaspoon Dijon mustard
  ¼   cup preshredded reduced-fat 4-cheese Mexican blend cheese

1. Preheat oven to 425°.
2. Place tortilla strips on a baking sheet lined with foil; lightly coat tortilla strips with cooking spray. Sprinkle strips with ½ teaspoon chili powder and ¼ teaspoon salt. Bake at 425° for 10 minutes or until crisp, and set aside.
3. Lightly spoon flour into a dry measuring cup; level with a knife. Combine flour, cornmeal, onion flakes, and ½ teaspoon chili powder in a shallow dish. Sprinkle fish with ¼ teaspoon salt; dredge in cornmeal mixture.
4. Heat 1 tablespoon oil in a large nonstick skillet over medium-high heat. Add fish; cook 3 minutes on each side or until browned and fish flakes easily when tested with a fork or until desired degree of doneness.

5. Combine romaine and next 4 ingredients in a large bowl. Combine juice, mustard, and ¼ teaspoon salt in a small bowl, stirring with a whisk. Gradually add 4 teaspoons oil, stirring constantly with a whisk. Drizzle juice mixture over lettuce mixture; toss gently to coat. Place 1½ cups salad mixture on each of 4 plates; sprinkle each serving with 1 tablespoon cheese. Place 1 fish fillet on each salad; top with 5 tortilla strips. Yield: 4 servings.

CALORIES 396 (30% from fat); FAT 13.3g (sat 2.4g, mono 5.7g, poly 3.6g); PROTEIN 40.5g; CARB 31.1g; FIBER 4.5g; CHOL 88mg; IRON 2.7mg; SODIUM 618mg; CALC 114mg

QUICK & EASY • MAKE AHEAD
Quick Carrot and Raisin Salad

Use prechopped red onion and carrots to save time in this no-cook dish. Prepare up to a day ahead, and serve with Spiced Roasted Chicken (recipe at right) or Pan-Seared Pork Chops with Applesauce (recipe at right).

⅓ cup raisins
¼ cup chopped red onion
¼ cup finely chopped fresh parsley
1½ tablespoons sliced almonds
1 pound matchstick-cut carrots
3 tablespoons fat-free mayonnaise
3 tablespoons fresh lemon juice
1½ teaspoons sugar
½ teaspoon ground cumin
½ teaspoon paprika
¼ teaspoon salt
¼ teaspoon ground cinnamon
¼ teaspoon bottled minced garlic

1. Combine first 5 ingredients in a large bowl.
2. Combine mayonnaise and remaining 7 ingredients in a small bowl, stirring with a whisk. Spoon dressing over carrot mixture; toss gently to coat. Cover and chill at least 30 minutes. Yield: 4 servings (serving size: 1¼ cup).

CALORIES 135 (16% from fat); FAT 2.4g (sat 0.2g, mono 1.1g, poly 0.5g); PROTEIN 2.4g; CARB 27.5g; FIBER 5g; CHOL 1mg; IRON 1.3mg; SODIUM 323mg; CALC 65mg

Spiced Roasted Chicken

While it's easy enough to buy a rotisserie chicken, roasting chicken at home allows you to control the sodium, flavorings, and quality of ingredients. Preparation is simple, while cooking is hands-off. Serve with Quick Carrot and Raisin Salad (recipe at left) and mashed potatoes.

1 (3¾-pound) whole roasting chicken
1 teaspoon dried oregano
1 teaspoon cumin seed, crushed
1 teaspoon bottled minced garlic
2 teaspoons olive oil
½ teaspoon salt
½ teaspoon ground cumin
Cooking spray

1. Preheat oven to 375°.
2. Remove and discard giblets and neck from chicken; trim excess fat. Starting at neck cavity, loosen skin from breasts and drumsticks by inserting fingers, gently pushing between skin and meat.
3. Combine oregano and next 5 ingredients in a small bowl. Rub seasoning mixture under loosened skin and over breasts and drumsticks. Tie ends of legs together with twine. Lift wing tips up and over back; tuck under chicken. Place chicken, breast side up, on a rack coated with cooking spray, and place rack in a roasting pan.
4. Bake at 375° for 40 minutes.
5. Increase oven temperature to 450° (do not remove chicken from oven); bake an additional 12 minutes or until a thermometer inserted in meaty part of thigh registers 165°. Remove chicken from pan; let stand 15 minutes. Remove skin from chicken; discard. Yield: 4 servings (serving size: about 5 ounces meat).

CALORIES 185 (31% from fat); FAT 6.4g (sat 1.3g, mono 2.9g, poly 1.2g); PROTEIN 29g; CARB 0.8g; FIBER 0.3g; CHOL 92mg; IRON 2.1mg; SODIUM 403mg; CALC 27mg

Pan-Seared Pork Chops with Applesauce

Homemade applesauce takes just minutes in the microwave, making a classic sweet-tart complement for pork chops.

4 cups sliced peeled Red Delicious apple (about 2)
¼ cup water
2 tablespoons brown sugar
1 tablespoon cider vinegar
⅛ teaspoon ground cinnamon
⅛ teaspoon salt
1 teaspoon canola oil
4 (4-ounce) boneless center-cut loin pork chops (about ½ inch thick)
¼ teaspoon salt
¼ teaspoon freshly ground black pepper

1. Combine first 5 ingredients in a medium microwave-safe bowl, and toss well. Cover with plastic wrap, and microwave at HIGH 12 minutes or until tender. Cool 5 minutes. Place apple mixture in a food processor, and process until smooth. Stir in ⅛ teaspoon salt.
2. Heat oil in a large nonstick skillet over medium-high heat. Sprinkle pork on both sides with ¼ teaspoon salt and pepper; add to pan. Cook 4 minutes on each side or until pork is done. Let stand 5 minutes. Serve with applesauce. Yield: 4 servings (serving size: 1 pork chop and 6 tablespoons applesauce).

CALORIES 251 (29% from fat); FAT 8.1g (sat 2.5g, mono 3.8g, poly 1.1g); PROTEIN 25.4g; CARB 18.6g; FIBER 1.5g; CHOL 62mg; IRON 1.1mg; SODIUM 278mg; CALC 35mg

Roasted Salmon with Fresh Vegetables

Bagged fresh green beans and fuss-free grape tomatoes, along with potato wedges, make up the vegetables and starch for this dish, all prepared in one pan. Because they take longer to cook, the potatoes cook alone for the first 10 minutes.

```
  2   teaspoons olive oil
 ½    teaspoon salt, divided
 ½    teaspoon freshly ground black
      pepper, divided
  1   (12-ounce) package prewashed,
      trimmed whole green beans
  1   (8-ounce) baking potato, cut
      lengthwise into 12 wedges
 24   grape or cherry tomatoes
  4   (6-ounce) salmon fillets (about
      1 inch thick)
  1   tablespoon fresh lemon juice
1¼    teaspoons Worcestershire sauce
      Lemon wedges (optional)
```

1. Preheat oven to 450°.
2. Combine oil, ¼ teaspoon salt, ¼ teaspoon pepper, beans, and potato in a medium bowl; toss to coat. Place potato on a jelly-roll pan lined with foil; bake at 450° for 10 minutes.
3. Reduce oven temperature to 425°. Add beans and tomatoes to pan; move potato mixture to one side of pan. Sprinkle fish with ¼ teaspoon salt and ¼ teaspoon pepper. Drizzle juice and Worcestershire sauce over fish. Add fish to pan. Bake at 425° for 18 minutes or until fish flakes easily when tested with a fork or until desired degree of doneness. Serve with lemon wedges, if desired. Yield: 4 servings (serving size: 1 salmon fillet and about 1 cup vegetables).

CALORIES 396 (36% from fat); FAT 15.7g (sat 3.5g, mono 7.4g, poly 3.6g); PROTEIN 39.6g; CARB 21.7g; FIBER 4.5g; CHOL 87mg; IRON 2.1mg; SODIUM 416mg; CALC 59mg

Sesame Chicken and Noodles

This simple, Asian-inspired pasta toss contains less fat and sodium than similar take-out fare without sacrificing its flavor. For added taste, toast the sesame seeds first.

```
  8   ounces uncooked spaghetti
 ½    cup fat-free, less-sodium chicken
      broth
 ¼    cup natural-style, reduced-fat
      creamy peanut butter (such as
      Smucker's)
  2   tablespoons sesame seeds, divided
  1   tablespoon brown sugar
  2   tablespoons rice vinegar
  2   tablespoons low-sodium soy sauce
  1   tablespoon fresh lime juice
 ½    teaspoon hot pepper sauce (such
      as Tabasco)
  2   teaspoons canola oil
 ¾    pound chicken breast tenders, cut
      into 1-inch pieces
 ¼    teaspoon salt
  2   cups matchstick-cut carrots,
      chopped (about 4 ounces)
1½    cups thinly sliced green onions
      (about 1 bunch)
```

1. Cook pasta according to package directions, omitting salt and fat. Drain, reserving 2 tablespoons cooking liquid.
2. Combine broth, peanut butter, 1½ tablespoons sesame seeds, and next 5 ingredients.
3. Heat oil in a large skillet over medium-high heat. Sprinkle chicken with salt. Add chicken to pan; sauté 3 minutes. Add carrots and onions; sauté 2 minutes or until chicken is done. Stir in broth mixture.
4. Add reserved cooking liquid and pasta to pan, tossing to coat. Top with 1½ teaspoons sesame seeds; serve immediately. Yield: 4 servings (serving size: 2 cups).

CALORIES 480 (23% from fat); FAT 12g (sat 1.7g, mono 6.2g, poly 3g); PROTEIN 33.5g; CARB 57.6g; FIBER 5.3g; CHOL 50mg; IRON 3.4mg; SODIUM 538mg; CALC 58mg

dinner tonight
A Saucy Boost

Fuss-free sauces boost these hearty dishes to a higher level of taste.

QUICK & EASY
Smothered Pork Chops with Thyme

First, sauté the chops, then make the flavorful gravy in the same pan.

TIME: 30 MINUTES

FLAVOR TIP: For heightened herbiness, substitute ½ teaspoon chopped fresh thyme for the dried.

```
  1   cup fat-free, less-sodium beef
      broth, divided
  2   tablespoons fat-free milk
  2   teaspoons all-purpose flour
  2   teaspoons Dijon mustard
 ½    teaspoon salt
 ¼    teaspoon freshly ground black
      pepper
  8   (2-ounce) boneless center-cut loin
      pork chops (about ¼ inch thick)
 ½    teaspoon paprika
 ¼    teaspoon dried thyme
      Cooking spray
  1   cup coarsely chopped onion
  1   tablespoon minced fresh parsley
```

1. Combine ¼ cup broth, milk, and next 4 ingredients in a small bowl; stir with a whisk. Set aside.
2. Sprinkle one side of each pork chop with paprika and thyme. Heat a large nonstick skillet over medium-high heat. Coat pan with cooking spray. Add half of pork to pan; sauté 1½ minutes on each side or until pork is done and lightly browned. Remove pork from pan. Repeat procedure with remaining pork. Reduce heat to medium. Add onion; sauté 4 minutes or until lightly golden. Add ¾ cup broth; bring to a boil. Cook 2 minutes. Add milk mixture, stirring with a whisk. Add pork, turning to coat; cook 1 minute. Sprinkle with parsley. Yield: 4 servings (serving size: 2 pork chops and ¼ cup sauce).

CALORIES 145 (34% from fat); FAT 5.5g (sat 1.9g, mono 2.5g, poly 0.4g); PROTEIN 17.2g; CARB 5.8g; FIBER 0.8g; CHOL 44mg; IRON 0.7mg; SODIUM 475mg; CALC 40mg

**Smothered Pork Chops
with Thyme**

Wild rice medley*

Tossed green salad

*Cook 1 (6.2-ounce) package fast-cooking long-grain and wild rice (such as Uncle Ben's) according to package directions, omitting salt and fat. Stir in ¼ cup chopped green onions, 2 tablespoons slivered almonds, and ¼ teaspoon dried thyme.

Game Plan

1. While rice cooks:
   • Prepare pork chops.
2. Combine rice with nuts, onions, and thyme.
3. Toss salad.

QUICK & EASY
Sirloin Steak with Tarragon-Garlic Sour Cream

The tangy sauce dresses up a steakhouse favorite. Packaged potato wedges round out the dish.

TIME: 40 MINUTES

QUICK TIP: Have the steak trimmed at the meat counter.

⅓ cup sour cream
¼ cup low-fat mayonnaise
2 tablespoons whole-grain Dijon mustard
1 teaspoon dried tarragon
1 teaspoon bottled minced garlic
½ teaspoon salt, divided
¼ teaspoon black pepper, divided
Cooking spray
1 (1-pound) boneless sirloin steak, trimmed
1 (20-ounce) package refrigerated red potato wedges (such as Simply Potatoes)

1. Combine first 5 ingredients in a small bowl; stir in ¼ teaspoon salt and ⅛ teaspoon pepper. Set aside.

2. Heat a large nonstick skillet over medium-high heat. Coat pan with cooking spray. Sprinkle both sides of steak with ¼ teaspoon salt and ⅛ teaspoon pepper; add steak to pan. Cook 5 minutes on each side or until desired degree of doneness. Remove from pan; let stand 5 minutes. Cut into ¼-inch-thick slices. Keep warm.

3. Wipe pan with a paper towel; return to heat. Recoat pan with cooking spray. Add potatoes; sauté 15 minutes or until browned and thoroughly heated, stirring occasionally. Serve with steak and sauce. Yield: 4 servings (serving size: 3 ounces steak, ⅔ cup potatoes, and 3 tablespoons sauce).

CALORIES 307 (32% from fat); FAT 11g (sat 4.8g, mono 3.6g, poly 0.4g); PROTEIN 26.4g; CARB 22.9g; FIBER 3.7g; CHOL 53mg; IRON 2.1mg; SODIUM 732mg; CALC 44mg

**Sirloin Steak with
Tarragon-Garlic Sour Cream**

Roasted baby carrots*

Low-fat vanilla ice cream with chocolate syrup

*Combine 1 pound baby carrots, 2 teaspoons olive oil, ½ teaspoon salt, ¼ teaspoon black pepper, and ⅛ teaspoon dried tarragon on a jelly-roll pan; toss gently to coat. Bake at 450° for 15 minutes or until carrots are lightly browned, stirring once.

Game Plan

1. While oven preheats:
   • Prep carrots.
2. While carrots roast:
   • Cook steak and potatoes.
3. Scoop ice cream into individual dishes; freeze until serving.

Angel Hair Pasta with Mussels and Red Pepper Sauce

Sweet red peppers help balance the naturally salty mussels and the slightly acidic tomatoes. See Saucy Dishes Menu 3 (page 26) for serving suggestions and game plan.

TIME: 37 MINUTES

8 ounces uncooked angel hair pasta
2 teaspoons olive oil
⅓ cup diced onion
1 garlic clove, minced
2 cups diced red bell pepper (about 2 medium)
½ teaspoon salt
Dash of ground red pepper
1 (14.5-ounce) can whole tomatoes, undrained and chopped
½ cup white wine
36 mussels (about 3 pounds), scrubbed and debearded
3 tablespoons chopped fresh parsley

1. Cook pasta according to package directions, omitting salt and fat. Drain; keep warm.

2. Heat oil in a large saucepan over medium-high heat. Add onion and garlic; sauté 5 minutes or until tender. Add bell pepper, salt, and ground red pepper; sauté 2 minutes. Add tomatoes and wine; bring to a boil. Reduce heat to low, and simmer 10 minutes. Add mussels, and increase heat to medium. Cover and simmer 7 minutes or until shells open. Discard any unopened shells. Serve mussel mixture over pasta; sprinkle with parsley. Yield: 4 servings (serving size: 9 mussels, about 1 cup pasta, and about 2 teaspoons parsley).

CALORIES 372 (18% from fat); FAT 7.4g (sat 1g, mono 2.6g, poly 1.3g); PROTEIN 24.9g; CARB 46.9g; FIBER 4.5g; CHOL 40mg; IRON 8.7mg; SODIUM 809mg; CALC 85mg

serves 4

Angel Hair Pasta with Mussels and Red Pepper Sauce (recipe on page 25)

Toasted French bread

Pound cake with strawberry-pepper sauce*

*Combine 3 tablespoons brown sugar, 1½ teaspoons balsamic vinegar, ⅛ teaspoon freshly ground black pepper, and 6 ounces frozen strawberries in a small saucepan; bring to a boil. Combine 1 tablespoon cornstarch and 1 tablespoon water, stirring with a whisk. Add to pan. Boil 1 minute, stirring constantly. Serve over sliced reduced-fat pound cake.

Game Plan

1. While pasta water comes to a boil:
- Prep ingredients for mussels.

2. While tomato mixture simmers:
- Prepare strawberry-pepper sauce.

3. While mussels cook:
- Cook pasta.
- Slice pound cake.

QUICK & EASY
Pork Medallions with Double-Apple Sauce

Half-and-half finishes the sauce of tart green Granny Smith apples and sweet cider, richly mellowing the flavors. If serving wine, chardonnay is a good match for this menu.

TOTAL TIME: 30 MINUTES

FLAVOR TIP: Crush dried herbs by hand to release extra aroma and flavor.

- 1 cup apple cider
- 2 large Granny Smith apples, peeled and each cut into 8 wedges (about 14 ounces)
- 1 (1-pound) pork tenderloin, trimmed and cut crosswise into 8 (½-inch-thick) slices
- ½ teaspoon salt
- ¼ teaspoon black pepper
- Cooking spray
- ½ cup half-and-half
- ½ teaspoon dried rosemary, crushed
- Chopped fresh parsley (optional)

1. Pour cider into a large nonstick skillet; bring to a boil. Add apples. Reduce heat, and simmer 5 minutes or until apples are barely tender. Remove apples from pan with a slotted spoon, and place apples in a medium bowl. Cook cider until reduced to ½ cup (about 3 minutes). Pour reduced cider over apples; set aside.

2. Sprinkle pork evenly with salt and pepper. Wipe pan clean with a damp paper towel. Heat pan over medium-high heat. Coat pan with cooking spray. Add pork to pan; cook 3 minutes on each side or until browned. Remove from heat. Add apple mixture, half-and-half, and rosemary. Garnish with parsley, if desired. Serve immediately. Yield: 4 servings (2 pork medallions, 4 apple wedges, and about ¼ cup sauce).

CALORIES 259 (26% from fat); FAT 7.5g (sat 3.5g, mono 2.8g, poly 0.6g); PROTEIN 25.2g; CARB 22.9g; FIBER 1.4g; CHOL 85mg; IRON 1.5mg; SODIUM 360mg; CALC 45mg

serves 4

Pork Medallions with Double-Apple Sauce

Lemon broccolini*

Egg noodles

*Steam 1 pound broccolini, covered, 5 minutes or until crisp-tender; drain. Combine 1 tablespoon extravirgin olive oil, 1 teaspoon grated lemon rind, 1 tablespoon fresh lemon juice, ¼ teaspoon salt, ¼ teaspoon crushed red pepper, and 1 minced garlic clove. Drizzle over broccolini; toss well to coat.

Game Plan

1. While water for noodles comes to a boil:
- Prepare broccolini, and set aside at room temperature.
- Cut apples into wedges.
- Slice pork into medallions.

2. While noodles cook:
- Prepare pork dish.

inspired vegetarian
Time for Lunch

A little advance work nets noonday bliss.

With a little bit of cooking on the weekend, you can prepare a variety of tasty, hearty lunches that are easily portioned and packed to go and reheated at work.

MAKE AHEAD
Carrot and Sweet Potato Soup with Cranberry Relish

Storing and transporting is easy: Place one cup soup, about one tablespoon relish, and 1½ teaspoons parsley in separate containers. To serve, reheat the soup; combine the relish and parsley, and garnish. Crisp breadsticks and a small wedge of sharp Cheddar cheese complete the meal.

RELISH:

- ¼ cup fresh cranberries, coarsely chopped
- 3 tablespoons fresh orange juice
- 1 tablespoon chopped shallots (1 medium)
- ½ teaspoon sugar

SOUP:

- 2 large carrots, peeled and cut into 2-inch pieces (about 4½ ounces)
- 1 large sweet potato, peeled and cut into 2-inch chunks (about ¾ pound)
- 1 small onion, cut into 8 wedges (about 14 ounces)
- 1 tablespoon olive oil
- 4 cups organic vegetable broth
- 1 teaspoon finely grated fresh ginger
- ¼ teaspoon salt
- ¼ teaspoon freshly ground black pepper

REMAINING INGREDIENT:

- 2 tablespoons chopped fresh flat-leaf parsley

1. To prepare relish, combine first 4 ingredients in a small bowl; set aside.

2. Preheat oven to 400°.

3. To prepare soup, combine carrot, sweet potato, and onion on a jelly-roll pan; drizzle with oil. Toss to coat. Bake at 400° for 30 minutes or until vegetables are tender and just beginning to brown, stirring after 15 minutes.

4. Place vegetables, broth, and ginger in a Dutch oven over medium-high heat; bring to a boil. Cover, reduce heat, and simmer 20 minutes.

5. Place half of vegetable mixture in a blender. Remove center piece of blender lid (to allow steam to escape); secure blender lid on blender. Place a clean towel over opening in blender lid (to avoid splatters). Blend until smooth. Pour pureed mixture into a large bowl; repeat procedure with remaining vegetable mixture. Stir in salt and pepper. Ladle 1 cup soup into each of 4 bowls. Stir parsley into relish. Top each serving with 1 tablespoon relish mixture. Yield: 4 servings.

CALORIES 144 (24% from fat); FAT 3.8g (sat 0.5g, mono 2.7g, poly 0.4g); PROTEIN 2.1g; CARB 25.7g; FIBER 3.4g; CHOL 0mg; IRON 0.8mg; SODIUM 763mg; CALC 44mg

QUICK & EASY

Falafel Pitas with Cucumber-Yogurt Dressing

Pack the cucumber-yogurt dressing in a separate container to serve with the sandwiches. Vegetable crudités such as bell pepper wedges and carrot or celery sticks will round out the meal. You can substitute fresh baby spinach for the arugula, if desired.

¼ cup minced red onion
1 tablespoon Dijon mustard
1 teaspoon ground cumin
½ teaspoon paprika
¼ teaspoon freshly ground black pepper
⅛ teaspoon salt
1 (15½-ounce) can chickpeas (garbanzo beans), rinsed and drained
1 (1-ounce) slice whole wheat bread, torn into pieces
1 large egg
1 large egg white
1½ tablespoons olive oil
2 (6-inch) whole wheat pitas, split
1 cup arugula
½ cup Cucumber-Yogurt Dressing

1. Place first 10 ingredients in a food processor; pulse 6 times or until well blended (mixture will be wet).

2. Heat oil in a large nonstick skillet over medium-high heat. Spoon about ⅓ cup chickpea mixture per patty into pan; cook 4 minutes on each side or until golden brown.

3. Line each pita half with ¼ cup arugula, add 1 patty to each pita half, and spoon 2 tablespoons Cucumber-Yogurt Dressing into each pita half. Yield: 4 servings (serving size: 1 filled pita half).

(Totals include Cucumber-Yogurt Dressing) CALORIES 280 (30% from fat); FAT 9.4g (sat 1.2g, mono 5g, poly 2.2g); PROTEIN 11.4g; CARB 40.1g; FIBER 7.3g; CHOL 53mg; IRON 3.3mg; SODIUM 592mg; CALC 81mg

MAKE AHEAD

CUCUMBER-YOGURT DRESSING:

1 cup plain fat-free yogurt
½ cup diced seedless cucumber
¼ cup minced red onion
1 teaspoon fresh lemon juice

1. Combine all ingredients in a small bowl. Cover and chill. Yield: about 1½ cups (serving size: 1 tablespoon).

CALORIES 8 (0% from fat); FAT 0g; PROTEIN 0.7g; CARB 1.6g; FIBER 0.1g; CHOL 0mg; IRON 0mg; SODIUM 9mg; CALC 20mg

QUICK & EASY • MAKE AHEAD

Spelt Salad with White Beans and Artichokes

Include a cluster of red grapes and crusty Italian bread to round out your meal.

1¼ cups uncooked spelt (farro), rinsed and drained
2½ cups water
⅓ cup chopped fresh mint
⅓ cup chopped fresh parsley
¼ cup minced red onion
3 tablespoons fresh lemon juice
2 tablespoons olive oil
¼ teaspoon salt
⅛ teaspoon freshly ground black pepper
1 (15-ounce) can navy beans, rinsed and drained
1 (14-ounce) can artichoke hearts, drained and chopped

1. Combine spelt and 2½ cups water in a medium saucepan; bring to a boil. Cover, reduce heat, and simmer 30 minutes or until tender and liquid is absorbed.

2. Combine cooked spelt, mint, and remaining ingredients in a large bowl, stirring well. Cover and store in refrigerator. Yield: 5 servings (serving size: 1 cup).

CALORIES 204 (29% from fat); FAT 6.5g (sat 0.8g, mono 4g, poly 0.9g); PROTEIN 7.4g; CARB 30.7g; FIBER 4.9g; CHOL 0mg; IRON 3.2mg; SODIUM 437mg; CALC 40mg

QUICK & EASY • MAKE AHEAD

Chunky Red Dal Soup

This savory, Moroccan-spiced soup gets a flavor kick from harissa, a hot condiment made by preserving chiles in salt. Look for it in Middle Eastern markets, or substitute any chile paste. Pack the soup in a microwave-safe container. Take with it a whole wheat pita, a carton of yogurt, and a handful of dried fruit and nuts in a zip-top plastic bag.

1½ teaspoons olive oil
½ cup chopped onion
1 teaspoon minced garlic
1½ teaspoons minced peeled fresh ginger
¾ teaspoon Spanish smoked paprika
½ teaspoon salt
¼ teaspoon ground cumin
⅛ teaspoon freshly ground black pepper
3 cups water
1 cup dried red lentils, rinsed and drained
1 cup canned chickpeas (garbanzo beans), rinsed and drained
1 (14.5-ounce) can diced tomatoes, undrained
1 tablespoon fresh lemon juice
1 teaspoon harissa
Chopped fresh cilantro (optional)

1. Heat oil in a large saucepan over medium heat. Add onion and garlic; cook 6 minutes or until tender, stirring frequently. Stir in ginger and next 4

Continued

ingredients; cook 1 minute. Add 3 cups water, lentils, chickpeas, and tomatoes; bring to a boil.

2. Cover, reduce heat, and simmer 30 minutes or until lentils are tender, stirring occasionally. Stir in lemon juice and harissa. Garnish with cilantro, if desired. Yield: 5 servings (serving size: 1 cup).

CALORIES 224 (8% from fat); FAT 2g (sat 0.3g, mono 1.1g, poly 0.4g); PROTEIN 12.9g; CARB 38.9g; FIBER 5.8g; CHOL 0mg; IRON 2.1mg; SODIUM 496mg; CALC 54mg

QUICK & EASY • MAKE AHEAD
Couscous Salad with Chickpeas and Tomatoes

Quick and easy to make, this salad keeps well and tastes best at room temperature—all of which make for an ideal weekday lunch. Pack it with cut-up fresh pineapple and biscotti.

  6 tablespoons organic vegetable broth (such as Swanson Certified Organic)
  6 tablespoons water
  ¾ cup uncooked couscous
  ¾ cup canned chickpeas (garbanzo beans), rinsed and drained
  6 tablespoons (1½ ounces) feta cheese, crumbled
  ⅓ cup chopped seeded plum tomato
  2 tablespoons chopped pitted kalamata olives
  2 tablespoons minced red onion
  2 tablespoons chopped fresh parsley
  1 tablespoon red wine vinegar
  1 tablespoon fresh lemon juice
  1 tablespoon extravirgin olive oil
  ⅛ teaspoon salt
Dash of freshly ground black pepper

1. Bring vegetable broth and 6 tablespoons water to a boil in a medium saucepan; gradually stir in couscous. Remove from heat; cover and let stand 10 minutes. Fluff with a fork.

2. Combine cooked couscous and remaining ingredients in a large bowl. Yield: 6 servings (serving size: ¾ cup).

CALORIES 181 (31% from fat); FAT 6.2g (sat 1.7g, mono 3.5g, poly 0.7g); PROTEIN 5.5g; CARB 25.8g; FIBER 2.7g; CHOL 6mg; IRON 0.9mg; SODIUM 373mg; CALC 56mg

reader recipes
Winning Creations

The second annual *Cooking Light* Ultimate Reader Recipe Contest showcases choice flavors and techniques.

With more than 4,000 entries for appetizer, side dish, entrée, and dessert recipes, only 12 innovative contestants made the cut for the second annual *Cooking Light* Ultimate Reader Recipe Contest. The finalists came to our Test Kitchens in Birmingham, Alabama, where they prepared their creations, which were judged by a panel of independent food professionals. Each category winner received a $5,000 cash prize, and the grand prize winner took home an additional $10,000 cash, plus $5,000 toward an active family vacation. Contest sponsors were Beef Checkoff, California raisins, Kerrygold cheeses and butters, and Muir Glen Organic tomato products.

Gloria Bradley, of Naperville, Illinois, developed tart, fresh, and sweet blueberry cupcakes with fresh lemon-laced cream cheese frosting to win the grand prize. The judges were impressed by the cupcakes' "terrific crumb," rich taste, and overall appearance. "The cupcakes were a great example of what a healthful dessert could and should be: moist, flavorful, and surprisingly rich," says contest judge David Bonom.

STAFF FAVORITE • MAKE AHEAD
Lemon-Scented Blueberry Cupcakes

GRAND PRIZE WINNER
CATEGORY WINNER—DESSERTS

"Lemon and blueberry flavors give these cupcakes a great taste. Blueberries or fresh, edible flowers make an easy, pretty decoration."

—Gloria Bradley, Naperville, Illinois

CUPCAKES:
 1½ cups (about 6¾ ounces) plus 2 tablespoons all-purpose flour, divided
 10 tablespoons granulated sugar
 1½ teaspoons baking powder
  ¼ teaspoon salt
  ⅛ teaspoon baking soda
  ¼ cup butter, melted
  1 large egg
  ½ cup low-fat buttermilk
  ½ cup 2% reduced-fat milk
  1 teaspoon grated lemon rind
  ¾ cup fresh or frozen blueberries, thawed

FROSTING:
  ¼ cup (2 ounces) ⅓-less-fat cream cheese, softened
  2 tablespoons butter, softened
  1 teaspoon grated lemon rind
  1 teaspoon vanilla extract
  ⅛ teaspoon salt
 1½ cups powdered sugar, sifted
  2 teaspoons fresh lemon juice
Fresh blueberries (optional)

1. Preheat oven to 350°.

2. Place 12 decorative paper muffin cup liners into muffin cups.

3. To prepare cupcakes, lightly spoon 1½ cups flour into dry measuring cups; level with a knife. Measure 1 tablespoon flour; level with a knife. Sift together 1½ cups flour plus 1 tablespoon flour, granulated sugar, and next 3 ingredients in a large bowl. Combine melted butter and egg in another large bowl; stir with a whisk. Add buttermilk, milk, and 1 teaspoon rind to butter mixture; stir with a whisk. Add buttermilk mixture to flour mixture, stirring just until moist. Toss blueberries with 1 tablespoon flour. Fold blueberries into batter. Spoon batter into prepared muffin cups. Bake at 350° for 25 minutes or until a wooden pick inserted in center comes out clean. Cool in pan 5 minutes on a wire rack; remove from pan. Cool completely on wire rack.

4. To prepare frosting, place cream cheese and next 4 ingredients in a bowl; beat with a mixer at medium speed just until blended. Gradually add powdered sugar (do not overbeat). Stir in juice. Spread frosting evenly over cupcakes; garnish with blueberries, if desired. Store, covered, in refrigerator. Yield: 1 dozen (serving size: 1 cupcake).

CALORIES 236 (29% from fat); FAT 7.7g (sat 4.6g, mono 2g, poly 0.4g); PROTEIN 3.7g; CARB 38.7g; FIBER 0.7g; CHOL 38mg; IRON 1mg; SODIUM 230mg; CALC 71mg

Argentine Black Bean Flatbread with Chimichurri Drizzle

CATEGORY WINNER—
STARTERS AND DRINKS

"Years ago, friends from Argentina invited me for dinner and served an unusual and tasty tostada. I have adapted that recipe into this flatbread."

—Erin Mylroie, St. George, Utah

    1 red bell pepper
    1 tablespoon cornmeal
Cooking spray
    1 tablespoon dry yeast
  ⅛ teaspoon sugar
    1 cup warm water (100° to 110°),
       divided
    3 cups all-purpose flour (about
       13½ ounces)
    1 teaspoon salt
 1½ cups Black Bean Spread
  ½ cup (2 ounces) finely grated fresh
       Parmesan cheese
  ¼ cup chopped fresh parsley
  ¼ cup chopped fresh cilantro
    2 tablespoons olive oil
    1 tablespoon fresh lemon juice
    2 teaspoons minced garlic

1. Preheat broiler.
2. Cut bell pepper in half lengthwise; discard seeds and membranes. Place pepper halves, skin sides up, on a foil-lined baking sheet; flatten with hand. Broil 12 minutes or until blackened. Place in a zip-top plastic bag; seal. Let stand 10 minutes. Peel and cut into 16 strips. Set aside.
3. Reduce oven temperature to 450°.
4. Sprinkle cornmeal over a baking sheet coated with cooking spray. Set aside.
5. Dissolve yeast and sugar in ½ cup warm water in a large bowl; let stand 5 minutes. Lightly spoon flour into dry measuring cups; level with a knife. Add ½ cup warm water, flour, and salt to yeast mixture, stirring until dough forms. Turn dough out onto a floured surface. Knead until smooth and elastic (about 10 minutes).
6. Place dough in a large bowl coated with cooking spray, turning to coat top. Cover and let rise in a warm place (85°), free from drafts, 1 hour or until doubled in size. (Gently press two fingers into dough. If indentation remains, dough has risen enough.) Roll dough into a 14 x 11–inch rectangle; place dough on prepared baking sheet. Spread 1½ cups Black Bean Spread over dough. Sprinkle with cheese. Bake at 450° for 13 minutes or until crust browns and cheese is bubbly. Cool 10 minutes.
7. Combine parsley and remaining 4 ingredients in a small bowl. Drizzle parsley mixture over cheese. Cut bread into 16 squares; garnish each square with 1 bell pepper strip. Yield: 16 servings (serving size: 1 square).

[Totals include Black Bean Spread] CALORIES 126 (19% from fat); FAT 2.7g (sat 0.7g, mono 1.5g, poly 0.3g); PROTEIN 4.3g; CARB 21g; FIBER 1.4g; CHOL 2mg; IRON 1.5mg; SODIUM 248mg; CALC 43mg

QUICK & EASY • MAKE AHEAD

BLACK BEAN SPREAD:
Use leftover spread as a dip with baked tortilla chips, a topping for a taco salad, or as a taco or burrito filler.

  ½ cup coarsely chopped onion
    1 (15-ounce) can 50%-less-sodium
       black beans, rinsed and drained
    1 (14.5-ounce) can organic fire-
       roasted diced tomatoes with green
       chiles, undrained (such as Muir
       Glen)

1. Combine all ingredients in a blender, and process until smooth. Yield: 3 cups (serving size: ½ cup).

CALORIES 54 (0% from fat); FAT 0g; PROTEIN 2.7g; CARB 10.7g; FIBER 2.4g; CHOL 0mg; IRON 0.8mg; SODIUM 303mg; CALC 25mg

WINE NOTE: Black beans have a delicious earthy character that tastes wonderful with an earthy Argentinean red wine. The most famous red grape of Argentina is malbec, which was brought to Argentina from the Bordeaux region of France more than a century ago. One tasty favorite that's well priced: Dona Paula Estate Malbec 2005 from Luján de Cuyo, Argentina ($16).

New-Fashioned Apple and Raisin Slaw

QUICK & EASY

CATEGORY WINNER—
SIDE DISHES AND SIDE SALADS

"This slaw is a healthier version of an original family recipe. It is creamy and delicious, and takes about five minutes to make."

—Kelly McWherter, Houston, Texas

  ½ cup light sour cream
    3 tablespoons reduced-fat
       mayonnaise
 1½ tablespoons white balsamic vinegar
    1 teaspoon sugar
  ½ teaspoon black pepper
  ¼ teaspoon salt
    2 cups unpeeled chopped Rome
       apple (about 1 medium)
    1 cup golden raisins
    1 (16-ounce) package cabbage-and-
       carrot coleslaw

1. Combine first 6 ingredients in a large bowl, stirring with a whisk. Add apple, raisins, and coleslaw; toss to combine. Yield: 8 servings (serving size: 1 cup).

CALORIES 120 (17% from fat); FAT 2.2g (sat 1.2g, mono 0.8g, poly 0.2g); PROTEIN 2.3g; CARB 25.3g; FIBER 3.3g; CHOL 0mg; IRON 0.8mg; SODIUM 162mg; CALC 31mg

Beef with Spicy Cocoa Gravy

"The unsweetened cocoa gives the broth a rich texture and heartiness."

—April Sims, Denton, Texas

1 tablespoon unsweetened cocoa
1 tablespoon ground coriander
1½ teaspoons garlic powder
1½ teaspoons ground cumin
1½ teaspoons ancho chile powder
1½ teaspoons paprika
1½ teaspoons dried oregano
⅛ teaspoon ground cinnamon
1½ pounds top round steak, trimmed and cut into 1-inch cubes
½ cup all-purpose flour
1 tablespoon olive oil
½ cup chopped onion
½ cup chopped green bell pepper
½ cup dry red wine
1 (14.5-ounce) can diced organic fire-roasted tomatoes, undrained
2 cups fat-free, less-sodium beef broth
1 teaspoon salt
⅛ teaspoon freshly ground black pepper
Fresh oregano sprigs (optional)

1. Combine first 8 ingredients in a large bowl. Add beef; toss to coat. Remove beef from bowl. Lightly spoon flour into a dry measuring cup; level with a knife. Add flour to cocoa mixture; stir with a whisk. Return beef to bowl; toss to coat. **2.** Heat oil in a Dutch oven over medium-high heat. Add beef mixture to pan; sauté 5 minutes, turning to brown on all sides. Remove beef from pan. Add onion and bell pepper to pan; sauté 5 minutes or until tender. Add wine and tomatoes; cook 3 minutes. Stir in broth, salt, and black pepper; return beef to pan. Cover, reduce heat, and simmer 1 hour and 10 minutes or until beef is tender, stirring occasionally. Garnish each serving with fresh oregano sprigs, if desired. Yield: 6 servings (serving size: about 1 cup).

CALORIES 263 (27% from fat); FAT 7.8g (sat 2.2g, mono 3.8g, poly 0.5g); PROTEIN 30g; CARB 15.3g; FIBER 2.3g; CHOL 56mg; IRON 3.7mg; SODIUM 731mg; CALC 37mg

lighten up
Cookie Cure

A revamped treat receives a thumbs-up from one of our editors and her spouse.

As a new doctor, Ben Downie doesn't have much time to bake, so he passed the recipe to his wife, *Cooking Light* editor Kathy Kitchens Downie. Both Ben and Kathy couldn't help but notice the recipe had copious amounts of butter, eggs, and chocolate. They both wanted a lighter cookie so Kathy brought the recipe to work.

The biggest challenge was trimming the chocolate. We cut the original's unsweetened chocolate and bittersweet chocolate back to two ounces of each, which trimmed 52 calories per cookie. To boost the overall flavor, they added a half-cup of fat-free unsweetened cocoa. And instead of the original's 1½ cups of bittersweet chocolate chips, they used ¼ cup semisweet chocolate minichips to save another 33 calories per serving.

Using 1½ tablespoons of butter saved 22 calories and 2.4 grams of fat. They also replaced seven eggs with 2½ cups egg substitute to slash the cholesterol.

MAKE AHEAD
Mudslide Cookies

1½ tablespoons butter
2 ounces bittersweet chocolate, coarsely chopped
2 ounces unsweetened chocolate, coarsely chopped
1 tablespoon instant coffee granules
1 tablespoon hot water
1 teaspoon vanilla extract
1½ cups all-purpose flour (about 6¾ ounces)
½ cup unsweetened cocoa
2 teaspoons baking powder
⅛ teaspoon salt
2½ cups sugar
½ cup egg substitute
2 large eggs
½ cup chopped walnuts
¼ cup semisweet chocolate minichips

1. Preheat oven to 350°. **2.** Place first 3 ingredients in a microwave-safe bowl; microwave at HIGH 1 minute or until chocolate is almost melted. Stir until smooth. Combine coffee granules and 1 tablespoon hot water, stirring until granules dissolve. Stir coffee and vanilla into chocolate mixture. **3.** Lightly spoon flour into dry measuring cups; level with a knife. Combine flour, cocoa, baking powder, and salt, stirring well with a whisk. Combine sugar, egg substitute, and eggs in a large bowl; beat with a mixer at high speed 6 minutes or until thick and pale. Gently stir ¼ of egg mixture into chocolate mixture; stir chocolate mixture into remaining egg mixture. Stir in flour mixture, nuts, and chocolate chips. **4.** Cover baking sheets with parchment paper. Drop dough by rounded tablespoonfuls 2 inches apart on prepared pans; with moist hands, gently press dough into ¼-inch-thick rounds. Bake at 350° for 15 minutes or until set. Cool 1 minute. Remove from pans; cool completely on wire racks. Yield: 30 cookies (serving size: 1 cookie).

CALORIES 142 (29% from fat); FAT 4.7g (sat 2g, mono 1g, poly 1.1g); PROTEIN 2.5g; CARB 25.2g; FIBER 1.3g; CHOL 16mg; IRON 1.1mg; SODIUM 59mg; CALC 29mg

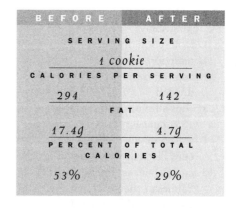

BEFORE	AFTER
SERVING SIZE	
1 cookie	
CALORIES PER SERVING	
294	142
FAT	
17.4g	4.7g
PERCENT OF TOTAL CALORIES	
53%	29%

Embrace the Cold

The reward: heading back inside for hot, tasty stews and braises.

Don't let the winter cold keep you inside; head out for some fun. And if you need added incentive, remember that when you come back inside, you can wrap your tingling hands around a bowl of steaming stew, or sit by the fire with creamy chowder. Spending time in the brisk air makes those dishes taste all the better.

Chicken Tagine with Lemon and Olives

A tagine is a terra-cotta pot with a conical lid used in Morocco. The stews that come from the pot are named for the cooking vessel, though you can cook them in a large skillet or Dutch oven. Serve with couscous or flatbread.

- 2 tablespoons fresh lemon juice
- 12 skinless, boneless chicken thighs
- ¼ cup all-purpose flour (about 1 ounce)
- ½ teaspoon salt
- ¼ teaspoon freshly ground black pepper
- ¼ teaspoon ground turmeric
- ⅛ teaspoon ground red pepper
- 2 teaspoons olive oil
- 2 cups chopped onion (about 2 medium)
- 1 teaspoon minced peeled fresh ginger
- 2 garlic cloves, minced
- 1 cup fat-free, less-sodium chicken broth
- ¼ cup pitted green olives, halved (about 12)
- 2 teaspoons grated lemon rind
- 1 (3-inch) cinnamon stick
- 2 tablespoons chopped fresh cilantro

1. Combine juice and chicken in a large zip-top plastic bag. Seal and marinate in refrigerator 30 minutes. Remove chicken from bag; discard marinade.
2. Pat chicken dry with paper towels. Dredge in flour; sprinkle with salt, black pepper, turmeric, and red pepper. Heat oil in a large nonstick skillet with high sides over medium-high heat. Add half of chicken; cook 3 minutes on each side or until lightly browned. Remove from pan. Repeat procedure with remaining chicken.
3. Add onion, ginger, and garlic to pan; sauté 5 minutes or until tender. Return chicken to pan. Add broth, olives, rind, and cinnamon stick; bring to a boil. Cover, reduce heat, and simmer 1 hour or until chicken is tender. Discard cinnamon stick; stir in cilantro. Yield: 6 servings (serving size: 2 chicken thighs and ⅓ cup sauce).

CALORIES 240 (34% from fat); FAT 9.1g (sat 1.6g, mono 4.4g, poly 2g); PROTEIN 28.6g; CARB 9.9g; FIBER 0.8g; CHOL 115mg; IRON 1.8mg; SODIUM 612mg; CALC 27mg

WINE NOTE: The fresh lemon and fruity olive oil lend this dish bright Mediterranean flavor, which calls for a high-acid white wine. However, the aromatic spices deserve a wine that's equally exotic. Try Moschofilero Boutari 2005 ($15), a widely available Greek wine that's made from the Moschofilero (mo-sko-feel-er-o) grape. It has a bold fragrance of citrus, melon, white flowers, and spice along with a nice balance of sweetness and grapefruit flavors.

Veal Osso Buco with Gremolata

Osso buco is a dish made with slow-braised veal shanks. Gremolata, a combination of parsley, lemon rind, and garlic, is a traditional finishing touch. Serve with polenta or mashed potatoes.

- 6 (8-ounce) veal shanks, trimmed
- ¾ teaspoon salt, divided
- ¼ teaspoon freshly ground black pepper
- ¼ cup all-purpose flour (about 1 ounce)
- 1 tablespoon butter, divided
- 1 cup finely chopped yellow onion (about 1 medium)
- ½ cup finely chopped carrot (about 1 medium)
- ½ cup finely chopped celery (about 1 stalk)
- 2 bacon slices, diced (uncooked)
- 1 cup dry white wine
- 1 cup fat-free, less-sodium beef broth
- 1 (14.5-ounce) can no-salt-added whole tomatoes, drained and chopped
- 1 cup chopped fresh flat-leaf parsley
- 1 teaspoon grated lemon rind
- 1 garlic clove, minced

1. Sprinkle veal with ¼ teaspoon salt and pepper; dredge in flour.
2. Melt 1½ teaspoons butter in a large Dutch oven over medium-high heat. Add 3 veal shanks, and cook 8 minutes, browning on all sides. Remove to a plate. Repeat procedure with 1½ teaspoons butter and remaining veal.
3. Add onion, carrot, celery, and bacon to pan; sauté 5 minutes or until vegetables are tender. Add wine; cook 5 minutes or until liquid almost evaporates. Add ½ teaspoon salt, broth, and tomatoes. Return veal to pan; bring to a boil. Cover, reduce heat, and simmer 2 hours or until veal is tender.
4. Combine parsley, rind, and garlic in a small bowl. Stir into osso buco; cook 10 minutes. Yield: 6 servings (serving size: 1 veal shank).

CALORIES 358 (32% from fat); FAT 12.5g (sat 4.2g, mono 4.5g, poly 1.3g); PROTEIN 49.2g; CARB 9.8g; FIBER 1.6g; CHOL 186mg; IRON 3.1mg; SODIUM 818mg; CALC 89mg

Beef Goulash

Hungary's national dish is a meat stew flavored with paprika and caraway seeds. Browning the meat first yields the most flavorful result. You can also serve over egg noodles.

1½ pounds boneless chuck roast, trimmed and cut into 1-inch pieces
¼ cup all-purpose flour (about 1 ounce)
1¼ teaspoons salt, divided
¾ teaspoon freshly ground black pepper, divided
1 tablespoon butter
4 cups chopped onion (about 2 large)
2 garlic cloves, minced
2 tablespoons paprika
1 tablespoon red wine vinegar
1 cup chopped plum tomato (about 3)
½ teaspoon caraway seeds, crushed
2 bay leaves
½ cup water
1 (14-ounce) can fat-free, less-sodium beef broth
2½ cups cubed peeled Yukon gold or red potato (about 1 pound)
1 tablespoon fresh lemon juice

1. Dredge beef in flour; sprinkle with ½ teaspoon salt and ¼ teaspoon pepper. Melt butter in a Dutch oven over medium-high heat. Add beef; cook 8 minutes, browning on all sides. Remove beef from pan.
2. Add onion and garlic to pan; sauté 10 minutes or until lightly browned. Stir in paprika and vinegar; cook 2 minutes. Return beef to pan. Add tomato, caraway seeds, and bay leaves; cook 3 minutes. Add ½ teaspoon salt, ¼ teaspoon pepper, ½ cup water, and broth; bring to a boil. Cover, reduce heat, and simmer 1 hour and 45 minutes. Add potato; cover and cook 1 hour and 15 minutes or until very tender. Stir in ¼ teaspoon salt, ¼ teaspoon pepper, and juice. Discard bay leaves. Yield: 8 servings (serving size: 1 cup).

CALORIES 242 (23% from fat); FAT 6.1g (sat 2.6g, mono 2.3g, poly 0.4g); PROTEIN 24.2g; CARB 22.4g; FIBER 2.5g; CHOL 47mg; IRON 2.8mg; SODIUM 517mg; CALC 31mg

---

French Country Lunch Menu
serves 6

Radicchio adds color and agreeable bitterness to the salad. Substitute peppery arugula for the radicchio or clementines for the oranges, if you prefer.

Rosemary-Scented Lentils and Sausage

Winter salad*

Syrah/Shiraz

*Combine 5 cups baby spinach leaves, 3 cups chopped radicchio, and 3 cups chopped endive in a large bowl. Combine 3 tablespoons red wine vinegar, 2 tablespoons extravirgin olive oil, 1 teaspoon Dijon mustard, ¼ teaspoon salt, and ¼ teaspoon freshly ground black pepper in a small bowl, stirring well with a whisk. Drizzle vinegar mixture over greens; toss well to combine. Top salad with ½ cup orange sections.

Rosemary-Scented Lentils and Sausage

To make this spicy dish even spicier, use hot Italian turkey sausage.

4 cups water
4 cups fat-free, less-sodium chicken broth
2 cups petite green lentils
2 teaspoons olive oil
2 cups minced yellow onion (about 1 large)
½ cup minced carrot (about 1 medium)
2 teaspoons minced fresh rosemary
2 garlic cloves, minced
½ pound Italian turkey sausage, casings removed
1 tablespoon tomato paste
½ teaspoon salt
¼ teaspoon freshly ground black pepper
⅛ teaspoon hot paprika
Dash of ground red pepper

1. Combine first 3 ingredients in a large saucepan over medium heat. Bring to a simmer. Cook 30 minutes or until almost tender.

---

2. Heat oil in a saucepan over medium-high heat. Add onion, carrot, rosemary, and garlic to pan. Sauté 10 minutes or until tender. Add sausage; cook 5 minutes, stirring to crumble. Add tomato paste and remaining 4 ingredients; cook 1 minute or until heated. Add sausage mixture to lentils; bring to a boil. Cook 30 minutes or until lentils are tender. Yield: 6 servings (serving size: about 1 cup).

CALORIES 341 (19% from fat); FAT 7g (sat 1.6g, mono 2.5g, poly 1.7g); PROTEIN 26.4g; CARB 43.6g; FIBER 7.7g; CHOL 33mg; IRON 5.8mg; SODIUM 731mg; CALC 38mg

---

Smoky Barbecue Chili
(pictured on page 225)

Cooking spray
2 cups chopped yellow onion
6 garlic cloves, coarsely chopped
2 to 3 pasilla chiles, stemmed and seeded
2 to 3 New Mexican dried red chiles, stemmed and seeded
2 chopped seeded chipotle chiles, canned in adobo sauce
2 cups fat-free, less-sodium chicken broth
1 tablespoon canola oil, divided
1¼ pounds top round, trimmed and cut into ½-inch pieces
1¼ pounds boneless pork loin, trimmed and cut into ½-inch pieces
1¾ cups no-salt-added tomato puree
½ cup water
2 tablespoons dark brown sugar
2 tablespoons cider vinegar
1 tablespoon honey mustard
1 tablespoon Worcestershire sauce
1 tablespoon molasses
½ teaspoon salt
2 (15-ounce) cans pinto beans, rinsed and drained

1. Heat a large nonstick skillet over medium-high heat. Coat pan with cooking spray. Add onion and garlic to pan; sauté 5 minutes. Add chiles; cook 2 minutes. Add broth; bring to a boil. Cover, reduce heat, and simmer 20 minutes or until chiles are tender. Cool slightly.

Place half of chile mixture in a blender. Remove center piece of blender lid (to allow steam to escape); secure blender lid on blender. Place a clean towel over opening in blender lid (to avoid spills). Blend until smooth. Pour into a medium bowl. Repeat procedure with remaining chile mixture.

2. Heat 1½ teaspoons oil in a Dutch oven over medium-high heat. Add beef; cook 7 minutes or until browned. Remove from pan. Heat 1½ teaspoons oil in pan. Add pork; cook 7 minutes or until browned. Add chile mixture and beef to pan. Stir in tomato puree and next 7 ingredients; bring to a boil. Partially cover, reduce heat, and simmer 1 hour or until tender, stirring occasionally. Stir in beans; cook 15 minutes. Yield: 8 servings (serving size: about 1 cup).

CALORIES 363 (26% from fat); FAT 10.4g (sat 3.4g, mono 4.8g, poly 1.2g); PROTEIN 38.1g; CARB 27.7g; FIBER 5.1g; CHOL 83mg; IRON 4.3mg; SODIUM 829mg; CALC 52mg

Braised Pork Roast with Fennel, Leeks, and Vermouth

1½ pounds boneless pork loin roast, trimmed
¼ cup all-purpose flour (about 1 ounce)
¾ teaspoon salt, divided
¼ teaspoon freshly ground black pepper
1 tablespoon olive oil
1 teaspoon fennel seeds, crushed
2 cups sliced leek (about 2 large)
2 cups sliced fennel bulb (about 2 large)
½ cup dry vermouth
1½ cups fat-free, less-sodium chicken broth

1. Dredge pork in flour, and sprinkle with ½ teaspoon salt and black pepper. Heat oil in a Dutch oven over medium-high heat. Add pork, and cook 8 minutes, browning on all sides. Remove from pan.
2. Add fennel seeds to pan; cook 30 seconds. Add leek and sliced fennel. Reduce heat to medium, and cook 10 minutes or until tender. Add vermouth, and cook

2 minutes or until liquid almost evaporates. Return pork to pan. Add broth, and bring to a boil. Cover, reduce heat, and simmer 1 hour and 45 minutes or until pork is tender. Stir in ¼ teaspoon salt. Cut pork into thin slices. Yield: 6 servings (serving size: 3 ounces pork and about ½ cup sauce).

CALORIES 290 (32% from fat); FAT 10.4g (sat 3.2g, mono 5.4g, poly 0.9g); PROTEIN 27.1g; CARB 16.2g; FIBER 3.2g; CHOL 67mg; IRON 2.5mg; SODIUM 499mg; CALC 77mg

Fish Chowder

4½ cups water
4 bay leaves
1½ pounds halibut fillets or other firm white fish, skinned
3 bacon slices (uncooked)
3½ cups cubed peeled baking potato
1½ cups chopped onion (about 1 large)
½ cup coarsely chopped carrot (about 1 medium)
1½ teaspoons dried thyme
1 teaspoon salt, divided
¾ teaspoon freshly ground black pepper, divided
4 cups 2% reduced-fat milk
1 tablespoon butter, cut into small pieces

1. Bring 4½ cups water and bay leaves to a simmer in a large skillet. Add fish; cover and simmer 10 minutes or until fish flakes easily when tested with a fork or until desired degree of doneness. Remove fish from pan with a slotted spoon. Cut fish into large pieces. Reserve 2½ cups cooking liquid and bay leaves.
2. Cook bacon in a Dutch oven over medium heat until crisp. Remove bacon from pan, reserving 1 teaspoon drippings in pan; crumble bacon, and set aside. Add potato, onion, and carrot to pan; cook over medium heat 10 minutes. Add reserved cooking liquid, bay leaves, thyme, ½ teaspoon salt, and ¼ teaspoon pepper; bring to a boil. Reduce heat; simmer 10 minutes. Add milk and butter; simmer 25 minutes until potatoes are tender (do not boil). Stir in fish, ½ teaspoon salt, and ½ teaspoon pepper. Discard bay leaves. Sprinkle with bacon.

Yield: 10 servings (serving size: 1 cup chowder and about 1 teaspoon bacon).

CALORIES 242 (32% from fat); FAT 8.6g (sat 3.5g, mono 3.1g, poly 1.1g); PROTEIN 21.8g; CARB 18.4g; FIBER 1.5g; CHOL 42mg; IRON 1.1mg; SODIUM 531mg; CALC 166mg

Hearty Minestrone with Barley, Sage, and Beans

1 teaspoon olive oil
2 cups finely chopped onion (about 1 medium)
½ cup finely chopped celery (about 1 stalk)
¼ cup finely chopped carrot (about 1 medium)
¼ cup thinly sliced green onions (about 4)
2 tablespoons finely chopped apple-wood-smoked bacon (about 1 ounce)
1 tablespoon chopped fresh flat-leaf parsley
1 tablespoon chopped fresh sage
½ teaspoon chopped fresh thyme
2 garlic cloves, minced
1¼ cups finely chopped Savoy cabbage
2 cups water
¼ teaspoon salt
¼ teaspoon freshly ground black pepper
3 (14-ounce) cans fat-free, less-sodium chicken broth
1 (16-ounce) can cannellini beans, rinsed and drained
1½ cups peeled Yukon gold potato (about 1 medium), cut into ½-inch cubes
½ cup uncooked pearl barley
2 cups green beans, cut into 1-inch pieces

1. Heat oil in a Dutch oven over medium-high heat. Add onion and next 8 ingredients; sauté 5 minutes. Add cabbage and next 5 ingredients; bring to a boil. Stir in potato and barley. Reduce heat, and simmer 20 minutes or until potatoes are tender. Stir in green beans; cook 5 minutes. Yield: 8 servings (serving size: about 1⅓ cups).

CALORIES 140 (16% from fat); FAT 2.5g (sat 0.7g, mono 1.2g, poly 0.4g); PROTEIN 6.2g; CARB 23.3g; FIBER 5.3g; CHOL 2mg; IRON 1.2mg; SODIUM 473mg; CALC 51mg

Pork Carnitas with Caramelized Onions and Chipotle

2   teaspoons chopped fresh oregano
1   teaspoon freshly ground black pepper
1½ pounds boneless Boston butt pork roast, trimmed and cut into 1-inch cubes
2   bay leaves
2   teaspoons olive oil
Cooking spray
2   cups chopped onion (about 2 medium)
6   garlic cloves, minced
1   teaspoon salt
½   teaspoon ground cumin
1   chopped chipotle chile, canned in adobo sauce
1   (14-ounce) can fat-free, less-sodium chicken broth
1   tablespoon chopped fresh cilantro
2   teaspoons fresh lime juice

1. Combine first 4 ingredients in a large zip-top plastic bag; seal and shake to coat pork. Refrigerate 8 hours or overnight.
2. Heat oil in a large nonstick skillet over medium-high heat. Remove pork from bag. Add pork to pan; cook 10 minutes, browning on all sides. Remove from pan.
3. Coat pan with cooking spray. Add onion and garlic; sauté 5 minutes or until lightly browned. Stir in salt, cumin, and chile. Return pork to pan, and add broth. Bring to a simmer; cover. Cook 2 hours or until pork is very tender. Remove from heat; discard bay leaves. Stir in cilantro and juice. Yield: 6 servings (serving size: ½ cup).

CALORIES 191 (35% from fat); FAT 7.4g (sat 2.2g, mono 3.7g, poly 0.8g); PROTEIN 21.7g; CARB 8.3g; FIBER 1.2g; CHOL 58mg; IRON 1.2mg; SODIUM 631mg; CALC 45mg

Monkfish in Saffron Broth over Baby Spinach and Red Potatoes

3   cups fresh baby spinach (about 2 ounces)
12 small red potatoes, quartered
4   cups fat-free, less-sodium chicken broth
1   cup dry white wine
1   cup quartered cherry tomatoes (about 16 medium)
¼   cup thinly sliced green onions (about 4)
1   garlic clove, minced
¼   teaspoon salt
¼   teaspoon freshly ground black pepper
¼   teaspoon saffron threads
1½ pounds boneless, skinless monkfish fillets, cut into 2-inch pieces

1. Place ½ cup spinach into each of 6 bowls; set aside.
2. Steam potatoes, covered, 10 minutes or until tender. Place 8 potato quarters into each bowl.
3. Combine broth and next 4 ingredients in a large nonstick skillet over medium-high heat. Bring to a boil, and cook until reduced to 3 cups (about 25 minutes). Add salt, pepper, and saffron to pan; cook 2 minutes. Reduce heat to medium; arrange fish pieces in a single layer in pan. Cover and cook 8 minutes or until fish flakes easily when tested with a fork or until desired degree of doneness. Divide fish evenly among bowls; spoon ½ cup broth mixture over each serving. Yield: 6 servings.

CALORIES 149 (12% from fat); FAT 1.9g (sat 0.4g, mono 0.3g, poly 0.8g); PROTEIN 20.5g; CARB 11.2g; FIBER 2.4g; CHOL 28mg; IRON 1.4mg; SODIUM 492mg; CALC 29mg

happy endings
Winter Shortcakes

The great American summer dessert turns into a cool-season standby.

Chocolate Shortcakes with Bananas and Caramel

SHORTCAKES:

1½ cups all-purpose flour (about 6¾ ounces)
½   cup sugar
⅓   cup unsweetened cocoa
1   teaspoon baking soda
½   teaspoon baking powder
¼   teaspoon salt
¼   cup chilled butter, cut into small pieces
½   cup fat-free buttermilk

FILLING:

¼   cup sugar
2   tablespoons water
2   tablespoons whipping cream
1   teaspoon butter
1   cup frozen reduced-calorie whipped topping, thawed
⅛   teaspoon unsweetened cocoa
2   bananas, peeled and cut into ¼-inch-thick slices (about 2 cups)

1. Preheat oven to 375°.
2. To prepare shortcakes, lightly spoon flour into dry measuring cups; level with a knife. Combine flour and next 5 ingredients in a large bowl, stirring with a whisk. Cut in ¼ cup butter with a pastry blender or 2 knives until mixture resembles coarse meal. Add buttermilk; stir just until moist. Knead lightly in bowl 5 or 6 times. Turn dough out onto a lightly floured surface; pat dough into an 8-inch circle on a baking sheet lined with parchment paper. Cut dough into 8 wedges, cutting into, but not through, dough. Bake at 375° for 18 minutes or until just firm to the touch. Remove from pan; cool on a wire rack. Place shortcake on a cutting board or work surface; cut along score lines with a serrated knife to form 8 wedges.
3. To prepare filling, combine ¼ cup sugar and 2 tablespoons water in a small saucepan over medium-high heat; stir gently just until sugar dissolves. Cook, without stirring, until pale golden (about 4 minutes), gently swirling pan if needed to cook sugar evenly. Remove from heat; add cream and 1 teaspoon butter, stirring with

a whisk until smooth. Cool 5 minutes.

4. Place whipped topping and ⅛ teaspoon cocoa in a medium bowl; fold just until combined. Split shortcakes in half horizontally using a serrated knife. Arrange about ¼ cup bananas over bottom half of each shortcake; top each serving with about 1 teaspoon caramel sauce, about 2 tablespoons whipped topping mixture, and top of shortcake. Drizzle ½ teaspoon caramel sauce over top of each shortcake. Yield: 8 servings (serving size: 1 filled shortcake).

CALORIES 285 (30% from fat); FAT 9.4g (sat 6.1g, mono 2.2g, poly 0.4g); PROTEIN 4.2g; CARB 49.4g; FIBER 2.6g; CHOL 22mg; IRON 1.7mg; SODIUM 323mg; CALC 50mg

---

MAKE AHEAD

Macaroon Shortcake with Roasted Pineapple

FILLING:

1 pineapple, peeled and cored
Cooking spray
2 tablespoons pineapple juice
1 tablespoon honey
½ teaspoon ground ginger
⅛ teaspoon ground cloves

SHORTCAKES:

1½ cups all-purpose flour (about 6¾ ounces)
¾ cup flaked sweetened coconut
1 teaspoon baking powder
¼ teaspoon salt
1 cup granulated sugar
¼ cup butter, softened
2 large egg whites
¼ teaspoon vanilla extract
½ cup 1% low-fat milk

REMAINING INGREDIENTS:

1¼ cups frozen reduced-calorie whipped topping, thawed
2 teaspoons powdered sugar

1. Preheat oven to 450°.

2. To prepare filling, cut pineapple lengthwise into quarters. Cut each quarter crosswise into ½-inch-thick slices. Arrange pineapple in a single layer on a jelly-roll pan coated with cooking spray. Combine juice, honey, ginger, and cloves; drizzle over pineapple. Bake at 450° for

20 minutes or until pineapple is lightly browned. Remove from oven; set aside.

3. Reduce oven temperature to 325°.

4. To prepare shortcakes, lightly spoon flour into dry measuring cups; level with a knife. Combine flour and next 3 ingredients, stirring well with a whisk. Place granulated sugar and butter in a large bowl; beat with a mixer at medium speed until well blended (about 5 minutes). Add egg whites, 1 at a time, beating well after each addition. Beat in vanilla. Add flour mixture and milk alternately to sugar mixture, beginning and ending with flour mixture. Pour batter into a 9-inch round cake pan coated with cooking spray. Bake at 325° for 40 minutes or until a wooden pick inserted in center comes out clean. Cool in pan 10 minutes on a wire rack; remove from pan. Cool completely on wire rack.

5. Place shortcake on a cutting board or work surface. Carefully split shortcake in half horizontally using a serrated knife. Place bottom half of shortcake on a platter; top with pineapple mixture, whipped topping, and top of shortcake. Sprinkle with powdered sugar. Yield: 10 servings (serving size: 1 wedge).

CALORIES 292 (24% from fat); FAT 7.8g (sat 5.6g, mono 1.3g, poly 0.3g); PROTEIN 3.8g; CARB 54g; FIBER 1.9g; CHOL 13mg; IRON 1.4mg; SODIUM 173mg; CALC 59mg

---

MAKE AHEAD

Ambrosia Shortcakes

SHORTCAKES:

2 cups all-purpose flour (about 9 ounces)
⅓ cup sugar
2 teaspoons baking powder
2 teaspoons grated orange rind
½ teaspoon baking soda
¼ teaspoon salt
¼ cup chilled butter, cut into small pieces
⅓ cup fat-free buttermilk
3 tablespoons frozen orange juice concentrate, thawed
1 tablespoon vanilla extract
Cooking spray
1 teaspoon water
1 large egg white, lightly beaten
1 teaspoon sugar

FILLING:

¼ cup fresh orange juice
¼ teaspoon cornstarch
¼ teaspoon vanilla extract
3 cups navel orange sections (about 2 large oranges)
1 cup chopped fresh pineapple
1 cup frozen reduced-calorie whipped topping, thawed
⅔ cup flaked sweetened coconut, toasted

1. Preheat oven to 375°.

2. To prepare shortcakes, lightly spoon flour into dry measuring cups; level with a knife. Combine flour and next 5 ingredients in a large bowl, stirring with a whisk; cut in butter with a pastry blender or 2 knives until mixture resembles coarse meal. Combine buttermilk, juice concentrate, and 1 tablespoon vanilla. Add buttermilk mixture to flour mixture; stir just until moist. Turn dough out onto a lightly floured surface; knead dough lightly 5 or 6 times. Let dough stand 10 minutes. Gently pat dough to a ½-inch thickness with lightly floured hands. Cut dough into 10 (2-inch) squares. Place squares 2 inches apart on a baking sheet coated with cooking spray.

3. Combine 1 teaspoon water and egg white. Brush egg white mixture over dough; sprinkle evenly with 1 teaspoon sugar. Bake at 375° for 13 minutes or until golden. Remove shortcakes from pan; cool on a wire rack.

4. To prepare filling, combine ¼ cup juice and cornstarch in a small saucepan over medium-high heat; bring to a boil. Cook 1 minute. Remove from heat, and stir in ¼ teaspoon vanilla. Combine orange sections and pineapple in a medium bowl. Drizzle cornstarch mixture over fruit; toss gently to combine. Cover and chill.

5. Split shortcakes in half horizontally using a serrated knife. Spoon about ¼ cup fruit mixture over bottom half of each shortcake; top each serving with about 1½ tablespoons whipped topping, about 1 tablespoon toasted coconut, and top of shortcake. Yield: 10 servings (serving size: 1 filled shortcake).

CALORIES 251 (26% from fat); FAT 7.3g (sat 5.1g, mono 1.3g, poly 0.3g); PROTEIN 4.2g; CARB 42.9g; FIBER 2.3g; CHOL 12mg; IRON 1.5mg; SODIUM 279mg; CALC 97mg

Apple-Cranberry Shortcakes

SHORTCAKES:
1¼ cups all-purpose flour (about
     5½ ounces)
¼ cup cornmeal
⅓ cup granulated sugar
1½ teaspoons baking powder
½ teaspoon ground cinnamon
¼ teaspoon salt
5 tablespoons chilled butter, cut
     into small pieces
6 tablespoons ice water
1 large egg white, lightly beaten
2 teaspoons granulated sugar

FILLING:
2 teaspoons butter
6 cups sliced peeled Gala or
     Braeburn apple (about 4 medium)
3 tablespoons brown sugar
½ cup fresh cranberries
¼ cup apple juice
¼ cup water
Dash of salt
1 cup frozen fat-free whipped
     topping, thawed
⅛ teaspoon ground cinnamon

1. Preheat oven to 375°.
2. To prepare shortcakes, lightly spoon flour into dry measuring cups; level with a knife. Place flour and next 5 ingredients in a food processor; pulse 2 or 3 times to combine. Add chilled butter; pulse 10 times or until mixture resembles coarse meal. With processor on, slowly add 6 tablespoons ice water through food chute, processing just until combined (do not form a ball).
3. Turn dough out onto a lightly floured surface; knead lightly 4 times with floured hands. Pat dough into a 14 x 4–inch rectangle on a large baking sheet lined with parchment paper. Cut dough into 8 even portions, cutting into, but not through, dough. Brush dough with egg white; sprinkle evenly with 2 teaspoons sugar. Bake at 375° for 15 minutes or until golden. Remove from pan; cool on a wire rack.
4. To prepare filling, melt 2 teaspoons butter in a large nonstick skillet over medium-high heat. Add apple, tossing to coat; sauté 4 minutes or until lightly browned. Stir in

brown sugar; sauté 2 minutes. Stir in cranberries, juice, ¼ cup water, and dash of salt. Reduce heat to low; simmer 5 minutes or until cranberries pop, stirring frequently.
5. Place whipped topping and ⅛ teaspoon cinnamon in a small bowl, and fold gently to combine. Place shortcake on a cutting board or work surface. Carefully split shortcake in half horizontally using a serrated knife. Place bottom half of shortcake on a platter; spread evenly with about ½ cup whipped topping mixture and apple mixture; top with shortcake top. Cut along score lines with a serrated knife to form 8 portions. Top each portion with 1 tablespoon whipped topping mixture. Yield: 8 servings (serving size: 1 filled shortcake).

CALORIES 278 (27% from fat); FAT 8.4g (sat 5.2g, mono 2.1g, poly 0.5g); PROTEIN 3.2g; CARB 48.2g; FIBER 2.3g; CHOL 21mg; IRON 1.3mg; SODIUM 256mg; CALC 69mg

Spiced Shortcakes with Sautéed Pears

SHORTCAKES:
2 cups all-purpose flour (about
     9 ounces)
⅓ cup regular oats
⅓ cup packed brown sugar
1 tablespoon baking powder
½ teaspoon salt
½ teaspoon ground cinnamon
¼ teaspoon ground ginger
¼ cup chilled butter, cut into small
     pieces
½ cup 1% low-fat milk
¼ cup water
Cooking spray
1 tablespoon water
1 large egg white, lightly beaten
1 teaspoon granulated sugar

FILLING:
5½ cups sliced peeled ripe Bosc pears
     (about 6 pears)
2 tablespoons fresh lemon juice
1 tablespoon butter
3 tablespoons brown sugar
1 teaspoon vanilla extract

REMAINING INGREDIENT:
2½ cups frozen fat-free vanilla yogurt

1. Preheat oven to 375°.
2. To prepare shortcakes, lightly spoon flour into dry measuring cups; level with a knife. Combine flour and next 6 ingredients in a large bowl, stirring with a whisk. Cut in ¼ cup butter with a pastry blender or 2 knives until butter pieces are pea-sized. Add milk and ¼ cup water; stir just until moist. Drop dough by level ¼ cup measures 2 inches apart onto a baking sheet coated with cooking spray. Flatten dough to ½-inch thickness using lightly floured hands. Let stand 5 minutes.
3. Combine 1 tablespoon water and egg white. Brush egg white mixture over dough; sprinkle evenly with granulated sugar. Bake at 375° for 15 minutes or until golden. Remove from pan; cool on a wire rack.
4. To prepare filling, combine pears and lemon juice; toss to coat. Melt 1 tablespoon butter in a large skillet over medium-high heat. Add pear mixture; sauté 2 minutes. Stir in 3 tablespoons brown sugar; bring to a boil. Reduce heat to low; simmer 5 minutes or until sauce thickens slightly, stirring occasionally. Remove from heat; stir in vanilla.
5. Split each shortcake in half horizontally using a serrated knife. Spoon about ⅓ cup pear mixture over bottom half of each shortcake; top each serving with top of shortcake and ¼ cup yogurt. Yield: 10 servings (serving size: 1 filled shortcake).

CALORIES 309 (19% from fat); FAT 6.4g (sat 3.8g, mono 1.6g, poly 0.4g); PROTEIN 6.6g; CARB 57.5g; FIBER 3.8g; CHOL 16mg; IRON 1.9mg; SODIUM 355mg; CALC 207mg

Pumpkin Shortcakes with Winter Fruit Compote

COMPOTE:
½ cup water
½ cup ruby port
¼ cup granulated sugar
2 star anise
1 (3-inch) cinnamon stick
1 (8-ounce) package dried mixed fruit

SHORTCAKES:
½ cup canned pumpkin
½ cup 1% low-fat milk
¼ cup water

2 cups all-purpose flour (about 9 ounces)
⅓ cup packed brown sugar
2 teaspoons baking powder
¾ teaspoon ground cinnamon
½ teaspoon salt
¼ teaspoon ground nutmeg
¼ cup chilled butter, cut into small
  pieces
Cooking spray
1 teaspoon granulated sugar

REMAINING INGREDIENT:
10 tablespoons crème fraîche

1. To prepare compote, combine first 5 ingredients in a medium saucepan over medium-high heat. Bring to a boil, stirring until sugar dissolves. Stir in fruit. Reduce heat to medium; simmer 5 minutes or until fruit is tender and liquid is slightly thick. Pour into a bowl; cover and chill at least 3 hours. Discard anise and cinnamon stick.

2. Preheat oven to 375°.

3. To prepare shortcakes, spoon pumpkin onto several layers of heavy-duty paper towels; spread to ½-inch thickness. Cover with additional paper towels; let stand 10 minutes. Scrape into a medium bowl using a rubber spatula. Add milk and ¼ cup water, stirring to combine.

4. Lightly spoon flour into dry measuring cups; level with a knife. Combine flour and next 5 ingredients in a large bowl, stirring with a whisk; cut in butter with a pastry blender or 2 knives until butter pieces are pea-sized. Add pumpkin mixture; stir just until moist. Drop dough by level ¼ cup measures 2 inches apart onto a baking sheet coated with cooking spray. Flatten dough to ½-inch thickness using lightly floured hands. Sprinkle evenly with 1 teaspoon granulated sugar. Bake at 375° for 15 minutes or until golden. Remove from pan; cool on a wire rack.

5. Split shortcakes in half horizontally using a serrated knife. Spoon about ¼ cup compote over bottom half of each shortcake; top each serving with 1 tablespoon crème fraîche and top of shortcake. Yield: 10 servings (serving size: 1 filled shortcake).

CALORIES 306 (30% from fat); FAT 10.3g (sat 6.3g, mono 2.8g, poly 0.5g); PROTEIN 4.2g; CARB 49g; FIBER 2.9g; CHOL 27mg; IRON 2.3mg; SODIUM 296mg; CALC 96mg

Pork Tenderloin Tonight

Four basic methods make this lean, quick-cooking cut of meat the highlight of easy, delicious meals.

One of the most versatile ingredients you can keep on hand for fast, easy weeknight meals is pork tenderloin. It's well suited to high-heat preparations that allow the meat to retain its moist tenderness as it cooks quickly.

We offer four general approaches: whole-roasted tenderloins; cutlets; and small strips and cubes. Roasting a one-pound tenderloin at 400° or higher takes just over 20 minutes. Sliced and pounded into cutlets, or trimmed into cubes and strips, pork tenderloin cooks quickly in the pan, browned and crusted outside yet juicy inside.

Pork and Vegetable Stir-Fry with Cashew Rice

(pictured on page 226)

¾ cup uncooked long-grain rice
⅓ cup chopped green onions
¼ cup dry-roasted cashews, salted
  and coarsely chopped
½ teaspoon salt
⅔ cup fat-free, less-sodium chicken
  broth
2 tablespoons cornstarch,
  divided
3 tablespoons low-sodium soy
  sauce, divided
2 tablespoons honey
1 (1-pound) pork tenderloin,
  trimmed and cut into ½-inch
  cubes
1 tablespoon canola oil,
  divided
2 cups sliced mushrooms (about
  4 ounces)
1 cup chopped onion
1 tablespoon grated peeled fresh
  ginger
2 garlic cloves, minced
2 cups sugar snap peas, trimmed
  (about 6 ounces)
1 cup chopped red bell pepper
  (about 1)

1. Cook rice according to package directions, omitting salt and fat. Stir in green onions, cashews, and salt; set aside, and keep warm.

2. Combine broth, 1 tablespoon cornstarch, 2 tablespoons soy sauce, and honey in a small bowl, and set aside.

3. Combine pork, 1 tablespoon cornstarch, and 1 tablespoon soy sauce in a bowl, tossing well to coat. Heat 2 teaspoons oil in a large nonstick skillet over medium-high heat. Add pork; sauté 4 minutes or until browned. Remove from pan.

4. Add 1 teaspoon oil to pan. Add mushrooms and 1 cup onion; sauté 2 minutes. Stir in ginger and garlic; sauté 30 seconds. Add peas and bell pepper; sauté 1 minute. Stir in pork; sauté 1 minute. Add broth mixture. Bring to a boil; cook 1 minute or until thick, stirring constantly. Serve over cashew rice. Yield: 4 servings (serving size: 1½ cups pork mixture and ½ cup cashew rice).

CALORIES 460 (23% from fat); FAT 11.8g (sat 2.5g, mono 6.2g, poly 2.3g); PROTEIN 31.8g; CARB 55.9g; FIBER 3.6g; CHOL 74mg; IRON 4.6mg; SODIUM 787mg; CALC 73mg

Fig and Blue Cheese-Stuffed Pork Tenderloin

An apple glaze and sweet dried figs complement the savory blue cheese in this simple yet refined dish. Serve with wild rice and steamed green beans.

  1 (1-pound) pork tenderloin, trimmed
  ½ cup dried figs, coarsely chopped
  ½ cup crumbled blue cheese
  ½ teaspoon salt
  ½ teaspoon freshly ground black pepper
    Cooking spray
  1 tablespoon apple jelly, melted

1. Preheat oven to 450°.

2. Cut pork in half lengthwise, cutting to, but not through, other side. Open halves, laying pork flat. Place pork between 2 sheets of heavy-duty plastic wrap; pound to ½-inch thickness using a meat mallet or small heavy skillet. Sprinkle figs and blue cheese over pork, leaving a ½-inch margin around edges. Roll up pork, jelly-roll fashion, starting with long side. Secure at 2-inch intervals with twine. Sprinkle pork with salt and pepper, and place on a foil-lined jelly-roll pan coated with cooking spray.

3. Bake at 450° for 20 minutes. Brush jelly over pork. Bake an additional 5 minutes or until a thermometer registers 160° (slightly pink). Let stand 10 minutes. Discard twine; cut pork into 12 (1-inch-thick) slices. Yield: 4 servings (serving size: 3 slices).

CALORIES 274 (30% from fat); FAT 9.2g (sat 4.6g, mono 3g, poly 0.6g); PROTEIN 28.4g; CARB 19.7g; FIBER 2.5g; CHOL 80mg; IRON 1.8mg; SODIUM 581mg; CALC 135mg

Mustard Herb-Crusted Pork Tenderloin

You can serve this comforting classic with a side of mashed potatoes and a vinaigrette-dressed mesclun salad. Substitute Parmigiano-Reggiano for the Romano cheese or try honey mustard in place of Dijon mustard, if you prefer.

  1 (½-ounce) slice white bread
  ¼ cup chopped fresh parsley
  3 tablespoons grated fresh Romano cheese
  2 teaspoons chopped fresh thyme
  1 (1-pound) pork tenderloin, trimmed
  ¼ teaspoon salt
  ⅛ teaspoon freshly ground black pepper
  2 tablespoons Dijon mustard
  ½ teaspoon fennel seeds, crushed
  1 garlic clove, minced
    Cooking spray

1. Preheat oven to 450°.

2. Place bread in a food processor; pulse 10 times or until coarse crumbs measure ¼ cup. Combine breadcrumbs, parsley, cheese, and thyme in a shallow dish. Sprinkle pork with salt and pepper. Combine mustard, fennel seeds, and garlic in a small bowl. Rub pork with mustard mixture; dredge in breadcrumb mixture.

3. Place pork on a jelly-roll pan coated with cooking spray. Bake at 450° for 25 minutes or until a thermometer registers 160° (slightly pink). Let stand 10 minutes. Cut crosswise into ¼-inch-thick slices. Yield: 4 servings (serving size: 3 ounces pork).

CALORIES 184 (30% from fat); FAT 6.2g (sat 2.3g, mono 2.7g, poly 0.4g); PROTEIN 25.8g; CARB 4.6g; FIBER 0.4g; CHOL 72mg; IRON 1.6mg; SODIUM 351mg; CALC 72mg

QUICK & EASY
Pork Fajitas with Mango

  1 tablespoon fresh lime juice
  1 teaspoon ground cumin
  1 (1-pound) pork tenderloin, trimmed and cut into ½-inch strips
    Cooking spray
  2 cups julienne-cut red bell pepper, (about 1 medium)
  2 cups julienne-cut green bell pepper, (about 1 medium)
  1 cup thinly sliced onion
  3 garlic cloves, minced
  1 tablespoon low-sodium soy sauce
  1 teaspoon sugar
  8 (8-inch) low-fat flour tortillas
  1½ cups diced mango (about 1)
  ¼ cup fat-free sour cream

1. Combine juice, cumin, and pork in a medium bowl, tossing well to coat. Let stand 5 minutes.

2. Heat a large nonstick skillet over medium-high heat. Coat pan with cooking spray. Add pork to pan; sauté 4 minutes or until done. Remove from pan.

3. Recoat pan with cooking spray. Add peppers and onion; cook 6 minutes or until tender. Add garlic and pork; cook 1 minute. Add soy sauce and sugar; cook 1 minute. Remove from heat.

4. Warm tortillas according to package directions. Serve pork mixture with tortillas, mango, and sour cream. Yield: 4 servings (serving size: 1½ cups pork mixture, 6 tablespoons mango, 1 tablespoon sour cream, and 2 tortillas).

CALORIES 410 (20% from fat); FAT 9.1g (sat 2.4g, mono 3.8g, poly 1.3g); PROTEIN 30g; CARB 51.6g; FIBER 4.1g; CHOL 76mg; IRON 3.8mg; SODIUM 579mg; CALC 147mg

Spicy Pork Parmesan Cutlets

Serve with angel hair pasta, a tossed green salad, and—if you're having wine—a glass of Italian red.

  1 (1-pound) pork tenderloin, trimmed
  2 tablespoons flour
  ¾ teaspoon salt, divided
  ⅛ teaspoon black pepper
  2 teaspoons olive oil, divided
    Cooking spray
  1 cup vertically sliced onion (about 1 medium)
  3 garlic cloves, thinly sliced
  1 cup tomato-and-basil pasta sauce
  ¼ teaspoon crushed red pepper
  3 tablespoons chopped fresh basil
  2 tablespoons grated Parmesan cheese

1. Preheat oven to 450°.

2. Cut pork crosswise into 12 (1-inch-thick) pieces. Place each piece between 2 sheets of heavy-duty plastic wrap; pound to ¼-inch thickness using a meat mallet or small heavy skillet. Combine flour, ½ teaspoon salt, and black pepper in a shallow dish. Dredge pork in flour mixture. Heat 1 teaspoon oil in a large nonstick skillet over medium-high heat.

Add half of pork; cook 2 minutes on each side or until browned. Remove pork from pan. Repeat with 1 teaspoon oil and remaining pork.

3. Coat pan with cooking spray. Add onion and ¼ teaspoon salt; sauté 2 minutes. Add garlic; sauté 5 minutes or until onions are golden brown. Stir in sauce and red pepper; cook 30 seconds. Remove from heat; stir in basil.

4. Place pork on a jelly-roll pan coated with cooking spray. Top each piece with about 1 tablespoon pasta sauce mixture and ½ teaspoon cheese. Bake at 450° for 5 minutes or until pork is done and cheese is melted. Yield: 4 servings (serving size: 3 cutlets).

CALORIES 227 (30% from fat); FAT 7.5g (sat 2.1g, mono 3.6g, poly 0.7g); PROTEIN 26.8g; CARB 12.6g; FIBER 1.8g; CHOL 76mg; IRON 2.2mg; SODIUM 734mg; CALC 90mg

WINE NOTE: These savory pork cutlets take much of their flavor from the tomato-basil sauce. Tomatoes are, of course, high in acidity, and basil has a distinct herbal tang. Both factors work well with a juicy, medium-bodied Italian red that's not too powerful or tannic. Italian Dolcettos fill the bill perfectly. A delicious wine: Conterno Fantino Dolcetto d'Alba "Bricco Bastia" 2005 ($21).

Pork Schnitzel with Noodles and Browned Cabbage

    4 ounces medium egg noodles
    ¼ cup reduced-fat sour cream
    4 teaspoons canola oil, divided
    6 cups shredded cabbage
    1 cup thinly sliced onion
    1 teaspoon sugar
    1 teaspoon salt, divided
    ¼ teaspoon black pepper, divided
    ⅓ cup fat-free, less-sodium chicken broth
    1 (1-pound) pork tenderloin, trimmed
    ¼ cup all-purpose flour
    3 large egg whites, lightly beaten
    ¾ cup dry breadcrumbs
Cooking spray
Lemon wedges (optional)
Chopped fresh parsley (optional)

1. Cook noodles according to package directions, omitting salt and fat. Drain. Combine noodles and sour cream in a large bowl, tossing well to coat.

2. Heat 1 teaspoon oil in a large nonstick skillet over medium heat. Add cabbage, onion, sugar, ½ teaspoon salt, and ⅛ teaspoon pepper to pan; cook 6 minutes or until cabbage is wilted, stirring occasionally. Add broth; cook 6 minutes or until cabbage is lightly browned. Stir cabbage mixture into noodle mixture. Wipe pan clean with a paper towel.

3. Cut pork crosswise into 12 (1-inch-thick) pieces. Place each piece between 2 sheets of heavy-duty plastic wrap; pound to ¼-inch thickness using a meat mallet or small, heavy skillet. Sprinkle pork evenly with ½ teaspoon salt and ⅛ teaspoon pepper. Place flour in a shallow dish. Place egg whites in a shallow dish. Place breadcrumbs in a shallow dish. Dredge 1 pork cutlet in flour. Dip in egg whites; dredge in breadcrumbs. Repeat with remaining pork, flour, egg whites, and breadcrumbs.

4. Heat 1 teaspoon oil in large nonstick skillet coated with cooking spray over medium heat; add 4 pieces pork to pan. Cook 3 minutes on each side or until pork is lightly browned and done. Remove pork from pan. Repeat procedure twice with 2 teaspoons oil and remaining pork. Serve with cabbage mixture, lemon wedges, and parsley, if desired. Yield: 4 servings (serving size: 3 pork cutlets and 1 cup cabbage mixture).

CALORIES 475 (25% from fat); FAT 13g (sat 3.5g, mono 5.6g, poly 2.8g); PROTEIN 36.8g; CARB 51.9g; FIBER 4.9g; CHOL 105mg; IRON 4.6mg; SODIUM 909mg; CALC 137mg

---

How to Trim Pork Tenderloin

However you prepare pork tenderloin, you'll need to trim off the "silver skin," or thin membrane on the meat's surface. First, slip the tip of a sharp paring or boning knife beneath the silver skin. Slice smoothly along the membrane as you pull it up and away from the meat.

. . . And Ready in Just About 20 Minutes

More than a week's worth of quick entrées to get dinner on the table in a flash.

QUICK & EASY

Mixed Greens Salad with Smoked Trout, Pistachios, and Cranberries

Raspberry vinegar adds a subtle sweetness. Substitute cider vinegar, if necessary.

    2 tablespoons raspberry vinegar
    2 tablespoons fat-free, less-sodium chicken broth
    1 tablespoon honey
    1 teaspoon extravirgin olive oil
    ¼ teaspoon freshly ground black pepper
    ¼ cup dried cranberries
    ⅓ cup (1½ ounces) goat cheese
    8 (½-ounce) slices French bread
    6 cups gourmet salad greens
    1 (7-ounce) smoked rainbow trout
    2 tablespoons dry-roasted pistachios

1. Preheat broiler.

2. Combine first 5 ingredients in a small bowl, stirring with a whisk. Add cranberries; let stand 5 minutes.

3. Spread about 1 teaspoon goat cheese on each bread slice. Arrange bread slices in a single layer on a baking sheet. Broil bread slices 1 minute.

4. Place 1½ cups salad greens on each of 4 plates. Top each serving with 1¾ ounces trout and 1½ teaspoons pistachios. Drizzle about 4 teaspoons dressing over each serving. Place 2 cheese toasts on each plate. Yield: 4 servings.

CALORIES 226 (33% from fat); FAT 9.9g (sat 3g, mono 3.7g, poly 2.2g); PROTEIN 17.4g; CARB 29.2g; FIBER 3.6g; CHOL 44mg; IRON 2.6mg; SODIUM 875mg; CALC 88mg

Chicken Panini with Fig Jam

¼ cup fig jam
1 (8-ounce) ciabatta, sliced horizontally
¼ cup crumbled blue cheese
2 tablespoons butter, softened
8 ounces sliced cooked chicken breast
⅛ teaspoon freshly ground black pepper
2 cups arugula leaves
1 teaspoon fresh lemon juice

1. Spread jam over cut side of top half of bread. Combine cheese and butter in a bowl, stirring until smooth. Spread cheese mixture over cut side of bottom half of bread. Arrange chicken evenly over cheese mixture; sprinkle with pepper. Place top half of bread, jam side down, over chicken.

2. Heat a large nonstick skillet over medium heat, and add sandwich to pan. Place a heavy cast-iron skillet on sandwich; cook 5 minutes or until both sides are browned, turning once.

3. Place arugula in a bowl. Drizzle juice over arugula; toss gently. Remove top bread half from sandwich. Arrange arugula mixture over chicken. Replace top bread half. Cut sandwich into 4 equal portions. Yield: 4 servings (serving size: ¼ sandwich).

CALORIES 381 (30% from fat); FAT 12.7g (sat 6.1g, mono 4.7g, poly 1g); PROTEIN 24.7g; CARB 42.6g; FIBER 1.2g; CHOL 70mg; IRON 2.6mg; SODIUM 591mg; CALC 71mg

Catfish Fajitas

1 pound catfish fillets, cut into 8 strips
2 teaspoons fajita seasoning
2 teaspoons olive oil
1 cup sliced red bell pepper
1 cup sliced green bell pepper
1 cup sliced onion
1 tablespoon chopped pickled jalapeño peppers
1 teaspoon bottled minced garlic
½ cup chopped plum tomato (about 2)
1 tablespoon low-sodium soy sauce
4 (8-inch) fat-free flour tortillas
½ cup bottled pico de gallo

1. Sprinkle both sides of fish evenly with fajita seasoning. Heat oil in a large non-stick skillet over medium-high heat. Add fish to pan; cook 2 minutes on each side or until fish flakes easily when tested with a fork. Remove fish from pan. Add bell peppers and next 3 ingredients to pan; cook 3 minutes, stirring occasionally. Add tomato; cook 2 minutes. Stir in soy sauce; cook 1 minute. Add fish; cook 1 minute or until thoroughly heated. Remove pan from heat.

2. Warm tortillas according to package directions. Spoon about 1 cup fish mixture down center of each tortilla; top each serving with 2 tablespoons pico de gallo. Serve immediately. Yield: 4 servings (serving size: 1 fajita).

CALORIES 334 (30% from fat); FAT 11.3g (sat 2.4g, mono 5.8g, poly 2.2g); PROTEIN 22.7g; CARB 35.3g; FIBER 3.7g; CHOL 53mg; IRON 2.2mg; SODIUM 908mg; CALC 29mg

Artichoke and Arugula Pizza with Prosciutto

Move the oven rack to the lowest level for a crisp crust on the pizza.

Cooking spray
1 tablespoon cornmeal
1 (13.8-ounce) can refrigerated pizza crust dough
2 tablespoons commercial pesto
¾ cup (3 ounces) shredded part-skim mozzarella cheese
1 (9-ounce) package frozen artichoke hearts, thawed and drained
1 ounce thinly sliced prosciutto
2 tablespoons shredded Parmesan cheese
1½ cups arugula leaves
1½ tablespoons fresh lemon juice

1. Position oven rack to lowest setting. Preheat oven to 500°.

2. Coat a baking sheet with cooking spray; sprinkle with cornmeal. Unroll dough onto prepared baking sheet, and pat into a 14 x 10–inch rectangle. Spread pesto evenly over dough, leaving a ½-inch border. Sprinkle mozzarella cheese over pesto. Place baking sheet on bottom oven rack; bake at 500° for 5 minutes. Remove pizza from oven.

3. Coarsely chop artichokes. Arrange artichokes on pizza; top with prosciutto. Sprinkle with Parmesan. Return pizza to bottom oven rack; bake an additional 6 minutes or until crust is browned.

4. Place arugula in a bowl. Drizzle juice over arugula; toss gently. Top pizza with arugula mixture. Cut pizza into 4 (7 x 5–inch) rectangles; cut each rectangle diagonally into 2 wedges. Yield: 4 servings (serving size: 2 wedges).

CALORIES 419 (28% from fat); FAT 13g (sat 4.4g, mono 6.4g, poly 0.6g); PROTEIN 20.1g; CARB 55.3g; FIBER 5.7g; CHOL 20mg; IRON 3.6mg; SODIUM 1,001mg; CALC 265mg

Cannellini-Stuffed Portobello Mushrooms

You can serve this dish with a tossed green salad.

4 (4-inch) portobello caps
Cooking spray
½ cup part-skim ricotta cheese
¼ teaspoon salt
¼ teaspoon garlic powder
¼ teaspoon dried rosemary, crushed
¾ cup bottled pasta sauce
1 (16-ounce) can cannellini beans, rinsed and drained
½ cup (2 ounces) preshredded part-skim mozzarella cheese

1. Preheat broiler.

2. Remove gills from undersides of mushrooms using a spoon; discard gills. Place caps, smooth side up, on a baking sheet coated with cooking spray; broil 2 minutes. Turn caps over; broil 2 minutes.

3. Combine ricotta, salt, garlic powder, and rosemary; stir well. Spread 2 tablespoons cheese mixture in each cap. Spoon 3 tablespoons pasta sauce over cheese mixture in each serving. Divide beans evenly among caps; sprinkle each with 2 tablespoons mozzarella. Broil 3 minutes or until cheese melts. Yield: 4 servings (serving size: 1 stuffed mushroom cap).

CALORIES 187 (29% from fat); FAT 6.1g (sat 3g, mono 1.1g, poly 0.8g); PROTEIN 13g; CARB 20.5g; FIBER 4.9g; CHOL 16mg; IRON 2mg; SODIUM 654mg; CALC 240mg

Scallops in Champagne Sauce

1½ tablespoons olive oil
1½ pounds sea scallops
1 cup sliced shiitake mushroom caps (about 4 ounces)
1½ tablespoons chopped shallots
½ cup Champagne or sparkling wine
1 tablespoon Dijon mustard
¼ teaspoon salt
¼ teaspoon dried tarragon
¼ cup reduced-fat sour cream

1. Heat oil in a large nonstick skillet over medium-high heat. Pat scallops dry with a paper towel. Add scallops to pan; cook 3 minutes on each side or until done. Remove from pan; keep warm.
2. Add mushrooms and shallots to pan; sauté 3 minutes or until liquid evaporates and mushrooms darken. Stir in Champagne, mustard, salt, and tarragon, scraping pan to loosen browned bits. Remove from heat; stir in sour cream. Serve with scallops. Yield: 4 servings (serving size: about 4 ounces scallops and 3 tablespoons sauce).

CALORIES 238 (33% from fat); FAT 8.6g (sat 2g, mono 3.9g, poly 1.1g); PROTEIN 30.3g; CARB 8.1g; FIBER 0.4g; CHOL 64mg; IRON 1.3mg; SODIUM 534mg; CALC 76mg

Balsamic-Plum Glazed Pork Chops

Port wine, plum preserves, and balsamic vinegar combine for the sweet and savory glaze.

1 teaspoon butter
4 (4-ounce) boneless center-cut loin pork chops (about ½ inch thick)
¾ teaspoon salt, divided
¼ teaspoon freshly ground black pepper
Cooking spray
2 tablespoons chopped shallots
1 teaspoon bottled minced garlic
¼ cup port wine
2 tablespoons balsamic vinegar
⅓ cup plum preserves
Chopped fresh parsley (optional)

1. Melt butter in a large nonstick skillet over medium-high heat. Sprinkle pork evenly with ½ teaspoon salt and pepper. Add pork to pan; cook 3½ minutes on each side. Remove from pan.
2. Coat pan with cooking spray. Add shallots and garlic; sauté 30 seconds. Add port and vinegar; cook 30 seconds, stirring occasionally. Stir in ¼ teaspoon salt and plum preserves; cook 30 seconds or until smooth, stirring constantly. Return pork to pan; cook 30 seconds or until desired degree of doneness, turning to coat. Sprinkle with parsley, if desired. Yield: 4 servings (serving size: 1 pork chop and about 1 tablespoon glaze).

CALORIES 281 (30% from fat); FAT 9.5g (sat 3.6g, mono 4.2g, poly 0.6g); PROTEIN 25.3g; CARB 20.5g; FIBER 0.1g; CHOL 71mg; IRON 0.8mg; SODIUM 508mg; CALC 31mg

Black Pepper Citrus Chicken

Be sure to use fresh, coarsely ground black pepper in this dish; finely ground will overpower the chicken.

1 tablespoon canola oil, divided
1¼ teaspoons freshly ground black pepper, divided
¼ teaspoon salt
4 (6-ounce) skinless, boneless chicken breast halves
1 cup vertically sliced onion
2 teaspoons bottled minced garlic
¼ cup white wine
2 tablespoons fresh orange juice
1 tablespoon fresh lemon juice
2 tablespoons chopped fresh parsley

1. Heat 1 teaspoon oil in a large nonstick skillet over medium-high heat. Sprinkle ½ teaspoon pepper and salt over chicken. Add chicken to pan; cook 2 minutes on each side or until browned. Remove chicken from pan; keep warm. Add 2 teaspoons oil to pan. Add onion and garlic to pan; sauté 2 minutes. Add wine; cook 1 minute. Return chicken to pan. Add ¾ teaspoon pepper and juices. Cover, reduce heat, and simmer 4 minutes or until chicken is done. Sprinkle with parsley. Yield: 4 servings (serving size: 1 chicken breast half and 2 tablespoons onion mixture).

CALORIES 240 (22% from fat); FAT 5.9g (sat 0.8g, mono 2.6g, poly 1.5g); PROTEIN 39.6g; CARB 3.8g; FIBER 0.5g; CHOL 99mg; IRON 1.5mg; SODIUM 259mg; CALC 29mg

Black-Eyed Peas and Rice with Andouille Sausage

Corn bread makes a nice accompaniment to round out this one-dish meal. Andouille sausage is a bit spicy. If you prefer a milder flavor, substitute regular chicken, turkey, or pork sausage.

1 (3½-ounce) bag boil-in-bag long-grain rice
1 teaspoon olive oil
½ cup prechopped onion
1 teaspoon bottled minced garlic
½ teaspoon Cajun seasoning
6 ounces chicken andouille sausage, sliced (such as Amy's)
1 cup fat-free, less-sodium chicken broth
1 (15-ounce) can black-eyed peas, rinsed and drained
1 (14.5-ounce) can no-salt-added diced tomatoes, undrained
1 teaspoon hot pepper sauce (such as Tabasco)
½ cup thinly sliced green onions

1. Place rice in an 8-inch square baking dish; cover with water. Microwave at HIGH 6 minutes; drain.
2. Heat oil in a large saucepan over medium heat. Add chopped onion, garlic, and Cajun seasoning to pan, and cook 2 minutes, stirring frequently. Stir in sausage, and cook 1 minute. Add rice, broth, peas, and tomatoes to pan; bring to a boil. Reduce heat, and simmer 4 minutes or until rice is tender. Stir in hot pepper sauce. Ladle about 1¼ cups mixture into each of 4 bowls, and sprinkle each serving with 2 tablespoons green onions. Yield: 4 servings.

CALORIES 251 (18% from fat); FAT 4.9g (sat 1.5g, mono 1.7g, poly 0.8g); PROTEIN 13.4g; CARB 37.7g; FIBER 5g; CHOL 46mg; IRON 3.3mg; SODIUM 714mg; CALC 102mg

Fettuccine Alfredo

Traditionally, this dish includes copious amounts of butter, cheese, and heavy cream.

For this new version—the first in a series of recipes we will revisit in honor of our 20th anniversary—we used butter, which has better flavor than margarine. We replaced fat-free milk with 1% low-fat milk, and used ⅓-less-fat cream cheese instead of light processed cream cheese. Both products offer a smidgen more fat for a big change in texture. The resulting dish rivals its traditional counterpart but still keeps the fat in check.

STAFF FAVORITE
Fettuccine Alfredo

    1   tablespoon butter
    2   garlic cloves, minced
    1   tablespoon all-purpose flour
 1⅓   cups 1% low-fat milk
 1¼   cups (5 ounces) grated fresh
        Parmigiano-Reggiano cheese,
        divided
    2   tablespoons ⅓-less-fat cream cheese
    ½   teaspoon salt
    4   cups hot cooked fettuccine
        (8 ounces uncooked pasta)
    2   teaspoons chopped fresh flat-leaf
        parsley
 Cracked black pepper

1. Melt butter in a medium saucepan over medium heat. Add garlic; cook 1 minute, stirring frequently. Stir in flour. Gradually add milk, stirring with a whisk. Cook 6 minutes or until mixture thickens, stirring constantly. Add 1 cup Parmigiano-Reggiano, cream cheese, and salt, stirring with a whisk until cheeses melt. Toss sauce with pasta. Sprinkle with ¼ cup Parmigiano-Reggiano cheese and parsley. Garnish with black pepper, if desired. Serve immediately. Yield: 4 servings (serving size: 1 cup).

CALORIES 399 (30% from fat); FAT 13.5g (sat 8g, mono 3.4g, poly 1.1g); PROTEIN 21.3g; CARB 48.9g; FIBER 2g; CHOL 34mg; IRON 2.1mg; SODIUM 822mg; CALC 451mg

Better with Butter

It may seem surprising to see *Cooking Light* extolling the virtues of butter. Although made up completely of fat—which accounts for almost all its calories—butter has a place in a healthful diet. This is partly because fat is satisfying, but mostly because when it comes to flavor, there's simply no substitute.

Think of butter as a very concentrated form of milk. About 21 pounds of milk are needed to create each pound of butter. First, fat is skimmed off the milk (that's the cream). Then the cream is churned until the fats and liquids separate to produce a semisolid fat (and that's what we know as butter).

The key to cooking with butter in light recipes is to use techniques that stretch it so you enjoy its benefits. So go ahead and dab some on—just do so sparingly. Your cooking, like butter itself, will be golden.

MAKE AHEAD • FREEZABLE
Sweet Potato Biscuits

Cutting in the butter makes for flaky, delicate biscuits. Be sure to stop cutting in the butter while there are still pebble-sized pieces. If you work it longer, the biscuits will be tough.

    2   cups all-purpose flour (about 9
        ounces)
    1   tablespoon sugar
    2   teaspoons baking powder
    ½   teaspoon salt
    5   tablespoons chilled unsalted
        butter, cut into small pieces
    1   cup pureed cooked sweet potatoes,
        cooled
    ⅓   cup fat-free milk
 Cooking spray

1. Preheat oven to 400°.
2. Lightly spoon flour into dry measuring cups; level with a knife. Combine flour, sugar, baking powder, and salt in a bowl. Cut in butter with a pastry blender or 2 knives until mixture resembles coarse meal. Combine sweet potato and milk in a small bowl; add potato mixture to flour mixture, stirring just until moist.
3. Turn dough out onto a lightly floured surface; knead lightly 5 times. Roll dough to a ¾-inch thickness; cut with a 2-inch biscuit cutter into 10 biscuits. Place biscuits on a baking sheet coated with cooking spray. Gather remaining dough. Roll to a ¾-inch thickness. Cut with a 2-inch biscuit cutter into 6 biscuits. Place biscuits on prepared baking sheet. Discard any remaining scraps.
4. Bake at 400° for 15 minutes or until lightly browned. Remove from pan; cool 5 minutes on wire racks. Serve warm or at room temperature. Yield: 16 servings (serving size: 1 biscuit).

CALORIES 124 (27% from fat); FAT 3.7g (sat 2.3g, mono 0.9g, poly 0.2g); PROTEIN 2.3g; CARB 20.1g; FIBER 1.3g; CHOL 10mg; IRON 1mg; SODIUM 173mg; CALC 47mg

QUICK & EASY • MAKE AHEAD
Maple Butter

Serve this butter chilled, or let it stand at room temperature 20 minutes. It's great with Sweet Potato Biscuits (recipe at left), corn bread, pancakes, or waffles.

    6   tablespoons butter, softened
    3   tablespoons maple syrup
    ⅛   teaspoon salt

1. Combine all ingredients in a small bowl; beat with a mixer at medium speed 1 minute or until smooth. Cover and chill until use. Yield: 24 servings (serving size: 1 teaspoon).

CALORIES 32 (79% from fat); FAT 2.8g (sat 1.8g, mono 0.7g, poly 0.1g); PROTEIN 0g; CARB 1.7g; FIBER 0g; CHOL 8mg; IRON 0mg; SODIUM 33mg; CALC 3mg

Salted vs. Unsalted

The difference between salted and unsalted butter is simple: about 80 milligrams of sodium per tablespoon. Salt acts as a preservative and prolongs the shelf life of butter. Most people use salted butter, and most of our recipes were tested with that variety, but some cooks prefer unsalted butter because it allows them to control the amount of salt in a dish and preserves the mellow sweetness of butter.

If you want unsalted butter, look for the phrase "sweet butter" or "unsalted." The term "sweet cream butter" is used for both salted and unsalted butter.

Butter, Defined

Clarified butter contains no water or milk solids, and can withstand temperatures as high as 400° without burning (regular butter burns at around 250°). To make clarified butter, simply melt butter, and remove the solids. What remains is pure milk fat that can be used to brown meats and seafood or to enrich sauces. Just don't use it as a spread: it's grainy when it cools. **Ghee** is similar to clarified butter, but the butter is browned to develop a nutty taste before the solids are skimmed off. It's popular in Indian cuisine for enriching sauces, finishing soups, or as a general cooking oil.

Storage Savvy

Air and bright light break down fat molecules and eventually turn butter rancid, which is why butter is best stored in cool, dark places—like refrigerators. Since fridge door temperatures vary considerably, skip the butter compartment and store butter near the back. And because butter tends to absorb odors, keep it covered and away from strong-smelling foods. In a cold refrigerator, a stick of salted butter in its original wrapping will keep for about 2 months (the salt acts as a preservative); unsalted butter, for 1½ months. Butter freezes well for up to 6 months.

At room temperature, butter maintains a soft, spreadable consistency. The best way to keep room-temperature butter is in a butter crock. These pots have a bell-shaped top encased by a tall base. Simply pack softened butter into the top, pour water into the base (change the water every few days), and place the top on the base, butter down. The water creates an airtight seal, keeping the butter from spoiling for up to a month.

Expert Opinion

We asked Shirley Corriher, a biochemist and author of *CookWise: The Hows and Whys of Successful Cooking,* to share some of her insights about butter.

Explain why butter tastes so great.
Everything that affects and creates butter's complex flavor is not clearly understood. Research that has been published to date only scratches the surface. This is one reason butter's flavor remains irreplaceable.

My friend Harold McGee (author of *On Food and Cooking*) explains that large compounds like carbohydrates, proteins, or fats are not nearly as flavorful as their smaller components—sugars, amino acids, and fatty acids. It is these small compounds in butter that send our taste receptors zinging.

From a food science standpoint, what makes butter so versatile for baking, sautéing, and enhancing flavors?
Butter is magic for browning. If you brush half of a chicken with oil and half with butter when you roast, the butter half becomes a magnificent rich brown while the oil half stays pale. The browning reaction requires protein and certain sugars, all of which are in butter.

But the marvelous golden brown colors are nothing compared to the flavors of heated butter. Browned butter, butter that is simply heated until it browns, provides a whole other realm of flavors.

For flaky pastry, solid fats are essential. In pastry, cold, firm, flat pieces of butter hold their shape in the hot oven long enough for the dough to begin to set both above and below the butter. It acts as a spacer, and so when the butter melts, steam in the dough puffs the pastry apart where the butter was, creating flakiness.

What kind of butter do you keep on hand for everyday use?
If I am testing recipes for *BakeWise,* my upcoming book, I use butter from the supermarket because I think that is the type of butter that most people will use. For personal use, I like European-style butters and cultured cream, which are quite flavorful and creamy.

How do you use premium butter?
I love popovers, and I feel they deserve the absolute best butter. The taste of real butter also elevates vegetables to extraordinary. I blanch, cool, chill, and reheat them with a little premium butter.

Do you prefer salted or unsalted butter?
I think salted butter tastes better. In baking, sometimes unsalted butter is desirable so that you can control the amount and taste of the salt.

Taste Testing

We sampled a dozen store brand and premium European-style butters side by side in a blind taste testing. Some were salted, others unsalted. We evaluated each based on flavor and texture.

Our unanimous favorite was salted Plugrá, a European-style butter. We preferred its natural, slightly sweet flavor and ultracreamy texture. You will certainly notice its superior flavor if you use it as a spread, to finish sauces, or to make a compound butter.

A close second was Land O' Lakes salted butter, which we routinely use in our Test Kitchens. We liked its flavor, clean finish, and smooth texture.

Eggs Benedict Florentine with Creamy Butter Sauce

Our version of this classic dish features scrambled eggs and sautéed spinach atop Canadian bacon slices and English muffins. It's topped with a creamy sauce that's finished with clarified butter, so it's reminiscent of hollandaise.

SAUCE:
- 1 tablespoon cornstarch
- ½ cup water
- ⅓ cup low-fat buttermilk
- 2 large eggs
- 2 tablespoons Clarified Butter (recipe at right)
- ½ teaspoon salt

EGGS:
- Cooking spray
- ½ teaspoon minced garlic
- ¼ teaspoon salt
- ¼ teaspoon freshly ground black pepper
- 6 large egg whites
- 4 large eggs

REMAINING INGREDIENTS:
- 6 cups fresh spinach, trimmed
- 8 English muffins, split and toasted
- 8 (½-ounce) slices Canadian bacon, each cut in half
- 3 tablespoons chopped fresh chives
- ¼ teaspoon freshly ground black pepper

1. To prepare sauce, place cornstarch in top of a double boiler. Combine ½ cup water, buttermilk, and 2 eggs, stirring well with a whisk. Add egg mixture to cornstarch; stir well. Cook over simmering water until thick and mixture reaches 160° (about 7 minutes), stirring constantly. Stir in Clarified Butter and ½ teaspoon salt. Remove from heat. Cover and keep warm.
2. To prepare eggs, heat a large nonstick skillet over medium heat. Coat pan with cooking spray. Add garlic to pan; cook 30 seconds, stirring frequently. Combine ¼ teaspoon salt, ¼ teaspoon pepper, egg whites, and 4 eggs, stirring well with a whisk. Add egg mixture to pan; cook 5 minutes or until set, stirring occasionally.

3. Place spinach in a large nonstick skillet over medium-high heat; cook 4 minutes or just until slightly wilted, stirring frequently. Place 2 muffin halves, cut sides up, on each of 8 plates. Place half a Canadian bacon slice on each muffin half, and top each serving with about ¼ cup spinach, about ¼ cup egg mixture, and about 2 tablespoons sauce. Sprinkle evenly with chives and ¼ teaspoon pepper. Serve immediately. Yield: 8 servings.

[Totals include Clarified Butter] CALORIES 264 (30% from fat); FAT 8.8g (sat 3.6g, mono 3g, poly 1.2g); PROTEIN 16.4g; CARB 29.9g; FIBER 0.4g; CHOL 174mg; IRON 3.7mg; SODIUM 714mg; CALC 155mg

Linguine with Spicy Crawfish Butter

The crawfish butter would also be good served over sautéed fish.

- 1 pound linguine
- Cooking spray
- ½ cup finely chopped onion
- 1 tablespoon Cajun seasoning
- ½ teaspoon ground red pepper
- ¼ teaspoon salt
- 3 garlic cloves, minced
- 7 tablespoons butter, softened
- 10 ounces frozen cooked peeled and deveined crawfish tail meat, thawed, rinsed, drained, and finely chopped
- ¼ cup chopped fresh flat-leaf parsley

1. Cook pasta according to package directions, omitting salt and fat. Drain.
2. Heat a small skillet over medium-high heat. Coat pan with cooking spray. Add onion to pan; sauté 3 minutes. Add Cajun seasoning, red pepper, salt, and garlic to pan; sauté 1 minute, and transfer to a large bowl. Add butter and crawfish to bowl; stir well to combine. Add hot pasta and parsley; toss well. Serve immediately. Yield: 8 servings (serving size: 1¼ cups).

CALORIES 327 (31% from fat); FAT 11.1g (sat 6.6g, mono 2.8g, poly 1g); PROTEIN 13.3g; CARB 43.8g; FIBER 2.1g; CHOL 64mg; IRON 2.2mg; SODIUM 373mg; CALC 29mg

Yukon Gold Potatoes Sautéed in Clarified Butter

Clarified butter flavors these potatoes and helps them turn an attractive golden brown color as they cook.

- 3 pounds Yukon gold potatoes, peeled and cut into 1½-inch pieces
- ¼ cup Clarified Butter (recipe below)
- 2 tablespoons chopped fresh flat-leaf parsley
- ½ teaspoon salt
- ¼ teaspoon freshly ground black pepper
- 1 garlic clove, minced

1. Place potatoes in a saucepan; cover with water. Bring to a boil. Reduce heat; simmer 2 minutes. Drain and let stand 2 minutes.
2. Heat Clarified Butter in a large nonstick skillet over medium-high heat. Add potatoes to pan; reduce heat to medium, and cook 20 minutes or until tender and browned, stirring occasionally. Stir in parsley and remaining ingredients; cook 30 seconds. Yield: 8 servings (serving size: about 1 cup).

[Totals include Clarified Butter] CALORIES 197 (29% from fat); FAT 6.4g (sat 4g, mono 1.8g, poly 0.2g); PROTEIN 4.1g; CARB 30.2g; FIBER 2.1g; CHOL 16mg; IRON 1.5mg; SODIUM 158mg; CALC 2mg

Clarified Butter

- ½ cup butter

1. Place butter in a medium saucepan over medium-low heat; cook 5 minutes or until completely melted. Skim solids off top with a spoon; discard solids. Slowly pour remaining butter out of pan, leaving remaining solids in pan; discard solids. Yield: about ⅓ cup (serving size: 1 teaspoon).

CALORIES 37 (100% from fat); FAT 4g (sat 2.6g, mono 1.2g, poly 0.2g); PROTEIN 0g; CARB 0g; FIBER 0g; CHOL 11mg; IRON 0mg; SODIUM 0mg; CALC 0mg

Dal with Ghee, Cumin, and Mustard Seeds

DAL:

3½ tablespoons Ghee, divided
1 cup finely chopped onion (about 1 medium)
¾ cup diced carrot (about 1 large)
1 tablespoon minced garlic (about 2 large cloves)
4 cups fat-free, less-sodium chicken broth
1 cup water
¼ cup finely chopped seeded jalapeño pepper (about 2)
1 tablespoon grated fresh ginger
2 teaspoons ground turmeric
2 teaspoons ground coriander
¾ teaspoon salt
1 pound yellow split peas
2 teaspoons brown mustard seeds
2 teaspoons cumin seeds

1. Heat 1½ teaspoons Ghee in a large saucepan over medium heat. Add onion, carrot, and garlic; cook 5 minutes. Stir in broth and next 7 ingredients; bring to a boil. Cover, reduce heat, and simmer 1 hour, stirring occasionally.
2. Place mustard and cumin seeds in a large nonstick skillet over medium heat; cook 1 minute or until toasted. Add 3 tablespoons Ghee; cook 1 minute or until seeds begin to pop. Stir into soup; serve immediately. Yield: 6 servings (serving size: about 1 cup).

[Totals include Ghee] CALORIES 387 (19% from fat); FAT 8.3g (sat 4.7g, mono 2.4g, poly 0.4g); PROTEIN 22.9g; CARB 57.7g; FIBER 2.4g; CHOL 19mg; IRON 4.2mg; SODIUM 567mg; CALC 41mg

GHEE:

½ cup butter

1. Place butter in a medium saucepan over medium-low heat. Cook 20 minutes or until solids have turned a nut brown, stirring occasionally. Skim solids from surface of melted butter; discard solids. Slowly pour butter out of pan, leaving solids in pan; discard solids. Yield: 6 tablespoons (serving size: 1 teaspoon).

CALORIES 37 (100% from fat); FAT 4.2g (sat 2.6g, mono 1.2g, poly 0.2g); PROTEIN 0g; CARB 0g; FIBER 0g; CHOL 11mg; IRON 0mg; SODIUM 0mg; CALC 0mg

---

Sole with Tarragon-Butter Sauce

4 (6-ounce) sole fillets
½ teaspoon salt, divided
¼ teaspoon freshly ground black pepper
Cooking spray
¾ cup dry white wine
¾ cup fat-free, less-sodium chicken broth
⅓ cup finely chopped shallots
1 tablespoon minced fresh garlic
5 teaspoons butter, cut into small pieces
1 tablespoon chopped fresh chives
1½ teaspoons chopped fresh tarragon

1. Sprinkle fish with ¼ teaspoon salt and pepper. Heat a large nonstick skillet over medium-high heat. Coat pan with cooking spray. Add 2 fish fillets to pan; cook 2 minutes on each side or until fish flakes easily when tested with a fork or until desired degree of doneness. Remove from pan; cover and keep warm. Repeat with remaining fish.
2. Add wine, broth, shallots, and garlic to pan; bring to a boil. Reduce heat, and simmer until reduced to about ½ cup

(about 10 minutes). Remove from heat; stir in ¼ teaspoon salt, butter, chives, and tarragon. Spoon sauce over fish; serve immediately. Yield: 4 servings (serving size: 1 fish fillet and 3 tablespoons sauce).

CALORIES 197 (30% from fat); FAT 6.6g (sat 3.4g, mono 1.6g, poly 1g); PROTEIN 29.4g; CARB 3.4g; FIBER 0.4g; CHOL 92mg; IRON 0.8mg; SODIUM 528mg; CALC 38mg

---

Chicken Kiev

3½ tablespoons butter, softened and divided
1 teaspoon finely chopped fresh dill
¾ teaspoon salt, divided
¼ teaspoon freshly ground black pepper
1 garlic clove, minced
4 (6-ounce) skinless, boneless chicken breast halves
2 tablespoons water
2 large egg whites
4½ (1-ounce) slices white bread
Cooking spray
1½ pounds baking potatoes, cut lengthwise into ¼-inch-thick wedges

1. Combine 2 tablespoons butter, dill, ⅛ teaspoon salt, pepper, and garlic in a small bowl, stirring well. Chill 1 hour.
2. Slice chicken breast halves lengthwise, cutting to, but not through, other side. Open halves, laying chicken flat. Place each chicken breast half between two sheets of plastic wrap; pound to ¼-inch thickness using a meat mallet or small heavy skillet.
3. Place about 1½ teaspoons butter mixture on small end of each chicken breast half, and roll up jelly-roll fashion. Tuck in sides, and secure each roll with wooden picks. Sprinkle chicken evenly with ½ teaspoon salt.
4. Combine 2 tablespoons water and egg whites in a shallow dish, stirring with a whisk. Place bread in a food processor; pulse 10 times or until coarse crumbs measure 3 cups. Microwave 2½ teaspoons butter at HIGH 15 seconds or until melted. Combine melted butter and
Continued

breadcrumbs in a shallow dish; toss well. Dip 1 chicken breast half in egg white mixture; dredge in breadcrumb mixture. Dip chicken breast half in egg white mixture again; dredge in breadcrumb mixture again. Repeat procedure with remaining chicken breast halves, egg white mixture, and breadcrumb mixture. Place chicken breast halves, seam sides down, in a jelly-roll pan coated with cooking spray. Cover and refrigerate 1 hour.

5. Preheat oven to 425°.

6. Bake chicken at 425° for 35 minutes or until chicken is done. Remove wooden picks before serving.

7. Place potatoes on a baking sheet coated with cooking spray; coat potatoes with cooking spray. Sprinkle potatoes with ⅛ teaspoon salt; toss. Bake at 425° for 40 minutes or until tender, turning once after 30 minutes. Transfer potatoes to a bowl, and toss with 2 teaspoons butter. Serve with chicken. Yield: 4 servings (serving size: 1 chicken breast half and about 1 cup potatoes).

CALORIES 413 (29% from fat); FAT 13.2g (sat 6.9g, mono 3.1g, poly 1.4g); PROTEIN 48.4g; CARB 23.4g; FIBER 4.7g; CHOL 125mg; IRON 3.5mg; SODIUM 856mg; CALC 77mg

---

MAKE AHEAD
Butterscotch Blondies
(pictured on page 226)

2   cups all-purpose flour (about 9 ounces)
2½ cups packed light brown sugar
2   teaspoons baking powder
½   teaspoon salt
10 tablespoons unsalted butter
¾   cup egg substitute
Cooking spray

1. Preheat oven to 350°.

2. Lightly spoon flour into dry measuring cups; level with a knife. Combine flour, sugar, baking powder, and salt in a large bowl.

3. Place butter in a small skillet over medium heat. Cook 6 minutes or until lightly browned, stirring occasionally. Pour into a small bowl, and cool 10 minutes. Combine butter and egg substitute,

stirring with a whisk. Pour butter mixture over flour mixture; stir just until moistened. Spoon batter into a 13 x 9–inch baking pan coated with cooking spray; smooth top with a spatula. Bake at 350° for 30 minutes or until a wooden pick inserted in center comes out clean. Cool in pan on a wire rack. Cut into 48 squares. Yield: 24 servings (serving size: 2 squares).

CALORIES 170 (25% from fat); FAT 4.8g (sat 3g, mono 1.2g, poly 0.2g); PROTEIN 1.9g; CARB 30.5g; FIBER 0.3g; CHOL 13mg; IRON 1.1mg; SODIUM 108mg; CALC 45mg

---

MAKE AHEAD
Cinnamon-Apple Cake

1¾ cups sugar, divided
¾   cup (6 ounces) block-style fat-free cream cheese, softened
½   cup butter, softened
1   teaspoon vanilla extract
2   large eggs
1½ cups all-purpose flour (about 6¾ ounces)
1½ teaspoons baking powder
¼   teaspoon salt
1   teaspoon ground cinnamon
3   cups chopped peeled Braeburn apple (about 2 large)
Cooking spray

1. Preheat oven to 350°.

2. Place 1½ cups sugar, cream cheese, butter, and vanilla in a large bowl; beat with a mixer at medium speed until well blended (about 4 minutes). Add eggs, 1 at a time, beating well after each addition. Lightly spoon flour into dry measuring cups; level with a knife. Combine flour, baking powder, and salt, stirring with a whisk. Add flour mixture to cream cheese mixture, beating at low speed until well blended.

3. Combine ¼ cup sugar and 1 teaspoon cinnamon. Combine 2 tablespoons cinnamon mixture and chopped apple in a bowl, and stir apple mixture into batter. Pour batter into a 9-inch springform pan coated with cooking spray. Sprinkle with remaining cinnamon mixture. Bake at 350° for 1 hour or until cake pulls away from sides of pan. Cool cake completely on a wire rack. Cut into 12 wedges, using

a serrated knife. Yield: 12 servings (serving size: 1 slice).

CALORIES 282 (28% from fat); FAT 8.7g (sat 5.2g, mono 2g, poly 0.4g); PROTEIN 4.8g; CARB 47.3g; FIBER 1.4g; CHOL 57mg; IRON 1.1mg; SODIUM 252mg; CALC 73mg

---

Polenta with Browned Butter and Mushroom Sauce

4   cups water
½   teaspoon salt
1   cup dry polenta
3   tablespoons butter, divided
¼   cup finely chopped shallots
1   (8-ounce) package presliced cremini mushrooms
1½ cups fat-free, less-sodium chicken broth
1   tablespoon fresh lemon juice
1½ teaspoons cornstarch
2   tablespoons finely chopped fresh chives
Chopped fresh chives (optional)

1. Combine 4 cups water and salt in a large saucepan over medium-high heat; bring to a boil. Gradually add polenta, stirring constantly with a whisk. Reduce heat, and cook 8 minutes or until thick, stirring frequently. Remove from heat. Add 1 tablespoon butter; stir until butter melts. Keep warm.

2. Melt 2 tablespoons butter in a large skillet over medium heat; cook 3 minutes or until lightly browned, stirring occasionally. Add shallots to pan, and cook 2 minutes or until browned, stirring frequently. Add mushrooms; cook 4 minutes or until lightly browned, stirring frequently. Combine broth, juice, and cornstarch in a small bowl, stirring until smooth. Stir broth mixture into mushroom mixture, and bring to a boil. Cook 1 minute, stirring constantly. Remove from heat, and stir in 2 tablespoons chives.

3. Place about ⅓ cup polenta in each of 8 bowls; top each serving with about ¼ cup mushroom mixture. Sprinkle each serving with chives, if desired. Yield: 8 servings.

CALORIES 136 (29% from fat); FAT 4.4g (sat 2.7g, mono 1.1g, poly 0.2g); PROTEIN 3.5g; CARB 21.3g; FIBER 2.6g; CHOL 11mg; IRON 0.7mg; SODIUM 253mg; CALC 19mg

Superfast Suppers

Here are our secrets for cooking a satisfying meal in 20 minutes or less.

So what are the secrets to success? We start with fresh, quick-cooking protein, such as fish fillets, pork chops, lamb chops, sausages, ground beef, chicken breast halves, or turkey cutlets. Then we often combine convenience products with a few fresh ingredients to brighten the result. Finally, we employ quick cooking methods, such as sautéing (cooking quickly over medium-high heat) or broiling, and pair the dishes with simple accompaniments to round out the meal.

QUICK & EASY
Spicy Honey-Brushed Chicken Thighs

Skinless, boneless thighs cook quickly and are more flavorful than white meat, so they need fewer ingredients.

- 2 teaspoons garlic powder
- 2 teaspoons chili powder
- 1 teaspoon salt
- 1 teaspoon ground cumin
- 1 teaspoon paprika
- ½ teaspoon ground red pepper
- 8 skinless, boneless chicken thighs
- Cooking spray
- 6 tablespoons honey
- 2 teaspoons cider vinegar

1. Preheat broiler.
2. Combine first 6 ingredients in a large bowl. Add chicken to bowl; toss to coat. Place chicken on a broiler pan coated with cooking spray. Broil chicken 5 minutes on each side.
3. Combine honey and vinegar in a small bowl, stirring well. Remove chicken from oven; brush ¼ cup honey mixture on chicken. Broil 1 minute. Remove chicken from oven, and turn over. Brush chicken with remaining honey mixture. Broil 1 minute or until chicken is done. Yield: 4 servings (serving size: 2 chicken thighs).

CALORIES 321 (31% from fat); FAT 11g (sat 3g, mono 4.1g, poly 2.5g); PROTEIN 28g; CARB 27.9g; FIBER 0.6g; CHOL 99mg; IRON 2.1mg; SODIUM 676mg; CALC 21mg

QUICK & EASY
Tilapia Piccata

Substitute most any flaky white fish, or use veal or chicken cutlets.

- 8 ounces uncooked orzo (about 1½ cups)
- ¾ cup grape tomatoes, halved
- 3 tablespoons chopped fresh parsley
- ½ teaspoon salt, divided
- ¼ teaspoon black pepper, divided
- 3 tablespoons all-purpose flour
- 4 (6-ounce) tilapia fillets
- 3 tablespoons butter, divided
- ¼ cup white wine
- 3 tablespoons fresh lemon juice
- 1 tablespoon drained capers

1. Cook pasta according to package directions, omitting salt and fat. Drain; stir in tomatoes, parsley, ¼ teaspoon salt, and ⅛ teaspoon pepper. Set aside, and keep warm.
2. Combine ¼ teaspoon salt, ⅛ teaspoon pepper, and flour in a large shallow dish. Dredge fish in flour mixture. Melt 1 tablespoon butter in a large nonstick skillet over medium-high heat. Add fish to pan; cook 1½ minutes on each side or until fish flakes easily when tested with a fork or until desired degree of doneness. Remove fish from pan; keep warm.
3. Add wine, juice, and capers to pan; cook 30 seconds. Remove from heat.

Add 2 tablespoons butter to pan; stir until butter melts. Serve fish with sauce and pasta mixture. Yield: 4 servings (serving size: 1 fillet, ¾ cup pasta mixture and about 1 tablespoon sauce).

CALORIES 461 (24% from fat); FAT 12.5g (sat 6.4g, mono 3.1g, poly 1.1g); PROTEIN 41.7g; CARB 45.3g; FIBER 2.6g; CHOL 108mg; IRON 1.6mg; SODIUM 512mg; CALC 30mg

QUICK & EASY
Chicken, Carrot, and Cucumber Salad

Serve with pita wedges or pita chips. Purchase pita chips or make your own by spraying pita wedges with cooking spray, sprinkling them with a little shredded Parmesan cheese, and baking them at 400° for about 10 minutes.

- 2 cups chopped cooked chicken breast (about 1 pound)
- 1¼ cups chopped seeded cucumber
- ½ cup matchstick-cut carrots
- ½ cup sliced radishes
- ⅓ cup chopped green onions
- ¼ cup light mayonnaise
- 2 tablespoons chopped fresh cilantro
- 1 teaspoon bottled minced garlic
- ¼ teaspoon salt
- ¼ teaspoon ground cumin
- ⅛ teaspoon black pepper
- 4 green leaf lettuce leaves
- 4 (6-inch) whole wheat pitas, each cut into 8 wedges

1. Combine first 5 ingredients in a large bowl. Combine mayonnaise and next 5 ingredients in a small bowl, stirring with a whisk. Add mayonnaise mixture to chicken mixture; stir until combined.
2. Place 1 lettuce leaf on each of 4 plates; top each leaf with about 1 cup chicken mixture. Place 8 pita wedges on each serving. Yield: 4 servings.

CALORIES 382 (25% from fat); FAT 10.4g (sat 2.1g, mono 2.7g, poly 4.3g); PROTEIN 40.7g; CARB 31.4g; FIBER 5.1g; CHOL 102mg; IRON 3mg; SODIUM 621mg; CALC 56mg

Shrimp and Scallop Arrabbiata

Arrabbiata is Italian for "angry" and often refers to the classic combination of tomatoes, pancetta, and hot pepper. Substitute bacon for the pancetta, if you prefer.

- 1 (9-ounce) package fresh linguine
- 2 tablespoons olive oil, divided
- 8 ounces peeled and deveined large shrimp
- 8 ounces bay scallops
- ¼ teaspoon salt
- 1 cup prechopped onion
- 2 teaspoons bottled minced garlic
- ¼ teaspoon fennel seeds, crushed
- ¼ teaspoon crushed red pepper
- 1 ounce pancetta, chopped
- 4 (14.5-ounce) cans organic stewed tomatoes, undrained (such as Muir Glen)
- 3 tablespoons chopped fresh basil

1. Cook pasta according to package directions, omitting salt and fat. Drain. Set aside, and keep warm.
2. Heat 1 tablespoon oil in a large non-stick skillet over medium-high heat. Add shrimp and scallops to pan; sprinkle with salt. Sauté 3 minutes or until almost done. Remove shrimp mixture from pan.
3. Heat 1 tablespoon oil in pan over medium-high heat. Add onion and next 4 ingredients; sauté 1 minute. Stir in tomatoes; bring to a boil. Cook 2 minutes, stirring occasionally. Return shrimp mixture to pan; cook 1 minute or until thoroughly heated. Remove from heat. Serve shrimp mixture over pasta. Sprinkle with basil. Yield: 4 servings (serving size: 1 cup pasta, 2 cups shrimp mixture, and 2 teaspoons basil).

CALORIES 480 (23% from fat); FAT 11.9g (sat 2.2g, mono 5.1g, poly 1.3g); PROTEIN 33.2g; CARB 55.4g; FIBER 5.7g; CHOL 110mg; IRON 4.2mg; SODIUM 718mg; CALC 59mg

Turkish Delight Menu
serves 4

This sandwich and salad combo is quick enough for weeknights.

Superfast Kofte

Couscous salad*

Orange wedges

*Bring 1 cup water to a boil in a medium saucepan; gradually stir in 1 cup couscous. Remove from heat; cover and let stand 5 minutes. Fluff with a fork. Combine couscous, ½ cup sliced radish, ½ cup crumbled feta, ¼ cup chopped red onion, 2 tablespoons chopped fresh parsley, 1 tablespoon chopped fresh mint, 1 tablespoon extravirgin olive oil, 2 teaspoons fresh lemon juice, ¼ teaspoon salt, and ¼ teaspoon freshly ground black pepper; toss gently.

Superfast Kofte

Kofte, Turkish meatballs often grilled on a stick, can be made from ground lamb, beef, or a combination.

- ½ cup prechopped white onion
- ⅓ cup dry breadcrumbs
- ¼ cup chopped fresh mint
- 2 tablespoons tomato paste
- 1 teaspoon bottled minced garlic
- ½ teaspoon salt
- ½ teaspoon ground cumin
- ¼ teaspoon ground cinnamon
- ¼ teaspoon ground red pepper
- ⅛ teaspoon ground allspice
- 1 pound lean ground round
- 1 large egg white, lightly beaten
- Cooking spray
- 8 (¼-inch-thick) slices plum tomato (about 2 tomatoes)
- 4 (6-inch) pitas, cut in half
- ¼ cup plain yogurt

1. Preheat broiler.
2. Combine first 12 ingredients in a large bowl; stir just until combined. Divide mixture into 8 equal portions; shape each portion into a 2-inch patty. Place patties on a jelly-roll pan coated with cooking spray. Broil 4 minutes on each side or until desired degree of doneness. Place 1 tomato slice and 1 patty in each pita half; top each half with 1½ teaspoons yogurt. Yield: 4 servings (serving size: 2 filled pita halves).

CALORIES 423 (24% from fat); FAT 11.4g (sat 4.3g, mono 4.3g, poly 0.9g); PROTEIN 31.6g; CARB 46.7g; FIBER 3.2g; CHOL 75mg; IRON 4.3mg; SODIUM 766mg; CALC 114mg

Thai Chicken Sauté

Use less hot sauce for milder flavor.

- 1 (3½-ounce) bag boil-in-bag rice
- 1½ pounds chicken breast tenders
- 1 tablespoon cornstarch
- 1 tablespoon fish sauce
- 4 teaspoons canola oil, divided
- 1 cup sliced onion
- 2 teaspoons bottled minced garlic
- 1 teaspoon bottled ground fresh ginger (such as Spice World)
- ½ cup light coconut milk
- 2 tablespoons Sriracha (hot chile sauce, such as Huy Fong)
- 1 tablespoon sugar
- 1 tablespoon fresh lime juice
- 2 tablespoons chopped fresh cilantro
- 4 lime wedges

1. Cook rice according to package directions, omitting salt and fat. Keep warm.
2. Toss chicken with cornstarch and fish sauce. Heat 1 tablespoon oil in a large nonstick skillet over medium-high heat. Add chicken to pan; sauté 5 minutes. Remove chicken from pan. Heat 1 teaspoon oil in pan. Add onion, garlic, and ginger; sauté 1 minute. Return chicken to pan; cook 1 minute or until done. Stir in coconut milk, Sriracha, sugar, and juice; cook 45 seconds or until thoroughly heated. Sprinkle each serving with 1½ teaspoons cilantro. Serve chicken mixture over rice with lime wedges. Yield: 4 servings (serving size: 1½ cups chicken mixture, ½ cup rice, and 1 lime wedge).

CALORIES 403 (24% from fat); FAT 10.8g (sat 3.1g, mono 4.3g, poly 2.4g); PROTEIN 42.6g; CARB 31.4g; FIBER 0.5g; CHOL 108mg; IRON 2.4mg; SODIUM 650mg; CALC 32mg

Filet Mignon with Sherry-Mushroom Sauce

  4 (4-ounce) beef tenderloin steaks, trimmed (1 inch thick)
 ½ teaspoon salt
 ¼ teaspoon black pepper
  2 teaspoons butter, divided
1½ cups presliced mushrooms
  2 tablespoons chopped shallots
  1 teaspoon bottled minced garlic
 ½ cup fat-free, less-sodium beef broth
 ¼ cup dry sherry
  2 teaspoons cornstarch
  2 teaspoons water

1. Sprinkle beef with salt and pepper. Melt 1 teaspoon butter in a large non-stick skillet over medium-high heat. Add beef to pan; cook 3½ minutes on each side or until desired degree of doneness. Remove beef from pan; keep warm.
2. Melt 1 teaspoon butter in pan. Add mushrooms, shallots, and garlic; sauté 3 minutes. Stir in broth and sherry. Combine cornstarch and 2 teaspoons water in a bowl, stirring until smooth. Add cornstarch mixture to pan; bring to a boil. Cook 1 minute, stirring constantly. Yield: 4 servings (serving size: 1 steak and about ¼ cup sauce).

CALORIES 219 (43% from fat); FAT 10.5g (sat 4.4g, mono 3.8g, poly 0.4g); PROTEIN 25.3g; CARB 3.3g; FIBER 0.4g; CHOL 76mg; IRON 3.3mg; SODIUM 420mg; CALC 12mg

Peach Spiced Lamb Chops

Use the same glaze for pork chops.

  1 tablespoon brown sugar
  1 teaspoon salt
  1 teaspoon onion powder
  1 teaspoon chili powder
  1 teaspoon paprika
 ½ teaspoon dried oregano
 ¼ teaspoon ground ginger
 ¼ teaspoon ground allspice
 ¼ teaspoon black pepper
  8 (4-ounce) bone-in lamb loin chops, trimmed
     Cooking spray
 ⅓ cup peach preserves

1. Combine first 9 ingredients in a small bowl; rub spice mixture evenly over both sides of lamb chops.
2. Heat a grill pan over medium-high heat. Coat pan with cooking spray. Add chops to pan, and cook 3½ minutes on each side. Brush each chop with about 1 teaspoon preserves. Turn chops over, and cook 1 minute. Brush chops with remaining preserves. Remove from heat. Yield: 4 servings (serving size: 2 chops).

CALORIES 361 (39% from fat); FAT 15.5g (sat 7g, mono 6.2g, poly 0.7g); PROTEIN 32.3g; CARB 21.8g; FIBER 0.4g; CHOL 103mg; IRON 3mg; SODIUM 690mg; CALC 37mg

Fettuccine with Bacon, Peas, and Parmesan

  1 (9-ounce) package fresh fettuccine pasta
  2 slices smoked center-cut bacon
 ½ cup prechopped onion
  2 teaspoons bottled minced garlic
  1 tablespoon chopped fresh thyme
 ½ cup frozen green peas
 ½ cup chopped green onions
 ⅓ cup half-and-half
  2 teaspoons butter
 ½ teaspoon salt
 ⅛ teaspoon black pepper
 ¼ cup shredded Parmesan cheese

1. Cook pasta according to package directions, omitting salt and fat. Drain pasta, reserving ¾ cup cooking liquid.
2. Cook bacon in a large nonstick skillet over medium heat until crisp. Remove bacon from pan, reserving drippings in pan; crumble bacon. Add ½ cup onion, garlic, and thyme to drippings in pan; sauté 2 minutes. Stir in peas; sauté 1 minute. Add green onions; sauté 1½ minutes. Add pasta, reserved cooking liquid, and half-and-half; cook 1 minute or until thoroughly heated, tossing to combine. Remove from heat. Add butter, salt, and pepper to pan; toss until butter melts. Sprinkle with crumbled bacon and Parmesan cheese. Yield: 4 servings (serving size: 1¼ cups).

CALORIES 313 (28% from fat); FAT 9.9g (sat 4.5g, mono 3.8g, poly 0.4g); PROTEIN 14.2g; CARB 43.1g; FIBER 3.7g; CHOL 22mg; IRON 0.7mg; SODIUM 747mg; CALC 145mg

8 Great Kitchen Shortcuts

1. Purchase prepared ingredients such as matchstick-cut carrots, presliced mushrooms, prechopped vegetable mixes, or bagged salad or slaw mixes.

2. Use a food processor to chop onions or shred cabbage.

3. Slice larger cuts of meat like pork tenderloin into medallions or thin strips to shorten cooking times.

4. Choose dual-duty ingredients such as olives, capers, or sun-dried tomatoes. Capers, for example, impart acid and a briny saltiness, allowing you to use fewer ingredients to achieve robust results.

5. Gather all the ingredients before you begin to cook.

6. Bring water to a boil more quickly by preheating the pan on the stove, starting with hot tap water, and covering the pot until the water reaches the boiling point.

7. While you wait for the oven to preheat or water to boil, prep the ingredients.

8. Pay a little extra at the fish counter to have your shrimp peeled and deveined.

Speedy Sides

When it comes to rounding out your plate, reach for wholesome, satisfying options. Our short list represents the choices we turn to time and again:
• Frozen mashed potatoes
• Refrigerated mashed sweet potatoes
• Presliced refrigerated potato wedges
• Fresh pasta
• Boil-in-bag rice
• Couscous
• Quick-cooking grits or polenta
• Bulgur
• Rice sticks or cellophane noodles
• Quick-cooking fresh vegetables such as green beans, zucchini, etc.

Shrimp Chalupa with Mango Salsa

This is our version of a Mexican dish in which tortilla dough is shaped like a boat and fried until crisp; in fact, *chalupa* means "boat" in Spanish. Regular chili powder is a blend that tastes mostly of cumin. Chipotle chile powder is pure ground dried chiles, and it packs a hot punch. For more heat use all chipotle powder, or tame the spice by substituting all chili powder.

1 cup chopped peeled mango
3 tablespoons prechopped red onion
2 tablespoons chopped fresh cilantro
1 tablespoon fresh lime juice
¾ teaspoon salt, divided
½ teaspoon chili powder
¼ teaspoon chipotle chile powder
32 large peeled, deveined shrimp (about 1¼ pounds)
1½ tablespoons olive oil, divided
8 (6-inch) corn tortillas

1. Combine first 4 ingredients in a bowl, and stir in ¼ teaspoon salt. Set aside.
2. Combine ½ teaspoon salt, chili powder, chipotle powder, and shrimp in a large bowl. Heat 1½ teaspoons oil in a large nonstick skillet over medium-high heat. Add shrimp to pan; cook 2 minutes on each side or until shrimp are done. Remove shrimp from pan; keep warm.
3. Wipe pan clean with a paper towel. Return pan to heat; add 1 teaspoon oil. Place 3 tortillas in pan; cook 30 seconds on each side or until tortillas puff slightly. Repeat procedure with 2 teaspoons oil and remaining tortillas.
4. Place 2 tortillas on each of 4 plates, and arrange 4 shrimp on each tortilla. Top each with about 2 tablespoons mango mixture, and serve immediately. Yield: 4 servings (serving size: 2 chalupas).

CALORIES 215 (30% from fat); FAT 7.2g (sat 0.9g, mono 3.9g, poly 1.4g); PROTEIN 13.7g; CARB 26.6g; FIBER 2.9g; CHOL 85mg; IRON 1.5mg; SODIUM 542mg; CALC 56mg

Sausage and Spinach Soup

Fresh herbs are added after the soup cooks so they'll retain their bright color and flavor. You can substitute 1 teaspoon dried herbs for each tablespoon fresh, but add them with the tomatoes. Serve with a toasted baguette.

10 ounces sweet turkey Italian sausage
Cooking spray
1 cup prechopped onion
2 teaspoons bottled minced garlic
½ cup water
1 (15-ounce) can cannellini beans, rinsed and drained
1 (14.5-ounce) can organic stewed tomatoes, undrained (such as Muir Glen)
1 (14-ounce) can fat-free, less-sodium chicken broth
2 cups baby spinach
1 tablespoon chopped fresh basil
2 teaspoons chopped fresh oregano
2 tablespoons grated fresh Romano cheese

1. Remove casings from sausage. Cook sausage in a large saucepan coated with cooking spray over high heat until browned, stirring to crumble. Add onion and garlic to pan; cook 2 minutes. Stir in ½ cup water, beans, tomatoes, and broth. Cover and bring to a boil. Uncover and cook 3 minutes or until slightly thick. Remove from heat, and stir in spinach, basil, and oregano. Ladle 1½ cups soup into each of 4 bowls, and sprinkle each serving with 1½ teaspoons cheese. Yield: 4 servings.

CALORIES 261 (30% from fat); FAT 8.6g (sat 2.8g, mono 2.7g, poly 2.5g); PROTEIN 20.9g; CARB 23.1g; FIBER 5.4g; CHOL 62mg; IRON 3.4mg; SODIUM 842mg; CALC 105mg

WINE NOTE: This delicious soup needs a wine that's crisp and medium-bodied, such as a California pinot gris (pinot grigio). The wine's crispness balances the richness of the sausage and the density of the beans. At the same time, the wine's body is substantial enough to stand up to the weight of those ingredients. Try Morgan Pinot Gris "R & D Franscioni Vineyard" 2006 (Santa Lucia Highlands, California), $18.

kitchen strategies
Cooking for a Picky Eater

Problem: California mom wants healthful recipes that will appeal to her finicky husband. Strategy: Fresh new dishes will broaden his palate.

Julie Mann, 40, of Berkeley, California, is an adventurous eater, but her husband, Aaron, 46, is more particular. He's comfortable with meat and potatoes, and though he enjoys avocados and corn, he picks around most other produce. Yet, he and Julie are both committed to nurturing an appreciation of healthful food in their daughter Ivy, 3.

We probed Aaron's specific likes and dislikes to create dishes the whole family will enjoy and develop guidelines Julie can use to expand her culinary repertoire. Much of what we learned from working with Aaron can apply to anyone who cooks for a finicky diner.

Broccoli with Red Pepper Flakes and Toasted Garlic
(pictured on page 228)

The bold, straightforward flavors of garlic and crushed red pepper make this classic Mediterranean broccoli dish appealing.

2 teaspoons olive oil
6 cups broccoli florets (about 1 head)
¼ teaspoon kosher salt
¼ teaspoon crushed red pepper
3 garlic cloves, thinly sliced
¼ cup water

1. Heat oil in a large nonstick skillet over medium-high heat. Add broccoli and next 3 ingredients. Sauté 2 minutes. Add ¼ cup water. Cover, reduce heat to low, and cook 2 minutes or until broccoli is crisp-tender. Yield: 4 servings (serving size: 1 cup).

CALORIES 53 (46% from fat); FAT 2.7g (sat 0.4g, mono 1.7g, poly 0.4g); PROTEIN 3.3g; CARB 6.4g; FIBER 3.2g; CHOL 0mg; IRON 1mg; SODIUM 147mg; CALC 55mg

Parmesan Chicken Paillards with Cherry Tomato Sauce

Paillards are boneless, skinless chicken breasts pounded flat and sautéed. A crust of Parmesan adds flavor.

4   (6-ounce) skinless, boneless chicken breast halves
½   teaspoon kosher salt, divided
½   teaspoon freshly ground black pepper, divided
¼   cup grated Parmesan cheese
1   tablespoon all-purpose flour
2   teaspoons olive oil, divided
Cooking spray
½   cup finely chopped onion
¼   cup fat-free, less-sodium chicken broth
1   tablespoon sherry vinegar
2   cups quartered cherry tomatoes
½   teaspoon dried oregano

1. Place each chicken breast half between 2 sheets of heavy-duty plastic wrap; pound to ½-inch thickness using a meat mallet or small heavy skillet. Sprinkle chicken with ¼ teaspoon salt and ¼ teaspoon pepper. Combine cheese and flour in a shallow dish. Dredge 1 side of each chicken breast half in cheese mixture.
2. Heat 1 teaspoon oil in a large nonstick skillet over medium-high heat. Add 2 chicken breast halves, cheese side down; cook 4 minutes on each side or until done. Repeat procedure with 1 teaspoon oil and remaining chicken breast halves. Remove from pan; keep warm.
3. Coat pan with cooking spray. Add onion; sauté 2 minutes. Stir in broth and vinegar; cook 1 minute or until liquid almost evaporates. Add tomatoes, oregano, ¼ teaspoon salt, and ¼ teaspoon pepper; cook 2 minutes. Yield: 4 servings (serving size: 1 chicken breast half and about ⅓ cup tomato mixture).

CALORIES 264 (20% from fat); FAT 5.9g (sat 1.8g, mono 2.6g, poly 0.9g); PROTEIN 42.6g; CARB 7.4g; FIBER 1.3g; CHOL 102mg; IRON 1.6mg; SODIUM 504mg; CALC 95mg

WINE NOTE: Try this recipe with the incredible Marchesi di Frescobaldi "Campo ai Sassi" Rosso di Montalcino 2004 (Montalcino, Tuscany, Italy), $20.

Penne with Pancetta, Spinach, and Buttery Crumb Topping

(pictured on page 228)

Pancetta is cured pork, similar in taste to bacon. The pancetta and cheesy sauce make this pasta dish a good vehicle for spinach. Serve with salad.

8   ounces French bread
Cooking spray
¾   cup (3 ounces) chopped pancetta
¾   cup chopped onion
2   teaspoons minced garlic
⅓   cup all-purpose flour (about 1½ ounces)
3¾ cups 2% reduced-fat milk, divided
¼   cup half-and-half
6   cups chopped fresh spinach
½   cup (2 ounces) grated fresh Parmigiano-Reggiano cheese
1¼ teaspoons salt
½   teaspoon black pepper
8   cups hot cooked penne (about 1 pound uncooked tube-shaped pasta)
¼   cup butter, melted

1. Preheat oven to 425°.
2. Place bread in a food processor; pulse 10 times or until coarse crumbs measure 4 cups; set aside.
3. Heat a large nonstick saucepan over medium-high heat. Coat with cooking spray. Add pancetta, onion, and garlic; sauté 5 minutes or until onion is tender. Lightly spoon flour into a dry measuring cup; level with a knife. Place flour in a small bowl; gradually add ¾ cup milk, stirring until smooth. Add flour mixture, 3 cups milk, and half-and-half to pan; bring to a boil, stirring constantly. Reduce heat, and simmer 2 minutes or until thick, stirring constantly. Add spinach; cook 1 minute. Remove from heat. Stir in cheese, salt, and pepper, stirring until cheese melts.
4. Place pasta in a large bowl. Add spinach mixture to pasta; toss well. Spoon mixture into a 13 x 9–inch baking dish coated with cooking spray. Combine breadcrumbs and butter; toss well. Sprinkle over pasta mixture.

5. Bake at 425° for 6 minutes or until crumbs are lightly browned. Yield: 8 servings (serving size: 1½ cups).

CALORIES 505 (29% from fat); FAT 16.1g (sat 7.9g, mono 5.6g, poly 1.6g); PROTEIN 19.5g; CARB 70.8g; FIBER 3.8g; CHOL 37mg; IRON 3.6mg; SODIUM 893mg; CALC 157mg

BLT Bread Salad

Substitute avocado for the tomatoes or add grilled chicken to make it an entrée.

⅓   cup nonfat buttermilk
2   tablespoons reduced-fat mayonnaise
2   teaspoons extravirgin olive oil
1   teaspoon white wine vinegar
1   teaspoon Dijon mustard
½   teaspoon freshly ground black pepper
⅛   teaspoon kosher salt
⅛   teaspoon ground red pepper
2   garlic cloves, minced
3   slices center-cut bacon
4   cups chopped plum tomato (about 6)
4   cups (1-inch) cubed Italian bread, toasted
3   cups torn romaine lettuce
1   cup vertically sliced onion

1. Combine first 9 ingredients in a large bowl, stirring with a whisk. Set aside.
2. Cook bacon in a large nonstick skillet over medium heat until crisp. Remove bacon from pan, reserving 2 teaspoons drippings. Crumble bacon, and set aside. Add reserved drippings to bowl; stir with a whisk. Add bacon and remaining ingredients; toss well. Yield: 4 servings (serving size: about 1½ cups).

CALORIES 247 (33% from fat); FAT 9.1g (sat 2.3g, mono 3.8g, poly 1.8g); PROTEIN 7.9g; CARB 34.8g; FIBER 3.7g; CHOL 7mg; IRON 2.3mg; SODIUM 517mg; CALC 111mg

Creole Shrimp Rémoulade over Baby Arugula

Rémoulade is a French condiment reminiscent of tartar sauce.

SHRIMP:

- 4 cups water
- 3 tablespoons ground red pepper
- 1 teaspoon mustard seeds
- 1 teaspoon dried thyme
- ¼ teaspoon kosher salt
- 1 bay leaf
- 1 pound medium shrimp, peeled and deveined

SAUCE:

- ¼ cup thinly sliced green onions
- 2 tablespoons finely chopped sweet onion
- 2 tablespoons reduced-fat mayonnaise
- 1 tablespoon Creole mustard
- 1 tablespoon ketchup
- 1 teaspoon white wine vinegar
- 1 teaspoon olive oil
- ½ teaspoon Worcestershire sauce
- ½ teaspoon hot sauce
- ⅛ teaspoon kosher salt

REMAINING INGREDIENT:

- 4 cups baby arugula

1. To prepare shrimp, combine first 6 ingredients in a large saucepan; bring to a boil. Add shrimp; cook 2 minutes. Drain, and rinse with cold water until cool. Drain; discard bay leaf.
2. To prepare sauce, combine green onions and next 9 ingredients in a large bowl; add shrimp, tossing to coat. Cover; chill 20 minutes. Arrange 1 cup arugula on each of 4 salad plates; top each serving with ½ cup shrimp mixture. Yield: 4 servings.

CALORIES 160 (24% from fat); FAT 4.3g (sat 0.8g, mono 1.2g, poly 1g); PROTEIN 23.8g; CARB 5.7g; FIBER 0.7g; CHOL 172mg; IRON 3.2mg; SODIUM 448mg; CALC 99mg

Roasted Cauliflower with Brown Butter

Roasted cauliflower has a savory caramelized crust and is tender and creamy inside. The roasting process coaxes maximum flavor from the cauliflower.

- 6 cups cauliflower florets (about 1 head)
- Cooking spray
- ¼ teaspoon salt
- ¼ teaspoon black pepper
- 2 teaspoons butter

1. Preheat oven to 400°.
2. Arrange cauliflower in a single layer on a baking sheet coated with cooking spray. Coat cauliflower florets with cooking spray; sprinkle with salt and pepper. Bake at 400° for 25 minutes, turning cauliflower twice.
3. Melt butter in a small skillet over medium heat; cook 3 minutes or until lightly browned. Combine cauliflower and browned butter in a bowl, and toss gently to coat. Yield: 4 servings (serving size: 1 cup).

CALORIES 53 (37% from fat); FAT 2.2g (sat 1.2g, mono 0.5g, poly 0.1g); PROTEIN 3g; CARB 7.5g; FIBER 1.3g; CHOL 5mg; IRON 0.9mg; SODIUM 183mg; CALC 45mg

Moo Shu Shrimp

This dish combines some of the ingredients for vegetable spring rolls with the assembly procedure for tacos.

- 2 teaspoons peanut oil, divided
- 1 tablespoon minced garlic, divided
- 1 pound small shrimp, peeled and deveined
- 2 cups thinly sliced mushrooms
- 1 cup shredded carrot
- ½ cup chopped green onions
- 6 cups Napa cabbage, shredded
- 2 tablespoons low-sodium soy sauce
- 1 tablespoon water
- 2 teaspoons cornstarch
- 1 teaspoon Sriracha (hot chile sauce, such as Huy Fong)
- 2 tablespoons hoisin sauce
- 8 (6-inch) flour tortillas

1. Heat 1 teaspoon oil in a large skillet over high heat. Add 1½ teaspoons garlic and shrimp; stir-fry 3 minutes or until shrimp are done. Remove shrimp from pan; keep warm.
2. Add 1 teaspoon oil to pan. Add 1½ teaspoons garlic and mushrooms; stir-fry 1 minute or until mushrooms are tender. Add carrot and onions; stir-fry 2 minutes. Stir in cabbage; cook 2 minutes or until wilted.
3. Combine soy sauce, 1 tablespoon water, cornstarch, and Sriracha in a small bowl, stirring with a whisk. Stir soy sauce mixture into cabbage mixture. Remove from heat; stir in shrimp, tossing to coat. Serve with hoisin sauce and tortillas. Yield: 4 servings (serving size: 1 cup shrimp mixture, 1½ teaspoons hoisin sauce, and 2 tortillas).

CALORIES 419 (21% from fat); FAT 9.8g (sat 2g, mono 3.8g, poly 2.6g); PROTEIN 32.4g; CARB 49.6g; FIBER 5g; CHOL 172mg; IRON 5.5mg; SODIUM 934mg; CALC 259mg

Cumin-Coriander Crusted Salmon

This heart-healthy entrée combines vibrant cumin, coriander seed, and cilantro. Letting the spiced fillets rest in the fridge melds the flavors.

- 2 tablespoons finely chopped fresh cilantro
- 1 tablespoon finely chopped shallots
- 1 teaspoon olive oil
- ½ teaspoon ground cumin
- ¼ teaspoon ground coriander
- ¼ teaspoon kosher salt
- ¼ teaspoon black pepper
- 4 (6-ounce) salmon fillets
- Cooking spray
- 4 lemon wedges

1. Combine first 7 ingredients in a small bowl, stirring to form a paste. Place fish, skin side down, in a shallow baking dish. Coat top of fish with cilantro mixture. Cover; refrigerate 1 hour.
2. Preheat oven to 400°.
3. Arrange fish on rack of a roasting pan coated with cooking spray, and place

rack in pan. Bake at 400° for 10 minutes or until fish flakes easily when tested with a fork or until desired degree of doneness. Serve with lemon wedges. Yield: 4 servings (serving size: 1 fish fillet and 1 lemon wedge).

CALORIES 289 (44% from fat); FAT 14.2g (sat 3.2g, mono 6.5g, poly 3.3g); PROTEIN 36.3g; CARB 1.9g; FIBER 0.4g; CHOL 87mg; IRON 0.7mg; SODIUM 200mg; CALC 29mg

Spicy Shrimp Tacos with Tomatillo Salsa

For even spicier salsa, use a habañero pepper. Leftover salsa makes a great dip for chips and veggies. Serve with red beans and rice, and garnish with cilantro.

SHRIMP:

    1 teaspoon chili powder
    ½ teaspoon ground red pepper
    ¼ teaspoon kosher salt
    3 garlic cloves, minced
    1 pound medium shrimp, peeled and deveined
    1 teaspoon olive oil

SALSA:

    ½ pound tomatillos, coarsely chopped
    ¼ cup chopped onion
    ¼ cup fat-free sour cream
    2 tablespoons chopped fresh cilantro
    2 tablespoons cider vinegar
    1 tablespoon fresh lime juice
    1 teaspoon sugar
    ⅛ teaspoon kosher salt
    1 avocado, peeled
    1 serrano chile, seeded and chopped

REMAINING INGREDIENT:

    8 (6-inch) corn tortillas

1. To prepare shrimp, combine first 5 ingredients in a bowl. Refrigerate 30 minutes. Heat oil in a large nonstick skillet over medium-high heat. Add shrimp; sauté 4 minutes or until done.
2. To prepare salsa, place tomatillos and next 9 ingredients in a food processor; process until smooth. Warm tortillas according to package directions. Divide

shrimp evenly among tortillas. Top each with about ¼ cup salsa; fold in half. Yield: 4 servings (serving size: 2 tacos).

CALORIES 323 (30% from fat); FAT 10.9g (sat 1.6g, mono 5.1g, poly 2.4g); PROTEIN 27.7g; CARB 31.2g; FIBER 5.4g; CHOL 175mg; IRON 3.6mg; SODIUM 373mg; CALC 126mg

dinner tonight
Steak for Supper

Four dishes sizzle with no-fuss evening choices.

Steak Menu 1
serves 4

Barbecued Flank Steak Sandwiches

Quick coleslaw*

Vegetable chips

*Combine 5 cups coleslaw mix, ¼ cup reduced-fat mayonnaise, 2 teaspoons fresh lemon juice, ½ teaspoon salt, and ½ teaspoon freshly ground black pepper in a bowl; toss to coat. Cover and chill 20 minutes before serving.

Game Plan

1. While grill pan heats:
  • Season steak.
2. While steak cooks:
  • Prepare slaw.
  • Slice onion.
  • Combine sauce ingredients.
3. While steak stands:
  • Cook onion.
  • Heat sauce.
4. Slice steak.
5. Assemble sandwiches.

Barbecued Flank Steak Sandwiches

Add smoky heat to this quick barbecue sauce with a dash of chipotle chile powder. Look for it in the spice section at the supermarket.

TOTAL TIME: 32 MINUTES

FLAVOR TIP: Substitute ⅛ teaspoon ground red pepper if you can't find chipotle chile powder for the sauce. Or you can omit it if you prefer a mellower flavor.

    Cooking spray
    1 (1-pound) flank steak, trimmed
    ½ teaspoon salt
    ¼ teaspoon freshly ground black pepper
    4 (¼-inch-thick) slices red onion
    ¼ cup ketchup
    2 tablespoons light brown sugar
    1 tablespoon cider vinegar
    1 tablespoon Worcestershire sauce
    ¼ teaspoon chipotle chile powder
    4 (3-ounce) hoagie rolls, split

1. Heat a grill pan over medium-high heat. Coat pan with cooking spray. Sprinkle steak evenly with salt and pepper. Add steak to pan; cook 6 minutes on each side or until desired degree of doneness. Remove steak from pan; let stand 10 minutes. Add onion to pan; cook 3 minutes on each side or until lightly browned. Remove from pan; cool.
2. Combine ketchup and next 4 ingredients in a large microwave-safe bowl, stirring well. Microwave at HIGH 1 minute or until thoroughly heated. Cut steak diagonally across grain into thin slices. Add steak to ketchup mixture; toss to coat. Divide steak mixture evenly among bottom halves of rolls; top each serving with one onion slice. Place top halves of rolls on sandwiches. Yield: 4 servings (serving size: 1 sandwich).

CALORIES 415 (19% from fat); FAT 8.6g (sat 3.5g, mono 2.2g, poly 1.4g); PROTEIN 32.5g; CARB 55.3g; FIBER 2.6g; CHOL 37mg; IRON 1.9mg; SODIUM 969mg; CALC 32mg

Steak Menu 2

serves 6

Flank Steak with Chunky Mojo Relish

Cuban black beans*

Pineapple sherbet

*Heat 2 teaspoons olive oil in a medium skillet over medium heat. Add ½ cup chopped onion and ½ teaspoon minced garlic to pan; cook 5 minutes, stirring occasionally. Stir in 2 (15-ounce) cans rinsed and drained black beans, ½ teaspoon hot sauce, and ¼ teaspoon salt; cook 2 minutes or until thoroughly heated, stirring frequently. Stir in ½ cup chopped plum tomato and 2 tablespoons chopped fresh cilantro.

Game Plan

1. While steak marinates:
   • Prepare orange and olive mixture.
   • Prepare black beans.
2. Cook steak.

QUICK & EASY

Flank Steak with Chunky Mojo Relish

Mojo is a garlicky, citrusy Caribbean sauce. Garnish with lime wedges and mint.

TOTAL TIME: 47 MINUTES (INCLUDES MARINATING TIME)

QUICK TIP: Purchase bottled citrus salad as a substitute for the oranges.

¼ cup fresh orange juice
2 tablespoons fresh lime juice
1 teaspoon minced garlic
1 teaspoon ground cumin
¾ teaspoon salt
½ teaspoon freshly ground black pepper
1 (1½-pound) flank steak, trimmed
2 cups diced, peeled orange (about 2 oranges)
3 tablespoons chopped fresh mint
¼ teaspoon hot pepper sauce (such as Tabasco)
6 pimiento-stuffed olives, minced
Cooking spray

1. Combine first 3 ingredients in a small bowl. Reserve 2 tablespoons juice mixture in a medium bowl; set aside. Add cumin, salt, and pepper to remaining juice mixture. Place steak in a shallow dish; brush evenly with spice mixture. Cover and chill 20 minutes.
2. Preheat broiler.
3. Add orange and next 3 ingredients to reserved juice mixture; toss gently.
4. Place steak on a broiler pan coated with cooking spray; brush remaining spice mixture over steak. Broil 6 minutes on each side or until desired degree of doneness. Let stand 5 minutes. Cut into thin slices. Serve with orange mixture. Yield: 6 servings (serving size: 3 ounces steak and 3 tablespoons orange mixture).

CALORIES 188 (30% from fat); FAT 6.2g (sat 2.4g, mono 2.5g, poly 0.3g); PROTEIN 24.6g; CARB 7.8g; FIBER 1.4g; CHOL 37mg; IRON 2mg; SODIUM 431mg; CALC 49mg

Steak Menu 3

serves 4

Flank Steak with Creamy Mushroom Sauce

Egg noodles

Buttered asparagus*

*Steam 1 pound trimmed asparagus, covered, 3 minutes or until crisp-tender; drain. Melt 1 tablespoon butter in a large skillet over medium-high heat. Add asparagus, ½ teaspoon salt, and ¼ teaspoon black pepper to pan; toss well. Cook 2 minutes or until thoroughly heated.

Game Plan

1. While broiler preheats:
   • Bring water to a boil.
   • Trim asparagus.
   • Steam asparagus.
   • Season steak.
2. While steak cooks:
   • Cook noodles.
   • Prepare sauce.
3. Sauté asparagus in butter.

QUICK & EASY

Flank Steak with Creamy Mushroom Sauce

This recipe calls for a gourmet mushroom mix, but most mushrooms will work.

TOTAL TIME: 23 MINUTES

1 (1-pound) flank steak, trimmed
½ teaspoon salt
½ teaspoon freshly ground black pepper
Cooking spray
½ cup chopped shallots
1 (4-ounce) package gourmet mushroom mix
⅓ cup water
2 teaspoons Dijon mustard
1 tablespoon Worcestershire sauce
½ teaspoon chopped fresh thyme
¼ cup fat-free sour cream

1. Preheat broiler.
2. Sprinkle steak evenly with salt and pepper. Place steak on a broiler pan coated with cooking spray. Broil 6 minutes on each side or until desired degree of doneness; let stand 10 minutes.
3. Heat a large nonstick skillet over medium heat. Coat pan with cooking spray. Add shallots to pan; cook 3 minutes, stirring occasionally. Add mushrooms. Cover and cook 4 minutes or until mushrooms are tender, stirring occasionally. Stir in ⅓ cup water, mustard, Worcestershire, and thyme. Cover and cook 2 minutes. Remove from heat; stir in sour cream.
4. Cut steak diagonally across grain into thin slices. Serve with mushroom sauce. Yield: 4 servings (serving size: 3 ounces steak and about ⅓ cup sauce).

CALORIES 186 (27% from fat); FAT 5.6g (sat 2.3g, mono 2.2g, poly 0.3g); PROTEIN 25.6g; CARB 7.5g; FIBER 0.5g; CHOL 38mg; IRON 2.1mg; SODIUM 443mg; CALC 49mg

QUICK & EASY

Stir-Fried Szechuan Steak on Rice

Dark sesame oil has a distinctive nutty flavor and aroma. You can find it in the Asian section of the grocery store.

TOTAL TIME: 31 MINUTES

QUICK TIP: Place steak in the freezer while rice cooks (about 15 minutes) and it will be easier to slice.

 1 (3½-ounce) bag boil-in-bag rice
 1 (1-pound) flank steak, trimmed
 1 teaspoon minced garlic (about 2 cloves)
 ½ teaspoon crushed red pepper
 ¼ cup low-sodium soy sauce
 2 teaspoons cornstarch
 1 teaspoon sugar
 2 teaspoons dark sesame oil
 2 cups fresh sugar snap peas, trimmed (about 8 ounces)
 ¼ cup chopped fresh cilantro
 3 tablespoons chopped dry-roasted peanuts

1. Cook rice according to package directions, omitting salt and fat. Set aside, and keep warm.
2. Cut steak diagonally across grain into 1-inch-thick slices. Combine steak, garlic,

and pepper in a bowl; toss well to coat. Combine soy sauce, cornstarch, and sugar in a small bowl, stirring with a whisk until smooth.
3. Heat oil in a large nonstick skillet over medium-high heat. Add sugar snap peas to pan, and stir-fry 1 minute. Add meat mixture to pan, and stir-fry 2 minutes. Add soy sauce mixture to pan; stir-fry 1 minute or until sauce is slightly thick. Place about ½ cup rice on each of 4 plates; top each serving with about 1¼ cups steak mixture. Sprinkle each serving with 1 tablespoon chopped cilantro and 2¼ teaspoons chopped peanuts. Yield: 4 servings.

CALORIES 363 (29% from fat); FAT 11.8g (sat 3.6g, mono 5.5g, poly 2g); PROTEIN 29.8g; CARB 31g; FIBER 2.1g; CHOL 37mg; IRON 3.4mg; SODIUM 641mg; CALC 64mg

inspired vegetarian

Culinary Adventures

These globe-spanning dishes bring the cuisines of the world to your table.

 These ethnic cuisines incorporate a tradition of showcasing vegetables, beans, and grains. Here we offer a week's worth of approachable vegetarian recipes based on world cuisines.

QUICK & EASY

Cuban Black Bean Patties with Pineapple Rice

You can prepare the patties in advance up to the point of dredging them in cornmeal; cover and refrigerate. Purchase precut, fresh pineapple in the produce section to save time.

RICE:

 1 (3½-ounce) bag boil-in-bag long-grain rice
 2 teaspoons butter
 1 cup diced fresh pineapple
 2 tablespoons chopped fresh cilantro
 ¼ teaspoon salt

PATTIES:

 2 cups rinsed, drained canned black beans (1 [15-ounce] can), divided
 ½ teaspoon bottled minced garlic
 ¼ teaspoon ground cumin
 ⅛ teaspoon salt
 1 large egg white
 ½ cup (2 ounces) shredded Monterey Jack cheese with jalapeño peppers
 ¼ cup chopped red onion
 ¼ cup cornmeal
 Cooking spray

ADDITIONAL INGREDIENT:

 ¼ cup reduced-fat sour cream

1. To prepare rice, cook rice according to package directions, omitting salt and fat. Drain; place rice in a large bowl. Melt butter in a nonstick skillet over medium-high heat. Add pineapple; sauté 4 minutes or just until pineapple begins to brown. Add pineapple mixture, cilantro, and ¼ teaspoon salt to rice in bowl; cover and keep warm. Wipe pan clean with paper towels.
2. To prepare patties, place 1½ cups beans, garlic, cumin, and ⅛ teaspoon salt in a bowl; partially mash with a fork. Place ½ cup beans and egg white in a food processor; process 30 seconds or until well combined. Add bean puree to bean mixture in bowl, and stir until combined. Add cheese and onion to bean mixture; stir until combined. Divide bean mixture into 4 equal portions, shaping each into a ½-inch-thick patty. Place cornmeal in a shallow dish. Dredge both sides of each patty in cornmeal.
3. Heat pan over medium-high heat. Coat pan with cooking spray. Add patties; cook 3 minutes on each side or until browned. Spoon about ½ cup rice onto each of 4 plates; top each serving with 1 patty and 1 tablespoon sour cream. Yield: 4 servings.

CALORIES 294 (27% from fat); FAT 8.7g (sat 5.4g, mono 1.7g, poly 0.2g); PROTEIN 10.2g; CARB 45g; FIBER 3.5g; CHOL 28mg; IRON 2mg; SODIUM 532mg; CALC 155mg

Open-Faced Jerk Vegetable Sandwiches

The vegetables can be assembled in advance and refrigerated overnight in a zip-top plastic bag. Preheat the broiler for the cheese toasts while you sauté the vegetables, and you'll save even more time.

- ⅛ teaspoon salt
- ⅛ teaspoon dried thyme
- ⅛ teaspoon ground cinnamon
- ⅛ teaspoon ground allspice
- ⅛ teaspoon black pepper
- ⅛ teaspoon ground red pepper
- 1½ cups (⅛-inch-thick) diagonally cut zucchini
- ½ onion, cut into ⅛-inch-thick slices
- 1 large red bell pepper, cut into ¼-inch-thick slices
- 1 teaspoon white wine vinegar
- 1 teaspoon olive oil, divided
  Cooking spray
- 3 tablespoons mango chutney
- 1 teaspoon light mayonnaise
- 4 (2-ounce) slices diagonally cut French bread
- 3 ounces thinly sliced Muenster cheese, cut into ⅛-inch-wide strips
- 1 cup gourmet salad greens

1. Combine first 6 ingredients in a large zip-top plastic bag. Add zucchini, onion, bell pepper, vinegar, and ½ teaspoon oil; seal and shake well to coat. Let stand 30 minutes, or refrigerate overnight.
2. Heat ½ teaspoon oil in a large non-stick skillet coated with cooking spray over medium-high heat. Add vegetable mixture, and sauté 5 minutes or until vegetables are tender and begin to brown. Remove vegetables from heat, and keep warm.
3. Preheat broiler.
4. Combine chutney and mayonnaise. Arrange bread slices on a baking sheet. Broil 1 minute or until lightly toasted on each side, and remove from heat. Spread each slice with about 1 tablespoon chutney mixture; top evenly with cheese. Broil 1 minute or until cheese melts. Place 1 cheese toast on each of 4 plates; top each serving with ¼ cup greens and ½ cup vegetable mixture. Yield: 4 servings (serving size: 1 sandwich).

CALORIES 316 (29% from fat); FAT 10.1g (sat 4.7g, mono 3.4g, poly 0.8g); PROTEIN 11.4g; CARB 45.4g; FIBER 3.8g; CHOL 21mg; IRON 2.3mg; SODIUM 761mg; CALC 221mg

Mexican Tomato-Bean Soup with Corn Dumplings

Prepare the dumpling dough while the soup simmers. Queso fresco is a mild, white Mexican cheese sold in tubs. You can substitute feta cheese.

SOUP:
- 2 teaspoons olive oil
- 1 cup chopped onion
- 1 tablespoon chili powder
- 2 teaspoons bottled minced garlic
- 2 cups organic vegetable broth (such as Swanson Certified Organic)
- 1 cup water
- ½ teaspoon dried oregano
- ¼ teaspoon salt
- ¼ teaspoon black pepper
- 1 (15½-ounce) can chickpeas (garbanzo beans), rinsed and drained
- 1 (14.5-ounce) can no-salt-added diced tomatoes, undrained

DUMPLINGS:
- ⅓ cup masa harina or cornmeal
- ⅛ teaspoon salt
- 3 tablespoons hot water
- 1 teaspoon olive oil

REMAINING INGREDIENTS:
- 2 tablespoons chopped fresh cilantro
- 1 tablespoon fresh lime juice
- ¼ cup (1 ounce) crumbled queso fresco

1. To prepare soup, heat 2 teaspoons oil in a Dutch oven over medium-high heat. Add onion; sauté 3 minutes or until tender. Add chili powder and garlic; sauté 30 seconds. Add broth and next 6 ingredients; bring to a boil. Cover, reduce heat, and simmer 20 minutes.
2. To prepare dumplings, combine masa harina and ⅛ teaspoon salt in a bowl. Add 3 tablespoons hot water and 1 teaspoon oil; stir until a soft dough forms (dough will be dry). Divide dough into 24 pieces, shaping each into a ball. Add dumplings to soup; cook, uncovered, 3 minutes or until dumplings float. Stir in cilantro and juice. Ladle 1 cup soup into each of 4 bowls; top each serving with 1 tablespoon queso fresco. Yield: 4 servings.

CALORIES 215 (23% from fat); FAT 5.5g (sat 1g, mono 3g, poly 1g); PROTEIN 7g; CARB 36.2g; FIBER 6.7g; CHOL 2mg; IRON 2mg; SODIUM 709mg; CALC 105mg

Dal with Cucumber Cream and Pita Chips

There are many ways to serve *dal*, an Indian dish of pureed lentils, peas, or beans. This version adds a cool, creamy cucumber topping to balance the spiciness.

PITA CHIPS:
- 2 (6-inch) whole wheat pitas

CUCUMBER CREAM:
- ½ cup fresh baby spinach
- ½ cup reduced-fat sour cream
- ½ cup finely chopped seeded peeled cucumber
  Dash of salt

DAL:
- 1 tablespoon olive oil
- 1½ teaspoons cumin seeds
- 1 teaspoon yellow mustard seeds
- 1 cup chopped onion
- 2 teaspoons bottled minced garlic
- ½ teaspoon crushed red pepper
- ¼ teaspoon ground turmeric
- ¼ teaspoon bottled ground fresh ginger (such as Spice World)
- 3 cups organic vegetable broth (such as Swanson Certified Organic)
- 1¼ cups dried lentils
- 1 cup water
- ½ cup chopped plum tomato
- ¼ teaspoon salt
- 2 teaspoons fresh lemon juice

1. Preheat oven to 350°.

2. To prepare pita chips, split pitas; cut each half into 8 wedges. Arrange wedges in a single layer on a baking sheet. Bake at 350° for 20 minutes or until crisp. Cool completely on baking sheet.

3. To prepare cucumber cream, place spinach and sour cream in a food processor; process until smooth. Place spinach mixture in a small bowl; stir in cucumber and dash of salt. Cover and chill at least 1 hour.

4. To prepare dal, heat oil in a large saucepan over medium-high heat. Add cumin seeds and mustard seeds; cook 2 minutes or until toasted, stirring frequently. Stir in onion, garlic, red pepper, turmeric, and ginger; cook 1 minute, stirring constantly. Stir in broth, lentils, and 1 cup water; bring to a boil. Cover, reduce heat, and simmer 30 minutes or until lentils are very tender, stirring occasionally. Uncover and simmer 20 minutes or until thick and creamy, stirring occasionally with a whisk. Remove from heat. Stir in tomato, ¼ teaspoon salt, and juice. Spoon about ¾ cup dal into each of 4 bowls; top each serving with 3 tablespoons cucumber cream and 8 pita chips. Yield: 4 servings.

CALORIES 384 (14% from fat); FAT 6g (sat 1.6g, mono 2.7g, poly 0.8g); PROTEIN 20.2g; CARB 63.3g; FIBER 21.1g; CHOL 7mg; IRON 6.3mg; SODIUM 708mg; CALC 81mg

Medianoche Grilled Cheese Sandwiches

The Spanish word for midnight is *medianoche*, and this type of sandwich is often enjoyed as a late-evening snack.

> 2 tablespoons Dijon mustard
> 1 tablespoon light mayonnaise
> ¼ teaspoon freshly ground black pepper
> 8 (1½-ounce) slices Hawaiian sweet bread
> 6 ounces reduced-fat Swiss cheese, thinly sliced
> 4 sandwich-cut dill pickles, cut in half crosswise
> 2 plum tomatoes, thinly sliced
> Cooking spray

1. Combine first 3 ingredients in a small bowl. Spread about 1½ teaspoons mustard mixture evenly over each bread slice. Divide cheese, pickles, and tomatoes evenly over 4 bread slices; top with remaining bread slices.

2. Heat a nonstick grill pan over medium-high heat. Coat pan with cooking spray. Add 1 sandwich to pan. Place a cast-iron or heavy skillet on top of sandwich; gently press to flatten. Cook 45 seconds on each side or until cheese melts and bread is toasted (leave cast-iron skillet on sandwich while it cooks). Repeat procedure with remaining sandwiches. Cut sandwiches in half diagonally. Yield: 4 servings (serving size: 1 sandwich).

CALORIES 381 (26% from fat); FAT 11.1g (sat 5.1g, mono 3.7g, poly 2.2g); PROTEIN 24.5g; CARB 44.5g; FIBER 2.1g; CHOL 34mg; IRON 2.5mg; SODIUM 722mg; CALC 549mg

Linguine with Two-Olive Marinara

This recipe's versatile sauce can also be spooned over cheese ravioli, used as a topping for pizza, or served with breadsticks as an appetizer.

> 2 teaspoons olive oil
> ⅔ cup chopped onion
> 2 teaspoons bottled minced garlic
> ¾ cup sliced pitted green olives (about 15)
> 1 (2¼-ounce) can sliced ripe olives, drained
> ¼ teaspoon sugar
> ¼ teaspoon crushed red pepper
> ¼ teaspoon black pepper
> ¼ teaspoon dried oregano
> ⅓ cup dry white wine
> 1 (28-ounce) can crushed tomatoes, undrained
> 10 ounces uncooked linguine
> ¾ cup (3 ounces) grated fresh Parmesan cheese
> 2 tablespoons chopped fresh parsley

1. Heat oil in a Dutch oven over medium-high heat. Add onion; sauté 3 minutes or until tender. Stir in garlic; sauté 1 minute. Add olives; sauté 30 seconds. Stir in sugar, red pepper, black pepper, and oregano; cook 1 minute, stirring constantly. Add wine; cook 30 seconds. Stir in tomatoes; bring to a boil. Reduce heat, and simmer 30 minutes. Remove from heat; keep warm.

2. Cook pasta according to package directions, omitting salt and fat. Drain. Arrange ⅔ cup pasta on each of 6 plates; top each serving with ½ cup sauce, 2 tablespoons cheese, and 1 teaspoon parsley. Yield: 6 servings.

CALORIES 338 (26% from fat); FAT 9.8g (sat 3g, mono 5g, poly 1g); PROTEIN 14.3g; CARB 48.9g; FIBER 4.3g; CHOL 10mg; IRON 3.7mg; SODIUM 808mg; CALC 246mg

Kisir

> 1¼ cups uncooked bulgur
> ½ cup fresh lemon juice (about 3 lemons)
> ¼ cup hot water
> 1 tablespoon extravirgin olive oil
> 1 teaspoon chile paste with garlic (such as sambal oelek)
> ½ teaspoon salt, divided
> ½ cup chopped green onions
> 1 cup chopped plum tomato (about 3 tomatoes)
> 1 cup chopped seeded peeled cucumber
> 2 tablespoons chopped fresh mint
> 2 tablespoons chopped fresh parsley
> 1 tablespoon chopped fresh dill
> 1 cup chopped green bell pepper
> 1 (15½-ounce) can chickpeas (garbanzo beans), rinsed and drained

1. Place bulgur in a large bowl.

2. Combine juice, ¼ cup hot water, oil, chile paste, and ¼ teaspoon salt; drizzle over bulgur, stirring to combine. Sprinkle onions evenly over bulgur mixture; layer tomato and cucumber over onions. Sprinkle with ¼ teaspoon salt, mint, parsley, and dill; top with bell pepper and chickpeas. Cover and chill 24 to 48 hours. Toss gently before serving. Yield: 4 servings (serving size: about 2 cups).

CALORIES 269 (17% from fat); FAT 5.2g (sat 0.5g, mono 3.3g, poly 0.9g); PROTEIN 9.8g; CARB 50.4g; FIBER 12.5g; CHOL 0mg; IRON 2.7mg; SODIUM 386mg; CALC 67mg

Great Family Gathering

Relatives scattered across the country maintain a long-standing tradition of food-centric reunions.

Cooking Light Associate Food Editor, Kathy Kitchens Downie, and her family get together for a family reunion each year. Follow some of their tips and you can plan one for your own family, too.

Friday Night Arrival Dinner Menu
serves 8

Cincinnati Chili

Southern Corn Bread with Molasses-Bourbon Butter

Mexican Hot Chocolate

Assorted sugar cookies or biscotti

Zinfandel

Sleep-in Saturday Breakfast Menu
serves 8

Smoked Salmon and Dill Tortilla

Cool Coffee Latte

Gingerbread Waffles

Bagels or cereal

Fresh fruit salad

Juice

Saturday Night Family Feast Menu
serves 8

Mushroom and Bacon-Stuffed Trout

Grits and Greens

Honey-Whole Wheat Bread

Carrot and Cucumber Salad

Steamed asparagus

King Cupcakes

Chardonnay or pinot noir

MAKE AHEAD • FREEZABLE
Cincinnati Chili

"At a Cincinnati reunion, we tried the city's famous cinnamon-laced chili over noodles with toppings. For our twist, we made an Indian spice mix—garam masala—spiked with black peppercorns."

Cooking spray
½ teaspoon salt, divided
1½ pounds ground sirloin
1½ cups chopped onion
2 teaspoons minced garlic
1 tablespoon canola oil
2 teaspoons Garam Masala
½ teaspoon ground cinnamon
¼ teaspoon ground red pepper
⅛ teaspoon ground nutmeg
2 tablespoons tomato paste
1 cup water
2 tablespoons red wine vinegar
1 (28-ounce) can diced tomatoes, undrained
2 (15.5-ounce) cans dark red kidney beans, rinsed, drained, and divided
1 (15.5-ounce) can light red kidney beans, rinsed and drained
3 tablespoons chopped onion
½ cup chopped fresh flat-leaf parsley

1. Heat a large Dutch oven over medium-high heat. Coat pan with cooking spray. Add ¼ teaspoon salt and beef to pan; cook 6 minutes or until browned, stirring to crumble. Transfer beef to a small bowl; keep warm.

2. Reduce heat to medium; recoat pan with cooking spray. Add 1½ cups onion to pan; cook 4 minutes, stirring frequently. Add garlic; cook 1 minute, stirring constantly. Add ¼ teaspoon salt, oil, and next 4 ingredients to pan; cook 1 minute or until fragrant, stirring constantly. Add tomato paste; cook 1 minute. Add 1 cup water, vinegar, and tomatoes to pan; bring to a boil. Reserve ½ cup dark red kidney beans. Add beef, remaining dark red kidney beans, and light red kidney beans to pan; cover, reduce heat, and simmer 30 minutes. Ladle 1¼ cups chili into each of 8 bowls. Top each serving with 1 tablespoon dark red kidney beans, about 1 teaspoon chopped onion, and 1 tablespoon parsley. Yield: 8 servings.

(Totals include Garam Masala) CALORIES 276 (20% from fat); FAT 6g (sat 1.7g, mono 2.7g, poly 1g); PROTEIN 26.5g; CARB 31.7g; FIBER 9.1g; CHOL 45mg; IRON 4.2mg; SODIUM 755mg; CALC 97mg

---

QUICK & EASY • MAKE AHEAD
GARAM MASALA:
Store leftovers in an airtight container up to two weeks. Use as a rub for salmon or chicken, or use sparingly to flavor curries.

3 tablespoons cumin seeds
2 tablespoons coriander seeds
1 tablespoon black peppercorns
8 cardamom pods
6 whole cloves

1. Combine all ingredients in a spice or coffee grinder; process until finely ground. Yield: ½ cup (serving size: 1 tablespoon).

CALORIES 16 (46% from fat); FAT 0.8g (sat 0.1g, mono 0.5g, poly 0.1g); PROTEIN 0.7g; CARB 2.3g; FIBER 1g; CHOL 0mg; IRON 2mg; SODIUM 5mg; CALC 34mg

Southern Corn Bread with Molasses-Bourbon Butter

"Corn bread is on the menu when we visit my grandmother. She swears by her cast-iron skillet, but you can also prepare this recipe in an eight-inch square baking pan coated with cooking spray. Molasses, creamy butter, and bourbon combine to make a delicious spread."

⅔ cup all-purpose flour (about 3 ounces)
1⅓ cups yellow cornmeal
1½ teaspoons baking powder
½ teaspoon baking soda
¼ teaspoon salt
1½ cups fat-free buttermilk
1 large egg, lightly beaten
5 tablespoons butter, softened and divided
2 teaspoons molasses
½ teaspoon bourbon
¼ teaspoon grated lemon rind

1. Preheat oven to 425°.
2. Lightly spoon flour into dry measuring cups; level with a knife. Combine flour and next 4 ingredients in a large bowl. Add buttermilk and egg; stir just until combined.
3. Place an 8-inch cast-iron skillet in oven 5 minutes, and remove from oven. Add 2½ tablespoons butter to pan; swirl to melt and lightly grease pan. Stir melted butter into batter. Pour batter into preheated pan. Bake at 425° for 20 minutes or until lightly browned and a wooden pick inserted in center comes out clean. Cool 5 minutes in pan. Cut into 8 wedges.
4. Combine 2½ tablespoons butter, molasses, bourbon, and rind in a small bowl; beat with a mixer at medium speed until combined (about 1 minute). Serve butter mixture with warm corn bread. Yield: 8 servings (serving size: 1 corn bread wedge and about 1 teaspoon butter mixture).

CALORIES 231 (30% from fat); FAT 7.8g (sat 4.7g, mono 2.1g, poly 0.4g); PROTEIN 5.4g; CARB 33.5g; FIBER 1g; CHOL 46mg; IRON 1.4mg; SODIUM 349mg; CALC 118mg

Mexican Hot Chocolate

"My father makes this hot chocolate accented with Mexican spices. We use good-quality chocolate our cousins bring from San Francisco. The leftovers are great chilled."

6 cups 1% low-fat milk, divided
¼ cup unsweetened cocoa
½ cup chopped semisweet chocolate
6 tablespoons brown sugar
¼ teaspoon ground nutmeg
2 cinnamon sticks, broken in half
1 vanilla bean, split lengthwise
1 cup miniature marshmallows
Ground red pepper (optional)
Additional cinnamon sticks (optional)

1. Combine 1 cup milk and cocoa in a small bowl; stir well with a whisk. Combine 5 cups milk, chocolate, sugar, nutmeg, and 2 cinnamon sticks in a large, heavy saucepan over medium heat. Scrape seeds from vanilla bean; add seeds and bean to milk. Add cocoa mixture to pan. Cook 25 minutes or until thoroughly heated and chocolate is melted, stirring frequently. Strain mixture through a fine sieve into a bowl; discard solids. Pour chocolate mixture into a pitcher. Serve with marshmallows. Garnish with ground red pepper and cinnamon sticks, if desired. Yield: 8 servings (serving size: ¾ cup chocolate and 2 tablespoons marshmallows).

CALORIES 198 (25% from fat); FAT 5.5g (sat 3.3g, mono 1.7g, poly 0.2g); PROTEIN 7g; CARB 32.8g; FIBER 1.6g; CHOL 7mg; IRON 1mg; SODIUM 107mg; CALC 242mg

Smoked Salmon and Dill Tortilla

"I always request authentic bagels and lox when my sister visits from New York City. In this recipe, I used smoked salmon to create a Spanish tortilla with buttery potatoes, onions, and dill. Serve with fresh fruit. Make this the night before, refrigerate, and serve at room temperature."

Cooking spray
2¼ pounds Yukon gold or red potatoes, thinly sliced (about 6 cups)
¾ cup egg substitute
½ cup chopped onion
1 tablespoon chopped fresh dill
¾ teaspoon salt
½ teaspoon freshly ground black pepper
5 large eggs, lightly beaten
⅔ cup (about 4 ounces) chopped smoked salmon
1½ tablespoons olive oil
½ cup light sour cream
Chopped fresh dill (optional)

1. Heat a large nonstick skillet over medium-high heat. Coat pan with cooking spray. Add potatoes to pan; lightly coat top of potatoes with cooking spray. Cook 8 minutes, turning frequently (don't let potatoes brown or crisp too much). Reduce heat to medium, and cook 20 minutes or until tender, stirring and turning frequently. Transfer potatoes to a bowl. Wipe pan with a paper towel.
2. Combine egg substitute and next 5 ingredients in a large bowl. Stir in salmon. Add potato, and stir gently to combine.
3. Heat oil in pan over medium-high heat. Add potato mixture; cook 1 minute, gently pressing down with a spatula to slightly flatten mixture. Reduce heat to medium-low; cook 15 minutes or until egg has completely set around edges and has just set in center of pan, gently shaking pan frequently. (Tortilla should easily move around pan.) Place a plate upside down on top of tortilla; invert onto plate. Carefully slide tortilla, cooked side up, into pan. Cook 5 minutes or until a knife inserted in center comes out clean, gently shaking pan occasionally. Carefully loosen tortilla with spatula; transfer to a serving platter. Cool at least 10 minutes. Cut into 8 wedges, and top with sour cream. Garnish with dill, if desired. Yield: 8 servings (serving size: 1 wedge and 1 tablespoon sour cream).

CALORIES 223 (29% from fat); FAT 7.3g (sat 2.2g, mono 3.3g, poly 0.8g); PROTEIN 12.4g; CARB 26.2g; FIBER 1.7g; CHOL 140mg; IRON 2.2mg; SODIUM 446mg; CALC 28mg

Cool Coffee Latte

"The Kitchenses drink coffee all day. Because the milk and coffee mixtures need to sit in the fridge overnight, start this the night before the big breakfast. This is best if you drink it within two days."

1¾ cups (5 ounces) good-quality medium roast coffee beans
5 cups cold water
4½ cups 1% low-fat milk
½ cup fat-free sweetened condensed milk
1 vanilla bean, split lengthwise

1. Place coffee beans in a food processor; process 45 seconds or until coffee is coarsely ground and no whole beans remain. Combine coffee and 5 cups cold water in a medium bowl, stirring to combine. Cover and refrigerate 8 hours or overnight.
2. Combine milks in a medium saucepan over medium heat. Scrape seeds from vanilla bean; add seeds and bean to milk mixture. Cook 8 minutes or until thoroughly heated (do not simmer), stirring occasionally. Remove from heat; cool to room temperature. Cover and refrigerate 8 hours or overnight.
3. Strain coffee mixture through a cheesecloth-lined fine sieve into a bowl. Discard cheesecloth and solids. Pour coffee mixture into a pitcher. (Yield is approximately 3 cups coffee extract.) Remove vanilla bean from milk mixture, and discard. Add milk mixture to coffee mixture just before serving; stir well to combine. Yield: 8 servings (serving size: about 1 cup).

CALORIES 114 (12% from fat); FAT 1.5g (sat 0.9g, mono 0.4g, poly 0.1g); PROTEIN 6.1g; CARB 18.6g; FIBER 0g; CHOL 8mg; IRON 0.1mg; SODIUM 91mg; CALC 221mg

Mushroom and Bacon-Stuffed Trout

"This simple recipe was inspired by a reunion years ago in Montana. It has a delicious toasted breadcrumb, bacon, and mushroom filling."

2 (1-ounce) slices white bread
Cooking spray
¾ cup chopped green onions (about 2 bunches)
¾ cup chopped onion
1 cup chopped cremini mushrooms (about 4 ounces)
2 teaspoons chopped fresh thyme
4 center-cut bacon slices, cooked and crumbled
8 (8-ounce) dressed whole rainbow trout
2 tablespoons fresh lemon juice
¾ teaspoon salt
½ teaspoon freshly ground black pepper
Lemon wedges (optional)
Thyme sprigs (optional)

1. Preheat oven to 350°.
2. Place bread in a food processor; pulse 2 times or until crumbly. Sprinkle crumbs on a baking sheet; bake at 350° for 5 minutes or until golden.
3. Increase oven temperature to 400°.
4. Heat a large nonstick skillet over medium-high heat. Coat pan with cooking spray. Add green onions and onion to pan; sauté 5 minutes. Add mushrooms; sauté 3 minutes or until mushrooms soften and most of liquid evaporates. Add chopped thyme; cook 30 seconds. Remove from heat. Combine mushroom mixture, breadcrumbs, and bacon in a bowl.
5. Open trout flat as you would a book. Drizzle trout evenly with juice; sprinkle evenly with salt and pepper. Spoon about ¼ cup mushroom mixture onto bottom half of each fish; fold over to cover with top half of fish. Arrange fish on a foil-lined broiler pan. Bake at 400° for 15 minutes or until fish flakes easily when tested with a fork or until desired degree or doneness. Garnish with lemon wedges and thyme sprigs, if desired.

Serve immediately. Yield: 8 servings (serving size: 1 stuffed trout).

CALORIES 294 (26% from fat); FAT 8.4g (sat 3.7g, mono 2.4g, poly 0.9g); PROTEIN 46.5g; CARB 8.2g; FIBER 0.9g; CHOL 102mg; IRON 3.7mg; SODIUM 436mg; CALC 34mg

Gingerbread Waffles

"My cousin Betsy and her husband developed these fluffy waffles for a family Champagne brunch. Serve with a dollop of lemon curd."

2 cups all-purpose flour (about 9 ounces)
1½ teaspoons baking powder
½ teaspoon baking soda
¼ teaspoon salt
¼ teaspoon ground cinnamon
1½ cups fat-free buttermilk
3 tablespoons canola oil
3 tablespoons molasses
2 teaspoons finely grated peeled fresh ginger
2 large egg yolks
1 (4-ounce) container applesauce
3 tablespoons minced crystallized ginger
2 large egg whites
Cooking spray

1. Lightly spoon flour into dry measuring cups; level with a knife. Combine flour and next 4 ingredients in a medium bowl; stir with a whisk. Combine buttermilk and next 5 ingredients in a small bowl. Add milk mixture to flour mixture, stirring just until combined. Stir in minced ginger.
2. Beat egg whites with a mixer at high speed until soft peaks form. Gently fold egg whites into batter.
3. Coat a waffle iron with cooking spray, and preheat. Spoon about ⅓ cup batter per 4-inch waffle onto hot waffle iron, spreading batter evenly to edges. Cook 5 minutes or until steaming stops, and repeat procedure with remaining batter. Yield: 9 servings (serving size: 2 waffles).

CALORIES 208 (26% from fat); FAT 6.1g (sat 0.7g, mono 3.2g, poly 1.7g); PROTEIN 5.8g; CARB 32.5g; FIBER 1g; CHOL 47mg; IRON 2mg; SODIUM 277mg; CALC 124mg

Grits and Greens

"Our Mississippi great-grandmother's grits recipe is revamped with sausage, onion, bell peppers, and wilted spinach. This would be a nice accompaniment to chicken or pork."

    6   ounces 50%-less-fat pork sausage
        (such as Jimmie Dean)
    1   cup chopped red bell pepper
    ½   cup grated onion
    ½   teaspoon salt, divided
    4   ounces fresh baby spinach (about
        5 cups)
    2   cups 1% low-fat milk
    1   (14-ounce) can fat-free,
        less-sodium chicken broth
  1¼   cups uncooked quick-cooking
        grits
    1   tablespoon butter, cut into pieces
    ½   teaspoon freshly ground black
        pepper
    ⅛   teaspoon ground red pepper
        Dash of ground nutmeg

1. Heat a large nonstick skillet over medium-high heat. Add sausage to pan; cook 4 minutes or until browned, stirring to crumble. Add bell pepper, onion, and ¼ teaspoon salt; sauté 3 minutes or until bell pepper is tender and sausage is done. Add spinach; cook 1 minute or until wilted. Remove pan from heat.
2. Combine milk and broth in a large saucepan; bring to a boil. Slowly add grits, stirring constantly. Cover, reduce heat, and simmer 5 minutes or until thick and grits are tender, stirring frequently. Stir in butter, black pepper, red pepper, and nutmeg. Remove from heat; stir in ¼ teaspoon salt and sausage mixture. Serve immediately. Yield: 8 servings (serving size: about ¾ cup grits).

CALORIES 198 (29% from fat); FAT 6.4g (sat 2.7g, mono 2.4g, poly 0.7g); PROTEIN 8.9g; CARB 26.6g; FIBER 1.8g; CHOL 21mg; IRON 2mg; SODIUM 425mg; CALC 93mg

Honey–Whole Wheat Bread

    ½   teaspoon sugar
    1   package dry yeast (about
        2¼ teaspoons)
    2   tablespoons warm water (100°
        to 110°)
    2   cups 1% low-fat milk
    ½   cup nonfat dry milk
    3   tablespoons canola oil
    3   tablespoons honey
    1   teaspoon salt
    2   cups plus 2 tablespoons all-purpose
        flour (about 9 ounces), divided
    2   cups bread flour (about 9½ ounces)
    2   cups whole wheat flour (about
        9½ ounces)
        Cooking spray

1. Dissolve sugar and yeast in warm water in a small bowl; let stand 15 minutes.
2. Combine 1% milk, dry milk, oil, honey, and salt in a medium, heavy saucepan over medium heat. Cook 5 minutes or until thoroughly warmed and dry milk dissolves, stirring occasionally. Remove from heat; cool to room temperature. Stir yeast mixture into milk mixture.
3. Lightly spoon 2 cups all-purpose flour, bread flour, and whole wheat flour into dry measuring cups; level with a knife. Place 2 cups all-purpose flour, bread flour, and whole wheat flour in a large bowl; stir with a whisk to combine. Add milk mixture to flour mixture; stir until a soft dough forms. Turn dough out onto a lightly floured surface. Knead until smooth and elastic (about 8 minutes); add enough of remaining all-purpose flour, 1 tablespoon at a time, to prevent dough from sticking to hands (dough will feel slightly sticky).
4. Place dough in a large bowl coated with cooking spray, turning to coat top. Cover and let rise in a warm place (85°), free from drafts, 55 minutes or until doubled in size. (Gently press two fingers into dough. If indentation remains, dough has risen enough.) Punch dough down; cover and let rest 15 minutes. Divide dough in half. Working with one

portion of dough at a time (cover remaining dough to prevent drying), roll dough into a 14 x 7–inch rectangle on a lightly floured surface. Roll up rectangle tightly, starting with a short edge, pressing firmly to eliminate air pockets; pinch seam and ends to seal. Place roll, seam side down, in an 8 x 4–inch loaf pan coated with cooking spray. Cover and let rise 30 minutes or until almost doubled in size.
5. Preheat oven to 400°.
6. Bake loaves at 400° for 10 minutes. Reduce oven temperature to 325° (do not remove loaves from oven); bake 50 minutes or until loaves are browned on bottom and sound hollow when tapped. Remove from pans; cool completely on wire racks. Yield: 2 loaves, 12 servings per loaf (serving size: 1 slice).

CALORIES 156 (14% from fat); FAT 2.5g (sat 0.4g, mono 1.2g, poly 0.7g); PROTEIN 5.5g; CARB 28.2g; FIBER 1.9g; CHOL 1mg; IRON 1.5mg; SODIUM 123mg; CALC 64mg

Carrot and Cucumber Salad

"For 10 years, my family lived in South Korea. This simple salad uses Korean kitchen staples—sesame, ground red pepper, garlic, and soy sauce."

    3   tablespoons low-sodium soy
        sauce
    2   tablespoons rice vinegar
    1   teaspoon sugar
    2   teaspoons canola oil
    2   teaspoons dark sesame oil
    ½   teaspoon minced garlic
    ¼   teaspoon ground red pepper
    2   cups chopped seeded cucumber
    1   (10-ounce) bag matchstick-cut
        carrots
    1   teaspoon sesame seeds, toasted

1. Combine first 7 ingredients in a large bowl, stirring well with a whisk. Add cucumber and carrot; toss well. Sprinkle with sesame seeds. Yield: 8 servings (serving size: ¾ cup).

CALORIES 47 (52% from fat); FAT 2.7g (sat 0.3g, mono 0.8g, poly 0.5g); PROTEIN 0.9g; CARB 5.4g; FIBER 1.4g; CHOL 0mg; IRON 0.3mg; SODIUM 227mg; CALC 19mg

King Cupcakes

"This dessert plays on the peanut butter and banana sandwich Elvis supposedly craved. Like him, our grandparents lived in Memphis, the site of many of our first get-together weekends."

CUPCAKES:
- ¼ cup butter, softened
- 1 cup granulated sugar
- ½ cup egg substitute
- ½ cup mashed ripe banana (about 1)
- 1 teaspoon vanilla extract
- 1¾ cups all-purpose flour (about 7¾ ounces)
- 1 teaspoon baking powder
- ¼ teaspoon salt
- ½ cup 1% low-fat milk

FROSTING:
- ¼ cup (2 ounces) ⅓-less-fat cream cheese, softened
- ¼ cup creamy peanut butter
- 3 tablespoons butter, softened
- 1½ cups powdered sugar
- ½ teaspoon vanilla extract
- Dash of salt
- 3 tablespoons chopped unsalted, dry-roasted peanuts

1. Preheat oven to 350°.
2. To prepare cupcakes, place ¼ cup butter and granulated sugar in a large bowl; beat with a mixer at medium speed until blended. Add egg substitute; beat well. Add banana and 1 teaspoon vanilla; beat 1 minute.
3. Lightly spoon flour into dry measuring cups; level with a knife. Combine flour, baking powder, and ¼ teaspoon salt in a bowl; stir with a whisk. Add flour mixture and milk alternately to sugar mixture, beginning and ending with flour mixture.
4. Line 12 muffin cups with paper liners; fill cups with batter. Bake at 350° for 20 minutes or until a wooden pick inserted in center comes out clean. Cool 5 minutes on a wire rack; remove from muffin cups, and cool completely on wire rack.
5. To prepare frosting, combine cream cheese, peanut butter, and 3 tablespoons butter in a medium bowl; beat until light and fluffy. Add powdered sugar, ½ teaspoon vanilla, and dash of salt. Spread frosting evenly over cupcakes; sprinkle evenly with peanuts. Yield: 12 cupcakes (serving size: 1 cupcake).

CALORIES 319 (32% from fat); FAT 11.4g (sat 5.6g, mono 3.4g, poly 1.3g); PROTEIN 5.6g; CARB 50g; FIBER 1.2g; CHOL 21mg; IRON 1.2mg; SODIUM 219mg; CALC 51mg

lighten up
Super Soup

A Scallop Chowder is revamped for a California lawyer with heart-healthy goals.

Patty Garcia of Sacramento, California, clipped the original version of Scallop Chowder from a newspaper three years ago. She and her husband, Jim, liked the idea of fresh thyme and Pernod (licorice-flavored liqueur) in a creamy, scallop-studded soup. However, since Jim had heart surgery, they have both altered their eating habits. So Garcia sent the recipe to *Cooking Light* for a healthful makeover.

BEFORE	AFTER
SERVING SIZE	
1 ¼ cups	
CALORIES PER SERVING	
909	349
FAT	
70.1g	8.1g
PERCENT OF TOTAL CALORIES	
69%	21%

Scallop Chowder

We liked the flavor of the clam juice in this soup, but you could substitute fat-free, less-sodium chicken broth.

- 2 teaspoons butter
- Cooking spray
- 1½ cups chopped onion (about 1 medium)
- ¼ cup chopped celery
- 1 teaspoon minced garlic
- 4½ cups (½-inch) cubed peeled Yukon gold or red potato (about 1½ pounds)
- 1¼ teaspoons kosher salt, divided
- 1 teaspoon freshly ground black pepper, divided
- ¼ cup all-purpose flour
- 2½ cups clam juice
- 2½ cups 2% reduced-fat milk
- 1 tablespoon Pernod (licorice-flavored liqueur)
- 1½ teaspoons chopped fresh thyme
- 1½ pounds sea scallops, cut into 1-inch chunks
- 1½ cups half-and-half
- ¼ cup chopped fresh chives

1. Melt butter in a Dutch oven coated with cooking spray over medium-high heat. Add onion and celery; sauté 5 minutes or until tender. Add garlic, and sauté 1 minute. Add potato, 1 teaspoon salt, and ¾ teaspoon pepper; cook 2 minutes. Lightly spoon flour into a dry measuring cup; level with a knife. Sprinkle flour over potato mixture, and cook 1 minute, stirring frequently. Add clam juice and milk; bring to a boil, stirring constantly. Cover, reduce heat, and simmer 20 minutes or until potato is tender. Partially mash potato using a potato masher. Stir in ¼ teaspoon salt, ¼ teaspoon pepper, Pernod, and thyme; simmer 10 minutes. Add scallops and half-and-half; cook 5 minutes or until scallops are done. Sprinkle with chives. Yield: 8 servings (serving size: about 1¼ cups chowder and 1½ teaspoons chives).

CALORIES 349 (21% from fat); FAT 8.1g (sat 4.6g, mono 2.2g, poly 0.2g); PROTEIN 33.8g; CARB 32.7g; FIBER 2.1g; CHOL 94mg; IRON 1.3mg; SODIUM 842mg; CALC 220mg

St. Patrick's Day Dinner

Irish Chef Darina Allen, cookbook author and owner of the Ballymaloe Cookery School in Cork, Ireland, shares simple recipes for a true Irish celebration.

St. Patrick's Day Dinner Menu

serves 6

Irish Colcannon and Thyme Leaf Soup

Farmhouse Crackers

Roasted Wild Salmon and Dill

Cut and Come Collards

Green Onion Champ

Mummy's Brown Soda Bread

Rhubarb Tart

Coffee or tea

Irish Colcannon and Thyme Leaf Soup

This soup reinterprets an Irish classic: colcannon, a dish of mashed potatoes and kale or cabbage. Garnish with extra thyme and black pepper.

2 tablespoons butter, divided
2½ cups diced peeled baking potato (about 14 ounces)
1 cup diced onion (about 4 ounces)
½ teaspoon salt, divided
½ teaspoon freshly ground black pepper, divided
3 cups fat-free, less-sodium chicken broth
2 cups water
3 tablespoons water
8 cups thinly sliced savoy cabbage (about 1 pound)
1 tablespoon chopped fresh thyme leaves

1. Melt 1 tablespoon butter in a large saucepan over medium heat. Add potato, onion, ¼ teaspoon salt, and ¼ teaspoon pepper. Cover and cook 6 minutes. Add broth and 2 cups water; bring to a boil. Cook 10 minutes or until potato is tender.

2. Combine 3 tablespoons water and 1 tablespoon butter in a large Dutch oven; bring to a simmer. Add cabbage and thyme. Cover and cook 5 minutes, stirring occasionally. Remove from heat; stir in ¼ teaspoon salt and ¼ teaspoon pepper.

3. Place half of potato mixture in a blender. Remove center piece of blender lid (to allow steam to escape); secure blender lid on blender. Place a clean towel over opening in blender lid (to avoid splatters). Blend until smooth. Pour into a large bowl. Repeat procedure with remaining potato mixture. Add potato mixture to cabbage mixture; cook over medium-low heat until thoroughly heated. Yield: 6 servings (serving size: 1⅓ cups).

CALORIES 130 (28% from fat); FAT 4.1g (sat 2.5g, mono 1.1g, poly 0.3g); PROTEIN 4.2g; CARB 21g; FIBER 4.5g; CHOL 10mg; IRON 0.9mg; SODIUM 442mg; CALC 48mg

WINE NOTE: Chardonnay has enough richness to mirror the roasted salmon, and its medium to full body complements one of Ireland's greatest culinary gifts: mashed potatoes. Even better, chardonnay and dill have a special flavor affinity. Here's a good-value, vibrant chardonnay that isn't too oaky: Chateau Ste. Michelle Chardonnay "Indian Wells" 2005 (Columbia Valley, Washington), $18.

STAFF FAVORITE • MAKE AHEAD

Farmhouse Crackers

1 cup whole wheat flour
1 cup all-purpose flour
½ teaspoon baking powder
½ teaspoon salt
2 tablespoons chilled butter, cut into small pieces
⅓ cup water
1 tablespoon whipping cream

1. Preheat oven to 300°.

2. Lightly spoon flours into dry measuring cups; level with a knife. Combine flours, baking powder, and salt in a large bowl; stir with a whisk. Cut in butter with a pastry blender or 2 knives until mixture resembles coarse meal. Add ⅓ cup water and cream; stir to form a stiff dough.

3. Roll dough into a 13-inch square on a baking sheet. Score dough into 16 equal squares. Pierce each cracker with a fork. Bake at 300° for 45 minutes or until crisp. Cool on pan. Yield: 16 crackers (serving size: 2 crackers).

CALORIES 139 (26% from fat); FAT 4g (sat 2.3g, mono 1g, poly 0.3g); PROTEIN 3.7g; CARB 22.9g; FIBER 2.3g; CHOL 10mg; IRON 1.3mg; SODIUM 200mg; CALC 26mg

---

QUICK & EASY

Roasted Wild Salmon and Dill

If wild salmon isn't in season, look for fresh-frozen (labeled "fish frozen at sea" or FAS) fish in stores, or order online from SeaBear Wild Salmon (www.seabear.com).

1 (2¼-pound) wild salmon fillet
Cooking spray
2 teaspoons olive oil
¾ teaspoon salt
½ teaspoon freshly ground black pepper
1 tablespoon chopped fresh dill
1 tablespoon grated lemon rind
8 (⅛-inch-thick) slices lemon

1. Preheat oven to 450°.

2. Place fish, skin side down, on a foil-lined baking sheet coated with cooking spray. Brush fish with oil; sprinkle with salt and pepper. Sprinkle dill and rind over fish; arrange lemon slices over fish. Bake at 450° for 10 minutes or until fish flakes easily when tested with a fork or until desired degree of doneness. Yield: 6 servings (serving size: about 4½ ounces).

CALORIES 192 (33% from fat); FAT 7g (sat 1.6g, mono 3.1g, poly 1.8g); PROTEIN 30g; CARB 0.3g; FIBER 0.2g; CHOL 70mg; IRON 0.9mg; SODIUM 369mg; CALC 60mg

QUICK & EASY
Cut and Come Collards

Darina Allen uses a heritage variety of kale called "cut and come" that isn't available in the States, so she suggests collard greens as a good substitute.

- 12 cups water
- 1 (16-ounce) package prewashed chopped collard greens
- 1¼ teaspoons salt, divided
- 1 tablespoon butter
- ½ teaspoon freshly ground black pepper

1. Bring 12 cups water to a boil in a large Dutch oven. Add greens and 1 teaspoon salt. Reduce heat, and simmer 25 minutes or until greens are tender; drain. Combine greens, ¼ teaspoon salt, butter, and pepper in a large bowl, stirring until butter melts. Yield: 6 servings (serving size: about ½ cup).

CALORIES 37 (54% from fat); FAT 2.2g (sat 1.2g, mono 0.5g, poly 0.2g); PROTEIN 1.7g; CARB 3.9g; FIBER 2.4g; CHOL 5mg; IRON 0.2mg; SODIUM 223mg; CALC 97mg

QUICK & EASY
Green Onion Champ

A bowl of buttery mashed potatoes—known as champ in Ireland—flecked with green onions "is comfort food at its best," says Allen.

- 7 cups cubed peeled Yukon gold potato (about 2½ pounds)
- 1¼ cups whole milk
- ¾ cup finely chopped green onions
- 3 tablespoons butter
- ¾ teaspoon salt
- ½ teaspoon freshly ground black pepper

1. Place potato in a large saucepan; cover with water. Bring to a boil. Reduce heat, and simmer 20 minutes or until potato is tender; drain.
2. Combine milk and onions in a small saucepan; bring to a simmer. Cook 3 minutes. Remove from heat.
3. Combine potato, milk mixture, butter, salt, and pepper in a bowl; beat with a mixer at medium speed until smooth. Yield: 6 servings (serving size: 1 cup).

CALORIES 242 (27% from fat); FAT 7.3g (sat 4.6g, mono 1.9g, poly 0.3g); PROTEIN 6.2g; CARB 36.8g; FIBER 2.8g; CHOL 20mg; IRON 1.7mg; SODIUM 372mg; CALC 70mg

Mummy's Brown Soda Bread

"My mother, Elizabeth O'Connell, now 82, still makes this soda bread every day," says Allen. Scoring a deep cross into the surface of the dough is called "blessing the bread." Because the bread uses baking soda as a leavener, it requires minimal kneading and no rising, so you can bake it just before supper and serve it warm.

- 2 cups all-purpose flour (about 9 ounces)
- 2 cups whole wheat flour (about 9½ ounces)
- 1½ teaspoons baking soda
- ¾ teaspoon salt
- 2 cups buttermilk
  Cooking spray

1. Preheat oven to 450°.
2. Lightly spoon flours into dry measuring cups; level with a knife. Combine flours, baking soda, and salt in a large bowl; stir with a whisk. Make a well in center of mixture. Add buttermilk to flour mixture; stir until blended (dough will be sticky). Turn dough out onto a generously floured surface; knead lightly 4 or 5 times. Shape dough into an 8-inch round loaf; place on a baking sheet coated with cooking spray. Cut a ¼-inch-deep X in top of dough.
3. Bake at 450° for 15 minutes. Reduce oven temperature to 400° (do not remove bread from oven); bake 15 minutes or until loaf sounds hollow when tapped. Cool on a wire rack. Yield: 1 loaf, 12 servings (serving size: 1 slice).

CALORIES 169 (10% from fat); FAT 1.9g (sat 0.9g, mono 0.1g, poly 0.2g); PROTEIN 6.2g; CARB 32.4g; FIBER 3g; CHOL 6mg; IRON 1.7mg; SODIUM 355mg; CALC 10mg

Rhubarb Tart

This showcases fresh rhubarb, which comes into season in March.

- ¼ cup all-purpose flour (about 1 ounce)
- 6 cups sliced fresh rhubarb
- ¾ cup sugar
- ½ (15-ounce) package refrigerated pie dough (such as Pillsbury)
- ½ cup frozen reduced-calorie whipped topping, thawed

1. Lightly spoon flour into a dry measuring cup; level with a knife. Combine flour, rhubarb, and sugar; toss well. Let stand 20 minutes, stirring occasionally.
2. Preheat oven to 350°.
3. Roll dough into an 11-inch circle. Fit dough into a 10-inch round removable-bottom tart pan. Press dough against bottom and sides of pan, and place in freezer 10 minutes. Spoon rhubarb mixture into crust. Bake at 350° for 55 minutes. Cool completely, and cut into wedges. Serve with whipped topping. Yield: 8 servings (serving size: 1 tart wedge and 1 tablespoon whipped topping).

CALORIES 237 (30% from fat); FAT 7.8g (sat 3.1g, mono 0.1g, poly 0.1g); PROTEIN 1.9g; CARB 40.1g; FIBER 1.8g; CHOL 3mg; IRON 0.4mg; SODIUM 117mg; CALC 83mg

---

About Rhubarb

Rhubarb is a long, celery-like vegetable generally cooked and eaten as a fruit. Its long stalks or ribs range in color from red to pink, and they're too tart to be eaten raw. In fact, rhubarb is usually cooked with a generous amount of sugar to balance its tartness. After sweetening, it makes delicious sauces, jams, and desserts, and is referred to as "pieplant" because of its popularity as a pie filling. You will often find it teamed with strawberries, ginger, or oranges.

Rhubarb is highly perishable, so it should be refrigerated in a plastic bag up to 3 days. It can also be blanched and frozen in freezer containers up to 6 months.

Cooking for a Prize

More winning creations from the Cooking Light Ultimate Reader Recipe Contest

In our January/February Reader Recipes column, we introduced you to the winners of the second annual *Cooking Light* Ultimate Reader Recipe Contest. This month we present more finalists from each of the four categories—starters, side dishes, entrées, and desserts—and their noteworthy dishes.

Baked Brie with Golden Raisin Compote

CATEGORY FINALIST—STARTERS AND DRINKS

"This flavorful appetizer is great because most of the prep work can take place before guests arrive. The Brie is rich enough to carry the appetizer with a tart and sweet compote. To ease slicing, keep Brie chilled until ready to use."

—Elizabeth Bennett, Mill Creek, Washington

6 cups chopped peeled Granny Smith apple (about 1½ pounds)
1 cup vertically sliced red onion (1 small)
1 cup golden raisins
⅓ cup white wine vinegar
¼ cup granulated sugar
¼ cup packed brown sugar
½ teaspoon ground cinnamon
½ teaspoon ground cardamom
¼ teaspoon salt
¼ teaspoon ground ginger
¼ teaspoon ground nutmeg
40 (¼-inch-thick) slices French bread baguette (about 8 ounces)
8 ounces Brie cheese, thinly sliced into 40 pieces
Thyme sprigs (optional)

1. Combine first 11 ingredients in a large saucepan; bring to a boil. Cover, reduce heat, and simmer 30 minutes, stirring occasionally. Uncover and cook 5 minutes or until slightly thick, stirring occasionally. Cool.

2. Preheat oven to 400°.

3. Spread 1½ tablespoons compote over each baguette slice; top each with 1 piece of cheese. Arrange slices on a large baking sheet. Bake at 400° for 5 minutes or until cheese melts. Garnish with thyme sprigs, if desired. Yield: 20 servings (serving size: 2 topped baguette slices).

CALORIES 132 (22% from fat); FAT 3.2g (sat 2g, mono 0.9g, poly 0.1g); PROTEIN 3.7g; CARB 23g; FIBER 1.1g; CHOL 11mg; IRON 0.7mg; SODIUM 178mg; CALC 31mg

Sesame-Crusted Beef Tenderloin Steaks with Pineapple, Mango, and Red Pepper Relish

CATEGORY FINALIST—ENTRÉES

"I like to serve this with long-grain and wild rice and steamed sugar snap peas for an elegant, healthy meal. I created this recipe to combine my love of steak with my kids' fondness for Asian foods."

—Teresa Ralston, New Albany, Ohio

RELISH:
½ cup finely chopped pineapple
½ cup finely chopped peeled mango
¼ cup finely chopped red bell pepper
2 tablespoons chopped fresh cilantro
½ teaspoon grated orange rind
1 tablespoon fresh orange juice
½ teaspoon crushed red pepper

REMAINING INGREDIENTS:
Cooking spray
½ teaspoon salt
½ teaspoon freshly ground black pepper
4 (4-ounce) beef tenderloin steaks (about 1 inch thick)
4 teaspoons black sesame seeds

1. To prepare relish, combine first 7 ingredients in a bowl; set aside.

2. Heat a grill pan over medium-high heat. Coat pan with cooking spray. Sprinkle salt and pepper evenly over steaks. Coat both sides of steak evenly with sesame seeds, pressing gently to adhere. Add steaks to pan; cook 3 minutes on each side or until desired degree of doneness. Serve with relish. Yield: 4 servings (serving size: 1 steak and about ⅓ cup relish).

CALORIES 226 (41% from fat); FAT 10.4g (sat 3.6g, mono 4g, poly 1.1g); PROTEIN 24.5g; CARB 8.1g; FIBER 1.4g; CHOL 71mg; IRON 3.8mg; SODIUM 349mg; CALC 44mg

MAKE AHEAD
Autumn Maple Cutout Cookies

CATEGORY FINALIST—DESSERTS

"Use real maple syrup for best results. I also like to use a maple leaf cookie cutter when I make these."

—Tracy Schuhmacher, Penfield, New York

¼ cup butter
2¼ cups all-purpose flour (about 10 ounces)
½ teaspoon baking powder
½ teaspoon ground cinnamon
¼ teaspoon baking soda
¼ teaspoon salt
⅛ teaspoon ground nutmeg
6 tablespoons granulated sugar
½ cup maple syrup
1 teaspoon maple flavoring
2 large egg whites, divided
⅓ cup chopped walnuts
2 tablespoons turbinado sugar or granulated sugar
Cooking spray

Continued

1. Melt butter in a small saucepan over low heat. Cook until milk solids stop crackling and turn amber (about 5 minutes), stirring occasionally. Transfer butter mixture to a small bowl, scraping pan to include milk solids. Cover and cool butter mixture in refrigerator 20 minutes or until soft and congealed but not firm.

2. Lightly spoon flour into dry measuring cups, and level with a knife. Combine flour and next 5 ingredients in a bowl, stirring with a whisk.

3. Combine chilled butter mixture and granulated sugar in a large bowl; beat with a mixer at medium speed until well blended (about 3 minutes). Add syrup, flavoring, and 1 egg white to butter mixture; beat at low speed 2 minutes or until well blended. Add flour mixture to butter mixture; beat at low speed until blended. Divide dough in half. Shape each portion into a ball; wrap in plastic wrap. Chill 1 hour or until firm.

4. Preheat oven to 350°.

5. Place walnuts and turbinado sugar in a food processor; pulse 15 times or until mixture is coarsely ground. Place 1 egg white in another small bowl; stir with a whisk.

6. Working with one portion of dough at a time (keep remaining dough chilled until use), roll dough to a ⅛-inch thickness on a floured surface, and cut with a 2½-inch round or decorative cutter. Place 24 cookies, evenly spaced, on a baking sheet coated with cooking spray. Gently brush tops of cookies with egg white; sprinkle evenly with half of walnut mixture. Bake at 350° for 12 minutes or until pale brown. Remove cookies from pan; cool completely on wire racks. Yield: 48 cookies (serving size: 2 cookies).

CALORIES 104 (27% from fat); FAT 3.1g (sat 1.3g, mono 0.7g, poly 0.9g); PROTEIN 1.8g; CARB 17.7g; FIBER 0.5g; CHOL 5mg; IRON 0.7mg; SODIUM 66mg; CALC 15mg

---

MAKE AHEAD

Theresa's Double-Tomato Soup

CATEGORY FINALIST—

SIDE DISHES AND SIDE SALADS

"I omitted the heavy cream that is usually found in tomato soups in order to make this recipe lighter. I don't miss it because pureeing creates a nice, creamy texture."

—Theresa Larsen, Redlands, California

    1 tablespoon butter
    1 cup chopped onion (1 medium)
    ¾ cup shredded carrot
    1 tablespoon minced garlic
    1 tablespoon minced shallots
    1 teaspoon sugar
    ¼ teaspoon freshly ground black
       pepper
    ⅛ teaspoon salt
   10 large basil leaves, divided
    3 drained sun-dried tomato halves,
       packed in oil with herbs (such as
       California Sun Dry brand)
    2 (14.5-ounce) cans organic diced
       tomatoes, undrained
    1 (14-ounce) can fat-free,
       less-sodium chicken broth

1. Melt butter in a large saucepan over medium heat. Add onion, carrot, garlic, and shallots to pan, and cook 5 minutes or until vegetables are tender, stirring frequently. Add sugar, pepper, salt, and 4 basil leaves, and cook 5 minutes. Add sun-dried tomatoes, diced tomatoes, and broth, and bring to a boil. Reduce heat, and simmer 1 hour. Remove from heat. Place half of soup in a blender. Remove center piece of blender lid (to allow steam to escape); secure blender lid on blender. Place a clean towel over opening in blender lid (to avoid splatters). Blend until smooth. Pour into a large bowl. Repeat procedure with remaining soup. Divide soup evenly among 6 bowls. Garnish each serving with 1 basil leaf. Yield: 6 servings (serving size: ¾ cup).

CALORIES 76 (30% from fat); FAT 2.5g (sat 1.3g, mono 0.7g, poly 0.1g); PROTEIN 2.2g; CARB 9.4g; FIBER 2g; CHOL 5mg; IRON 1.1mg; SODIUM 229mg; CALC 14mg

---

enlightened cook

Creole Cuisine with Heart

Chef Tory McPhail reintroduces a healthful lunch lineup at the landmark Commander's Palace in post-Katrina New Orleans.

When Commander's Palace reopened in October 2006—more than a year after Hurricane Katrina struck—Good & Hearty items returned, as well.

The restaurant's Good & Hearty program is a joint project with the Ochsner Clinic Foundation. Several years ago, New Orleans cardiologist Richard Milani, M.D., approached the Brennan family, longtime owners of Commander's Palace, seeking a culinary partner in the city's ongoing campaign against heart disease. They received him with open arms, and now Chef Tony McPhail and his staff prepare Good & Hearty dishes for the restaurant's patrons. Good & Hearty dishes account for one of every three daily special orders.

Gulf Fish en Papillote

En papillote is the French term for food baked in a parchment paper packet; it's a favorite way of preparing fish in New Orleans.

    1 cup matchstick-cut carrots
    1 cup vertically sliced red onion
    ¾ cup (2-inch) julienne-cut celery
    ½ cup red bell pepper strips
    1 teaspoon chopped fresh chervil
    1 teaspoon chopped fresh tarragon
    ¼ teaspoon salt, divided
    ¼ teaspoon freshly ground black
       pepper, divided
    2 (6-ounce) white sea bass fillets
    2 teaspoons butter
    ¼ cup dry white wine

1. Preheat oven to 350°.

2. Combine first 6 ingredients, ⅛ teaspoon salt, and ⅛ teaspoon pepper in a medium bowl.

3. Sprinkle fish evenly with ⅛ teaspoon salt and ⅛ teaspoon pepper. Cut 2 (15-inch) squares of parchment paper. Fold each square in half, and open each. Place 1½ cups vegetable mixture near each fold. Top each serving with 1 fillet, 1 teaspoon butter, and 2 tablespoons wine. Fold paper; seal edges with narrow folds. Place packets on a jelly-roll pan. Bake at 350° for 18 minutes or until parchment is puffy. Place on plates, and cut open. Serve immediately. Yield: 2 servings (serving size: 1 fillet and about 1½ cups vegetable mixture).

CALORIES 264 (26% from fat); FAT 7.6g (sat 3.3g, mono 1.7g, poly 1.6g); PROTEIN 33.2g; CARB 15.4g; FIBER 3.8g; CHOL 80mg; IRON 1.2mg; SODIUM 518mg; CALC 77mg

Grilled Beef Panzanella with Port Wine Vinaigrette

If the weather isn't conducive to grilling outdoors, use a grill pan for the beef in this main dish salad. Open a bottle of pinot noir to accompany this dish.

VINAIGRETTE:
2 tablespoons port
1 tablespoon cider vinegar
1 tablespoon extravirgin olive oil
1½ teaspoons light-colored corn syrup
½ teaspoon chopped fresh thyme
⅛ teaspoon salt
Dash of freshly ground black pepper

SALAD:
3½ cups (½-inch) cubed French bread (4 ounces bread)
Cooking spray
2 cups chopped tomato
3 tablespoons finely chopped onion
2 tablespoons chopped fresh basil
2 tablespoons grated fresh pecorino Romano cheese
¼ teaspoon freshly ground black pepper
4 (4-ounce) beef tenderloin steaks, trimmed (1 inch thick)
¼ teaspoon salt

1. Prepare grill.
2. Preheat oven to 350°.
3. To prepare vinaigrette, combine first 7 ingredients in a small bowl; stir with a whisk.
4. To prepare salad, arrange bread cubes in a single layer on a baking sheet. Lightly coat bread cubes with cooking spray. Bake at 350° for 18 minutes or until toasted. Combine bread, tomato, and next 4 ingredients in a large bowl. Drizzle vinaigrette over bread mixture; toss gently to coat. Sprinkle beef with ¼ teaspoon salt. Place beef on grill rack coated with cooking spray; grill 3 minutes on each side or until medium-rare or desired degree of doneness. Serve beef over salad. Yield: 4 servings (serving size: 1 steak and 1 cup salad).

CALORIES 418 (33% from fat); FAT 15.5g (sat 4.7g, mono 6.9g, poly 0.8g); PROTEIN 29.9g; CARB 35.9g; FIBER 2.8g; CHOL 75mg; IRON 3.5mg; SODIUM 668mg; CALC 95mg

Roasted Butternut Squash with Herbed Vinaigrette

McPhail frequently roasts vegetables to deepen their flavors.

DRESSING:
2 tablespoons white balsamic vinegar
1 tablespoon olive oil
1 tablespoon finely chopped shallots
¼ teaspoon chopped fresh thyme
¼ teaspoon salt

SALAD:
1⅓ cups cubed peeled butternut squash
1 cup cubed peeled sweet potato
½ cup green beans
½ cup wax beans
4 cups trimmed arugula
¼ cup vertically sliced sweet onion
¼ teaspoon salt
⅛ teaspoon freshly ground black pepper

1. Preheat oven to 350°.
2. To prepare dressing, combine first 5 ingredients in a small bowl, stirring well with a whisk.
3. To prepare salad, combine 1 tablespoon dressing, squash, and sweet potato in a medium bowl; toss well. Place squash mixture on a jelly-roll pan or roasting pan in a single layer. Bake at 350° for 15 minutes. Add green beans and wax beans; bake an additional 10 minutes. Cool slightly. Combine squash mixture, remaining dressing, arugula, and remaining ingredients in a large bowl, and toss well. Yield: 4 servings (serving size: 1¼ cups).

CALORIES 122 (28% from fat); FAT 3.8g (sat 0.5g, mono 2.7g, poly 0.4g); PROTEIN 2.6g; CARB 21.5g; FIBER 4.2g; CHOL 0mg; IRON 1.5mg; SODIUM 312mg; CALC 99mg

Herb-Crusted Pork Tenderloin

A judicious amount of butter is used to brown the pork and sauté the shallots and garlic, resulting in a robust dish with minimal fat. Use all spinach, if you prefer. Roast an extra head of garlic, which you can spread on a sliced baguette.

1 whole garlic head
6 shallots, quartered (about ¼ pound)
2 tablespoons butter, divided
1 (1-pound) pork tenderloin, trimmed
1¼ teaspoons chopped fresh thyme, divided
¾ teaspoon salt, divided
½ teaspoon freshly ground black pepper, divided
2 cups (½-inch) cubed peeled sweet potato
1¼ cups sliced cremini mushrooms
½ cup fat-free, less-sodium chicken broth
⅓ cup dry white wine
3 cups baby spinach
3 cups trimmed arugula

Continued

1. Preheat oven to 350°.

2. Remove white papery skin from garlic head (do not peel or separate cloves). Wrap garlic head and each shallot separately in foil. Bake at 350° for 1 hour; cool 10 minutes. Separate cloves; squeeze to extract garlic pulp. Discard skins.

3. Place 1 tablespoon butter in a microwave-safe bowl. Microwave at HIGH 15 seconds or until melted. Rub butter over pork; sprinkle with 1 teaspoon thyme, ¼ teaspoon salt, and ¼ teaspoon pepper. Heat a large ovenproof nonstick skillet over medium-high heat. Add pork; cook 5 minutes, browning on all sides. Place pan in oven; bake at 350° for 20 minutes or until a thermometer registers 160° (slightly pink). Remove pork from pan; cover with foil. Let stand 10 minutes.

4. While pork stands, melt 1 tablespoon butter in pan over medium-high heat. Add shallots and garlic; sauté 2 minutes. Stir in potato; sauté 2 minutes. Stir in mushrooms, ½ teaspoon salt, and ¼ teaspoon pepper; sauté 2 minutes. Stir in broth and wine; bring to a boil. Cover, reduce heat, and simmer 6 minutes or until potato is tender. Stir in spinach, arugula, and ¼ teaspoon thyme; cook 1 minute or until greens are slightly wilted. Cut pork crosswise into 12 pieces. Serve pork over potato mixture. Yield: 4 servings (serving size: 3 pieces pork and ¾ cup potato mixture).

CALORIES 289 (31% from fat); FAT 9.9g (sat 5g, mono 3.2g, poly 0.7g); PROTEIN 27.9g; CARB 22.4g; FIBER 3.9g; CHOL 89mg; IRON 3.2mg; SODIUM 665mg; CALC 90mg

Can Fish?

You bet. Choose canned tuna and salmon for an easy, economical way to work more beneficial omega-3 fatty acids into your diet.

MAKE AHEAD
Curried Potato Salad with Tuna

Madras curry powder, a hot-pepper variation of the familiar Indian spice blend, adds a kick to this salad.

1½ pounds cubed peeled Yukon gold potato
2 tablespoons cider vinegar
⅓ cup golden raisins
1 tablespoon chopped shallots
1 (6-ounce) can albacore tuna in water, drained and flaked
3 tablespoons reduced-fat mayonnaise
2 tablespoons plain low-fat yogurt
2 tablespoons mango chutney
1½ teaspoons Madras curry powder
½ teaspoon salt
¼ teaspoon freshly ground black pepper
¼ cup sliced almonds, toasted

1. Place potatoes in a medium saucepan; cover with water. Bring to a boil. Reduce heat. Simmer 20 minutes or until tender; drain. Cool. Combine potatoes and vinegar in a large bowl, tossing to coat. Add raisins, shallots, and tuna.

2. Combine mayonnaise and next 5 ingredients in a bowl, stirring with a whisk. Add mayonnaise mixture to potato mixture; toss to coat. Chill 1 hour. Stir in almonds. Yield: 6 servings (serving size: about ¾ cup).

CALORIES 199 (17% from fat); FAT 3.8g (sat 0.6g, mono 1.5g, poly 0.7g); PROTEIN 8.6g; CARB 33.1g; FIBER 2.3g; CHOL 8mg; IRON 1.7mg; SODIUM 429mg; CALC 29mg

QUICK & EASY
Tuna-Garbanzo Salad

Inspired by Spanish tapas, this salad spotlights premium tuna. Bonito del Norte or albacore packed in oil are good choices for this recipe.

2 quarts water
1 teaspoon salt
2 cups (1-inch) cut green beans (about ½ pound)
¼ cup finely chopped shallots (about 2 medium)
2 fire-roasted piquillo peppers, chopped
1 garlic clove, minced
1 (15-ounce) can chickpeas (garbanzo beans), rinsed and drained
3 tablespoons light mayonnaise
2 tablespoons sherry vinegar
1 teaspoon Spanish smoked paprika
4 cups arugula
1 (7.8-ounce) jar premium tuna, packed in oil, drained and flaked
¼ cup (1 ounce) grated fresh Parmesan cheese
8 (1-ounce) slices French bread

1. Preheat broiler.

2. Bring 2 quarts water and salt to a boil. Add green beans; cook 4 minutes or until beans are crisp-tender. Drain and rinse with cold water; drain. Combine green beans, shallots, peppers, garlic, and chickpeas in a large bowl.

3. Combine mayonnaise, vinegar, and paprika in a small bowl, stirring well. Add mayonnaise mixture to bean mixture; toss gently to combine. Arrange 1 cup arugula on each of 4 plates; top each serving with about 1 cup bean mixture. Divide tuna evenly among plates.

4. Sprinkle cheese evenly over bread slices; place bread on a baking sheet. Broil 2 minutes or until lightly toasted. Serve toasts with salad. Yield:4 servings (serving size: about 2 cups salad and 2 toasts).

CALORIES 391 (26% from fat); FAT 11.5g (sat 2.2g, mono 2.8g, poly 3.6g); PROTEIN 23.7g; CARB 46.5g; FIBER 6.2g; CHOL 23mg; IRON 3.5mg; SODIUM 1,052mg; CALC 198mg

QUICK & EASY

Wasabi Salmon Burgers with Edamame-Cilantro Pesto

For a little extra calcium in your diet, remove only the skin and leave the bones in the sockeye salmon.

½ cup soft tofu (about 4 ounces)
1 (7-ounce) can red sockeye salmon, drained, skin and bones discarded
1 (6-ounce) can skinless, boneless pink salmon in water, drained
¼ cup chopped fresh chives
2 teaspoons Dijon mustard
½ teaspoon wasabi paste
⅛ teaspoon freshly ground black pepper
1 large egg white, lightly beaten
½ cup panko (Japanese breadcrumbs)
1 teaspoon canola oil
4 curly leaf lettuce leaves
4 hamburger buns with sesame seeds
4 (¼-inch-thick) slices tomato
4 (¼-inch-thick) slices sweet or red onion
½ cup Edamame-Cilantro Pesto

1. Place tofu on several layers of heavy-duty paper towels. Cover with additional paper towels; let stand 5 minutes. Place tofu in a large bowl. Add salmon to bowl; mash with a fork to crumble. Add chives and next 4 ingredients; mix well. Divide mixture into 4 equal portions, shaping each into a ½-inch-thick patty. Place panko in a shallow dish; dredge patties in panko.
2. Heat oil in a large nonstick skillet over medium-high heat. Add patties to pan; cook 3 minutes on each side or until

golden brown. Place 1 lettuce leaf on bottom half of each bun; top each serving with 1 tomato slice, 1 patty, and 1 onion slice. Spread 2 tablespoons Edamame-Cilantro Pesto over each serving; top with top halves of buns. Yield: 4 servings (serving size: 1 burger).

(Totals include Edamame-Cilantro Pesto) CALORIES 345 (32% from fat); FAT 12.2g (sat 1.9g, mono 3.7g, poly 3.1g); PROTEIN 22.9g; CARB 35.4g; FIBER 3.3g; CHOL 32mg; IRON 3.1mg; SODIUM 844mg; CALC 250mg

QUICK & EASY • MAKE AHEAD

EDAMAME-CILANTRO PESTO:

2 cups cilantro leaves
1 cup frozen blanched shelled edamame (green soy beans), thawed
½ cup water
1½ teaspoons canola oil
1 teaspoon green curry paste
1 teaspoon fish sauce
½ teaspoon salt
1 large garlic clove, peeled

1. Place all ingredients in a food processor; process until smooth. Yield: 1 cup (serving size: 2 tablespoons).

CALORIES 35 (44% from fat); FAT 1.7g (sat 0.1g, mono 0.5g, poly 0.3g); PROTEIN 2.2g; CARB 2.6g; FIBER 1g; CHOL 0mg; IRON 0.5mg; SODIUM 226mg; CALC 17mg

QUICK & EASY

Spinach Salad with Tuna and Grape Tomatoes

A lemony vinaigrette, enriched with extra-virgin olive oil, ties the flavors together.

2 tablespoons champagne vinegar
1 tablespoon finely chopped shallots
1 tablespoon extravirgin olive oil
1½ teaspoons grated lemon rind
¼ teaspoon freshly ground black pepper
⅛ teaspoon salt
5 cups baby spinach
5 cups torn red leaf lettuce
2 cups halved grape tomatoes
2 (6-ounce) cans albacore tuna in water, drained and flaked

1. Combine first 6 ingredients in a large bowl; stir well with a whisk. Add spinach and remaining ingredients; toss well. Yield: 4 servings (serving size: about 2½ cups salad).

CALORIES 140 (36% from fat); FAT 5.6g (sat 1g, mono 3g, poly 1.2g); PROTEIN 16.2g; CARB 7.4g; FIBER 2.7g; CHOL 24mg; IRON 2.7mg; SODIUM 345mg; CALC 77mg

Twice-Baked Salmon Potatoes

Pair these spuds with a green salad. We tested this recipe with hot-smoked salmon fillets, but the canned variety will work fine.

4 large baking potatoes
½ cup sliced green onions
½ cup reduced-fat sour cream
⅓ cup fat-free milk
3½ tablespoons butter, softened
3 tablespoons prepared horseradish
½ teaspoon salt
½ teaspoon freshly ground black pepper
1 (4.5-ounce) package hot-smoked salmon
¼ cup (1 ounce) grated fresh Parmesan cheese

1. Preheat oven to 450°.
2. Bake potatoes at 450° for 50 minutes or until done; cool slightly.
3. Reduce oven temperature to 400°.
4. Cut each potato in half lengthwise, and scoop out pulp, leaving ¼-inch-thick shells. Combine potato pulp, onions, and next 7 ingredients in a large bowl, stirring until blended. Spoon potato mixture into shells. Sprinkle cheese evenly over potatoes. Bake at 400° for 15 minutes or until thoroughly heated. Yield: 4 servings (serving size: 1 potato).

CALORIES 508 (30% from fat); FAT 16.9g (sat 10.1g, mono 3.6g, poly 0.7g); PROTEIN 21.6g; CARB 69.2g; FIBER 7.6g; CHOL 64mg; IRON 3.7mg; SODIUM 867mg; CALC 200mg

Salmon

Canned salmon is an excellent source of omega-3 fatty acids—one (four-ounce) portion contains up to 2.2 grams. Because there's no significant difference in omega-3 levels among salmon varieties, let flavor and texture guide your choices.

There are three main types of canned salmon: pink, sockeye, and king. Pink salmon has the lightest color and mildest flavor. Sockeye has brighter salmon color and flavor. King salmon, a premium fish, also called chinook, is prized for its succulent texture and supreme flavor.

Salmon is usually packed in its cooking liquid or water, but check the label to be sure. Many varieties of canned salmon contain bones and skin unless labeled "boneless, skinless." The label should also indicate if the salmon is wild. Canned salmon allows you to serve wild salmon year-round, especially when fresh is expensive and hard to find.

Tuna

Many kinds of tuna are available in cans or tins, glass jars, or pouches.

Pouches and glass jars allow the pure tuna flavor to shine. Most canned tuna is packed in water, broth, olive oil, or canola oil. Read the labels closely to determine whether any ingredients, such as salt or broth, have been added, and which type and cut of fish are contained.

Tuna varieties offer differing amounts of omega-3 fatty acids. Albacore, often labeled "white meat tuna," has the most: One (four-ounce) serving packed in water delivers 1.06 grams, while you'll get 0.5 gram from the same size serving of albacore packed in oil. Since omega-3s *are* oils, they don't disperse when the fish is packed in water, and draining the water allows most of these beneficial fatty acids to remain in the fish. But tuna packed in oil provides an environment where the fish's natural oils mix with the packing oil, so when the can is drained, some of the omega-3 oils are lost.

Hot-Smoked Salmon Quesadillas

Cotija is a salty aged Mexican cheese.

- ¾ cup finely chopped red onion
- ¼ cup chopped fresh cilantro
- ⅔ cup no-salt-added whole-kernel corn, drained
- 2 tablespoons fresh lime juice
- 1 jalapeño pepper, seeded and minced
- 1 (15-ounce) can black beans, rinsed and drained
- 1 (4.5-ounce) package hot-smoked salmon, flaked
- ¾ cup (3 ounces) shredded Monterey Jack cheese
- ⅓ cup (1½ ounces) grated cotija cheese
- 6 (10-inch) flour tortillas, divided
- Cooking spray
- ¾ cup halved grape tomatoes
- ½ cup diced peeled avocado
- ¼ cup reduced-fat sour cream
- 1 tablespoon fresh lime juice
- ⅛ teaspoon salt
- Cilantro sprigs (optional)
- Lime wedges (optional)

1. Combine first 7 ingredients, stirring well. Combine cheeses. Divide half of cheese mixture evenly among 3 tortillas. Top each with about 1⅓ cups bean mixture. Sprinkle evenly with remaining cheese. Top with 3 tortillas.

2. Heat a large nonstick skillet over medium-high heat. Coat pan with cooking spray. Place 1 quesadilla in pan; cook 4 minutes on each side or until golden. Remove and keep warm. Wipe skillet clean with paper towels. Repeat procedure with cooking spray and remaining quesadillas. Cut each quesadilla in half; cut each half into 3 wedges.

3. Combine tomatoes and next 4 ingredients; toss gently. Serve with quesadillas. Garnish with cilantro sprigs and lime wedges, if desired. Yield: 6 servings (serving size: 3 quesadilla wedges and ¼ cup avocado mixture).

CALORIES 422 (31% from fat); FAT 14.3g (sat 5.6g, mono 5.1g, poly 1.5g); PROTEIN 21.1g; CARB 46.6g; FIBER 10g; CHOL 38mg; IRON 1.2mg; SODIUM 957mg; CALC 157mg

Soup and Sandwich Menu
serves 4

Salty, smoky salmon and tangy goat cheese offset sweet notes from the corn and roasted pepper.

Sweet Corn Chowder with Hot-Smoked Salmon

Roasted pepper and goat cheese sandwiches*

Chardonnay

*Heat a medium skillet over medium-high heat. Coat pan with cooking spray. Add 4 (¼-inch-thick) red onion slices to pan; sauté 4 minutes or until crisp-tender. Remove from pan. Spread 1 tablespoon soft goat cheese on 2 pieces of toasted white country bread; top each with 2 onion slices. Arrange ½ cup arugula on each; top each with ⅓ cup bottled roasted red bell pepper. Top with remaining bread slices, and cut in half.

Sweet Corn Chowder with Hot-Smoked Salmon

The fish, used in place of the bacon often found in traditional chowder recipes, adds heart-healthy fats and protein. Great made ahead, this soup gets even better with time.

- 1 tablespoon butter
- 2 cups chopped onion
- 3 cups fat-free, less-sodium chicken broth
- 1½ cups cubed peeled baking potato
- 1½ cups fresh corn kernels
- 1 (15-ounce) can no-salt-added cream-style corn
- ¼ teaspoon freshly ground black pepper
- ⅛ teaspoon ground red pepper
- 2 (4.5-ounce) packages hot-smoked salmon, flaked
- 4 teaspoons chopped fresh chives

1. Melt butter in a large saucepan over medium-high heat. Add onion; sauté 4 minutes. Add broth and potato; bring to a boil. Reduce heat, and simmer 10 minutes or until potato is tender. Add corn kernels and cream-style corn; cook 5 minutes. Stir in peppers. Ladle 1¼ cups chowder into each of 4 soup bowls. Divide salmon evenly among bowls. Garnish each serving with 1 teaspoon chives. Yield: 4 servings.

CALORIES 310 (21% from fat); FAT 7.4g (sat 2.6g, mono 2.3g, poly 1.2g); PROTEIN 18.6g; CARB 45.5g; FIBER 6g; CHOL 22mg; IRON 1.8mg; SODIUM 832mg; CALC 43mg

---

QUICK & EASY
Crisp Greens with Tonnato Dressing

This dressing is inspired by Italian *tonnato*, a sauce made from pureed tuna.

DRESSING:
- ¼ cup reduced-fat mayonnaise
- ¼ cup fat-free, less-sodium chicken broth
- 2 tablespoons red wine vinegar
- 1 tablespoon fresh lemon juice
- ½ teaspoon salt
- ¼ teaspoon freshly ground black pepper
- Dash of ground red pepper
- 2 garlic cloves, chopped
- 1 (6-ounce) can light tuna in olive oil, drained

SALAD:
- 8 cups torn romaine lettuce
- 1 cup peeled sliced cucumber
- 8 green bell pepper rings
- 8 red bell pepper rings
- 2 plum tomatoes, cut into ¼-inch-thick slices
- ¼ cup finely chopped red onion
- 4 teaspoons capers, drained

1. To prepare dressing, place first 9 ingredients in a blender; process until smooth, scraping sides.
2. To prepare salad, combine lettuce and next 4 ingredients in a large bowl; add dressing, tossing gently to coat. Place about 2½ cups salad on each of 4 plates. Sprinkle each serving with 1 tablespoon onion and 1 teaspoon capers. Yield: 4 servings.

CALORIES 141 (37% from fat); FAT 5.8g (sat 1.1g, mono 0.5g, poly 1.5g); PROTEIN 10.2g; CARB 14.7g; FIBER 4.9g; CHOL 15mg; IRON 2.1mg; SODIUM 666mg; CALC 66mg

---

then & now
Italian Cream Cake

Italian cream cake first appeared in Cooking Light *in November 1995, after winning high ratings in our Test Kitchens for its rich flavor and moist texture.*

Readers, staffers included, have long considered Italian Cream Cake their go-to cake for special occasions.

The original three-layer version called for light butter and butter extract—which we shy away from now—and yielded 20 thin servings. To update this classic, we scaled back to two layers, reduced the amount of pecans, and toasted them for more intensity. The savings in fat and calories allowed us to use regular butter for more flavor. We also switched from all-purpose flour to cake flour, which yields tall, tender layers.

Swirled with cream cheese frosting, this reborn cake renders a satisfying 16 servings, so everyone has a little more to celebrate at your next party.

STAFF FAVORITE • MAKE AHEAD
Italian Cream Cake

CAKE:
- Cooking spray
- 2 teaspoons cake flour
- ⅓ cup butter, softened
- 1¼ cups granulated sugar
- 2 large egg yolks
- 2 cups cake flour (about 8 ounces)
- 1 teaspoon baking soda
- ¼ teaspoon salt
- 1 cup low-fat buttermilk
- ¼ cup finely chopped pecans, toasted
- 1 teaspoon coconut extract
- 1 teaspoon vanilla extract
- 6 large egg whites

FROSTING:
- 1 tablespoon butter
- ½ cup (5 ounces) ⅓-less-fat cream cheese
- 3½ cups powdered sugar
- 1 teaspoon vanilla extract

1. Preheat oven to 350°.
2. To prepare cake, coat bottoms of 2 (9-inch) round cake pans with cooking spray (do not coat sides of pans). Line bottoms of pans with wax paper. Coat wax paper with cooking spray, and dust with 2 teaspoons flour; set aside.
3. Place ⅓ cup butter in a large bowl; beat with a mixer at medium speed until creamy. Gradually add granulated sugar, beating well. Add egg yolks, one at a time, beating well after each addition.
4. Lightly spoon 2 cups flour into dry measuring cups; level with a knife. Combine 2 cups flour, baking soda, and salt; stir well. Add flour mixture and buttermilk alternately to butter mixture, beginning and ending with flour mixture. Stir in pecans, coconut extract, and 1 teaspoon vanilla.
5. Beat egg whites with a mixer at high speed until stiff peaks form, using clean, dry beaters (do not overbeat). Fold egg whites into batter; pour batter into prepared pans. Bake at 350° for 23 minutes or until a wooden pick inserted in center comes out clean. Cool in pans 5 minutes on a wire rack. Loosen cake layers from sides of pans; remove from pans. Remove and discard wax paper. Cool completely.
6. To prepare frosting, place 1 tablespoon butter and cream cheese in a large bowl; beat with a mixer at high speed until fluffy. Gradually add powdered sugar, beating at low speed until smooth (do not overbeat). Add 1 teaspoon vanilla; beat well.
7. Place 1 cake layer on a plate; spread with one-third of frosting. Top with other cake layer. Spread remaining frosting over top and sides of cake. Yield: 16 servings (serving size: 1 slice).

CALORIES 322 (25% from fat); FAT 8.8g (sat 4.6g, mono 2.8g, poly 0.8g); PROTEIN 4.7g; CARB 56.6g; FIBER 0.5g; CHOL 45mg; IRON 1.4mg; SODIUM 221mg; CALC 33mg

Salt of the Earth

Prized first as a commodity and now for its taste, salt enhances the quality of an array of dishes.

From a culinary perspective, salt is indispensable. It comes in many varieties—everything from artisanal sea salts to traditional table salt—and it enhances and rounds out the flavors of almost every other ingredient it touches, even sweets. In essence, salt makes food taste more like itself.

But because there is a proven link between eating too much salt and high blood pressure, many people have to watch their sodium intake. The Institute of Medicine, American Heart Association, and U.S. Department of Agriculture all recommend that healthy people consume less than 2,300 milligrams of sodium each day, but many Americans far exceed this amount. Packaged, processed, and take-out foods are notoriously high in sodium and contribute heavily to the problem. Fortunately, cooking for yourself makes it much easier to control the amount of sodium you take in. That's good because salt plays a crucial role in a healthful diet; it helps regulate the body's fluid balance, so it's actually necessary for survival.

At *Cooking Light*, we've found that it doesn't take a lot of salt to achieve its many culinary benefits. Using small amounts of salt in a strategic way helps flavors bloom without overloading on sodium. Used judiciously, salt brightens flavors, balances the bitterness of certain foods, acts as a preservative, and tenderizes. Learn how thoughtful use of this ingredient can truly enhance many of the favorite foods you cook.

MAKE AHEAD • FREEZABLE
Sweet and Salty Peanut Chocolate Chunk Cookies

Coarse-grained sea salt doesn't melt into the batter, so you experience a crunchy burst with every bite. Use any other nut you like in place of peanuts.

- ⅓ cup coarsely chopped unsalted, dry-roasted peanuts
- 1 cup all-purpose flour (about 4½ ounces)
- ½ teaspoon baking powder
- ¼ teaspoon baking soda
- ½ cup granulated sugar
- ½ cup packed brown sugar
- ¼ cup unsalted butter, softened
- 1 teaspoon vanilla extract
- 1 large egg
- ⅓ cup semisweet chocolate chips
- ½ teaspoon coarse sea salt
- Cooking spray

1. Preheat oven to 350°.

2. Place nuts in a small baking pan. Bake at 350° for 8 minutes or until lightly toasted; cool.

3. Lightly spoon flour into a dry measuring cup; level with a knife. Combine flour, baking powder, and baking soda, stirring well with a whisk.

4. Place sugars and butter in a large bowl; beat with a mixer at medium speed until well blended (about 2 minutes). Add vanilla and egg; beat until combined. Add flour mixture to sugar mixture; beat at low speed until well blended. Stir in peanuts, chocolate chips, and salt.

5. Drop dough by teaspoonfuls 2 inches apart onto baking sheets coated with cooking spray. Bake at 350° for 10 minutes or until edges are lightly browned. Cool on pans 5 minutes. Remove cookies from pans; cool completely on wire racks. Yield: 38 cookies (serving size: 1 cookie).

CALORIES 61 (35% from fat); FAT 2.4g (sat 1.2g, mono 0.8g, poly 0.3g); PROTEIN 0.9g; CARB 9.2g; FIBER 0.3g; CHOL 9mg; IRON 0.3mg; SODIUM 48mg; CALC 9mg

STAFF FAVORITE • MAKE AHEAD
Classic Gravlax

Serve this buttery-soft cured salmon as an appetizer on brown bread with fresh dill, Dijon mustard, thinly sliced cucumbers, and grated lemon rind. We found that high-quality wild salmon yields the best results.

- ⅓ cup fine sea salt
- ⅓ cup sugar
- 2 tablespoons grated lemon rind
- ¼ teaspoon whole white peppercorns, crushed
- 1 (1½-pound) center-cut salmon fillet, unskinned and cut in half crosswise
- 2 cups fresh dill sprigs

1. Combine first 4 ingredients. Sprinkle one-third of salt mixture in bottom of an 8-inch square baking dish. Arrange 1 salmon half, skin side down, in dish. Sprinkle with one-third salt mixture and dill. Top with remaining salmon half, skin side up. Spread remaining salt mixture over top of salmon. Cover loosely with plastic wrap. Place a cast-iron skillet or other heavy object on top of salmon to weigh it down; refrigerate 24 hours.

2. Remove skillet; set aside. Uncover salmon; carefully turn salmon stack over. Cover loosely with plastic wrap. Place skillet on top of salmon, and refrigerate 24 hours.

3. Remove skillet; set aside. Uncover salmon; carefully turn salmon stack over. Cover loosely with plastic wrap. Place skillet on top of salmon, and refrigerate 12 hours. Scrape off and discard dill and salt mixture; discard liquid. Rinse salmon. Cut salmon into ⅛-inch-thick slices. Discard skin. Yield: 12 appetizer servings (serving size: about 2 ounces).

CALORIES 48 (41% from fat); FAT 2.2g (sat 0.5g, mono 0.9g, poly 0.5g); PROTEIN 6g; CARB 0.7g; FIBER 0g; CHOL 14mg; IRON 0.1mg; SODIUM 397mg; CALC 4mg

Homemade Seasoning Blends

Preparing your own blends allows you to control the amount of salt in them, and they taste fresher and more intense than many commercial blends.

QUICK & EASY
Herb-Seasoned Salt

This gremolata-like finishing salt offers a great way to use up leftover bits of herbs. Try it with rosemary, thyme, or oregano in place of parsley. Use it on grilled shrimp, chicken, or fish.

2 tablespoons finely chopped fresh flat-leaf parsley
1 teaspoon grated lemon rind
½ teaspoon kosher salt
⅛ teaspoon freshly ground black pepper
1 garlic clove, minced

1. Combine all ingredients. Yield: 4 servings (serving size: about 1¾ teaspoons).

CALORIES 2 (0% from fat); FAT 0g; PROTEIN 0.1g; CARB 0.5g; FIBER 0.2g; CHOL 0mg; IRON 0.1mg; SODIUM 236mg; CALC 5mg

QUICK & EASY • MAKE AHEAD
Spice-Seasoned Salt

Sprinkle this heady blend over steaks, burgers, tuna, chicken, or pork before grilling, sautéing, or broiling. Make a double batch and store in an airtight container up to one month.

2 teaspoons kosher salt
2 teaspoons ancho chile powder
1. teaspoon ground cumin
½ teaspoon ground coriander
⅛ teaspoon freshly ground black pepper

1. Combine all ingredients. Yield: 8 servings (serving size: about ¾ teaspoon).

CALORIES 2 (45% from fat); FAT 0.1g; PROTEIN 0.1g; CARB 0.2g; FIBER 0.1g; CHOL 0mg; IRON 0.1mg; SODIUM 471mg; CALC 2mg

Salt-Crusted Herbed Cornish Hen

A mixture of kosher salt and water with the consistency of wet sand is packed onto Cornish hen halves to form a hard crust that is chipped off once cooked. The resulting bird is moist, tender, and flavorful. Garnish with extra herbs and lemon slices.

1 (1½-pound) Cornish hen
1 tablespoon fresh lemon juice
2 teaspoons chopped fresh oregano
2 teaspoons chopped fresh thyme
1 teaspoon olive oil
¼ teaspoon freshly ground black pepper
1 garlic clove, minced
Cooking spray
1 cup water
1 (3-pound) box kosher salt

1. Preheat oven to 375°.
2. Remove and discard giblets and neck from hen. Split hen in half lengthwise. Trim excess fat. Starting at neck cavity, loosen skin from breast and drumsticks by inserting fingers, gently pushing between skin and meat. Combine juice and next 5 ingredients; rub herb mixture under loosened skin and rub over breast and drumsticks.
3. Line a jelly-roll pan with foil; coat foil with cooking spray. Combine 1 cup water and salt. For each hen half, pat 1 cup salt mixture into a ½-inch-thick oval shape on pan. Coat each salt oval with cooking spray; top each oval with 1 hen half, breast side up. Lightly coat hen halves with cooking spray; pack remaining salt mixture evenly over hen halves.
4. Bake at 375° for 35 minutes or until a thermometer registers 165°. Tap salt to loosen; discard salt mixture. Discard skin. Yield: 2 servings (serving size: 1 hen half).

CALORIES 211 (33% from fat); FAT 7.7g (sat 1.7g, mono 3.4g, poly 1.5g); PROTEIN 32.3g; CARB 1.7g; FIBER 0.2g; CHOL 146mg; IRON 1.3mg; SODIUM 793mg; CALC 32mg

MAKE AHEAD
Golden Buttermilk Cake with Strawberries

Salt enhances the flavor of baked goods, in this case underscoring the silky taste of the butter and buttermilk. We used unsalted butter here to better control the amount of salt in the recipe. For a more colorful topping, use equal amounts of strawberries, blueberries, blackberries, and raspberries.

1 cup cake flour (about 4 ounces)
1 teaspoon baking powder
½ teaspoon baking soda
¼ teaspoon salt
⅓ cup granulated sugar
¼ cup unsalted butter, softened
¼ cup egg substitute
⅔ cup low-fat buttermilk
1 teaspoon vanilla extract
Cooking spray
1 teaspoon powdered sugar
4 cups sliced strawberries
1 tablespoon granulated sugar

1. Preheat oven to 350°.
2. Lightly spoon flour into a dry measuring cup; level with a knife. Combine flour, baking powder, baking soda, and salt, stirring with a whisk.
3. Place ⅓ cup granulated sugar and butter in a medium bowl; beat with a mixer at medium speed until well blended. Add egg substitute; beat just until combined. Add flour mixture and buttermilk alternately to sugar mixture, beginning and ending with flour mixture; beat well after each addition. Stir in vanilla (batter will be thick).
4. Spoon batter into an 8-inch round cake pan coated with cooking spray. Bake at 350° for 22 minutes or until a wooden pick inserted in center comes out clean. Cool in pan on a wire rack 10 minutes. Remove from pan; cool completely on wire rack. Sift powdered sugar over top of cake.
5. Combine berries and 1 tablespoon granulated sugar; toss to coat. Let stand 15 minutes. Serve berry mixture with cake. Yield: 8 servings (serving size: 1 cake slice and ½ cup berry mixture).

CALORIES 193 (29% from fat); FAT 6.3g (sat 3.8g, mono 1.5g, poly 0.4g); PROTEIN 3.5g; CARB 31.4g; FIBER 2g; CHOL 16mg; IRON 1.8mg; SODIUM 253mg; CALC 75mg

Garlic-Thyme Focaccia

Two kinds of salt add flavor and crunch. For a spicy variation, infuse the oil with ½ teaspoon crushed red pepper along with the garlic; strain through a sieve before brushing the flavored oil onto the dough.

　1　teaspoon sugar
　1　package dry yeast (about
　　　2¼ teaspoons)
　1　cup warm water (100° to 110°)
　½　teaspoon fine sea salt
2⅓　cups plus 2 tablespoons
　　　all-purpose flour, divided (about
　　　11¼ ounces)
　Cooking spray
　1　tablespoon olive oil
　2　garlic cloves, thinly sliced
　1　tablespoon chopped fresh
　　　thyme
　¾　teaspoon coarse sea salt

1. Dissolve sugar and yeast in 1 cup warm water in a large bowl; let stand 5 minutes. Stir in fine sea salt. Lightly spoon flour into dry measuring cups and spoons; level with a knife. Add 2 cups plus 2 tablespoons flour to yeast mixture, stirring to form a soft dough. Turn dough out onto a floured surface. Knead dough until smooth and elastic (about 8 minutes); add enough remaining flour, 1 tablespoon at a time, to prevent dough from sticking to hands.
2. Place dough in a large bowl coated with cooking spray, turning to coat top. Cover and let rise in a warm place (85°), free from drafts, 45 minutes or until doubled in size. (Gently press two fingers into dough. If indentation remains, dough has risen enough.)
3. Heat oil in a small skillet over medium-low heat. Add garlic; cook 5 minutes or until fragrant. Remove garlic from oil with a slotted spoon; discard garlic, and remove pan from heat.
4. Place dough on a baking sheet coated with cooking spray; pat into a 12 x 8–inch rectangle. Brush garlic oil over dough; sprinkle with thyme. Cover and let rise 25 minutes or until doubled in size.
5. Preheat oven to 425°.

6. Make indentations in top of dough using handle of a wooden spoon or your fingertips; sprinkle dough evenly with coarse sea salt. Bake at 425° for 14 minutes or until lightly browned. Remove from pan; cool on a wire rack. Yield: 10 servings (serving size: 1 piece).

CALORIES 128 (12% from fat); FAT 1.7g (sat 0.2g, mono 1g, poly 0.3g); PROTEIN 3.5g; CARB 24.2g; FIBER 1.1g; CHOL 0mg; IRON 1.6mg; SODIUM 289mg; CALC 7mg

Salt-Roasted Shrimp with Lemon-Honey Dipping Sauce

Roasting shrimp atop a bed of hot rock salt cooks the shrimp evenly and helps hold in moisture. Because the shrimp are cooked unpeeled, the salt doesn't permeate, and the results are tender and juicy.

　1　(4-pound) box rock salt
　24　unpeeled jumbo shrimp (about
　　　1½ pounds)
　2　teaspoons grated lemon rind
　⅓　cup fresh lemon juice (about
　　　4 lemons)
　2　tablespoons minced green onions
　2　tablespoons honey
　1　teaspoon low-sodium soy sauce
　⅛　teaspoon ground red pepper
　1　garlic clove, minced

1. Preheat oven to 400°.
2. Pour salt in an even layer in a shallow roasting pan or large cast-iron skillet. Place pan in oven at 400° for 30 minutes or until salt is very hot. Arrange shrimp in a single layer over salt. Cover with foil; bake at 400° for 5 minutes or until shrimp are done.
3. Combine rind and remaining 6 ingredients; serve sauce with shrimp. Yield: 8 appetizer servings (serving size: 3 shrimp and 1 tablespoon sauce).

CALORIES 111 (12% from fat); FAT 1.5g (sat 0.3g, mono 0.2g, poly 0.6g); PROTEIN 17.4g; CARB 6.4g; FIBER 0.2g; CHOL 129mg; IRON 2.1mg; SODIUM 225mg; CALC 48mg

Sesame–Sea Salt Breadsticks

Fleur de sel is a popular sea salt; substitute any other type of sea salt, if you prefer. Pressed into the exterior of the sticks, the coarse grains add savory texture.

　½　teaspoon sugar
　1　package dry yeast (about
　　　2¼ teaspoons)
　1　cup warm water (100° to 110°)
1¼　teaspoons fleur de sel, divided
2½　cups plus 2 tablespoons
　　　all-purpose flour, divided (about
　　　11⅓ ounces)
　3　tablespoons sesame seeds, toasted
　Cooking spray
　1　tablespoon yellow cornmeal

1. Dissolve sugar and yeast in 1 cup warm water in a large bowl; let stand 5 minutes. Stir in ¼ teaspoon salt. Lightly spoon flour into dry measuring cups and spoons; level with a knife. Add 2 cups plus 2 tablespoons flour and sesame seeds to yeast mixture; stir to form a soft dough. Turn dough out onto a floured surface. Knead until smooth and elastic (about 8 minutes); add enough of remaining flour, 1 tablespoon at a time, to prevent dough from sticking to hands (dough will feel sticky).
2. Place dough in a large bowl coated with cooking spray, turning to coat top. Cover and let rise in a warm place (85°), free from drafts, 45 minutes or until doubled in size. (Gently press two fingers into dough. If indentation remains, dough has risen enough.) Punch dough down; cover and let rest 5 minutes.
3. Preheat oven to 375°.
4. Divide dough into 4 equal portions. Working with one portion at a time (cover remaining dough to prevent drying), roll portion into a 10 x 5–inch rectangle on a floured surface. Sprinkle with ¼ teaspoon salt; gently roll salt into dough with a rolling pin. Cut dough into 8 (10-inch-long) strips. Gently pick up both ends of each strip; gently twist dough. Place dough twists 1 inch apart on baking sheets coated with cooking spray and sprinkled with cornmeal.

Repeat procedure three times with remaining dough and ¾ teaspoon salt.
5. Bake at 375° for 12 minutes or until lightly browned on bottom. Remove from pan; cool on wire racks. Yield: 32 breadsticks (serving size: 2 breadsticks).

CALORIES 88 (10% from fat); FAT 1g (sat 0.1g, mono 0.3g, poly 0.4g); PROTEIN 2.6g; CARB 16.9g; FIBER 0.9g; CHOL 0mg; IRON 1.2mg; SODIUM 181mg; CALC 6mg

QUICK & EASY
Endive, Romaine, and Radicchio Salad

A sprinkling of salt softens the bitter notes of endive and radicchio.

    3 cups (½-inch) sliced Belgian
       endive (about 6 heads)
    3 cups torn romaine lettuce
    3 cups torn radicchio
    ½ teaspoon kosher salt
    1 tablespoon red wine vinegar
    ½ teaspoon Dijon mustard
    ⅛ teaspoon freshly ground black
       pepper
    1 garlic clove, minced
    2 teaspoons olive oil
    ¼ cup (1 ounce) grated fresh
       Parmesan cheese

1. Combine first 3 ingredients in a large bowl. Sprinkle with salt; toss gently. Combine vinegar, mustard, pepper, and garlic in a small bowl; add oil, stirring with a whisk. Drizzle dressing over greens; toss gently to coat. Sprinkle with cheese. Yield: 6 servings (serving size: 1⅓ cups salad and 2 teaspoons cheese).

CALORIES 47 (56% from fat); FAT 2.9g (sat 1.1g, mono 1.5g, poly 0.3g); PROTEIN 2.7g; CARB 2.9g; FIBER 1.4g; CHOL 3mg; IRON 0.6mg; SODIUM 254mg; CALC 83mg

Spring Break

Zesty citrus and tropical fruits forecast the bright days ahead.

If you're in a yearning-for-spring mood, it's time to give your taste buds a tropical getaway, courtesy of flavorful citrus and tropical fruits. There's no need to search for rare exotica. Mangoes, papayas, pineapple, carambola (star fruit), and more appear regularly at most grocery stores, thanks to crops from California, Florida, Hawaii, and Mexico. Along with energizing tastes and colors, these fruits host nutritional perks. Even better, they're easy to incorporate into dishes from breakfast to entrées to desserts.

QUICK & EASY
Fish Tacos with Papaya-Coconut Salsa

Serve with a side of black beans.

SALSA:
  1½ cups chopped peeled papaya
    1 cup finely chopped red bell
       pepper
    ⅓ cup chopped red onion
    2 tablespoons unsweetened coconut,
       toasted
    2 tablespoons fresh lime juice
    1 tablespoon chopped fresh cilantro
    2 teaspoons minced seeded jalapeño
       pepper (about 1 small)
    ¼ teaspoon salt

FISH:
    1 pound red snapper fillets or other
       firm white fish
    2 tablespoons fresh lime juice
    ¼ teaspoon salt
    ¼ teaspoon freshly ground black
       pepper
    ⅓ cup panko (Japanese breadcrumbs)
    2 tablespoons canola oil

REMAINING INGREDIENTS:
    8 (6-inch) yellow corn tortillas
    2 cups finely shredded red cabbage
    8 teaspoons reduced-fat sour cream
    8 lime wedges

1. To prepare salsa, combine first 8 ingredients; let stand 30 minutes.
2. To prepare fish, place fish in a shallow dish; drizzle with 2 tablespoons juice. Cover and marinate in refrigerator 30 minutes, turning fish occasionally.
3. Remove fish from marinade, discarding marinade; pat fish dry with paper towels. Sprinkle fish with ¼ teaspoon salt and black pepper. Dredge fish in panko, gently pressing to adhere. Heat oil in a large nonstick skillet over medium-high heat. Add fish to pan; cook 4 minutes on each side or until fish flakes easily when tested with a fork or until desired degree of doneness. Cut fish into chunks.
4. Heat tortillas according to package directions. Divide fish evenly among tortillas. Top each with ¼ cup cabbage, ⅓ cup salsa, 1 teaspoon sour cream, and 1 lime wedge. Serve immediately. Yield: 4 servings (serving size: 2 tacos).

CALORIES 394 (30% from fat); FAT 13.3g (sat 3.4g, mono 4.8g, poly 3.3g); PROTEIN 29g; CARB 41.2g; FIBER 6.1g; CHOL 47mg; IRON 1.5mg; SODIUM 482mg; CALC 182mg

BEER NOTE: Lager is the white wine of beer—perfect with spicy foods or fish dishes. Pop open a Caribbean Red Stripe Lager ($7.50 for a six-pack), with its subtle aromas of sweet malt, grain, and fresh hay. It's delicate, yet refreshing against the jalapeño heat. The light, fluffy texture is also a nice contrast to the crunch of the fish.

Piña Colada Cheesecake Bars

CRUST:

1 cup graham cracker crumbs
2 tablespoons coconut flour or all-purpose flour
2 tablespoons turbinado sugar
½ teaspoon ground ginger
2 tablespoons butter, melted
1 tablespoon canola oil
1 tablespoon water
Cooking spray

FILLING:

1 cup 2% low-fat cottage cheese
½ cup sugar
¼ cup (2 ounces) block-style fat-free cream cheese, softened
1½ tablespoons grated lemon rind
1 tablespoon fresh lemon juice
1 tablespoon pineapple juice
½ teaspoon vanilla extract
Dash of salt
¾ cup egg substitute

REMAINING INGREDIENTS:

1 cup chopped fresh pineapple
¼ cup unsweetened shredded coconut, toasted

1. Preheat oven to 350°.
2. To prepare crust, combine first 4 ingredients in a bowl. Add butter, oil, and 1 tablespoon water; toss well. Press mixture into bottom of an 8-inch square baking pan coated with cooking spray. Bake at 350° for 10 minutes. Cool completely on a wire rack.
3. To prepare filling, place cottage cheese and next 7 ingredients in a food processor, and process until smooth. Add egg substitute, and process until blended. Spread cheese mixture over cooled crust. Bake at 350° for 33 minutes or until set. Cool 10 minutes on a wire rack. Refrigerate 2 hours or until thoroughly chilled. Top with pineapple and coconut. Cut into 16 bars. Yield: 16 servings (serving size: 1 bar).

CALORIES 117 (35% from fat); FAT 4.6g (sat 2.2g, mono 1.2g, poly 0.7g); PROTEIN 4.1g; CARB 15.4g; FIBER 0.9g; CHOL 6mg; IRON 0.5mg; SODIUM 142mg; CALC 27mg

Carrot-Pineapple Slaw

This salad is a delicious match for grilled pork tenderloin or pork chops.

1 cup diced fresh pineapple
½ cup raisins
1 (10-ounce) package matchstick-cut carrots
2 tablespoons canola oil
2 tablespoons fresh lemon juice
2 tablespoons maple syrup
1 tablespoon fresh pineapple juice
2 tablespoons chopped fresh flat-leaf parsley
¼ teaspoon salt
⅛ teaspoon black pepper

1. Combine first 3 ingredients in a large bowl. Combine oil and next 3 ingredients, stirring with a whisk. Add oil mixture to carrot mixture; toss well. Add parsley, salt, and pepper; toss well. Cover and chill. Yield: 6 servings (serving size: about 1 cup).

CALORIES 130 (34% from fat); FAT 4.9g (sat 0.4g, mono 2.8g, poly 1.5g); PROTEIN 1g; CARB 22.7g; FIBER 2.3g; CHOL 0mg; IRON 0.6mg; SODIUM 132mg; CALC 32mg

Frozen Lemonade with Coconut Rum

1½ cups ice cubes, crushed
3 tablespoons frozen lemonade concentrate
2 tablespoons coconut rum (such as Malibu)
Lime wedge (optional)

1. Place ice, concentrate, and rum in a blender; blend until slushy. Garnish with lime wedge, if desired. Yield: 1 serving (serving size: about 1 cup).

CALORIES 172 (0% from fat); FAT 0.1g (sat 0g, mono 0g, poly 0.1g); PROTEIN 0.2g; CARB 25.8g; FIBER 0.1g; CHOL 0mg; IRON 0.4mg; SODIUM 2mg; CALC 4mg

Coconut Pancakes with Orange-Mango Compote

The compote is a delicious topping for pancakes, French toast, or oatmeal.

COMPOTE:

1½ cups chopped peeled cored red apple (about 1 medium)
1 cup chopped peeled mango (about 1 medium)
1 cup water
1 teaspoon grated orange rind
⅓ cup chopped orange sections
2 tablespoons light brown sugar
¼ teaspoon ground cinnamon
1 tablespoon cornstarch
1 tablespoon water
1½ teaspoons fresh lime juice

PANCAKES:

¾ cup all-purpose flour (about 3⅓ ounces)
⅓ cup coconut flour or all-purpose flour (about 1 ounce)
1½ teaspoons baking powder
1½ teaspoons granulated sugar
¼ teaspoon salt
1 cup light coconut milk
¼ cup fat-free milk
1 tablespoon canola oil
1 large egg

1. To prepare compote, combine first 7 ingredients in a large saucepan; bring to a boil. Cover, reduce heat, and cook 8 minutes or until fruit is tender. Combine cornstarch, 1 tablespoon water, and lime juice in a small bowl, stirring with a whisk; stir into fruit mixture; bring to a boil. Cook 1 minute or until slightly thickened, stirring constantly. Remove from heat.
2. To prepare pancakes, lightly spoon flours into dry measuring cups, and level with a knife. Combine flours, baking powder, granulated sugar, and salt in a large bowl. Combine coconut milk, fat-free milk, oil, and egg in a small bowl, stirring with a whisk. Add milk mixture to flour mixture, stirring with a whisk (batter will be thick).
3. Pour about ¼ cup batter per pancake onto a hot nonstick griddle or nonstick skillet; spread gently with a spatula.

Cook 2 minutes or until tops are covered with bubbles and edges looked cooked. Carefully turn pancakes over; cook 2 minutes or until bottoms are lightly browned. Serve with compote. Yield: 4 servings (serving size: 2 pancakes and about ½ cup compote).

CALORIES 330 (25% from fat); FAT 9.3g (sat 4.3g, mono 2.6g, poly 1.3g); PROTEIN 7.5g; CARB 57.6g; FIBER 8.4g; CHOL 53mg; IRON 2.4mg; SODIUM 377mg; CALC 163mg

Pork Tenderloin Kebabs

Pineapple stars in the marinade and the skewers. Serve these with Mango Salsa (recipe at right) and basmati rice.

    ¾ cup low-sodium soy sauce
    ¼ cup honey
    ¼ cup pineapple juice
    ¼ cup fresh lime juice (about 2 limes)
    1½ tablespoons grated peeled fresh
        ginger
    1 tablespoon olive oil
    2 teaspoons minced garlic
    ¼ teaspoon five-spice powder
    ½ teaspoon freshly ground black
        pepper
    2 pounds pork tenderloin, trimmed
        and cut into 32 pieces
    32 (1-inch) cubes fresh pineapple
        (about 1 medium)
    16 (1-inch) pieces red onion (about
        1 small)
    Cooking spray

1. Combine first 9 ingredients in a large zip-top plastic bag; add pork. Seal bag, and marinate in refrigerator 1 hour, turning occasionally.
2. Prepare grill.
3. Remove pork from bag, reserving ½ cup marinade. Thread 4 pork pieces, 4 pineapple cubes, and 2 onion pieces alternately onto each of 8 (12-inch) skewers. Place kebabs on grill rack coated with cooking spray; grill 10 minutes or until done, turning and basting occasionally with reserved marinade. Yield: 8 servings (serving size: 1 kebab).

CALORIES 247 (21% from fat); FAT 5.9g (sat 1.7g, mono 2.9g, poly 0.6g); PROTEIN 26.1g; CARB 21.9g; FIBER 1.2g; CHOL 67mg; IRON 1.8mg; SODIUM 635mg; CALC 26mg

Grilled Chicken, Mango, and Jícama Salad with Tequila-Lime Vinaigrette

(pictured on page 227)

CHICKEN:

    ¼ cup fresh orange juice
    ¼ cup low-sodium soy sauce
    2 teaspoons minced garlic
    ¾ teaspoon chili powder
    6 (6-ounce) skinless, boneless
        chicken breast halves

VINAIGRETTE:

    ¼ cup chopped fresh cilantro
    ¼ cup fresh orange juice
    2 tablespoons fresh lime juice
    2 tablespoons tequila
    2 tablespoons extravirgin olive oil
    1½ teaspoons honey
    ¼ teaspoon freshly ground black
        pepper
    ⅛ teaspoon ground red pepper
    Dash of salt

TORTILLA STRIPS:

    4 (6-inch) yellow corn tortillas,
        cut into ½-inch-wide strips
    Cooking spray
    ½ teaspoon ground cumin
    ¼ teaspoon salt
    ¼ teaspoon paprika
    Dash of ground red
        pepper

REMAINING INGREDIENTS:

    ½ teaspoon salt
    1 cup (3 x ¼–inch) strips peeled
        jícama
    1 cup thinly sliced peeled mango
        (about 1 large)
    1 (5-ounce) bag mixed baby greens

1. To prepare chicken, combine first 5 ingredients in a large zip-top plastic bag. Seal and marinate in refrigerator 2 hours, turning bag occasionally.
2. To prepare vinaigrette, combine cilantro and next 8 ingredients in a small bowl; stir with a whisk. Chill until ready to use.
3. Preheat oven to 350°.
4. To prepare tortilla strips, place strips in a large bowl. Coat with cooking spray; toss. Combine cumin and next

3 ingredients. Sprinkle over strips; toss well. Spread strips in a single layer on a baking sheet. Bake at 350° for 8 minutes or until almost crisp. Remove strips from oven; cool. (Tortilla strips will crisp as they cool.)
5. Prepare grill.
6. Remove chicken from bag, discarding marinade. Sprinkle chicken with ½ teaspoon salt. Place chicken on grill rack coated with cooking spray, and grill 5 minutes on each side or until done. Cut chicken into ½-inch slices. Combine jícama, mango, and greens in a large bowl. Pour vinaigrette over jícama mixture, and toss to coat. Place 1⅓ cups jícama mixture on each of 6 plates, and top each serving with 1 sliced chicken breast half. Top evenly with tortilla strips. Yield: 6 servings.

CALORIES 330 (20% from fat); FAT 7.3g (sat 1.3g, mono 3.9g, poly 1.1g); PROTEIN 41.9g; CARB 20.1g; FIBER 3g; CHOL 99mg; IRON 2.3mg; SODIUM 737mg; CALC 71mg

QUICK & EASY
Mango Salsa

This all-purpose relish is good with pork, chicken, and flank steak.

    2½ cups chopped peeled mango
        (about 3 medium)
    ⅓ cup chopped red onion
    ¼ cup chopped fresh cilantro
    1½ tablespoons minced seeded
        jalapeño pepper
    1½ teaspoons grated peeled fresh
        ginger
    1 tablespoon fresh lime juice

1. Combine all ingredients in a bowl. Let stand 30 minutes before serving. Yield: 8 servings (serving size: ⅓ cup).

CALORIES 37 (5% from fat); FAT 0.2g (sat 0g, mono 0.1g, poly 0g); PROTEIN 0.4g; CARB 9.7g; FIBER 1.1g; CHOL 0mg; IRON 0.1mg; SODIUM 1mg; CALC 8mg

Zesty Citrus Chicken

The chicken marinates in citrus juice so the meat stays tender. A touch of coconut flour adds tropical flavor to the breading. Use all-purpose flour instead, if you prefer.

    6 limes
    ½ cup fresh lemon juice (about
       4 lemons)
    6 (6-ounce) skinless, boneless
       chicken breast halves
    ⅓ cup all-purpose flour (about
       2¼ ounces)
    ¼ cup coconut flour or all-purpose
       flour (about 1 ounce)
    2 teaspoons paprika
    1 teaspoon salt
    1 teaspoon freshly ground black
       pepper
    1 tablespoon olive oil, divided
 Cooking spray
    ⅓ cup packed brown sugar
    ¼ cup fat-free, less-sodium chicken
       broth
   12 thin orange slices

1. Grate rind from limes, reserving 2 tablespoons rind; set aside. Squeeze juice from limes to equal ¾ cup.
2. Combine lime juice, lemon juice, and chicken in a large zip-top plastic bag. Seal and marinate in refrigerator 2 hours, turning bag occasionally.
3. Preheat oven to 350°.
4. Remove chicken from bag, reserving 2 tablespoons marinade. Pat chicken dry with paper towels. Lightly spoon flours into dry measuring cups; level with a knife. Combine flours, paprika, salt, and pepper in a shallow dish. Dredge chicken in flour mixture. Heat 1½ teaspoons oil in a large nonstick skillet coated with cooking spray over medium-high heat. Add 3 chicken breast halves; cook 2 minutes on each side or until lightly browned. Place chicken in a 13 x 9–inch baking dish coated with cooking spray. Repeat procedure with 1½ teaspoons oil and remaining chicken.
5. Combine lime rind and brown sugar; sprinkle over chicken. Combine reserved marinade and broth; drizzle around chicken. Top each chicken breast half with 2 orange slices. Bake at 350° for 25 minutes or until chicken is done. Place chicken on a serving platter. Strain any remaining liquid in dish through a fine mesh sieve over a bowl. Discard solids. Spoon sauce over chicken. Yield: 6 servings (serving size: 1 chicken breast half and about 1 tablespoon sauce).

CALORIES 332 (14% from fat); FAT 5.1g (sat 1.2g, mono 2.2g, poly 0.8g); PROTEIN 41.5g; CARB 29.9g; FIBER 3.8g; CHOL 99mg; IRON 2.2mg; SODIUM 533mg; CALC 56mg

---

QUICK & EASY
Carambola-Papaya Salad with Honey-Mint Dressing

Carambola (kehr-ahm-BOH-lah) is a juicy, sweet-tart fragrant fruit that derives its other name—star fruit—from its shape when sliced crosswise. The skin is edible, so there's no need to peel the fruit.

    1 tablespoon chopped fresh mint
    1 tablespoon fresh pineapple juice
    1 tablespoon fresh lime juice
    1 teaspoon honey
  1¼ cups diced peeled papaya
  1¼ cups cubed fresh pineapple
    1 carambola (star fruit), cut
       crosswise into ¼-inch slices
       (about 5 ounces)
    ¼ cup coarsely chopped macadamia
       nuts, lightly toasted
 Mint sprigs (optional)

1. Combine first 4 ingredients in a small bowl.
2. Combine papaya, pineapple, and carambola in a large bowl. Drizzle honey mixture over fruit, and toss gently to coat. Sprinkle with macadamia nuts. Garnish with mint sprigs, if desired. Yield: 6 servings (serving size: ⅔ cup fruit and 2 teaspoons nuts).

CALORIES 77 (51% from fat); FAT 4.4g (sat 0.7g, mono 3.3g, poly 0.1g); PROTEIN 1g; CARB 10.3g; FIBER 1.9g; CHOL 0mg; IRON 0.3mg; SODIUM 2mg; CALC 17mg

---

in season
Hearty Greens

As winter winds down, these nutritious, full-bodied veggies are at their best.

QUICK & EASY • MAKE AHEAD
Vegetable Lo Mein with Edamame and Mustard Greens

Mustard greens' peppery bite contrasts with tender, fresh Asian egg noodles. If you can't find them, substitute fresh pasta such as vermicelli or spaghetti.

    ½ cup boiling water
    ¼ cup dried wood ear mushrooms
    2 quarts water
    3 cups chopped mustard greens
    1 (14-ounce) package fresh Chinese
       egg noodles
    ¼ cup low-sodium soy sauce, divided
    1 tablespoon dark sesame oil
    2 tablespoons canola oil
    1 tablespoon grated peeled fresh
       ginger
  1¼ cups (¼-inch-thick) red bell
       pepper strips (about 1 medium)
    ¾ cup chopped green onions
    1 garlic clove, minced
  1½ cups frozen shelled edamame
       (green soybeans), thawed
    3 tablespoons hoisin sauce

1. Combine ½ cup boiling water and mushrooms in a bowl; cover and let stand 15 minutes. Drain mushrooms in a sieve over a bowl, reserving soaking liquid. Remove and discard stems. Chop mushroom caps; set aside.
2. Bring 2 quarts water to a boil in a Dutch oven. Add greens, and cook 1 minute or until greens wilt. Remove greens from water with a slotted spoon. Plunge greens into ice water; drain and squeeze dry. Set greens aside.
3. Return water in pan to a boil. Add noodles, and cook 2 minutes or until done. Drain and rinse with cold water, and drain well. Place noodles in a large bowl. Add 1 tablespoon soy sauce and sesame oil, tossing to coat, and set aside.

4. Heat canola oil in a wok or large non-stick skillet over medium-high heat. Add ginger; stir-fry 5 seconds. Add mush-rooms, bell pepper, onions, and garlic; stir-fry 2 minutes or until bell pepper is crisp-tender. Stir in greens and edamame; stir-fry 30 seconds. Stir in reserved mushroom soaking liquid, noo-dle mixture, 3 tablespoons soy sauce, and hoisin sauce; cook 2 minutes or until thoroughly heated. Yield: 6 servings (serving size: 1⅓ cups).

CALORIES 339 (26% from fat); FAT 9.8g (sat 1g, mono 4.1g, poly 3.2g); PROTEIN 15.8g; CARB 47g; FIBER 4.9g; CHOL 0mg; IRON 2.1mg; SODIUM 710mg; CALC 73mg

Black-Eyed Pea Cakes with Collard Greens

This novel approach to a classic Southern combination calls for a good sturdy skillet to sauté the cakes. To make this vegetar-ian, cook the greens in vegetable broth.

GREENS:
1½ teaspoons canola oil
½ cup chopped onion
2 garlic cloves, minced
8 cups chopped collard greens (about 12 ounces)
2 cups fat-free, less-sodium chicken broth
½ cup chopped red bell pepper
1 tablespoon cider vinegar
½ teaspoon sugar
¼ teaspoon salt

PEA CAKES:
1 teaspoon olive oil
¼ cup chopped green onions
½ teaspoon grated lemon rind
½ teaspoon minced fresh thyme
1 garlic clove, minced
2½ cups canned black-eyed peas, rinsed, drained, and divided
1 tablespoon dry breadcrumbs
1 tablespoon chopped fresh parsley
2 teaspoons Dijon mustard
½ teaspoon freshly ground black pepper
¼ teaspoon ground red pepper
¼ cup cornmeal
1 tablespoon canola oil

1. To prepare greens, heat 1½ teaspoons canola oil in a Dutch oven over medium-high heat. Add ½ cup onion and 2 garlic cloves; sauté 5 minutes or until onion is tender. Add greens and next 5 ingredi-ents; bring to a boil. Reduce heat; sim-mer 45 minutes or until greens are ten-der, stirring occasionally.
2. To prepare pea cakes, heat olive oil in a large nonstick skillet over medium-high heat. Add green onions, rind, thyme, and 1 garlic clove to pan; sauté 1 minute or until garlic is golden brown. Place garlic mixture, 1¼ cups peas, breadcrumbs, and next 4 ingredients in a food processor; pulse until well blended. Combine pea mixture and 1¼ cups peas in a bowl, stirring well. Divide mixture into 8 equal portions, shaping each into a ½-inch-thick patty. Place cornmeal in a shallow dish; carefully dredge pea cakes in cornmeal. Place pea cakes on a baking sheet; refrigerate 15 minutes.
3. Heat 1 tablespoon canola oil in skillet over medium-high heat. Add pea cakes; cook 2 minutes on each side or until gol-den and thoroughly heated. Serve over collard greens. Yield: 4 servings (serving size: 2 pea cakes and ½ cup greens).

CALORIES 267 (27% from fat); FAT 8.1g (sat 0.9g, mono 4.2g, poly 2.3g); PROTEIN 12.1g; CARB 38.5g; FIBER 9.5g; CHOL 0mg; IRON 2.5mg; SODIUM 768mg; CALC 156mg

Pan-Asian Repast Menu
serves 6

The refreshing salad provides textural contrast.

Chicken and Potatoes over Sautéed Spinach

Asian salad*

Pineapple chunks with ground red pepper

*Combine 6 cups chopped romaine let-tuce heart, 1 cup grated carrot, 1 cup chopped cucumber, and 1 cup halved grape tomatoes in a large bowl. Combine ¼ cup rice wine vinegar, 2 tablespoons soy sauce, 1½ teaspoons miso, 1 teaspoon minced garlic, and 1 teaspoon grated peeled fresh ginger in a small bowl. Add 1 tablespoon sesame oil and 1 teaspoon peanut oil, stirring constantly with a whisk. Drizzle dressing over greens; toss gently.

Chicken and Potatoes over Sautéed Spinach

This recipe exemplifies the Chinese tech-nique of red cooking—braising meat in a flavorful combination of soy sauce, ginger, alcohol, and spices. Serve in shallow rimmed soup bowls so you can enjoy all the broth. Sautéed mustard greens would also be good with this dish.

4 cups thinly sliced leek (about 4 large)
1 cup thinly sliced celery
6 tablespoons low-sodium soy sauce
¼ cup julienne-cut peeled fresh ginger
¼ cup dry vermouth or dry sherry
2 teaspoons sugar
1 teaspoon five-spice powder
1 (14-ounce) can fat-free, less-sodium chicken broth
1½ pounds skinless, boneless chicken thighs, cut into thirds
1½ pounds peeled white potatoes, cut into 1-inch pieces
¼ cup chopped fresh cilantro
½ teaspoon freshly ground black pepper
2 teaspoons canola oil
1 teaspoon dark sesame oil
2 (10-ounce) packages fresh spinach

1. Combine first 8 ingredients in a large Dutch oven over medium-high heat; bring to a boil. Add chicken; return to a boil. Cover, reduce heat, and simmer 10 minutes, stirring occasionally.
2. Add potatoes; return to a simmer. Cover and cook 25 minutes or until potatoes are tender, stirring occasionally. Stir in cilantro and pepper.
3. Heat oils in a large skillet over medium-high heat. Add half of spinach; cook 1 minute, tossing constantly. Add remaining spinach; cook 2 minutes or until spinach wilts, tossing constantly. Serve chicken mixture over spinach. Yield: 6 servings (serving size: 1⅓ cups chicken mixture and about ⅓ cup spinach).

CALORIES 343 (20% from fat); FAT 7.6g (sat 1.5g, mono 2.7g, poly 2.2g); PROTEIN 29.6g; CARB 39.4g; FIBER 6.1g; CHOL 94mg; IRON 6.2mg; SODIUM 846mg; CALC 170mg

Winter Greens, Asiago, and Anchovy Pizza

Anchovies and raisins, a popular eastern Mediterranean pairing, bring a salty sweetness to this calcium-rich pizza. Use any combination of cool-weather greens you like—collard greens, kale, or mustard greens.

Cooking spray
1 cup sliced red onion (about 1 medium)
3 tablespoons raisins
3 garlic cloves, minced
2 canned anchovy fillets, minced
3 cups loosely packed baby spinach (about 3 ounces)
3 cups chopped turnip greens (about 5 ounces)
¼ teaspoon salt
¼ teaspoon crushed red pepper
1 (10-ounce) Italian cheese-flavored thin pizza crust (such as Boboli)
¾ cup (3 ounces) shredded part-skim mozzarella cheese
½ cup (2 ounces) grated Asiago cheese

1. Preheat oven to 400°.
2. Heat a large nonstick skillet over medium heat. Coat pan with cooking spray. Add onion, and cook 10 minutes or until tender, stirring occasionally. Add raisins, garlic, and anchovies; cook 2 minutes, stirring frequently. Add spinach and greens; cover and cook 4 minutes or until spinach and greens wilt. Uncover and cook 3 minutes or until liquid evaporates. Stir in salt and pepper. Cool slightly.
3. Place crust on a baking sheet. Sprinkle crust evenly with mozzarella; top evenly with spinach mixture. Sprinkle Asiago evenly over spinach mixture. Bake at 400° for 12 minutes or until cheese melts and begins to brown. Cut pizza into 8 wedges. Yield: 4 servings (serving size: 2 wedges).

CALORIES 391 (30% from fat); FAT 13.1g (sat 5.9g, mono 3.3g, poly 3g); PROTEIN 20g; CARB 49.6g; FIBER 3.9g; CHOL 26mg; IRON 4.3mg; SODIUM 833mg; CALC 528mg

Sweet Potato, Sausage, and Kale Soup

This version of a traditional Portuguese soup uses sweet potatoes in place of white potatoes.

2 tablespoons olive oil
4 cups chopped onion (about 2 large)
1 teaspoon salt, divided
½ teaspoon crushed red pepper
6 garlic cloves, thinly sliced
1 pound sweet turkey Italian sausage
8 cups coarsely chopped peeled sweet potato (about 2¼ pounds)
5 cups water
4 cups fat-free, less-sodium chicken broth
1 (16-ounce) package prewashed torn kale
1 (16-ounce) can cannellini beans or other white beans, rinsed and drained

1. Heat oil in a large Dutch oven over medium-high heat. Add onion; sauté 5 minutes. Add ½ teaspoon salt, pepper, and garlic; sauté 1 minute. Remove casings from sausage; add sausage to pan. Cook 5 minutes or until sausage is lightly browned, stirring to crumble. Add potato, 5 cups water, and broth; bring to a boil. Reduce heat, and simmer 8 minutes. Gradually add kale; cook 10 minutes or until tender. Stir in ½ teaspoon salt and beans; cook 5 minutes or until thoroughly heated. Yield: 10 servings (serving size: about 1¾ cups).

CALORIES 254 (29% from fat); FAT 8.2g (sat 2.1g, mono 3.4g, poly 1.4g); PROTEIN 14.2g; CARB 34.8g; FIBER 6.9g; CHOL 27mg; IRON 2.9mg; SODIUM 797mg; CALC 132mg

Slow-Braised Collard Greens

This basic Southern preparation for greens would work well with turnip or mustard greens, too; cook about 15 minutes less if substituting those more delicate greens.

3 applewood-smoked bacon slices
½ cup chopped onion
½ teaspoon crushed red pepper
¼ teaspoon salt
1 (16-ounce) package prewashed torn collard greens
1 cup fat-free, less-sodium chicken broth
½ cup water
¼ cup dry white wine
1½ tablespoons white vinegar

1. Cook bacon in a Dutch oven over medium heat until crisp. Remove bacon from pan; crumble. Add onion to drippings in pan; cook 2 minutes, stirring frequently. Add pepper, salt, and greens; cook 2 minutes or until greens begin to wilt, stirring constantly. Stir in bacon, broth, and remaining ingredients. Cover, reduce heat, and simmer 1 hour or until greens are tender. Yield: 6 servings (serving size: ⅔ cup).

CALORIES 60 (39% from fat); FAT 2.6g (sat 0.9g, mono 1g, poly 0.4g); PROTEIN 4.2g; CARB 6.3g; FIBER 3.1g; CHOL 5mg; IRON 0.3mg; SODIUM 289mg; CALC 116mg

White Bean and Collard Greens Soup

1 tablespoon olive oil
1 cup finely chopped yellow onion
3 garlic cloves, minced
½ cup pinot grigio or other light white wine
½ teaspoon freshly ground black pepper
¼ teaspoon salt
4 cups finely shredded collard greens (about 6 ounces)
2 teaspoons minced fresh thyme
2 (14-ounce) cans fat-free, less-sodium chicken broth
1 (15.5-ounce) can Great Northern beans, rinsed and drained

1. Heat oil in a Dutch oven over medium-high heat. Add onion and garlic; sauté 5 minutes or until onion is tender. Add wine, pepper, and salt. Reduce heat; simmer 5 minutes or until liquid almost evaporates. Add greens, thyme, and broth. Cover, reduce heat, and simmer 8 minutes or until greens are tender. Add beans; simmer 5 minutes or until thoroughly heated. Yield: 4 servings (serving size: 1¼ cups).

CALORIES 139 (26% from fat); FAT 4g (sat 0.6g, mono 2.6g, poly 0.6g); PROTEIN 7.6g; CARB 19.6g; FIBER 5.5g; CHOL 0mg; IRON 1.7mg; SODIUM 388mg; CALC 111mg

---

QUICK & EASY

Italian Turkey Sausage and Escarole Soup

This one-dish meal makes it to the table in less than 30 minutes. Use spicy Italian sausage for extra heat and Asiago cheese for a nutty finish.

  8 ounces sweet turkey Italian sausage
  2 teaspoons olive oil
  ¾ cup finely chopped onion
  1 garlic clove, minced
  1 cup water
  1 cup uncooked small seashell pasta
  1 cup chopped seeded plum tomato
  1 teaspoon dried Italian seasoning
  ¼ teaspoon freshly ground black pepper
  3 (14-ounce) cans fat-free, less-sodium chicken broth
  4 cups torn escarole (about 3 ounces)
  2 tablespoons grated fresh Parmesan cheese

1. Remove casings from sausage. Heat oil in a Dutch oven over medium-high heat. Add sausage, onion, and garlic; cook 4 minutes, stirring to crumble. Stir in 1 cup water and next 5 ingredients; bring to a boil. Reduce heat; stir in escarole. Simmer 10 minutes or until escarole and pasta are tender. Top with cheese. Yield: 6 servings (serving size: 1⅓ cups soup and 1 teaspoon cheese).

CALORIES 184 (31% from fat); FAT 6.3g (sat 1.7g, mono 2.8g, poly 1.6g); PROTEIN 12.9g; CARB 19.4g; FIBER 3.3g; CHOL 33mg; IRON 2mg; SODIUM 648mg; CALC 67mg

---

new ingredient
Chai Time

Enliven your palate and your cooking with the fragrant, versatile spice blends in this ancient Indian tea.

Chai Latte Brownies

  ¼ cup 1% low-fat milk
  3 cardamom pods, crushed
  3 whole allspice, crushed
  3 whole cloves
  1 (1-inch) cinnamon stick
  ¼ cup semisweet chocolate chips
  ¼ cup butter
  2 large eggs
  1½ cups all-purpose flour (about 6¾ ounces)
  1 cup granulated sugar
  ½ cup unsweetened cocoa
  ⅓ cup packed brown sugar
  1 teaspoon baking powder
  ½ teaspoon salt
Cooking spray

1. Preheat oven to 350°.
2. Combine first 5 ingredients in a small saucepan; bring to a boil. Cover, remove from heat, and let stand 15 minutes. Strain milk mixture through a fine sieve into a large microwave-safe bowl; discard solids. Add chocolate chips and butter to milk mixture; microwave at HIGH 20 seconds or until chips and butter melt, stirring until smooth. Cool slightly; add eggs, stirring with a whisk.
3. Lightly spoon flour into dry measuring cups; level with a knife. Combine flour and next 5 ingredients in a medium bowl, stirring with a whisk. Add flour mixture to chocolate mixture, stirring just until combined. Spread evenly into a 9-inch square baking pan coated with cooking spray. Bake at 350° for 30 minutes or until center is set. Cool 10 minutes in pan on a wire rack. Cut into 20 pieces. Yield: 20 servings (serving size: 1 brownie).

CALORIES 130 (26% from fat); FAT 3.8g (sat 1.9g, mono 1.5g, poly 0.2g); PROTEIN 2.2g; CARB 23.5g; FIBER 1.1g; CHOL 27mg; IRON 1mg; SODIUM 110mg; CALC 29mg

---

QUICK & EASY

Oatmeal-Chai Buttermilk Pancakes

Serve with apple butter, dusted with powdered sugar, or drizzled with honey. For convenience, make the batter the night before, cover, and refrigerate.

  1½ cups 1% low-fat milk
  12 whole cloves
  8 cardamom pods, crushed
  1 (3-inch) cinnamon stick, broken
  1 (1-inch) piece peeled fresh ginger, coarsely chopped
  2 teaspoons black tea leaves (such as Darjeeling or Assam)
  1 cup low-fat buttermilk
  1 tablespoon butter, melted
  1½ teaspoons vanilla extract
  2 large eggs, lightly beaten
  ½ cup all-purpose flour (about 2¼ ounces)
  3 tablespoons brown sugar
  1 teaspoon baking soda
  1 teaspoon baking powder
  ½ teaspoon salt
  2 cups regular oats

1. Combine first 5 ingredients in a small saucepan over medium heat. Cover and cook 15 minutes. Remove from heat; stir in tea leaves, and steep 2 minutes. Strain mixture through a sieve into a large bowl; discard solids. Stir in buttermilk; cool to room temperature. Add butter, vanilla, and eggs; stir well with a whisk.
2. Lightly spoon flour into a dry measuring cup; level with a knife. Combine flour and next 4 ingredients. Add flour mixture to milk mixture; stir until combined. Stir in oats. Cover and let stand 15 minutes. Pour about ¼ cup batter per pancake onto a hot nonstick griddle or nonstick skillet. Cook 2 minutes or until tops are covered with bubbles and edges look cooked. Carefully turn pancakes over; cook 2 minutes or until bottoms are lightly browned. Yield: 6 servings (serving size: 2 pancakes).

CALORIES 249 (24% from fat); FAT 6.6g (sat 2.7g, mono 2g, poly 0.8g); PROTEIN 10.6g; CARB 37.8g; FIBER 2.8g; CHOL 80mg; IRON 2.3mg; SODIUM 589mg; CALC 199mg

Chai

Use this basic chai recipe as a starting point, then alter it to suit your preferences. You might add black peppercorns, vanilla bean seeds, or star anise, for instance.

1½ cups water
7 cardamom pods, crushed
6 whole cloves
4 white peppercorns
1 (½-inch) piece peeled fresh ginger, coarsely chopped
1 cinnamon stick, broken
1 cup whole milk
1 tablespoon black tea leaves (such as Darjeeling or Assam)
¼ cup honey

1. Combine first 6 ingredients in a medium saucepan; bring to a boil. Cover, reduce heat, and simmer 15 minutes. Add milk and tea; simmer 4 minutes (do not boil). Strain through a fine sieve into a small bowl; discard solids. Add honey to tea mixture, stirring until well blended. Yield: 2 servings (serving size: about 1 cup).

CALORIES 202 (18% from fat); FAT 4g (sat 2.3g, mono 1g, poly 0.2g); PROTEIN 4.1g; CARB 40.4g; FIBER 0.1g; CHOL 12mg; IRON 0.2mg; SODIUM 58mg; CALC 129mg

Chai-Spiced Winter Squash Puree

10 cups (1-inch) cubed peeled butternut squash (about 3¾ pounds)
2 tablespoons olive oil
½ teaspoon salt
¼ teaspoon ground cinnamon
¼ teaspoon freshly ground black pepper
⅛ teaspoon ground ginger
⅛ teaspoon ground cardamom
⅛ teaspoon ground cumin
Dash of white pepper
Dash of ground cloves
2 large shallots, peeled and quartered
1 large onion, cut into 1-inch pieces
¼ cup water
1 tablespoon brown sugar

1. Preheat oven to 375°.
2. Combine first 12 ingredients in a large bowl, tossing well to coat. Place squash mixture on a foil-lined jelly-roll pan. Bake at 375° for 50 minutes or until tender. Place squash mixture, ¼ cup water, and sugar in a food processor; process until smooth. Serve immediately. Yield: 6 servings (serving size: about ¾ cup).

CALORIES 204 (22% from fat); FAT 4.9g (sat 0.7g, mono 3.4g, poly 0.6g); PROTEIN 3.5g; CARB 41.9g; FIBER 6.7g; CHOL 0mg; IRON 2.3mg; SODIUM 212mg; CALC 155mg

Chai-Brined Pork Tenderloin with Spiced Apple Chutney

Chai spices bring a new twist to this classic combination of apples, onions, and pork.

BRINE:
2 teaspoons black tea leaves (such as Darjeeling or Assam)
3 cups unsweetened apple juice
3 tablespoons kosher salt
3 tablespoons brown sugar
½ teaspoon black peppercorns, crushed
6 whole cloves
1 bay leaf
3 cups cold water
2 (1-pound) pork tenderloins, trimmed

CHUTNEY:
2 cups unsweetened apple juice
2 teaspoons black tea leaves
1 teaspoon butter
1 teaspoon olive oil
1½ cups diced onion
4 cups diced peeled Rome apple (about 3 large)
½ cup golden raisins
2 tablespoons brown sugar
1 tablespoon cider vinegar
1 teaspoon minced peeled fresh ginger
½ teaspoon kosher salt
¼ teaspoon coarsely ground black pepper
⅛ teaspoon ground cardamom
⅛ teaspoon ground cinnamon
Dash of ground cloves

REMAINING INGREDIENTS:
1 teaspoon olive oil
½ teaspoon white peppercorns, crushed
½ teaspoon black peppercorns, crushed
Cooking spray

1. To prepare brine, place 2 teaspoons tea leaves on a double layer of cheesecloth. Gather edges of cheesecloth together, and tie securely.
2. Combine 3 cups apple juice and next 5 ingredients in a large saucepan, and bring to a boil. Cook 1 minute, and remove from heat. Add cheesecloth bag; cover and steep 5 minutes. Discard cheesecloth bag. Add 3 cups water, and cool to room temperature. Pour liquid into a large heavy-duty zip-top plastic bag. Add pork tenderloins to bag; seal and marinate in refrigerator 8 hours or overnight, turning bag occasionally.
3. To prepare chutney, bring 2 cups juice to a boil in a large saucepan. Remove from heat. Stir in 2 teaspoons tea leaves, and steep 2 minutes. Strain juice mixture through a sieve into a bowl; discard solids. Reserve juice mixture.
4. Heat butter and 1 teaspoon oil in pan over medium-low heat. Add onion; cook 20 minutes or until golden brown, stirring frequently. Stir in apple; cook 5 minutes. Add reserved juice mixture, raisins, and next 8 ingredients. Bring mixture to a boil over medium-high heat; reduce heat to medium. Cook 30 minutes or until apple is tender and mixture is thick. Remove from heat.
5. Preheat oven to 350°.
6. Remove pork from bag; discard brine. Pat pork dry with paper towels. Brush pork with 1 teaspoon oil; sprinkle on all sides with white peppercorns and ½ teaspoon black peppercorns. Place pork on a broiler pan coated with cooking spray. Bake at 350° for 40 minutes or until a thermometer registers 160° (slightly pink). Place pork on a platter, and let stand 5 minutes. Cut pork across grain into thin slices. Serve with chutney. Yield: 8 servings (serving size: 3 ounces pork and about ⅓ cup chutney).

CALORIES 242 (20% from fat); FAT 5.5g (sat 1.8g, mono 2.5g, poly 0.5g); PROTEIN 17.9g; CARB 31.2g; FIBER 1.7g; CHOL 50mg; IRON 1.6mg; SODIUM 412mg; CALC 29mg

Five Signs of Spring

Tender, delicate vegetables are welcome harbingers of the season.

Of all the produce of spring, a handful of vegetables really signals the season: asparagus, spring onions, baby artichokes, green peas, and fava beans. Each is a delicate but tasty addition to any dish it graces. But their time is short, so you'll want to make use of them while they're abundant and inexpensive.

Pappardelle with Lemon, Baby Artichokes, and Asparagus

Pappardelle is a wide, flat pasta. If you can't find it, use fettuccine. Be sure to grate the rind before you juice the lemon.

- 12 ounces uncooked pappardelle (wide ribbon pasta)
- 2¼ cups cold water, divided
- ¼ cup fresh lemon juice (about 2 lemons)
- 24 baby artichokes (about 2 pounds)
- 3 tablespoons extravirgin olive oil, divided
- 1 pound asparagus, trimmed and cut diagonally into 1-inch pieces
- 2 tablespoons chopped fresh flat-leaf parsley
- 1 tablespoon grated lemon rind
- 1 teaspoon chopped fresh thyme
- ½ teaspoon salt
- ½ teaspoon freshly ground black pepper
- 1¼ cups (5 ounces) grated fresh Parmigiano-Reggiano cheese

1. Cook pasta according to package directions, omitting salt and fat. Drain pasta, reserving ½ cup cooking liquid. Set pasta aside; keep warm.

2. Combine 2 cups water and juice in a medium bowl. Working with 1 artichoke at a time, cut off stem to within ¼-inch of base; peel stem. Remove bottom leaves and tough outer leaves, leaving tender heart and bottom; trim about 1 inch from top of artichoke. Cut each artichoke in half lengthwise. Place artichoke halves in lemon water.

3. Heat 1 tablespoon oil in a large skillet over medium heat. Drain artichokes well; pat dry. Add artichokes to pan. Cover and cook 8 minutes, stirring occasionally; uncover. Increase heat to medium-high; cook 2 minutes or until artichokes are golden, stirring frequently. Place artichokes in a large bowl.

4. Place pan over medium heat; add ¼ cup water and asparagus to pan. Cover and cook 5 minutes or until crisp-tender. Add asparagus, parsley, and rind to artichokes; toss well. Add pasta, reserved cooking liquid, 2 tablespoons oil, thyme, salt, and pepper to artichoke mixture; toss well. Place 2 cups pasta mixture into each of 6 shallow bowls; top each serving with about 3 tablespoons cheese. Yield: 6 servings.

CALORIES 411 (28% from fat); FAT 12.6g (sat 4g, mono 6.4g, poly 1.3g); PROTEIN 20.2g; CARB 59.5g; FIBER 12.2g; CHOL 15mg; IRON 3.9mg; SODIUM 644mg; CALC 217mg

MAKE AHEAD
Fresh Pea Soup with Mint

Serve warm or at room temperature for a first course or with a salad for a light meal.

- 2 teaspoons butter
- 1 cup coarsely chopped green onions
- 4 cups shelled green peas (about 4 pounds unshelled)
- 3 cups fat-free, less-sodium chicken broth
- 2 cups water
- 1 tablespoon fresh lemon juice
- ¼ teaspoon salt
- ¼ teaspoon freshly ground black pepper
- 1 tablespoon extravirgin olive oil
- 2 tablespoons thinly sliced mint
- Cracked black pepper (optional)

1. Melt butter in a large saucepan over medium heat. Add onions to pan; cook 3 minutes, stirring occasionally. Add peas, broth, and 2 cups water; bring to a boil. Reduce heat, and simmer 10 minutes or until peas are very tender, stirring occasionally. Remove from heat; let stand 15 minutes. Stir in juice, salt, and ¼ teaspoon pepper.

2. Place half of pea mixture in a blender; process until smooth. Pour pureed mixture into a large bowl. Repeat procedure with remaining pea mixture. Strain half of pureed mixture through a sieve into a large bowl, reserving liquid; discard solids. Return liquid to pureed soup mixture. Ladle about ¾ cup soup into each of 6 bowls; drizzle each with ½ teaspoon oil. Sprinkle each serving with 1 teaspoon mint. Garnish with cracked pepper, if desired. Yield: 6 servings.

CALORIES 161 (30% from fat); FAT 5.3g (sat 1.4g, mono 2.9g, poly 0.7g); PROTEIN 8.6g; CARB 20.8g; FIBER 7.7g; CHOL 3mg; IRON 2.6mg; SODIUM 311mg; CALC 56mg

Spring Onion and Morel Galette

Morels, the wild mushrooms that are a member of the truffle family, have a distinctive smoky, nutty essence.

PASTRY:

 1 cup all-purpose flour (about 4½ ounces)
⅔ cup cake flour (about 2⅔ ounces)
½ teaspoon salt
 3 tablespoons chilled butter, cut into small pieces
½ cup fat-free sour cream
 1 tablespoon fresh lemon juice
 3 tablespoons ice water

FILLING:

1¼ pounds spring onions
Cooking spray
 2 cups fresh morel mushrooms, halved lengthwise (about 4 ounces)
¼ teaspoon salt
¼ teaspoon freshly ground black pepper
½ cup (2 ounces) grated Gruyère cheese

1. To prepare pastry, lightly spoon flours into dry measuring cups; level with a knife. Combine flours and ½ teaspoon salt in a medium bowl. Cut in butter with a pastry blender or 2 knives until mixture resembles coarse meal. Combine sour cream and juice in a bowl, stirring well. Stir sour cream mixture into flour mixture. Sprinkle surface with 3 tablespoons ice water, 1 tablespoon at a time; toss with a fork until moist and crumbly (do not form a ball).

2. Gently press mixture into a 4-inch circle on plastic wrap; cover. Chill 20 minutes. Slightly overlap 2 sheets of plastic wrap on a slightly damp surface. Unwrap and place chilled dough on plastic wrap. Cover dough with 2 additional sheets of overlapping plastic wrap. Roll dough, still covered, into a 12-inch circle (about ¼-inch thick). Place dough in freezer 5 minutes or until plastic wrap can be easily removed. Remove top sheets of plastic wrap; place dough, plastic wrap side up, onto a baking sheet lined with parchment paper. Remove remaining plastic wrap.

3. Preheat oven to 400°.

4. To prepare filling, cut white parts of onions into thin slices, reserving green tops. Heat a large nonstick skillet over medium-high heat. Coat pan with cooking spray. Add sliced onions to pan; sauté 15 minutes or until golden. Add mushrooms to pan; cook 5 minutes or until moisture evaporates. Remove from heat. Cut green tops of onions into slices. Add tops, ¼ teaspoon salt, and pepper to pan; stir to combine. Spread onion mixture evenly over dough, leaving a 2-inch border; sprinkle cheese evenly over onion mixture. Fold edges of dough toward center, pressing gently to seal (dough will only partially cover onion mixture). Place pan on bottom rack in oven; bake at 400° for 25 minutes or until browned. Yield: 8 servings (serving size: 1 wedge).

CALORIES 195 (32% from fat); FAT 6.9g (sat 4.1g, mono 1.9g, poly 0.4g); PROTEIN 6.6g; CARB 27.3g; FIBER 2.5g; CHOL 20mg; IRON 2.5mg; SODIUM 308mg; CALC 148mg

Skillet-Roasted Chicken with Baby Artichokes and Olives

The quick roasting method in step 2 speedily cooks the chicken.

 1 (4-pound) whole roasting chicken
 2 teaspoons canola oil
 1 (14-ounce) can fat-free, less-sodium chicken broth, divided
½ teaspoon salt, divided
½ teaspoon freshly ground black pepper, divided
 3 cups water
 3 tablespoons fresh lemon juice
18 baby artichokes
 1 tablespoon extravirgin olive oil
 1 cup dry white wine
 1 teaspoon all-purpose flour
¼ cup capers, rinsed and drained
16 picholine olives, pitted
 3 cups hot cooked white rice

1. Preheat oven to 500°.

2. Split chicken in half lengthwise. Heat canola oil in a large stainless steel skillet over high heat. Place chicken, skin side down, in pan; place pan in oven. Cook chicken at 500° for 10 minutes; remove from oven. Carefully turn chicken over; pour 1½ cups broth over chicken. Return pan to oven; cook 25 minutes or until a thermometer inserted in meaty part of thigh registers 165°. Remove chicken from pan; let stand 10 minutes. Remove skin from chicken; discard skin. Sprinkle chicken with ¼ teaspoon salt and ¼ teaspoon pepper; cut chicken into thin slices. Cover and keep warm. Reserve pan drippings.

3. Combine 3 cups water and juice in a large bowl. Working with 1 artichoke at a time, cut off stem to within ¼-inch of base; peel stem. Remove bottom leaves and tough outer leaves, leaving tender heart and bottom; trim about 1 inch from top of artichoke. Cut each artichoke lengthwise into quarters. Place artichoke quarters in lemon water.

4. Heat olive oil in a large skillet over medium heat. Drain artichokes well; pat dry. Add artichokes to pan. Cover and cook 10 minutes or until tender; uncover. Increase heat to high; cook 2 minutes or until artichokes are golden, stirring frequently. Place artichokes in a medium bowl; sprinkle with ¼ teaspoon salt and ¼ teaspoon pepper.

5. Place a zip-top plastic bag inside a 2-cup glass measure. Pour chicken drippings into bag; let stand 10 minutes (fat will rise to top). Seal bag; carefully snip off 1 bottom corner of bag. Place pan over medium-high heat. Drain drippings into pan, stopping before fat layer reaches opening; discard fat. Stir in wine. Bring to a boil; cook until reduced to 1 cup (about 8 minutes).

6. Combine 2 tablespoons broth and flour, stirring until smooth. Add flour mixture to drippings; bring to a boil. Reduce heat to medium-low. Add artichokes, capers, and olives; cook 2 minutes or until thoroughly heated, stirring frequently. Serve with chicken and rice. Yield: 6 servings (serving size: 3 ounces chicken, about ⅓ cup sauce, and ½ cup rice).

CALORIES 393 (27% from fat); FAT 11.7g (sat 2.4g, mono 5.8g, poly 2.4g); PROTEIN 32.1g; CARB 41.7g; FIBER 9.8g; CHOL 71mg; IRON 4.6mg; SODIUM 787mg; CALC 104mg

Grilled Asparagus with Almond Gremolata

Closely watch the asparagus on the grill; the cook time will vary according to the size of the spears. If using a grill basket, make sure to preheat it.

⅓ cup sliced almonds, toasted and coarsely chopped
⅓ cup chopped fresh parsley
2 teaspoons grated lemon rind
3 tablespoons fresh lemon juice
2 tablespoons chopped fresh chives
1 tablespoon capers, drained and chopped
½ teaspoon chopped fresh thyme
½ teaspoon chopped fresh oregano
1 garlic clove, minced
¼ teaspoon salt, divided
¼ teaspoon freshly ground black pepper, divided
2 pounds fresh asparagus, trimmed
Cooking spray

1. Combine first 9 ingredients in a small bowl. Stir in ⅛ teaspoon salt and ⅛ teaspoon pepper.
2. Prepare grill.
3. Arrange asparagus on a grill rack coated with cooking spray; grill 8 minutes or until crisp-tender, turning twice. Sprinkle asparagus with ⅛ teaspoon salt and ⅛ teaspoon pepper. Divide asparagus evenly among 6 plates, and top each serving with about 2 tablespoons parsley mixture. Yield: 6 servings.

CALORIES 65 (40% from fat); FAT 2.9g (sat 0.3g, mono 1.7g, poly 0.8g); PROTEIN 4.8g; CARB 8.2g; FIBER 4g; CHOL 0mg; IRON 3.7mg; SODIUM 156mg; CALC 59mg

---

Blanching Basics

Blanching cooks vegetables just enough to heighten their flavor, intensify the color, and preserve freshness. To blanch is simply to cook food briefly in boiling water and submerge it in ice water to stop the cooking process. Blanch delicate spring ingredients like fava beans or green peas and pat them dry before putting them in the freezer, where they will keep up to two months.

Grilled Lamb Skewers with Warm Fava Bean Salad

The bright, fresh taste and textures of this salad complement grilled beef, chicken, or fish as well. If using wooden skewers, soak them in water 30 minutes before grilling.

4 cups shelled fava beans (about 8 pounds unshelled)
1½ teaspoons extravirgin olive oil
1 tablespoon chopped fresh mint
1 teaspoon grated lemon rind
2 tablespoons fresh lemon juice
1 teaspoon salt, divided
½ teaspoon freshly ground black pepper, divided
2 tablespoons water
1½ pounds leg of lamb, trimmed and cut into 1-inch cubes
Cooking spray
6 lemon wedges

1. Cook fava beans in boiling water 1 minute or until tender. Drain and rinse with cold water. Drain. Remove tough outer skins from beans, and discard skins.
2. Combine oil, mint, rind, juice, ½ teaspoon salt, and ¼ teaspoon pepper in a medium bowl, stirring with a whisk. Heat 2 tablespoons water in a medium saucepan over medium-high heat, and add beans to pan. Cook 2 minutes or until beans are thoroughly heated. Add beans to juice mixture, and toss to coat.
3. Prepare grill.
4. Thread lamb onto 12 (8-inch) skewers. Coat lamb with cooking spray; sprinkle evenly with ½ teaspoon salt and ¼ teaspoon pepper. Place skewers on grill rack coated with cooking spray; grill 7 minutes or until lamb is done, turning occasionally. Serve with salad and lemon wedges. Yield: 6 servings (serving size: 2 skewers, ½ cup salad, and 1 lemon wedge).

CALORIES 284 (33% from fat); FAT 10.3g (sat 4.3g, mono 4.5g, poly 0.7g); PROTEIN 24.8g; CARB 23g; FIBER 6.3g; CHOL 53mg; IRON 3.1mg; SODIUM 442mg; CALC 51mg

---

Flatbread with Asparagus and Spring Onions

This dough can be made ahead through the first rise, then punched down and refrigerated. If you don't have a pizza peel, use the back of a baking sheet to transfer the dough onto your preheated stone.

FLATBREAD:
Dash of sugar
1 package dry yeast (about 2¼ teaspoons)
¾ cup plus 3 tablespoons warm water (100° to 110°), divided
2 cups plus 3 tablespoons bread flour, divided (about 10⅔ ounces)
1 tablespoon extravirgin olive oil
½ teaspoon salt
Cooking spray
2 tablespoons cornmeal, divided

TOPPINGS:
2½ teaspoons extravirgin olive oil
1 garlic clove, minced
4 cups thinly sliced spring onions (about 2½ pounds)
¼ teaspoon salt
3 cups (1-inch pieces) asparagus (about 1 pound)
¾ cup (3 ounces) fontina cheese, shredded

1. To prepare flatbread, dissolve sugar and yeast in ¼ cup water in a large bowl; let stand 5 minutes. Lightly spoon flour into dry measuring cups and spoons; level with a knife. Add ¼ cup flour to yeast mixture, stirring with a spoon. Cover and let stand 30 minutes (mixture will be bubbly); uncover. Add ½ cup plus 3 tablespoons water to yeast mixture. Add 1¾ cups flour, 1 tablespoon oil, and ½ teaspoon salt, stirring until a soft dough forms. Turn dough out onto a floured surface. Knead until smooth and elastic (about 10 minutes); add enough of remaining flour, 1 tablespoon at a time, to prevent dough from sticking to hands (dough will feel sticky).
2. Place dough in a large bowl coated with cooking spray, turning to coat top. Cover and let rise in a warm place (85°), free from drafts, 1 hour or until doubled
Continued

in size. (Gently press two fingers into dough. If indentation remains, dough has risen enough.)

3. Punch dough down, and divide in half. Working with 1 portion at a time (cover remaining dough to prevent drying), roll dough into a 12-inch circle on a floured surface. Place dough circle on a pizza peel sprinkled with 1 tablespoon cornmeal.

4. Place a pizza stone on bottom rack in oven. Preheat oven to 500°.

5. To prepare toppings, combine 2½ teaspoons oil and garlic in a bowl; let stand 30 minutes.

6. Heat a large nonstick skillet over medium heat. Coat pan with cooking spray. Add onions and ¼ teaspoon salt to pan. Cover and cook 20 minutes, stirring occasionally. Uncover and cook 3 minutes or until golden, stirring frequently.

7. Cook asparagus in boiling water 2 minutes or until crisp-tender. Drain; rinse with cold water. Drain.

8. Brush dough circle with half of garlic mixture; arrange half of asparagus and onion mixture over dough, leaving a ½-inch border. Top with half of cheese. Slide dough onto preheated pizza stone. Bake at 500° for 9 minutes or until lightly browned. Repeat procedure with remaining dough, cornmeal, garlic mixture, asparagus, onion mixture, and cheese. Serve immediately. Yield: 2 flatbreads; 6 servings per flatbread (serving size: 1 slice).

CALORIES 145 (27% from fat); FAT 4.4g (sat 1.7g, mono 2.2g, poly 0.4g); PROTEIN 6.5g; CARB 21.7g; FIBER 2.5g; CHOL 8mg; IRON 1.9mg; SODIUM 210mg; CALC 72mg

Sugar Snap and Green Peas with Lemon and Mint

    3   quarts water
 2½   cups shelled green peas (about
        2 pounds unshelled)
 3½   cups sugar snap peas, trimmed
        (about ¾ pound)
 1½   tablespoons butter
  ½   teaspoon salt
  ¼   teaspoon freshly ground black
        pepper
    2   tablespoons chopped fresh mint
    2   teaspoons grated lemon rind

1. Bring 3 quarts water to a boil in an 8-quart stockpot or Dutch oven. Add green peas to boiling water; cook 1 minute. Add sugar snap peas; cook 2 minutes or until crisp-tender. Drain and pat dry.

2. Melt butter in a large skillet over medium heat. Add pea mixture, salt, and pepper to pan; cook 3 minutes, stirring occasionally. Remove from heat; stir in mint and rind. Yield: 6 servings (serving size: about ¾ cup).

CALORIES 99 (28% from fat); FAT 3.1g (sat 1.8g, mono 0.8g, poly 0.2g); PROTEIN 4.7g; CARB 13.1g; FIBER 4.6g; CHOL 8mg; IRON 2.3mg; SODIUM 220mg; CALC 48mg

Salmon with Sweet Pea Cream

Puree fresh green peas with half-and-half and broth for a smooth sauce.

    Cooking spray
    4   green onions, thinly sliced
    3   garlic cloves, minced
    2   cups shelled green peas (about
        2 pounds unshelled)
    1   cup fat-free, less-sodium chicken
        broth
  ½   teaspoon salt, divided
  ¼   cup half-and-half
    1   tablespoon chopped fresh dill
    4   (6-ounce) salmon fillets, skinned
  ¼   teaspoon freshly ground black
        pepper
    2   cups hot cooked long-grain white
        rice
    Dill sprigs (optional)

1. Heat a large nonstick skillet over medium heat. Coat pan with cooking spray. Add onions to pan; cook 1 minute, stirring frequently. Add garlic to pan; cook 30 seconds. Add green peas to pan; cook 1 minute, stirring frequently. Add broth and ¼ teaspoon salt, and bring to a simmer. Cook 4 minutes or until peas are tender. Transfer pea mixture to a food processor, and process 2 minutes or until smooth. Strain mixture through a sieve into a bowl, reserving liquid; discard solids. Stir in half-and-half and chopped dill. Cover and keep warm.

2. Wipe pan clean with paper towels. Place pan over medium-high heat. Coat pan with cooking spray. Sprinkle fish evenly with ¼ teaspoon salt and pepper. Add fish to pan; cook 2½ minutes. Carefully turn fish over; cook 5 minutes or until fish flakes easily when tested with a fork or until desired degree of doneness. Serve with pea mixture and rice. Garnish with dill sprigs, if desired. Yield: 4 servings (serving size: ½ cup rice, 1 salmon fillet, and ¼ cup sauce).

CALORIES 405 (29% from fat); FAT 12.9g (sat 3.7g, mono 5.4g, poly 2.7g); PROTEIN 38.2g; CARB 33.9g; FIBER 3.8g; CHOL 86mg; IRON 2.7mg; SODIUM 495mg; CALC 72mg

WINE NOTE: Consider serving this with a German spätlese riesling. Try the Pfeffingen "Ungsteiner Herrenberg" Riesling Spätlese 2004 from Pfalz, Germany ($20).

kitchen strategies
Table for Two (or More)

Problem: A Texas physician seeks recipes she can adjust to serve varying numbers of diners. Strategy: Quick dishes that are easy to double or halve.

Cooking for two doesn't necessarily mean less work than cooking for a larger group. Recipes most often serve four to six people, and it can be tricky determining how to cut a recipe down, what to leave out, and what to substitute. Robin Eickhoff, 39, a San Antonio physician, cooks for her husband, Tom, and herself for most of the year. But when her stepsons visit or when another family or couple come over for dinner, she might need to cook for four to eight people.

We've created a batch of recipes with Eickhoff and her family in mind—quick, easy, and healthful fare with adjustable serving amounts. (Some even provide lunch the next day.) We offer instructions to increase the smaller dishes to feed four or more people and to scale back the larger recipes to serve just two.

Slow-Cooked Chile Con Carne

To trim this recipe to two servings, omit one can of beans and use only one cup of broth. Cut the remaining ingredients in half.

Cooking spray
1½   cups chopped onion (about 1 medium)
2   garlic cloves, minced
1   pound sirloin, cut into 1-inch cubes
2½ cups diced plum tomato (about 6)
1   tablespoon chili powder
2   teaspoons ground cumin
1   teaspoon dried oregano
1   (15-ounce) can pinto beans, rinsed and drained
1   (15-ounce) can black beans, rinsed and drained
1   (14-ounce) can fat-free, less-sodium beef broth
¼   teaspoon salt

1. Heat a large nonstick skillet over medium-high heat. Coat pan with cooking spray. Add onion, garlic, and beef to pan; cook 5 minutes or until beef is browned, stirring occasionally. Combine beef mixture and next 7 ingredients in a 3½- to 4-quart electric slow cooker. Cover and cook on HIGH 3½ hours or until beef is tender. Uncover; cook 30 minutes or until slightly thick. Stir in salt. Yield: 4 servings (serving size: 1½ cups).

CALORIES 291 (19% from fat); FAT 6g (sat 1.9g, mono 2g, poly 0.3g); PROTEIN 34g; CARB 28.2g; FIBER 8.9g; CHOL 49mg; IRON 4.2mg; SODIUM 752mg; CALC 92mg

Chicken Potpie

To serve three, use 1½ tablespoons flour, cut the phyllo stack into quarters, and scale remaining ingredients down by half. Bake the potpies in three (10-ounce) ramekins. (Tuck one quarter of phyllo sheets on top of each ramekin; discard remaining quarter.) Bake 15 minutes or until tops are golden. To reduce prep time, look for prechopped vegetables in the supermarket.

2   tablespoons butter
2   tablespoons olive oil
3   cups diced red potato (about 1 pound)
2   cups diced onion
2   cups sliced mushrooms (about 8 ounces)
1   cup diced celery
1   cup diced carrot
¼   cup chopped fresh parsley
2   teaspoons chopped fresh thyme
2½ tablespoons all-purpose flour
3   cups fat-free milk
½   cup fat-free, less-sodium chicken broth
2   cups chopped cooked chicken breast (about 12 ounces)
1   cup frozen green peas
1   teaspoon salt
½   teaspoon freshly ground black pepper
6   (14 x 9–inch) sheets frozen phyllo dough, thawed
Cooking spray

1. Preheat oven to 375°.
2. Melt butter in a large saucepan over medium-high heat; add oil. Add potato and next 6 ingredients, and sauté 5 minutes. Reduce heat to low; sprinkle flour over vegetables. Cook 5 minutes, stirring frequently. Stir in milk and broth. Increase heat to medium-high; bring to a boil. Reduce heat, and simmer 5 minutes or until thickened. Add chicken, peas, salt, and pepper.
3. Spoon mixture into a 2-quart baking dish. Place 1 phyllo sheet on a large cutting board or work surface (cover remaining dough to keep from drying); lightly spray with cooking spray. Repeat layers with cooking spray and remaining phyllo. Place phyllo layers loosely on top of mixture in dish. Place dish on a baking sheet. Bake at 375° for 20 minutes or until top is golden. Yield: 6 servings.

CALORIES 354 (29% from fat); FAT 11.2g (sat 3.8g, mono 5.3g, poly 1.2g); PROTEIN 24.2g; CARB 40g; FIBER 4.4g; CHOL 52mg; IRON 2.5mg; SODIUM 680mg; CALC 209mg

Individual Chocolate Soufflé Cakes

To serve four, use five teaspoons flour and double the remaining ingredients. Doubling the flour would make the base too heavy.

Cooking spray
4½   tablespoons granulated sugar, divided
1   tablespoon all-purpose flour
1½ tablespoons Dutch process cocoa
2   tablespoons fat-free milk
¼   teaspoon vanilla extract
1   large egg white
1   teaspoon powdered sugar

1. Preheat oven to 350°.
2. Coat 2 (6-ounce) ramekins with cooking spray; sprinkle each with ¾ teaspoon granulated sugar.
3. Combine 2 tablespoons granulated sugar, flour, cocoa, and milk in a small saucepan over medium heat. Cook 2 minutes, stirring until smooth. Spoon chocolate mixture into a medium bowl; cool 4 minutes. Stir in vanilla.
4. Place egg white in a medium bowl; beat with a mixer at high speed until soft peaks form. Add 2 tablespoons granulated

Continued

sugar, 1 teaspoon at a time, beating until stiff peaks form (do not overbeat). Gently stir ¼ of egg white mixture into chocolate mixture; gently fold in remaining egg white mixture. Spoon mixture into prepared dishes. Sharply tap dishes 2 or 3 times to level. Place dishes on a baking sheet; bake at 350° for 15 minutes or until puffy and set. Sprinkle each soufflé with ½ teaspoon powdered sugar. Serve immediately. Yield: 2 servings (serving size: 1 soufflé).

CALORIES 152 (4% from fat); FAT 0.6g (sat 0.3g, mono 0.2g, poly 0g); PROTEIN 3.5g; CARB 35.3g; FIBER 1.4g; CHOL 0mg; IRON 0.8mg; SODIUM 35mg; CALC 26mg

Roasted Flank Steak with Olive Oil–Herb Rub

To serve two, use two (4-ounce) beef tenderloin steaks instead of flank steak, reduce the herbs to ½ teaspoon each, and omit the broth.

 2 teaspoons olive oil
 1 teaspoon chopped fresh thyme
 1 teaspoon chopped fresh oregano
 1 teaspoon chopped fresh parsley
 ⅛ teaspoon grated lemon rind
 1 garlic clove, minced
 ½ teaspoon salt
 ¼ teaspoon freshly ground black pepper
 1 (1½-pound) flank steak, trimmed
Cooking spray
 ¼ cup dry red wine
 ¼ cup fat-free, less-sodium beef broth
Thyme sprigs (optional)

1. Preheat oven to 400°.
2. Combine first 6 ingredients in a small bowl; set aside.
3. Sprinkle salt and pepper over steak. Heat a large ovenproof skillet over medium-high heat. Coat pan with cooking spray. Add steak to pan; cook 1 minute on each side or until browned. Add wine and broth; cook 1 minute. Spread herb mixture over steak; place pan in oven. Bake at 400° for 10 minutes or until desired degree of doneness. Let stand 10 minutes before cutting steak

diagonally across grain into thin slices. Serve with pan sauce. Garnish with fresh thyme sprigs, if desired. Yield: 6 servings (serving size: 3 ounces steak and about 1 tablespoon sauce).

CALORIES 167 (38% from fat); FAT 7g (sat 2.5g, mono 3.3g, poly 0.4g); PROTEIN 23.9g; CARB 0.5g; FIBER 0.1g; CHOL 37mg; IRON 1.6mg; SODIUM 266mg; CALC 21mg

Turkey Mini Meat Loaves

Feed six by doubling the ingredients and shaping the mixture into one eight by four-inch loaf. Bake time may increase to about 45 to 50 minutes; use a thermometer to check for internal temperature of 165°.

Cooking spray
 ½ cup chopped onion
 3 tablespoons dry breadcrumbs
 1 tablespoon chopped fresh parsley
 1 teaspoon Worcestershire sauce
 ¼ teaspoon salt
 ¼ teaspoon dried oregano
 ⅛ teaspoon freshly ground black pepper
 8 ounces ground turkey breast
 1 large egg white, lightly beaten
 3 tablespoons ketchup, divided
 ¼ teaspoon hot pepper sauce (such as Tabasco)

1. Preheat oven to 350°.
2. Heat a small skillet over medium-high heat. Coat pan with cooking spray. Add onion to pan; sauté 5 minutes or until lightly browned. Remove from heat; cool slightly.
3. Combine onion, breadcrumbs, and next 7 ingredients in a large bowl. Stir in 2 tablespoons ketchup. Spoon about ½ cup meat mixture into each of 3 muffin cups coated with cooking spray; place muffin pan on a baking sheet. Combine 1 tablespoon ketchup and hot pepper sauce in a small bowl. Brush ketchup mixture over meat loaf tops. Bake at 350° for 30 minutes or until a thermometer registers 165°. Yield: 3 servings (serving size: 1 loaf).

CALORIES 142 (10% from fat); FAT 1.5g (sat 0.4g, mono 0.1g, poly 0.2g); PROTEIN 20.2g; CARB 12g; FIBER 0.8g; CHOL 30mg; IRON 1.2mg; SODIUM 508mg; CALC 28mg

Comforting Classics Menu
serves 3

This menu's appeal lies in its simple, straightforward flavors; however, if you want bolder taste, stir ½ teaspoon chipotle chile powder into the potatoes.

Turkey Mini Meat Loaves

Smashed cheddar new potatoes*

Green salad

*Place 1½ pounds quartered new potatoes in a medium saucepan; cover with water. Bring to a boil; reduce heat, and simmer 20 minutes or until tender. Drain. Place potatoes in a medium bowl. Add ¾ cup 2% reduced-fat milk, ⅓ cup shredded extrasharp white Cheddar cheese, 1 tablespoon butter, ½ teaspoon salt, and ½ teaspoon freshly ground black pepper; mash with a potato masher to desired consistency.

Halibut Tacos with Yogurt-Lime Sauce

For two servings, use a ¾-pound fillet, and halve the remaining ingredients. Top the tacos with bottled salsa, if desired. For heat, add ⅛ teaspoon ground red pepper to yogurt mixture.

 1½ pounds skinless halibut fillets
 ¼ cup fresh lime juice (about 3 limes), divided
 ½ teaspoon salt
 ¼ teaspoon freshly ground black pepper
 1 cup plain fat-free yogurt
 1 teaspoon sugar
 ¼ teaspoon salt
 ⅛ teaspoon chili powder
Cooking spray
 8 (6-inch) corn tortillas
 1 10-ounce package shredded cabbage (about 2 cups)
 1 peeled avocado, cut into 16 slices
 ¼ cup chopped fresh cilantro

1. Place fish in a shallow bowl, and cover with 3 tablespoons juice, ½ teaspoon salt, and pepper. Cover and refrigerate 20 minutes.

2. Combine 1 tablespoon juice, yogurt, sugar, ¼ teaspoon salt, and chili powder. Cover and chill.

3. Heat a large nonstick skillet over medium-high heat. Coat pan with cooking spray. Add fish and marinade to pan. Cover and cook 8 minutes or until fish flakes easily when tested with a fork or until desired degree of doneness. Cut fish into 8 equal pieces.

4. Warm tortillas according to package directions. Top each tortilla with about 2 ounces fish, ¼ cup shredded cabbage, 2 tablespoons yogurt mixture, 2 avocado slices, and 1½ teaspoons cilantro. Yield: 4 servings (serving size: 2 tacos).

CALORIES 405 (21% from fat); FAT 9.5g (sat 1.4g, mono 4.3g, poly 2.4g); PROTEIN 43.8g; CARB 37.4g; FIBER 5.8g; CHOL 56mg; IRON 2.9mg; SODIUM 683mg; CALC 311mg

Pork Tenderloin, Pasta, and Peas Menu
serves 4

Substitute soba or lo mein noodles for udon, if you prefer.

Hoisin Pork Tenderloin

Udon noodle toss*

Steamed sugar snap peas

*Heat 1 tablespoon canola oil in a large nonstick skillet over medium-high heat. Add 1 cup red bell pepper strips, ½ cup matchstick-cut carrots, and 2 minced garlic cloves; sauté 3 minutes. Add 4 cups hot cooked udon noodles, 2 tablespoons chopped fresh cilantro, 2 tablespoons low-sodium soy sauce, 2 tablespoons fresh lime juice, and 2 teaspoons dark sesame oil; toss to coat.

Serving Solution

Freeze tablespoons of ingredients such as tomato paste, chicken or beef broth, chipotle chiles and adobo, and pesto in ice cube trays. Once solid, pop them out and store them in zip-top plastic bags for convenient small servings.

Hoisin Pork Tenderloin

To prepare two servings, replace the pork tenderloin with two (four-ounce) boneless pork chops, and reduce the marinade ingredients by half. Sprinkle each pork chop with one teaspoon sesame seeds for the last five to 10 minutes of cooking.

- ¼ cup hoisin sauce
- 2 tablespoons sliced green onions
- 2 tablespoons low-sodium soy sauce
- 1 tablespoon rice wine vinegar
- 2 garlic cloves, minced
- 1 (1-pound) pork tenderloin, trimmed
- Cooking spray
- 1 tablespoon sesame seeds

1. Combine first 5 ingredients in a large zip-top plastic bag; add pork to bag. Seal and marinate in refrigerator 2 hours, turning bag once.

2. Preheat oven to 425°.

3. Remove pork from bag, reserving marinade. Place pork on rack of a broiler pan or roasting pan coated with cooking spray; place rack in pan. Bake at 425° for 15 minutes. Sprinkle pork with sesame seeds; bake an additional 5 minutes or until a thermometer registers 160° (slightly pink). Place pork on a cutting board; let stand 10 minutes. Cut into ½-inch-thick slices.

4. Pour reserved marinade into a small saucepan; bring to a boil. Cook until reduced to ⅓ cup (about 2 minutes); serve with pork. Yield: 4 servings (serving size: 3 ounces pork and about 4 teaspoons sauce).

CALORIES 194 (27% from fat); FAT 5.8g (sat 1.7g, mono 2.2g, poly 1.1g); PROTEIN 25.4g; CARB 8.7g; FIBER 0.9g; CHOL 68mg; IRON 2mg; SODIUM 574mg; CALC 37mg

Presenting Pork Chops

Two cuts—bone-in and boneless—in four flavorful recipes make satisfying suppers.

Pork Chops Menu 1
serves 4

Pan-Seared Pork Chops with Red Currant Sauce (recipe on page 90)

Mushroom-barley pilaf*

Arugula salad with balsamic vinaigrette

*Cook 1 cup quick-cooking barley according to package directions, omitting salt and fat. Heat 1 tablespoon olive oil in a large saucepan over medium-high heat. Add 1 cup chopped onion and 1 (8-ounce) package presliced mushrooms; sauté 4 minutes. Stir in 2 minced garlic cloves; sauté 1 minute. Add ¼ cup dry sherry; cook until liquid almost evaporates. Stir in barley; cook 2 minutes or until thoroughly heated. Season with ½ teaspoon salt and ¼ teaspoon freshly ground black pepper.

Game Plan

1. While barley cooks:
- Prepare mushroom mixture for pilaf, and keep warm.

2. Prep ingredients for pork chops.

3. Cook pork chops.

4. Assemble and dress salad.

Pan-Seared Pork Chops with Red Currant Sauce

Tart cider vinegar balances the sweet currant jelly in this full-bodied, glossy sauce. See Pork Chops Menu 1 (page 89) for menu and game plan.

TOTAL TIME: 35 MINUTES

FLAVOR TIP: For brighter taste, substitute ½ teaspoon chopped fresh thyme for the dried herb on the chops.

- 2   teaspoons olive oil
- 4   (6-ounce) bone-in center-cut loin pork chops, trimmed (about ½ inch thick)
- 1   teaspoon ground coriander
- ¾   teaspoon salt, divided
- ¼   cup chopped shallots
- ¼   teaspoon dried thyme
- 2   garlic cloves, minced
- 2   tablespoons cider vinegar
- 1   cup fat-free, less-sodium beef broth
- ⅓   cup red currant jelly
- ¼   teaspoon freshly ground black pepper
- 1   teaspoon cornstarch
- 1   teaspoon water
- Chopped fresh chives (optional)

1. Heat oil in a large nonstick skillet over medium-high heat. Sprinkle pork with coriander and ½ teaspoon salt. Add pork to pan; cook 3 minutes on each side. Remove from pan. Add shallots, thyme, garlic, and ¼ teaspoon salt to pan; sauté 1 minute. Stir in vinegar; cook 15 seconds or until liquid almost evaporates. Stir in broth; bring to a boil. Cook until reduced to ⅔ cup (about 3 minutes). Add jelly and pepper; cook 2 minutes or until jelly melts.

2. Combine cornstarch and 1 teaspoon water in a small bowl. Add cornstarch mixture to pan; bring to a boil. Cook 1 minute, stirring constantly. Add pork to pan; cook 1 minute or until thoroughly heated. Garnish pork with chives, if desired. Yield: 4 servings (serving size: 1 pork chop and about 3 tablespoons sauce).

CALORIES 361 (32% from fat); FAT 12.6g (sat 4.1g, mono 6.3g, poly 1g); PROTEIN 39.4g; CARB 20.4g; FIBER 0.2g; CHOL 105mg; IRON 1.3mg; SODIUM 631mg; CALC 48mg

Pork Chops Menu 2
serves 4
Barbecue-Rubbed Pork Chops

Cheddar grits*

Cucumber–red onion salad

*Bring 2 cups fat-free milk and 1¼ cups water to a boil in a medium saucepan over medium-high heat. Slowly add ¾ cup quick-cooking grits, stirring well with a whisk. Cover, reduce heat, and simmer 5 minutes or until thick, stirring occasionally. Remove from heat. Add 1 cup reduced-fat shredded sharp Cheddar cheese, 1 tablespoon butter, ½ teaspoon salt, and ⅛ teaspoon freshly ground black pepper, stirring until cheese melts.

Game Plan

1. While milk mixture comes to a boil:
  • Prepare pork chop rub.
2. Grill pork chops.
3. While grits simmer:
  • Assemble salad.

Barbecue-Rubbed Pork Chops

This bold, zesty rub is made up of seven spices. Turn up the heat by using hot paprika or ¼ teaspoon ground red pepper.

TOTAL TIME: 35 MINUTES

- 1   tablespoon light brown sugar
- 1   teaspoon salt
- 1   teaspoon paprika
- 1   teaspoon chili powder
- ¾   teaspoon garlic powder
- ¾   teaspoon ground cumin
- ¼   teaspoon dry mustard
- ⅛   teaspoon ground allspice
- ⅛   teaspoon ground red pepper
- 4   (6-ounce) bone-in center-cut loin pork chops, trimmed (about ½ inch thick)
- Cooking spray

1. Combine first 9 ingredients; rub over both sides of pork. Heat a grill pan over medium-high heat. Coat pan with cooking spray. Add pork; cook 2 minutes on each side. Reduce heat to medium, and cook 8 minutes or until done, turning occasionally. Remove from pan; let stand 5 minutes. Yield: 4 servings (serving size: 1 pork chop).

CALORIES 277 (34% from fat); FAT 10.5g (sat 3.8g, mono 4.7g, poly 0.8g); PROTEIN 38.8g; CARB 4.3g; FIBER 0.5g; CHOL 105mg; IRON 1.4mg; SODIUM 669mg; CALC 48mg

Pork Chops Menu 3
serves 4
Spiced Chops with Mango-Mint Salsa

Roasted sweet potatoes*

Sautéed baby spinach

*Cut 2 (8-ounce) peeled sweet potatoes in half lengthwise; cut each half lengthwise into 6 wedges. Combine sweet potatoes, 1 tablespoon olive oil, ½ teaspoon salt, ½ teaspoon ground cumin, and ⅛ teaspoon ground red pepper in a bowl; toss gently to coat. Place wedges on a baking sheet; bake at 425° for 25 minutes or until tender.

Game Plan

1. While oven preheats:
  • Cut potatoes, and coat with spice mixture.
2. While potatoes bake:
  • Prepare salsa.
  • Cook pork.
  • Sauté spinach.

Spiced Chops with Mango-Mint Salsa

Allspice and mango bring Caribbean flair to this dish. The salsa, redolent of mint, also packs a bit of heat thanks to a dusting of crushed red pepper. A Jamaican beer, such as Red Stripe, would complement this meal.

TOTAL TIME: 35 MINUTES

FLAVOR TIP: To tweak the taste of the salsa, use lime juice and rind instead of lemon. Or substitute chopped papaya for the mango, if you prefer; look for ripe, golden-yellow papaya that yields slightly to finger pressure.

¾ teaspoon chili powder
¼ teaspoon salt
⅛ teaspoon ground allspice
4 (4-ounce) boneless center-cut loin pork chops, trimmed
Cooking spray
1½ cups finely chopped peeled mango
2 tablespoons chopped fresh mint
½ teaspoon grated lemon rind
1 tablespoon fresh lemon juice
2 teaspoons sugar
¼ teaspoon crushed red pepper

1. Combine first 3 ingredients in a small bowl; sprinkle evenly over pork.
2. Heat a large nonstick skillet over medium-high heat. Coat pan with cooking spray. Add pork; cook 4 minutes on each side or until done.
3. Combine mango and remaining 5 ingredients in a medium bowl. Serve with pork. Yield: 4 servings (serving size: 1 pork chop and about ⅓ cup salsa).

CALORIES 222 (29% from fat); FAT 7.1g (sat 2.6g, mono 3.2g, poly 0.5g); PROTEIN 26.1g; CARB 13.2g; FIBER 1.3g; CHOL 70mg; IRON 0.9mg; SODIUM 201mg; CALC 36mg

---

Pork Chops Menu 4
serves 4

Pork Chops Stuffed with Feta and Spinach

Herbed pita*

Yogurt drizzled with honey and cinnamon

*Cut 2 (6-inch) pitas into 8 wedges. Lightly coat pita wedges with cooking spray. Sprinkle with ¼ teaspoon dried basil, ¼ teaspoon dried coriander, ⅛ teaspoon salt, and ⅛ teaspoon dried thyme. Place pita wedges on a baking sheet; bake at 425° for 8 minutes or until toasted.

Game Plan

1. Preheat oven.
2. Bake pita.
3. While broiler preheats:
  • Prepare feta stuffing.
4. Stuff and broil pork chops.

Pork Chops Stuffed with Feta and Spinach

Lemon juice and rind add a citrusy tang to the Greek-inspired filling.

TOTAL TIME: 42 MINUTES

Cooking spray
4 garlic cloves, minced and divided
½ teaspoon salt, divided
¼ teaspoon freshly ground black pepper, divided
5 sun-dried tomatoes, packed without oil, diced
1 (10-ounce) package frozen chopped spinach, thawed, drained, and squeezed dry
¼ cup (1 ounce) crumbled reduced-fat feta cheese
3 tablespoons (1½-ounces) block-style fat-free cream cheese
½ teaspoon grated lemon rind
4 (4-ounce) boneless center-cut loin pork chops, trimmed
2 tablespoons fresh lemon juice
2 teaspoons Dijon mustard
¼ teaspoon dried oregano

1. Preheat broiler.
2. Heat a large nonstick skillet over medium-high heat. Coat pan with cooking spray. Add 2 garlic cloves; sauté 1 minute. Add ¼ teaspoon salt, ⅛ teaspoon pepper, tomatoes, and spinach; sauté until moisture evaporates. Remove from heat; stir in cheeses and rind.
3. Cut a horizontal slit through thickest portion of each pork chop to form a pocket. Stuff about ¼ cup spinach mixture into each pocket. Sprinkle ¼ teaspoon salt and ⅛ teaspoon pepper over pork. Arrange pork on rack of a broiler pan or roasting pan coated with cooking spray; place rack in pan. Combine 2 garlic cloves, juice, mustard, and oregano in a bowl; stir well. Brush half of mustard mixture over pork. Broil 6 minutes; turn chops. Brush remaining mixture over pork; broil 2 minutes or until done. Yield: 4 servings (serving size: 1 pork chop).

CALORIES 232 (33% from fat); FAT 8.6g (sat 3.4g, mono 3.1g, poly 0.7g); PROTEIN 32.1g; CARB 7.2g; FIBER 2.8g; CHOL 73mg; IRON 2.5mg; SODIUM 640mg; CALC 186mg

---

lighten up
All-Star Carrot Cake

A volleyball champ scores with the revitalization of her grandmother's special dessert.

As a member of her high school volleyball team, Emma Olgard of Spokane, Washington, understands the importance of maintaining a healthy lifestyle. And she knows nutrition plays a key role in performing well. Her interest in food went one step further when she began preparing meals for her family three days a week to earn money to buy a car for her 16th birthday. She loved cooking and baking so much that she asked her grandmother, Myrna, for the recipe of her favorite dessert, carrot cake.

With eight ounces of full-fat cream cheese, a pound of powdered sugar, and a cup each of vegetable oil, butter, and pecans, the cake was overloaded with calories and fat.

Our first move was to replace the cup of vegetable oil with three tablespoons of heart-healthy canola oil. To compensate for the loss of liquid, we increased the crushed pineapple to 1½ cups. Since nuts and coconut add plenty of flavor in small amounts, we reduced the amount of pecans to ⅓ cup and that of flaked coconut by half. For the frosting, we trimmed 4⅓ cups powdered sugar down to 3 cups to reduce calories. Instead of using full-fat cream cheese, we combined the ⅓-less-fat version with 2 tablespoons of butter to mimic the original frosting's richness.

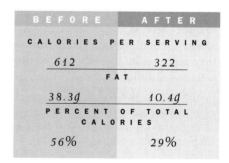

BEFORE	AFTER
CALORIES PER SERVING	
612	322
FAT	
38.3g	10.4g
PERCENT OF TOTAL CALORIES	
56%	29%

Continued

Carrot Cake

CAKE:

1½ cups all-purpose flour (about 6¾ ounces)

1⅓ cups granulated sugar

½ cup sweetened flaked coconut

⅓ cup chopped pecans

2 teaspoons baking soda

1 teaspoon salt

2 teaspoons ground cinnamon

3 tablespoons canola oil

2 large eggs, lightly beaten

2 cups grated carrot

1½ cups canned crushed pineapple, drained

Cooking spray

FROSTING:

2 tablespoons butter, softened

1 (8-ounce) block ⅓-less-fat cream cheese, softened

3 cups powdered sugar

2 teaspoons vanilla extract

Additional grated carrot (optional)

1. Preheat oven to 350°.

2. To prepare cake, lightly spoon flour into dry measuring cups; level with a knife. Combine flour and next 6 ingredients in a large bowl; stir well with a whisk. Combine oil and eggs; stir well. Stir egg mixture, 2 cups carrot, and pineapple into flour mixture. Spoon batter into a 13 x 9–inch baking pan coated with cooking spray. Bake at 350° for 35 minutes or until a wooden pick inserted in center comes out clean. Cool completely on a wire rack.

3. To prepare frosting, combine butter and cream cheese in a large bowl. Beat with a mixer at medium speed until smooth. Beat in powdered sugar and vanilla just until smooth. Spread frosting over top of cake. Garnish each serving with grated carrot, if desired. Yield: 16 servings (serving size: 1 piece).

CALORIES 322 (29% from fat); FAT 10.4g (sat 4.2g, mono 3.2g, poly 1.5g); PROTEIN 4.1g; CARB 54.4g; FIBER 1.4g; CHOL 40mg; IRON 1mg; SODIUM 403mg; CALC 29mg

Your New Old Favorites

We lend pizzazz to readers' go-to weeknight meals: tacos, pasta, and casseroles.

When a reader posted the question "What are the three most repeated dinners in your household?" on the CookingLight.com bulletin boards, it hit a nerve. At one point, the thread had 72 posts and more than 4,000 views. And it piqued not only readers' interest but ours, as well. We know that when a recipe finds its way to the table time and again, it often becomes a lifetime favorite. But what is it, we wondered, that shifts a dish from a first-time experiment to a reliable standby?

To find out, we began looking through the posts for common themes. Patsy Kreitman, 36, a working mother of two boys in Parsippany, New Jersey, admitted that she doesn't have time or energy to try out new dishes regularly, and that one-dish meals or casseroles are repeats in her house. Jean Zurn, a 39-year-old accountant from Brooklyn, New York, likes dishes in which she can "change one ingredient and make a lot of difference," as with enchiladas, a staple on her table. In her post, Kay Deis, an active 61-year-old retiree in Dadeville, Alabama, revealed that she and her husband have a penchant for pasta. In fact, we found that pasta, casseroles, and wraps or tacos populated nearly everyone's list.

Thai Beef Tacos with Lime-Cilantro Slaw
(pictured on page 230)

Tacos go Asian with crunchy cabbage slaw and steak flavored with ginger and fish sauce. Packaged coleslaw and matchstick carrots speed preparation. Serve with lime wedges and cilantro sprigs, if desired.

STEAK:

1 tablespoon sugar

1½ teaspoons minced peeled fresh ginger

1½ teaspoons fish sauce

½ teaspoon chili garlic sauce (such as Lee Kum Kee)

¼ teaspoon freshly ground black pepper

2 garlic cloves, minced

1 pound flank steak, trimmed

Cooking spray

SLAW:

¼ cup fresh lime juice

2 tablespoons rice wine vinegar

1 tablespoon sugar

1½ teaspoons minced peeled fresh ginger

1½ teaspoons fish sauce

½ teaspoon chili garlic sauce

2 garlic cloves, minced

3 cups packaged angel hair slaw

2 cups packaged matchstick-cut carrots

¼ cup sliced green onions

½ cup chopped fresh cilantro

REMAINING INGREDIENT:

8 (6-inch) fat-free flour tortillas

1. To prepare flank steak, combine first 6 ingredients in a large zip-top plastic bag. Add steak to bag; seal and marinate in refrigerator 20 minutes, turning occasionally.

2. Prepare grill or broiler.

3. Remove steak from bag; discard marinade. Place steak on grill rack or broiler pan coated with cooking spray; cook 5 minutes on each side or until desired degree of doneness. Let stand 5 minutes. Cut steak diagonally across grain into thin slices.

4. To prepare slaw, combine juice and next 6 ingredients in a large bowl. Add slaw and next 3 ingredients; toss well to combine.

5. Divide steak evenly among tortillas; spoon about ½ cup slaw onto each tortilla. Fold in half; serve immediately. Yield: 4 servings (servings size: 2 tacos).

CALORIES 431 (24% from fat); FAT 11.5g (sat 3.9g, mono 5g, poly 1.4g); PROTEIN 31g; CARB 50.8g; FIBER 5.1g; CHOL 42mg; IRON 4.3mg; SODIUM 871mg; CALC 157mg

Margarita Fish Tacos with Chipotle-Lime Mayo and Arugula

This versatile dish would be good with chicken or shrimp. To turn it into a salad, omit the tortillas and add chopped jicama and avocado.

    2   tablespoons tequila
  1½   tablespoons grated orange rind
    1   tablespoon grated lime rind
    2   teaspoons sugar
    2   teaspoons warm water
    1   pound halibut fillets
    ¼   teaspoon salt
    ¼   teaspoon freshly ground black
        pepper
    1   teaspoon olive oil
    ¼   cup reduced-fat mayonnaise
    1   tablespoon finely chopped fresh
        cilantro
    1   tablespoon fresh lime juice
  1½   teaspoons finely chopped chipotle
        chile, canned in adobo sauce
        (about 1 chile)
    8   (6-inch) corn tortillas
    2   cups trimmed arugula

1. Combine first 5 ingredients in a large zip-top plastic bag. Add fish to bag; seal and marinate in refrigerator 30 minutes, turning occasionally. Remove fish from

bag; discard marinade. Pat fish dry; sprinkle with salt and pepper. Heat oil in a large nonstick skillet over medium-high heat. Add fish; cook 4 minutes on each side or until fish flakes easily when tested with a fork or until desired degree of doneness. Break fish into chunks.

2. Combine mayonnaise, cilantro, juice, and chipotle.

3. Warm tortillas according to package directions. Divide fish evenly among tortillas; top each tortilla with ¼ cup arugula and about 2 teaspoons mayonnaise mixture. Fold in half. Yield: 4 servings (serving size: 2 tacos).

CALORIES 272 (23% from fat); FAT 6.9g (sat 1g, mono 2.1g, poly 2.5g); PROTEIN 26g; CARB 24g; FIBER 2.6g; CHOL 36mg; IRON 1.2mg; SODIUM 367mg; CALC 97mg

QUICK & EASY
Buffalo Tacos

Tacos have broad appeal, making them a good dish in which to try a new ingredient. Buffalo tastes like beef but has less saturated fat. It's available in many supermarkets—at the meat counter or in the frozen section. Substitute ground beef or turkey.

    1   teaspoon canola oil
    1   cup chopped onion (about
        1 small)
    3   garlic cloves, minced
    1   pound lean ground buffalo
    ⅓   cup tomato paste
    ½   teaspoon salt
    ½   teaspoon dried oregano
    ½   teaspoon ground cumin
    ¼   to ½ teaspoon ground red pepper
    2   cups water
    8   (6-inch) corn tortillas
    1   cup chopped tomato
    1   cup chopped iceberg lettuce
    ½   cup (2 ounces) shredded reduced-
        fat Cheddar cheese
    ¼   cup sliced ripe olives
    ¼   cup reduced-fat sour cream

1. Heat oil in a large nonstick skillet over medium heat. Add onion, garlic, and buffalo; cook 5 minutes or until buffalo is done, stirring to crumble. Add tomato paste and next 4 ingredients; stir well to combine. Stir in 2 cups water; bring to a

boil. Reduce heat, and simmer 20 minutes or until thick.

2. Warm tortillas according to package directions. Spoon about ¼ cup meat mixture onto each tortilla; top each tortilla with 2 tablespoons chopped tomato, 2 tablespoons lettuce, 1 tablespoon cheese, 1½ teaspoons olives, and 1½ teaspoons sour cream. Fold in half. Yield: 4 servings (serving size: 2 tacos).

CALORIES 389 (30% from fat); FAT 12.8g (sat 5.2g, mono 4.1g, poly 1.7g); PROTEIN 33.3g; CARB 37.4g; FIBER 5.5g; CHOL 72mg; IRON 4.9mg; SODIUM 686mg; CALC 255mg

Spinach-Feta Calzone Casserole

Readers love a one-dish meal; this updated casserole is a cross between a vegetarian calzone and the classic Greek dish spanakopita.

DOUGH:

    1   package dry yeast (about
        2¼ teaspoons)
    ¾   cup warm water (100° to 110°)
    1   teaspoon olive oil
    2   cups all-purpose flour (about
        9 ounces)
    ½   teaspoon salt
  Cooking spray

FILLING:

    1   tablespoon olive oil, divided
    5   garlic cloves, thinly sliced and
        divided
    2   cups thinly vertically sliced onion
        (about 1 medium)
    ¼   teaspoon salt
    ¼   teaspoon crushed red pepper
    2   pounds coarsely chopped fresh
        spinach
    ¾   cup (3 ounces) crumbled feta
        cheese

1. To prepare dough, dissolve yeast in ¾ cup warm water in a small bowl; let stand 5 minutes. Stir in 1 teaspoon oil. Lightly spoon flour into dry measuring cups; level with a knife. Combine flour and ½ teaspoon salt in a large bowl; add yeast mixture, stirring until dough forms. Turn
Continued

dough out onto a lightly floured surface. Knead until smooth and elastic (about 6 minutes). Place dough in a large bowl coated with cooking spray, turning to coat top. Cover and let rise in a warm place (85°), free from drafts, for 1½ hours or until doubled in size. (Gently press two fingers into dough. If indentation remains, dough has risen enough.)

2. Punch dough down; cover and let rest 5 minutes. Roll dough into a 12-inch square; fit dough into an 8-inch square baking pan coated with cooking spray, allowing excess dough to hang over edges of dish.

3. Preheat oven to 425°.

4. To prepare filling, combine 1 teaspoon oil and 2 garlic cloves; set aside.

5. Heat 2 teaspoons oil in a Dutch oven over medium-high heat. Add 3 garlic cloves and onion; sauté 5 minutes or until onion is tender and lightly browned. Spoon onion mixture into a large bowl. Stir in ¼ teaspoon salt and pepper; keep warm. Add half of spinach to pan; cook 1 minute or until spinach begins to wilt, stirring frequently. Add remaining spinach; cook 5 minutes or until spinach wilts. Place spinach in a colander; press until barely moist. Add spinach and cheese to onion mixture, stirring until well combined.

6. Brush dough with half of garlic-oil mixture; top with spinach mixture. Fold excess dough over filling to cover; brush with remaining garlic-oil mixture. Bake at 425° for 30 minutes or until golden. Let stand 10 minutes. Yield: 6 servings.

CALORIES 275 (23% from fat); FAT 7.1g (sat 2.7g, mono 2.9g, poly 0.9g); PROTEIN 11.7g; CARB 43.2g; FIBER 5.4g; CHOL 13mg; IRON 6.5mg; SODIUM 576mg; CALC 240mg

WINE NOTE: Feta cheese is incredibly wine friendly, suitable with white, rosé, or even lighter reds. And a sauvignon blanc, like Chateau Ste. Michelle Columbia Valley ($10), is ideal with the Mediterranean flavors of Spinach-Feta Calzone Casserole. The wine's tangy acidity acts like a squeeze of lemon to punch up the flavors, while the salty cheese emphasizes the citrus fruit notes of the wine.

Stovetop Sausage Mac and Cheese

It seems everyone loves mac and cheese. This quick and easy pasta toss combines three types of cheese, plus sausage, for creamy yet hearty texture and flavor. For a more colorful version, stir in spinach.

    4 ounces chicken and sun-dried
         tomato sausage (such as
         Gerhard's), chopped
 1 ¼ cups fat-free milk
    2 tablespoons all-purpose flour
    ¾ cup (3 ounces) shredded reduced-
         fat sharp Cheddar cheese
    ⅓ cup (about 1⅓ ounces) shredded
         Monterey Jack cheese
    ¼ cup (2 ounces) ⅓-less-fat cream
         cheese
    ½ teaspoon onion powder
    ¼ teaspoon garlic salt
    5 cups hot cooked elbow macaroni
         (about 8 ounces uncooked pasta)
Chopped fresh parsley (optional)

1. Heat a large nonstick saucepan over medium-high heat. Add sausage; sauté 4 minutes or until browned. Combine milk and flour in a small bowl, stirring well with a whisk. Add milk mixture to pan; bring to a boil, stirring constantly. Reduce heat to medium. Stir in cheeses, onion powder, and garlic salt; cook 3 minutes or until cheeses melt, stirring constantly. Stir in pasta. Garnish with parsley, if desired. Serve immediately. Yield: 4 servings (serving size: about 1¼ cups).

CALORIES 433 (29% from fat); FAT 13.9g (sat 7.8g, mono 3.8g, poly 0.9g); PROTEIN 23.6g; CARB 53.1g; FIBER 2.7g; CHOL 56mg; IRON 2.4mg; SODIUM 538mg; CALC 340mg

Chicken Stroganoff Pasta

Stroganoff usually consists of thin slices of beef in a mushroom–sour cream sauce and served over noodles or rice pilaf. This version keeps the classic flavors but uses chicken in place of beef and incorporates sage for a twist.

    1 tablespoon butter
 1 ½ cups chopped onion (about
         1 medium)
    2 teaspoons finely chopped fresh sage
 1 ¼ teaspoons salt, divided
    ¼ teaspoon freshly ground black
         pepper, divided
    1 (8-ounce) package presliced
         mushrooms
    ¼ cup all-purpose flour (about 1
         ounce)
    1 teaspoon paprika
    1 pound skinless, boneless chicken
         breasts
    1 tablespoon olive oil
    ½ cup fat-free, less-sodium chicken
         broth
    2 tablespoons sherry
    1 cup reduced-fat sour cream
    1 tablespoon all-purpose flour
    5 cups hot cooked wide egg noodles
         (about 8 ounces uncooked pasta)
    ¼ cup chopped fresh parsley

1. Melt butter in a large nonstick skillet over medium-high heat. Add onion; sauté 5 minutes or until tender. Add sage, ¼ teaspoon salt, ⅛ teaspoon pepper, and mushrooms; sauté 5 minutes or until mushrooms begin to brown. Spoon mixture into a large bowl.

2. Combine ¼ cup flour and paprika in a shallow dish. Cut each chicken breast

A small change can add much-needed variety to beloved staple dishes.

half in half lengthwise; cut crosswise into ¼-inch strips. Dredge chicken strips in flour mixture; shake off excess flour mixture. Heat oil in pan over medium-high heat. Add chicken; sprinkle with ¼ teaspoon salt and ⅛ teaspoon pepper. Sauté 4 minutes or until chicken is done. Add chicken to mushroom mixture.

3. Add broth and sherry to pan, scraping pan to loosen browned bits. Reduce heat to medium-low. Place sour cream in a small bowl; sprinkle with 1 tablespoon flour. Stir with a whisk until combined. Stir sour cream mixture and ¾ teaspoon salt into broth mixture. Stir in chicken mixture; cook 1 minute or until thoroughly heated. Add noodles and parsley; stir well to combine. Yield: 6 servings (serving size: about 1⅔ cups).

CALORIES 427 (28% from fat); FAT 13.5g (sat 5.7g, mono 4.7g, poly 1.6g); PROTEIN 28.7g; CARB 47g; FIBER 3g; CHOL 101mg; IRON 3.4mg; SODIUM 625mg; CALC 96mg

Peanut Fettuccine with Shrimp, Carrots, and Snow Peas

For an authentic Asian touch, use wide, flat rice noodles.

- 8 ounces uncooked fettuccine
- ¼ cup creamy peanut butter
- 1 tablespoon peanut oil, divided
- 4 cups snow peas, trimmed
- 2 cups packaged matchstick-cut carrots
- 1 tablespoon grated peeled fresh ginger
- 3 garlic cloves, thinly sliced
- ¾ cup fat-free, less-sodium chicken broth, divided
- 1 pound peeled and deveined medium shrimp
- 1 tablespoon sugar
- 2 tablespoons low-sodium soy sauce
- 2 teaspoons chili garlic sauce
- ¼ cup minced fresh cilantro

1. Cook pasta according to package directions, omitting salt and fat. Drain in a colander over a bowl, reserving ½ cup cooking liquid. Set pasta aside. Combine reserved liquid and peanut butter in a small bowl, stirring with a whisk until combined. Set aside.

2. Heat 2 teaspoons oil in a large nonstick skillet over medium-high heat. Add snow peas and carrots; stir-fry 3 minutes. Stir in ginger and garlic; stir-fry 2 minutes or until vegetables are tender. Add ¼ cup broth; cook 1 minute. Spoon carrot mixture into a large bowl; keep warm. Add 1 teaspoon oil to pan. Add shrimp; stir-fry 2 minutes or until shrimp are done. Add shrimp to carrot mixture; keep warm.

3. Combine ½ cup broth, sugar, soy sauce, and chili sauce in a small bowl, stirring with a whisk until sugar dissolves. Add soy sauce mixture and peanut butter mixture to pan. Reduce heat; simmer 3 minutes or until slightly thick. Add pasta to pan, tossing to coat. Stir in shrimp mixture; cook 2 minutes or until thoroughly heated, tossing to coat. Sprinkle with cilantro. Yield: 6 servings (serving size: 1½ cups).

CALORIES 352 (25% from fat); FAT 9.8g (sat 1.9g, mono 3.9g, poly 2.9g); PROTEIN 25.6g; CARB 41.5g; FIBER 4.2g; CHOL 115mg; IRON 4.4mg; SODIUM 419mg; CALC 89mg

then & now

Beef Stroganoff

Legend has it this dish was created for 19th-century Russian general Count Alexander Stroganov, and it eventually became a dinner-party standby for American home cooks in the 1950s and 1960s.

The recipe's longevity is no surprise; its combination of thinly sliced beef, mushrooms, and noodles in a creamy sauce has broad and comforting appeal.

When our recipe for this classic first ran in September/October 1988, it called for beef-flavored bouillon granules and hot water, as well as margarine. Our current interpretation uses fat-free, less-sodium beef broth, butter, and cremini instead of white mushrooms for deeper flavor. The new recipe also calls for browning the steak for less time than the original, which produces more tender results.

Beef Stroganoff

- 1 pound boneless sirloin steak, trimmed
- Cooking spray
- 3 cups sliced cremini mushrooms (about 8 ounces)
- ½ cup chopped onion
- 1 tablespoon butter
- 2 tablespoons all-purpose flour
- 1 cup fat-free, less-sodium beef broth
- ¼ cup dry sherry
- ½ teaspoon salt
- ⅛ teaspoon freshly ground black pepper
- ¾ cup reduced-fat sour cream
- 4 cups hot cooked egg noodles (8 ounces uncooked)
- 3 tablespoons minced fresh flat-leaf parsley
- Fresh parsley sprigs (optional)

1. Cut beef diagonally across grain into ¼-inch-wide strips; cut strips into 2-inch pieces.

2. Heat a large nonstick skillet over medium-high heat. Coat pan with cooking spray. Add beef to pan; sauté 2 minutes or until lightly browned. Remove beef from pan; place in a medium bowl, and keep warm. Add mushrooms and onion to pan; sauté 4 minutes. Add mushroom mixture to beef.

3. Melt butter in pan over medium heat. Add flour. Cook 1 minute, stirring with a whisk. Gradually add broth, stirring constantly. Cook 1 minute or until thick and bubbly, stirring constantly.

4. Add beef mixture, sherry, salt, and pepper to pan; bring to a boil. Reduce heat, and simmer 4 minutes. Remove from heat; let stand 30 seconds. Stir in sour cream.

5. Combine noodles and minced parsley. Serve beef mixture over noodles. Garnish with parsley sprigs, if desired. Yield: 6 servings (serving size: about ⅔ cup beef mixture and ⅔ cup noodles).

CALORIES 352 (30% from fat); FAT 11.7g (sat 5.3g, mono 3.9g, poly 1g); PROTEIN 24.2g; CARB 36g; FIBER 1.8g; CHOL 87mg; IRON 3.1mg; SODIUM 355mg; CALC 40mg

Creative Cooks

With inspiration ranging from Ireland to Asia, here are more *Cooking Light* Ultimate Reader Recipe Contest finalist entries.

In January/February and March, we highlighted the 2006 *Cooking Light* Ultimate Reader Recipe Contest winning and finalists' recipes, featuring varied flavors and techniques. This month we offer an impressive range of recipes from the remaining finalists.

Grilled Skirt Steak and Mesclun Salad with Miso Dressing

CATEGORY FINALIST—ENTRÉES

"Miso paste can be found in most Asian grocery stores. The darker the paste, the saltier and stronger the flavor. For a lower-fat option, substitute flank steak."

—Melissa Iwai, Brooklyn, New York

DRESSING:

1 tablespoon rice wine vinegar
1 tablespoon low-sodium soy sauce
2 teaspoons canola oil
2 teaspoons miso (soybean paste)
½ teaspoon sugar
½ teaspoon sesame oil

SALAD:

2½ tablespoons chopped green onions
2 tablespoons low-sodium soy sauce
2 teaspoons rice wine vinegar
½ teaspoon sugar
2 teaspoons minced garlic cloves
1 (1-pound) skirt steak
Cooking spray
8 cups gourmet salad greens
2 tomatoes, each cut into 8 wedges (about 1 pound)
½ English cucumber, thinly sliced
2 teaspoons sesame seeds, toasted

1. To prepare dressing, combine first 6 ingredients in a bowl, stirring with a whisk until smooth. Set aside.

2. To prepare steak, combine onions and next 4 ingredients in a large zip-top plastic bag. Add steak to bag; seal. Marinate in refrigerator 1 hour, turning occasionally.

3. Prepare grill.

4. Remove steak from bag; discard marinade. Place steak on grill rack coated with cooking spray; cook 5 minutes on each side or until desired degree of doneness. Let stand 5 minutes. Cut steak diagonally across grain into thin slices. Place steak in a medium bowl. Drizzle with half of dressing; toss well.

5. Place salad greens in a large bowl. Drizzle with remaining dressing; toss well. Place about 1 cup salad mixture on each of 4 plates. Top each serving with 3 ounces steak, 4 tomato wedges, and one quarter of cucumber slices. Sprinkle each serving with ½ teaspoon sesame seeds. Yield: 4 servings.

CALORIES 275 (47% from fat); FAT 14.5g (sat 4.6g, mono 6.3g, poly 2.8g); PROTEIN 26.2g; CARB 10.7g; FIBER 4.1g; CHOL 51mg; IRON 4.6mg; SODIUM 621mg; CALC 102mg

WINE NOTE: When layering potent flavors like the savory soy and chargrilled smoke of Grilled Skirt Steak and Mesclun Salad with Miso Dressing, the wine should have similar complexity. A supple syrah, like Gloria Ferrer Syrah 2002 ($19), resonates with this dish: It has just enough tannin to stand up to the steak, and the ripe blackberry and smoky flavors are amplified by the savory elements.

Poached Pear and Greens Salad

CATEGORY FINALIST—SIDE DISHES AND SIDE SALADS

"I made a poached pear dessert and thought the pears would be delightful in a salad. If white balsamic vinegar is not available, Champagne vinegar works well, too."

—Margee Berry, Trout Lake, Washington

2 cups water
1 (750-milliliter) bottle riesling or other slightly sweet white wine
1 (2-inch) piece vanilla bean, split lengthwise
3 peeled cored firm Bartlett pears (about 1 pound)
2 (2-inch) lemon rind strips
2 (2-inch) orange rind strips
8 cups mixed salad greens
8 (⅛-inch-thick) slices red onion, separated into rings
½ cup golden California raisins
½ cup (2 ounces) crumbled goat cheese
2 tablespoons extravirgin olive oil
2 tablespoons white balsamic vinegar
2 teaspoons honey Dijon mustard

1. Combine 2 cups water and wine in a large saucepan over medium heat. Scrape seeds from vanilla bean; add seeds, bean, and next 3 ingredients to pan; bring to a boil. Reduce heat, and simmer 15 minutes or until pears are tender. Drain and cool; discard bean and rinds. Cut pears in half lengthwise, and cut into thin wedges.

2. Place 1 cup greens on each of 8 plates. Top each serving with 1 red onion slice, 1 tablespoon raisins, ⅓ cup pears, and 1 tablespoon cheese.

3. Combine oil, vinegar, and mustard in a small bowl; stir with a whisk until smooth. Drizzle about 1 teaspoon dressing over each salad. Serve immediately. Yield: 8 servings.

CALORIES 136 (34% from fat); FAT 5.2g (sat 1.6g, mono 2.8g, poly 0.5g); PROTEIN 2.9g; CARB 22g; FIBER 3.7g; CHOL 3mg; IRON 1.4mg; SODIUM 56mg; CALC 56mg

Chocolate Chip Irish Cream Pound Cake

CATEGORY FINALIST—DESSERTS

"This cake is even better on the second day."

—Anna Ginsberg, Austin, Texas

```
¼   cup semisweet chocolate
     minichips
1   teaspoon cake flour
2¾  cups cake flour (about 11 ounces)
1   teaspoon baking powder
½   teaspoon salt
¾   cup fat-free cream cheese,
     softened
10  tablespoons butter, softened
1   cup granulated sugar
1   cup packed brown sugar
1   teaspoon vanilla extract
3   large eggs
¾   cup Irish cream liqueur
    Baking spray with flour
2   tablespoons powdered sugar
```

1. Preheat oven to 325°.

2. Combine chocolate chips and 1 teaspoon flour in a small bowl; toss.

3. Lightly spoon 2¾ cups flour into dry measuring cups; level with a knife. Sift together flour, baking powder, and salt.

4. Place cream cheese and butter in a bowl; beat with a mixer at high speed to blend. Add granulated sugar, brown sugar, and vanilla; beat until blended. Add eggs, 1 at a time; beat well after each addition. Beat at high speed 1 minute. With mixer on low, add flour mixture and liqueur alternately to sugar mixture, beginning and ending with flour mixture; beat well after each addition. Fold in chocolate chips. Pour batter into a 12-cup Bundt pan coated with baking spray. Bake at 325° for 55 minutes or until a wooden pick inserted in center comes out clean. Cool 10 minutes on a wire rack; remove from pan. Cool completely on wire rack. Sift powdered sugar over cake. Yield: 16 servings (serving size: 1 slice).

CALORIES 308 (30% from fat); FAT 10.1g (sat 5.9g, mono 2.5g, poly 0.5g); PROTEIN 5g; CARB 48.9g; FIBER 0.6g; CHOL 59mg; IRON 2.3mg; SODIUM 231mg; CALC 60mg

Smoked Salmon and Cheese Mini Twice-Baked Potatoes

CATEGORY FINALIST— STARTERS AND DRINKS

"I love Ireland and the country's wonderful food. When I think of Irish food, the first items that come to mind are potatoes, salmon, and cheese."

—Abigail McMahon, Sherman Oaks, California

```
6   small Yukon gold or red potatoes
     (about 2 pounds)
1   teaspoon olive oil
½   teaspoon salt, divided
    Cooking spray
2   tablespoons fat-free milk
1   tablespoon butter
½   teaspoon black pepper
½   cup (2 ounces) finely grated white
     Cheddar cheese
2   tablespoons finely chopped
     smoked salmon (1 ounce)
```

1. Preheat oven to 400°.

2. Rub potatoes with oil; sprinkle with ¼ teaspoon salt. Place potatoes on a jelly-roll pan coated with cooking spray. Bake at 400° for 35 minutes or until tender. Remove from oven; cool 10 minutes.

3. Cut potatoes in half crosswise; cut off a small portion of rounded edge so potato will stand upright. Carefully scoop out about 1 teaspoon pulp from each half, leaving shells intact. Combine potato pulp, milk, butter, pepper, cheese, and ¼ teaspoon salt in a bowl. Spoon about 1 heaping teaspoon potato mixture into each potato shell. Arrange stuffed potatoes on a jelly-roll pan; top each with ½ teaspoon chopped salmon. Bake at 400° for 15 minutes or until thoroughly heated. Yield: 12 servings (serving size: 1 stuffed potato half).

CALORIES 96 (27% from fat); FAT 2.9g (sat 1.7g, mono 0.6g, poly 0.1g); PROTEIN 3.5g; CARB 13.6g; FIBER 0.9g; CHOL 8mg; IRON 0.7mg; SODIUM 159mg; CALC 37mg

Easter Dinner

This festive meal is a pleasure to host because you do most of the preparation in advance.

Easter Dinner Menu
serves 8

Shrimp and Bacon Deviled Eggs

Sun-Dried Tomato and Herb-Stuffed Leg of Lamb

Asparagus with Olive Gremolata

Roasted Potatoes with Herb Vinaigrette

Hot Cross Buns

Almond Jelly Roll with Raspberry Filling

WINE NOTE: Syrah, which is rich and mouth-filling with an earthy, meaty character, perfectly underscores the luscious meatiness of lamb. A terrific syrah bargain: Grand Archer Syrah 2003 from Sonoma County, California ($20).

STAFF FAVORITE • MAKE AHEAD
Shrimp and Bacon Deviled Eggs

Instant potato flakes give the filling body. You can prepare this a day ahead; cover with plastic wrap, and refrigerate.

```
8   hard-cooked large eggs
¼   cup instant potato flakes
¼   cup fat-free mayonnaise
1   tablespoon chopped fresh chives
2   teaspoons Dijon mustard
¼   teaspoon salt
⅛   teaspoon freshly ground black
     pepper
⅛   teaspoon ground red pepper
½   cup cooked medium shrimp, peeled
     and chopped (about 4 ounces)
2   tablespoons chopped fresh parsley
3   center-cut bacon slices, cooked
     and crumbled
```

Continued

1. Cut eggs in half lengthwise; remove yolks. Place 4 yolks in a medium bowl; reserve remaining yolks for another use. Add potato flakes and next 6 ingredients to yolks; stir well. Stir in shrimp and parsley. Spoon about 1 rounded tablespoon shrimp mixture into each egg white half. Sprinkle with bacon. Yield: 8 servings (serving size: 2 stuffed egg halves).

CALORIES 83 (40% from fat); FAT 3.7g (sat 1.2g, mono 1.5g, poly 0.6g); PROTEIN 8.8g; CARB 3.2g; FIBER 0.3g; CHOL 127mg; IRON 0.7mg; SODIUM 295mg; CALC 23mg

MAKE AHEAD
Sun-Dried Tomato and Herb-Stuffed Leg of Lamb

Stuff and roll the roast the day before; remove from the refrigerator, and let stand at room temperature 30 minutes before cooking.

  1 cup boiling water
 ⅓ cup sun-dried tomatoes, packed without oil
Cooking spray
 ⅓ cup finely chopped shallots
  4 garlic cloves, minced and divided
  2 teaspoons finely chopped fresh rosemary, divided
1¼ teaspoons salt, divided
 ¾ teaspoon black pepper, divided
  1 (1½-ounce) slice sourdough bread
  1 (2½-pound) rolled boneless leg of lamb

1. Combine 1 cup boiling water and tomatoes in a bowl; let stand 30 minutes or until soft. Drain and chop.
2. Preheat oven to 425°.
3. Heat a large nonstick skillet over medium-high heat. Coat pan with cooking spray. Add shallots; sauté 3 minutes or until tender. Add tomatoes and 2 garlic cloves; sauté 1 minute. Stir in 1 teaspoon rosemary, ¼ teaspoon salt, and ¼ teaspoon pepper.
4. Place bread in a food processor; pulse 25 times or until coarse crumbs measure ¾ cup. Stir crumbs into shallot mixture.
5. Unroll roast; trim fat. Place roast between 2 sheets of heavy-duty plastic wrap; pound to ¾-inch thickness using a meat mallet or small heavy skillet. Sprinkle roast with ½ teaspoon salt and ¼ teaspoon pepper. Spread breadcrumb mixture over roast. Reroll roast; secure at 1-inch intervals with twine. Combine 1 teaspoon rosemary, ½ teaspoon salt, ¼ teaspoon pepper, and 2 minced garlic cloves; rub over roast.
6. Place roast on rack of a broiler pan coated with cooking spray. Bake at 425° for 30 minutes. Remove roast from oven; cover loosely with foil. Bake an additional 20 minutes or until a thermometer registers 145° (medium-rare) or until desired degree of doneness. Let roast stand 15 minutes before slicing. Yield: 8 servings (serving size: about 3 ounces).

CALORIES 231 (48% from fat); FAT 12.4g (sat 5g, mono 5.2g, poly 0.9g); PROTEIN 23.1g; CARB 5.8g; FIBER 0.6g; CHOL 77mg; IRON 2.2mg; SODIUM 506mg; CALC 22mg

QUICK & EASY • MAKE AHEAD
Asparagus with Olive Gremolata

Steam the asparagus and prepare the gremolata a day in advance; refrigerate separately. Allow both to come to room temperature before serving.

GREMOLATA:
 ½ cup picholine olives, pitted (about 2 ounces)
 ½ cup chopped fresh flat-leaf parsley
  1 tablespoon grated lemon rind
 ¼ teaspoon salt
  2 garlic cloves, minced

REMAINING INGREDIENTS:
2½ pounds trimmed asparagus spears, steamed and chilled
 ¼ teaspoon freshly ground black pepper

1. To prepare gremolata, place olives in a food processor; pulse 3 times or until finely chopped. Add parsley, lemon rind, salt, and garlic. Pulse 2 times or until mixture is combined. Serve gremolata over asparagus; sprinkle with pepper. Yield: 8 servings.

CALORIES 41 (29% from fat); FAT 1.3g (sat 0.2g, mono 0.8g, poly 0.2g); PROTEIN 3.4g; CARB 6.4g; FIBER 3.4g; CHOL 0mg; IRON 3.3mg; SODIUM 189mg; CALC 46mg

QUICK & EASY • MAKE AHEAD
Roasted Potatoes with Herb Vinaigrette

To get a head start, quarter the potatoes, and toss with half of the olive oil and 1 teaspoon lemon juice (to prevent browning). Refrigerate overnight in a zip-top plastic bag. Bring to room temperature before roasting.

  3 tablespoons olive oil, divided
  3 pounds small red potatoes, quartered (about 24)
Cooking spray
  1 teaspoon salt, divided
 ½ teaspoon black pepper, divided
  3 garlic cloves, minced
  2 tablespoons chopped fresh chives
  3 tablespoons white wine vinegar
  1 tablespoon Dijon mustard
1½ teaspoons chopped fresh tarragon

1. Preheat oven to 400°.
2. Combine 1½ tablespoons oil and potatoes on a large jelly-roll pan coated with cooking spray, tossing to coat. Sprinkle with ½ teaspoon salt and ¼ teaspoon pepper. Bake at 400° for 40 minutes or until tender, stirring after 25 minutes. Add garlic; toss well. Bake an additional 5 minutes or until potatoes are done.
3. Combine 1½ tablespoons oil, ½ teaspoon salt, ¼ teaspoon pepper, chives, and remaining 3 ingredients, stirring with a whisk. Drizzle over potatoes; toss gently. Yield: 8 servings (serving size: ¾ cup).

CALORIES 172 (29% from fat); FAT 5.5g (sat 0.8g, mono 3.8g, poly 0.7g); PROTEIN 3.5g; CARB 27.8g; FIBER 3g; CHOL 0mg; IRON 1.4mg; SODIUM 353mg; CALC 24mg

Hot Cross Buns

Wrap cooked, cooled buns in foil, and freeze; thaw at room temperature. Reheat at 300° for 20 minutes. Unwrap; pipe on glaze while buns are warm.

BUNS:

⅓ cup granulated sugar
1 package dry yeast (about 2¼ teaspoons)
¾ cup warm whole milk (100° to 110°)
4 cups all-purpose flour, divided (about 18 ounces)
6 tablespoons butter, melted
¾ teaspoon salt
½ teaspoon ground cinnamon
2 large eggs, lightly beaten
½ cup golden raisins
Cooking spray

GLAZE:

1 cup powdered sugar
⅛ teaspoon ground cinnamon
2 tablespoons whole milk

1. To prepare buns, dissolve granulated sugar and yeast in warm milk in a large bowl; let stand 5 minutes.
2. Lightly spoon flour into dry measuring cups; level with a knife. Add 3¾ cups flour, butter, and next 3 ingredients to milk mixture, stirring until a soft dough forms.
3. Turn dough out onto a lightly floured surface. Knead in raisins. Knead dough until smooth and elastic (about 6 minutes); add enough of remaining flour, 1 tablespoon at a time, to prevent dough from sticking to hands.
4. Place dough in a large bowl coated with cooking spray, turning to coat top. Cover and let rise in a warm place (85°), free from drafts, 45 minutes or until doubled in size. (Press two fingers into dough. If indentation remains, dough has risen enough.) Punch dough down; cover and let rest 5 minutes.
5. Divide dough into 20 equal portions; roll each portion into a ball. Place balls in a 9-inch square baking pan coated with cooking spray. Cover and let rise 45 minutes or until doubled in size.

6. Preheat oven to 350°.
7. Uncover and bake at 350° for 20 minutes or until golden. Cool in pan 5 minutes on a wire rack. Remove from pan.
8. To prepare glaze, combine powdered sugar and ⅛ teaspoon cinnamon, stirring well with a whisk. Stir in 2 tablespoons milk. Spoon glaze into a zip-top plastic bag. Seal bag; snip a tiny hole in 1 corner of bag. Pipe a cross on top of each warm roll. Yield: 20 rolls (serving size: 1 roll).

CALORIES 185 (22% from fat); FAT 4.5g (sat 2.6g, mono 1.2g, poly 0.3g); PROTEIN 3.8g; CARB 32.2g; FIBER 1g; CHOL 31mg; IRON 1.5mg; SODIUM 126mg; CALC 23mg

Almond Jelly Roll with Raspberry Filling

Almond paste makes the cake a bit sticky, so be sure to coat the wax paper in the pan with cooking spray and dust with flour before spooning in the batter. Combining the almond paste and sugar in a blender or food processor helps incorporate the paste into the batter without lumps. This cake can be made a day in advance; just wrap it in plastic wrap, and store in the fridge.

CAKE:

¾ cup granulated sugar
¼ cup almond paste
Cooking spray
⅔ cup plus 2 teaspoons all-purpose flour, divided (about 3 ounces)
1 teaspoon baking powder
⅛ teaspoon salt
4 large eggs
1 teaspoon vanilla extract
¼ cup powdered sugar, divided

REMAINING INGREDIENTS:

⅔ cup seedless raspberry jam
½ cup whipping cream
¼ cup powdered sugar
Fresh raspberries (optional)

1. Preheat oven to 350°.
2. To prepare cake, combine granulated sugar and almond paste in a blender or food processor; process until well blended. Set aside.

3. Coat a 15 x 10–inch jelly-roll pan with cooking spray. Line bottom of pan with wax paper. Coat paper well with cooking spray. Dust with 2 teaspoons flour; set aside.
4. Lightly spoon ⅔ cup flour into dry measuring cups; level with a knife. Combine flour, baking powder, and salt in a medium bowl, stirring with a whisk.
5. Place eggs in a large bowl, and beat with a mixer at high speed until pale and fluffy (about 4 minutes). Gradually add granulated sugar mixture and vanilla, beating at medium speed until smooth (about 3 minutes). Sift half of flour mixture over egg mixture; fold in. Repeat procedure with remaining flour mixture. Spread batter evenly into prepared pan. Bake at 350° for 10 minutes or until cake springs back when touched lightly in center. Loosen cake from sides of pan, and turn out onto a dishtowel dusted with 2 tablespoons powdered sugar; carefully peel off wax paper. Sprinkle cake with 2 tablespoons powdered sugar; cool 1 minute. Starting at narrow end, roll up cake and towel together. Place, seam side down, on a wire rack; cool completely (about 30 minutes).
6. Unroll cake carefully; remove towel. Spread jam over cake, leaving a ½-inch margin around edges. Reroll cake; place, seam side down, on a platter.
7. Place cream and ¼ cup powdered sugar in a medium bowl; beat with a mixer at high speed until stiff peaks form. Cut cake into 8 slices with a serrated knife. Top each slice with whipped cream and raspberries, if desired. Yield: 8 servings (servings size: 1 slice cake and 1 tablespoon whipped cream).

CALORIES 321 (28% from fat); FAT 10.1g (sat 4.4g, mono 3.8g, poly 1g); PROTEIN 5.2g; CARB 53.9g; FIBER 0.6g; CHOL 126mg; IRON 1.1mg; SODIUM 139mg; CALC 71mg

Tasty Packages

Cooking in a parchment or foil packet creates light, simple springtime specialties.

Cooking en papillote—steaming small portions of food in a wrapper—is a classic technique. And, the best part is that it's a solution for busy weeknight dinners and entertaining. There's something inherently festive about opening a packet at the table to free a cloud of fragrant steam. Use our easy recipes and tips, and you'll know how to create your own quick entrées to enjoy fresh spring produce all season long.

New Orleans–Style Shrimp

(pictured on page 231)

- 3 tablespoons Worcestershire sauce
- 2 tablespoons fresh lemon juice
- 1 tablespoon butter, melted
- 2 teaspoons chopped fresh rosemary
- 2 teaspoons chopped garlic
- ½ teaspoon dried thyme
- ½ teaspoon hot pepper sauce
- ¼ teaspoon freshly ground black pepper
- ¼ teaspoon ground red pepper
- 2 pounds unpeeled large shrimp
- 2 lemons, cut into ¼-inch slices
- 4 teaspoons butter

1. Combine first 11 ingredients in a large bowl; toss well. Cover and marinate in refrigerator 30 minutes.
2. Preheat oven to 425°.
3. Fold 4 (16 x 12–inch) sheets of heavy-duty aluminum foil in half crosswise. Open foil. Remove shrimp mixture from bowl; reserve marinade. Place about 2¼ cups shrimp mixture on half of each foil sheet. Drizzle marinade evenly over shrimp. Top each serving with 1 teaspoon butter. Fold foil over shrimp; tightly seal edges.
4. Place packets on a baking sheet. Bake at 425° for 20 minutes. Let stand 10 minutes. Place on plates. Unfold packets carefully; peel shrimp, and serve immediately. Yield: 4 servings (serving size: 1 packet).

CALORIES 323 (30% from fat); FAT 10.7g (sat 4.9g, mono 2.3g, poly 1.8g); PROTEIN 46.4g; CARB 8.9g; FIBER 0.8g; CHOL 363mg; IRON 6.5mg; SODIUM 513mg; CALC 156mg

Champagne and Orange-Steamed Lobster Tails en Papillote

- 8 orange slices
- 4 (5-ounce) lobster tails
- 2 tablespoons butter, cut into small pieces
- ¼ cup chopped fennel fronds
- ¾ cup dry Champagne or sparkling wine
- ¼ teaspoon kosher salt

1. Preheat oven to 425°.
2. Cut 4 (15 x 24–inch) pieces of parchment paper. Fold in half crosswise. Draw a large heart half on each piece, with fold of paper being center of heart. Cut out heart, and open. Layer 2 orange slices, 1 lobster tail, 1½ teaspoons butter, and 1 tablespoon fennel fronds near fold of each piece of parchment. Spoon 3 tablespoons Champagne over each serving. Starting at top of heart, fold edges of parchment, sealing edges with narrow folds. Twist end tip to secure tightly. Place packets on a baking sheet. Bake at 425° for 12 minutes. Remove from oven; let stand 5 minutes. Carefully open 1 packet. Remove meat from lobster tail; coarsely chop. Return meat to lobster tail shell; place on plate. Drizzle packet juices over serving; repeat with remaining packets. Sprinkle evenly with salt. Yield: 4 servings.

CALORIES 290 (26% from fat); FAT 8.5g (sat 4g, mono 2g, poly 1.3g); PROTEIN 37.8g; CARB 8.8g; FIBER 0.8g; CHOL 143mg; IRON 2.1mg; SODIUM 480mg; CALC 105mg

Chicken Baked in Coconut-Curry Sauce

- ½ cup coconut milk
- ¼ cup fat-free, less-sodium chicken broth
- 2 teaspoons minced garlic
- 1 to 1½ teaspoons red curry paste
- 4 (6-ounce) skinless, boneless chicken breast halves
- ¾ teaspoon kosher salt
- ½ teaspoon freshly ground black pepper
- 2 zucchini, halved lengthwise and thinly sliced (about 2 cups)
- 1 cup thinly sliced yellow squash (about 2 small)
- 1 cup (¼-inch-thick) red bell pepper strips (about 1 large)
- ½ cup diagonally cut green onions
- 4 teaspoons chopped fresh cilantro
- 4 lime wedges

1. Preheat oven to 425°.
2. Combine first 4 ingredients in a medium bowl; stir with a whisk.
3. Place chicken breast halves between 2 sheets of heavy-duty plastic wrap; pound each piece to an even thickness using a meat mallet or small heavy skillet. Sprinkle salt and pepper evenly over both sides of chicken.
4. Fold 4 (16 x 12–inch) sheets of heavy-duty aluminum foil in half crosswise. Open foil; layer ½ cup zucchini, ¼ cup squash, ¼ cup bell pepper, 2 tablespoons green onions, and 1 chicken breast half on half of each foil sheet. Spoon 3 tablespoons of coconut milk mixture over each serving. Fold foil over chicken and vegetables; tightly seal edges.
5. Place packets on a baking sheet. Bake at 425° for 22 minutes. Remove from oven; let stand 5 minutes. Place on plates. Unfold packets carefully, and sprinkle each serving with 1 teaspoon cilantro. Garnish with lime wedges. Serve immediately. Yield: 4 servings (serving size: 1 packet and 1 lime wedge).

CALORIES 278 (27% from fat); FAT 8.4g (sat 5.9g, mono 0.8g, poly 0.6g); PROTEIN 41.7g; CARB 8.4g; FIBER 2.3g; CHOL 99mg; IRON 2.8mg; SODIUM 523mg; CALC 57mg

Feta, Herb, and Sun-Dried Tomato–Stuffed Chicken

Sun-dried tomatoes and fresh basil temper tangy feta in a savory chicken breast stuffing.

    2   cups water
    ½   cup sun-dried tomatoes, packed without oil
    ½   cup (2 ounces) crumbled feta cheese
    2   teaspoons chopped fresh basil
    1   teaspoon chopped fresh oregano
    ½   teaspoon minced garlic
    ¾   teaspoon freshly ground black pepper, divided
    4   (6-ounce) skinless, boneless chicken breasts
    ½   teaspoon kosher salt
    2   tablespoons butter
    ½   teaspoon grated lemon rind
    ¼   cup fat-free, less-sodium chicken broth
    2   teaspoons thinly sliced fresh basil (optional)

1. Preheat oven to 425°.
2. Bring 2 cups water to a boil in a small saucepan; add tomatoes. Remove from heat; cover and let stand 5 minutes. Drain and cut into thin strips. Combine tomatoes, cheese, next 3 ingredients, and ¼ teaspoon pepper in a small bowl.
3. Place chicken breast halves between 2 sheets of heavy-duty plastic wrap, and pound each piece to an even thickness using a meat mallet or small heavy skillet. Cut a horizontal slit through one side of each chicken breast half to form a deep pocket. Stuff ¼ cup tomato mixture into each pocket. Sprinkle both sides of chicken with salt and ½ teaspoon pepper.
4. Fold 4 (16 x 12–inch) sheets of heavy-duty aluminum foil in half crosswise. Open foil; place 1½ teaspoons butter on half of each foil sheet. Lay one stuffed chicken breast half on top of each portion of butter. Place ⅛ teaspoon grated lemon rind on top of each stuffed chicken breast half, and drizzle each serving with 1 tablespoon broth. Fold foil over chicken, and tightly seal edges. Place packets on a baking sheet. Bake at 425° for 20 minutes. Remove from oven, and

let stand 5 minutes. Unfold packets carefully, and cut each chicken breast half into thin slices. Garnish each serving with ½ teaspoon sliced basil, if desired. Serve immediately. Yield: 4 servings (serving size: 1 packet).

CALORIES 311 (29% from fat); FAT 10.1g (sat 5.7g, mono 2g, poly 0.7g); PROTEIN 43g; CARB 8.2g; FIBER 2.5g; CHOL 121mg; IRON 1.6mg; SODIUM 572mg; CALC 77mg

Mediterranean Mahimahi in Parchment with Couscous

If you can't find mahimahi, use tuna. The fish and couscous combo creates a savory one-dish meal.

    1   cup water
    ¾   cup uncooked couscous
    1   cup halved grape tomatoes
    ¼   cup chopped pitted kalamata olives
    2   tablespoons minced red onion
    2   tablespoons chopped fresh parsley
    1   tablespoon fresh lemon juice
    2   teaspoons chopped fresh oregano
    1   teaspoon minced garlic
    7   teaspoons extravirgin olive oil, divided
    1¼   teaspoons freshly ground black pepper, divided
    ¾   teaspoon kosher salt, divided
    4   (6-ounce) mahimahi or other firm white fish fillets
    12   thin lemon slices (about 1½ lemons)

1. Preheat oven to 425°.
2. Bring 1 cup water to a boil in a medium saucepan; gradually stir in couscous. Remove from heat; cover and let stand 5 minutes. Fluff with a fork. Place couscous, tomatoes, and next 6 ingredients in a large bowl. Add 1 tablespoon oil, ¼ teaspoon pepper, and ¼ teaspoon salt; toss to combine. Set aside.
3. Cut 4 (15 x 24–inch) pieces of parchment paper. Fold in half crosswise. Draw a large heart half on each piece, with fold of paper being center of heart. Cut out heart, and open. Sprinkle both sides of fillets with ½ teaspoon salt and 1 teaspoon pepper. Place 1 fillet near fold of each piece of parchment. Top each fillet with

3 lemon slices; drizzle 1 teaspoon oil over each serving. Starting at top of heart, fold edges of parchment, sealing edges with narrow folds. Twist end tip to secure tightly. Place packets on a baking sheet. Bake at 425° for 12 minutes. Place on plates; cut open. Serve immediately with couscous. Yield: 4 servings (serving size: 1 packet and 1 cup couscous mixture).

CALORIES 466 (28% from fat); FAT 14.4g (sat 2.1g, mono 9.3g, poly 2.1g); PROTEIN 47.6g; CARB 33.9g; FIBER 3g; CHOL 80mg; IRON 2.8mg; SODIUM 696mg; CALC 72mg

Soy-Ginger Steamed Halibut with Vegetables

Use precut vegetables from the produce aisle to save time.

    ¼   cup low-sodium soy sauce
    ¼   cup fresh lime juice
    1   tablespoon minced peeled fresh ginger
    2½   teaspoons minced seeded jalapeño (1 small)
    ½   cup shredded carrot
    ¼   cup diagonally cut green onions
    1   cup sugar snap peas, trimmed
    1   cup thinly sliced shiitake mushrooms (about 2 ounces)
    1   cup julienne-cut red bell pepper (1 large)
    4   (6-ounce) halibut fillets, skinned
    8   ounces buckwheat soba noodles
    ¼   cup chopped fresh cilantro

1. Preheat oven to 425°.
2. Combine first 4 ingredients, stirring with a whisk. Set aside.
3. Fold 4 (16 x 12–inch) sheets of heavy-duty aluminum foil in half crosswise. Open foil; layer 2 tablespoons carrot, 1 tablespoon onions, ¼ cup sugar snap peas, ¼ cup mushrooms, and ¼ cup bell pepper on half of each foil sheet. Dip fish fillets in soy mixture, turning to coat evenly. Place one fillet on each mound of vegetables. Spoon remaining soy mixture over servings. Fold foil over fish; tightly seal edges. Place packets on a baking sheet. Bake at 425° for 13 minutes. Remove from oven; let stand 3 minutes.

Continued

4. While packets bake, cook soba according to package directions, omitting salt and fat. Drain and rinse with cold water; drain. Place 1 cup soba on each of 4 plates. Top each serving with contents of 1 packet. Sprinkle each serving with 1 tablespoon cilantro. Serve immediately. Yield: 4 servings.

CALORIES 439 (10% from fat); FAT 5.1g (sat 0.6g, mono 1.8g, poly 1.8g); PROTEIN 44.1g; CARB 53.1g; FIBER 5.5g; CHOL 54mg; IRON 3.6mg; SODIUM 504mg; CALC 129mg

WINE NOTE: Soy, which is salty, and jalapeños, which have a fiery heat, both need a fruity wine to cushion their impact. A California riesling works well. Most California rieslings are very fruity and less crisp than their European counterparts. Try Jekel Riesling 2005 from Monterey ($13).

Salmon en Papillote with Dill-Yogurt Sauce

Use a dry white wine if you don't have vermouth on hand. Serve with a salad.

YOGURT SAUCE:
- ½ cup grated seeded peeled cucumber
- ¾ cup plain low-fat yogurt
- 1 tablespoon chopped fresh dill
- 1 teaspoon fresh lemon juice
- ¼ teaspoon minced garlic
- ¼ teaspoon pepper
- ⅛ teaspoon kosher salt

REMAINING INGREDIENTS:
- 2 cups thinly sliced fennel bulb (about 1 medium)
- ½ cup thinly sliced leek (about 1 small)
- 2 teaspoons extravirgin olive oil
- 4 (6-ounce) salmon fillets, skinned
- 1 teaspoon kosher salt
- ½ teaspoon freshly ground black pepper
- ¼ cup dry vermouth
- Chopped fresh dill (optional)

1. To prepare yogurt sauce, place cucumber on several layers of paper towels; cover with additional paper towels. Let cucumber stand 5 minutes, pressing down occasionally. Combine cucumber and next 4 ingredients in a small bowl. Stir in ¼ teaspoon pepper and ⅛ teaspoon salt. Cover and refrigerate 1 hour.
2. Preheat oven to 425°.
3. Cut 4 (15 x 24–inch) pieces of parchment paper. Fold in half crosswise. Draw a large heart half on each piece, with fold of paper being center of heart. Cut out heart, and open. Place about ½ cup fennel near fold of each piece of parchment. Top each serving with 2 tablespoons leek and ½ teaspoon oil. Sprinkle fish evenly with 1 teaspoon salt and ½ teaspoon pepper. Place 1 fillet on each serving. Drizzle 1 tablespoon vermouth over each serving. Starting at top of heart, fold edges of parchment, sealing edges with narrow folds. Twist end tip to secure tightly. Place packets on a baking sheet. Bake at 425° for 15 minutes. Remove from oven, and let stand 5 minutes. Place on plates; cut open. Garnish with chopped fresh dill, if desired. Serve immediately with yogurt sauce. Yield: 4 servings (serving size: 1 packet and about ⅓ cup yogurt sauce).

CALORIES 358 (41% from fat); FAT 16.2g (sat 3.9g, mono 7.5g, poly 3.4g); PROTEIN 39.7g; CARB 9.9g; FIBER 2.2g; CHOL 90mg; IRON 1.4mg; SODIUM 675mg; CALC 144mg

Steamed Trout with Chive-Tarragon Butter

Substitute fresh thyme or rosemary for the tarragon, if you wish.

- 1½ tablespoons butter
- 1 teaspoon chopped fresh chives
- ¾ teaspoon minced garlic
- ¼ teaspoon chopped fresh tarragon
- ⅛ teaspoon grated lemon rind
- ½ teaspoon kosher salt, divided
- ½ teaspoon freshly ground black pepper, divided
- 4 (8-ounce) dressed whole trout fillets
- 4 lemon wedges

1. Combine first 5 ingredients in a small microwave-safe bowl. Microwave at HIGH 30 seconds. Stir in ¼ teaspoon salt and ¼ teaspoon pepper. Set aside.
2. Preheat oven to 425°.
3. Cut 4 (15 x 24–inch) pieces of parchment paper. Fold in half crosswise. Draw a large heart half on each piece, with fold of paper being center of heart. Cut out heart, and open. Place 1 fillet near fold of each piece of parchment. Squeeze 1 lemon wedge over each fillet. Brush butter mixture evenly over fillets; sprinkle evenly with ¼ teaspoon salt and ¼ teaspoon pepper. Starting at top of heart, fold edges of parchment, sealing edges with narrow folds. Twist end tip to secure tightly. Place packets on a baking sheet. Bake at 425° for 12 minutes. Place on plates; cut open. Serve immediately. Yield: 4 servings (serving size: 1 packet).

CALORIES 358 (34% from fat); FAT 13.6g (sat 7g, mono 3.6g, poly 1.1g); PROTEIN 58.4g; CARB 0.9g; FIBER 0.1g; CHOL 143mg; IRON 4.6mg; SODIUM 436mg; CALC 34mg

---

Parchment Pointers

Parchment baking paper has been treated with an acid and coated with silicone (similar to silicone baking sheet liners) to render a sturdy, burn-resistant, nonstick paper impervious to liquids.

• For these recipes, our Test Kitchens recommend parchment paper—bleached or unbleached—sold on a roll since you may need larger dimensions than parchment sold in separate sheets.

• Don't substitute wax paper for parchment when steaming. Wax paper tears easily, and more importantly, it will burn and eventually leak liquids.

• Parchment paper can safely be used in an oven at temperatures up to 450°.

• The parchment will be puffy and slightly browned when the dish is nearly done.

• Parchment paper also makes an excellent nonstick liner for baking sheets or cake pans. Layer crepes, single-serving cuts of meat, or baked goods in parchment sheets for freezing; you can easily separate what you need when it's time to defrost.

Eggs

Their virtuosity figures into many foods, from sauces and soups to cakes and cookies.

While nutritionists appreciate the egg's dietary virtues, cooks are inspired by its versatility. Not only are eggs triumphant solo—poached, scrambled, or fried—but they're an impressive team player, too. In baking, this important ingredient contributes structure, color, flavor, and richness. It lightens and leavens, binds, thickens, adds moisture, and glazes. To keep fat concerns in check, we often use a combination of whole eggs and egg whites with great success. Learn how moderate use of this key ingredient is crucial in a variety of recipes.

MAKE AHEAD

Black and White Angel Food Cake

(pictured on page 229)

Place leftover yolks in an airtight container, cover with a thin layer of water, and refrigerate for up to two days; use them to make custards, such as our Cinnamon Crème Anglaise (recipe on page 104).

CAKE:

- 1 cup cake flour (about 4 ounces)
- 1½ cups granulated sugar, divided
- ½ teaspoon cream of tartar
- ¼ teaspoon salt
- 12 large egg whites
- 1 teaspoon fresh lemon juice
- ½ teaspoon vanilla extract
- 2 tablespoons unsweetened dark cocoa (such as Hershey's Special Dark)

GLAZE:

- 1½ cups powdered sugar
- 2 tablespoons tub light cream cheese, softened
- 1 tablespoon 1% low-fat milk
- 1 teaspoon vanilla extract
- ¾ teaspoon unsweetened dark cocoa (such as Hershey's Special Dark)

TOPPING:

Sliced strawberries (optional)

1. Preheat oven to 325°.

2. To prepare cake, lightly spoon flour into a dry measuring cup; level with a knife. Combine flour and ¾ cup granulated sugar, stirring with a whisk; set aside.

3. Place cream of tartar, salt, and egg whites in a large bowl; beat with a mixer at high speed until foamy. Add ¾ cup granulated sugar, 1 tablespoon at a time, beating until stiff peaks form. Beat in juice and ½ teaspoon vanilla. Sift flour mixture over egg white mixture, ¼ cup at a time; fold in after each addition.

4. Spoon half of batter into an ungreased 10-inch tube pan, spreading evenly. Break air pockets by cutting through batter with a knife. Sift 2 tablespoons cocoa over remaining batter; fold in. Spoon cocoa batter evenly over top of vanilla batter; break air pockets by cutting through cocoa layer with a knife. Bake at 325° for 55 minutes or until cake springs back when lightly touched. Invert pan; cool completely. Loosen cake from sides of pan using a narrow metal spatula. Invert cake onto a plate.

5. To prepare glaze, place powdered sugar, cream cheese, milk, and 1 teaspoon vanilla in a medium bowl; beat with a mixer at medium speed until smooth. Drizzle half of glaze over cake.

6. Add ¾ teaspoon cocoa to remaining glaze; stir well to combine. Drizzle glaze over cake. Refrigerate 5 minutes or until glaze is set. Garnish with strawberries, if desired. Yield: 12 servings (serving size: 1 slice).

CALORIES 210 (3% from fat); FAT 0.6g (sat 0.3g, mono 0.1g, poly 0.1g); PROTEIN 4.7g; CARB 47.3g; FIBER 0.5g; CHOL 1mg; IRON 0.8mg; SODIUM 111mg; CALC 9mg

Easy Caesar Salad

Old-fashioned Caesar salad dressing recipes typically call for raw egg yolks, but the yolks in this version are cooked. They're heated with the other dressing ingredients so there's less risk of the yolks scrambling.

- 1 tablespoon olive oil
- 2 garlic cloves, crushed
- 3 ounces French bread, cut into ½-inch cubes (about 3½ cups)
- 1 tablespoon fresh lemon juice
- 1 tablespoon red wine vinegar
- 1 tablespoon water
- ¼ teaspoon Dijon mustard
- ⅛ teaspoon salt
- 3 canned anchovy fillets, patted dry and finely chopped
- 1 large egg yolk
- 1 (10-ounce) package chopped romaine lettuce
- ¼ cup (1 ounce) grated fresh Parmesan cheese
- ½ teaspoon freshly ground black pepper

1. Heat oil in a small saucepan over medium heat. Stir in garlic. Remove pan from heat; let stand 5 minutes. Remove garlic from oil with a slotted spoon; discard garlic.

2. Preheat broiler.

3. Place bread on a baking sheet. Drizzle bread with 1½ teaspoons oil; toss to coat. Arrange bread in an even layer. Broil 6 inches from heat 2 minutes or until lightly browned, stirring after 1 minute. Turn oven off. Place pan on middle oven rack; close oven door.

4. Add juice and next 6 ingredients to oil in pan. Cook over medium heat 30 seconds or until mixture is thick and begins to
Continued

bubble around edges, stirring constantly. Pour mixture into a small bowl; cool to room temperature.

5. Place lettuce in a large bowl. Add egg mixture, cheese, and pepper; toss gently to coat. Add bread; toss gently to combine. Serve immediately. Yield: 6 servings (serving size: about 1⅓ cups).

CALORIES 102 (44% from fat); FAT 5g (sat 1.5g, mono 2.6g, poly 0.6g); PROTEIN 4.7g; CARB 9.8g; FIBER 1.5g; CHOL 39mg; IRON 1.1mg; SODIUM 306mg; CALC 94mg

Cinnamon Crème Anglaise

Egg yolks thicken this classic French stovetop custard sauce. Drizzle it over fresh fruit or cakes. Keep leftovers in the refrigerator for up to three days.

    2   cups 1% low-fat milk
    ⅓   cup sugar
    1   (3-inch) cinnamon stick
    4   large egg yolks

1. Combine milk, sugar, and cinnamon stick in a small, heavy saucepan over medium-low heat; cook 5 minutes or just until sugar dissolves and mixture is hot, stirring occasionally.
2. Place egg yolks in a medium bowl; stir with a whisk until blended. Gradually add about half of hot milk mixture, stirring constantly with a whisk (leave cinnamon in pan). Add egg mixture to milk mixture in pan. Cook over medium-low heat 6 minutes or until mixture is thick and coats back of a spoon, stirring constantly with a wooden spoon (do not boil).
3. Strain sauce through a fine sieve into a bowl; discard cinnamon. Place bowl of sauce in a large ice-filled bowl 15 minutes or until sauce is room temperature, stirring occasionally. Cover and chill. Yield: 8 servings (serving size: ¼ cup).

CALORIES 85 (31% from fat); FAT 2.9g (sat 1.2g, mono 1.2g, poly 0.4g); PROTEIN 3.3g; CARB 11.6g; FIBER 0g; CHOL 105mg; IRON 0.3mg; SODIUM 35mg; CALC 87mg

Cream Puffs with Ice Cream and Caramel

Eggs are a critical leavening agent for cream puffs, making the batter rise and expand. Piercing the cooked puffs allows steam to escape so the texture is almost hollow. A stand mixer is crucial; the batter is too thick to beat with a hand mixer. Freeze completely cooled cream puffs for up to one month. Cream puffs are also good with savory fillings, such as chicken or shrimp salad.

    1   cup bread flour (about 4¾ ounces)
    1   cup water
    3   tablespoons butter
    ¼   teaspoon salt
    3   large egg whites
    2   large eggs
    2   cups vanilla low-fat ice cream
    ½   cup fat-free caramel sundae syrup

1. Preheat oven to 425°.
2. Cover a large, heavy baking sheet with parchment paper; set aside.
3. Lightly spoon flour into a dry measuring cup; level with a knife. Set aside.
4. Combine 1 cup water, butter, and salt in a large, heavy saucepan over medium-high heat; bring to a boil, stirring occasionally with a wooden spoon. Add flour, stirring well until mixture is smooth and pulls away from sides of pan. Cook 30 seconds, stirring constantly. Remove from heat. Place dough in bowl of a stand mixer. Add egg whites and eggs, 1 at a time, beating at medium speed with a paddle attachment until well combined. Beat 2 minutes at medium speed.
5. Scoop dough by ¼ cupfuls into 8 mounds 2 inches apart onto prepared pan. Bake at 425° for 20 minutes. Reduce oven temperature to 350° (do not remove pan from oven); bake an additional 30 minutes. Turn oven off. Pierce top of each cream puff with a knife; return pan to oven. Cool cream puffs in closed oven 20 minutes. Remove from oven; cool completely on a wire rack.

6. Split cream puffs in half horizontally. Fill each puff with ¼ cup ice cream and 1 tablespoon syrup. Yield: 8 servings (serving size: 1 filled cream puff).

CALORIES 229 (27% from fat); FAT 6.8g (sat 3.6g, mono 1.6g, poly 0.5g); PROTEIN 7g; CARB 34.6g; FIBER 0.9g; CHOL 67mg; IRON 1mg; SODIUM 213mg; CALC 61mg

Pasta Carbonara Florentine

Whisked eggs and Parmesan cheese are stirred into a skillet of just-cooked pasta to form a rich, creamy sauce. The spinach adds color and a subtly earthy flavor twist.

    Cooking spray
    ½   teaspoon salt, divided
    1   (6-ounce) package bagged prewashed baby spinach
    6   slices center-cut bacon, chopped
    1   cup finely chopped onion
    2   tablespoons dry white wine
    8   ounces uncooked spaghetti
    ½   cup (2 ounces) grated fresh Parmesan cheese
    ½   teaspoon freshly ground black pepper
    1   large egg
    1   large egg white
    3   tablespoons chopped fresh parsley

1. Heat a large nonstick skillet over medium heat. Coat pan with cooking spray. Add ¼ teaspoon salt and spinach; cook 1 minute or until spinach wilts, stirring constantly. Place spinach in a bowl.
2. Add bacon to pan; cook 3 minutes or until crisp, stirring frequently. Remove bacon from pan, reserving 2 teaspoons drippings in pan; set bacon aside. Add onion to pan; cook 2 minutes or until tender, stirring frequently. Add wine; cook 1 minute or until liquid is reduced by half. Remove from heat; keep warm.
3. Cook pasta according to package directions, omitting salt and fat. Drain well, reserving 1 tablespoon cooking liquid. Immediately add pasta and reserved cooking liquid to onion mixture in skillet. Add spinach and bacon; stir well to combine. Place skillet over low heat.

4. Combine ¼ teaspoon salt, cheese, pepper, egg, and egg white, stirring with a whisk. Add to pasta mixture, tossing well to coat. Cook 1 minute. Remove from heat. Sprinkle with parsley. Serve immediately. Yield: 4 servings (serving size: 1 cup).

CALORIES 387 (26% from fat); FAT 11.3g (sat 5g, mono 4.3g, poly 1.2g); PROTEIN 19.5g; CARB 52.2g; FIBER 4.5g; CHOL 74mg; IRON 4.2mg; SODIUM 822mg; CALC 231mg

QUICK & EASY
Green Onion Egg Drop Soup

Egg drop soup is often garnished with just a few sliced green onions, but this version uses a generous amount for a rich flavor. Whisked eggs are stirred into simmering broth to thicken the soup and create delicate ribbons.

    3 cups fat-free, less-sodium chicken broth
    1 cup water
    ½ cup thinly sliced green onions
    ⅓ cup thinly sliced shiitake mushroom caps
 1½ teaspoons low-sodium soy sauce
    ¼ teaspoon grated peeled fresh ginger
    2 large egg whites
    1 large egg
Dash of freshly ground black pepper

1. Combine first 6 ingredients in a medium saucepan over medium-high heat; bring to a boil. Reduce heat, and simmer 3 minutes.
2. Combine egg whites and egg, stirring with a whisk. Pour egg mixture into simmering broth mixture; stir once. Cook 1 minute. Remove from heat; stir in pepper. Serve immediately. Yield: 4 cups (serving size: 1 cup).

CALORIES 44 (27% from fat); FAT 1.3g (sat 0.4g, mono 0.5g, poly 0.2g); PROTEIN 4.4g; CARB 3.2g; FIBER 0.8g; CHOL 53mg; IRON 0.4mg; SODIUM 455mg; CALC 19mg

Deli Dinner Menu
serves 4

The slaw tastes better if you prepare it in advance. "Cornichon" is the French word for "gherkin," a small pickle.

Egg Salad BLTs

Slaw with feta*

Cornichons

*Combine 1 tablespoon white wine vinegar, 1 tablespoon fresh lemon juice, 1 tablespoon extravirgin olive oil, 1 teaspoon sugar, ½ teaspoon salt, and ½ teaspoon freshly ground black pepper. Combine 4 cups packaged angel hair slaw, ½ cup chopped green onions, and ⅓ cup crumbled feta cheese. Drizzle dressing over slaw; toss to combine.

Egg Salad BLTs

    ¼ cup fat-free mayonnaise
    3 tablespoons thinly sliced green onions
    3 tablespoons reduced-fat sour cream
    2 teaspoons whole-grain Dijon mustard
    ½ teaspoon freshly ground black pepper
    ¼ teaspoon grated lemon rind
    8 hard-cooked large eggs
    8 (1½-ounce) slices peasant bread or firm sandwich bread, toasted
    4 center-cut bacon slices, cooked and cut in half crosswise
    8 (¼-inch-thick) slices tomato
    4 large Boston lettuce leaves

1. Combine first 6 ingredients in a medium bowl, stirring well.
2. Cut 2 eggs in half lengthwise; reserve 2 yolks for another use. Coarsely chop remaining egg whites and whole eggs. Add eggs to mayonnaise mixture; stir gently to combine.
3. Arrange 4 bread slices on a cutting board or work surface. Top each with ½ cup egg mixture, 2 bacon pieces, 2 tomato slices, 1 lettuce leaf, and 1 bread slice. Serve immediately. Yield: 4 servings (serving size: 1 sandwich).

CALORIES 371 (28% from fat); FAT 11.7g (sat 4.1g, mono 4.4g, poly 1.4g); PROTEIN 21.9g; CARB 44g; FIBER 2.4g; CHOL 329mg; IRON 4mg; SODIUM 892mg; CALC 70mg

BEER NOTE: With an Egg Salad BLT sandwich, reach for a Samuel Adams Pale Ale ($7). The bready yeast and malt flavors are balanced with bitter hops that add some welcome snap to the meal. A cold, characterful American pale ale is also a more thirst-quenching choice than wine.

QUICK & EASY
Pesto and Prosciutto Poached Egg Sandwiches

Our method of poaching eggs produces great results. Break the raw eggs into custard cups, then set them in simmering water. Because the eggs cook inside the cups, they come out perfectly round. Use pasteurized eggs for safety, or cook regular eggs eight minutes or until well done.

    4 pasteurized large eggs
Cooking spray
    4 teaspoons commercial pesto
    4 teaspoons water
    4 multigrain English muffins, lightly toasted
    1 ounce very thin slices prosciutto
    ¼ teaspoon freshly ground black pepper

1. Add water to a large skillet, filling two-thirds full; bring to a boil. Reduce heat; simmer. Break 1 egg into each of 4 (8-ounce) custard cups coated with cooking spray. Place cups in simmering water. Cover pan; cook 4 minutes or until yolk is just set or until desired degree of doneness. Remove custard cups from water.
2. Combine pesto and 4 teaspoons water. Spread 1 teaspoon pesto mixture on cut side of each of 4 English muffin halves, and top evenly with prosciutto.
3. Run a small rubber spatula around outside edge of each custard cup; slide 1 egg onto each prosciutto-topped muffin half. Sprinkle eggs evenly with pepper, and drizzle each with 1 teaspoon pesto mixture. Top with remaining muffin halves, cut side down. Serve immediately. Yield: 4 servings (serving size: 1 sandwich).

CALORIES 270 (31% from fat); FAT 9.4g (sat 2.7g, mono 3.9g, poly 1.2g); PROTEIN 15.2g; CARB 31.5g; FIBER 2g; CHOL 219mg; IRON 3.2mg; SODIUM 522mg; CALC 194mg

Japanese Home Cooking

Uncomplicated techniques and a few special ingredients are all it takes to create this healthful cuisine.

MAKE AHEAD • FREEZABLE
Vegetarian Dashi

Dashi is a soup stock used extensively in Japanese cuisine. Traditionally, the stock is made with bonito (fish flakes); this vegetarian version combines shiitake mushrooms with kelp (dried seaweed or konbu) to impart a similar robust flavor. These two ingredients are strained, leaving a clear broth void of calories, fat, and other nutrients (that's why there's no nutrition information below). If you are in a pinch for time, substitute commercial mushroom broth (such as Pacific Natural Foods Organic Mushroom Broth) for the dashi, since the overall flavor is of mushrooms, not kelp.

8½ cups water, divided
  2 cups dried shiitake mushrooms, coarsely chopped (about 2 ounces)
  1 ounce dried kelp (about 5 [7-inch] pieces)

1. Place 8 cups water and mushrooms in a Dutch oven; bring to a boil. Reduce heat, and simmer 45 minutes. Add ½ cup water and kelp; bring to a boil. Remove from heat. Drain mixture in a colander over a bowl, reserving mushrooms for another use; discard kelp. Store dashi in an airtight container in refrigerator up to 1 week. Yield: 5 cups.

Soba Noodle Bowl with Egg

Browning the omelet gives it a wonderful toasted flavor.

1½ tablespoons canola oil, divided
  1 cup drained no-salt-added whole-kernel corn
  4 large eggs, lightly beaten
  1 cup vertically sliced onion (about 1 medium)
  1 cup thinly sliced fresh shiitake mushroom caps
  5 cups Vegetarian Dashi (recipe at left)
  2 cups torn spinach
  2 tablespoons low-sodium soy sauce
2½ teaspoons mirin (sweet rice wine)
  8 ounces soba (buckwheat noodles), cooked
Sliced green onions (optional)

1. Heat 1 tablespoon oil in a large non-stick skillet over medium-high heat. Combine corn and eggs in a small bowl, stirring with a whisk; pour into pan. Loosen omelet with a spatula, tilting pan to allow uncooked egg mixture to come in contact with pan. (Mixture will puff and bubble.) Cook 2 minutes or until browned on bottom. Cut omelet into quarters, using a spatula. Turn each quarter over; cook until set.
2. Transfer omelet to a cutting board; cut into 1-inch pieces.
3. Heat 1½ teaspoons oil in a Dutch oven over medium-high heat. Add 1 cup onion and mushrooms; sauté 4 minutes. Add Vegetarian Dashi and next 4 ingredients. Reduce heat; cook 4 minutes or until spinach wilts. Stir in omelet pieces. Garnish with green onions, if desired. Yield: 4 servings (serving size: 2 cups).

CALORIES 397 (25% from fat); FAT 11.2g (sat 2g, mono 5.4g, poly 2.5g); PROTEIN 18.8g; CARB 59.7g; FIBER 1.8g; CHOL 240mg; IRON 2.9mg; SODIUM 795mg; CALC 63mg

MAKE AHEAD • FREEZABLE
Spicy Cucumber Noodle Salad with Edamame

This cool noodle salad has a spicy-hot zip from the chile paste in the mayonnaise. A similar spread is tucked into some varieties of sushi.

  8 ounces uncooked soba (buckwheat noodles)
  1 cup frozen shelled edamame (green soybeans)
  1 cup diced English cucumber
  ¼ cup thinly sliced green onions
  ¼ cup reduced-fat mayonnaise
  1 tablespoon rice vinegar
  2 teaspoons white miso (soybean paste)
  1 teaspoon low-sodium soy sauce
  1 teaspoon chile paste with garlic (such as sambal oelek)
  1 teaspoon dark sesame oil
1¼ cups fresh bean sprouts

1. Cook soba in boiling water 2 minutes; add edamame. Bring to a boil; cook 2 minutes. Drain; rinse with cold water. Drain; cool. Place soba mixture in a bowl. Add cucumber and onions.
2. Combine mayonnaise and next 5 ingredients; stir with a whisk. Pour over soba mixture; toss well. Top with bean sprouts. Yield: 6 servings (serving size: about ¾ cup salad and about ¼ cup sprouts).

CALORIES 198 (19% from fat); FAT 4.2g (sat 0.9g, mono 1.1g, poly 1.9g); PROTEIN 9.7g; CARB 33.9g; FIBER 0.9g; CHOL 0mg; IRON 2mg; SODIUM 502mg; CALC 40mg

---

Simple Sides

Create your own mix-and-match menus using these recipes and easy side dishes like steamed green beans dressed with dark sesame oil and toasted sesame seeds. Other accompaniments include vinegar and sugar-marinated cucumber slices; shiitake mushrooms sautéed in sesame oil, mirin, and low-sodium soy sauce; and steamed asparagus tossed with lemon juice, sesame oil, and low-sodium soy sauce.

Zen Temple Dumplings

"Zen" refers to a style of Buddhism (most Buddhists are vegetarian), and this dish is representative of what Zen Buddhist monks might eat at temples throughout Japan—hence the temple reference in the recipe title. Enjoy them as an appetizer or a main course with a side of vegetables or tofu. The dumplings can be prepared up to a month in advance: Place uncooked dumplings on a baking sheet and freeze; store in zip-top freezer bags. To serve, steam the frozen dumplings for about 10 minutes or until the wonton wrappers are translucent.

DUMPLINGS:

1½ teaspoons coarsely chopped peeled fresh ginger
2 garlic cloves, peeled
1 cup (2-inch) slices asparagus (about ½ pound)
¼ cup (1-inch) pieces green onions
1 (8-ounce) can whole water chestnuts, drained and coarsely chopped
1 (8-ounce) package mushrooms, stems removed
2 teaspoons dark sesame oil
1½ teaspoons low-sodium soy sauce
¼ teaspoon kosher salt
36 wonton wrappers
Cooking spray

SAUCE:

⅓ cup low-sodium soy sauce
1 tablespoon minced green onions
2 tablespoons rice vinegar
2 teaspoons dark sesame oil

1. To prepare dumplings, drop ginger and garlic through food chute with food processor on; process until minced. Add asparagus, ¼ cup green onion pieces, and water chestnuts; pulse 4 times or until chopped. Add mushrooms and next 3 ingredients; pulse 4 times or until mixture is finely chopped.
2. Working with 1 wonton wrapper at a time (cover remaining wrappers with a damp towel to keep from drying), spoon about 2 teaspoons mushroom mixture in center of wrapper. Moisten edges of wrapper with water. Bring 2 opposite corners together. Press edges together with fingertips to seal, forming a triangle. Place on a baking sheet coated with cooking spray; lightly cover with a towel or plastic wrap. Repeat procedure with remaining wonton wrappers and mushroom mixture.
3. Add water to a Dutch oven to a depth of 1 inch; bring to a boil. Coat a metal vegetable steamer with cooking spray. Arrange 9 dumplings in steamer, slightly overlapping. Steam dumplings, covered, 8 minutes or until tender. Remove dumplings from steamer; cover and keep warm. Repeat procedure with remaining dumplings.
4. To prepare sauce, combine ⅓ cup soy sauce and remaining 3 ingredients. Drizzle over dumplings. Yield: 9 servings (serving size: 4 dumplings and 2 teaspoons sauce).

CALORIES 138 (18% from fat); FAT 2.7g (sat 0.4g, mono 0.9g, poly 1.1g); PROTEIN 5.2g; CARB 23.7g; FIBER 2.3g; CHOL 3mg; IRON 2.1mg; SODIUM 585mg; CALC 28mg

Basic Japanese White Rice

Perfect Japanese rice is pearly white and sticky enough to pick up with chopsticks.

1½ cups uncooked short-grain rice (sushi rice)
1¾ cups water

1. Place rice in a fine mesh strainer. Rinse with cold running water, gently stirring rice until water runs clear (about 1 minute).
2. Combine rice and 1¾ cups water in a heavy, medium saucepan; let stand 1 hour. Bring to a boil; cover, reduce heat, and simmer 10 minutes. Remove from heat. Let stand, covered, 10 minutes. Yield: 5 servings (serving size: 1 cup).

CALORIES 215 (1% from fat); FAT 0.3g (sat 0.1g, mono 0.1g, poly 0.1g); PROTEIN 3.9g; CARB 47.5g; FIBER 1.7g; CHOL 0mg; IRON 2.5mg; SODIUM 1mg; CALC 2mg

Vegetable Maki

These maki (rice rolled in nori) are easy to prepare once you master the rolling technique.

5 cups Basic Japanese White Rice (recipe at left)
2 tablespoons rice vinegar
2 teaspoons sugar
½ teaspoon kosher salt
1 cup finely chopped fresh shiitake mushrooms (about 2½ ounces)
½ cup finely chopped carrot
2 tablespoons sesame seeds, toasted
1 tablespoon low-sodium soy sauce
1 tablespoon mirin (sweet rice wine)
6 nori (seaweed) sheets
6 tablespoons Ponzu Sauce (recipe on page 108)

1. Place Basic Japanese White Rice in a bowl. Combine vinegar, sugar, and salt; sprinkle over rice, tossing gently with a wooden spoon.
2. Combine mushrooms and next 4 ingredients in a small bowl; set aside.
3. Cut off 1 quarter of each nori sheet along short end. Place 1 nori sheet, shiny side down, on a sushi mat covered with plastic wrap, with long end toward you. Pat about ¾ cup rice mixture evenly over nori with moist hands, leaving a 1-inch border on nearest end. Sprinkle about 3 tablespoons mushroom mixture over rice. Lift edge of nori closest to you; fold over filling. Lift bottom edge of sushi mat; keeping mat and plastic wrap free, roll toward top edge, pressing firmly on sushi roll. Continue rolling to top edge; press mat to seal sushi roll. Let rest, seam side down, 5 minutes. Cut about ½-inch from each end of roll; discard trimmings. Cut roll crosswise into 5 pieces. Repeat procedure with remaining nori, rice, and mushroom mixture. Serve with Ponzu Sauce. Yield: 6 servings (serving size: 5 maki pieces and 1 tablespoon sauce).

CALORIES 254 (6% from fat); FAT 1.7g (sat 0.1g, mono 0.1g, poly 0.1g); PROTEIN 5.2g; CARB 51.4g; FIBER 2.1g; CHOL 0mg; IRON 2.8mg; SODIUM 522mg; CALC 9mg

Silken Tofu with Ponzu Sauce

Custardy, cool tofu is a refreshing dish that is often served as part of a larger menu.

- 1 pound light silken tofu, drained and cut into 11 (½-inch-thick) slices
- ¼ cup Ponzu Sauce (recipe below)
- ¼ cup thinly sliced green onions
- ¼ cup shredded nori (seaweed)

1. Place tofu in a single layer in a large dish; drizzle with Ponzu Sauce. Cover and marinate in refrigerator 1 hour. Sprinkle with onions and nori. Yield: 4 servings (serving size: about 3 slices and about 1 tablespoon sauce).

CALORIES 53 (12% from fat); FAT 0.7g (sat 0.1g, mono 0.1g, poly 0.4g); PROTEIN 7.6g; CARB 3.6g; FIBER 0.3g; CHOL 0mg; IRON 1.3mg; SODIUM 365mg; CALC 37mg

Ponzu Sauce

The tangy soy-based sauce is traditionally made with a citrus fruit and may have been inspired by visitors from Holland during the 17th century. Fresh lemon juice and orange juice give this sauce a citrus snap.

- ½ cup low-sodium soy sauce
- ¼ cup fresh orange juice
- 2 tablespoons fresh lemon juice
- 1 tablespoon water
- 1 tablespoon mirin (sweet rice wine)
- ⅛ teaspoon crushed red pepper

1. Combine all ingredients in a bowl. Cover and chill. Yield: 1 cup (serving size: 1 tablespoon).

CALORIES 9 (0% from fat); FAT 0g; PROTEIN 0.5g; CARB 1.5g; FIBER 0.1g; CHOL 0mg; IRON 0.2mg; SODIUM 267mg; CALC 2mg

20 Minute Dishes

From sandwiches to stir-fry, pasta to pork, here are simple, fresh, and easy meals you can make superfast.

Pork Chops Marsala

Serve with mashed potatoes. Garnish with thyme sprigs, if desired.

- 6 tablespoons all-purpose flour, divided
- 4 (4-ounce) boneless center-cut loin pork chops (about ½ inch thick)
- Cooking spray
- ⅓ cup minced shallots (about 2)
- 2 teaspoons bottled minced garlic
- 1 (8-ounce) package presliced mushrooms
- 2 teaspoons chopped fresh thyme
- 1 cup fat-free, less-sodium chicken broth
- ¼ cup Marsala wine or dry sherry
- ¼ teaspoon salt
- ¼ teaspoon black pepper

1. Heat a large nonstick skillet over medium-high heat. Place ¼ cup flour in a shallow dish. Dredge pork in flour. Coat pan with cooking spray. Add pork to pan; cook 4 minutes on each side or until browned. Remove pork from pan.
2. Add shallots, garlic, and mushrooms to pan; sauté 3 minutes or until moisture evaporates. Add 2 tablespoons flour and thyme to pan, and cook 1 minute, stirring well. Combine broth and Marsala, stirring until smooth. Gradually add broth mixture to pan, stirring constantly with a whisk; bring to a boil. Reduce heat, and simmer 2 minutes or until sauce thickens.
3. Return pork to pan; cook 2 minutes or until desired degree of doneness, turning to coat. Sprinkle with salt and pepper. Yield: 4 servings (serving size: 1 pork chop and ½ cup sauce).

CALORIES 242 (25% from fat); FAT 6.8g (sat 2.5g, mono 2.9g, poly 0.6g); PROTEIN 27g; CARB 15.4g; FIBER 1.1g; CHOL 67mg; IRON 2.1mg; SODIUM 299mg; CALC 44mg

Tuscan Tuna Sandwiches

Fennel, basil, and capers give this supper Italian flair. Toasted bread adds a nice texture, but it's an optional step.

- ¼ cup finely chopped fennel bulb
- ¼ cup prechopped red onion
- ¼ cup chopped fresh basil
- 2 tablespoons drained capers
- 2 tablespoons fresh lemon juice
- 2 tablespoons extravirgin olive oil
- ¼ teaspoon black pepper
- 2 (6-ounce) cans solid white tuna in water, drained
- 1 (4-ounce) jar chopped roasted red bell peppers, drained
- 8 (1-ounce) slices sourdough bread, toasted

1. Combine first 9 ingredients in a bowl, stirring well. Spoon ½ cup tuna mixture on each of 4 bread slices. Top each serving with 1 bread slice. Cut each sandwich in half diagonally. Yield: 4 servings (serving size: 1 sandwich).

CALORIES 292 (31% from fat); FAT 10g (sat 1.6g, mono 5.6g, poly 1.7g); PROTEIN 25.2g; CARB 24.3g; FIBER 3.3g; CHOL 36mg; IRON 2.4mg; SODIUM 878mg; CALC 85mg

Lemon Basil Shrimp and Pasta

Substitute chopped cooked chicken for a variation on this one-dish meal. Serve with focaccia or crusty baguette. To speed up preparation, use fresh pasta (available in the supermarket's refrigerated section), which cooks more quickly than dried. Check the package directions for the cook time and add the shrimp during the last three minutes.

- 3 quarts water
- 8 ounces uncooked spaghetti
- 1 pound peeled and deveined large shrimp
- ¼ cup chopped fresh basil
- 3 tablespoons drained capers
- 2 tablespoons extravirgin olive oil
- 2 tablespoons fresh lemon juice
- ½ teaspoon salt
- 2 cups baby spinach

1. Bring 3 quarts water to a boil in a Dutch oven. Add pasta; cook 8 minutes. Add shrimp to pan; cook 3 minutes or until shrimp are done and pasta is al dente. Drain. Place pasta mixture in a large bowl. Stir in basil and next 4 ingredients. Place ½ cup spinach on each of 4 plates; top each serving with 1½ cups pasta mixture. Yield: 4 servings.

CALORIES 397 (22% from fat); FAT 9.6g (sat 1.5g, mono 5.3g, poly 1.8g); PROTEIN 31g; CARB 44.9g; FIBER 2.4g; CHOL 172mg; IRON 5.4mg; SODIUM 666mg; CALC 88mg

QUICK & EASY

Sweet and Sour Chicken

Cut the chicken into pieces while you wait for the pan to heat. Serve over long-grain white rice.

- 1 tablespoon olive oil
- 1 tablespoon bottled minced garlic
- 1 teaspoon bottled ground fresh ginger (such as Spice World)
- ¼ teaspoon crushed red pepper
- 1½ pounds skinless, boneless chicken breasts, cut into ½-inch pieces
- ¾ cup chopped onion
- ½ cup chopped celery
- ½ cup chopped red bell pepper
- 1 (15¼-ounce) can pineapple chunks in juice, undrained
- ⅓ cup reduced-sodium soy sauce
- 2 tablespoons dry sherry
- 1½ tablespoons cornstarch
- 2 teaspoons brown sugar
- ¼ cup dry-roasted chopped cashews

1. Heat oil in a large nonstick skillet over medium-high heat. Add garlic, ginger, red pepper, and chicken to pan; sauté 5 minutes or until chicken is done. Remove chicken mixture from pan; set aside.
2. Add onion, celery, and bell pepper to pan, and sauté 4 minutes or until crisp-tender. Drain pineapple, reserving ½ cup juice. Add 1 cup pineapple chunks to pan; cook 30 seconds. Reserve remaining pineapple for another use. Combine reserved ½ cup juice, soy sauce, sherry, cornstarch, and sugar in a bowl, stirring with a whisk until smooth.

3. Return chicken mixture to pan. Stir in juice mixture; bring to boil. Cook 1 minute. Sprinkle with cashews. Yield: 4 servings (serving size: about 1 cup).

CALORIES 388 (27% from fat); FAT 11.6g (sat 2.4g, mono 6.2g, poly 2g); PROTEIN 41.5g; CARB 28.9g; FIBER 2.1g; CHOL 101mg; IRON 2.7mg; SODIUM 858mg; CALC 58mg

QUICK & EASY

Spicy Tilapia with Pineapple-Pepper Relish

Fresh pineapple chunks, now widely available in supermarkets, speed the prep for this relish. Serve with coconut rice (substitute light coconut milk for some of the water to cook it). Round out menu with a romaine lettuce salad tossed with lime dressing.

- 2 teaspoons canola oil
- 1 teaspoon Cajun seasoning
- ¼ teaspoon kosher salt
- ¼ teaspoon ground red pepper
- 4 (6-ounce) tilapia fillets
- 1½ cups chopped fresh pineapple chunks
- ⅓ cup chopped onion
- ⅓ cup chopped plum tomato
- 2 tablespoons rice vinegar
- 1 tablespoon chopped fresh cilantro
- 1 small jalapeño pepper, seeded and chopped
- 4 lime wedges

1. Heat oil in a large nonstick skillet over medium-high heat. Combine Cajun seasoning, salt, and red pepper in a small bowl. Sprinkle fish evenly with spice mixture. Add fish to pan, and cook 2 minutes on each side or until fish flakes easily when tested with a fork or until desired degree of doneness.
2. Combine pineapple and next 5 ingredients in a large bowl, stirring gently. Serve pineapple mixture with fish. Garnish with lime wedges. Yield: 4 servings (serving size: 1 fillet, about ½ cup relish, and 1 lime wedge).

CALORIES 228 (22% from fat); FAT 5.5g (sat 1.2g, mono 2.2g, poly 1.4g); PROTEIN 34.9g; CARB 11.2g; FIBER 1.5g; CHOL 85mg; IRON 1.2mg; SODIUM 328mg; CALC 29mg

QUICK & EASY

Herbed Lamb Chops with Pomegranate Reduction

Add a side of couscous.

- Cooking spray
- 8 (3-ounce) lamb rib chops, trimmed
- ½ teaspoon black pepper
- ¼ teaspoon salt
- ¼ teaspoon chopped fresh thyme
- ¾ cup pomegranate juice
- 1 teaspoon Dijon mustard
- ½ teaspoon honey
- 2 tablespoons minced shallots
- 1 teaspoon bottled minced garlic
- 1 teaspoon cornstarch
- 1 teaspoon water
- 1 tablespoon chopped fresh chives
- ⅛ teaspoon salt
- ⅛ teaspoon black pepper

1. Preheat broiler.
2. Coat a foil-lined baking sheet with cooking spray. Place lamb on prepared pan. Sprinkle lamb evenly with ½ teaspoon pepper, ¼ teaspoon salt, and thyme. Broil 5 minutes on each side.
3. Combine juice, mustard, and honey in a small bowl. Heat a small saucepan over medium-high heat. Coat pan with cooking spray. Add shallots and garlic to pan; sauté 1 minute. Stir in juice mixture; bring to a boil. Reduce heat, and cook until reduced to ½ cup (about 5 minutes). Combine cornstarch and water in a small bowl; stir until smooth. Add cornstarch mixture to pan; bring to a boil. Cook 1 minute, stirring constantly. Remove from heat; stir in chives, ⅛ teaspoon salt, and ⅛ teaspoon pepper. Serve with lamb. Yield: 4 servings (serving size: 2 lamb chops and 2 tablespoons sauce).

CALORIES 264 (57% from fat); FAT 16.6g (sat 8g, mono 6.5g, poly 0.6g); PROTEIN 18.6g; CARB 9.2g; FIBER 0.2g; CHOL 65mg; IRON 1.6mg; SODIUM 307mg; CALC 27mg

Willett's Way

Harvard-based researcher Walter Willett, MD, has devoted his career to helping people eat better. Here's what he recommends for you.

Walter Willett, MD, DRPH, is a world-renowned researcher, chairperson of the Harvard School of Public Health's department of nutrition, leader of the country's most influential epidemiological study, and an outspoken health advocate who challenges the government to change policies that affect the way we eat.

Willett is responsible for the science that underlies many of the changes in how we eat—or, at least, how we should eat to be healthy. Much of our public awareness can be credited to Willett and his team of researchers.

One of his main campaigns has been to change the U.S. Department of Agriculture's food guide pyramid. Although Willett was instrumental in shaping the current federal government dietary guidelines and says they're an improvement over the old Food Guide Pyramid, he doesn't think they go far enough. Instead, he advocates his Healthy Eating Pyramid, which emphasizes plentiful whole grains, plant oils, fruits and vegetables, nuts and legumes; moderate lean proteins (from fish, poultry, and eggs); modest dairy consumption; and occasionally enjoying red meat, butter, and simple carbohydrates. He also believes most people need a daily multivitamin "for insurance," to protect against shortfalls of B vitamins, folic acid, and vitamin D.

Grilled Herb Chicken with Roma Tomato Sauce

Red wine and balsamic vinegar dress up a simple sauce of tomatoes, onion, and garlic. Serve over multigrain pasta.

    1   tablespoon olive oil
    ⅓   cup finely chopped onion
    1   garlic clove, minced
    2¼ cups chopped seeded plum tomato
        (about 1 pound)
    ½   cup dry red wine
    2   teaspoons balsamic vinegar
    1   teaspoon salt, divided
    ¼   teaspoon freshly ground black
        pepper, divided
    2   tablespoons chopped fresh basil,
        divided
    1   tablespoon chopped fresh thyme
    4   (6-ounce) skinless, boneless
        chicken breasts
  Cooking spray

1. Heat oil in a medium saucepan over medium heat. Add onion and garlic; cook 3 minutes or until tender, stirring occasionally. Stir in tomato, wine, vinegar, ½ teaspoon salt, and ⅛ teaspoon pepper; bring to a boil. Reduce heat, and simmer 10 minutes or until thick, stirring occasionally. Remove from heat; stir in 1 tablespoon basil.
2. Prepare grill.
3. Combine thyme, 1 tablespoon basil, ½ teaspoon salt, and ⅛ teaspoon pepper in a small bowl. Coat chicken with cooking spray; sprinkle with thyme mixture. Place chicken on grill rack coated with cooking spray; grill 5 minutes on each side or until done. Serve with tomato mixture. Yield: 4 servings (serving size: 1 chicken breast half and about ⅓ cup tomato mixture).

CALORIES 200 (30% from fat); FAT 6.7g (sat 1.4g, mono 3.8g, poly 1.1g); PROTEIN 27g; CARB 7.1g; FIBER 1.7g; CHOL 70mg; IRON 1.5mg; SODIUM 652mg; CALC 36mg

Roasted Chicken Thighs Provençal

This recipe uses skinned, bone-in chicken thighs, which are meaty and succulent. Roasting the vegetables and chicken in one pan makes this an easy, one-dish meal. If you can't find niçoise olives, use kalamatas.

    3   pounds small red potatoes,
        quartered
    4   plum tomatoes, seeded and each
        cut into 6 wedges
    3   carrots, peeled and cut into 1-inch
        chunks
  Cooking spray
    1   tablespoon olive oil
    1½ tablespoons chopped fresh
        rosemary, divided
    2   teaspoons chopped fresh thyme,
        divided
    1   teaspoon salt, divided
    ½   teaspoon freshly ground black
        pepper, divided
    6   (6-ounce) skinless chicken thighs
   24   niçoise olives
  Rosemary sprigs (optional)

1. Preheat oven to 425°.
2. Place first 3 ingredients on a jelly-roll pan coated with cooking spray. Drizzle vegetable mixture with oil; sprinkle with 1 tablespoon chopped rosemary, 1 teaspoon thyme, ¾ teaspoon salt, and ¼ teaspoon pepper. Toss gently, and spread in a single layer on pan. Bake at 425° for 30 minutes. Remove vegetable mixture from pan, and keep warm.
3. Sprinkle chicken with 1½ teaspoons chopped rosemary, 1 teaspoon thyme, ¼ teaspoon salt, and ¼ teaspoon pepper. Add chicken and olives to pan. Bake at 425° for 35 minutes or until chicken is done. Garnish with rosemary sprigs, if desired. Yield: 6 servings (serving size: 1 chicken thigh, 1⅔ cups vegetable mixture, and 4 olives).

CALORIES 519 (36% from fat); FAT 20.6g (sat 4.7g, mono 10g, poly 4g); PROTEIN 38.5g; CARB 43.5g; FIBER 5.5g; CHOL 121mg; IRON 3.7mg; SODIUM 786mg; CALC 67mg

Espresso Soy Milk Shake

Willett is a fan of soy milk and ice cream. This shake is a way to enjoy the benefits of caffeine, which may help lower your risk of diabetes and Parkinson's disease.

2 tablespoons fat-free chocolate syrup
2⅛ teaspoons instant espresso granules or instant coffee granules, divided
1½ cups vanilla soy ice cream (such as Soy Dreams)
½ cup low-fat plain soy milk

1. Combine syrup and ⅛ teaspoon espresso granules in a small bowl, stirring well. Using a spoon, drizzle half of syrup mixture around inside rim of 2 small narrow glasses. Combine 2 teaspoons espresso granules, ice cream, and milk in a blender; process until smooth. Pour 1 cup ice cream mixture into each glass. Serve immediately. Yield: 2 servings.

CALORIES 290 (34% from fat); FAT 10.9g (sat 2.3g, mono 2.1g, poly 5.5g); PROTEIN 3.1g; CARB 43.9g; FIBER 1g; CHOL 0mg; IRON 0.9mg; SODIUM 243mg; CALC 81mg

Cherry-Blackberry Crumble

Canola oil is a good alternative to traditional butter in the topping.

⅓ cup whole wheat pastry flour
½ cup regular oats
5 tablespoons brown sugar, divided
¼ cup sliced almonds
3 tablespoons canola oil
2 tablespoons cornstarch
½ teaspoon finely grated lemon rind
1 tablespoon fresh lemon juice
⅛ teaspoon salt
2 (12-ounce) packages frozen pitted Bing cherries, thawed
1 (12-ounce) package frozen blackberries, thawed
Cooking spray

1. Preheat oven to 375°.

2. Lightly spoon flour into a dry measuring cup; level with a knife. Combine flour, oats, 2 tablespoons sugar, almonds, and oil in a small bowl, stirring until blended.
3. Combine 3 tablespoons sugar, cornstarch, and next 5 ingredients in a large bowl. Toss gently to combine. Spoon fruit mixture into an 8-inch square baking dish coated with cooking spray. Sprinkle with oat mixture. Bake at 375° for 35 minutes or until bubbly. Yield: 8 servings (serving size: 1 cup).

CALORIES 220 (31% from fat); FAT 7.5g (sat 0.6g, mono 4.2g, poly 2.2g); PROTEIN 3.2g; CARB 35.5g; FIBER 5.8g; CHOL 0mg; IRON 1.1mg; SODIUM 39mg; CALC 44mg

Honey and Toasted Pistachio Muffins

Each of these homemade muffins contains almost three grams of fiber. Flaxseed meal provides a nutty flavor, fiber, and omega-3 fatty acids. Look for it in health-food stores and large supermarkets; it's also available online (at www.bobsredmill.com).

1 cup whole wheat flour (about 4¾ ounces)
1 cup all-purpose flour (about 4½ ounces)
¼ cup flaxseed meal
1¼ teaspoons baking soda
⅛ teaspoon salt
⅛ teaspoon ground nutmeg
⅛ teaspoon ground allspice
1 cup buttermilk
½ cup packed brown sugar
2 tablespoons canola oil
2 large eggs, lightly beaten
¼ cup golden raisins
Cooking spray
3 tablespoons finely chopped pistachios
2 tablespoons honey

1. Preheat oven to 350°.
2. Lightly spoon flours into dry measuring cups; level with a knife. Combine flours and next 5 ingredients in a medium bowl, and stir well with a whisk. Make a well in center of mixture. Combine buttermilk, sugar, oil, and eggs; add to flour

mixture, stirring just until moist. Stir in raisins. Spoon batter into 12 muffin cups coated with cooking spray. Sprinkle evenly with pistachios. Bake at 350° for 15 minutes or until muffins spring back when touched lightly in center. Remove muffins from pans immediately; cool on a wire rack. Drizzle honey evenly over tops of muffins. Yield: 12 servings (serving size: 1 muffin).

CALORIES 198 (28% from fat); FAT 6.2g (sat 1.1g, mono 2.4g, poly 2g); PROTEIN 5.2g; CARB 31.9g; FIBER 2.6g; CHOL 38mg; IRON 1.5mg; SODIUM 197mg; CALC 28mg

Walnut-Green Bean Salad

The nutty flavor in this salad comes from walnut oil, which contains heart-healthy monounsaturated fat. Look for it in most large supermarkets along with other oils, or substitute extravirgin olive oil. Serve the salad as a first course or a side, or add shredded chicken or shrimp to make it an entrée.

2 tablespoons walnut oil
1½ tablespoons rice vinegar
1 tablespoon water
1 teaspoon honey
½ teaspoon salt
½ teaspoon Dijon mustard
¼ teaspoon freshly ground black pepper
1 cup uncooked bulgur
1 cup boiling water
½ teaspoon salt
1 pound diagonally cut green beans (about 4 cups)
2 cups halved grape tomatoes
⅓ cup chopped fresh parsley
½ cup vertically sliced red onion

1. Combine first 7 ingredients in a small bowl; stir with a whisk until blended.
2. Combine bulgur and 1 cup boiling water in a large bowl. Cover and let stand 30 minutes; drain. Stir in salt.
3. Steam beans, covered, 5 minutes or until tender. Drain and plunge beans into ice water; drain. Place beans in a large bowl. Add bulgur, tomatoes, parsley, onion, and oil mixture; toss gently to combine. Serve at room temperature, or
Continued

cover and chill. Yield: 8 servings (serving size: 1 cup).

CALORIES 165 (28% from fat); FAT 5.1g (sat 0.5g, mono 1.1g, poly 3.1g); PROTEIN 4.9g; CARB 28.1g; FIBER 7.7g; CHOL 0mg; IRON 1.9mg; SODIUM 415mg; CALC 47mg

Harissa Salmon

HARISSA:
½ teaspoon caraway seeds
Cooking spray
2 garlic cloves, minced
½ teaspoon ground coriander
½ cup bottled roasted red bell pepper, drained
½ teaspoon chile paste with garlic (such as sambal oelek)
¼ teaspoon salt

RICE:
1½ cups uncooked instant brown rice
½ teaspoon ground cumin
½ teaspoon grated lemon rind
¼ cup chopped fresh cilantro
¼ teaspoon salt

SALMON:
4 (6-ounce) salmon fillets
¼ teaspoon salt

REMAINING INGREDIENT:
Lemon slices (optional)

1. To prepare harissa, place caraway seeds in a small skillet over medium heat. Cook 2 minutes or until fragrant, stirring frequently. Remove from pan. Coat pan with cooking spray. Add garlic; cook 2 minutes or until tender. Add coriander; cook 1 minute. Combine caraway seeds, garlic mixture, bell pepper, chile paste, and ¼ teaspoon salt in a blender or mini food processor; process until smooth.
2. To prepare rice, cook rice, cumin, and rind, according to package directions, omitting salt and fat. Remove from heat; add cilantro and ¼ teaspoon salt. Toss gently. Cover and keep warm.
3. Preheat oven to 400°.
4. To prepare salmon, heat a large oven-proof nonstick skillet over medium-high heat. Coat pan with cooking spray. Sprinkle fish with ¼ teaspoon salt. Add

to pan; cook 2 minutes or until lightly browned. Turn fish over; spread harissa evenly over fish. Bake at 400° for 7 minutes or until fish flakes easily when tested with a fork or until desired degree of doneness. Serve with rice. Garnish with lemon slices, if desired. Yield: 4 servings (serving size: 1 fillet and 1½ cups rice).

CALORIES 451 (28% from fat); FAT 14.2g (sat 3.1g, mono 5.7g, poly 3.3g); PROTEIN 40.4g; CARB 37.8g; FIBER 2.2g; CHOL 87mg; IRON 1.6mg; SODIUM 633mg; CALC 29mg

Seared Scallops with Citrus Ginger Sauce

The key to getting a good brown crust is to pat the scallops dry before cooking, sear them in a very hot cast-iron skillet, and, while they cook, only move them to turn them over. Serve over rice noodles.

2 teaspoons roasted sesame oil, divided
4 (1-inch) diagonally cut green onions
1 teaspoon peanut oil
1½ pounds medium sea scallops
¼ teaspoon salt, divided
¼ cup fresh orange juice
¼ cup mirin (sweet rice wine)
2 tablespoons lemon juice
2 tablespoons low-sodium soy sauce
¼ teaspoon grated fresh ginger
¼ teaspoon crushed red pepper
1 teaspoon water
½ teaspoon cornstarch

1. Heat 1 teaspoon sesame oil in a large cast-iron or heavy skillet over high heat. Add onions; sauté 1 minute or until wilted. Remove from pan; set aside.
2. Add 1 teaspoon sesame oil and peanut oil to pan. Pat scallops dry with paper towels; sprinkle with ⅛ teaspoon salt. Add scallops to pan; cook 2 minutes or until golden brown. Turn scallops; reduce heat to medium, and cook 1 minute or until scallops are done. Remove scallops from pan; keep warm.
3. Add orange juice, next 5 ingredients, and ⅛ teaspoon salt to pan; bring to a boil. Reduce heat, and simmer 3 minutes. Combine 1 teaspoon water and

cornstarch; stir into sauce. Cook 30 seconds or until sauce begins to thicken. Add scallops to pan; toss to coat. Top with onions. Yield: 4 servings (serving size: about 4 ounces).

CALORIES 296 (15% from fat); FAT 5.1g (sat 0.5g, mono 1.5g, poly 1.4g); PROTEIN 41.9g; CARB 16.7g; FIBER 0.5g; CHOL 91mg; IRON 1mg; SODIUM 885mg; CALC 77mg

Sesame Noodles with Broccoli

Nuts and seeds are a good source of protein and healthful fats.

SAUCE:
2 tablespoons tahini (sesame seed paste)
2 tablespoons water
2 tablespoons rice wine vinegar
2 tablespoons low-sodium soy sauce
1½ tablespoons dark sesame oil
2 teaspoons honey
½ teaspoon salt
½ teaspoon grated peeled fresh ginger
½ teaspoon chile paste with garlic (such as sambal oelek)
2 garlic cloves, minced

NOODLES:
8 ounces uncooked whole wheat spaghetti
5 cups broccoli florets
2 cups matchstick-cut carrots
¾ cup thinly sliced green onions
⅓ cup chopped fresh cilantro
3 tablespoons sesame seeds, toasted
¼ teaspoon salt

1. To prepare sauce, combine first 10 ingredients in a small bowl; stir with a whisk.
2. To prepare noodles, cook pasta in a large pot of boiling water 5 minutes, omitting salt and fat. Add broccoli, and cook 1 minute. Add carrots; cook 1 minute. Drain; place in a large bowl. Sprinkle with onions and remaining 3 ingredients. Drizzle with sauce; toss well. Serve immediately. Yield: 4 servings (serving size: 2 cups).

CALORIES 401 (31% from fat); FAT 13.7g (sat 2g, mono 4.9g, poly 5.9g); PROTEIN 14.9g; CARB 62.7g; FIBER 13.6g; CHOL 0mg; IRON 4.1mg; SODIUM 798mg; CALC 119mg

Fiery & Cool

When the temperature rises, follow the lead of cultures around the world and balance spicy dishes with cool sides and condiments.

African Ground Nut Stew with Sour Cream–Chive Topping

1 cup fat-free sour cream
¼ cup minced fresh chives
2 teaspoons canola oil
1¼ cups thinly sliced yellow onion
¾ cup chopped red bell pepper
3 garlic cloves, minced
1 cup chopped unsalted, dry-roasted peanuts
1 teaspoon salt
½ to 1 teaspoon crushed red pepper
4 cups (1-inch) cubed peeled sweet potatoes (about 1½ pounds)
2½ cups quartered small red potatoes (about 1 pound)
2½ cups organic vegetable broth (such as Swanson Certified Organic)
1 (28-ounce) can diced tomatoes, undrained

1. Combine sour cream and chives in a small bowl; cover. Refrigerate 2 hours.
2. Heat oil in a Dutch oven over medium-high heat. Add onion and bell pepper; sauté 3 minutes or until tender. Add garlic; sauté 30 seconds. Stir in peanuts, salt, and crushed red pepper; sauté 2 minutes. Add potatoes, broth, and tomatoes; bring to a boil. Cover, reduce heat, and simmer 1 hour and 10 minutes or until potatoes are tender. Place 1⅔ cups stew into each of 6 bowls; top each serving with about 2½ tablespoons sour cream mixture. Yield: 6 servings.

CALORIES 416 (30% from fat); FAT 14g (sat 1.9g, mono 6.9g, poly 4.5g); PROTEIN 14.1g; CARB 62g; FIBER 10g; CHOL 7mg; IRON 2.4mg; SODIUM 882mg; CALC 175mg

Chipotle Pork Soft Tacos with Pineapple Salsa

Pork, a common taco filling throughout Latin America, takes well to spices. A slightly sweet fruit salsa helps balance the heat. Serve with lime wedges.

SALSA:
2 cups minced pineapple
1 cup minced apple
¼ cup minced shallots
2 tablespoons chopped cilantro
1 tablespoon fresh lime juice
½ teaspoon ground cumin
¼ teaspoon salt

TACOS:
1 tablespoon canola oil
1 cup thinly sliced yellow onion
2 garlic cloves, minced
1½ pounds pork tenderloin, halved lengthwise and cut crosswise into thin strips
½ cup fat-free, less-sodium chicken broth
1 tablespoon cider vinegar
1 teaspoon dried oregano
1 teaspoon ground cumin
½ teaspoon salt
½ teaspoon freshly ground black pepper
12 cherry tomatoes, quartered
2 chipotle chiles, canned in adobo sauce, chopped (about 2 tablespoons)
12 (6-inch) corn tortillas, warmed

1. To prepare salsa, combine first 7 ingredients in a medium bowl; stir until well blended. Cover and chill.
2. To prepare tacos, heat oil in a large nonstick skillet over medium heat. Add onion to pan; cook 2 minutes or until tender. Add garlic; cook 30 seconds. Add pork; cook 4 minutes or until pork loses its pink color, stirring occasionally. Stir in broth and next 7 ingredients. Cover, reduce heat, and simmer 10 minutes. Uncover and simmer 10 minutes or until liquid almost evaporates. Warm tortillas according to package directions. Serve pork mixture with tortillas and salsa. Yield: 6 servings (serving size: 2 tortillas, ⅔ cup pork mixture, and ½ cup salsa).

CALORIES 391 (19% from fat); FAT 8.3g (sat 1.8g, mono 3.6g, poly 2g); PROTEIN 29.3g; CARB 50.8g; FIBER 6.9g; CHOL 74mg; IRON 3.6mg; SODIUM 420mg; CALC 161mg

Jerk Chicken

Serve with sautéed okra and tomatoes.

CHICKEN:
⅓ cup diced yellow onion
¼ cup finely chopped green onions
2 tablespoons cider vinegar
2 teaspoons brown sugar
1 teaspoon dried thyme
1 teaspoon freshly ground black pepper
¾ teaspoon ground allspice
½ teaspoon ground nutmeg
2 garlic cloves, chopped
1 habanero pepper, quartered
6 (6-ounce) skinless, boneless chicken breast halves
½ teaspoon salt
Cooking spray

PLANTAINS:
2 soft black plantains (about 1 pound)
½ cup light coconut milk
1 tablespoon butter
¼ teaspoon salt

1. To prepare chicken, place first 10 ingredients in a food processor; pulse 30 times or until finely chopped. Spoon onion mixture into a large zip-top plastic bag. Add chicken to bag; seal. Marinate in refrigerator overnight, turning bag occasionally.

Continued

2. Prepare grill.

3. Remove chicken from bag; discard marinade. Sprinkle chicken with ½ teaspoon salt. Place chicken on a grill rack coated with cooking spray; grill 6 minutes on each side or until done.

4. To prepare plantains, peel plantains, and cut into 1-inch pieces. Cook plantains in boiling water 20 minutes or until tender; drain. Combine plantains, coconut milk, butter, and ¼ teaspoon salt in a medium bowl; mash to desired consistency. Place ⅓ cup plantain mixture on each of 6 plates; top each serving with 1 chicken breast half. Yield: 6 servings.

CALORIES 276 (17% from fat); FAT 5.3g (sat 2.8g, mono 1g, poly 0.6g); PROTEIN 40.4g; CARB 14.9g; FIBER 1.8g; CHOL 104mg; IRON 1.8mg; SODIUM 427mg; CALC 36mg

Szechuan Spicy Noodles with Carrot-Cucumber Relish

RELISH:
- 1 cup shredded seeded peeled cucumber
- ¼ teaspoon salt
- 1 cup shredded carrot
- 1 tablespoon seasoned rice vinegar
- 2 teaspoons sugar
- ½ teaspoon dark sesame oil

NOODLES:
- 8 ounces udon noodles (thick, round fresh Japanese wheat noodles)
- ½ cup fat-free, less-sodium chicken broth
- ¼ cup natural-style peanut butter (such as Smucker's)
- 2 tablespoons low-sodium soy sauce
- 1 tablespoon chile paste with garlic (such as sambal oelek)

Cooking spray
- ⅓ cup thinly sliced green onions
- 1 tablespoon minced peeled fresh ginger
- 6 ounces ground pork
- 2 garlic cloves, minced

1. To prepare relish, place cucumber in a colander; sprinkle with salt. Toss well. Drain 1 hour. Place cucumber on several layers of paper towels, and cover with additional paper towels. Let stand 5 minutes, pressing down occasionally. Combine cucumber, carrot, vinegar, sugar, and oil in a medium bowl; stir until well blended. Cover and chill 1 hour.

2. To prepare noodles, cook noodles according to package directions, omitting salt and fat. Drain and set aside.

3. Combine broth, peanut butter, soy sauce, and chile paste in a small bowl; stir well with a whisk. Heat a large non-stick skillet over medium-high heat; coat pan with cooking spray. Add onions, ginger, and pork to pan; sauté 5 minutes or until pork loses its pink color. Add garlic to pan; sauté 30 seconds. Pour broth mixture into pan; bring to a simmer, and cook 1 minute or until slightly thick. Pour pork mixture over noodles; toss well. Serve with relish. Yield: 4 servings (serving size: 1 cup noodle mixture and 6 tablespoons relish).

CALORIES 246 (37% from fat); FAT 10.1g (sat 2.1g, mono 4.4g, poly 2.7g); PROTEIN 16.5g; CARB 23.2g; FIBER 2.4g; CHOL 23mg; IRON 1.2mg; SODIUM 624mg; CALC 38mg

Comfort for Company Menu
serves 6

This fresh twist on a meat-and-potatoes meal makes a great choice for an informal dinner party. If you like even more spice, add a chopped chipotle chile to the sweet potatoes.

Chile-Rubbed Steak with Corn and Red Pepper Relish

Cheddar sweet potatoes*

Argentine Malbec wine

*Place 1½ pounds cubed peeled sweet potatoes in a saucepan, and cover with water; bring to a boil. Reduce heat, and simmer 15 minutes or until tender. Drain; return potatoes to pan. Add 1 cup 1% low-fat milk, ½ cup shredded Cheddar cheese, and ½ cup chopped green onions. Mash to desired consistency. Cook over medium heat 2 minutes or until thoroughly heated, stirring constantly.

Chile-Rubbed Steak with Corn and Red Pepper Relish

For spicier steaks, increase the ground red pepper by ¼ teaspoon or more.

RELISH:
- 1 teaspoon olive oil
- 3 ears corn
- 1 red bell pepper
Cooking spray
- ½ cup finely chopped red onion
- ¼ cup finely chopped fresh cilantro
- 1 tablespoon fresh lime juice
- 1 teaspoon brown sugar
- ¼ teaspoon salt

STEAK:
- ½ teaspoon onion powder
- ½ teaspoon salt
- ½ teaspoon ground cumin
- ½ teaspoon brown sugar
- ½ teaspoon dried oregano
- ½ teaspoon Spanish smoked paprika
- ¼ teaspoon garlic powder
- ¼ teaspoon ground red pepper
- ⅛ teaspoon black pepper
- 6 (4-ounce) beef tenderloin steaks (about 1 inch thick)

1. Prepare grill.

2. To prepare relish, brush oil over corn and bell pepper. Place corn and bell pepper on grill rack coated with cooking spray; grill 20 minutes or until lightly browned, turning every 5 minutes. Place bell pepper in a zip-top plastic bag; seal. Let stand 10 minutes. Remove pepper from bag; peel and chop. Place pepper in a large bowl.

3. Cut kernels from ears of corn to measure 2½ cups; add to bell pepper. Stir in onion and next 4 ingredients.

4. To prepare steak, combine onion powder and next 8 ingredients; rub mixture evenly over steaks. Place steaks on a grill rack coated with cooking spray; grill 5 minutes on each side or until desired degree of doneness. Serve with relish. Yield: 6 servings (serving size: 1 steak and about ⅓ cup relish).

CALORIES 190 (29% from fat); FAT 6.2g (sat 1.6g, mono 2.1g, poly 0.1g); PROTEIN 24.5g; CARB 12.4g; FIBER 1.8g; CHOL 60mg; IRON 3.2mg; SODIUM 351mg; CALC 11mg

Indonesian Beef Curry with Coconut Rice

CURRY:
Cooking spray
1½ pounds lean top round, cut into thin slices
1½ tablespoons canola oil
½ cup thinly sliced shallots
2 tablespoons minced peeled fresh ginger
6 garlic cloves, thinly sliced
2 serrano chiles, thinly sliced
2 teaspoons ground coriander
1½ teaspoons ground cumin
¾ teaspoon salt
½ teaspoon ground cloves
½ teaspoon freshly ground black pepper
3 cardamom pods, crushed
1 (3-inch) cinnamon stick
1 cup organic vegetable broth
1 tablespoon fresh lime juice

RICE:
1¼ cups water
1 cup uncooked basmati rice
1 cup light coconut milk
¼ teaspoon salt

1. To prepare curry, heat a large skillet over medium-high heat. Coat with cooking spray. Place half of beef in skillet; cook 1 minute on each side. Remove beef from pan. Keep warm. Repeat.
2. Reduce heat to medium; add oil to pan. Add shallots, ginger, garlic, and chiles; cook 4 minutes, stirring occasionally. Stir in coriander and next 6 ingredients; cook 30 seconds, stirring constantly. Return beef to pan. Add broth; bring to a simmer. Cover, reduce heat, and simmer 35 minutes or until beef is tender. Uncover; cook 10 minutes or until sauce is thick. Discard cinnamon stick; stir in juice.
3. To prepare rice, bring 1¼ cups water and remaining 3 ingredients to a boil. Cover, reduce heat, and simmer 18 minutes. Remove from heat. Let stand, covered, 5 minutes. Fluff with a fork. Place ⅔ cup rice onto each of 6 plates; top each serving with ½ cup curry. Yield: 6 servings.

CALORIES 280 (30% from fat); FAT 9.4g (sat 3.4g, mono 3.4g, poly 1.2g); PROTEIN 27.9g; CARB 18.6g; FIBER 1g; CHOL 64mg; IRON 3.1mg; SODIUM 536mg; CALC 26mg

Pork Vindaloo with Raita

RAITA:
1½ cups plain low-fat yogurt
¾ cup chopped seeded peeled cucumber
¾ cup chopped seeded tomato
¼ teaspoon salt
1 teaspoon garam masala

VINDALOO:
1½ cups thinly sliced sweet onion
2 teaspoons grated peeled fresh ginger
1 teaspoon dry mustard
1 teaspoon ground cumin
¾ teaspoon salt
½ teaspoon ground coriander
½ teaspoon ground cinnamon
½ teaspoon ground turmeric
½ teaspoon black pepper
½ to 1 teaspoon ground red pepper
¼ teaspoon ground cloves
2 tablespoons cider vinegar
2 garlic cloves, minced
1½ pounds boneless pork loin, cut into ¾-inch cubes
Cooking spray
1 cup chopped seeded tomato

REMAINING INGREDIENT:
4½ cups hot cooked basmati rice

1. To prepare raita, spoon yogurt onto several layers of heavy-duty paper towels; spread to ½-inch thickness. Cover with additional paper towels; let stand 5 minutes. Scrape into a bowl using a rubber spatula. Stir in cucumber and next 3 ingredients; cover and refrigerate.
2. To prepare vindaloo, combine onion and next 13 ingredients in a large bowl; marinate in refrigerator 30 minutes.
3. Heat a large Dutch oven over medium-high heat. Coat pan with cooking spray. Add pork mixture; sauté 7 minutes or until lightly browned. Stir in 1 cup tomato. Cover, reduce heat, and simmer 30 minutes or until pork is tender, stirring occasionally. Serve with raita and rice. Yield: 6 servings (serving size: ½ cup vindaloo, ¼ cup raita, and ¾ cup rice).

CALORIES 378 (19% from fat); FAT 8g (sat 2.8g, mono 2.9g, poly 0.6g); PROTEIN 30.2g; CARB 44.1g; FIBER 2.1g; CHOL 70mg; IRON 2.9mg; SODIUM 479mg; CALC 118mg

Coconut-Chile Snapper with a Caribbean Bean Puree

Black beans and banana form the base for the cool component of this dish.

PUREE:
2 teaspoons canola oil
¼ cup minced shallots
1 garlic clove, minced
¾ cup thinly sliced banana (about 1 banana)
1 cup canned black beans, rinsed and drained
½ cup organic vegetable broth (such as Swanson Certified Organic), divided
1 tablespoon fresh lime juice
1½ teaspoons ground cumin
¼ teaspoon salt

SNAPPER:
1 cup shredded carrot (about 1 carrot)
1 cup light coconut milk
2 teaspoons chili powder
¼ teaspoon salt
2 jalapeños, minced
4 (6-ounce) red snapper fillets, skinned

1. To prepare puree, heat oil in a large nonstick skillet over medium heat. Add shallots and garlic; cook 2 minutes or until tender, stirring occasionally. Add banana; cook 2 minutes, stirring occasionally. Stir in beans, ¼ cup broth, juice, cumin, and ¼ teaspoon salt; cover and simmer 5 minutes or until liquid is absorbed. Place banana mixture and ¼ cup broth in a food processor; process until smooth.
2. To prepare snapper, combine carrot and next 4 ingredients in a large nonstick skillet over medium-high heat; bring to a simmer. Add fish to pan; cover and simmer 7 minutes or until fish flakes easily when tested with a fork or until desired degree of doneness. Yield: 4 servings (serving size: 1 fillet, ¼ cup bean puree, and about 3 tablespoons coconut sauce).

CALORIES 312 (24% from fat); FAT 8.2g (sat 3.5g, mono 1.8g, poly 1.5g); PROTEIN 39.1g; CARB 22.5g; FIBER 4.7g; CHOL 63mg; IRON 2.1mg; SODIUM 709mg; CALC 97mg

More for Your Calories

Here are some smart tips to pack extra nutrition into every bite.

Herbed Bread–Stuffed Tomatoes

(pictured on page 231)

The bread and tomatoes in this recipe supply about 20 percent of the day's fiber, while the touch of sharp Parmesan boosts a serving to provide 10 percent of daily calcium needs.

  6 ripe firm plum tomatoes (about
      1½ pounds), cut in half lengthwise
  ½ teaspoon kosher salt, divided
  ¼ teaspoon freshly ground black
      pepper
  4 ounces whole wheat bread (about
      2 slices), toasted and cut into
      ½-inch cubes
1½ tablespoons extravirgin olive oil
  1 tablespoon minced fresh basil
  1 teaspoon minced fresh oregano
  ½ teaspoon minced fresh thyme
  1 teaspoon minced garlic
  2 tablespoons grated fresh Parmesan
      cheese

1. Preheat oven to 375°.
2. Scoop pulp and seeds from tomato halves into a sieve over a bowl; press with a spoon. Reserve ¼ cup liquid in bowl. Discard pulp mixture.
3. Place tomato halves, cut sides up, in an 11 x 7–inch baking dish. Sprinkle with ¼ teaspoon salt and pepper. Place bread in a bowl; drizzle with tomato liquid. Stir in ¼ teaspoon salt, oil, basil, oregano, thyme, and garlic. Fill tomato halves with bread stuffing, pressing gently. Sprinkle each with ½ teaspoon cheese. Bake at 375° for 12 minutes or until thoroughly heated. Yield: 4 servings (serving size: 3 tomato halves).

CALORIES 151 (46% from fat); FAT 7.7g (sat 1.2g, mono 4g, poly 0.8g); PROTEIN 6.7g; CARB 16.6g; FIBER 5.3g; CHOL 2mg; IRON 1.3mg; SODIUM 423mg; CALC 95mg

White Chocolate, Strawberry, and Oatmeal Cookies

Dried strawberries lend fiber, color, and subtle sweetness.

  ¾ cup all-purpose flour (about
      3⅓ ounces)
  1 cup regular oats
  ½ teaspoon baking soda
  ¼ teaspoon salt
  ¾ cup packed brown sugar
  ¼ cup butter, softened
  1 teaspoon vanilla extract
  1 large egg
  ¾ cup coarsely chopped dried
      strawberries
  ⅓ cup premium white chocolate
      chips (such as Ghirardelli)
Cooking spray

1. Preheat oven to 350°.
2. Lightly spoon flour into dry measuring cups; level with a knife. Combine flour, oats, baking soda, and salt; stir with a whisk. Place sugar and butter in the bowl of a stand mixer; beat at medium speed until well blended (about 3 minutes). Add vanilla and egg; beat well. Gradually add flour mixture, beating until blended. Add strawberries and chips; beat at low speed just until blended.
3. Drop dough by tablespoonfuls 2 inches apart onto baking sheets coated with cooking spray. Bake at 350° for 12 minutes or until lightly browned. Remove from oven; cool on pan 1 minute. Remove cookies from pan; cool completely on wire racks. Yield: 2 dozen (serving size: 1 cookie).

CALORIES 98 (30% from fat); FAT 3.3g (sat 2.1g, mono 0.6g, poly 0.2g); PROTEIN 1.2g; CARB 16g; FIBER 0.6g; CHOL 14mg; IRON 0.5mg; SODIUM 73mg; CALC 11mg

Sesame Green Beans

  1 pound green beans, trimmed
  ½ teaspoon peanut oil
  ½ teaspoon rice vinegar
  ¼ teaspoon salt
  ¼ teaspoon freshly ground black
      pepper
  ¼ teaspoon dark sesame oil
  1 garlic clove, minced
2½ teaspoons sesame seeds, toasted

1. Steam beans, covered, 8 minutes or until crisp-tender. Drain and plunge beans into ice water; drain. Place beans in a large bowl. Add peanut oil and next 5 ingredients; toss to coat. Sprinkle with sesame seeds; toss well. Serve at room temperature or chilled. Yield: 4 servings (serving size: 1 cup).

CALORIES 54 (30% from fat); FAT 1.8g (sat 0.3g, mono 0.7g, poly 0.7g); PROTEIN 2.4g; CARB 8.9g; FIBER 4.2g; CHOL 0mg; IRON 1.4mg; SODIUM 153mg; CALC 46mg

Lemony Chickpea Dip

Canned chickpeas offer fiber; rinsing and draining them reduces sodium.

  ⅓ cup fat-free sour cream
  ¼ cup water
  2 tablespoons fresh lemon juice
  1 tablespoon olive oil
  ½ teaspoon ground cumin
  ½ teaspoon hot paprika
  ½ teaspoon hot sauce
  ¼ teaspoon salt
  1 (19-ounce) can chickpeas
      (garbanzo beans), rinsed and
      drained
  2 garlic cloves, peeled
  2 tablespoons chopped fresh
      cilantro

1. Place all ingredients except cilantro in a food processor; process until smooth. Transfer chickpea mixture to a bowl. Stir in cilantro. Yield: 1½ cups (serving size: 2 tablespoons dip).

CALORIES 40 (38% from fat); FAT 1.7g (sat 0.2g, mono 1g, poly 0.4g); PROTEIN 1.3g; CARB 5.3g; FIBER 1.2g; CHOL 0mg; IRON 0.4mg; SODIUM 115mg; CALC 15mg

Banana Nut Muffins with Oatmeal Streusel

Whole wheat flour and oatmeal offer whole grains. The prudent amount of walnuts adds fiber, vitamin E, and unsaturated fats. English walnuts (the most common variety in supermarkets) provide nearly 20 percent of an adequate daily intake of heart-healthy omega-3 fats per serving.

MUFFINS:

- 1½ cups all-purpose flour (about 6¾ ounces)
- ½ cup whole wheat flour (about 2½ ounces)
- ⅔ cup packed brown sugar
- 2 teaspoons baking powder
- ¼ teaspoon ground cinnamon
- ¼ teaspoon salt
- 1 cup mashed ripe banana (about 2 bananas)
- ¾ cup 1% low-fat milk
- 3 tablespoons canola oil
- ½ teaspoon vanilla extract
- 1 large egg, lightly beaten
- ¼ cup chopped walnuts, toasted

STREUSEL:

- 6 tablespoons regular oats
- 5 tablespoons all-purpose flour (about 1½ ounces)
- 2 tablespoons brown sugar
- 2 tablespoons butter, softened
- ¼ teaspoon ground cinnamon

1. Preheat oven to 375°.

2. To prepare muffins, lightly spoon 1½ cups all-purpose flour and whole wheat flour into dry measuring cups; level with a knife. Combine flours and next 4 ingredients in a large bowl; make a well in center of mixture. Combine banana and next 4 ingredients in a bowl; stir well. Add to flour mixture. Stir just until moistened; fold in walnuts. Place 12 muffin cup liners in muffin cups. Spoon batter into 12 muffin cups.

3. To prepare streusel, combine oats and remaining 4 ingredients in a small bowl. Blend with a pastry blender or 2 knives until mixture resembles coarse meal. Sprinkle streusel over batter. Bake at 375° for 22 minutes or until a wooden pick inserted in center comes out clean. Yield: 12 muffins (serving size: 1 muffin).

CALORIES 241 (30% from fat); FAT 8.1g (sat 1.9g, mono 3.1g, poly 2.5g); PROTEIN 4.6g; CARB 38.9g; FIBER 2.1g; CHOL 23mg; IRON 1.8mg; SODIUM 164mg; CALC 89mg

Cantaloupe–Chicken Salad Sandwiches with Creamy Tarragon Dressing

Adding fruit to a chicken salad boosts fiber and vitamin C (a serving of this recipe provides almost one-third of the daily recommended value).

- ¼ cup thinly sliced green onions
- ¼ cup reduced-fat mayonnaise
- 2 tablespoons white wine vinegar
- 1 teaspoon minced fresh tarragon
- ¼ teaspoon kosher salt
- ⅛ teaspoon freshly ground black pepper
- 2 cups (½-inch) cubes cooked chicken breast (about 1 pound)
- 1½ cups (½-inch) cubes cantaloupe
- ⅓ cup chopped celery
- 4 cups mixed salad greens
- 1⅓ cups thinly sliced cucumber
- 6 (6-inch) whole wheat pitas, cut in half

1. Combine first 6 ingredients in a bowl; stir with a whisk. Add chicken, cantaloupe, and celery; stir gently. Cover and chill 30 minutes.

2. Divide salad greens and cucumber slices evenly among pita halves. Spoon about ⅓ cup chicken salad into each pita half. Serve immediately. Yield: 6 servings (serving size: 2 filled pita halves).

CALORIES 262 (13% from fat); FAT 3.8g (sat 0.6g, mono 0.6g, poly 1.5g); PROTEIN 18.6g; CARB 42g; FIBER 6g; CHOL 25mg; IRON 3.2mg; SODIUM 667mg; CALC 44mg

WINE NOTE: This fabulous sandwich goes well with a glass of chilled white wine. The cantaloupe's fresh fruitiness calls for a wine that's equally fresh and fruity, without any toasty oak flavors to get in the way. A dry riesling is ideal. Trefethen Estate Dry Riesling 2005 from Napa Valley, California ($20), is excellent.

Grilled Flank Steak with Tomato, Avocado, and Cucumber Salad

STEAK:

- 1 (2¼-pound) flank steak, trimmed
- 2 tablespoons fresh lime juice
- ½ teaspoon freshly ground black pepper
- ¼ teaspoon kosher salt
- Cooking spray

SALAD:

- 2 cups grape tomatoes
- 2 cups torn Bibb lettuce
- 1½ cups (½-inch) diced peeled avocado
- ⅓ cup vertically sliced red onion
- 1 cucumber (about ¾ pound), peeled, halved lengthwise, seeded, and cut into ¼-inch-thick slices
- 2 tablespoons chopped fresh cilantro
- 3 tablespoons fresh lime juice
- 1½ teaspoons minced seeded serrano chile
- 1½ teaspoons extravirgin olive oil
- ¼ teaspoon kosher salt
- ¼ teaspoon freshly ground black pepper

1. To prepare steak, place steak in a large shallow dish. Drizzle with 2 tablespoons juice, and sprinkle with ½ teaspoon pepper; rub into steak. Cover; let steak stand at room temperature for 20 minutes, turning occasionally.

2. Prepare grill.

3. Remove steak from dish; discard marinade. Sprinkle steak with ¼ teaspoon salt. Place steak on a grill rack coated with cooking spray; grill 8 minutes on each side or until desired degree of doneness. Let stand 10 minutes before cutting into thin slices.

4. To prepare salad, combine tomatoes and next 4 ingredients in a large bowl. Combine cilantro and remaining 5 ingredients. Drizzle cilantro mixture over cucumber mixture; toss gently. Serve with steak. Yield: 8 servings (serving size: 3 ounces steak and ¾ cup salad).

CALORIES 232 (48% from fat); FAT 12.4g (sat 3.7g, mono 6.2g, poly 1g); PROTEIN 24.9g; CARB 6.4g; FIBER 2.4g; CHOL 38mg; IRON 2.2mg; SODIUM 173mg; CALC 36mg

Toasted Millet with Parmesan

This dish is similar to grits or polenta and pairs well with steak or grilled pork. For al dente texture, simmer only 15 minutes. A serving of this dish offers more than 10 percent of a day's fiber, a dose of iron, and filling protein.

1   cup uncooked millet
3   cups water
½   teaspoon salt
½   cup (2 ounces) grated fresh Parmesan cheese
1   tablespoon fresh lemon juice
2   teaspoons butter
½   teaspoon chopped fresh thyme
¼   teaspoon black pepper

1. Place millet in a large nonstick skillet over medium heat; cook 4 minutes or until toasted, stirring constantly.
2. Combine millet, 3 cups water, and salt in a large saucepan; bring to a boil. Reduce heat, and simmer 20 minutes. Remove from heat; cover and let stand 10 minutes. Stir in cheese and remaining ingredients. Yield: 5 servings (serving size: about ½ cup).

CALORIES 200 (25% from fat); FAT 5.5g (sat 2.6g, mono 1.4g, poly 1g); PROTEIN 7.5g; CARB 29.8g; FIBER 3.5g; CHOL 11mg; IRON 1.3mg; SODIUM 374mg; CALC 96mg

Chicken Vegetable Potpie

Invest a little time in a flaky homemade whole wheat crust, and cut prep time by using precooked chicken breast, bottled minced garlic, and sliced button mushrooms. Frozen edamame (green soybeans) add another dose of fiber and good-for-you unsaturated fat.

CRUST:
¾   cup all-purpose flour (about 3⅓ ounces)
½   cup whole wheat flour (about 2⅓ ounces)
¼   teaspoon kosher salt
⅛   teaspoon ground red pepper
¼   cup vegetable shortening
4   to 5 tablespoons ice water

FILLING:
2   cups (½-inch) cubes red potato
1   tablespoon water
Cooking spray
1   cup sliced leek (about 1 large)
¼   cup chopped celery
1   small garlic clove, minced
1   cup sliced mushrooms
½   cup all-purpose flour (about 2¼ ounces)
2   cups fat-free, less-sodium chicken broth
2   cups diced cooked chicken breast (about 1 pound)
1   cup frozen shelled edamame (green soybeans), thawed
½   cup thinly sliced carrot
¼   teaspoon minced fresh thyme
¾   teaspoon kosher salt
¼   teaspoon freshly ground black pepper

1. To prepare crust, lightly spoon ¾ cup all-purpose flour and whole wheat flour into dry measuring cups; level with a knife. Place flours, salt, and red pepper in a food processor; pulse 2 times. Add shortening; pulse 4 times or just until mixture resembles coarse meal. Transfer mixture to a bowl. Sprinkle ice water, 1 tablespoon at a time, over flour mixture; toss with a fork until moist and crumbly (do not form a ball). Press mixture gently into a 4-inch circle on plastic wrap; cover. Chill 30 minutes.
2. Preheat oven to 400°.
3. To prepare filling, place potato in a shallow microwave-safe bowl; add 1 tablespoon water. Lightly cover with wax paper. Microwave at HIGH 2 minutes or until crisp-tender, stirring once.
4. Heat a medium saucepan over medium heat. Coat pan with cooking spray. Add leek, celery, and garlic; cook 4 minutes. Add mushrooms; cook 3 minutes. Lightly spoon ½ cup flour into a dry measuring cup; level with a knife. Place flour in a medium bowl; add broth, stirring with a whisk. Stir broth mixture into leek mixture; bring to a boil, stirring constantly. Reduce heat, and simmer 8 minutes. Stir in potato, chicken, and remaining 5 ingredients. Spoon into an 11 x 7–inch baking dish coated with cooking spray.

5. Slightly overlap 2 sheets of plastic wrap on a slightly damp surface. Unwrap and place chilled dough on plastic wrap. Cover dough with 2 additional sheets of overlapping plastic wrap. Roll dough, still covered, into a 12 x 8–inch rectangle. Remove top sheets of plastic wrap. Place dough, plastic wrap side up, over filling. Remove top sheets of plastic wrap. Tuck in overlapping edges of dough. Cut 3 (1-inch) slits in top of dough. Bake at 400° for 25 minutes or until crust is browned and filling is bubbly. Remove from oven. Let stand 10 minutes before serving. Cut into 6 portions. Yield: 6 servings.

CALORIES 383 (26% from fat); FAT 11.1g (sat 3.5g, mono 3.1g, poly 3.5g); PROTEIN 27.1g; CARB 44g; FIBER 5.2g; CHOL 46mg; IRON 3.1mg; SODIUM 864mg; CALC 48mg

---

Take Two

What's the most nutrient-dense food in each of these pairs?

Diet soda or skim milk?

While a diet soda has few, if any, calories, milk has more nutrients. An 80-calorie, 8-ounce cup of fat-free milk contains nearly 30 percent of the RDA for calcium, 8 grams of high-quality protein, almost a third of the daily needs for riboflavin, about one-tenth of the needed potassium, and a bit of magnesium.

One-percent low-fat cottage cheese or canned salmon?

While cottage cheese has just 1 gram of fat per half-cup and salmon nearly 7 grams per 4-ounce serving, the fish is more nutrient dense. Salmon contains about three times more calcium (courtesy of its small bones) and four times more potassium, plus omega-3 fats and iron.

Brown rice or bulgur?

A half-cup of bulgur (75 calories) outshines the same amount of brown rice (108 calories) with twice the fiber, twice the iron, and a bit more protein. Both have similar amounts of B vitamins and minerals.

My Old Kentucky Home

Even if you can't attend the Derby, our recipes can take you there.

Classic Mint Juleps

This lightly sweetened concoction is a classic that has been enjoyed throughout the South since long before the first Kentucky Derby. This rendition won our Test Kitchens' top score.

    1 cup sugar
    1 cup water
   16 mint sprigs, lightly crushed
    8 cups finely crushed ice
    1 cup bourbon
  Mint sprigs (optional)

1. Bring sugar and 1 cup water to a boil in a small saucepan. Cook 4 minutes or until sugar dissolves. Remove sugar syrup from heat; cool completely. Place 2 crushed mint sprigs in bottom of each of 8 glasses. Add 1 cup crushed ice, 2 tablespoons sugar syrup, and 2 tablespoons bourbon to each glass. Garnish with mint sprigs, if desired. Yield: 8 servings.

CALORIES 170 (0% from fat); PROTEIN 0g; CARB 25g; FIBER 0g; CHOL 0mg; IRON 0mg; SODIUM 0mg; CALC 0mg

SPIRIT NOTE: Bourbon is America's original spirit, made primarily from corn with varying amounts of wheat, barley, and rye. Wild Turkey 80 ($18) may sound like your grandfather's whiskey, but this smooth yet rich bourbon with caramel sweetness, vanilla aromas, and a touch of spice is a superb foundation for a mint julep. For a lighter-bodied, fruitier, and gentler style, choose a bourbon with a lot of wheat, like Maker's Mark ($23).

Asparagus-Apple Salad with Blue Cheese Vinaigrette

Featuring the contrasting elements of apples (a Kentucky crop), asparagus, and blue cheese, this salad rounds out a Derby Day menu.

   ¼ cup (1 ounce) crumbled blue cheese
   2 tablespoons chopped fresh parsley
   2 tablespoons white vinegar
   1 tablespoon water
   1 teaspoon sugar
   2 teaspoons Dijon mustard
   1 teaspoon extravirgin olive oil
   ¼ teaspoon salt
   ¼ teaspoon freshly ground black pepper
   2 cups (2-inch) diagonally cut asparagus
   4 cups torn butter lettuce
   2 cups thinly sliced Gala apple

1. Combine first 9 ingredients, stirring with a whisk.
2. Cook asparagus in boiling water 1 minute. Drain and rinse with cold running water; drain. Combine asparagus, lettuce, and apple in a large bowl. Drizzle with vinaigrette, and toss gently to coat. Yield: 8 servings (serving size: 1 cup).

CALORIES 58 (29% from fat); FAT 1.9g (sat 0.8g, mono 0.5g, poly 0.2g); PROTEIN 2.1g; CARB 9.6g; FIBER 1g; CHOL 3mg; IRON 1.2mg; SODIUM 159mg; CALC 43mg

Kentucky Chocolate Nut Tartlets

Chocolate, pecans, and bourbon fill petite versions of the state's favorite pie.

PASTRY:

    1 cup all-purpose flour (about 4½ ounces)
  1½ tablespoons sugar
   ½ teaspoon salt
   ⅛ teaspoon baking powder
    2 tablespoons vegetable shortening
    4 to 5 tablespoons ice water
  Cooking spray

FILLING:

    3 tablespoons semisweet chocolate chips
    3 tablespoons chopped pecans, toasted
  2½ tablespoons sugar
  3½ tablespoons light-colored corn syrup
    1 tablespoon egg substitute
    1 tablespoon bourbon
    1 teaspoon all-purpose flour
   ½ teaspoon vanilla extract
  Dash of salt
    2 teaspoons bourbon (optional)

1. To prepare pastry, lightly spoon flour into a dry measuring cup; level with a knife. Place flour and next 3 ingredients in a food processor; pulse 3 times. Add shortening; pulse 4 or 5 times or just until combined. Place flour mixture in a bowl. Gradually sprinkle ice water over flour mixture; toss until moistened. Turn dough out onto a lightly floured surface, and gently knead 3 or 4 times. Press mixture into a 4-inch disk. Place between 2 sheets of plastic wrap; chill 30 minutes.
2. Preheat oven to 375°.
3. Roll dough into an 11-inch circle; remove plastic wrap. Cut dough into 18 circles using a 2½-inch cutter. (Reroll any remaining pieces of dough.) Fit dough into miniature nonstick muffin cups coated with cooking spray. Gently press dough into bottom and up sides of cups.
4. To prepare filling, divide chocolate
Continued

and pecans evenly among muffin cups. Combine 2½ tablespoons sugar and next 6 ingredients in a small bowl; stir well with a whisk. Divide sugar mixture evenly among cups. Bake at 375° for 15 minutes or until pastry is lightly browned and filling is set. Run a knife around each tartlet; remove from pan. Lightly brush tartlets with 2 teaspoons bourbon, if desired. Cool completely. Yield: 1½ dozen (serving size: 1 tartlet).

CALORIES 74 (32% from fat); FAT 2.8g (sat 0.7g, mono 1.1g, poly 0.7g); PROTEIN 1.1g; CARB 12.6g; FIBER 0.4g; CHOL 0mg; IRON 0.5mg; SODIUM 83mg; CALC 5mg

Spoon Bread

This soufflé-like corn bread is enjoyed in the South and adorns many a Kentucky Derby spread.

- ¾ cup stone-ground yellow cornmeal
- 1 teaspoon sugar
- 1 teaspoon salt
- ¼ teaspoon freshly ground black pepper
- 2½ cups 1% low-fat milk
- ¼ teaspoon hot sauce
- 2 large egg yolks, lightly beaten
- 1 tablespoon butter
- ½ teaspoon baking powder
- 3 large egg whites
- Cooking spray

1. Preheat oven to 350°.
2. Combine first 4 ingredients in a large saucepan; stir in milk and hot sauce. Cook over medium heat until thick (about 15 minutes), stirring constantly. Place egg yolks in a medium bowl. Spoon ½ cup hot cornmeal mixture into egg yolks. Stir egg yolk mixture into remaining cornmeal mixture. Add butter, stirring until butter melts.
3. Place baking powder and egg whites in a medium bowl; beat with a mixer at high speed until stiff peaks form. Fold one-fourth of egg white mixture into cornmeal mixture. Fold remaining egg white mixture into cornmeal mixture. Gently spoon mixture into an 11 x 7–inch baking dish coated with cooking

spray. Bake at 350° for 40 minutes or until lightly browned and puffy. Serve immediately. Yield: 8 servings.

CALORIES 108 (32% from fat); FAT 3.8g (sat 1.7g, mono 1.4g, poly 0.4g); PROTEIN 5.5g; CARB 13.3g; FIBER 0.9g; CHOL 58mg; IRON 0.6mg; SODIUM 402mg; CALC 118mg

Hickory Grilled Beef with Henry Bain Sauce

The zesty sauce, created in 1881 by Henry Bain, headwaiter of the Louisville Pendennis Club, is also great with grilled steak, pork, or chicken. Major Grey's chutney is a thick, chunky, spicy Indian condiment; look for it in the supermarket near the steak sauces.

SAUCE:
- ⅔ cup no-salt-added ketchup
- ½ cup Major Grey's chutney
- ⅓ cup bottled chili sauce (such as Heinz)
- ¼ cup steak sauce (such as A1)
- ¼ cup low-sodium Worcestershire sauce
- ½ teaspoon hot sauce

BEEF:
- 4 cups hickory wood chips
- 2 cups water
- Cooking spray
- 1 (3¼-pound) beef tenderloin, trimmed
- 1 teaspoon freshly ground black pepper
- ½ teaspoon salt

1. To prepare sauce, combine first 6 ingredients; cover and chill.
2. To prepare beef, soak wood chips in water 1 hour.
3. Remove grill rack; set aside. Prepare grill for indirect grilling, heating one side to medium-high and leaving one side with no heat.
4. Place half of wood chips on hot coals. Place a disposable aluminum foil pan on unheated side of grill. Pour 2 cups water in pan. Coat grill rack with cooking spray; place on grill.
5. Sprinkle beef evenly with pepper and salt. Place beef on grill rack over foil pan on unheated side. Close lid; cook

55 minutes or until a thermometer registers 135° or until desired degree of doneness. Add additional wood chips halfway through cooking time. Remove beef from grill. Cover lightly with foil; let stand 15 minutes. Cut beef across grain into thin slices. Serve with sauce. Yield: 12 servings (serving size: 3 ounces beef and about 2½ tablespoons sauce).

CALORIES 219 (28% from fat); FAT 6.7g (sat 2.6g, mono 2.7g, poly 0.3g); PROTEIN 24.3g; CARB 13.7g; FIBER 0.1g; CHOL 67mg; IRON 1.7mg; SODIUM 636mg; CALC 17mg

Crunchy Chow-Chow

Legend has it that Chinese workers brought a version of this condiment to America in the 1800s. The relish became a favorite in the South, where it's served with all kinds of meats and atop field peas. Store in the refrigerator up to two weeks in a glass or plastic bowl (they won't react with the vinegar).

- 1 cup finely chopped red bell pepper
- 1 cup finely chopped green bell pepper
- 1 cup finely chopped cucumber
- 1 cup fresh corn kernels
- 1 cup finely chopped onion
- 1 cup finely chopped green tomato
- 1 cup finely chopped carrot
- 1 tablespoon salt
- 1 jalapeño pepper, seeded and finely chopped
- 6 tablespoons sugar
- 6 tablespoons cider vinegar
- 3 tablespoons water
- 1 teaspoon ground turmeric
- ¼ teaspoon celery seed

1. Combine first 9 ingredients in a glass bowl. Cover and refrigerate 8 hours. Drain well.
2. Combine vegetable mixture, sugar, and remaining ingredients in a large saucepan. Cook over medium heat 5 minutes or just until heated. Serve chilled or at room temperature. Yield: 5 cups (serving size: ¼ cup).

CALORIES 35 (5% from fat); FAT 0.2g (sat 0g, mono 0g, poly 0.1g); PROTEIN 0.7g; CARB 8.2g; FIBER 1g; CHOL 0mg; IRON 0.3mg; SODIUM 185mg; CALC 8mg

Kentucky Burgoo

Most Kentuckians can't imagine Derby Day without this thick meat and vegetable stew. Variations abound, using all kinds of meats such as lamb, veal, and game. Pass hot sauce at the table for those who want to add a little zip.

    1 tablespoon canola oil, divided
    1 pound boneless sirloin steak, cut
       into 1-inch cubes
    ½ pound pork tenderloin, cut into
       1-inch cubes
    ½ pound skinless, boneless chicken
       breast, cut into 1-inch pieces
  3½ cups water, divided
    ½ teaspoon salt
    ½ teaspoon freshly ground black
       pepper, divided
    1 (14-ounce) can less-sodium beef
       broth
    1 cup (1-inch) pieces onion
    1 cup (1-inch) pieces green bell
       pepper
    1 cup (1-inch) pieces carrot
    3 garlic cloves, minced
  2½ cups (½-inch) cubed peeled
       baking potato (about 12 ounces)
    1 cup fresh or frozen lima beans
    1 cup fresh or frozen corn
       kernels
    1 cup fresh or frozen cut okra
    1 tablespoon chopped fresh or
    1 teaspoon dried thyme
    1 tablespoon chopped fresh parsley
    2 tablespoons dark brown sugar
    3 tablespoons cider vinegar
    2 tablespoons tomato paste
    1 tablespoon Worcestershire sauce
    1 (14.5-ounce) can diced tomatoes,
       undrained
       Chopped fresh parsley (optional)

1. Heat 1½ teaspoons oil in a large Dutch oven over medium-high heat. Add half of beef, pork, and chicken; sauté 5 minutes or until browned. Remove beef mixture from pan; repeat procedure with 1½ teaspoons oil and remaining beef, pork, and chicken. Add 3 cups water, salt, ¼ teaspoon black pepper, and broth to pan, scraping pan to loosen browned bits. Add beef mixture, onion, bell pepper, carrot, and garlic to

pan; bring to a boil. Reduce heat, and simmer, uncovered, 1 hour or until beef is tender, stirring occasionally.
2. Add ½ cup water, potato, and next 5 ingredients; bring to a boil. Reduce heat, and simmer 30 minutes or until potato is tender. Stir in ¼ teaspoon black pepper, sugar, and next 4 ingredients; simmer 30 minutes or until mixture is thick. Sprinkle with additional parsley, if desired. Yield: 8 servings (serving size: about 1¼ cups).

CALORIES 302 (25% from fat); FAT 8.4g (sat 2.4g, mono 4.1g, poly 1.2g); PROTEIN 29g; CARB 28.2g; FIBER 4.7g; CHOL 72mg; IRON 3.4mg; SODIUM 417mg; CALC 78mg

STAFF FAVORITE • MAKE AHEAD
Bourbon Caramel Sauce

This silky sauce, which earned our Test Kitchens' top rating, capitalizes on bourbon's oaky spirit. It's delicious over low-fat vanilla ice cream, pound cake, or bread pudding. Cover the surface of any leftovers with plastic wrap (to prevent a skin from forming).

  1½ cups sugar
    ⅔ cup water
    2 teaspoons light-colored corn
       syrup
    ¼ cup evaporated low-fat milk
    ¼ cup fat-free half-and-half
    1 tablespoon butter
    3 tablespoons bourbon

1. Sprinkle sugar in an even layer in a large, heavy saucepan. Combine ⅔ cup water and syrup; pour over sugar. Cook over medium-high heat until sugar dissolves (about 4 minutes), stirring gently. Cook 20 minutes or until golden (do not stir). Remove from heat. Gradually stir in milk, half-and-half, and butter using a long-handled wooden spoon (mixture will bubble vigorously). Cook over low heat until mixture is smooth, stirring constantly. Remove from heat. Stir in bourbon. Serve warm. (Mixture thickens as it cools.) Yield: 1⅓ cups (serving size: about 1 tablespoon).

CALORIES 90 (8% from fat); FAT 0.8g (sat 0.5g, mono 0.2g, poly 0g); PROTEIN 0.3g; CARB 20.2g; FIBER 0g; CHOL 3mg; IRON 0mg; SODIUM 14mg; CALC 13mg

Hot Brown Sandwiches

In 1923, this Louisville classic was created by Chef Fred Schmidt at the Brown Hotel.

SAUCE:
    1 tablespoon butter
  1½ tablespoons all-purpose flour
  1¾ cups 1% low-fat milk
    ½ cup (2 ounces) shredded sharp
       Cheddar cheese
    3 tablespoons grated fresh Parmesan
       cheese
    2 teaspoons Marsala or cream sherry
    ¼ teaspoon salt
    ¼ teaspoon freshly ground black
       pepper
    ¼ teaspoon paprika
    ¼ teaspoon Worcestershire sauce
    ⅛ teaspoon ground red pepper

REMAINING INGREDIENTS:
    6 (1½-ounce) slices hearty white
       bread (such as Pepperidge Farm),
       toasted and cut in half diagonally
    ¾ pound shredded cooked turkey
       breast
   12 (¼-inch-thick) slices tomato
    2 tablespoons grated fresh Parmesan
       cheese
    6 bacon slices, cooked and crumbled

1. Preheat broiler.
2. To prepare sauce, melt butter in a medium saucepan over medium heat. Gradually add flour, stirring with a whisk; cook 1 minute, stirring constantly. Gradually add milk, stirring with a whisk; bring to a boil, stirring constantly. Reduce heat, and simmer 2 minutes, stirring constantly. Add Cheddar and next 7 ingredients, stirring until cheeses melt. Remove from heat.
3. Arrange 2 toast halves in bottom of each of 6 gratin dishes or ovenproof plates. Arrange 2 ounces turkey over each serving. Top each serving with about ⅓ cup sauce, 2 tomato slices, and 1 teaspoon Parmesan. Broil 2 minutes or until bubbly. Sprinkle each serving with about 1 tablespoon bacon. Yield: 6 servings (serving size: 1 sandwich).

CALORIES 353 (29% from fat); FAT 11.3g (sat 5.4g, mono 3.2g, poly 0.7g); PROTEIN 29.7g; CARB 31.7g; FIBER 1.7g; CHOL 75mg; IRON 3mg; SODIUM 764mg; CALC 260mg

Beaten Biscuits

The proper texture for this bread lies between a traditional biscuit and a cracker, which a food processor helps to achieve.

2½   cups all-purpose flour (about 11¼ ounces)
 1   teaspoon sugar
 ½   teaspoon salt
 ½   teaspoon baking powder
 ¼   cup vegetable shortening, chilled
 ½   cup cold 1% low-fat milk
 ⅓   cup ice water

1. Preheat oven to 400°.
2. Lightly spoon flour into dry measuring cups; level with a knife. Place flour, sugar, salt, and baking powder in a food processor; pulse 4 times. Add shortening; pulse 6 times or until well blended. Add milk and ⅓ cup ice water; process 1½ minutes. (Dough should have a shiny appearance.) Turn dough out onto a lightly floured surface. Cover and let stand 5 minutes.
3. Uncover dough; roll to about ½-inch thickness. Cut dough with a 2-inch round cutter. (Reroll scraps.) Place dough circles on a baking sheet. Pierce tops of dough circles with a fork. Bake at 400° for 18 minutes or until lightly browned. Yield: 2 dozen (serving size: 1 biscuit).

CALORIES 69 (29% from fat); FAT 2.2g (sat 0.6g, mono 0.7g, poly 0.6g); PROTEIN 1.5g; CARB 10.4g; FIBER 0.4g; CHOL 0mg; IRON 0.6mg; SODIUM 62mg; CALC 14mg

lighten up
Splendid Spinach-Cheese Bake

A California reader seeks our help to trim down her go-to brunch specialty.

Joyce Keil, of San Mateo, California, has a family favorite recipe for Spinach-Cheese Bake. This original recipe's short ingredient list belied its heavy nutrition profile. One pound of cheese, one-quarter cup butter, three eggs, and a cup of whole milk contributed a hefty amount of fat and most of the dish's calories. One serving contained more than half of a day's worth of saturated fat as well as one-third of the dietary cholesterol for someone on a 2,000-calorie diet, according to the USDA's Dietary Guidelines for Americans and the American Heart Association.

Reducing the fat and maintaining the casserole's delicate taste and light texture was challenging. Most of the flavor and fat came from the butter and four cups of Monterey Jack cheese. We reduced the butter to one tablespoon, which was melted and used to grease the pan and maintain the casserole's buttery flavor. And we reduced the total amount of cheese and substituted a lower-fat version to keep fat in check: We combined ¾ cup Monterey Jack cheese with 1¼ cups of more assertive-tasting reduced-fat sharp Cheddar cheese. These changes cut more than 13 grams of fat (nearly 9 grams saturated) and 135 calories per portion. The butter, cheese, and eggs contributed most of the original's cholesterol count, but by using less butter, mostly reduced-fat cheese, and 1 cup of fat-free and cholesterol-free egg substitute, we slashed 89 milligrams of cholesterol per serving. Adding a bit more spinach improved the fiber and iron content. And to compensate for this addition, we increased the flour-milk mixture with minimal extra calories by using fat-free milk instead of whole. Adding a little mustard and a few spices further boosted the savory quality of the casserole.

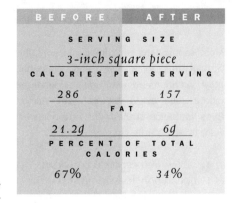

BEFORE	AFTER
SERVING SIZE	
3-inch square piece	
CALORIES PER SERVING	
286	157
FAT	
21.2g	6g
PERCENT OF TOTAL CALORIES	
67%	34%

Spinach-Cheese Bake

You can assemble the casserole in less than 10 minutes by using preshredded cheeses.

 1   tablespoon butter, melted
     Cooking spray
 2   (6-ounce) packages fresh baby spinach
1¼   cups (5 ounces) shredded reduced-fat sharp Cheddar cheese
 ¾   cup (3 ounces) shredded Monterey Jack cheese
1⅓   cups all-purpose flour (about 5¾ ounces)
1½   cups fat-free milk
 1   cup egg substitute
 1   teaspoon salt
 1   teaspoon baking powder
 2   teaspoons Dijon mustard
 ¼   teaspoon freshly ground black pepper
 ⅛   teaspoon ground nutmeg
 ⅛   teaspoon ground red pepper

1. Preheat oven to 350°.
2. Pour butter into bottom of a 13 x 9–inch baking dish coated with cooking spray; tilt dish to coat. Place spinach evenly in bottom of dish; sprinkle evenly with cheeses.
3. Lightly spoon flour into dry measuring cups; level with a knife. Combine flour and remaining 8 ingredients in a medium bowl; stir with a whisk until blended. Pour milk mixture over cheese. Bake at 350° for 40 minutes or until lightly browned. Serve immediately. Yield: 12 servings.

CALORIES 157 (34% from fat); FAT 6g (sat 3.7g, mono 1.7g, poly 0.4g); PROTEIN 10.8g; CARB 15.1g; FIBER 1.6g; CHOL 18mg; IRON 2.6mg; SODIUM 494mg; CALC 263mg

Rubs and Sauces for the Grill

Rely on these all-purpose formulas to quickly flavor grilled meat and vegetables.

Try our versatile rubs and sauces on everything from fish, chicken, and beef to vegetables. We'll bet you use them on grilled fare all summer long.

QUICK & EASY • MAKE AHEAD
Cajun Blackening Dry Rub

Try this fiery rub on white-fleshed fish fillets such as catfish or snapper, or chicken breasts or shrimp. You can sprinkle it on burgers of any variety, turkey to beef—or over lightly oiled corn on the cob.

2½ tablespoons paprika
 1 tablespoon kosher salt
1½ teaspoons ground cumin
1½ teaspoons dried thyme
 1 teaspoon freshly ground black pepper
 ½ teaspoon garlic powder
 ½ teaspoon ground red pepper

1. Combine all ingredients. Store in an airtight container up to 2 weeks. Yield: about ⅓ cup (serving size: 1 teaspoon).

CALORIES 5 (36% from fat); FAT 0.2g (sat 0g, mono 0g, poly 0.1g); PROTEIN 0.2g; CARB 0.9g; FIBER 0.6g; CHOL 0mg; IRON 0.4mg; SODIUM 354mg; CALC 6mg

QUICK & EASY • MAKE AHEAD
Texas Barbecue Dry Rub

Because the sugar in this sweet-savory blend can burn, it's best on meats that cook for extended times over low heat, such as brisket, ribs, or leg of lamb. Try it on spit-roasted whole turkey or chicken—or any meat cooked over indirect heat, such as brined pork chops. In cooler months, use it on meats braised in the slow cooker.

 2 tablespoons chili powder
 2 tablespoons brown sugar
 2 teaspoons salt
 2 teaspoons freshly ground black pepper
 1 teaspoon dry mustard
 1 teaspoon ground cumin
 ¼ teaspoon ground red pepper

1. Combine all ingredients. Store in an airtight container up to 2 weeks. Yield: about ⅓ cup (serving size: 1 teaspoon).

CALORIES 9 (10% from fat); FAT 0.1g (sat 0g, mono 0g, poly 0g); PROTEIN 0.1g; CARB 2g; FIBER 0.3g; CHOL 0mg; IRON 0.2mg; SODIUM 296mg; CALC 4mg

QUICK & EASY • MAKE AHEAD
Asian Dry Rub

Spicy meat skewers are popular street vendor fare in Asia. This potent rub approximates that flavor; it's best on dark-meat chicken, strong-flavored fish like salmon or sardines, or any cut of pork. Or sprinkle over thickly sliced tomatoes, set them over an unheated section of the grill, and allow them to smoke for a few minutes.

 4 teaspoons dried basil
 4 teaspoons dried mint
 2 teaspoons salt
 2 teaspoons ground ginger
 2 teaspoons paprika
1½ teaspoons ground red pepper
 1 teaspoon freshly ground black pepper
 ½ teaspoon garlic powder

1. Combine all ingredients. Store in an airtight container up to 2 weeks. Yield: about ⅓ cup (serving size: 1 teaspoon).

CALORIES 4 (23% from fat); FAT 0.1g (sat 0g, mono 0g, poly 0g); PROTEIN 0.2g; CARB 0.7g; FIBER 0.3g; CHOL 0mg; IRON 0.3mg; SODIUM 296mg; CALC 9mg

QUICK & EASY
Greek Wet Rub
(pictured on page 233)

Try this aromatic combo on lamb chops, white-fleshed fish, shrimp, or any poultry. Or use it to season lamb and red onion kebabs.

 ¼ cup fresh oregano leaves
 2 tablespoons chopped fresh rosemary
 3 tablespoons olive oil
 2 teaspoons grated lemon rind
 1 tablespoon fresh lemon juice
 2 teaspoons salt
 4 garlic cloves, minced

1. Place all ingredients in a mini food processor; process until finely chopped. Yield: about ⅓ cup (serving size: 1½ teaspoons).

CALORIES 36 (95% from fat); FAT 3.8g (sat 0.5g, mono 2.7g, poly 0.4g); PROTEIN 0.1g; CARB 0.8g; FIBER 0.2g; CHOL 0mg; IRON 0.1mg; SODIUM 430mg; CALC 8mg

QUICK & EASY
Miso Wet Rub

Miso is Japanese fermented soybean paste used to flavor many dishes, in addition to the familiar soup at sushi restaurants. There are dozens of varieties. Look for yellow miso, a mild, somewhat earthy, and almost sweet version that is often available in the produce section of large supermarkets. Try this thick rub on salmon fillets, dark-meat chicken, pork, or tofu steaks.

 ⅓ cup yellow miso
 2 tablespoons rice vinegar
 2 tablespoons honey
 1 tablespoon minced peeled fresh ginger
 ¼ teaspoon ground red pepper

Continued

1. Combine all ingredients, stirring well with a whisk. Yield: ½ cup (serving size: 2 teaspoons).

CALORIES 23 (16% from fat); FAT 0.4g (sat 0g, mono 0.1g, poly 0.3g); PROTEIN 0.9g; CARB 4.4g; FIBER 0.2g; CHOL 0mg; IRON 0mg; SODIUM 329mg; CALC 0mg

Korean Barbecue Wet Rub

One of the most popular Korean dishes is *bulgogi*, thin slices of beef that are soaked in a sweet-salty marinade and grilled. Here is a traditional-tasting rub that goes on just before the food is grilled. It's great on salmon, steaks, pork tenderloin, dark-meat chicken, or any game bird, such as duck or quail.

- ¼ cup packed brown sugar
- 2 teaspoons low-sodium soy sauce
- 2 teaspoons dark sesame oil
- 1 teaspoon salt
- 4 garlic cloves, minced

1. Combine all ingredients. Refrigerate in an airtight container up to 1 week. Yield: about 3 tablespoons (serving size: 1½ teaspoons).

CALORIES 53 (27% from fat); FAT 1.6g (sat 0.2g, mono 0.6g, poly 0.6g); PROTEIN 0.2g; CARB 9.8g; FIBER 0.1g; CHOL 0mg; IRON 0.3mg; SODIUM 457mg; CALC 12mg

Pesto Vinaigrette

Here's the taste of a summer herb favorite in a light drizzle that's perfect over fish and veggies just off the grill. We loved it with thickly sliced, grilled eggplant and Vidalia onion.

- ½ cup fresh basil leaves
- ⅓ cup extravirgin olive oil
- 3 tablespoons white wine vinegar
- 2 tablespoons water
- 2 tablespoons pine nuts, toasted
- 2 tablespoons grated Parmigiano-Reggiano cheese
- ½ teaspoon salt
- ½ teaspoon black pepper
- 2 garlic cloves

1. Place all ingredients in a food processor; process until smooth. Refrigerate in an airtight container up to 1 week. Yield: ⅔ cup (serving size: 2 teaspoons).

CALORIES 51 (97% from fat); FAT 5.5g (sat 0.8g, mono 3.6g, poly 0.9g); PROTEIN 0.5g; CARB 0.4g; FIBER 0.1g; CHOL 1mg; IRON 0.2mg; SODIUM 88mg; CALC 14mg

Red Onion Chutney

This East Indian sauce is a tasty condiment for grilled burgers, fish, beef, chicken, or pork.

- 2 cups finely chopped red onion
- ½ cup red wine vinegar
- ⅓ cup packed brown sugar
- 1 tablespoon minced peeled fresh ginger
- 1 teaspoon mustard seeds
- ½ teaspoon crushed red pepper
- ¼ teaspoon salt
- ⅛ teaspoon ground cloves

1. Bring all ingredients to a boil in a medium saucepan. Cover, reduce heat, and simmer 15 minutes. Uncover and cook 10 minutes or until liquid almost evaporates. Refrigerate in an airtight container up to 2 weeks. Yield: 1 cup (serving size: 2 tablespoons).

CALORIES 72 (3% from fat); FAT 0.2g (sat 0g, mono 0.1g, poly 0.1g); PROTEIN 0.5g; CARB 17.8g; FIBER 0.7g; CHOL 0mg; IRON 0.4mg; SODIUM 81mg; CALC 23mg

Chile Finishing Oil

Drizzle on steaks, chicken, tofu, or vegetables the moment they come off the fire. You can also brush the spicy oil over pizza dough, or use it to make a fiery salad dressing. Keep leftovers in the refrigerator.

- ½ cup canola oil
- 1 teaspoon cumin seeds
- 8 dried hot red chiles
- 4 garlic cloves, crushed

1. Combine all ingredients in a small saucepan, and cook over medium heat 3 minutes or until garlic is lightly browned. Remove from heat, and cool 15 minutes. Place mixture in a blender or mini food processor, and process until smooth. Strain mixture through a sieve into a bowl, and discard solids. Refrigerate in an airtight container up to 10 days. Yield: ⅓ cup (serving size: 1 teaspoon).

CALORIES 41 (100% from fat); FAT 4.7g (sat 0.3g, mono 2.8g, poly 1.4g); PROTEIN 0g; CARB 0g; FIBER 0g; CHOL 0mg; IRON 0mg; SODIUM 0mg; CALC 0mg

Plum Barbecue Sauce

Drape this zesty sauce over food after it's cooked, or brush it on during the last minute or two of cook time. Serve with grilled chicken, pork tenderloin, or burgers. Or add to a slow cooker with pork or beef roast. Smoky chipotle chile powder is a fine substitute for smoked paprika.

- 1¾ cups chopped plums (about 6)
- 1 cup ketchup
- ¼ cup finely chopped shallots
- ¼ cup maple syrup
- 2½ tablespoons red wine vinegar
- 2 teaspoons Dijon mustard
- 1 teaspoon smoked paprika
- ½ teaspoon freshly ground black pepper
- ¼ teaspoon ground red pepper

1. Combine all ingredients in a medium saucepan; bring to a boil. Cover, reduce heat, and simmer 5 minutes. Uncover and cook 15 minutes or until thick, stirring occasionally. Cool 10 minutes. Place mixture in a food processor; process until smooth. Refrigerate in an airtight container up to 2 weeks. Yield: 2 cups (serving size: 2 tablespoons).

CALORIES 41 (4% from fat); FAT 0.2g (sat 0g, mono 0.1g, poly 0.1g); PROTEIN 0.5g; CARB 10.2g; FIBER 0.5g; CHOL 0mg; IRON 0.3mg; SODIUM 176mg; CALC 9mg

Milk & Cream

These culinary staples lend velvety texture and subtle taste to a satisfying range of applications.

Aside from being the beverage of choice for washing down cookies, milk is crucial to many cooking applications, from velvety custards to creamy casseroles. Over the years, we've learned that all types of milk products have a place in the pages of *Cooking Light.* Depending on the role milk plays in a particular dish, we may call for low-fat milk or perhaps a higher-fat product such as whipping cream or half-and-half.

For example, if we're making a white béchamel sauce, we can use a low-fat or fat-free product because the sauce will be thickened with flour, which mitigates the thinner texture of a lower-fat milk. On the other hand, if we want to round out the flavors of a pan sauce and add silky texture, a touch of whipping cream or half-and-half is appropriate.

Pasta Primavera

A combination of equal parts milk and cream, half-and-half creates a silky, full-bodied sauce. This makes a lovely vegetarian entrée for spring.

 2 cups green beans, trimmed and halved crosswise
 2 cups broccoli florets
 ½ cup (1-inch) slices asparagus (about 2 ounces)
 6 ounces uncooked fettuccine
 1 tablespoon olive oil
 1 cup chopped onion
 2 teaspoons minced fresh garlic
 ⅛ teaspoon crushed red pepper
 ½ cup fresh or frozen green peas
 1 cup grape tomatoes, halved
 ⅔ cup half-and-half
 1 teaspoon cornstarch
 ¾ teaspoon salt
 ¼ cup chopped fresh basil
 ¼ cup (1 ounce) shaved Parmigiano-Reggiano cheese

1. Cook beans in boiling water 1 minute. Add broccoli and asparagus; cook 2 minutes or until vegetables are crisp-tender. Remove vegetables from pan with a slotted spoon; place in a large bowl. Return water to a boil. Add pasta; cook 10 minutes or until al dente. Drain and add to vegetable mixture.
2. Heat oil in a large nonstick skillet over medium-high heat. Add onion, and sauté 2 minutes. Add garlic and red pepper; sauté 3 minutes or until onion begins to brown. Add peas, and sauté 1 minute. Add tomatoes; sauté 2 minutes. Combine half-and-half and cornstarch, stirring with a whisk. Reduce heat to medium. Add half-and-half mixture and salt to pan; cook 1 minute or until thick, stirring constantly. Pour sauce over pasta mixture; toss gently to coat. Sprinkle with basil and cheese. Serve immediately. Yield: 4 servings (serving size: 2 cups pasta mixture, 1 tablespoon basil, and 1 tablespoon cheese).

CALORIES 338 (29% from fat); FAT 10.8g (sat 4.7g, mono 4.4g, poly 0.8g); PROTEIN 13.7g; CARB 49.6g; FIBER 7.1g; CHOL 20mg; IRON 2.9mg; SODIUM 607mg; CALC 205mg

WINE NOTE: Sauvignon blanc is a good option to pair with Pasta Primavera since the fresh "green" quality mirrors vegetables perfectly. But because this is a cream-based pasta primavera, opt instead for a pinot blanc. Rounder and more mellow than sauvignon blanc, pinot blanc is loaded with floral and citrus character. Try Robert Sinskey Pinot Blanc 2005 Los Carneros, California ($18).

Raisin-Honey Milk Bread

The fat from the whole milk keeps the bread moist, and its natural sugars (along with the honey) create a golden crust.

 1 cup warm whole milk (100° to 110°)
 ¼ cup honey, divided
 1 package dry yeast (about 2¼ teaspoons)
 2 large egg yolks, lightly beaten
 3½ cups all-purpose flour, divided (about 15¾ ounces)
 1 cup raisins
 1 teaspoon salt
 Cooking spray

1. Combine milk, 1 tablespoon honey, and yeast in a large bowl, stirring with a whisk; let stand 5 minutes. Stir in 3 tablespoons honey and yolks.
2. Lightly spoon flour into dry measuring cups; level with a knife. Combine 3 cups flour, raisins, and salt in a large bowl. Add milk mixture, stirring until a soft dough forms. Turn dough out onto a lightly floured surface. Knead until smooth and elastic (about 8 minutes); add enough of remaining flour, 1 tablespoon at a time, to prevent dough from sticking to hands (dough will feel sticky).
3. Place dough in a large bowl coated with cooking spray, turning to coat top. Cover dough, and let rise in a warm place (85°), free from drafts, 1 hour and 15 minutes or until doubled in size. (Gently press two fingers into dough. If indentation remains, dough has risen enough.) Punch dough down; cover and let rest 5 minutes. Shape dough into a 9 x 4–inch oval; place on a baking sheet coated with cooking spray. Cover and let rise 55 minutes or until doubled in size.
4. Preheat oven to 350°.
5. Bake at 350° for 30 minutes or until browned and loaf sounds hollow when tapped. Cool on a wire rack 20 minutes before cutting into 16 slices. Yield: 16 servings (serving size: 1 slice).

CALORIES 160 (8% from fat); FAT 1.4g (sat 0.5g, mono 0.4g, poly 0.2g); PROTEIN 4.1g; CARB 33.3g; FIBER 1.5g; CHOL 27mg; IRON 1.7mg; SODIUM 158mg; CALC 27mg

Chocolate-Mint Pudding

Unless milk is stabilized with a thickener such as flour or cornstarch, it will "break," or curdle, when it becomes too hot; that's why it's important to go no higher than 180 degrees at the beginning of step one.

- 3 cups fat-free milk
- ½ cup packed fresh mint leaves (about ½ ounce)
- ⅔ cup sugar
- ¼ cup cornstarch
- 3 tablespoons unsweetened cocoa
- ⅛ teaspoon salt
- 3 large egg yolks, lightly beaten
- ½ teaspoon vanilla extract
- 2 ounces semisweet chocolate, chopped
- Mint sprigs (optional)

1. Heat milk over medium-high heat in a small, heavy saucepan to 180° or until tiny bubbles form around edge (do not boil). Remove from heat; add ½ cup mint. Let stand 15 minutes; strain milk mixture through a sieve into a bowl. Discard solids. Return milk to pan; stir in sugar, cornstarch, cocoa, and salt. Return pan to medium heat; bring to a boil, stirring constantly with a whisk until thick.
2. Place egg yolks in a medium bowl; gradually add half of hot milk mixture, stirring constantly with a whisk. Add egg mixture to pan; bring to a boil, stirring constantly. Cook 1 minute or until thick. Remove from heat; add vanilla and chocolate, stirring until chocolate melts. Pour pudding into a bowl; cover surface of pudding with plastic wrap. Chill. Garnish with mint sprigs, if desired. Yield: 6 servings (serving size: about ⅔ cup).

CALORIES 227 (25% from fat); FAT 6.4g (sat 3.2g, mono 2.5g, poly 0.4g); PROTEIN 6.7g; CARB 39.4g; FIBER 1.2g; CHOL 105mg; IRON 1.1mg; SODIUM 106mg; CALC 173mg

Banana-Coconut Ice Cream

The added creaminess of two percent milk (as opposed to fat-free or one percent) makes rich ice cream with few ice crystals.

- 1½ cups 2% reduced-fat milk
- 1 cup cream of coconut
- ⅓ cup sugar
- 1½ cups mashed ripe banana (about 3 bananas)

1. Combine first 3 ingredients in a medium bowl, stirring until sugar dissolves. Stir in banana; cover and chill.
2. Pour mixture into freezer can of an ice-cream freezer; freeze according to manufacturer's instructions. Spoon ice cream into a freezer-safe container; cover and freeze 1 hour or until firm. Yield: 8 servings (serving size: about ⅔ cup).

CALORIES 203 (27% from fat); FAT 6g (sat 4.6g, mono 0.8g, poly 0.2g); PROTEIN 2g; CARB 37.2g; FIBER 1.1g; CHOL 3mg; IRON 0.1mg; SODIUM 38mg; CALC 58mg

Angel Food Cake Stuffed with Whipped Cream and Berries

BERRIES:
- 2 cups fresh raspberries
- 1½ cups fresh blackberries
- 1½ cups fresh blueberries
- ¼ cup granulated sugar
- 2 tablespoons fresh orange juice

CAKE:
- 1 cup cake flour (about 4 ounces)
- 1 cup powdered sugar, divided
- ½ teaspoon ground ginger
- ¾ cup granulated sugar
- 12 large egg whites
- 1 teaspoon cream of tartar
- ½ teaspoon salt
- 2 tablespoons fresh orange juice

WHIPPED CREAM:
- ¾ cup whipping cream, chilled
- ½ vanilla bean, split lengthwise
- ¾ cup powdered sugar

REMAINING INGREDIENTS:
- 2 tablespoons powdered sugar
- Grated orange rind (optional)

1. To prepare berries, combine first 5 ingredients; toss to combine. Cover and chill 1 hour.
2. Preheat oven to 375°.
3. To prepare cake, place a rack in lower third of oven. Lightly spoon flour into a dry measuring cup; level with a knife. Sift together flour, ½ cup powdered sugar, and ginger in a medium bowl. Sift together ½ cup powdered sugar and ¾ cup granulated sugar in another bowl. Place egg whites in a large bowl; beat with a mixer at high speed until foamy. Add cream of tartar and salt; beat until soft peaks form. Add powdered and granulated sugar mixture, 1 tablespoon at a time, beating until stiff peaks form. Sift flour mixture over egg white mixture, ¼ cup at a time; fold in. Fold in 2 tablespoons juice.
4. Spoon batter into an ungreased 10-inch tube pan, spreading evenly. Break air pockets by cutting through batter with a knife. Bake at 375° for 30 minutes or until cake springs back when lightly touched. Invert pan; cool completely. Loosen cake from sides of pan using a narrow metal spatula. Invert cake onto a plate.
5. Cut 1 inch off top of cake using a serrated knife; set top of cake aside. Hollow out bottom of cake using a small knife, leaving a 1-inch-thick shell; reserve torn cake for another use.
6. To prepare whipped cream, place cream in a medium bowl; beat with a mixer at high speed until soft peaks form. Scrape seeds from vanilla bean into bowl; discard pod. Gradually add ¾ cup powdered sugar, beating at high speed until stiff peaks form.
7. Spoon all but 1 cup of berry mixture into cake shell; top with whipped cream. Replace top of cake; sprinkle with 2 tablespoons powdered sugar. Serve immediately with additional berry mixture; garnish with orange rind, if desired. Yield: 12 servings (serving size: 1 stuffed cake slice and 4 teaspoons berry mixture).

CALORIES 269 (20% from fat); FAT 6g (sat 3.5g, mono 1.6g, poly 0.4g); PROTEIN 5.2g; CARB 50.2g; FIBER 2.9g; CHOL 20mg; IRON 1.2mg; SODIUM 149mg; CALC 26mg

Anatomy of Milk

- Raw cow's milk is about 87 percent water, 5 percent sugar, 3½ percent protein, and just under 4 percent fat.
- Because fat is lighter than water, unhomogenized milk separates so that cream rises to the top; when skimmed off, the milk that's left is almost fat-free.
- One cup of milk contains about 102 milligrams of sodium.
- Ninety-eight percent of milk in the United States is vitamin D-fortified; one cup of fortified milk contains 25 percent of the Daily Value for vitamin D.
- When fat is removed from milk, vitamin A is removed, too. That's why two percent, one percent, and fat-free milk are most often fortified with this vitamin. One cup of fortified milk contains 10 percent of the Daily Value for vitamin A.
- One cup of milk also provides 20 percent of the Daily Value for phosphorous.

Milk Varieties

With none of its inherent fat removed, **whole milk** is thick and rich. Each eight-ounce glass has 146 calories, 7.9 grams of fat, and 276 milligrams of calcium. Whole milk is recommended as a beverage for children under the age of two, but in most cases is considered too high in fat for adults and older children. It can, however, play an important role in cooking. It adds silky texture to sauces and soups, flavor and texture to baked goods, and golden gloss to doughs and crusts.

An eight-ounce glass of **two percent (reduced-fat) milk** contains 121 calories, 4.7 grams of fat, and 297 milligrams of calcium, while the same serving of **one percent,** or **low-fat, milk** has 102 calories, 2.6 grams of fat, and 300 milligrams of calcium.

When considering which milk to drink, the question is simply how much you value the increased creaminess of the two percent milk over the reduction in calories and fat of one percent or fat-free milk. When cooking, the decision is often more clear. For example, when making ice cream, you may need more fat for better results. The fat in the milk not only lends fullness of flavor but also interferes with the formation of ice crystals so the ice cream is rendered velvety smooth.

Other dishes, like the flour-thickened sauce in Stovetop Mac and Cheese (recipe on page 147), rely on other ingredients or techniques for texture and are dependent on milk mostly for flavor and liquidity. So a lower-fat milk works fine in these cases.

Fat-free milk is many people's milk beverage of choice. Also called skim milk, it contains no fat, only 83 calories, and 306 milligrams of calcium per eight-ounce glass. Lower-fat milks have more calcium per cup than whole milk. Use fat-free milk on cereal, in coffee, as a drink—and to make certain dishes, such as puddings and cheese sauces, where the milk provides background flavor, and other ingredients, such as flour or cornstarch, lend texture.

Whipping cream (or heavy whipping cream) has 51 calories and 5.6 grams of fat per tablespoon. When beaten, whipping cream doubles in volume to create a classic dessert topping. (Neither light whipping cream nor light cream contains enough fat to hold its shape when whipped.) Whipping cream is the only type of milk that won't curdle when brought to a boil. Use it to enrich sauces and soups, adding just a bit at a time.

Half-and-half is a mixture of equal parts milk and cream, and weighs in with only 20 calories and 1.7 grams of fat per tablespoon. Use it to finish sauces and soups, but add it off the stove or over lower heat to prevent it from curdling.

Buttermilk was traditionally the liquid that remained after butter was churned from cream. Today, buttermilk is made by adding bacteria cultures to fat-free, low-fat, or whole milk. Buttermilk has a thick consistency and tart flavor. It's often used for cakes, biscuits, pancakes, and quick breads.

Acidophilus milk is whole, reduced-fat, or fat-free milk with friendly *Lactobacillus acidophilus* bacteria added to it. The bacteria is believed to benefit the digestive tract, much the same way yogurt does.

In the Process

For reasons of safety, nutrition, and appearance, almost all milk sold in the United States is homogenized, pasteurized, and vitamin fortified.

Pasteurization is the required process of heating raw milk at a high temperature (about 162 degrees) for a short time to retard spoilage and extend shelf life—without diminishing its nutritional value.

Ultra High Temperature Processing (UHT) refers to a technique in which the milk is treated for one to three seconds at a much higher temperature (about 265 to 300 degrees), and the milk is packed in sterile aseptic containers to give it a non-refrigerated shelf life of three months with no loss of nutrients.

Homogenization is essentially emulsification—the fat globules are broken down and dispersed, via centrifuge, through the milk so they can no longer separate. It's what makes milk smooth and creamy.

Vitamins are often added to milk. Most milk is fortified with vitamin D, a nutrient essential to the absorption of calcium. Vitamin A is often added to two percent, one percent, and skim milk to replace vitamin A lost when the fat is removed.

Hot Milk

When heating milk, several concerns may arise. First, milk and half-and-half tend to "break," or curdle, if heated to a boil so add these products over low heat or off the heat. Our recipes typically call for warming these milks to no higher than 180 degrees.

Milk and milk-based mixtures (such as chowder) also tend to scorch on the bottom. To prevent this, use a heavy pan to evenly distribute the heat, and rinse it with water before adding the milk. The water creates a barrier that helps keep the milk's proteins from sticking to the pan. To stop milk from forming a skin as it's heated (which is caused by evaporation on the surface), keep the pan partially covered.

STAFF FAVORITE

Stovetop Mac and Cheese

Low-fat milk works well in this application.

1¼ cups uncooked elbow macaroni (about 6 ounces)
1 cup 1% low-fat milk
2 tablespoons all-purpose flour
1¼ cups (5 ounces) shredded reduced-fat sharp Cheddar cheese
½ teaspoon salt
⅛ teaspoon freshly ground black pepper
1 (1½-ounce) slice white bread
1 tablespoon butter, melted

1. Cook pasta according to package directions, omitting salt and fat. Drain.
2. Combine milk and flour in a medium saucepan, stirring with a whisk. Cook over medium heat 2 minutes or until thick, stirring constantly with a whisk. Add cheese, salt, and pepper, stirring with a whisk until smooth. Add pasta; toss to coat. Let stand 4 minutes.
3. Place bread in a food processor, and pulse 10 times or until crumbs measure 1¼ cups.
4. Heat a large nonstick skillet over medium heat. Add breadcrumbs, and cook 5 minutes or until lightly browned, stirring occasionally. Stir in butter; cook 2 minutes, stirring occasionally. Sprinkle breadcrumb mixture over pasta mixture. Yield: 4 servings (serving size: ¾ cup).

CALORIES 334 (30% from fat); FAT 11g (sat 6.5g, mono 2.8g, poly 0.8g); PROTEIN 17.7g; CARB 40.3g; FIBER 1.7g; CHOL 30mg; IRON 2.1mg; SODIUM 661mg; CALC 417mg

Family Favorite

A retired teacher prepares her signature salty-sweet Indian condiment to welcome her son home from Iraq.

Sue Barker, of Rogers, Arkansas, adores the vibrant flavors of Indian cuisine and often integrates Indian spices into her cooking. So when her 22-year-old son, Evan, an army medic, returned from Iraq last year, she prepared one of his favorite dishes: Tomato Chutney with Baked Pita Chips. "Every time he comes home, he wants Indian food," says Barker, a retired schoolteacher.

Barker created the chutney 15 years ago to satisfy a hankering for healthful, yet tasty, Indian fare. The result was an impressive fusion of sweet, sour, and spicy ingredients.

QUICK & EASY

Tomato Chutney with Baked Pita Chips

The versatile chutney also makes a zingy spread on turkey sandwiches, or serve it with grilled chicken.

6 (6-inch) pitas
Cooking spray
1 teaspoon kosher salt
2 teaspoons canola oil
1 teaspoon cumin seeds
1 teaspoon mustard seeds
1 cup chopped onion (about 1 medium)
1 tablespoon minced peeled fresh ginger
2 garlic cloves, minced
1 jalapeño pepper, seeded and finely chopped
1 teaspoon curry powder
1 teaspoon ground turmeric
2 (14.5-ounce) cans no-salt-added diced tomatoes, undrained
½ cup chopped fresh cilantro
⅓ cup raisins
2 tablespoons sugar

1. Preheat oven to 400°.
2. Split pitas, and cut each half into 8 wedges. Arrange wedges on a large baking sheet. Lightly coat wedges with cooking spray, and sprinkle with salt. Bake at 400° for 7 minutes or until crisp.
3. Heat oil in a large saucepan over medium-high heat. Add cumin seeds and mustard seeds to pan; sauté 1 minute or until mustard seeds begin to pop. Add onion, ginger, garlic, and jalapeño to pan; sauté 3 minutes or until onion is tender. Stir in curry and turmeric; cook 30 seconds. Stir in tomatoes. Cover, reduce heat, and simmer 15 minutes. Uncover and cook 5 minutes or until mixture begins to thicken. Stir in cilantro, raisins, and sugar. Cool to room temperature. Serve with chips. Yield: 12 servings (serving size: about ¼ cup chutney and about 8 chips).

CALORIES 131 (7% from fat); FAT 1g (sat 0.1g, mono 0.6g, poly 0.3g); PROTEIN 4.5g; CARB 25.9g; FIBER 1.6g; CHOL 0mg; IRON 2.2mg; SODIUM 147mg; CALC 31mg

Fiesta Rice

"This rice complements any Mexican meal, especially enchiladas. The roasted corn is delicious, and the nuttiness of the brown rice enhances the flavor."
—Maro Desjardins, Tulsa, Oklahoma

2 teaspoons olive oil
1 (10-ounce) package frozen whole-kernel corn, thawed
1 tablespoon butter
1 cup chopped green onions
1½ cups uncooked brown rice
1 teaspoon ground cumin
1 teaspoon minced garlic
2 cups fat-free, less-sodium chicken broth
⅛ teaspoon freshly ground black pepper
Dash of salt
1 (14.5-ounce) can diced tomatoes with chiles, undrained
1 (15-ounce) can black beans, rinsed and drained
½ cup chopped fresh cilantro
1 tablespoon fresh lime juice

1. Heat oil in a medium saucepan over medium-high heat. Add corn to pan; cook 10 minutes or until corn starts to brown, stirring occasionally. Remove from pan. Set aside.

2. Melt butter in pan. Add onions; sauté 5 minutes or until tender. Stir in rice, cumin, and garlic; cook 1 minute. Add broth, pepper, salt, and tomatoes to pan; bring to a boil. Cover, reduce heat, and simmer 45 minutes, stirring occasionally. Remove from heat; stir in corn and beans. Cover and let stand 10 minutes. Stir in cilantro and juice. Yield: 8 servings (serving size: 1 cup).

CALORIES 226 (16% from fat); FAT 3.9g (sat 1.3g, mono 1.7g, poly 0.7g); PROTEIN 6.6g; CARB 43.5g; FIBER 4.9g; CHOL 4mg; IRON 2.1mg; SODIUM 354mg; CALC 52mg

Asparagus Soup with Cheese Croutons

"Green peppercorns have a clean, mild flavor that goes well with fresh vegetables, and they blend nicely with the soup."
—Chris Pancerella Gayman,
Carlisle, Pennsylvania

1   (14-ounce) can fat-free, less-sodium chicken broth
1   pound asparagus, trimmed and cut into 2-inch pieces
1½ teaspoons butter
1   teaspoon olive oil
¼   cup thinly sliced shiitake mushrooms
8   (½-ounce) slices French bread
Cooking spray
¼   cup (1 ounce) shredded Gouda cheese
¼   cup cooked brown rice
¼   teaspoon freshly ground green peppercorns
⅛   teaspoon sea salt

1. Place broth and asparagus in a medium saucepan over medium-high heat; bring to a simmer. Cook 8 minutes or until asparagus is tender. Remove from heat.
2. Heat butter and oil in a small skillet over medium-high heat. Add sliced mushrooms to pan; cook 3 minutes or until mushrooms begin to brown. Set aside.
3. Preheat broiler.
4. Place bread on a baking sheet covered with foil; coat bread with cooking spray. Broil 2 minutes or until golden brown. Turn bread over, and sprinkle evenly with cheese. Broil 2 minutes or until cheese bubbles.
5. Pour asparagus mixture into a blender. Add rice, peppercorns, and salt; puree until smooth. Ladle ½ cup soup into each of 8 bowls; top evenly with mushrooms. Top each serving with 1 crouton. Yield: 8 servings.

CALORIES 86 (27% from fat); FAT 2.6g (sat 1.2g, mono 0.9g, poly 0.1g); PROTEIN 4.3g; CARB 11.9g; FIBER 1.9g; CHOL 6mg; IRON 0.9mg; SODIUM 234mg; CALC 64mg

Quick and Easy Pansit

"Pansit is a traditional Filipino dish similar to pad thai. I adapted this dish from my extended family's authentic pansit recipe, incorporating ingredients readily available at local supermarkets."
—Kimberly Rackett,
Franklin Square, New York

1   (8-ounce) package uncooked wide rice sticks (rice-flour noodles)
1   teaspoon canola oil
1   cup chopped onion
2   garlic cloves, minced
1   (8-ounce) package presliced mushrooms
2   cups cubed cooked chicken breast (about 10 ounces)
1   cup matchstick-cut carrots
1   cup frozen peas (about 4 ounces)
1   (9-ounce) package frozen French-cut green beans
1   tablespoon sesame seeds
2   tablespoons low-sodium soy sauce
1   tablespoon sesame oil
¼   teaspoon freshly ground black pepper

1. Cook noodles according to package directions, omitting salt and fat. Drain and set aside.
2. Heat canola oil in a large nonstick skillet over medium-high heat. Add onion, garlic, and mushrooms to pan; sauté 5 minutes or until tender. Add chicken, carrots, peas, and beans; cook 3 minutes or until thoroughly heated. Stir in sesame seeds, soy sauce, sesame oil, pepper, and noodles. Serve immediately. Yield: 6 servings (serving size: 2 cups).

CALORIES 303 (17% from fat); FAT 5.7g (sat 1g, mono 1.9g, poly 2.4g); PROTEIN 21.1g; CARB 45.1g; FIBER 4.8g; CHOL 40mg; IRON 2.3mg; SODIUM 275mg; CALC 51mg

Mediterranean Mix Menu
serves 4

Chicken, Peppers, Onions, and Mushrooms with Marsala Wine

Greek salad*

Crusty Italian bread

*Combine 4 cups torn romaine lettuce, ½ cup thinly sliced red onion, ½ cup thinly sliced cucumber, ½ cup halved cherry tomatoes, and ½ cup crumbled feta cheese in a large bowl. Combine 1 tablespoon lemon juice, 2 teaspoons red wine vinegar, ½ teaspoon dried oregano, and ¼ teaspoon salt in a small bowl. Gradually add 1 tablespoon extravirgin olive oil, stirring constantly with a whisk. Drizzle oil mixture over salad; toss well.

Chicken, Peppers, Onions, and Mushrooms with Marsala Wine

"This quick, easy sautéed dish is delicious with a Greek salad."
—Dessie DeVito, Waltham, Massachusetts

Cooking spray
1½ pounds chicken breast tenders
1½ cups thinly sliced onion
1   cup thinly vertically sliced red bell pepper (about 1 medium)
2   tablespoons olive oil
½   teaspoon salt
½   teaspoon black pepper
1   (8-ounce) package presliced exotic mushroom blend (such as shiitake, cremini, and oyster)
3   tablespoons Marsala wine

1. Heat a large nonstick skillet over medium-high heat. Coat pan with
Continued

cooking spray. Add chicken to pan; sauté 7 minutes or until chicken is done. Remove chicken from pan. Add onion and bell pepper to pan; sauté 5 minutes or until onion starts to brown. Add oil, salt, black pepper, and mushrooms to pan; sauté 3 minutes or until mushrooms are tender and onion starts to caramelize. Add wine and chicken to pan, and cook 1 minute or until thoroughly heated. Serve immediately. Yield: 4 servings (serving size: 1¾ cups).

CALORIES 295 (28% from fat); FAT 9.2g (sat 1.6g, mono 5.4g, poly 1.3g); PROTEIN 41.8g; CARB 8.9g; FIBER 1.8; CHOL 99mg; IRON 1.8mg; SODIUM 411mg; CALC 33mg

inspired vegetarian
Cinco de Mayo

Commemorate this Mexican holiday with our authentic, mostly prep-ahead menu.

Cinco de Mayo Menu
serves 8

Drinks

Strawberry Agua Fresca

Amaretto Margaritas

Starters

Mushroom and Fontina Quesadillas
or
Vegetarian Taquitos

Black Bean and Avocado Salsa

Mango Salsa

Cumin Chips

Entrées

Black Bean, Corn, and Zucchini Enchiladas

Grilled Peppers, Squash, and Onions

Desserts

Mexican Chocolate Soufflés
or
Pineapple-Lime Sorbet

Strawberry Agua Fresca

Prepare this early on the day of the party; chill until your guests arrive.

- 4 cups quartered fresh strawberries (about 2 pints)
- 6 cups cold water, divided
- ¼ cup sugar
- 2 tablespoons chopped fresh mint
- 4 teaspoons fresh lime juice

1. Place strawberries, 2 cups water, sugar, and mint in a blender; process 2 minutes or until smooth. Strain mixture through a sieve into a pitcher; discard solids. Add 4 cups water and juice; refrigerate. Serve over ice. Yield: 8 servings (serving size: about 1 cup).

CALORIES 52 (5% from fat); FAT 0.3g (sat 0g, mono 0g, poly 0.1g); PROTEIN 0.6g; CARB 13g; FIBER 1.8g; CHOL 0mg; IRON 0.5mg; SODIUM 1mg; CALC 17mg

Amaretto Margaritas

Amaretto provides an interesting twist on the traditional margarita's orange curaçao liqueur. We start with a homemade sweet-and-sour mix that can be prepared several days in advance and refrigerated. When guests arrive, add the remaining ingredients. To serve in salt-rimmed glasses, pour sea salt on a small plate. Rub the rim of each glass with a lime wedge, and then dip the rim in the salt.

- ¾ cup sugar
- ¾ cup water
- 1½ cups fresh lime juice (about 9 limes)
- 1 cup tequila
- ¾ cup orange juice
- ½ cup amaretto (almond-flavored liqueur)
- 8 lime slices

1. Combine sugar and ¾ cup water in a small saucepan; bring to a boil. Reduce heat; simmer 5 minutes or until sugar dissolves. Remove from heat; cool completely. Stir in lime juice.
2. Combine sugar mixture, tequila, orange juice, and amaretto in a pitcher. Serve over ice. Garnish with lime slices. Yield: 8 servings (serving size: ½ cup margarita and 1 lime slice).

CALORIES 209 (0% from fat); FAT 0.1g (sat 0g, mono 0g, poly 0.1g); PROTEIN 0.4g; CARB 31g; FIBER 0.2g; CHOL 0mg; IRON 0.1mg; SODIUM 2mg; CALC 9mg

SPIRIT NOTE: The most important words in choosing a tequila are "100 percent agave." Unless you spot this phrase on the label, you're getting as little as 51 percent agave, with lots of sugar added to make up the difference. An exceptional value is 1800 Reposado ($24). "Reposado" indicates the tequila was "rested" in oak, imparting flavors of citrus zest and butterscotch, which complement the nutty amaretto in this innovative margarita.

Mushroom and Fontina Quesadillas

Substitute Monterey Jack cheese for fontina, if you wish. Chop the vegetables in advance; refrigerate. Finish the recipe just before serving.

- Cooking spray
- 1 tablespoon finely chopped red onion
- 1 tablespoon finely chopped jalapeño pepper
- 2½ cups finely chopped portobello mushroom caps
- 4 cups finely chopped shiitake mushrooms
- ¼ teaspoon salt
- 4 (8-inch) whole wheat flour tortillas
- ¼ cup (1 ounce) shredded fontina cheese

1. Heat a large nonstick skillet over medium-high heat. Coat pan with cooking spray. Add onion and jalapeño; sauté 2 minutes. Add mushrooms and salt; sauté 5 minutes or until moisture evaporates. Remove mushroom mixture from pan; keep warm.
2. Wipe pan clean with paper towels. Return pan to heat; add 1 tortilla. Cook

1 minute; turn tortilla over. Arrange about ⅓ cup mushroom mixture over half of tortilla; top with 1 tablespoon cheese. Fold in half; cook 30 seconds on each side or until cheese melts and tortilla is golden. Repeat procedure with remaining tortillas, mushroom mixture, and cheese. Cut each quesadilla into 4 wedges. Yield: 8 servings (serving size: 2 wedges).

CALORIES 58 (48% from fat); FAT 3.1g (sat 0.7g, mono 0.3g, poly 0.1g); PROTEIN 3.8g; CARB 5.5g; FIBER 2.1g; CHOL 4mg; IRON 0.7mg; SODIUM 232mg; CALC 0.7mg

MAKE AHEAD
Vegetarian Taquitos

Taquito (ta-KEE-toe) means "little taco." These savory filled corn tortillas are rolled in cigar-shaped bundles. You can prepare and refrigerate the filling the night before; allow it to stand at room temperature for 30 minutes before assembling the taquitos. Use tongs to dip the tortillas into the simmering broth.

FILLING:
- 1 teaspoon canola oil
- ½ cup finely chopped onion
- 1 teaspoon minced garlic
- 1½ cups veggie ground round (such as Yves Veggie Cuisine)
- ¼ teaspoon salt
- ¼ teaspoon cumin
- ¼ teaspoon ground red pepper
- 1 (4.5-ounce) can chopped green chiles, undrained

REMAINING INGREDIENTS:
- 2 cups organic vegetable broth (such as Swanson Certified Organic)
- 16 (6-inch) corn tortillas
- ⅔ cup (about 2½ ounces) shredded reduced-fat sharp Cheddar cheese, divided
- Cooking spray

1. To prepare filling, heat oil in a large nonstick skillet over medium-high heat. Add onion and garlic; sauté 3 minutes or until onion is tender. Add veggie ground round and next 4 ingredients; cook 5 minutes.

2. Preheat oven to 425°.

3. Bring broth to a boil in a large saucepan. Reduce heat, and simmer. Working with 1 tortilla at a time, carefully dip tortilla into broth 2 seconds using tongs; place softened tortilla on a paper towel. Spoon about 1 tablespoon filling across lower third of tortilla; top with 2 teaspoons cheese. Roll up; place rolled tortilla on a baking sheet coated with cooking spray. Lightly spray rolled tortilla with cooking spray. Repeat procedure with remaining tortillas, filling, and cheese.

4. Bake at 425° for 13 minutes or until rolls are crisp. Yield: 8 servings (serving size: 2 taquitos).

CALORIES 185 (21% from fat); FAT 4.3g (sat 1.3g, mono 0.4g, poly 1.5g); PROTEIN 13g; CARB 25.8g; FIBER 4.8g; CHOL 6mg; IRON 1.4mg; SODIUM 412mg; CALC 159mg

QUICK & EASY • MAKE AHEAD
Black Bean and Avocado Salsa

This is best if prepared an hour before serving. It's great with Cumin Chips (recipe at right).

- 2 cups chopped seeded tomato
- 1 cup diced peeled avocado
- ½ cup chopped red onion
- 2 tablespoons chopped fresh cilantro
- 2 tablespoons fresh lime juice
- 1 tablespoon finely chopped seeded jalapeño pepper
- ⅛ teaspoon salt
- 1 (15-ounce) can black beans, rinsed and drained
- Lime wedges (optional)

1. Combine first 8 ingredients in a medium bowl; toss gently. Cover and chill 30 minutes before serving. Garnish with lime wedges, if desired. Yield: 3½ cups (serving size: ¼ cup).

CALORIES 43 (48% from fat); FAT 2.3g (sat 0.4g, mono 1.4g, poly 0.3g); PROTEIN 1.6g; CARB 5.8g; FIBER 2.2g; CHOL 0mg; IRON 0.6mg; SODIUM 107mg; CALC 12mg

QUICK & EASY • MAKE AHEAD
Mango Salsa

For a less spicy version, discard seeds and ribs from the jalapeño before chopping. If made in advance, stir the salsa just before serving.

- 2 cups diced peeled mango (about 2 mangoes)
- 2 cups diced seeded tomato
- 2 tablespoons chopped red onion
- 2 tablespoons chopped fresh cilantro
- 2 tablespoons diced jalapeño pepper
- 2 tablespoons fresh lime juice
- 1 teaspoon sugar
- ¼ teaspoon salt

1. Combine all ingredients in a medium bowl; toss gently. Cover and chill. Yield: 4 cups (serving size: ½ cup).

CALORIES 45 (0% from fat); FAT 0.2g (sat 0g, mono 0.1g, poly 0.1g); PROTEIN 0.7g; CARB 11.6g; FIBER 1.5g; CHOL 0mg; IRON 0.2mg; SODIUM 77mg; CALC 11mg

MAKE AHEAD
Cumin Chips

If you can find blue corn tortillas, they'll add color to the table. Prepare the chips a day or two ahead, and store in an airtight container.

- 4 teaspoons fresh lime juice
- 2 teaspoons canola oil
- ½ teaspoon ground cumin
- 12 (6-inch) corn tortillas
- Cooking spray
- ¼ teaspoon salt

1. Preheat oven to 375°.

2. Combine first 3 ingredients in a small bowl. Brush each tortilla with juice mixture. Cut each tortilla into 6 wedges. Arrange wedges in a single layer on 2 baking sheets coated with cooking spray. Sprinkle evenly with salt. Bake at 375° for 30 minutes or until crisp, turning chips and rotating pans every 10 minutes. Yield: 8 servings (serving size: 9 chips).

CALORIES 42 (34% from fat); FAT 1.6g (sat 0.1g, mono 0.7g, poly 0.5g); PROTEIN 0.8g; CARB 7g; FIBER 0.8g; CHOL 0mg; IRON 0.1mg; SODIUM 78mg; CALC 9mg

Black Bean, Corn, and Zucchini Enchiladas

1 teaspoon canola oil
2 cups diced zucchini
1 (10-ounce) package frozen whole-kernel corn
1 (15-ounce) can black beans, rinsed and drained
3 cups Enchilada Sauce, divided
Cooking spray
8 (8-inch) whole wheat tortillas
2 cups (8 ounces) shredded reduced-fat Cheddar cheese, divided

1. Preheat oven to 350°.
2. Heat oil in a large nonstick skillet over medium-high heat. Add zucchini and corn; sauté 5 minutes or until vegetables are tender. Remove from heat, and stir in beans.
3. Spread 1 cup Enchilada Sauce in bottom of a 13 x 9–inch baking dish coated with cooking spray. Spoon about ½ cup zucchini mixture down center of 1 tortilla; sprinkle with 2 tablespoons cheese, and roll up. Place seam-side down in baking dish. Repeat procedure with remaining tortillas, zucchini mixture, and 14 tablespoons cheese. Spread 2 cups sauce evenly over enchiladas.
4. Cover with foil; bake at 350° for 30 minutes. Uncover; top with 1 cup cheese. Bake, uncovered, 10 minutes or until cheese melts. Yield: 8 servings (serving size: 1 enchilada).

(Totals include Enchilada Sauce) CALORIES 348 (27% from fat); FAT 4.2g (sat 1.8g, mono 1.5g, poly 1.5g); PROTEIN 16g; CARB 47.2g; FIBER 7g; CHOL 20mg; IRON 3.3mg; SODIUM 878mg; CALC 260mg

MAKE AHEAD
ENCHILADA SAUCE:

1 teaspoon canola oil
½ cup diced red onion
1 teaspoon minced garlic
½ cup organic vegetable broth
1 tablespoon chili powder
1 tablespoon honey
1 teaspoon ground cumin
½ teaspoon salt
1 (28-ounce) can crushed tomatoes, undrained

1. Heat oil in a large saucepan over medium heat. Add onion and garlic; sauté 5 minutes or until onion is tender. Stir in broth and remaining ingredients. Reduce heat, and simmer 30 minutes. Yield: 3 cups (serving size: about ⅓ cup).

CALORIES 37 (19% from fat); FAT 0.8g (sat 0.1g, mono 0.4g, poly 0.2g); PROTEIN 1g; CARB 7.4g; FIBER 1.1g; CHOL 0mg; IRON 1.2mg; SODIUM 341mg; CALC 36mg

Grilled Peppers, Squash, and Onions

2 teaspoons olive oil
½ teaspoon salt
¼ teaspoon ground cumin
¼ teaspoon freshly ground black pepper
2 red bell peppers, cut into 2-inch pieces (about 2 cups)
2 yellow bell peppers, cut into 2-inch pieces (about 2 cups)
2 small zucchini, quartered lengthwise
2 small yellow squash, quartered lengthwise
1 red onion, cut into 1-inch-thick slices
Cooking spray

1. Combine all ingredients except cooking spray in a zip-top plastic bag; seal and shake well. Marinate in refrigerator 2 hours or overnight.
2. Preheat grill.
3. Arrange vegetables in a single layer on grill rack coated with cooking spray. Grill 10 minutes or until browned, turning vegetables occasionally. Yield: 8 servings (serving size: about 1 cup).

CALORIES 55 (26% from fat); FAT 1.6g (sat 0.3g, mono 0.9g, poly 0.4g); PROTEIN 2g; CARB 2.2g; FIBER 10.2g; CHOL 3mg; IRON 0mg; SODIUM 0.8mg; CALC 82mg

Mexican Chocolate Soufflés

You can omit the small amount of coffee liqueur without drastically changing the flavor. Contemporary Mexican chefs often add ground red pepper to their chocolate desserts; leave it out if you want a more traditional taste.

Cooking spray
3 tablespoons granulated sugar
½ cup granulated sugar
¼ cup unsweetened cocoa
2 tablespoons all-purpose flour
1 teaspoon ground cinnamon
⅛ teaspoon salt
⅛ teaspoon ground red pepper (optional)
¾ cup fat-free milk
3 ounces bittersweet chocolate, chopped
1 teaspoon vanilla extract
1 teaspoon coffee-flavored liqueur (such as Kahlúa)
1 large egg yolk, lightly beaten
¼ teaspoon cream of tartar
6 large egg whites
2 tablespoons granulated sugar
Powdered sugar (optional)

1. Preheat oven to 375°.
2. Coat 8 (6-ounce) ramekins with cooking spray; sprinkle with 3 tablespoons granulated sugar.
3. Combine ½ cup granulated sugar, cocoa, flour, cinnamon, salt, and pepper, if desired, in a medium saucepan. Gradually add milk, stirring with a whisk until smooth. Bring to a boil over medium-high heat; cook 1 minute, stirring constantly. Remove from heat; add chocolate, stirring with a whisk until smooth. Place chocolate mixture in a large bowl; stir in vanilla, liqueur, and egg yolk.
4. Place cream of tartar and egg whites in another large bowl; beat with a mixer at high speed until foamy. Add 2 tablespoons granulated sugar, 1 tablespoon at a time, beating until stiff peaks form.

Gently stir one-third of egg white mixture into chocolate mixture; gently fold in remaining egg white mixture. Spoon evenly into prepared ramekins; sharply tap ramekins 2 or 3 times on counter to level. Place ramekins on a baking sheet.

5. Bake at 375° for 30 minutes or until puffy and set. Sprinkle with powdered sugar, if desired. Serve immediately. Yield: 8 servings.

CALORIES 178 (28% from fat); FAT 5.6g (sat 2.7g, mono 1.9g, poly 0.2g); PROTEIN 5.3g; CARB 30.7g; FIBER 1.9g; CHOL 26mg; IRON 0.9mg; SODIUM 90mg; CALC 41mg

---

MAKE AHEAD •FREEZABLE

Pineapple-Lime Sorbet

Jazz up this fresh, icy treat with a splash of tequila. If you're making this ahead stir the pineapple in just before serving.

1½ cups sugar
2 cups water
6½ tablespoons fresh lime juice, divided
1¼ cups unsweetened pineapple juice
1 tablespoon grated lime rind
½ cup finely chopped fresh pineapple

1. Combine sugar, 2 cups water, and 2½ tablespoons lime juice in a medium saucepan; bring to a boil. Reduce heat, and simmer 5 minutes or until sugar dissolves. Remove from heat. Place sugar mixture in an airtight container, and chill.

2. Stir in ¼ cup lime juice, pineapple juice, and rind. Pour mixture into freezer can of an ice-cream freezer; freeze according to manufacturer's instructions, adding pineapple during last 10 minutes. Yield: 8 servings (serving size: ½ cup).

CALORIES 172 (0% from fat); FAT 0.1g (sat 0g, mono 0g, poly 0.1g); PROTEIN 0.2g; CARB 44.4g; FIBER 0.2g; CHOL 0mg; IRON 0.2mg; SODIUM 1mg; CALC 8mg

---

dinner tonight

Speedy Shrimp

Tender and juicy, shrimp is a quick pick for a fresh meal.

Shrimp Menu 1
serves 4

Grilled Teriyaki Shrimp Kebabs

Mashed sweet potatoes*

Grilled asparagus

*Microwave 1 (24-ounce) package refrigerated mashed sweet potatoes according to package directions. Stir in 1 teaspoon butter, 1 teaspoon maple syrup, and ¼ teaspoon salt. Sprinkle with ½ teaspoon toasted sesame seeds.

Game Plan

1. Prepare mashed sweet potatoes; keep warm.
2. Prepare kebabs.
3. Grill kebabs and asparagus.

QUICK & EASY

Grilled Teriyaki Shrimp Kebabs

You can brush this versatile sauce over cubed skinless, boneless chicken breasts or thighs. Or use it as a dipping sauce with spring rolls.

TIME: 40 MINUTES

QUICK TIP: Use cubed pineapple from the supermarket produce section. It costs a bit more, but it's worth the time you'll save putting this supper together.

SAUCE:
¼ cup low-sodium teriyaki sauce
1 tablespoon sesame seeds, toasted

KEBABS:
48 large peeled and deveined shrimp (about 1½ pounds)
32 (1-inch) pieces cubed fresh pineapple (about ¾ pound)
1 red onion, cut into 8 wedges
Cooking spray

1. Prepare grill.
2. To prepare sauce, combine teriyaki sauce and sesame seeds in a small bowl.
3. To prepare kebabs, thread 6 shrimp, 4 pineapple chunks, and 1 onion wedge alternately onto each of 8 (10-inch) skewers. Brush kebabs with teriyaki mixture. Place kebabs on a grill rack coated with cooking spray; grill 8 minutes or until shrimp are done, turning once. Yield: 4 servings (serving size: 2 kebabs).

CALORIES 254 (14% from fat); FAT 4g (sat 0.7g, mono 0.8g, poly 1.6g); PROTEIN 35.6g; CARB 17.6g; FIBER 1.9g; CHOL 259mg; IRON 4.6mg; SODIUM 514mg; CALC 110mg

---

Shrimp Menu 2
serves 4

Shrimp Caesar Salad

Sun-dried tomato garlic breadsticks*

Fresh strawberries with vanilla yogurt

*Unroll 1 (11-ounce) can refrigerated soft breadstick dough. Combine 2 tablespoons chopped oil-packed sun-dried tomatoes and 1 teaspoon minced garlic. Spread mixture from center to 1 short end of dough; fold other half of dough over tomato mixture, pinching ends to seal. Cut dough along perforations to form 8 breadsticks. Twist each breadstick; place on a baking sheet coated with cooking spray. Bake at 375° for 15 minutes.

Game Plan

1. Assemble breadsticks.
2. While breadsticks bake:
• Prepare salad.
• Slice strawberries.

Shrimp Caesar Salad

Precooked shrimp speed up preparation. If you purchase raw shrimp, cook them in boiling water for two minutes or until done. Sriracha Thai hot sauce adds spicy heat to the dressing; omit it for a mild dish. Serve with sauvignon blanc.

TIME: 30 MINUTES

QUICK TIP: Keep cooked peeled shrimp in the freezer for speedy, no-cook main dish salads. Thaw shrimp under cold running water.

DRESSING:
- 2 tablespoons light mayonnaise
- 2 tablespoons water
- 2 tablespoons fresh lemon juice
- 1 teaspoon grated Parmesan cheese
- ¼ teaspoon freshly ground black pepper
- ¼ teaspoon Sriracha (hot chile sauce, such as Huy Fong)
- ⅛ teaspoon Worcestershire sauce
- 2 garlic cloves, minced

SALAD:
- ¾ cup fat-free seasoned croutons
- 2 tablespoons grated Parmesan cheese
- 1½ pounds medium shrimp, cooked and peeled
- 1 (10-ounce) package chopped romaine lettuce
- 3 tablespoons pine nuts, toasted
  Chopped fresh chives (optional)

1. To prepare dressing, combine first 8 ingredients, stirring with a whisk.
2. To prepare salad, combine croutons and next 3 ingredients in a large bowl. Add dressing; toss well to coat. Top with pine nuts. Garnish with chives, if desired. Serve immediately. Yield: 4 servings (serving size: 3 cups salad and 2¼ teaspoons pine nuts).

CALORIES 295 (29% from fat); FAT 9.4g (sat 1.7g, mono 2.1g, poly 4g); PROTEIN 38.6g; CARB 12.2g; FIBER 1.8g; CHOL 261mg; IRON 5.2mg; SODIUM 462mg; CALC 149mg

Shrimp Menu 3
serves 4

Asian Rice with Shrimp and Snow Peas

Spicy-sweet cantaloupe salad*

Iced green tea

*Combine 3 cups cubed cantaloupe, 2 teaspoons chopped seeded jalapeño, and 2 teaspoons chopped fresh mint in a medium bowl. Combine 2 tablespoons fresh orange juice, 1 teaspoon sugar, and 1 teaspoon fresh lime juice, stirring until sugar dissolves. Pour juice mixture over cantaloupe mixture; toss. Chill 30 minutes.

Game Plan

1. Prepare salad.
2. While salad chills:
- • Cook rice.
3. While rice cooks:
- • Boil water to cook shrimp and snow peas.
- • Trim snow peas, and chop green onions.

Asian Rice with Shrimp and Snow Peas

Take leftovers of this dish to work the next day for a terrific lunch.

TIME: 40 MINUTES

SHOPPING TIP: "Easy peel" deveined raw shrimp costs half as much as peeled and deveined shrimp. If you use it, add 5 minutes to the prep time.

- 1 cup uncooked long-grain rice
- 1 cup water
- 1 cup fat-free, less-sodium chicken broth
- 3 tablespoons low-sodium soy sauce
- 3 tablespoons rice vinegar
- 1 tablespoon dark sesame oil
- 2 teaspoons bottled chopped garlic
- 1 teaspoon hot sauce
- 2 cups snow peas, trimmed (about 6 ounces)
- 1½ pounds large peeled and deveined shrimp
- ½ cup diagonally cut green onions
- 4 teaspoons slivered almonds, toasted

1. Combine first 3 ingredients in a medium saucepan; bring to a boil. Cover, reduce heat, and simmer 20 minutes or until liquid is absorbed.
2. Combine soy sauce and next 4 ingredients in a large bowl; stir with a whisk. Set aside.
3. Cook snow peas and shrimp in boiling water 2 minutes or until shrimp are done. Drain. Add snow peas, shrimp, green onions, and rice to soy mixture; toss well to combine. Top with almonds. Serve immediately. Yield: 4 servings (serving size: 2 cups rice mixture and 1 teaspoon almonds).

CALORIES 334 (20% from fat); FAT 7.6g (sat 1.2g, mono 1.9g, poly 3.5g); PROTEIN 38.9g; CARB 25.4g; FIBER 2.3g; CHOL 259mg; IRON 5.7mg; SODIUM 776mg; CALC 129mg

menu of the month
Graduation Celebration

Relatives, friends, and the guest of honor will enjoy this fresh spring luncheon. You'll enjoy its ease.

Graduation Celebration Menu
serves 12

Cucumber-Buttermilk Vichyssoise

Chipotle Grilled Pork Tenderloin with Strawberry-Avocado Salsa

Haricots Verts, Radish, and Watercress Salad

Pine Nut and Lemon Orzo

Cheese Muffins

Rhubarb Spritzers

Frozen Blackberry-Lemon Chiffon Pie

Cucumber-Buttermilk Vichyssoise

Our version of this French classic adds cucumber and buttermilk to the familiar potato soup. Prepare it in advance, and refrigerate or freeze. It will keep frozen for up to a month, but you'll need to puree it again after it's thawed.

- 2 teaspoons olive oil
- 1 cup chopped Vidalia or other sweet onion
- 2 garlic cloves, minced
- 6½ cups chopped seeded peeled English cucumber (about 3)
- 3 cups cubed peeled baking potato (about 1¼ pounds)
- 3 (14-ounce) cans fat-free, less-sodium chicken broth, divided
- 3 cups buttermilk
- 1 tablespoon fresh lemon juice
- ½ teaspoon salt
- ¼ teaspoon white pepper
  Thinly sliced cucumber

1. Heat oil in a large Dutch oven over medium heat. Add onion and garlic to pan; cook 8 minutes or until onion is tender, stirring occasionally.
2. Add chopped cucumber, potato, and 2 cans broth to pan; bring to a boil. Cover, reduce heat, and simmer 20 minutes or until potato is very tender, stirring occasionally.
3. Place one-third of potato mixture in a blender. Remove center piece of blender lid (to allow steam to escape); secure blender lid on blender. Place a clean towel over opening in blender lid (to avoid splatters). Blend until smooth. Pour into a large bowl. Repeat procedure twice with remaining potato mixture. Cool.
4. Add 1 can chicken broth, buttermilk, juice, salt, and pepper to cooled potato mixture, stirring well. Cover and chill. Garnish with sliced cucumber. Yield: 12 servings (serving size: about 1 cup).

CALORIES 100 (27% from fat); FAT 3g (sat 1.4g, mono 0.6g, poly 0.1g); PROTEIN 4.4g; CARB 14.4g; FIBER 1.5g; CHOL 9mg; IRON 0.7mg; SODIUM 331mg; CALC 22mg

Chipotle Grilled Pork Tenderloin with Strawberry-Avocado Salsa

If pressed for time, grill the pork a day ahead, refrigerate, and serve it at room temperature; slice the pork just before serving.

PORK:
- ¼ cup minced chipotle chile, canned in adobo sauce
- 3 tablespoons fresh lime juice
- 1½ cups (¼-inch-thick) slices onion
- 2 garlic cloves, crushed
- 3 (1-pound) pork tenderloins, trimmed
- 1 teaspoon salt
  Cooking spray

SALSA:
- 5 cups quartered strawberries (about 2 quarts)
- 1⅓ cups chopped peeled avocado (about 1 large)
- ¼ cup thinly sliced green onions
- ¼ cup chopped fresh cilantro
- 3 tablespoons fresh lime juice
- ½ teaspoon salt

1. To prepare pork, combine first 4 ingredients in a large zip-top plastic bag. Add pork; seal and marinate in refrigerator 2 hours, turning bag occasionally.
2. Prepare grill.
3. Remove pork from bag; discard marinade. Sprinkle pork evenly with 1 teaspoon salt. Place pork on a grill rack coated with cooking spray. Grill 20 minutes or until a thermometer registers 155° (slightly pink), turning occasionally. Let stand 10 minutes; cut into slices.
4. To prepare salsa, combine strawberries and remaining 5 ingredients in a medium bowl; toss gently. Serve immediately with pork. Yield: 12 servings (serving size: 3 ounces pork and about ⅓ cup salsa).

CALORIES 180 (33% from fat); FAT 6.6g (sat 1.8g, mono 3.2g, poly 0.8g); PROTEIN 23.3g; CARB 6.6g; FIBER 2.2g; CHOL 63mg; IRON 1.7mg; SODIUM 348mg; CALC 19mg

Haricots Verts, Radish, and Watercress Salad

Haricots verts is French for green beans and refers to a short, slim, tender kind of green bean. If you can't find them, substitute regular green beans, and cook them just a little longer.

- 3 pounds haricots verts, trimmed
- 4 cups trimmed watercress (about 4 ounces)
- 1 cup sliced radishes
- 2 tablespoons extravirgin olive oil
- 1 tablespoon white wine vinegar
- 1 tablespoon water
- 1 tablespoon Dijon mustard
- 1 teaspoon salt
- ¼ teaspoon freshly ground black pepper

1. Steam beans, covered, 6 minutes or until crisp-tender. Rinse beans with cold water; drain. Chill.
2. Combine beans, watercress, and radishes in a large bowl; toss gently. Combine oil and remaining 5 ingredients in a small bowl, stirring well with a whisk. Drizzle vinegar mixture over watercress mixture; toss gently. Serve immediately. Yield: 12 servings (serving size: 1 cup).

CALORIES 51 (42% from fat); FAT 2.4g (sat 0.3g, mono 1.7g, poly 0.3g); PROTEIN 1.8g; CARB 7.4g; FIBER 4.2g; CHOL 0mg; IRON 0.6mg; SODIUM 235mg; CALC 72mg

Pine Nut and Lemon Orzo

If you make the orzo ahead, keep it refrigerated, and toss with the dressing mixture, parsley, and pine nuts just before serving.

- 4 cups uncooked orzo (rice-shaped pasta; about 1½ pounds)
- 2 tablespoons grated lemon rind
- ¾ cup fresh lemon juice (about 4 medium lemons)
- 1 teaspoon salt
- ¾ teaspoon freshly ground black pepper
- 3 tablespoons extravirgin olive oil
- ¾ cup chopped fresh flat-leaf parsley
- ½ cup pine nuts, toasted

Continued

1. Cook pasta according to package directions, omitting salt and fat. Drain.
2. Combine rind, juice, salt, and pepper in a large bowl. Slowly add oil to juice mixture, stirring constantly with a whisk. Add pasta to juice mixture; toss to coat. Cool to room temperature. Stir in parsley and pine nuts. Yield: 12 servings (serving size: 1 cup).

CALORIES 280 (26% from fat); FAT 8.1g (sat 1g, mono 3.6g, poly 2.6g); PROTEIN 8.7g; CARB 44.8g; FIBER 2.3g; CHOL 0mg; IRON 2.4mg; SODIUM 202mg; CALC 19mg

MAKE AHEAD
Cheese Muffins

Be sure to splurge on freshly shredded Parmigiano-Reggiano for these muffins because the flavor is superior. Serve any leftover muffins with soup or a salad for a light lunch.

    1   cup plus 1 tablespoon (4¼ ounces) fresh finely shredded Parmigiano-Reggiano cheese, divided
    2¼ cups all-purpose flour (about 10 ounces)
    3   tablespoons sugar
    2   teaspoons baking powder
    ½   teaspoon baking soda
    ½   teaspoon salt
    ¼   teaspoon freshly ground black pepper
    1¾ cups 1% low-fat milk
    2½ tablespoons canola oil
    1   large egg, lightly beaten
        Cooking spray

1. Preheat oven to 350°.
2. Place 3 tablespoons cheese in a small bowl; set aside. Lightly spoon flour into dry measuring cups; level with a knife. Combine flour, remaining cheese, sugar, and next 4 ingredients in a medium bowl, stirring with a whisk. Make a well in center of mixture. Combine milk, oil, and egg; add to flour mixture, stirring just until moist.
3. Spoon batter into 15 muffin cups coated with cooking spray. Sprinkle evenly with reserved 3 tablespoons cheese. Bake at 350° for 20 minutes or until muffins spring back when touched lightly in center. Remove muffins from pans immediately; place on a wire rack. Yield: 15 servings (serving size: 1 muffin).

CALORIES 176 (30% from fat); FAT 5.9g (sat 1.9g, mono 2.6g, poly 1.1g); PROTEIN 7g; CARB 23.5g; FIBER 0.7g; CHOL 24mg; IRON 1.3mg; SODIUM 379mg; CALC 191mg

MAKE AHEAD
Rhubarb Spritzers

Fresh rhubarb works best for this recipe, but frozen will do in a pinch. Its characteristically tart taste combines well with lime juice and sugar for a refreshing springtime beverage. You can add sparkling wine instead of water for adults.

    2½ cups water
    ¾   cup sugar
    2   pounds rhubarb, cut into 1-inch pieces
    2   tablespoons fresh lime juice
    1   (25-ounce) bottle sparkling water, chilled
    12 lime slices

1. Combine first 3 ingredients in a large saucepan; bring to a boil. Cover, reduce heat, and simmer 10 minutes. Strain mixture through a sieve into a bowl, pressing rhubarb with back of spoon to remove as much liquid as possible. Discard solids. Cool to room temperature. Stir in juice. Cover and chill.
2. Stir in sparkling water just before serving. Garnish with lime slices. Yield: 12 servings (serving size: ⅔ cup spritzer and 1 lime slice).

CALORIES 74 (0% from fat); FAT 0g; PROTEIN 0.1g; CARB 19.4g; FIBER 0.5g; CHOL 0mg; IRON 0mg; SODIUM 3mg; CALC 8mg

MAKE AHEAD • FREEZABLE
Frozen Blackberry-Lemon Chiffon Pie

Fresh seasonal berries lend both vibrant color and taste to this pie, but frozen berries will work, as well.

    1½ cups graham cracker crumbs (about 12 cookie sheets)
    3   tablespoons butter, melted
    2   tablespoons 2% reduced-fat milk
        Cooking spray
    3   cups blackberries
    ¼   cup fresh lemon juice
    ¼   teaspoon salt
    4   large egg whites
    1   cup plus 2 tablespoons sugar
    6   tablespoons water
        Fresh blackberries (optional)
        Mint sprigs (optional)

1. Combine first 3 ingredients in a bowl; toss with a fork until moist. Press into bottom and up sides of a 9-inch springform pan coated with cooking spray.
2. Place 3 cups blackberries and lemon juice in a blender; process until smooth. Strain mixture through a sieve into a bowl; discard solids.
3. Place salt and egg whites in a large bowl; beat with a mixer at high speed until foamy. Combine sugar and 6 tablespoons water in a medium saucepan; bring to a boil. Cook, without stirring, until a thermometer registers 250°. Gradually pour hot sugar syrup into egg white mixture, beating at medium speed, then at high speed, until stiff peaks form. Gently fold in blackberry mixture; pour into prepared crust. Cover; freeze 8 hours or overnight. Let stand 5 minutes at room temperature before serving. Garnish with fresh blackberries and mint, if desired. Yield: 12 servings.

CALORIES 166 (22% from fat); FAT 4.1g (sat 2g, mono 1.2g, poly 0.6g); PROTEIN 2.6g; CARB 30.9g; FIBER 2.2g; CHOL 8mg; IRON 0.6mg; SODIUM 153mg; CALC 18mg

kitchen strategies
Fix and Freeze

Problem: A stay-at-home mom struggles to find time to put together dinner for her family. Strategy: We offer a variety of make-ahead fare that allows her to cook when it's convenient.

Chickpea, Chard, and Tomato Stew

Serve this full-flavored stew with salad and crusty French bread or garlic toast.

    2   teaspoons olive oil
    1   cup chopped onion
    3   garlic cloves, minced
    1   pound ground chicken
    ¼   cup no-salt-added tomato paste
    2   (15½-ounce) cans chickpeas
        (garbanzo beans), rinsed and
        drained
    4   cups chopped Swiss chard
    2   cups chopped tomato
    1   cup water
    1   teaspoon chili powder
    ½   teaspoon cumin
    ½   teaspoon kosher salt
    3   (14-ounce) cans fat-free,
        less-sodium chicken broth

1. Heat oil in a large Dutch oven over medium-high heat. Add onion and garlic; sauté 1 minute. Add chicken; sauté 4 minutes. Add tomato paste; cook 1 minute. Partially mash chickpeas with a potato masher. Add chickpeas, chard, and remaining ingredients; bring to a boil. Reduce heat, and simmer 15 minutes. Cool completely. Place chickpea mixture in an airtight container or heavy-duty zip-top plastic bag; freeze.
2. Thaw chickpea mixture overnight in refrigerator. Reheat chickpea mixture in microwave or place mixture in a large saucepan; bring to a boil. Reduce heat; simmer 5 minutes. Yield: 8 servings (serving size: 1½ cups).

CALORIES 161 (17% from fat); FAT 3g (sat 0.2g, mono 1.4g, poly 1g); PROTEIN 18g; CARB 16.6g; FIBER 3.9g; CHOL 33mg; IRON 1.8mg; SODIUM 610mg; CALC 40mg

Chinese Chicken and Mushroom Lettuce Cups

Stir cilantro into the filling after thawing to keep the flavor bright. Use Bibb lettuce leaves instead of Boston for the cups, if you prefer. This appetizer can be served warm or at room temperature. Serve with chili garlic sauce.

SERVING SOLUTION: You can also use the thawed chicken mixture as a tasty filling for mini-pita sandwiches.

    1   teaspoon sesame oil
    3   garlic cloves, minced
    3   cups minced cremini mushrooms
        (about 8 ounces)
    1   cup minced shiitake mushroom
        caps (about 2½ ounces)
    1   pound ground chicken breast
    3   cups shredded napa (Chinese)
        cabbage
    ¼   teaspoon kosher salt
    ⅛   teaspoon crushed red pepper
    1   (8-ounce) can whole water
        chestnuts, drained and minced
    1   cup minced green onions
    2   tablespoons oyster sauce
    2   tablespoons low-sodium soy
        sauce
    ¼   cup chopped fresh cilantro
    24 Boston lettuce leaves

1. Heat oil in a large nonstick skillet over medium heat. Add garlic, and cook 2 minutes. Add mushrooms and chicken; cook 8 minutes, stirring occasionally. Add cabbage, salt, pepper, and water chestnuts; cook 5 minutes or until cabbage wilts. Remove from heat, and stir in onions, oyster sauce, and soy sauce. Cool completely. Place in an airtight container or heavy-duty zip-top plastic bag; freeze.
2. Thaw chicken mixture overnight in refrigerator or microwave at MEDIUM 10 minutes. Bring to room temperature, or microwave at HIGH until warm, if desired. Stir in cilantro. Spoon about 3 tablespoons chicken mixture into each lettuce leaf with a slotted spoon. Yield: 8 servings (serving size: 3 lettuce cups).

CALORIES 103 (13% from fat); FAT 1.5g (sat 0.3g, mono 0.4g, poly 0.5g); PROTEIN 15.3g; CARB 7.4g; FIBER 2.3g; CHOL 33mg; IRON 1.4mg; SODIUM 270mg; CALC 44mg

Chili Verde

This popular New Mexican dish is essentially a green chile stew often made with pork.

    1   teaspoon canola oil
    ¼   teaspoon salt
    ½   teaspoon black pepper, divided
    2   pounds boneless pork shoulder
        (Boston butt), trimmed and cut
        into 1-inch pieces
    3   cups chopped onion (about 2)
    ¼   cup chopped seeded Anaheim chile
    2   tablespoons chopped seeded
        jalapeño pepper (about 1)
    2   garlic cloves, crushed
    3   cups fat-free, less-sodium chicken
        broth
    2   teaspoons dried oregano
    1   teaspoon ground cumin
    1   teaspoon ground coriander
    5   (11-ounce) cans whole tomatillos,
        drained and chopped
    ¼   cup chopped fresh cilantro
    6   cups hot cooked long-grain rice
    8   lime wedges

1. Preheat oven to 400°.
2. Heat oil in a large Dutch oven over medium-high heat. Sprinkle salt and ¼ teaspoon black pepper over pork. Add pork to pan; cook 8 minutes or until browned. Remove from pan. Add onion, chile peppers, and garlic; sauté 5 minutes. Return pork to pan. Add ¼ teaspoon black pepper, broth, and next 4 ingredients; bring to a boil. Cover and bake at 400° for 1 hour. Stir in cilantro. Cover and bake an additional 30 minutes or until pork is tender. Cool completely. Place mixture in an airtight container or a heavy-duty zip-top plastic bag; freeze.
3. Thaw pork mixture overnight in refrigerator. Reheat in microwave or place mixture in a large saucepan over medium heat and cook until thoroughly heated, stirring frequently. Serve over rice. Garnish with lime wedges. Yield: 8 servings (serving size: ¾ cup rice, 1 cup pork mixture, and 1 lime wedge).

CALORIES 437 (30% from fat); FAT 14.5g (sat 3.8g, mono 5.6g, poly 1.3g); PROTEIN 28.9g; CARB 46.2g; FIBER 6.3g; CHOL 81mg; IRON 4.3mg; SODIUM 591mg; CALC 65mg

Moussaka

EGGPLANT:

3 peeled eggplants, cut into ½-inch-thick slices (about 3 pounds)
1 teaspoon kosher salt
Cooking spray
¼ teaspoon freshly ground black pepper

MEAT MIXTURE:

1 teaspoon olive oil
1¼ cups minced onion (about 1 large)
4 garlic cloves, minced
1 pound ground chicken breast
½ cup uncooked bulgur
1½ tablespoons minced fresh mint
¼ teaspoon freshly ground black pepper
⅛ teaspoon kosher salt
⅛ teaspoon ground allspice
1 (28-ounce) can diced tomatoes, undrained

TOPPING:

1 tablespoon butter
2 tablespoons all-purpose flour
1 cup fat-free milk
2 garlic cloves, crushed
½ cup (2 ounces) feta cheese
¼ teaspoon ground nutmeg
1 cup plain low-fat yogurt

1. Preheat oven to 425°.
2. To prepare eggplant, place eggplant on several layers of paper towels; sprinkle evenly with 1 teaspoon salt. Cover with additional paper towels; let stand 10 minutes, pressing down occasionally. Lightly coat slices with cooking spray; sprinkle with ¼ teaspoon pepper. Arrange eggplant in a single layer on 2 baking sheets. Bake at 425° for 8 minutes. Turn eggplant slices over. Rotate baking sheets; bake an additional 8 minutes.
3. To prepare meat mixture, heat oil in a large nonstick skillet over medium-high heat. Add onion, 4 garlic cloves, and chicken; sauté 6 minutes or until chicken is done. Stir in bulgur and next 5 ingredients; bring to a boil. Cover, reduce heat, and simmer 20 minutes. Remove from heat; cool completely.

4. To prepare topping, melt butter in a medium saucepan over medium heat. Add flour, stirring with a whisk until well blended. Gradually add milk, stirring with a whisk until blended. Add 2 garlic cloves; bring to a boil. Reduce heat to low; cook 2 minutes or until thick, stirring constantly with a whisk. Pour milk mixture into a food processor; add feta and nutmeg. Process until smooth; stir in yogurt.
5. Coat 2 (8-inch) square baking dishes with cooking spray. Divide half of eggplant slices between dishes; top each with 1 cup meat mixture. Repeat procedure with remaining eggplant and remaining meat mixture. Pour 1¼ cups topping mixture over each. Bake at 425° for 35 minutes or until top is bubbling. Yield: 2 casseroles, 4 servings each.

CALORIES 230 (20% from fat); FAT 5.1g (sat 2.7g, mono 1.3g, poly 0.4g); PROTEIN 20g; CARB 29.4g; FIBER 9.4g; CHOL 48mg; IRON 1.3mg; SODIUM 581mg; CALC 167mg

Shredded Beef and Mushroom Ragu

1 cup hot water
2 cups dried porcini mushrooms (about 2 ounces)
¾ teaspoon kosher salt, divided
½ teaspoon black pepper
4 beef short ribs, trimmed (about 1½ pounds)
1 tablespoon all-purpose flour
2 teaspoons olive oil
4 cups thinly sliced cremini mushrooms (about 8 ounces)
2 cups thinly sliced onion (about 1 medium)
1 tablespoon tomato paste
1 teaspoon chopped fresh thyme
4 garlic cloves, crushed
1 cup dry red wine
1 cup fat-free, less-sodium beef broth

1. Preheat oven to 350°.
2. Combine 1 cup hot water and porcini mushrooms in a small bowl; let stand 10 minutes. Drain mushrooms through a fine sieve into a bowl, reserving liquid. Chop mushrooms; set aside.

3. Sprinkle ½ teaspoon salt and pepper over ribs; dredge ribs in flour. Heat oil in a large Dutch oven over medium-high heat. Add ribs to pan; cook 12 minutes, browning on all sides. Remove ribs from pan. Add porcini mushrooms, cremini mushrooms, and next 4 ingredients to pan; cook 12 minutes or until mushrooms are tender. Add wine, scraping pan to loosen brown bits. Add mushroom liquid and broth; bring to a boil. Add ribs to pan; cover. Place pan in oven; bake at 350° for 2½ hours or until ribs are tender. Let stand 10 minutes. Remove meat from bones; discard bones, fat, and gristle. Shred meat with 2 forks; return meat to pan. Stir in ¼ teaspoon salt. Cool completely. Place mixture in an airtight container or a heavy-duty zip-top plastic bag; freeze.
4. Thaw meat mixture overnight in refrigerator. Place mixture in a large saucepan over medium heat; cook until thoroughly heated, stirring frequently. Yield: 6 servings (serving size: ¾ cup).

CALORIES 331 (46% from fat); FAT 17g (sat 6.8g, mono 7.9g, poly 0.7g); PROTEIN 30.4g; CARB 11.1g; FIBER 3.1g; CHOL 79mg; IRON 5.1mg; SODIUM 366mg; CALC 29mg

Arugula Pesto

2 cups trimmed arugula (about 2 ounces)
2 cups fresh spinach leaves (about 2 ounces)
¼ cup (1 ounce) grated fresh Parmesan cheese
2 tablespoons pine nuts
1 tablespoon extravirgin olive oil
2 teaspoons white wine vinegar
1 teaspoon minced garlic (about 1 large clove)
1 teaspoon crushed red pepper
¼ teaspoon salt

1. Place all ingredients in a food processor; process until smooth. Drop pesto by tablespoonfuls onto a jelly-roll pan lined with wax paper. Cover with plastic wrap; freeze until solid. Store frozen pesto in an airtight container in freezer up to 2 months.

2. Thaw in refrigerator. Yield: 6 servings (serving size: 2 tablespoons).

CALORIES 62 (78% from fat); FAT 5.4g (sat 1.1g, mono 2.5g, poly 1.4g); PROTEIN 2.1g; CARB 1.9g; FIBER 0.7g; CHOL 3mg; IRON 0.6mg; SODIUM 163mg; CALC 54mg

---

MAKE AHEAD • FREEZABLE

Sausage and Pepper Calzones

Coat your fingertips with flour as you crimp the calzones to prevent the dough from sticking. Use mild Italian chicken sausage, if desired.

DOUGH:
2¾ cups all-purpose flour, divided (about 12⅓ ounces)
1 cup warm water (100° to 110°)
1 package dry yeast (about 2¼ teaspoons)
Dash of sugar
1 tablespoon extravirgin olive oil
¾ teaspoon kosher salt
Cooking spray

FILLING:
1 teaspoon olive oil
2 cups thinly sliced red bell pepper (about 2)
1 cup chopped onion (about 1)
2 garlic cloves, minced
1 pound chicken apple sausage (such as Gerhard's), cut into ¼-inch slices
¾ cup (3 ounces) shredded part-skim mozzarella cheese
½ cup no-salt-added tomato sauce
¼ cup 2% low-fat cottage cheese
2 tablespoons grated fresh Parmesan cheese
1 teaspoon dried oregano
½ teaspoon kosher salt
¼ teaspoon crushed red pepper

1. To prepare dough, lightly spoon flour into dry measuring cups; level with a knife. Combine ½ cup flour, 1 cup warm water, yeast, and sugar in a large bowl; let stand 15 minutes. Gradually add 1¾ cups flour, 1 tablespoon oil, and ¾ teaspoon salt; stir until a soft dough forms. Knead until smooth and elastic (about 8 minutes); add enough of remaining flour,

1 tablespoon at a time, to prevent dough from sticking to hands.
2. Place dough in a large bowl coated with cooking spray, turning to coat top. Cover and let rise in a warm place (85°), free from drafts, 1 hour or until doubled in size. (Gently press two fingers into dough. If indentation remains, dough has risen enough.)
3. To prepare filling, heat 1 teaspoon oil over medium-high heat in a large non-stick skillet. Add bell pepper, onion, garlic, and sausage; sauté 10 minutes or until tender. Spoon mixture into a bowl; cool slightly. Add mozzarella and remaining 6 ingredients to sausage mixture; stir well.
4. Preheat oven to 450°.
5. Punch dough down; cover and let rest 5 minutes. Divide into 8 equal portions. Roll each portion into a 6-inch circle on a lightly floured surface. Spoon about ½ cup sausage mixture onto half of each circle, leaving a ½-inch border. Fold dough over filling; crimp edges of dough with fingers to seal. Place calzones on a large baking sheet lined with foil and coated with cooking spray. Pierce tops of dough once with a fork. Lightly coat calzones with cooking spray. Bake at 450° for 14 minutes or until browned. Remove from oven. Cool completely on a wire rack.
6. Coat a sheet of foil with cooking spray. Place 1 calzone on coated side of foil; seal. Repeat procedure with remaining calzones and cooking spray. Place calzones in a heavy-duty zip-top plastic bag; freeze.
7. Preheat oven to 450°.
8. To reheat, place foil-wrapped, frozen calzones on a large baking sheet. Bake at 450° for 40 minutes or until thoroughly heated. Yield: 8 servings (serving size: 1 calzone).

CALORIES 327 (30% from fat); FAT 10.7g (sat 3.5g, mono 2.4g, poly 0.6g); PROTEIN 16.3g; CARB 42g; FIBER 4g; CHOL 49mg; IRON 3.2mg; SODIUM 680mg; CALC 124mg

---

then & now

Make-Ahead Breakfast Casserole

Our readers love the convenience of a make-ahead dish, and this casserole, which ran in our November/December 1988 issue, is an all-time favorite.

MAKE AHEAD

Make-Ahead Breakfast Casserole

8 ounces ciabatta bread, cut into 1-inch cubes
Cooking spray
1 pound turkey breakfast sausage
½ cup chopped green onions
1¼ cups fat-free milk
1 cup (4 ounces) reduced-fat shredded sharp Cheddar cheese
2 large eggs, lightly beaten
1 (8-ounce) carton egg substitute
2 tablespoons chopped fresh parsley

1. Preheat oven to 400°.
2. Arrange bread cubes in a single layer on a baking sheet. Bake at 400° for 8 minutes or until toasted.
3. Heat a medium skillet over medium-high heat. Coat pan with cooking spray. Add sausage to pan; cook 6 minutes or until browned, stirring to crumble. Combine sausage, bread, and onions in a large bowl. Combine milk, cheese, eggs, and egg substitute in a medium bowl, stirring with a whisk. Add milk mixture to bread mixture, tossing to coat bread. Spoon mixture into a 2-quart baking dish coated with cooking spray. Cover and refrigerate 8 hours or overnight.
4. Preheat oven to 350°.
5. Uncover casserole. Bake at 350° for 50 minutes or until set and lightly browned. Sprinkle with parsley; serve immediately. Yield: 6 servings (serving size: about 1 cup).

CALORIES 344 (28% from fat); FAT 10.8g (sat 4.2g, mono 2.2g, poly 1g); PROTEIN 28.7g; CARB 26.4g; FIBER 1g; CHOL 123mg; IRON 3.3mg; SODIUM 983mg; CALC 227mg

Raspberry Rhapsody

Beautiful and delicate fresh raspberries resonate in these fine finales.

Fresh raspberry season, when supermarket produce aisles and farmers' markets offer locally grown berries, is gratifyingly long, beginning in late spring, peaking around July, and continuing into September in warmer regions. We're all familiar with the standard red raspberry, and you may have seen the slightly less common black variety. But cultivated raspberries also come in a rainbow of hues, from the deepest purple, orange, and pink to gold and white (look for these at farmers' markets and gourmet stores).

QUICK & EASY • MAKE AHEAD
Raspberry Coulis

Coulis (koo-LEE) is a French term for a puree and sauce. This one can be served over ice cream or low-fat brownies.

4½   cups fresh raspberries (about 1½ pints)
2½   cups water, divided
¾   cup sugar
¼   cup fresh lime juice (about 4 limes)
2   tablespoons cornstarch

1. Place raspberries and 1 cup water in a blender; process until smooth. Strain raspberry mixture through a fine sieve into a bowl; discard solids. Combine raspberry puree, 1½ cups water, and sugar in a small saucepan. Combine juice and cornstarch in a small bowl, stirring with a whisk until blended. Add cornstarch mixture to raspberry mixture; bring to a boil over medium heat. Cook 5 minutes or until thick, stirring constantly. Strain through a fine sieve into a bowl; discard solids. Cool. Cover and chill. Yield: about 3½ cups (serving size: ¼ cup).

CALORIES 61 (3% from fat); FAT 0.2g (sat 0g, mono 0g, poly 0.1g); PROTEIN 0.3g; CARB 15.3g; FIBER 1.7g; CHOL 0mg; IRON 0.2mg; SODIUM 0mg; CALC 7mg

QUICK & EASY • MAKE AHEAD
Raspberry Refrigerator Jam

12   cups fresh raspberries (about 4 pints), divided
2¼   cups sugar, divided
¾   cup warm water (100° to 110°)
1   (1.75-ounce) package pectin

1. Place 9 cups raspberries in a blender; process until smooth. Strain mixture through a fine sieve into a large bowl, pressing lightly with back of a spoon; discard seeds. Add 3 cups raspberries to bowl; partially mash raspberries with a spoon. Stir in 1½ cups sugar.
2. Combine ¾ cup warm water and pectin in a small saucepan, stirring to dissolve. Stir in ¾ cup sugar; bring to a boil over medium heat, stirring constantly. Remove from heat; add pectin mixture to raspberry mixture in bowl, stirring until combined. Cool to room temperature. Mixture will thicken as it cools. Spoon into airtight containers; cover and chill 8 hours or overnight. Yield: 4 cups (serving size: 2 tablespoons).

CALORIES 74 (1% from fat); FAT 0.1g (sat 0g, mono 0g, poly 0.1g); PROTEIN 0.3g; CARB 18.3g; FIBER 1.4g; CHOL 0mg; IRON 0.2mg; SODIUM 0mg; CALC 6mg

MAKE AHEAD
Raspberry Phyllo Tarts

1   (2.1-ounce) package mini phyllo shells (such as Athens)
3   tablespoons reduced-fat graham cracker crumbs (about 1¼ cookie sheets)
1   tablespoon butter, melted
1   teaspoon sugar
1½   tablespoons honey
4   ounces fat-free cream cheese, softened
45   fresh raspberries (about ½ pint)

1. Preheat oven to 350°.
2. Place shells on a baking sheet. Bake at 350° for 5 minutes or until crisp. Cool on a wire rack.
3. Combine crumbs, butter, and sugar in a small bowl. Spoon ½ teaspoon crumb mixture into each prepared shell.
4. Combine honey and cream cheese in a small bowl; beat with a mixer at medium speed until smooth. Spoon 1 teaspoon cheese mixture into each shell. Top each shell with 3 raspberries. Sprinkle tops of tarts with 1 tablespoon crumb mixture. Yield: 15 servings (serving size: 1 tart).

CALORIES 49 (37% from fat); FAT 2g (sat 0.6g, mono 0.8g, poly 0.3g); PROTEIN 1.3g; CARB 6.7g; FIBER 0.7g; CHOL 3mg; IRON 0.3mg; SODIUM 65mg; CALC 21mg

MAKE AHEAD
Raspberry Thumbprint Cookies

¾   cup (3 ounces) grated almond paste
⅔   cup sugar
5   tablespoons butter, softened
¼   teaspoon vanilla extract
1   large egg white
1¼   cups all-purpose flour (about 5½ ounces)
¼   teaspoon salt
6   tablespoons Raspberry Refrigerator Jam (recipe at left)

1. Preheat oven to 325°.
2. Line 2 large baking sheets with parchment paper; secure to baking sheets with masking tape.
3. Place first 3 ingredients in a bowl; beat with a mixer at medium speed 4 minutes or until light and fluffy. Add vanilla and egg white; beat well.
4. Lightly spoon flour into dry measuring cups; level with a knife. Add flour and salt to almond paste mixture; beat at low speed until well blended. Turn dough out onto a lightly floured surface, and shape dough into 36 (1-inch) balls. Place balls 1 inch apart on prepared baking sheets, and press thumb into center of each cookie, leaving an indentation. Bake at 325° for 10 minutes or until golden.
5. Remove cookies from pans; cool on wire racks. Spoon about ½ teaspoon Raspberry Refrigerator Jam into center of each cookie. Yield: 3 dozen (serving size: 1 cookie).

(Totals include Raspberry Refrigerator Jam) CALORIES 61 (34% from fat); FAT 2.3g (sat 1.1g, mono 0.8g, poly 0.2g); PROTEIN 0.8g; CARB 9.5g; FIBER 0.4g; CHOL 4mg; IRON 0.3mg; SODIUM 29mg; CALC 6mg

Chocolate Raspberry Tart with White Chocolate Cream

CRUST:
- 1 tablespoon sugar
- 1 teaspoon unsweetened cocoa
- 6 chocolate graham cracker sheets
- 1 ounce bittersweet chocolate, chopped
- Dash of salt
- 1 large egg white
- Cooking spray

FILLING:
- 1 cup fat-free milk
- 2 tablespoons sugar
- 2 large egg yolks
- 1 envelope unflavored gelatin
- 3 ounces premium white baking chocolate, chopped
- 1 cup frozen reduced-calorie whipped topping (such as Light Cool Whip), thawed

TOPPING:
- 4 cups fresh raspberries (about 1½ pints)
- ½ cup apple jelly
- 1 tablespoon fresh lemon juice
- Chocolate curls (optional)
- Mint leaves (optional)

1. Preheat oven to 350°.

2. To prepare crust, place first 5 ingredients in a food processor; process until fine crumbs form.

3. Place egg white in a small bowl; beat with a fork until frothy. Add 3 tablespoons of beaten egg white through food chute with food processor on; process just until combined. Discard any remaining egg white. Press crumb mixture into a 9-inch round removable-bottom tart pan or a 9-inch springform pan coated with cooking spray. Bake at 350° for 7 minutes. Cool completely on a wire rack.

4. To prepare filling, combine milk, 2 tablespoons sugar, and egg yolks in a small saucepan. Sprinkle gelatin evenly over milk mixture. Let stand 5 minutes. Cook over medium heat 5 minutes or until gelatin dissolves and mixture begins to thicken, stirring constantly.

Remove from heat; add white chocolate, stirring until chocolate melts and mixture is smooth. Scrape white chocolate mixture into a medium bowl. Place bowl in a larger ice-filled bowl until mixture cools and thickens (about 4 minutes), stirring constantly (do not allow gelatin mixture to set). Gently stir ¼ cup whipped topping into white chocolate mixture; gently fold in remaining whipped topping. Scrape into prepared crust using a rubber spatula; spread evenly to edge of crust. Cover pan with plastic wrap; chill at least 1 hour.

5. To prepare topping, place raspberries in a large bowl. Remove plastic wrap from tart pan; remove sides of tart pan. Heat jelly in a small saucepan until melted, stirring constantly. Remove from heat; stir in juice. Drizzle jelly mixture over raspberries; toss gently to coat. Spoon raspberry mixture evenly over filling. Refrigerate, uncovered, 15 minutes. Garnish with chocolate curls and mint leaves, if desired. Yield: 12 servings (serving size: 1 wedge).

CALORIES 184 (29% from fat); FAT 6g (sat 3.1g, mono 0.6g, poly 0.3g); PROTEIN 3.6g; CARB 30.5g; FIBER 3.1g; CHOL 36mg; IRON 0.5mg; SODIUM 90mg; CALC 60mg

Raspberry-Ginger Sorbet

The ginger adds a spicy note that nicely contrasts the sweetness of the raspberries and the tang of lemon.

- ¾ cup sugar
- ¾ cup water
- 1 tablespoon grated peeled fresh ginger
- 2 teaspoons grated lemon rind
- 6 cups fresh raspberries (about 2 pints)

1. Combine first 4 ingredients in a medium saucepan. Bring to a boil over medium-high heat, and cook 1 minute or until sugar dissolves.

2. Place sugar mixture and raspberries in a food processor, and process until smooth. Press mixture through a fine sieve over a large bowl, and discard seeds. Cool completely.

3. Pour mixture into freezer can of an ice-cream freezer, and freeze according to manufacturer's instructions. Spoon sorbet into a freezer-safe container; cover and freeze 1 hour or until firm. Remove sorbet from freezer 10 minutes before serving. Yield: 4 cups (serving size: ½ cup).

CALORIES 115 (1% from fat); FAT 0; PROTEIN 1.2g; CARB 27.9g; FIBER 2.5g; CHOL 0mg; IRON 0.8mg; SODIUM 2mg; CALC 13mg

superfast
20 Minute Dishes

From kebabs to steaks, salad to sandwiches, here are simple, fresh, and easy meals you can make superfast.

Pesto Halibut Kebabs

Serve this dish with Israeli couscous tossed with toasted sliced almonds, dried cranberries, and chopped fresh parsley.

- 1½ pounds halibut, cut into 1-inch pieces
- 1 large red bell pepper, cut into 1-inch pieces
- 3 tablespoons prepared basil pesto
- 2 tablespoons white wine vinegar
- ½ teaspoon salt
- Cooking spray

1. Preheat broiler.

2. Place fish and bell pepper in a shallow dish. Drizzle pesto and vinegar over fish mixture; toss to coat. Let stand 5 minutes.

3. Thread fish and pepper alternately onto each of 4 (12-inch) skewers; sprinkle evenly with salt. Place skewers on a jelly-roll pan coated with cooking spray. Broil 8 minutes or until desired degree of doneness, turning once. Yield: 4 servings (serving size: 1 skewer).

CALORIES 239 (30% from fat); FAT 7.9g (sat 1.2g, mono 2.3g, poly 2.9g); PROTEIN 36.3g; CARB 4g; FIBER 1.2g; CHOL 55mg; IRON 1.8mg; SODIUM 514mg; CALC 104mg

Open-Faced Turkey Patty Melt

Substitute ground chicken or ground sir-loin for the turkey, if you prefer. Pair sand-wiches with vegetable chips.

   1   teaspoon olive oil
   1   cup vertically sliced Vidalia or
        other sweet onion
   ¼   cup part-skim ricotta cheese
  1½   teaspoons Worcestershire sauce
   ½   teaspoon black pepper
   1   pound ground turkey breast
   1   large egg white, lightly beaten
Cooking spray
   4   (1-ounce) slices reduced-fat Swiss
        cheese
   4   slices light rye bread
   ¼   cup country-style Dijon mustard

1. Heat oil in a large nonstick skillet over medium heat. Add onion to pan. Cook 5 minutes or until lightly browned; stir occasionally. Transfer onion to a bowl.
2. Preheat broiler.
3. Combine cheese and next 4 ingredi-ents. Divide turkey mixture into 4 equal portions, shaping each into a ½-inch-thick patty. Return pan to medium heat. Coat pan with cooking spray. Add pat-ties to pan; cook 4 minutes or until brown. Turn patties over; cook 1 minute. Top each patty with 1 cheese slice; cook 3 minutes or until cheese melts and pat-ties are done.
4. Place bread slices in a single layer on a baking sheet; broil 2 minutes or until toasted. Spread 1 tablespoon mustard on each bread slice; top each serving with 1 patty. Divide onion mixture evenly among sandwiches. Yield: 4 servings (serving size: 1 sandwich).

CALORIES 348 (23% from fat); FAT 9g (sat 4g, mono 2.2g, poly 2.6g); PROTEIN 43.4g; CARB 22.4g; FIBER 1.5g; CHOL 50mg; IRON 2.1mg; SODIUM 848mg; CALC 325mg

Pineapple Chicken Salad Pitas

  2½   cups chopped cooked chicken
        breast (about 1 pound)
   ½   cup matchstick-cut carrots
   ⅓   cup sliced almonds, toasted
   ⅓   cup light mayonnaise
   ¼   cup finely chopped green onions
   ¼   cup plain fat-free yogurt
   1   tablespoon Worcestershire sauce
   ½   teaspoon garlic powder
   ¼   teaspoon salt
   ¼   teaspoon black pepper
   1   (8-ounce) can crushed pineapple
        in juice, drained
   4   (6-inch) whole wheat pitas, each
        cut in half
   8   romaine lettuce leaves

1. Combine first 11 ingredients in a large bowl, stirring well. Line each pita half with 1 lettuce leaf; fill each half with ⅓ cup chicken mixture. Yield: 4 servings (serving size: 2 stuffed pita halves).

CALORIES 471 (30% from fat); FAT 15.5g (sat 2.5g, mono 5.4g, poly 6.2g); PROTEIN 36.8g; CARB 48.8g; FIBER 7.2g; CHOL 82mg; IRON 3.9mg; SODIUM 776mg; CALC 98mg

Sautéed Snapper with Plum Tomatoes and Spinach

If you can't find snapper, purchase anoth-er mild, firm white fish, such as cod or halibut.

   1   tablespoon olive oil, divided
   4   (6-ounce) snapper fillets
   ¼   teaspoon salt
   ¼   teaspoon black pepper
  1½   cups diced plum tomato (about
        6 tomatoes)
   2   teaspoons bottled minced garlic
   ¼   cup dry white wine
   3   cups baby spinach leaves

1. Heat 1½ teaspoons oil in a large non-stick skillet over medium-high heat. Sprinkle fish evenly with salt and pep-per. Add fish to pan; cook 2 minutes on each side. Remove fish from pan.
2. Heat 1½ teaspoons oil in pan over medium-high heat. Add tomato and gar-lic; sauté 1 minute. Stir in wine; simmer 2 minutes. Add spinach to pan; cook 1 minute or just until spinach wilts. Return fish to pan. Spoon tomato mixture over fish; cook 1 minute or until fish flakes easily when tested with a fork or until desired degree of doneness. Yield: 4 servings (serving size: 1 fillet and about ½ cup spinach mixture).

CALORIES 225 (24% from fat); FAT 5.9g (sat 1g, mono 2.9g, poly 1.3g); PROTEIN 36.5g; CARB 5.2g; FIBER 1.7g; CHOL 63mg; IRON 1.3mg; SODIUM 280mg; CALC 90mg

Steaks with Tuscan-Style Cannellini Salad

Cannellini, large white kidney beans, are common in Tuscan dishes. You can use any white bean, such as Great Northern or navy beans.

   2   cups chopped plum tomato (about
        ½ pound)
   2   tablespoons balsamic vinegar
   1   tablespoon chopped fresh rosemary
   1   tablespoon chopped fresh parsley
   2   teaspoons bottled minced garlic
   1   teaspoon extravirgin olive oil
   1   (16-ounce) can cannellini beans,
        rinsed and drained
   ¾   teaspoon salt, divided
   ¾   teaspoon cracked black pepper,
        divided
   4   (4-ounce) beef tenderloin steaks,
        trimmed (1 inch thick)
Cooking spray

1. Combine first 7 ingredients in a large bowl, stirring well. Sprinkle ¼ teaspoon salt and ¼ teaspoon pepper over bean mixture; stir to combine.
2. Heat a grill pan over medium-high heat. Sprinkle steaks evenly with ½ tea-spoon salt and ½ teaspoon pepper. Coat pan with cooking spray. Add steaks to pan; cook 3 minutes on each side or until desired degree of doneness. Serve with bean mixture. Yield: 4 servings (serving size: 1 steak and ½ cup bean mixture).

CALORIES 291 (35% from fat); FAT 11.2g (sat 3.9g, mono 4.8g, poly 0.9g); PROTEIN 27.7g; CARB 18.2g; FIBER 4.6g; CHOL 71mg; IRON 3.4mg; SODIUM 700mg; CALC 59mg

Spicy Chicken and Snow Peas

Look for chile paste with garlic on the Asian aisle of large supermarkets.

  1 (3½-ounce) bag boil-in-bag long-grain rice
  2 tablespoons sugar
  3 tablespoons low-sodium soy sauce
  2 tablespoons rice vinegar
  2 teaspoons chile paste with garlic (such as sambal oelek)
  1 teaspoon bottled ground fresh ginger (such as Spice World)
    Cooking spray
  1 teaspoon dark sesame oil
1½ cups matchstick-cut carrots
  1 cup thinly sliced red bell pepper
  2 cups chopped cooked chicken breast
  2 cups snow peas, trimmed
  ¼ teaspoon salt
  ⅓ cup unsalted, dry-roasted peanuts

1. Cook rice according to package directions, omitting salt and fat. Keep warm.
2. Combine sugar and next 4 ingredients in a small bowl. Heat a large nonstick skillet over medium-high heat. Coat pan with cooking spray. Add oil. Add carrots and pepper to pan; sauté 2 minutes. Add chicken and peas; sauté 1 minute. Transfer chicken mixture to a large bowl; stir in salt.
3. Return pan to heat. Add soy sauce mixture; bring to a boil. Cook until reduced to ¼ cup (about 1½ minutes), stirring constantly. Arrange about ½ cup rice on each of 4 plates; top each serving with about 1¼ cups chicken mixture. Drizzle 1 tablespoon sauce over each serving; sprinkle each serving with about 4 teaspoons peanuts. Yield: 4 servings.

CALORIES 293 (30% from fat); FAT 9.9g (sat 1.8g, mono 4.3g, poly 3g); PROTEIN 27.3g; CARB 24.7g; FIBER 3.8g; CHOL 60mg; IRON 2.4mg; SODIUM 667mg; CALC 48mg

Sweet Talk

Everything you need to know about cooking with spring's sweet onions

Grilled Tuna with White Bean and Charred Onion Salad
(pictured on page 232)

The addition of tuna makes this an entrée, but you can omit it to create a side salad.

TUNA:
  1 tablespoon grated lemon rind
  2 tablespoons fresh lemon juice
  ½ teaspoon Dijon mustard
  ½ teaspoon olive oil
  ¼ teaspoon freshly ground black pepper
  1 garlic clove, minced
  4 (6-ounce) tuna steaks
    Cooking spray

SALAD:
  1 Vidalia or other sweet onion, cut into ¼-inch-thick slices
  3 tablespoons red wine vinegar
  1 tablespoon olive oil
  ¼ teaspoon salt
  ¼ teaspoon freshly ground black pepper
  ¼ teaspoon Dijon mustard
  1 garlic clove, minced
  ½ cup chopped seeded peeled cucumber
  ¼ cup chopped flat-leaf parsley
  1 tablespoon capers
  1 (15-ounce) can cannellini beans, rinsed and drained
  6 cups mixed salad greens

1. Prepare grill.
2. To prepare tuna, combine first 6 ingredients in a large zip-top plastic bag. Add tuna to bag; seal. Marinate in refrigerator 30 minutes, turning once. Remove tuna from bag; discard marinade. Place tuna on a grill rack coated with cooking spray; grill 2 minutes on each side or until desired degree of doneness.
3. To prepare salad, place onion slices on grill rack coated with cooking spray; grill 5 minutes on each side or until tender. Cool and chop.
4. Combine vinegar and next 5 ingredients in a large bowl, stirring with a whisk until blended. Add onion, cucumber, parsley, capers, and beans to vinegar mixture; toss to coat. Arrange 1½ cups salad greens on each of 4 plates. Top each serving with about ½ cup onion mixture and 1 tuna steak. Yield: 4 servings.

CALORIES 383 (27% from fat); FAT 12.7g (sat 2.7g, mono 5.5g, poly 3.3g); PROTEIN 44g; CARB 21.9g; FIBER 6.6g; CHOL 63mg; IRON 4.6mg; SODIUM 515mg; CALC 110mg

Onion Pissaladière

Anchovies are a traditional ingredient in this French tart, but omit them, if you prefer.

  1 tablespoon olive oil
10 cups thinly sliced Vidalia or other sweet onion (about 4 large)
  8 canned anchovy fillets in oil, drained
  2 teaspoons minced fresh thyme
  ¼ teaspoon freshly ground black pepper
  1 (13.8-ounce) can refrigerated pizza dough
    Cooking spray
  ⅓ cup niçoise olives, pitted and coarsely chopped
    Thyme sprigs (optional)

1. Heat oil in a large nonstick skillet over medium heat. Add onion and anchovies to pan. Cover and cook 25 minutes or until onion is very tender, stirring occasionally. Uncover and cook 10 minutes or until onion is golden brown, stirring frequently. Stir in 2 teaspoons thyme and pepper. Keep warm.
2. Preheat oven to 400°.
3. Press dough into a 15 x 10–inch jelly-roll pan coated with cooking spray. Bake at 400° for 15 minutes or until lightly browned. Remove from oven. Arrange onion mixture evenly over crust; top with olives. Cut into squares. Garnish with thyme sprigs, if desired. Serve immediately. Yield: 8 servings (serving size: 1 square).

CALORIES 194 (23% from fat); FAT 4.9g (sat 0.5g, mono 2.9g, poly 1.1g); PROTEIN 6.2g; CARB 31.1g; FIBER 2g; CHOL 3mg; IRON 1.7mg; SODIUM 585mg; CALC 31mg

Chicken and Onion Kebabs with Onion-Mint Raita

Raita is a yogurt-based sauce used in Indian cuisine. Grated sweet onion adds depth to this version, which is also nice with lamb. Make it up to a day ahead, and it will only improve as the flavors meld.

KEBABS:

2 teaspoons grated lemon rind
3 tablespoons fresh lemon juice
2 tablespoons chopped fresh mint
1 teaspoon olive oil
1 garlic clove, minced
4 (6-ounce) skinless, boneless chicken breast halves, cut into 1-inch pieces
1 Vidalia or other sweet onion, cut into 1-inch pieces
2 cups (½-inch-thick) slices zucchini, each halved
½ teaspoon salt
¼ teaspoon freshly ground black pepper
Cooking spray

RAITA:

1 cup plain yogurt
¼ cup grated fresh sweet onion
2 tablespoons chopped fresh mint
2 teaspoons grated lemon rind
½ teaspoon salt
⅛ teaspoon freshly ground black pepper
⅛ teaspoon ground red pepper
1 garlic clove, minced

1. To prepare kebabs, combine first 5 ingredients in a large zip-top plastic bag. Add chicken to bag, and seal. Marinate in refrigerator 1 hour, turning occasionally. Add onion and zucchini to bag; toss well.
2. Prepare grill.
3. Remove chicken and onion mixture from bag; discard marinade. Thread chicken, onion, and zucchini alternately onto each of 8 (12-inch) skewers. Sprinkle kebabs evenly with ½ teaspoon salt and ¼ teaspoon black pepper. Place kebabs on grill rack coated with cooking spray, and grill 10 minutes or until chicken is done, turning occasionally.
4. To prepare raita, combine yogurt and remaining 7 ingredients in a bowl, stirring well. Cover and chill. Serve with kebabs. Yield: 4 servings (serving size: 2 kebabs and ¼ cup raita).

CALORIES 226 (20% from fat); FAT 4.9g (sat 1.9g, mono 1.8g, poly 0.6g); PROTEIN 33.1g; CARB 12g; FIBER 2g; CHOL 82mg; IRON 2mg; SODIUM 710mg; CALC 125mg

WINE NOTE: Onion is such a piquant, dominant flavor that it often makes wines taste hollow or dull. But sweet onions such as Vidalia or Maui pair wonderfully with a fresh, bold, well-chilled white wine. Given the mint and lemon in this dish, try a lively sauvignon blanc. Many California sauvignon blancs have citrus and mint flavors, mirroring the flavors precisely, and the wine is dramatic enough to stand up to the flavor of onions. A great bet: Raymond Sauvignon Blanc Reserve 2005 Napa Valley, California ($14).

MAKE AHEAD
Pickled Onions

Add these onions to salads and sandwiches, or serve them on a relish tray as a spicy-sweet appetizer. They will keep up to three weeks in the refrigerator.

2 large Vidalia or other sweet onions, thinly sliced (about 2 pounds)
1 cup rice vinegar
1 cup water
½ cup sugar
1 teaspoon black peppercorns
1 teaspoon whole cloves
1 teaspoon mustard seeds
½ teaspoon whole allspice
¼ teaspoon salt

1. Cook onion in boiling water 2 minutes. Drain and plunge onion into ice water; drain. Place cooked onion in a large glass bowl.
2. Combine vinegar and remaining 7 ingredients in a medium saucepan; bring mixture to a boil. Cover, reduce heat, and simmer 5 minutes. Pour vinegar mixture over onion. Cool. Cover and refrigerate overnight. Yield: about 9 servings (serving size: ½ cup).

CALORIES 18 (0% from fat); FAT 0g; PROTEIN 0.3g; CARB 4.5g; FIBER 0.5g; CHOL 0mg; IRON 0.1mg; SODIUM 8mg; CALC 8mg

MAKE AHEAD
Caramelized Onion Marmalade

This sweet-tart spread makes a delicious topping for bruschetta or pizza; it's also a nice complement to grilled flank steak, chicken, or pork.

1 tablespoon butter
3 tablespoons brown sugar
10 cups thinly sliced sweet onion (about 4 large)
4 garlic cloves, minced
2 tablespoons red wine vinegar
¾ teaspoon salt
⅛ teaspoon freshly ground black pepper

1. Melt butter in a large nonstick skillet over medium heat. Add sugar to pan; cook 1 minute or until sugar dissolves. Add onion and garlic. Cover and cook 30 minutes or until onion is very tender, stirring occasionally. Add vinegar to onion mixture. Cook, uncovered, 10 minutes or until golden brown, stirring frequently. Stir in salt and pepper. Yield: 12 servings (serving size: 2 tablespoons).

CALORIES 44 (20% from fat); FAT 1g (sat 0.6g, mono 0.3g, poly 0.1g); PROTEIN 0.5g; CARB 8.8g; FIBER 0.7g; CHOL 3mg; IRON 0.2mg; SODIUM 157mg; CALC 16mg

---

Selection and Storage

Sweet onions are light in color, only slightly golden. Since they have high water content, they bruise easily. Look for firm onions with no blemishes. Give each a gentle squeeze; it should be firm to the touch. Because mild onions are lower in sulfur (a natural preservative) than regular onions, they have a shorter shelf life and keep a month or more stored in a cool, dry place.

Grilled Onion and Potato Salad

Use a grill basket or thread the potatoes and onions onto skewers before grilling to prevent them from falling through the grate. Dress the vegetables while still warm so they absorb the tangy dressing mixture. Serve at room temperature or chilled.

    2   pounds small red potatoes,
        halved
    2   teaspoons olive oil
    ⅛   teaspoon salt
    ⅛   teaspoon freshly ground black
        pepper
    2   Vidalia or other sweet onions,
        cut into ½-inch-thick slices
        (about 1 pound)
Cooking spray
    2   tablespoons sherry vinegar
    2   tablespoons fat-free, low-sodium
        chicken broth
    1   tablespoon olive oil
    ½   teaspoon salt
    ¼   teaspoon freshly ground black
        pepper
    1   garlic clove, minced
    ¼   cup chopped fresh flat-leaf
        parsley

1. Prepare grill.
2. Place potatoes in a large saucepan. Cover with cold water to 2 inches above potatoes; bring to a boil. Cover, reduce heat, and simmer 8 minutes or until almost tender. Drain and rinse with cold water; drain. Combine potatoes, 2 teaspoons oil, and next 3 ingredients in a large bowl, tossing gently to coat. Arrange potatoes and onion in a single layer on grill rack coated with cooking spray; grill 10 minutes or until potatoes are tender, turning once.
3. Combine vinegar and next 5 ingredients in a large bowl, stirring with a whisk. Add potato mixture to vinegar mixture; toss gently to coat. Let stand 20 minutes. Stir in parsley. Yield: 8 servings (serving size: ¾ cup).

CALORIES 132 (20% from fat); FAT 3g (sat 0.4g, mono 2.1g, poly 0.4g); PROTEIN 2.8g; CARB 24.1g; FIBER 2.8g; CHOL 0mg; IRON 1.1mg; SODIUM 200mg; CALC 28mg

from the pantry
Peppercorn Primer

Discover why the peppercorn's zingy, herby, and earthy variations earn it space in the spice rack.

Black Pepper Shrimp

This Vietnamese-inspired meal is at its best with freshly ground black pepper.

    ¾   cup organic vegetable broth
    1   tablespoon cornstarch
    2   tablespoons low-sodium soy sauce
    1   tablespoon sherry
    1   teaspoon brown sugar
    1   to 3 teaspoons chile paste (such as
        sambal oelek)
    ½   teaspoon freshly ground black
        pepper
    ¼   teaspoon salt
    1   tablespoon canola oil
    2   teaspoons grated peeled fresh
        ginger
    2   garlic cloves, minced
    2   cups (½-inch) slices bok choy
        (about 4½ ounces)
    1   cup sliced shiitake mushrooms
    ¼   cup chopped green onions
    1½ pounds peeled and deveined large
        shrimp
    4   cups hot cooked rice

1. Combine first 8 ingredients in a medium bowl, and stir with a whisk. Set aside.
2. Heat oil in a wok or large nonstick skillet over medium-high heat. Add ginger and garlic; stir-fry 30 seconds. Add bok choy, mushrooms, onions, and shrimp. Stir-fry 3 minutes or until bok choy begins to wilt. Add broth mixture to pan; bring to a boil. Cover, reduce heat, and simmer 10 minutes or until vegetables are tender and shrimp are done. Serve over rice. Yield: 4 servings (serving size: ¾ cup shrimp mixture and 1 cup rice).

CALORIES 465 (14% from fat); FAT 7.1g (sat 1g, mono 2.7g, poly 2.4g); PROTEIN 40.5g; CARB 57.3g; FIBER 2.1g; CHOL 259mg; IRON 6.8mg; SODIUM 831mg; CALC 149mg

Berry and Black Pepper Sauce

Cracked black peppercorns add a pungent undertone to this fruit sauce.

    ½   cup fresh orange juice (about
        2 oranges)
    1½ teaspoons cornstarch
    2   cups fresh berries (blackberries,
        raspberries, blueberries, or
        strawberries)
    1   tablespoon sugar
    ½   teaspoon cracked black pepper

1. Combine juice and cornstarch in a small saucepan; bring to a boil, stirring constantly. Stir in berries, sugar, and pepper. Reduce heat, and simmer 8 minutes or until thick. Yield: 7 servings (serving size: ¼ cup).

CALORIES 36 (8% from fat); FAT 0.3g (sat 0g, mono 0g, poly 0.1g); PROTEIN 0.6g; CARB 8.5g; FIBER 2.4g; CHOL 0mg; IRON 0.3mg; SODIUM 1mg; CALC 11mg

Pepper-Crusted Salmon with Soy Drizzle

Sweet soy sauce (*kecap manis*) is an Indonesian condiment made with palm sugar; it's available in Asian supermarkets.

    1   tablespoon sesame seeds
    1   tablespoon freshly ground green
        peppercorns
    1   tablespoon freshly ground black
        pepper
    2   teaspoons grated orange rind
    ½   teaspoon sea salt
    4   (6-ounce) salmon fillets
Cooking spray
    4   teaspoons sweet soy sauce

1. Preheat oven to 400°.
2. Combine first 5 ingredients in a shallow dish. Dredge both sides of salmon in peppercorn mixture.
3. Heat a large ovenproof skillet over medium heat. Coat pan with cooking spray. Add salmon; cook 2 minutes on each side. Bake at 400° for 6 minutes or
Continued

until fish flakes easily when tested with a fork or until desired degree of doneness. Drizzle fillets evenly with soy sauce. Yield: 4 servings (serving size: 1 fillet and 1 teaspoon soy sauce).

CALORIES 297 (43% from fat); FAT 14.3g (sat 3.3g, mono 6.1g, poly 3.7g); PROTEIN 37.5g; CARB 2.2g; FIBER 1g; CHOL 87mg; IRON 1.1mg; SODIUM 723mg; CALC 54mg

Pan-Seared Beef Filet with Green Peppercorn Sauce

Serve with creamy mashed potatoes and a green salad.

    4 (4-ounce) beef tenderloin steaks, trimmed (1 inch thick)
    ½ teaspoon freshly ground black pepper
    ¼ teaspoon kosher salt
       Cooking spray
    ¼ cup finely chopped shallots (about 2 medium)
    ½ cup dry red wine
    ¾ cup fat-free, less-sodium beef broth
    1 teaspoon freshly ground green peppercorns
    1 teaspoon cornstarch
    1 teaspoon water
    1 teaspoon butter

1. Sprinkle steaks with black pepper and salt. Heat a large nonstick skillet over medium-high heat. Coat pan with cooking spray. Add steaks; cook 3 minutes on each side or until desired degree of doneness. Remove from pan; keep warm.
2. Add shallots to pan; sauté 30 seconds. Stir in wine; cook 2 minutes or until liquid almost evaporates. Stir in broth and green pepper; cook 2 minutes. Combine cornstarch and 1 teaspoon water in a small bowl. Add cornstarch mixture to pan; bring to a boil. Cook 1 minute or until slightly thick, stirring constantly. Remove from heat; add butter, stirring until butter melts. Spoon sauce evenly over steaks. Yield: 4 servings (serving size: 1 steak and 2 tablespoons sauce).

CALORIES 197 (38% from fat); FAT 8.4g (sat 3.3g, mono 3.2g, poly 0.4g); PROTEIN 25.9g; CARB 3.3g; FIBER 0.3g; CHOL 78mg; IRON 2.1mg; SODIUM 274mg; CALC 36mg

Cracked Pepper-Seed Bread

Robust, piquant black peppercorns are balanced by the clean freshness of green peppercorns.

    1   package dry yeast (about 2¼ teaspoons)
    2   cups warm water (100° to 110°)
    ¼   cup honey
    1   tablespoon canola oil
    1½   teaspoons salt, divided
    5¼   cups bread flour (about 25 ounces), divided
    ½   cup wheat bran
    5   tablespoons sunflower seed kernels, divided
    5   tablespoons sesame seeds, divided
    2¼   teaspoons cracked black peppercorns, divided
    2¼   teaspoons cracked green peppercorns, divided
         Cooking spray
    1   large egg, beaten

1. Dissolve yeast in 2 cups warm water in a large bowl; let stand 5 minutes. Add honey, oil, and ½ teaspoon salt, stirring with a whisk. Lightly spoon flour into dry measuring cups; level with a knife. Add 3 cups flour and bran to yeast mixture, stirring until combined. Cover and let stand in a warm place (85°), free from drafts, 1 hour or until small bubbles appear on surface.
2. Add 1 teaspoon salt, 2 cups flour, ¼ cup sunflower seeds, ¼ cup sesame seeds, 1½ teaspoons black pepper, and 1½ teaspoons green pepper; stir until dough forms. Turn dough out onto a floured surface. Knead until smooth and elastic (about 8 minutes); add enough of remaining flour, 1 tablespoon at a time, to prevent dough from sticking to hands (dough will feel tacky). Place dough in a large bowl coated with cooking spray, turning to coat top. Cover and let rise in a warm place (85°), free from drafts, 45 minutes or until doubled in size. (Gently press two fingers into dough. If indentation remains, dough has risen enough.) Punch dough down; cover and let rest 5 minutes.

3. Divide dough in half; place each half in an 8 x 4–inch loaf pan coated with cooking spray. Cover and let rise in a warm place (85°), free from drafts, 45 minutes or until doubled in size.
4. Preheat oven to 400°.
5. Brush loaf tops with egg; sprinkle tops evenly with 1 tablespoon sunflower seeds, 1 tablespoon sesame seeds, ¾ teaspoon black pepper, and ¾ teaspoon green pepper. Bake at 400° for 35 minutes or until loaves are browned on bottom and sound hollow when tapped. Remove loaves from pans, and cool on wire racks. Cut each loaf into 8 slices. Yield: 2 loaves, 8 servings per loaf (serving size: 1 slice).

CALORIES 199 (19% from fat); FAT 4.1g (sat 0.5g, mono 1.5g, poly 1.9g); PROTEIN 7.3g; CARB 35.9g; FIBER 2.4g; CHOL 13mg; IRON 2.7mg; SODIUM 232mg; CALC 35mg

Mashed Potatoes with White Pepper, Leeks, and Garlic

    5   cups cubed peeled Yukon gold potato (about 2 pounds)
         Cooking spray
    ½   cup chopped leek (about 1 medium)
    1   garlic clove, minced
    ½   cup 2% reduced-fat milk
    3   tablespoons butter, softened
    1   teaspoon salt
    ½   teaspoon ground white pepper

1. Place potato in a saucepan; cover with water. Bring to a boil. Reduce heat, and simmer 20 minutes or until tender. Drain; return potato to pan.
2. Heat a large nonstick skillet over medium heat. Coat pan with cooking spray. Add leek and garlic; cook 2 minutes or until tender, stirring occasionally.
3. Add milk and butter to potato; beat with a mixer at medium speed until smooth. Stir in leek mixture, salt, and pepper. Serve warm. Yield: 6 servings (serving size: ⅔ cup).

CALORIES 190 (29% from fat); FAT 6.1g (sat 3.8g, mono 1.6g, poly 0.2g); PROTEIN 4.4g; CARB 28.8g; FIBER 1.9g; CHOL 17mg; IRON 1.5mg; SODIUM 454mg; CALC 31mg

Summer Cookbook

Take advantage of the bounty of this, the freshest season of all. Here we offer 45 recipes that make the most of the tastiest vegetables, the sweetest fruits, and the most fragrant herbs of the year.

Starters & Drinks

These appetizers and beverages offer scrumptious ways to begin any get-together.

MAKE AHEAD
Clam Dip with Bacon

Serve this dip cold with a platter of crudités and pita chips.

- 10 tablespoons reduced-fat sour cream
- 10 tablespoons reduced-fat mayonnaise
- ¼ cup fresh lemon juice (about 2 lemons)
- 2 tablespoons chopped green onions
- 2 tablespoons chopped fresh parsley
- 1½ teaspoons prepared horseradish
- ¾ teaspoon Worcestershire sauce
- ⅛ teaspoon salt
- ⅛ teaspoon freshly ground black pepper
- 2 (6.5-ounce) cans chopped clams, drained
- 2 center-cut bacon slices, cooked and crumbled

1. Combine all ingredients in a medium bowl, stirring with a whisk; cover and chill at least 1 hour. Yield: 16 servings (serving size: 2 tablespoons).

CALORIES 47 (54% from fat); FAT 2.8g (sat 1.1g, mono 0.8g, poly 0.7g); PROTEIN 2.9g; CARB 2.7g; FIBER 0.1g; CHOL 10mg; IRON 2.6mg; SODIUM 134mg; CALC 21mg

QUICK & EASY
Cucumber Tea Sandwiches with Mint-Chile Butter

Use this recipe as a template, and customize according to your preferences. Try adding watercress, baby lettuce greens, or thinly sliced poached chicken breast.

- 6 tablespoons butter, softened
- 3 tablespoons chopped fresh mint
- ¼ teaspoon salt
- 1 serrano chile, seeded and finely chopped
- 12 (1-ounce) slices white sandwich bread
- 1½ cups thinly sliced English cucumber
- 1 tablespoon fresh lime juice

1. Combine first 4 ingredients, stirring until well combined.
2. Trim crusts from bread; discard crusts. Spread each bread slice with about 1½ teaspoons butter mixture. Place cucumber in a small bowl, and drizzle with lime juice; toss to coat. Arrange cucumber slices in an even layer over buttered sides of 6 bread slices; top with remaining bread slices, buttered side down. Cut sandwiches diagonally into quarters. Yield: 12 servings (serving size: 2 sandwich quarters).

CALORIES 89 (63% from fat); FAT 6.2g (sat 3.6g, mono 1.5g, poly 0.2g); PROTEIN 1.2g; CARB 7.9g; FIBER 0.4g; CHOL 15mg; IRON 0.4mg; SODIUM 163mg; CALC 25mg

QUICK & EASY
Watermelon-Feta Salad with Fresh Herbs

With peak-season produce, you don't need many flavor embellishments—in this case, just a little cheese, a squeeze of fresh lemon juice, and a sprinkling of salt.

- 6 cups (½-inch) cubed seedless watermelon
- 2 cups chopped trimmed watercress (about 1 bunch)
- ¾ cup (3 ounces) crumbled reduced-fat feta cheese
- ½ cup thinly sliced red onion
- ¼ cup thinly sliced fresh basil
- 3 tablespoons thinly sliced fresh mint
- 3 tablespoons fresh lemon juice
- ¼ teaspoon salt

1. Place all ingredients in a large bowl; toss gently to combine. Serve immediately. Yield: 6 servings (serving size: about 1 cup).

CALORIES 79 (21% from fat); FAT 1.8g (sat 1g, mono 0.5g, poly 0.2g); PROTEIN 4.4g; CARB 14.1g; FIBER 1g; CHOL 5mg; IRON 0.5mg; SODIUM 290mg; CALC 57mg

WINE NOTE: There's no better match for this refreshing watermelon salad than a chilled dry rosé. Both are cold, pink, crisp, and fruity—a magical marriage. Two good choice rosés, one still, the other sparkling: Robert Hall Rosé de Robles 2005 from Paso Robles, California ($15) and Korbel Brut Rosé Sparkling Wine (nonvintage) from California ($11).

Artichokes with Roasted Garlic–Wine Dip

Add the roasted garlic in two stages—half is cooked with wine and broth to soften the flavor, and the rest is added at the end for a more potent taste. If you plan to serve the remaining wine with this first course, choose a crisp, acidic pinot grigio or sauvignon blanc, which pairs well with artichokes. Otherwise, any dry white will work.

    2 whole garlic heads
    4 artichokes (about 3½ pounds)
    ½ cup dry white wine
    1 cup organic vegetable broth (such
       as Swanson Certified Organic)
    1 tablespoon butter
    ¼ teaspoon kosher salt
    Chopped fresh parsley (optional)

1. Preheat oven to 400°.
2. Remove white papery skin from garlic heads (do not peel or separate cloves). Wrap each head separately in foil. Bake at 400° for 45 minutes; cool 10 minutes. Separate cloves; squeeze to extract pulp. Discard skins.
3. Cut off stems of artichokes, and remove bottom leaves. Trim about ½ inch from tops of artichokes. Place artichokes, stem ends down, in a large Dutch oven filled two-thirds with water; bring to a boil. Cover, reduce heat, and simmer 45 minutes or until a leaf near center of each artichoke pulls out easily. Remove artichokes from pan.
4. Combine half of garlic pulp and wine in a small saucepan; bring to a boil. Cook 2 minutes. Add broth; cook until reduced to ½ cup (about 8 minutes). Remove from heat; stir in butter and salt. Pour mixture into a blender; add remaining half of garlic pulp. Remove center piece of blender lid (to allow steam to escape); secure blender lid on blender. Place a clean towel over opening in blender lid (to avoid splatters). Blend until smooth. Sprinkle dip with parsley, if desired. Serve dip with warm artichokes. Yield: 4 servings (serving size: 1 artichoke and 3 tablespoons dip).

CALORIES 135 (21% from fat); FAT 3.1g (sat 1.9g, mono 0.7g, poly 0.2g); PROTEIN 5.2g; CARB 19.8g; FIBER 7.2g; CHOL 8mg; IRON 1.9mg; SODIUM 403mg; CALC 84mg

---

Blackberry Limeade

(pictured on page 236)

This summer cooler is great to bring along on a picnic or to serve at a backyard party.

    6 cups water, divided
    3 cups fresh blackberries
    1 cup sugar
    ⅔ cup fresh lime juice (about 4
       limes)
    8 thin lime slices
    Fresh blackberries (optional)

1. Place 1 cup water and 3 cups blackberries in a blender; process until smooth. Press blackberry puree through a sieve into a large pitcher; discard seeds. Add 5 cups water, sugar, and juice to pitcher; stir until sugar dissolves. Place 1 lime slice and a few blackberries, if desired, into each of 8 glasses; pour about 1 cup limeade over each serving. Yield: 8 servings.

CALORIES 125 (2% from fat); FAT 0.3g (sat 0g, mono 0g, poly 0.2g); PROTEIN 0.8g; CARB 31.9g; FIBER 0.7g; CHOL 0mg; IRON 0.4mg; SODIUM 5mg; CALC 22mg

---

Rosé Sangría

Use a sparkling rosé, such as one from southern France or Spain, for this refreshing, summery drink. Combine all the ingredients except the wine up to a day in advance; stir in wine just before serving so the sangría doesn't lose its fizz.

    1 large orange
    1 cup quartered fresh strawberries
       (about 10)
    1 cup fresh raspberries
    ½ cup Cointreau or Triple Sec
       (orange-flavored liqueur)
    ½ cup fresh orange juice (about
       2 large oranges)
    1 tablespoon sugar
    1 (750-milliliter) bottle sparkling
       rosé wine, chilled
    8 cups ice cubes

1. Cut orange into thin slices; cut each slice into quarters. Combine orange, strawberries, and next 4 ingredients in a large pitcher; stir gently until sugar dissolves. Cover and chill at least 1 hour. Stir in wine. Place 1 cup ice into each of 8 tall glasses; pour about ¾ cup sangría over each serving. Serve immediately. Yield: 8 servings.

CALORIES 155 (2% from fat); FAT 0.3g (sat 0g, mono 0g, poly 0.1g); PROTEIN 0.8g; CARB 16.9g; FIBER 2g; CHOL 0mg; IRON 0.6mg; SODIUM 6mg; CALC 26mg

---

Golden Beet, Peach, and Goat Cheese Salad with Champagne Vinaigrette

If you can find striped Chioggia beets, combine them with the golden beets for a more colorful salad.

    2   pounds golden beets
    1½   cups julienne-cut firm ripe white
         peaches (about 8 ounces)
    1   cup thinly sliced red onion
    2   tablespoons Champagne vinegar
    2   tablespoons chopped fresh basil
    1   tablespoon finely chopped shallots
    1   tablespoon extravirgin olive oil
    2   teaspoons sugar
    ½   teaspoon salt
    ¼   teaspoon freshly ground black
         pepper
    ½   cup (2 ounces) crumbled reduced-
         fat goat cheese

1. Leave root and 1-inch stem on beets; scrub with a brush. Place beets in a medium saucepan; cover with water. Bring to a boil. Cover, reduce heat, and simmer 30 minutes or until tender. Drain and rinse with cold water; drain. Cool. Trim off beet roots and stems; rub off skins. Cut beets into ¼-inch-thick slices. Place beet slices in a large bowl; add peaches and onion.
2. Combine vinegar and next 6 ingredients, stirring with a whisk. Drizzle over salad; toss gently to coat. Sprinkle with cheese. Yield: 6 servings (serving size: about 1 cup).

CALORIES 107 (29% from fat); FAT 3.5g (sat 1g, mono 1.7g, poly 0.3g); PROTEIN 2.9g; CARB 17.3g; FIBER 3.7g; CHOL 2mg; IRON 1mg; SODIUM 320mg; CALC 25mg

Citrus-Ginger Sparkler

4 ounces peeled fresh ginger, grated
6 cups fresh orange juice (about
   6 pounds oranges)
½ cup fresh lemon juice (about
   3 medium lemons)
¼ cup sugar
2 cups sparkling water, chilled

1. Place ginger on several layers of damp cheesecloth. Gather edges of cheesecloth; squeeze cheesecloth bag over a small bowl to extract about ¼ cup ginger juice. Discard pulp.
2. Combine ginger juice, orange juice, lemon juice, and sugar in a large pitcher; stir until sugar dissolves. Chill at least 2 hours. Stir in sparkling water; serve immediately. Yield: 8 servings (serving size: about 1 cup).

CALORIES 114 (3% from fat); FAT 0.4g (sat 0g, mono 0.1g, poly 0.1g); PROTEIN 1.4g; CARB 27.6g; FIBER 0.5g; CHOL 0mg; IRON 0.4mg; SODIUM 2mg; CALC 22mg

Grilled Vegetable, Arugula, and Yellow Tomato Salad

Use spinach or gourmet mixed salad greens in place of arugula, if you prefer.

2 large red bell peppers (about
   12 ounces)
Cooking spray
1 large Vidalia or other sweet
   onion, cut into ¼-inch-thick
   slices (about 10 ounces)
6 cups loosely packed trimmed
   arugula (about 10 ounces)
3 yellow tomatoes, each cut into
   8 wedges (about 12 ounces)
2 tablespoons finely chopped
   shallots
2 tablespoons white balsamic vinegar
1 tablespoon extravirgin olive oil
1 tablespoon honey
1 teaspoon Dijon mustard
½ teaspoon salt
¼ teaspoon freshly ground black
   pepper

1. Prepare grill.
2. Cut bell peppers in half lengthwise; discard seeds and membranes. Place bell pepper halves, skin sides down, on grill rack coated with cooking spray. Grill 5 minutes on each side or until blackened. Place in a zip-top plastic bag; seal. Let stand 10 minutes. Peel and cut bell peppers into strips.
3. Place onion on grill; grill 7 minutes on each side or until tender. Cool 5 minutes; cut onion slices in half.
4. Combine bell peppers, onion, arugula, and tomatoes in a large bowl; toss gently to combine.
5. Combine shallots and remaining 6 ingredients, stirring with a whisk. Drizzle dressing over salad; toss gently to coat. Serve immediately. Yield: 6 servings (serving size: 1⅔ cups).

CALORIES 88 (28% from fat); FAT 2.7g (sat 0.4g, mono 1.7g, poly 0.5g); PROTEIN 2.2g; CARB 15.8g; FIBER 2.5g; CHOL 0mg; IRON 1mg; SODIUM 230mg; CALC 55mg

Herbed Ricotta and Tomato Bruschetta

For the best flavor, seek out juicy, home-grown or farmers' market tomatoes. This is a good starter to prepare when you have the grill going for an entrée, but you can also toast the bread under the broiler.

¼ cup whole milk ricotta cheese
2 teaspoons finely chopped fresh
   chives
2 teaspoons finely chopped fresh
   mint
1 teaspoon finely chopped fresh
   tarragon
1 teaspoon fresh lemon juice
¼ teaspoon freshly ground black
   pepper
4 teaspoons finely chopped fresh
   flat-leaf parsley, divided
8 (1-ounce) slices country-style
   bread
1 garlic clove, halved
1½ teaspoons extravirgin olive oil
1 large ripe tomato, cut into 8
   (¼-inch-thick) slices (about
   8 ounces)
⅛ teaspoon salt

1. Prepare grill.
2. Combine first 6 ingredients; stir in 1 tablespoon parsley.
3. Place bread slices on grill rack; grill 1 minute on each side or until lightly browned. Rub one side of each bread slice with cut sides of garlic. Discard garlic. Brush oil evenly over garlic-rubbed sides of bread slices. Spread 1½ teaspoons ricotta mixture over each bread slice; top each serving with 1 tomato slice. Sprinkle salt and 1 teaspoon parsley evenly over tomatoes. Serve immediately. Yield: 8 servings (serving size: 1 piece).

CALORIES 102 (24% from fat); FAT 2.7g (sat 0.8g, mono 0.9g, poly 0.2g); PROTEIN 3.4g; CARB 15.7g; FIBER 1.2g; CHOL 4mg; IRON 1mg; SODIUM 224mg; CALC 37mg

Fig, Prosciutto, and Gorgonzola Salad

Balsamic vinegar reduces to a syrupy glaze that glistens atop this simple first course.

⅓ cup balsamic vinegar
2 tablespoons honey
¼ teaspoon salt
⅛ teaspoon freshly ground black
   pepper
2 ounces very thin slices prosciutto,
   cut into ⅛-inch-wide strips
12 large dark-skinned fresh figs,
   halved (such as Black Mission,
   Celeste, or Brown Turkey, about
   1 pound)
¾ cup (3 ounces) crumbled
   Gorgonzola cheese

1. Combine first 4 ingredients in a small saucepan; bring to a boil. Reduce heat, and simmer until reduced to ¼ cup (about 8 minutes). Cool.
2. Heat a large nonstick skillet over medium-high heat. Add prosciutto; sauté 3 minutes or until lightly browned.
3. Arrange 4 fig halves on each of 6 salad plates. Divide prosciutto evenly over servings. Sprinkle each serving with 2 tablespoons cheese; drizzle with 2 teaspoons balsamic reduction. Serve immediately. Yield: 6 servings.

CALORIES 196 (27% from fat); FAT 5.8g (sat 3.1g, mono 1.2g, poly 0.3g); PROTEIN 6.6g; CARB 32.8g; FIBER 3.7g; CHOL 19mg; IRON 0.8mg; SODIUM 481mg; CALC 124mg

Main Dishes

Everyday entrées take on flavorful new presence paired with fresh-from-the-garden ingredients.

QUICK & EASY
Grilled Salmon with Roasted Corn Relish
(pictured on page 235)

This entire dish is prepared on the grill.

    4 Anaheim chiles
  Cooking spray
    2 shucked ears corn
    1 cup diced tomato
  ¼ cup chopped fresh cilantro
    6 tablespoons fresh lime juice
    1 teaspoon salt, divided
  ½ teaspoon freshly ground black
       pepper, divided
    1 teaspoon ground cumin
    4 (6-ounce) skinless salmon fillets

1. Prepare grill.
2. Place chiles on grill rack coated with cooking spray; grill 5 minutes on each side or until blackened. Place chiles in a heavy-duty zip-top plastic bag; seal. Let stand 5 minutes. Peel chiles; cut in half lengthwise. Discard seeds and membranes. Cut chiles into ¼-inch strips.
3. Place corn on grill rack coated with cooking spray; grill 10 minutes or until lightly browned, turning occasionally. Cool slightly. Cut kernels from cobs.
4. Combine chiles, corn, tomato, cilantro, and juice; toss gently. Add ½ teaspoon salt and ¼ teaspoon pepper.
5. Combine ½ teaspoon salt, ¼ teaspoon pepper, and cumin, stirring well. Rub spice mixture evenly over both sides of fish. Place fish on grill rack coated with cooking spray; grill 4 minutes on each side or until fish flakes easily when tested with a fork or until desired degree of doneness. Serve with relish. Yield: 4 servings (serving size: 1 fillet and ¾ cup relish).

CALORIES 304 (33% from fat); FAT 11.3g (sat 2.6g, mono 4.8g, poly 2.9g); PROTEIN 33.9g; CARB 18.1g; FIBER 2.7g; CHOL 80mg; IRON 1.7mg; SODIUM 671mg; CALC 39mg

STAFF FAVORITE
Fiery Flank Steak with Tomato Jam

Make jam to capitalize on a bumper crop of summer tomatoes. Prepare the jam up to two days ahead.

JAM:

    6 large ripe tomatoes, cored and cut
       in half crosswise (about 4 pounds)
  ⅓ cup sugar
  ⅓ cup grated onion
    3 garlic cloves, minced
    2 jalapeño peppers, minced
  ¼ cup chopped fresh cilantro
    3 tablespoons fresh lime juice
  ¼ teaspoon salt

STEAK:

    1 tablespoon grated lime rind
  ⅓ cup fresh lime juice
    2 teaspoons olive oil
    2 jalapeño peppers, minced
    2 garlic cloves, minced
    2 pounds flank steak, trimmed
  ½ teaspoon salt
  Cooking spray

REMAINING INGREDIENT:
  Lemon slices (optional)

1. To prepare jam, grate tomatoes, flesh side down, over a large bowl to form 5½ cups pulp; discard skins. Combine pulp, sugar, and next 3 ingredients in a medium saucepan; bring to a boil. Reduce heat, and simmer until reduced to 2¼ cups (about 20 minutes), stirring occasionally. Cool to room temperature. Stir in cilantro, 3 tablespoons juice, and ¼ teaspoon salt.
2. To prepare steak, combine rind and next 4 ingredients in a large zip-top plastic bag. Add steak; seal. Marinate in refrigerator 8 hours or overnight, turning bag occasionally.
3. Prepare grill.
4. Remove steak from bag; discard marinade. Sprinkle both sides of steak evenly with ½ teaspoon salt. Place steak on a grill rack coated with cooking spray; grill 3 minutes on each side or until desired degree of doneness. Let stand 5 minutes. Cut steak diagonally across grain into thin slices. Serve with jam. Garnish with lemon slices, if desired. Yield: 8 servings (serving size: 3 ounces steak and about ¼ cup jam).

CALORIES 258 (31% from fat); FAT 8.8g (sat 3.5g, mono 3.5g, poly 0.6g); PROTEIN 26.3g; CARB 19.3g; FIBER 3.1g; CHOL 40mg; IRON 2.5mg; SODIUM 161mg; CALC 57mg

WINE NOTE: Tomato Jam captures the rich flavor of summer tomatoes, a classic partner for high-acid red wines. For a sure bet, reach for Chianti or an affordable barbera, like Michele Chiarlo Barbera d'Asti Le Orme 2004 ($13). This bright wine has tart cranberry flavors and the vibrant acidity that tomatoes demand.

QUICK & EASY
Chile-Rubbed Steak Tacos

For a festive party presentation, set out a buffet with toppings like salsa, sour cream, shredded cheese, grilled peppers and onions, guacamole, and chopped tomato.

    2 tablespoons chili powder
    1 teaspoon garlic powder
  ¾ teaspoon kosher salt
  ½ teaspoon crushed red pepper
  ½ teaspoon black pepper
  ¼ teaspoon ground cinnamon
  1½ pounds flank steak, trimmed
  Cooking spray
  12 (6-inch) corn tortillas
    6 lime wedges

1. Prepare grill.
2. Combine first 6 ingredients in a bowl; stir well with a fork. Rub mixture evenly over both sides of steak; let stand 10 minutes.
3. Place steak on a grill rack coated with cooking spray; grill 8 minutes on each side or until desired degree of doneness. Remove steak from grill; let stand 5 minutes. Cut steak diagonally across grain into thin slices. Heat tortillas according to package directions. Place 1½ ounces steak in center of each tortilla; fold in half. Serve with lime wedges. Yield: 6 servings (serving size: 2 tacos and 1 lime wedge).

CALORIES 256 (27% from fat); FAT 7.6g (sat 2.4g, mono 2.1g, poly 2.1g); PROTEIN 27g; CARB 20.8g; FIBER 2.8g; CHOL 37mg; IRON 2.2mg; SODIUM 366mg; CALC 60mg

Marinated Chicken Cooked Under a Brick

¼ cup chopped shallots
1 teaspoon grated lemon rind
3 tablespoons fresh lemon juice
2 tablespoons balsamic vinegar
2 tablespoons honey
1 tablespoon Dijon mustard
1 tablespoon olive oil
1 tablespoon chopped fresh rosemary
2 teaspoons chopped fresh thyme
2 teaspoons low-sodium soy sauce
6 garlic cloves, minced
1 (4-pound) whole chicken
Cooking spray
½ teaspoon salt
¼ teaspoon freshly ground black
   pepper

1. Combine first 11 ingredients in a 13 x 9–inch baking dish.
2. Remove and discard giblets and neck from chicken. Trim excess fat. With a sharp knife or kitchen shears, remove wings at first joint; discard wings. Split chicken in half lengthwise. Remove and discard skin; pierce entire surface of chicken with a fork. Place chicken in dish, turning to coat. Cover and refrigerate 8 hours or overnight, turning occasionally.
3. Remove chicken from dish; discard marinade. Coat chicken with cooking spray; sprinkle chicken evenly with salt and pepper.
4. Prepare grill for indirect grilling, heating one side to medium-high and leaving one side with no heat. Maintain temperature at 400°.
5. Wrap 2 bricks with aluminum foil. Place chicken, breast side down, on grill rack coated with cooking spray on unheated side. Place 1 prepared brick on each chicken half. Cover and grill 1 hour or until a thermometer inserted into thickest part of thigh registers 165°. Carefully remove hot bricks; remove chicken from grill. Let chicken stand 5 minutes. Carve chicken. Yield: 4 servings (serving size: about 4 ounces).

CALORIES 247 (36% from fat); FAT 9.8g (sat 2.6g, mono 3.8g, poly 2.2g); PROTEIN 35.6g; CARB 1.7g; FIBER 0.1g; CHOL 106mg; IRON 1.8mg; SODIUM 420mg; CALC 20mg

Fava Bean and Grilled Shrimp Salad in Radicchio Cups

Removing the skins from fresh-shelled favas is a necessary task that's worth the effort.

1½ cups shelled fava beans (about
    2 pounds unshelled)
1   pound peeled and deveined
    medium shrimp
2   tablespoons extravirgin olive oil,
    divided
½   teaspoon salt, divided
¼   teaspoon freshly ground black
    pepper, divided
Cooking spray
2   tablespoons fresh lemon juice
1   garlic clove, minced
3   tablespoons chopped fresh flat-
    leaf parsley
4   radicchio leaves

1. Cook beans in boiling water 1 minute; drain. Plunge beans into ice water; drain. Remove tough outer skins from beans; discard skins. Place beans in a large bowl; set aside.
2. Prepare grill.
3. Thread shrimp evenly onto 6 (12-inch) skewers; brush with 1 teaspoon oil. Sprinkle shrimp evenly with ¼ teaspoon salt and ⅛ teaspoon pepper. Place skewers on a grill rack coated with cooking spray; grill 1½ minutes on each side or until shrimp are done. Cool slightly; remove shrimp from skewers. Add shrimp to beans.
4. Combine 5 teaspoons oil, ¼ teaspoon salt, ⅛ teaspoon pepper, juice, and garlic in a small bowl, stirring with a whisk. Drizzle juice mixture over shrimp mixture; toss to coat. Stir in parsley.
5. Place 1 radicchio leaf on each of 4 salad plates; spoon 1 cup shrimp mixture into each leaf. Yield: 4 servings.

CALORIES 378 (23% from fat); FAT 9.6g (sat 1.5g, mono 5.4g, poly 1.8g); PROTEIN 38g; CARB 35.4g; FIBER 14.3g; CHOL 172mg; IRON 6.8mg; SODIUM 474mg; CALC 125mg

Grilled Chicken with Tomato Salad

Sweet grape tomatoes work well in this summer salad, but you can use yellow pear or cherry tomatoes, as well.

CHICKEN:
½   cup finely chopped onion
2   tablespoons fresh lemon juice
2   garlic cloves, minced
12 chicken thighs (about 3½
    pounds), skinned
½   teaspoon salt
½   teaspoon freshly ground black
    pepper
Cooking spray

SALAD:
2   cups grape tomatoes, halved
2   tablespoons chopped fresh flat-
    leaf parsley
2   tablespoons diced red onion
2   tablespoons white wine vinegar
1   tablespoon capers, drained
2   teaspoons extravirgin olive oil
¼   teaspoon salt
¼   teaspoon freshly ground black
    pepper
1   garlic clove, minced

1. To prepare chicken, combine first 3 ingredients in a large zip-top plastic bag. Add chicken to bag; seal. Marinate in refrigerator 2 hours, turning occasionally.
2. Prepare grill.
3. Remove chicken from bag; discard marinade. Sprinkle chicken evenly with ½ teaspoon salt and ½ teaspoon pepper. Place chicken on a grill rack coated with cooking spray; grill 9 minutes on each side or until done.
4. To prepare salad, combine tomatoes and remaining 8 ingredients in a large bowl; toss well. Serve with chicken. Yield: 6 servings (serving size: 2 chicken thighs and about ⅓ cup salad).

CALORIES 351 (31% from fat); FAT 12.2g (sat 2.9g, mono 4.6g, poly 2.8g); PROTEIN 52.8g; CARB 4.9g; FIBER 1g; CHOL 220mg; IRON 3.1mg; SODIUM 565mg; CALC 42mg

Tandoori-Spiced Grilled Shrimp with Mint-Cilantro Chutney

This recipe makes a generous amount of the fresh herb chutney. Serve extra with cumin-spiced rice, samosas, or other Indian-inspired dishes. Serve the shrimp skewers with basmati rice or naan (Indian flatbread) heated on the grill.

SHRIMP:

½ teaspoon coriander seeds
½ teaspoon fennel seeds
½ teaspoon cumin seeds
½ cup plain fat-free yogurt
1 tablespoon brown sugar
1 tablespoon fresh lemon juice
¼ teaspoon ground cardamom
¼ teaspoon ground cinnamon
¼ teaspoon ground cloves
¼ teaspoon ground red pepper
32 peeled and deveined large shrimp (about 1 pound)
1 large Vidalia or other sweet onion, cut into 16 wedges
16 (1-inch) pieces green bell pepper
16 cherry tomatoes
1 teaspoon olive oil
Cooking spray

CHUTNEY:

½ cup loosely packed fresh mint leaves
½ cup loosely packed fresh cilantro leaves
½ cup chopped onion
2 tablespoons fresh lemon juice
1 teaspoon ground cumin
¼ teaspoon salt
1 serrano chile, seeded and chopped
1 garlic clove

1. To prepare shrimp, combine first 3 ingredients in a small skillet over medium heat; cook 2 minutes or until fragrant, stirring constantly. Cool. Place spice mixture in a spice or coffee grinder; process until finely ground.
2. Combine spice mixture, yogurt, and next 6 ingredients in a large zip-top plastic bag. Add shrimp to bag; seal. Toss to coat. Marinate in refrigerator 1 hour, turning bag occasionally.
3. Prepare grill.
4. Combine onion wedges, bell pepper, and tomatoes in a large bowl. Drizzle with oil; toss to coat.
5. Remove shrimp from bag; discard marinade. Thread 4 shrimp, 2 tomatoes, 2 onion wedges, and 2 bell pepper pieces alternately onto each of 8 (10-inch) skewers. Lightly coat skewers with cooking spray. Place skewers on grill rack coated with cooking spray. Grill 4 minutes on each side or until done.
6. To prepare chutney, combine mint and remaining 7 ingredients in a food processor; process until smooth. Serve with shrimp. Yield: 4 servings (serving size: 2 skewers and 2½ tablespoons chutney).

CALORIES 194 (17% from fat); FAT 3.6g (sat 0.6g, mono 1.2g, poly 1g); PROTEIN 25.3g; CARB 15.2g; FIBER 3.2g; CHOL 173mg; IRON 4.9mg; SODIUM 334mg; CALC 123mg

Lemon-Tarragon Grilled Pork Chops

¾ cup water
2 tablespoons sugar
2 tablespoons kosher salt
¼ cup chopped fresh tarragon
1 tablespoon grated lemon rind
¼ cup fresh lemon juice
4 (6-ounce) bone-in center-cut pork chops (about ½ inch thick)
¼ teaspoon freshly ground black pepper
Cooking spray

1. Combine first 3 ingredients in a bowl, stirring with a whisk until sugar and salt dissolve. Pour water mixture into a large zip-top plastic bag. Add tarragon, rind, juice, and pork chops to bag; seal. Marinate in refrigerator 2 hours, turning bag occasionally.
2. Prepare grill.
3. Remove pork from bag; discard marinade. Sprinkle pork evenly with pepper. Place pork on a grill rack coated with cooking spray. Grill 3 minutes on each side or until desired degree of doneness. Yield: 4 servings (serving size: 1 pork chop).

CALORIES 174 (35% from fat); FAT 6.8g (sat 2.5g, mono 3.1g, poly 0.5g); PROTEIN 25.5g; CARB 0.9g; FIBER 0.1g; CHOL 69mg; IRON 0.7mg; SODIUM 333mg; CALC 28mg

Asian-Style Beef Tenderloin Salad

Purple-tinged Thai basil has a distinct, aromatic flavor that would be delicious in place of the regular basil called for in this salad. Fish sauce is a condiment available at Asian markets. If you can't find fish sauce, substitute low-sodium soy sauce.

DRESSING:

1 tablespoon fresh lime juice
1 tablespoon rice vinegar
1½ teaspoons Sriracha (hot chile sauce, such as Huy Fong)
1 teaspoon granulated sugar
1 teaspoon fish sauce
¼ teaspoon sesame oil

SALAD:

2 (6-ounce) beef tenderloin steaks, trimmed (1 inch thick)
¼ teaspoon salt
⅛ teaspoon freshly ground black pepper
Cooking spray
6 cups torn red leaf lettuce
1½ cups thinly sliced English cucumber
¼ cup chopped fresh cilantro
¼ cup thinly sliced shallots (about 2 small)
2 tablespoons thinly sliced fresh basil

1. To prepare dressing, combine first 6 ingredients in a small bowl, stirring well with a whisk.
2. Prepare grill.
3. To prepare salad, sprinkle both sides of steak with salt and pepper. Place steak on a grill rack coated with cooking spray; grill 4 minutes on each side or until desired degree of doneness. Let stand 5 minutes. Cut steak diagonally across grain into thin slices.
4. Combine lettuce and remaining 4 ingredients in a large bowl. Add steak to bowl. Drizzle salad mixture with dressing mixture; toss to coat. Serve immediately. Yield: 4 servings (serving size: 2 cups).

CALORIES 168 (37% from fat); FAT 6.9g (sat 2.5g, mono 2.6g, poly 0.4g); PROTEIN 19.4g; CARB 6.4g; FIBER 1g; CHOL 54mg; IRON 3.2mg; SODIUM 363mg; CALC 35mg

Cocktel de Camarones
Shrimp Cocktail

2 cups fat-free, less-sodium chicken broth
5 tablespoons fresh lime juice, divided
1 sprig fresh oregano
1½ pounds peeled and deveined medium shrimp
1 cup ice
1 cup tomato juice
2 teaspoons Mexican-style hot sauce
1 cup diced onion
1 cup chopped seeded tomato
1 cup chopped peeled English cucumber
½ teaspoon freshly ground black pepper
¼ teaspoon salt
1 tablespoon chopped fresh cilantro
¾ cup diced peeled avocado
6 lime wedges

1. Combine broth, 1 tablespoon lime juice, and oregano in a large saucepan; bring to a simmer. Cook 5 minutes. Discard oregano. Add shrimp to pan; cook 3 minutes or until done.
2. Transfer shrimp mixture to a large bowl. Stir in ice, tomato juice, and hot sauce. Let stand 1 minute or until ice melts. Stir in ¼ cup lime juice, onion, tomato, cucumber, pepper, and salt. Cool. Cover and chill.
3. Stir in cilantro. Divide shrimp mixture evenly among 6 bowls; top with avocado. Garnish with lime wedges. Yield: 6 servings (serving size: 4 ounces shrimp, ⅔ cup broth mixture, 2 tablespoons avocado, and 1 lime wedge).

CALORIES 185 (24% from fat); FAT 5g (sat 0.9g, mono 2.1g, poly 1.2g); PROTEIN 25.3g; CARB 10g; FIBER 2.4g; CHOL 172mg; IRON 3.5mg; SODIUM 519mg; CALC 85mg

WINE NOTE: One wine has a lot to match in this bold shrimp cocktail. Lime, tomato, hot sauce, shrimp, avocado—they all impact wine differently. With so many elements at play, serve a simple, dry, refreshing white that's flexible with all sorts of seafood. One of the best is albariño from Spain. Try Nora Albariño 2005 from Rias Baixas, Spain ($15).

Cumin, Honey, and Mint–Marinated Lamb Chops

The natural sugar in the honey helps the chops caramelize on the grill.

¼ cup chopped fresh mint
1 tablespoon balsamic vinegar
2 teaspoons ground cumin
1 teaspoon dry mustard
2 teaspoons honey
½ teaspoon salt
½ teaspoon freshly ground black pepper
8 (4-ounce) lamb loin chops, about 1 inch thick, trimmed
Cooking spray

1. Combine first 7 ingredients in a small bowl, stirring well. Place lamb in a single layer in a shallow dish; rub spice mixture evenly over both sides of lamb. Cover and refrigerate 4 hours.
2. Prepare grill.
3. Place lamb on a grill rack coated with cooking spray. Grill 4 minutes on each side or until desired degree of doneness. Serve immediately. Yield: 4 servings (serving size: 2 chops).

CALORIES 223 (50% from fat); FAT 12.3g (sat 5.5g, mono 4.7g, poly 0.5g); PROTEIN 22.4g; CARB 4.4g; FIBER 0.6g; CHOL 72mg; IRON 2.6mg; SODIUM 353mg; CALC 27mg

Feed-a-Crowd Menu
serves 8
Jerk Pork Tenderloin with Pineapple-Plum Relish

Coconut rice*

Stewed turnip greens

*Heat 2 tablespoons olive oil in a large saucepan over medium-high heat. Add 2 cups uncooked basmati rice; sauté 1 minute. Stir in 2 cups fat-free, less-sodium chicken broth, 1 (14-ounce) can coconut milk, and 1 teaspoon salt; bring to a boil. Cover, reduce heat, and simmer 20 minutes or until liquid is absorbed. Stir in ½ cup chopped green onions.

Jerk Pork Tenderloin with Pineapple-Plum Relish

PORK:

1½ cups chopped green onions
¼ cup red wine vinegar
3 tablespoons brown sugar
2 tablespoons olive oil
2 tablespoons fresh lime juice
2 tablespoons low-sodium soy sauce
1 teaspoon salt
1 teaspoon ground allspice
¾ teaspoon dried thyme
¼ teaspoon ground cinnamon
¼ teaspoon freshly ground black pepper
2 garlic cloves, peeled
1 habanero pepper
2 (1-pound) pork tenderloins, trimmed
Cooking spray

RELISH:

2 cups finely chopped pineapple
¾ cup finely chopped ripe plum (about 3 medium)
2 tablespoons chopped fresh mint
1 tablespoon cider vinegar
1 tablespoon honey
2 teaspoons grated peeled fresh ginger
1 teaspoon low-sodium soy sauce

1. To prepare pork, combine first 13 ingredients in a blender; process until smooth. Place green onion mixture in a large zip-top bag. Add pork to bag; seal. Marinate in refrigerator 8 hours or overnight, turning occasionally.
2. Prepare grill.
3. Remove pork from bag; discard marinade. Place pork on a grill rack coated with cooking spray; grill 23 minutes or until a thermometer registers 155° or until desired degree of doneness. Let pork stand 10 minutes. Cut pork into ½-inch-thick slices.
4. To prepare relish, combine pineapple and remaining 6 ingredients in a bowl, stirring well. Serve with pork. Yield: 8 servings (serving size: 3 ounces pork and about ⅓ cup relish).

CALORIES 154 (24% from fat); FAT 4.1g (sat 1.4g, mono 1.8g, poly 0.4g); PROTEIN 17.5g; CARB 11.7g; FIBER 0.5g; CHOL 48mg; IRON 1.1mg; SODIUM 101mg; CALC 13mg

Smoked Flank Steak

Hickory wood chips impart a savory note, though you can experiment with other types of wood.

    2   teaspoons ground cumin
    2   teaspoons Spanish smoked paprika
    ½   teaspoon kosher salt
    ½   teaspoon ground coriander
    ⅛   teaspoon ground red pepper
    4   garlic cloves, minced
    1   (1½-pound) flank steak, trimmed
    2   cups hickory wood chips
    2   cups water
    Cooking spray

1. Combine first 6 ingredients in a small bowl, stirring well. Place steak in a shallow dish; rub spice mixture evenly over both sides of steak. Cover and refrigerate 8 hours or overnight.
2. Soak wood chips in water 1 hour; drain.
3. Prepare grill for indirect grilling, heating one side to low and leaving one side with no heat. Maintain temperature at 200° to 225°.
4. Place wood chips on hot coals. Place a disposable aluminum foil pan on unheated side of grill. Pour 2 cups water in pan. Coat grill rack with cooking spray; place on grill. Place steak on grill rack over foil pan on unheated side. Close lid; grill 1 hour and 5 minutes or until steak is medium-rare or until desired degree of doneness, turning once. Remove steak from grill; cover and let stand 5 minutes. Cut steak diagonally across grain into thin slices. Yield: 6 servings (serving size: 3 ounces).

CALORIES 166 (38% from fat); FAT 7g (sat 2.8g, mono 2.7g, poly 0.3g); PROTEIN 22.9g; CARB 1.3g; FIBER 0.5g; CHOL 45mg; IRON 1.8mg; SODIUM 205mg; CALC 23mg

Sides

Add color and variety to your meals with recipes from simple to spectacular.

Thai Summer Slaw

Prepare slaw and dressing one day ahead, and store separately in the refrigerator.

SLAW:

    3   cups thinly sliced napa (Chinese) cabbage
    ½   cup (⅛-inch) julienne-cut yellow squash
    ½   cup (⅛-inch) julienne-cut zucchini
    ½   cup (⅛-inch) julienne-cut red bell pepper
    ½   cup (⅛-inch) julienne-cut yellow bell pepper
    ½   cup (⅛-inch) julienne-cut seeded peeled cucumber
    ½   cup shredded carrot
    ½   cup chopped fresh cilantro
    ¼   cup thinly sliced green onions
    ¼   cup grated radishes
    1   minced seeded jalapeño pepper

DRESSING:

    3   tablespoons fresh lime juice
    1   tablespoon fish sauce
    1   tablespoon water
    1½ teaspoons sugar
    ½   teaspoon chile paste with garlic (such as sambal oelek)

1. To prepare slaw, combine first 11 ingredients in a large bowl.
2. To prepare dressing, combine juice and remaining 4 ingredients in a small bowl; stir with a whisk until sugar dissolves. Drizzle over slaw; toss well to coat. Serve immediately. Yield: 10 servings (serving size: about ½ cup).

CALORIES 20 (5% from fat); FAT 0.1g (sat 0g, mono 0g, poly 0.1g); PROTEIN 0.9g; CARB 4.6g; FIBER 1.1g; CHOL 0mg; IRON 0.2mg; SODIUM 156mg; CALC 28mg

Corn and Summer Vegetable Sauté

Use parsley or chives in place of cilantro, if you prefer. Garnish with chives.

    1   tablespoon canola oil
    ½   cup chopped green onions (about 4)
    1   garlic clove, minced
    1   cup sliced fresh okra (about 4 ounces)
    1   cup chopped red bell pepper (about 1)
    1   finely chopped seeded jalapeño pepper
    1   cup fresh corn kernels (about 2 ears)
    1   (15-ounce) can black beans, rinsed and drained
    ⅓   cup minced fresh cilantro
    ⅛   teaspoon salt
    ⅛   teaspoon freshly ground black pepper

1. Heat oil in a large nonstick skillet over medium-high heat. Add onions and garlic; sauté 1 minute. Add okra; sauté 3 minutes. Reduce heat to medium. Add bell pepper and jalapeño; cook 5 minutes. Add corn; cook 5 minutes. Stir in beans; cook 2 minutes. Stir in cilantro; sprinkle with salt and black pepper. Yield: 6 servings (serving size: ⅔ cup).

CALORIES 90 (27% from fat); FAT 2.7g (sat 0.2g, mono 1.5g, poly 0.9g); PROTEIN 3.7g; CARB 15.9g; FIBER 4.8g; CHOL 0mg; IRON 1.2mg; SODIUM 232mg; CALC 43mg

---

Choice Ingredient: Napa Cabbage

Napa's broad leaves and mellow sweetness stand up to nearly any cooking method—grated raw, sliced and stir-fried, or spiced and picked as kimchi, often found on Korean menus.

When purchasing, first check the name; napa may also be listed as celery cabbage or Chinese cabbage. Then pick a head that seems heavy for its size and does not appear dry or cracked.

Mediterranean Stuffed Eggplant

Look for panko, coarse Japanese breadcrumbs, in most supermarkets in the Asian foods section or with the other breadcrumbs.

    3 medium eggplants
       Cooking spray
    4 teaspoons olive oil, divided
 1½ cups chopped onion
    1 cup chopped red bell pepper
    1 cup chopped green bell pepper
  ¼ cup dry white wine
    1 tablespoon chopped fresh
       oregano
    1 tablespoon chopped fresh basil
    6 plum tomatoes, chopped
    3 garlic cloves, minced
    1 medium zucchini, chopped
    1 medium summer squash, chopped
 1½ teaspoons salt, divided
  ¼ teaspoon freshly ground black
       pepper
  ¾ cup (3 ounces) crumbled feta
       cheese
 1¼ cups panko (Japanese
       breadcrumbs), divided
       Chopped fresh parsley (optional)

1. Preheat oven to 350°.
2. Cut each eggplant in half lengthwise. Scoop out pulp, leaving ¼-inch-thick shells; reserve pulp. Place eggplant shells, skin sides down, on a baking sheet coated with cooking spray; bake at 350° for 15 minutes.
3. Chop eggplant pulp into ½-inch pieces. Heat 1 tablespoon oil in a large nonstick skillet over medium-high heat. Add chopped eggplant to pan, and sauté 8 minutes or until eggplant begins to brown. Place eggplant in a bowl. Coat pan with cooking spray. Add onion, and sauté 5 minutes or until tender. Stir in red bell pepper and next 8 ingredients; sauté 6 minutes. Return eggplant to pan. Stir in 1¼ teaspoons salt and black pepper; sauté 5 minutes. Remove from heat; stir in cheese and ¼ cup panko. Cool slightly. Spoon about 1 cup eggplant mixture into each eggplant shell.
4. Combine 1 cup panko, 1 teaspoon oil, and ¼ teaspoon salt. Sprinkle panko

mixture evenly over stuffed eggplants. Lightly coat with cooking spray. Bake at 350° for 20 minutes or until thoroughly heated and tops begin to brown. Sprinkle with parsley, if desired. Yield: 6 servings (serving size: 1 stuffed eggplant half).

CALORIES 237 (32% from fat); FAT 8.4g (sat 3.4g, mono 3.2g, poly 0.8g); PROTEIN 9g; CARB 35.9g; FIBER 12.2g; CHOL 17mg; IRON 1.5mg; SODIUM 842mg; CALC 147mg

---

MAKE AHEAD

Peach Chutney

(pictured on page 234)

Pair this sweet and slightly hot condiment with grilled chicken or pork, or curry dishes. It can also perk up a turkey or ham sandwich. Store in the refrigerator for up to one week.

    5 cups chopped peeled peaches
       (about 1¾ pounds)
 1½ cups finely chopped red onion
  ½ cup packed brown sugar
  ½ cup white wine vinegar
    3 tablespoons minced peeled fresh
       ginger
  ½ teaspoon salt
    1 minced seeded jalapeño pepper
  ½ cup chopped fresh cilantro
    2 tablespoons fresh lime juice

1. Combine first 6 ingredients in a saucepan; bring to a boil. Cover, reduce heat, and simmer 45 minutes. Stir in jalapeño. Simmer, uncovered, 5 minutes. Remove from heat; stir in cilantro and juice. Cool to room temperature. Yield: 4 cups (serving size: ¼ cup).

CALORIES 57 (2% from fat); FAT 0.1g (sat 0g, mono 0g, poly 0.1g); PROTEIN 0.6g; CARB 14.4g; FIBER 1.5g; CHOL 0mg; IRON 0.4mg; SODIUM 78mg; CALC 14mg

Peak-season produce offers many colorful opportunities for the plate and the palate.

Red and Yellow Pepper Gratin

Fresh breadcrumbs enhance the texture of this dish. If you don't have sourdough, any white bread will do.

  ½ cup boiling water
  ¼ cup sun-dried tomatoes, packed
       without oil
    1 teaspoon chopped fresh thyme
  ½ teaspoon salt
  ½ teaspoon Hungarian sweet paprika
  ¼ teaspoon freshly ground black
       pepper
    2 large red bell peppers, cut into
       ¼-inch strips
    1 large yellow bell pepper, cut into
       ¼-inch strips
    1 small zucchini, halved lengthwise
       and thinly sliced (about ½ cup)
    1 small yellow squash, halved
       lengthwise and thinly sliced
       (about ½ cup)
    1 medium yellow onion, peeled,
       halved lengthwise, and thinly
       sliced (about ¾ cup)
    2 teaspoons olive oil, divided
       Cooking spray
 1½ ounces sourdough bread
    2 tablespoons grated fresh
       Parmigiano-Reggiano cheese

1. Combine ½ cup boiling water and sun-dried tomatoes in a bowl; let stand 30 minutes or until soft. Drain and cut tomatoes into ¼-inch strips.
2. Preheat oven to 400°.
3. Combine tomatoes and next 9 ingredients in a large bowl. Drizzle with 1 teaspoon oil; toss gently. Spoon mixture into an 11 x 7–inch baking dish coated with cooking spray. Bake at 400° for 45 minutes or until vegetables are tender, stirring every 15 minutes. Remove from oven.
4. Place bread in a food processor; pulse 10 times or until coarse crumbs measure about 1 cup. Add 1 teaspoon oil and cheese; pulse to combine. Sprinkle breadcrumb mixture over vegetables. Bake at 400° for 20 minutes or until breadcrumbs are golden brown. Yield: 6 servings.

CALORIES 94 (34% from fat); FAT 3.5g (sat 0.7g, mono 1.7g, poly 0.7g); PROTEIN 3.4g; CARB 14.9g; FIBER 1.6g; CHOL 1mg; IRON 1.2mg; SODIUM 327mg; CALC 57mg

Korean Cucumber Salad

Use a mandoline or food processor to slice the cucumber uniformly thin. Salting the cucumber causes it to wilt and draws out excess moisture. It also gives the dish a pickled quality similar to kimchi, Korea's spicy and pungent fermented cabbage condiment.

- 3½ cups (1/16-inch-thick) slices English cucumber (about 1 large)
- 2 teaspoons kosher salt
- 2 tablespoons minced green onions
- 1 tablespoon rice vinegar
- 1 teaspoon sugar
- ½ teaspoon crushed red pepper
- ½ teaspoon dark sesame oil

1. Combine cucumber and salt, tossing well. Let stand at room temperature 20 minutes. Drain and squeeze dry.
2. Combine cucumber, onions, and remaining ingredients. Serve chilled or at room temperature. Yield: 8 servings (serving size: about ¼ cup).

CALORIES 12 (30% from fat); FAT 0.4g (sat 0.1g, mono 0.1g, poly 0.1g); PROTEIN 0.3g; CARB 2g; FIBER 0.5g; CHOL 0mg; IRON 0.1mg; SODIUM 119mg; CALC 7mg

Roasted Tomato Relish with Thyme

This makes a fine accompaniment with grilled fish, chicken, or beef, or serve it as a topping for bruschetta.

- 12 plum tomatoes, halved lengthwise and seeded (about 2 pounds)
- 2 tablespoons olive oil, divided
- ¼ teaspoon freshly ground black pepper
- 2 large shallots, peeled
- 1 tablespoon balsamic vinegar
- 1 teaspoon chopped fresh thyme
- ½ teaspoon sugar
- ¼ teaspoon salt
- 1 garlic clove, minced

1. Preheat oven to 350°.
2. Place tomatoes, cut sides down, on a foil-lined baking sheet. Brush with 1 tablespoon oil; sprinkle with pepper.

Bake at 350° for 50 minutes. Wrap shallots in foil; add to baking sheet. Bake an additional 40 minutes or until tomatoes are lightly charred and shallots are soft. Cool 10 minutes.
3. Chop tomatoes and shallots; place in a medium bowl. Add 1 tablespoon oil, vinegar, and remaining ingredients to bowl; toss well. Yield: about 1 cup (serving size: about 2 tablespoons).

CALORIES 61 (55% from fat); FAT 3.7g (sat 0.5g, mono 2.7g, poly 0.4g); PROTEIN 1.4g; CARB 6.9g; FIBER 1.2g; CHOL 0mg; IRON 0.5mg; SODIUM 78mg; CALC 11mg

Smoky Tomatillo Salsa

For even smokier taste, add ¼ teaspoon Spanish smoked paprika to this mixture. Serve with tortilla chips, grilled chicken, or pork.

- 2 garlic cloves
- 2 jalapeño peppers
- 1 green bell pepper, halved and seeded
- 1 pound tomatillos, husks and stems removed
- Cooking spray
- 1 cup coarsely chopped onion
- ⅓ cup chopped fresh cilantro
- 3 tablespoons chopped green onions
- 2 tablespoons fresh lime juice
- ½ teaspoon sugar
- ½ teaspoon salt

1. Prepare grill.
2. Thread garlic cloves onto a 6-inch skewer. Arrange skewer, peppers, and tomatillos on a grill rack coated with cooking spray; grill 8 minutes or until blackened, turning frequently. Remove seeds from jalapeño peppers. Combine garlic, peppers, tomatillos, 1 cup onion, and remaining ingredients in a food processor; process until finely chopped. Yield: 7 servings (serving size: about ⅓ cup).

CALORIES 41 (15% from fat); FAT 0.7g (sat 0.1g, mono 0.1g, poly 0.3g); PROTEIN 1.2g; CARB 8.6g; FIBER 2.1g; CHOL 0mg; IRON 0.6mg; SODIUM 171mg; CALC 19mg

Grilled Eggplant Salad

Assemble this up to three hours ahead.

- 1 (1-pound) eggplant, cut crosswise into ½-inch-thick slices
- Cooking spray
- 2 cups coarsely chopped tomato
- ¼ cup (1 ounce) crumbled feta cheese
- 2 tablespoons chopped fresh basil
- 1 tablespoon red wine vinegar
- 1 tablespoon balsamic vinegar
- 2 teaspoons capers
- 1 teaspoon extravirgin olive oil
- ¼ teaspoon dried oregano
- ¼ teaspoon freshly ground black pepper
- ⅛ teaspoon salt
- 1 garlic clove, minced

1. Prepare grill.
2. Lightly coat both sides of eggplant slices with cooking spray. Place eggplant on grill rack coated with cooking spray; grill 5 minutes on each side or until tender. Cool; cut each eggplant slice into quarters. Combine eggplant, tomato, and remaining ingredients in a large bowl; toss gently. Yield: 4 servings (serving size: 1¼ cups).

CALORIES 86 (39% from fat); FAT 3.7g (sat 1.6g, mono 1.3g, poly 0.4g); PROTEIN 3.5g; CARB 12g; FIBER 5g; CHOL 8mg; IRON 0.9mg; SODIUM 243mg; CALC 67mg

Grilled Corn Succotash

- 4 ears shucked corn
- Cooking spray
- 4 cups water
- 1 cup shelled lima beans
- 2 cups (1-inch) cut green beans (about ½ pound)
- 1½ tablespoons butter
- 1 cup chopped onion
- 2 garlic cloves, minced
- 1 cup halved grape tomatoes
- ¼ cup chopped fresh basil
- 1½ tablespoons fresh lemon juice
- 1 tablespoon balsamic vinegar
- ¾ teaspoon salt
- ¼ teaspoon freshly ground black pepper

1. Prepare grill.

2. Place corn on grill rack coated with cooking spray; cook 10 minutes or until lightly browned, turning every 2 minutes. Cool corn. Cut kernels from ears of corn.

3. Bring 4 cups water to a boil in a large saucepan. Add lima beans; cook 20 minutes. Add green beans; cook 2 minutes. Drain beans, and rinse with cold water; drain well.

4. Melt butter in a large nonstick skillet over medium-high heat. Add onion and garlic; cook, stirring occasionally, 5 minutes or until onion is lightly browned. Stir in corn, and cook 2 minutes. Add beans; cook 2 minutes. Remove from heat. Stir in tomatoes and remaining ingredients. Yield: 6 servings (serving size: 1 cup).

CALORIES 140 (24% from fat); FAT 3.8g (sat 2g, mono 1g, poly 0.6g); PROTEIN 5.1g; CARB 25g; FIBER 5.3g; CHOL 8mg; IRON 1.5mg; SODIUM 338mg; CALC 36mg

Desserts

The season's best fruits and herbs star in these finales.

STAFF FAVORITE • MAKE AHEAD

Lemon Pound Cake with Cherry Compote

This recipe received our Test Kitchens' highest rating. The sauce is delicious served over ice cream, as well.

CAKE:

   Cooking spray
  3 cups plus 2 tablespoons all-purpose flour (about 13²⁄₃ ounces), divided
  2 teaspoons baking powder
  ½ teaspoon baking soda
  ½ teaspoon salt
  2 cups granulated sugar
  ¾ cup butter, softened
  2 large eggs
  1 cup low-fat buttermilk
  1 tablespoon grated fresh lemon rind
  3 tablespoons fresh lemon juice
  1 teaspoon chopped fresh mint
  1 tablespoon powdered sugar

COMPOTE:

  4 cups pitted sweet cherries (about 1½ pounds)
  ¼ cup granulated sugar
  2 tablespoons water
  2 teaspoons cornstarch
  ¼ teaspoon almond extract

1. Preheat oven to 350°.

2. To prepare cake, coat a 10-inch tube pan with cooking spray; dust with 2 tablespoons flour.

3. Lightly spoon 3 cups flour into dry measuring cups; level with a knife. Combine 3 cups flour, baking powder, baking soda, and salt in a bowl, stirring well with a whisk. Combine 2 cups granulated sugar and butter in a large bowl; beat with a mixer at medium speed until light and fluffy. Add eggs, 1 at a time, beating well after each addition. Add flour mixture to sugar mixture alternately with buttermilk, beating at low speed, beginning and ending with flour mixture. Add rind, juice, and mint; beat just until blended.

4. Spoon batter into prepared pan; sharply tap pan once on counter to remove air bubbles. Bake at 350° for 45 minutes or until a wooden pick inserted in center comes out clean. Cool in pan 10 minutes on a wire rack; remove from pan. Cool completely on a wire rack. Sift powdered sugar over top of cake. Cut cake into 16 slices.

5. To prepare compote, combine cherries and next 3 ingredients in a medium saucepan; bring to a boil. Cook 1 minute, stirring constantly. Remove from heat; stir in extract. Cool. Serve with cake. Yield: 16 servings (serving size: 1 slice cake and ¼ cup compote).

CALORIES 319 (28% from fat); FAT 9.9g (sat 5.8g, mono 2.6g, poly 0.6g); PROTEIN 4.4g; CARB 54.8g; FIBER 1.6g; CHOL 50mg; IRON 1.5mg; SODIUM 260mg; CALC 68mg

MAKE AHEAD • FREEZABLE

Mint Julep Granita

Infuse a simple sugar syrup with the taste of fresh mint and combine it with bourbon for a slushy Southern-accented dessert.

  3 cups water
  1½ cups sugar
  ⅔ cup finely chopped fresh mint
  1 cup bourbon
  8 lime wedges
  Mint sprigs (optional)

1. Combine 3 cups water and sugar in a medium saucepan; bring to a boil, stirring until sugar dissolves. Stir in chopped mint. Remove from heat; cool completely.

2. Strain sugar mixture through a sieve into a 13 x 9–inch baking dish; discard solids. Stir in bourbon. Cover and freeze 8 hours or until firm. Remove mixture from freezer; let stand 15 minutes. Scrape entire mixture with a fork until fluffy. Place about ½ cup granita in each of 8 small bowls or glasses; serve with lime wedges. Garnish with mint sprigs, if desired. Yield: 8 servings.

CALORIES 211; (0% from fat); FAT 0g; PROTEIN 0.2g; CARB 38g; FIBER 0.3g; CHOL 0mg; IRON 0.5mg; SODIUM 2mg; CALC 9mg

---

Mint

If mint is growing in your garden, you may be wondering how to use it—bushels of it—fast. This fresh-smelling plant is synonymous with vigorous growth and spreading. Fortunately, mint is versatile. You can mix mint into a mojito or julep, toss it into salads, and oven-roast it with lamb chops or salmon fillets.

When shopping for mint, note that plants with smaller leaves tend to be more flavorful and fragrant. Look for firm stalks with leaf tips that point upward. Pluck a leaf, rub it between your fingers, and sniff; the aroma should be strong and pleasant. To extend the life of fresh mint by a few days, wrap sprigs in a damp paper towel and store in the refrigerator in a plastic bag.

Fresh Cherry Smoothie

Come summer, a cherry pitter is a wise, inexpensive investment. You can use it to pit olives, as well.

    2   cups pitted sweet cherries
 1½   cups ice
 1½   cups plain fat-free yogurt
   ¼   cup honey

1. Combine all ingredients in a blender; process until smooth. Serve immediately. Yield: 4 servings (serving size: 1 cup).

CALORIES 168 (5% from fat); FAT 0.9g (sat 0.3g, mono 0.2g, poly 0.2g); PROTEIN 6.2g; CARB 36.5g; FIBER 1.7g; CHOL 2mg; IRON 0.5mg; SODIUM 72mg; CALC 195mg

Roasted Nectarines with Buttermilk Custard

Roasting the nectarines concentrates their natural sugar. Peaches or plums also roast well.

SAUCE:
   ⅛   teaspoon salt
    4   egg yolks
   ⅓   cup sugar
    1   cup 1% low-fat milk
    2   tablespoons low-fat buttermilk
   ¼   teaspoon vanilla extract

NECTARINES:
    6   nectarines, halved and pitted
        (about 2 pounds)
Cooking spray
    1   tablespoon sugar
Verbena sprigs (optional)

1. To prepare sauce, combine salt and egg yolks in a medium bowl. Gradually add ⅓ cup sugar, beating 2 minutes with a mixer at medium-high speed.
2. Heat 1 cup milk over medium heat in a small, heavy saucepan to 180° or until tiny bubbles form around edge (do not boil). Gradually add hot milk to sugar mixture, stirring constantly. Return milk mixture to pan; cook over medium-low heat 5 minutes or until slightly thick and mixture coats back of a spoon, stirring

constantly (do not boil). Remove from heat. Stir in buttermilk and vanilla. Place pan in a large ice-filled bowl until mixture cools completely, stirring occasionally. Spoon mixture into a bowl. Cover and chill.
3. Preheat oven to 400°.
4. To prepare nectarines, place nectarines, cut sides up, in a 13 x 9–inch baking dish coated with cooking spray. Sprinkle nectarines evenly with 1 tablespoon sugar. Bake at 400° for 25 minutes or until nectarines are soft and lightly browned. Serve with chilled sauce. Garnish with verbena sprigs, if desired. Yield: 6 servings (serving size: 2 nectarine halves and ¼ cup sauce).

CALORIES 176 (17% from fat); FAT 3.4g (sat 1.4g, mono 1.4g, poly 0.5g); PROTEIN 4.3g; CARB 32.8g; FIBER 1g; CHOL 138mg; IRON 0.7mg; SODIUM 80mg; CALC 70mg

Late-Harvest Riesling Sorbet with Berries

The late-harvest version of the wine has a higher sugar content than standard riesling. Fresh lime juice offsets the sweetness in our refreshing dessert. Use a combination of any fresh berries you have on hand.

SORBET:
 1⅔   cups late-harvest riesling
   ½   cup water
   ½   cup sugar
   ¼   cup fresh lime juice

BERRIES:
    1   cup blackberries
    1   cup blueberries
   ½   cup raspberries
    2   tablespoons sugar
    3   tablespoons late-harvest riesling
   ½   teaspoon grated lime rind

1. To prepare sorbet, combine first 4 ingredients in a small saucepan over medium heat; cook 3 minutes or until sugar dissolves, stirring occasionally. Increase heat to medium-high; bring to a boil. Cook 30 seconds. Pour mixture into a bowl; cool. Cover and chill 1 hour.
2. Pour mixture into freezer can of an ice-cream freezer; freeze according to

manufacturer's instructions. Spoon sorbet into a freezer-safe container; cover and freeze 2 hours or until firm.
3. To prepare berries, combine blackberries and remaining 5 ingredients; toss gently. Cover and chill. Serve sorbet topped with berries. Yield: 6 servings (serving size: about ⅔ cup sorbet and about ⅓ cup berries).

CALORIES 125 (2% from fat); FAT 0.3g (sat 0g, mono 0g, poly 0.1g); PROTEIN 0.8g; CARB 30.7g; FIBER 2.5g; CHOL 0mg; IRON 0.6mg; SODIUM 6mg; CALC 18mg

Glazed Cherry-Cheese Turnovers

 1½   cups pitted sweet cherries,
        coarsely chopped
   ⅓   cup granulated sugar
    1   tablespoon cornstarch
    2   tablespoons water
    1   teaspoon grated fresh orange rind
   ¼   teaspoon almond extract
   ½   cup powdered sugar, divided
   ¼   cup (2 ounces) ⅓-less-fat cream
        cheese, softened
   ½   teaspoon vanilla extract
  16   (14 x 9–inch) sheets frozen phyllo
        dough, thawed
Cooking spray
    1   teaspoon orange juice

1. Combine cherries and granulated sugar in a medium saucepan over medium heat; bring to a boil. Reduce heat, and simmer 10 minutes, stirring occasionally. Combine cornstarch and 2 tablespoons water, stirring until smooth. Add cornstarch mixture to cherry mixture; bring to a boil. Cook 1 minute, stirring constantly. Remove from heat; stir in rind and almond extract. Cool.
2. Preheat oven to 400°.
3. Combine 3 tablespoons powdered sugar, cheese, and vanilla in a small bowl, stirring until well blended.
4. Place 1 phyllo sheet on a large cutting board or work surface (cover remaining dough to keep from drying); lightly coat with cooking spray. Repeat layers 3 times. Gently press layers together. Using a sharp knife or a pizza cutter, cut each phyllo stack crosswise into 4 (9 x 3½–inch) strips. Spoon 1 teaspoon cream cheese mixture

onto one short end of each strip. Spoon 1 level tablespoonful cherry mixture on top of cream cheese mixture, leaving a 1-inch border. Fold one corner of edge with 1-inch border over mixture, forming a triangle; continue folding back and forth into a triangle to end of strip. Repeat procedure with remaining phyllo, cooking spray, cream cheese, and cherry mixture.

5. Place triangles, seam sides down, on a large baking sheet coated with cooking spray; lightly coat triangles with cooking spray. Bake at 400° for 10 minutes or until golden. Cool on wire racks 5 minutes. Combine 5 tablespoons powdered sugar and juice in a small bowl, stirring until smooth. Drizzle juice mixture over turnovers. Yield: 16 servings (serving size: 1 turnover).

CALORIES 108 (17% from fat); FAT 2g (sat 0.8g, mono 0.8g, poly 0.2g); PROTEIN 1.9g; CARB 20.6g; FIBER 0.7g; CHOL 3mg; IRON 0.7mg; SODIUM 106mg; CALC 7mg

MAKE AHEAD
Cheese Blintzes with Fresh Fruit Salsa

Prepare the salsa and assemble the blintzes up to two hours ahead of serving time.

SALSA:
⅔ cup diced peeled ripe mango
⅔ cup sliced strawberries
⅔ cup sliced banana
3 tablespoons mango chutney

BLINTZES:
1 cup part-skim ricotta cheese
3 tablespoons powdered sugar
1 teaspoon vanilla extract
8 (9-inch) packaged French crepes
Cooking spray
2 teaspoons butter, melted

1. To prepare salsa, combine first 4 ingredients in a bowl; toss gently. Cover and chill.

2. Preheat oven to 450°.

3. To prepare blintzes, combine ricotta, sugar, and vanilla, stirring well. Spoon 2 tablespoons cheese mixture in center of each crepe; fold sides and ends over. Place seam side down in a 13 x 9–inch

baking dish coated with cooking spray. Brush butter over crepes. Bake at 450° for 6 minutes or until lightly browned. Serve salsa over crepes. Yield: 4 servings (serving size: 2 crepes and about ¼ cup salsa).

CALORIES 252 (29% from fat); FAT 8.1g (sat 4.3g, mono 2g, poly 0.3g); PROTEIN 9.8g; CARB 35.5g; FIBER 2g; CHOL 34mg; IRON 0.6mg; SODIUM 195mg; CALC 182mg

QUICK & EASY • MAKE AHEAD
Fresh Blueberry Sauce

Serve this sauce chilled over low-fat pound cake or ice cream. It's also nice warm over pancakes or waffles for breakfast.

1 cup water
¾ cup sugar
1 cup fresh blueberries
1 teaspoon butter
1 teaspoon fresh lemon juice
½ teaspoon vanilla extract
⅛ teaspoon ground nutmeg

1. Combine 1 cup water and sugar in a small saucepan over medium-high heat; bring to a boil. Cook 5 minutes or until sugar dissolves, stirring constantly. Add blueberries and remaining ingredients to pan; return to boil. Reduce heat to medium; cook 4 minutes or until berries pop, stirring occasionally. Remove from heat. Yield: 12 servings (serving size: about 3 tablespoons).

CALORIES 59 (6% from fat); FAT 0.4g (sat 0.2g, mono 0.1g, poly 0g); PROTEIN 0.1g; CARB 14.3g; FIBER 0.3g; CHOL 1mg; IRON 0mg; SODIUM 2mg; CALC 1mg

MAKE AHEAD
Peach-Blackberry Soup

Firm, slightly underripe peaches work well in this recipe.

1 cup riesling
2 pounds fresh peaches, peeled and sliced (about 5 cups)
1 (3-inch) cinnamon stick
3 tablespoons honey
2 teaspoons fresh lemon juice
¼ teaspoon vanilla extract
1 cup fresh blackberries
Fresh mint leaves (optional)

1. Combine first 3 ingredients in a medium saucepan over medium-high heat; bring to a boil. Cover, reduce heat to low, and simmer 10 minutes or until peaches are tender. Remove from heat; cool. Discard cinnamon stick.

2. Place half of peach mixture in a blender or food processor; process until smooth. Pour pureed mixture into a large bowl; repeat procedure with remaining peach mixture. Stir in honey, juice, and vanilla. Chill for 1 hour.

3. Ladle ½ cup soup into each of 6 small bowls; top each serving with about 2½ tablespoons blackberries. Garnish with mint leaves, if desired. Yield: 6 servings.

CALORIES 135 (3% from fat); FAT 0.5g (sat 0g, mono 0.1g, poly 0.2g); PROTEIN 1.8g; CARB 26.7g; FIBER 3.5g; CHOL 0mg; IRON 0.6mg; SODIUM 1mg; CALC 17mg

MAKE AHEAD • FREEZABLE
Blackberry-Buttermilk Sherbet

Straining the blackberry mixture is optional but worth the effort for the smoothest, creamiest texture.

2½ cups blackberries (about 12 ounces)
½ cup sugar
1¼ cups low-fat buttermilk

1. Combine blackberries and sugar in a blender or food processor; process until smooth. Strain blackberry mixture through a fine sieve into a bowl; discard solids. Stir in buttermilk.

2. Pour mixture into freezer can of an ice-cream freezer; freeze according to manufacturer's instructions. Spoon sherbet into a freezer-safe container; cover and freeze 4 hours or until firm. Yield: 6 servings (serving size: about ½ cup).

CALORIES 113 (6% from fat); FAT 0.8g (sat 0.3g, mono 0g, poly 0.2g); PROTEIN 2.7g; CARB 25.1g; FIBER 3.1g; CHOL 3mg; IRON 0.4mg; SODIUM 57mg; CALC 70mg

Summer Fruit Upside-Down Cornmeal Cake

The wooden pick test isn't accurate for this cake since the fruit makes it appear wet when it's really done. Look for cake to brown slightly as your best visual cue for doneness. Serve warm with low-fat vanilla ice cream.

    1   cup (¼-inch-thick) nectarine slices
    1   cup blueberries
    1   cup raspberries
    1   teaspoon fresh lemon juice
        Cooking spray
    1   tablespoon butter, melted
    1   cup plus 1 tablespoon sugar, divided
 1¼   cups all-purpose flour (5½ ounces)
    ½   cup stone ground yellow cornmeal
 1½   teaspoons baking powder
    ¼   teaspoon salt
    5   tablespoons butter, softened
    2   large eggs
    1   teaspoon vanilla extract

1. Preheat oven to 350°.
2. Combine first 4 ingredients in a medium bowl; toss gently. Coat a 9-inch cake pan with cooking spray. Brush pan with melted butter. Sprinkle evenly with 1 tablespoon sugar. Pour nectarine mixture into pan in an even layer; set aside.
3. Lightly spoon flour into dry measuring cups; level with a knife. Combine flour, cornmeal, baking powder, and salt in a bowl, stirring well with a whisk.
4. Combine 1 cup sugar and softened butter in a large bowl; beat with a mixer at medium speed until well combined. Add eggs, 1 at a time, beating well after each addition. Beat in vanilla. Add flour mixture to butter mixture; beat just until combined.
5. Spoon batter evenly over fruit mixture. Bake at 350° for 40 minutes or until cake is set and light brown. Cool in pan on a wire rack 5 minutes. Place a plate upside down on top of cake pan; invert cake onto plate. Serve warm or at room temperature. Yield: 12 servings (serving size: 1 wedge).

CALORIES 221 (28% from fat); FAT 6.8g (sat 3.9g, mono 1.8g, poly 0.4g); PROTEIN 3.2g; CARB 37.4g; FIBER 1.2g; CHOL 50mg; IRON 1.1mg; SODIUM 163mg; CALC 46mg

---

dinner tonight
From the Grill

Cooked over the flame, chicken, fish, and beef make for swift suppers.

From the Grill Menu 1
serves 4

Grilled Chicken and Tapenade Sandwiches

Grilled vegetable skewers*

Cubed cantaloupe drizzled with Port

*Cut 2 zucchini, 1 red bell pepper, and 1 red onion into 1½-inch pieces. Thread vegetables alternately onto 4 skewers, brush with olive oil, and sprinkle with ½ teaspoon kosher salt and ¼ teaspoon freshly ground black pepper. Grill 15 minutes or until crisp-tender and lightly charred. Brush evenly with 1 tablespoon balsamic vinegar just before serving.

Game Plan

1. Prepare topping for sandwiches.
2. While topping stands:
  • Prepare vegetable skewers.
  • Grill chicken and vegetables.
3. While chicken stands:
  • Add cheese and remaining ingredients to topping.
4. Once slightly cooled, cut chicken into thin slices, and assemble sandwiches.

Grilled Chicken and Tapenade Sandwiches

Robust olives, balsamic vinegar, and feta cheese convey Mediterranean flavors.
TOTAL TIME: 39 MINUTES

 1½   cups diced seeded tomato
    2   tablespoons balsamic vinegar
    2   tablespoons finely chopped pitted kalamata olives
    1   tablespoon chopped fresh basil
    1   tablespoon chopped fresh flat-leaf parsley
    1   teaspoon chopped fresh oregano
    ½   teaspoon minced garlic
    5   teaspoons extravirgin olive oil, divided
    1   pound skinless, boneless chicken breast
    ½   teaspoon kosher salt, divided
    ½   teaspoon freshly ground black pepper
        Cooking spray
    ¼   cup (1 ounce) crumbled feta cheese
    4   (2-ounce) ciabatta sandwich rolls, halved

1. Combine first 7 ingredients in a small bowl. Add 2 teaspoons oil; toss gently to combine. Let stand 15 minutes.
2. Prepare grill.
3. Brush chicken evenly with 1 tablespoon oil, and sprinkle with ¼ teaspoon salt and pepper. Place chicken on a grill rack coated with cooking spray; grill 6 minutes on each side or until done. Remove from grill. Let stand 5 minutes before cutting into thin slices.
4. Add cheese and ¼ teaspoon salt to tomato mixture; stir gently to combine. Arrange sliced chicken evenly on bottom halves of rolls. Top each serving with one-fourth of tomato mixture, and cover with top halves of rolls. Serve immediately. Yield: 4 servings (serving size: 1 sandwich).

CALORIES 369 (30% from fat); FAT 12.3g (sat 3g, mono 7g, poly 1.6g); PROTEIN 33.2g; CARB 30.1g; FIBER 1.5g; CHOL 79mg; IRON 2.7mg; SODIUM 815mg; CALC 63mg

From the Grill Menu 2

serves 4

**Grilled Salmon with
Apricot-Mustard Glaze**

Parmesan-spinach orzo pilaf*

Pineapple chunks with
chopped fresh mint

*Prepare 8 ounces orzo according to package directions, omitting salt and fat. Add 3 ounces fresh baby spinach and 1½ teaspoons bottled minced garlic; stir well to combine. Cover and let stand 4 minutes, stirring twice to slightly wilt spinach. Add ½ teaspoon kosher salt and ½ teaspoon freshly ground black pepper. Just before serving, stir in ¼ cup grated fresh Parmesan cheese.

Game Plan

1. Season salmon fillets.
2. While salmon refrigerates:
   • Prepare glaze.
3. While glaze simmers:
   • Boil water for orzo.
   • Grate cheese for orzo.
4. While salmon grills:
   • Cook orzo.
5. Combine orzo and remaining pilaf ingredients.

QUICK & EASY
Grilled Salmon with Apricot-Mustard Glaze

TOTAL TIME: 39 MINUTES

SALMON:

4 (6-ounce) salmon fillets (about 1 inch thick)
1½ teaspoons minced garlic
½ teaspoon kosher salt
¼ teaspoon freshly ground black pepper

GLAZE:

¼ cup apricot nectar
¼ cup apricot preserves
1 tablespoon Dijon mustard
1½ teaspoons white wine vinegar
1½ teaspoons honey
¼ teaspoon kosher salt
¼ teaspoon freshly ground black pepper

REMAINING INGREDIENT:
Cooking spray

1. Prepare grill.
2. To prepare fish, sprinkle fillets with garlic, ½ teaspoon salt, and ¼ teaspoon pepper. Cover and refrigerate 15 minutes.
3. To prepare glaze, combine nectar and next 6 ingredients in a small saucepan; bring to a boil. Reduce heat, and simmer until reduced to ¼ cup (about 10 minutes). Remove from heat; set aside.
4. Place fillets, skin side up, on grill rack coated with cooking spray. Grill 2 minutes; carefully turn over, and grill 4 minutes or until fish flakes easily when tested with a fork or until desired degree of doneness. Brush each fillet with 1 tablespoon glaze; grill 30 seconds. Yield: 4 servings (serving size: 1 fillet).

CALORIES 342 (34% from fat); FAT 13.1g (sat 3.1g, mono 5.7g, poly 3.2g); PROTEIN 36.4g; CARB 18.1g; FIBER 0.2g; CHOL 87mg; IRON 0.7mg; SODIUM 482mg; CALC 25mg

From the Grill Menu 3

serves 4

Chile-Spiced Tenderloin Steaks

Toasted corn and tomato salad*

Flour tortilla

*Whisk together 2 tablespoons lime juice, 1 tablespoon olive oil, 1 teaspoon bottled minced garlic, ¼ teaspoon salt, and ¼ teaspoon hot sauce in a small bowl. Toast 1 cup fresh corn in dry skillet 2 minutes or until golden, stirring frequently. Toss corn with 1 cup halved cherry tomatoes, ½ cup diced red bell pepper, ½ cup diced red onion, and 1 teaspoon fresh oregano in a medium bowl. Stir in juice mixture. Let stand 15 minutes. Toss gently before serving.

Game Plan

1. Combine marinade ingredients, and let steaks stand.
2. Prepare toasted corn and tomato salad:
   • Combine all ingredients; cover and let stand.
3. While salad stands:
   • Grill steaks.
4. While steaks rest:
   • Toss salad gently.

QUICK & EASY
Chile-Spiced Tenderloin Steaks

Ancho chile powder is found in the spice aisle of most supermarkets. Use bottled minced garlic to save a little prep time. Serve with lime wedges.

TOTAL TIME: 35 MINUTES

3 tablespoons fresh lime juice
2 teaspoons minced garlic
1 teaspoon ancho chile powder
1 teaspoon dried oregano
¾ teaspoon kosher salt
½ teaspoon ground cumin
½ teaspoon ground coriander
½ teaspoon freshly ground black pepper
¼ teaspoon ground red pepper
4 (4-ounce) beef tenderloin steaks (about 1 inch thick)
Cooking spray

1. Prepare grill.
2. Combine first 9 ingredients in a small bowl, and rub marinade mixture evenly over both sides of steaks. Let steaks stand at room temperature 15 minutes. Remove steaks from marinade, and discard remaining marinade. Place steaks on a grill rack coated with cooking spray; grill 5 minutes on each side or until desired degree of doneness. Remove from grill, and let stand 5 minutes. Yield: 4 servings (serving size: 1 steak).

CALORIES 173 (35% from fat); FAT 6.8g (sat 2.6g, mono 2.7g, poly 0.3g); PROTEIN 24.5g; CARB 2g; FIBER 0.4g; CHOL 67mg; IRON 1.9mg; SODIUM 424mg; CALC 29mg

Harvest Treat

A Washington State farmer develops a delicious meal with nectarines from her orchard.

Sliced Steak with Nectarines and Arugula

Because of their thin skins, nectarines don't require peeling for this salad.

  2 teaspoons olive oil
  2 garlic cloves, crushed
  1 (1¼-pound) flank steak, trimmed and cut into ⅛-inch-thick slices
  1 teaspoon kosher salt
  ½ teaspoon black pepper
  ½ teaspoon crushed red pepper
  1 (5-ounce) bag arugula
    Cooking spray
  ⅓ cup thinly sliced shallots (about 1 large)
  3 tablespoons balsamic vinegar
  2 nectarines, pitted and cut into ¼-inch wedges (about ⅔ pound)
  4 teaspoons fresh lemon juice
  1 ounce Parmigiano-Reggiano cheese, shaved into thin strips

1. Place oil and garlic in a large nonstick skillet over medium heat; cook 4 minutes or until garlic is lightly browned, stirring occasionally. Remove garlic with a slotted spoon, and discard. Increase heat to medium-high.
2. Sprinkle steak evenly with salt and peppers. Add steak to pan; sauté 1 minute or until desired degree of doneness. Transfer steak to a large bowl. Add arugula to bowl; toss well.
3. Wipe pan dry with a paper towel. Coat pan with cooking spray. Reduce heat to medium. Add shallots and vinegar to pan; cook 2 minutes or until shallots are soft, stirring occasionally. Add nectarine to pan; cook 30 seconds, tossing to coat. Add nectarine mixture and juice to steak mixture; toss gently. Serve with cheese. Yield: 5 servings (serving size: about 1¾ cups salad and 1 tablespoon cheese).

CALORIES 248 (33% from fat); FAT 9.1g (sat 3.6g, mono 4g, poly 0.6g); PROTEIN 27.5g; CARB 14g; FIBER 1.1g; CHOL 41mg; IRON 2.3mg; SODIUM 534mg; CALC 142mg

---

Steak and Potatoes Menu
serves 4

Cooking the steaks on a grill pan and purchasing precut potatoes help this meal come together quickly for busy weeknights.

Espresso-Grilled Tenderloin Steaks

Roasted potato wedges*

Sautéed green beans

*Preheat oven to 450°. Combine 1 (20-ounce) package of refrigerated red potato wedges (such as Simply Potatoes), 2 tablespoons olive oil, ¾ teaspoon salt, ¼ teaspoon ground cumin, and ¼ teaspoon ground red pepper on a jelly-roll pan. Bake at 450° for 20 minutes or until browned, stirring once. Garnish with parsley sprigs, if desired.

QUICK & EASY
Espresso-Grilled Tenderloin Steaks

"This recipe can be prepared year-round and served with almost any side dish."
—Michaela Rosenthal, Woodland Hills, California

    Cooking spray
  1 teaspoon finely ground espresso
  1 teaspoon light brown sugar
  1 teaspoon steak seasoning (such as McCormick Grill Mates seasoning blends)
  4 (4-ounce) beef tenderloin steaks, trimmed (1 inch thick)

1. Heat a grill pan over medium-high heat. Coat pan with cooking spray. Combine espresso, brown sugar, and seasoning in a small bowl; rub mixture evenly over both sides of steaks. Add steaks to pan; cook 4 minutes on each side or until desired degree of doneness. Yield: 4 servings (serving size: 1 steak).

CALORIES 190 (45% from fat); FAT 9.5g (sat 3.7g, mono 3.9g, poly 0.4g); PROTEIN 23.5g; CARB 1.1g; FIBER 0g; CHOL 71mg; IRON 1.5mg; SODIUM 245mg; CALC 18mg

---

QUICK & EASY
Thyme-Garlic Roasted Asparagus

"I created this hassle-free asparagus recipe, and my guests love it every time."
—Lynda Bennett, Belvedere, California

  3 garlic cloves, minced
    Cooking spray
  1 pound asparagus, trimmed
  1 teaspoon olive oil
  ½ teaspoon dried thyme
  ¼ teaspoon salt

1. Preheat oven to 400°.
2. Spread garlic in an 11 x 7–inch baking dish coated with cooking spray. Arrange asparagus in an even layer over garlic; drizzle with oil. Combine thyme and salt; sprinkle over asparagus. Bake at 400° for 15 minutes or until asparagus is crisp-tender, turning once. Yield: 4 servings.

CALORIES 45 (24% from fat); FAT 1.2g (sat 0.2g, mono 0.9g, poly 0.1g); PROTEIN 2.6g; CARB 5.8g; FIBER 2.6g; CHOL 0mg; IRON 0.6mg; SODIUM 146mg; CALC 31mg

---

QUICK & EASY
Cherry Tomato Salad with Walnut-Tarragon Dressing

"I use walnut oil to bring a subtle nutty flavor and depth to vinaigrette."
—Caroline Markunas, New York, New York

  1 tablespoon balsamic vinegar
  1 tablespoon Dijon mustard
  2 teaspoons toasted walnut oil
  ¼ teaspoon salt
  ⅛ teaspoon freshly ground black pepper
  3 cups halved cherry tomatoes (about 1½ pounds)
  1½ tablespoons finely chopped walnuts, toasted
  1½ teaspoons chopped fresh tarragon

1. Combine first 5 ingredients in a large bowl, stirring with a whisk. Add tomatoes, walnuts, and tarragon, tossing to coat. Yield: 6 servings (serving size: ½ cup).

CALORIES 53 (54% from fat); FAT 3.2g (sat 0.3g, mono 0.6g, poly 2.2g); PROTEIN 1.5g; CARB 5.9g; FIBER 1.5g; CHOL 0mg; IRON 0.5mg; SODIUM 168mg; CALC 18mg

Chicken and Sausage Gumbo

"I grew up in New Orleans and love Cajun and Creole dishes. I modified many of my family's recipes to make them healthier."

—Marian Wright, Houston, Texas

- ¼ cup all-purpose flour (about 1 ounce)
- 2 tablespoons olive oil
- 2½ cups finely chopped yellow onion (1 large)
- 1½ cups finely chopped green bell pepper (1 large)
- 1 cup finely chopped celery
- 3 garlic cloves, minced
- 1½ pounds skinless, boneless chicken breast, cut into 1½-inch pieces
- 8 ounces light smoked sausage, cut into 1-inch pieces (such as Healthy Choice)
- 2 (14½-ounce) cans no-salt-added organic diced tomatoes, undrained
- 2 (14-ounce) cans fat-free, less-sodium chicken broth
- ¼ teaspoon Worcestershire sauce
- 2 bay leaves
- ½ teaspoon salt
- ½ teaspoon black pepper
- ¼ teaspoon hot sauce
- 3 cups hot cooked rice

1. Place flour in a large Dutch oven over medium heat; cook 20 minutes or until light brown, stirring constantly with a whisk. (If flour browns too fast, remove pan from heat; stir constantly until it cools down.) Remove flour from pan, and set aside.

2. Add oil to pan. Stir in onion, bell pepper, and celery; cook 10 minutes or until onion is tender, stirring frequently. Stir in garlic; cook 30 seconds. Remove onion mixture from pan; set aside.

3. Increase heat to medium-high; add chicken and sausage to pan. Cook 4 minutes or until chicken is done; return onion mixture to pan. Remove pan from heat. Sprinkle browned flour over chicken mixture; stir well. Return pan to medium heat. Drain 1 can tomatoes; stir in 1 can drained tomatoes and 1 can undrained tomatoes. Cook 2 minutes, stirring constantly. Add broth, Worcestershire, and bay leaves; bring to a boil, stirring constantly. Cover, reduce heat, and simmer 30 minutes, stirring occasionally. Discard bay leaves. Stir in salt, black pepper, and hot sauce. Serve over rice. Yield: 6 servings (serving size: 1⅔ cups gumbo and ½ cup rice).

CALORIES 419 (20% from fat); FAT 9.2g (sat 2.1g, mono 4.2g, poly 1.1g); PROTEIN 35.8g; CARB 44.2g; FIBER 3.3g; CHOL 82mg; IRON 3.5mg; SODIUM 888mg; CALC 42mg

---

QUICK & EASY • MAKE AHEAD

Couscous-Garbanzo Salad

"This delicious salad is a great side dish for grilled fish or chicken."

—Trisha Kruse, Eagle, Idaho

- 1 cup organic vegetable broth
- 1 cup uncooked couscous
- 2 cups chopped seeded tomato (about 2 medium)
- 1 cup diced cucumber (about 1)
- 1 cup thinly sliced green onions (about 6)
- ½ cup grated carrot (1 medium)
- ½ cup diced red bell pepper
- 1 (15½-ounce) can chickpeas (garbanzo beans), drained
- 2 tablespoons extravirgin olive oil
- 2 tablespoons red wine vinegar
- 1 tablespoon fresh lemon juice
- 2 teaspoons chopped fresh oregano
- 1 teaspoon minced garlic
- ½ teaspoon salt
- ¼ teaspoon freshly ground black pepper
- ¼ teaspoon crushed red pepper

1. Bring broth to a boil in a medium saucepan, and gradually stir in couscous. Remove from heat; cover and let stand 5 minutes. Place couscous in a large bowl, and cool completely. Fluff with a fork. Stir in tomato and next 5 ingredients; toss well. Combine oil and remaining 7 ingredients in a small bowl; stir with a whisk. Add vinegar mixture to couscous mixture just before serving; toss gently. Yield: 10 servings (serving size: about ¾ cup).

CALORIES 132 (24% from fat); FAT 3.5g (sat 0.4g, mono 2.2g, poly 0.7g); PROTEIN 4g; CARB 21.4g; FIBER 3g; CHOL 0mg; IRON 0.9mg; SODIUM 246mg; CALC 29mg

---

then & now

Chocolate Chip Cookies

Low-fat desserts have always been welcome in the pages of Cooking Light.

Traci Michaelson's recipe for Chewy Chocolate Chip Cookies, included in our Reader Recipes column of January/February 1998, was no exception. We caught up with Michaelson, who agreed to try our new-and-improved recipe. The verdict in our Test Kitchens: our highest rating.

STAFF FAVORITE • MAKE AHEAD
FREEZABLE

Chocolate Chip Cookies

Store up to a week in an airtight container.

- 2¼ cups all-purpose flour (about 10 ounces)
- 1 teaspoon baking soda
- ¼ teaspoon salt
- 1 cup packed brown sugar
- ¾ cup granulated sugar
- ½ cup butter, softened
- 1 teaspoon vanilla extract
- 2 large egg whites
- ¾ cup semisweet chocolate chips
- Cooking spray

1. Preheat oven to 350°.

2. Lightly spoon flour into dry measuring cups; level with a knife. Combine flour, baking soda, and salt, stirring with a whisk.

3. Combine sugars and butter in a large bowl; beat with a mixer at medium speed until well blended. Add vanilla and egg whites; beat 1 minute. Add flour mixture and chips; beat until blended.

4. Drop dough by level tablespoons 2 inches apart onto baking sheets coated with cooking spray. Bake at 350° for 10 minutes or until lightly browned. Cool on pans 2 minutes. Remove from pans; cool completely on wire racks. Yield: 4 dozen (serving size: 1 cookie).

CALORIES 88 (31% from fat); FAT 3g (sat 1.8g, mono 0.5g, poly 0.1g); PROTEIN 1g; CARB 14.6g; FIBER 0.2g; CHOL 5mg; IRON 0.4mg; SODIUM 56mg; CALC 5mg

Sweet Stuff

Learn how different sugars enhance desserts, entrées, breads, and accompaniments.

Sugar is indispensable to cooking. It often performs more than one role in a given recipe.

It also plays multiple roles in baking. At the simplest level, it imparts sweetness. Beyond that, it helps create a light, tender crumb: When creamed with butter for a cake batter, sugar's hard crystal surfaces create pockets that trap air and expand during cooking, yielding a fluffy, tender final product. It also attracts and holds moisture, so cakes, cookies, and quick breads stay fresher longer. Sugar inhibits the development of gluten (tough, elastic proteins) to keep cakes and quick breads tender, as opposed to chewier biscuits or yeast breads that typically don't include much (if any) sugar. It helps with browning, creating golden crusts on coffeecakes and cookies, and crystallizing on brownies, pound cakes, and cookies to form crunchy, crackled tops.

When sugar is heated, it goes through a series of chemical reactions called caramelization. What starts as one-note sweet, white granulated sugar becomes nutty, amber-hued caramel—the basis of many dessert sauces or the syrupy topping for flan or crème caramel. When combined with liquid ingredients, sugar lowers the freezing point—so ice cream and sorbet stay velvety smooth and creamy and don't form solid ice.

Sugar can also be key in dishes other than desserts because it balances bitter and sour tastes. For example, coffee is too bitter sans sugar for many people. Because of its balancing effects, sugar is often added to tart salad dressings and tomato-based sauces (such as barbecue sauce) to soften the acidity. It's sprinkled over vegetables as they sauté, or meat as it's browned, to add rich color and deepen the flavor.

MAKE AHEAD
Bittersweet Brownies

¼ cup boiling water
1 tablespoon instant espresso granules or 2 tablespoons instant coffee granules
¼ cup bittersweet chocolate chips
6 tablespoons butter, melted
½ teaspoon vanilla extract
1 large egg, lightly beaten
1 large egg white, lightly beaten
1½ cups all-purpose flour (about 6¾ ounces)
1⅓ cups granulated sugar
½ cup unsweetened cocoa
1 teaspoon baking powder
¼ teaspoon salt
Cooking spray
2 teaspoons powdered sugar (optional)

1. Preheat oven to 350°.
2. Combine ¼ cup boiling water and espresso in a medium bowl. Add chocolate chips, stirring until chocolate melts; cool slightly. Stir in butter, vanilla, egg, and egg white.
3. Lightly spoon flour into dry measuring cups; level with a knife. Combine flour and next 4 ingredients, stirring with a whisk. Add coffee mixture to flour mixture, stirring just until moist. Spoon batter into a 9-inch square baking pan coated with cooking spray. Bake at 350° for 25 minutes or until a wooden pick inserted in center comes out clean. Cool in pan on a wire rack. Sprinkle with powdered sugar, if desired. Yield: 16 servings (serving size: 1 brownie).

CALORIES 171 (31% from fat); FAT 5.8g (sat 3.4g, mono 1.4g, poly 0.3g); PROTEIN 2.5g; CARB 29.3g; FIBER 1.2g; CHOL 25mg; IRON 1.1mg; SODIUM 107mg; CALC 26mg

MAKE AHEAD • FREEZABLE
Brown Sugar–Pecan Shortbread

Dark brown sugar adds rich caramel notes to these cookies; turbinado sugar provides crunch. If you don't want to bake all of the cookies at once, freeze one dough log for up to two months. Slice frozen dough, and bake; if the dough is too hard to slice, let it stand at room temperature for 10 to 15 minutes.

1½ cups all-purpose flour (about 6¾ ounces)
¼ cup cornstarch
3 tablespoons finely chopped pecans, toasted
⅛ teaspoon salt
½ cup butter, softened
½ cup packed dark brown sugar
¼ cup ice water
2 tablespoons turbinado sugar

1. Lightly spoon flour into dry measuring cups; level with a knife. Combine flour and next 3 ingredients, stirring well with a whisk. Place butter and brown sugar in a medium bowl; beat with a mixer at medium speed until light and fluffy (about 1 minute). Gradually add flour mixture, beating at low speed. (Mixture will appear crumbly.) Sprinkle ice water over flour mixture; beat at low speed just until combined. Shape dough into 2 (6-inch-long) logs; wrap each log in plastic wrap. Chill logs 1 hour or until very firm.
2. Preheat oven to 350°.
3. Line baking sheets with parchment paper. Unwrap dough; cut each log into 16 slices using a serrated knife. Place dough circles 1 inch apart on prepared baking sheets. Sprinkle tops evenly with turbinado sugar, gently pressing into dough. Bake at 350° for 18 minutes or until lightly browned. Remove from baking sheets; cool on a wire rack. Yield: 32 cookies (serving size: 1 cookie).

CALORIES 70 (44% from fat); FAT 3.4g (sat 1.9g, mono 1g, poly 0.3g); PROTEIN 0.7g; CARB 9.4g; FIBER 0.2g; CHOL 8mg; IRON 0.4mg; SODIUM 31mg; CALC 5mg

Vietnamese Caramelized Pork and Rice Noodle Salad

Brown sugar patted onto the pork caramelizes on the grill, creating crunchy blackened bits.

DRESSING:

¾ cup water
4½ tablespoons granulated sugar
3 tablespoons rice vinegar
2 tablespoons fresh lime juice
1½ tablespoons fish sauce
2 teaspoons minced peeled fresh ginger
¾ teaspoon Sriracha (hot chile sauce)
3 garlic cloves, minced

SALAD:

1 (6-ounce) package rice vermicelli
1 pound pork tenderloin, trimmed
2 teaspoons fish sauce
1 teaspoon Sriracha (hot chile sauce)
¼ teaspoon garlic powder
¼ teaspoon salt
¼ teaspoon freshly ground black pepper
3 tablespoons brown sugar
Cooking spray
2 cups thinly sliced red leaf lettuce
1 cup matchstick-cut peeled English cucumber
1 cup matchstick-cut carrot
1 cup bean sprouts
¼ cup chopped fresh basil
¼ cup chopped fresh cilantro
3 tablespoons chopped fresh mint
½ cup chopped dry-roasted peanuts
Lime wedges (optional)

1. To prepare dressing, combine first 8 ingredients in a small saucepan; cook over medium heat 5 minutes or just until sugar dissolves. Remove from heat; cool.
2. To prepare salad, place vermicelli in a large bowl. Cover with boiling water. Let stand 20 minutes or until tender. Drain and rinse with cold water; drain.
3. Prepare grill.
4. Cut tenderloin in half lengthwise. Cut each piece in half crosswise. Place each pork piece between 2 sheets of plastic wrap; pound to an even thickness using a meat mallet or small heavy skillet.

Combine 2 teaspoons fish sauce and 1 teaspoon Sriracha; drizzle over pork. Sprinkle evenly with garlic powder, salt, and pepper. Pat brown sugar onto pork.
5. Place pork on a grill rack coated with cooking spray. Grill 12 minutes or until slightly pink in center, turning pieces occasionally to prevent burning. Place pork on a cutting board; let stand 5 minutes. Cut across grain into very thin slices.
6. Combine vermicelli, lettuce, and next 6 ingredients in a large bowl. Pour dressing over salad; toss well. Top with pork and nuts. Serve with lime wedges, if desired. Yield: 6 servings (serving size: 1⅔ cups salad, about 2 ounces pork, and 4 teaspoons peanuts).

CALORIES 342 (22% from fat); FAT 8.3g (sat 1.9g, mono 3.7g, poly 1.9g); PROTEIN 19.9g; CARB 47.6g; FIBER 2.7g; CHOL 43mg; IRON 1.9mg; SODIUM 821mg; CALC 48mg

Bacon and Brown Sugar-Braised Collard Greens

Cooking collard greens in a lightly sweetened braising liquid curbs their bitter bite.

2 bacon slices
1 cup chopped onion
1 garlic clove, minced
2 cups water
2 tablespoons cider vinegar
1 tablespoon brown sugar
½ teaspoon salt
½ teaspoon ground red pepper
1 (16-ounce) package prewashed torn collard greens

1. Cook bacon in a Dutch oven over medium-high heat until crisp. Remove bacon from pan, reserving drippings in pan. Crumble bacon; set aside. Add onion and garlic to pan; cook over medium heat 5 minutes or until tender, stirring occasionally. Stir in crumbled bacon, 2 cups water, and next 4 ingredients. Gradually add greens. Cover, reduce heat, and simmer 1 hour or until tender. Yield: 8 servings (serving size: ½ cup).

CALORIES 60 (42% from fat); FAT 2.8g (sat 0.9g, mono 1.2g, poly 0.4g); PROTEIN 2.3g; CARB 7.2g; FIBER 2.4g; CHOL 4mg; IRON 0.2mg; SODIUM 208mg; CALC 90mg

Caramel Layer Cake

Work quickly to spread the frosting on the cake before it begins to set. We call for light brown sugar in the cake to lend a subtly sweet flavor, but dark brown in the frosting to provide a contrasting rich caramel flavor. You can use light brown sugar for both the cake and frosting, if you prefer.

CAKE:

Cooking spray
1 tablespoon cake flour
1 cup packed light brown sugar
7 tablespoons butter, softened
½ cup egg substitute
2 cups cake flour (about 8 ounces)
1 teaspoon baking powder
½ teaspoon baking soda
¼ teaspoon salt
1 cup fat-free milk

FROSTING:

½ cup packed dark brown sugar
3 tablespoons butter
1 teaspoon vanilla extract
⅛ teaspoon salt
1 (14-ounce) can sweetened condensed milk

1. Preheat oven to 350°.
2. To prepare cake, coat 2 (8-inch) round cake pans with cooking spray; line bottoms of pans with wax paper. Lightly coat wax paper with cooking spray; dust pans with 1 tablespoon flour. Set aside.
3. Place light brown sugar and 7 tablespoons butter in a large mixing bowl; beat with a mixer at medium speed 3 minutes or until well blended. Add egg substitute; beat well. Lightly spoon 2 cups flour into dry measuring cups; level with a knife. Combine flour, baking powder, baking soda, and ¼ teaspoon salt, stirring well with a whisk. Add flour mixture to sugar mixture alternately with 1 cup milk, beginning and ending with flour mixture.
4. Spoon batter into prepared pans. Sharply tap pans once on counter to remove air bubbles. Bake at 350° for 25 minutes or until a wooden pick inserted in center comes out clean. Cool in pans
Continued

10 minutes on a wire rack; remove from pans. Remove wax paper; discard. Cool cakes completely on wire rack.

5. To prepare frosting, combine dark brown sugar and remaining 4 ingredients in a medium, heavy saucepan over medium heat; bring to a boil. Cook 2 minutes or until mixture is thick, stirring constantly.

6. Place 1 cake layer on a plate; spread with ⅓ cup frosting. Top with remaining cake layer. Spread remaining frosting over top and sides of cake. Yield: 16 servings (serving size: 1 slice).

CALORIES 298 (29% from fat); FAT 9.7g (sat 6g, mono 2.5g, poly 0.5g); PROTEIN 5g; CARB 48.5g; FIBER 0.3g; CHOL 28mg; IRON 1.9mg; SODIUM 238mg; CALC 136mg

STAFF FAVORITE

Whole Wheat Cinnamon Rolls

Brown sugar sweetens the filling, and powdered sugar dissolves into a milky glaze that's drizzled over the top.

DOUGH:

1½ packages dry yeast (about 3¼ teaspoons)
¾ cup warm fat-free milk (100° to 110°)
¼ cup warm water (100° to 110°)
¼ cup butter, softened
¼ cup honey
½ teaspoon salt
1½ teaspoons fresh lemon juice
1 large egg, lightly beaten
1 large egg white, lightly beaten
2½ cups all-purpose flour, divided (about 11¼ ounces)
1½ cups whole wheat flour (about 7 ounces)
Cooking spray

FILLING:

¼ cup packed brown sugar
1½ tablespoons ground cinnamon
⅛ teaspoon ground nutmeg
⅓ cup raisins

GLAZE:

¾ cup powdered sugar, sifted
¾ teaspoon vanilla extract
5 teaspoons fat-free milk

1. To prepare dough, dissolve yeast in warm milk and ¼ cup warm water in a large bowl; let stand 5 minutes or until foamy. Add butter and next 5 ingredients; stir well. Lightly spoon flours into dry measuring cups; level with a knife. Add 2 cups all-purpose flour and whole wheat flour, stirring until a soft dough forms. Turn dough out onto a floured surface. Knead until smooth and elastic (about 8 minutes); add enough of remaining all-purpose flour, 1 tablespoon at a time, to prevent dough from sticking to hands (dough will feel sticky). Place dough in a large bowl coated with cooking spray, turning to coat top. Cover and let rise in a warm place (85°), free from drafts, 1 hour or until doubled in size. (Gently press two fingers into dough. If indentation remains, dough has risen enough.) Punch dough down; roll into a 16 x 12–inch rectangle on a floured surface. Coat surface of dough with cooking spray.

2. To prepare filling, combine brown sugar, cinnamon, and nutmeg; sprinkle over dough, leaving a ½-inch border. Sprinkle raisins over dough, pressing gently into dough. Roll up rectangle tightly, starting with a long edge, pressing firmly to eliminate air pockets; pinch seam to seal. Cut dough into 16 rolls. Place rolls, cut sides up, in a 13 x 9–inch baking pan coated with cooking spray. Cover and let rise 45 minutes or until doubled in size.

3. Preheat oven to 375°.

4. Uncover rolls. Bake at 375° for 22 minutes or until lightly browned. Cool in pan on a wire rack.

5. To prepare glaze, place powdered sugar and vanilla in a small bowl. Add 5 teaspoons milk, 1 teaspoon at a time, stirring to form a thick glaze. Drizzle glaze evenly over rolls. Yield: 16 servings (serving size: 1 roll).

CALORIES 209 (16% from fat); FAT 3.7g (sat 2g, mono 0.9g, poly 0.3g); PROTEIN 5.1g; CARB 40.4g; FIBER 2.6g; CHOL 21mg; IRON 2mg; SODIUM 111mg; CALC 39mg

Grilled Peaches with Amaretto-Pecan Caramel Sauce

Caramel is nothing more than melted, browned sugar; we add water to hasten the melting process and reduce the risk of burning the sugar.

1 cup granulated sugar
⅓ cup water
½ cup apple cider
2 tablespoons amaretto (almond-flavored liqueur)
1 teaspoon chilled butter
⅓ cup chopped pecans, toasted
6 firm ripe peaches, halved and pitted (about 3 pounds)
1 tablespoon brown sugar
¼ teaspoon salt
Cooking spray

1. Prepare grill.

2. Combine granulated sugar and ⅓ cup water in a medium, heavy saucepan over medium-high heat; cook until sugar dissolves, stirring gently to dissolve sugar evenly. Continue cooking 8 minutes or until golden brown (do not stir); gently tilt pan and swirl mixture to evenly brown. Remove from heat. Slowly add cider, amaretto, and butter, stirring constantly with a long-handled wooden spoon (mixture will bubble vigorously). Cook over medium-low heat 5 minutes or until smooth. Stir in pecans. Remove from heat.

3. Sprinkle cut sides of peaches evenly with brown sugar and salt. Place peaches, cut sides up, on a grill rack coated with cooking spray; grill 2 minutes on each side or until tender. Serve warm with sauce. Yield: 6 servings (serving size: 2 peach halves and about 3 tablespoons sauce).

CALORIES 269 (19% from fat); FAT 5.8g (sat 0.8g, mono 3g, poly 1.6g); PROTEIN 2g; CARB 55g; FIBER 3g; CHOL 2mg; IRON 0.6mg; SODIUM 106mg; CALC 17mg

Sugar's versatility makes it crucial to savory applications as well as desserts.

Michael Pollan's Dilemma

An author known for his food expertise faces the challenge of many parents: learning to entice a particular eater at home.

Michael Pollan spends a lot of time thinking about food. The author of *The Omnivore's Dilemma*, which explores the ethics, economics, and environmental issues related to how our food is produced, Pollan also loves the simple pleasures of cooking and eating. He will try just about anything and clearly enjoys trying new cuisines, especially as prepared at the tables of friends and restaurants in Berkeley, California—locally known as Gourmet Gulch—where he lives.

But dinner at home, which he shares with his wife, artist Judith Belzer, and their son, Isaac, 14, isn't always so simple—or enjoyable. Pollan may have investigated the complexities of big agribusiness, the organic industry, family farms, and hunting and foraging his own food, but he's still working to come up with meals his teenage son will enjoy. Here are a few of his favorite entrées.

QUICK & EASY
Chicken Skewers with Soy-Mirin Marinade

Isaac enjoys Japanese-style grilled specialties. This marinade would also pair nicely with salmon. Serve with sautéed snow peas.

- ⅓ cup mirin (sweet rice wine)
- ⅓ cup low-sodium soy sauce
- 1 teaspoon dark sesame oil
- 1½ pounds skinless, boneless chicken breast, cut lengthwise into 1-inch strips
- 1 large red bell pepper, cut into 8 pieces
- 1 large green bell pepper, cut into 8 pieces
- Cooking spray
- 2 tablespoons sesame seeds, toasted
- 3 cups hot cooked rice

1. Combine first 3 ingredients in a large bowl; add chicken to bowl, and toss to coat. Let stand 15 minutes, turning chicken occasionally.
2. Prepare grill.
3. Remove chicken from bowl, reserving marinade. Place marinade in a small saucepan; bring to a boil. Cook until reduced to ¼ cup (about 5 minutes). Thread chicken and bell peppers on 8 (12-inch) wooden skewers. Brush skewers with marinade. Place skewers on grill rack coated with cooking spray. Grill 4 minutes on each side or until done, brushing occasionally with remaining marinade. Remove from grill; sprinkle with sesame seeds. Serve with rice. Yield: 4 servings (serving size: 2 skewers and ¾ cup rice).

CALORIES 463 (17% from fat); FAT 8.5g (sat 1.8g, mono 2.4g, poly 1.9g); PROTEIN 44.9g; CARB 44.5g; FIBER 3.1g; CHOL 108mg; IRON 4.6mg; SODIUM 814mg; CALC 46mg

Italian-Style Grilled Steak

The family enjoyed a steak dish similar to this on a family trip to Italy. Drizzling the cooked steak with olive oil is a traditional finishing touch, so this dish calls for your best-quality oil. Freeze the beef for 10 to 15 minutes to make it easier to slice. Garnish with fresh rosemary or thyme sprigs.

- 1 (1-pound) beef rib-eye steak, trimmed
- 1 tablespoon finely chopped fresh rosemary
- 1 tablespoon finely chopped fresh thyme
- 2 tablespoons fresh lemon juice
- 1 garlic clove, minced
- ½ teaspoon kosher salt
- ¼ teaspoon freshly ground black pepper
- Cooking spray
- 4 cups hot cooked spaghetti (about 4 ounces uncooked pasta)
- 4 teaspoons extravirgin olive oil

1. Cut beef across grain into ¼-inch-thick slices. Combine beef, rosemary, thyme, lemon juice, and garlic in a large zip-top plastic bag; seal. Marinate beef in refrigerator 1 hour, turning occasionally.
2. Prepare grill.
3. Remove beef from bag, discarding marinade. Sprinkle beef with salt and pepper. Place beef on grill rack coated with cooking spray; grill 1 minute on each side or until desired degree of doneness. Serve with pasta. Drizzle oil over beef and pasta. Yield: 4 servings (serving size: 3 ounces steak, 1 cup pasta, and 1 teaspoon oil).

CALORIES 489 (41% from fat); FAT 22.2g (sat 7.3g, mono 10.5g, poly 1.4g); PROTEIN 36.6g; CARB 33.8g; FIBER 1.7g; CHOL 126mg; IRON 3.8mg; SODIUM 300mg; CALC 37mg

QUICK & EASY
Garlic-Herb Roasted Rack of Lamb

Pollan chooses high-quality grass-fed meats from local producers. The mustardy rub enhances the flavor of the meat.

- 2 tablespoons fresh lemon juice
- 2 tablespoons chopped fresh thyme
- 1 tablespoon chopped fresh flat-leaf parsley
- 1 tablespoon Dijon mustard
- 1 garlic clove, minced
- 1 (1½-pound) French-cut rack of lamb (8 ribs)
- ½ teaspoon salt
- ¼ teaspoon freshly ground black pepper
- Cooking spray

1. Preheat oven to 425°.
2. Combine first 5 ingredients in a small bowl; stir with a whisk.
3. Sprinkle lamb evenly with salt and pepper; rub lamb evenly with herb mixture. Place on a jelly-roll pan or broiler pan coated with cooking spray. Bake at 425° for 35 minutes or until a thermometer registers 145° (medium-rare). Cover with foil; let stand 10 minutes before serving. Cut rack into 8 pieces. Yield: 4 servings (serving size: 2 chops).

CALORIES 293 (48% from fat); FAT 15.7g (sat 5.6g, mono 6.3g, poly 1.4g); PROTEIN 34.2g; CARB 1.3g; FIBER 0.3g; CHOL 112mg; IRON 3.1mg; SODIUM 463mg; CALC 29mg

inspired vegetarian
Supper for Two

A week's worth of entrées, with fresh ideas for leftover ingredients.

Cooking for two is certainly easier than cooking for a large group, but the whole business of leftovers can be tricky. To help solve the dilemma of extra servings and ingredients, we've tailored a week's worth of meatless entrées that serve just two. Two platefuls, two bowlfuls, just two portions every time.

Tomato and Parmesan Strata

2 (1-ounce) slices whole wheat bread, cut into 1-inch cubes
Cooking spray
½ cup chopped onion
2 cups baby spinach leaves
1 garlic clove, minced
½ teaspoon chopped fresh thyme
¼ teaspoon salt
⅛ teaspoon black pepper
3 large egg whites, lightly beaten
1 large egg, lightly beaten
1 cup chopped seeded plum tomato (about 2 medium)
2 tablespoons grated fresh Parmesan cheese

1. Preheat oven to 375°.
2. Place bread cubes in a 1½-quart baking dish coated with cooking spray.
3. Heat a large nonstick skillet over medium-high heat. Coat pan with cooking spray. Add onion to pan; sauté 3 minutes or until tender. Add spinach and garlic; sauté 2 minutes or until spinach wilts. Remove from heat.
4. Combine thyme, salt, black pepper, egg whites, and egg in a medium bowl; stir with a whisk. Stir in spinach mixture and tomato. Pour egg mixture over bread cubes in baking dish; sprinkle with cheese.
5. Bake at 375° for 20 minutes or until set; let stand 5 minutes. Yield: 2 servings (serving size: about 2 cups).

CALORIES 186 (29% from fat); FAT 5.9g (sat 2g, mono 1.6g, poly 0.5g); PROTEIN 16.9g; CARB 18g; FIBER 5.3g; CHOL 112mg; IRON 2.3mg; SODIUM 684mg; CALC 183mg

Orange-Glazed Tofu Triangles with Sesame Rice

Adding a weight (such as a cutting board) while the tofu drains on paper towels presses liquid out, which results in a crispier exterior when cooked on the grill pan. Buy water-packed tofu, not the silken variety.

1 (12.3-ounce) package water-packed extrafirm light tofu
2 tablespoons orange juice
1 tablespoon low-sodium soy sauce, divided
1½ teaspoons rice vinegar
1 teaspoon honey
½ teaspoon chili garlic sauce, divided
¼ teaspoon grated peeled fresh ginger
¼ teaspoon salt, divided
Cooking spray
1 teaspoon dark sesame oil
½ cup frozen green peas, thawed
½ cup grated carrot
¼ cup thinly sliced green onions
1 cup hot cooked long-grain rice
1 tablespoon sesame seeds, toasted

1. Cut tofu in half crosswise; reserve one tofu half for another use. Cut tofu half lengthwise into 3 (¾-inch-thick) slices; cut each slice in half diagonally. Arrange tofu pieces in a single layer on several layers of heavy-duty paper towels. Cover tofu with additional paper towels; place a cutting board on top of tofu, and let stand 15 minutes.
2. Combine juice, 1½ teaspoons soy sauce, vinegar, honey, ¼ teaspoon chili garlic sauce, and ginger in a shallow dish, stirring with a whisk. Remove cutting board and paper towels from tofu; sprinkle ⅛ teaspoon salt over tofu. Add tofu slices to juice mixture in dish, turning to coat. Cover and marinate at room temperature 30 minutes, turning tofu slices after 15 minutes.
3. Heat a grill pan over medium heat. Coat pan with cooking spray. Drain tofu; discard marinade. Add tofu to pan; cook 3 minutes or until lightly browned. Turn tofu over; cook 2 minutes. Set aside; keep warm.
4. Heat oil in a medium nonstick skillet over medium heat. Add peas, carrot, and onions; cook 2 minutes. Stir in 1½ teaspoons soy sauce, ¼ teaspoon chili garlic sauce, and ⅛ teaspoon salt. Add rice; cook 2 minutes or until thoroughly heated. Stir in sesame seeds. Place 1 cup rice mixture on each of 2 plates, and arrange 3 tofu pieces on each. Yield: 2 servings.

CALORIES 275 (18% from fat); FAT 5.5g (sat 0.5g, mono 1g, poly 1.4g); PROTEIN 13.6g; CARB 41.3g; FIBER 4.6g; CHOL 0mg; IRON 3.2mg; SODIUM 660mg; CALC 62mg

Sweet and Sour Tofu

Serve with a spinach and mushroom salad sprinkled with toasted chopped almonds. Be sure to purchase water-packed tofu; the silken is not firm enough for the draining step when it is weighted down with the cutting board.

1 (12.3-ounce) package water-packed extrafirm light tofu
1 teaspoon canola oil
¼ teaspoon salt, divided
¼ teaspoon minced peeled fresh ginger
1 red bell pepper, cut into ¼-inch strips (about 1½ cups)
¾ cup unsweetened pineapple juice, divided
1 teaspoon cornstarch
2 tablespoons lemon juice
1½ tablespoons low-sodium soy sauce
1 teaspoon sugar
¼ teaspoon chili garlic sauce (such as Lee Kum Kee)
2 tablespoons chopped fresh cilantro
1 tablespoon thinly sliced green onions
1½ cups hot cooked long-grain rice

1. Cut tofu into 6 pieces. Arrange tofu pieces in a single layer on several layers of heavy-duty paper towels. Cover tofu with additional paper towels; place a cutting board on top of tofu, and let stand 15 minutes. Remove cutting board and paper towels. Cut tofu pieces into ¼-inch cubes; set aside.

2. Heat oil in a nonstick skillet over medium-high heat. Add tofu; sprinkle with ⅛ teaspoon salt. Cook 8 minutes, stirring frequently. Transfer tofu to a plate. Add ginger and bell pepper to pan; sauté 2 minutes or until crisp-tender.

3. Combine 2 teaspoons pineapple juice and cornstarch in a small bowl; set aside. Add remaining pineapple juice to pan. Stir in ⅛ teaspoon salt, lemon juice, soy sauce, sugar, and chili garlic sauce. Add cornstarch mixture; stir well. Bring to a boil; cook 1 minute. Return tofu to pan, stirring gently to coat. Stir in cilantro and onions. Spoon ¾ cup rice onto each of 2 serving plates; top each serving with 1½ cups tofu mixture. Yield: 2 servings.

CALORIES 334 (13% from fat); FAT 5g (sat 0.6g, mono 2g, poly 1.8g); PROTEIN 15.6g; CARB 57.3g; FIBER 4.3g; CHOL 0mg; IRON 2.9mg; SODIUM 853mg; CALC 78mg

QUICK & EASY
Mushroom Ravioli with Parmesan-Chive Sauce

Freeze leftover wonton wrappers in heavy-duty zip-top bags.

RAVIOLI:

½ (8-ounce) package button mushrooms
½ (6-ounce) package presliced portobello mushrooms
1 teaspoon olive oil
1 teaspoon butter
2 tablespoons finely chopped shallots
⅛ teaspoon salt
14 wonton wrappers
1 teaspoon cornstarch

SAUCE:

½ cup 1% low-fat milk
1 tablespoon all-purpose flour
2 tablespoons grated fresh Parmesan cheese
1 tablespoon chopped fresh chives
⅛ teaspoon salt
Dash of freshly ground black pepper

REMAINING INGREDIENT:

Fresh chives (optional)

1. To prepare ravioli, place mushrooms in food processor; pulse 10 times or until finely chopped. Heat oil and butter in a large nonstick skillet over medium-high heat. Add shallots, and sauté 2 minutes. Add mushrooms and ⅛ teaspoon salt; cook 5 minutes or until moisture evaporates, stirring occasionally.

2. Working with one wonton wrapper at a time (cover remaining wrappers with a damp towel to keep them from drying), spoon about 2 teaspoons mushroom mixture into center of each wrapper. Moisten edges of dough with water; bring two opposite corners together. Pinch edges together to seal, forming a triangle. Place ravioli on a large baking sheet sprinkled with cornstarch.

3. To prepare sauce, combine milk and flour in a small saucepan over medium-low heat; stir with a whisk. Cook 4 minutes or until slightly thickened, stirring frequently. Remove from heat; stir in cheese, 1 tablespoon chives, ⅛ teaspoon salt, and pepper. Set aside; keep warm.

4. Cook ravioli in boiling water 2 minutes or until tender. Drain. Serve with sauce. Garnish with fresh chives, if desired. Yield: 2 servings (serving size: 7 ravioli and 3 tablespoons sauce).

CALORIES 334 (22% from fat); FAT 8.2g (sat 3.5g, mono 3.3g, poly 0.8g); PROTEIN 17.3g; CARB 48.7g; FIBER 2.5g; CHOL 18mg; IRON 3mg; SODIUM 896mg; CALC 410mg

---

Dinner for Two Menu
serves 2

A light salad provides contrast to the heady, robust Moroccan stew.

Vegetarian Harira

Carrot and cucumber salad*

Baked pita wedges

*Using a vegetable peeler, shave 1 medium peeled carrot into ribbons. Shave 1 (6-inch) piece English cucumber to yield ¾ cup ribbons. Combine ribbons in a medium bowl. Combine 1 tablespoon fresh lemon juice, 2 teaspoons extravirgin olive oil, ⅛ teaspoon salt, and ⅛ teaspoon ground red pepper, stirring with a whisk. Drizzle juice mixture over ribbons; toss to coat.

MAKE AHEAD
Vegetarian Harira

Several spices give this chickpea and lentil soup rich flavor without lamb, the traditional meat used in the Moroccan dish. Pair the soup with baked pita wedges. Freeze the leftover mushroom broth to use in place of water in homemade vegetable soups.

1 tablespoon canola oil
½ cup chopped onion
¼ cup chopped celery
1 cup warm water
Pinch of saffron threads
¼ teaspoon salt, divided
⅛ teaspoon minced peeled fresh ginger
⅛ teaspoon ground red pepper
⅛ teaspoon ground cinnamon
1 garlic clove, minced
1 cup organic mushroom broth (such as Pacific Natural Foods)
¾ cup chopped seeded plum tomato
¼ cup dried small red lentils
1 (15-ounce) can no-salt-added chickpeas (garbanzo beans), drained
1½ tablespoons chopped fresh cilantro
1½ tablespoons chopped fresh parsley

1. Heat oil in a large saucepan over medium heat. Add onion and celery to pan; sauté 4 minutes or until tender. Combine 1 cup warm water and saffron; let stand 2 minutes. Add ⅛ teaspoon salt, ginger, red pepper, cinnamon, and garlic to pan; cook 1 minute. Add saffron mixture, broth, tomato, lentils, and chickpeas; bring to a boil. Reduce heat, and simmer 20 minutes or until lentils are tender. Stir in cilantro, parsley, and ⅛ teaspoon salt. Yield: 2 servings (serving size: 1½ cups).

CALORIES 323 (25% from fat); FAT 8.9g (sat 0.6g, mono 4.3g, poly 2.5g); PROTEIN 14.8g; CARB 47.2g; FIBER 9.7g; CHOL 0mg; IRON 3.8mg; SODIUM 611mg; CALC 95mg

Onion and Fresh Herb Omelet with Mixed Greens

Add whole fresh strawberries and whole wheat toast for an easy weeknight brunch or light supper during the week.

OMELET:

- ½ cup egg substitute
- ¼ cup fat-free milk
- 1½ teaspoons minced fresh parsley
- ½ teaspoon minced fresh thyme
- ¼ teaspoon salt
- ⅛ teaspoon freshly ground black pepper
- 1 large egg, lightly beaten
- ¼ cup all-purpose flour (about 1 ounce)
- Cooking spray
- 2 cups vertically sliced onion
- 1 garlic clove, crushed

SALAD:

- 3 cups loosely packed gourmet salad greens
- 1½ teaspoons red wine vinegar
- 1 teaspoon extravirgin olive oil
- 2 tablespoons crumbled goat cheese
- 1½ teaspoons sliced almonds, toasted

1. To prepare omelet, combine first 7 ingredients in a small bowl, stirring with a whisk. Lightly spoon flour into a dry measuring cup; level with a knife. Add flour to egg mixture; stir well.
2. Heat a large nonstick skillet over medium-high heat. Coat pan with cooking spray. Add onion to pan; sauté 7 minutes or until browned. Add garlic; sauté 1 minute. Pour egg mixture over onion mixture in pan. Reduce heat, and cook 3 minutes or until set. Loosen omelet with a spatula, and fold in half; cook 1 minute. Cut omelet in half; place one half on each of 2 plates.
3. To prepare salad, combine salad greens, vinegar, and oil; toss well. Arrange 1½ cups greens on top of each serving; top each serving with 1 tablespoon cheese and ¾ teaspoon almonds. Yield: 2 servings.

CALORIES 291 (30% from fat); FAT 9.8g (sat 2.7g, mono 4.3g, poly 2g); PROTEIN 18g; CARB 33.8g; FIBER 4.7g; CHOL 110mg; IRON 4.2mg; SODIUM 507mg; CALC 189mg

Tempeh with Curried Cashew Sauce

Once opened, *tempeh* (TEHM-pay), otherwise known as "mildly fermented soybean cakes," can be frozen in an airtight container up to one year from the sell-by date. Soy tempeh's chewy texture soaks up the flavor of the rich cashew sauce. Serve over long-grain brown rice, if you wish.

TEMPEH:

- 2 tablespoons rice vinegar
- 2 tablespoons low-sodium soy sauce
- 1½ tablespoons honey
- 1½ teaspoons finely chopped peeled fresh ginger
- 1 garlic clove, minced
- 1 (8-ounce) package organic tempeh, cut into ½-inch cubes

SAUCE:

- 1 teaspoon olive oil
- 2 tablespoons coarsely chopped unsalted cashews
- ½ cup chopped onion
- ¼ teaspoon curry powder
- 1 garlic clove, minced
- ¼ cup 2% reduced-fat milk
- 2 tablespoons hot water
- ⅛ teaspoon salt

REMAINING INGREDIENT:

- 1 (6-inch) whole wheat pita, cut into 4 wedges

1. To prepare tempeh, heat a medium saucepan over medium-high heat. Add first 5 ingredients to pan, stirring with a whisk. Add tempeh; bring to a boil. Cook 3 minutes or until liquid is almost evaporated, stirring frequently. Place tempeh mixture in a medium bowl; cover and keep warm.
2. To prepare sauce, heat oil in a small saucepan over medium-high heat. Add cashews to pan; cook 2 minutes or until lightly browned. Add onion to pan; sauté 3 minutes or until tender. Add curry powder and 1 garlic clove to pan; cook 1 minute, stirring constantly. Remove from heat. Stir in milk.
3. Place cashew mixture, 2 tablespoons hot water, and salt in a blender. Remove center piece of blender lid (to allow steam to escape); secure blender lid on blender. Place a clean towel over opening in blender lid (to avoid splatters). Blend until smooth, scraping sides. Add cashew sauce to tempeh in bowl; toss gently to coat. Serve with pita wedges. Yield: 2 servings (serving size: about 1 cup tempeh mixture and 2 pita wedges).

CALORIES 414 (28% from fat); FAT 12.9g (sat 3.5g, mono 4.2g, poly 1g); PROTEIN 30.7g; CARB 48.2g; FIBER 9.6g; CHOL 2mg; IRON 5.3mg; SODIUM 778mg; CALC 248mg

entertaining
Fabulous Fish Soups

As the weather warms, serve these light soups for casual gatherings.

In seaports around the world—in countries from Brazil to India to Vietnam—fish soup takes pride of place at family tables and other gatherings. Simple, authentic, and full of flavor, fish soup is well-suited to entertaining wherever you are. As early summer approaches, fish makes a light base for soups that won't require much effort or a battery of equipment to prepare.

Fish stock—the backbone for many of these recipes—is less time-consuming to prepare than beef or chicken stock. At the market, buy whole fish, have the fishmonger fillet it, and take the bones along with the fillets. You can freeze the bones until you're ready to use them, or make the stock ahead of time. The stock freezes well, and it's great for making pasta dishes, sauces, and more.

To prepare for your party, get a jump on the cooking. Make the soup up to a day ahead, leaving out the fish. As the soup reheats, add the fish to cook just before serving. Round out the menu with a tossed green salad and a simple side dish, such as hot cooked herbed rice or crusty bread.

Armed with these recipes, a stockpot, wooden spoon, blender, and sieve, you have the elements for superb soup and a great casual gathering.

Mussel Soup with Green Curry

The soup is moderately spicy, but you can use more or less chile, depending on your taste. Serve with sticky rice.

CURRY PASTE:
- 1½ teaspoons coriander seeds
- 1½ teaspoons cumin seeds
- ½ teaspoon black peppercorns
- 2 whole cloves
- 1 cup chopped fresh cilantro
- ½ cup chopped peeled fresh lemongrass (about 2 stalks)
- 2 tablespoons grated peeled fresh ginger
- 1 tablespoon Thai fish sauce (such as Three Crabs)
- 1 tablespoon dark sesame oil
- 2 teaspoons grated lime rind
- 5 garlic cloves, peeled
- 4 shallots, halved (about ¼ pound)
- 1 serrano chile
- ¼ cup water

SOUP:
- 1½ teaspoons dark sesame oil
- 4 cups water
- 1 cup dry white wine
- 1 (8-ounce) bottle clam juice
- 60 mussels (about 1½ pounds), scrubbed and debearded
- ⅓ cup chopped fresh cilantro

1. To prepare curry paste, heat a small, heavy skillet over medium-high heat. Add first 4 ingredients to pan; cook 1 minute or until fragrant, stirring frequently. Place spice mixture in a spice or coffee grinder; process mixture until finely ground.

2. Place ground spices, 1 cup cilantro, and next 8 ingredients in a food processor; process until chopped, scraping sides. With processor on, slowly pour ¼ cup water through food chute; process until smooth.

3. To prepare soup, heat 1½ teaspoons oil in a large Dutch oven over medium-high heat. Add curry paste to pan; sauté 3 minutes. Add 4 cups water, wine, and clam juice; bring to a boil. Reduce heat, and simmer 30 minutes; add mussels. Cover and cook over medium-high heat 5 minutes or until mussels open; discard any unopened shells. Sprinkle with ⅓ cup cilantro. Serve immediately. Yield: 6 servings (serving size: about 1¼ cups).

CALORIES 238 (28% from fat); FAT 7.5g (sat 1.3g, mono 2.4g, poly 2.5g); PROTEIN 20.7g; CARB 14.6g; FIBER 1.1g; CHOL 46mg; IRON 7.9mg; SODIUM 784mg; CALC 88mg

---

QUICK & EASY
Greek-Style Clam Soup

For casual entertaining, make the broth ahead of time, through step one, and just reheat it to cook the clams.

- 2 tablespoons olive oil
- 1 cup chopped onion
- ½ teaspoon salt
- 5 garlic cloves, minced
- 3 cups chopped seeded peeled tomato
- 3 cups water
- 1 cup dry white wine
- 2 (8-ounce) bottles clam juice
- 30 littleneck clams, scrubbed (about 2 pounds)
- ⅓ cup chopped fresh parsley
- ¼ cup chopped fresh oregano
- 2 tablespoons fresh lemon juice
- 3 cups hot cooked orzo (about 1½ cups uncooked rice-shaped pasta)
- 6 tablespoons crumbled feta cheese

1. Heat oil in a large Dutch oven over medium-high heat. Add onion, salt, and garlic; sauté 4 minutes. Stir in tomato; cook 8 minutes, stirring occasionally. Stir in 3 cups water, wine, and clam juice; bring to a boil. Reduce heat, and simmer 6 minutes.

2. Add clams to pan. Cover and cook 10 minutes or until clams open; discard any unopened shells. Remove from heat. Stir in parsley, oregano, and lemon juice. Place ½ cup pasta in each of 6 soup bowls; ladle 5 clams and about 1 cup broth over each serving. Top each serving with 1 tablespoon cheese. Yield: 6 servings.

CALORIES 306 (23% from fat); FAT 7.9g (sat 2.3g, mono 3.9g, poly 0.8g); PROTEIN 14g; CARB 39.8g; FIBER 2.7g; CHOL 26mg; IRON 8.7mg; SODIUM 511mg; CALC 122mg

---

Cioppino

According to legend, Portuguese and Italian immigrants who settled in the San Francisco Bay area created *cioppino* (chuh-PEE-noh).

STOCK:
- 1½ teaspoons olive oil
- 1½ cups sliced celery
- ¾ cup sliced carrot
- 2 tablespoons tomato paste
- 3 garlic cloves, minced
- 1 onion, peeled and quartered
- 8 thyme sprigs
- 1 bunch parsley
- 1 pound fish bones
- 5 cups water

SOUP:
- 2 tablespoons olive oil
- 1 cup finely chopped carrot
- 1½ cups thinly sliced onion
- 4 garlic cloves, minced
- 2 cups chopped seeded peeled tomato
- 2 tablespoons tomato paste
- ½ teaspoon saffron threads, crushed
- 1 teaspoon sugar
- ½ teaspoon salt
- ½ cup pinot noir or other spicy dry red wine
- 30 mussels (about 1¼ pounds), scrubbed and debearded
- 3 (6-ounce) red snapper or other firm white fish fillets, cut into 1-inch pieces
- ⅓ cup chopped fresh parsley
- 2 tablespoons chopped fresh oregano
- 1 tablespoon chopped fresh thyme
- 6 lemon wedges

1. To prepare stock, heat 1½ teaspoons oil in a large Dutch oven over medium-high heat. Add celery and next 4 ingredients; sauté 4 minutes. Add thyme, parsley, and bones. Pour 5 cups water over mixture; bring to a boil. Reduce heat, and simmer 30 minutes. Strain stock through a sieve into a bowl; discard solids.

2. To prepare soup, wipe pan dry with a paper towel. Heat 2 tablespoons oil in pan over medium-high heat. Add 1 cup
Continued

carrot, onion, and 4 garlic cloves; sauté 4 minutes. Stir in tomato and next 4 ingredients; cook 1 minute. Add wine; bring to a boil. Cook 8 minutes or until liquid almost evaporates. Stir in stock; bring to a boil. Stir in mussels and fish. Cover and cook over medium-high heat 4 minutes or until mussels open and fish flakes easily when tested with a fork or until desired degree of doneness; discard any unopened shells. Remove from heat; stir in ⅓ cup parsley, oregano, and thyme. Serve immediately with lemon wedges. Yield: 6 servings (serving size: about 1½ cups soup and 1 lemon wedge).

CALORIES 268 (30% from fat); FAT 9g (sat 1.4g, mono 4.8g, poly 1.6g); PROTEIN 28.7g; CARB 14.8g; FIBER 2.4g; CHOL 54mg; IRON 4.5mg; SODIUM 594mg; CALC 90mg

Soupe au Verte with Goat Cheese Toasts

Use halibut for this herbed dish only if you can buy it fresh. Otherwise, use another firm white fish, like snapper.

STOCK:

    6   cups water
 1½   cups chopped celery
    ½   cup chopped carrot
    2   bay leaves
    1   large onion, quartered
    1   bunch fresh parsley
    1   pound fish bones

SOUP:

    2   bacon slices
    1   tablespoon butter
    2   cups chopped onion
    2   cups cubed peeled Yukon gold or
        red potato
    1   cup chopped carrot
    2   teaspoons sugar
 1¼   teaspoons salt, divided
    1   cup dry white wine
    1   (16-ounce) package frozen green
        peas
    1   cup half-and-half
    2   tablespoons chopped fresh mint
    8   (6-ounce) halibut fillets
    ½   teaspoon freshly ground black
        pepper
  Cooking spray

TOASTS:

    1   teaspoon butter, softened
    ¼   cup (1 ounce) crumbled goat
        cheese
    8   (½-ounce) slices French bread
    2   teaspoons finely chopped parsley
    ¼   teaspoon freshly ground black
        pepper

REMAINING INGREDIENT:

 2½   tablespoons chopped fresh parsley

1. To prepare stock, combine first 7 ingredients in a large Dutch oven; bring to a boil. Reduce heat, and simmer 30 minutes. Strain stock through a fine sieve into a bowl; discard solids.
2. Preheat oven to 450°.
3. To prepare soup, wipe pan dry with a paper towel. Cook bacon in pan over medium heat until crisp. Remove bacon from pan; crumble and set aside. Increase heat to medium-high; add butter to drippings in pan, and melt. Add 2 cups onion, potato, 1 cup carrot, sugar, and 1 teaspoon salt; sauté 5 minutes. Add wine; cook until wine is reduced to ½ cup (about 8 minutes). Add stock and peas; bring to a boil. Reduce heat, and simmer 10 minutes or until potato and carrot are tender. Cool slightly. Place half of vegetable mixture in a blender. Remove center piece of blender lid (to allow steam to escape); secure blender lid on blender. Place a clean towel over opening in blender lid (to avoid splatters). Process until smooth, scraping sides. Pour pureed vegetable mixture into a large bowl. Repeat procedure with remaining vegetable mixture. Strain vegetable mixture through a sieve into pan; discard solids. Stir in half-and-half and mint; cook over medium-low heat until thoroughly heated, stirring occasionally.
4. Sprinkle fish with ¼ teaspoon salt and ½ teaspoon pepper. Place fish on a jelly-roll pan coated with cooking spray. Bake at 450° for 20 minutes or until fish flakes easily when tested with a fork or until desired degree of doneness.
5. Preheat broiler.
6. To prepare toasts, spread butter and goat cheese evenly over bread slices. Place on a baking sheet. Broil 1 minute or until cheese melts. Sprinkle toasts evenly

with 2 teaspoons parsley and ¼ teaspoon pepper.
7. Place 1 fillet in each of 8 shallow soup bowls. Ladle 1 cup soup over each fillet; sprinkle evenly with bacon and 2½ tablespoons parsley. Serve each with 1 toast. Yield: 8 servings.

CALORIES 422 (23% from fat); FAT 10.9g (sat 4.7g, mono 3.4g, poly 1.7g); PROTEIN 43.3g; CARB 29.3g; FIBER 4.2g; CHOL 78mg; IRON 3.5mg; SODIUM 706mg; CALC 169mg

Vatapa

A classic Brazilian soup, this dish offers a harmonious balance of tangy, sweet, and spicy flavors. For an added traditional touch, try sprinkling the soup with chopped peanuts just before serving. If you can't find a Brazilian lager, Mexican beer, such as Dos Equis, works well in its place.

STOCK:

    6   cups water
    1   cup chopped onion
    ¾   cup chopped carrot
    1   tablespoon grated peeled fresh
        ginger
    4   garlic cloves, minced
    1   pound fish bones

SOUP:

  Cooking spray
    1   cup chopped onion
    1   tablespoon brown sugar
    1   teaspoon salt
    1   tablespoon grated peeled fresh
        ginger
    3   garlic cloves, minced
    1   serrano chile, seeded and finely
        chopped
    3   cups chopped seeded peeled
        tomato
    1   (12-ounce) bottle beer
    1   (13.5-ounce) can light coconut
        milk
    1   pound grouper or other firm
        white fish fillets, cut into 1-inch
        pieces
    ⅓   cup chopped fresh cilantro
    1   tablespoon fresh lime juice
    3   cups hot cooked basmati rice
    6   lime wedges

1. To prepare stock, combine first 6 ingredients in a large Dutch oven; bring to a boil. Reduce heat, and simmer 30 minutes. Strain stock through a fine sieve into a bowl; discard solids.

2. To prepare soup, wipe pan dry with a paper towel. Heat pan over medium-high heat. Coat pan with cooking spray. Add 1 cup onion, sugar, and salt; sauté 3 minutes. Add 1 tablespoon ginger, 3 garlic cloves, and chile; sauté 30 seconds. Stir in stock, tomato, and beer; bring to a boil. Cook until reduced to 6 cups (about 15 minutes). Stir in coconut milk; bring to a boil. Reduce heat, and simmer 20 minutes, stirring occasionally. Add fish; cook 5 minutes over medium-high heat or until fish flakes easily when tested with a fork or until desired degree of doneness. Stir in cilantro and juice. Serve with rice and lime wedges. Yield: 6 servings (serving size: about 1⅓ cups soup, ½ cup rice, and 1 lime wedge).

CALORIES 241 (17% from fat); FAT 4.5g (sat 3.5g, mono 0.2g, poly 0.4g); PROTEIN 18.4g; CARB 32.1g; FIBER 1.8g; CHOL 28mg; IRON 1.6mg; SODIUM 464mg; CALC 50mg

menu of the month
Pool Party

Gather the gang and dive into dinner with this no-fuss lineup.

Poolside Buffet Menu
serves 6

Watermelon Cooler

Red Pepper Hummus

Cucumber Salad with Rice Vinegar Dressing

New Potato Salad

Polynesian Flank Steak

Strawberry-Chocolate Tart

MAKE AHEAD
Watermelon Cooler
(pictured on page 233)

Make this drink ahead of time, and keep refrigerated up to three days.

8 cups chopped seedless watermelon (about 3¼ pounds)
1 cup fresh lime juice (about 6 limes)
½ cup sugar
½ cup water
Dash of salt

1. Place half of watermelon in a blender; process until smooth. Strain watermelon through a sieve into a pitcher; discard solids. Repeat procedure with remaining watermelon. Stir in lime juice, sugar, ½ cup water, and dash of salt. Serve over ice. Yield: 6 servings (serving size: 1 cup).

CALORIES 136 (2% from fat); FAT 0.3g (sat 0g, mono 0.1g, poly 0.1g); PROTEIN 1.4g; CARB 35.4g; FIBER 1g; CHOL 0mg; IRON 0.5mg; SODIUM 28mg; CALC 20mg

---

MAKE AHEAD
Red Pepper Hummus

For convenience, prepare the dip up to three days in advance and refrigerate in an airtight container. Serve with pita wedges and bell pepper strips.

1 red bell pepper
2½ tablespoons fresh lemon juice
1 tablespoon tahini (sesame seed paste)
½ teaspoon freshly ground black pepper
¼ teaspoon salt
¼ teaspoon ground cumin
1 (19-ounce) can chickpeas (garbanzo beans), rinsed and drained
1 garlic clove, quartered

1. Preheat broiler.

2. Cut bell pepper in half lengthwise; discard seeds and membranes. Place pepper halves, skin sides up, on a foil-lined baking sheet; flatten with hand. Broil 10 minutes or until blackened. Place in a zip-top plastic bag; seal. Let stand 10 minutes. Peel.

---

3. Place bell pepper and remaining ingredients in a food processor; process until smooth. Yield: 6 servings (serving size: ⅓ cup).

CALORIES 94 (29% from fat); FAT 3g (sat 0.2g, mono 1.1g, poly 1.6g); PROTEIN 3.7g; CARB 14.1g; FIBER 3.7g; CHOL 0mg; IRON 1.3mg; SODIUM 209mg; CALC 30mg

---

QUICK & EASY • MAKE AHEAD
Cucumber Salad with Rice Vinegar Dressing

3 cups thinly sliced seeded peeled cucumber (about 2 medium)
3 tablespoons rice vinegar
2 teaspoons dark sesame oil
1 teaspoon sugar
½ teaspoon salt
2 tablespoons chopped green onions
1½ tablespoons chopped unsalted, dry-roasted peanuts

1. Combine first 5 ingredients in a medium bowl; toss to coat cucumber. Sprinkle with onions and peanuts before serving. Yield: 6 servings (serving size: ½ cup salad, 1 teaspoon green onions, and ¾ teaspoon peanuts).

CALORIES 42 (60% from fat); FAT 2.8g (sat 0.4g, mono 1.2g, poly 1g); PROTEIN 1g; CARB 3.7g; FIBER 0.7g; CHOL 0mg; IRON 0.3mg; SODIUM 199mg; CALC 12mg

---

QUICK & EASY • MAKE AHEAD
New Potato Salad

1½ pounds small red potatoes
½ cup finely chopped red bell pepper
⅓ cup finely chopped celery
5 tablespoons low-fat mayonnaise
¼ cup minced shallots
¼ cup chopped green onions
2 tablespoons white wine vinegar
1 tablespoon Dijon mustard
½ teaspoon salt
½ teaspoon freshly ground black pepper

1. Place potatoes in a saucepan; cover with water. Bring to a boil. Reduce heat; simmer 15 minutes or until tender. Drain and rinse with cold water; drain. Cool. Cut potatoes into quarters. Combine
Continued

potatoes and remaining ingredients in a large bowl; toss gently to coat. Yield: 6 servings (serving size: about ¾ cup).

CALORIES 113 (15% from fat); FAT 1.9g (sat 0.5g, mono 0g, poly 0.1g); PROTEIN 2.6g; CARB 22.2g; FIBER 2.5g; CHOL 0mg; IRON 1.1mg; SODIUM 351mg; CALC 21mg

Polynesian Flank Steak

Turning the steak on the grill about every five minutes helps keep the marinade from scorching as the meat cooks.

⅓ cup pineapple juice
⅓ cup low-sodium soy sauce
¼ cup thinly sliced green onions
1 tablespoon minced peeled fresh ginger
1 tablespoon honey
1 garlic clove, minced
1½ pounds flank steak
Cooking spray

1. Combine first 6 ingredients in a large zip-top plastic bag; add steak to bag. Seal and marinate in refrigerator 3 hours, turning once.
2. Prepare grill.
3. Remove steak from bag, reserving marinade. Place steak on grill rack coated with cooking spray; grill 20 minutes or until desired degree of doneness, turning and basting frequently with reserved marinade. Let stand 10 minutes before cutting diagonally across grain into thin slices. Yield: 6 servings (serving size: 3 ounces steak).

CALORIES 188 (30% from fat); FAT 6.3g (sat 2.6g, mono 2.5g, poly 0.3g); PROTEIN 24.8g; CARB 6.2g; FIBER 0.2g; CHOL 42mg; IRON 1.7mg; SODIUM 396mg; CALC 24mg

MAKE AHEAD
Strawberry-Chocolate Tart

CRUST:

1¾ cups regular oats
¼ cup sugar
¼ teaspoon salt
3½ tablespoons chilled butter, cut into small pieces
2 tablespoons water
Cooking spray

FILLING:

2 cups fat-free milk
½ cup sugar
⅓ cup unsweetened cocoa
2 tablespoons cornstarch
1 teaspoon vanilla extract
¼ teaspoon salt
⅓ cup semisweet chocolate chips

REMAINING INGREDIENT:

2½ cups sliced strawberries

1. Preheat oven to 400°.
2. To prepare crust, place first 3 ingredients in a food processor; process until finely ground (about 30 seconds). Add butter; pulse 3 times or until combined. Add 2 tablespoons water; pulse until dough forms. Press oat mixture into bottom and up sides of a 9-inch round removable-bottom tart pan coated with cooking spray. Bake at 400° for 18 minutes or until browned. Cool completely on a wire rack.
3. To prepare filling, combine milk and next 5 ingredients in a medium saucepan, stirring with a whisk until well combined. Bring to a boil over medium-high heat; reduce heat, and simmer 4 minutes or until thick, stirring constantly. Remove from heat; add chocolate chips, stirring until chips melt. Pour into cooled crust; cool 10 minutes on wire rack. Carefully remove tart from pan; cool completely on wire rack. Arrange strawberry slices, spokelike, on top of custard, working from outside of pan to center. Cover loosely with parchment paper coated with cooking spray; chill 8 hours or overnight. Yield: 8 servings (serving size: 1 slice).

CALORIES 270 (30% from fat); FAT 9g (sat 4.3g, mono 3.3g, poly 0.6g); PROTEIN 6.1g; CARB 45.7g; FIBER 4.3g; CHOL 14mg; IRON 2.1mg; SODIUM 213mg; CALC 82mg

sound bites

Whole-Grain Salads

Grains perk up salads and harmonize with your favorite fresh ingredients.

With their nutty taste, mild flavor, and chewy texture, grains are a fitting canvas for salads because they go well with the bright, fresh flavors of summer.

Use the recipes here as a basis for making your own grain salads. Once you get started, you'll see a world of possibilities.

MAKE AHEAD
Sesame Brown Rice Salad with Shredded Chicken and Peanuts

Cook the brown rice in plenty of water so it won't be sticky. Serve with lime wedges.

1 cup long-grain brown rice
2 cups shredded cooked chicken breast
½ cup shredded carrot
⅓ cup sliced green onions
¼ cup dry-roasted peanuts, divided
1 tablespoon chopped fresh cilantro, divided
½ teaspoon salt
2 tablespoons fresh lime juice
4 teaspoons canola oil
1 teaspoon dark sesame oil
2 garlic cloves, minced

1. Cook rice according to package directions, omitting salt and fat. Transfer rice to a large bowl; fluff with a fork. Cool. Add chicken, carrot, onions, 2 tablespoons peanuts, 2 teaspoons cilantro, and salt to rice; toss to combine.
2. Combine juice and remaining 3 ingredients in a small bowl. Drizzle oil mixture over rice mixture; toss to combine. Place 1½ cups salad on each of 4 plates. Sprinkle each serving with 1½ teaspoons peanuts and ¼ teaspoon cilantro. Yield: 4 servings.

CALORIES 393 (30% from fat); FAT 13.3g (sat 2g, mono 6.3g, poly 4g); PROTEIN 27.8g; CARB 40.2g; FIBER 4g; CHOL 60mg; IRON 1.7mg; SODIUM 424mg; CALC 44mg

Wild Rice and Summer Succotash Salad

Cooking times for wild rice vary. In general, cook one cup rice in three cups water, though you may need to add a little more water before the rice is done.

⅓ cup red wine vinegar
¼ cup chopped fresh flat-leaf parsley
¼ cup Dijon mustard
3 tablespoons chopped fresh basil leaves
2 tablespoons chopped green onions
1½ teaspoons chopped fresh thyme
½ teaspoon kosher salt
¼ teaspoon freshly ground black pepper
1 garlic clove, minced
3 tablespoons extravirgin olive oil
3 cups water
1 cup wild rice
1 cup (1-inch) cut green beans (about ¼ pound)
1 cup frozen baby lima beans
1 cup finely chopped red bell pepper
1 cup finely chopped celery
1 cup finely chopped red onion
1 cup diced plum tomato
6 romaine lettuce leaves
3 tablespoons slivered almonds, toasted

1. Combine first 9 ingredients in a bowl, stirring well with a whisk. Gradually add oil to vinegar mixture, stirring constantly.
2. Bring 3 cups water to a boil in a medium saucepan. Add rice to pan. Cook, covered, 45 minutes or until tender. Drain. Place rice in a large bowl. Add ¼ cup vinegar mixture; toss well. Cool.
3. Cook green beans and lima beans in boiling water 4 minutes or until tender. Drain. Rinse with cold water; drain. Add beans, remaining vinegar mixture, bell pepper, celery, onion, and tomato to rice mixture; toss well. Line each of 6 plates with 1 lettuce leaf; top each with about 1½ cups salad mixture. Sprinkle each serving with 1½ teaspoons almonds. Yield: 6 servings.

CALORIES 342 (30% from fat); FAT 11.3g (sat 1.4g, mono 7.3g, poly 1.7g); PROTEIN 13.6g; CARB 50.1g; FIBER 10.6g; CHOL 0mg; IRON 3.9mg; SODIUM 443mg; CALC 98mg

Barley, Roasted Vegetables, and Feta Salad

SALAD:
4 cups water
1 cup uncooked pearl barley
2 red bell peppers, cut into wedges
1 medium peeled eggplant, cut into ½-inch-thick slices
Cooking spray
1 medium zucchini, halved lengthwise
1 medium yellow squash, halved lengthwise
¼ teaspoon kosher salt
¼ teaspoon freshly ground black pepper
¼ cup chopped fresh parsley
¼ cup chopped fresh mint
2 tablespoons chopped fresh dill
1 teaspoon grated orange rind
2 garlic cloves, minced

DRESSING:
⅓ cup red wine vinegar
5 teaspoons extravirgin olive oil
½ teaspoon kosher salt

REMAINING INGREDIENT:
⅓ cup crumbled feta cheese

1. Preheat oven to 400°.
2. To prepare salad, bring 4 cups water to a boil in a large saucepan. Add barley. Cover, reduce heat, and simmer 45 minutes or until tender. Let barley stand, covered, 5 minutes. Spoon barley into a large bowl.
3. Place peppers and eggplant on one jelly-roll pan coated with cooking spray; place zucchini and squash on another jelly-roll pan coated with cooking spray. Coat vegetables with cooking spray; sprinkle with ¼ teaspoon salt and black pepper. Place pan with squash on top rack in oven and pan with eggplant on middle rack. Bake at 400° for 12 minutes or until squash and zucchini are tender. Remove pan with squash, and move pan with eggplant to top rack. Bake peppers and eggplant an additional 8 minutes or until tender. Cool. Cut vegetables into ½-inch pieces. Add vegetables, parsley, and next 4 ingredients to barley; toss gently.

4. To prepare dressing, combine vinegar, oil, and ½ teaspoon salt, stirring well with a whisk. Add dressing to barley mixture; toss. Sprinkle with cheese. Yield: 6 servings (serving size: 1½ cups salad and about 2½ teaspoons cheese).

CALORIES 320 (29% from fat); FAT 10.3g (sat 3g, mono 5.3g, poly 1.4g); PROTEIN 11.1g; CARB 50.5g; FIBER 15.2g; CHOL 11mg; IRON 3.7mg; SODIUM 512mg; CALC 129mg

Black Rice, Spinach, Salmon, and Mango Salad

1½ cups black rice
Cooking spray
1 (8-ounce) salmon fillet (about ½ inch thick)
¼ cup fresh lime juice
1 teaspoon kosher salt
1 teaspoon ground cumin
1 teaspoon grated peeled fresh ginger
1 garlic clove, minced
2½ tablespoons canola oil
3 cups diced peeled mango (about 2 medium)
1 cup halved grape tomatoes
½ cup thinly sliced green onions
½ cup finely chopped green bell pepper
1 (6-ounce) package fresh baby spinach

1. Rinse rice, and drain well. Cook rice in boiling water 35 minutes or until al dente; drain. Cool.
2. Heat a nonstick skillet over medium-high heat. Coat pan with cooking spray. Add salmon; cook 3 minutes on each side or until fish flakes easily when tested with a fork or until desired degree of doneness. Cool; break into bite-sized pieces.
3. Combine juice and next 4 ingredients in a large bowl, stirring well with a whisk. Gradually add oil to juice mixture, stirring constantly. Add rice, mango, tomatoes, onions, pepper, and spinach; toss gently. Place 1 cup rice mixture in each of 6 bowls; top each with 1 ounce salmon. Yield: 6 servings.

CALORIES 320 (28% from fat); FAT 10.1g (sat 1.3g, mono 4.9g, poly 3g); PROTEIN 13g; CARB 46.1g; FIBER 3.1g; CHOL 19mg; IRON 2.2mg; SODIUM 361mg; CALC 59mg

Toasted Quinoa, Snow Peas, Tomatoes, and Mozzarella Salad

Quinoa grains are covered with a naturally occurring bitter substance called saponin. Although processors remove most of this soapy substance by washing or polishing the grain, it is important that quinoa be thoroughly rinsed in several changes of clean water before it's cooked. For added flavor, toast it before cooking.

1½ cups uncooked quinoa, rinsed and drained
3 cups water
1 cup diagonally cut snow peas
¾ cup (3 ounces) diced fresh mozzarella cheese
½ cup chopped red onion
½ cup chopped seedless cucumber
¼ cup chopped fresh mint
2 tablespoons chopped fresh basil
1 pint cherry tomatoes, halved
1 teaspoon grated lemon rind
¼ cup fresh lemon juice
1½ tablespoons Dijon mustard
4 teaspoons extravirgin olive oil
¾ teaspoon kosher salt
¼ teaspoon freshly ground black pepper
¼ teaspoon hot pepper sauce

1. Heat a medium saucepan over medium-high heat. Add quinoa to pan; cook 5 minutes or until toasted, stirring frequently. Add 3 cups water to pan; bring to a boil. Cover, reduce heat, and cook 15 minutes or until tender. Fluff with a fork; cool. Place quinoa in a large bowl. Add peas and next 6 ingredients.
2. Combine rind and remaining 6 ingredients in a small bowl, stirring with a whisk. Add juice mixture to quinoa mixture; toss gently to coat. Yield: 6 servings (serving size: 1½ cups).

CALORIES 265 (29% from fat); FAT 8.6g (sat 2.5g, mono 3.5g, poly 1.5g); PROTEIN 9.1g; CARB 35.1g; FIBER 4.8g; CHOL 11mg; IRON 3.8mg; SODIUM 368mg; CALC 138mg

Toasted Millet and Confetti Vegetable Salad with Sesame and Soy Dressing

Dating back to biblical times, millet is a tiny, rounded, pale golden (though some strains are red) grain. Although it remains a staple in African and Asian diets, it is less widely consumed in America.

DRESSING:
3 tablespoons rice vinegar
1 tablespoon cold water
1 tablespoon low-sodium soy sauce
1 teaspoon grated peeled fresh ginger
1 teaspoon canola oil
½ teaspoon dark sesame oil
½ teaspoon salt
1 garlic clove, minced

SALAD:
1 cup uncooked millet
2 cups water
3 tablespoons chopped walnuts
1 tablespoon low-sodium soy sauce
1 cup diced carrot
1 cup chopped fresh cilantro
½ cup finely chopped red bell pepper
½ cup finely chopped green bell pepper
½ cup thinly sliced green onions
1 tablespoon finely chopped seeded jalapeño pepper

1. To prepare dressing, combine first 8 ingredients in a small bowl.
2. To prepare salad, heat a medium saucepan over medium-high heat. Add millet to pan; cook 5 minutes or until golden, stirring frequently. Add 2 cups water; bring to a boil. Cover, reduce heat, and simmer 20 minutes. Remove from heat; let stand, covered, 10 minutes. Fluff with a fork. Cool completely.
3. Heat a small saucepan over medium-high heat. Add nuts; cook 3 minutes or until lightly toasted, stirring occasionally. Add 1 tablespoon soy sauce; cook 30 seconds, stirring constantly.
4. Cook carrot in boiling water 3 minutes or until tender. Drain; rinse with cold water. Drain. Combine millet, carrot, cilantro, bell peppers, onions, and jala-peño in a large bowl. Drizzle dressing over millet mixture; toss well. Top with walnuts. Yield: 4 servings (serving size: 1¾ cups salad and 2 teaspoons nuts).

CALORIES 238 (28% from fat); FAT 7.3g (sat 0.8g, mono 1.7g, poly 3.9g); PROTEIN 7.3g; CARB 42.1g; FIBER 5.6g; CHOL 0mg; IRON 4.5mg; SODIUM 587mg; CALC 35mg

Storage and Handling

Grains have a long shelf life—up to a year—if they're stored properly. The fats in grains can turn rancid over time. Any grain you use should have a pleasant, nutty aroma when you open the container. If it smells strong or sour, it's rancid and should be discarded. Store grains in airtight containers in a cool, dark place. If you live in a hot, humid climate, keep them in the refrigerator. In general, you can store cooked grains, tightly covered, in the refrigerator up to five days; grains with a chewy texture (wild, brown, and black rice, barley, and bulgur) can be frozen without turning mushy.

Rinse **wild rice** in a strainer before cooking to clean any chaff. Soaking the rice overnight can shorten cooking time by about 20 minutes but also results in milder-tasting rice. Use 3 cups water per 1 cup uncooked wild rice.

Quinoa must be rinsed in three changes of cold water in order to remove the saponin (a bitter-tasting, naturally occurring insect repellent); be sure to drain well before cooking. Use 2 cups water per 1 cup uncooked quinoa.

Soaking **barley** in water overnight will slash its cooking time almost in half. Cook in plenty of water—3 cups per 1 cup uncooked barley.

For extra flavor, toast 1 cup **millet** in a dry skillet before cooking it in 2 cups water.

When using **brown** or **black rice** in salads, cook it in plenty of water (2½ to 3 cups per 1 cup medium-grain rice), and drain it like pasta. This keeps the grains from sticking together.

Better Baked Limas

A creamy Pennsylvania Dutch specialty trims down and shapes up.

BEFORE	AFTER
SERVING SIZE	
²/₃ cup	
CALORIES PER SERVING	
383	241
FAT	
19.6g	6g
PERCENT OF TOTAL CALORIES	
46%	22%

Mom's Pennsylvania Dutch Beans

1 pound dried baby lima beans
4 cups water
1½ teaspoons salt, divided
Cooking spray
1 cup chopped yellow onion
1 teaspoon minced garlic
½ cup fat-free, less-sodium chicken broth
⅓ cup packed light brown sugar
3 tablespoons butter, cut into pieces
1 tablespoon molasses
2 teaspoons dry mustard
1 cup light sour cream (such as Daisy)

1. Sort and wash beans; place in a large Dutch oven. Cover with water to 2 inches above beans; bring to a boil. Cook 2 minutes; remove from heat. Cover and let stand 1 hour. Drain beans; return to pan. Add 4 cups water and 1 teaspoon salt; bring to a boil. Reduce heat, and simmer 1 hour. Drain and set aside.
2. Preheat oven to 350°.
3. Wipe pan dry with paper towel. Heat pan over medium-high heat. Coat pan with cooking spray. Add onion to pan; sauté 5 minutes or until tender. Add garlic to pan; sauté 30 seconds. Combine beans, ½ teaspoon salt, onion mixture, broth, and next 4 ingredients in a 13 x 9-inch baking dish coated with cooking spray. Bake at 350° for 1 hour. Remove from oven; stir in sour cream. Serve immediately. Yield: 10 servings (serving size: about ⅔ cup).

CALORIES 241 (22% from fat); FAT 6g (sat 3.9g, mono 0.9g, poly 0.3g); PROTEIN 10.7g; CARB 37g; FIBER 8.5g; CHOL 9mg; IRON 2.9mg; SODIUM 213mg; CALC 49mg

20 Minute Dishes

From salad to saté, poultry to pasta, here are simple, fresh, and easy meals you can make superfast.

QUICK & EASY
Spicy Basque-Style Chicken

Smoked paprika is a traditional ingredient in Spanish cuisine. Serve this dish with saffron rice to soak up the tasty sauce.

1 teaspoon smoked paprika
¼ teaspoon black pepper
1 pound skinless, boneless chicken breast tenders
2 teaspoons olive oil
2 teaspoons bottled minced garlic
¼ cup sliced green olives
2 (10-ounce) cans diced tomatoes and green chiles, undrained
¼ cup finely chopped prosciutto
2 tablespoons chopped fresh parsley

1. Combine paprika and pepper; sprinkle evenly over chicken. Heat oil in a large nonstick skillet over medium-high heat. Add chicken to pan; cook 4 minutes. Add garlic to pan; cook 30 seconds. Turn chicken over. Add olives and tomatoes to pan; bring to a boil. Reduce heat, and simmer 6 minutes.
2. Remove chicken from pan. Increase heat to medium-high; cook sauce 2 minutes, stirring occasionally. Serve sauce with chicken, and sprinkle with prosciutto and parsley. Yield: 4 servings (serving size: 3 ounces chicken, about ½ cup sauce, 1 tablespoons prosciutto, and 1½ teaspoons parsley).

CALORIES 264 (31% from fat); FAT 9g (sat 1.6g, mono 4g, poly 2.2g); PROTEIN 36.2g; CARB 8g; FIBER 0.3g; CHOL 94mg; IRON 1.4mg; SODIUM 876mg; CALC 92mg

QUICK & EASY
Beef Saté with Peanut Dipping Sauce

Flank steak cooks quickly when thinly sliced. The dipping sauce is inspired by traditional Indonesian condiments that often accompany this dish.

1 (3½-ounce) bag boil-in-bag long-grain rice
1 (1-pound) flank steak, trimmed
2 tablespoons hoisin sauce
¼ teaspoon salt
Cooking spray
2 tablespoons chopped fresh cilantro
2 tablespoons light coconut milk
1½ tablespoons creamy peanut butter
1 tablespoon low-sodium soy sauce
1 teaspoon sugar
1 teaspoon fresh lime juice
½ teaspoon red curry paste

1. Preheat broiler.
2. Cook rice according to package directions, omitting salt and fat. Drain; cover and keep warm.
3. Cut steak diagonally across grain into ¼-inch-thick slices. Combine steak and hoisin in a bowl; toss to coat. Thread steak onto 8 (8-inch) skewers; sprinkle evenly with salt. Place skewers on a broiler pan coated with cooking spray; broil 3 minutes on each side or until desired degree of doneness. Sprinkle skewers with cilantro.
4. Combine coconut milk and remaining 5 ingredients in a bowl, stirring until smooth. Serve with skewers and rice. Yield: 4 servings (serving size: 2 skewers, ½ cup rice, and about 1 tablespoon peanut sauce).

CALORIES 306 (28% from fat); FAT 9.4g (sat 3.4g, mono 3.8g, poly 1.2g); PROTEIN 27.6g; CARB 26.4g; FIBER 1g; CHOL 37mg; IRON 2.8mg; SODIUM 503mg; CALC 30mg

Chicken Cobb Salad
(pictured on page 234)

Serve this salad with a chilled summer soup or sandwich for a light and refreshing meal.

Cooking spray
1½ pounds skinless, boneless chicken breast cutlets
¼ teaspoon salt
¼ teaspoon black pepper
8 cups mixed greens
1 cup cherry tomatoes, halved
⅓ cup diced peeled avocado
2 tablespoons sliced green onions
⅓ cup fat-free Italian dressing
2 tablespoons crumbled blue cheese
1 bacon slice, cooked and crumbled

1. Heat a large nonstick skillet over medium-high heat. Coat pan with cooking spray. Sprinkle chicken with salt and pepper. Add chicken to pan; cook 5 minutes on each side or until done. Cut into ½-inch slices.
2. Combine greens, tomatoes, avocado, and onions in a large bowl. Drizzle greens mixture with dressing; toss gently to coat. Arrange about 2 cups greens mixture on each of 4 salad plates. Top each serving with 4 ounces chicken, 1½ teaspoons cheese, and about ½ teaspoon bacon. Yield: 4 servings.

CALORIES 263 (27% from fat); FAT 8g (sat 2.4g, mono 3.2g, poly 1.4g); PROTEIN 37.9g; CARB 8.9g; FIBER 3.7g; CHOL 99mg; IRON 2.6mg; SODIUM 606mg; CALC 89mg

Penne with Asparagus, Spinach, and Bacon

8 ounces uncooked penne pasta
2 bacon slices
½ cup chopped sweet onion
2½ cups (1-inch) slices asparagus (about 1 pound)
1½ cups fat-free, less-sodium chicken broth
4 cups bagged baby spinach leaves
½ cup (2 ounces) preshredded Parmesan cheese, divided
¼ teaspoon black pepper

1. Cook pasta according to package directions, omitting salt and fat. Drain; keep warm.
2. Cook bacon in a large nonstick skillet over medium heat until crisp. Remove bacon from pan; crumble. Add onion to drippings in pan; sauté 1 minute. Add asparagus and broth to pan; bring to a boil. Reduce heat, and simmer 5 minutes or until asparagus is crisp-tender. Add pasta, spinach, ¼ cup cheese, and pepper to pan; toss well. Sprinkle with ¼ cup cheese and bacon. Yield: 4 servings (serving size: about 1½ cups pasta mixture and 1 tablespoon cheese).

CALORIES 363 (25% from fat); FAT 10.2g (sat 4.2g, mono 3.6g, poly 0.8g); PROTEIN 17.8g; CARB 49.1g; FIBER 4.6g; CHOL 18mg; IRON 4.3mg; SODIUM 501mg; CALC 239mg

Spiced Chicken Thighs with Yogurt Sauce

The yogurt sauce's cooling effect balances the heat of the chicken.

1 cup uncooked couscous
1 teaspoon ground cumin
1 teaspoon ground coriander
1 teaspoon ground turmeric
¼ teaspoon ground ginger
¼ teaspoon ground red pepper
½ teaspoon salt, divided
8 skinless, boneless chicken thighs (about 1½ pounds)
Cooking spray
¼ cup chopped fresh cilantro
1 teaspoon bottled minced garlic
1 (6-ounce) carton plain fat-free yogurt
Cilantro sprigs (optional)

1. Cook couscous according to package directions, omitting salt and fat.
2. Combine cumin and next 4 ingredients in a bowl; stir in ¼ teaspoon salt. Sprinkle spice mixture over chicken. Heat a large nonstick skillet over medium heat. Coat pan with cooking spray. Add chicken to pan; cook 6 minutes on each side or until done.
3. Combine ¼ teaspoon salt, chopped cilantro, garlic, and yogurt in a bowl, stirring well. Serve with chicken and couscous. Garnish with cilantro sprigs, if desired. Yield: 4 servings (serving size: 2 chicken thighs, about ¼ cup yogurt mixture, and ½ cup couscous).

CALORIES 335 (31% from fat); FAT 11.7g (sat 3.3g, mono 4.4g, poly 2.7g); PROTEIN 32.6g; CARB 22.5g; FIBER 1.5g; CHOL 100mg; IRON 2.2mg; SODIUM 425mg; CALC 111mg

Linguine with Garlicky Clams and Peas

Fresh linguine from the supermarket's refrigerated section cooks quickly, so this dish comes together in a flash. Crusty bread and a tossed green salad will round out the meal.

1 (9-ounce) package fresh linguine
2 tablespoons olive oil
1½ teaspoons bottled minced garlic
3 (6½-ounce) cans chopped clams, undrained
1 cup organic vegetable broth (such as Swanson Certified Organic)
¼ cup dry white wine
¼ teaspoon crushed red pepper
1 cup frozen green peas
½ cup (2 ounces) preshredded Parmesan cheese
2 tablespoons chopped fresh basil

1. Cook pasta according to package directions, omitting salt and fat. Drain; keep warm.
2. Heat oil in a large nonstick skillet over medium-high heat. Add garlic to pan; sauté 1 minute. Drain clams, reserving clams and ½ cup juice. Add reserved clam juice, broth, wine, and pepper to pan; bring to a boil. Reduce heat, and simmer 5 minutes, stirring occasionally. Add clams and peas to pan; cook 2 minutes or until thoroughly heated. Add pasta to pan; toss well. Sprinkle with cheese and basil. Yield: 4 servings (serving size: 1½ cups pasta mixture, 2 tablespoons cheese, and 1½ teaspoons basil).

CALORIES 368 (29% from fat); FAT 11.9g (sat 3g, mono 6.9g, poly 0.9g); PROTEIN 19.8g; CARB 46.5g; FIBER 4.3g; CHOL 24mg; IRON 1.9mg; SODIUM 961mg; CALC 166mg

Sandwich Sampler

Based on American standbys, these updated combinations satisfy when it's hot.

Consider hot dogs, BLTs, grilled cheese, and wraps, and it's clear Americans have a special love affair with the sandwich. It's estimated that we each consume 198 sandwiches annually; that's more than 45 billion collectively.

Englishwoman Elizabeth Leslie introduced the sandwich to Americans in her 1840 cookbook *Directions for Cookery,* and by the early 1900s, inexpensive, presliced, commercially sold bread was available and sandwiches were the standard lunch of America's working class. This tradition has grown over the decades with the increase in two-income households that value the sandwich's ease, convenience, and portability.

Sandwiches make terrific warm-weather fare because they require little or no cooking. And since you probably have about 99 sandwiches left to eat this year, you can fill the bill with any of these creative, healthful renditions.

QUICK & EASY
Little Italy Chicken Pitas with Sun-Dried Tomato Vinaigrette

(pictured on page 237)

Use oil from the sun-dried tomatoes to prepare the vinaigrette for this zesty sandwich.

- 2 tablespoons balsamic vinegar
- 1½ tablespoons sun-dried tomato oil
- 1 tablespoon chopped drained oil-packed sun-dried tomatoes
- ¼ teaspoon freshly ground black pepper
- 1 garlic clove, minced
- 4 cups shredded cooked chicken breast (about ¾ pound)
- 1 cup chopped tomato (about 1 medium)
- ½ cup (2 ounces) grated Asiago cheese
- ¼ cup thinly sliced fresh basil
- 6 (6-inch) pitas, cut in half
- 3 cups mixed baby greens

1. Combine first 5 ingredients in a large bowl. Stir in chicken, tomato, cheese, and basil. Line each pita half with ¼ cup greens. Divide chicken mixture evenly among pita halves. Yield: 6 servings (serving size: 2 stuffed pita halves).

CALORIES 342 (24% from fat); FAT 9.1g (sat 2.8g, mono 4.2g, poly 1.3g); PROTEIN 26.4g; CARB 37.3g; FIBER 2.4g; CHOL 56mg; IRON 2.7mg; SODIUM 397mg; CALC 162mg

QUICK & EASY
Spicy Southwestern Chicken Sandwiches

Rich, buttery avocado and sweet red bell pepper balance the spiciness from the chipotles in this flavorful sandwich.

- ¼ cup reduced-fat mayonnaise
- 1 tablespoon fresh lime juice
- 1 teaspoon finely chopped fresh cilantro
- 1 teaspoon adobo sauce
- ½ teaspoon chopped chipotle chile, canned in adobo sauce
- 2 garlic cloves, minced
- 4 cups shredded cooked chicken breast (about ¾ pound)
- ¼ cup chopped red bell pepper
- ¼ cup chopped avocado
- 8 (1-ounce) slices sourdough bread, toasted
- 8 (⅛-inch-thick) slices tomato
- 4 romaine lettuce leaves

1. Combine first 6 ingredients in a large bowl. Stir in chicken, pepper, and avocado. Divide chicken mixture evenly among 4 bread slices; top each with 2 tomato slices and 1 lettuce leaf. Cover with remaining 4 bread slices. Yield: 4 servings (serving size: 1 sandwich).

CALORIES 347 (22% from fat); FAT 8.4g (sat 2g, mono 3.1g, poly 2.4g); PROTEIN 31.8g; CARB 33.9g; FIBER 2.7g; CHOL 72mg; IRON 2.6mg; SODIUM 555mg; CALC 61mg

QUICK & EASY
Hot Dogs "Run Through the Garden"

Chicago residents love their hot dogs with the works, or "run through the garden." "Sport" peppers are small, pickled hot peppers. You can substitute pickled banana or jalapeño peppers. Baked potato chips round out the meal.

- 7 hot dog buns
- 2 quarts water
- 7 97% fat-free beef franks (such as Hebrew National)
- 1 cup finely diced white onion
- 1 cup diced tomato
- ½ cup sweet pickle relish
- ⅓ cup prepared mustard
- 14 sport peppers

1. Preheat oven to 350°.
2. Wrap buns in foil; bake at 350° for 10 minutes or until thoroughly heated. Remove from oven, and keep warm.
3. Bring 2 quarts water to a simmer in a large saucepan. Add franks; simmer 5 minutes or until thoroughly heated. Drain well. Place 1 frank in each heated bun. Top each frank with about 2 tablespoons onion, about 2 tablespoons tomato, about 1 tablespoon relish, and about 2 teaspoons mustard. Serve with peppers. Yield: 7 servings (serving size: 1 hot dog and 2 peppers).

CALORIES 225 (21% from fat); FAT 5.3g (sat 1.8g, mono 1.9g, poly 0.7g); PROTEIN 10.7g; CARB 36.3g; FIBER 2.8g; CHOL 15mg; IRON 3mg; SODIUM 1,187mg; CALC 76mg

All-American Grilled Cheese with a Twist

8 (1-ounce) slices country white bread
2 cups (4 ounces) shredded sharp Cheddar cheese
8 (¼-inch) slices plum tomato (about 2 tomatoes)
¼ cup thinly sliced fresh basil
Cooking spray

1. Place 4 bread slices on a work surface; arrange ½ cup cheese on each slice. Top each slice with 2 tomato slices and 1 tablespoon basil. Top with remaining 4 bread slices.
2. Heat a large nonstick skillet over medium heat. Coat pan with cooking spray. Add sandwiches to pan; cook 4 minutes or until lightly browned. Turn sandwiches over; cover and cook 2 minutes or until cheese melts. Yield: 4 servings (serving size: 1 sandwich).

CALORIES 247 (38% from fat); FAT 10.5g (sat 6.3g, mono 3.4g, poly 0.6g); PROTEIN 11.6g; CARB 30g; FIBER 3.2g; CHOL 30mg; IRON 1.1mg; SODIUM 464mg; CALC 233mg

Fried Green Tomato BLTs

A Southern favorite, fried green tomatoes lend a delightful twist to this sandwich. The tomatoes take center stage over the bacon in this version.

8 slices 40%-less-fat bacon
⅓ cup yellow cornmeal
¼ cup finely shredded Parmesan cheese
¼ teaspoon freshly ground black pepper
12 (¼-inch-thick) slices green tomato (about 2 tomatoes)
2 teaspoons olive oil, divided
Cooking spray
¼ cup reduced-fat mayonnaise
8 (1-ounce) slices country white bread, toasted
8 red leaf lettuce leaves

1. Cook bacon in a large nonstick skillet over medium heat until crisp. Remove bacon from pan, reserving 2 teaspoons drippings. Set bacon and drippings aside.
2. Combine cornmeal, cheese, and pepper in a shallow dish. Dredge tomato slices in cornmeal mixture. Heat 1 teaspoon reserved drippings and 1 teaspoon oil in a large nonstick skillet coated with cooking spray over medium-high heat. Cook 6 tomato slices 2 minutes on each side or until lightly browned. Repeat procedure with 1 teaspoon bacon drippings, 1 teaspoon oil, and 6 tomato slices.
3. Spread 1 tablespoon mayonnaise over each of 4 bread slices. Top each slice with 2 lettuce leaves, 3 tomato slices, and 2 bacon slices. Top with remaining 4 bread slices. Serve immediately. Yield: 4 servings (serving size: 1 sandwich).

CALORIES 380 (31% from fat); FAT 13g (sat 3.9g, mono 6g, poly 2.3g); PROTEIN 14.6g; CARB 54.1g; FIBER 5.1g; CHOL 16mg; IRON 2.6mg; SODIUM 889mg; CALC 105mg

Shrimp Rémoulade Po'boys

RÉMOULADE SAUCE:
⅓ cup reduced-fat mayonnaise
2 tablespoons finely chopped onion
2 tablespoons finely chopped celery
2 tablespoons finely chopped green bell pepper
1 tablespoon prepared horseradish
2 tablespoons ketchup
2 teaspoons lemon juice
2 teaspoons Worcestershire sauce
1 teaspoon minced fresh basil
⅛ teaspoon freshly ground black pepper
1 small garlic clove, minced

REMAINING INGREDIENTS:
24 large shrimp, peeled and deveined
Cooking spray
4 (3-ounce) French bread loaves, sliced horizontally
1 cup chopped iceberg lettuce
1 cup chopped tomato

1. To prepare sauce, combine first 11 ingredients in a medium bowl. Chill.
2. Prepare grill.
3. Thread shrimp onto 4 (10-inch) skewers. Place skewers on grill rack coated with cooking spray; grill 2 minutes on each side or until shrimp are done.
4. Preheat oven to 350°.
5. Hollow out bread halves, leaving 1-inch-thick shells. Place bread on a baking sheet; bake at 350° for 5 minutes. Place ¼ cup lettuce, ¼ cup tomato, and 6 shrimp in bottom half of each loaf. Spoon ¼ cup sauce over each sandwich. Cover with top bread halves. Yield: 4 servings (serving size: 1 sandwich).

CALORIES 290 (17% from fat); FAT 5.4g (sat 1.3g, mono 1.5g, poly 2.2g); PROTEIN 14.1g; CARB 46.5g; FIBER 3.2g; CHOL 64mg; IRON 3.5mg; SODIUM 799mg; CALC 91mg

WINE NOTE: This sandwich needs a summer white with enough body and bite to cut through the spicy mayo. Willamette Valley Vineyards Pinot Gris 2006 ($15) offers crisp pear and apple flavors, honeysuckle aromas, and a lush body, making it a favorite with shellfish.

Lobster Wraps with Lemon Mayonnaise

LEMON MAYONNAISE:
¼ cup light mayonnaise
2 tablespoons chopped fresh chives
1 teaspoon fresh lemon juice
⅛ teaspoon freshly ground black pepper

REMAINING INGREDIENTS:
¾ cup chopped seeded tomato (about 1 medium)
4 (4-ounce) lobster tails, cooked and chopped
4 (2.8-ounce) whole wheat flatbreads (such as Flatout)
8 Bibb lettuce leaves

1. To prepare lemon mayonnaise, combine first 4 ingredients; stir well.
2. Combine lemon mayonnaise, tomato, and lobster; stir well. Divide lobster mixture evenly among flatbreads. Top each serving with 2 lettuce leaves. Roll up jelly-roll fashion. Yield: 4 servings (serving size: 1 wrap).

CALORIES 371 (21% from fat); FAT 8.6g (sat 1g, mono 1.5g, poly 0.6g); PROTEIN 31g; CARB 41.7g; FIBER 3.6g; CHOL 113mg; IRON 0.7mg; SODIUM 1,098mg; CALC 66mg

Cheese

Learn about our go-to varieties of this multifaceted, much-loved staple.

No matter how tasty a dish may be, it's almost always better with cheese—whether it's a tangy feta on a green salad, salty Parmesan with juicy fruit, melted fontina on pizza, or pungent blue cheese with figs. In fact, some of our best-selling issues have featured cheese on the cover.

There are hundreds of specific cheese varieties, ranging in flavor from sweet and nutty to bitter and acidic, so we focus here on the ones we turn to most often. We frequently use certain cheeses because they deliver big flavor in small doses, such as Parmigiano-Reggiano, sharp or extrasharp Cheddar, goat, feta, Gruyère, blue, and smoked cheeses. We also use more subtly flavored cheeses such as Brie or fontina when their superior melting qualities benefit the dish. The following tips and recipes will show you how to use these different cheeses to success, to both enhance the recipes in which they're used and to allow the cheese the spotlight as an ingredient.

Ham and Gruyère Potato Gratin

We prefer the richness of Gruyère for this gratin, but you can also substitute any type of Swiss cheese. Try a mandoline or the slicing blade of a food processor to create uniformly thin potato slices. You can use a skewer to check the tenderness of the potatoes as the gratin bakes.

2½ cups 1% low-fat milk
2 tablespoons all-purpose flour
¾ teaspoon salt
½ teaspoon black pepper
2 teaspoons butter
½ cup finely chopped onion
1 cup (4 ounces) shredded Gruyère cheese, divided
2 pounds Yukon Gold potatoes, cut into ⅛-inch-thick slices (about 6½ cups)
Cooking spray
4 ounces less-sodium reduced-fat ham, chopped

1. Preheat oven to 350°.
2. Combine first 4 ingredients, stirring with a whisk; set aside.
3. Heat butter in a medium saucepan over medium heat. Add onion; cook 3 minutes or until tender, stirring frequently. Stir in milk mixture; bring to a boil. Cook 2 minutes, stirring constantly. Remove from heat; add ½ cup cheese, stirring until smooth.
4. Arrange half of potatoes in an 11 x 7–inch baking dish coated with cooking spray. Pour half of sauce over potatoes; top evenly with ham. Top with remaining potatoes and remaining sauce; sprinkle evenly with ½ cup cheese.
5. Cover with foil coated with cooking spray. Bake at 350° for 40 minutes. Uncover and bake an additional 45 minutes or until potatoes are tender and cheese is golden brown. Remove from oven; let stand 5 minutes before serving. Yield: 8 servings.

CALORIES 226 (29% from fat); FAT 7.2g (sat 4g, mono 2.3g, poly 0.4g); PROTEIN 12.7g; CARB 26.9g; FIBER 1.6g; CHOL 29mg; IRON 1.4mg; SODIUM 455mg; CALC 242mg

Caramelized Onion, Swiss Chard, and Fontina Cheese Strata

Inspired by the flavors of French onion soup, this strata also features a layer of crumbled tofu.

Cooking spray
3 cups thinly sliced Vidalia or other sweet onion
8 cups coarsely chopped Swiss chard (about 1 pound)
½ teaspoon salt, divided
1⅓ cups fat-free milk
1 cup egg substitute
¼ teaspoon freshly ground black pepper
⅛ teaspoon crushed red pepper
Dash of ground nutmeg
12 ounces French bread, cut into ½-inch cubes (about 10 cups)
¾ cup drained, crumbled water-packed firm tofu
1 cup (4 ounces) shredded fontina cheese

1. Heat a large nonstick skillet over medium heat. Coat pan with cooking spray. Add onion; cook 12 minutes or until browned, stirring frequently. Add chard; cook 5 minutes or until chard wilts, stirring frequently. Remove from heat; stir in ¼ teaspoon salt. Cool.
2. Combine ¼ teaspoon salt, milk, and next 5 ingredients in a large bowl; toss well to coat. Place half of bread mixture in an 11 x 7–inch baking dish coated with cooking spray. Top evenly with tofu, half of chard mixture, and ½ cup cheese. Top evenly with remaining bread mixture, remaining chard mixture, and ½ cup cheese. Cover with foil coated with cooking spray. Refrigerate 8 hours or overnight.
3. Preheat oven to 350°.
4. Remove strata from refrigerator; let stand at room temperature 15 minutes. Bake strata, covered, at 350° for 30 minutes. Uncover and bake an additional 15 minutes or until set. Let stand 10 minutes before serving. Yield: 8 servings.

CALORIES 262 (29% from fat); FAT 8.3g (sat 3.5g, mono 2.1g, poly 1.1g); PROTEIN 16.3g; CARB 31.3g; FIBER 3.1g; CHOL 18mg; IRON 3.3mg; SODIUM 717mg; CALC 240mg

Bacon-Cheddar Corn Muffins

Use extrasharp cheese for the most intense flavor. These muffins are great for breakfast or with soup; split and toast leftovers.

Cooking spray
1½ cups all-purpose flour (about 6¾ ounces)
½ cup yellow cornmeal
1 teaspoon baking powder
1 teaspoon baking soda
1 teaspoon sugar
½ teaspoon salt
1 cup fat-free milk
2 tablespoons lemon juice
2 tablespoons butter, melted
1 large egg, lightly beaten
½ cup (2 ounces) shredded extrasharp Cheddar cheese
4 center-cut bacon slices, cooked and crumbled

1. Preheat oven to 400°.
2. Place 12 paper muffin cup liners in muffin cups. Coat liners with cooking spray; set aside.
3. Lightly spoon flour into dry measuring cups; level with a knife. Combine flour and next 5 ingredients in a large bowl; make a well in center of mixture.
4. Combine milk and juice in a medium bowl; let stand 2 minutes (milk will curdle). Add butter and egg; stir well. Add to flour mixture, stirring just until moist. Stir in cheese and bacon. Spoon batter evenly into prepared muffin cups. Bake at 400° for 17 minutes or until muffins spring back when touched lightly in center. Remove muffins from pans immediately; place on a wire rack. Yield: 12 servings (serving size: 1 muffin).

CALORIES 142 (30% from fat); FAT 4.8g (sat 2.6g, mono 1.5g, poly 0.3g); PROTEIN 5.2g; CARB 19.1g; FIBER 0.6g; CHOL 30mg; IRON 1.1mg; SODIUM 342mg; CALC 88mg

Bruschetta with Peach Salsa and Melted Brie

Place the cheese in the freezer for about 20 minutes for easier cutting. To make in advance, you can prepare and refrigerate the salsa up to a day ahead.

2 cups chopped peeled peaches (about 4)
¾ cup finely chopped red bell pepper (about 1)
¼ cup chopped green onions
2 tablespoons chopped fresh cilantro
1 tablespoon sugar
1 tablespoon fresh lime juice
Dash of ground red pepper
1 (8-ounce) French bread baguette, cut into 24 slices
4 ounces chilled Brie cheese, cut into 24 pieces

1. Preheat broiler.
2. Combine first 7 ingredients; set aside.
3. Arrange bread slices in an even layer on a baking sheet. Top each bread slice with 1 piece of cheese; broil 3 minutes or until cheese melts and bread is toasted. Remove pan from oven. Top each bread slice with about 1½ tablespoons salsa; serve immediately. Yield: 12 servings (serving size: 2 topped bread slices).

CALORIES 100 (24% from fat); FAT 2.7g (sat 1.7g, mono 0.8g, poly 0.1g); PROTEIN 4g; CARB 15.9g; FIBER 1g; CHOL 9mg; IRON 0.8mg; SODIUM 183mg; CALC 22mg

Melon and Prosciutto Salad with Parmigiano-Reggiano

This colorful appetizer would be a fine addition to an antipasto spread. Parmigiano-Reggiano provides nutty contrast to sweet melons and mirrors the taste of salty prosciutto.

3 cups (½-inch) cubed honeydew melon (about ½ medium melon)
3 cups (½-inch) cubed cantaloupe (about 1 medium melon)
2 tablespoons thinly sliced fresh mint
1 teaspoon fresh lemon juice
¼ teaspoon freshly ground black pepper
2 ounces thinly sliced prosciutto, cut into thin strips
½ cup (2 ounces) shaved fresh Parmigiano-Reggiano cheese
Cracked black pepper (optional)
Mint sprigs (optional)

1. Combine first 5 ingredients, tossing gently. Arrange melon mixture on a serving platter. Arrange prosciutto evenly over melon mixture; sprinkle with cheese. Garnish with cracked black pepper and mint sprigs, if desired. Yield: 8 servings (serving size: about ¾ cup).

CALORIES 87 (30% from fat); FAT 2.9g (sat 1.5g, mono 0.5g, poly 0.1g); PROTEIN 5.3g; CARB 11.1g; FIBER 0.6g; CHOL 11mg; IRON 0.4mg; SODIUM 271mg; CALC 94mg

Measure for Measure

Type of cheese	Yield	Weight
Solid (goat, feta, or blue cheese)	¼ cup	2 ounces
	⅓ cup	about 3 ounces
	½ cup	4 ounces
	⅔ cup	about 5 ounces
	¾ cup	6 ounces
	1 cup	8 ounces
Shredded or crumbled cheese	¼ cup	1 ounce
	⅓ cup	about 1½ ounces
	½ cup	2 ounces
	⅔ cup	about 2½ ounces
	¾ cup	3 ounces
	1 cup	4 ounces

Asparagus Ribbons with Lemon and Goat Cheese

Creamy goat cheese crowns a refreshingly bracing salad. Because the asparagus is shaved, it doesn't have to be cooked.

    1   pound large asparagus spears,
        trimmed
 1½   cups cherry tomatoes, halved
    2   tablespoons finely chopped fresh
        chives
    2   tablespoons fresh lemon juice
    2   teaspoons extravirgin olive oil
   ½   teaspoon freshly ground black
        pepper
   ½   teaspoon Dijon mustard
   ¼   teaspoon sugar
   ¼   teaspoon salt
   ½   cup (2 ounces) crumbled goat
        cheese

1. Hold each asparagus spear by the tip end. Shave asparagus into ribbons with a vegetable peeler to measure 3 cups. Reserve tips for another use. Combine asparagus and tomatoes in a bowl.
2. Combine chives and next 6 ingredients, stirring with a whisk. Drizzle over asparagus mixture, tossing gently to coat. Top with goat cheese. Yield: 8 servings (serving size: ½ cup).

CALORIES 47 (54% from fat); FAT 2.8g (sat 1.2g, mono 1.3g, poly 0.2g); PROTEIN 2.7g; CARB 3.7g; FIBER 1.4g; CHOL 3mg; IRON 1.3mg; SODIUM 105mg; CALC 26mg

How to Make Asparagus Ribbons

Shave asparagus into ribbons with a vegetable peeler to measure 3 cups.

Parmesan Soufflé with Fresh Fines Herbes

Although chervil is a traditional component of fines herbes, oregano is more readily available and makes a tasty substitute. Serve as a side dish or a light dinner with a green salad.

        Cooking spray
    2   tablespoons dry breadcrumbs
   ¼   cup minced shallots (about 1
        large)
   ⅓   cup all-purpose flour (about 1½
        ounces)
   ½   teaspoon salt
   ¼   teaspoon freshly ground black
        pepper
 1¼   cups 1% low-fat milk
   ⅓   cup dry white wine
    1   large egg yolk, lightly beaten
   ½   cup (2 ounces) grated fresh
        Parmigiano-Reggiano cheese
    2   tablespoons chopped fresh parsley
    2   tablespoons chopped fresh chives
    1   teaspoon chopped fresh oregano
        or chervil
   ¼   teaspoon chopped fresh tarragon
        (optional)
    6   large egg whites
        Dash of cream of tartar

1. Preheat oven to 350°.
2. Lightly coat a 2-quart soufflé dish with cooking spray; sprinkle breadcrumbs over bottom and sides of dish. Set aside.
3. Heat a medium saucepan over medium-high heat. Coat pan with cooking spray. Add shallots; sauté 2 minutes or until tender. Remove shallots from pan; set aside.
4. Lightly spoon flour into a dry measuring cup; level with a knife. Combine flour, salt, and pepper in saucepan. Gradually add milk, stirring with a whisk until blended; stir in wine. Bring to a boil over medium-high heat, stirring constantly; cook 1 minute or until thick. Remove from heat.
5. Place egg yolk in a medium bowl, and gradually stir about one-fourth of hot milk mixture into egg yolk, stirring constantly with a whisk. Add to remaining hot milk mixture, stirring constantly. Cook 30 seconds, stirring constantly;

remove from heat. Add cheese; stir until smooth. Stir in shallots, parsley, chives, oregano, and tarragon, if desired. Spoon cheese mixture into a large bowl.
6. Place egg whites and cream of tartar in a large bowl; beat with a mixer at high speed until stiff peaks form. Gently stir one-fourth of egg white mixture into cheese mixture; gently fold in remaining egg white mixture. Spoon into prepared dish. Bake at 350° for 55 minutes or until puffy, golden, and set. Serve immediately. Yield: 6 servings.

CALORIES 129 (30% from fat); FAT 4.3g (sat 2.3g, mono 1.3g, poly 0.3g); PROTEIN 10.7g; CARB 11.6g; FIBER 0.4g; CHOL 44mg; IRON 0.9mg; SODIUM 440mg; CALC 186mg

Strawberry, Mint, and Goat Cheese Salad

Serve over mixed greens or fresh baby spinach for a colorful side salad or starter. You can chill goat cheese in the freezer for five minutes to make crumbling it easier.

    3   cups quartered strawberries (about
        1 pound)
    1   tablespoon chopped fresh mint
    1   tablespoon balsamic vinegar
   ¼   teaspoon freshly ground black
        pepper
   ½   cup (2 ounces) crumbled goat
        cheese

1. Combine first 4 ingredients; toss gently. Cover and chill 1 hour. Sprinkle evenly with cheese. Serve immediately. Yield: 6 servings (serving size: about ½ cup).

CALORIES 52 (38% from fat); FAT 2.2g (sat 1.4g, mono 0.5g, poly 0.2g); PROTEIN 2.3g; CARB 6.3g; FIBER 1.6g; CHOL 4mg; IRON 0.5mg; SODIUM 36mg; CALC 26mg

Lamb Pitas with Feta Sauce

Herbed lamb patties are topped with zingy feta-yogurt sauce in this Greek-inspired sandwich. For tender lamb, avoid overworking the meat mixture.

- ½ cup toasted wheat germ
- 2 tablespoons chopped fresh mint
- 2 tablespoons chopped fresh cilantro
- 1 tablespoon chopped fresh oregano
- 1 tablespoon sherry vinegar
- 1 teaspoon ground cumin
- ½ teaspoon salt
- ¼ teaspoon ground red pepper
- ⅛ teaspoon ground allspice
- 3 garlic cloves, minced
- ¾ pound lean ground lamb
- Cooking spray
- ½ cup (2 ounces) crumbled reduced-fat feta cheese
- ¼ cup plain fat-free yogurt
- 20 (¼-inch-thick) slices cucumber
- 10 romaine lettuce leaves
- 10 (¼-inch-thick) slices tomato
- 5 (6-inch) whole wheat pitas, cut in half

1. Preheat broiler.
2. Combine first 10 ingredients in a large bowl. Add lamb; stir just until combined. Divide mixture into 10 equal portions, shaping each into a ¼-inch-thick oval patty. Place patties on a broiler pan coated with cooking spray. Broil 2 minutes on each side or until done.
3. Combine cheese and yogurt in a small bowl; set aside.
4. Arrange 1 patty, 2 cucumber slices, 1 lettuce leaf, and 1 tomato slice in each pita half. Drizzle each pita half with about 1½ teaspoons cheese mixture. Serve immediately. Yield: 5 servings (serving size: 2 stuffed pita halves).

CALORIES 400 (32% from fat); FAT 14.3g (sat 5.4g, mono 4.6g, poly 2.1g); PROTEIN 26.1g; CARB 45.8g; FIBER 7.2g; CHOL 54mg; IRON 4.2mg; SODIUM 774mg; CALC 87mg

Fig and Gorgonzola Tart

Even when fresh figs are coming into season, this tart works best with dried figs; their rich, concentrated sweetness is complemented by the sharpness of the blue cheese. Serve warm or at room temperature, as an appetizer or dessert with a glass of port.

CRUST:
- 1¼ cups all-purpose flour (about 5½ ounces)
- 1 tablespoon sugar
- Dash of salt
- ¼ cup chilled butter, cut into small pieces
- 2 tablespoons ice water
- Cooking spray

FILLING:
- 12 dried Black Mission figs, stems removed
- ¼ cup fig preserves
- 1 tablespoon hot water
- ½ cup (2 ounces) crumbled Gorgonzola or other blue cheese

1. To prepare crust, lightly spoon flour into dry measuring cups; level with a knife. Place flour, sugar, and salt in a food processor; pulse 2 times or until combined. Add butter; pulse 15 times or until mixture resembles cornmeal. With processor on, slowly add 2 tablespoons ice water, 1 tablespoon at a time, through food chute, processing just until blended (do not allow dough to form a ball). Press into bottom and up sides of a 9-inch tart pan coated with cooking spray. Cover and refrigerate 30 minutes.
2. Preheat oven to 375°.
3. Place pan on a baking sheet. Bake at 375° for 20 minutes (crust will be very lightly browned at edges). Cool slightly.
4. To prepare filling, place figs in a bowl; add enough boiling water to cover fruit. Cover and let stand 15 minutes or until figs are soft. Drain well; chop figs. Combine preserves and 1 tablespoon hot water in a medium bowl. Stir in chopped figs. Spoon fig mixture into crust, and spread in an even layer. Bake at 375° for 10 minutes or until heated. Cool on a wire rack 5 minutes. Sprinkle tart with cheese. Yield: 8 servings (serving size: 1 wedge).

CALORIES 246 (31% from fat); FAT 8.4g (sat 5.2g, mono 1.5g, poly 0.4g); PROTEIN 4.5g; CARB 40.4g; FIBER 3.3g; CHOL 21mg; IRON 1.5mg; SODIUM 159mg; CALC 88mg

Smoked Cheddar–Stuffed Mushrooms

The strong flavor of smoked Cheddar cheese goes a long way in these savory bite-sized appetizers. Dicing (instead of shredding) the cheese allows for little melted pockets in the filling.

- Cooking spray
- ¼ cup minced shallots (about 1 large)
- 1 garlic clove, minced
- 40 button mushrooms (about 1 pound)
- ¼ cup dry breadcrumbs
- 2 tablespoons chopped fresh parsley
- ½ teaspoon salt
- ½ teaspoon freshly ground black pepper
- 2 ounces smoked Cheddar cheese, diced
- 1 teaspoon olive oil
- 1 teaspoon water

1. Preheat oven to 400°.
2. Heat a small nonstick skillet over medium-high heat. Coat pan with cooking spray. Add shallots and garlic; sauté 2 minutes or until tender. Place shallot mixture in a medium bowl.
3. Remove stems from mushrooms; chop stems. Add chopped stems, breadcrumbs, and next 4 ingredients to shallot mixture; toss with a fork until blended. Add oil and 1 teaspoon water; stir well.
4. Spoon about 1 teaspoon filling into each mushroom cap. Arrange mushrooms, filling side up, on a baking sheet. Bake at 400° for 20 minutes or until filling begins to brown and cheese melts. Serve warm. Yield: 10 servings (serving size: 4 mushrooms).

CALORIES 51 (44% from fat); FAT 2.5g (sat 1.1g, mono 0.9g, poly 0.2g); PROTEIN 2.7g; CARB 4.6g; FIBER 0.3g; CHOL 6mg; IRON 0.4mg; SODIUM 176mg; CALC 51mg

Corn Bread for a Crew

This slimmed-down recipe proves to be a crowd-pleaser.

Jane McDowell of St. Helens, Oregon, received the recipe for a green chile-and-cheese-enhanced corn bread from a colleague at an office potluck more than 15 years ago. Because it made a large quantity, it was good for potlucks, but the calorie-rich corn bread wasn't suitable for everyday meals. She attempted lightening the recipe at home, but wasn't pleased with the results. McDowell sent the recipe to *Cooking Light* in order to bring one of her favorite dishes back into her repertoire.

Keeping the texture tender and moist while reducing fat and calories was the main challenge. We halved the amount of fat, using richer-flavored butter in place of the margarine. Creaming the butter with sugar helped promote a lighter texture (instead of stirring in melted butter, as many corn bread recipes require). This change trimmed 40 calories and nearly five grams of fat per slice. Since we reduced the fat so drastically, we added a bit of nonfat buttermilk along with a little baking soda in place of some of the baking powder to promote a delicate crumb. Using less baking powder, which contains a dose of sodium, along with cutting the salt in half helped lower the overall sodium to a more manageable 480 milligrams per slice. We used a combination of two large eggs and egg substitute, shaving another gram of fat and 26 milligrams of cholesterol per serving. Finally, we omitted the mild-flavored Monterey Jack cheese and full-fat Cheddar from the original and used all reduced-fat extrasharp Cheddar cheese—and were able to add a bit more—to offer more complex flavor.

BEFORE	AFTER
SERVING SIZE	
1 piece	
CALORIES PER SERVING	
245	175
FAT	
12.1g	5.4g
PERCENT OF TOTAL CALORIES	
44%	28%

MAKE AHEAD

Chile-Cheese Corn Bread

⅓ cup butter, softened
2 tablespoons sugar
½ cup egg substitute
⅓ cup nonfat buttermilk
2 large eggs
¾ cup all-purpose flour (about 3⅓ ounces)
1¾ cups cornmeal
1½ teaspoons baking soda
1½ teaspoons baking powder
¾ teaspoon salt
¾ cup (3 ounces) shredded reduced-fat extrasharp Cheddar cheese
1 (14¾-ounce) can cream-style corn
1 (4½-ounce) can chopped green chiles, undrained
Cooking spray

1. Preheat oven to 375°.
2. Combine butter and sugar in a large bowl. Beat with a mixer at medium speed until light and fluffy. Add egg substitute, buttermilk, and eggs, beating at low speed until well combined.
3. Lightly spoon flour into dry measuring cups, and level with a knife. Combine flour and next 4 ingredients in a medium bowl, and stir with a whisk. Add flour mixture to buttermilk mixture, stirring just until combined. Fold in cheese, corn, and chiles. Pour batter into a 13 x 9–inch baking pan coated with cooking spray. Bake at 375° for 45 minutes or until a wooden pick inserted in center comes out clean. Remove from oven, and cool 5 minutes in pan. Yield: 16 servings (serving size: 1 piece).

CALORIES 175 (28% from fat); FAT 5.4g (sat 3.2g, mono 1.2g, poly 0.3g); PROTEIN 5.5g; CARB 25.6g; FIBER 1.1g; CHOL 39mg; IRON 1mg; SODIUM 480mg; CALC 88mg

Muffin Mastery

A Toronto doctor creates hearty muffins to boost her active early morning routine.

Charlotte Moore from Toronto regularly starts her day before 5 A.M. Her mornings often consist of training with the Toronto Argonaut Rowing Club or distance running in preparation for her first marathon. She sought a hearty but not heavy breakfast to fuel her workouts and keep her energy levels up at work.

"My ideal breakfast would be something requiring little preparation, with plenty of complex carbohydrates, fiber, and some protein. These muffins fill the bill." With the right combination of bananas, wheat bran, dried pineapple, dates, and walnuts, Moore's Morning Glory Muffins are a speedy breakfast that is not only nutrient-dense but also tasty.

MAKE AHEAD

Morning Glory Muffins

Substitute apricots or raisins for chopped pitted dates, if you like. The dried fruits, nuts, oatmeal, wheat bran, and whole wheat flour contribute plenty of fiber to each muffin. Complete your breakfast with fat-free yogurt and fruit.

Cooking spray
1 cup whole wheat flour (about 4¾ ounces)
½ cup all-purpose flour (about 2¼ ounces)
1 cup regular oats
¾ cup packed brown sugar
1 tablespoon wheat bran
2 teaspoons baking soda
¼ teaspoon salt
1 cup plain fat-free yogurt
1 cup mashed ripe banana (about 2)
1 large egg, lightly beaten
1 cup chopped pitted dates
¾ cup chopped walnuts
½ cup chopped dried pineapple
3 tablespoons ground flaxseed (about 2 tablespoons whole)

Continued

1. Preheat oven to 350°.

2. Place 18 muffin cup liners in muffin cups; coat liners with cooking spray.

3. Lightly spoon flours into dry measuring cups, and level with a knife. Combine flours and next 5 ingredients in a large bowl; stir with a whisk. Make a well in center of mixture. Combine yogurt, banana, and egg; add to flour mixture, stirring just until moist. Fold in dates, walnuts, and pineapple. Spoon batter into prepared muffin cups. Sprinkle evenly with flaxseed. Bake at 350° for 20 minutes or until muffins spring back when touched lightly in center. Remove muffins from pans immediately; cool on a wire rack. Yield: 18 servings (serving size: 1 muffin).

CALORIES 186 (21% from fat); FAT 4.4g (sat 0.5g, mono 0.7g, poly 2.8g); PROTEIN 4.2g; CARB 35.2g; FIBER 3.4g; CHOL 12mg; IRON 1.2mg; SODIUM 190mg; CALC 42mg

Thai Chicken Lettuce Cups

"I find most Asian lettuce wraps overpowering, so I came up with this entrée because I love light and fresh Thai flavors."

—Amy Sokol, San Antonio, Texas

1½ pounds skinless, boneless chicken breast, coarsely chopped
3 tablespoons fat-free, less-sodium chicken broth
1 teaspoon minced peeled fresh ginger
½ cup chopped water chestnuts
¼ cup chopped red onion
¼ cup sliced green onions
¼ cup chopped fresh cilantro
¼ cup fresh lime juice
2 tablespoons fish sauce
1 tablespoon sugar
⅛ teaspoon salt
12 Bibb lettuce leaves
¼ cup chopped peanuts
4 teaspoons sliced serrano chile (about 2)

1. Place chicken in a food processor; pulse until coarsely ground.

2. Heat a large nonstick skillet over medium heat. Add chicken, broth, and ginger to pan; cook 8 minutes or until chicken is done, stirring frequently. Drain well, and transfer to a large bowl. Add water chestnuts and next 7 ingredients to bowl; toss well. Place ⅓ cup chicken mixture into each lettuce leaf. Serve with peanuts and serrano. Yield: 6 servings (serving size: 2 filled cups, 2 teaspoons peanuts, and about ½ teaspoon serrano).

CALORIES 170 (29% from fat); FAT 5.4g (sat 1.1g, mono 2.3g, poly 1.5g); PROTEIN 22.3g; CARB 8.2g; FIBER 1.3g; CHOL 54mg; IRON 1.3mg; SODIUM 577mg; CALC 31mg

Rigatoni Mediterranean

"This is an easy and delicious meal. Allowing this entrée to stand about 20 minutes after baking allows the flavors to meld."

—Lorraine Fina Stevenski, Clearwater, Florida

1 pound uncooked rigatoni
¼ cup olive oil, divided
5½ cups diced peeled eggplant (about 1 pound)
6 garlic cloves, minced
2 cups thinly sliced Walla Walla or other sweet onion (about 1 large)
1 large zucchini, halved lengthwise and thinly sliced (about 2 cups)
¾ cup thinly sliced green onions (about 6)
¼ cup chopped fresh basil
1 teaspoon dried Italian seasoning
½ teaspoon salt
½ teaspoon freshly ground black pepper
1 (28-ounce) can organic crushed tomatoes, undrained
2 cups (8 ounces) shredded part-skim mozzarella cheese
Cooking spray
½ cup (2 ounces) grated fresh Parmesan cheese

1. Preheat oven to 350°.

2. Cook pasta according to package directions, omitting salt and fat. Drain and set aside.

3. Heat 2 tablespoons oil in a large nonstick skillet over medium-high heat. Add eggplant to pan, and sauté 6 minutes or until lightly browned. Drain on a paper towel-lined plate.

4. Heat 2 tablespoons oil in pan over medium heat. Add garlic to pan, and cook 30 seconds, stirring constantly. Add sweet onion, zucchini, and green onions to pan; cook 6 minutes or until tender, stirring occasionally. Add basil and next 4 ingredients to pan; bring to a boil. Cover, reduce heat, and simmer 15 minutes.

5. Combine pasta, eggplant, and tomato mixture in a large bowl; stir in mozzarella. Transfer pasta mixture to a 13 x 9–inch baking dish coated with cooking spray. Sprinkle evenly with Parmesan cheese. Cover and bake at 350° for 15 minutes; uncover and bake an additional 5 minutes. Yield: 10 servings (serving size: about 2 cups).

CALORIES 346 (29% from fat); FAT 11g (sat 4g, mono 5.3g, poly 0.8g); PROTEIN 15.7g; CARB 45.7g; FIBER 5g; CHOL 17mg; IRON 2.5mg; SODIUM 397mg; CALC 224mg

MAKE AHEAD
Cinnamon Roll Dessert

"My family loves this dessert; it's like one giant cinnamon roll."

—Gaelen McNamara, Haslett, Michigan

ROLL:

1 package dry yeast (about 2¼ teaspoons)
1 teaspoon granulated sugar
¼ cup warm water (100° to 110°)
3 cups sifted cake flour (about 11 ounces), divided
½ cup granulated sugar
1 teaspoon salt
1 cup warm low-fat buttermilk (100° to 110°)
1 large egg
1¾ cups all-purpose flour (about 7¾ ounces), divided
½ cup raisins
Cooking spray
¾ cup packed brown sugar
2 teaspoons ground cinnamon
4 teaspoons unsweetened cocoa
3 tablespoons butter, melted and divided

- ½ cup powdered sugar
- 2 tablespoons (1 ounce) ⅓-less-fat cream cheese, softened
- ½ teaspoon vanilla extract
- 2 teaspoons fat-free milk

1. To prepare roll, dissolve yeast and 1 teaspoon granulated sugar in ¼ cup warm water in a small bowl; let yeast mixture stand 5 minutes.

2. Combine 2 cups cake flour, ½ cup granulated sugar, and salt in a large bowl. Add buttermilk and egg; beat with a mixer at medium-low speed 30 seconds. Add yeast mixture; beat 1 minute. Add 1 cup cake flour, and beat 1 minute. Lightly spoon all-purpose flour into dry measuring cups; level with a knife. Stir 1 cup all-purpose flour into cake flour mixture to form a soft dough. Turn dough out onto a floured surface. Sprinkle surface of dough with raisins. Knead until smooth and elastic (about 8 minutes); add enough of remaining all-purpose flour, 1 tablespoon at a time, to prevent dough from sticking to hands.

3. Place dough in a large bowl coated with cooking spray, turning to coat top. Cover and let rise in a warm place (85°), free from drafts, 1½ hours or until doubled in size. (Gently press two fingers into dough. If indentation remains, dough has risen enough.) Punch dough down. Divide into 3 pieces. Cover and let stand 5 minutes (dough will feel sticky).

4. Combine brown sugar, cinnamon, and cocoa in a small bowl. Working with one portion of dough at a time (cover remaining dough to prevent drying), roll dough into a 16 x 6–inch rectangle on a lightly floured surface. Brush surface of dough with 1 tablespoon butter, and sprinkle with one-third of brown sugar mixture. Roll up tightly, starting with a long edge, pressing firmly to eliminate air pockets; pinch seam and ends to seal. Braid the 3 rolls, pinching ends to seal. Place braid in a 9-inch springform pan coated with cooking spray, forming a ring. Cover and let rise 1 hour or until doubled in size.

5. Preheat oven to 350°.

6. Uncover dough, and bake at 350° for 25 minutes. Lightly cover with foil; bake 20 minutes or until golden brown and loaf sounds hollow when tapped. Cool 10 minutes in pan on a wire rack. Remove from pan; cool on wire rack.

7. To prepare glaze, place powdered sugar, cream cheese, and vanilla in a medium bowl; beat with a mixer at low speed just until blended. Stir in fat-free milk. Drizzle over bread. Cool to room temperature before serving. Cut into wedges. Yield: 16 servings (serving size: 1 wedge).

CALORIES 253 (12% from fat); FAT 3.4g (sat 1.9g, mono 0.8g, poly 0.3g); PROTEIN 4.6g; CARB 51.5g; FIBER 1.4g; CHOL 21mg; IRON 2.7mg; SODIUM 195mg; CALC 45mg

Quick Eggplant and Tomato Sauté

"Eggplant has always been my favorite vegetable. I experimented with this sauté by adding peppers and garlic."

—Kathy Moss, Siloam Springs, Arkansas

- 2 tablespoons olive oil
- 2 cups chopped red onion (1 large)
- 1 cup chopped yellow bell pepper (about 1)
- 1 cup chopped red bell pepper (about 1)
- 2 teaspoons minced garlic
- 5½ cups diced peeled eggplant (about 1 pound)
- ½ teaspoon kosher salt
- ½ teaspoon freshly ground black pepper
- 1 (14½-ounce) can organic diced tomatoes, undrained

1. Heat oil in a large nonstick saucepan over medium-high heat. Add onion and bell peppers; sauté 3 minutes. Add garlic, and sauté 1 minute. Add eggplant, salt, black pepper, and tomatoes; stir to combine. Cover, reduce heat, and simmer 5 minutes. Yield: 12 servings (serving size: ½ cup).

CALORIES 46 (47% from fat); FAT 2.4g (sat 0.3g, mono 1.7g, poly 0.3g); PROTEIN 1g; CARB 5.5g; FIBER 2.1g; CHOL 0mg; IRON 0.4mg; SODIUM 160mg; CALC 8mg

inspired vegetarian
Shell Beans and Peas

Luscious, creamy, and tender, they're ideal for warm-weather meals.

We all eagerly anticipate fresh summer produce. In particular, vegetarians welcome fresh peas and shell beans. Because they contain more protein than any other plant food and are good sources of soluble fiber, vitamins, and minerals, legumes are an indispensable staple of meatless cuisine. Unlike their dried counterparts, though, fresh peas and beans don't require presoaking or long cook times. And unlike canned beans and peas, fresh are low in sodium.

Stock up on fresh peas and shell beans throughout the summer. Try them in these easy recipes, then blanch and freeze some extra to enjoy later.

Veggie Plate Menu
serves 8

Visit your local farmers' market, and let peak produce inspire your meal.

Simple Garlicky Lima Beans

Corn sauté*

Sliced tomatoes

Corn bread

*Melt 2 tablespoons butter in a large skillet over medium-high heat. Add ½ cup sliced shallots and 2 minced garlic cloves to pan; sauté 2 minutes. Add 4 cups fresh corn kernels, ½ teaspoon salt, and ½ teaspoon freshly ground black pepper; sauté 3 minutes. Remove from heat. Stir in ⅓ cup finely chopped green onions and 2 teaspoons lime rind.

Simple Garlicky
Lima Beans

This is a delicious, basic way to cook any kind of fresh shell bean or pea. You can add these cooked beans to salads. For another variation, drizzle with olive oil and lemon juice, and sprinkle with crushed red pepper or a few shavings of Parmesan cheese.

      4 cups fresh lima beans
    2½ cups water
      1 tablespoon olive oil
      2 garlic cloves, crushed
      3 thyme sprigs
      1 bay leaf
      ½ teaspoon sea salt
      ¼ teaspoon freshly ground black
         pepper

1. Sort and wash beans; drain. Combine beans and next 5 ingredients in a medium saucepan. Bring to a boil. Cover, reduce heat, and simmer 20 minutes or until tender. Discard thyme sprigs and bay leaf. Stir in salt and pepper. Yield: 8 servings (serving size: ½ cup).

CALORIES 105 (21% from fat); FAT 2.4g (sat 0.4g, mono 1.3g, poly 0.5g); PROTEIN 5.4g; CARB 16.2g; FIBER 3.9g; CHOL 0mg; IRON 2.5mg; SODIUM 152mg; CALC 30mg

Marinated Lady Peas

A light, lemony vinaigrette complements the delicate flavor of lady peas.

      4 cups fresh lady peas
      2 tablespoons fresh lemon juice
      2 tablespoons white wine vinegar
    1½ tablespoons extravirgin olive oil
      ½ teaspoon salt
      2 garlic cloves, minced
      ¼ cup sliced shallots
      3 tablespoons chopped fresh parsley
      ⅛ teaspoon freshly ground black
         pepper

1. Sort and wash peas; cook peas in boiling water 20 minutes or until tender. Drain.
2. Combine juice and next 4 ingredients in a large bowl. Add peas, shallots, parsley,

and pepper; toss well. Cover and chill. Yield: 8 servings (serving size: ½ cup).

CALORIES 100 (26% from fat); FAT 2.9g (sat 0.4g, mono 1.9g, poly 0.4g); PROTEIN 2.4g; CARB 16.4g; FIBER 4.2g; CHOL 0mg; IRON 1mg; SODIUM 159mg; CALC 101mg

Fresh Peas with Spicy
Pepper Relish

The lightly pickled relish will keep up to two days in the refrigerator.

RELISH:
      1 cup diced red bell pepper
      ½ cup diced onion
      2 tablespoons chopped fresh
         parsley
      1 tablespoon cider vinegar
      2 teaspoons minced seeded
         jalapeño pepper
      ½ teaspoon sugar
      ¼ teaspoon dry mustard
      ¼ teaspoon salt

PEAS:
      3 cups fresh black-eyed peas
      2 teaspoons olive oil
      1 cup chopped onion
      ¼ teaspoon minced garlic
    2½ cups organic vegetable broth
         (such as Swanson Certified
         Organic)
      ½ teaspoon ground cumin
      ½ teaspoon Spanish smoked paprika
      ¼ teaspoon ground red pepper
      ¼ teaspoon salt
      1 bay leaf

1. To prepare relish, combine first 8 ingredients in a bowl. Cover and chill.
2. To prepare peas, sort and wash peas; set aside. Heat oil in a medium saucepan over medium-high heat. Add 1 cup onion and garlic to pan; sauté 5 minutes. Stir in peas, broth, and remaining 5 ingredients; bring to a boil. Cover, reduce heat, and simmer 20 minutes or until peas are tender. Discard bay leaf. Serve with relish. Yield: 6 servings (serving size: ⅔ cup peas and 2 tablespoons relish).

CALORIES 113 (16% from fat); FAT 2g (sat 0.3g, mono 1.2g, poly 0.3g); PROTEIN 2.9g; CARB 21.3g; FIBER 4.8g; CHOL 0mg; IRON 1.2mg; SODIUM 440mg; CALC 106mg

Cranberry
Bean-Vegetable Soup
with Pesto

PESTO:
    1½ teaspoons pine nuts
      1 garlic clove, peeled
      2 teaspoons olive oil
      1 cup fresh basil leaves
      2 tablespoons fresh grated Parmesan
         cheese
    Dash of salt

SOUP:
      3 cups fresh cranberry beans
      2 teaspoons olive oil
      1 cup thinly sliced leek (about 1
         large)
      ½ cup diced carrot
      1 garlic clove, minced
      4 cups water
      1 cup diced zucchini
      1 cup diced yellow squash
      1 (14.5-ounce) can diced tomatoes,
         undrained
      ½ teaspoon salt
      ¼ teaspoon freshly ground black
         pepper

1. To prepare pesto, drop pine nuts and 1 garlic clove through food chute with food processor on; process until minced. Add 2 teaspoons oil; pulse 3 times or until combined. Add basil, cheese, and dash of salt; process 30 seconds or until finely minced, scraping sides of bowl once. Set aside.
2. To prepare soup, sort and wash beans; set aside. Heat 2 teaspoons oil in a Dutch oven over medium-high heat. Add leek, carrot, and minced garlic clove to pan; sauté 4 minutes or until leek is tender. Add 4 cups water and beans; bring to a boil. Cover, reduce heat, and simmer 25 minutes or until beans are tender.
3. Add zucchini, squash, and tomatoes to pan; simmer, uncovered, 10 minutes or until vegetables are tender.
4. Stir in ½ teaspoon salt and pepper. Ladle 1¼ cups soup into each of 6 bowls; top each serving with 1¼ teaspoons pesto. Yield: 6 servings.

CALORIES 195 (19% from fat); FAT 4.2g (sat 0.8g, mono 2.3g, poly 0.8g); PROTEIN 10.5g; CARB 30.9g; FIBER 11.3g; CHOL 1mg; IRON 2.9mg; SODIUM 325mg; CALC 108mg

Pink-Eyed Peas with Smoked Paprika

Field peas are often cooked with bacon or ham. In this vegetarian version, Spanish smoked paprika mimics the taste of bacon.

3 cups fresh pink-eyed peas (about 1 pound)
1 tablespoon butter
½ cup finely chopped onion
2 garlic cloves, minced
1 jalapeño pepper, seeded and minced
3 cups organic vegetable broth (such as Swanson Certified Organic)
½ teaspoon freshly ground black pepper
¼ teaspoon Spanish smoked paprika

1. Sort and wash peas.
2. Heat butter in a large saucepan over medium-high heat. Add onion, garlic, and jalapeño to pan; sauté 3 minutes or until onion is tender. Add peas, broth, pepper, and paprika; bring to a boil. Reduce heat, and simmer 50 minutes or until peas are tender, stirring occasionally. Yield: 4 servings (serving size: about ¾ cup).

CALORIES 147 (20% from fat); FAT 3.3g (sat 1.9g, mono 0.8g, poly 0.3g); PROTEIN 3.6g; CARB 25.6g; FIBER 6g; CHOL 8mg; IRON 1.4mg; SODIUM 453mg; CALC 147mg

MAKE AHEAD
Fresh Pea Salad with Radishes, Tomatoes, and Mint

Chickpeas, black-eyed peas, or lady peas could also be used in this salad.

1½ cups fresh pink-eyed peas
3 tablespoons fresh lemon juice
1 tablespoon rice wine vinegar
1 tablespoon olive oil
2 cups grape or cherry tomatoes, halved
1 cup thinly sliced radishes (about 8)
¼ cup chopped fresh mint
¼ teaspoon salt
¼ teaspoon freshly ground black pepper
Mint sprigs (optional)

1. Sort and wash peas; place in a small saucepan. Cover with water to 2 inches above peas; bring to a boil. Cover, reduce heat, and simmer 20 minutes or until tender. Drain.
2. Combine juice, vinegar, and oil in a small bowl; stir well with a whisk.
3. Combine peas, tomatoes, and next 4 ingredients in a medium bowl. Drizzle juice mixture over salad, tossing to coat. Cover and chill. Garnish with mint sprigs, if desired. Yield: 6 servings (serving size: ⅔ cup).

CALORIES 217 (22% from fat); FAT 5.4g (sat 0.7g, mono 2.4g, poly 1.6g); PROTEIN 10.2g; CARB 34g; FIBER 9.6g; CHOL 0mg; IRON 3.5mg; SODIUM 145mg; CALC 65mg

Three Bean Salad with Almonds and Pecorino

Crisp green beans team up with the buttery limas in this tangy salad. Substitute pink-eyed peas for the lima beans, if you like. Toast almonds in a 350° oven for 8 minutes or until golden. This salad is especially tasty served warm.

1½ cups fresh lima beans
½ pound fresh yellow wax beans, trimmed and cut into 2-inch pieces
½ pound fresh green beans, trimmed and cut into 2-inch pieces
3 tablespoons sherry or red wine vinegar
2 teaspoons olive oil
¼ teaspoon salt
¼ teaspoon freshly ground black pepper
¼ cup (about 1 ounce) shaved fresh pecorino Romano cheese
2 tablespoons slivered almonds, toasted

1. Sort and wash lima beans; place in a small saucepan. Cover with water to 2 inches above beans, and bring to a boil. Cover, reduce heat, and simmer 20 minutes or until tender. Drain.
2. Cook wax and green beans in boiling water 5 minutes or until tender. Drain and plunge beans into ice water; drain.
3. Combine lima, wax, and green beans in a large bowl. Add vinegar, oil, salt, and pepper; toss well. Top with cheese and almonds. Yield: 6 servings (serving size: about 1 cup bean mixture, about 2 teaspoons cheese, and 1 teaspoon almonds).

CALORIES 127 (31% from fat); FAT 4.4g (sat 1.2g, mono 2.2g, poly 0.7g); PROTEIN 6.7g; CARB 15.6g; FIBER 5g; CHOL 3mg; IRON 2.3mg; SODIUM 185mg; CALC 102mg

QUICK & EASY
Chana Masala

This light version of a favorite dish from northern India is a delicious way to use fresh chickpeas. Serve it with basmati rice and plain yogurt.

1½ cups fresh chickpeas (garbanzo beans)
2 teaspoons olive oil
1 cup chopped onion
1 tablespoon minced peeled fresh ginger
1 garlic clove, minced
⅛ teaspoon salt
⅛ teaspoon ground cumin
⅛ teaspoon ground red pepper
¾ cup organic vegetable broth (such as Swanson Certified Organic)
½ cup chopped seeded tomato
2 tablespoons chopped fresh cilantro
⅛ teaspoon garam masala

1. Sort and wash chickpeas, and place in a large saucepan. Cover with water to 2 inches above chickpeas; bring to a boil. Cook 5 minutes or until tender. Drain.
2. Heat oil in a large nonstick skillet over medium heat. Add onion, ginger, and garlic to pan; cook 5 minutes, stirring occasionally. Stir in salt, cumin, and pepper; cook 1 minute. Add chickpeas, broth, and tomato; cook 5 minutes or until liquid almost evaporates. Remove from heat; stir in cilantro and garam masala. Yield: 4 servings (serving size: ½ cup).

CALORIES 146 (19% from fat); FAT 3.1g (sat 0.3g, mono 1.7g, poly 0.3g); PROTEIN 5.9g; CARB 23.1g; FIBER 4.7g; CHOL 0mg; IRON 1.2mg; SODIUM 228mg; CALC 51mg

dinner tonight
Rotisserie Chicken

Versatile and convenient, prepared poultry makes quick work of supper.

Rotisserie Chicken Menu 1
serves 4

Asian Chicken, Noodle, and Vegetable Salad

Wonton crisps*

Cucumber spears

*Stack 12 wonton wrappers; cut in half diagonally. Arrange wonton halves in a single layer on a foil-lined baking sheet. Coat with cooking spray; sprinkle with ¼ teaspoon kosher salt. Bake at 375° for 10 minutes or until lightly browned.

Game Plan

1. While noodles cook:
   • Prepare chili sauce mixture for salad.
   • Cut cucumber spears.
2. While oven preheats:
   • Cut and season wonton wrappers.
   • Chop vegetables.
3. While wonton crisps bake:
   • Assemble salad.

Asian Chicken, Noodle, and Vegetable Salad

Mix the dark meat with the breast meat, if you like.

TOTAL TIME: 38 MINUTES

QUICK TIP: Spend less time chopping by purchasing matchstick-cut carrots and chopped green bell pepper from the supermarket produce section.

    6 ounces uncooked rice noodles
    2 cups cubed skinless, boneless
       rotisserie chicken breast
    ½ cup matchstick-cut carrots
    ½ cup chopped green bell pepper
    ⅓ cup chopped green onions
       (about 3)
    ¼ cup canned sliced water chestnuts,
       drained
    ¼ cup Thai sweet chili sauce (such
       as Mae Ploy)
    2 tablespoons canola oil
 1½ tablespoons rice wine vinegar
 1½ tablespoons fresh lemon juice
    2 teaspoons low-sodium soy sauce
    ½ teaspoon grated peeled fresh
       ginger
    2 tablespoons chopped unsalted,
       dry-roasted peanuts

1. Prepare noodles according to package directions. Drain and cool. Combine noodles, chicken, and next 4 ingredients in a large bowl; toss well.
2. Combine chili sauce and next 5 ingredients in a small bowl, stirring with a whisk. Drizzle chili sauce mixture over noodle mixture; toss gently to coat. Sprinkle with peanuts. Serve immediately. Yield: 4 servings (serving size: 2 cups).

CALORIES 373 (29% from fat); FAT 11.9g (sat 1.5g, mono 6.1g, poly 3.4g); PROTEIN 23.6g; CARB 43.7g; FIBER 1.8g; CHOL 60mg; IRON 2.1mg; SODIUM 368mg; CALC 37mg

---

Rotisserie Chicken Menu 2
serves 4

Chicken and Bacon Roll-Ups

Sweet potato chips

Mixed berry parfaits*

*Combine 2 cups blueberries and 2 cups sliced strawberries in a medium bowl. Combine ½ cup vanilla yogurt, 1 tablespoon honey, and ¼ teaspoon grated lemon rind in a small bowl. Place ½ cup fruit mixture in each of 4 parfait glasses. Spoon 2 tablespoons yogurt mixture into each glass. Top each serving with ½ cup fruit mixture. Garnish with fresh mint sprigs, if desired.

Game Plan

1. Assemble parfaits, and refrigerate.
2. Make mayonnaise mixture.
3. Shred chicken and lettuce, chop tomato.
4. Assemble wraps.

Chicken and Bacon Roll-Ups

Ripe summer tomatoes are essential here. Cut the wraps in half crosswise to serve. For smoky taste, try an applewood-smoked bacon (such as Nueske's).

TOTAL TIME: 35 MINUTES

FLAVOR TIP: Substitute 1 teaspoon chopped fresh basil or chives for tarragon in the mayonnaise mixture, if you prefer.

    ½ cup reduced-fat mayonnaise
    1 teaspoon minced fresh tarragon
    2 teaspoons fresh lemon juice
    4 (2.8-ounce) whole wheat
       flatbreads (such as Flatout)
    2 cups shredded romaine lettuce
    2 cups chopped tomato (about
       2 medium)
    4 center-cut bacon slices, cooked
       and drained
    2 cups shredded skinless, boneless
       rotisserie chicken breast

1. Combine first 3 ingredients in a small bowl. Spread 2 tablespoons mayonnaise mixture over each flatbread. Top each with ½ cup lettuce, ½ cup tomato, 1 bacon slice, crumbled, and ½ cup chicken. Roll up. Yield: 4 servings (serving size: 1 wrap).

CALORIES 433 (27% from fat); FAT 13g (sat 2.6g, mono 2g, poly 0.9g); PROTEIN 34.8g; CARB 44.2g; FIBER 5.5g; CHOL 66mg; IRON 3.1mg; SODIUM 925mg; CALC 49mg

Rotisserie Chicken Menu 3

serves 4

Chicken Chilaquiles

Lime-cilantro coleslaw*

Watermelon wedges

*Combine 3 tablespoons fresh lime juice, 1 tablespoon extravirgin olive oil, and 2 teaspoons sugar in a small bowl. Combine ¼ cup chopped green onions, ¼ cup chopped fresh cilantro, and 1 (12-ounce) package coleslaw in a large bowl. Drizzle juice mixture over coleslaw mixture; toss well to coat.

Game Plan

1. While oven preheats:
- Combine chicken mixture.
- Prepare tomatillo mixture.
- Assemble casserole.
2. While casserole bakes:
- Mix coleslaw.
- Slice and refrigerate watermelon.

QUICK & EASY
Chicken Chilaquiles

For even more heat, add ¼ teaspoon ground red pepper to the tomatillo mixture.

TOTAL TIME: 45 MINUTES

QUICK TIP: Purchase grated fresh Parmesan cheese from the supermarket.

- 2 cups shredded skinless, boneless rotisserie chicken breast
- ½ cup chopped green onions
- ½ cup (2 ounces) shredded Monterey Jack cheese with jalapeño peppers, divided
- 2 tablespoons grated Parmesan cheese
- 1 teaspoon chili powder
- ¼ teaspoon salt
- ¼ teaspoon black pepper
- ¾ cup 1% low-fat milk
- ¼ cup chopped fresh cilantro
- 1 (11-ounce) can tomatillos, drained
- 1 (4.5-ounce) can chopped green chiles, drained
- 12 (6-inch) corn tortillas
Cooking spray

1. Preheat oven to 375°.
2. Combine chicken, onions, ¼ cup Monterey Jack cheese, Parmesan, chili powder, salt, and pepper in a medium bowl. Place milk and next 3 ingredients in a food processor or blender; process until smooth.
3. Heat tortillas according to package directions. Pour ⅓ cup tomatillo mixture into bottom of an 11 x 7–inch baking dish coated with cooking spray. Arrange 4 tortillas in dish, and top with half of chicken mixture. Repeat layers with remaining tortillas and chicken mixture, ending with tortillas.
4. Pour remaining tomatillo mixture over tortillas; sprinkle with ¼ cup Monterey Jack cheese. Bake at 375° for 20 minutes or until bubbly. Yield: 4 servings (serving size: 1½ cups).

CALORIES 347 (28% from fat); FAT 10.9g (sat 4.5g, mono 2.9g, poly 1.9g); PROTEIN 30.9g; CARB 33.3g; FIBER 5.9g; CHOL 79mg; IRON 1.5mg; SODIUM 560mg; CALC 272mg

Rotisserie Chicken Menu 4

serves 4

Chicken, Rice, and Tropical Fruit Salad

Herbed green beans*

Iced tea

*Cook 1 pound trimmed green beans in boiling water 7 minutes or until crisp-tender. Drain. Place green beans in a medium bowl. Add 1 tablespoon minced fresh tarragon, 1 tablespoon minced fresh flat-leaf parsley, 2 teaspoons extravirgin olive oil, ¼ teaspoon salt, and ⅛ teaspoon freshly ground black pepper; toss well.

Game Plan

1. While rice cooks:
- Chop pineapple and mango.
- Halve grapes.
- Prepare mint mixture.
2. Assemble salad, and refrigerate.
3. While beans cook:
- Chop herbs for beans.

QUICK & EASY • MAKE AHEAD
Chicken, Rice, and Tropical Fruit Salad

TOTAL TIME: 39 MINUTES

QUICK TIP: Look for peeled, cored, and cubed fresh pineapple in the produce section of your supermarket.

- 1 cup uncooked basmati rice
- 2 cups cubed skinless, boneless rotisserie chicken breast
- 1 cup cubed fresh pineapple
- 1 cup jarred sliced peeled mango, drained and chopped
- ½ cup seedless red grapes, halved
- ¼ cup sliced almonds, toasted
- 2 tablespoons finely chopped fresh mint
- 1½ tablespoons fresh lemon juice
- 1½ tablespoons canola oil
- ¼ teaspoon salt
- ¼ teaspoon freshly ground black pepper
- 4 romaine lettuce leaves
Mint sprigs (optional)

Continued

1. Cook rice according to package directions, omitting salt and fat. Cool. Combine rice and next 5 ingredients.
2. Combine chopped mint, juice, oil, salt, and pepper in a small bowl, stirring with a whisk. Drizzle mint mixture over rice mixture; toss well. Cover and chill. Place 1 lettuce leaf on each of 4 plates. Spoon 1½ cups rice mixture onto each lettuce leaf. Garnish with mint sprigs, if desired. Yield: 4 servings.

CALORIES 346 (30% from fat); FAT 11.5g (sat 1.4g, mono 6.2g, poly 3g); PROTEIN 25.5g; CARB 36.1g; FIBER 2.8g; CHOL 60mg; IRON 1.6mg; SODIUM 199mg; CALC 45mg

happy endings
Ices Are Nice

The snow cone grows up in these chilly treats.

Remember how great a snow cone tasted when you were a kid—how the frozen sweetness cooled you down and perked you up on a hot summer day? Those bubblegum and blue raspberry sugar-coated ice flakes are still fine for kids. And with flavors fit for an adult, frozen ice is a great summer dessert.

"Water ices," or granitas in Italian, are flavorful, coarsely textured ice crystals. Stirred while freezing, the "ice"—often little more than fruit juice and sugar—develops into a refreshing, flaky slush. Ices are pretty to look at and a delight to eat, especially after dinner on a warm evening.

Part of the dessert's appeal is that it's so versatile. It can be a sophisticated end to a fancy dinner or provide down-home cool comfort at any time of day. And ices couldn't be easier to prepare. They're most commonly made from sweetened fruit juices, but you can use coffee, pureed fruit, even wine and liqueurs. And you don't need an ice-cream maker; just combine a few ingredients in a baking dish, and pop it in the freezer. A perfectly textured slush is ready in a few hours. Best of all, ices are fun to eat—like a snow cone, but all grown up.

Apricot Ice with Roasted Almonds

For a special presentation, place a few slices of fresh apricot in the bottom of a small serving dish, and top with this delicious ice. The ice will keep in the freezer up to three days. Garnish with curls of lemon rind.

 3 tablespoons fresh lemon juice (about 1 lemon)
 2 tablespoons sugar
 ⅛ teaspoon salt
 ⅛ teaspoon almond extract
 1 (11.5-ounce) can apricot nectar
 ¼ cup finely chopped honey-roasted almonds

1. Combine first 5 ingredients in an 8-inch baking dish, stirring until sugar dissolves. Cover and freeze 45 minutes. Stir nectar mixture with a fork every 45 minutes until completely frozen and slushy (about 3 hours).
2. Remove nectar mixture from freezer; scrape mixture with a fork until fluffy. Top with almonds. Serve immediately. Yield: 4 servings (serving size: ½ cup ice and 1 tablespoon almonds).

CALORIES 128 (31% from fat); FAT 4.5g (sat 0.4g, mono 2.9g, poly 0.9g); PROTEIN 2.2g; CARB 21.1g; FIBER 1.8g; CHOL 0mg; IRON 2mg; SODIUM 89mg; CALC 25mg

Honeydew Bellini Ice

The traditional Bellini combines peaches and the Italian sparkling wine prosecco, a combo made famous at Harry's Bar in Venice, Italy. This version uses pureed fresh honeydew melon and will end an alfresco dinner with flair.

 2 cups cubed honeydew melon
 ¼ cup sugar
 2 teaspoons fresh lemon juice
 1 cup prosecco or sparkling white wine

1. Combine first 3 ingredients in a blender; process until smooth and sugar dissolves. Stir in prosecco; pour into an

11 x 7–inch baking dish. Cover and freeze 45 minutes. Stir with a fork every 45 minutes until completely frozen and slushy (about 4 hours). Remove melon mixture from freezer; scrape mixture with a fork until fluffy. Yield: 6 servings (serving size: ½ cup).

CALORIES 80 (1% from fat); FAT 0.1g (sat 0g, mono 0g, poly 0g); PROTEIN 0.4g; CARB 13.9g; FIBER 0.5g; CHOL 0mg; IRON 0.2mg; SODIUM 12mg; CALC 7mg

Orange and Cream Ice

This cool concoction is a grown-up version of the Fifty-Fifty treat sold on ice-cream trucks in the 1960s. Prepare and freeze the ices separately up to three days ahead.

 ½ teaspoon finely grated orange rind
 2 cups fresh orange juice (about 7 oranges)
 2 tablespoons sugar
 2 tablespoons fresh lemon juice
 1 cup 2% reduced-fat milk
 4 teaspoons sugar
 ¼ teaspoon vanilla extract

1. Combine first 4 ingredients in a medium bowl; stir until sugar dissolves. Pour into an 11 x 7–inch baking dish. Cover and freeze 45 minutes. Stir with a fork every 45 minutes until completely frozen and slushy (about 3 hours).
2. Combine milk, 4 teaspoons sugar, and vanilla in a small bowl, stirring until sugar dissolves. Cover and freeze 45 minutes. Stir with a fork every 30 to 45 minutes until completely frozen and slushy (about 2 hours).
3. To serve, remove orange mixture and milk mixture from freezer; stir each mixture with a fork until fluffy. Spoon orange ice into 6 small dishes; top with cream ice. Yield: 6 servings (serving size: ½ cup orange ice and about 3 tablespoons vanilla ice).

CALORIES 86 (10% from fat); FAT 1g (sat 0.5g, mono 0.3g, poly 0.1g); PROTEIN 2g; CARB 18g; FIBER 0.2g; CHOL 3mg; IRON 0.2mg; SODIUM 21mg; CALC 59mg

PAN-SEARED SCALLOPS WITH LEMON
PREP TIME: 5 MIN. TOTAL TIME: 20 MIN.
SERVES 4

- 1 pound sea scallops, tough muscles removed
  Coarse salt and freshly ground pepper, to taste
- 1 tablespoon extra-virgin olive oil, plus more as needed
- 1 lemon, cut into wedges

Pat scallops dry with paper towels, and season with salt and pepper. Heat oil in a skillet over medium-high heat. Add half the scallops to skillet, and cook, flipping once, until golden brown and cooked through, about 3 minutes per side. Transfer to a plate. Repeat with remaining scallops, adding more oil to the skillet as needed. Serve immediately, with lemon wedges on the side.

RICOTTA TART WITH CHOCOLATE AND KUMQUATS
PREP TIME: 10 MIN. TOTAL TIME: 60 MIN.
SERVES 6 TO 8

FOR THE CRUST
- 5 ounces chocolate wafers (about 24 cookies)
- 4 tablespoons unsalted butter, melted
- 1 tablespoon granulated sugar
  Pinch of salt

FOR THE FILLING
- 1½ cups ricotta (12 ounces)
- ½ cup heavy cream
- 2 tablespoons granulated sugar
- ⅛ teaspoon ground cinnamon
- 5 kumquats, thinly sliced crosswise
- 1 ounce bittersweet chocolate, coarsely chopped

1. For the crust: Preheat oven to 400°. Pulse wafers in a food processor until fine crumbs form. Transfer to a bowl, and stir in butter, sugar, and salt. Press into bottom and up sides of a 9-inch tart pan. Bake for 10 minutes. Let cool.
2. For the filling: Beat together ricotta, cream, sugar, and cinnamon until fluffy. Fold in half the kumquats and half the chocolate. Pour into cooled crust. Top with remaining kumquats and chocolate. Refrigerate for at least 30 minutes (or overnight) before serving.

KALE, WHITE BEAN, AND PROSCIUTTO CROSTINI
PREP TIME: 5 MIN. TOTAL TIME: 15 MIN.
SERVES 4

- 3 tablespoons extra-virgin olive oil, plus more for drizzling
- 2 tablespoons red-wine vinegar
  Coarse salt and freshly ground pepper
- 1 can (14½ ounces) cannellini beans, drained and rinsed
- 2 ounces thinly sliced prosciutto, cut into 2-inch pieces
- 2 garlic cloves, thinly sliced
- ¼ teaspoon red-pepper flakes
- ½ cup dry white wine
- ½ bunch kale (about 8 ounces), stems removed, leaves torn into 1-inch pieces
- ½ baguette, cut into ½-inch slices

1. Whisk together 2 tablespoons oil, the vinegar, ¼ teaspoon salt, and pepper to taste. Add beans, and toss to coat.
2. Arrange prosciutto in a single layer in a large sauté pan. Cook over medium-high heat, turning occasionally, until golden and crisp, about 5 minutes. Drain on paper towels.
3. Add remaining tablespoon oil, the garlic, and red-pepper flakes to pan, and cook over medium heat for 1 minute. Add wine and kale. Cover, and cook, stirring once, until wilted. Stir in bean mixture and prosciutto, and season with salt and pepper. Spoon onto baguette slices, and drizzle with oil.

ROASTED SPAGHETTI SQUASH WITH HERBS
PREP TIME: 10 MIN. TOTAL TIME: 65 MIN.
SERVES 4

- 1 spaghetti squash (about 4 pounds), halved lengthwise, seeds removed
- 1 tablespoon extra-virgin olive oil, plus more for brushing
- 1 tablespoon packed light-brown sugar
  Coarse salt and freshly ground pepper
- ½ cup grated Parmesan cheese (about 2½ ounces)
- ½ cup chopped fresh flat-leaf parsley
- ½ cup chopped fresh cilantro
- ¼ cup blanched hazelnuts (1 ounce), toasted and coarsely chopped

1. Preheat oven to 400°. Brush cut sides of squash with oil, and sprinkle with sugar and salt and pepper to taste. Place squash, cut sides down, on a rimmed baking sheet. Roast until tender, about 45 minutes. Let cool slightly on sheet on a wire rack, about 10 minutes.
2. Scrape squash with a fork to remove flesh in long strands. Place in a large bowl. Add oil, Parmesan, parsley, cilantro, hazelnuts, 1 teaspoon salt, and pepper to taste. Toss, and serve immediately.

KALE, WHITE BEAN, AND PROSCIUTTO CROSTINI

PAN-SEARED SCALLOPS WITH LEMON

ROASTED SPAGHETTI SQUASH WITH HERBS

RICOTTA TART WITH CHOCOLATE AND KUMQUATS

Espresso Ice with Anise Cream

Sambuca is a potent Italian liqueur traditionally enjoyed with a garnish of whole coffee beans. If you don't care for its licorice flavor, simply omit it.

1½ cups boiling water
¼ cup packed light brown sugar
1 tablespoon instant espresso granules
1¼ cups vanilla light ice cream, softened
¼ cup frozen fat-free whipped topping, thawed
1½ teaspoons sambuca (anise-flavored liqueur)

1. Combine first 3 ingredients in an 8-inch baking dish, stirring until sugar and espresso dissolve. Cover and freeze 45 minutes. Stir with a fork every 45 minutes until completely frozen (about 4 hours).
2. Remove espresso mixture from freezer; scrape mixture with a fork until fluffy. Combine ice cream, whipped topping, and liqueur. Serve over espresso ice. Yield: 4 servings (serving size: about ½ cup ice and about ¼ cup cream).

CALORIES 150 (21% from fat); FAT 3.5g (sat 1.6g, mono 0g, poly 0g); PROTEIN 2g; CARB 26.9g; FIBER 0g; CHOL 22mg; IRON 0.3mg; SODIUM 37mg; CALC 75mg

Sangría Ice

This frozen version of the Spanish beverage made with red wine and fruit earned our Test Kitchens' highest rating.

1 cup cabernet sauvignon or other dry red wine
1 cup water
1 (16-ounce) package frozen mixed berries
1 orange, thinly sliced
⅔ cup fresh orange juice (about 3 oranges)
¼ cup sugar
6 orange slices

1. Combine first 4 ingredients in a large bowl. Cover and chill 8 hours. Remove orange; discard. Press berry mixture through a sieve over a bowl; discard solids. Combine berry mixture, juice, and sugar in an 8-inch dish, stirring until sugar dissolves. Cover and freeze 45 minutes. Stir with a fork every 45 minutes until completely frozen and slushy (about 4 hours).
2. Remove berry mixture from freezer; scrape mixture with a fork until fluffy. Garnish with orange slices. Yield: 6 servings (serving size: about ¾ cup ice and 1 orange slice).

CALORIES 132 (4% from fat); FAT 0.7g (sat 0.1g, mono 0.1g, poly 0.2g); PROTEIN 1g; CARB 26.2g; FIBER 3.2g; CHOL 0mg; IRON 0.4mg; SODIUM 4mg; CALC 31mg

Rum-Spiked Golden Pineapple Ice

This combination of tropical flavors would be welcome at a pool party.

½ cup water
⅓ cup packed brown sugar
2½ cups pineapple juice (3 [6-ounce] cans)
4 teaspoons dark rum

1. Combine ½ cup water and sugar in a saucepan; bring to a boil. Cook over medium-high heat 2 minutes or until sugar dissolves, stirring constantly. Remove from heat; cool. Stir in juice and rum. Pour mixture into an 11 x 7-inch baking dish; cover and freeze 45 minutes. Stir pineapple mixture with a fork every 45 minutes until completely frozen and slushy (about 4 hours).
2. Remove pineapple mixture from freezer; scrape mixture with a fork until fluffy. Yield: 6 servings (serving size: ½ cup).

CALORIES 112 (1% from fat); FAT 0.1g (sat 0g, mono 0g, poly 0g); PROTEIN 0.3g; CARB 26.3g; FIBER 0.2g; CHOL 0mg; IRON 0.5mg; SODIUM 6mg; CALC 28mg

Blackberry Ice

A touch of rosewater, which is available at Middle Eastern markets and specialty food stores, enhances the flavor of the berries. If you can't find it, omit it. Prepare this up to three days ahead.

1½ cups water
½ cup sugar
1 pound blackberries (fresh or frozen)
¼ teaspoon finely grated lemon rind
1 tablespoon fresh lemon juice
¼ teaspoon rosewater

1. Combine 1½ cups water and sugar in a small saucepan, and bring to a boil. Cook over medium-high heat 2 minutes or until sugar dissolves, stirring constantly. Remove from heat; cool. Pour into a blender. Add blackberries and remaining ingredients; process until smooth. Strain mixture through a fine sieve into a bowl, and discard solids. Pour mixture into an 11 x 7-inch baking dish; cover and freeze 45 minutes. Stir with a fork every 45 minutes until completely frozen and slushy (about 3 hours).
2. Remove blackberry mixture from freezer, and scrape with a fork until fluffy. Yield: 8 servings (serving size: about ½ cup).

CALORIES 85 (2% from fat); FAT 0.2g (sat 0g, mono 0g, poly 0.1g); PROTEIN 0.7g; CARB 21.6g; FIBER 2.9g; CHOL 0mg; IRON 0.5mg; SODIUM 1mg; CALC 18mg

Where There's Smoke

Bill and Cheryl Jamison haunt America's BBQ joints for the hottest regional styles. Light up the grill, and bring your favorite home.

True slow-smoked barbecue is all-American food that inspires pride in those who champion various regional styles. Friendly rivalries flourish in different corners of the country about the best meats, the proper methods of cooking, the nature of sauces, the tastiest accompaniments, even whether you should eat it with your hands or a fork. Bill and Cheryl Jamison have crisscrossed the country and eaten at countless barbecue joints to research their cookbooks. These are some of their favorite styles of 'cue. It's time you joined the fun as we look at five capitals of the craft that claim to have the best. Try their recipes, adapted for home cooks, for each style of barbecue and sides. It's creative fare that invites experimentation and innovation.

MAKE AHEAD
Kansas City Dry Rub

Use this sweet, smoky blend on steaks, pork tenderloin, pork chops, or chicken. Store in an airtight container up to one month.

- ¼ cup paprika
- 2 tablespoons Spanish smoked paprika
- 2 tablespoons freshly ground black pepper
- 1 tablespoon brown sugar
- 2 teaspoons kosher salt
- 2 teaspoons garlic powder
- 1½ teaspoons chili powder
- ½ teaspoon celery salt

1. Combine all ingredients. Yield: ¾ cup (serving size: 1½ teaspoons).

CALORIES 5 (0% from fat); FAT 0g; PROTEIN 0.1g; CARB 1.1g; FIBER 0.2g; CHOL 0mg; IRON 0.1mg; SODIUM 178mg; CALC 3mg

MAKE AHEAD
Kansas City Barbeque Sauce

Thick, tomato-rich Kansas City sauces are sweeter than those from other barbeque regions. While commercial renditions can overdo the sugar, this version (inspired by the scrumptious Gates Original) balances sweet with spice.

- 1 cup plus 2 tablespoons ketchup
- 1 cup water
- ⅓ cup cider vinegar
- ¼ cup packed brown sugar
- 1 tablespoon onion powder
- 1 tablespoon chili powder
- 1 tablespoon freshly ground black pepper
- 1½ tablespoons molasses
- ¾ teaspoon ground celery seed
- ½ teaspoon smoked salt (such as McCormick)

1. Combine all ingredients in a large saucepan; bring to a boil over medium heat. Reduce heat; simmer 25 minutes or until slightly thick. Yield 2½ cups (serving size: about 2 tablespoons).

CALORIES 31 (3% from fat); FAT 0.1g (sat 0g, mono 0g, poly 0g); PROTEIN 0.3g; CARB 7.8g; FIBER 0.2g; CHOL 0mg; IRON 0.3mg; SODIUM 198mg; CALC 12mg

Kansas City Barbecued Chicken

Meaty chicken leg quarters stay moister on the grill than chicken breasts and are a perfect vehicle for the sauce.

- 4 cups hickory wood chips
- 8 (10-ounce) bone-in chicken leg-thigh quarters
- ¼ cup Kansas City Dry Rub (recipe at left)
- 2 cups water
- Cooking spray
- 1½ cups Kansas City Barbecue Sauce (recipe at left)

1. Soak wood chips in water 1 hour; drain well.

2. Loosen skin from thighs and drumsticks by inserting fingers, gently pushing between skin and meat. Rub Kansas City Dry Rub evenly under loosened skin; let stand at room temperature 30 minutes.

3. Remove grill rack; set aside. Prepare grill for indirect grilling, heating one side to medium-high and leaving one side with no heat.

4. Pierce bottom of a disposable aluminum foil pan several times with tip of a knife. Place pan on heated side of grill; add half of wood chips to pan. Place another disposable aluminum foil pan (do not pierce pan) on unheated side of grill. Pour 2 cups water in pan. Coat grill rack with cooking spray; place grill rack on grill.

5. Place chicken on grill rack on unheated side. Close lid; cook 1½ hours. Add additional wood chips halfway through cooking time. Turn chicken over; cover and cook 30 minutes or until a thermometer registers 165°. Remove chicken from grill; let stand 10 minutes. Remove and discard skin.

6. Bring sauce to a simmer in a small saucepan. Brush chicken with ½ cup sauce. Serve chicken with remaining sauce. Yield: 8 servings (serving size: 1 chicken leg-thigh quarter and 2 tablespoons sauce).

CALORIES 294 (33% from fat); FAT 10.9g (sat 2.9g, mono 3.9g, poly 2.5g); PROTEIN 35g; CARB 12.7g; FIBER 0.4g; CHOL 119mg; IRON 2.1mg; SODIUM 591mg; CALC 36mg

KC-Style Potato Salad

3 pounds red potatoes, cut into
  $1/2$-inch pieces
3 tablespoons Kansas City Dry Rub
  (recipe on page 194)
$1 1/2$ teaspoons salt, divided
$1/4$ cup Kansas City Barbecue Sauce
  (recipe on page 194)
3 tablespoons canola oil
2 tablespoons cider vinegar
2 teaspoons prepared mustard
1 cup finely chopped celery
$1/2$ cup finely chopped onion
$1/4$ cup finely chopped fresh parsley
$1/2$ teaspoon black pepper

1. Place potatoes in a large saucepan;
cover with water. Stir in Kansas City
Dry Rub and 1 teaspoon salt. Bring to a
boil. Reduce heat; simmer 15 minutes or
until tender. Drain.
2. Combine Kansas City Barbecue
Sauce, oil, vinegar, and mustard in a
large bowl; stir with a whisk. Add warm
potatoes, and toss to coat. Add $1/2$ teaspoon salt, celery, onion, parsley, and
pepper; toss to combine. Let stand 20
minutes; serve at room temperature.
Yield: 8 servings (serving size: 1 cup).

CALORIES 187 (27% from fat); FAT 5.6g (sat 0.4g, mono 3.1g,
poly 1.7g); PROTEIN 3.6g; CARB 31g; FIBER 3.5g; CHOL 0mg;
IRON 1.5mg; SODIUM 342mg; CALC 33mg

Memphis Barbecue Sauce

Memphis offers sauces that occupy the
middle ground between other styles.
These blends provide moderate amounts
of sweet, heat, and tang, which add up to
a lot of flavor.

1 cup ketchup
$3/4$ cup white vinegar
2 tablespoons brown sugar
2 tablespoons Worcestershire sauce
2 tablespoons prepared mustard
1 tablespoon onion powder
$1/2$ teaspoon freshly ground black
  pepper
$1/4$ teaspoon salt
$1/8$ teaspoon ground red pepper

1. Combine all ingredients in a medium
saucepan; bring to a simmer. Cook 5
minutes; serve warm. Yield: 2 cups (serving size: 2 tablespoons).

CALORIES 25 (4% from fat); FAT 0.1g (sat 0g, mono 0.1g, poly 0g);
PROTEIN 0.4g; CARB 6.4g; FIBER 0.2g; CHOL 0mg; IRON 0.3mg;
SODIUM 247mg; CALC 10mg

Memphis Pork and
Coleslaw Sandwiches
(pictured on page 239)

You'll need to start the pork and soak the
wood chunks a day ahead; you can make
the slaw a day in advance as well.

PORK:

8 hickory wood chunks (about
  4 pounds)
2 tablespoons paprika
1 tablespoon freshly ground black
  pepper
1 tablespoon turbinado sugar
$1 1/2$ teaspoons kosher salt
$1 1/2$ teaspoons garlic powder
$1 1/2$ teaspoons onion powder
$1 1/2$ teaspoons dry mustard
1 (5-pound) bone-in pork shoulder
  (Boston butt)
$1/3$ cup white vinegar
1 tablespoon Worcestershire sauce
1 teaspoon canola oil
1 (12-ounce) can beer
2 cups water
Cooking spray

SLAW:

$1/4$ cup finely chopped onion
$1 1/2$ tablespoons prepared mustard
$1 1/2$ tablespoons white vinegar
1 tablespoon reduced-fat
  mayonnaise
$1 1/2$ teaspoons granulated sugar
$1/4$ teaspoon salt
6 cups chopped green cabbage

REMAINING INGREDIENTS:

13 hamburger buns
$1 2/3$ cups Memphis Barbecue Sauce
  (recipe at left)

1. To prepare pork, soak wood chunks in
water about 16 hours; drain.

2. Combine paprika and next 6 ingredients; reserve 1 tablespoon paprika mixture. Rub half of remaining paprika mixture onto pork. Place in a large zip-top
plastic bag; seal and refrigerate overnight.
3. Remove pork from refrigerator; let
stand at room temperature 30 minutes.
Rub remaining paprika mixture (except 1
tablespoon reserved) onto pork.
4. Combine reserved 1 tablespoon
paprika mixture, $1/3$ cup vinegar, Worcestershire, oil, and beer in a small
saucepan; cook over low heat 5 minutes
or until warm.
5. Remove grill rack; set aside. Prepare
grill for indirect grilling, heating one side
to medium-low and leaving one side with
no heat. Maintain temperature at 225°.
Pierce bottom of a disposable aluminum
foil pan several times with a knife. Place
pan on heated side of grill; add half of
wood chunks to pan. Place another disposable aluminum foil pan (do not pierce
pan) on unheated side of grill. Pour 2
cups water in pan. Coat grill rack with
cooking spray; place grill rack on grill.
6. Place pork on grill rack on unheated
side. Close lid; cook $4 1/2$ hours or until a
thermometer registers 170°, gently
brushing pork with beer mixture every
hour (avoid brushing off sugar mixture).
Add additional wood chunks halfway
through cooking time. Discard any
remaining beer mixture.
7. Preheat oven to 250°.
8. Remove pork from grill. Wrap pork in
several layers of aluminum foil, and place
in a baking pan. Bake at 250° for 2 hours
or until a thermometer registers 195°.
Remove from oven. Let stand, still
wrapped, 1 hour or until pork easily pulls
apart. Unwrap pork; trim and discard fat.
Shred pork with 2 forks.
9. While pork bakes, prepare slaw.
Combine onion and next 5 ingredients
in a large bowl. Add cabbage, and toss to
coat. Cover and chill 3 hours before
serving. Serve pork and slaw on buns
with Memphis Barbecue Sauce. Yield: 13
servings (serving size: 1 bun, 3 ounces
pork, about $1/3$ cup slaw, and about $1 1/2$
tablespoons sauce).

CALORIES 387 (35% from fat); FAT 15.2g (sat 5.1g, mono 6.3g,
poly 2.2g); PROTEIN 26.6g; CARB 33.7g; FIBER 2.3g; CHOL 74mg;
IRON 3.5mg; SODIUM 843mg; CALC 120mg

Texas-Style Smoked Brisket

In Texas, barbecue is about the beef—if there's any sauce, it's a thin, spicy pan sauce using the meat drippings. Look for a flat-cut brisket, which will be a fairly even thickness, and leave the fat layer on for the best results.

BRISKET:

- 1 tablespoon brown sugar
- 1 tablespoon smoked paprika
- 1 tablespoon freshly ground black pepper
- 1½ teaspoons kosher salt
- 1½ teaspoons onion powder
- 1 (7-ounce) can chipotle chiles in adobo sauce
- 1 cup chopped onion
- ¼ cup cider vinegar
- ¼ cup Worcestershire sauce
- 1 (12-ounce) can beer
- 1 (4½-pound) flat-cut brisket (about 3 inches thick)
- 8 hickory wood chunks (about 4 pounds)
- 2 cups water
- Cooking spray
- 2 cups (½-inch) sliced onion
- 2 tablespoons pickled jalapeño peppers

SAUCE:

- 1 cup fat-free, less-sodium beef broth
- 2 tablespoons Worcestershire sauce
- 1 tablespoon cider vinegar
- 1 tablespoon ketchup
- 1 tablespoon pickled jalapeño liquid

1. To prepare brisket, combine first 5 ingredients. Place 2 tablespoons sugar mixture in a blender. Set aside remaining sugar mixture.

2. Remove 2 chiles and 2 tablespoons sauce from can; add to blender. Reserve remaining chiles and sauce for another use. Add chopped onion and next 3 ingredients to blender; process until smooth. Combine brisket and chipotle mixture in a 2-gallon zip-top plastic bag; seal. Marinate in refrigerator 24 hours, turning occasionally.

3. Soak wood chunks in water about 16 hours; drain. Remove brisket from bag, discarding marinade. Pat brisket dry, and rub with remaining sugar mixture. Let brisket stand at room temperature 30 minutes.

4. Remove grill rack; set aside. Prepare grill for indirect grilling, heating one side to medium-low and leaving one side with no heat. Maintain temperature at 225°.

5. Pierce bottom of a disposable aluminum foil pan several times with tip of a knife. Place pan on heated side of grill; add half of wood chunks to pan. Place another disposable aluminum foil pan (do not pierce pan) on unheated side of grill. Pour 2 cups water in pan. Coat grill rack with cooking spray, and place on grill.

6. Place brisket on grill rack on unheated side. Close lid; cook 3½ hours or until a meat thermometer registers 170°. Add additional wood chunks halfway through cooking time.

7. Preheat oven to 250°.

8. Remove brisket from grill. Place sliced onion and jalapeño on a large sheet of aluminum foil. Top with brisket; seal tightly. Place foil-wrapped brisket in a large baking pan. Bake at 250° for 1½ hours or until thermometer registers 190°. Remove from oven. Let stand, still wrapped, 1 hour. Unwrap brisket, reserving juices, onion, and jalapeño; trim and discard fat. Cut brisket across grain into thin slices.

9. To prepare sauce, finely chop sliced onion and jalapeño; set aside. Place brisket juices in a zip-top plastic bag inside a 2-cup glass measure; let stand 10 minutes (fat will rise to the top). Seal bag; carefully snip off 1 bottom corner of bag. Drain ½ cup drippings into a saucepan, stopping before fat layer reaches opening; discard fat and remaining drippings. Add onion, jalapeño, broth, and remaining 4 ingredients to pan; cook over medium heat 5 minutes or until thoroughly heated. Yield: 10 servings (serving size: about 3 ounces brisket and about 3½ tablespoons sauce).

CALORIES 243 (33% from fat); FAT 9g (sat 2.9g, mono 3.9g, poly 0.4g); PROTEIN 29.5g; CARB 8.2g; FIBER 0.7g; CHOL 86mg; IRON 3.2mg; SODIUM 530mg; CALC 27mg

BEER NOTE: Smoky brisket calls for a smoky beer. Although the Lone Star State makes some excellent brews (any of which would pair well with Texas barbecue), try Germany's Aecht Schlenkerla Maerzen beer, which has an alluring aroma of bacon and smoked sausage from the use of smoked barley. Its full body and gentle malt sweetness balance the spicy sauce. At 16.9 ounces, one bottle ($4) is enough to share.

Long-Cooked Collards with Cane Syrup

Try this hearty side with Memphis-style barbecue. Cane syrup is a common Southern sweetener used in everything from cookies to vegetables. If you can't find it, use its close cousin, molasses, or honey. Pepper vinegar offsets the syrup's sweetness.

- 2 cups chopped onion
- 2 garlic cloves, minced
- 1 bacon slice, chopped
- 4 cups water
- 4 cups fat-free, less-sodium chicken broth
- ¼ cup cider vinegar
- 2 tablespoons cane syrup
- 1½ teaspoons coarsely ground black pepper
- ¼ teaspoon salt
- 2½ pounds packaged prewashed torn collard greens
- Hot pepper vinegar (optional)

1. Cook first 3 ingredients in a large Dutch oven over medium-high heat 6 minutes or until tender. Add 4 cups water and next 5 ingredients; bring to a boil. Gradually add greens. Cover, reduce heat, and simmer 45 minutes, stirring occasionally. Uncover; cook 1 hour or until very tender. Serve with pepper vinegar, if desired. Yield: 8 servings (serving size: 1 cup).

CALORIES 99 (18% from fat); FAT 2g (sat 0.6g, mono 0.7g, poly 0.5g); PROTEIN 5.5g; CARB 16.9g; FIBER 6.3g; CHOL 2mg; IRON 0.8mg; SODIUM 328mg; CALC 228mg

Brunswick Stew

In North Carolina, you'll find Brunswick stew is a common barbecue accompaniment, though it's hearty enough to be a main dish. Traditionally, it might include everything harvested on the farm and a few items from the woods (particularly squirrel), but this version limits the meats to chicken and pork.

2 bacon slices, chopped
1/2 pound boneless pork loin, trimmed and cut into 1/2-inch cubes
3/4 pound skinless, boneless chicken breasts
3/4 pound skinless, boneless chicken thighs
4 cups fat-free, less-sodium chicken broth
1 cup water
1 1/2 cups mashed cooked peeled baking potato (about 3/4 pound)
1 cup chopped onion
3/4 cup (1-inch) sliced green beans
3/4 cup fresh corn kernels
1 tablespoon Worcestershire sauce
1 1/2 teaspoons prepared mustard
1 teaspoon coarsely ground black pepper
3/4 teaspoon salt
1/4 teaspoon ground red pepper
1 (10-ounce) package frozen baby lima beans, thawed

1. Cook bacon in a Dutch oven over medium-high heat until crisp. Add pork; sauté 5 minutes or until lightly browned. Add chicken; sauté 2 minutes. Add broth and 1 cup water; bring to a boil. Cover, reduce heat, and simmer 50 minutes or until pork is tender.
2. Remove chicken from pan; shred with 2 forks. Return chicken to pan; add potato and remaining ingredients. Bring to a simmer; simmer, uncovered, 45 minutes or until slightly thick, stirring occasionally. Yield: 8 servings (serving size: 1 1/4 cups).

CALORIES 290 (21% from fat); FAT 6.9g (sat 2.1g, mono 2.7g, poly 1.2g); PROTEIN 30.6g; CARB 35.9g; FIBER 4.2g; CHOL 81mg; IRON 2.6mg; SODIUM 597mg; CALC 49mg

Carolina Pulled Pork with Lexington Red Sauce

You'll need to start this recipe a day ahead to allow ample time for the wood chunks to soak and the flavors of the dry rub to penetrate the meat. Slow, low-heat cooking is key to tender pork that shreds easily. While the pork is still warm, shred it into uneven shards, mixing together some of the crisp, dark outer meat with the moister interior meat.

PORK:
8 hickory wood chunks (about 4 pounds)
2 tablespoons turbinado sugar
2 tablespoons coarsely ground black pepper
2 tablespoons paprika
1 1/2 teaspoons salt
1/2 teaspoon ground red pepper
1 (5-pound) bone-in pork shoulder (Boston butt)
1 cup cider vinegar
2 1/4 cups water, divided
1 teaspoon salt
1 teaspoon canola oil
Cooking spray

SAUCE:
1 cup cider vinegar
1/3 cup ketchup
1/4 cup water
2 teaspoons granulated sugar
1/2 teaspoon salt
1/2 teaspoon freshly ground black pepper
1/4 teaspoon crushed red pepper

1. To prepare pork, soak wood chunks in water about 16 hours; drain.
2. Combine turbinado sugar and next 4 ingredients; reserve 2 tablespoons sugar mixture. Rub half of remaining sugar mixture onto pork. Place in a large zip-top plastic bag; seal and refrigerate pork overnight.
3. Remove pork from refrigerator, and let stand at room temperature 30 minutes. Rub remaining sugar mixture (except reserved 2 tablespoons) onto pork.

4. Combine reserved 2 tablespoons sugar mixture, 1 cup vinegar, 1/4 cup water, 1 teaspoon salt, and oil in a small saucepan; cook over low heat 10 minutes or until sugar dissolves.
5. Remove grill rack; set aside. Prepare grill for indirect grilling, heating one side to medium-low and leaving one side with no heat. Maintain temperature at 225°. Pierce bottom of a disposable aluminum foil pan several times with the tip of a knife. Place pan on heated side of grill; add half of wood chunks to pan. Place another disposable aluminum foil pan (do not pierce pan) on unheated side of grill. Pour 2 cups water in pan. Coat grill rack with cooking spray, and place on grill.
6. Place pork on grill rack on unheated side. Close lid, and cook 4 1/2 hours or until a thermometer registers 170°, gently brushing pork with vinegar mixture every hour (avoid brushing off sugar mixture). Add additional wood chunks halfway through cooking time. Discard any remaining vinegar mixture.
7. Preheat oven to 250°.
8. Remove pork from grill. Wrap pork in several layers of aluminum foil, and place in a baking pan. Bake at 250° for 2 hours or until a thermometer registers 195°. Remove from oven. Let stand, still wrapped, 1 hour or until pork easily pulls apart. Unwrap pork; trim and discard fat. Shred pork with 2 forks.
9. To prepare sauce, combine 1 cup vinegar, ketchup, and remaining 5 ingredients in a small saucepan; bring to a boil. Cook until reduced to 1 1/4 cups (about 5 minutes). Serve sauce warm or at room temperature with pork. Yield: 13 servings (serving size: 3 ounces pork and about 1 1/2 tablespoons sauce).

CALORIES 230 (50% from fat); FAT 12.9g (sat 4.6g, mono 5.8g, poly 1.3g); PROTEIN 21.4g; CARB 4.7g; FIBER 0.3g; CHOL 74mg; IRON 1.6mg; SODIUM 692mg; CALC 31mg

Santa Maria Smoked Tri-Tip

Flavorful tri-tip steak is a cut of beef also known as bottom sirloin or sirloin tip.

  3 cups hickory wood chips
  1 teaspoon kosher salt
  1 teaspoon freshly ground black pepper
  1/2 teaspoon garlic powder
  1 (2 1/4-pound) tri-tip steak, trimmed
  Cooking spray
  2 cups Santa Maria Salsa (recipe at right)
  Cilantro sprigs (optional)

1. Soak wood chips in water 1 hour; drain well.
2. Combine salt, pepper, and garlic powder; sprinkle evenly over steak. Let stand at room temperature 30 minutes.
3. Remove grill rack; set aside. Prepare grill, heating one side to high and one side to medium. Place wood chips on hot coals on medium-heat side of grill; heat wood chips 10 minutes. Coat grill rack with cooking spray; place on grill.
4. Lightly coat steak with cooking spray. Place steak on grill rack over high-heat side of grill; grill 6 minutes, turning 3 times. Place steak on grill rack over medium-heat side of grill; grill 40 minutes or until a thermometer registers 140° (medium-rare) or until desired degree of doneness. Remove steak from grill; let stand 10 minutes. Cut steak diagonally across grain into thin slices. Serve with Santa Maria Salsa; garnish with cilantro sprigs, if desired. Yield: 8 servings (serving size: 3 ounces steak and 1/4 cup salsa).

CALORIES 259 (46% from fat); FAT 13.1g (sat 4.8g, mono 6.9g, poly 0.5g); PROTEIN 30.9g; CARB 2.6g; FIBER 0.7g; CHOL 66mg; IRON 3.9mg; SODIUM 544mg; CALC 26mg

WINE NOTE: Tri-tip from California's Santa Ynez Valley goes naturally with a full-throttle merlot from the same region. Gainey Merlot 2004 (Santa Ynez Valley, California), $26, has enough structure to stand up to the steak, the char-smokiness of the wood chips, and the pungency of the salsa.

Santa Maria Salsa

This sprightly, crunchy relish is a California original that's served with smoked steak.

  2 (14.5-ounce) cans fire-roasted diced tomatoes with green chiles, undrained (such as Muir Glen)
  1 cup finely chopped celery
  1/2 cup finely chopped onion
  1 1/2 teaspoons white vinegar
  1/2 teaspoon kosher salt
  1/2 teaspoon freshly ground black pepper
  1/2 teaspoon Worcestershire sauce
  1/4 teaspoon garlic powder
  1/4 teaspoon hot pepper sauce (such as Tabasco)

1. Drain 1 can tomatoes. Combine drained tomatoes, undrained tomatoes, and remaining ingredients; cover and chill at least 30 minutes before serving. Yield: 4 cups (serving size: 1/4 cup).

CALORIES 10 (9% from fat); FAT 0.1g (sat 0g, mono 0g, poly 0g); PROTEIN 0.4g; CARB 2.4g; FIBER 0.6g; CHOL 0mg; IRON 0.2mg; SODIUM 236mg; CALC 13mg

Texas Peach Cobbler

This dessert tops fruit with a biscuit-like topping. The batter goes into the dish first, then rises up through the fruit as it bakes.

FILLING:
  4 cups sliced peeled ripe peaches (about 2 pounds)
  2 tablespoons granulated sugar
  1 teaspoon fresh lemon juice
  1/4 teaspoon vanilla extract

BATTER:
  6 tablespoons butter
  1 1/4 cups all-purpose flour (about 5 1/2 ounces)
  3/4 cup granulated sugar
  2 teaspoons baking powder
  1/8 teaspoon salt
  Dash of ground cinnamon
  1 cup 1% low-fat milk
  1/2 teaspoon vanilla extract
  1 tablespoon turbinado sugar

1. Preheat oven to 350°.
2. To prepare filling, combine first 4 ingredients in a medium bowl; set aside.
3. To prepare batter, place butter in an 8-inch square baking dish. Place dish in oven 5 minutes or until butter melts. Lightly spoon flour into dry measuring cups; level with a knife. Combine flour and next 4 ingredients in a medium bowl. Combine milk and 1/2 teaspoon vanilla; add milk mixture to flour mixture, stirring just until moist. Spoon batter over butter, spreading evenly (do not stir). Spoon peach mixture over batter, gently pressing peaches into batter. Bake at 350° for 40 minutes. Sprinkle with turbinado sugar, and bake an additional 10 minutes or until crust is golden. Yield: 8 servings.

CALORIES 294 (28% from fat); FAT 9.3g (sat 5.7g, mono 2.4g, poly 0.5g); PROTEIN 4.2g; CARB 51g; FIBER 2.2g; CHOL 24mg; IRON 1.3mg; SODIUM 235mg; CALC 118mg

then & now
Peach-Blueberry Cobbler

Midsummer brings an abundance of juicy peaches and blueberries.

In our July/August 1998 issue, we offered a Peach-Blueberry Cobbler as a way to make use of these seasonal treasures. Our new and improved version of this recipe makes a few changes to highlight the flavor even more deliciously. We've omitted the original's 1/4 teaspoon of cinnamon, as the spice tends to overpower the flavor of the delicate fruit. We also switched from cornstarch to flour to thicken the filling and create a more pleasing consistency. But the biggest change is in the topping. The original recipe called for rolling and cutting the dough. This time we created easy, tender, fluffy drop biscuits to top the fruit by increasing the amount of sugar and using butter instead of margarine. Finally, we crowned the cobbler with a sprinkling of turbinado sugar so you enjoy a sweet crunch with each bite. For a special treat, add a scoop of low-fat vanilla ice cream.

Peach-Blueberry Cobbler

(pictured on page 238)

FILLING:

½ cup granulated sugar
2 tablespoons all-purpose flour
½ teaspoon grated lemon rind
¼ teaspoon salt
3 cups chopped peeled peaches
(about 2 pounds)
2 cups fresh blueberries
1 tablespoon fresh lemon juice
Cooking spray

TOPPING:

1⅓ cups all-purpose flour (about 6
ounces)
⅓ cup granulated sugar
½ teaspoon baking powder
¼ teaspoon salt
3 tablespoons chilled butter, cut
into small pieces
⅔ cup low-fat buttermilk
1½ tablespoons turbinado sugar

1. Preheat oven to 400°.
2. To prepare filling, combine first 4
ingredients in a large bowl. Add peaches,
blueberries, and juice. Spoon mixture
into an 8-inch square baking dish coated
with cooking spray. Bake at 400° for 15
minutes.
3. To prepare topping, lightly spoon 1⅓
cups flour into dry measuring cups; level
with a knife. Combine 1⅓ cups flour, ⅓
cup granulated sugar, baking powder,
and ¼ teaspoon salt, stirring with a
whisk. Cut in butter with a pastry
blender or 2 knives until mixture resembles coarse meal. Add buttermilk; stir
just until moist.
4. Remove dish from oven; drop dough
onto peach mixture to form 8 rounds.
Sprinkle dough evenly with turbinado
sugar. Bake at 400° for 25 minutes or
until bubbly and golden. Yield: 8 servings (serving size: ½ cup cobbler and 1
biscuit).

CALORIES 259 (17% from fat); FAT 4.9g (sat 2.9g, mono 1.2g,
poly 0.4g); PROTEIN 3.9g; CARB 52.1g; FIBER 2.4g; CHOL 12mg;
IRON 1.3mg; SODIUM 230mg; CALC 52mg

Color Your Palate

Bright and vibrant produce boasts a rich array of beneficial antioxidants and nutrients.

Like many great ideas, the concept that vibrantly colored produce is good for you was born in a mundane setting. In the early 1990s, two coworkers at the USDA's Human Nutrition Research Center on Aging at Tufts University in Boston were car-pooling to work. As neuroscientist James Joseph, PhD, remembers it, a colleague mentioned a test, called ORAC (Oxygen Radical Absorbency Capacity), that meas-ures antioxidant activity in body tissues. (In the body, antioxidants are compounds that sacrifice themselves to save healthy cells from damage. They can be vitamins, minerals, or other compounds that help prevent or inhibit cell damage.) Chemist and nutritionist Ronald Prior, PhD, the second carpool member, wondered if he could try another version of the test on food.

In 1996, Prior "turned his lab into a salad bar and started measuring antioxidant levels for all kinds of fruits and vegetables," says Joseph. "It turns out the fruits and vegetables with the highest ORAC levels were the most colorful."

Every time you add blue and purple to your plate in the form of eggplant, blueberries, or plums, your body benefits from disease-fighting antioxidants called ellagitannins, anthocyanins, and proanthocyanidins. Add orange with carrots, cantaloupe, or apri-cots, and you tap into beta-carotene, one of the most powerful antioxidants. Cap it off with red tomatoes, and you'll gain lycopene, an antioxidant that may protect the heart and prevent prostate cancer.

Even though the many names scientists give these beneficial compounds seem complex, the message is simple: Eat a variety of different-colored fruits and vegeta-bles daily to ensure you obtain the widest diversity of vitamins, minerals, and other antioxidants.

Spinach Salad with Grilled Red Onion Rings and Sesame Vinaigrette

The lutein from the spinach and the flavonols from the onion bolster the nutri-tion of this side dish.

1 large red onion, cut crosswise into
12 (¼-inch-thick) rings (about
10 ounces)
2 teaspoons dark sesame oil, divided
1½ tablespoons fresh lemon juice
1 tablespoon low-sodium soy sauce
1 tablespoon honey
10 cups baby spinach leaves (about
10 ounces)
¼ teaspoon freshly ground black
pepper
⅛ teaspoon salt
1 tablespoon sesame seeds, toasted

1. Prepare grill.
2. Combine onion and ½ teaspoon oil, tossing to coat. Arrange onion on a grill rack; grill 9 minutes or until browned and tender, turning frequently.
3. Combine 1½ teaspoons oil, juice, soy sauce, and honey in a small bowl, stirring with a whisk.
4. Place spinach in a large bowl; sprinkle with pepper and salt. Add onions. Drizzle oil mixture over spinach mix-ture, tossing gently to coat. Sprinkle with sesame seeds. Yield: 6 servings (serving size: 2 cups).

CALORIES 56 (35% from fat); FAT 2.2g (sat 0.3g, mono 0.9g,
poly 0.9g); PROTEIN 1.7g; CARB 8.1g; FIBER 1.8g; CHOL 0mg;
IRON 1.7mg; SODIUM 176mg; CALC 53mg

Broccoli Mac and Cheese Gratin

Blanched broccoli boosts the nutritional profile of a familiar cheesy pasta main dish. Besides lending color to the recipe, the green vegetable adds fiber, folate, and vitamin C.

    4   cups uncooked medium seashell
        pasta (about 12 ounces)
    6   cups broccoli florets (about 1
        pound)
    1   tablespoon olive oil, divided
    2   garlic cloves, minced
   1/3 cup finely chopped onion
  3 3/4 cups 1% low-fat milk, divided
   1/3 cup all-purpose flour (about
        1 1/2 ounces)
    1   cup (4 ounces) shredded fontina
        cheese
   1/2 cup (2 ounces) grated Asiago
        cheese
  1 1/4 teaspoons salt
   1/4 teaspoon freshly ground black
        pepper
   1/8 teaspoon ground red pepper
Dash of ground nutmeg
Cooking spray
    2   (1-ounce) slices white bread

1. Preheat oven to 400°.
2. Cook pasta in boiling water 8 minutes; add broccoli. Cook 3 minutes or until pasta is done. Drain.
3. Heat 2 teaspoons oil in a Dutch oven over medium heat. Add garlic to pan; cook 45 seconds. Transfer garlic mixture to a small bowl; set aside.
4. Add 1 teaspoon oil to pan; stir in onion. Cook 1 minute, stirring frequently. Remove from heat; stir in 3 cups milk. Lightly spoon flour into a dry measuring cup; level with a knife. Combine 3/4 cup milk and flour in a small bowl, stirring with a whisk. Add flour mixture to onion mixture. Return pan to medium-high heat, stirring constantly with a whisk; bring to a boil. Cook 1 minute or until thick, stirring constantly with a whisk. Remove from heat; stir in fontina and next 5 ingredients. Add pasta mixture to milk mixture, tossing gently to coat. Pour into a 13 x 9–inch baking dish coated with cooking spray.

5. Place garlic mixture and bread in a food processor; pulse 15 times or until fine crumbs measure 1 cup. Sprinkle breadcrumb mixture over pasta mixture. Bake at 400° 18 minutes or until top is brown. Yield: 8 servings (serving size: 1 1/2 cups).

CALORIES 360 (26% from fat); FAT 10.4g (sat 5.2g, mono 3.4g, poly 0.7g); PROTEIN 19g; CARB 48.7g; FIBER 3.2g; CHOL 27mg; IRON 2.4mg; SODIUM 708mg; CALC 341mg

Grilled Rack of Lamb with Three-Onion Jam

The flavonoid antioxidants found in onions are also found in broccoli, tea, and apples. This subtly sweet jam is a good complement for assertive lamb, and it's also nice on burgers.

JAM:

  1 1/2 cups halved pearl onions
  1 1/2 cups 1-inch pieces peeled shallots
    1   cup chopped red onion
    2   teaspoons butter
    2   teaspoons olive oil
   1/4 cup packed brown sugar
   1/4 cup fat-free, less-sodium chicken
        broth
   1/4 teaspoon salt
   1/4 teaspoon coarsely ground black
        pepper
    1   tablespoon red wine vinegar
    2   teaspoons chopped fresh thyme

LAMB:

   1/2 teaspoon coarsely ground black
        pepper
   1/4 teaspoon salt
    2   (1 1/2-pound) French-cut racks
        of lamb (8 ribs each), trimmed
Cooking spray

1. To prepare jam, combine first 6 ingredients in a large saucepan over medium-high heat; cook 10 minutes or until onions are tender, stirring frequently. Reduce heat to medium; cook 5 minutes or until golden. Add broth, 1/4 teaspoon salt, and 1/4 teaspoon pepper; simmer 20 minutes. Stir in vinegar and thyme; simmer 8 minutes or until liquid evaporates. Remove from heat; keep warm.

2. Prepare grill.
3. To prepare lamb, sprinkle 1/2 teaspoon pepper and 1/4 teaspoon salt over lamb. Place lamb on a grill rack coated with cooking spray; grill 4 minutes, turning once. Reduce heat to medium; grill lamb 10 minutes on each side or until desired degree of doneness. Let rest 10 minutes before cutting into chops. Serve lamb chops with onion jam. Yield: 8 servings (serving size: 2 lamb chops and 3 tablespoons jam).

CALORIES 336 (35% from fat); FAT 13.1g (sat 4.7g, mono 5.5g, poly 1.2g); PROTEIN 27.4g; CARB 29.4g; FIBER 0.4g; CHOL 80mg; IRON 3.3mg; SODIUM 249mg; CALC 35mg

MAKE AHEAD

Lemon-Chive Potato Salad

White-fleshed potatoes and onions offer at least two types of antioxidants, which may enhance immune function. Cover this dish and refrigerate it for a minimum of four hours to allow the flavors to adequately meld.

  4 1/2 cups (1/2-inch) cubed peeled
        baking potato (about 2 pounds)
   1/3 cup finely chopped onion
   1/2 cup light mayonnaise
   1/4 cup chopped fresh chives
    3   tablespoons fresh lemon juice
   1/2 teaspoon salt
   1/2 teaspoon freshly ground black
        pepper
   1/2 cup thinly sliced radishes

1. Place potato in a large saucepan, and cover with water. Bring to a boil. Reduce heat, and simmer 15 minutes or until tender. Drain. Cool; cover and chill. Stir in onion.
2. Combine mayonnaise and next 4 ingredients in a small bowl, stirring with a whisk. Add mayonnaise mixture to potato mixture; toss gently to coat. Cover and refrigerate 4 hours or overnight. Sprinkle radishes over potato mixture just before serving. Yield: 8 servings (serving size: about 2/3 cup).

CALORIES 137 (14% from fat); FAT 2.1g (sat 0.5g, mono 0.4g, poly 1.1g); PROTEIN 2.4g; CARB 28g; FIBER 2g; CHOL 0mg; IRON 0.5mg; SODIUM 286mg; CALC 11mg

Berry-Season Brunch Menu
serves 6

Capitalize on a leisurely summer Sunday.

Almond-Buttermilk Hotcakes with Blackberry-Grape Sauce

Minty raspberry sparkler*

Canadian bacon

*Combine ¼ cup sugar and ¼ cup water in a small, heavy saucepan, and bring to a boil, stirring until sugar dissolves. Add 2 mint sprigs to pan; let stand 5 minutes. Remove mint, and discard. Combine sugar mixture, 3 cups fresh raspberries, and 2 tablespoons fresh lemon juice in a blender, and process until smooth. Strain mixture through a sieve into a bowl, and discard solids. Spoon 3 tablespoons raspberry mixture into each of 6 wineglasses; top each serving with ½ cup chilled Champagne.

Almond-Buttermilk Hotcakes with Blackberry-Grape Sauce

The sauce offers sources of antioxidants that may protect against cancer and improve mental function.

SAUCE:

3 tablespoons seedless blackberry jam
¼ teaspoon grated lemon rind
2 tablespoons fresh lemon juice
1 tablespoon water
1 teaspoon cornstarch
1 cup seedless red grapes, halved lengthwise
1½ cups fresh blackberries

HOTCAKES:

1½ cups all-purpose flour (about 6¾ ounces)
¼ cup sliced almonds, toasted
1¼ teaspoons baking powder
1 teaspoon baking soda
¼ teaspoon freshly ground nutmeg
⅛ teaspoon salt
1⅓ cups nonfat buttermilk
½ cup packed brown sugar
⅓ cup water
2 tablespoons canola oil
1 large egg, lightly beaten
Cooking spray

1. To prepare sauce, combine first 5 ingredients in a small saucepan over medium heat, and stir with a whisk. Add grapes to pan; bring to a boil. Reduce heat, and simmer 1 minute or until slightly thick. Stir in blackberries. Remove from heat, and keep warm.

2. To prepare hotcakes, lightly spoon flour into dry measuring cups; level with a knife. Combine flour and next 5 ingredients in a large bowl, stirring with a whisk. Combine buttermilk and next 4 ingredients; add to flour mixture, stirring until smooth.

3. Pour about ¼ cup batter per pancake onto a hot nonstick griddle or nonstick skillet coated with cooking spray. Cook 2 minutes or until tops are covered with bubbles and edges looked cooked. Carefully turn pancakes over; cook 2 minutes or until bottoms are lightly browned. Repeat procedure with remaining batter. Serve hotcakes with sauce. Yield: 6 servings (serving size: 2 hotcakes and about ¼ cup sauce).

CALORIES 342 (21% from fat); FAT 8.1g (sat 0.8g, mono 4.4g, poly 2.2g); PROTEIN 7.8g; CARB 61.7g; FIBER 3.5g; CHOL 36mg; IRON 2.6mg; SODIUM 435mg; CALC 171mg

Super Sizzler Menu
serves 4

Latin flavors infuse this menu.

Spiced Tilapia with Roasted Pepper–Tomatillo Sauce

Saffron and cilantro rice*

Steamed green beans

*Heat 1 tablespoon olive oil in a large saucepan over medium-high heat. Add ½ cup chopped onion and 2 minced garlic cloves to pan; sauté 2 minutes. Add 1 cup long-grain white rice to pan; sauté 1 minute. Stir in 2 cups fat-free, less-sodium chicken broth and ⅛ teaspoon crushed saffron threads; bring to a boil. Cover, reduce heat, and simmer 20 minutes or until liquid is absorbed. Stir in ⅓ cup chopped fresh cilantro, 1 tablespoon fresh lime juice, and ¼ teaspoon salt.

Spiced Tilapia with Roasted Pepper–Tomatillo Sauce

This sauce supplies vitamin C, vitamin E, and a little lycopene.

SAUCE:

1 large red bell pepper
2 teaspoons canola oil
1 cup finely chopped tomatillo
¼ teaspoon salt
1 garlic clove, minced
2 tablespoons chopped fresh cilantro
1 teaspoon rice vinegar
1 teaspoon honey

FISH:

2 tablespoons flour
2 teaspoons chili powder
½ teaspoon dried oregano
¼ teaspoon ground cumin
4 (6-ounce) tilapia fillets
¼ teaspoon salt
¼ teaspoon freshly ground black pepper
2 teaspoons canola oil
Cilantro sprigs (optional)

1. Preheat broiler.

2. To prepare sauce, cut bell pepper in half lengthwise; discard seeds and membranes. Place pepper halves, skin sides up, on a foil-lined baking sheet; flatten with hand. Broil 15 minutes or until blackened. Place in a zip-top plastic bag; seal. Let stand 10 minutes. Peel and cut into chunks.

3. Heat 2 teaspoons oil in a large nonstick skillet over medium heat. Add tomatillo to pan; cook 6 minutes or until tender. Add ¼ teaspoon salt and garlic to pan; cook 1 minute. Transfer mixture to a blender or food processor. Add bell pepper, chopped cilantro, vinegar, and honey. Remove center piece of blender lid (to allow steam to escape); secure blender lid on blender. Place a clean towel over opening in blender lid (to avoid splatters). Blend until smooth; set aside. Wipe pan with a paper towel.

4. To prepare fish, combine flour, chili powder, oregano, and cumin in a shallow dish; stir with a whisk. Sprinkle fish

Continued

evenly with ¼ teaspoon salt and pepper; dredge in flour mixture.

5. Heat 2 teaspoons oil in pan over medium-high heat. Add fish to pan, and cook 2 minutes or until lightly browned. Carefully turn fish over, and cook 4 minutes or until fish flakes easily when tested with a fork or until desired degree of doneness. Serve fish with sauce. Garnish with cilantro sprigs, if desired. Yield: 4 servings (serving size: 1 fillet and about ¼ cup sauce).

CALORIES 239 (32% from fat); FAT 8.5g (sat 1.6g, mono 4g, poly 2.4g); PROTEIN 34.3g; CARB 7.4g; FIBER 1.6g; CHOL 73mg; IRON 1.4mg; SODIUM 382mg; CALC 27mg

Grilled Eggplant Stack

Antioxidants in the eggplant may promote healthy aging and memory.

    1 (1-pound) eggplant, cut crosswise
       into ½-inch-thick slices
    ¾ teaspoon salt, divided
    ¼ cup balsamic vinegar
    ¼ cup dry red wine
    1 tablespoon brown sugar
    1 small zucchini (about 4 ounces)
    1 small yellow squash (about 4
       ounces)
    1 large red bell pepper, quartered
       lengthwise and seeded
    1 teaspoon olive oil
    ¼ teaspoon freshly ground black
       pepper
    ¼ cup (2 ounces) goat cheese
    1 tablespoon chopped fresh basil
    1 teaspoon chopped fresh oregano

1. Place eggplant slices in a colander. Sprinkle evenly with ½ teaspoon salt; toss well. Let stand 10 minutes. Rinse slices thoroughly; dry with paper towels.
2. Combine vinegar, wine, and sugar in a small saucepan over medium heat; bring to a boil. Reduce heat, and simmer until reduced to ¼ cup (about 8 minutes).
3. Prepare grill.
4. Trim ends from zucchini and squash; cut each lengthwise into 4 (¼-inch-thick) slices. Flatten pepper pieces with hand. Brush eggplant, zucchini, squash, and pepper pieces with oil; sprinkle with

¼ teaspoon salt and black pepper. Place pepper pieces, skin side down, eggplant, zucchini, and squash on a grill rack; grill 8 minutes or until tender, turning once.
5. Combine cheese, basil, and oregano.
6. To assemble stack, place 1 eggplant slice on a plate; top with one-fourth of cheese mixture. Lay one strip of squash and one strip of zucchini side by side. Drizzle with 1½ teaspoons balsamic mixture. Top with one pepper piece. Top with one eggplant slice and drizzle with 1½ teaspoons balsamic mixture. Repeat procedure three times with remaining eggplant, cheese, squash, zucchini, peppers, and balsamic mixture. Let stand 5 minutes before serving. Yield: 4 servings (serving size: 1 stack).

CALORIES 117 (35% from fat); FAT 4.6g (sat 2.3g, mono 1.5g, poly 0.4g); PROTEIN 5.4g; CARB 15.5g; FIBER 5.3g; CHOL 7mg; IRON 1.2mg; SODIUM 211mg; CALC 49mg

MAKE AHEAD
Tomato Marmalade

Both the cooked tomato and the oil render the fruit's lycopene more easily absorbed by the body. Serve this as a condiment with roasted lamb or chicken, or as a sandwich spread.

    2 tablespoons olive oil
    1 cup finely chopped onion
    1 tablespoon minced garlic
    7 cups chopped seeded tomato
       (about 3 pounds)
    ½ cup sugar
    ½ cup fresh lemon juice
    3 tablespoons molasses
    2 tablespoons tomato paste
    ¼ teaspoon ground red pepper
    ⅛ teaspoon ground allspice
    ⅛ teaspoon ground cloves
    ½ teaspoon salt, divided
    ¼ teaspoon freshly ground black
       pepper

1. Heat oil in a large saucepan over medium heat. Add onion to pan; cook 4 minutes or until tender. Add garlic; cook 1 minute. Add tomato; cook 4 minutes. Stir in sugar, next 6 ingredients, and ¼ teaspoon salt; bring to a boil. Reduce heat, and simmer until mixture thickens

and is reduced to 2½ cups (about 65 minutes). Stir in ¼ teaspoon salt and black pepper. Yield: 2½ cups (serving size: about 1½ tablespoons).

CALORIES 46 (23% from fat); FAT 1.2g (sat 0.2g, mono 0.8g, poly 0.2g); PROTEIN 0.6g; CARB 9.1g; FIBER 0.8g; CHOL 0mg; IRON 0.3mg; SODIUM 59mg; CALC 13mg

Cherry Tomato Spaghetti with Toasted Pine Nuts
(pictured on page 239)

The tomatoes offer lycopene, vitamin C, and fiber.

    2 (1-ounce) slices sandwich bread
    1½ tablespoons olive oil, divided
    1 teaspoon garlic powder, divided
    3 cups red cherry tomatoes
    3 garlic cloves, thinly sliced
    8 ounces uncooked spaghetti
    ¼ cup chopped fresh basil
    3 tablespoons pine nuts, toasted
    ½ teaspoon salt
    ¼ teaspoon freshly ground black
       pepper

1. Place bread in a food processor; pulse 10 times or until coarse crumbs measure 1 cup. Add 1½ teaspoons oil and ½ teaspoon garlic powder; pulse to combine.
2. Heat a large nonstick skillet over medium heat. Add breadcrumb mixture to pan; cook 2 minutes or until lightly toasted. Remove from pan; set aside.
3. Heat 1 teaspoon oil in pan. Add tomatoes to pan; cook 3 minutes or until tomatoes begin to wrinkle. Sprinkle with ½ teaspoon garlic powder and garlic; cook 30 seconds. Cover, and reduce heat to low.
4. Cook pasta according to package directions, omitting salt and fat. Add pasta, 2 teaspoons oil, basil, pine nuts, salt, and pepper to tomato mixture, stirring to combine. Toss pasta with breadcrumbs; serve immediately. Yield: 4 servings (serving size: 2 cups).

CALORIES 365 (28% from fat); FAT 11.2g (sat 1.2g, mono 5.1g, poly 3.2g); PROTEIN 11.2g; CARB 56.4g; FIBER 3.5g; CHOL 0mg; IRON 3.3mg; SODIUM 395mg; CALC 39mg

Sunshine Smoothie

½ cup chopped peeled mango
1½ cups chopped peeled apricots
   (about 4 small)
 1 cup chopped cantaloupe
⅔ cup chopped peeled nectarine
   (about 1 medium)
¼ cup mango nectar (such as Jumex)
⅛ teaspoon grated lemon rind
 1 (6-ounce) carton lemon low-fat
   yogurt
 1 cup ice cubes

1. Place mango in a zip-top plastic bag;
seal. Freeze 1 hour.
2. Combine apricots and next 5 ingredients in a blender; process until smooth. Add mango and ice; process until smooth. Yield: 4 servings (serving size: about 1 cup).

CALORIES 104 (8% from fat); FAT 0.9g (sat 0.4g, mono 0.3g, poly 0.1g); PROTEIN 3.4g; CARB 22.5g; FIBER 3g; CHOL 2mg; IRON 0.4mg; SODIUM 36mg; CALC 86mg

superfast suppers
20 Minute Dishes

From salad to stir-fry, lamb to shrimp, here are simple, fresh, and easy meals you can make superfast.

Cherry-Glazed Pan-Seared Lamb Chops

Cooking spray
 2 teaspoons dried rosemary
½ teaspoon salt
½ teaspoon black pepper, divided
 8 (4-ounce) lamb loin chops,
   trimmed
 2 teaspoons bottled minced garlic
½ cup fat-free, less-sodium beef
   broth
½ cup cherry preserves
¼ cup balsamic vinegar
Parsley sprigs (optional)

1. Heat a large nonstick skillet over medium-high heat. Coat pan with cooking spray. Combine rosemary, salt, and ¼ teaspoon pepper in a small bowl, stirring well. Rub spice mixture evenly over both sides of lamb. Add lamb to pan; cook 5 minutes on each side. Remove lamb from pan. Wipe pan clean with paper towels.
2. Return pan to medium heat; recoat with cooking spray. Add garlic to pan; cook 30 seconds. Add ¼ teaspoon pepper and broth; cook 1 minute, scraping pan to loosen browned bits. Stir in preserves and vinegar; cook 3 minutes or until slightly thick. Return lamb to pan; turn to coat. Cook 1 minute or until desired degree of doneness. Garnish with parsley sprigs, if desired. Yield: 4 servings (serving size: 2 lamb chops and 3 tablespoons glaze).

CALORIES 370 (43% from fat); FAT 17.6g (sat 7.4g, mono 7.4g, poly 1.3g); PROTEIN 22.6g; CARB 29.2g; FIBER 0.4g; CHOL 84mg; IRON 1.8mg; SODIUM 422mg; CALC 29mg

Seared Scallops with Lemon Orzo

Cooking spray
½ cup prechopped onion
 1 cup uncooked orzo (rice-shaped
   pasta)
 1 cup fat-free, less-sodium chicken
   broth
½ cup dry white wine
¼ teaspoon dried thyme
 2 tablespoons chopped fresh chives
 2 tablespoons fresh lemon juice
 2 teaspoons olive oil
1½ pounds sea scallops
¼ teaspoon salt
¼ teaspoon black pepper

1. Heat a medium saucepan over medium-high heat. Coat pan with cooking spray. Add onion to pan; sauté 3 minutes. Stir in pasta, broth, wine, and thyme; bring to a boil. Cover, reduce heat, and simmer 15 minutes or until liquid is absorbed and pasta is al dente. Stir in chives and lemon juice. Keep warm.
2. Heat oil in a large cast-iron skillet over medium-high heat. Sprinkle scallops evenly with salt and pepper. Add scallops to pan; cook 3 minutes on each side or until desired degree of doneness. Serve with pasta mixture. Yield: 4 servings (serving size: 4½ ounces scallops and about ¾ cup pasta mixture).

CALORIES 480 (10% from fat); FAT 5.1g (sat 1.7g, mono 1.9g, poly 0.7g); PROTEIN 60.9g; CARB 45.5g; FIBER 2.2g; CHOL 122mg; IRON 1.1mg; SODIUM 875mg; CALC 95mg

Coconut Curried Pork, Snow Pea, and Mango Stir-Fry

Red curry powder is a blend of coriander, cumin, chiles, and cardamom. Serve with lime wedges, if desired.

 2 (3½-ounce) bags boil-in-bag
   long-grain rice
 1 (1-pound) pork tenderloin,
   trimmed
 1 tablespoon canola oil
 1 teaspoon red curry powder
 1 cup snow peas
⅓ cup light coconut milk
 1 tablespoon fish sauce
 1 teaspoon red curry paste
 1 cup bottled mango, cut into
   ½-inch pieces
½ cup sliced green onions, divided
 2 tablespoons shredded coconut

1. Prepare rice according to package directions, omitting salt and fat; drain.
2. Cut pork into 1-inch cubes. Heat oil in a large nonstick skillet over medium-high heat. Sprinkle pork evenly with curry powder. Add pork and snow peas to pan; stir-fry 3 minutes.
3. Combine coconut milk, fish sauce, and curry paste, stirring well. Add milk mixture to pan; bring to a simmer. Stir in mango and ¼ cup onions; cook 1 minute or until thoroughly heated. Remove from heat. Place 1 cup rice on each of 4 plates; top each serving with 1¼ cups pork mixture. Sprinkle each serving with 1 tablespoon onions and 1½ teaspoons coconut. Yield: 4 servings.

CALORIES 429 (20% from fat); FAT 9.7g (sat 3.5g, mono 3.9g, poly 1.6g); PROTEIN 29.7g; CARB 54.8g; FIBER 2.3g; CHOL 74mg; IRON 4mg; SODIUM 454mg; CALC 38mg

Spanish-Style Halibut

1 slice applewood-smoked bacon
½ teaspoon salt
½ teaspoon smoked paprika
¼ teaspoon black pepper
4 (6-ounce) skinless halibut fillets
2 teaspoons bottled minced garlic
1 (6-ounce) package fresh baby
   spinach

1. Cook bacon in a large nonstick skillet over medium heat until crisp. Remove bacon from pan, reserving drippings in pan. Crumble bacon; set aside.
2. Combine salt, paprika, and black pepper in a small bowl. Sprinkle spice mixture evenly over fish. Add fish to drippings in pan, and cook 3 minutes on each side or until fish flakes easily when tested with a fork or until desired degree of doneness. Remove fish from pan, and keep warm.
3. Add garlic to pan, and cook 1 minute, stirring frequently. Stir in bacon. Add spinach to pan, and cook 1 minute or until spinach begins to wilt. Serve with fish. Yield: 4 servings (serving size: 1 fillet and ½ cup spinach mixture).

CALORIES 214 (21% from fat); FAT 5.1g (sat 1g, mono 2.7g, poly 1.3g); PROTEIN 37.4g; CARB 2.4g; FIBER 1.2g; CHOL 57mg; IRON 2.9mg; SODIUM 475mg; CALC 124mg

Gnocchi with Shrimp, Asparagus, and Pesto

2 quarts water
1 (16-ounce) package vacuum-packed gnocchi (such as Vigo)
4 cups (1-inch) slices asparagus
   (about 1 pound)
1 pound peeled and deveined large
   shrimp, coarsely chopped
1 tablespoon water
1 cup basil leaves
2 tablespoons pine nuts, toasted
2 tablespoons preshredded
   Parmesan cheese
2 teaspoons fresh lemon juice
2 teaspoons bottled minced garlic
4 teaspoons extravirgin olive oil
¼ teaspoon salt

1. Bring 2 quarts water to a boil in a Dutch oven. Add gnocchi to pan; cook 4 minutes or until done (gnocchi will rise to surface). Remove gnocchi with a slotted spoon; place in a large bowl. Add asparagus and shrimp to pan; cook 5 minutes or until shrimp are done. Drain. Add shrimp mixture to gnocchi.
2. Place 1 tablespoon water, basil, and next 4 ingredients in a food processor; process until smooth, scraping sides. Drizzle oil through food chute with food processor on; process until well blended. Add salt and basil mixture to shrimp mixture; toss to coat. Serve immediately. Yield: 4 servings (serving size: 2 cups).

CALORIES 355 (24% from fat); FAT 9.3g (sat 1.6g, mono 4.5g, poly 2.5g); PROTEIN 26.5g; CARB 42.7g; FIBER 3g; CHOL 170mg; IRON 5.7mg; SODIUM 894mg; CALC 108mg

Herbed Greek Chicken Salad

Serve with toasted pita wedges.

1 teaspoon dried oregano
½ teaspoon garlic powder
¾ teaspoon black pepper, divided
½ teaspoon salt, divided
   Cooking spray
1 pound skinless, boneless chicken
   breast, cut into 1-inch cubes
5 teaspoons fresh lemon juice,
   divided
1 cup plain fat-free yogurt
2 teaspoons tahini (sesame-seed
   paste)
1 teaspoon bottled minced garlic
8 cups chopped romaine lettuce
1 cup peeled chopped English
   cucumber
1 cup grape tomatoes, halved
6 pitted kalamata olives, halved
¼ cup (1 ounce) crumbled feta cheese

1. Combine oregano, garlic powder, ½ teaspoon pepper, and ¼ teaspoon salt in a bowl. Heat a nonstick skillet over medium-high heat. Coat pan with cooking spray. Add chicken and spice mixture; sauté until chicken is done. Drizzle with 1 tablespoon juice; stir. Remove from pan.
2. Combine 2 teaspoons juice, ¼ teaspoon salt, ¼ teaspoon pepper, yogurt, tahini, and garlic in a small bowl; stir well. Combine lettuce, cucumber, tomatoes, and olives. Place 2½ cups of lettuce mixture on each of 4 plates. Top each serving with ½ cup chicken mixture and 1 tablespoon cheese. Drizzle each serving with 3 tablespoons yogurt mixture. Yield: 4 servings.

CALORIES 243 (29% from fat); FAT 7.7g (sat 2.3g, mono 2.9g, poly 1.6g); PROTEIN 29.7g; CARB 13.4g; FIBER 3.5g; CHOL 70mg; IRON 2.5mg; SODIUM 578mg; CALC 216mg

kitchen strategies

Meal Plan

Problem: With dinner undecided most days, a busy Colorado reader makes too many trips to the supermarket. Strategy: Think strategically and shop once for dishes that will feed the family all week long.

Mention meal planning, and people often say they don't have the time. Julie Curtin, of Denver, has as full a schedule as anyone. But she knows she's wasting time by not planning meals.

By staying on top of inventory, planning what dishes she'll prepare during the coming week, and making a comprehensive grocery list of the ingredients she needs, Curtin can make one shopping trip a week that will replenish her cupboards and provide meals for seven days.

To accomplish this goal, we suggest ways to develop effective menus. One important tactic is to choose meals with crossover potential.

We've developed a week's worth of dinners for Curtin and her family. Some of the recipes use extra ingredients from other meals, but put them to work in a different dish, so the Curtins don't feel like they're simply eating leftovers.

Of course, the Curtins wouldn't want to eat this same menu every week; it's the general approach that matters. A little extra planning will allow Curtin to spend less time shopping and more time enjoying meals with her family.

Shrimp and
Lemon Skewers

Serve over rice, and cook extra rice for the Broccoli and Chicken Stir-Fried Rice.

     1   tablespoon extravirgin olive oil
     1   tablespoon balsamic vinegar
    ¾   teaspoon grated lemon rind
    1½ teaspoons fresh lemon juice
    ⅛   teaspoon kosher salt
    ⅛   teaspoon freshly ground black
         pepper
     3   garlic cloves, minced
    40 large shrimp, peeled and deveined
         (about 1½ pounds)
    16 ¼-inch-thick lemon slices
         Cooking spray
         Parsley sprigs (optional)

1. Combine first 7 ingredients in a large zip-top plastic bag. Add shrimp to bag; seal. Marinate in refrigerator 30 minutes. Remove shrimp from bag, reserving marinade. Thread 5 shrimp and 2 lemon slices onto each of 8 (12-inch) wooden skewers.
2. Prepare grill.
3. Place skewers on grill rack coated with cooking spray; grill 3 minutes on each side or until shrimp are done, basting occasionally with reserved marinade. Garnish with parsley sprigs, if desired. Yield: 4 servings (serving size: 2 skewers).

CALORIES 195 (16% from fat); FAT 3.4g (sat 0.6g, mono 0.7g, poly 1.2g); PROTEIN 35.2g; CARB 7.5g; FIBER 2.6g; CHOL 259mg; IRON 4.5mg; SODIUM 260mg; CALC 122mg

Grilled Corn
with Lime Butter

Serve with Hoisin and Lime–Marinated Grilled Chicken (page 206) or Blackened Grilled Flank Steak (page 206).

     8   ears shucked corn
         Cooking spray
     1   tablespoon butter, softened
     1   teaspoon grated lime rind
    ¼   teaspoon salt
    ¼   teaspoon ground red pepper

1. Prepare grill.
2. Place corn on grill rack coated with cooking spray; grill 12 minutes or until done, turning occasionally. Combine butter, rind, salt, and pepper in a bowl. Serve with corn. Yield: 8 servings (serving size: 1 ear corn and about ½ teaspoon butter).

CALORIES 90 (25% from fat); FAT 2.5g (sat 1.1g, mono 0.7g, poly 0.6g); PROTEIN 2.9g; CARB 17.2g; FIBER 2.5g; CHOL 4mg; IRON 0.5mg; SODIUM 96mg; CALC 3mg

Broccoli and Chicken
Stir-Fried Rice

Slightly browning the broccoli deepens the taste of the dish.

    1½ tablespoons canola oil
     8   cups broccoli florets (about
         2 bunches)
     2   cups vertically sliced onion
         (about 1)
    ½   cup fat-free, less-sodium chicken
         broth, divided
     2   cups cooked long-grain rice
     1   tablespoon minced garlic
     2   teaspoons minced peeled fresh
         ginger
    ½   teaspoon crushed red pepper
     2   Hoisin and Lime–Marinated
         Grilled Chicken breast halves,
         thinly sliced (recipe on page 206)
     2   tablespoons low-sodium soy sauce
     2   tablespoons oyster sauce
     1   tablespoon rice wine vinegar
     1   teaspoon cornstarch
    ¼   teaspoon salt

1. Heat oil in a large nonstick skillet over medium-high heat. Add broccoli and onion; sauté 5 minutes. Add ¼ cup broth; cover and cook 3 minutes. Remove broccoli mixture from pan.
2. Place pan over medium-high heat. Add rice; cook 5 minutes, stirring occasionally. Add broccoli mixture, garlic, ginger, pepper, and chicken; toss well.
3. Combine ¼ cup broth, soy sauce, oyster sauce, vinegar, and cornstarch; add to pan. Bring to a boil; cook 1 minute. Stir in salt. Yield: 4 servings (serving size: 2 cups).

CALORIES 345 (23% from fat); FAT 8.7g (sat 1g, mono 3.8g, poly 2.2g); PROTEIN 27.4g; CARB 38.4g; FIBER 5.2g; CHOL 49mg; IRON 3.2mg; SODIUM 872mg; CALC 97mg

Steak Wraps with
Blue Cheese and
Caramelized Onions

These wraps use extra beef from the Blackened Grilled Flank Steak (page 206).

     1   teaspoon olive oil
     5   cups thinly sliced onion (about 2)
    ¼   teaspoon freshly ground black
         pepper
    ⅛   teaspoon salt
    ¼   cup fat-free, less-sodium chicken
         broth
     2   tablespoons balsamic vinegar
     1   teaspoon sugar
     6   ounces Blackened Grilled Flank
         Steak (recipe on page 206)
     1   cup cannellini beans or other
         white beans, drained
     4   (8-inch) fat-free flour tortillas
     4   cups chopped romaine lettuce
     1   cup cooked long-grain rice
    ½   cup (2 ounces) crumbled blue
         cheese

1. Heat oil in a large nonstick skillet over medium heat. Add onion, pepper, and salt; cook 5 minutes, stirring occasionally. Add broth; cook 5 minutes or until liquid evaporates. Stir in vinegar and sugar; cook 5 minutes. Add Blackened Grilled Flank Steak to pan; cook 3 minutes or until thoroughly heated. Set steak mixture aside; keep warm.
2. Mash beans with a fork until smooth. Warm tortillas according to package directions. Spread ¼ cup beans over each tortilla, leaving 1-inch borders. Top each tortilla with 1 cup lettuce, ¼ cup rice, and 2 tablespoons cheese. Divide steak mixture evenly among tortillas; roll up. Yield: 4 servings (serving size: 1 wrap).

CALORIES 431 (19% from fat); FAT 9g (sat 3.9g, mono 3g, poly 0.9g); PROTEIN 26.3g; CARB 60.3g; FIBER 7.5g; CHOL 31mg; IRON 4mg; SODIUM 792mg; CALC 172mg

Zucchini, Sausage, and Feta Casserole

This pasta casserole combines pantry ingredients with fresh produce for a hearty dish. Any leftovers are even better the next day as the flavors have time to meld.

2½ cups uncooked ziti (short tube-shaped pasta)
8 ounces chicken sausage
Cooking spray
1 teaspoon olive oil
5 cups thinly sliced zucchini (about 1½ pounds)
2 cups vertically sliced onion (about 1)
½ teaspoon kosher salt
¼ teaspoon freshly ground black pepper
3 garlic cloves, minced
½ cup fat-free, less-sodium chicken broth
2 teaspoons all-purpose flour
½ cup (2 ounces) crumbled feta cheese
½ cup (2 ounces) shredded part-skim mozzarella cheese

1. Preheat oven to 400°.
2. Cook pasta in boiling water 5 minutes, omitting salt and fat; drain.
3. Remove casings from sausage. Heat a large nonstick skillet over medium-high heat. Coat pan with cooking spray. Add sausage to pan; cook until browned, stirring to crumble. Remove from pan. Heat oil in pan. Add zucchini, onion, salt, pepper, and garlic. Cook 10 minutes or until vegetables are tender and zucchini begins to brown, stirring occasionally.
4. Combine broth and flour in a small bowl, stirring with a whisk. Add broth mixture to pan; cook 1 minute. Combine zucchini mixture, pasta, sausage, and feta cheese in a large bowl; toss well. Spoon pasta mixture into an 11 x 7–inch baking dish coated with cooking spray. Sprinkle evenly with mozzarella cheese. Bake at 400° for 20 minutes or until bubbly and lightly browned. Yield: 6 servings (serving size: 1 cup).

CALORIES 284 (27% from fat); FAT 8.6g (sat 4.6g, mono 1.9g, poly 0.6g); PROTEIN 16.9g; CARB 35.3g; FIBER 2.6g; CHOL 35mg; IRON 2mg; SODIUM 433mg; CALC 160mg

Blackened Grilled Flank Steak

Serve with Grilled Corn with Lime Butter (page 205) and a simple green salad.

1 tablespoon garlic powder
2 teaspoons ground cumin
2 teaspoons hot paprika
2 teaspoons dried oregano
1 teaspoon kosher salt
1 teaspoon freshly ground black pepper
½ teaspoon ground red pepper
1 (2-pound) flank steak, trimmed
Cooking spray

1. Combine first 7 ingredients; rub spice mixture over both sides of steak. Cover and refrigerate 3 hours.
2. Prepare grill.
3. Place steak on grill rack coated with cooking spray; grill 5 minutes on each side or until desired degree of doneness. Let stand 10 minutes. Cut steak diagonally across grain into thin slices. Yield: 8 servings (serving size: 3 ounces).

CALORIES 160 (32% from fat); FAT 5.7g (sat 2.3g, mono 2.2g, poly 0.2g); PROTEIN 24.1g; CARB 1.4g; FIBER 0.5g; CHOL 37mg; IRON 1.9mg; SODIUM 287mg; CALC 29mg.

MAKE AHEAD
Corn and Clam Chowder

Use extra corn from Grilled Corn with Lime Butter (page 205).

2 bacon slices, chopped
1 cup minced onion (about 1)
2 cups clam juice, divided
2 cups fat-free, less-sodium chicken broth
2 cups diced Yukon gold potato
2 cups corn kernels
2 cups littleneck clams (about 1 pound)
¾ cup low-fat buttermilk
2 tablespoons whipping cream
1 tablespoon chopped fresh flat-leaf parsley
⅛ teaspoon black pepper

1. Cook bacon in a large Dutch oven over medium heat 5 minutes or until crisp. Remove bacon from pan, reserving 1 teaspoon drippings in pan. Add onion to drippings in pan; cook 5 minutes or until browned. Add 1 cup clam juice, scraping pan to loosen browned bits. Add 1 cup clam juice and broth; bring to a boil. Add potato; simmer 10 minutes.
2. Add corn and clams to pan; bring to a boil. Reduce heat, and simmer 5 minutes or until shells open. Discard unopened shells. Remove from heat; stir in buttermilk and remaining 3 ingredients. Sprinkle with bacon. Yield: 4 servings (serving size: 2 cups chowder and about 1 teaspoon bacon).

CALORIES 348 (27% from fat); FAT 10.4g (sat 4g, mono 3.4g, poly 1.4g); PROTEIN 24.5g; CARB 40g; FIBER 3.7g; CHOL 63mg; IRON 17.5mg; SODIUM 709mg; CALC 132mg

Hoisin and Lime–Marinated Grilled Chicken

Save two breast halves from this dish to use later in Broccoli and Chicken Stir-Fried Rice (page 205).

¼ cup hoisin sauce
2 tablespoons low-sodium soy sauce
1 tablespoon grated peeled fresh ginger
2 teaspoons dark sesame oil
1 teaspoon grated lime rind
½ teaspoon kosher salt
8 garlic cloves, minced
6 (6-ounce) skinless, boneless chicken breast halves
Cooking spray

1. Combine first 7 ingredients in a large zip-top plastic bag. Add chicken to bag; seal. Marinate in refrigerator 2 hours, turning bag occasionally.
2. Prepare grill.
3. Remove chicken from bag; discard marinade. Place chicken on grill rack coated with cooking spray, and grill 5 minutes on each side or until chicken is done. Yield: 6 servings (serving size: 1 chicken breast half).

CALORIES 243 (17% from fat); FAT 4.5g (sat 0.9g, mono 0.6g, poly 0.7g); PROTEIN 39.9g; CARB 6.4g; FIBER 0.4g; CHOL 99mg; IRON 1.5mg; SODIUM 618mg; CALC 24mg

From Farm to Table

Whether you stock up at a farmers' market, supermarket, or neighbor's garden, here are great ways to bring summer produce to the table.

Farmers' markets spotlight everyday produce like cucumbers, zucchini, and eggplant—nothing too fancy. In fact, these are items we've become accustomed to seeing in supermarkets year-round. But it's important to remember that these humble fruits and vegetables do indeed have a natural peak season—summer—when they look and taste amazing.

WINE NOTE: With vegetables we often think white wine, but grilled eggplant's smoky flavor and pleasantly bitter skin marries well with medium-bodied, rustic reds. Try a Tuscan blend like Tenuta di Arceno PrimaVoce 2003 ($20). The wine's cherry fruit has hints of leather and earth to amplify the herbal flavors of rosemary and thyme, while its vivid acidity balances the creamy aïoli.

STAFF FAVORITE
Grilled Eggplant Sandwiches with Red Onion and Aïoli

Use a sliced loaf of good-quality Italian bread; its dense texture stands up to grilling. Sprinkle eggplant with salt; let it stand, applying pressure periodically, and rinse before grilling to leach excess moisture and bitterness.

AÏOLI:
- ¼ cup light mayonnaise
- 1 tablespoon extravirgin olive oil
- 1 tablespoon fresh lemon juice
- 1 garlic clove, minced

SANDWICHES:
- 1 (1-pound) eggplant, cut crosswise into ¼-inch-thick slices
- 1 tablespoon kosher salt
- 1 teaspoon chopped fresh thyme
- 1 teaspoon chopped fresh parsley
- ½ teaspoon chopped fresh rosemary
- Cooking spray
- 4 (½-inch-thick) slices red onion
- 8 (½-inch-thick) slices Italian bread
- 8 (¼-inch-thick) slices tomato
- 2 cups lightly packed arugula leaves

1. To prepare aïoli, combine first 4 ingredients in a small bowl, stirring well. Cover and chill.

2. To prepare sandwiches, arrange eggplant in a single layer on several layers of heavy-duty paper towels. Sprinkle both sides of eggplant with salt; cover with additional paper towels. Let stand 30 minutes, pressing down occasionally. Rinse eggplant with cold water. Drain; pat dry.

3. Prepare grill.

4. Combine thyme, parsley, and rosemary in a small bowl, stirring well. Lightly coat eggplant slices with cooking spray; sprinkle with herb mixture.

5. Arrange eggplant and onion on grill rack coated with cooking spray; grill 2 minutes on each side or until vegetables are tender and lightly browned. Remove from heat, and keep warm. Arrange bread slices in a single layer on grill rack coated with cooking spray, and grill 1 minute on each side or until toasted.

6. Spread about 2 teaspoons aïoli over 1 side of each of 4 bread slices; divide eggplant and onion evenly among bread slices. Place 2 tomato slices on each sandwich; top each serving with ½ cup arugula. Spread about 2 teaspoons aïoli over 1 side of each remaining 4 bread slices; place on top of sandwiches. Yield: 4 servings (serving size: 1 sandwich).

CALORIES 352 (30% from fat); FAT 11.7g (sat 1.3g, mono 5.9g, poly 3.6g); PROTEIN 8.2g; CARB 53.3g; FIBER 7g; CHOL 5mg; IRON 2.9mg; SODIUM 749mg; CALC 81mg

MAKE AHEAD
Corn and Fingerling Potato Chowder with Applewood-Smoked Bacon

As the name implies, fingerling potatoes have a narrow shape, similar to a finger. These baby white potatoes contain less starch than russet potatoes; waxy small red potatoes make a good stand-in.

- 2 slices applewood-smoked bacon
- 1¾ cups diced onion
- 3½ cups fresh corn kernels (about 7 ears)
- 1 teaspoon chopped fresh thyme
- 2 garlic cloves, minced
- 2 cups fat-free, less-sodium chicken broth
- ½ cup 2% reduced-fat milk
- ½ cup half-and-half
- 8 ounces (¼-inch-thick) rounds fingerling potato slices
- ¼ teaspoon salt
- ¼ teaspoon freshly ground black pepper
- Thyme sprigs (optional)

1. Cook bacon in a large Dutch oven over medium heat until crisp. Remove bacon from pan; crumble. Add onion to drippings in pan; cook 8 minutes or until tender, stirring occasionally. Add corn, chopped thyme, and garlic to pan; cook 30 seconds, stirring constantly. Stir in broth, milk, half-and-half, and potatoes; bring to a simmer. Cover and cook 10 minutes or until potatoes are tender, stirring occasionally.

Continued

2. Transfer 2 cups potato mixture to a blender. Remove center piece of blender lid (to allow steam to escape); secure blender lid on blender. Place a clean towel over opening in blender lid (to avoid splatters). Blend until smooth; return pureed mixture to pan. Stir in salt and pepper; sprinkle with crumbled bacon. Garnish with thyme sprigs, if desired. Yield: 5 servings (serving size: about 1 cup).

CALORIES 186 (27% from fat); FAT 5.5g (sat 2.7g, mono 1.2g, poly 0.4g); PROTEIN 7.6g; CARB 27.8g; FIBER 3.4g; CHOL 18mg; IRON 1.1mg; SODIUM 398mg; CALC 84mg

Salmon with Cucumber Salad and Dill Sauce

(pictured on page 240)

Prepare the sauce up to one day ahead, and refrigerate. Wild salmon is available in many fish markets and grocery stores; its rich, vivid flavor will only make the dish better.

    6 tablespoons fat-free sour cream
    2 tablespoons plus 1 teaspoon finely chopped fresh dill, divided
    3 tablespoons rice vinegar, divided
 1½ tablespoons finely chopped shallots
    ¼ teaspoon grated lemon rind
    2 teaspoons fresh lemon juice
    1 garlic clove, minced
    4 (6-ounce) salmon fillets (about 1 inch thick)
    ¼ teaspoon salt
    ¼ teaspoon freshly ground black pepper
      Cooking spray
    ¼ cup dry white wine
    1 English cucumber (about 1 pound)

1. Combine sour cream, 2 tablespoons dill, 2 tablespoons vinegar, shallots, rind, juice, and garlic in a bowl, stirring well; cover and chill.
2. Sprinkle fish evenly with salt and pepper. Heat a large nonstick skillet over medium-high heat. Coat pan with cooking spray. Add fish to pan, and cook 3 minutes. Turn fish over, and cook

1 minute. Remove from heat. Add wine; cover and let stand 3 minutes or until fish flakes easily when tested with a fork or until desired degree of doneness.
3. Using a vegetable peeler, shave cucumber lengthwise into ribbons to yield about 2 cups. Combine cucumber, 1 tablespoon rice vinegar, and 1 teaspoon dill in a bowl; toss gently to coat. Place about ½ cup cucumber mixture on each of 4 plates; top each serving with 1 fillet and 2 tablespoons sour cream mixture. Yield: 4 servings.

CALORIES 347 (49% from fat); FAT 18.7g (sat 3.7g, mono 6.6g, poly 6.7g); PROTEIN 35.4g; CARB 7.2g; FIBER 0.9g; CHOL 102mg; IRON 1mg; SODIUM 283mg; CALC 68mg

Ginger, Beef, and Green Bean Stir-Fry

Fresh green beans and bell peppers combine with chili garlic and hoisin sauces for a quick and tasty entrée.

    3 tablespoons low-sodium soy sauce
    4 teaspoons cornstarch
    1 tablespoon hoisin sauce
    2 to 3 teaspoons chili garlic sauce (such as Lee Kum Kee)
    1 (14-ounce) can fat-free, less-sodium chicken broth
    2 teaspoons dark sesame oil, divided
    ¼ cup finely chopped green onions
    2 tablespoons minced peeled fresh ginger
    3 garlic cloves, minced
    1 pound boneless sirloin steak, cut into ¼-inch strips
    5 cups (2-inch) cut green beans (about 1¼ pounds)
    1 cup red bell pepper strips
    ¾ cup (2-inch) slices green onion tops
    2 cups hot cooked white rice

1. Combine first 5 ingredients in a bowl, stirring well with a whisk. Set aside.
2. Heat 1 teaspoon oil in a large nonstick skillet over medium-high heat. Add chopped green onions, ginger, and garlic to pan; sauté 30 seconds. Add beef to pan, and sauté 4 minutes or until browned. Remove from pan.

3. Wipe pan dry with a paper towel. Add 1 teaspoon oil to pan; heat over medium-high heat. Add beans and pepper to pan. Cover and cook 3 minutes. Uncover and cook 3 minutes, stirring frequently. Add green onion tops; sauté 1 minute. Return beef mixture to pan. Stir in broth mixture; bring to a boil. Cook 1 minute, stirring constantly. Remove from heat. Serve with rice. Yield: 4 servings (serving size: 1¾ cups beef mixture and ½ cup rice).

CALORIES 440 (35% from fat); FAT 17.2g (sat 6.3g, mono 7.2g, poly 1.7g); PROTEIN 29g; CARB 41.8g; FIBER 7.7g; CHOL 53mg; IRON 3.9mg; SODIUM 745mg; CALC 142mg

Charred Summer Vegetables

Serve with simple grilled pork, chicken, or fish.

      Cooking spray
 2½ cups fresh corn kernels (about 5 ears)
    2 cups chopped green beans (about 8 ounces)
    1 cup chopped zucchini (about 4 ounces)
    1 cup chopped red bell pepper
    2 tablespoons finely chopped shallots
    2 tablespoons fresh lemon juice
    1 tablespoon chopped fresh flat-leaf parsley
    4 teaspoons extravirgin olive oil
    ½ teaspoon salt
    ½ teaspoon chopped fresh thyme
    ¼ teaspoon freshly ground black pepper

1. Heat a 12-inch cast-iron skillet over high heat. Coat pan with cooking spray. Add corn and next 3 ingredients to pan; stir to combine. Cover and cook 5 minutes. Combine shallots and remaining 6 ingredients in a bowl, stirring well. Add shallot mixture to corn mixture; toss to coat. Yield: 6 servings (serving size: ⅔ cup).

CALORIES 102 (28% from fat); FAT 3.2g (sat 0.3g, mono 1.7g, poly 0.3g); PROTEIN 3.3g; CARB 18.5g; FIBER 2.7g; CHOL 0mg; IRON 0.8mg; SODIUM 210mg; CALC 31mg

Fresh Corn Tart with Chipotle Cream

Meatless Soyrizo adds a mildly spicy and earthy flavor, similar to traditional Spanish chorizo. Substitute chorizo, if you prefer. Serve with a green salad.

CREAM:

¼ cup light sour cream
2 teaspoons fresh lime juice
1 teaspoon minced chipotle chile, canned in adobo sauce
1 teaspoon water

TART:

Cooking spray
1½ cups chopped onion
⅔ cup chopped seeded poblano chile
6 ounces meatless Spanish sausage (such as Soyrizo)
3½ cups corn kernels (about 7 ears)
3 garlic cloves, minced
2 cups water
½ teaspoon salt
¾ cup dry polenta
½ cup (2 ounces) shredded part-skim mozzarella cheese, divided
2 tablespoons chopped fresh cilantro

1. To prepare cream, combine first 4 ingredients in a bowl, stirring well. Cover and chill.
2. Preheat oven to 400°.
3. To prepare tart, heat a 10-inch cast-iron skillet over medium-high heat. Coat pan with cooking spray. Add onion to pan; sauté 5 minutes. Add poblano chile to pan; sauté 5 minutes. Remove casings from sausage. Add sausage to pan; sauté 2 minutes, stirring to crumble. Add corn and garlic to pan; sauté 5 minutes or until lightly browned. Remove corn mixture from pan.
4. Wipe pan dry with a paper towel. Recoat pan with cooking spray, and set pan aside.
5. Combine 2 cups water and salt in a saucepan over medium-high heat; bring to a boil. Gradually stir in polenta; cook 5 minutes or until thick, stirring constantly. Remove from heat, and stir in 1½ cups corn mixture. Pour polenta mixture into prepared pan. Sprinkle ¼ cup cheese evenly over polenta mixture; top with remaining corn mixture. Sprinkle ¼ cup cheese over top.
6. Bake at 400° for 25 minutes or until lightly browned. Let stand 5 minutes, and cut into wedges. Sprinkle with cilantro. Serve with chipotle cream. Yield: 6 servings (serving size: 1 wedge, 2 teaspoons chipotle cream, and 1 teaspoon cilantro).

CALORIES 295 (31% from fat); FAT 10.2g (sat 2.8g, mono 4g, poly 2.8g); PROTEIN 13.1g; CARB 42.4g; FIBER 6.2g; CHOL 10mg; IRON 3.5mg; SODIUM 686mg; CALC 164mg

---

QUICK & EASY
Grilled Halibut with Sweet Pepper and Balsamic Salad

This sweet pepper salad pairs well with halibut, snapper, or other firm, white-fleshed fish. You can also serve it with sautéed chicken breast or grilled pork tenderloin.

2 red bell peppers
2 yellow bell peppers
Cooking spray
3 tablespoons finely chopped fresh parsley, divided
3 tablespoons finely chopped fresh chives, divided
2 tablespoons white balsamic vinegar
1 tablespoon extravirgin olive oil
1 tablespoon capers
1 teaspoon finely chopped fresh marjoram
¾ teaspoon salt, divided
½ teaspoon freshly ground black pepper, divided
1 garlic clove, minced
4 (6-ounce) halibut fillets

1. Prepare grill.
2. Cut bell peppers in half lengthwise; discard seeds and membranes. Place pepper halves, skin sides down, on a cutting board or work surface; flatten with hand. Place pepper halves on a grill rack coated with cooking spray; grill 12 minutes or until blackened. Place in a zip-top plastic bag; seal. Let stand 10 minutes. Peel and cut into strips.
3. Combine bell peppers, 2 tablespoons parsley, 2 tablespoons chives, vinegar, oil, capers, marjoram, ¼ teaspoon salt, ¼ teaspoon black pepper, and garlic; toss gently to coat.
4. Sprinkle fish evenly with ½ teaspoon salt and ¼ teaspoon black pepper. Place fish on grill rack coated with cooking spray; grill 6 minutes on each side or until fish flakes easily when tested with a fork or until desired degree of doneness. Sprinkle fish with 1 tablespoon parsley and 1 tablespoon chives. Serve with bell pepper mixture. Yield: 4 servings (serving size: 1 fillet and ½ cup bell pepper mixture).

CALORIES 248 (26% from fat); FAT 7.2g (sat 1g, mono 3.7g, poly 1.6g); PROTEIN 35.4g; CARB 8.9g; FIBER 2.4g; CHOL 52mg; IRON 2.2mg; SODIUM 599mg; CALC 109mg

---

Oven-Roasted Tomato and Chèvre Bruschetta

Plum tomatoes work well for this tasty appetizer because they have fewer seeds than larger varieties. You can bake the tomatoes up to three days ahead. Keep them refrigerated, but allow them to come to room temperature before serving.

12 plum tomatoes, halved lengthwise
Cooking spray
½ teaspoon kosher salt
24 (½-inch-thick) slices diagonally-cut French bread baguette
1 tablespoon extravirgin olive oil
1 garlic clove, halved
½ cup (4 ounces) soft goat cheese
3 tablespoons thinly sliced fresh basil

1. Preheat oven to 350°.
2. Arrange tomatoes, skin side down, in a single layer on a jelly-roll pan coated with cooking spray. Sprinkle evenly with salt; coat lightly with cooking spray. Bake at 350° for 2 hours. Turn oven off; cool tomatoes in closed oven at least 1 hour. Remove roasted tomatoes from baking sheet.
3. Preheat oven to 400°.
4. Arrange bread slices in a single layer on a baking sheet; brush evenly with oil. Bake at 400° for 14 minutes or until
Continued

toasted. Rub each bread slice with cut sides of garlic; discard garlic. Spread about 1 teaspoon cheese on each bread slice; top each serving with 1 tomato half. Sprinkle each serving with about ½ teaspoon basil. Yield: 12 servings (serving size: 2 bruschetta).

CALORIES 131 (29% from fat); FAT 4.2g (sat 1.8g, mono 1.7g, poly 0.5g); PROTEIN 5g; CARB 18.5g; FIBER 1.7g; CHOL 4mg; IRON 1.2mg; SODIUM 304mg; CALC 43mg

in season
A Slice of Summer

Eight fresh recipes offer good reasons to make room in the fridge for a watermelon.

Watermelon boasts an unbeatable combination: It's colorful, sweet, crunchy, refreshing, and portable. In addition to quenching thirst—watermelon is 92 percent water—it provides hefty doses of vitamin C, vitamin A, potassium, and lycopene (a disease-fighting antioxidant found in red fruits and vegetables).

QUICK & EASY
Picante Three-Melon Salad

This dish deftly balances sweet, salty, tart, and spicy tastes. Use jalapeño pepper instead of serrano for slightly less heat.

    3   cups red cubed seeded
        watermelon
    3   cups yellow cubed seeded
        watermelon
    3   cups cubed honeydew melon
    ½   cup chopped white onion
    2   tablespoons chopped fresh
        cilantro
    2½ teaspoons finely chopped seeded
        serrano chile (about 1)
    1   teaspoon grated lime rind
    3   tablespoons fresh lime juice
    ½   teaspoon salt
    ¼   teaspoon chili powder
    ⅛   to ¼ teaspoon minced chipotle
        chile, canned in adobo sauce

1. Combine first 6 ingredients in a large bowl. Combine rind and remaining 4 ingredients in a small bowl. Pour juice mixture over melon mixture; toss well. Let stand 15 minutes before serving. Yield: 8 servings (serving size: 1 cup).

CALORIES 63 (4% from fat); FAT 0.3g (sat 0.1g, mono 0.1g, poly 0.1g); PROTEIN 1.2g; CARB 16g; FIBER 1.2g; CHOL 0mg; IRON 0.4mg; SODIUM 162mg; CALC 15mg

MAKE AHEAD
Pickled Watermelon Rind

Use the rind to prepare this versatile condiment to serve with Chilled Seared Shrimp with Watermelon Pickle (page 211), grilled chicken, smoked pork, or ham and biscuits. A six-pound watermelon yields about two pounds of rind. Keep rind fully submerged in pickling liquid, and leave the cheesecloth bag of spices in with the pickled rind so the flavor intensifies with time. Refrigerate up to two weeks.

    1   (6-pound) watermelon
    6   cups water
    2   tablespoons salt, divided
    1   teaspoon pickling spice
    3   (¼-inch) slices fresh ginger
    2   whole cloves
    2   whole allspice
    1   (3-inch) cinnamon stick
    1¼ cups sugar
    1   cup white vinegar

1. Carefully remove and discard outer green layer from watermelon rind using a vegetable peeler. Reserve watermelon pulp for another use. Cut rind into ½-inch pieces. Bring 6 cups water and 5 teaspoons salt to a boil in a large saucepan over medium-high heat. Add rind to pan. Reduce heat, and simmer 15 minutes or until crisp-tender. Drain rind. Place in a large bowl.
2. Place pickling spice, ginger, cloves, allspice, and cinnamon on a double layer of cheesecloth. Gather edges of cheesecloth together; tie securely. Combine cheesecloth bag, 1 teaspoon salt, sugar, and vinegar in saucepan; bring to a boil, stirring until sugar dissolves. Pour hot vinegar mixture over rind. Cool to room temperature. Cover and chill 12 hours.

3. Strain rind mixture through a sieve into a saucepan; return solids to bowl. Bring liquid to a boil; carefully pour over solids. Chill at least 8 hours before serving. Yield: 10 servings (serving size: about ¼ cup).

CALORIES 35 (0% from fat); FAT 0g; PROTEIN 1.1g; CARB 7.9g; FIBER 0g; CHOL 0mg; IRON 0mg; SODIUM 175mg; CALC 26mg

MAKE AHEAD
Basil-Infused Watermelon Lemonade

Basil and watermelon provide bright, sweet flavor in this refreshing beverage. Serve well chilled or over ice.

    1   cup water
    ¾   cup sugar
    1   cup thinly sliced fresh basil
    8   cups cubed seeded watermelon
    ½   cup fresh lemon juice (about
        3 lemons)

1. Combine 1 cup water and sugar in a small saucepan; bring to a boil. Reduce heat, and simmer 5 minutes or until sugar dissolves. Remove from heat. Stir in basil; chill 1 hour. Strain sugar mixture through a sieve into a bowl, and discard basil.
2. Place watermelon in a blender; process until smooth. Strain watermelon puree through a fine sieve into a large bowl, reserving liquid; discard solids. Combine watermelon liquid, sugar mixture, and juice in a pitcher; chill. Yield: 5 servings (serving size: 1 cup).

CALORIES 197 (2% from fat); FAT 0.4g (sat 0g, mono 0.1g, poly 0.2g); PROTEIN 1.8g; CARB 50.8g; FIBER 1.4g; CHOL 0mg; IRON 0.9mg; SODIUM 4mg; CALC 33mg

Chilled Seared Shrimp with Watermelon Pickle

This recipe uses both the Pickled Watermelon Rind and its tasty pickling liquid. Toss the shrimp mixture occasionally as it chills to evenly distribute the liquid. Serve over mixed greens for a light lunch.

- ½ teaspoon ground coriander
- ¼ teaspoon salt
- ⅛ teaspoon ground red pepper
- 1 pound peeled and deveined large shrimp
- 1 tablespoon olive oil
- 1 cup thinly sliced halved English cucumber
- ½ cup Pickled Watermelon Rind, drained and sliced (recipe on page 210)
- ⅓ cup Pickled Watermelon Rind pickling liquid
- ⅓ cup thinly sliced red onion
- 1 tablespoon cider vinegar

1. Place first 4 ingredients in a bowl; toss well. Heat oil in a large nonstick skillet over medium-high heat. Add shrimp mixture to pan, and cook 2 minutes on each side or until done. Remove from heat; cool 10 minutes.

2. Combine shrimp, cucumber, and remaining ingredients in a large bowl; toss well. Chill 1 hour. Yield: 4 servings (serving size: 1 cup).

CALORIES 212 (23% from fat); FAT 5.4g (sat 0.9g, mono 2.8g, poly 1.1g); PROTEIN 23.9g; CARB 16.1g; FIBER 0.4g; CHOL 172mg; IRON 2.9mg; SODIUM 491mg; CALC 79mg

Watermelon and Lime Granita

Make this in a spare moment on the weekend, then serve later in the week for a no-fuss dessert.

- ½ cup sugar
- ½ cup water
- 4 cups cubed seedless watermelon
- ½ cup fresh lime juice (about 5 limes)
- Lime wedges (optional)

1. Place sugar and ½ cup water in a small saucepan over medium-high heat; bring to a boil. Reduce heat, and simmer 3 minutes. Remove from heat. Place sugar mixture in a small bowl; cool 10 minutes. Cover and chill at least 30 minutes.

2. Place sugar mixture, watermelon, and juice in a blender; process until smooth. Pour watermelon mixture into an 11 x 7-inch baking dish; cover and freeze 3 hours. Stir well. Cover and freeze at least 2 hours or overnight. Remove mixture from freezer, and let stand at room temperature 10 minutes. Scrape entire mixture with a fork until fluffy. Serve with lime wedges, if desired. Yield: 6 servings (serving size: ½ cup).

CALORIES 100 (2% from fat); FAT 0.2g (sat 0g, mono 0g, poly 0.1g); PROTEIN 0.7g; CARB 26g; FIBER 0.5g; CHOL 0mg; IRON 0.3mg; SODIUM 2mg; CALC 11mg

Marinated Grilled Chicken Breast with Watermelon-Jalapeño Salsa

Watermelon makes a nice foil for the earthy spices in the marinade.

- 1 tablespoon chopped fresh oregano
- 1 tablespoon extravirgin olive oil
- 1 teaspoon chili powder
- ¾ teaspoon ground cumin
- ½ teaspoon salt
- 3 garlic cloves, minced
- 4 (6-ounce) skinless, boneless chicken breast halves
- Cooking spray
- 2 cups (½-inch) cubed seeded watermelon
- 1 cup (½-inch) cubed peeled ripe mango
- ¼ cup finely chopped red onion
- 2 tablespoons chopped fresh cilantro
- 2 tablespoons finely chopped seeded jalapeño pepper (about 1 small)
- 1 tablespoon fresh lime juice
- ½ teaspoon sugar
- ¼ teaspoon salt

1. Combine first 6 ingredients in a large zip-top plastic bag. Add chicken to bag; seal. Marinate in refrigerator up to 4 hours, turning bag occasionally.

2. Prepare grill.

3. Place chicken on a grill rack coated with cooking spray. Grill 5 minutes on each side or until done. Combine watermelon and remaining 7 ingredients. Serve watermelon mixture with chicken. Yield: 4 servings (serving size: 1 chicken breast half and 1 cup salsa).

CALORIES 304 (25% from fat); FAT 8.3g (sat 1.8g, mono 4.1g, poly 1.4g); PROTEIN 40.7g; CARB 15.9g; FIBER 1.5g; CHOL 108mg; IRON 1.8mg; SODIUM 540mg; CALC 44mg

Watermelon Salad with Parmigiano-Reggiano

Salt in the dressing and cheese heightens the sweetness of the watermelon.

- 3 cups (1½-inch) cubed seeded orange watermelon
- 3 cups (1½-inch) cubed seeded yellow watermelon
- 1 cup chopped seeded plum tomato (about 4)
- ½ cup Pickled Watermelon Rind (recipe on page 210), drained
- ⅓ cup thinly sliced shallots
- 1 tablespoon chopped fresh mint
- 1 teaspoon grated lemon rind
- 2 tablespoons fresh lemon juice
- 1 tablespoon extravirgin olive oil
- ¾ teaspoon salt
- ¼ cup (1 ounce) grated Parmigiano-Reggiano cheese

1. Combine first 6 ingredients in a large bowl; toss gently. Combine lemon rind, juice, oil, and salt in a small bowl, stirring with a whisk. Pour juice mixture over watermelon mixture; toss gently to coat. Sprinkle with cheese. Yield: 8 servings (serving size: 1 cup salad and 1½ teaspoons cheese).

CALORIES 111 (24% from fat); FAT 3g (sat 0.9g, mono 1.6g, poly 0.3g); PROTEIN 2.9g; CARB 20.1g; FIBER 1.1g; CHOL 3mg; IRON 0.6mg; SODIUM 328mg; CALC 65mg

Ginger-Soy Marinated Tuna Steaks with Sesame-Watermelon Relish

If yellow or orange watermelon isn't available, any variety will work.

TUNA:

- ¾ cup fresh orange juice (about 3 oranges)
- ½ cup chopped green onions
- ¼ cup fresh lemon juice (about 2 lemons)
- ¼ cup low-sodium soy sauce
- 3 tablespoons grated peeled fresh ginger
- 1 tablespoon sugar
- 1 tablespoon Sriracha (hot chile sauce, such as Huy Fong)
- 3 garlic cloves, minced
- 4 (6-ounce) tuna steaks (about ¾ inch thick)

RELISH:

- 1 cup diced seeded orange watermelon
- 1 cup diced seeded yellow watermelon
- 1 cup diced seeded red watermelon
- 3 tablespoons thinly sliced green onions
- 2 tablespoons chopped fresh basil
- 2 teaspoons seasoned rice vinegar
- 1 tablespoon fresh lemon juice
- 1 teaspoon sugar
- ½ teaspoon grated peeled fresh ginger
- ¼ teaspoon salt
- ¼ teaspoon dark sesame oil

REMAINING INGREDIENTS:

Cooking spray
- 1 teaspoon toasted sesame seeds (optional)

1. To prepare tuna, combine first 8 ingredients in a large zip-top plastic bag. Add fish to bag; seal. Marinate in refrigerator 30 minutes, turning occasionally.
2. To prepare relish, combine watermelons and next 8 ingredients in a large bowl. Cover and chill.

3. Prepare grill.
4. Remove fish from bag; discard marinade. Place fish on grill rack coated with cooking spray; cook 3 minutes on each side or until medium-rare or desired degree of doneness. Serve with relish. Sprinkle with sesame seeds, if desired. Yield: 4 servings (serving size: 1 tuna steak and ¾ cup relish).

CALORIES 293 (27% from fat); FAT 8.8g (sat 2.2g, mono 2.9g, poly 2.6g); PROTEIN 40.7g; CARB 11.3g; FIBER 0.7g; CHOL 65mg; IRON 2.2mg; SODIUM 269mg; CALC 29mg

menu of the month
Take It Outside

These breezy recipes guarantee a delicious picnic that's easy on the cook.

Perfectly Portable Menu
serves 4

Gingery Limeade

White Bean Dip with Rosemary and Sage

Purchased breadsticks

Fruited Chicken Salad Over Couscous
or
Artichoke-Bacon Chicken Salad Sandwiches

Cinnamon-Almond Cookies

QUICK & EASY • MAKE AHEAD
Gingery Limeade

Tote chilled limeade in a thermos. Grated ginger adds zip, but you can omit it for a classic version.

- ¾ cup sugar
- ¼ cup boiling water
- 1½ teaspoons grated peeled fresh ginger
- 1½ teaspoons grated lime rind
- ¾ cup fresh lime juice (about 4 limes)
- 2½ cups cold water
- 4 lime slices (optional)

1. Combine first 4 ingredients in a small bowl, stirring with a whisk until sugar dissolves. Strain mixture through a sieve into a pitcher. Add juice and 2½ cups cold water. Chill completely. Serve with lime slices, if desired. Yield: 4 servings (serving size: about 1 cup).

CALORIES 158 (1% from fat); FAT 0.1g (sat 0g, mono 0g, poly 0g); PROTEIN 0.2g; CARB 41.9g; FIBER 0.3g; CHOL 0mg; IRON 0.1mg; SODIUM 1mg; CALC 5.7mg

QUICK & EASY • MAKE AHEAD
White Bean Dip with Rosemary and Sage

Prepare the dip up to a day in advance to give the flavors a chance to meld. In addition to pita wedges, you can serve crudités for dipping.

- 2 tablespoons fresh lemon juice
- 1 tablespoon extravirgin olive oil
- 2 teaspoons minced fresh rosemary
- 2 teaspoons minced fresh sage
- ¼ teaspoon freshly ground black pepper
- 2 garlic cloves, chopped
- 1 (19-ounce) can cannellini beans or other white beans, rinsed and drained
- 4 (6-inch) pitas, each cut into 6 wedges

Sage sprig (optional)

1. Place first 7 ingredients in a food processor; process until smooth. Serve with pita wedges. Garnish with sage sprig, if desired. Yield: 8 servings (serving size: about 3 tablespoons dip and 3 pita wedges).

CALORIES 128 (13% from fat); FAT 1.9g (sat 0.3g, mono 1.3g, poly 0.3g); PROTEIN 5.1g; CARB 22.6g; FIBER 2.1g; CHOL 0mg; IRON 1.9mg; SODIUM 161mg; CALC 35mg

Choice Ingredient: Cannellini Beans

Often referred to as white kidney beans, cannellinis are a nutritious staple of Italian cuisine. Each one-cup serving supplies 229 micrograms of folate, 80 milligrams of magnesium, and a third of your recommended daily intake of fiber. Cannellinis are earthy, nutty, buttery, and slightly sweet. Select either dried beans, which triple in size when cooked (one cup dried will yield three cups cooked), or the canned variety. Because of their meaty texture, the beans maintain their shape, making them an attractive addition to salads, stews, pastas, and soups.

QUICK & EASY • MAKE AHEAD

Fruited Chicken Salad Over Couscous

Either pack the couscous separately, or line the bottom of a large portable container with the couscous and top with the chicken mixture. Prepare this salad just a few hours in advance; if made too far ahead, the fruit becomes watery. Purchase precut fruit for easier preparation.

 ¾   cup water
 ¼   cup orange juice
 ¼   teaspoon curry powder
 ¼   teaspoon salt
 ¾   cup uncooked couscous
 ¼   cup orange juice
 1   tablespoon extravirgin olive oil
 1   tablespoon honey
 ½   teaspoon curry powder
 ¼   teaspoon salt
 ⅛   teaspoon freshly ground black pepper
 2   cups chopped skinless, boneless rotisserie chicken breast
 2   cups honeydew melon cubes
 1   cup seedless red grapes, halved
 ½   cup thinly sliced fresh basil
 ½   cup chopped green onions
 3   tablespoons sliced almonds, toasted
 1   (11-ounce) can mandarin oranges in light syrup, drained

1. Combine first 4 ingredients in a small saucepan over high heat. Bring to a boil; gradually stir in couscous. Remove from heat; cover and let stand 5 minutes. Fluff with a fork.
2. Combine ¼ cup orange juice, oil, and next 4 ingredients, stirring with a whisk. Stir 1 tablespoon dressing into couscous mixture, and set remaining dressing aside.
3. Combine chicken and remaining 6 ingredients in a large bowl. Drizzle remaining dressing over salad; toss gently to coat. Serve salad over couscous. Yield: 4 servings (serving size: about 1½ cups salad and ¾ cup couscous).

CALORIES 361 (17% from fat); FAT 7g (sat 0.7g, mono 4g, poly 1.1g); PROTEIN 20.4g; CARB 56.7g; FIBER 4.8g; CHOL 30mg; IRON 1.3mg; SODIUM 488mg; CALC 70mg

QUICK & EASY • MAKE AHEAD

Artichoke-Bacon Chicken Salad Sandwiches

Chicken salad makes a good sourdough sandwich with arugula, artichoke hearts, and bacon.

 ⅓   cup plain low-fat yogurt
 ¼   cup light mayonnaise
 ¾   teaspoon chopped fresh rosemary
 ¼   teaspoon freshly ground black pepper
 1   garlic clove, minced
 2   cups shredded skinless, boneless rotisserie chicken breast
 1   cup drained canned artichoke hearts, chopped
 4   bacon slices, cooked and crumbled
 2   cups trimmed arugula
 8   (1½-ounce) slices sourdough bread, toasted

1. Combine first 5 ingredients in a large bowl. Stir in chicken, artichoke hearts, and bacon. Divide arugula evenly over 4 bread slices; top each slice with ¾ cup chicken mixture and 1 bread slice. Yield: 4 servings (serving size: 1 sandwich).

CALORIES 439 (25% from fat); FAT 12.4g (sat 2.6g, mono 3.4g, poly 4.2g); PROTEIN 34.3g; CARB 47.6g; FIBER 2.9g; CHOL 73mg; IRON 5.1mg; SODIUM 886mg; CALC 146mg

MAKE AHEAD

Cinnamon-Almond Cookies

These delicately spiced shape-and-bake cookies are crisp on the outside and chewy on the inside. Store extra cookies in an airtight container.

COOKIES:

 ⅓   cup butter, softened
 ½   cup granulated sugar
 ¼   cup slivered almonds, toasted
 1½ cups sifted cake flour (about 5¼ ounces)
 ⅔   cup powdered sugar
 ¼   teaspoon salt
 ¼   teaspoon ground cinnamon
 ¼   teaspoon ground cloves
 ¼   cup ice water
     Cooking spray

TOPPING:

 2   teaspoons powdered sugar
 ⅛   teaspoon ground cinnamon

1. To prepare cookies, place butter and granulated sugar in a medium bowl; beat with a mixer at medium speed until well blended (about 2 minutes).
2. Place almonds in a spice or coffee grinder; process until finely ground. Combine flour, ground almonds, ⅔ cup powdered sugar, salt, ¼ teaspoon cinnamon, and cloves. Add flour mixture to butter mixture; beat until just combined. Add ¼ cup ice water; beat at low speed until moist. Gently press mixture into a ball; wrap in plastic wrap. Refrigerate 1 hour or until thoroughly chilled.
3. Preheat oven to 300°.
4. Shape dough into 30 (1-inch) balls. Place balls 2 inches apart on a baking sheet coated with cooking spray. Bake at 300° for 25 minutes. Cool on a wire rack.
5. To prepare topping, combine 2 teaspoons powdered sugar and ⅛ teaspoon cinnamon. Sprinkle sugar mixture evenly over cooled cookies. Yield: 30 servings (serving size: 1 cookie).

CALORIES 65 (35% from fat); FAT 2.5g (sat 1.3g, mono 0.8g, poly 0.2g); PROTEIN 0.6g; CARB 10.2g; FIBER 0.2g; CHOL 5mg; IRON 0.4mg; SODIUM 34mg; CALC 4mg

Movers &
Taste Shapers

How a nutritionist, a cookbook author, and a community activist have helped improve the way we eat.

You may not know them, but Marion Nestle, Jeanne Jones, and Olga Fusté have changed how we eat. These nutrition leaders have influenced public policy regarding food, pioneered innovative low-fat cuisine, and revamped traditional Latino foods to help prevent health problems. Whether in the classroom or the kitchen, these innovators point the way to eating smart, living well—and enjoying the simple luxury of a good meal.

Stuffed Piquillo Peppers

Nestle enjoys Spanish-style tapas, appetizer-sized portions that allow her to reasonably savor a variety of flavors at a single meal. Piquillos are small, red, spicy-sweet roasted Spanish peppers; look for them in gourmet groceries, or order them online from La Tienda (www.tienda.com).

1½ cups water
  ½   cup long-grain brown rice
  ⅛   teaspoon saffron threads, crushed
  2   garlic cloves, minced
  ¼   cup chopped fresh flat-leaf parsley
  ½   teaspoon freshly ground black
      pepper
  ¼   teaspoon salt
  1   (14.5-ounce) can diced tomatoes,
      drained
  10 piquillo peppers (about
      1 [7.76-ounce] jar)
Cooking spray
  ¼   cup (1 ounce) shredded Manchego
      cheese
Flat-leaf parsley sprigs (optional)

1. Combine first 4 ingredients in a small saucepan; bring to a boil. Cover, reduce heat, and simmer 40 minutes or until done. Stir in chopped parsley, black pepper, salt, and tomatoes. Cook 3 minutes. Remove from heat.

2. Preheat oven to 400°.

3. Spoon about 3 tablespoons rice mixture into each piquillo pepper. Place stuffed peppers in an 8-inch square baking dish coated with cooking spray. Sprinkle evenly with cheese. Bake at 400° for 10 minutes or until peppers are thoroughly heated. Garnish with parsley sprigs, if desired. Yield: 5 servings (serving size: 2 stuffed peppers).

CALORIES 109 (17% from fat); FAT 2g (sat 1.2g, mono 0.2g, poly 0.2g); PROTEIN 3.4g; CARB 17.9g; FIBER 1.2g; CHOL 4mg; IRON 0.8mg; SODIUM 442mg; CALC 84mg

QUICK & EASY • MAKE AHEAD
Fresh Corn Salad
(pictured on page 242)

Fresh, sweet summer corn requires no cooking, which makes this a particularly appealing warm-weather side dish.

  ¾   cup light sour cream
  1   teaspoon Worcestershire
      sauce
  ¾   teaspoon seasoned salt
  3   cups fresh corn kernels (about
      5 ears)
  1   cup finely chopped red bell
      pepper
  1   cup finely chopped green
      onions

1. Combine first 3 ingredients in a large bowl, stirring with a whisk. Add corn and remaining ingredients, stirring to combine. Cover and refrigerate at least 2 hours before serving. Yield: 8 servings (serving size: about ½ cup).

CALORIES 112 (21% from fat); FAT 2.6g (sat 1.3g, mono 0.3g, poly 0.5g); PROTEIN 4g; CARB 22.2g; FIBER 3.1g; CHOL 8mg; IRON 0.8mg; SODIUM 94mg; CALC 13mg

Halibut with Caper Sauce

Jeanne Jones likes to serve this South American–inspired dish over rice with chopped parsley.

  2   tablespoons fresh lime juice
  4   (6-ounce) halibut fillets
  1   teaspoon olive oil
  1   cup thinly vertically sliced onion
      (about 1 medium)
  2   cups diced seeded tomato (about 2)
  ¼   cup jarred diced pimiento,
      divided
  2   tablespoons capers
  1   tablespoon finely chopped seeded
      jalapeño pepper
  ¼   teaspoon salt
  ¼   cup water
  4   lime wedges

1. Combine juice and fish in a zip-top plastic bag; seal. Marinate in refrigerator 2 hours, turning once.
2. Heat oil in a large skillet over medium heat. Add onion to pan; cook 8 minutes or until tender, stirring frequently. Increase heat to medium-high. Stir in tomato, 2 tablespoons pimiento, capers, jalapeño, and salt. Cover and cook 5 minutes. Add ¼ cup water and fish; cover and cook fish 3 minutes on each side. Uncover and cook 3 minutes or until fish flakes easily when tested with a fork or until desired degree of doneness. Place 1 fillet on each of 4 plates. Top each serving with ¼ cup sauce. Sprinkle each with 1½ teaspoons remaining pimiento. Garnish with lime wedges. Yield: 4 servings.

CALORIES 232 (21% from fat); FAT 5.4g (sat 0.8g, mono 2.2g, poly 1.5g); PROTEIN 36.7g; CARB 7.9g; FIBER 1.7g; CHOL 54mg; IRON 2mg; SODIUM 372mg; CALC 99mg

Spirited Bread Pudding

"In many Latin American countries, there seems to be a bakery on every corner," Fusté explains. "Leftover French bread finds its way into this bread pudding. Topped with caramelized sugar and cut in wedges like a cake, this is a dressed-up version of the homey classic." If you don't have a kitchen blowtorch to caramelize the sugar in step four, simply sift two tablespoons powdered sugar over the top of the baked pudding.

    1   tablespoon butter, softened
    2   tablespoons brown sugar
    2   tablespoons coarsely chopped
        walnuts
    2   cups fat-free milk
    1   (8-ounce) loaf French bread, cut
        into ½-inch cubes
    ½   cup granulated sugar
  1½   tablespoons butter, melted
    ½   teaspoon vanilla extract
    ⅛   teaspoon salt
    2   large eggs, lightly beaten
    ¼   cup golden raisins
  1½   tablespoons cognac
    ½   teaspoon grated orange rind
    2   tablespoons granulated sugar
        Orange rind strips (optional)

1. Preheat oven to 350°.
2. Spread softened butter evenly into bottom of an 8-inch round cake pan, and sprinkle with brown sugar and walnuts. Set prepared pan aside.
3. Combine milk and bread in a large bowl. Let stand 15 minutes, occasionally pressing on bread to soak up milk. Add ½ cup granulated sugar, melted butter, vanilla, salt, and eggs; stir with a wooden spoon 1 minute or until bread cubes break apart. Stir in raisins, cognac, and ½ teaspoon grated rind. Pour bread mixture into prepared pan. Place pan in a 13 x 9–inch baking pan; add hot water to larger pan to a depth of 1 inch. Bake at 350° for 50 minutes or until a knife inserted in center comes out clean. Remove cake pan from water. Let stand 5 minutes. Invert onto a serving platter.
4. Sift 2 tablespoons granulated sugar evenly over pudding. Holding a kitchen blowtorch about 3 inches from surface of pudding, heat sugar, moving torch back

and forth, until sugar is completely melted and caramelized (about 1 minute). Serve warm. Garnish with orange rind strips, if desired. Yield: 8 servings (serving size: 1 wedge).

CALORIES 255 (25% from fat); FAT 7g (sat 3g, mono 2g, poly 1.4g); PROTEIN 6.6g; CARB 40.7g; FIBER 1.2g; CHOL 64mg; IRON 1.1mg; SODIUM 295mg; CALC 111mg

MAKE AHEAD
Little Empañadas with Potatoes and Chorizo
Empañaditas con Papas y Chorizo

These mini-empañadas, which would be at home on a Spanish tapas platter, are an example of how Nestle makes a meal from appetizer portions. Mexican chorizo is made with fresh pork (as opposed to Spanish-style chorizo made with smoked pork).

    2   cups all-purpose flour (about
        9 ounces)
    1   tablespoon sugar
    1   teaspoon baking powder
    ½   teaspoon salt, divided
    3   tablespoons chilled butter, cut
        into small pieces
    9   tablespoons ice water, divided
    1   teaspoon cider vinegar
    2   ounces fresh chorizo
    2   cups diced Yukon gold potato
        (about 8 ounces)
    ¼   teaspoon hot paprika
        Cooking spray
    1   large egg white, lightly beaten

1. Lightly spoon flour into dry measuring cups; level with a knife. Place flour, sugar, baking powder, and ¼ teaspoon salt in a food processor; pulse 2 times or until combined. Add butter; pulse 4 times or until mixture resembles coarse meal. With processor on, slowly add ½ cup ice water and vinegar through food chute, processing just until combined (do not form a ball). Gently press mixture into 2 (5-inch) circles on plastic wrap; cover. Chill 1 hour.
2. Remove chorizo from casings. Cook chorizo in a large nonstick skillet over medium-high heat until browned, stirring to crumble.

3. Place potato in a saucepan; cover with water. Bring to a boil. Reduce heat, and simmer 8 minutes or until tender; drain. Place in a large bowl; mash with a potato masher. Add chorizo, paprika, and ¼ teaspoon salt; stir until well combined.
4. Preheat oven to 425°.
5. Remove dough from refrigerator, and halve each disc. Place 1 dough portion between 2 sheets of wax paper. Roll into a ¼-inch thickness; cut 2 (3-inch) circles with a biscuit cutter. Repeat procedure with remaining dough portions. Combine excess dough, roll to ¼-inch-thickness, and cut 4 (3-inch) circles with a biscuit cutter. Working with 1 circle at a time (cover remaining circles with a damp towel to prevent drying), spoon 1 tablespoon potato mixture into center of circle, and fold dough over filling. Press edges together with a fork to seal. Place empañadita on a large baking sheet coated with cooking spray. Combine 1 tablespoon water and egg white. Lightly brush tops of empañaditas with egg mixture. Bake at 425° for 20 minutes or until lightly browned. Yield: 12 empañaditas (serving size: 1 empañadita).

CALORIES 144 (31% from fat); FAT 4.9g (sat 2.5g, mono 1.6g, poly 0.4g); PROTEIN 4.1g; CARB 20.5g; FIBER 0.8g; CHOL 12mg; IRON 1.3mg; SODIUM 222mg; CALC 27mg

QUICK & EASY
Ricotta Raspberry Canapés

Fresh ricotta's creaminess is key to this recipe. You can find it in gourmet supermarkets, or make your own.

   12   (½-ounce) slices whole wheat
        peasant bread
    1   cup fresh ricotta cheese
    ½   teaspoon freshly ground black
        pepper
    2   cups fresh raspberries
    2   tablespoons honey
        Mint sprigs (optional)

1. Preheat oven to 300°.
2. Cut each bread slice in half; place on a baking sheet. Bake at 300° for 7 minutes
Continued

or until lightly toasted. Remove from oven; cool completely.

3. Combine ricotta and pepper in a small bowl. Spread about 2 teaspoons cheese mixture on each toast. Top each toast with 2 or 3 raspberries; drizzle evenly with honey. Garnish with mint sprigs, if desired. Serve immediately. Yield: 12 servings (serving size: 2 canapés).

CALORIES 96 (32% from fat); FAT 3.4g (sat 1.8g, mono 1g, poly 0.3g); PROTEIN 4.1g; CARB 13.2g; FIBER 2.3g; CHOL 11mg; IRON 0.8mg, SODIUM 93mg; CALC 63mg

---

Indian Menu for Eight
serves 8

Turkey Curry

Summer squash sauté*

Basmati rice

*Melt 2 tablespoons butter in a large non-stick skillet over medium-high heat. Add 3 cups julienne-cut zucchini, 3 cups julienne-cut yellow squash, 1 cup red bell pepper strips, 1 cup vertically sliced onion, ½ teaspoon salt, and ½ teaspoon freshly ground black pepper; sauté 5 minutes. Remove from heat, and sprinkle with 2 tablespoons chopped fresh cilantro.

QUICK & EASY
Turkey Curry

Jones often serves this dish at parties with basmati rice and a selection of chutneys, raisins, bell peppers, tomato, pineapple, papaya, and roasted almonds. Leftovers are even better the next day.

  2 tablespoons butter
  3 cups finely chopped peeled Golden Delicious apple (about 2)
  2 cups finely chopped onion (about 1 large)
  2 garlic cloves, minced
  1 tablespoon curry powder
  ½ teaspoon salt
  ¼ teaspoon ground red pepper
  ½ cup fat-free milk
  2 tablespoons cornstarch
  2 cups fat-free, less-sodium chicken broth
  6 cups chopped cooked turkey breast (about 1 pound)
  1½ tablespoons fresh lemon juice

1. Melt butter in a large Dutch oven over medium-low heat. Add apple, onion, and garlic to pan. Cover and cook 12 minutes or until onion is tender. Add curry powder, salt, and pepper to pan. Combine milk and cornstarch in a small bowl, stirring with a whisk; add to pan. Stir in broth. Reduce heat, and cook 4 minutes or until slightly thick, stirring constantly. Add turkey and juice to pan; cook 5 minutes or until turkey is thoroughly heated. Yield: 8 servings (serving size: 1 cup).

CALORIES 143 (21% from fat); FAT 3.4g (sat 2g, mono 0.9g, poly 0.3g); PROTEIN 18.3g; CARB 9.7g; FIBER 1.2g; CHOL 55mg; IRON 1.2mg; SODIUM 316mg; CALC 37mg

---

Stuffed Eye of Round

Fusté's husband prepares this dish for special occasions. The colorful, savory filling uses Spanish chorizo to lend a lovely smoked flavor.

FILLING:

  ⅓ cup diced bottled pimiento
  2 tablespoons capers
  5 large green olives, chopped
  4 ounces lean smoked ham, diced
  2 ounces Spanish chorizo, diced
  1 hard-cooked large egg, finely chopped

BEEF:

  1 (3-pound) boneless eye-of-round roast, trimmed
  ½ teaspoon salt
  ½ teaspoon ground cumin
  ½ teaspoon dried thyme
  ⅛ teaspoon freshly ground black pepper
  3 garlic cloves, chopped
  1 teaspoon olive oil
  2 cups water
  1 cup chopped onion
  6 small red potatoes, quartered
  1 (8-ounce) can no-salt-added tomato sauce
  1 bay leaf

1. To prepare filling, combine first 6 ingredients; set aside.

2. To prepare beef, cut a 2½-inch-wide horizontal slit into end of roast, and cut through to other end to form a deep pocket using a long, thin knife. Spoon filling into pocket, and pack using handle of a wooden spoon (the roast will be very full). Secure open end of roast with twine ½ inch from edge. Combine salt, cumin, thyme, pepper, and garlic; rub over roast.

3. Heat oil in a 6-quart Dutch oven over medium-high heat. Add roast to pan; cook 5 minutes, browning on all sides. Add 2 cups water and remaining ingredients to pan; reduce heat to medium-low. Cover and cook 2 hours or until roast is tender, turning roast after 1 hour.

4. Transfer meat to a cutting board or work surface. Using a slotted spoon, transfer potatoes to a platter; keep warm. Simmer liquid in pan until reduced to 1 cup (about 15 minutes). Discard bay leaf.

5. Remove twine before cutting roast into 12 slices. Yield: 12 servings (serving size: 1 stuffed roast slice, 4 teaspoons sauce, and 2 potato quarters).

CALORIES 268 (27% from fat); FAT 8.1g (sat 2.7g, mono 3.6g, poly 0.6g); PROTEIN 29.8g; CARB 17g; FIBER 1.9g; CHOL 84mg; IRON 2.6mg; SODIUM 435mg; CALC 19mg

---

Sweet Rice Pudding
Arroz con Dulce

"This is a traditional dessert for parties and special occasions," says Olga Fusté. "In tropical climates, this dish is frequently made with coconut milk."

  2 cups water
  1 tablespoon butter
  ¼ teaspoon salt
  1 (2-inch) cinnamon stick
  1 cup uncooked Arborio or other short-grain rice
  2½ cups fat-free milk
  ⅓ cup sugar
  2 teaspoons grated lime rind
  ½ cup golden raisins
  1 teaspoon vanilla extract

1. Combine first 4 ingredients in a large saucepan; bring to a boil. Stir in rice. Reduce heat to medium, and cook 10 minutes or until liquid is almost absorbed, stirring occasionally. Discard cinnamon stick. Stir in milk, sugar, and rind; bring to a boil over medium heat, stirring frequently. Reduce heat to medium-low, and cook 25 minutes or until mixture thickens and becomes creamy, stirring frequently. Remove from heat. Stir in raisins and vanilla. Yield: 6 servings (serving size: ⅔ cup pudding).

CALORIES 254 (8% from fat); FAT 2.3g (sat 1.4g, mono 0.7g, poly 0.1g); PROTEIN 6.1g; CARB 52.2g; FIBER 1.5g; CHOL 7mg; IRON 1.7mg; SODIUM 172mg; CALC 135mg

---

QUICK & EASY
Puerto Rican Cabbage Salad

Cabbage is one of the most widely used vegetables in Latin American cuisines. Fusté enjoys this slaw with rice and beans or fish tacos.

    7   cups very thinly sliced green cabbage
    ½   cup grated carrot
    2   tablespoons finely chopped onion
    1   tablespoon minced fresh cilantro
    ¼   cup fresh lime juice
    1   tablespoon cider vinegar
  1½   teaspoons extravirgin olive oil
    ¼   teaspoon salt
    ¼   teaspoon freshly ground black pepper

1. Combine first 4 ingredients in a large bowl. Combine juice and remaining 4 ingredients, stirring well with a whisk. Drizzle juice mixture over cabbage mixture; toss well to combine. Cover and chill 15 minutes. Yield: 8 servings (serving size: ¾ cup).

CALORIES 29 (31% from fat); FAT 1g (sat 0.1g, mono 0.6g, poly 0.2g); PROTEIN 1g; CARB 5.1g; FIBER 1.7g; CHOL 0mg; IRON 0.4mg; SODIUM 87mg; CALC 32mg

---

QUICK & EASY
Doña Carmen's Garlic Rice

Fusté was greatly influenced by her mentor, Doña Carmen. This recipe of Carmen's turns ordinary rice into a simple yet flavorful side.

  1½   teaspoons olive oil
    2   cups uncooked long-grain rice
    6   garlic cloves, crushed
  3¼   cups water
  1½   teaspoons salt

1. Heat oil in a medium saucepan over medium heat. Add rice and garlic to pan; cook 3 minutes, stirring frequently. Stir in 3¼ cups water and salt; bring to a simmer. Cover, reduce heat to medium-low, and cook 20 minutes or until liquid is absorbed. Fluff with a fork before serving. Yield: 8 servings (serving size: about ⅔ cup).

CALORIES 180 (6% from fat); FAT 1.2g (sat 0.2g, mono 0.7g, poly 0.2g); PROTEIN 3.4g; CARB 37.7g; FIBER 0.7g; CHOL 0mg; IRON 2mg; SODIUM 443mg; CALC 17mg

---

QUICK & EASY • MAKE AHEAD
Spanish Almonds

Although these olive oil–roasted almonds contain a high percentage of fat, it's the heart-healthy unsaturated kind. Plus, they offer protein and fiber, which makes them a smart snack, according to Nestle.

    1   tablespoon extravirgin olive oil
    ½   teaspoon Spanish smoked paprika
    ½   teaspoon salt
    ¼   teaspoon ground cumin
    ½   pound whole blanched almonds

1. Preheat oven to 300°.
2. Combine all ingredients in a large bowl; spread evenly in a single layer on a parchment-lined baking sheet. Bake at 300° for 35 minutes. Remove from oven; cool to room temperature. Yield: 2 cups (serving size: 2 tablespoons).

CALORIES 91 (80% from fat); FAT 8.1g (sat 0.7g, mono 5.3g, poly 1.8g); PROTEIN 3.1g; CARB 2.9g; FIBER 1.5g; CHOL 0mg; IRON 0.6mg; SODIUM 77mg; CALC 31mg

---

then & now
Easy Refrigerator Pickles

Food stylist Kathleen Kanen has been with Cooking Light since 1988, and prepared and styled thousands of recipes for photography.

Easy Refrigerator Pickles, a reader recipe first published in our July/August 1989 issue, is one of her favorites. In this new rendition, she trimmed the sugar by one-quarter cup and bumped the salt up from a half-teaspoon to three-quarters of a teaspoon. She also added a smidgen of black pepper, crushed red pepper, and some sliced garlic. These changes yielded a tastier pickle with a blend of crisp, sweet, and sour flavors and just 20 milligrams more sodium per serving than the original.

MAKE AHEAD
Easy Refrigerator Pickles

    6   cups thinly sliced pickling cucumbers (about 2 pounds)
    2   cups thinly sliced onion
  1½   cups white vinegar
    ¾   cup sugar
    ¾   teaspoon salt
    ½   teaspoon mustard seeds
    ½   teaspoon celery seeds
    ½   teaspoon ground turmeric
    ½   teaspoon crushed red pepper
    ¼   teaspoon freshly ground black pepper
    4   garlic cloves, thinly sliced

1. Place 3 cups cucumber in a medium glass bowl; top with 1 cup onion. Repeat layers.
2. Combine vinegar and remaining 8 ingredients in a small saucepan; stir well. Bring to a boil; cook 1 minute. Pour over cucumber mixture; cool. Cover and chill at least 4 days. Yield: 7 cups (serving size: ¼ cup).
NOTE: Pickles may be stored in the refrigerator up to one month.

CALORIES 28 (10% from fat); FAT 0.1g (sat 0g, mono 0g, poly 0.1g); PROTEIN 0.3g; CARB 7g; FIBER 0.3g; CHOL 0mg; IRON 0.1mg; SODIUM 64mg; CALC 7mg

A World of Burgers

Use our tips and recipes to add innovative twists to the all-American standby.

Burgers are the standby for backyard cookouts. With these recipes, you can go beyond the basic burger and create your own masterpiece with flavorful meats, robust seasonings, and unique ingredients.

International flavors mesh well within burgers. Rosemary, oregano, and feta cheese are tucked into ground lamb to create a Greek version that's nested inside pita bread. Italian herbs, mozzarella cheese, and pasta sauce team up in a burger reminiscent of a meatball sub.

Choose different breads for more diversity. Aside from those called for in these recipes, try focaccia, Hawaiian bread rolls, sourdough bread, Texas toast, English muffins, or garlic toast. Or go bunless and serve the meat patties over rice, orzo, couscous, egg noodles, or spaghetti.

QUICK & EASY
Greek Lamb Burgers

Fresh rosemary, oregano, and lemon rind harmonize with the richness of lamb and feta cheese. If you don't want to make the sauce, serve with a drizzle of plain, fat-free yogurt. Tuck tomato slices and lettuce leaves into the pita pockets, if desired. Serve with fresh fruit and lemonade.

- ½ cup (2 ounces) crumbled reduced-fat feta cheese
- 1 tablespoon chopped fresh rosemary
- 2 teaspoons grated lemon rind
- 2 teaspoons chopped fresh oregano
- ½ teaspoon salt
- 3 garlic cloves, minced
- ¾ pound lean ground lamb
- ¾ pound ground turkey breast
- Cooking spray
- 3 (6-inch) pitas, cut in half
- 6 tablespoons Easy Tzatziki Sauce (page 221)

1. Prepare grill.
2. Combine first 8 ingredients. Divide mixture into 6 equal portions, shaping each into a ½-inch-thick patty.
3. Place patties on a grill rack coated with cooking spray; grill 6 minutes on each side or until a thermometer registers 165°. Remove from grill; let stand 5 minutes.

Place 1 patty in each pita half; drizzle each serving with 1 tablespoon Easy Tzatziki Sauce. Yield: 6 servings (serving size: 1 stuffed pita half).

CALORIES 275 (34% from fat); FAT 10.3g (sat 4.4g, mono 3.6g, poly 0.8g); PROTEIN 25.9g; CARB 19.1g; FIBER 0.8g; CHOL 62mg; IRON 1.9mg; SODIUM 576mg; CALC 78mg

QUICK & EASY
Saté Burgers

Peanuts, cilantro, brown sugar, lime juice, and fish sauce create the flavors of the Indonesian meat skewers called saté. Using equal amounts of ground turkey and pork keeps these burgers lean. Serve on a bed of brown rice with spinach and lime wedges.

- ½ cup chopped fresh cilantro
- ¼ cup finely chopped unsalted dry-roasted peanuts
- 2 tablespoons fresh lime juice
- 1½ tablespoons brown sugar
- 1½ tablespoons fish sauce
- 1½ teaspoons ground cumin
- ½ teaspoon salt
- ¼ teaspoon hot pepper sauce (such as Tabasco)
- 3 garlic cloves, minced
- ¾ pound ground pork
- ¾ pound ground turkey breast
- Cooking spray

1. Prepare grill.
2. Combine first 11 ingredients. Divide mixture into 6 equal portions, shaping each into a ½-inch-thick patty.
3. Place patties on a grill rack coated with cooking spray; grill 7 minutes on each side or until a thermometer registers 165°. Remove from grill; let stand 5 minutes. Yield: 6 servings (serving size: 1 patty).

CALORIES 166 (41% from fat); FAT 7.5g (sat 2.1g, mono 3.1g, poly 1.3g); PROTEIN 20.1g; CARB 4.9g; FIBER 0.8g; CHOL 49mg; IRON 0.7mg; SODIUM 599mg; CALC 16mg

QUICK & EASY
Italian Meatball Burgers

These saucy, family-friendly burgers might be best eaten with a knife and fork.

- 8 ounces sweet turkey Italian sausage
- 1 teaspoon dried oregano
- 1 teaspoon dried basil
- ½ teaspoon salt
- ½ teaspoon fennel seeds, crushed
- ⅛ teaspoon garlic powder
- 1 pound ground sirloin
- Cooking spray
- 2 ounces fresh mozzarella cheese, thinly sliced
- 6 (2-ounce) Italian bread rolls, split
- ¾ cup tomato-basil pasta sauce (such as Muir Glen organic)

1. Prepare grill.
2. Remove casings from sausage. Combine sausage and next 6 ingredients. Divide mixture into 6 equal portions, shaping each into a ½-inch-thick patty.
3. Place patties on a grill rack coated with cooking spray; grill 5 minutes. Turn patties over; grill 2 minutes. Divide cheese evenly over patties, and grill 5 minutes or until a thermometer registers 165°. Remove from grill; let stand 5 minutes.
4. Place rolls, cut sides down, on grill rack; grill 1 minute or until toasted. Place 1 patty on bottom half of each roll; top each serving with 2 tablespoons sauce and top half of roll. Yield: 6 servings (serving size: 1 burger).

CALORIES 375 (33% from fat); FAT 13.9g (sat 5.3g, mono 4.4g, poly 1.7g); PROTEIN 28.1g; CARB 32.7g; FIBER 1.8g; CHOL 80mg; IRON 4.5mg; SODIUM 894mg; CALC 130mg

Southwestern Turkey-Cheddar Burgers with Grilled Onions

Wheat germ adds a nuttiness that complements the turkey and spices. For more spicy heat, use Monterey Jack cheese with jalapeño peppers.

¾ cup finely chopped Maui or other sweet onion
⅓ cup wheat germ
1½ teaspoons ancho chile powder
¾ teaspoon ground cumin
½ teaspoon salt
¼ teaspoon ground red pepper
1½ pounds ground turkey breast
Cooking spray
4 ounces extrasharp Cheddar cheese, thinly sliced
6 (½-inch-thick) slices Maui or other sweet onion
6 (2-ounce) Kaiser rolls, split
6 tablespoons Chipotle-Poblano Ketchup (recipe on page 221)

1. Prepare grill.
2. Combine first 7 ingredients in a large bowl. Divide mixture into 6 equal portions, shaping each into a ½-inch-thick patty.
3. Place patties on a grill rack coated with cooking spray; grill 5 minutes. Turn patties over; grill 2 minutes. Divide cheese evenly over patties; grill 5 minutes or until a thermometer registers 165°. Remove from grill; let stand 5 minutes.
4. Place onion slices on grill rack coated with cooking spray; grill 4 minutes on each side or until browned and tender.
5. Place rolls, cut sides down, on grill rack; grill 1 minute or until toasted. Place 1 patty on bottom half of each roll; top each serving with 1 onion slice, 1 tablespoon Chipotle-Poblano Ketchup, and top half of roll. Yield: 6 servings (serving size: 1 burger).

CALORIES 395 (24% from fat); FAT 10.7g (sat 4.8g, mono 2.5g, poly 1.6g); PROTEIN 32.8g; CARB 42.6g; FIBER 3.3g; CHOL 54mg; IRON 3.4mg; SODIUM 853mg; CALC 211mg

Sun-Dried Tomato Beef Burgers

For the best results, look for soft, pliable sun-dried tomatoes in the produce section near the fresh tomatoes. If you want more tomato flavor and a bit of heat, serve with Chipotle-Poblano Ketchup (page 221). Toasted English muffin halves would also make great buns.

½ cup sun-dried tomatoes, packed without oil
¼ cup minced shallots
2 tablespoons Dijon mustard
1 tablespoon balsamic vinegar
1 teaspoon paprika
½ teaspoon salt
½ teaspoon freshly ground black pepper
1½ pounds ground sirloin
1 garlic clove, minced
Cooking spray
6 (2-ounce) Kaiser rolls, split
6 (⅛-inch-thick) red onion slices
6 romaine lettuce leaves

1. Place tomatoes in a bowl; cover with boiling water. Let stand 30 minutes or until soft. Drain and finely chop.
2. Prepare grill.
3. Combine tomatoes, shallots, and next 7 ingredients. Divide mixture into 6 equal portions, shaping each into a ½-inch-thick patty.
4. Place patties on a grill rack coated with cooking spray; grill 5 minutes on each side or until a thermometer registers 160°. Remove from grill; let stand 5 minutes.
5. Place rolls, cut sides down, on grill rack; grill 1 minute or until toasted. Place 1 patty on bottom half of each roll; top each serving with 1 onion slice, 1 lettuce leaf, and top half of roll. Yield: 6 servings (serving size: 1 burger).

CALORIES 381 (30% from fat); FAT 12.7g (sat 4.3g, mono 4.9g, poly 1.4g); PROTEIN 29g; CARB 36.2g; FIBER 2.4g; CHOL 72mg; IRON 4.8mg; SODIUM 722mg; CALC 81mg

Korean Barbecue Burgers

These burgers are based on *bulgogi*, a traditional Korean barbecue specialty of marinated sirloin. If you prefer more authentic flavor, just top with a splash of rice vinegar and kimchi, the spicy-hot pickled vegetable condiment available at Asian markets. Serve with rice crackers.

½ cup chopped green onions
3 tablespoons low-sodium soy sauce
1½ tablespoons brown sugar
1½ tablespoons minced peeled fresh ginger
1 tablespoon dark sesame oil
½ teaspoon freshly ground black pepper
2 garlic cloves, minced
1½ pounds ground sirloin
Cooking spray
6 (1½-ounce) whole wheat hamburger buns, split
6 red leaf lettuce leaves
6 tablespoons thinly sliced radishes

1. Prepare grill.
2. Combine first 8 ingredients. Divide mixture into 6 equal portions, shaping each into a ½-inch-thick patty.
3. Place patties on a grill rack coated with cooking spray; grill 6 minutes on each side or until a thermometer registers 160°. Remove from grill; let patties stand 5 minutes.
4. Place buns, cut sides down, on grill rack; grill 1 minute or until toasted. Place 1 patty on bottom half of each bun; top each serving with 1 lettuce leaf, 1 tablespoon radishes, and top half of bun. Yield: 6 servings (serving size: 1 burger).

CALORIES 343 (38% from fat); FAT 14.4g (sat 4.7g, mono 5.7g, poly 2.3g); PROTEIN 26.7g; CARB 27.4g; FIBER 3.7g; CHOL 72mg; IRON 3.8mg; SODIUM 534mg; CALC 72mg

Apricot Turkey Burgers

Chopped chickpeas and tangy dried apricots keep these Moroccan-spiced burgers moist. For a more unusual offering, fold one into flatbread such as FlatOut, Indian naan, or Middle Eastern lavash.

¾ cup drained canned chickpeas (garbanzo beans)
½ cup dried apricots, chopped
⅓ cup minced shallots
½ teaspoon salt
½ teaspoon ground ginger
½ teaspoon ground cumin
½ teaspoon ground cinnamon
⅛ teaspoon ground red pepper
1½ pounds ground turkey
   Cooking spray
6 (1½-ounce) multigrain hamburger buns, split
6 tablespoons Easy Tzatziki Sauce (recipe on page 221)

1. Prepare grill.
2. Place chickpeas in a food processor; pulse 3 times or until chopped. Combine chickpeas, apricots, and next 7 ingredients. Divide mixture into 6 equal portions, shaping each into a ½-inch-thick patty.
3. Place patties on a grill rack coated with cooking spray; grill 6 minutes on each side or until a thermometer registers 165°. Remove from grill; let stand 5 minutes.
4. Place buns, cut sides down, on grill rack; grill 1 minute or until toasted. Place 1 patty on bottom half of each bun; top each serving with 1 tablespoon Easy Tzatziki Sauce and top half of bun. Yield: 6 servings (serving size: 1 burger).

CALORIES 320 (26% from fat); FAT 9.2g (sat 2.3g, mono 3.6g, poly 2.3g); PROTEIN 24.9g; CARB 35.4g; FIBER 4.6g; CHOL 53mg; IRON 3.5mg; SODIUM 541mg; CALC 89mg

Tuna Sushi Burgers

Some of the tuna is pureed to help bind the burgers; the rest is finely chopped to create texture. Wet your hands before shaping the patties to keep the mixture from sticking.

1½ pounds tuna steaks, finely chopped and divided
⅓ cup minced green onions
1½ tablespoons seasoned rice vinegar
1½ tablespoons low-sodium soy sauce
1 tablespoon minced peeled fresh ginger
¾ teaspoon sugar
   Cooking spray

1. Prepare grill.
2. Place ¾ cup tuna in a food processor; process until smooth. Combine pureed tuna, remaining tuna, onions, and next 4 ingredients. Divide mixture into 6 equal portions using wet hands, shaping each into a ½-inch-thick patty.
3. Place patties on a grill rack coated with cooking spray; grill 2 minutes. Turn patties over; grill 1 minute or until desired degree of doneness. Remove from grill; let stand 5 minutes. Yield: 6 servings (serving size: 1 patty).

CALORIES 166 (29% from fat); FAT 5.4g (sat 1.4g, mono 1.8g, poly 1.6g); PROTEIN 25.8g; CARB 2.2g; FIBER 0.2g; CHOL 42mg; IRON 1.3mg; SODIUM 251mg; CALC 13mg

Swedish Meatball Burgers

You can also perch the patties atop egg noodles.

⅓ cup finely chopped onion
2 tablespoons chopped fresh parsley
1½ tablespoons white wine vinegar
1 tablespoon paprika
1 tablespoon brown sugar
1 teaspoon salt
⅛ teaspoon ground allspice
⅛ teaspoon ground nutmeg
1½ pounds ground veal
   Cooking spray
6 (2-ounce) potato sandwich rolls (such as Cobblestone Mill), split
6 tablespoons fat-free sour cream

1. Prepare grill.
2. Combine first 9 ingredients. Divide mixture into 6 equal portions, shaping each into a ½-inch-thick patty.
3. Place patties on a grill rack coated with cooking spray; grill 5 minutes on each side or until a thermometer registers 160°. Remove from grill, and let stand 5 minutes.
4. Place rolls, cut sides down, on grill rack; grill 1 minute or until toasted. Place 1 patty on bottom half of each roll; top each serving with 1 tablespoon sour cream and top half of roll. Yield: 6 servings (serving size: 1 burger).

CALORIES 326 (29% from fat); FAT 10.6g (sat 3.2g, mono 4.3g, poly 1.9g); PROTEIN 25.5g; CARB 31.9g; FIBER 1.5g; CHOL 89mg; IRON 2.1mg; SODIUM 718mg; CALC 45mg

Jamaican Chicken Burgers

Mashed plantains bind and moisten these island-inspired burgers. Be sure to choose ripe plantains with black skins; they're tender and slightly sweet. Commercial Pickapeppa sauce—a tangy, sweet Jamaican condiment found near the steak sauces in most supermarkets—would be a fitting accompaniment, as is our Chipotle-Poblano Ketchup (recipe on page 221).

1 cup thinly sliced soft black plantain (about 1 medium)
¼ cup chopped green onions
1 tablespoon cider vinegar
1 tablespoon Worcestershire sauce
1 teaspoon dried thyme
½ teaspoon ground allspice
½ teaspoon salt
¼ teaspoon ground red pepper
1½ pounds ground chicken breast
   Cooking spray
6 (2-ounce) onion sandwich buns, split
6 (⅛-inch-thick) slices red onion
12 (¼-inch-thick) slices tomato

1. Prepare grill.
2. Cook plantain in boiling water 15 minutes or until very tender. Drain; place in a large bowl. Mash plantain with a

fork until smooth; cool 5 minutes. Stir in green onions and next 7 ingredients. Divide mixture into 6 equal portions, shaping each into a ½-inch-thick patty.
3. Place patties on a grill rack coated with cooking spray; grill 4 minutes on each side or until a thermometer registers 165°. Remove from grill, and let stand 5 minutes.
4. Place buns, cut sides down, on grill rack; grill 1 minute or until toasted. Place 1 patty on bottom half of each bun; top each serving with 1 red onion slice, 2 tomato slices, and top half of bun. Yield: 6 servings (serving size: 1 burger).

CALORIES 313 (16% from fat); FAT 5.5g (sat 1.3g, mono 2.4g, poly 1g); PROTEIN 25.3g; CARB 40.9g; FIBER 3.3g; CHOL 50mg; IRON 3.1mg; SODIUM 578mg; CALC 93mg

---

MAKE AHEAD
Chipotle-Poblano Ketchup

Two types of chiles provide smoky heat to this sauce, which goes with any type of meat or poultry burger. It's also great with oven fries or chicken fingers.

    1 poblano chile (about 5 ounces)
    1 cup ketchup
    2 tablespoons minced seeded
       chipotle chiles, canned in adobo
       sauce (about 2 chiles)
    ½ teaspoon ground cumin

1. Preheat broiler.
2. Pierce poblano 2 times with the tip of a knife. Place poblano on a foil-lined baking sheet; broil 10 minutes or until blackened, turning occasionally. Place in a zip-top plastic bag; seal. Let stand 15 minutes. Peel and discard skins. Cut a lengthwise slit in poblano; discard seeds and stem. Finely chop poblano.
3. Combine poblano and remaining ingredients. Refrigerate in an airtight container up to 2 weeks. Yield: 1¼ cups (serving size: 1 tablespoon).

CALORIES 15 (12% from fat); FAT 0.2g (sat 0g, mono 0g, poly 0.1g); PROTEIN 0.3g; CARB 3.6g; FIBER 0.4g; CHOL 0mg; IRON 0.2mg; SODIUM 150mg; CALC 3mg

---

QUICK & EASY • MAKE AHEAD
Ginger-Honey Mustard

Sweet and pungent, this condiment enlivens poultry or fish burgers.

    1   cup Dijon mustard
    ¼   cup honey
    1½ tablespoons dry mustard
    1½ tablespoons minced peeled fresh
        ginger
    ⅛   teaspoon hot pepper sauce (such
        as Tabasco)

1. Combine all ingredients. Refrigerate in an airtight container up to 2 weeks. Yield: 1¼ cups (serving size: 1 tablespoon).

CALORIES 16 (11% from fat); FAT 0.2g (sat 0.1g, mono 0g, poly 0g); PROTEIN 0.2g; CARB 3.7g; FIBER 0.1g; CHOL 0mg; IRON 0.1mg; SODIUM 156mg; CALC 2mg

---

QUICK & EASY • MAKE AHEAD
Easy Tzatziki Sauce

Serve this tangy, creamy Greek sauce with lamb or beef, or any burger with Mediterranean or Middle Eastern spices. It's also a good dip for vegetable sticks or soft pita wedges. For a pretty embellishment, float a rosemary sprig on top of the dip.

    ¾   cup plain low-fat yogurt
    2   tablespoons grated peeled seeded
        cucumber
    1½ teaspoons minced fresh onion
    ⅛   teaspoon salt
    ⅛   teaspoon freshly ground black
        pepper

1. Combine all ingredients. Refrigerate in an airtight container up to 2 days. Yield: about ¾ cup (serving size: 1 tablespoon).

CALORIES 10 (18% from fat); FAT 0.2g (sat 0.1g, mono 0.1g, poly 0g); PROTEIN 0.8g; CARB 1.2g; FIBER 0g; CHOL 1mg; IRON 0mg; SODIUM 35mg; CALC 28mg

---

reader recipes
Successful Experiment

A grade-schooler invents a delightful salad with fresh fruit, yogurt, and jam.

As a self-described "scientist cook," seven-year-old Cyrus Johnson often experiments with unique food combinations to create new dishes for his family. "Science cooking means you never use a real recipe," explains the second grader from Portland, Oregon. "You just make up inventions and taste them."

That's how he developed his Majiggy (short for "thingamajiggy") Fruit Salad. "It was a summer evening, and we needed something like an appetizer. I went into the kitchen and looked in the fridge. Then I thought, well, we have enough fruit, so I decided to make a fruit salad." He added plain yogurt and raspberry jam to dress up the dish and received glowing reviews from his grandparents.

"He thinks of what he does as experimenting," says his mother, Robin. "He always has a hypothesis (usually 'it will be delicious') and then finds out whether he's right." But, as for the verdict on his Majiggy Fruit Salad, Cyrus says, "It's very fruitish. It is also very organic, sort of tart, and sweet." And just as his hypothesis predicted, it's delicious.

QUICK & EASY
Majiggy Fruit Salad

    ¼ cup plain fat-free yogurt
    2 tablespoons seedless raspberry jam
    3 cups sliced peaches (about 2)
    2 cups fresh blueberries
    2 cups sliced apricots (about 2)
    ½ cup grapes (about 14)

1. Combine yogurt and jam in a small bowl. Combine peaches and remaining 3 ingredients in a large bowl. Add yogurt mixture to bowl, and toss gently to coat. Yield: 4 servings (serving size: 1½ cups).

CALORIES 86 (3% from fat); FAT 0.3g (sat 0g, mono 0g, poly 0.1g); PROTEIN 1.2g; CARB 21.5g; FIBER 2g; CHOL 0mg; IRON 0.3mg; SODIUM 6mg; CALC 19mg

Indian-Spiced
Baked Potato Cakes

"I wanted to spice up potato cakes to go with a simple grilled chicken. This recipe is versatile, and you can substitute any spice combination you prefer."

—Phillip Kwun, New York, New York

  1   teaspoon canola oil
  ½   teaspoon mustard seeds
  ½   teaspoon cumin seeds
  1   teaspoon kosher salt
4½   cups peeled shredded baking
       potato (about 2 pounds)
  2   tablespoons chopped fresh parsley
  2   tablespoons canola oil
  ¼   teaspoon ground turmeric
  ¼   teaspoon freshly ground black
       pepper
Dash of ground red pepper
Cooking spray
  5   tablespoons light sour cream

1. Preheat oven to 400°.
2. Heat 1 teaspoon oil in a small skillet over medium heat. Add mustard and cumin seeds to pan; cook 2 minutes or until mustard seeds pop, stirring constantly. Remove from heat. Place spice mixture and salt in a mortar; crush seeds with pestle. Set aside.
3. Gently squeeze potato to remove excess moisture. Combine potato, spice mixture, parsley, and next 4 ingredients in a large bowl. Divide mixture into 10 (⅓-cup) portions; place on a baking sheet coated with cooking spray. Flatten to ½-inch thickness. Bake at 400° for 16 minutes or until golden. Turn over; bake an additional 5 minutes. Serve with sour cream. Yield: 5 servings (serving size: 2 potato cakes and 1 tablespoon sour cream).

CALORIES 257 (29% from fat); FAT 8.2g (sat 1.5g, mono 3.9g, poly 2g); PROTEIN 6g; CARB 40.4g; FIBER 4.4g; CHOL 0mg; IRON 2.3mg; SODIUM 405mg; CALC 39mg

---

Asian Chicken Slaw

"I came up with this recipe after a long workout when I wanted a quick, light meal. Now I often eat it for lunch or omit the chicken and serve it as a side for dinner."

—Jaime Horn, Florence, South Carolina

SLAW:

2½   cups shredded cooked chicken
       breast (about 1 pound)
  ¾   cup finely chopped celery
  ½   cup chopped sugar snap peas
  ½   cup chopped red bell pepper
  ¼   cup finely chopped onion
  1   (10-ounce) package angel hair
       slaw
  1   (8-ounce) can sliced water
       chestnuts, drained

DRESSING:

  ¼   cup cider vinegar
  ¼   cup rice wine vinegar
  2   tablespoons sugar
  1   teaspoon salt
  2   teaspoons low-sodium soy sauce
  ¼   teaspoon garlic powder
  ¼   teaspoon freshly ground black
       pepper

REMAINING INGREDIENTS:

  ¼   cup slivered almonds, toasted
  1   teaspoon sesame seeds, toasted

1. To prepare slaw, combine first 7 ingredients in a large bowl.
2. To prepare dressing, combine cider vinegar and next 6 ingredients in a small bowl; stir with a whisk. Pour dressing over slaw; toss to coat. Cover and chill 1 hour. Sprinkle with almonds and sesame seeds before serving. Yield: 6 servings (serving size: about 1½ cups).

CALORIES 152 (22% from fat); FAT 3.7g (sat 0.5g, mono 1.9g, poly 0.9g); PROTEIN 11.5g; CARB 18.5g; FIBER 4.5g; CHOL 24mg; IRON 1mg; SODIUM 585mg; CALC 32mg

---

Florentine Frittata with
Bruschetta Toppings

"I came up with this recipe as a high-protein vegetarian dish."

—Kimberly Lindstrom,
Shoreline, Washington

1½   cups coarsely chopped plum
       tomato
  1   tablespoon chopped fresh basil
  2   teaspoons balsamic vinegar
  1   teaspoon olive oil
  ⅛   teaspoon crushed red pepper
  1   garlic clove, minced
  ½   teaspoon salt, divided
1½   cups (6 ounces) fat-free ricotta
       cheese
  ¼   teaspoon black pepper
  4   large eggs, lightly beaten
  4   large egg whites, lightly beaten
Cooking spray
  1   cup chopped red onion
  1   (8-ounce) package presliced
       mushrooms
  3   cups bagged baby spinach leaves

1. Preheat oven to 350°.
2. Combine first 6 ingredients and ¼ teaspoon salt in a small bowl. Set aside.
3. Combine ricotta, black pepper, ¼ teaspoon salt, eggs, and egg whites in a medium bowl.
4. Heat a nonstick skillet over medium-high heat. Coat pan with cooking spray. Add onion; sauté 2 minutes. Add mushrooms; sauté 2 minutes. Add spinach; sauté 1 minute. Stir in egg mixture. Wrap handle of pan with foil. Bake at 350° for 20 minutes or until a wooden pick inserted in center comes out clean. Top with tomato mixture. Yield: 6 servings (serving size: 1 wedge and about ¼ cup tomato mixture).

CALORIES 118 (33% from fat); FAT 4.3g (sat 1.2g, mono 1.8g, poly 0.7g); PROTEIN 12.2g; CARB 7.8g; FIBER 1.5g; CHOL 143mg; IRON 1.4mg; SODIUM 328mg; CALC 131mg

Pasta and Salad Supper Menu
serves 6

Garden Shrimp Pasta

Tossed salad with avocado and cashews*

Crusty French bread

*Combine 4 cups red leaf lettuce, 2 cups torn Bibb lettuce, 2 cups julienne-cut yellow bell pepper, 1½ cups chopped peeled avocado, ⅓ cup coarsely chopped cashews, and ⅓ cup chopped green onions; toss gently. Combine 2 tablespoons white wine vinegar, 1½ tablespoons fresh lime juice, 1 tablespoon extravirgin olive oil, ½ teaspoon salt, and ¼ teaspoon freshly ground black pepper, stirring well. Drizzle vinegar mixture over lettuce mixture; toss gently.

QUICK & EASY
Garden Shrimp Pasta

"You could make this dish vegetarian by substituting tofu for shrimp."

—Debi Dudley, Salt Lake City, Utah

2   tablespoons olive oil
1   teaspoon chopped fresh oregano
1   teaspoon grated lemon rind
1   teaspoon grated orange rind
¼   teaspoon crushed red pepper
¼   teaspoon salt
2   pounds medium peeled and deveined shrimp
8   ounces uncooked angel hair pasta
5   cups chopped seeded tomato (about 1½ pounds)
¼   cup thinly sliced fresh basil
¼   cup thinly sliced fresh mint
2   tablespoons red wine vinegar
1   tablespoon olive oil
2   teaspoons spicy brown mustard
1   teaspoon sugar
½   teaspoon grated lemon rind
1   teaspoon fresh lemon juice
⅛   teaspoon salt
⅛   teaspoon freshly ground black pepper
¾   cup (3 ounces) crumbled feta cheese

1. Combine first 7 ingredients in a large bowl; toss well. Heat a large nonstick skillet over medium-high heat. Add shrimp mixture to pan; sauté 6 minutes or until done. Remove from heat; set aside.
2. Cook pasta according to package directions, omitting salt and fat. Place pasta in a large bowl; add tomato, basil, and mint.
3. Combine vinegar and next 7 ingredients in a small bowl. Pour over pasta mixture, and toss to coat. Place about 1¾ cups pasta mixture on each of 6 plates. Top each serving with about 3 ounces shrimp mixture and 2 tablespoons cheese. Yield: 6 servings.

CALORIES 420 (29% from fat); FAT 13.6g (sat 3.8g, mono 6.2g, poly 2.5g); PROTEIN 39g; CARB 35.4g; FIBER 3.1g; CHOL 242mg; IRON 5.7mg; SODIUM 560mg; CALC 181mg

dinner tonight
Fish and Shellfish

Choose no-fuss seafood for speedy and nutritious suppers.

Fish and Shellfish Menu 1
serves 6

Garlic-and-Herb Oven-Fried Halibut

Red potatoes with herbed vinaigrette*

Steamed broccoli

*Place 1½ pounds quartered red potatoes in a medium saucepan. Cover with cold water; bring to a boil. Cook 8 minutes or until tender; drain. Cool. Combine 2 tablespoons white wine vinegar, 1 tablespoon extravirgin olive oil, ¼ teaspoon salt, and ¼ teaspoon black pepper in a large bowl, stirring well. Add potatoes, ¼ cup sliced green onions, and 2 teaspoons chopped fresh parsley to vinegar mixture; toss.

Game Plan

1. While oven preheats:
  • Cook potatoes.
  • Prepare fish.
2. While fish cooks:
  • Finish potatoes.
  • Steam broccoli.

QUICK & EASY
Garlic-and-Herb Oven-Fried Halibut

Coat fillets with crumbs and bake at a high temperature for a crisp texture similar to fried fish. Fresh herbs and other seasonings heighten the flavor.

TOTAL TIME: 42 MINUTES

1   cup panko (Japanese breadcrumbs)
1   tablespoon chopped fresh basil
1   tablespoon chopped fresh flat-leaf parsley
½   teaspoon onion powder
1   large garlic clove, minced
2   large egg whites, lightly beaten
1   large egg, lightly beaten
2   tablespoons all-purpose flour
6   (6-ounce) halibut fillets
¾   teaspoon salt
¼   teaspoon black pepper
2   tablespoons olive oil, divided
Cooking spray

1. Preheat oven to 450°.
2. Combine first 5 ingredients in a shallow dish. Combine egg whites and egg in a shallow dish. Place flour in a shallow dish. Sprinkle fish with salt and pepper. Dredge fish in flour. Dip in egg mixture; dredge in panko mixture.
3. Heat 1 tablespoon oil in a large nonstick skillet over medium-high heat. Add 3 fish fillets; cook 2½ minutes on each side or until browned. Place fish on a broiler pan coated with cooking spray. Repeat procedure with 1 tablespoon oil and remaining fish. Bake at 450° for 6 minutes or until fish flakes easily when tested with a fork or until desired degree of doneness. Yield: 6 servings (serving size: 1 fillet).

CALORIES 293 (29% from fat); FAT 9.6g (sat 1.4g, mono 4.9g, poly 1.8g); PROTEIN 39.4g; CARB 9.2g; FIBER 0.5g; CHOL 90mg; IRON 1.8mg; SODIUM 446mg; CALC 89mg

Fish and Shellfish
Menu 2

serves 4

Bacon, Arugula, and Shrimp Salad

Quinoa pilaf*

Lemon sorbet

*Heat 2 teaspoons canola oil in a medium saucepan. Add ½ cup chopped onion and 2 minced garlic cloves to pan; sauté 3 minutes. Add 1½ cups dry quinoa to pan; sauté 1 minute. Stir in 3 cups fat-free, less-sodium chicken broth; bring to a boil. Cover, reduce heat, and simmer 20 minutes or until liquid is absorbed. Remove from heat; fluff with a fork. Stir in ¼ cup toasted slivered almonds and ¼ cup thinly sliced green onions.

Game Plan

1. Prepare quinoa.
2. While quinoa cooks:
   • Toast almonds.
   • Slice green onions.
   • Cook bacon.
   • Cook shrimp.
3. Toss salad.

QUICK & EASY
Bacon, Arugula, and Shrimp Salad

Arugula is a peppery salad green. If you can't find it, substitute another green with similar bite, such as watercress. Or simply use mixed salad greens.

TOTAL TIME: 34 MINUTES

```
 2    slices center-cut bacon
1½    pounds peeled and deveined
      large shrimp
 5    cups arugula leaves (about
      2½ ounces)
 1    cup halved cherry tomatoes
 2    tablespoons plain low-fat yogurt
 2    tablespoons balsamic vinegar
 2    teaspoons extravirgin olive oil
¼    teaspoon black pepper
```

1. Cook bacon in a large nonstick skillet over medium heat until crisp. Remove bacon from pan, reserving 1 teaspoon drippings in pan. Crumble bacon, and set aside. Add shrimp to drippings in pan; sauté 5 minutes or until done. Using a slotted spoon, transfer shrimp to a large bowl. Add arugula and tomatoes to shrimp; toss gently.
2. Combine yogurt, vinegar, oil, and pepper in a small bowl, stirring well with a whisk. Drizzle vinegar mixture over shrimp mixture; toss gently to combine. Place 2¼ cups salad mixture on each of 4 plates; divide crumbled bacon evenly among salads. Yield: 4 servings.

CALORIES 247 (28% from fat); FAT 7.8g (sat 1.8g, mono 3.3g, poly 1.7g); PROTEIN 36.8g; CARB 5.4g; FIBER 0.8g; CHOL 263mg; IRON 4.5mg; SODIUM 332mg; CALC 135mg

---

Fish and Shellfish
Menu 3

serves 4

Spiced Salmon with Mustard Sauce

Sautéed spinach*

Couscous

*Melt 1 tablespoon butter in a large nonstick skillet over medium-high heat. Add 2 minced garlic cloves to pan; sauté 1 minute. Add 12 cups fresh trimmed spinach to pan; sauté 3 minutes or until spinach begins to wilt. Sprinkle with ½ teaspoon salt and ¼ teaspoon freshly ground black pepper.

Game Plan

1. While broiler preheats:
   • Bring water to a boil for couscous.
   • Prepare salmon.
2. While salmon cooks:
   • Prepare couscous.
   • Prepare spinach.

QUICK & EASY
Spiced Salmon with Mustard Sauce

Butter-sautéed spinach makes a nice side dish, but any wilted greens will do.

TOTAL TIME: 30 MINUTES

```
 2    teaspoons whole-grain mustard
 1    teaspoon honey
¼    teaspoon ground turmeric
¼    teaspoon ground red pepper
⅛    teaspoon garlic powder
¼    teaspoon salt
 4    (6-ounce) salmon fillets
      Cooking spray
```

1. Preheat broiler.
2. Combine first 6 ingredients in a small bowl, stirring well with a fork. Rub mustard mixture evenly over fillets. Place fillets, skin sides down, on a jelly-roll pan coated with cooking spray. Broil 8 minutes or until fish flakes easily when tested with a fork or until desired degree of doneness. Yield: 4 servings (serving size: 1 fillet).

CALORIES 324 (53% from fat); FAT 18.9g (sat 3.7g, mono 6.6g, poly 6.7g); PROTEIN 34g; CARB 2.9g; FIBER 0.1g; CHOL 100mg; IRON 0.8mg; SODIUM 268mg; CALC 22mg.

Smoky Barbecue Chili, page 32

Butterscotch Blondies,
page 46

Pork and Vegetable Stir-Fry with
Cashew Rice, page 37

Grilled Chicken, Mango, and Jícama Salad
with Tequila-Lime Vinaigrette, page 77

Broccoli with Red Pepper Flakes and Toasted Garlic, page 50

Penne with Pancetta, Spinach, and Buttery Crumb Topping, page 51

Black and White Angel Food Cake,
page 103

Thai Beef Tacos with
Lime-Cilantro Slaw, page 92

New Orleans–Style Shrimp, page 100

Herbed Bread–Stuffed
Tomatoes, page 116

Grilled Tuna with White Bean and
Charred Onion Salad, page 143

Watermelon
Cooler, page 173

Greek Wet Rub, page 123

Peach Chutney, page 155

Chicken Cobb Salad,
page 178

Grilled Salmon with Roasted Corn
Relish, page 150

Blackberry Limeade, page 148

Little Italy Chicken Pitas with Sun-Dried Tomato Vinaigrette, page 179

Peach-Blueberry Cobbler, page 199

Cherry Tomato Spaghetti with Toasted
Pine Nuts, page 202

Memphis Pork and Coleslaw
Sandwiches, page 195

Mixed Greens and Nectarine Salad,
page 259

Salmon with Cucumber Salad and Dill Sauce,
page 208

Frozen Peanut Butter Pie, page 268

Fresh Corn Salad, page 214

Pasta with Lemon Cream Sauce,
Asparagus, and Peas, page 260

Cornmeal, Jalapeño, and Fresh Corn Scones, page 301

Cornflake-Crusted Halibut with Chile-Cilantro Aïoli, page 271

Chicken and Root Vegetable Potpie,
page 285

Fresh Orange Sorbet, page 271

Mini Crab Cakes with Herbed Aïoli,
page 291

Fudgy Mocha-Toffee Brownies,
page 272

Adreena Barmakian and
Jayne Cohen's Apple Pie, page 312

Chicken and Asparagus in
White Wine Sauce, page 334

Chicken, Pasta, and Chickpea Stew,
page 326

Brunswick Stew, page 306

Spinach and Ricotta–Stuffed Shells,
page 327

Porcini-Dusted Chicken Scaloppine, page 324

Potato-Sour Cream Biscuits, page 352

Pear-Cranberry Pie with Oatmeal Streusel, page 356

Moroccan Chickpea Stew, page 384

Bourbon-Pecan Tart with Chocolate Drizzle, page 357

Roast Turkey with Truffle Gravy, page 343;
Basic Cranberry Sauce, page 353; Potato-Sour Cream
Biscuits, page 352; Wild Rice Stuffing, page 349; Green
Beans with Bacon, page 348; Mashed Roots, page 350

Watercress, Frisée, and Grapefruit Salad
with Curry Vinaigrette, page 342

Oils

We rely on a few favorites for flavor and versatility. Learn how to get the most from them.

Cooking oils are indispensable. They lubricate food, distribute heat, facilitate browning, create tenderness in baked goods, and provide a smooth, rich mouthfeel. Many also impart their own characteristic flavors to the dishes to which they're added. Bruschetta brushed with extravirgin olive oil gains fruity, "green" nuances, while a salad tossed with walnut oil vinaigrette takes on toasty notes. Other oils—notably regular olive oil and canola oil—taste more neutral, so they allow the flavors of the food to shine.

QUICK & EASY
Stir-Fried Shrimp with Spicy Orange Sauce

Neutral-tasting canola oil allows the flavors of orange juice, honey, ginger, and chiles to shine. It can also withstand the heat of stir-frying in this tasty take on sweet-and-sour shrimp. Serve over rice or udon noodles.

1½ pounds peeled and deveined large shrimp
1 tablespoon cornstarch
¼ cup fresh orange juice
2 tablespoons low-sodium soy sauce
2 tablespoons honey
1 tablespoon rice wine vinegar
1 tablespoon chile paste with garlic (such as sambal oelek)
2 tablespoons canola oil
1 tablespoon minced peeled fresh ginger
3 garlic cloves, minced
⅓ cup chopped green onions

1. Place shrimp in a medium bowl. Sprinkle with cornstarch; toss well to coat. Set aside.
2. Combine juice and next 4 ingredients, stirring with a whisk; set aside.
3. Heat oil in a large nonstick skillet over medium-high heat. Add ginger and garlic to pan; stir-fry 15 seconds or until fragrant. Add shrimp mixture; stir-fry 3 minutes. Add juice mixture and onions; cook 2 minutes or until sauce is thick and shrimp are done, stirring frequently. Serve immediately. Yield: 4 servings (serving size: ¾ cup).

CALORIES 301 (30% from fat); FAT 10g (sat 1.1g, mono 4.6g, poly 3.2g); PROTEIN 35.3g; CARB 16.8g; FIBER 0.5g; CHOL 259mg; IRON 4.4mg; SODIUM 621mg; CALC 103mg

STAFF FAVORITE
Bagna Cauda Bruschetta

This sublime starter (pronounced BAHN-yah KOW-dah broo-SKEH-tah) depends on the richness of extravirgin olive oil. The dish is based on the classic Northern Italian appetizer of warm olive oil, anchovies, and garlic that's usually served with vegetable dippers. Here, the potent dip is drizzled onto bread and then topped with a colorful mix of grilled vegetables.

1 (8-ounce) baguette, sliced crosswise into 24 pieces
1 zucchini
1 red bell pepper, quartered
Cooking spray
1 tablespoon fresh lemon juice
¼ teaspoon salt
5 garlic cloves, minced
3 canned anchovy fillets, rinsed and minced
¼ cup extravirgin olive oil
2 tablespoons chopped fresh flat-leaf parsley

1. Preheat broiler.
2. Arrange baguette slices in an even layer on a baking sheet. Broil 1 minute or until toasted. Cool completely on baking sheet.
3. Prepare grill or grill pan.
4. Cut zucchini lengthwise into 3 equal pieces. Arrange zucchini pieces and bell pepper quarters, skin sides down, in a single layer on grill rack or grill pan coated with cooking spray, and grill 3 minutes on each side or until lightly browned and crisp-tender. Chop zucchini and bell pepper; cover and keep warm.
5. Place juice, salt, garlic, and anchovies in a small food processor; process 30 seconds or until mixture forms a paste. Add oil; pulse 10 times or until combined. Spoon mixture into a small saucepan; bring to a simmer over medium-high heat. Remove from heat; stir in parsley.
6. Place 2 baguette slices on each of 12 plates. Drizzle each slice with about ½ teaspoon oil mixture, and top with about 1 tablespoon vegetables. Serve immediately. Yield: 12 servings.

CALORIES 99 (44% from fat); FAT 4.8g (sat 0.7g, mono 3.4g, poly 0.7g); PROTEIN 2.4g; CARB 13g; FIBER 0.8g; CHOL 1mg; IRON 0.8mg; SODIUM 211mg; CALC 9mg

MAKE AHEAD
Quinoa, Corn, and Tomato Salad with Chive-Infused Oil

Brightly colored flavored oil coats the quinoa grains and lends the salad fresh chive flavor. Refrigerate leftover oil. Garnish with whole fresh chives.

1½ cups water
1 cup uncooked quinoa
1 cup fresh corn kernels (about 2 ears)
1 cup cherry tomatoes, halved
¼ cup finely chopped fresh flat-leaf parsley
2 tablespoons Chive-Infused Oil
2 tablespoons fresh lime juice
2 tablespoons white wine vinegar
¼ teaspoon salt
1 garlic clove, minced

Continued

1. Combine 1½ cups water and quinoa in a medium saucepan; bring to a boil. Cover, reduce heat, and simmer 10 minutes or until liquid is absorbed. Remove from heat; let stand 10 minutes. Fluff with a fork.

2. Combine quinoa, corn, tomatoes, and parsley in a medium bowl. Combine Chive-Infused Oil and remaining 4 ingredients, stirring with a whisk. Drizzle over salad; toss well to coat. Let stand 10 minutes before serving. Yield: 6 servings (serving size: ⅔ cup).

(Totals include Chive-Infused Oil) CALORIES 179 (34% from fat); FAT 6.7g (sat 0.7g, mono 4.1g,poly 1.3g); PROTEIN 5.2g; CARB 26.1g; FIBER 2.4g; CHOL 0mg; IRON 2.2mg; SODIUM 145mg; CALC 20mg

QUICK & EASY • MAKE AHEAD

CHIVE-INFUSED OIL:
¾ cup extravirgin olive oil
½ cup (1-inch) slices fresh chives
½ teaspoon salt

1. Place all ingredients in a blender; pulse 6 times or until chives are very finely minced. Strain mixture through a fine sieve into a bowl, and discard solids. Store in refrigerator in an airtight container up to 2 weeks. Yield: ¾ cup (serving size: 1½ teaspoons).

CALORIES 63 (100% from fat); FAT 7g (sat 1g, mono 5.4g, poly 0.6g); PROTEIN 0g; CARB 0g; FIBER 0g; CHOL 0mg; IRON 0mg; SODIUM 49mg; CALC 0mg

STAFF FAVORITE • MAKE AHEAD
Port-Fig Napoleons with Walnut Oil and Honey Cream

This pastry is suited for any season because it uses dried fruit. Walnut oil adds a distinctive nutty essence to the crisp phyllo layers and the fig mixture. Use a pizza cutter to glide easily through the phyllo dough.

PHYLLO:
Cooking spray
6 (14 x 9–inch) sheets frozen phyllo dough, thawed
1 tablespoon walnut oil, divided
2 tablespoons powdered sugar, divided

FIGS:
½ cup port or other sweet red wine
18 dried figs, stems removed, thinly sliced
1 (2-inch) cinnamon stick
1 tablespoon walnut oil
Dash of salt

CREAM:
½ cup (4 ounces) ⅓-less-fat cream cheese, softened
2 tablespoons fresh orange juice
1 tablespoon honey

REMAINING INGREDIENT:
1 tablespoon powdered sugar

1. Preheat oven to 350°.
2. To prepare phyllo, line a large baking sheet with parchment paper; coat paper with cooking spray. Place 1 phyllo sheet on paper (cover remaining dough to keep from drying); lightly brush with ½ teaspoon oil. Sprinkle with 1 teaspoon powdered sugar. Repeat layers five times with 5 phyllo sheets, 2½ teaspoons oil, and 5 teaspoons powdered sugar. Cut phyllo stack lengthwise into 3 equal strips; make 5 crosswise cuts to form 18 pieces.
3. Coat another sheet of parchment paper with cooking spray; cover phyllo pieces with paper, coated side down. Place another baking sheet on top of phyllo to weigh it down. Bake at 350° for 15 minutes or until golden brown and crisp. Carefully remove top baking sheet and top piece of parchment. Cool phyllo pieces on a wire rack.
4. To prepare figs, combine port, figs, and cinnamon stick in a saucepan over medium-high heat; bring to a boil. Remove from heat; cover and let stand 10 minutes. Remove figs with a slotted spoon; set aside. Discard cinnamon stick. Bring port to a boil over medium-high heat, and cook until reduced to about 2 tablespoons (about 2 minutes). Remove from heat; stir in reserved figs, 1 tablespoon oil, and salt. Cool to room temperature.
5. To prepare cream, combine cream cheese, juice, and honey in a small bowl; beat with a mixer at low speed 30 seconds or until smooth. Cover and chill 30 minutes.

6. Place 1 phyllo piece on each of 6 dessert plates. Top each serving with about 2 teaspoons cream and about 1 tablespoon fig mixture. Repeat layers once, and top each serving with 1 phyllo piece. Sprinkle evenly with 1 tablespoon powdered sugar. Serve immediately. Yield: 6 servings (serving size: 1 Napoleon).

CALORIES 312 (30% from fat); FAT 10.3g (sat 3.5g, mono 2.8g, poly 3.3g); PROTEIN 4.7g; CARB 52.2g; FIBER 5.8g; CHOL 14mg; IRON 1.7mg; SODIUM 168mg; CALC 110mg

WINE NOTE: You'll need some port to prepare this recipe, so make it a bottle you can enjoy right alongside this richly layered and wonderfully textured dessert. A tawny port, like Dow's 10 Years Tawny ($31), provides ample sweetness. And wood aging imparts tawnies with nutty, dried fruit, and treacle flavors that echo those found in the dessert.

Barley Risotto with Summer Vegetables

Regular olive oil is a good choice for sautéing vegetables—it adds a mild olive oil flavor and can stand up to higher-heat cooking. It also coats the barley grains so they don't clump. Try other summer vegetables in this satisfying side dish, such as corn, zucchini, or even lima beans.

6 cups water
1½ teaspoons salt
2 tablespoons olive oil, divided
1 cup finely chopped yellow squash
1 cup finely chopped orange bell pepper
1 cup (½-inch) cut green beans
½ cup minced shallots
2 garlic cloves, minced
1¼ cups uncooked pearl barley
½ cup dry white wine
2 cups chopped seeded peeled tomato (about 2 medium)
¼ cup chopped fresh basil
½ cup (2 ounces) crumbled goat cheese

1. Combine 6 cups water and salt in a medium saucepan; bring to a simmer (do not boil). Keep warm over low heat.

2. Heat 2 teaspoons oil in a large non-stick skillet over medium-high heat. Add squash, bell pepper, and beans to pan; sauté 6 minutes or until tender. Set aside.

3. Heat 4 teaspoons oil in a large saucepan over medium heat. Add shallots and garlic to pan; cook 3 minutes, stirring frequently. Add barley; cook 2 minutes, stirring constantly. Stir in wine; cook 2 minutes or until liquid is nearly absorbed, stirring constantly. Add water mixture, ½ cup at a time, stirring constantly until each portion of water is absorbed before adding the next (about 45 minutes total). Add squash mixture, and cook 2 minutes, stirring constantly. Remove from heat, and stir in tomato and basil. Top with goat cheese. Yield: 6 servings (serving size: 1⅓ cups risotto and about 1½ tablespoons cheese).

CALORIES 262 (28% from fat); FAT 8.2g (sat 2.7g, mono 4g, poly 0.9g); PROTEIN 7.9g; CARB 42g; FIBER 8.9g; CHOL 7mg; IRON 2.2mg; SODIUM 653mg; CALC 67mg

MAKE AHEAD • FREEZABLE
Ginger-Carrot Muffins

Canola oil creates a moist, tender crumb; its mild taste doesn't interfere with the sweetness of carrots and currants or the ginger's bite. Be careful not to overmix the batter, as doing so can make the muffins tough.

Cooking spray
2 cups all-purpose flour (about 9 ounces)
½ cup sugar
2 teaspoons baking soda
1 teaspoon ground ginger
¼ teaspoon salt
½ cup fat-free sour cream
¼ cup canola oil
¼ cup 1% low-fat milk
1 teaspoon vanilla extract
2 large egg whites, lightly beaten
1 large egg, lightly beaten
3 cups grated carrot (about 6 medium)
½ cup dried currants
¼ cup chopped pecans, toasted

1. Preheat oven to 350°.
2. Place 18 paper muffin cup liners in muffin cups; coat liners with cooking spray. Set aside.
3. Lightly spoon flour into dry measuring cups; level with a knife. Combine flour and next 4 ingredients in a large bowl, stirring with a whisk. Make a well in center of mixture. Combine sour cream and next 5 ingredients, stirring well with a whisk; add to flour mixture, stirring just until moist. Add carrot, currants, and pecans; stir just until combined.
4. Spoon batter into prepared muffin cups. Bake at 350° for 25 minutes or until muffins spring back when touched lightly in center. Remove muffins from pans immediately, and place on a wire rack. Yield: 18 servings (serving size: 1 muffin).

CALORIES 143 (30% from fat); FAT 4.8g (sat 0.5g, mono 2.6g, poly 1.4g); PROTEIN 3g; CARB 22.4g; FIBER 1.3g; CHOL 12mg; IRON 0.9mg; SODIUM 207mg; CALC 27mg

QUICK & EASY
Mixed Greens and Nectarine Salad
(pictured on page 240)

For a delicious fall salad, substitute sliced pears or apples.

4 cups gourmet salad greens
2 cups thinly sliced nectarines (about 2)
¼ cup Walnut Oil Vinaigrette

1. Place greens and nectarines in a large bowl. Drizzle with Walnut Oil Vinaigrette; toss gently to coat. Yield: 4 servings (serving size: about 1 cup).

(Totals include Walnut Oil Vinaigrette) CALORIES 83 (31% from fat); FAT 2.9g (sat 0.3g, mono 0.6g, poly 1.8g); PROTEIN 1.5g; CARB 14.1g; FIBER 1.7g; CHOL 0mg; IRON 1mg; SODIUM 132mg; CALC 31mg

MAKE AHEAD
WALNUT OIL VINAIGRETTE:
¼ cup red wine vinegar
2 tablespoons minced shallots
2 tablespoons walnut oil
2 tablespoons honey
1 tablespoon fresh lemon juice
½ teaspoon salt
¼ teaspoon freshly ground black pepper

1. Combine all ingredients, stirring with a whisk. Store in refrigerator up to 1 week. Yield: ⅔ cup (serving size: about 1 tablespoon).

CALORIES 39 (62% from fat); FAT 2.7g (sat 0.3g, mono 0.6g, poly 1.7g); PROTEIN 0.1g; CARB 4g; FIBER 0g; CHOL 0mg; IRON 0.1mg; SODIUM 118mg; CALC 1mg

QUICK & EASY • MAKE AHEAD
Sesame-Ginger Sauce

Drizzle this all-purpose Asian condiment over steamed vegetables, or use it as a tasty dipping sauce for pot stickers or spring rolls.

2 tablespoons rice wine vinegar
2 tablespoons low-sodium soy sauce
1 tablespoon water
1 tablespoon dark sesame oil
1 teaspoon minced peeled fresh ginger
¼ teaspoon crushed red pepper
1 garlic clove, minced

1. Combine all ingredients, stirring well with a whisk. Yield: ½ cup (serving size: 1 tablespoon).

CALORIES 19 (85% from fat); FAT 1.8g (sat 0.3g, mono 0.7g, poly 0.7g); PROTEIN 0.2g; CARB 0.5g; FIBER 0.1g; CHOL 0mg; IRON 0.1mg; SODIUM 134mg; CALC 1mg

QUICK & EASY • MAKE AHEAD
FREEZABLE
Asian Basil Pesto

The deep, toasty notes of dark sesame oil enhance this Asian version of the classic Italian sauce. Toss with rice noodles, or dollop on fish or chicken. You can also stir a few tablespoons into a simple meat and vegetable stir-fry.

2 cups fresh Thai basil leaves
2 tablespoons dry-roasted peanuts
1½ tablespoons dark sesame oil
1 tablespoon fish sauce
1 tablespoon rice wine vinegar
1 tablespoon sugar
1 teaspoon crushed red pepper
2 garlic cloves

Continued

1. Place all ingredients in a food processor; process until smooth. Press plastic wrap onto surface of pesto. Store in refrigerator up to 1 week. Yield: ½ cup (serving size: 1 tablespoon).

CALORIES 45 (72% from fat); FAT 3.6g (sat 0.5g, mono 1.5g, poly 1.4g); PROTEIN 0.9g; CARB 2.9g; FIBER 0.6g; CHOL 0mg; IRON 0.4mg; SODIUM 189mg; CALC 20mg

---

QUICK & EASY • MAKE AHEAD
Salsa Crudo

Juicy summer tomatoes pair beautifully with fruity extravirgin olive oil in this Italian-style uncooked sauce that is delicious on pasta, grilled bread, chicken, or fish.

  4 cups chopped tomato
  ¼ cup minced fresh basil
  2 tablespoons extravirgin olive oil
  1 tablespoon balsamic vinegar
  ½ teaspoon salt
  ¼ teaspoon freshly ground black pepper
  2 garlic cloves, minced

1. Combine all ingredients; let stand 30 minutes. Yield: 4 cups (serving size: about ⅓ cup).

CALORIES 36 (63% from fat); FAT 2.5g (sat 0.4g, mono 1.8g, poly 0.3g); PROTEIN 0.6g; CARB 3.2g; FIBER 0.7g; CHOL 0mg; IRON 0.3mg; SODIUM 104mg; CALC 5mg

---

well equipped
Fresh Squeezed

Presses, reamers, trumpets, and juicers turn citrus into delightful dishes.

Sometimes the most overlooked ingredients and gadgets in the kitchen turn out the most amazing flavors. Take the ubiquitous lemon, lime, orange, or grapefruit, for instance. Each can brighten the flavor of dressings and soups, add a tangy zip to desserts and cookies, and finish sauces and salsas to perfection. And, when it comes to balancing flavors in a dish, fresh citrus works wonders. All you need to get the job done is a citrus reamer or manual juicer.

MAKE AHEAD
Mixed Citrus Marmalade

Tart marmalade is delicious on scones or breakfast breads. This recipe produces classic British-style bitter marmalade. If you prefer less bitterness, use only half the grapefruit rind.

  2 large thin-skinned oranges
  2 red grapefruit (about 2 pounds)
  1 lemon
  2 cups sugar
  2 cups water
  ⅛ teaspoon kosher salt

1. Carefully remove rind from fruit using a vegetable peeler; discard white pith. Cut rind from 1 orange, 1 grapefruit, and lemon into 1 x ¼-inch strips. Discard remaining rind. Section fruit; cut into 1-inch pieces. Discard seeds; reserve juice.
2. Combine all ingredients in a large saucepan; bring to a boil. Reduce heat, and simmer 1 hour or until thick, stirring occasionally. Cool. Pour into airtight containers. Yield: 3 cups (serving size: 2 tablespoons).
NOTE: Store marmalade in the refrigerator up to 3 weeks.

CALORIES 77 (0% from fat); FAT 0g; PROTEIN 0.2g; CARB 20.2g; FIBER 0.9g; CHOL 0mg; IRON 0.1mg; SODIUM 10mg; CALC 9mg

---

MAKE AHEAD
Lemon Panna Cotta

Puree mixed summer berries to sauce this cool dessert.

  2 cups plain low-fat yogurt
  1 cup whole milk
  ½ cup sugar
  1 (2-inch) piece vanilla bean, split lengthwise
  1½ teaspoons unflavored gelatin
  ¼ cup fresh lemon juice (about 2 lemons)

1. Spoon yogurt onto several layers of heavy-duty paper towels; spread to ½-inch thickness. Cover with additional paper towels; let stand 15 minutes. Scrape into a medium bowl using a rubber spatula; set aside.

---

2. Combine milk and sugar in a medium saucepan over medium-high heat; stir well with a whisk. Scrape seeds from vanilla bean; add seeds and bean to milk. Cook 3 minutes or until sugar dissolves, stirring frequently.
3. Remove pan from heat. Remove and discard vanilla bean. Add milk mixture to drained yogurt, and stir until well blended.
4. Sprinkle gelatin over juice in a small microwave-safe bowl. Let stand for 5 minutes. Microwave at HIGH for 30 seconds, stirring every 10 seconds until gelatin dissolves. Stir gelatin mixture thoroughly into yogurt mixture. Pour about ½ cup panna cotta mixture into each of 8 ramekins or custard cups. Cover and chill at least 6 hours or overnight. Serve in cups, or invert onto individual plates. Yield: 8 servings (serving size: 1 panna cotta).

CALORIES 109 (16% from fat); FAT 1.9g (sat 1.2g, mono 0.5g, poly 0.1g); PROTEIN 4.6g; CARB 18.9g; FIBER 0g; CHOL 7mg; IRON 0.1mg; SODIUM 56mg; CALC 147mg

---

Pasta with Lemon Cream Sauce, Asparagus, and Peas
(pictured on page 243)

If long fusilli isn't available in your market, linguine works just as well. Garnish with chopped parsley or chives, if desired.

  8 ounces uncooked long fusilli (twisted spaghetti)
  1¾ cups (1½-inch) slices asparagus (about ½ pound)
  1 cup frozen green peas, thawed
  1 tablespoon butter
  1 garlic clove, minced
  1 cup organic vegetable broth
  1 teaspoon cornstarch
  ⅓ cup heavy cream
  3 tablespoons fresh lemon juice (about 1 lemon)
  ½ teaspoon salt
  ¼ teaspoon freshly ground black pepper
Dash of ground red pepper
Coarsely ground black pepper (optional)
Lemon slices (optional)

1. Cook pasta according to package directions, omitting salt and fat. Add asparagus during last minute of cooking time. Place peas in a colander. Drain pasta mixture over peas; set aside.

2. Melt butter in a skillet over medium-high heat. Add garlic to pan; sauté 1 minute. Combine broth and cornstarch in a small bowl; stir until well blended. Add broth mixture to pan; bring to a boil. Cook 1 minute or until thick, stirring constantly. Remove from heat. Stir in cream and next 4 ingredients. Add pasta mixture to broth mixture; toss gently to coat. Garnish with coarsely ground black pepper and lemon slices, if desired. Serve immediately. Yield: 4 servings (serving size: about 1½ cups).

CALORIES 351 (29% from fat); FAT 11.2g (sat 6.7g, mono 2.9g, poly 0.5g); PROTEIN 11.5g; CARB 52.9g; FIBER 4.9g; CHOL 35mg; IRON 3.6mg; SODIUM 471mg; CALC 49mg

MAKE AHEAD
Lime-Mint Shortbread

These cookies are delicious as an accompaniment to an afternoon cup of tea. The dough can also be pressed into mini cupcake tins, baked, and filled with store-bought lemon or lime curd.

⅓ cup powdered sugar
5 tablespoons butter, softened
1 teaspoon grated lime rind
2 tablespoons fresh lime juice (about 1 lime)
½ teaspoon lemon extract
1¼ cups all-purpose flour (about 5½ ounces)
1 tablespoon finely chopped fresh mint
Cooking spray
2 teaspoons powdered sugar

1. Preheat oven to 350°.

2. Combine first 5 ingredients in a large bowl; beat with a mixer at medium speed until well blended.

3. Lightly spoon flour into dry measuring cups; level with a knife. Add flour and mint to butter mixture; stir just until combined. Turn dough out onto a floured surface; knead lightly 5 times.

4. Pat dough into an 8-inch circle on a baking sheet coated with cooking spray. Cut dough into 12 wedges, cutting into but not through dough. Crimp edges of dough with a fork. Bake at 350° for 25 minutes or until golden. Sprinkle with 2 teaspoons powdered sugar. Yield: 12 servings (serving size: 1 wedge).

CALORIES 105 (42% from fat); FAT 4.9g (sat 3g, mono 1.2g, poly 0.2g); PROTEIN 1.4g; CARB 14g; FIBER 0.4g; CHOL 13mg; IRON 0.7mg; SODIUM 34mg; CALC 5mg

MAKE AHEAD
Glazed Lemon Buttermilk Cake

This cake is great with a cup of morning coffee or mixed berries and a scoop of sorbet for dessert.

CAKE:
3 tablespoons grated lemon rind (about 2 lemons)
3 tablespoons fresh lemon juice (about 1 lemon)
Cooking spray
2 tablespoons granulated sugar
3 cups all-purpose flour (13½ ounces)
1 teaspoon baking powder
¾ teaspoon salt
½ teaspoon baking soda
½ cup butter, softened
1½ cups granulated sugar
½ to 1 teaspoon lemon extract
3 large eggs
1 cup low-fat buttermilk

LEMON GLAZE:
1 cup powdered sugar
1½ tablespoons fresh lemon juice
1 tablespoon low-fat buttermilk
1 teaspoon grated lemon rind (optional)

1. Preheat oven to 350°.

2. To prepare cake, combine 3 tablespoons rind and 3 tablespoons juice in a small bowl. Set aside.

3. Coat a 10-inch Bundt pan with cooking spray; dust with 2 tablespoons granulated sugar.

4. Lightly spoon flour into dry measuring cups, and level with a knife. Combine flour, baking powder, salt, and baking soda in a large bowl, stirring well with a whisk.

5. Place butter in a large bowl; beat with a mixer at medium speed until light and fluffy. Gradually add rind mixture, 1½ cups granulated sugar, and extract, beating until well blended. Add eggs, 1 at a time, beating well after each addition. Add flour mixture and 1 cup buttermilk alternately to sugar mixture, beating at low speed, beginning and ending with flour mixture.

6. Spoon batter into prepared pan. Bake at 350° for 45 minutes or until a wooden pick inserted in center comes out clean. Cool in pan 10 minutes on a wire rack; remove from pan. Cool completely on wire rack.

7. To prepare glaze, combine powdered sugar, 1½ tablespoons juice, and 1 tablespoon buttermilk in a small bowl, stirring until smooth. Drizzle glaze over warm cake. Garnish with 1 teaspoon grated lemon rind once glaze is set, if desired. Yield: 16 servings (serving size: 1 slice).

CALORIES 267 (24% from fat); FAT 7g (sat 4g, mono 1.9g, poly 0.4g); PROTEIN 4.3g; CARB 47.3g; FIBER 0.8g; CHOL 56mg; IRON 1.3mg; SODIUM 252mg; CALC 46mg

QUICK & EASY • MAKE AHEAD
Citrusade with Lemon, Lime, and Grapefruit

For a sweeter beverage, use ¾ cup sugar. Fresh citrus slices and mint sprigs add visual appeal to a glass or pitcher of this thirst-quenching drink.

¾ cup water
⅔ to ¾ cup sugar
1 cup fresh grapefruit juice (about 3 grapefruit)
1 tablespoon grated lemon rind
¼ cup fresh lemon juice (about 2 lemons)
2½ cups ice water
2 tablespoons fresh lime juice (about 1 lime)
5 lemon slices (optional)
5 lime slices (optional)
5 mint sprigs (optional)

1. Combine ¾ cup water and sugar in a saucepan over medium-high heat; cook
Continued

until sugar dissolves, stirring frequently. Cool. Stir in grapefruit juice and next 4 ingredients. Garnish with lemon slices, lime slices, and mint sprigs, if desired. Yield: 5 servings (serving size: 1 cup).

CALORIES 128 (0% from fat); FAT 0.1g (sat 0g, mono 0g, poly 0g); PROTEIN 0.3g; CARB 33g; FIBER 0.3g; CHOL 0mg; IRON 0.1mg; SODIUM 4mg; CALC 11mg

Orange-Sesame Salad Dressing

Try this dressing tossed with fresh baby spinach.

½ cup fresh orange juice (about 2 large oranges)
⅓ cup rice wine vinegar
2 tablespoons sesame seeds
1 tablespoon Chinese hot mustard
1 teaspoon sugar
¼ teaspoon kosher salt
1 garlic clove, minced
2 tablespoons canola oil
1 teaspoon dark sesame oil

1. Combine first 7 ingredients in a medium bowl. Slowly drizzle oils into juice mixture, stirring constantly with a whisk. Yield: 1½ cups (serving size: 4 teaspoons).

CALORIES 27 (77% from fat); FAT 2.3g (sat 0.2g, mono 1.2g, poly 0.8g); PROTEIN 0.2g; CARB 1.2g; FIBER 0.1g; CHOL 0mg; IRON 0.2mg; SODIUM 45mg; CALC 11mg

Tomatillo-Lime Salsa

Serve with tortilla chips or grilled flank steak or chicken.

1 pound tomatillos
2 to 3 tablespoons fresh lime juice (about 1 lime)
1 jalapeño pepper, seeded and minced
½ cup chopped onion
½ cup chopped fresh cilantro
1 teaspoon kosher salt

1. Discard husks and stems from tomatillos. Place tomatillos, juice, and

pepper in a food processor; pulse until tomatillos are coarsely chopped. Add onion, cilantro, and salt; pulse until combined. Yield: 2 cups (serving size: 2 tablespoons).

CALORIES 12 (23% from fat); FAT 0.3g (sat 0g, mono 0.1g, poly 0.1g); PROTEIN 0.4g; CARB 2.5g; FIBER 0.7g; CHOL 0mg; IRON 0.2mg; SODIUM 118mg; CALC 4mg

Simple Seviche

Acid in the juice "cooks" the fish in this no-cook starter.

½ cup chopped fresh cilantro
½ cup fresh orange juice (about 2 large oranges)
⅓ cup vertically sliced red onion
¼ cup fresh lime juice (about 2 limes)
¼ cup fresh lemon juice (about 2 lemons)
1 tablespoon canola oil
2 teaspoons hot sauce
½ pound mahimahi or other firm white fish, cut into ½-inch pieces
1 avocado, peeled and diced
1 jalapeño pepper, seeded and minced

1. Combine all ingredients in a large bowl, and toss well. Refrigerate for 30 minutes before serving. Yield: 6 servings (serving size: ½ cup).

CALORIES 113 (61% from fat); FAT 7.7g (sat 0.7g, mono 4.6g, poly 0.8g); PROTEIN 8.2g; CARB 6.4g; FIBER 1.2g; CHOL 28mg; IRON 1.4mg; SODIUM 45mg; CALC 13mg

superfast
20 Minute Dishes

From stew to steak, chops to salads, here are simple, fresh, and easy meals you can make superfast.

Romaine and Turkey Salad with Creamy Avocado Dressing

Chop oven-roasted turkey breast from the deli counter into chunks for a quick start on this salad.

¼ cup low-fat buttermilk
1 tablespoon light mayonnaise
1 tablespoon fresh lime juice
½ teaspoon salt
⅛ teaspoon ground red pepper
1 garlic clove, peeled
½ ripe peeled avocado, seeded and coarsely mashed
8 (½-ounce) slices diagonally cut French bread (about ½ inch thick)
¼ cup (1 ounce) preshredded Parmesan cheese
4 cups bagged chopped romaine lettuce
2 cups diced roasted turkey breast (about 8 ounces)
½ cup thinly sliced green onions
2 tablespoons chopped fresh cilantro

1. Combine first 7 ingredients in a blender, and process until smooth, scraping sides. Set aside.
2. Preheat broiler.
3. Arrange bread slices in a single layer on a baking sheet. Sprinkle 1½ teaspoons cheese on each bread slice. Broil bread slices 2 minutes or until lightly browned.
4. Combine lettuce and remaining 3 ingredients in a large bowl. Drizzle buttermilk mixture over lettuce mixture; toss gently to coat. Serve with cheese toasts. Yield: 4 servings (serving size: about 1½ cups salad and 2 cheese toasts).

CALORIES 260 (28% from fat); FAT 8g (sat 2.4g, mono 3.5g, poly 1g); PROTEIN 24.2g; CARB 22.8g; FIBER 4g; CHOL 53mg; IRON 2.6mg; SODIUM 694mg; CALC 171mg

Chicken Puttanesca with Angel Hair Pasta

We add olives, capers, and crushed red pepper to bottled pasta sauce for a quick variation on the traditional version.

    8   ounces uncooked angel hair pasta
    2   teaspoons olive oil
    4   (6-ounce) skinless, boneless
        chicken breast halves
    ½   teaspoon salt
    2   cups tomato-basil pasta sauce
        (such as Muir Glen Organic)
    ¼   cup pitted and coarsely chopped
        kalamata olives
    1   tablespoon capers
    ¼   teaspoon crushed red pepper
    ¼   cup (1 ounce) preshredded
        Parmesan cheese
        Chopped fresh basil or basil sprigs
        (optional)

1. Cook pasta according to package directions, omitting salt and fat. Drain and keep warm.
2. Heat oil in a large nonstick skillet over medium-high heat. Cut chicken into 1-inch pieces. Add chicken to pan; sprinkle evenly with salt. Cook chicken 5 minutes or until lightly browned, stirring occasionally. Stir in pasta sauce, olives, capers, and pepper; bring to a simmer. Cook 5 minutes or until chicken is done, stirring frequently. Arrange 1 cup pasta on each of 4 plates; top each with 1½ cups chicken mixture. Sprinkle each serving with 1 tablespoon cheese. Garnish with chopped basil or basil sprigs, if desired. Yield: 4 servings.

CALORIES 530 (21% from fat); FAT 12.4g (sat 2.8g, mono 6.6g, poly 2g); PROTEIN 51.8g; CARB 55g; FIBER 2.1g; CHOL 104mg; IRON 4.2mg; SODIUM 971mg; CALC 165mg

Pork Chops with Ancho Chile Rub and Raspberry Glaze

Ancho chile powder, made from dried poblano peppers, adds a mild heat, which is mellowed by the sweetness of the preserves in the glaze.

    2   teaspoons ancho chile powder
    ½   teaspoon salt
    ¼   teaspoon dried thyme
    4   (6-ounce) bone-in center-cut pork
        chops (about ½ inch thick)
        Cooking spray
    ¼   cup fat-free, less-sodium beef broth
    2   tablespoons seedless raspberry
        preserves

1. Combine first 3 ingredients in a small bowl, stirring well. Rub spice mixture evenly over pork. Heat a large nonstick skillet over medium heat. Coat pan with cooking spray. Add pork to pan, and cook 3 minutes on each side or until desired degree of doneness. Remove from pan, and keep warm.
2. Add broth to pan, and cook 30 seconds, scraping pan to loosen browned bits. Increase heat to medium-high. Add preserves to pan; cook 1 minute or until slightly thick, stirring constantly with a whisk. Brush pork with glaze. Yield: 4 servings (serving size: 1 pork chop and 1½ tablespoons glaze).

CALORIES 187 (29% from fat); FAT 6g (sat 2g, mono 2.9g, poly 1.1g); PROTEIN 25.2g; CARB 6.8g; FIBER 0.2g; CHOL 70mg; IRON 0.1mg; SODIUM 398mg; CALC 1mg

Cioppino-Style Seafood Stew

Inspired by the famed San Francisco meal-in-a-bowl, this comes together with minimal fuss. Serve it with Parmesan toast.

    1½ tablespoons olive oil
    ½   cup prechopped onion
    1½ teaspoons bottled minced garlic
    ¼   teaspoon crushed red pepper
    1   pound mussels, scrubbed and
        debearded
    8   ounces sea scallops
    8   ounces peeled and deveined
        medium shrimp
    ½   cup clam juice
    ¼   cup chopped fresh flat-leaf parsley
    1   (14.5-ounce) can diced tomatoes,
        undrained

1. Heat oil in a Dutch oven over medium-high heat. Add onion, garlic, and pepper to pan; sauté 2 minutes. Add mussels, scallops, and shrimp to pan; sauté 1 minute. Stir in clam juice, parsley, and tomatoes; bring to a boil. Cover, reduce heat, and simmer 10 minutes or until mussels open; discard any unopened shells. Yield: 4 servings (serving size: 2 cups).

CALORIES 289 (29% from fat); FAT 9.3g (sat 1.5g, mono 4.8g, poly 1.7g); PROTEIN 36.2g; CARB 13.8g; FIBER 1.5g; CHOL 138mg; IRON 6.4mg; SODIUM 726mg; CALC 88mg

Pepper and Garlic-Crusted Tenderloin Steaks with Port Sauce

Serve with long-grain and wild rice pilaf and steamed green beans. Although these steaks are simple enough for weeknights, they're good for company, as well.

    2   teaspoons black peppercorns
    ½   teaspoon salt
    3   garlic cloves, minced
    4   (4-ounce) beef tenderloin steaks,
        trimmed (1 inch thick)
        Cooking spray
    ¼   cup port wine
    ¼   cup canned beef broth
    1   tablespoon chopped fresh thyme

1. Place peppercorns in a small zip-top plastic bag; seal. Crush peppercorns using a meat mallet or small heavy skillet. Combine peppercorns, salt, and garlic in a bowl; rub evenly over steaks.
2. Heat a large nonstick skillet over medium-high heat. Coat pan with cooking spray. Add steaks to pan. Reduce heat; cook 4 minutes on each side or until desired degree of doneness. Remove steaks from pan. Cover and keep warm.
3. Add port and broth to pan, stirring to loosen browned bits. Cook until reduced to ¼ cup (about 3 minutes). Place 1 steak on each of 4 plates; drizzle each serving with 1 tablespoon sauce. Sprinkle each serving with ¾ teaspoon thyme. Yield: 4 servings.

CALORIES 205 (33% from fat); FAT 7.4g (sat 2.7g, mono 3g, poly 0.3g); PROTEIN 25.5g; CARB 6g; FIBER 0.4g; CHOL 76mg; IRON 2.1mg; SODIUM 389mg; CALC 36mg

Thai Shrimp Salad with Spicy-Sour Dressing

Sriracha, a Thai hot sauce, adds a spicy kick to this noodle salad. Use less or omit it, if you prefer. If you can't find fish sauce, substitute low-sodium soy sauce.

  4 ounces uncooked linguine
 12 ounces peeled and deveined medium shrimp
 ½   cup fresh lime juice
  1 tablespoon sugar
  1 tablespoon Sriracha (hot chile sauce, such as Huy Fong)
  1 teaspoon fish sauce
  4 cups torn romaine lettuce
 1¼ cups vertically sliced red onion
 ¼   cup matchstick-cut carrots
 ½   cup chopped fresh mint leaves
 ¼   cup chopped fresh cilantro
 ⅓   cup chopped dry-roasted cashews, unsalted

1. Cook pasta according to package directions, omitting salt and fat. Add shrimp to pan during last 3 minutes of cook time. Drain and rinse with cold water. Drain.
2. Combine juice and next 3 ingredients in a large bowl, stirring until sugar dissolves. Add pasta mixture, lettuce, and next 4 ingredients to juice mixture; toss to coat. Place about 2 cups pasta mixture on each of 4 plates. Sprinkle each serving with 4 teaspoons cashews. Yield: 4 servings.

CALORIES 305 (19% from fat); FAT 6.5g (sat 1.3g, mono 3.3g, poly 1.4g); PROTEIN 23g; CARB 37.6g; FIBER 2.9g; CHOL 166mg; IRON 5.8mg; SODIUM 414mg; CALC 88mg

Ah, Sake!

Japanese rice wine is a multipurpose ingredient at home in Western and Asian recipes.

If you're fond of Japanese food, you've likely enjoyed a bottle of sake with the meal. Or maybe you've ordered a trendy "saketini" cocktail at a bar. That's about all most Americans know about sake (pronounced sah-kee or sah-kay). But the 6,800-year-old style of Japanese rice wine is finding more fans in the United States as bars, restaurants, and wineshops have begun to offer a range of premium sakes from Japanese and a handful of U.S. producers.

Sake, like beer, is brewed from grain yet has the variety, complexity, and subtlety of wine. The good stuff is best sipped cold to appreciate the flavors, which range from sweet to dry and fruity to yeasty.

While sake is wonderful to sip, you also can use it in cooking. Japanese cooks reach for sake to balance sweet and salty flavors, to tenderize meat in marinades, and as a pickling agent. Sake is handy to downplay strong, fishy odors and to highlight a dish's delicate flavors and aromas.

You can use any sake you find at the supermarket (look for it near wine or beer) or wineshop to prepare these recipes. Once you've tried these, next time you buy sake, you may get two bottles—one to sip and another with which to cook.

Warm Oranges in Sake Cream with Sesame Brittle

For a more colorful dessert, prepare the brittle with half regular sesame seeds and half black sesame seeds. The brittle can be made up to two days in advance and stored in an airtight container.

BRITTLE:
  Cooking spray
 ½   cup granulated sugar
 ¼   cup water
  2 tablespoons sesame seeds

SAKE CREAM:
 ½   cup sake
  2 tablespoons butter
  1 tablespoon brown sugar
  Dash of salt
  1 tablespoon heavy cream
  3 cups orange sections (about 6 oranges)

REMAINING INGREDIENT:
  3 cups vanilla fat-free ice cream

1. To prepare brittle, line a baking sheet with foil; coat foil with cooking spray.
2. Combine granulated sugar and ¼ cup water in a small saucepan over medium-high heat. Cook until sugar dissolves, stirring gently to dissolve sugar evenly. Cook 4 minutes or until golden (do not stir). Remove from heat; carefully stir in sesame seeds. Rapidly spread mixture onto prepared baking sheet. Cool completely; break into small pieces.
3. To prepare sake cream, combine sake, butter, brown sugar, and salt in a medium saucepan over medium-high heat; bring to a boil. Cook until reduced to ¼ cup (about 4 minutes). Remove from heat; stir in cream. Gently stir in orange segments. Serve over ice cream; sprinkle with brittle. Yield: 6 servings (serving size: ½ cup sake cream, ½ cup ice cream, and ½ ounce brittle).

CALORIES 239 (25% from fat); FAT 6.7g (sat 3.3g, mono 2g, poly 1g); PROTEIN 4.7g; CARB 37.2g; FIBER 2.5g; CHOL 13mg; IRON 0.4mg; SODIUM 100mg; CALC 124mg

QUICK & EASY

Cornflake-Crusted Halibut with Chile-Cilantro Aïoli

(pictured on page 244)

This recipe first ran in March 2004 in Dinner Tonight, one of our most popular columns. It received our Test Kitchens' highest rating when we first tasted it and remains a staff favorite. Serve with steamed green beans and rice tossed with cilantro and chopped red bell pepper.

AÏOLI:

    2 tablespoons minced fresh cilantro
    3 tablespoons fat-free mayonnaise
    1 serrano chile, seeded and minced
    1 garlic clove, minced

FISH:

    1 cup fat-free milk
    1 large egg white, lightly beaten
    2 cups cornflakes, finely crushed
  ¼ cup all-purpose flour (about
       1 ounce)
  ½ teaspoon salt
  ¼ teaspoon pepper
    2 tablespoons olive oil
    4 (6-ounce) halibut fillets
    4 lemon wedges

1. To prepare aïoli, combine first 4 ingredients, stirring well.
2. To prepare fish, combine milk and egg white in a shallow dish, stirring well with a whisk. Combine cornflakes, flour, salt, and pepper in another shallow dish.
3. Heat oil in a large nonstick skillet over medium-high heat. Dip fish in milk mixture, and dredge in cornflake mixture. Add fish to pan, and cook 4 minutes on each side or until fish flakes easily when tested with a fork or until desired degree of doneness. Serve fish with aïoli and lemon wedges. Yield: 4 servings (serving size: 1 fish fillet, about 1 tablespoon aïoli, and 1 lemon wedge).

CALORIES 367 (27% from fat); FAT 11.2g (sat 1.6g, mono 6.3g, poly 1.9g); PROTEIN 40.8g; CARB 25.1g; FIBER 2.2g; CHOL 56mg; IRON 2.4mg; SODIUM 645mg; CALC 166mg

Best Yeast Bread

Hawaiian Bubble Bread

This irresistible sweet yeast bread is a staff favorite. Dough is shaped into balls—"bubbles"—and layered into a tube pan. Cut the bread into slices, or simply let diners pull apart the bubbles.

    1 teaspoon sugar
    1 package quick-rise yeast (about
       2¼ teaspoons)
    1 cup warm water (100° to 110°)
    1 cup sliced ripe banana
  ½ cup pineapple-orange-banana
       juice concentrate, undiluted
  ½ cup honey
    2 tablespoons butter, melted
    5 cups bread flour, divided (about
       23¾ ounces)
    1 teaspoon salt
  Cooking spray
  ¼ cup cream of coconut
    2 tablespoons pineapple-orange-
       banana juice concentrate,
       undiluted
  ½ cup sifted powdered sugar

1. Dissolve sugar and yeast in 1 cup warm water, and let stand 5 minutes.
2. Combine banana, ½ cup juice concentrate, honey, and butter in a blender; process until smooth, and set aside.
3. Lightly spoon flour into dry measuring cups; level with a knife. Combine 2 cups flour and salt in large bowl, stirring well. Add yeast mixture and banana mixture to flour mixture, stirring until well blended. Add 2¾ cups flour, stirring to form a soft dough.
4. Turn dough out onto a lightly floured surface; knead until smooth and elastic (about 8 minutes). Add enough of remaining flour, 1 tablespoon at a time, to prevent dough from sticking to hands.
5. Place dough in a large bowl coated with cooking spray, turning to coat top. Cover and let rise in a warm place (85°), free from drafts, 1½ hours or until doubled in size. Punch dough down. Turn out onto a lightly floured surface; let rest 5 minutes. Form dough into 1½-inch balls (about 30 balls) on a lightly floured surface. Layer balls in a 10-inch tube pan coated with cooking spray; set aside.

6. Combine cream of coconut and 2 tablespoons juice concentrate in bowl; stir well. Pour 3 tablespoons juice mixture over dough; set remaining juice mixture aside. Cover dough, and let rise 1½ hours or until doubled in size.
7. Preheat oven to 350°.
8. Uncover dough, and bake at 350° for 30 minutes or until loaf sounds hollow when tapped. Cool in pan for 20 minutes. Remove from pan; place on a wire rack. Stir powdered sugar into remaining juice mixture. Drizzle powdered sugar mixture over top of warm bread. Yield: 18 servings (serving size: 1 slice).

CALORIES 210 (9% from fat); FAT 2.2g (sat 1.1g, mono 0.4g, poly 0.3g); PROTEIN 4.9g; CARB 43g; FIBER 1.3g; CHOL 3mg; IRON 1.8mg; SODIUM 143mg; CALC 8mg

Best Ice Cream/Sorbet

MAKE AHEAD • FREEZABLE

Fresh Orange Sorbet

(pictured on page 246)

This sorbet has been a fixture for staffers since it was first tested. It's a standby for special occasions.

  2½ cups water
    1 cup sugar
  Orange rind strips from 2 oranges
  2⅔ cups fresh orange juice
  ⅓ cup fresh lemon juice
  Grated orange rind (optional)
  Mint sprigs (optional)

1. Combine 2½ cups water and sugar in a saucepan; bring to a boil. Add rind strips to pan. Reduce heat, and simmer 5 minutes. Strain sugar mixture through a sieve into a bowl; discard solids. Cool completely.
2. Add orange juice and lemon juice to sugar mixture; stir well. Pour mixture into freezer can of an ice-cream freezer; freeze according to manufacturer's instructions. Spoon sorbet into a freezer-safe container; cover and freeze 1 hour or until firm. Garnish with grated rind and mint sprigs, if desired. Yield: 12 servings (serving size: ½ cup).

CALORIES 91 (0% from fat); FAT 0g; PROTEIN 0.4g; CARB 23.1g; FIBER 0.2g; CHOL 0mg; IRON 0.1mg; SODIUM 1mg; CALC 5mg

Garlic Fries

An enormously popular story with readers, "Out of the Frying Pan Into the Oven" appeared in April 2002. In it we lightened many popular and traditionally fat-laden foods. These fries stand out. First, they're roasted at high heat until crisp and golden. Then you toss them in melted butter, grated Parmesan cheese, and chopped fresh parsley for a tasty finishing touch.

    4   teaspoons canola oil
    ¾   teaspoon salt
    3   pounds peeled baking potatoes, cut into ¼-inch-thick strips
Cooking spray
    2   tablespoons butter
    8   garlic cloves, minced (about 5 teaspoons)
    2   tablespoons finely chopped fresh parsley
    2   tablespoons freshly grated Parmesan cheese

1. Preheat oven to 400°.
2. Combine first 3 ingredients in a large zip-top plastic bag, tossing to coat. Arrange potatoes in a single layer on a baking sheet coated with cooking spray. Bake at 400° for 50 minutes or until potatoes are tender and golden brown, turning after 20 minutes.
3. Place butter and garlic in a large non-stick skillet, and cook over low heat 2 minutes, stirring constantly. Add potatoes, parsley, and Parmesan cheese to pan; toss to coat. Serve immediately. Yield: 6 servings.

CALORIES 256 (27% from fat); FAT 7.7g (sat 3.3g, mono 2g, poly 2g); PROTEIN 5.9g; CARB 42.3g; FIBER 3.5g; CHOL 12mg; IRON 1.9mg; SODIUM 386mg; CALC 55mg

MAKE AHEAD
Coconut Banana Bread with Lime Glaze

This recipe originally appeared on the cover of our September 2003 issue and remains one of our best banana breads.

    2   cups all-purpose flour (about 9 ounces)
    ¾   teaspoon baking soda
    ½   teaspoon salt
    1   cup granulated sugar
    ¼   cup butter, softened
    2   large eggs
 1 ½   cups mashed ripe banana (about 3 bananas)
    ¼   cup plain low-fat yogurt
    3   tablespoons dark rum
    ½   teaspoon vanilla extract
    ½   cup flaked sweetened coconut
Cooking spray
    1   tablespoon flaked sweetened coconut
    ½   cup powdered sugar
 1 ½   tablespoons fresh lime or lemon juice

1. Preheat oven to 350°.
2. Lightly spoon flour into dry measuring cups; level with a knife. Combine flour, baking soda, and salt, stirring with a whisk.
3. Place granulated sugar and butter in a large bowl; beat with a mixer at medium speed until well blended. Add eggs, 1 at a time, beating well after each addition. Add banana, yogurt, rum, and vanilla; beat until blended. Add flour mixture; beat at low speed just until moist. Stir in ½ cup coconut. Spoon batter into a 9 x 5–inch loaf pan coated with cooking spray; sprinkle with 1 tablespoon coconut. Bake at 350° for 1 hour or until a wooden pick inserted in center comes out clean. Cool in pan 10 minutes on a wire rack; remove from pan. Combine powdered sugar and juice, stirring with a whisk; drizzle over warm bread. Cool completely on wire rack. Yield: 1 loaf, 16 servings (serving size: 1 slice).

CALORIES 193 (21% from fat); FAT 4.6g (sat 2.8g, mono 1.1g, poly 0.3g); PROTEIN 2.9g; CARB 35g; FIBER 1.1g; CHOL 35mg; IRON 1mg; SODIUM 179mg; CALC 15mg

MAKE AHEAD
Fudgy Mocha-Toffee Brownies
(pictured on page 247)

These gooey bars are as rich as anything you'll find in a bakery. They're a welcome treat in a lunch box, as a weeknight dessert, or any time you need a sweet treat.

Cooking spray
    2   tablespoons instant coffee granules
    ¼   cup hot water
    ¼   cup butter
    ¼   cup semisweet chocolate chips
 1 ½   cups all-purpose flour (about 6¾ ounces)
 1 ⅓   cups sugar
    ½   cup unsweetened cocoa
    1   teaspoon baking powder
    ½   teaspoon salt
    1   teaspoon vanilla extract
    2   large eggs
    ¼   cup toffee chips

1. Preheat oven to 350°.
2. Coat bottom of a 9-inch square baking pan with cooking spray.
3. Combine coffee granules and ¼ cup hot water, stirring until coffee granules dissolve.
4. Combine butter and semisweet chocolate chips in a small microwave-safe bowl. Microwave at HIGH 1 minute or until butter melts; stir until chocolate is smooth.
5. Lightly spoon flour into dry measuring cups; level with a knife. Combine flour, sugar, unsweetened cocoa, baking powder, and salt in a large bowl, stirring with a whisk. Combine coffee mixture, butter mixture, vanilla extract, and eggs in a medium bowl, stirring with a whisk. Add coffee mixture to flour mixture; stir just until combined. Spread evenly into prepared pan. Sprinkle evenly with toffee chips. Bake at 350° for 22 minutes. Cool on a wire rack. Yield: 20 servings.

CALORIES 145 (30% from fat); FAT 4.8g (sat 2.4g, mono 1.8g, poly 0.3g); PROTEIN 2.2g; CARB 24.9g; FIBER 1.1g; CHOL 30mg; IRON 0.9mg; SODIUM 121mg; CALC 23mg

Best Pork
Pan-Roasted Pork Loin with Leeks
Lombo di Maiale Coi Porri

Leeks, a mild, sweet member of the onion family, are cooked slowly along with the pork until they're very tender. This recipe earned its status as a favorite because the time-honored Italian technique and straightforward flavor are so reliable.

    4   large leeks (about 2¼ pounds)
    ½   cup water
    1   tablespoon butter, divided
    ½   teaspoon salt, divided
    ½   teaspoon pepper, divided
    1   (2-pound) boneless pork loin, trimmed
    ½   cup dry white wine
        Chopped fresh parsley (optional)

1. Remove roots and tough upper leaves from leeks. Cut each leek in half lengthwise. Cut each half crosswise into ½-inch-thick slices (you should have about 6 cups). Soak in cold water to loosen dirt.
2. Combine leeks, ½ cup water, 1 teaspoon butter, ¼ teaspoon salt, and ¼ teaspoon pepper in a large Dutch oven or deep sauté pan over medium-high heat. Cook 10 minutes or until leek wilts. Pour leek mixture into a bowl.
3. Heat remaining 2 teaspoons butter in pan over medium-high heat. Add pork to pan. Cook 5 minutes, turning to brown on all sides. Add remaining ¼ teaspoon salt, remaining ¼ teaspoon pepper, and wine to pan; cook 15 seconds, scraping pan to loosen browned bits. Return leek mixture to pan. Cover, reduce heat, and simmer 2 hours or until pork is tender. Remove pork from pan. Increase heat to reduce leek sauce if too watery. Cut pork into ¼-inch-thick slices. Serve with leek mixture. Garnish with parsley, if desired. Yield: 6 servings (serving size: about 3 ounces pork and about 2½ tablespoons leek mixture).

CALORIES 246 (39% from fat); FAT 10.7g (sat 4.2g, mono 4.4g, poly 1.1g); PROTEIN 24.8g; CARB 12.1g; FIBER 1g; CHOL 73mg; IRON 2.8mg; SODIUM 306mg; CALC 60mg

Late Summer Menu
serves 8

Fresh produce stars in this simple supper. Start the potatoes while the grill preheats. The beans and pork chops will cook in a flash.

Green and Yellow Bean Salad with Chunky Tomato Dressing and Feta Cheese

Smashed red potatoes*

Grilled pork chops

*Place 2½ pounds quartered small red potatoes in a medium saucepan. Cover with water to 3 inches above potatoes; bring to a boil. Reduce heat, and cook 15 minutes or until tender; drain. Return pan to heat. Add ⅔ cup 2% reduced-fat milk and 2 tablespoons butter to pan; cook 1 minute or until heated. Add potatoes to pan; mash with a potato masher to desired consistency. Stir in ⅓ cup sour cream, ¼ cup chopped green onions, 1 teaspoon salt, and ½ teaspoon freshly ground black pepper.

Best Salad
QUICK & EASY
Green and Yellow Bean Salad with Chunky Tomato Dressing and Feta Cheese

Buy the freshest beans you can find for this simple dish. Then combine them with sherry vinegar, extravirgin olive oil, fresh basil, and good-quality feta cheese for a stellar summer salad.

    4   cups water
    ¾   pound wax beans, trimmed
    ¾   pound green beans, trimmed
    2   cups chopped tomato
    1   tablespoon sherry vinegar
    2   teaspoons extravirgin olive oil
    ½   teaspoon salt
    ¼   teaspoon freshly ground black pepper
    ½   cup thinly sliced fresh basil
    ½   cup (2 ounces) crumbled feta cheese

1. Bring 4 cups water to a boil in a medium saucepan. Cook beans in boiling water 5 minutes or until crisp-tender. Drain and rinse with cold water; drain.
2. Combine tomato and next 4 ingredients in a bowl. Divide beans evenly among 8 plates. Top each serving with ¼ cup tomato mixture. Sprinkle each serving with 1 tablespoon sliced basil and 1 tablespoon cheese. Yield: 8 servings.

CALORIES 67 (39% from fat); FAT 2.9g (sat 1.3g, mono 1.2g, poly 0.3g); PROTEIN 3g; CARB 8.7g; FIBER 2.3g; CHOL 6mg; IRON 1.1mg; SODIUM 246mg; CALC 73mg

Best Grain Side Dish
Creamed Corn with Bacon and Leeks

The combination of sweet corn and smoky bacon gives this uncomplicated dish sublime flavor. It's a delicious way to put fresh end-of-summer corn to use.

    6   ears corn
    2   cups 1% low-fat milk
    1   tablespoon cornstarch
    1   teaspoon sugar
    ½   teaspoon salt
    ¼   teaspoon freshly ground black pepper
    4   slices bacon
    1   cup chopped leek

1. Cut kernels from ears of corn to measure 3 cups. Using dull side of a knife blade, scrape milk and remaining pulp from cobs into a bowl. Place 1½ cups kernels, low-fat milk, cornstarch, sugar, salt, and pepper in a food processor; process until smooth, scraping sides.
2. Cook bacon in a large cast-iron skillet over medium heat until crisp, turning once. Remove bacon from pan, reserving 1 teaspoon drippings in pan; crumble bacon. Add leek to pan, and cook 2 minutes or until tender, stirring constantly. Add pureed corn mixture, remaining 1½ cups corn kernels, and corn milk mixture to pan; bring to a boil. Reduce heat, and simmer 3 minutes or until slightly thick, stirring constantly. Sprinkle with crumbled bacon just before serving. Yield: 6 servings (serving size: ⅔ cup).

CALORIES 151 (27% from fat); FAT 4.6g (sat 1.7g, mono 1.9g, poly 0.8g); PROTEIN 7g; CARB 23.1g; FIBER 2.4g; CHOL 9mg; IRON 0.8mg; SODIUM 325mg; CALC 111mg

Best Chicken Dish
Roasted Chicken with Onions, Potatoes, and Gravy

This recipe first ran in the May 2005 issue in a column that profiled Chuck Williams, founder of Williams-Sonoma.

      1   (4-pound) roasting chicken
  1¼   teaspoons salt, divided
   ¾   teaspoon freshly ground black pepper, divided
      4   oregano sprigs
      1   lemon, quartered
      1   celery stalk, cut into 2-inch pieces
Cooking spray
      2   tablespoons butter, melted
      2   pounds medium yellow onions, peeled and each cut into 8 wedges
      2   pounds small red potatoes, cut into (1-inch) wedges
   ¼   cup all-purpose flour (about 1 ounce)
      1   (14-ounce) can fat-free, less-sodium chicken broth, divided
Lemon wedges (optional)
Oregano sprigs (optional)

1. Preheat oven to 425°.
2. Remove and discard giblets and neck from chicken. Trim excess fat. Starting at neck cavity, loosen skin from breast and drumsticks by inserting fingers, gently pushing between skin and meat. Combine ½ teaspoon salt and ½ teaspoon black pepper; rub under loosened skin and over breast and drumsticks. Place oregano sprigs, quartered lemon, and celery pieces into body cavity. Lift wing tips up and over back; tuck under chicken. Tie legs together with string. Place chicken, breast side up, on the rack of a broiler pan coated with cooking spray.
3. Combine ½ teaspoon salt, remaining ¼ teaspoon pepper, butter, onions, and potatoes in a bowl; toss well to coat. Arrange mixture around chicken on rack. Place rack in pan. Bake at 425° for 20 minutes. Reduce oven temperature to 325° (do not remove pan from oven); bake an additional 1 hour and 10 minutes or until onions and potatoes are tender and a thermometer inserted into meaty part of chicken thigh registers

165°. Set chicken, onions, and potatoes aside; cover and keep warm.
4. Place a zip-top plastic bag inside a 2-cup glass measure. Pour pan drippings into bag; let stand 10 minutes (fat will rise to the top). Seal bag; carefully snip off 1 bottom corner of bag. Drain drippings into a small saucepan, stopping before fat layer reaches opening; discard fat. Combine remaining ¼ teaspoon salt, flour, and ½ cup chicken broth in a small bowl, stirring with a whisk. Add flour mixture and remaining chicken broth to saucepan. Bring to a boil over medium-high heat. Reduce heat to medium; cook 5 minutes or until gravy thickens, stirring frequently with a whisk. Carve chicken; serve with gravy and onion mixture. Garnish with lemon wedges and oregano sprigs, if desired. Yield: 6 servings (serving size: about 4 ounces chicken, 1⅓ cups onion mixture, and ⅓ cup gravy).

CALORIES 430 (24% from fat); FAT 11.6g (sat 4.5g, mono 3.8g, poly 2g); PROTEIN 36.9g; CARB 43.7g; FIBER 5.2g; CHOL 113mg; IRON 3.4mg; SODIUM 753mg; CALC 71mg

Best Pie/Cobbler
MAKE AHEAD
Coconut-Peach Cobbler with Bourbon-Pecan Ice Cream

We love this dessert because you can make all the components ahead and assemble at the last minute.

ICE CREAM:
      4   cups vanilla low-fat ice cream, softened
   ¼   cup chopped pecans, toasted
   ¼   cup bourbon

CRUST:
      2   cups all-purpose flour (about 9 ounces)
      3   tablespoons granulated sugar
      1   tablespoon baking powder
   ¼   teaspoon salt
   ½   cup flaked sweetened coconut, toasted
      6   tablespoons chilled butter, cut into small pieces
   ½   cup evaporated fat-free milk
      2   large egg yolks

FILLING:
    11   cups sliced peeled peaches (about 4 pounds)
      1   cup packed brown sugar
      6   tablespoons all-purpose flour
   ¼   teaspoon ground nutmeg
Dash of salt
Cooking spray
      1   tablespoon granulated sugar

1. To prepare ice cream, combine vanilla ice cream, chopped pecans, and bourbon in a bowl; cover and freeze mixture at least 3 hours.
2. To prepare crust, lightly spoon 2 cups flour into dry measuring cups; level with a knife. Place 2 cups flour, 3 tablespoons granulated sugar, baking powder, and ¼ teaspoon salt in a food processor; pulse 2 times or until blended. Add coconut and butter; pulse 10 times or until mixture resembles coarse meal. Combine milk and egg yolks. Remove 1 tablespoon milk mixture; set aside. With processor on, slowly pour remaining milk mixture through food chute; pulse 5 times or just until blended. Gently press mixture into a 6-inch square on heavy-duty plastic wrap; cover with additional plastic wrap. Chill at least 30 minutes. Roll dough, still covered, into a 14 x 10–inch rectangle.
3. Preheat oven to 350°.
4. To prepare filling, combine sliced peeled peaches, brown sugar, 6 tablespoons flour, nutmeg, and dash of salt in a large bowl; spoon into a 13 x 9–inch baking dish coated with cooking spray. Remove one sheet of plastic wrap from dough; place dough on peach mixture, pressing to edge of dish. Remove remaining sheet of plastic wrap; brush dough with reserved milk mixture. Cut 6 (2-inch) slits in dough, and sprinkle with 1 tablespoon granulated sugar. Bake at 350° for 35 minutes or until golden. Let stand 30 minutes on a wire rack. Serve with bourbon-pecan ice cream. Yield: 16 servings (serving size: 1 piece cobbler and ¼ cup bourbon-pecan ice cream).

CALORIES 310 (26% from fat); FAT 9g (sat 4.8g, mono 2.8g, poly 0.8g); PROTEIN 5.1g; CARB 52.9g; FIBER 3.1g; CHOL 44mg; IRON 1.5mg; SODIUM 242mg; CALC 145mg

MAKE AHEAD
Chunky Two-Bean and Beef Chili

Nothing hits the spot on a blustery cold day like a pot of hot chili. This recipe is a favorite because we love the chunks of meat, subtle spicy heat from the jalapeño peppers, and depth of flavor from the red wine. Reduce the ground red pepper by half if you prefer a milder version.

    1 tablespoon canola oil, divided
  Cooking spray
1½ pounds beef stew meat
  ¾ teaspoon salt
1½ cups chopped onion
  ½ cup chopped green bell pepper
    1 tablespoon minced fresh garlic
    2 teaspoons finely chopped
        jalapeño pepper
  ⅔ cup cabernet sauvignon or dry red
        wine
1½ tablespoons brown sugar
    2 tablespoons tomato paste
1½ teaspoons ancho chile powder
    1 teaspoon dried oregano
    1 teaspoon ground red pepper
  ½ teaspoon chili powder
  ¼ teaspoon ground cumin
  ¼ teaspoon ground coriander
  ⅛ teaspoon ground cinnamon
    1 (28-ounce) can whole tomatoes,
        undrained and chopped
    1 (15-ounce) can dark red kidney
        beans, rinsed and drained
    1 (15-ounce) can hot chili beans
  Reduced-fat sour cream (optional)

1. Heat 1 teaspoon canola oil in a large Dutch oven coated with cooking spray over medium-high heat. Sprinkle beef with salt. Add half of beef to pan; sauté 8 minutes or until browned. Remove from pan. Repeat procedure with remaining beef.
2. Add remaining 2 teaspoons oil, onion, and bell pepper to pan; sauté 3 minutes. Add garlic and jalapeño; sauté 1 minute. Add wine, scraping pan to loosen browned bits. Return beef to pan. Stir in sugar and remaining ingredients except sour cream; bring to a boil. Cover, reduce heat, and simmer 1½ hours or until beef

is tender, stirring occasionally. Garnish with sour cream, if desired. Yield: 6 servings (serving size: about 1⅓ cups).

CALORIES 390 (26% from fat); FAT 11.4g (sat 3.2g, mono 4.8g, poly 1.1g); PROTEIN 31.3g; CARB 37.5g; FIBER 10.1g; CHOL 71mg; IRON 5mg; SODIUM 825mg; CALC 94mg

Best Pasta Dish
QUICK & EASY
Cavatappi with Spinach, Beans, and Asiago Cheese

A great weeknight dinner you can prepare at a moment's notice, this pasta offers lots of variations. Use whatever pasta, canned beans, or cheese you happen to have on hand.

    8 cups coarsely chopped spinach
        leaves
    4 cups hot cooked cavatappi (about
        6 ounces uncooked spiral-shaped
        pasta)
  ½ cup (2 ounces) shredded Asiago
        cheese
    2 tablespoons olive oil
  ¼ teaspoon salt
  ¼ teaspoon freshly ground black
        pepper
    1 (19-ounce) can cannellini beans
        or other white beans, rinsed and
        drained
    2 garlic cloves, crushed
  Cracked black pepper (optional)

1. Combine first 8 ingredients in a large bowl; toss well. Sprinkle with cracked black pepper, if desired. Yield: 4 servings (serving size: 2 cups).

CALORIES 401 (27% from fat); FAT 12g (sat 3.4g, mono 6.2g, poly 1.2g); PROTEIN 18.8g; CARB 54.7g; FIBER 6.7g; CHOL 10mg; IRON 6.4mg; SODIUM 464mg; CALC 306mg

WINE NOTE: With the simple flavors of this dish, look for a light, refreshing Italian pinot grigio that also has northern Italian heritage. Bollini Pinot Grigio Trentino 2005 ($15) has flavors of white peach and nectarine. The juicy, refreshing quality is perfect against the dry texture of the beans and the slightly bitter spinach, while the rather full body matches the olive oil's fruity richness.

Best Soup
Baked Potato Soup

    4 baking potatoes (about 2½
        pounds)
  ⅔ cup all-purpose flour (about 3
        ounces)
    6 cups 2% reduced-fat milk
    1 cup (4 ounces) reduced-fat
        shredded extrasharp Cheddar
        cheese, divided
    1 teaspoon salt
  ½ teaspoon freshly ground black
        pepper
    1 cup reduced-fat sour cream
  ¾ cup chopped green onions,
        divided
    6 slices bacon, cooked and
        crumbled
  Cracked black pepper (optional)

1. Preheat oven to 400°.
2. Pierce potatoes with a fork; bake at 400° for 1 hour or until tender. Cool. Peel potatoes; coarsely mash.
3. Lightly spoon flour into dry measuring cups; level with a knife. Place flour in a large Dutch oven; gradually add milk, stirring with a whisk until blended. Cook over medium heat until thick and bubbly (about 8 minutes). Add mashed potatoes, ¾ cup cheese, salt, and ½ teaspoon pepper, stirring until cheese melts. Remove from heat.
4. Stir in sour cream and ½ cup onions. Cook over low heat 10 minutes or until thoroughly heated (do not boil). Ladle 1½ cups soup into each of 8 bowls. Sprinkle each serving with 1½ teaspoons cheese, 1½ teaspoons onions, and about 1 tablespoon bacon. Garnish with cracked pepper, if desired. Yield: 8 servings.

CALORIES 329 (30% from fat); FAT 10.8g (sat 5.9g, mono 3.5g, poly 0.7g); PROTEIN 13.6g; CARB 44.5g; FIBER 2.8g; CHOL 38mg; IRON 1.1mg; SODIUM 587mg; CALC 407mg

Best Rice Recipe
Risotto with Porcini Mushrooms and Mascarpone

1½ cups boiling water
½ cup dried porcini mushrooms (about ½ ounce)
1 (14-ounce) can less-sodium beef broth
Cooking spray
1 cup uncooked Arborio rice or other short-grain rice
¾ cup chopped shallots
2 garlic cloves, minced
½ cup dry white wine
¼ cup (1 ounce) grated Parmigiano-Reggiano cheese
¼ cup (1 ounce) mascarpone cheese
1 tablespoon chopped fresh or 1 teaspoon dried thyme
½ teaspoon salt
½ teaspoon freshly ground black pepper

1. Combine 1½ cups boiling water and mushrooms; let stand 10 minutes or until soft. Drain through a colander over a bowl. Reserve 1¼ cups soaking liquid; chop mushrooms.
2. Bring reserved soaking liquid and broth to a simmer in a small saucepan (do not boil). Keep broth mixture warm over low heat.
3. Heat a large saucepan over medium-high heat. Coat pan with cooking spray. Add rice, shallots, and garlic to pan; sauté 5 minutes. Add wine; cook until liquid evaporates (about 2 minutes).
4. Add 1 cup broth mixture to rice mixture; cook over medium heat 5 minutes or until the liquid is nearly absorbed, stirring occasionally. Add remaining broth mixture, ½ cup at a time, stirring occasionally until each portion of broth mixture is absorbed before adding next (about 25 minutes total). Add mushrooms, Parmigiano-Reggiano and mascarpone cheeses, thyme, salt, and pepper; stir gently just until cheeses melt. Serve warm. Yield: 4 servings (serving size: 1 cup).

CALORIES 198 (28% from fat); FAT 6.1g (sat 3.2g, mono 1g, poly 0.3g); PROTEIN 8.9g; CARB 27g; FIBER 1.2g; CHOL 15mg; IRON 1.9mg; SODIUM 449mg; CALC 113mg

Top Chefs

Three former Cooking Light *columnists reflect on the evolution and growing popularity of meatless cuisine.*

Deborah Madison, Peter Berley, and Steven Petusevsky—a trio of onetime *Cooking Light* Inspired Vegetarian authors—have been influential in transforming vegetarian cuisine in America to its Technicolor present, filled with seasonal produce and ethnic dishes that appeal to everyone.

Deborah's Late Summer Dinner Menu
serves 4

Potato-Leek Gratin

Sautéed Fennel with Lemon and Pepper

Steamed Zucchini with Herb Sauce

Pancake Soufflé with Caramelized Apples

Potato-Leek Gratin

"This is the simplest way I know to make a potato gratin. Simmering the vegetables in the milk precooks them somewhat, shortening time in the oven and flavoring the milk, as well. You can easily vary this gratin by substituting some of the potatoes with other root vegetables, such as celery root, turnips, rutabagas, or parsnips."

—Deborah Madison

4 cups 2% reduced-fat milk
2 cups thinly sliced leek (about 2 large)
1 teaspoon salt
¼ teaspoon freshly ground black pepper
3 pounds baking potato, peeled and cut into ¼-inch-thick slices
2 thyme sprigs
1 bay leaf
1 garlic clove, minced
Cooking spray
1 cup (4 ounces) shredded Gruyère cheese

1. Preheat oven to 375°.
2. Place first 8 ingredients in a Dutch oven; bring to a boil. Cover, reduce heat, and simmer 10 minutes or until potato is tender. Discard thyme and bay leaf.
3. Spoon half of potato mixture into a 13 x 9–inch baking dish coated with cooking spray. Sprinkle with ½ cup cheese. Top with remaining potato mixture and ½ cup cheese. Bake at 375° for 1 hour or until golden brown. Let stand 10 minutes before serving. Yield: 6 servings.

CALORIES 362 (24% from fat); FAT 9.6g (sat 5.6g, mono 2.8g, poly 0.6g); PROTEIN 15.2g; CARB 55g; FIBER 4.5g; CHOL 33mg; IRON 1.5mg; SODIUM 555mg; CALC 426mg

The Seasonal Chef

Deborah Madison's roots in the vegetarian kitchen stretch back to the groundbreaking restaurant Greens in San Francisco. When it opened in 1979, Greens was the first restaurant in the country to serve vegetarian fare in a high-end setting. In her 1999 and 2000 columns for *Cooking Light*, Madison included colorful produce and complex ethnic recipes to create vegetarian dishes that would entice even meat eaters.

Today, her cooking is informed by what's in season in Santa Fe, New Mexico, where she lives. Her book, *Local Flavors*, explains that visiting farmers' markets allows shoppers to taste the freshest produce, know what's in season, and get to know the people growing their food.

While Madison finds people are embracing varied styles of eating that fit their personal food philosophies, she recalls when vegetarians weren't accommodated at most restaurants. Now with many chefs exploring the range of flavors and textures vegetables offer, this is less of an issue.

Sautéed Fennel with Lemon and Pepper

Fennel seeds and fennel fronds (the feathery tops of the bulb) both underscore this vegetable's clean anise flavor. Fennel is also called anise.

¼ teaspoon fennel seeds
1 teaspoon chopped fennel fronds
½ teaspoon sea salt
¼ teaspoon grated lemon rind
¼ teaspoon freshly ground black pepper
5½ cups (½-inch-thick) slices fennel bulb (about 2 small bulbs)
2 teaspoons extravirgin olive oil

1. Cook fennel seeds in a small saucepan over medium heat 1 minute or until toasted. Place seeds in a small zip-top bag; crush with a rolling pin.
2. Combine fennel seeds, fennel fronds, salt, rind, and pepper in a large bowl.
3. Steam fennel slices, covered, 5 minutes or until tender. Drain. Add fennel and oil to fennel frond mixture; toss well. Yield: 4 servings (serving size: 1¼ cups).

CALORIES 57 (39% from fat); FAT 2.5g (sat 0.3g, mono 1.7g, poly 0.2g); PROTEIN 1.5g; CARB 8.7g; FIBER 3.7g; CHOL 0mg; IRON 0.9mg; SODIUM 349mg; CALC 60mg

Steamed Zucchini with Herb Sauce

If you can find an heirloom zucchini called Costata Romanesca, you're in for a treat. When cut crosswise, it makes a pretty scalloped slice. Otherwise, use standard zucchini.

¼ cup finely chopped fresh parsley
3 tablespoons finely chopped shallots
1 tablespoon chopped fresh basil
1 tablespoon chopped capers
2 teaspoons extravirgin olive oil
2 teaspoons grated lemon rind
1 teaspoon chopped fresh oregano
1 teaspoon fresh lemon juice
¼ teaspoon sea salt
6 cups (¼-inch-thick) slices zucchini (about 2 pounds)

1. Combine first 9 ingredients in a large bowl; set aside.
2. Steam zucchini, covered, 4 minutes or until crisp-tender. Add to parsley mixture in bowl; toss gently to coat. Yield: 4 servings (serving size: about ¾ cup).

CALORIES 65 (39% from fat); FAT 2.8g (sat 0.4g, mono 1.9g, poly 0.4g); PROTEIN 3.1g; CARB 9.6g; FIBER 2.9g; CHOL 0mg; IRON 1.2mg; SODIUM 233mg; CALC 47mg

Pancake Soufflé with Caramelized Apples

The batter can be whipped up in a blender a few hours in advance, and the apples can be caramelized ahead of time, as well. Just combine the batter and apples in the skillet, and pop it in the oven as you sit down to dinner; it will be puffed and glorious by the time you're ready for dessert.

2½ tablespoons butter, divided
3 cups sliced peeled Granny Smith apple (about 1 pound)
2 tablespoons sugar
¼ cup sugar
½ cup all-purpose flour (about 2¼ ounces)
¾ cup fat-free milk
½ teaspoon vanilla extract
⅛ teaspoon salt
2 large eggs
2 large egg whites

1. Preheat oven to 350°.
2. Melt 1 tablespoon butter in a large nonstick skillet over medium-high heat. Add apple and 2 tablespoons sugar to pan; sauté 7 minutes or until lightly browned. Reduce heat, and cook 5 minutes or until browned, stirring occasionally. Remove from heat.
3. Melt 1½ tablespoons butter in an 8-inch cast-iron skillet, tipping pan quickly until butter coats sides of pan. Pour melted butter and ¼ cup sugar into a blender. Lightly spoon flour into a dry measuring cup; level with a knife. Add flour and remaining 5 ingredients to blender; process until smooth. Pour batter into prepared skillet. Top evenly with apple mixture. Bake at 350° for 35 minutes or until a wooden pick inserted in center comes out clean. Cut into wedges. Serve immediately. Yield: 4 servings (serving size: 1 wedge).

CALORIES 307 (29% from fat); FAT 9.8g (sat 5.3g, mono 2.8g, poly 0.7g); PROTEIN 8.7g; CARB 47.8g; FIBER 2.6g; CHOL 125mg; IRON 1.4mg; SODIUM 213mg; CALC 72mg

Peter's Make-Ahead Dips and Snacks Menu
serves 12

Walnut-Fennel Dip

Butternut Squash Spread with Pepitas

Garlic Pita Chips

Vegetable crudités

Spinach and Shiitake Mushroom Phyllo Turnovers

Walnut-Fennel Dip

This dip can be prepared up to two days in advance. Serve with crudités such as bell pepper strips, broccoli florets, and baby carrots.

2 teaspoons olive oil
1 cup finely chopped fennel bulb
1 cup chopped Rio or other sweet onion
¼ cup chopped shallots
½ teaspoon salt
½ teaspoon fresh thyme leaves
⅛ teaspoon crushed red pepper
3 garlic cloves, halved
1 cup water
⅓ cup chopped walnuts, toasted
2 tablespoons lemon juice
1 tablespoon chopped fresh parsley

1. Heat oil in a large nonstick skillet over medium-high heat. Add fennel and next 6 ingredients to pan; sauté 8 minutes or until vegetables are tender. Add 1 cup water; bring to a boil. Cover, reduce heat, and simmer 8 minutes. Uncover and simmer until liquid evaporates (about 4 minutes). Remove from heat; cool.
2. Place fennel mixture, walnuts, and juice in a food processor; pulse 10 times or until combined (mixture will not be smooth). Spoon into a medium bowl;

Continued

sprinkle with parsley. Serve warm or chilled. Yield: 1½ cups (serving size: 2 tablespoons).

CALORIES 44 (61% from fat); FAT 3g (sat 0.3g, mono 0.9g, poly 1.7g); PROTEIN 1g; CARB 4.3g; FIBER 1.1g; CHOL 0mg; IRON 0.3mg; SODIUM 110mg; CALC 20mg

The Flexible Chef

In the 1990s, author and cooking teacher Peter Berley was drawn to a macrobiotic diet that advocates eating a balance of whole grains and locally grown, seasonal vegetables as a way to cure allergies and asthma. It worked, but he found that style of eating too rigid. Through the process of training to become a chef and teaching cooking classes, he settled on a more flexible approach to eating.

Studying the way vegetables are used in Italy allowed him to create dishes that use fewer ingredients but have more vibrant flavors. He often uses the same ingredient in several ways to build its flavor, a strategy he employed as the Inspired Vegetarian columnist in 2002.

His latest book, *The Flexitarian Table: Inspired Flexible Meals for Meat Lovers, Vegetarians and Everyone in Between*, is based on what he considers the future of vegetarian cuisine, in which people adopt a vegetable-friendly way of eating—no matter their dietary identity.

Butternut Squash Spread with Pepitas

Add a few tablespoons of water when pureeing the squash mixture to achieve a creamy consistency, if necessary.

1½   cups (½-inch) cubed peeled butternut squash (about 1 pound)
1   teaspoon olive oil
Cooking spray
½   cup diced onion
1½   teaspoons chopped fresh sage
¼   teaspoon salt
⅛   teaspoon freshly ground black pepper
2   garlic cloves, minced
Dash of crushed red pepper
¼   cup chopped sun-dried tomatoes, packed without oil
2   tablespoons unsalted pumpkinseed kernels, toasted

1. Place squash in a medium saucepan; cover with water 2 inches above squash. Bring to a boil; cover, reduce heat, and cook 15 minutes or until tender. Drain.
2. Heat oil in a large nonstick skillet coated with cooking spray over medium-high heat. Add onion to pan; sauté 4 minutes or until tender. Add sage and next 4 ingredients; sauté 2 minutes. Cool.
3. Place squash, onion mixture, and tomatoes in a food processor; process until smooth. Spoon into a medium bowl; sprinkle with pumpkinseed kernels. Yield: 1½ cups (serving size: 2 tablespoons).

CALORIES 26 (21% from fat); FAT 0.6g (sat 0.1g, mono 0.3g, poly 0.2g); PROTEIN 0.8g; CARB 5.1g; FIBER 0.9g; CHOL 0mg; IRON 0.4mg; SODIUM 74mg; CALC 15mg

Garlic Pita Chips

These can be made a day or two in advance and are great to have on hand for snacking. Store in zip-top bags.

6   (6-inch) pitas
Cooking spray
½   teaspoon garlic salt
¼   teaspoon freshly ground black pepper

1. Preheat oven to 350°.
2. Coat one side of each pita with cooking spray. Sprinkle pitas evenly with garlic salt and pepper. Cut each pita into 8 wedges; arrange wedges in a single layer on a jelly-roll pan coated with cooking spray. Bake at 350° for 20 minutes or until crisp. Yield: 4 dozen chips (serving size: 4 chips).

CALORIES 80 (0% from fat); FAT 0g; PROTEIN 3.5g; CARB 16.5g; FIBER 0.5g; CHOL 0mg; IRON 1.4mg; SODIUM 120mg; CALC 20mg

Spinach and Shiitake Mushroom Phyllo Turnovers

These turnovers can be assembled and frozen until you are ready to bake them.

1   teaspoon olive oil
2   cups diced shiitake mushroom caps (about 8 ounces)
1   cup chopped onion
3   garlic cloves, minced
1   (12.3-ounce) package reduced-fat firm tofu, drained
1   tablespoon yellow miso (soybean paste)
1   tablespoon lemon juice
⅛   teaspoon sea salt
⅛   teaspoon freshly ground black pepper
3   (6-ounce) packages fresh baby spinach
36   (14 x 9–inch) sheets frozen phyllo dough, thawed (1 pound)
Cooking spray

1. Heat oil in a large nonstick skillet over medium-high heat. Add mushrooms, onion, and garlic to pan; sauté 10 minutes or until tender. Remove from heat.
2. Place tofu in a large bowl. Add miso, juice, salt, and pepper; mash with a fork until combined. Add mushroom mixture to tofu mixture, and stir until combined.
3. Heat a large nonstick skillet over medium heat. Add 1 bag spinach to pan; cook until wilted (about 7 minutes), stirring frequently. Drain. Repeat procedure with remaining 2 bags spinach. Add spinach to tofu mixture; stir until well combined. Cool.

4. Preheat oven to 400°.

5. Place 3 phyllo sheets on a large cutting board or work surface (cover remaining dough to keep from drying); lightly coat phyllo with cooking spray. Cut stack into 4 (3½-inch-wide) strips. Spoon about 1 rounded tablespoon spinach mixture onto one end of each strip. Fold one corner of the end over mixture, forming a triangle; keep folding back and forth into a triangle to the end of strip. Repeat with each strip. Place triangles, seam sides down, on a baking sheet. Lightly coat tops with cooking spray. Repeat procedure with remaining phyllo sheets and filling. Bake at 400° for 12 minutes or until golden. Yield: 4 dozen (serving size: 2 turnovers).

CALORIES 77 (18% from fat); FAT 1.5g (sat 0.3g, mono 0.8g, poly 0.3g); PROTEIN 3.2g; CARB 12.5g; FIBER 1.1g; CHOL 0mg; IRON 1.5mg; SODIUM 161mg; CALC 29mg

---

Steven's Easy Family Dinner Menu
serves 6

Pasta with White Beans, Greens, and Lemon

Mediterranean Chopped Salad

Yogurt Parfaits with Walnuts, Dates, and Honey

Pasta with White Beans, Greens, and Lemon

1 pound uncooked orecchiette
2 tablespoons extravirgin olive oil
Cooking spray
3 garlic cloves, minced
¾ cup chopped sun-dried tomatoes, packed without oil
¼ teaspoon crushed red pepper
1 (15-ounce) can cannellini beans, rinsed and drained
3 cups trimmed arugula or baby spinach
1 cup fresh basil leaves, coarsely chopped (about 1 [1-ounce] package)
1 tablespoon grated lemon rind
3 tablespoons fresh lemon juice
1 teaspoon kosher salt
5 tablespoons pine nuts, toasted
¼ cup (1 ounce) grated Parmesan cheese

1. Cook pasta according to package directions, omitting salt and fat. Drain. Place pasta in a large bowl; drizzle with oil, tossing to coat.

2. Heat a large Dutch oven over medium-high heat. Coat pan with cooking spray. Add garlic to pan; sauté 1 minute or until garlic begins to brown. Add pasta mixture, tomatoes, pepper, and beans; cook 2 minutes, stirring constantly. Stir in arugula, basil, rind, juice, and salt; cook 1 minute or until arugula wilts. Spoon 1½ cups pasta mixture into each of 6 shallow bowls; top each serving with 2½ teaspoons pine nuts and 2 teaspoons cheese. Serve immediately. Yield: 6 servings.

CALORIES 438 (25% from fat); FAT 12.2g (sat 2g, mono 4.7g, poly 3.2g); PROTEIN 16.2g; CARB 68.2g; FIBER 5.5g; CHOL 3mg; IRON 4.4mg; SODIUM 623mg; CALC 132mg

---

The Practical Chef

When Steven Petusevsky had to create a vegetarian-friendly menu for a 300-seat restaurant in Miami in 1989, he knew plain brown rice and steamed vegetables wouldn't work. So he drew on his formal chef's training and background at Whole Foods Market and upscale hotels. He made coleslaw with sea vegetables, crafted burgers from grain and soy, and prepared faux veal piccata using seitan (a protein-rich food made from wheat gluten and water).

As it was when he wrote for *Cooking Light* in 1998, his cooking these days is rooted in the whole-grain and vegetable-centered cooking styles found along the Mediterranean in countries such as Greece, Italy, and Spain. He runs Market Salamander in Palm Beach, Florida, which he stocks with locally made goat cheese and produce.

"As long as vegetarian cuisine is delicious and appealing, it has a high level of acceptance," he says. "It's not about labeling something; it's about serving fabulous food."

Mediterranean Chopped Salad

2 cups chopped red bell pepper
2 cups chopped zucchini
1 cup chopped yellow or orange bell pepper
1 cup chopped seeded tomato
⅓ cup chopped red onion
¼ cup minced fresh flat-leaf parsley
2 tablespoons red wine vinegar
1 tablespoon extravirgin olive oil
1 teaspoon kosher salt
½ teaspoon black pepper
6 cups chopped romaine lettuce

1. Combine first 10 ingredients in a large bowl; toss well. Cover and chill up to 1 hour. Arrange 1 cup lettuce on each of 6 small plates; top each serving with 2 cups bell pepper mixture. Serve immediately. Yield: 6 servings.

CALORIES 67 (38% from fat); FAT 2.8g (sat 0.4g, mono 1.7g, poly 0.5g); PROTEIN 2.4g; CARB 10.4g; FIBER 3.4g; CHOL 0mg; IRON 1.4mg; SODIUM 328mg; CALC 38mg

---

Yogurt Parfaits with Walnuts, Dates, and Honey

2 (16-ounce) containers vanilla low-fat yogurt
6 tablespoons chopped dates
¼ cup chopped walnuts, toasted
3 tablespoons honey
Ground cinnamon (optional)

1. Spoon yogurt onto several layers of heavy-duty paper towels; spread to ½-inch thickness. Cover with additional towels; let stand 5 minutes. Scrape yogurt into a bowl using a rubber spatula.

2. Spoon ½ cup drained yogurt into each of 6 parfait glasses; top each serving with 1 tablespoon dates, 2 teaspoons walnuts, and 1½ teaspoons honey. Cover and chill 1 hour. Sprinkle with cinnamon, if desired. Yield: 6 servings.

CALORIES 224 (21% from fat); FAT 5.2g (sat 1.5g, mono 1g, poly 2.4g); PROTEIN 8.5g; CARB 38.3g; FIBER 1.3g; CHOL 7mg; IRON 0.4mg; SODIUM 100mg; CALC 270mg

All In Good Time

Problem: An Arizona reader struggles to cook and serve entrées and sides at the same time for company. Strategy: We make preparing multiple dishes manageable with two menus that prove the value of planning.

For Janis Milham of Scottsdale, Arizona, entertaining is about "community and conversation." But when she's cooking for company, she often feels harried.

It's a common dilemma for hosts. Successful entertaining depends on careful planning and preparation. To set main and side dishes on the table at the same time, Milham will need to choose a manageable menu, partially prepare some dishes in advance, and cook others simultaneously. We've developed two menus that put these principles to work. We've also provided a recipe for hors d'oeuvres to buy Milham time before dinner. This approach gives her better control, which means less stress, more time with guests, and a more enjoyable evening for everyone.

Casual Supper Menu
serves 6

Pecorino–Black Pepper Breadsticks

Creamy Artichoke Dip

Chicken Breasts with Gorgonzola-Tomato Salsa

Sautéed Broccoli and Mushrooms

Spicy Potato Wedges

WINE NOTE: This full-flavored menu needs a dramatic wine to stand up to the powerful flavors of black pepper and gorgonzola, plus the vegetable flavors of artichoke and broccoli. In general, when a menu goes in many directions like this, a wise choice is a bracing, fresh white that has acidity to counterbalance a wealth of food flavors. A sauvignon blanc works well. Try Veramonte Sauvignon Blanc Reserva 2006 from Chile ($11).

MAKE AHEAD

Pecorino-Black Pepper Breadsticks

Offered with Creamy Artichoke Dip (recipe below), this savory snack satisfies peckish guests while dinner cooks. You can bake these ahead of time, cool completely, and store at room temperature up to two days.

⅓ cup all-purpose flour (about 1½ ounces)
¼ cup whole wheat flour (about 1¼ ounces)
¼ cup grated fresh pecorino Romano cheese
¾ teaspoon baking powder
½ teaspoon freshly ground black pepper
5 tablespoons water
1 teaspoon extravirgin olive oil
Cooking spray

1. Preheat oven to 450°.
2. Lightly spoon flours into dry measuring cups; level with a knife. Combine flours, cheese, baking powder, and pepper in a medium bowl. Add 5 tablespoons water and oil; stir until dough forms. Turn dough out onto a floured surface; knead lightly 4 or 5 times. Divide dough into 18 equal portions, shaping each portion into an 8-inch rope. Place ropes on a baking sheet coated with cooking spray.
3. Bake at 450° for 10 minutes or until bottoms are golden brown. Remove from oven; cool on a wire rack. Yield: 6 servings (serving size: 3 breadsticks).

CALORIES 64 (27% from fat); FAT 1.9g (sat 0.7g, mono 0.8g, poly 0.7g); PROTEIN 2.7g; CARB 9.3g; FIBER 0.8g; CHOL 3mg; IRON 0.6mg; SODIUM 113mg; CALC 74mg

---

MAKE AHEAD

Creamy Artichoke Dip

Serve with Pecorino–Black Pepper Breadsticks (recipe above). To make this the night before, combine dip ingredients, spoon into the baking dish, cover, and refrigerate. Let stand at room temperature for 30 minutes before baking.

½ cup (4 ounces) block-style fat-free cream cheese, softened
¼ cup reduced-fat mayonnaise
3 tablespoons grated fresh Parmesan cheese
2 teaspoons minced garlic
2 teaspoons fresh lemon juice
½ teaspoon hot pepper sauce (such as Tabasco)
¼ teaspoon kosher salt
¼ teaspoon freshly ground black pepper
2 (9-ounce) packages frozen artichoke hearts (about 2 cups), thawed and chopped
Cooking spray

1. Preheat oven to 350°.
2. Combine first 8 ingredients in a large bowl; stir until well blended. Stir in artichoke hearts. Spoon artichoke mixture into an 8-inch square baking dish coated with cooking spray. Bake at 350° for 30 minutes or until artichoke mixture is hot and begins to brown. Serve warm. Yield: 6 servings (serving size: about ⅓ cup).

CALORIES 72 (30% from fat); FAT 2.4g (sat 0.8g, mono 0.2g, poly 0g); PROTEIN 5.7g; CARB 8.3g; FIBER 4.1g; CHOL 5mg; IRON 0.5mg; SODIUM 352mg; CALC 129mg

---

STAFF FAVORITE

Chicken Breasts with Gorgonzola-Tomato Salsa

Combine the salsa ingredients—except the cheese—up to a few hours before dinner, and store at room temperature.

2 cups chopped tomato
⅓ cup minced red onion
⅓ cup finely chopped fresh basil
2 teaspoons extravirgin olive oil
1 teaspoon kosher salt, divided
6 (6-ounce) skinless, boneless chicken breast halves
¼ teaspoon freshly ground black pepper
Cooking spray
3 tablespoons crumbled Gorgonzola cheese

1. Combine tomato, onion, basil, oil, and ½ teaspoon salt in a medium bowl. Let stand at room temperature.

2. Place each chicken breast half between 2 sheets of heavy-duty plastic wrap; pound each to 1-inch thickness using a meat mallet or small heavy skillet. Sprinkle both sides of chicken with ½ teaspoon salt and pepper.

3. Heat a large nonstick skillet over medium-high heat. Coat pan with cooking spray. Add 3 chicken breast halves to pan; cook 4 minutes on each side or until chicken is browned and done. Remove from pan; keep warm. Repeat procedure with remaining chicken.

4. Stir cheese into tomato mixture. Place 1 chicken breast half on each of 6 plates; top each serving with about ⅓ cup salsa. Yield: 6 servings.

CALORIES 178 (28% from fat); FAT 5.6g (sat 1.8g, mono 2.2g, poly 0.9g); PROTEIN 27.2g; CARB 3.5g; FIBER 1.1g; CHOL 74mg; IRON 1.1mg; SODIUM 426mg; CALC 43mg

---

Logistics Lesson

1. Design a menu that allows dishes to be cooked at different times—some in advance, some later.

2. Devise a game plan. Read recipes over carefully to determine when dishes need to be cooked, where they'll cook, and how much space they'll require. Then sketch out a schedule of what needs to be done, who will do it, and when.

3. Organize ingredients. Have ingredients prepped and easily accessible when it comes time to cook last-minute dishes.

4. Keep appetites in check. Provide guests with light hors d'oeuvres so they won't be overly hungry or impatient for dinner.

5. Work ahead whenever possible. Some dishes must be cooked last minute. Others can be prepared in advance and reheated just before serving. And some dishes have components that can be made ahead. The more work you do in advance, the less pressure you'll face as dinner approaches.

6. Use the stove efficiently. Some foods won't require your immediate attention, such as roasts and braises, which frees you to cook other dishes at the same time on the stovetop.

Sautéed Broccoli and Mushrooms

Because this dish cools down swiftly, prepare just before serving.

    1 tablespoon olive oil
    4 cups sliced mushrooms (about
       ½ pound)
    ¼ cup sliced shallots (about 1)
    ¼ cup dry sherry
    4 cups broccoli florets (about
       1 bunch)
    ½ teaspoon kosher salt
    ½ cup fat-free, less-sodium chicken
       broth
    ¼ teaspoon freshly ground black
       pepper

1. Heat oil in a large Dutch oven over medium-high heat. Add mushrooms and shallots to pan; sauté 10 minutes or until mushrooms are lightly browned. Stir in sherry; cook 2 minutes or until liquid evaporates, stirring frequently.
2. Add broccoli and salt to pan; stir well. Stir in broth; bring to a boil. Cover and cook 5 minutes or until broccoli is crisp-tender. Stir in pepper. Yield: 6 servings (serving size: about ¾ cup).

CALORIES 63 (39% from fat); FAT 2.7g (sat 0.4g, mono 1.7g, poly 0.4g); PROTEIN 4.2g; CARB 6.4g; FIBER 2.2g; CHOL 0mg; IRON 0.9mg; SODIUM 212mg; CALC 29mg

---

Spicy Potato Wedges

This simple side dish is mostly hands-off, which lets you cook other dishes on the stovetop at the same time.

    2½ pounds Yukon gold potatoes, each
        cut lengthwise into 8 wedges
    1½ tablespoons canola oil
    ½   teaspoon kosher salt
    ½   teaspoon garlic powder
    ¼   teaspoon ground red pepper
        Cooking spray

1. Preheat oven to 425°.
2. Combine potatoes and oil in a large bowl, tossing well to coat. Combine salt, garlic powder, and pepper in a small

---

bowl. Sprinkle salt mixture over potatoes, tossing well to coat. Arrange potatoes in a single layer on two baking sheets coated with cooking spray. Bake at 425° for 25 minutes. Turn potato wedges over, and rotate pans; bake an additional 20 minutes or until golden brown. Yield: 6 servings (serving size: about 6 ounces potato wedges).

CALORIES 164 (20% from fat); FAT 3.7g (sat 0.3g, mono 2.1g, poly 1.1g); PROTEIN 3.2g; CARB 29.9g; FIBER 4.6g; CHOL 0mg; IRON 1mg; SODIUM 168mg; CALC 17mg

---

Company's Coming Menu
serves 6

Pecorino-Black Pepper Breadsticks
(page 280)

Creamy Artichoke Dip
(page 280)

Braised Lamb Shanks with Orange and Olives

Mashed Potatoes and Turnips

Haricots Verts with Shallots and Pancetta

Braised Lamb Shanks with Orange and Olives

While this dish takes more than three hours to complete, it can be left unattended much of the time. Nestle the lamb shanks in the pan so they're surrounded by cooking liquid.

    1 tablespoon olive oil
    6 (12-ounce) lamb shanks, trimmed
    ½ teaspoon kosher salt
    ¼ teaspoon freshly ground black
       pepper
    ¼ cup all-purpose flour (about 1
       ounce)
    6 garlic cloves, peeled and crushed
    ½ cup fresh orange juice (about 2
       oranges)
    ½ cup dry white wine
    4 cups fat-free, less-sodium beef
       broth
    1 tablespoon minced fresh thyme
    1 tablespoon tomato paste
    1 tablespoon grated orange rind
    4 kalamata olives, pitted and
       quartered lengthwise

Continued

1. Preheat oven to 350°.

2. Heat oil in a large Dutch oven over medium-high heat. Sprinkle lamb with salt and pepper. Place flour in a shallow dish. Dredge lamb in flour, turning to coat; shake off excess flour. Add 2 shanks to pan; cook 2½ minutes on each side or until browned. Remove from pan. Repeat procedure twice with remaining lamb shanks.

3. Add garlic to pan; sauté 1 minute. Add orange juice, scraping pan to loosen browned bits. Stir in wine; bring to a boil. Cook 3 minutes. Stir in broth, thyme, and tomato paste; return to a boil. Remove from heat.

4. Add lamb to pan; cover and bake at 350° for 2 hours. Stir in rind and olives; bake an additional 30 minutes or until lamb is very tender. Place lamb on a platter; keep warm.

5. Place a large zip-top plastic bag inside a 4-cup glass measure. Pour cooking liquid into bag; let stand 10 minutes (fat will rise to the top). Seal bag; carefully snip off 1 bottom corner of bag. Drain cooking liquid and olives into pan, stopping before fat layer reaches opening; discard fat. Bring cooking liquid to a boil over medium-high heat; cook until reduced to 2 cups (about 20 minutes). Yield: 6 servings (serving size: 1 shank and ⅓ cup sauce).

CALORIES 473 (27% from fat); FAT 14.2g (sat 5.2g, mono 6.5g, poly 0.9g); PROTEIN 73.2g; CARB 8.6g; FIBER 0.6g; CHOL 228mg; IRON 5.9mg; SODIUM 666mg; CALC 38mg

Mashed Potatoes and Turnips

      2   whole cloves
      ½   onion, peeled
      1   pound peeled baking potato, cut into 1-inch pieces
      1   pound peeled turnips, cut into 1-inch pieces
      ¼   cup (1 ounce) finely grated Parmesan cheese
      ¼   cup reduced-fat sour cream
      ½   teaspoon kosher salt
      ¼   teaspoon freshly ground black pepper

1. Push cloves into onion. Place onion, potato, and turnips in a large saucepan; cover with water. Bring to a boil. Reduce heat, and simmer 20 minutes or until potato and turnips are tender; drain. Discard onion and cloves. Return potato mixture to pan.

2. Add cheese, sour cream, salt, and pepper to pan; mash with a potato masher to desired consistency. Yield: 6 servings (serving size: about ⅔ cup).

CALORIES 117 (18% from fat); FAT 2.4g (sat 1.4g, mono 0.3g, poly 0.1g); PROTEIN 3.7g; CARB 20.9g; FIBER 2.8g; CHOL 8mg; IRON 0.5mg; SODIUM 268mg; CALC 83mg

QUICK & EASY
Haricots Verts with Shallots and Pancetta

Chill the pancetta to make it easier to mince. Add ¼ teaspoon freshly ground black pepper to finished beans, if desired.

      Cooking spray
      ½   cup minced pancetta (about 2 ounces)
      ¼   cup thinly sliced shallots
      ¼   cup fat-free, less-sodium chicken broth
      1   tablespoon balsamic vinegar
      1   pound haricots verts, trimmed
      ⅛   teaspoon kosher salt

1. Heat a Dutch oven over medium-high heat. Coat pan with cooking spray. Add pancetta and shallots to pan; sauté 5 minutes or until pancetta is crisp and shallots are tender and lightly browned. Add broth and vinegar to pan, scraping pan to loosen browned bits. Add beans to pan, tossing to coat. Cover and cook 7 minutes or until beans are crisp-tender. Remove from heat; stir in salt. Yield: 6 servings (serving size: about 1⅓ cups).

CALORIES 64 (44% from fat); FAT 3.1g (sat 1.4g, mono 0g, poly 0.1g); PROTEIN 3g; CARB 7g; FIBER 2.6g; CHOL 7mg; IRON 0.9mg; SODIUM 219mg; CALC 30mg

---

Prep List for Casual Supper Menu (page 280)

One day ahead

For hors d'oeuvres:
- Prepare breadsticks.
- Combine ingredients for artichoke dip; spoon into baking dish. Cover dip, and refrigerate.

A few hours ahead

For chicken:
- Chop tomato, red onion, and basil; combine salsa ingredients except for cheese.
- Measure cheese.
- Pound chicken breasts; refrigerate.

For broccoli:
- Slice shallots and mushrooms; chop broccoli. Store in separate containers.
- Measure sherry and chicken broth; store in separate containers.

30 minutes before guests arrive
- Bake artichoke dip.

1 hour before supper
- Preheat oven.
- Cut potato wedges; coat with oil and seasoning.

45 minutes before supper
- Place potatoes in oven.

20 minutes before supper
- Cook first 3 chicken breast halves.
- Turn potatoes.
- Sauté mushrooms and shallots.

12 minutes before supper
- Tent cooked chicken breast halves loosely with foil to keep warm.
- Cook second 3 chicken breast halves.
- Add sherry to mushroom mixture.

8 minutes before supper
- Add broccoli and broth to mushrooms.
- Stir cheese into salsa.

From Our Kitchens to Yours

Gleaned from testing thousands of healthful recipes, here are 10 principles that can bolster your cooking.

Eggs cost just 65 cents per dozen, the Scarsdale Diet was hip, and Ben and Jerry's introduced their Cherry Garcia ice cream flavor when the first issues of *Cooking Light* arrived on newsstands. Today we're still going strong, striving to stay on top of culinary and scientific advances in healthful eating so we can bring more flavor and enjoyment to our recipes—and ultimately to your table.

In looking back over 20 years of recipe testing and food development, we noted that while some principles have remained constant (such as heeding the American Dietetic Association's [ADA] nutrition guidelines), we've created or adapted others, and the concept of what makes a recipe healthful and flavorful continues to evolve. To mark our 20th anniversary, we share here our 10 most important cooking practices.

Cumin-Crusted Pot Roast with Sweet Potatoes and Parsnips

1½ tablespoons instant minced onion
1 tablespoon cumin seeds
1 teaspoon dried oregano
½ teaspoon garlic powder
½ teaspoon freshly ground black pepper
1¼ teaspoons salt, divided
3 pounds boneless chuck roast, trimmed
Cooking spray
4 small onions, each cut into 8 wedges
4 garlic cloves, thinly sliced
2 tablespoons balsamic vinegar
1 (14-ounce) can fat-free, less-sodium beef broth
1 (14.5-ounce) can diced tomatoes, drained
3 cups (½-inch) cubed peeled sweet potatoes
2 cups chopped peeled parsnips
2 cups (½-inch) pieces green bell pepper
⅓ cup chopped fresh parsley

1. Preheat oven to 350°.
2. Combine first 5 ingredients in a spice or coffee grinder; process until finely ground. Stir in ½ teaspoon salt. Lightly coat roast with cooking spray; rub spice mixture over roast.
3. Heat a Dutch oven over medium-high heat. Coat pan with cooking spray. Add roast to pan, and cook 6 minutes, turning to brown on all sides. Remove roast from pan. Add onions to pan; sauté 3 minutes or until lightly browned. Add garlic, and sauté 1 minute. Add vinegar, broth, and tomatoes; bring to a boil. Return roast to pan; cover. Bake at 350° for 2 hours, turning roast after 1 hour.
4. Add potatoes, parsnips, and bell pepper to pan; cover and bake an additional 1 hour or until vegetables are tender. Remove roast from pan, and let stand 15 minutes. Shred meat with 2 forks. Stir ¾ teaspoon salt and parsley into vegetable mixture. Serve roast with vegetable mixture and cooking liquid. Yield: 8 servings (serving size: 3 ounces roast, about 1 cup vegetable mixture, and about ⅓ cup cooking liquid).

CALORIES 324 (33% from fat); FAT 11.8g (sat 3.9g, mono 5.4g, poly 0.5g); PROTEIN 28.8g; CARB 25.3g; FIBER 5.2g; CHOL 82mg; IRON 5mg; SODIUM 591mg; CALC 70mg

Vietnamese Chicken Salad

This crunchy salad embodies the culinary philosophy of balancing contrasting tastes of sweet, sour, salty, and bitter. Increased availability of ethnic ingredients, such as fish sauce, means you can create authentic dishes without a separate trip to a specialty market. Packaged angel hair slaw and matchstick-cut carrots speed preparation.

1 pound skinless, boneless chicken breast
1½ cups chopped green onions, divided
¼ cup fresh lime juice
3 tablespoons sugar
1 garlic clove, minced
2 tablespoons fish sauce
6 cups thinly sliced green cabbage
1 cup matchstick-cut carrot
¾ cup (3 x ⅛–inch) julienne-cut red bell pepper
¾ cup (3 x ⅛–inch) julienne-cut yellow bell pepper
½ cup finely chopped dry roasted peanuts
⅓ cup chopped fresh basil
⅓ cup chopped fresh mint
⅓ cup chopped fresh cilantro

1. Place chicken and ½ cup green onions in a medium saucepan; cover with water. Bring to a boil over medium-high heat; cover, reduce heat, and simmer 5 minutes. Remove from heat; let stand 10 minutes. Drain and discard green onions. Place chicken on a work surface or cutting board, and shred with 2 forks.
2. Combine juice, sugar, and garlic in a small microwave-safe bowl. Cover with plastic wrap; microwave at HIGH 20 seconds or until sugar melts. Cool to room temperature; stir in fish sauce.
3. Combine 1 cup onions, chicken, cabbage, and remaining 7 ingredients in a large bowl. Drizzle with juice mixture; toss well to coat. Cover and let stand 5 minutes before serving. Yield: 6 servings (serving size: about 1½ cups).

CALORIES 215 (25% from fat); FAT 6g (sat 1g, mono 2.6g, poly 1.9g); PROTEIN 22.4g; CARB 20.4g; FIBER 4.6g; CHOL 44mg; IRON 2mg; SODIUM 625mg; CALC 90mg

10 Principles of Healthy Cooking

1. Incorporate Healthful Fats

Using less fat is just part of the picture when it comes to healthful eating. In fact, the years have brought dramatic changes in how health experts view fats. Back in the late 1980s, the concept that some fatty foods might be healthful was a fairly new idea. Now, though, monounsaturated and polyunsaturated fats, found in foods like salmon, avocados, many oils, and nuts, are considered healthful. When these types of fats replace unhealthy saturated and trans fats, they can help reduce harmful LDL cholesterol levels and may lower your risk of stroke and heart disease.

2. All Foods Have a Place in a Healthful Diet

We've never declared certain foods off-limits, but in the early days of our magazine, we avoided high-fat ingredients (especially those high in saturated fat) such as butter, cream, and bacon. The keys are moderation and balance. Indulging in a high-fat treat every now and then won't harm you, so long as your overall diet is healthful—what you eat at one meal isn't as important as the balance of what you eat over a few days or a week.

3. Cook from a Global Pantry

In the early years of *Cooking Light,* ethnic fare seemed a foreign concept to most cooks, though we often spotlighted other cuisines as ways to relish flavorful, low-fat food. Now, once-exotic dishes like pad thai, Indian curries, and Mexican moles have become mainstream, thanks to broader availability of ingredients for these dishes. One great benefit of the availability of global ingredients is you can learn to use them in everyday applications. These concentrated sauces and robust herbs offer ways to add flavor with minimal effort and little or no fat.

4. Seek Quality Ingredients

Splurging on top-notch ingredients can boost taste. A light shaving of the highest quality Parmesan, Parmigiano-Reggiano, imparts maximum flavor. And using a splash of authentic, aged balsamic vinegar makes a world of difference, providing intense yet sweet sharpness.

5. Embellish Convenience Products with Fresh Ones

Our readers are busier than ever. We now include well-chosen convenience products to help speed preparation on busy nights. But there are limitations for some of these products. For a soup made with canned beans and canned tomatoes, for example, we're likely to add fresh herbs, lightly sautéed celery, a squeeze of fresh lemon juice, or a sprinkling of freshly grated cheese. That way, you reap the benefits of time-saving ingredients as well as the spark of the fresh ones.

6. Boost Nutrition by Adding Healthful Ingredients

We look for ways to enhance a dish's nutritional benefits, such as adding whole wheat flour to muffins or wheat germ to a piecrust. Such additions don't alter the texture or taste of the finished dish, but they add fiber, vitamins, antioxidants, or other nutrients.

7. Bake with Precision

Baking requires accuracy to create chemical reactions that ensure cakes stay moist, cookies become crisp, and breads rise. Light baking necessitates even more care, as there's less margin for error when there's less fat to cover up mistakes. Be sure to use the correct equipment—a spouted measuring cup for liquid ingredients and flat measuring cups for dry ingredients. When measuring dry ingredients, weighing them is the most accurate course. Or lightly spoon the item into cups or spoons, and level off excess with the flat side of a knife. For wet ingredients, pour liquid into a spouted measuring cup, place cup on counter, and bend down to check the measurement at eye level.

8. Use a Combination-Fat Approach

In our test kitchens, we've discovered that using only fat-free products in recipes affects flavor and texture. For example, a cheesecake made with egg substitute and fat-free cream cheese has a too-tangy taste and slick appearance and mouthfeel. But using a combination of fat-free and reduced-fat cream cheese, along with a whole egg or two, yields a more luscious, creamy dessert that's still much lower in calories and fat than traditional versions.

9. Balance Ingredients for Harmonious Flavor

When there's less fat to smooth out the taste in a recipe, other salty, sour, or sweet flavors may come to the forefront and overpower the dish. Consider low-fat salad dressings. In traditional vinaigrettes, the ratio of oil to acid might be two to one. In a light vinaigrette, though, the ratio is much lower. If we didn't compensate for that loss of oil with, say, a sweet touch of honey or maple syrup, the dressing would be too tart. Adjusting the sweet component in the dressing rounds out the flavors so the vinaigrette tastes balanced.

10. Brown or Toast to Maximize Flavor

Often, how you cook food is as important as the ingredients you use. For example, we've found toasting spices and nuts heightens their flavor, as does browning meat before braising. Toasting nuts intensifies their nuttiness so you can use fewer. The same principle works for meat—browning creates a caramelized crust that builds flavor in the overall dish.

Chicken and Root Vegetable Potpie

(pictured on page 245)

In the magazine's early days, we shied away from indulgent ingredients like puff pastry. Now, though, we understand that these items can fit into a healthful diet.

    3   cups fat-free, less-sodium chicken broth
 1½   cups frozen green peas, thawed
    1   cup (½-inch) cubed peeled baking potato
    1   cup (½-inch) cubed peeled sweet potato
    1   cup (½-inch) cubed peeled celeriac (celery root)
    1   cup (½-inch-thick) slices parsnip
    1   (10-ounce) package frozen pearl onions
    1   pound skinless, boneless chicken breast, cut into bite-sized pieces
  ⅔   cup all-purpose flour (about 3 ounces), divided
 1½   cups fat-free milk
  ¼   cup chopped fresh parsley
    2   tablespoons chopped fresh thyme
 1½   teaspoons salt
    1   teaspoon freshly ground black pepper
        Cooking spray
    1   sheet frozen puff pastry dough, thawed

1. Preheat oven to 400°.
2. Bring broth to a boil in a large Dutch oven. Add peas and next 5 ingredients; cover, reduce heat, and simmer 6 minutes. Add chicken; cook 5 minutes or until chicken is done. Remove chicken and vegetables from broth with a slotted spoon; place in a large bowl.
3. Increase heat to medium. Lightly spoon flour into dry measuring cups; level with a knife. Place all but 1 tablespoon flour in a medium bowl; gradually add milk, stirring with a whisk until well blended. Add milk mixture to broth; cook 5 minutes or until thick, stirring frequently. Stir in chicken mixture, parsley, thyme, salt, and pepper. Spoon mixture into an 11 x 7–inch baking dish coated with cooking spray.

4. Sprinkle 1 tablespoon flour on a work surface; roll dough into a 13 x 9–inch rectangle. Place dough over chicken mixture, pressing to seal at edges of dish. Cut small slits into dough to allow steam to escape; coat dough lightly with cooking spray. Place dish on a foil-lined baking sheet. Bake at 400° for 16 minutes or until pastry is browned and filling is bubbly. Yield: 8 servings.

CALORIES 388 (30% from fat); FAT 13g (sat 2g, mono 3g, poly 7.1g); PROTEIN 21.9g; CARB 45.7g; FIBER 4.4g; CHOL 34mg; IRON 3mg; SODIUM 790mg; CALC 115mg

Spinach-Apple Salad with Maple-Bacon Vinaigrette

Reduced-fat vinaigrettes can be tricky—too little oil, and the dressing may be too tart. Adding a sweet element (maple syrup) and a sharp/bitter element (mustard) helps achieve harmony.

    1   tablespoon maple syrup
    1   teaspoon red wine vinegar
  ¼   teaspoon Dijon mustard
    1   tablespoon extravirgin olive oil
    1   tablespoon chopped fresh chives
  ¼   teaspoon salt
  ¼   teaspoon freshly ground black pepper
    2   slices center-cut bacon, cooked and crumbled
 2½   cups julienne-cut Granny Smith apple (about 1 apple)
  ¼   cup thinly vertically sliced red onion
    1   (6-ounce) package fresh baby spinach

1. Combine first 3 ingredients in a small bowl, stirring well with a whisk. Gradually add oil, stirring with a whisk until well blended. Add chives, salt, pepper, and bacon; stir with a whisk until well blended.
2. Combine apple, onion, and spinach in a large bowl. Drizzle with vinaigrette; toss to coat. Serve immediately. Yield: 6 servings (serving size: about 1 cup).

CALORIES 63 (43% from fat); FAT 3g (sat 0.6g, mono 2g, poly 0.3g); PROTEIN 1.5g; CARB 8.7g; FIBER 1.9g; CHOL 2mg; IRON 1.1mg; SODIUM 192mg; CALC 26mg

Glazed Cinnamon-Raisin Tea Bread

Ground flaxseed, found in the baking or organic foods aisle, enhances this loaf with iron, vitamin E, and omega-3 fatty acids. For best results, measure the flour, sugars, and ground flaxseed the same way. Toasting the nuts heightens their flavor so we can call for less.

BREAD:
  ½   cup raisins
  ½   cup golden raisins
    2   cups hot water
  ¾   cup fat-free buttermilk
  ½   cup granulated sugar
  ¼   cup canola oil
  ½   teaspoon almond extract
    1   large egg, lightly beaten
    1   large egg white, lightly beaten
 1½   cups all-purpose flour (about 6¾ ounces)
  ¼   cup ground flaxseed
    1   teaspoon ground cinnamon
  ¾   teaspoon baking powder
  ¼   teaspoon baking soda
  ¼   teaspoon salt
  ⅛   teaspoon ground nutmeg
        Cooking spray

GLAZE:
  ½   cup powdered sugar
    2   teaspoons 1% low-fat milk
    2   teaspoons apple juice
    2   tablespoons sliced almonds, toasted

1. Preheat oven to 350°.
2. To prepare bread, cover raisins with 2 cups hot water in a medium bowl; cover and let stand 5 minutes. Drain.
3. Combine buttermilk and next 5 ingredients in a large bowl; stir with a whisk until well blended. Stir in raisins.
4. Lightly spoon flour into dry measuring cups; level with a knife. Combine flour and next 6 ingredients, stirring with a whisk. Add flour mixture to buttermilk mixture, stirring just until moist. Spoon batter into an 8 x 4–inch loaf pan coated with cooking spray. Bake at 350° for 45 minutes or until a wooden pick inserted *Continued*

in center comes out clean. Cool in pan 10 minutes on a wire rack; remove from pan. Cool completely on wire rack.

5. To prepare glaze, combine powdered sugar, 1% milk, and juice, stirring until smooth. Drizzle glaze evenly over bread; immediately sprinkle with almonds. Yield: 16 servings (serving size: 1 slice).

CALORIES 167 (29% from fat); FAT 5.3g (sat 0.5g, mono 2.6g, poly 1.8g); PROTEIN 3.1g; CARB 27.9g; FIBER 1.4g; CHOL 13mg; IRON 1mg; SODIUM 120mg; CALC 45mg

QUICK AND EASY
Cavatappi with Prosciutto and Parmesan

This simple pasta toss relies on a few well-chosen, high-quality ingredients. Ensure success with Italian imports: extravirgin olive oil; buttery imported prosciutto from Parma; and nutty, complex Parmigiano-Reggiano, also from Parma.

½ pound uncooked cavatappi
Cooking spray
1 garlic clove, minced
2 tablespoons extravirgin olive oil
1 tablespoon finely chopped fresh parsley
½ teaspoon salt
½ teaspoon freshly ground black pepper
1 ounce very thin slices prosciutto, cut into thin strips
¼ cup (1 ounce) shaved fresh Parmigiano-Reggiano cheese

1. Cook pasta according to package directions, omitting salt and fat. Drain in a colander over a bowl, reserving 3 tablespoons cooking liquid.
2. Heat pan over medium heat. Coat pan with cooking spray. Add garlic, and sauté 1 minute. Remove from heat. Add reserved 3 tablespoons cooking liquid and pasta to pan; let stand 2 minutes. Stir in oil and next 4 ingredients; sprinkle with cheese. Serve immediately. Yield: 4 servings (serving size: 1 cup pasta mixture and 1 tablespoon cheese).

CALORIES 313 (30% from fat); FAT 10.4g (sat 2.7g, mono 5.6g, poly 0.8g); PROTEIN 12.4g; CARB 43g; FIBER 1.9g; CHOL 11mg; IRON 2.1mg; SODIUM 555mg; CALC 103mg

Crisp Salmon with Lemony Spinach and Potatoes

All you need to round out this nutritious meal is a whole-grain dinner roll. Salmon and olive oil provide heart-healthy monounsaturated fat; the salmon also contributes omega-3 fatty acids. Japanese-style breadcrumbs, known as panko, are now widely available in supermarkets, and we often use them to create a crunchy crust on oven-fried fish and poultry.

2 large peeled baking potatoes, cut into 1-inch pieces (about 2¼ pounds)
⅓ cup fat-free buttermilk
¾ teaspoon salt, divided
¾ teaspoon black pepper, divided
1 teaspoon grated lemon rind, divided
2 teaspoons lemon juice
⅓ cup panko (Japanese breadcrumbs)
½ teaspoon instant minced onion
½ teaspoon dried oregano
¼ teaspoon paprika
4 (6-ounce) salmon fillets (about 1 inch thick)
1 tablespoon olive oil, divided
2 garlic cloves, minced
2 (6-ounce) packages fresh baby spinach
Oregano sprigs (optional)

1. Preheat oven to 400°.
2. Place potatoes in a saucepan, and cover with water; bring to a boil. Reduce heat, and simmer 15 minutes or until tender; drain. Return potatoes to pan. Add buttermilk, ½ teaspoon salt, ¼ teaspoon pepper, ½ teaspoon lemon rind, and juice; mash with a potato masher. Keep warm.
3. Combine panko, onion, dried oregano, paprika, and ¼ teaspoon pepper in a shallow bowl. Sprinkle salmon evenly with ¼ teaspoon salt. Dredge in panko mixture.
4. Heat 2 teaspoons oil in a large nonstick ovenproof skillet over medium-high heat. Add fish to pan; cook 2 minutes on one side or until browned. Turn fish over; place skillet in oven. Bake at 400° for 6 minutes or until fish flakes

easily when tested with a fork or until desired degree of doneness.
5. While fish cooks, heat 1 teaspoon oil in a large nonstick skillet over medium heat. Add garlic; cook 1 minute, stirring constantly. Gradually add spinach, turning frequently; cook 3 minutes or until spinach wilts. Stir in ½ teaspoon rind and ¼ teaspoon pepper. Arrange ½ cup spinach mixture on each of 4 plates; top each with ¾ cup potato mixture and 1 fillet. Garnish with oregano sprigs, if desired. Serve immediately. Yield: 4 servings.

CALORIES 514 (29% from fat); FAT 16.8g (sat 3.6g, mono 8.1g, poly 3.6g); PROTEIN 43.6g; CARB 48.1g; FIBER 5.5g; CHOL 87mg; IRON 4.9mg; SODIUM 703mg; CALC 127mg

Roast Chicken with Mushroom-Barley Stuffing

Instead of traditional bread stuffing, we've boosted the nutritional profile by using barley. Dried porcini can be pricey, but their deep earthy flavor is crucial.

1 cup dried porcini mushrooms (about 1 ounce)
1 cup boiling water
1 (4-pound) roasting chicken
1¼ teaspoons salt, divided
½ teaspoon black pepper, divided
4 thyme sprigs
1 small onion, quartered
¼ cup all-purpose flour (about 1 ounce)
2 cups fat-free, less-sodium chicken broth, divided
1 tablespoon olive oil
¼ cup chopped shallots
2 (8-ounce) packages presliced button mushrooms
1 cup water
1 cup uncooked quick-cooking barley
2 teaspoons chopped fresh thyme
1½ teaspoons sherry vinegar

1. Combine porcini and 1 cup boiling water; cover and let stand 45 minutes.
2. Preheat oven to 425°.
3. Remove and discard giblets and neck from chicken. Trim excess fat. Starting at

neck cavity, loosen skin from breast and drumsticks by inserting fingers, gently pushing between skin and meat. Rub ¼ teaspoon salt and ¼ teaspoon pepper under loosened skin and over breast and drumsticks. Lift wing tips up and over back; tuck under chicken. Stuff thyme sprigs and onion into body cavity. Tie ends of legs together with twine. Place chicken on a rack in a roasting pan. Bake at 425° for 1 hour or until a thermometer inserted into meaty part of thigh registers 165°. Remove chicken from pan; cover and keep warm.

4. Drain porcini in a colander over a bowl; reserve ⅔ cup liquid. Chop porcini.

5. Place a zip-top plastic bag inside a 2-cup glass measure. Pour chicken drippings into bag; let stand 10 minutes (fat will rise to the top). Seal bag; carefully snip off 1 bottom corner of bag. Drain drippings into a small saucepan, stopping before fat layer reaches opening; discard fat. Lightly spoon flour into a dry measuring cup; level with a knife. Add flour to drippings, stirring with a whisk until smooth; cook 1 minute over medium heat, stirring constantly. Add ⅓ cup mushroom soaking liquid and 1½ cups broth, stirring with a whisk; cook 8 minutes or until thick, stirring frequently with a whisk. Stir in ½ teaspoon salt; cover and keep warm.

6. Heat oil in a medium saucepan over medium-high heat. Add shallots to pan; sauté 3 minutes. Add porcini and button mushrooms; sauté 4 minutes or until tender. Stir half of mushroom mixture into gravy; cover and keep warm. Add ½ cup broth, ½ teaspoon salt, ¼ teaspoon pepper, ⅓ cup mushroom soaking liquid, 1 cup water, and barley to remaining mushroom mixture in medium saucepan. Bring to a boil; reduce heat, and simmer 10 minutes or until barley is tender. Stir in chopped thyme and vinegar. Remove and discard skin from chicken. Serve chicken with stuffing and gravy. Yield: 6 servings (serving size: 4 ounces meat, about ½ cup stuffing, and ⅓ cup gravy).

CALORIES 386 (26% from fat); FAT 11.1g (sat 2.6g, mono 4.7g, poly 2.5g); PROTEIN 38g; CARB 32.6g; FIBER 7.5g; CHOL 89mg; IRON 4.2mg; SODIUM 739mg; CALC 31mg

QUICK & EASY
Pasta with Vodka Cream Sauce

Although the dish uses canned tomatoes and broth for convenience, it tastes fresh because of the basil stirred in at the end.

½ pound uncooked penne pasta
1 tablespoon olive oil
½ cup finely chopped onion
1 teaspoon salt, divided
¼ teaspoon crushed red pepper
1 garlic clove, minced
½ cup vodka
¼ cup fat-free, less-sodium chicken broth
1 (14.5-ounce) can no-salt-added diced tomatoes, undrained
¼ cup whipping cream
3 tablespoons thinly sliced fresh basil

1. Cook pasta according to package directions, omitting salt and fat. Drain and keep warm.

2. Heat oil in a large nonstick skillet over medium-high heat. Add onion to pan; sauté 4 minutes or until tender. Add ¼ teaspoon salt, pepper, and garlic; sauté 1 minute. Add vodka; bring to a boil. Reduce heat, and simmer 3 minutes or until liquid is reduced by about half. Stir in ½ teaspoon salt, broth, and tomatoes; bring to a boil. Reduce heat, and simmer 8 minutes. Place tomato mixture in a blender. Remove center piece of blender lid (to allow steam to escape); secure blender lid on blender. Place a clean towel over opening in blender lid (to avoid splatters). Process until smooth. Return tomato mixture to pan; stir in cream. Cook 2 minutes over medium heat, stirring constantly. Remove from heat. Stir in pasta, ¼ teaspoon salt, and basil. Serve immediately. Yield: 4 servings (serving size: 1 cup).

CALORIES 354 (25% from fat); FAT 9.9g (sat 3.9g, mono 4.1g, poly 0.6g); PROTEIN 8.5g; CARB 48.6g; FIBER 3.1g; CHOL 20mg; IRON 1.2mg; SODIUM 662mg; CALC 36mg

STAFF FAVORITE • MAKE AHEAD
Lemon-Lime Layer Cake

To create a nutritionally sound cake that's moist and tender with luscious frosting, we use a combination of full-fat (butter), reduced-fat (⅓-less-fat cream cheese), and fat-free (egg substitute) ingredients. As with any baked good—especially one that's light—measure all ingredients carefully.

CAKE:
Cooking spray
1½ cups granulated sugar
½ cup butter, softened
¾ cup egg substitute
1 tablespoon grated lemon rind
1 tablespoon grated lime rind
1 tablespoon fresh lime juice
2¼ cups all-purpose flour (about 10 ounces)
1½ teaspoons baking powder
1 teaspoon baking soda
½ teaspoon salt
1⅓ cups low-fat buttermilk

ICING:
1 teaspoon grated lemon rind
1 teaspoon grated lime rind
1 teaspoon fresh lime juice
1 (8-ounce) package ⅓-less-fat cream cheese, softened
2½ cups powdered sugar, sifted (about 10 ounces)

Continued

1. Preheat oven to 350°.

2. To prepare cake, coat 2 (9-inch) round cake pans with cooking spray; line bottoms of pans with wax paper. Coat wax paper with cooking spray.

3. Place granulated sugar and butter in a large bowl; beat with a mixer at medium speed until well blended (about 5 minutes). Add egg substitute and next 3 ingredients; beat well. Lightly spoon flour into dry measuring cups; level with a knife. Combine flour, baking powder, baking soda, and salt, stirring well with a whisk. Add flour mixture and buttermilk alternately to sugar mixture, beginning and ending with flour mixture. Spoon batter into prepared pans; tap pans once on countertop to remove air bubbles.

4. Bake at 350° for 30 minutes or until a wooden pick inserted in center comes out clean. Cool in pans on a wire rack 10 minutes; remove cakes from pans. Carefully peel off wax paper. Cool completely on wire racks coated with cooking spray.

5. To prepare icing, place 1 teaspoon lemon rind and next 3 ingredients in a medium bowl; beat with a mixer at medium speed until smooth (about 1 minute). Gradually add powdered sugar, beating at low speed just until blended (do not overbeat). Cover and chill 30 minutes.

6. Place 1 cake layer on a plate; spread with ½ cup icing. Top with remaining cake layer. Spread remaining icing over top and sides of cake. Chill 1 hour. Store cake loosely covered in refrigerator. Yield: 16 servings (serving size: 1 slice).

CALORIES 319 (28% from fat); FAT 10g (sat 6.1g, mono 2.7g, poly 0.6g); PROTEIN 5.6g; CARB 52.8g; FIBER 0.6g; CHOL 28mg; IRON 1.2mg; SODIUM 334mg; CALC 78mg

dinner tonight
Chili Time

Choose from three styles to warm up any autumn evening.

Chili Menu 1
serves 4

Beef and Beer Chili

Jack and red pepper quesadillas*

Mixed green salad with bottled cilantro dressing

*Coat 1 side of each of 4 (6-inch) whole wheat tortillas with cooking spray. Place tortillas, coated side down, on a large baking sheet. Sprinkle each tortilla with 2 tablespoons shredded Monterey Jack cheese, 2 tablespoons chopped bottled roasted red bell peppers, 1 tablespoon chopped cilantro, and 2 teaspoons sliced green onions. Fold each tortilla in half. Bake at 400° for 5 minutes or until cheese melts. Cut into wedges.

Game Plan

1. While oven preheats for quesadillas:
- Chop ingredients for chili.

2. While chili simmers:
- Assemble quesadillas.

3. While quesadillas bake:
- Toss salad.

Beef and Beer Chili

Cornmeal helps thicken the chili to a satisfying consistency. Serve with a chilled lager.

TOTAL TIME: 41 MINUTES

MAKE-AHEAD TIP: Prepare an extra batch of the chili; freeze in single-serving zip-top plastic bags up to three months. Thaw overnight in the refrigerator, and reheat in the microwave.

1½ cups chopped red onion (about 1 medium)
1 cup chopped red bell pepper (about 1 small)
8 ounces extralean ground beef
2 garlic cloves, minced
1½ tablespoons chili powder
2 teaspoons ground cumin
1 teaspoon sugar
½ teaspoon salt
½ teaspoon dried oregano
1 (19-ounce) can red kidney beans, rinsed and drained
1 (14.5-ounce) can no-salt-added diced tomatoes, undrained
1 (14-ounce) can low-sodium beef broth
1 (12-ounce) bottle beer (such as Budweiser)
1 tablespoon yellow cornmeal
1 tablespoon fresh lime juice

1. Combine first 4 ingredients in a large Dutch oven over medium-high heat. Cook 5 minutes or until beef is browned, stirring to crumble. Stir in chili powder, cumin, sugar, and salt; cook 1 minute. Add oregano and next 4 ingredients; bring to a boil. Reduce heat, and simmer 15 minutes. Stir in cornmeal; cook 5 minutes. Stir in juice. Yield: 4 servings (serving size: 1½ cups).

CALORIES 261 (20% from fat); FAT 5.7g (sat 2.1g, mono 2g, poly 0.2g); PROTEIN 18.3g; CARB 30.3g; FIBER 8.3g; CHOL 30mg; IRON 3.7mg; SODIUM 799mg; CALC 74mg

Chili Menu 2

serves 4

Pork and Hominy Chili

Strawberry agua fresca*

Blue corn tortilla chips

*Combine 2 cups quartered strawberries, 1 cup cold water, 2 tablespoons sugar, and 1 tablespoon chopped fresh mint in a blender; process 2 minutes or until smooth. Strain strawberry mixture through a sieve into a bowl; discard solids. Add 2 cups cold water and 2 teaspoons fresh lemon juice; chill. Serve over ice.

Game Plan

1. Trim and chop pork and vegetables.
2. While pork and vegetables sauté:
   • Quarter strawberries for agua fresca.
3. While chili simmers:
   • Blend ingredients for agua fresca; chill.

QUICK & EASY
Pork and Hominy Chili

TOTAL TIME: 30 MINUTES

FLAVOR TIP: Substitute turkey or chicken breast for the pork, if you prefer.

    2 teaspoons canola oil
    8 ounces boneless center-cut pork
       chops, trimmed and cubed
    1 cup chopped onion (about 1
       medium)
    ¾ cup chopped green bell pepper
    2 teaspoons bottled minced garlic
    1 tablespoon chili powder
    2 teaspoons ground cumin
    ¼ teaspoon salt
    ¼ teaspoon freshly ground black
       pepper
    ⅛ teaspoon ground red pepper
    ¼ cup no-salt-added tomato paste
    1 (15.5-ounce) can golden hominy,
       rinsed and drained
    1 (14.5-ounce) can no-salt-added
       diced tomatoes, undrained
    1 (14-ounce) can fat-free,
       less-sodium chicken broth
    ¼ cup light sour cream

1. Heat oil in a large saucepan over medium-high heat. Add pork to pan; sauté 5 minutes or until lightly browned. Add onion, bell pepper, and garlic; sauté 5 minutes or until tender. Stir in chili powder and next 4 ingredients. Cook 1 minute, stirring constantly. Stir in tomato paste, hominy, tomatoes, and broth; bring to a boil. Reduce heat, and simmer 10 minutes. Serve with sour cream. Yield: 4 servings (serving size: about 1½ cups chili and 1 tablespoon sour cream).

CALORIES 238 (29% from fat); FAT 7.8g (sat 2.5g, mono 3g, poly 1.3g); PROTEIN 17.6g; CARB 24.6g; FIBER 5.2g; CHOL 33mg; IRON 2.1mg; SODIUM 650mg; CALC 61mg

Chili Menu 3

serves 4

Moroccan Chickpea Chili

Orange–green olive salad*

Lavash

*Combine 2 tablespoons honey, 1½ tablespoons fresh lemon juice, 1 tablespoon extravirgin olive oil, ¼ teaspoon ground cumin, and a dash of salt in a small bowl. Arrange 4 cups fresh baby spinach on a serving platter. Cut 4 peeled navel oranges into ¼-inch-thick slices; arrange over spinach. Drizzle with honey mixture; sprinkle with 2 tablespoons chopped green olives.

Game Plan

1. Chop vegetables for chili.
2. While vegetables sauté:
   • Prep remaining chili ingredients.
3. While chili simmers:
   • Prepare salad.

QUICK & EASY
Moroccan Chickpea Chili

This recipe proves you don't need meat to make a hearty chili.

TOTAL TIME: 36 MINUTES

    2   teaspoons olive oil
    1   cup chopped onion
    ¾   cup chopped celery
    ½   cup chopped carrot
    1   teaspoon bottled minced garlic
    2   teaspoons ground cumin
    2   teaspoons paprika
    1   teaspoon ground ginger
    ½   teaspoon ground turmeric
    ¼   teaspoon freshly ground black
        pepper
    ¼   teaspoon salt
    ⅛   teaspoon ground cinnamon
    ⅛   teaspoon ground red pepper
    1½ cups water
    2   tablespoons no-salt-added tomato
        paste
    2   (15½-ounce) cans chickpeas
        (garbanzo beans), rinsed and
        drained
    1   (14.5-ounce) can no-salt-added
        diced tomatoes, undrained
    2   tablespoons chopped fresh
        cilantro
    1   tablespoon fresh lemon juice

1. Heat oil in a large saucepan over medium-high heat. Add onion, celery, carrot, and garlic to pan; sauté 5 minutes. Stir in cumin and next 7 ingredients; cook 1 minute, stirring constantly. Add 1½ cups water, tomato paste, chickpeas, and tomatoes; bring to a boil. Cover, reduce heat, and simmer 20 minutes. Stir in cilantro and juice. Yield: 4 servings (serving size: 1½ cups).

CALORIES 215 (23% from fat); FAT 5.5g (sat 0.4g, mono 2.9g, poly 1.9g); PROTEIN 7.7g; CARB 36.3g; FIBER 9.8g; CHOL 0mg; IRON 3.4mg; SODIUM 534mg; CALC 102mg

Club Class

This California-based *Cooking Light* Supper Club pushes its culinary boundaries by turning monthly gatherings into learning experiences.

Long-standing *Cooking Light* Supper Clubs stay together because members share interests. Beyond a love of good food, for example, the tie that binds the Sacramento-based Kitchen Table Cooking Club is learning. Each monthly get-together has become a kind of culinary class.

The first *Cooking Light* Supper Club started in 1999 in Northern California. Today, hundreds of Supper Clubs gather around the world. Clubs typically unite through postings on the CookingLight.com bulletin board, then meet regularly to cook and eat recipes from the magazine. Many clubs begin by cooking recipes from the current issue of the magazine, progressing to internationally or seasonally themed menus. As a group's repertoire begins to expand, they may eventually branch out and start preparing recipes from other sources. Inevitably, the personalities of members determine the character of their respective clubs. In the case of the Kitchen Table group, the members' strong desire to develop culinary acumen sets their club's course.

Maria Everly cofounded the club six years ago. Since then, the group has explored cuisines from Moroccan to Cajun, techniques from braising to preparing a brunoise (a very fine dice of vegetables), and cookbooks from noted chefs.

Club members' duties revolve. The host picks the theme and is responsible for cooking the main dish; she assigns the rest of the meal to other members. But it's more than just a well-orchestrated potluck. "Often, the host will assign each person a research project—to investigate where the dish came from, the chef who developed the recipe, or any special or seasonal ingredients," says club member Dina Guillen. "Then we share what we learned."

Wine Country Menu
serves 6

Champagne Pomegranate Cocktail

Mixed Greens Salad with Pears, Goat Cheese, and Fig Vinaigrette

Mini Crab Cakes with Herbed Aïoli

Cedar Plank–Grilled Salmon with Avocado-Orange Salsa
or
Rosemary-Scented Cornish Hens with Red Wine Reduction

Roasted Asparagus with Dijon-Lemon Sauce

Farro with Wild Mushrooms

Raspberry Frozen Yogurt

QUICK & EASY
Champagne Pomegranate Cocktail

4 cups crushed ice
2 cups pomegranate juice
½ cup ginger ale
¼ cup brandy
1 (750-milliliter) bottle Champagne or sparkling wine
Pomegranate seeds (optional)

1. Combine first 5 ingredients in a pitcher. Pour about 1 cup Champagne mixture into each of 8 glasses. Garnish with seeds, if desired. Yield: 8 servings.

CALORIES 125 (0% from fat); FAT 0g; PROTEIN 0.3g; CARB 11.7g; FIBER 0g; CHOL 0mg; IRON 0.1mg; SODIUM 9mg; CALC 10mg

---

Mixed Greens Salad with Pears, Goat Cheese, and Fig Vinaigrette

The vinaigrette's sweet-tart taste makes it well suited as a marinade for grilled or roasted pork and chicken.

6 cups mixed salad greens
1½ cups thinly sliced, cored Bosc pear (about 1)
¼ cup (1 ounce) crumbled goat cheese
6 tablespoons Fig Vinaigrette

1. Place 1 cup greens on each of 6 plates; top each serving with ¼ cup pear and 2 teaspoons goat cheese. Drizzle 1 tablespoon vinaigrette over each serving; serve immediately. Yield: 6 servings.

(Totals include Fig Vinaigrette) CALORIES 84 (28% from fat); FAT 2.6g (sat 0.9g, mono 1.2g, poly 0.3g); PROTEIN 2.3g; CARB 14.2g; FIBER 3g; CHOL 2mg; IRON 1.1mg; SODIUM 95mg; CALC 57mg

FIG VINAIGRETTE:

½ cup balsamic vinegar
5 dried Black Mission figs, stemmed and coarsely chopped
6 tablespoons water
1 tablespoon fresh lemon juice
2 tablespoons minced shallots
1 teaspoon minced fresh thyme
1 garlic clove, minced
1 tablespoon extravirgin olive oil
¼ teaspoon salt

1. Combine vinegar and figs in a small saucepan over high heat, and bring to a boil. Reduce heat, and simmer until reduced to ⅓ cup (about 5 minutes). Combine fig mixture, 6 tablespoons water, and lemon juice in a blender, and process until smooth.
2. Place fig mixture in a small bowl. Stir in shallots, thyme, and garlic. Add oil and salt; stir well with a whisk. Yield: about ⅔ cup (serving size: 1 tablespoon).

CALORIES 46 (27% from fat); FAT 1.4g (sat 0.2g, mono 1g, poly 0.2g); PROTEIN 0.4g; CARB 8.3g; FIBER 1g; CHOL 0mg; IRON 0.2mg; SODIUM 64mg; CALC 17mg

Mini Crab Cakes with Herbed Aïoli

(pictured on page 247)

Garnish these delicate cakes with chives, and serve with lemon wedges.

AÏOLI:

- ½ cup reduced-fat mayonnaise
- 2 teaspoons chopped fresh chives
- 2 teaspoons chopped fresh parsley
- 2 teaspoons fresh lemon juice
- 1 garlic clove, minced

CRAB CAKES:

- ¼ cup finely chopped red bell pepper
- 3 tablespoons reduced-fat mayonnaise
- 1 tablespoon chopped fresh chives
- 1 tablespoon chopped fresh parsley
- 2 teaspoons Dijon mustard
- 2 teaspoons fresh lemon juice
- 1 teaspoon Worcestershire sauce
- ½ teaspoon freshly ground black pepper
- ¾ cup panko (Japanese breadcrumbs)
- 1 pound lump crabmeat, shell pieces removed
- 1 teaspoon canola oil
- Cooking spray

1. Preheat oven to 350°.
2. To prepare aïoli, combine first 5 ingredients in a small bowl; set aside.
3. To prepare crab cakes, combine bell pepper and next 7 ingredients in a large bowl; stir well with a whisk. Add panko and crabmeat; toss gently. Divide crab mixture into 12 equal portions, shaping each into a 1-inch-thick patty.
4. Heat oil in a large ovenproof skillet coated with cooking spray over medium-high heat. Add patties; cook 2 minutes. Carefully turn patties over. Place pan in oven; bake at 350° for 6 minutes. Yield: 6 servings (serving size: 2 crab cakes and about 1 tablespoon aïoli).

CALORIES 150 (34% from fat); FAT 5.6g (sat 0.3g, mono 0.5g, poly 0.2g); PROTEIN 17.2g; CARB 9.9g; FIBER 0.5g; CHOL 56mg; IRON 0.5mg; SODIUM 567mg; CALC 59mg

Cedar Plank–Grilled Salmon with Avocado-Orange Salsa

- 1 (15 x 6½ x ⅜–inch) cedar grilling plank
- ¼ cup maple syrup
- 2 tablespoons Cointreau (orange-flavored liqueur)
- 1 teaspoon grated orange rind
- ½ teaspoon salt, divided
- ¼ teaspoon freshly ground black pepper, divided
- 6 (6-ounce) salmon fillets (about 1 inch thick)
- 1 cup orange sections (about 2 oranges)
- ¾ cup diced peeled avocado (about 1)
- ¼ cup fresh orange juice (about 1 orange)
- 2 tablespoons finely chopped red onion
- 2 tablespoons finely chopped red bell pepper
- 1 tablespoon finely chopped fresh chives
- 1 tablespoon fresh lime juice

1. Immerse and soak plank in water 1 hour; drain.
2. Prepare grill.
3. Combine syrup, Cointreau, and rind in a small saucepan; bring to a boil. Cook until reduced to ¼ cup (about 3 minutes). Cool 5 minutes. Sprinkle ¼ teaspoon salt and ⅛ teaspoon black pepper over fish; brush fish with syrup mixture.
4. Place plank on grill rack, and grill 3 minutes or until lightly charred. Carefully turn plank over, and place fish on charred side of plank. Cover and grill 12 minutes or until fish flakes easily when tested with a fork or until desired degree of doneness.
5. Combine ¼ teaspoon salt, ⅛ teaspoon black pepper, orange sections, and remaining 6 ingredients in a medium bowl; serve with fish. Yield: 6 servings (serving size: 1 salmon fillet and ¼ cup salsa).

CALORIES 425 (46% from fat); FAT 21.5g (sat 4.2g, mono 8.4g, poly 7.1g); PROTEIN 34.8g; CARB 19.8g; FIBER 2.2g; CHOL 100mg; IRON 1.1mg; SODIUM 298mg; CALC 55mg

WINE NOTE: Salmon works with many white wines, but when the nutty, woodsy flavor of a charred cedar plank is factored in, serve a California chardonnay. It, too, has nutty woodsy flavors, and a creamy, citrusy chardonnay will also mirror the creaminess of the avocado and the citrusiness of the orange. Try Geyser Peak Winery Chardonnay 2005 from Alexander Valley, California ($13).

Entertain with Ease Menu

serves 6

Try this menu for your next dinner party.

Rosemary-Scented Cornish Hens with Red Wine Reduction

Double walnut rice pilaf*

Sautéed Broccolini

*Heat 2 teaspoons olive oil in a large saucepan over medium-high heat. Add ¼ cup chopped fresh shallots to pan; sauté 3 minutes. Add 2 minced garlic cloves; sauté 1 minute. Add 1 cup uncooked long-grain rice; sauté 1 minute. Stir in 2 cups fat-free, less-sodium chicken broth; bring to a boil. Cover, reduce heat, and cook 20 minutes or until liquid is absorbed. Stir in 2 tablespoons chopped fresh chives and 2 tablespoons toasted walnut oil. Top with ¼ cup toasted walnuts.

Rosemary-Scented Cornish Hens with Red Wine Reduction

The hens need only a small drizzle of the intensely flavorful sauce.

- 3 (1¼-pound) Cornish hens
- 3 tablespoons stone-ground mustard
- 2 teaspoons minced fresh rosemary
- ¾ teaspoon kosher salt
- ½ teaspoon freshly ground black pepper
- 5 garlic cloves, minced and divided
- Cooking spray
- ½ cup dry red wine
- ½ cup fat-free, less-sodium chicken broth
- 2 tablespoons fresh lemon juice
- 2 teaspoons honey

Continued

1. Remove and discard giblets and necks from hens; trim excess fat. Split hens in half lengthwise. Starting at neck cavity, loosen skin from hens by inserting fingers, gently pushing between skin and meat. Combine mustard, rosemary, salt, pepper, and 3 garlic cloves to form a paste; rub mustard mixture under loosened skin. Place hen halves, meaty sides up, on a broiler pan coated with cooking spray. Chill 30 minutes.

2. Preheat oven to 425°.

3. Bake hens at 425° for 30 minutes or until a thermometer registers 165°. Place hens on a platter; keep warm.

4. Place a zip-top plastic bag inside a 2-cup glass measure. Pour drippings from pan into bag; let stand 10 minutes (fat will rise to the top). Seal bag; snip off 1 bottom corner of bag. Drain drippings into a nonstick skillet, stopping before fat layer reaches opening; discard fat.

5. Add wine to drippings in pan; bring to a boil over medium-high heat. Cook until reduced to ¼ cup (about 3 minutes). Stir in broth, juice, honey, and 2 garlic cloves; cook until reduced to ¼ cup (about 2 minutes). Remove mixture from heat.

6. Remove skin from hens; discard. Drizzle each hen with 2 teaspoons wine mixture. Serve immediately. Yield: 6 servings (serving size: ½ hen).

CALORIES 345 (25% from fat); FAT 9.5g (sat 2.4g, mono 3g, poly 2.3g); PROTEIN 57.3g; CARB 3.7g; FIBER 0.2g; CHOL 258mg; IRON 2.3mg; SODIUM 565mg; CALC 42mg

QUICK & EASY
Roasted Asparagus with Dijon-Lemon Sauce

2 pounds asparagus spears, trimmed
4 teaspoons extravirgin olive oil, divided
½ teaspoon kosher salt
2 garlic cloves, minced
1 teaspoon grated lemon rind
2 tablespoons fresh lemon juice
½ teaspoon Dijon mustard
¼ teaspoon freshly ground black pepper
1 tablespoon chopped fresh parsley

1. Preheat oven to 425°.

2. Combine asparagus, 2 teaspoons oil, salt, and garlic in a large bowl, tossing well to coat. Arrange asparagus mixture in a single layer on a baking sheet. Bake at 425° for 12 minutes or until crisp-tender.

3. Combine 2 teaspoons oil, rind, juice, mustard, and pepper in a small bowl, stirring with a whisk. Arrange asparagus on a platter; drizzle juice mixture over asparagus. Sprinkle with parsley. Yield: 6 servings.

CALORIES 60 (50% from fat); FAT 3.3g (sat 0.5g, mono 2.2g, poly 0.6g); PROTEIN 3.4g; CARB 6.8g; FIBER 3.3g; CHOL 0mg; IRON 3.3mg; SODIUM 166mg; CALC 40mg

Farro with Wild Mushrooms

Farro is a type of wheat. It's popular in Italy, especially cooked in a pilaf that highlights its firm, chewy texture.

2 cups hot water
¾ cup dried porcini mushrooms (about ¾ ounce)
1 tablespoon olive oil
2 cups sliced cremini mushrooms
2 cups chopped onion
3 garlic cloves, minced
1 cup farro
½ cup dry red wine
1 teaspoon chopped fresh thyme
¼ teaspoon kosher salt
¼ teaspoon freshly ground black pepper
1 (14-ounce) can fat-free, less-sodium beef broth
6 tablespoons grated Parmigiano-Reggiano cheese

1. Place 2 cups hot water and porcini mushrooms in a small bowl; cover and let stand 20 minutes or until tender. Drain mushrooms in a fine sieve over a bowl, reserving liquid. Coarsely chop porcini.

2. Heat oil in a large saucepan over medium-high heat. Add porcini mushrooms, cremini mushrooms, onion, and garlic to pan; sauté 6 minutes. Stir in farro, and cook 1 minute, stirring occasionally. Add wine; cook 1 minute

or until most of liquid evaporates. Add reserved mushroom liquid, thyme, salt, pepper, and broth; bring to a boil. Reduce heat, and simmer 45 minutes or until most of liquid evaporates, stirring occasionally. Remove from heat; stir in cheese. Yield: 6 servings (serving size: ¾ cup).

CALORIES 178 (23% from fat); FAT 4.5g (sat 1.2g, mono 2.1g, poly 0.3g); PROTEIN 7.6g; CARB 29.6g; FIBER 1.8g; CHOL 4mg; IRON 2.2mg; SODIUM 309mg; CALC 84mg

STAFF FAVORITE • MAKE AHEAD
FREEZABLE
Raspberry Frozen Yogurt

This light, refreshing dessert makes an ideal finish for a multicourse meal. Serve with biscotti.

2 cups vanilla low-fat yogurt
½ cup whole milk
¼ cup sugar
1 (10-ounce) package frozen raspberries in light syrup, thawed
Fresh raspberries (optional)

1. Combine first 3 ingredients in a large bowl; stir until sugar dissolves.

2. Place thawed raspberries in a blender; process until smooth. Strain puree through a fine sieve over a bowl. Discard seeds. Add puree to yogurt mixture.

3. Pour raspberry mixture into freezer can of an ice-cream freezer; freeze according to manufacturer's instructions. Spoon into a freezer-safe container; cover and freeze 1 hour or until firm. Garnish with fresh raspberries, if desired. Yield: 8 servings (serving size: ½ cup).

CALORIES 100 (12% from fat); FAT 1.3g (sat 0.8g, mono 0.3g, poly 0.1g); PROTEIN 3.8g; CARB 18.6g; FIBER 0.5g; CHOL 5mg; IRON 0.2mg; SODIUM 47mg; CALC 124mg

Farewell Summer

Step out to the patio, and savor one last alfresco supper.

End-of-Summer Supper Menu
serves 8

Tomato Tapenade

Grilled Blue Cheese Burgers

Black Bean, Rice, and Sweet Corn Salad

Greens Tossed with Sherry-Fig Vinaigrette

Zinfandel

Snickerdoodles

Iced coffee

MAKE AHEAD
Tomato Tapenade

Make the oil and oven-dried tomato mixture up to two days ahead and refrigerate; let it stand at room temperature for about 15 minutes before serving.

- ½ cup pitted kalamata olives
- 2 teaspoons chopped fresh rosemary
- 2 teaspoons chopped fresh oregano
- 4 garlic cloves, minced
- 2½ pounds plum tomatoes, halved and seeded
- Cooking spray
- 2 tablespoons olive oil
- ¼ teaspoon pepper
- 24 (½-ounce) slices French bread, toasted
- 2 tablespoons thinly sliced fresh basil

1. Preheat oven to 300°.
2. Combine first 5 ingredients on a jelly-roll pan coated with cooking spray. Drizzle tomato mixture with oil; toss to coat. Arrange tomatoes in a single layer, cut sides up. Bake at 300° for 2 hours and 15 minutes. Cool and coarsely chop. Stir in pepper. Serve on bread slices, and garnish with basil. Yield: 8 servings (serving size: about 5 tablespoons tomato mixture, 3 bread slices, and about ½ teaspoon basil).

CALORIES 196 (27% from fat); FAT 5.9g (sat 0.8g, mono 4.1g, poly 0.8g); PROTEIN 5.2g; CARB 33.3g; FIBER 2.4g; CHOL 0mg; IRON 2.1mg; SODIUM 411mg; CALC 15mg

---

STAFF FAVORITE • MAKE AHEAD
Grilled Blue Cheese Burgers

Shape the patties the night before, and chill until you're ready to grill. Set out lettuce, sliced tomato, thin red onion rings, Dijon mustard, and reduced-fat mayonnaise so guests can build their own burgers.

- 2 (1-ounce) slices country white bread
- 2 tablespoons fat-free milk
- ½ teaspoon salt
- ½ teaspoon pepper
- 2 pounds lean ground sirloin
- ½ cup (2 ounces) crumbled blue cheese
- Cooking spray
- 8 hamburger rolls, halved

1. Prepare grill.
2. Place bread in a food processor; process 30 seconds or until finely ground. Place breadcrumbs in a large bowl. Add milk to breadcrumbs; toss with a fork to moisten. Add salt, pepper, and beef to breadcrumb mixture, stirring just until combined. Divide meat mixture into 16 equal portions, shaping each into a 3½-inch patty. Spoon 1 tablespoon cheese in center of each of 8 patties; top each with 1 patty, pinching edges to seal.
3. Place patties on grill rack coated with cooking spray; grill 4 minutes on each side or until desired degree of doneness. Remove from heat; keep warm.
4. Lightly coat cut sides of rolls with cooking spray; place cut sides down on grill rack, and grill 30 seconds or until toasted. Serve patties on toasted rolls with desired toppings. Yield: 8 servings (serving size: 1 burger).

CALORIES 355 (34% from fat); FAT 13.3g (sat 5.4g, mono 4.9g, poly 1.5g); PROTEIN 24.6g; CARB 32.2g; FIBER 1.4g; CHOL 61mg; IRON 4mg; SODIUM 621mg; CALC 135mg

---

WINE NOTE: Enjoy a bottle of American zinfandel with this menu. Pietra Santa Zinfandel 2003 ($16) is loaded with jammy blackberry and raspberry fruit, along with smoky oak and hints of Chinese five spice that go great with grilled flavors.

MAKE AHEAD
Black Bean, Rice, and Sweet Corn Salad

- 1 cup water
- 1 teaspoon salt, divided
- ½ cup long-grain rice
- 6 tablespoons fresh lime juice (about 2 large limes)
- 2 tablespoons extravirgin olive oil
- ¼ teaspoon freshly ground black pepper
- 1 garlic clove, minced
- 1 cup rinsed and drained canned black beans
- 1 cup fresh corn kernels (about 2 ears)
- ¼ cup chopped fresh cilantro

1. Combine 1 cup water and ½ teaspoon salt in a large, heavy saucepan; bring to a boil. Add rice to pan. Cover, reduce heat, and simmer 20 minutes or until liquid is absorbed. Fluff with a fork.
2. Combine ½ teaspoon salt, juice, oil, pepper, and garlic in a large bowl. Add rice and beans; toss to coat. Let stand 15 minutes or until completely cool. Stir in corn and cilantro. Yield: 8 servings (serving size: about ⅓ cup).

CALORIES 111 (30% from fat); FAT 3.7g (sat 0.5g, mono 2.6g, poly 0.5g); PROTEIN 2.8g; CARB 18.5g; FIBER 2.2g; CHOL 0mg; IRON 1.1mg; SODIUM 387mg; CALC 16mg

Greens Tossed with Sherry-Fig Vinaigrette

Serve the extra dressing with grilled seafood or pork tenderloin.

½ cup chopped prosciutto
½ cup diced red onion
8 cups torn romaine lettuce
1 (6-ounce) package fresh baby spinach
1 cup Sherry-Fig Vinaigrette

1. Cook prosciutto in a medium skillet over medium heat 3 minutes or until crisp. Add onion to pan; cook 1 minute. Combine prosciutto mixture, romaine, and spinach in a large bowl. Add 1 cup Sherry-Fig Vinaigrette; toss well. Yield: 8 servings (serving size: 2 cups).

(Totals include Sherry-Fig Vinaigrette) CALORIES 71 (28% from fat); FAT 2.2g (sat 0.6g, mono 0.1g, poly 0.6g); PROTEIN 4.1g; CARB 9.4g; FIBER 1.9g; CHOL 9mg; IRON 1.4mg; SODIUM 266mg; CALC 54mg

SHERRY-FIG VINAIGRETTE:
1 garlic clove
⅓ cup sherry wine vinegar
¼ cup fresh orange juice
2 teaspoons grapeseed oil
2 teaspoons sugar
1 teaspoon dried rosemary
½ teaspoon black pepper
¼ teaspoon kosher salt
1 (15-ounce) can whole figs in syrup, drained

1. With food processor on, drop garlic through food chute; process until finely chopped. Add vinegar and remaining ingredients; process until smooth. Yield: 1½ cups (serving size: 1 tablespoon).

CALORIES 16 (23% from fat); FAT 0.4g (sat 0g, mono 0.1g, poly 0.3g); PROTEIN 0.1g; CARB 3.1g; FIBER 0.4g; CHOL 0mg; IRON 0.1mg; SODIUM 20mg; CALC 6mg

---

Snickerdoodles

¾ cup granulated sugar
⅔ cup light brown sugar
½ cup butter, softened
1 teaspoon vanilla extract
1 large egg
1½ cups all-purpose flour (about 6¾ ounces)
1 teaspoon baking powder
½ teaspoon ground cinnamon
¼ teaspoon salt
⅓ cup granulated sugar
1½ teaspoons ground cinnamon
Cooking spray

1. Preheat oven to 400°.
2. Combine first 3 ingredients in a medium bowl; beat with a mixer at medium speed until light and fluffy. Beat in vanilla and egg.
3. Lightly spoon flour into dry measuring cups; level with a knife. Combine flour, baking powder, ½ teaspoon cinnamon, and salt, stirring well with a whisk. Add flour mixture to butter mixture, and beat just until combined. Shape dough into 30 balls.
4. Combine ⅓ cup granulated sugar and 1½ teaspoons cinnamon in a small shallow dish. Roll balls in sugar mixture, and place 2 inches apart on baking sheets coated with cooking spray. Bake at 400° for 8 minutes or until tops crack. Cool on pans 1 minute. Remove from pans; cool on a wire rack. Yield: 30 cookies (serving size: 1 cookie).

CALORIES 99 (30% from fat); FAT 3.3g (sat 2g, mono 0.9g, poly 0.2g); PROTEIN 0.9g; CARB 16.9g; FIBER 0.3g; CHOL 15mg; IRON 0.5mg; SODIUM 59mg; CALC 17mg

---

on hand
Secrets of Saffron

This exotic ingredient gives dishes vivid color and distinctive taste.

Saffron enchants with its luminous red-orange color, delicate bittersweet flavor, and honeylike fragrance. Cuisines around the world prize the spice, and contemporary chefs admire it, too.

High-quality, 100 percent pure red saffron threads cost about $12 for approximately two teaspoons, and it's a delicious investment. Saffron is remarkably versatile in cooking, as our recipes demonstrate.

Saffron Kulfi

Kulfi is South Asian ice cream. This dessert, which requires no special equipment, earned our highest rating.

2 tablespoons water
⅛ teaspoon saffron threads, crushed
¾ cup whipping cream
⅛ teaspoon salt
⅛ teaspoon ground cardamom
⅛ teaspoon ground cinnamon
1 (14-ounce) can fat-free sweetened condensed milk
1 (12-ounce) can evaporated fat-free milk

1. Combine 2 tablespoons water and saffron in a small microwave-safe bowl; microwave at HIGH 20 seconds.
2. Combine saffron mixture and remaining ingredients in an 8-inch square baking dish, stirring with a whisk. Cover with plastic wrap; freeze 8 hours or overnight. Let soften slightly at room temperature before serving. Yield: 10 servings (serving size: ½ cup).

CALORIES 246 (25% from fat); FAT 6.7g (sat 4.2g, mono 1.9g, poly 0.3g); PROTEIN 7.5g; CARB 38.5g; FIBER 0g; CHOL 33mg; IRON 0.1mg; SODIUM 136mg; CALC 264mg

Swedish Saffron Bread

Traditionally served in Sweden on December 13 to commemorate St. Lucia, this light, rich-tasting bread is great anytime and makes a fitting accompaniment for breakfast or brunch.

    1   cup hot water
    ½   cup golden raisins
    ¼   cup dried currants
    ¼   cup sugar, divided
    ½   teaspoon saffron threads, crushed
    1   package dry yeast (about 2¼ teaspoons)
    1   cup warm 2% reduced-fat milk (100° to 110°)
    3⅓ cups all-purpose flour, divided (about 15 ounces)
    1   teaspoon salt
    ½   teaspoon ground cinnamon
    3   tablespoons butter, melted
    2   large eggs, divided and lightly beaten
        Cooking spray

1. Combine first 3 ingredients. Cover and let stand 10 minutes or until raisins and currants plump. Drain and set aside.
2. Dissolve 1 tablespoon sugar, saffron, and yeast in milk in a small bowl; let stand 5 minutes. Lightly spoon flour into dry measuring cups; level with a knife. Combine 3 cups flour, 3 tablespoons sugar, salt, and cinnamon in a large bowl. Add raisins, currants, yeast mixture, butter, and 1 egg to flour mixture; stir until dough forms a ball.
3. Turn dough out onto a lightly floured surface. Knead until smooth and elastic (about 10 minutes); add enough of remaining flour, 1 tablespoon at a time, to prevent dough from sticking to hands.
4. Place dough in a large bowl coated with cooking spray, turning to coat top. Cover and let rise in a warm place (85°), free from drafts, 1 hour or until doubled in size. (Gently press two fingers into dough. If indentation remains, dough has risen enough.) Punch dough down. Turn out onto a lightly floured surface; knead 3 times.
5. Divide dough into 3 equal portions, shaping each portion into a 16-inch rope. Place ropes lengthwise on a baking sheet coated with cooking spray (do not stretch); pinch ends together at one end to seal. Braid ropes; pinch loose ends to seal. Cover and let rise 1 hour or until doubled in size.
6. Preheat oven to 375°.
7. Gently brush dough with 1 egg. Bake at 375° for 25 minutes or until loaf sounds hollow when tapped. Remove from pan; cool on a wire rack. Yield: 16 servings (serving size: 1 slice).

CALORIES 164 (19% from fat); FAT 3.4g (sat 1.8g, mono 0.9g, poly 0.3g); PROTEIN 4.4g; CARB 29.3g; FIBER 1.2g; CHOL 33mg; IRON 1.6mg; SODIUM 180mg; CALC 32mg

Lamb with Dates, Apricots, and Saffron over Couscous

Middle Eastern–style stews often combine meat, spices, and fruit.

    1   teaspoon olive oil
    1   (1-pound) boneless leg of lamb, trimmed and cubed
    ½   teaspoon salt, divided
    ¼   teaspoon freshly ground black pepper, divided
    1   cup chopped onion
    ¼   cup fresh orange juice (about 1 large orange)
    6   garlic cloves, minced
    ½   teaspoon ground cumin
    ½   teaspoon ground coriander
    ¼   teaspoon saffron threads, crushed
    1½ cups fat-free, less-sodium beef broth
    1½ cups (¼-inch-thick) slices carrot
    ½   cup dried apricots, cut into ¼-inch-thick strips
    ½   cup halved pitted dates
    2   tablespoons chopped fresh mint
    2   cups hot cooked couscous

1. Heat oil in a medium saucepan over medium-high heat. Add lamb, ¼ teaspoon salt, and ⅛ teaspoon pepper to pan; sauté 8 minutes or until browned. Remove from pan.
2. Add onion, juice, and garlic to pan; cook until liquid evaporates, scraping pan to loosen browned bits. Stir in cumin, coriander, and saffron; cook 15 seconds. Return lamb to pan. Stir in broth; bring to a boil. Cover, reduce heat, and simmer 30 minutes. Stir in carrot, apricots, and dates. Cover and cook 18 minutes or until carrot is tender. Remove from heat; stir in ¼ teaspoon salt, ⅛ teaspoon pepper, and mint. Serve over couscous. Yield: 4 servings (serving size: 1 cup lamb mixture and ½ cup couscous).

CALORIES 416 (16% from fat); FAT 7.5g (sat 2.6g, mono 3.4g, poly 0.5g); PROTEIN 29.4g; CARB 57.7g; FIBER 5.5g; CHOL 73mg; IRON 3.6mg; SODIUM 584mg; CALC 70mg

Mussels with Saffron, Tomato, and Wine over Linguine

Saffron, tomato, and shellfish balance well. Garnish with mint sprigs, if desired.

    2   tablespoons butter
    ¼   cup chopped shallots
    3   garlic cloves, minced
    ¼   teaspoon saffron threads, crushed
    1   (14.5-ounce) can no-salt-added diced tomatoes, undrained
    ½   cup dry white wine
    ¼   cup chopped fresh parsley
    ⅛   teaspoon freshly ground black pepper
    1   (8-ounce) bottle clam juice
    2   pounds mussels, scrubbed and debearded
    4   cups hot cooked linguine (about 8 ounces uncooked pasta)

1. Melt butter in a Dutch oven over medium-high heat. Add shallots and garlic to pan; sauté 1½ minutes. Add saffron and tomatoes; cook 2 minutes. Stir in wine, parsley, pepper, and juice; bring to a boil. Cook 4 minutes. Add mussels. Cover and cook 6 minutes or until shells open; discard any unopened shells. Serve over pasta. Yield: 4 servings (serving size: 2¼ cups mussels, ¾ cup sauce, and 1 cup pasta).

CALORIES 487 (22% from fat); FAT 11.6g (sat 4.8g, mono 2.6g, poly 1.6g); PROTEIN 36.4g; CARB 58.7g; FIBER 3.7g; CHOL 80mg; IRON 11.8mg; SODIUM 866mg; CALC 110mg

Saffron-Marinated Pork Tenderloin with Grilled Pepper Relish

Saffron lends the pork subtle flavor.

PORK:
- ⅓ cup sliced shallots
- ⅓ cup chopped fresh basil
- 1 tablespoon fresh lemon juice
- 2 teaspoons olive oil
- 2 teaspoons paprika
- 1 teaspoon ground cumin
- ¼ teaspoon saffron threads, crushed
- 3 garlic cloves, thinly sliced
- 1 (1-pound) pork tenderloin, trimmed
- ¾ teaspoon salt
- ¼ teaspoon freshly ground black pepper
- Cooking spray

RELISH:
- 2 (¼-inch-thick) slices red onion
- 1 large red bell pepper
- 1 large green bell pepper
- 1 tablespoon chopped fresh basil
- 1 teaspoon sugar
- 2 teaspoons sherry vinegar
- ¼ teaspoon salt

1. To prepare pork, combine first 9 ingredients in a large zip-top plastic bag; seal. Marinate in refrigerator 24 hours, turning occasionally.

2. Prepare grill.

3. Remove pork from bag; discard marinade. Sprinkle pork with ¾ teaspoon salt and black pepper. Place pork on a grill rack coated with cooking spray. Grill 18 minutes or until a thermometer registers 155° (slightly pink), turning occasionally. Let stand 10 minutes before cutting into slices.

4. To prepare relish, place onion and bell peppers on grill rack coated with cooking spray. Grill onion 4 minutes on each side or until tender. Grill peppers 12 minutes or until blackened, turning occasionally. Place peppers in a large zip-top plastic bag; seal. Let stand 10 minutes. Peel peppers; cut in half lengthwise. Discard seeds and membranes. Chop onion and peppers. Combine onion, peppers, basil, and remaining 3 ingredients in a medium bowl. Serve relish with pork. Yield: 4 servings (serving size: 3 ounces pork and ½ cup relish).

CALORIES 208 (12% from fat); FAT 6.6g (sat 1.7g, mono 3.4g, poly 0.9g); PROTEIN 25.6g; CARB 11.7g; FIBER 2.7g; CHOL 74mg; IRON 2.5mg; SODIUM 653mg; CALC 39mg

Chicken Biryani

Biryani is a Middle Eastern and South Asian dish that usually mixes rice, vegetables, aromatic spices, and meat or poultry.

- 1 tablespoon butter
- 1 cup chopped onion
- 1 tablespoon grated peeled fresh ginger
- 3 garlic cloves, minced
- 1 teaspoon ground cumin
- ½ teaspoon ground allspice
- ¼ teaspoon saffron threads, crushed
- ¼ teaspoon ground cardamom
- ½ cup chopped tomato
- ½ cup golden raisins
- 1 finely chopped serrano chile
- 1½ pounds skinless, boneless chicken thighs, cut into 1-inch pieces
- 2 tablespoons fresh lime juice
- ¼ teaspoon salt
- 1 cup basmati rice
- 2 cups water
- ¼ cup chopped fresh cilantro

1. Melt butter in a large saucepan over medium-high heat. Add onion, ginger, and garlic to pan; sauté 5 minutes or until lightly browned. Stir in cumin, allspice, saffron, and cardamom; cook 15 seconds. Stir in tomato, raisins, and serrano; cook 1 minute. Add chicken; cook 5 minutes, stirring frequently. Add juice and salt; cook 30 seconds. Add rice; cook 1½ minutes, stirring frequently. Stir in 2 cups water; bring to a boil. Cover, reduce heat, and simmer 12 minutes or until liquid is absorbed. Remove from heat; let stand 10 minutes. Sprinkle with cilantro. Yield: 4 servings (serving size: about 1⅓ cups).

CALORIES 386 (12% from fat); FAT 5.3g (sat 2.4g, mono 1.4g, poly 0.7g); PROTEIN 42.5g; CARB 41.7g; FIBER 2.3g; CHOL 106mg; IRON 2.4mg; SODIUM 730mg; CALC 57mg

STAFF FAVORITE
Paella Valencia

Valencia is a Spanish coastal city where this dish is particularly revered.

- 1 tablespoon olive oil
- ¾ pound peeled and deveined large shrimp
- ¾ teaspoon salt, divided
- ¼ teaspoon freshly ground black pepper, divided
- ½ cup thinly sliced Spanish chorizo sausage (about 2 ounces)
- 2 (2-ounce) skinless, boneless chicken thighs, quartered
- 1 cup chopped onion
- 3 garlic cloves, minced
- ½ cup chopped tomato
- 1 tablespoon capers, drained
- ¼ teaspoon saffron threads, crushed
- 1 cup Arborio rice or other short-grain rice
- ⅔ cup white wine
- 1 (14-ounce) can fat-free, less-sodium chicken broth
- ½ cup frozen green peas
- ¼ cup water
- 18 mussels (about ¾ pound), scrubbed and debearded
- 2½ tablespoons chopped bottled roasted red bell pepper
- 2 tablespoons chopped fresh cilantro

1. Heat oil in a large nonstick skillet over medium-high heat. Sprinkle shrimp with ¼ teaspoon salt and ⅛ teaspoon black pepper. Add shrimp to pan; sauté 4 minutes or until shrimp are done. Place shrimp in a medium bowl. Add chorizo to pan, and cook 1 minute or until browned. Add chorizo to bowl.

2. Sprinkle chicken with ¼ teaspoon salt and ⅛ teaspoon black pepper. Add chicken to pan, and cook 2 minutes on each side or until browned. Add onion and garlic to pan; cook 2 minutes or until tender, stirring frequently. Stir in tomato, capers, and saffron; cook 1 minute. Add ¼ teaspoon salt, rice, wine, and broth to pan; bring to a boil. Cover, reduce heat, and simmer 25 minutes or until rice is tender.

3. Add shrimp mixture, peas, ¼ cup water, and mussels to pan. Cover and cook 8 minutes over medium heat or until mussels open; discard any unopened shells. Remove from heat, and stir in bell pepper and cilantro. Let stand 3 minutes. Yield: 6 servings (serving size: 1⅔ cups).

CALORIES 304 (29% from fat); FAT 9.6g (sat 2.5g, mono 4.2g, poly 1.6g); PROTEIN 30.3g; CARB 22g; FIBER 1.6g; CHOL 139mg; IRON 4.5mg; SODIUM 901mg; CALC 65mg

Clams and Shrimp in Saffron Fennel Broth

Pernod, fennel, and tarragon combine to give the broth a light licorice taste. Crushing the fennel seeds helps release their flavor.

- 1   tablespoon olive oil
- ½   cup finely chopped shallots
- ½   teaspoon saffron threads, crushed
- ¼   teaspoon fennel seeds, crushed
- 2   garlic cloves, minced
- 3   cups clam juice
- 2   tablespoons Pernod (licorice-flavored liqueur)
- 2   tablespoons tomato paste
- 1   tablespoon chopped fresh tarragon
- ¼   teaspoon salt
- ⅛   teaspoon freshly ground black pepper
- ¾   pound red potatoes, cut into ½-inch cubes
- 1   fennel bulb, cut into 12 wedges
- 24   littleneck clams
- ¾   pound peeled and deveined medium shrimp

1. Heat oil in a large saucepan over medium heat. Add shallots, saffron, fennel seeds, and garlic to pan; cook 4 minutes or until tender. Add clam juice, Pernod, and tomato paste; bring to a boil. Reduce heat, and simmer 15 minutes.
2. Stir in tarragon, salt, pepper, potatoes, and fennel bulb; cover and cook 10 minutes. Add clams; cover and cook 10 minutes. Stir in shrimp. Cover and

cook 2 minutes or until clams open and shrimp are done; discard any unopened shells. Yield: 4 servings (serving size: 2¼ cups).

CALORIES 284 (18% from fat); FAT 5.7g (sat 0.8g, mono 2.8g, poly 1.1g); PROTEIN 28.5g; CARB 29.2g; FIBER 4.1g; CHOL 153mg; IRON 11.6mg; SODIUM 733mg; CALC 144mg

Risotto Milanese

This classic Italian dish is traditionally served with veal shanks, though it would also make a fine side for braised short ribs, roasted and grilled fish, or beef tenderloin.

- ¼   teaspoon saffron threads
- 2   (14-ounce) cans fat-free, less-sodium chicken broth
- 2   teaspoons unsalted butter
- 3   tablespoons finely chopped shallots
- 3   tablespoons finely chopped prosciutto (about 1 ounce)
- 2   garlic cloves, minced
- 1   cup Arborio rice or other short-grain rice
- ⅓   cup white wine
- ¼   cup (1 ounce) grated fresh Parmesan cheese
- ⅛   teaspoon freshly ground black pepper

1. Combine saffron and broth in a small saucepan; bring to a simmer (do not boil). Keep warm over low heat.
2. Melt butter in a large saucepan over medium-high heat. Add shallots, prosciutto, and garlic to pan; sauté 2 minutes or until shallots are tender. Add rice; cook 1 minute, stirring constantly. Stir in wine; cook 2 minutes or until liquid is nearly absorbed, stirring constantly.
3. Add broth mixture, ½ cup at a time, stirring constantly until each portion of broth is absorbed before adding the next (about 25 minutes total). Remove from heat; stir in cheese and pepper. Serve immediately. Yield: 4 servings (serving size: about ¾ cup).

CALORIES 152 (25% from fat); FAT 4.2g (sat 2.4g, mono 1.3g, poly 0.3g); PROTEIN 7.4g; CARB 20.5g; FIBER 1.2g; CHOL 14mg; IRON 0.9mg; SODIUM 524mg; CALC 75mg

reader recipes
Your Very Best

From appetizers to entrées and sides to desserts, these creations showcase our readers' top efforts.

Some of the most popular recipes in our 20-year history have come from readers. In our January/February 1989 issue under the headline "Recipe Exchange," we first featured reader recipes for Cornish hen, pickled cauliflower, apple crisp, and bean soup. In time, that column blossomed into the popular Reader Recipes feature.

To come up with this list, we combed through old issues and polled our staff to select favorite reader-created go-to casseroles, impressive desserts, special appetizers, and more. We retested the recipes to ensure that ingredients were still available, cook times were correct, and—most importantly—that they still deserve top billing. And now, we share them with you. From side dishes to main dishes, dips to desserts, these recipes represent your finest.

STAFF FAVORITE
Angel Biscuits

We like these biscuits straight from the oven with a drizzle of honey or spoonful of jam.

- 1   package dry yeast (about 2¼ teaspoons)
- ½   cup warm water (100° to 110°)
- 5   cups all-purpose flour (about 22½ ounces)
- ¼   cup sugar
- 1   teaspoon baking powder
- 1   teaspoon baking soda
- 1   teaspoon salt
- ½   cup vegetable shortening
- 2   cups low-fat buttermilk
- Cooking spray
- 1   tablespoon butter, melted

1. Dissolve yeast in ½ cup warm water in a small bowl, and let stand 5 minutes.
2. Lightly spoon flour into dry measuring cups; level with a knife. Combine flour
Continued

and next 4 ingredients in a large bowl. Cut in shortening with a pastry blender or 2 knives until mixture resembles coarse meal. Add yeast mixture and buttermilk to flour mixture; stir just until moist. Cover and chill 1 hour.

3. Preheat oven to 450°.

4. Turn dough out onto a heavily floured surface; knead lightly 5 times. Roll dough to a ½-inch thickness; cut with a 2½-inch biscuit cutter. Place biscuits on a baking sheet coated with cooking spray. Brush melted butter over biscuit tops. Bake at 450° for 12 minutes or until golden. Yield: 2 dozen (serving size: 1 biscuit).

CALORIES 154 (29% from fat); FAT 5g (sat 1.5g, mono 1.5g, poly 1.1g); PROTEIN 3.6g; CARB 23.2g; FIBER 0.8g; CHOL 3mg; IRON 1.3mg; SODIUM 198mg; CALC 36mg

---

STAFF FAVORITE
Easy Corn Casserole

We published this casserole created by Kansas reader Peg Tantillo in our June 1996 issue. Making the most of convenience products, this dish comes together quickly as an ideal side for chili, spicy pork, or chicken. The original called for low-calorie margarine; we updated it with butter for a smoother, richer taste.

  ¼ cup egg substitute
  ¼ cup butter, melted
  1 (8¾-ounce) can no-salt-added whole-kernel corn, drained
  1 (8¾-ounce) can no-salt-added cream-style corn
  1 (8½-ounce) package corn muffin mix
  1 (8-ounce) carton plain fat-free yogurt
  Cooking spray

1. Preheat oven to 350°.

2. Combine first 6 ingredients in a medium bowl; stir well. Pour into an 8-inch square baking dish coated with cooking spray. Bake at 350° for 45 minutes or until set. Yield: 8 servings.

CALORIES 238 (35% from fat); FAT 9.2g (sat 4.8g, mono 3g, poly 0.6g); PROTEIN 4.9g; CARB 35.2g; FIBER 1.5g; CHOL 16mg; IRON 1.3mg; SODIUM 327mg; CALC 43mg

---

Cambodian Summer Rolls

Novato, California, reader Cathy Jo Belford sent us this Asian-inspired appetizer for the April 2002 column. The fresh herbs, sweet shrimp, slight spicy heat, and crisp lettuce offer well-balanced taste and texture.

ROLLS:

  6 cups water
 36 unpeeled medium shrimp (about 1 pound)
  4 ounces uncooked rice noodles
 12 (8-inch) round sheets rice paper
  ¼ cup hoisin sauce
  3 cups shredded red leaf lettuce
  ¼ cup thinly sliced fresh basil
  ¼ cup thinly sliced fresh mint

DIPPING SAUCE:

  ⅓ cup low-sodium soy sauce
  ¼ cup water
  2 tablespoons sugar
  2 tablespoons chopped fresh cilantro
  2 tablespoons fresh lime juice
  1 teaspoon minced peeled fresh ginger
  1 teaspoon chile paste with garlic (such as sambal oelek)
  1 garlic clove, minced

1. To prepare rolls, bring 6 cups water to a boil in a large saucepan. Add shrimp to pan; cook 3 minutes or until done. Drain and rinse with cold water; drain. Peel shrimp; chill.

2. Place noodles in a large bowl; cover with boiling water. Let stand 8 minutes; drain.

3. Add cold water to a large, shallow dish to a depth of 1 inch. Place 1 rice paper sheet in water. Let stand 2 minutes or until soft. Place rice paper sheet on a flat surface.

4. Spread 1 teaspoon hoisin sauce in center of sheet; top with 3 shrimp, ¼ cup lettuce, about 2½ tablespoons noodles, 1 teaspoon basil, and 1 teaspoon mint. Fold sides of sheet over filling, roll up jelly-roll fashion, and gently press seam to seal. Place roll, seam side down, on a serving platter; cover to keep from drying. Repeat procedure with remaining

---

rice paper, hoisin sauce, shrimp, lettuce, noodles, basil, and mint.

5. To prepare dipping sauce, combine soy sauce and remaining 7 ingredients in a small bowl; stir with a whisk. Yield: 12 servings (serving size: 1 roll and about 1½ tablespoons sauce).

CALORIES 131 (6% from fat); FAT 0.9g (sat 0.1g, mono 0.1g, poly 0.2g); PROTEIN 6.7g; CARB 24.1g; FIBER 0.8g; CHOL 36mg; IRON 1mg; SODIUM 379mg; CALC 37mg

---

STAFF FAVORITE • MAKE AHEAD
FREEZABLE
Peanut Butter Pie

Mary Frances Noveh from River Ridge, Louisiana, sent us this dessert recipe, which first appeared in December 2001. She noted it was like a "peanut butter and chocolate candy bar." We loved the results, and since it makes two pies, you can share one with a friend and keep the other for yourself. Several tasters in our Test Kitchens enjoy serving this pie frozen.

  1 cup powdered sugar
  1 cup natural-style, reduced-fat creamy peanut butter (such as Smucker's)
  1 (8-ounce) block ⅓-less-fat cream cheese, softened
  1 (14-ounce) can fat-free sweetened condensed milk
 12 ounces frozen fat-free whipped topping, thawed
  2 (6-ounce) reduced-fat graham cracker crusts
 20 teaspoons fat-free chocolate sundae syrup

1. Combine first 3 ingredients in a large bowl; beat with a mixer at medium speed until smooth. Add milk; beat until combined. Fold in whipped topping. Divide mixture evenly between crusts; chill 8 hours or until set (pies will have a soft, fluffy texture). Cut into wedges; drizzle with chocolate syrup. Yield: 20 servings (serving size: 1 wedge and 1 teaspoon syrup).

CALORIES 302 (30% from fat); FAT 10g (sat 3.8g, mono 3.3g, poly 2.8g); PROTEIN 6.9g; CARB 45.8g; FIBER 1g; CHOL 11mg; IRON 0.6mg; SODIUM 252mg; CALC 59mg

Risotto with Fresh Mozzarella, Grape Tomatoes, and Basil

3 tablespoons balsamic vinegar
4½ cups fat-free, less-sodium chicken broth
2 tablespoons extravirgin olive oil, divided
2 cups chopped leek
1½ cups Arborio rice or other medium-grain rice
⅓ cup dry white wine
¼ cup half-and-half
1 teaspoon salt
¼ teaspoon freshly ground black pepper
1 cup halved grape tomatoes
¼ cup chopped fresh basil
5 ounces fresh mozzarella cheese, finely diced

1. Place vinegar in a small, heavy saucepan; bring to a boil over medium heat. Cook until slightly syrupy and reduced to 1 tablespoon (about 4 minutes). Set aside.
2. Bring broth to a simmer in a medium saucepan (do not boil). Keep warm.
3. Heat 1 tablespoon oil in a large saucepan over medium-high heat. Add leek to pan; sauté 3 minutes or until tender. Add rice; cook 2 minutes, stirring constantly. Stir in wine, and cook 1 minute or until liquid is nearly absorbed, stirring constantly. Stir in 1 cup broth; cook 5 minutes or until liquid is nearly absorbed, stirring constantly. Reduce heat to medium. Add remaining broth, ½ cup at a time, stirring constantly until each portion of broth is absorbed before adding the next (about 25 minutes total). Stir in half-and-half, salt, and pepper; cook 2 minutes. Remove from heat; stir in tomatoes, basil, and cheese. Place about 1 cup risotto into each of 6 shallow serving bowls; drizzle each serving with ½ teaspoon balsamic syrup and ½ teaspoon oil. Yield: 6 servings.

CALORIES 378 (29% from fat); FAT 12.1g (sat 5.2g, mono 4.1g, poly 1g); PROTEIN 13.2g; CARB 51.6g; FIBER 1.6g; CHOL 24mg; IRON 1.3mg; SODIUM 777mg; CALC 178mg

Ginger Cookies

Originally appearing in our March/April 1993 issue, these gingersnap cookies created by Elizabeth Graubard of Palm Harbor, Florida, have stood the test of time. We swapped flavorful butter for the original's margarine and still love the snappy flavor and crisp texture.

6 tablespoons butter, softened
⅔ cup plus 3 tablespoons sugar, divided
¼ cup molasses
1 large egg
2 cups all-purpose flour (about 9 ounces)
2 teaspoons baking soda
1 teaspoon ground ginger
1 teaspoon ground cinnamon
½ teaspoon ground mace
Cooking spray

1. Place butter in a large bowl; beat with a mixer at medium speed until fluffy. Gradually add ⅔ cup sugar, beating at medium speed until light and well blended. Add molasses and egg; beat well.
2. Lightly spoon flour into dry measuring cups, and level with a knife. Combine flour and next 4 ingredients, stirring with a whisk. Gradually add flour mixture to butter mixture, stirring until well blended. Divide dough in half. Wrap each portion in plastic wrap, and freeze 30 minutes.
3. Preheat oven to 350°.
4. Shape each portion of dough into 26 (1-inch) balls. Roll balls in 3 tablespoons sugar, and place 2 inches apart on baking sheets coated with cooking spray. Flatten cookies with bottom of a glass to ½-inch thickness. Bake at 350° for 12 minutes or until lightly browned. Remove from pans, and cool completely on wire racks. Yield: 52 cookies (serving size: 1 cookie).

CALORIES 48 (28% from fat); FAT 1.5g (sat 0.9g, mono 0.4g, poly 0.1g); PROTEIN 0.6g; CARB 8.2g; FIBER 0.2g; CHOL 8mg; IRON 0.3mg; SODIUM 60mg; CALC 6mg

Seared Beef Tenderloin Mini Sandwiches with Mustard-Horseradish Sauce

We received the recipe for these great-tasting appetizers from Susan Wambui Thiong'o in Nairobi, Kenya, in 2004. You can substitute peppery arugula for the watercress, if you prefer.

⅔ cup fat-free sour cream
¼ cup Dijon mustard
2 tablespoons minced fresh tarragon
2 tablespoons prepared horseradish
1 (1½-pound) beef tenderloin, trimmed
½ teaspoon freshly ground black pepper
Cooking spray
2 tablespoons fresh lemon juice
3 cups trimmed watercress (about 1 bunch)
1 (8-ounce) French bread baguette, cut diagonally into 16 slices
2 tablespoons capers
½ cup (2 ounces) shaved fresh Parmesan cheese

1. Combine first 4 ingredients, stirring well with a whisk. Cover and chill.
2. Secure beef at 2-inch intervals with twine. Sprinkle beef with pepper. Heat a large nonstick skillet over medium-high heat. Coat pan with cooking spray. Add beef to pan; cook 15 minutes or until desired degree of doneness, turning frequently. Let stand 15 minutes. Cut into 16 slices. Sprinkle with juice.
3. Arrange watercress evenly on bread slices. Place 1 beef slice and about 1 tablespoon chilled sauce over each bread slice. Arrange capers and cheese evenly over sauce. Yield: 16 servings (serving size: 1 open-faced sandwich).

CALORIES 136 (33% from fat); FAT 5g (sat 1.8g, mono 1.5g, poly 0.3g); PROTEIN 12.6g; CARB 10g; FIBER 0.6g; CHOL 25mg; IRON 1.7mg; SODIUM 314mg; CALC 94mg

Something to Celebrate

Chicago neighbors join *Cooking Light* to enjoy a special event with a garden-inspired menu perfect for end-of-summer entertaining.

WINE NOTE: This menu boasts bright, acidic flavors and fresh herbs in both the Herbed Goat Cheese and the Lemon-Parsley Pesto, so you'll want a high-acid white that won't go flat against these zippy flavors. Try a Vermentino, made from an Italian grape of the same name found in Liguria and Tuscany. Campo al Mare Vermentino 2005 ($17) has melon and peach flavors delicate enough for goat cheese with an herbal, sagelike edge of its own.

The 2007 *Cooking Light* FitHouse represents several milestones: It was built during our 20th anniversary year; it will be among the first homes in Chicago to qualify for the city's green-building guidelines; and its state-of-the-art kitchen, three outdoor spaces, and top floor penthouse make the home ideally suited for entertaining. What better way to celebrate it than with a party?

Celebration Menu
serves 8

Herbed Goat Cheese

Grilled Vegetable Salad

Tossed green salad

Salmon Skewers with Lemon-Parsley Pesto

Cornmeal, Jalapeño, and Fresh Corn Scones

Grilled Nectarines and Plums with Vanilla Bean Syrup

Vermentino (white wine)

Do It Ahead

Two days ahead:
• Prepare and refrigerate Herbed Goat Cheese.

One day ahead:
• Trim and cut vegetables for Grilled Vegetable Salad.

• Bake Cornmeal, Jalapeño, and Fresh Corn Scones; cool and store in an airtight container.

Two hours ahead:
• Prepare syrup and whipped topping for Grilled Nectarines and Plums with Vanilla Bean Syrup.

• Shave Parmigiano-Reggiano cheese.

MAKE AHEAD
Herbed Goat Cheese

This is a simple make-ahead recipe, ideal for summer entertaining. The longer the cheese refrigerates, the more flavor it absorbs from the herbs. You can leave it to marinate for up to two days. For optimal flavor, let the goat cheese stand at room temperature about 10 minutes before serving.

  ⅓ cup chopped fresh basil
  1 teaspoon grated lemon rind
  2 tablespoons fresh lemon juice
  1 tablespoon extravirgin olive oil
  2 teaspoons chopped fresh oregano
  ¼ teaspoon salt
  ¼ teaspoon freshly ground black pepper
  2 garlic cloves, minced
  1 (3-ounce) package goat cheese
  1 (8-ounce) French baguette, cut into 16 slices, toasted

1. Combine first 8 ingredients in a small bowl, stirring well. Coat cheese evenly with basil mixture, pressing gently to adhere. Cover and refrigerate at least 2 hours. Serve cheese with baguette slices. Yield: 8 servings (serving size: ¾ ounce cheese and 2 bread slices).

CALORIES 122 (30% from fat); FAT 4g (sat 1.8g, mono 1.9g, poly 0.2g); PROTEIN 4.6g; CARB 17.8g; FIBER 0.6g; CHOL 5mg; IRON 1.2mg; SODIUM 296mg; CALC 21mg

Grilled Vegetable Salad

Similar to an antipasto plate, this composed salad combines brightly colored grilled vegetables with fresh herbs and cheese in place of a traditional vinaigrette. Serve this warm or at room temperature.

  5 plum tomatoes, quartered and seeded
  1½ pounds Japanese eggplant, trimmed and halved lengthwise
  1 large red onion, cut into ½-inch-thick slices
  1 red bell pepper, halved and seeded
  1 yellow bell pepper, halved and seeded
  1 tablespoon extravirgin olive oil
  ¼ teaspoon salt
  ¼ teaspoon freshly ground black pepper
  Cooking spray
  3 tablespoons chopped fresh flat-leaf parsley
  2 garlic cloves, minced
  ¼ cup (1 ounce) shaved Parmigiano-Reggiano cheese

1. Prepare grill.
2. Arrange first 5 ingredients in a single layer on a baking sheet. Brush vegetables evenly with oil; sprinkle with salt and pepper. Place eggplant, onion, and peppers in a single layer on grill rack coated with cooking spray. Grill 4 minutes on each side or until charred. Remove from grill. Place peppers in a large zip-top plastic bag; seal. Let stand 10 minutes.

Peel peppers, and cut into thin strips. Cut eggplant into ½-inch pieces.

3. Arrange tomatoes, skin side down, on grill rack coated with cooking spray. Grill 2 minutes on each side or until soft. Arrange tomatoes alternately with other vegetables on a serving platter. Combine parsley and garlic; sprinkle evenly over vegetables. Garnish with cheese. Yield: 8 servings (serving size: about 1 cup vegetables and about 1½ teaspoons cheese).

CALORIES 80 (33% from fat); FAT 2.9g (sat 0.9g, mono 1.5g, poly 0.3g); PROTEIN 3.4g; CARB 12.2g; FIBER 3.7g; CHOL 2mg; IRON 0.6mg; SODIUM 138mg; CALC 56mg

STAFF FAVORITE • QUICK & EASY
Salmon Skewers with Lemon-Parsley Pesto

Prepare this dish just before grilling so the pesto maintains its color.

- ½ cup (2 ounces) freshly grated Parmigiano-Reggiano cheese
- ½ cup fresh flat-leaf parsley leaves
- ¼ cup fresh basil leaves
- ¼ cup capers, drained
- 2 teaspoons grated lemon rind
- 2 teaspoons fresh lemon juice
- 1 garlic clove, minced
- 2½ tablespoons extravirgin olive oil, divided
- 2 pounds skinless, boneless salmon fillets, cut into 1-inch chunks
- ½ teaspoon salt, divided
- ¼ teaspoon freshly ground black pepper
- Cooking spray
- 4 cups hot cooked orzo
- Parsley sprigs (optional)
- Lemon wedges (optional)

1. Prepare grill.

2. Place first 7 ingredients in a food processor. Add 1½ tablespoons oil; process until smooth, scraping sides. Set aside.

3. Thread fish evenly onto 16 skewers. Brush fish with 1 tablespoon oil; sprinkle evenly with ¼ teaspoon salt and pepper. Arrange skewers on grill rack coated with cooking spray; grill 1 minute on each side or until desired degree of doneness. Remove from grill, and keep warm.

4. Combine orzo and ¼ teaspoon salt; toss well. Place ½ cup orzo on each of 8 plates; arrange 2 skewers on each plate. Top each serving with about 1 tablespoon herb mixture. Garnish with parsley sprigs and lemon wedges, if desired. Yield: 8 servings.

CALORIES 407 (28% from fat); FAT 12.7g (sat 2.6g, mono 5.5g, poly 3g); PROTEIN 29.2g; CARB 43.3g; FIBER 2.1g; CHOL 58mg; IRON 3mg; SODIUM 398mg; CALC 87mg

MAKE AHEAD
Cornmeal, Jalapeño, and Fresh Corn Scones

(pictured on page 244)

If you want to tame the heat, reduce the amount of pepper or omit it.

- 1¾ cups all-purpose flour (about 7¾ ounces)
- ¾ cup cornmeal
- 1 tablespoon baking powder
- 1 teaspoon kosher salt
- 4½ tablespoons chilled butter, cut into small pieces
- ½ cup fresh corn kernels (about 1 ear)
- 2 tablespoons finely chopped seeded jalapeño pepper
- 1 cup nonfat buttermilk
- Cooking spray

1. Preheat oven to 400°.

2. Lightly spoon flour into dry measuring cups; level with a knife. Combine flour, cornmeal, baking powder, and salt in a medium bowl, stirring with a whisk. Cut in butter with a pastry blender or 2 knives until mixture resembles coarse meal. Stir in corn and pepper. Add buttermilk, stirring just until moist (dough will be slightly sticky).

3. Turn dough out onto a lightly floured surface; knead lightly 2 or 3 times with lightly floured hands. Pat dough into a 9-inch circle on a baking sheet coated with cooking spray. Cut dough into 12 wedges, cutting into, but not through, dough. Bake at 400° for 25 minutes or until lightly browned. Cool on a wire rack. Yield: 12 servings (serving size: 1 scone).

CALORIES 150 (29% from fat); FAT 4.8g (sat 2.8g, mono 1.2g, poly 0.3g); PROTEIN 3.6g; CARB 23.5g; FIBER 2.1g; CHOL 12mg; IRON 1.3mg; SODIUM 304mg; CALC 99mg

STAFF FAVORITE
Grilled Nectarines and Plums with Vanilla Bean Syrup

Grilling heightens the fruit's sweetness and flavor. Slightly firm fruit will stand up to the heat; if you're using ripe fruit, take it from the grill just a few minutes sooner than directed. Garnish with mint sprigs.

- 2 cups water
- ⅓ cup honey
- 1 (3-inch) vanilla bean, split lengthwise
- ¼ cup frozen fat-free whipped topping, thawed
- 2 tablespoons mascarpone cheese
- 1 tablespoon honey
- 4 nectarines, halved and pitted
- 4 plums, halved and pitted
- Cooking spray
- 2 cups cherries, halved and pitted
- 2 tablespoons sliced almonds, toasted and chopped

1. Prepare grill.

2. Combine 2 cups water and ⅓ cup honey in a small saucepan over medium-high heat. Scrape seeds from vanilla bean, and add seeds to honey mixture. Discard bean. Bring to a boil. Cook until reduced to 1¼ cups (about 15 minutes). Combine whipped topping, cheese, and 1 tablespoon honey, stirring until smooth. Set aside.

3. Lightly coat both sides of nectarines and plums with cooking spray. Place nectarines and plums, cut side down, on a grill rack coated with cooking spray. Grill 2 minutes on each side or until soft. Place 1 nectarine half and 1 plum half in each of 8 shallow bowls. Top each serving with ¼ cup cherries; drizzle each with 2 tablespoons honey mixture. Spoon 2 teaspoons cheese mixture over each serving; sprinkle each serving with ¾ teaspoon nuts. Yield: 8 servings.

CALORIES 173 (24% from fat); FAT 4.6g (sat 1.9g, mono 1.6g, poly 0.5g); PROTEIN 2.1g; CARB 33.7g; FIBER 2g; CHOL 9mg; IRON 0.5mg; SODIUM 6mg; CALC 21mg

20 Minute Dishes

From chicken to steak, soup to salad, here are simple, fresh, and easy meals you can make superfast.

QUICK & EASY

Braised Chicken with Red Potatoes and Tarragon Broth

Serve this one-dish meal with a green salad and crusty bread.

- 2 teaspoons olive oil
- ⅓ cup finely chopped shallots (about 2 small)
- 1 pound skinless, boneless chicken breast halves, cut into bite-sized pieces
- 2½ cups fat-free, less-sodium chicken broth
- ½ cup dry white wine
- 1 teaspoon chopped fresh tarragon
- ½ teaspoon salt
- ¼ teaspoon freshly ground black pepper
- 1 (12-ounce) package red potato wedges (such as Simply Potatoes), cut into ½-inch pieces
- 2 tablespoons chopped fresh flat-leaf parsley

1. Heat oil in a large saucepan over medium-high heat. Add shallots to pan; sauté 1 minute. Add chicken to pan; sauté 2 minutes or until browned. Add broth, wine, tarragon, salt, and pepper; bring to a boil. Simmer 5 minutes, stirring occasionally. Add potatoes; simmer 5 minutes or until potatoes are tender. Remove from heat; stir in parsley. Yield: 4 servings (serving size: 1¼ cups).

CALORIES 227 (15% from fat); FAT 3.9g (sat 0.7g, mono 2.1g, poly 0.6g); PROTEIN 29.2g; CARB 16.2g; FIBER 1.8g; CHOL 66mg; IRON 1.6mg; SODIUM 831mg; CALC 33mg

QUICK & EASY

Southwestern Pork Soup

Substitute chicken for pork in this dish, if you prefer. Pink beans are similar to pinto beans, but smaller; if you can't find pink beans, substitute pintos. Add Cheddar corn bread and orange slices to round out the meal.

Cooking spray
- 1 cup prechopped onion
- ⅔ cup prechopped green bell pepper
- 1 tablespoon bottled minced garlic
- 1 jalapeño pepper, seeded and minced
- 1 pound pork tenderloin, trimmed and cut into bite-sized pieces
- 2 cups fat-free, less-sodium chicken broth
- 2 teaspoons chili powder
- 1 teaspoon ground cumin
- ½ teaspoon salt
- ¼ teaspoon black pepper
- 1 (15-ounce) can pink beans, rinsed and drained
- 1 (14-ounce) can diced tomatoes, undrained
- 2 tablespoons chopped fresh cilantro
- 1 cup diced avocado

1. Heat a small nonstick Dutch oven over medium heat. Coat pan with cooking spray. Add onion, bell pepper, garlic, and jalapeño to pan; sauté 2 minutes. Add pork; cook 3 minutes. Add broth and next 6 ingredients; bring to a boil. Partially cover, reduce heat, and simmer 6 minutes or until pork is done, stirring occasionally. Remove from heat, and stir in cilantro. Serve with avocado. Yield: 4 servings (serving size: about 1¾ cups soup and ¼ cup avocado).

CALORIES 310 (30% from fat); FAT 10.5g (sat 2.4g, mono 5.5g, poly 1.4g); PROTEIN 30.6g; CARB 24.5g; FIBER 8.3g; CHOL 74mg; IRON 3.7mg; SODIUM 911mg; CALC 82mg

STAFF FAVORITE • QUICK & EASY

Flank Steak and Edamame with Wasabi Dressing

Wasabi paste, Japanese horseradish, has a distinctive flavor.

- 1 (1-pound) flank steak, trimmed
- 2 tablespoons plus 2 teaspoons low-sodium soy sauce, divided
- ½ teaspoon salt
- ½ teaspoon pepper
Cooking spray
- 2 teaspoons dark sesame oil
- 1 tablespoon bottled ground fresh ginger (such as Spice World)
- 2 teaspoons bottled minced garlic
- 1 (10-ounce) package frozen shelled edamame (green soybeans), thawed
- ¼ cup rice vinegar
- 2 teaspoons wasabi paste

1. Heat a grill pan over medium-high heat. Rub steak with 2 teaspoons soy sauce; sprinkle with salt and pepper. Coat pan with cooking spray. Add steak to pan. Cook 5 minutes on each side or until desired degree of doneness. Remove from pan; let stand 10 minutes. Cut steak diagonally across grain into ½-inch-thick slices.

2. Heat oil in a large nonstick skillet over medium heat. Add ginger and garlic; sauté 1 minute, stirring occasionally. Add 2 tablespoons soy sauce and edamame to pan; cook 2 minutes.

3. Combine vinegar and wasabi paste in a bowl, stirring until smooth. Place ½ cup edamame mixture on each of 4 plates. Top each serving with 3 ounces steak; drizzle each with 1 tablespoon vinegar mixture. Yield: 4 servings.

CALORIES 253 (42% from fat); FAT 11.9g (sat 3g, mono 3.7g, poly 3.9g); PROTEIN 27.7g; CARB 5.9g; FIBER 0.1g; CHOL 28mg; IRON 2.8mg; SODIUM 653mg; CALC 64mg

Braised Halibut with Bacon and Mushrooms

Smoky bacon complements slightly sweet halibut. If you can't find fresh halibut, substitute snapper.

  1   (3½-ounce) bag boil-in-bag long-grain rice
  4   applewood-smoked bacon slices
  ⅓   cup prechopped onion
  1   tablespoon chopped fresh thyme
  8   ounces presliced mushrooms
  2   teaspoons olive oil
  4   (6-ounce) halibut fillets
  ½   teaspoon salt
  ¼   teaspoon pepper
  1   cup dry white wine
  2   tablespoons chopped fresh parsley

1. Cook rice according to package directions, omitting salt and fat. Drain and keep warm.
2. Cook bacon in a large nonstick skillet over medium heat until crisp. Remove bacon from pan; crumble. Add onion, thyme, and mushrooms to drippings in pan; sauté 3 minutes. Remove mushroom mixture from pan.
3. Heat oil in pan over medium heat. Sprinkle fish with salt and pepper. Add fish to pan, and cook 2 minutes on each side or until browned. Return mushroom mixture to pan. Stir in wine, and cook 3 minutes or until fish flakes easily when tested with a fork or until desired degree of doneness. Sprinkle with crumbled bacon and parsley. Serve over rice. Yield: 4 servings (serving size: 1 fillet, 6 tablespoons mushroom mixture, and ½ cup rice).

CALORIES 388 (26% from fat); FAT 11.1g (sat 2.7g, mono 5.2g, poly 2.1g); PROTEIN 43.1g; CARB 27.3g; FIBER 1.3g; CHOL 64mg; IRON 3.2mg; SODIUM 617mg; CALC 103mg

Sicilian Chicken

Sicilian olives are large green olives marinated in herbs; you can substitute Spanish manzanilla olives. Accompany with orzo pasta and Chianti, if you're pouring wine.

  4   (6-ounce) skinless, boneless chicken breast halves
  ½   teaspoon salt
  ½   teaspoon pepper
  1   tablespoon olive oil
  3   tablespoons all-purpose flour
  ½   cup dry white wine
  ½   cup sliced Sicilian olives
  ¼   cup golden raisins
  1   tablespoon balsamic vinegar
  1   teaspoon dried oregano
  1   (14.5-ounce) can diced no-salt-added tomatoes, undrained
  ¼   cup chopped fresh basil

1. Place each chicken breast half between 2 sheets of heavy-duty plastic wrap; pound each to ½-inch thickness using a meat mallet or heavy skillet. Sprinkle both sides of chicken breast halves with salt and pepper.
2. Heat oil in a large nonstick skillet over medium-high heat. Place flour in a shallow dish; dredge chicken in flour. Add chicken to pan; cook 3 minutes on each side or until lightly browned. Add wine; cook 1 minute. Add olives and next 4 ingredients; bring to a boil. Reduce heat, and simmer 8 minutes or until chicken is done. Sprinkle with basil. Yield: 4 servings (serving size: 1 chicken breast half and about 6 tablespoons sauce).

CALORIES 304 (20% from fat); FAT 6.8g (sat 1.2g, mono 3.9g, poly 1g); PROTEIN 41.3g; CARB 18.2g; FIBER 2.6g; CHOL 99mg; IRON 2.5mg; SODIUM 671mg; CALC 59mg

Sautéed Escarole, Corn, and White Bean Salad

Escarole's bitter flavor mellows when cooked. Combine it with fresh corn and white beans for a refreshing dish.

  2   heads escarole, quartered lengthwise and rinsed
      Cooking spray
  2   ounces pancetta, chopped
  1   zucchini, quartered and cut into julienne strips
  1   garlic clove, minced
  1   cup fresh corn kernels
  ½   cup chopped fresh flat-leaf parsley
  1   (15-ounce) can navy beans, rinsed and drained
  2   tablespoons red wine vinegar
  1   teaspoon extravirgin olive oil
  ½   teaspoon pepper

1. Heat a large nonstick skillet over medium-high heat. Add escarole to pan; cook 3 minutes or until wilted, turning frequently. Trim white stem end from each escarole quarter; roughly chop.
2. Wipe pan with a paper towel. Return pan to medium-high heat. Coat pan with cooking spray. Add pancetta, zucchini, and garlic to pan; cook 2 minutes or until zucchini is tender. Add corn; cook 1 minute. Combine escarole, corn mixture, parsley, and beans in a large bowl. Add vinegar, oil, and pepper; toss well to coat. Serve immediately. Yield: 4 servings (serving size: about 1¾ cups).

CALORIES 210 (31% from fat); FAT 7.2g (sat 2.4g, mono 3.1g, poly 1g); PROTEIN 12.6g; CARB 32.7g; FIBER 14.4g; CHOL 10mg; IRON 4.1mg; SODIUM 634mg; CALC 199mg .

Herbed Basmati Rice

"This is the glue that holds my marriage together," jokes Projects Editor Mary Simpson Creel as she fluffs the grains in a bowl of Herbed Basmati Rice.

Like many readers, she's enjoyed this side dish since we first published it in April 1997 and prepares it so often that her husband, Terry, has nicknamed it "Wife Rice." Creel made several flavor-boosting adjustments over the years. She doubled the amount of uncooked rice to increase the serving size from ½ cup to ⅔ cup, now our standard for grain side dishes. To boost the overall flavor, Creel uses a mixture of chicken broth and water instead of only water. She also cooks the rice in a skillet instead of a saucepan, which offers more surface area for the rice to sauté and trims the cooking time by about five minutes. Using a bit less fat to sauté the rice enables her to add toasted pine nuts and Parmesan cheese.

We think these changes make a good accompaniment outstanding. Add a little chopped rotisserie chicken or cooked shrimp, and you can promote this side dish to an entrée.

STAFF FAVORITE • QUICK & EASY
Herbed Basmati Rice

    1   teaspoon olive oil
    Cooking spray
    1   cup uncooked basmati rice
    1   garlic clove, minced
    1   cup water
    1   cup fat-free, less-sodium chicken
        broth
    ¼   teaspoon salt
    ¼   cup chopped green onions
    ¼   cup pine nuts, toasted
    3   tablespoons grated fresh Parmesan
        cheese
    1   tablespoon chopped fresh basil
    1   teaspoon chopped fresh thyme
    ½   teaspoon freshly ground black
        pepper

1. Heat oil in a medium skillet coated with cooking spray over medium-high heat. Add rice and garlic to pan; sauté 2 minutes or until rice is lightly toasted. Add 1 cup water, broth, and salt to pan; bring to a boil. Cover, reduce heat, and simmer 15 minutes or until liquid is absorbed and rice is tender. Remove from heat; let stand 5 minutes. Stir in onions and remaining ingredients. Yield: 6 servings (serving size: ⅔ cup).

CALORIES 182 (27% from fat); FAT 5.4g (sat 0.8g, mono 1.8g, poly 2.1g); PROTEIN 4g; CARB 31.9g; FIBER 1.5g; CHOL 2mg; IRON 1.5mg; SODIUM 203mg; CALC 37mg

Potato Casserole, Perfected

A Washington State mother seeks a trimmed-down version of a vintage family favorite.

Janelle Youngren, of Vancouver, Washington, received this potato casserole recipe from her late grandmother-in-law, Kitty, who first prepared it after a bingo night with friends 25 years ago. Since then, the side dish has become a staple at family get-togethers. "I asked Granny for the recipe, but once I saw the list of ingredients, I knew it needed work to make it better for you," Youngren says.

The cheesy classic needed to slim down in calories, fat, and sodium. We reduced the original version's one cup of margarine to 2 tablespoons of richer, creamier butter—one tablespoon in the casserole and one mixed with the crushed cornflake cereal topping. We switched from full-fat sour cream and processed cheese to light versions of both, which maintained the casserole's smooth, creamy quality. We also used a low-fat, lower-sodium condensed cream of chicken soup and omitted the original recipe's half-teaspoon of salt to keep the overall sodium at a more reasonable level for a side dish.

STAFF FAVORITE
Hash Brown Casserole

    ¾   cup chopped onion
    ½   teaspoon paprika
    ½   teaspoon freshly ground black
        pepper
    1   (32-ounce) package frozen
        Southern-style hash brown
        potatoes, diced
    2   tablespoons butter, melted and
        divided
    1   (10¾-ounce) can condensed
        reduced-fat, reduced-sodium
        cream of chicken soup, undiluted
        (such as Campbell's Healthy
        Request)
    8   ounces light processed cheese,
        cubed (such as Velveeta Light)
    1   (8-ounce) carton light sour cream
        (such as Daisy)
    Cooking spray
    2   cups cornflakes, coarsely crushed

1. Preheat oven to 350°.
2. Combine first 4 ingredients and 1 tablespoon butter in a large bowl; toss well.
3. Combine soup and cheese in a medium microwave-safe bowl. Microwave at HIGH 6 minutes or until cheese melts, stirring every 2 minutes. Stir in sour cream. Pour cheese mixture over potato mixture, and stir well. Spread mixture evenly in a 13 x 9–inch baking dish coated with cooking spray.
4. Combine cornflakes and 1 tablespoon butter; sprinkle evenly over top of potato mixture. Bake at 350° for 1 hour. Yield: 12 servings (serving size: about ½ cup).

CALORIES 181 (30% from fat); FAT 6g (sat 3.8g, mono 0.9g, poly 0.3g); PROTEIN 7.1g; CARB 25.5g; FIBER 1.5g; CHOL 21mg; IRON 1.7mg; SODIUM 494mg; CALC 11mg

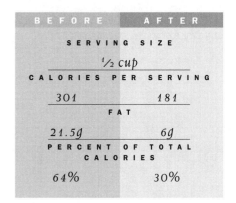

BEFORE	AFTER
SERVING SIZE	
½ cup	
CALORIES PER SERVING	
301	181
FAT	
21.5g	6g
PERCENT OF TOTAL CALORIES	
64%	30%

Bowls Of Comfort

Nothing provides wintertime satisfaction quite like a helping of a simple favorite.

The short, busy days and long, chilly nights of the colder months call for food that soothes. Slow-cooked roasts, soups, stews, puddings, and porridges provide comfort to the core.

Chances are you have lifelong connections with your favorite comfort foods. They provide pleasant associations, perhaps memories of home and family. They're typically simple, unpretentious, and deeply satisfying, especially this time of year.

We've collected a variety of dishes representing regional American favorites, from Yankee Pot Roast of New England to Black-Eyed Pea Stew, a variation of Hoppin' John of the Carolinas. Whether you grew up with these foods or are trying them for the first time, you'll appreciate their homespun flavor. And many of these dishes grow even tastier with time, once the flavors have melded. So make a batch one night, and then enjoy it again later in the week to savor contentment by the bowlful.

MAKE AHEAD
Split Pea Soup

5½ cups water
4 cups organic vegetable broth (such as Swanson Certified Organic)
2 cups green split peas
¾ cup finely chopped yellow onion
6 ounces diced Canadian bacon (about 1 cup)
1 cup finely chopped carrot
1 cup thinly sliced celery
½ teaspoon freshly ground black pepper
⅛ teaspoon salt
1 tablespoon fresh lemon juice

1. Combine first 5 ingredients in a large Dutch oven over medium-high heat; bring to a simmer. Cover, reduce heat, and simmer 1 hour, stirring occasionally.
2. Stir in carrot, celery, pepper, and salt. Simmer, uncovered, 45 minutes or until peas are tender and soup thickens, stirring occasionally. Remove from heat; stir in juice. Yield: 6 servings (serving size: 1¼ cups).

CALORIES 310 (6% from fat); FAT 2.1g (sat 0.7g, mono 0.9g, poly 0.2g); PROTEIN 23.5g; CARB 50.1g; FIBER 1.2g; CHOL 14mg; IRON 2.7mg; SODIUM 864mg; CALC 27mg

Baked Louisiana Dirty Rice and Beans

This spicy casserole, an old New Orleans favorite, traditionally features chicken livers and gizzards. This version substitutes juicy chicken thighs. Brown rice adds a nutty, earthy taste.

1 tablespoon olive oil
1 cup finely chopped green bell pepper
¾ cup finely chopped red onion
½ cup finely chopped celery
½ pound skinless, boneless chicken thighs, cut into ½-inch cubes
1 cup uncooked long-grain brown rice
2½ cups fat-free, less-sodium chicken broth
½ cup thinly sliced green onions
2 teaspoons minced fresh thyme
1 teaspoon salt
½ teaspoon freshly ground black pepper
⅛ to ¼ teaspoon ground red pepper
2 garlic cloves, minced
1 (15-ounce) can red kidney beans, rinsed and drained

1. Preheat oven to 350°.
2. Heat oil in a large Dutch oven over medium heat. Add bell pepper, red onion, and celery to pan; cook 4 minutes or until vegetables are tender, stirring occasionally. Add chicken; cook 3 minutes or until lightly browned. Stir in rice; cook 30 seconds. Add broth and remaining ingredients; bring to a simmer. Cover and bake at 350° for 1 hour and 15 minutes or until liquid is absorbed and rice is tender. Yield: 6 servings (serving size: about 1 cup).

CALORIES 250 (22% from fat); FAT 6.2g (sat 1.3g, mono 3g, poly 1.3g); PROTEIN 13.5g; CARB 34.9g; FIBER 4.8g; CHOL 25mg; IRON 1.7mg; SODIUM 741mg; CALC 42mg

Rice Pudding

Short-grain, starchy white rice, such as Arborio, provides silky texture and creamy consistency for this satisfying dessert.

2 cups cooked Arborio rice or other short-grain rice
3½ cups fat-free milk
⅓ cup sugar
¼ cup nonfat dry milk
¼ teaspoon salt
2 large eggs, lightly beaten
¼ cup golden raisins
1 teaspoon vanilla extract
1 teaspoon ground cinnamon

1. Combine first 5 ingredients in a large saucepan over medium heat; bring to a simmer. Simmer 30 minutes, stirring occasionally.
2. Place eggs in a medium bowl. Gradually add half of rice mixture to eggs, stirring constantly with a whisk. Return egg mixture to pan over medium-low heat; cook 2 minutes, stirring constantly. Remove from heat; stir in raisins and vanilla. Spoon ½ cup pudding into each of 8 bowls. Sprinkle ⅛ teaspoon cinnamon over each serving. Yield: 8 servings.

CALORIES 176 (7% from fat); FAT 1.4g (sat 0.4g, mono 0.5g, poly 0.2g); PROTEIN 7.6g; CARB 33g; FIBER 0.8g; CHOL 54mg; IRON 1.1mg; SODIUM 160mg; CALC 151mg

STAFF FAVORITE • MAKE AHEAD

Black-Eyed Pea Stew

This stew is a cousin of Hoppin' John, a Southern dish made with black-eyed peas and rice. Beer pairs well with this dish.

- 2 cups dried black-eyed peas
- 1 tablespoon peanut oil
- ¾ cup finely chopped yellow onion
- 8 ounces turkey kielbasa, halved lengthwise and cut into ½-inch pieces
- 4 cups organic vegetable broth (such as Swanson Certified Organic)
- 1 teaspoon salt
- ½ teaspoon crushed red pepper
- ½ teaspoon freshly ground black pepper
- 2 bay leaves
- 1 tablespoon cider vinegar
- 1 (28-ounce) can no-salt-added diced tomatoes
- 1 (10-ounce) bag prewashed mustard greens

1. Sort and wash peas; set aside.

2. Heat oil in a large saucepan over medium heat. Add onion to pan; cook 3 minutes or until tender. Add sausage; cook 4 minutes or until lightly browned.

3. Stir in broth; bring to a simmer, scraping pan to loosen browned bits. Stir in peas, salt, peppers, and bay leaves. Cover and simmer 45 minutes or until peas begin to soften. Uncover and cook 15 minutes or until liquid begins to thicken.

4. Stir in vinegar, tomatoes, and mustard greens; simmer 10 minutes or until peas are tender, stirring occasionally. Discard bay leaves. Yield: 8 servings (serving size: about 1 cup).

CALORIES 235 (19% from fat); FAT 5g (sat 1.1g, mono 2.4g, poly 0.9g); PROTEIN 15.5g; CARB 33.7g; FIBER 6.6g; CHOL 17mg; IRON 4.4mg; SODIUM 830mg; CALC 81mg

MAKE AHEAD

Brunswick Stew

(pictured on page 250)

From 19th-century Virginia, this stew originally included squirrel meat (we opt here for chicken). Although the stew is sometimes thickened with stale bread cubes, this version uses flour to give it body and features garlic bread on the side.

- Cooking spray
- 1 cup chopped red bell pepper
- ¾ cup chopped yellow onion
- ½ cup chopped celery
- 1 tablespoon peanut oil
- 1 tablespoon all-purpose flour
- 1 pound skinless, boneless chicken thighs, cut into ½-inch pieces
- 2 cups fat-free, less-sodium chicken broth
- 2 tablespoons no-salt-added tomato paste
- 1 teaspoon dried thyme
- ½ teaspoon salt
- ½ teaspoon hot pepper sauce (such as Tabasco)
- 1 (10-ounce) package frozen whole-kernel corn, thawed
- 1 (10-ounce) package frozen baby lima beans, thawed
- 6 (1-ounce) slices Italian bread, toasted
- 2 garlic cloves, halved

1. Heat a large Dutch oven over medium-high heat. Coat pan with cooking spray. Add bell pepper, onion, and celery to pan; cook 5 minutes, stirring occasionally. Add oil to pan. Combine flour and chicken in a medium bowl, tossing to coat. Add chicken to pan; cook 2 minutes or until lightly browned. Gradually stir in broth; bring to a boil. Cook 1 minute or until slightly thick, stirring constantly. Add tomato paste and next 5 ingredients to pan. Cover, reduce heat, and simmer 30 minutes.

2. Rub bread slices with cut sides of garlic; discard garlic. Serve bread with stew. Yield: 6 servings (serving size: 1 cup stew and 1 slice bread).

CALORIES 319 (26% from fat); FAT 9.2g (sat 2.2g, mono 3.5g, poly 2.6g); PROTEIN 22.4g; CARB 38g; FIBER 5.8g; CHOL 50mg; IRON 3.2mg; SODIUM 596mg; CALC 58mg

MAKE AHEAD

Yankee Pot Roast

Yankee cooks traditionally add the vegetables partway through the cooking process, which helps keep them from breaking down.

- 1 teaspoon canola oil
- 2 pounds boneless chuck roast, trimmed
- Cooking spray
- 1 cup chopped yellow onion
- 4 cups fat-free, less-sodium beef broth
- 1 tablespoon whole-grain Dijon mustard
- 1 teaspoon salt
- 1 teaspoon dried thyme
- ½ teaspoon freshly ground black pepper
- ½ teaspoon dried sage
- 2 bay leaves
- 2½ cups (1-inch) cubed peeled rutabaga (about 1 pound)
- 2½ cups (1-inch) cubed peeled parsnip (about 1 pound)
- 1½ cups (1-inch-thick) slices carrot (about 8 ounces)
- 2 cups (1-inch) cubed peeled baking potato (about 1 pound)
- Thyme sprigs (optional)

1. Preheat oven to 300°.

2. Heat oil in a large Dutch oven over medium-high heat. Add beef to pan, browning on all sides (about 8 minutes). Remove from pan. Coat pan with cooking spray. Add onion to pan; sauté 5 minutes or until onion begins to brown. Stir in broth, scraping pan to loosen browned bits. Reduce heat; add mustard and next 5 ingredients. Return roast to pan; bring to a simmer.

3. Cover and bake at 300° for 1½ hours. Stir in rutabaga, parsnip, and carrot. Bake, covered, 1 hour. Stir in potato;

cover and bake 30 minutes or until roast and vegetables are very tender. Discard bay leaves. Garnish with thyme sprigs, if desired. Yield: 8 servings (serving size: about 1¼ cups).

CALORIES 325 (28% from fat); FAT 10.2g (sat 3.3g, mono 4.6g, poly 0.7g); PROTEIN 28.7g; CARB 29.3g; FIBER 5.8g; CHOL 79mg; IRON 4.3mg; SODIUM 642mg; CALC 72mg

Breakfast Gathering Menu
serves 6

Multigrain Breakfast Porridge

Hard-boiled eggs

Fresh fruit salad

Orange juice and coffee

MAKE AHEAD
Multigrain Breakfast Porridge

This dish features rolled oats and wheat berries, products of the Montana-Dakotas region.

4½ cups water
½ cup uncooked wheat berries (hard winter wheat), rinsed
¾ teaspoon salt
¾ cup regular oats
3 tablespoons uncooked quick-cooking grits
¾ cup fat-free milk
¼ cup maple syrup
½ cup chopped walnuts, toasted

1. Combine first 3 ingredients in a large saucepan over medium-high heat; bring to a simmer. Cover, reduce heat, and simmer 20 minutes.
2. Stir in oats; simmer, uncovered, 12 minutes, stirring frequently. Stir in grits; simmer 5 minutes, stirring frequently.
3. Stir in milk and syrup; simmer 1 minute or until porridge thickens, stirring constantly. Remove from heat. Serve with walnuts. Yield: 6 servings (serving size: about ½ cup porridge and 4 teaspoons walnuts).

CALORIES 219 (28% from fat); FAT 6.9g (sat 0.6g, mono 1.6g, poly 4.3g); PROTEIN 7.7g; CARB 34g; FIBER 3.6g; CHOL 0mg; IRON 1.1mg; SODIUM 312mg; CALC 55mg

Reheating Tips

Some of these dishes will thicken considerably after being refrigerated. To reheat leftovers, thin them with additional liquid from the recipe (fat-free milk for Multigrain Breakfast Porridge at left for instance) or water. Start with a tablespoon or two, adding more liquid as it heats until you reach the desired consistency.

Reheat portions in the microwave or in a saucepan over medium heat. When reheating on the stovetop, stir the mixture frequently to prevent scorching on the bottom.

inspired vegetarian

Caribbean Cuisine

Island fare is soulful, nourishing, and reflects a delectable mix of cultural history.

Ethnic diversity permeates the Caribbean's 7,000-plus islands that extend from Florida to Venezuela. Due to its colorful history, this region is a melting pot of cuisines, and many islands offer numerous delectable vegetarian dishes. The phrase "fusion food" perfectly describes it as it developed from the influences of native people and European, African, and Asian immigrants.

Herbs like thyme, spices such as ginger, allspice, and nutmeg, and hot pepper pastes and sauces give these vegetarian dishes lots of flavor, thus eliminating the need for excessive butter, oil, and cream. Ripe tropical fruits like guava and mango sweeten cakes, bread puddings, and pies, while nuts add protein to savory dishes and richness to desserts.

The recipes here reflect the amalgam of cuisines you'll find in the Caribbean. Made with ingredients that are available in most large supermarkets, they'll give you a taste of the islands from the comfort of your own kitchen.

Mixed Vegetable Coo-Coo with Tomato Sauce

Coo-coo, the Caribbean rendition of soft polenta, traditionally hails from Barbados.

SAUCE:
Cooking spray
½ cup chopped onion
½ cup chopped red bell pepper
¾ teaspoon dried oregano
¼ teaspoon kosher salt
¼ teaspoon black pepper
1 large garlic clove, minced
¼ cup organic vegetable broth (such as Swanson Certified Organic)
1 teaspoon dark brown sugar
⅛ teaspoon ground allspice
2 cups canned crushed tomatoes, undrained

COO-COO:
2 cups cornmeal
1 teaspoon kosher salt
7 cups water
2 cups frozen whole-kernel corn, thawed
1 cup frozen cut okra, thawed
2 tablespoons butter

1. To prepare sauce, heat a small saucepan over medium heat. Coat pan with cooking spray. Add onion and next 5 ingredients to pan; cook 5 minutes, stirring occasionally. Stir in broth and next 3 ingredients. Partially cover, reduce heat, and simmer 20 minutes, stirring occasionally.
2. To prepare coo-coo, place cornmeal and 1 teaspoon salt in a large saucepan. Gradually add 7 cups water, stirring constantly with a whisk. Bring to a boil. Reduce heat to medium, and cook 15 minutes, stirring frequently. Add corn and okra; cook 2 minutes or until thoroughly heated, stirring constantly. Remove from heat. Place butter in a small skillet over medium heat; cook 2 minutes or until browned. Add butter to coo-coo; stir well. Serve sauce over coo-coo. Yield: 6 servings (serving size: about 1 cup coo-coo and ⅔ cup tomato sauce).

CALORIES 299 (16% from fat); FAT 5.4g (sat 2.6g, mono 1.4g, poly 0.8g); PROTEIN 7.9g; CARB 58.2g; FIBER 7.7g; CHOL 10mg; IRON 3.6mg; SODIUM 561mg; CALC 78mg

Haitian Rice and Beans

Rice and bean dishes are prepared on almost every island in the Caribbean because they make an easy, nourishing, inexpensive meal. Adding kidney beans to the rice is typical of Haiti, as is the use of shallots.

      2   tablespoons olive oil
      2   cups chopped shallots (about 9 large)
  1½   cups chopped green bell pepper
      1   teaspoon dried oregano
      3   garlic cloves, minced
      ¼   cup organic vegetable broth (such as Swanson Certified Organic)
      2   teaspoons balsamic vinegar
      ½   teaspoon kosher salt, divided
      3   cups water
      1   tablespoon minced chipotle chile, canned in adobo sauce
  1½   cups uncooked long-grain white rice
      1   (15-ounce) can red kidney beans, rinsed and drained

1. Heat oil in a large nonstick skillet over medium-high heat. Add shallots, bell pepper, oregano, and garlic to pan; cook 12 minutes or until vegetables are tender, stirring frequently. Remove from heat. Stir in broth, vinegar, and ¼ teaspoon salt. Cover and set aside.
2. Bring 3 cups water and chile to a boil in a medium saucepan; add rice. Cover, reduce heat, and simmer 18 minutes or until liquid is absorbed. Remove from heat; fluff with a fork. Stir in ¼ teaspoon salt and beans. Spoon 1 cup rice mixture onto each of 6 serving plates; top each serving with about ¼ cup shallot mixture. Yield: 6 servings.

CALORIES 290 (16% from fat); FAT 5.1g (sat 0.8g, mono 3.4g, poly 0.7g); PROTEIN 7g; CARB 54.2g; FIBER 4.1g; CHOL 0mg; IRON 3.4mg; SODIUM 352mg; CALC 53mg

Black-Eyed Pea Patties with Garlic Pepper Salsa

Black-eyed peas were introduced in the Caribbean by African slaves. Somewhat drier than other legumes, they're ivory-gray in color with a black "eye" at the inner curve. They go by many names, including gungo and pigeon peas. These patties can be shaped an hour in advance; cover and refrigerate.

      3   garlic cloves, minced
      2   serrano chiles, seeded and finely chopped
      2   (16-ounce) cans black-eyed peas, rinsed and well drained
      ⅓   cup finely chopped red bell pepper
      6   tablespoons chopped fresh cilantro, divided
  1½   teaspoons ground cumin
      ½   teaspoon kosher salt, divided
      1   large egg, lightly beaten
      1   tablespoon olive oil, divided
      2   cups chopped tomato
      2   teaspoons fresh lime juice

1. Combine garlic and chiles in a large bowl. Place 1 teaspoon garlic mixture in a small bowl; set aside. Add peas to garlic mixture in large bowl; mash with a potato masher. Add bell pepper, ¼ cup cilantro, cumin, ¼ teaspoon salt, and egg, stirring until well blended. Divide mixture into 12 equal portions (about ¼ cup each), shaping each into a ½-inch-thick patty.
2. Heat 1½ teaspoons oil in a large nonstick skillet over medium-high heat. Add 6 patties; cook 4 minutes on each side or until browned. Repeat procedure with 1½ teaspoons olive oil and remaining patties.
3. Add 2 tablespoons cilantro, ¼ teaspoon salt, tomato, and lime juice to reserved garlic mixture in bowl; stir well. Serve with patties. Yield: 6 servings (serving size: 2 patties and ⅓ cup salsa).

CALORIES 119 (29% from fat); FAT 3.9g (sat 0.7g, mono 2g, poly 0.7g); PROTEIN 6.1g; CARB 16g; FIBER 4.1g; CHOL 35mg; IRON 1.5mg; SODIUM 435mg; CALC 37mg

BEER NOTE: Sometimes it's fun to conjure a little sunshine with your autumn meals. And these salsa-laced patties mark the perfect occasion to enjoy a refreshing Caribbean beer like Red Stripe Lager ($7.50/six-pack) from Jamaica. Beers that are developed alongside spicy cuisine tend to be light-bodied, balanced, and neutral, making this beer a good choice with the patties' serrano peppers and cumin.

Chayote Gratin

Chayote (chi-OH-tay) is a pale green fruit popular in Jamaica; it's also called mirliton in Louisiana and other Southern states. The soft, watery flesh tastes similar to zucchini and surrounds a soft, oval, white seed.

          Cooking spray
      6   cups cubed peeled chayote (about 2¼ pounds)
      ¼   cup water
      ½   teaspoon olive oil
      1   cup chopped onion
      ¼   cup finely chopped celery
      ¼   cup finely chopped green bell pepper
  1¼   teaspoons chopped fresh thyme
      ½   teaspoon kosher salt
      1   (1-ounce) slice whole wheat bread
      2   tablespoons grated fresh Parmesan cheese
  1½   teaspoons butter, melted

1. Heat a large nonstick skillet over medium-high heat. Coat pan with cooking spray. Add chayote to pan; sauté 10 minutes or until crisp-tender. Reduce heat to low; add ¼ cup water. Cover and cook 10 minutes or until tender. Place chayote in a large bowl and mash with a potato masher. Drain mashed chayote in a fine sieve 30 minutes, reserving pulp.
2. Preheat oven to 350°.
3. Heat oil in a large nonstick skillet coated with cooking spray over medium-high heat. Add onion, celery, pepper, and thyme to pan; sauté 10 minutes or until vegetables are tender. Add chayote

pulp and salt, stirring to combine. Spoon mixture into an 8-inch square baking dish coated with cooking spray.

4. Place bread in a food processor; pulse 10 times or until fine crumbs measure ½ cup. Combine crumbs and cheese in a small bowl; stir in butter. Sprinkle crumb mixture evenly over chayote mixture. Bake at 350° for 25 minutes or until golden. Yield: 12 servings (serving size: ½ cup).

CALORIES 38 (28% from fat); FAT 1.2g (sat 0.5g, mono 0.3g, poly 0.1g); PROTEIN 1.6g; CARB 6g; FIBER 1.9g; CHOL 2mg; IRON 0.4mg; SODIUM 119mg; CALC 38mg

Spiced Rum-Glazed Plantains

In Cuba, plantains are eaten as a savory side dish in the same way Americans enjoy sweet potatoes. Wait until the plantain skins have blackened to guarantee the fruit is sweet and tender.

3   pounds ripe plantains
Cooking spray
⅓   cup fresh orange juice
¼   cup packed dark brown sugar
2½ tablespoons dark rum
1   tablespoon lime juice
½   teaspoon grated peeled fresh ginger
⅛   teaspoon grated whole nutmeg
2   tablespoons chilled butter, cut into small pieces
½   teaspoon kosher salt

1. Preheat oven to 350°.
2. Peel plantains; diagonally cut into ½-inch-thick slices. Arrange plantain slices in a single layer on a jelly-roll pan coated with cooking spray. Combine orange juice and next 5 ingredients in a small bowl; stir with a whisk. Pour juice mixture over plantains. Dot with butter, and sprinkle with salt. Bake at 350° for 30 minutes. Gently turn plantains over using tongs; bake an additional 10 minutes or until lightly browned. Yield: 12 servings (serving size: ½ cup).

CALORIES 183 (11% from fat); FAT 2.3g (sat 1.4g, mono 0.5g, poly 0.2g); PROTEIN 1.6g; CARB 41.5g; FIBER 2.6g; CHOL 5mg; IRON 0.8mg; SODIUM 98mg; CALC 9mg

West Indian Vegetable Curry

Hindu immigrant workers brought wet and dry curry mixtures to Trinidad and Tobago. Here a habanero pepper is added for a brief time while the mixture simmers to impart subtle heat without overpowering the dish. Calabaza, also called West Indian pumpkin, has a brilliant orange, firm, sweet flesh, much like acorn or butternut squash. This vegetable dish is often served over rice or with coo-coo, a Caribbean dish similar to polenta.

1   tablespoon olive oil
Cooking spray
1   cup chopped yellow onion
1   cup chopped red bell pepper
¼   cup chopped green onions
1   tablespoon chopped fresh thyme
1½ teaspoons curry powder
1   teaspoon kosher salt
3   garlic cloves, minced
2   cups organic vegetable broth (such as Swanson Certified Organic), divided
1⅓ cups (¼-inch-thick) slices carrot
1   habanero pepper
3   cups cubed peeled calabaza or hubbard squash (about 1 pound)
1½ cups chopped plum tomato
2   zucchini, halved lengthwise and sliced (about 3 cups)

1. Heat oil in a large Dutch oven coated with cooking spray over medium-high heat. Add yellow onion and next 6 ingredients to pan; sauté 5 minutes or until vegetables are tender. Add 1 cup broth, scraping pan to loosen browned bits. Add 1 cup broth and carrot; sauté 5 minutes.
2. Pierce habanero with a fork; add to pan. Stir in squash, tomato, and zucchini; bring to a boil. Reduce heat, and simmer 10 minutes. Discard habanero; simmer 15 minutes or until vegetables are tender. Yield: 7 servings (serving size: 1 cup).

CALORIES 105 (21% from fat); FAT 2.5g (sat 0.4g, mono 1.5g, poly 0.4g); PROTEIN 2.6g; CARB 21.1g; FIBER 5.7g; CHOL 0mg; IRON 1.4mg; SODIUM 465mg; CALC 64mg

Puerto Rican Guava Bread Pudding

Guava paste is a firm, sticky, rose-colored sweet sold in bricks or canned.

PUDDING:
1¼ cups 1% low-fat milk
1   (12-ounce) can evaporated fat-free milk
2   large egg whites, lightly beaten
1   large egg, lightly beaten
⅓   cup packed dark brown sugar
⅓   cup dark rum
½   teaspoon ground cinnamon
½   teaspoon grated peeled fresh ginger
⅛   teaspoon grated whole nutmeg
12 ounces French bread, cut into 1-inch cubes, toasted (about 8 cups)
Cooking spray

SAUCE:
¾   cup water, divided
1   tablespoon lime juice
8   ounces guava paste, cut into small pieces

1. To prepare pudding, combine first 4 ingredients in a large bowl; stir well with a whisk. Stir in sugar, rum, cinnamon, ginger, and nutmeg. Add bread; toss gently to coat. Spoon mixture into an 11 x 7-inch baking dish coated with cooking spray. Cover and chill 1 hour.
2. Preheat oven to 350°.
3. Place baking dish in a roasting pan; add hot water to pan to a depth of 1 inch. Cover and bake at 350° for 15 minutes. Uncover and bake an additional 15 minutes or until a knife inserted in center comes out clean. Let stand 15 minutes.
4. To prepare sauce, combine ¼ cup water, juice, and guava paste in a small saucepan over low heat. Cook 10 minutes or until paste is melted, stirring frequently. Remove from heat; stir in ½ cup water. Serve with pudding. Yield: 12 servings (serving size: 1 pudding piece and about 1½ tablespoons sauce).

CALORIES 208 (6% from fat); FAT 1.5g (sat 0.4g, mono 0.6g, poly 0.3g); PROTEIN 6g; CARB 39g; FIBER 1g; CHOL 19mg; IRON 1.1mg; SODIUM 245mg; CALC 127mg

Apple Pie Day

Every October, amateur bakers in a New Hampshire town turn out for a friendly baking contest to celebrate the local crop.

New Englanders take great pride in their apples and, especially, their apple pies. Take the example of the Who Makes the Best Apple Pie Party, hosted every October by Bonnie Hunt of Holderness, New Hampshire. This friendly competition strives to determine who makes the best apple pie in town, and it's held at Hunt's restored Victorian farmhouse overlooking White Oak Pond, and close by Squam Lake of *On Golden Pond* fame.

Bonnie's Best Apple Pie Contest Menu
serves 12

Barbara's Peppery Pecans

Autumn Salad with Red Wine Vinaigrette

Grilled Pork Tenderloin

Swiss Baked Potatoes

Chunky Spiced Applesauce

Corn Bread Bites

Apple pie

Apple cider, beer, riesling, coffee

WINE NOTE: This terrific autumn menu has riesling written all over it. In Europe, riesling is the historic match for pork and potatoes, and it's equally delicious with applesauce and corn muffins. Best of all, riesling's breezy freshness and vivacity add a "lightness" to the rich main dish. Choose a German riesling at the spätlese level of ripeness, such as Selbach-Oster Zeltinger Sonnenuhr Riesling Spätlese 2005 from the Mosel-Saar-Ruwer, about $25.

MAKE AHEAD
Barbara's Peppery Pecans

You can keep these pecans in an airtight container up to one week. They're delicious with cocktails or as part of a cheese plate with sharp Cheddar and sliced apples.

> 1 tablespoon sugar
> 1 tablespoon Worcestershire sauce
> 1 teaspoon kosher salt
> 1 teaspoon butter, melted
> ¼ teaspoon ground red pepper
> ¼ teaspoon ground cinnamon
> 1 pound pecan halves
> Cooking spray

1. Preheat oven to 325°.
2. Combine all ingredients except cooking spray in a large bowl, tossing well to coat. Spread mixture evenly on a jelly-roll pan coated with cooking spray. Coat nuts with cooking spray. Bake at 325° for 15 minutes, stirring every 5 minutes. Remove from oven; cool completely. Store in an airtight container. Yield: 3½ cups (serving size: about 2 tablespoons).

CALORIES 99 (94% from fat); FAT 10.3g (sat 1g, mono 5.8g, poly 3.1g); PROTEIN 1.3g; CARB 2.1g; FIBER 1.4g; CHOL 0mg; IRON 0.4mg; SODIUM 65mg; CALC 11mg

Autumn Salad with Red Wine Vinaigrette

This recipe is similar to a salad Hunt traditionally serves at her annual gathering, using Asian pears and Macoun apples.

> 2 tablespoons extravirgin olive oil
> 2 tablespoons red wine vinegar
> ½ teaspoon sugar
> ½ teaspoon minced garlic
> ¼ teaspoon paprika
> ¼ teaspoon dry mustard
> ⅛ teaspoon salt
> Dash of dried basil
> Dash of ground red pepper
> 5 cups mixed salad greens
> 4 cups torn romaine lettuce
> 2½ cups cubed Asian pear (about 1 large)
> 2 cups chopped Granny Smith apple (about 1 large)
> ½ cup thinly sliced red onion
> ¼ cup (1 ounce) crumbled goat cheese

1. Combine first 9 ingredients in a bowl, stirring with a whisk.
2. Combine salad greens, romaine lettuce, pear, apple, and onion in a large bowl. Drizzle with vinaigrette, and toss well to coat. Sprinkle with cheese. Yield: 12 servings (serving size: about 1 cup salad and 1 teaspoon cheese).

CALORIES 48 (60% from fat); FAT 3.2g (sat 0.8g, mono 2g, poly 0.3g); PROTEIN 1g; CARB 4.7g; FIBER 1.4g; CHOL 2mg; IRON 0.4mg; SODIUM 40mg; CALC 19mg

MAKE AHEAD
Grilled Pork Tenderloin

If it's too cold to grill, you can roast the tenderloins at 425° for 20 minutes or until a thermometer registers 160°; let stand 10 minutes before slicing.

> 1 cup olive oil
> 1 cup orange juice
> ¼ cup chopped green onions
> 2 teaspoons ground white pepper
> 2 teaspoons salt, divided
> 3 (1-pound) pork tenderloins, trimmed
> Cooking spray

1. Combine first 4 ingredients in a large zip-top plastic bag. Add 1 teaspoon salt and pork to bag; seal and shake well. Marinate in refrigerator 2 hours, turning bag occasionally.

2. Prepare grill.

3. Remove pork from bag, and discard marinade. Sprinkle pork evenly with 1 teaspoon salt. Place pork on grill rack coated with cooking spray; grill 20 minutes or until a thermometer registers 160° (slightly pink). Let stand 10 minutes before cutting into thin slices. Yield: 14 servings (serving size: 3 ounces pork).

CALORIES 176 (35% from fat); FAT 6.9g (sat 1.9g, mono 3.7g, poly 0.6g); PROTEIN 25.7g; CARB 1.1g; FIBER 0.1g; CHOL 72mg; IRON 1.4mg; SODIUM 234mg; CALC 8mg

Swiss Baked Potatoes

This homey gratin partners nicely with pork or other grilled meats.

- 6 baking potatoes, peeled and thinly sliced (about 3½ pounds)
- Cooking spray
- 1¼ cups thinly sliced onion (about 1 medium)
- 1½ teaspoons freshly ground black pepper
- ¾ teaspoon salt
- ½ cup (2 ounces) shredded Gruyère cheese
- 2 tablespoons butter, chilled and cut into small pieces
- ¾ cup fat-free, less-sodium beef broth

1. Preheat oven to 375°.

2. Arrange one-third of potato slices in bottom of a shallow 2-quart baking dish coated with cooking spray. Top with one-third of onion slices. Sprinkle with ½ teaspoon pepper, ¼ teaspoon salt, and one-third of cheese. Repeat layers twice, ending with cheese. Dot with butter. Pour broth over potato mixture. Coat top with cooking spray. Cover with foil, and bake at 375° for 30 minutes. Uncover and bake an additional 30 minutes or until tender. Yield: 12 servings (serving size: ⅔ cup).

CALORIES 106 (30% from fat); FAT 3.5g (sat 2.1g, mono 1g, poly 0.2g); PROTEIN 3.2g; CARB 15.9g; FIBER 1.6g; CHOL 10mg; IRON 0.8mg; SODIUM 208mg; CALC 58mg

MAKE AHEAD
Chunky Spiced Applesauce

Cranberries lend this applesauce an appealing rosiness. For best flavor, use a variety of apples, such as Golden Delicious, Braeburn, Cortland, and Rome. You can prepare this recipe up to one day ahead. Serve with Grilled Pork Tenderloin (page 310).

- 10 cups cubed peeled apple (about 3 pounds)
- ½ lemon
- 2 cups fresh cranberries
- 1 cup sugar
- ½ cup maple syrup
- ⅓ cup water
- ½ teaspoon ground cinnamon
- Dash of freshly grated nutmeg

1. Place apple in a large bowl; cover with cold water. Squeeze juice from lemon half into bowl; place lemon half in bowl. Set aside.

2. Combine cranberries and remaining 5 ingredients in a Dutch oven; bring to a boil, stirring occasionally. Cook 3 minutes or until cranberries pop.

3. Drain apple, and discard lemon. Add apple to pan. Cover, reduce heat, and simmer 25 minutes or until apple is soft. Uncover, bring to a boil, and cook 15 minutes. Mash apple mixture with a potato masher. Pour into serving dish, and cover and chill at least 2 hours. Yield: 7 cups (serving size: about ½ cup).

CALORIES 124 (0% from fat); FAT 0.2g (sat 0g, mono 0g, poly 0.1g); PROTEIN 0.3g; CARB 32.5g; FIBER 2.6g; CHOL 0mg; IRON 0.3mg; SODIUM 2mg; CALC 14mg

MAKE AHEAD • FREEZABLE
Corn Bread Bites

This recipe also makes a dozen muffins in a standard muffin tin; bake 17 minutes or until golden brown. You also can double the recipe and freeze the extra muffins up to one month. If you do this, prepare the muffins in two batches so the baking powder doesn't lose its effectiveness while the extra batter waits for the first batch to be turned out of the pans.

- ⅔ cup all-purpose flour (about 3 ounces)
- ½ cup yellow cornmeal
- 1 tablespoon sugar
- 1½ teaspoons baking powder
- ¼ teaspoon salt
- ½ cup (2 ounces) shredded sharp Cheddar cheese
- ½ cup reduced-fat sour cream
- ¼ cup thinly sliced green onions
- 1 (8¾-ounce) can cream-style corn
- Dash of hot sauce
- 1 large egg, lightly beaten
- Cooking spray

1. Preheat oven to 375°.

2. Lightly spoon flour into dry measuring cups; level with a knife. Combine flour and next 4 ingredients in a large bowl. Combine cheese and next 5 ingredients in a small bowl; stir with a whisk. Add to flour mixture; stir just until moistened.

3. Divide batter evenly among 36 miniature muffin cups coated with cooking spray. Bake at 375° for 10 minutes or until golden brown. Cool in pans 2 minutes on wire racks; remove from pans. Cool completely on wire racks. Yield: 12 servings (serving size: 3 muffins).

CALORIES 108 (28% from fat); FAT 3.4g (sat 1.9g, mono 0.5g, poly 0.1g); PROTEIN 3.7g; CARB 15.5g; FIBER 0.8g; CHOL 28mg; IRON 0.8mg; SODIUM 221mg; CALC 89mg

MAKE AHEAD
Susan Brackett's First Prize Apple Pie

The judges awarded the top honors to Susan Brackett for her crumb-topped pie. Brackett used Cortland apples, but any tart apple will do. We found Pink Lady apples do nicely.

CRUST:

- 1½ cups all-purpose flour (about 6¾ ounces)
- ¼ teaspoon salt
- ¼ teaspoon baking powder
- 2 tablespoons chilled butter, cut into small pieces
- 2 tablespoons vegetable shortening
- 1 teaspoon vinegar
- 7 tablespoons ice water

Continued

FILLING:

⅓ cup granulated sugar
2 tablespoons all-purpose flour
½ teaspoon ground cinnamon
½ teaspoon ground nutmeg
⅛ teaspoon salt
7 cups thinly sliced peeled Pink Lady apple (about 7 medium)
Cooking spray

TOPPING:

6 tablespoons all-purpose flour (about 1¾ ounces)
3 tablespoons brown sugar
3 tablespoons chilled butter, cut into small pieces

1. To prepare crust, lightly spoon 1½ cups four into dry measuring cups; level with a knife. Combine 1½ cups flour, ¼ teaspoon salt, and baking powder in a medium bowl; cut in 2 tablespoons butter and shortening with a pastry blender or 2 knives until mixture resembles coarse meal. Sprinkle surface with vinegar and ice water, 1 tablespoon at a time, tossing with a fork until dough is moist and crumbly (do not form a ball). Gently press dough into a 4-inch circle on 2 sheets of overlapping heavy-duty plastic wrap, and cover with 2 additional sheets of overlapping plastic wrap. Roll dough, still covered, into a 12-inch circle. Chill dough 30 minutes or until plastic wrap can be easily removed.

2. Preheat oven to 425°.

3. To prepare filling, combine granulated sugar and next 4 ingredients in a small bowl. Sprinkle sugar mixture over apple; toss well to coat.

4. Remove top sheets of plastic wrap from dough circle; fit dough, plastic wrap side up, into a 10-inch deep-dish pie plate coated with cooking spray, letting dough extend over edge of plate. Remove remaining plastic wrap. Fold edges under; flute. Spoon filling into crust.

5. To prepare topping, combine 6 tablespoons flour and brown sugar in a medium bowl. Cut in 3 tablespoons butter with a pastry blender or 2 knives until mixture is crumbly. Sprinkle topping mixture over apple mixture. Bake at 425° for 10 minutes. Reduce heat to 350° (do not remove pie from oven); bake an

additional 40 minutes. Yield: 10 servings (serving size: 1 wedge).

CALORIES 246 (31% from fat); FAT 8.5g (sat 4.6g, mono 2.2g, poly 1.1g); PROTEIN 2.9g; CARB 40.6g; FIBER 2.6g; CHOL 15mg; IRON 1.4mg; SODIUM 143mg; CALC 22mg

---

MAKE AHEAD

Adreena Barmakian and Jayne Cohen's Apple Pie

(pictured on page 248)

Barmakian and Cohen teamed up to create this traditional pie. They used Cortland apples; we found that Pacific Rose apples also work well.

2½ cups all-purpose flour (about 11¼ ounces)
¾ teaspoon salt
6 tablespoons chilled butter, cut into small pieces
2 tablespoons vegetable shortening, cut into small pieces
1 tablespoon fresh lemon juice
¾ cup ice water
2½ cups thinly sliced peeled Braeburn apple (about 1 pound)
2½ cups thinly sliced peeled Cortland apple (about 1 pound)
1 cup sugar
¼ cup all-purpose flour (about 1 ounce)
¼ teaspoon ground cinnamon
⅛ to ¼ teaspoon ground allspice
Cooking spray
1 tablespoon chilled butter, cut into small pieces
½ teaspoon vanilla extract
1 tablespoon whole milk

1. Lightly spoon 2½ cups flour into dry measuring cups; level with a knife. Combine 2½ cups flour and salt in a large bowl, and cut in 6 tablespoons butter and shortening with a pastry blender or 2 knives until mixture resembles coarse meal. Add lemon juice. Sprinkle surface with ice water, 1 tablespoon at a time, and toss with a fork until moist and crumbly. Shape dough into a ball, and wrap in plastic wrap. Chill 1 hour.

2. Divide dough into 2 equal portions. Gently press each portion into a 1-inch-thick circle on heavy-duty plastic wrap; cover and freeze 10 minutes.

3. Preheat oven to 350°.

4. Place sliced apples in a large bowl. Combine sugar, ¼ cup flour, cinnamon, and allspice in a small bowl. Sprinkle sugar mixture over apples, and toss well to coat.

5. Roll 1 dough portion into a 12-inch circle on a lightly floured surface. Fit into a 9-inch pie plate coated with cooking spray, allowing dough to extend over edge. Roll remaining dough portion into a 10-inch circle on a lightly floured surface. Spoon apple mixture into prepared pie plate, and dot with 1 tablespoon butter. Drizzle apple mixture with vanilla. Top with 10-inch dough circle. Press edges of dough together. Fold edges under, and flute. Brush surface of dough with milk. Cut 3 (1-inch) slits in top of dough to allow steam to escape. Bake at 350° for 1 hour or until apples are tender. Yield: 10 servings (serving size: 1 slice).

CALORIES 326 (30% from fat); FAT 10.8g (sat 6g, mono 2.8g, poly 1.2g); PROTEIN 3.8g; CARB 54.1g; FIBER 2.3g; CHOL 21mg; IRON 1.7mg; SODIUM 233mg; CALC 14mg

---

MAKE AHEAD

Marie Colbath's Apple Pie

2½ cups all-purpose flour (about 11¼ ounces)
1¼ teaspoons kosher salt, divided
½ cup plus 1 tablespoon chilled butter, cut into small pieces and divided
10 tablespoons ice water
8 cups sliced peeled McIntosh apple (about 3 pounds)
1 tablespoon lemon juice
½ cup packed brown sugar
¼ cup plus 1 tablespoon granulated sugar, divided
3 tablespoons all-purpose flour
1⅛ teaspoons ground cinnamon, divided
Cooking spray
1 egg white, lightly beaten

1. Preheat oven to 425°.

2. Lightly spoon 2½ cups flour into dry measuring cups; level with a knife. Combine 2½ cups flour and 1 teaspoon salt in a large bowl; cut in ½ cup butter with a pastry blender or 2 knives until mixture resembles coarse meal. Sprinkle surface with ice water, 1 tablespoon at a time; toss with a fork until moist and crumbly (do not form a ball).

3. Divide dough in half. Gently press each half into a 4-inch circle on 2 sheets of overlapping heavy-duty plastic wrap; cover with 2 additional sheets of overlapping plastic wrap. Chill 30 minutes.

4. Roll 1 dough half, still covered, into a 12-inch circle. Roll remaining dough half, still covered, into an 11-inch circle. Chill 30 minutes.

5. Combine apple and juice in a bowl. Combine brown sugar, ¼ cup granulated sugar, 3 tablespoons flour, 1 teaspoon cinnamon, and ¼ teaspoon salt in a small bowl. Sprinkle sugar mixture over apple mixture; toss well to coat.

6. Remove top 2 sheets of plastic wrap from 12-inch dough circle; fit dough, plastic wrap side up, into a 9-inch deep-dish pie plate coated with cooking spray, allowing dough to extend over edge. Remove remaining plastic wrap. Spoon filling into dough, and dot with 1 tablespoon butter; brush edges of dough lightly with water.

7. Remove top 2 sheets of plastic wrap from 11-inch dough circle; place, plastic wrap side up, over filling. Remove remaining plastic wrap. Press edges of dough together. Fold edges under, and flute. Cut 4 (1-inch) slits in top of dough to allow steam to escape.

8. Combine 1 tablespoon granulated sugar and ⅛ teaspoon cinnamon in a small bowl. Brush top and edges of dough with egg white; sprinkle with sugar mixture. Place pie on a baking sheet. Bake at 425° for 25 minutes. Reduce oven temperature to 350° (do not remove pie from oven); bake an additional 30 minutes or until golden. Shield pie with foil, if necessary. Cool on a wire rack. Yield: 10 servings (serving size: 1 wedge).

CALORIES 327 (29% from fat); FAT 10.7g (sat 6.6g, mono 2.7g, poly 0.6g); PROTEIN 4.2g; CARB 55.2g; FIBER 3.2g; CHOL 27mg; IRON 2mg; SODIUM 319mg; CALC 26mg

Fiber Fundamentals

Its multiple healthful benefits can be enjoyed with a few easy strategies and these delicious recipes.

Fall favorites like hearty stews with beans, barley, or lentils, and desserts with fresh apples and pears, are satisfying and naturally abundant in fiber. Not only are high-fiber foods tasty, but they also help to control hunger, lower cholesterol, and maintain digestive health.

The American Dietetic Association (ADA) recommends eating 20 to 35 grams of fiber daily. But estimates show most of us fall short of that, consuming only about 14 grams daily. Yet boosting your fiber intake is easier than you may think, and fall is a great time to switch out typical staples with hearty higher-fiber versions. Swap white English muffins for 100 percent whole wheat versions, corn flakes for bran breakfast cereal or oatmeal, white rice for whole wheat couscous or bulgur, and juice for fresh fruit. Little changes like these add up to a big difference.

"The trick is to think in groups of 10—getting 10 grams in the morning, 10 at lunch, and 10 at dinner," says Dawn Jackson Blatner, RD, a Chicago-based spokesperson for the ADA. You can start by simply adding snacks like carrot sticks, a fresh piece of fruit, or popcorn to round out your meals.

Hearty Quinoa with Sautéed Apples and Almonds

Besides providing fiber, quinoa packs more protein than any other grain. Almost one-fifth of your daily fiber needs are met in one serving of this side. Use a little curry powder in place of the cinnamon, if desired, for a more complex flavor. Prepare this simple dish to serve with a roast chicken or pork tenderloin.

   1   cup uncooked quinoa
   2   teaspoons olive oil, divided
   ¾   cup chopped onion
   ¾   cup finely diced carrot (about 2)
   1   garlic clove, minced
   2   cups organic vegetable broth (such as Swanson Certified Organic)
   ¼   teaspoon salt
   ¼   teaspoon ground cinnamon
   1½ cups finely diced unpeeled Granny Smith apple (about 1)
   3   tablespoons slivered almonds, toasted
   ⅛   teaspoon freshly ground black pepper

1. Place quinoa in a fine sieve; place sieve in a large bowl. Cover quinoa with water. Using your hands, rub grains together for 30 seconds; rinse and drain. Repeat procedure twice. Drain well.

2. Heat 1 teaspoon oil in a saucepan over medium-high heat. Add onion, carrot, and garlic to pan; sauté 5 minutes or until onion is tender and carrot begins to brown. Stir in quinoa, broth, salt, and cinnamon; bring to a boil. Cover, reduce heat, and simmer 20 minutes or until liquid is absorbed. Remove from heat. Fluff with a fork; keep warm.

3. Heat 1 teaspoon oil in a nonstick skillet over medium-high heat. Add apple to pan; sauté 7 minutes or until apple begins to brown. Add apple, almonds, and pepper to quinoa, tossing to combine. Serve warm. Yield: 4 servings (serving size: 1 cup).

CALORIES 258 (26% from fat); FAT 7.4g (sat 0.8g, mono 3.9g, poly 1.9g); PROTEIN 7.4g; CARB 42.4g; FIBER 5.1g; CHOL 0mg; IRON 4.5mg; SODIUM 464mg; CALC 60mg

Pear Crisp with Oat Streusel Topping

This fall favorite acquires its fiber from unpeeled juicy pears, sweet raisins, and regular oats, and it provides one-fourth of your day's fiber in one portion.

CRISP:

7¾ cups cubed Bartlett or Anjou pears
1 cup golden raisins
1 tablespoon all-purpose flour
1 tablespoon fresh lemon juice
½ teaspoon ground cinnamon
¼ teaspoon salt
Cooking spray

TOPPING:

½ cup all-purpose flour (about 2¼ ounces)
1 cup regular oats
¼ cup packed brown sugar
⅛ teaspoon ground cinnamon
Dash of salt
¼ cup chilled butter, cut into small pieces
½ cup frozen fat-free whipped topping, thawed

1. Preheat oven to 375°.
2. To prepare crisp, place first 6 ingredients in a large bowl; toss to combine. Spoon mixture into an 11 x 7–inch baking dish coated with cooking spray.
3. To prepare topping, lightly spoon ½ cup flour into a dry measuring cup; level with a knife. Place ½ cup flour and next 4 ingredients in a small bowl; stir to combine. Cut in butter with a pastry blender or 2 knives until mixture resembles very coarse meal. Sprinkle oat mixture evenly over pear mixture. Bake at 375° for 50 minutes or until browned on top. Serve with whipped topping. Yield: 8 servings (serving size: about 1 cup and 1 tablespoon whipped topping).

CALORIES 303 (20% from fat); FAT 6.8g (sat 3.8g, mono 1.8g, poly 0.6g); PROTEIN 3.7g; CARB 60g; FIBER 6.9g; CHOL 15mg; IRON 1.7mg; SODIUM 142mg; CALC 40mg

Winter Squash Casserole

Any winter squash would work in this spicy-sweet side dish. Though you start with a lot of squash, it cooks down in the preliminary roasting. Even the small amounts of currants and pecans contribute to the dish's hefty 8.4 grams of fiber per serving.

10 cups (1-inch) cubed peeled butternut squash (about 8 pounds)
2 teaspoons olive oil
¼ cup fresh orange juice
2 tablespoons brown sugar
2 tablespoons brandy
1 tablespoon butter
½ teaspoon ground cinnamon
¼ teaspoon salt
¼ cup dried currants
Cooking spray
2 tablespoons all-purpose flour
2 tablespoons whole wheat flour
2 tablespoons chilled butter, cut into small pieces
3 tablespoons chopped pecans

1. Preheat oven to 400°.
2. Arrange squash pieces in a single layer on a jelly-roll pan. Drizzle with oil, stirring to coat. Bake at 400° for 1 hour and 20 minutes or until squash is tender and beginning to brown, stirring every 20 minutes.
3. Transfer squash to a bowl. Add juice and next 5 ingredients. Mash with a potato masher until combined and fairly smooth. Stir in currants. Scrape squash mixture into an 8-inch square baking dish coated with cooking spray.
4. Combine flours in a small bowl; cut in chilled butter with a pastry blender or 2 knives until mixture resembles coarse meal. Stir in pecans. Sprinkle pecan mixture evenly over squash mixture. Bake at 400° for 30 minutes or until thoroughly heated and topping begins to brown. Serve warm. Yield: 8 servings (serving size: about ¾ cup).

CALORIES 245 (29% from fat); FAT 7.8g (sat 3.1g, mono 3.1g, poly 1g); PROTEIN 3.9g; CARB 44.8g; FIBER 8.4g; CHOL 11mg; IRON 3mg; SODIUM 116mg; CALC 158mg

Red Lentil Dal with Charred Onions

Quick-cooking red lentils don't need to be pureed since they break down as they cook. Lentils are a great source of protein, as well as fiber. This recipe gives 20 percent of your daily fiber goal. Serve over brown rice with a side of broccoli for a vegetarian meal.

1 tablespoon olive oil, divided
1 onion, cut into ¼-inch-thick slices
1 teaspoon mustard seeds
½ teaspoon coriander seeds
½ teaspoon cumin seeds
1 whole clove
¼ teaspoon ground cinnamon
⅛ teaspoon ground cardamom
1 dried hot red chile
1 tablespoon minced peeled fresh ginger
1 garlic clove, minced
4 cups organic vegetable broth (such as Swanson Certified Organic)
1 cup dried small red lentils
1 (14.5-ounce) can no-salt-added diced tomatoes, undrained
¼ cup chopped fresh cilantro
1 tablespoon fresh lime juice

1. Heat 1 teaspoon oil in a large, heavy cast-iron skillet over medium-high heat. Add onion to pan; cook 2 minutes or until charred. Carefully turn over onion, and cook 4 minutes or until blackened and charred. Remove from heat. Coarsely chop; set aside.
2. Combine mustard seeds and next 3 ingredients in a small skillet over medium heat. Cook 1½ minutes or until fragrant, stirring frequently. Remove from heat. Combine mustard mixture, cinnamon, cardamom, and chile in a spice or coffee grinder. Pulse until ground.
3. Heat 2 teaspoons oil in a small Dutch oven over medium-high heat. Add ginger and garlic to pan; sauté 1 minute. Stir in spices; sauté 1 minute. Add broth, lentils, and tomatoes to pan; bring to a boil. Cover, reduce heat, and simmer 30 minutes, stirring occasionally. Uncover; add onion, and cook 10 minutes. Stir in

cilantro and juice. Yield: 7 servings (serving size: 1 cup).

CALORIES 149 (17% from fat); FAT 2.8g (sat 0.3g, mono 1.6g, poly 0.3g); PROTEIN 8.4g; CARB 23.6g; FIBER 5.5g; CHOL 0mg; IRON 2.1mg; SODIUM 354mg; CALC 33mg

MAKE AHEAD • FREEZABLE

Ham and Bean Soup

Soak the beans and chop the vegetables the night before to shave prep time. Measure one-quarter cupfuls of seven varieties of dried beans to use in place of the 12-ounce variety mix. A serving contributes more than one-third of your daily fiber needs.

1 (12-ounce) package variety dried seven-bean mix
Cooking spray
1 cup chopped onion (1 medium)
3 garlic cloves, minced
4 cups fat-free, less-sodium chicken broth
1 cup chopped carrot (about 2)
1 cup chopped celery (3 ribs)
1 cup chopped green bell pepper
1 cup chopped red bell pepper
¼ cup chopped fresh flat-leaf parsley
2 tablespoons chopped fresh basil
1 tablespoon chopped fresh oregano
1 tablespoon chopped fresh thyme
¾ teaspoon kosher salt
½ teaspoon freshly ground black pepper
1 smoked ham hock (about 4 ounces)
1 (14-ounce) can crushed tomatoes, undrained
1 bay leaf
1 tablespoon fresh lemon juice

1. Sort and wash beans; place in a large Dutch oven. Cover with water to 2 inches above beans; cover and let stand 8 hours. Drain beans.
2. Heat a large Dutch oven over medium-high heat. Coat pan with cooking spray. Add onion and garlic to pan; sauté 3 minutes. Add beans, broth, and remaining ingredients except juice; bring to a boil. Cover, reduce heat, and simmer 2½ hours. Remove ham hock from pan; cool slightly. Remove ham from bones; finely chop and return meat to pan. Discard bones, skin, and fat. Discard bay leaf. Stir in juice. Yield: 8 servings (serving size: about 1⅓ cups).

CALORIES 231 (18% from fat); FAT 4.5g (sat 1.4g, mono 1.7g, poly 0.8g); PROTEIN 15.6g; CARB 33.8g; FIBER 10.9g; CHOL 15mg; IRON 4.1mg; SODIUM 478mg; CALC 87mg

QUICK & EASY

Multigrain Pilaf

Roasted buckwheat groats—called "kasha"—lend this pilaf a nutty flavor. Kasha is available in the kosher section of most grocery stores. Serve this side, which provides about 10 percent of daily fiber needs in one serving, with roasted duck.

1 teaspoon olive oil
1 cup chopped onion
3 garlic cloves, minced
2⅓ cups organic vegetable broth (such as Swanson Certified Organic)
⅓ cup uncooked kasha (buckwheat groats)
⅓ cup uncooked pearl barley
⅓ cup uncooked bulgur
½ teaspoon kosher salt
1 bay leaf
¼ cup chopped pecans, toasted
⅛ teaspoon freshly ground black pepper

1. Heat oil in a 2-quart saucepan over medium-high heat. Add onion and garlic to pan; sauté 3 minutes or until onion is tender.
2. Add broth and next 5 ingredients to pan; bring to a boil. Cover, reduce heat, and simmer 15 minutes or until liquid is absorbed. Remove from heat. Discard bay leaf. Fluff with a fork; stir in pecans and pepper. Yield: 7 servings (serving size: ½ cup).

CALORIES 115 (31% from fat); FAT 4g (sat 0.4g, mono 2.3g, poly 1.1g); PROTEIN 2.7g; CARB 18.4g; FIBER 3.7g; CHOL 0mg; IRON 0.6mg; SODIUM 327mg; CALC 16mg

QUICK & EASY

Steamed Brussels Sprouts and Cauliflower with Walnuts

This quick and versatile side dish is good with roasts or chicken. A serving boasts nearly one-fourth of daily fiber needs while the walnuts add a dose of heart-healthy unsaturated fat.

6 tablespoons coarsely chopped walnuts
2¼ cups trimmed Brussels sprouts (about 1 pound), halved
3 cups cauliflower florets
½ teaspoon kosher salt
¼ teaspoon freshly ground black pepper
½ teaspoon fresh lemon juice

1. Place walnuts in a small skillet over medium heat; cook 3 minutes or until walnuts are lightly browned, shaking pan frequently. Remove from heat.
2. Steam Brussels sprouts, covered, 10 minutes or until tender. Add cauliflower to pan; steam, covered, 2 minutes or just until tender. Drain. Place Brussels sprouts, cauliflower, salt, pepper, and juice in a medium bowl; toss to combine. Sprinkle evenly with walnuts. Yield: 6 servings (serving size: about ¾ cup).

CALORIES 104 (30% from fat); FAT 3.5g (sat 0.4g, mono 0.5g, poly 2.5g); PROTEIN 6.4g; CARB 15.2g; FIBER 6.3g; CHOL 0mg; IRON 1.8mg; SODIUM 222mg; CALC 68mg

The Whole Truth

When a label reads "made with whole grains," it doesn't mean it offers a good deal of fiber. If a product isn't 100 percent whole grain, it's a safe bet most of the fiber has been removed in processing. A food that is "made with whole grains" is likely produced with mostly low-fiber refined flours and a few higher-fiber whole grain flours. Look for the first few ingredients to include whole wheat, rye, oatmeal, millet, quinoa, or whole cornmeal. Visit www.wholegrainscouncil.org to discover more high-fiber, whole-grain sources.

Roasted Pumpkin and Sweet Potato Pilau

Pilau (or pilaf) typically consists of meats or vegetables added to a grain, and is an ideal way to add more fiber to your diet with whole grains like wild rice, brown rice, or bulgur. Serve with pork chops and green beans. This hearty side's pumpkin, potato, and brown rice offer about 10 percent of your daily fiber needs.

     2   cups (½-inch) cubed peeled fresh pumpkin (about 12 ounces)
    1½   cups (½-inch) cubed peeled sweet potato (about 1 medium)
         Cooking spray
     2   teaspoons olive oil
     1   cup diced onion (1 small)
    ⅓   cup diced celery (about 1 rib)
     2   teaspoons minced garlic
     4   cups fat-free, less-sodium chicken broth
     1   cup brown rice
     2   teaspoons chopped fresh sage
    ½   teaspoon freshly ground black pepper
    ¼   teaspoon salt
     1   bay leaf

1. Preheat oven to 400°.
2. Arrange pumpkin and sweet potato in an even layer on a jelly-roll pan coated with cooking spray. Bake at 400° for 35 minutes or until vegetables are tender and just begin to brown, stirring after 18 minutes. Remove from oven, and set aside.
3. Heat oil in a large saucepan over medium-high heat. Add onion, celery, and garlic to pan; sauté 3 minutes or until onion is tender. Stir in broth and remaining 5 ingredients; bring to a boil. Cover, reduce heat, and simmer 50 minutes or until rice is done and liquid is almost absorbed. Remove from heat; discard bay leaf. Add pumpkin mixture; stir gently to combine. Yield: 6 servings (serving size: about ¾ cup).

CALORIES 200 (11% from fat); FAT 2.5g (sat 0.4g, mono 1.4g, poly 0.5g); PROTEIN 5.9g; CARB 38.8g; FIBER 3g; CHOL 0mg; IRON 1.3mg; SODIUM 428mg; CALC 45mg

---

Sweet and Spicy Baked Beans

To quick-soak the beans, cover with water to 2 inches above beans; bring to a boil. Cook 2 minutes; remove from heat. Cover and let stand 1 hour. Then continue the recipe with preheating the oven. Just one serving of this new twist on a familiar side goes a long way toward helping you reach your daily fiber goal.

     1   pound dried navy beans
     4   slices bacon, cut into ½-inch pieces
     1   cup diced onion (1 small)
     1   tablespoon tomato paste
    ⅓   cup light molasses
    ¼   cup packed dark brown sugar
     3   tablespoons minced jalapeño pepper (about 1)
     1   teaspoon dry mustard
    ¼   teaspoon ground red pepper
     5   cups water, divided
     1   teaspoon salt

1. Sort and wash beans; place in a large Dutch oven. Cover with water to 2 inches above beans; cover and let stand 8 hours or overnight. Drain beans.
2. Preheat oven to 350°.
3. Cook bacon in a Dutch oven over medium heat 5 minutes or just until crisp. Remove bacon from pan, reserving 1 tablespoon drippings in pan; return bacon to pan. Add onion to pan; cook 5 minutes or until onion begins to brown, stirring frequently. Add tomato paste; cook 2 minutes, stirring frequently. Stir in molasses and next 4 ingredients. Stir in beans and 4 cups water. Increase heat to medium-high; bring mixture to a boil. Cover and bake at 350° for 3 hours. Stir in 1 cup water. Cover and bake an additional 1 hour or until beans are tender, but not falling apart, and liquid is almost absorbed. Remove from oven; stir in salt. Yield: 10 servings (serving size: ½ cup).

CALORIES 233 (12% from fat); FAT 3.1g (sat 1g, mono 1.2g, poly 0.6g); PROTEIN 9.8g; CARB 42.7g; FIBER 11.3g; CHOL 4mg; IRON 3.2mg; SODIUM 316mg; CALC 107mg

---

sidetracked
Sweet Beneath the Surface

Earthy and scrumptious, root vegetables round out a meal.

Once considered humble and plain, root vegetables such as parsnips, celeriac (celery root), sweet potatoes, beets, and turnips are now prized by savvy cooks for their earthy flavors and sturdy textures, making them ideally suited for the heartier meals of fall and winter.

Although they offer satisfying substance and sweetness, most root vegetables are low in calories and virtually fat-free. They're also sources of vitamins A and C, potassium, calcium, iron, and fiber. A bonus: Most are also easy on the grocery budget.

Glazed Parsnips, Carrots, and Pearl Onions

Add more water, ¼ cup at a time, if needed to make vegetables tender.

    3½   cups (¼-inch) diagonally cut carrot
     2   cups (¼-inch) diagonally cut parsnip
     2   cups frozen pearl onions (about 10 ounces)
     1   cup water
    ½   cup dry white wine
     2   tablespoons sugar
    1½   tablespoons butter
     1   tablespoon white wine vinegar
     1   teaspoon salt
    ⅛   teaspoon freshly ground black pepper

1. Combine all ingredients in a large nonstick skillet; bring to a boil. Cook 12 minutes or until vegetables are tender and liquid is slightly syrupy, stirring frequently. Yield: 6 servings (serving size: about ¾ cup).

CALORIES 156 (19% from fat); FAT 3.2g (sat 1.9g, mono 0.8g, poly 0.2g); PROTEIN 2.3g; CARB 31.5g; FIBER 4.9g; CHOL 8mg; IRON 0.9mg; SODIUM 485mg; CALC 64mg

Sweet Potato Ravioli with Lemon-Sage Brown Butter

Serve with ham, roasted pork loin, Cornish hen, or venison.

    1 (1-pound) sweet potato
    2 tablespoons grated fresh Parmesan
       cheese
   ½   teaspoon salt, divided
   ¼   teaspoon ground cinnamon
   ⅛   teaspoon ground nutmeg
   24 wonton wrappers
    1 large egg white, lightly beaten
    6 quarts water
       Cooking spray
    3 tablespoons butter
    1 tablespoon chopped fresh sage
    1 tablespoon fresh lemon juice
   ⅛   teaspoon freshly ground black
       pepper
       Sage sprigs (optional)

1. Preheat oven to 400°.
2. Pierce potato several times with a fork; place on a foil-lined baking sheet. Bake at 400° for 40 minutes or until tender. Cool. Peel potato; mash. Combine potato, cheese, ¼ teaspoon salt, cinnamon, and nutmeg in a small bowl.
3. Working with 1 wonton wrapper at a time (cover remaining wrappers with a damp towel to keep them from drying), spoon 1 tablespoon potato mixture into center of wrapper. Brush edges of dough with egg white; bring 2 opposite corners to center. Press edges together to seal, forming a triangle.
4. Bring 6 quarts water to a boil. Add 8 ravioli; cook 2 minutes or until done. Remove ravioli from pan with a slotted spoon. Lightly coat cooked wontons with cooking spray; keep warm. Repeat procedure with remaining ravioli.
5. Melt butter in a small skillet over high heat. Add chopped sage to pan; cook 1 minute or until butter is lightly browned. Stir in ¼ teaspoon salt, juice, and pepper. Drizzle butter mixture over ravioli. Garnish with sage sprigs, if desired. Yield: 8 servings (serving size: 3 ravioli).

CALORIES 159 (17% from fat); FAT 5.1g (sat 3g, mono 1.3g, poly 0.4g); PROTEIN 4.1g; CARB 24.3g; FIBER 1.9g; CHOL 15mg; IRON 1.3mg; SODIUM 356mg; CALC 45mg

Honey and Herb-Roasted Root Vegetables

This versatile side dish showcases the natural sweetness of the vegetables.

   1½ cups sliced fennel bulb (about 1
       small bulb)
   1½ cups (½-inch) cubed peeled
       butternut squash
   1¼ cups (½-inch) cubed red potato
    1 cup (½-inch) cubed peeled turnip
    1 cup (½-inch-thick) slices parsnip
    1 tablespoon olive oil
   ¾   teaspoon salt
   ½   teaspoon chopped fresh thyme
   ¼   teaspoon freshly ground black
       pepper
    6 garlic cloves, peeled
    3 large shallots, peeled and halved
       Cooking spray
    1 tablespoon honey
   1½ teaspoons cider vinegar

1. Preheat oven to 450°.
2. Combine first 11 ingredients in a large bowl; toss well. Arrange vegetable mixture in a single layer on a jelly-roll pan coated with cooking spray. Bake at 450° for 25 minutes or until vegetables are browned and tender. Place vegetable mixture in a large bowl. Add honey and vinegar, and toss well. Yield: 4 servings (serving size: about ⅔ cup).

CALORIES 181 (19% from fat); FAT 3.8g (sat 0.5g, mono 2.5g, poly 0.5g); PROTEIN 3.6g; CARB 36.2g; FIBER 6.4g; CHOL 0mg; IRON 1.8mg; SODIUM 496mg; CALC 104mg

Selection and Storage

Look for root vegetables that are smooth, firm, and heavy for their size. Avoid bruised, shriveled, or cracked vegetables. Purchase carrots and beets with unwilted green tops attached whenever possible; this indicates freshness. Remove tops before storing.

Store potatoes, sweet potatoes, and onions in a cool, dry, dark place. Keep carrots, parsnips, beets, turnips, and celeriac (celery root) unwashed in a plastic bag in the refrigerator. Wash root vegetables just before using.

Roasted Beet and Shallot Salad over Wilted Beet Greens and Arugula

Use beets with fresh green tops attached, or substitute Swiss chard for beet greens, if you prefer. Serve with pan-roasted salmon or trout, lamb chops, or beef tenderloin.

   1½ pounds beets
    8 shallots, peeled and halved
       Cooking spray
    1 tablespoon balsamic vinegar
    1 teaspoon grated orange rind
    2 teaspoons olive oil, divided
   ½   teaspoon salt, divided
    1 teaspoon sugar
    2 teaspoons cider vinegar
    5 cups trimmed arugula (about 5
       ounces)
    2 tablespoons chopped walnuts,
       toasted

1. Preheat oven to 425°.
2. Trim beets, reserving greens. Wrap beets in foil. Place beets and shallots on a baking sheet coated with cooking spray. Coat shallots with cooking spray. Bake at 425° for 25 minutes or until shallots are lightly browned. Remove shallots from pan. Return beets to oven; bake an additional 35 minutes or until beets are tender. Cool. Peel beets; cut into ½-inch wedges. Place beets, shallots, vinegar, rind, 1 teaspoon oil, and ¼ teaspoon salt in a large bowl; toss well.
3. Heat 1 teaspoon oil in a large nonstick skillet over medium-high heat. Add reserved beet greens to pan; sauté 1 minute or until greens begin to wilt. Stir in sugar, cider vinegar, and ¼ teaspoon salt; cook 30 seconds, stirring constantly. Remove pan from heat. Add arugula; stir just until wilted. Place about 1 cup greens mixture on each of 4 plates. Sprinkle each serving with 1½ teaspoons walnuts; top each serving with ¾ cup beet mixture. Yield: 4 servings.

CALORIES 127 (31% from fat); FAT 4.3g (sat 0.5g, mono 2g, poly 1.4g); PROTEIN 4.3g; CARB 19.4g; FIBER 4.6g; CHOL 0mg; IRON 1.8mg; SODIUM 393mg; CALC 81mg

Spicy Roasted Potato Wedges

Serve with flank steak, pork tenderloin, or roasted chicken.

    1   tablespoon olive oil
    1   teaspoon dried oregano
    ¾   teaspoon salt
    ½   teaspoon paprika
    ⅛   teaspoon crushed red pepper
    4   red potatoes, each cut into 8
        wedges (about 2 pounds)
      Cooking spray
    2   tablespoons grated fresh Parmesan
        cheese

1. Preheat oven to 450°.
2. Combine first 6 ingredients in a large bowl; toss well. Arrange potatoes in a single layer on a baking sheet coated with cooking spray. Bake at 450° for 30 minutes or until golden. Sprinkle potatoes with cheese, and bake an additional 2 minutes or until cheese melts. Yield: 6 servings (serving size: about 1 cup).

CALORIES 137 (20% from fat); FAT 3g (sat 0.6g, mono 1.8g, poly 0.3g); PROTEIN 3.6g; CARB 24.4g; FIBER 2.8g; CHOL 2mg; IRON 1.3mg; SODIUM 330mg; CALC 38mg

Celery Root and Potato Röstis

Rösti (RAW-stee) is a Swiss-German term describing a dish, usually shredded potatoes, served crisp and golden. Celery root lends this version distinctive flavor. Serve with steak, pork tenderloin, or omelets.

    2   cups shredded peeled baking
        potato (about 1 pound)
    2   cups shredded peeled celeriac
        (celery root; about ½ pound)
    ½   cup finely chopped onion
    3   tablespoons all-purpose flour
    2   tablespoons chopped fresh chives
    1   teaspoon chopped fresh thyme
    ¾   teaspoon salt
    ⅛   teaspoon freshly ground black
        pepper
    1   large egg white, lightly beaten
   2½   tablespoons butter, divided
      Fat-free sour cream (optional)

1. Preheat oven to 425°.
2. Combine first 9 ingredients in a large bowl; toss well. Divide potato mixture into 8 (½-cup) portions, shaping each into a ½-inch-thick patty.
3. Melt 4 teaspoons butter in a large non-stick skillet over medium-high heat. Add 4 patties to pan; cook 5 minutes on each side or until golden. Place on a baking sheet. Repeat procedure with 3½ teaspoons butter and remaining patties.
4. Bake patties at 425° for 8 minutes or until thoroughly heated. Serve with sour cream, if desired. Yield: 8 servings (serving size: 1 rösti).

CALORIES 147 (31% from fat); FAT 5g (sat 3.1g, mono 1.3g, poly 0.3g); PROTEIN 3.2g; CARB 23.2g; FIBER 2.4g; CHOL 13mg; IRON 0.7mg; SODIUM 375mg; CALC 28mg

kitchen strategies
Making Budget

Problem: A North Carolina clan needs to keep grocery costs low. Strategy: Shop smart, and cook from scratch.

When you have three kids, as do Dinah Riggs and her husband, Doug, feeding the family takes a bite out of the budget. "Packaged foods like fish sticks can cost an arm and a leg," says Dinah. And while the Riggses, who live in Charlotte, North Carolina, want to be economical, they still want enjoyable meals. Dinah has a few cash-saving tactics but seeks more advice. To help with her goal, we offer smart shifts that can lead to big savings.

STAFF FAVORITE
Slow-Cooked Tuscan Pork with White Beans

An inexpensive cut of pork becomes rich and tender when braised. Creamy beans make the dish hearty and satisfying. If you prefer to use an electric slow cooker to prepare this meal, just combine pre-soaked beans and remaining ingredients in cooker; cover and cook on HIGH for eight hours.

    2   cups dried navy beans
    1   tablespoon minced fresh sage,
        divided
    2   teaspoons kosher salt, divided
    1   teaspoon ground fennel seeds
    8   garlic cloves, minced and divided
   2½   pounds boneless pork shoulder
        (Boston butt), trimmed
    4   cups water
    2   bay leaves

1. Sort and wash beans, and place in a large Dutch oven. Cover with water to 2 inches above beans; cover and let stand 8 hours. Drain beans.
2. Preheat oven to 275°.
3. Combine 2 teaspoons sage, 1 teaspoon salt, fennel seeds, and 3 garlic cloves. Rub sage mixture over pork. Place pork, beans, 1 teaspoon sage, 1 teaspoon salt, 5 garlic cloves, 4 cups water, and bay leaves in Dutch oven, and bring to a boil. Cover and bake at 275° for 4 hours or until pork is very tender. Discard bay leaves. Pull pork apart into chunks, and serve with bean mixture. Yield: 8 servings (serving size: about 3 ounces pork and 1 cup bean mixture).

CALORIES 391 (25% from fat); FAT 11g (sat 3.6g, mono 4.7g, poly 1.6g); PROTEIN 39.6g; CARB 32.7g; FIBER 12.9g; CHOL 95mg; IRON 4.7mg; SODIUM 584mg; CALC 109mg

Spicy Shrimp and Fettuccine

We used dried basil, but you can substitute 2 tablespoons fresh basil, if desired.

    8   ounces uncooked fettuccine
    1   tablespoon olive oil
    ½   teaspoon crushed red pepper
    4   garlic cloves, minced
    1   pound large shrimp, peeled and
        deveined
    2   cups chopped plum tomato
        (about 5)
    2   tablespoons reduced-fat sour
        cream
    1   tablespoon tomato paste
    1   teaspoon dried basil
    ½   teaspoon kosher salt
    ¼   cup freshly grated Parmesan
        cheese

1. Cook pasta according to package directions, omitting salt and fat. Drain.
2. Heat oil in a Dutch oven over medium-high heat. Add pepper and garlic to pan; sauté 1 minute. Add shrimp; sauté 1 minute. Stir in tomato and next 4 ingredients; bring to a boil. Reduce heat, and simmer 5 minutes. Stir in pasta; cook 1 minute or until thoroughly heated.
3. Place 1½ cups pasta mixture on each of 4 plates; top each serving with 1 tablespoon cheese. Serve immediately. Yield: 4 servings.

CALORIES 414 (19% from fat); FAT 8.7g (sat 2.5g, mono 3.5g, poly 1.3g); PROTEIN 34.1g; CARB 49.4g; FIBER 3.3g; CHOL 180mg; IRON 5.1mg; SODIUM 494mg; CALC 153mg

Fresh Vegetable Barley

Look for barley in bulk bins at natural food markets. Feta won't break the bank, and like other strong cheeses such as Parmesan, a little goes a long way.

  1   teaspoon olive oil
  ¾ cup chopped onion (about 1 small)
  1   garlic clove, minced
  ¾ cup uncooked pearl barley
 1¾ cups Homemade Chicken Stock (page 320)
 1½ cups chopped zucchini (about 1)
 1½ cups halved cherry tomatoes
  ¼ teaspoon kosher salt
  ¼ teaspoon freshly ground black pepper
  2   tablespoons crumbled feta cheese
     Chopped fresh parsley (optional)

1. Heat oil in a large saucepan over medium-high heat. Add onion and garlic; sauté 2 minutes. Add barley; cook 1 minute. Stir in Homemade Chicken Stock; bring to a boil. Cover, reduce heat, and simmer 30 minutes. Stir in zucchini, tomatoes, salt, and pepper; cover and cook 5 minutes. Ladle 1 cup barley mixture into each of 4 bowls. Top each serving with 1½ teaspoons feta and parsley, if desired. Yield: 4 servings.

CALORIES 177 (17% from fat); FAT 3.3g (sat 0.9g, mono 1.1g, poly 0.3g); PROTEIN 6.2g; CARB 31.4g; FIBER 7.7g; CHOL 5mg; IRON 1.5mg; SODIUM 187mg; CALC 64mg

Roast Garlic-Lemon Chicken

Rotisserie chicken from the supermarket deli can be a convenient and inexpensive option. But roasting your own bird allows you to control the quality of the ingredients, the overall flavor profile, and the amount of sodium. Cooking a chicken breast-side down helps keep the white meat juicy. Reserve carcass and juices in the broiler pan to make Homemade Chicken Stock (page 320).

  1 (4-pound) whole chicken
  1 teaspoon kosher salt
  ½ teaspoon freshly ground black pepper
  8 garlic cloves, peeled
  1 small lemon, quartered

1. Preheat oven to 400°.
2. Remove and discard giblets and neck from chicken. Trim excess fat. Starting at neck cavity, loosen skin from breast and drumsticks by inserting fingers, gently pushing between skin and meat.
3. Combine salt and pepper in a small bowl. Rub salt mixture under loosened skin. Lift wing tips up and over back, and tuck under chicken. Place garlic and lemon in body cavity. Place chicken, breast side down, on a broiler pan. Bake at 400° for 1 hour or until a thermometer inserted in meaty part of thigh registers 165°. Let stand 10 minutes. Discard skin. Yield: 4 servings (serving size: 5 ounces meat).

CALORIES 170 (23% from fat); FAT 4.4g (sat 1.1g, mono 1.3g, poly 1.1g); PROTEIN 30.4g; CARB 0.4g; FIBER 0.1g; CHOL 99mg; IRON 1.3mg; SODIUM 580mg; CALC 19mg

---

Ways to Save

- **Buy in bulk.** Steel-cut oats bought from the bulk bin, for instance, are $.89 per pound, while a tin runs $3.35 a pound. Rice, lentils, beans, and chickpeas are also great bulk savers, as well as large bags of rice.
- **Buy seasonal.** Eating seasonal produce is more than just fresh and delicious; it saves money. Cucumbers in season are generally bargains. But out of season, they have to travel from afar and can cost several dollars per pound. Stay attuned to the seasons so you can buy the fruits and veggies that are most economical—and freshest as a bonus.
- **Stock your pantry.** Having plenty of inexpensive staples on hand, such as beans, rice, lentils, canned tomatoes, and tomato paste, lets you turn to the convenience of the cupboards rather than make an expensive trip to the store.
- **Shop for bargains.** Check your local grocery store's weekly circular or look for specials at the store, then plan meals around the items that are on sale. Buy-one, get-one-free deals in particular can help the bottom line.

- **Make your own.** Few of us have time to cook everything from scratch, but some foods are worth the extra effort. Homemade trail mix can save you 50 percent over the premade packages, and cooking and freezing your own beans will save you several dollars—ounce for ounce—over canned beans.
- **Compare apples to apples.** Compare the prices of similar items carefully. Make sure you're comparing pound per pound and serving per serving.
- **Surf the Web.** Many food manufacturers offer product coupons online. Go to a search page, such as Google.com or Yahoo.com, and type in the phrase "grocery coupons" to get started. Many grocery chains also advertise specials and offer coupons on their Web sites.
- **Plant an herb garden.** Fresh herbs from the supermarket cost about $2 an ounce and often aren't used before they wither. Consider growing herbs in your backyard or in windowsill pots. Herbs don't require much maintenance, and you can snip exactly the amount needed for a recipe.

Braised Chicken with Chickpeas and Tomatoes

1 cup dried chickpeas (garbanzo beans)
4 cups water
1 cup thinly sliced onion (about 1), divided
6 garlic cloves, chopped
1 bay leaf
2 teaspoons olive oil
4 chicken drumsticks, skinned (about 1¼ pounds)
4 chicken thighs, skinned (about 1¾ pounds)
2 tablespoons all-purpose flour
¼ cup white wine vinegar
2 cups chopped plum tomato (about 5)
½ cup Homemade Chicken Stock (recipe at right)
½ teaspoon salt
½ teaspoon freshly ground black pepper
Lemon wedges (optional)

1. Sort and wash chickpeas; place in a large Dutch oven. Cover with water to 2 inches above chickpeas; cover and let stand 8 hours. Drain chickpeas.
2. Place 1½ cups chickpeas, 4 cups water, ½ cup onion, garlic, and bay leaf in pan; bring to a boil. (Reserve leftover chickpeas for another use.) Cover, reduce heat, and simmer 45 minutes or until beans are just tender. Drain chickpea mixture in a colander over a bowl, reserving ½ cup cooking liquid. Set chickpea mixture aside.
3. Heat oil in pan over medium-high heat. Dredge chicken in flour. Add chicken to pan; cook 6 minutes, browning on all sides. Remove from pan.
4. Add ½ cup onion to pan. Sauté 4 minutes or until tender. Add vinegar, scraping pan to loosen browned bits. Cook 1 minute or until liquid evaporates.
5. Add tomato, Homemade Chicken Stock, and reserved cooking liquid to pan. Add chickpea mixture, and bring to a boil. Place chicken on top of chickpeas, and sprinkle with salt and pepper. Cover, reduce heat, and simmer 40 minutes or until chicken is done and chickpeas are tender. Discard bay leaf. Serve with lemon wedges, if desired. Yield: 8 servings (serving size: 1 chicken leg or thigh and ¾ cup bean mixture).

CALORIES 261 (34% from fat); FAT 9.8g (sat 2.4g, mono 3.9g, poly 2.3g); PROTEIN 27.7g; CARB 14.8g; FIBER 3.2g; CHOL 82mg; IRON 2.6mg; SODIUM 244mg; CALC 36mg

---

Cajun Creation Menu
serves 6

Hints of spicy heat in the salad mirror the taste of the entrée.

Red Beans and Rice with Smoked Turkey Sausage

Salad with spicy pecans*

Garlic bread

*Melt 2 teaspoons butter in a skillet over medium heat. Add 3 tablespoons chopped pecans, 1 tablespoon brown sugar, and ¼ teaspoon salt-free Cajun seasoning; cook 3 minutes or until toasted, stirring occasionally. Combine 3 tablespoons red wine vinegar, 1 tablespoon extravirgin olive oil, 1 teaspoon spicy brown mustard, ½ teaspoon hot sauce, and ¼ teaspoon salt. Drizzle over 6 cups torn romaine lettuce and ½ cup thinly sliced red onion; toss to coat. Top with pecans.

Red Beans and Rice with Smoked Turkey Sausage

A classic Louisiana way to feed a lot of people for a little money, this dish is as easy on the pocket as it is on the palate.

2 cups dried small red beans
1 teaspoon olive oil
2 cups chopped onion (about 1 large)
3 garlic cloves, minced
10 cups water
2 tablespoons salt-free Cajun seasoning
¾ teaspoon kosher salt
2 bay leaves
¾ pound smoked turkey sausage, thinly sliced
3 cups hot cooked long-grain rice
Chopped green onions (optional)

1. Sort and wash beans; place in a large Dutch oven. Cover with water to 2 inches above beans; cover and let stand 8 hours. Drain beans.
2. Heat oil in pan over medium-high heat. Add 2 cups onion and garlic to pan; sauté 4 minutes. Stir in beans, 10 cups water, and next 4 ingredients; bring to a boil. Reduce heat, and simmer 1½ hours or until bean mixture thickens. Serve over rice. Garnish with green onions, if desired. Yield: 6 servings (serving size: 1 cup bean mixture and ½ cup rice).

CALORIES 428 (14% from fat); FAT 6.7g (sat 2.1g, mono 2g, poly 1.1g); PROTEIN 25.9g; CARB 67.5g; FIBER 5.6g; CHOL 30mg; IRON 11.6mg; SODIUM 842mg; CALC 129mg

---

MAKE AHEAD • FREEZABLE
Homemade Chicken Stock

This recipe yields 48 ounces of stock. The same amount of canned broth would cost about $4.32.

Bones from a cooked (4-pound) chicken
5 whole peppercorns
3 quarts water
2 parsley sprigs (optional)
1 onion, quartered

1. Preheat oven to 400°.
2. Split carcass in half lengthwise. Place carcass halves in bottom of broiler pan with juices from Roast Garlic-Lemon Chicken (page 319).
3. Bake at 400° for 1 hour, turning bones once after 30 minutes.
4. Scrape bones, juices, and browned bits into a large Dutch oven. Add peppercorns, 3 quarts water, parsley, if desired, and onion to pan. Bring to a boil over medium-high heat. Reduce heat, and simmer 2 hours; skim surface occasionally, discarding solids.
5. Strain stock through a sieve into a bowl; discard solids. Cool to room temperature. Cover and chill 8 to 24 hours. Skim fat from surface; discard. Refrigerate stock in an airtight container up to 5 days, or freeze up to 3 months. Yield: 8 servings (serving size: ¾ cup).

CALORIES 5 (54% from fat); FAT 0.3g (sat 0.1g, mono 0.1g, poly 0.1g); PROTEIN 0.6g; CARB 0.1g; FIBER 0g; CHOL 2mg; IRON 0mg; SODIUM 9mg; CALC 8mg

Standout Stew

A Pennsylvania writer and her family crave the richness of this hearty beef ragoût.

Come fall, Christina Wilson of Lansdowne, Pennsylvania, relies on this cool-weather standby. Wilson first created her Autumn Cranberry Beef Stew at her husband Ben's request. He's a "very meat-and-potatoes type of guy," says Wilson. With ingredients she had at the ready, she combined beef, dark beer, thyme, pearl onions, and mushrooms to develop a hearty broth, adding cranberry sauce to add sweetness to the rich dish.

Autumn Cranberry Beef Stew

1   teaspoon dried thyme
½   teaspoon salt
½   teaspoon freshly ground black pepper
1   (3-pound) boneless chuck roast, trimmed and cut into 2-inch cubes
Cooking spray
1   cup chopped onion
1   cup fat-free, less-sodium beef broth
2   bay leaves
1   (12-ounce) Guinness Stout
1   (10-ounce) package frozen pearl onions, thawed
1   (8-ounce) package button mushrooms, quartered
¼   cup water
2   tablespoons all-purpose flour
¾   cup whole-berry cranberry sauce
8   cups hot cooked egg noodles (about 1 pound)
Chopped fresh thyme (optional)

1. Combine first 3 ingredients in a small bowl; sprinkle over beef. Heat a Dutch oven over medium-high heat. Coat pan with cooking spray. Add beef to pan; cook 6 minutes, turning to brown on all sides. Add chopped onion, broth, bay leaves, and stout; bring to a boil. Cover, reduce heat, and simmer 2 hours or until beef is tender, stirring occasionally. Stir in pearl onions and mushrooms; cook, covered, 15 minutes, stirring occasionally.
2. Combine ¼ cup water and flour in a small bowl. Add flour mixture and cranberry sauce to pan. Cook 5 minutes. Discard bay leaves. Serve with noodles. Garnish with fresh thyme, if desired. Yield: 10 servings (serving size: about ¾ cup stew and ¾ cup noodles).

CALORIES 479 (27% from fat); FAT 14.6g (sat 4.8g, mono 6.3g, poly 1.1g); PROTEIN 39.5g; CARB 43.7g; FIBER 2.6g; CHOL 138mg; IRON 6.3mg; SODIUM 239mg; CALC 35mg

Bourbon-Glazed Salmon

"I created this recipe after tasting the bourbon salmon from my local grocery seafood counter. Mine has received rave reviews, even from picky eaters."
—Esther Maples, Harlem, Georgia

3   tablespoons brown sugar
3   tablespoons bourbon
2   tablespoons low-sodium soy sauce
1   tablespoon grated peeled fresh ginger
1   tablespoon fresh lime juice
3   garlic cloves, minced
¼   teaspoon freshly ground black pepper
4   (6-ounce) skinless salmon fillets
Cooking spray
¼   cup thinly sliced green onions
1   tablespoon sesame seeds, toasted

1. Combine first 7 ingredients in a large zip-top plastic bag. Add fish to bag; seal. Marinate in refrigerator 1½ hours, turning occasionally.
2. Heat a large nonstick skillet over medium-high heat. Coat pan with cooking spray. Add fish and marinade to pan; cook fish 4 minutes on each side or until fish flakes easily when tested with a fork or until desired degree of doneness. Place 1 fillet on each of 4 plates; drizzle each serving with about 2 teaspoons sauce. Sprinkle each serving with 1 tablespoon green onions and ¾ teaspoon sesame seeds. Yield: 4 servings.

CALORIES 353 (36% from fat); FAT 14.1g (sat 3.2g, mono 6g, poly 3.6g); PROTEIN 37.4g; CARB 13g; FIBER 0.3g; CHOL 87mg; IRON 4.3mg; SODIUM 281mg; CALC 41mg

Hillary's Black Bean-Smoked Chile Spread

"Hillary, my neighbor, shared this recipe with me. I immediately spotted a keeper. The interesting blend of the black beans and spices and the subtle nip of the chipotle chiles make this spread enjoyable as a topping for chicken or focaccia, or as a dip with baked chips."
—Lois Murray, Locust Grove, Virginia

1   tablespoon olive oil
½   cup chopped onion
1   teaspoon ground cumin
½   teaspoon ground coriander
½   cup water
¼   cup chopped fresh cilantro, divided
¼   cup sliced green onions
1   tablespoon fresh lime juice
1   teaspoon chopped chipotle chile, canned in adobo sauce
¼   teaspoon kosher salt
1   (15-ounce) can black beans, rinsed and drained

1. Heat oil in a small skillet over medium heat. Add chopped onion, cumin, and coriander to pan; cook 10 minutes, stirring occasionally. Place onion mixture, ½ cup water, 2 tablespoons cilantro, green onions, and remaining 4 ingredients in a food processor; process until smooth. Garnish with 2 tablespoons cilantro. Yield: 12 servings (serving size: 2 tablespoons).

CALORIES 27 (47% from fat); FAT 1.4g (sat 0.2g, mono 0.8g, poly 0.1g); PROTEIN 1g; CARB 4.5g; FIBER 1.5g; CHOL 0mg; IRON 0mg; SODIUM 153mg; CALC 12mg

Jollof Barley Casserole

"Jollof rice is a West African casserole of rice and various meats."
—Nikolina Jonah, Frankfort, Kentucky

1½ teaspoons paprika
¾ teaspoon salt
¼ teaspoon white pepper
¼ teaspoon freshly ground black pepper
1 pound skinless, boneless chicken thighs, cut into (2-inch) pieces
1 pound veal stew meat
Cooking spray
1½ cups finely chopped onion
1 cup finely chopped green bell pepper
¾ teaspoon dried thyme
¼ teaspoon ground red pepper
1 bay leaf
1½ cups uncooked pearl barley
2½ cups fat-free, less-sodium chicken broth
1 cup finely chopped tomato
1 (10-ounce) can no-salt-added tomato puree

1. Preheat oven to 350°.
2. Combine first 4 ingredients in a small bowl. Sprinkle chicken and veal evenly with 1¾ teaspoons spice mixture. Heat a large Dutch oven over medium-high heat. Coat pan with cooking spray. Add chicken and veal to pan; cook 5 minutes, turning to brown on all sides. Remove chicken mixture from pan; keep warm.
3. Reduce heat to medium. Add onion and bell pepper to pan; cook 5 minutes, stirring frequently. Add remaining spice mixture, thyme, red pepper, and bay leaf to pan; cook 1 minute, stirring occasionally. Add barley; cook 1 minute, stirring constantly. Add broth, tomato, and tomato puree; bring to a boil. Stir in chicken mixture. Cover and simmer 10 minutes, stirring occasionally.
4. Bake at 350° for 1 hour or until barley is tender. Let stand 10 minutes; discard bay leaf. Yield: 8 servings (serving size: about 1 cup).

CALORIES 369 (21% from fat); FAT 8.5g (sat 2.3g, mono 3g, poly 1.6g); PROTEIN 35.5g; CARB 37.5g; FIBER 8g; CHOL 102mg; IRON 3.2mg; SODIUM 434mg; CALC 44mg

Classic Combo Menu
serves 6

Instead of pork chops and applesauce, try this tasty pairing.

Lightened Waldorf Salad

Pan-fried pork chops*

Wilted spinach with bacon

*Place ½ cup panko in a shallow dish. Place ⅓ cup all-purpose flour in another shallow dish. Place 1 beaten egg in another shallow dish. Sprinkle 6 (4-ounce) center-cut boneless pork chops with 1 teaspoon salt and ½ teaspoon freshly ground black pepper. Heat 1½ tablespoons olive oil in a large skillet over medium-high heat. Dredge pork in flour; dip in egg. Dredge in panko. Place pork in pan; cook 3 minutes on each side or until done.

QUICK & EASY • MAKE AHEAD
Lightened Waldorf Salad

"I developed this recipe to cut down on the fat content of the original Waldorf salad, which was dressed with heavy mayonnaise."
—M. Georgene Laffey, Pinehurst, North Carolina

½ cup raisins
½ cup apple juice
1 cup finely chopped celery
1 cup chopped Granny Smith apple
¼ cup coarsely chopped walnuts, toasted
2 tablespoons fat-free mayonnaise
2 tablespoons fat-free apple-flavored yogurt

1. Combine raisins and apple juice in a microwave-safe bowl; microwave at HIGH 30 seconds. Let stand 2 minutes; drain. Combine raisins, celery, apple, and walnuts in a medium bowl. Stir in mayonnaise and yogurt. Yield: 6 servings (serving size: ½ cup).

CALORIES 93 (31% from fat); FAT 3.2g (sat 0.2g, mono 0.7g, poly 2g); PROTEIN 2g; CARB 16.1g; FIBER 1.6g; CHOL 1mg; IRON 0.5mg; SODIUM 60mg; CALC 25mg

MAKE AHEAD
Cake with Orange Sauce

"Here is a fabulous dessert that dates back to my childhood in Minneapolis in the 1940s."
—Elizabeth Stommel, Falmouth, Massachusetts

CAKE:
1 cup sugar
½ cup butter, softened
1 large egg
2 teaspoons grated orange rind
1¾ cups all-purpose flour (about 7¾ ounces)
1 teaspoon baking powder
1 teaspoon baking soda
⅛ teaspoon salt
1 cup fat-free buttermilk
⅓ cup finely chopped walnuts
Cooking spray

SAUCE:
1 cup sugar
1 cup fresh orange juice (about 3 oranges)
3 tablespoons fresh lemon juice

1. Preheat oven to 350°.
2. To prepare cake, place 1 cup sugar and butter in a large bowl; beat with a mixer at medium speed until well blended (about 5 minutes). Add egg; beat well. Beat in rind. Lightly spoon flour into dry measuring cups; level with a knife. Combine flour, baking powder, baking soda, and salt, stirring well. Add flour mixture and buttermilk alternately to sugar mixture, beginning and ending with flour mixture. Stir in walnuts.
3. Pour into an 8-inch square baking pan coated with cooking spray. Bake at 350° for 30 minutes or until a wooden pick inserted in center comes out clean. Cool in pan on a wire rack 10 minutes. Remove from pan. Cool completely on rack.
4. To prepare sauce, combine sugar and juices in a saucepan over medium-high heat; bring to a boil. Cook until reduced to 1 cup (about 15 minutes). Cool. Serve over cake. Yield: 16 servings (serving size: 1 cake square and 1 tablespoon sauce).

CALORIES 308 (30% from fat); FAT 10.4g (sat 5.2g, mono 2.4g, poly 2g); PROTEIN 3.9g; CARB 51.5g; FIBER 0.8g; CHOL 38mg; IRON 1.1mg; SODIUM 250mg; CALC 61mg

Natural Selection

A Seattle forager combs the Northwest woods in search of elusive, delectable mushrooms.

Forager Jeremy Faber estimates that he drives 80,000 miles a year, roughly the equivalent of traveling from his home in Seattle to Miami and back once a month for a year. But Faber stays entirely in the Northwest, heading to the forested mountains, foothills, coasts, and anywhere else he might find luscious wild mushrooms. Faber interprets the sky, terrain, and flora like a treasure map, following clues that might lead to a trove of wild mushrooms and other edible finds.

While edible wild mushrooms number in the hundreds, many are unremarkable and hardly worth the effort. Foragers focus instead on "choice edibles" such as yellow and white chanterelles, lobster mushrooms, porcinis, and matsutakes.

MAKE AHEAD
Beef Braised with Red Wine and Mushrooms

Add a teaspoon or two of ground dried porcini mushrooms along with the broth and red wine to give the dish an extra layer of mushroom flavor. Meaty, earthy-tasting mushrooms such as porcini or black trumpet are ideal. Serve over egg noodles or rice.

½ cup dried porcini mushrooms (about ½ ounce)
1 cup boiling water
1¼ pounds lean beef stew meat, cut into 1-inch cubes
¾ teaspoon salt, divided
½ teaspoon freshly ground black pepper, divided
2 tablespoons olive oil
1 cup pearl onions (about 16)
6 cups chopped cremini mushrooms (about 1 pound)
1½ cups (¼-inch) slices carrot (about 2 large)
1½ cups fat-free, less-sodium beef broth
½ cup dry red wine
4 thyme sprigs
3 garlic cloves, crushed
2 bay leaves
1 tablespoon water
2 teaspoons cornstarch

1. Combine porcini mushrooms and 1 cup boiling water in a small bowl; let stand 30 minutes. Strain mushrooms through a sieve into a bowl, reserving liquid. Chop mushrooms; set aside.
2. Sprinkle beef with ¼ teaspoon salt and ¼ teaspoon pepper. Heat oil in a large Dutch oven over medium-high heat. Add half of beef to pan; sauté 5 minutes or until lightly browned on all sides. Remove beef from pan with a slotted spoon; place in a bowl. Repeat procedure with remaining beef.
3. Add onions to pan; sauté 3 minutes or until lightly browned. Add cremini mushrooms and carrot; sauté 3 minutes or until mushrooms are tender. Add beef, porcini mushrooms, porcini liquid, ½ teaspoon salt, ¼ teaspoon pepper, broth, and next 4 ingredients; bring to a boil. Cover, reduce heat, and simmer 1½ hours or until beef is tender. Uncover and cook 20 minutes, stirring occasionally.
4. Combine 1 tablespoon water and cornstarch in a small bowl. Add cornstarch mixture to pan; bring to a boil. Cook 1 minute or until liquid thickens. Discard thyme sprigs and bay leaves. Yield: 4 servings (serving size: 1¼ cups).

CALORIES 307 (30% from fat); FAT 10.3g (sat 3.8g, mono 4.3g, poly 0.6g); PROTEIN 33.5g; CARB 19.9g; FIBER 3.5g; CHOL 88mg; IRON 4.8mg; SODIUM 716mg; CALC 47mg

QUICK & EASY
Wild Mushroom Spread

A mushroom blend will bring complex flavor to this hors d'oeuvre. We used a mixture of wild and cultivated mushrooms (lobster, oyster, shiitake, cremini, and button).

2 teaspoons olive oil
½ cup finely chopped shallots (about 2 large)
3½ cups finely chopped wild or cultivated mushrooms (about 12 ounces)
½ cup (4 ounces) ⅓-less-fat cream cheese, softened
2 tablespoons dry sherry
2 tablespoons minced fresh flat-leaf parsley
½ teaspoon salt
⅛ teaspoon freshly ground black pepper
16 (½-ounce) slices diagonally cut French bread baguette (about ½ inch thick)

1. Heat oil in a large nonstick skillet over medium heat. Add shallots to pan; cook 3 minutes or until tender, stirring occasionally. Add mushrooms; cook 7 minutes or until liquid evaporates, stirring occasionally. Place mushroom mixture in a medium bowl. Place half of mushroom mixture, cream cheese, and sherry in a food processor; process until smooth. Add pureed mixture to remaining mushroom mixture. Stir in parsley, salt, and pepper. Serve with baguette slices. Yield: 8 servings (serving size: 2 baguette slices and 2 tablespoons spread).

CALORIES 140 (28% from fat); FAT 4.4g (sat 2.1g, mono 0.7g, poly 0.4g); PROTEIN 5.6g; CARB 20.6g; FIBER 1g; CHOL 10mg; IRON 1.3mg; SODIUM 399mg; CALC 17mg

Wild Versus Cultivated

Mushrooms that grow in the wilderness are wild, of course. Other mushrooms—grown in controlled climates for commercial sale—are cultivated. Yet cultivated mushrooms are sometimes mislabeled as wild on restaurant menus and store shelves. Portobello, shiitake, cremini, and oyster mushrooms are some of the more popular cultivated varieties (most oyster mushrooms sold in retail stores are cultivated, though wild oyster mushrooms are sometimes sold in gourmet grocery stores and farmers' markets). These varieties have been labeled "exotic" by the USDA to distinguish them from true wild mushrooms.

Dried wild mushrooms need to be reconstituted in hot water for about 30 minutes. They're a viable substitute for fresh wild mushrooms, particularly in dishes such as soups, stews, and braises, where their texture will not be noticeably different from fresh mushrooms.

Generally speaking, wild mushrooms are more flavorful than their cultivated counterparts and are preferable in these recipes. But because fresh wild mushrooms aren't always available, consider the following alternatives:

- **For chopped wild mushrooms:** Chopped portobello or cremini mushrooms
- **For porcini:** Portobello, cremini, and shiitake have meaty flavor that approaches the deep taste of porcini.
- **For chanterelles:** Oyster or hen of the woods mushrooms offer similar tenderness, yet milder flavor. Chanterelles are also sometimes cultivated.
- **For fresh wild mushrooms:** Use a blend of cultivated mushrooms and reconstituted dried wild mushrooms. The dried mushrooms will bring an earthiness to the mix.

Fines Herbes Omelet with Wild Mushrooms

Chanterelle or oyster mushrooms would complement this omelet. Chervil is a traditional component of fines herbes; if it's available, add ¼ teaspoon to the mix.

Cooking spray
3 cups sliced wild or cultivated mushrooms (about ½ pound)
3 tablespoons fat-free milk, divided
2 tablespoons fat-free sour cream
2 tablespoons (1 ounce) fat-free cream cheese, softened
¼ teaspoon salt, divided
⅛ teaspoon freshly ground black pepper
1 tablespoon thinly sliced green onions
1 teaspoon minced fresh chives
1 teaspoon minced fresh flat-leaf parsley
¼ teaspoon minced fresh tarragon
4 large egg whites, lightly beaten
2 large eggs, lightly beaten

1. Heat a large nonstick skillet over medium-high heat. Coat pan with cooking spray. Add mushrooms to pan; sauté 6 minutes or until moisture evaporates and mushrooms begin to brown. Remove from heat.
2. Combine 1 tablespoon milk, sour cream, cream cheese, ⅛ teaspoon salt, and pepper in a medium bowl; stir well with a whisk. Add mushrooms to milk mixture; stir well. Combine 2 tablespoons milk, ⅛ teaspoon salt, onions, and remaining 5 ingredients in a bowl; stir well.
3. Heat pan over medium-high heat. Coat pan with cooking spray. Spread egg mixture evenly in pan; cook 3 minutes or until center is set. Top with mushroom mixture. Carefully loosen omelet with a spatula; fold in half. Cut omelet in half. Yield: 2 servings (serving size: ½ omelet).

CALORIES 172 (31% from fat); FAT 5.9g (sat 1.9g, mono 2g, poly 0.9g); PROTEIN 20.8g; CARB 9.5g; FIBER 1.3g; CHOL 214mg; IRON 1.6mg; SODIUM 584mg; CALC 112mg

Porcini-Dusted Chicken Scaloppine

(pictured on page 251)

This dish puts dried porcini mushroom powder to use as a flavorful coating for chicken cutlets. If fresh porcini or chanterelle mushrooms are available, use them for the sauce. Serve with steamed haricots verts and garlic mashed potatoes.

½ cup dried porcini mushrooms (about ½ ounce)
4 (6-ounce) skinless, boneless chicken breast halves
½ teaspoon salt, divided
¼ teaspoon freshly ground black pepper, divided
1 tablespoon olive oil, divided
2 tablespoons minced shallots (about 1)
1 garlic clove, minced
3 cups sliced wild or cultivated mushrooms (about ½ pound)
½ cup dry white wine
½ cup fat-free, less-sodium chicken broth
3 tablespoons reduced-fat sour cream
1 tablespoon minced fresh flat-leaf parsley

1. Place porcini mushrooms in a spice or coffee grinder; process until finely ground. Cut chicken breasts in half horizontally. Sprinkle chicken with ¼ teaspoon salt and ⅛ teaspoon pepper. Sprinkle both sides of chicken with porcini powder, shaking off excess powder.
2. Heat 1 teaspoon oil in a large nonstick skillet over medium-high heat. Add 4 chicken pieces to pan; cook 1½ minutes on each side or until chicken is lightly browned and done. Remove chicken from pan; keep warm. Repeat procedure with 1 teaspoon oil and remaining chicken pieces.
3. Heat 1 teaspoon oil over medium heat. Add shallots and garlic to pan; cook 1 minute, stirring frequently. Add 3 cups mushrooms; cook 5 minutes or until liquid evaporates, stirring occasionally. Stir in wine, scraping pan to loosen browned bits. Increase heat to medium-high; cook 2 minutes or until liquid almost evaporates. Add broth to pan;

simmer until liquid is reduced to ¼ cup (about 5 minutes). Stir in sour cream; cook 1 minute. Remove from heat; stir in ¼ teaspoon salt, ⅛ teaspoon pepper, and parsley. Yield: 4 servings (serving size: 2 chicken pieces and about 1½ tablespoons sauce).

CALORIES 269 (25% from fat); FAT 7.3g (sat 2g, mono 3.1g, poly 1g); PROTEIN 43.2g; CARB 6.1g; FIBER 1.4g; CHOL 104mg; IRON 2.6mg; SODIUM 469mg; CALC 49mg

Wild Mushroom and Root Vegetable Sauté

Firmer mushrooms such as porcini, lobster, or matsutake are preferable in this recipe, though it's versatile enough for most any type. We enjoyed pleasing results with a mix of lobster and cremini.

    1 tablespoon olive oil, divided
    1 cup chopped onion
  3½ cups (¼-inch) diced Yukon gold
       potato (about 1 pound)
    1 cup (¼-inch) diced carrot (about
       1 large)
   ½ teaspoon salt, divided
   ¼ teaspoon freshly ground black
       pepper, divided
    1 teaspoon butter
    6 cups chopped wild or cultivated
       mushrooms (about 1 pound)
    1 tablespoon chopped fresh parsley

1. Heat 2 teaspoons oil in a large nonstick skillet over medium-high heat. Add onion to pan; sauté 3 minutes or until tender. Add potato, carrot, ¼ teaspoon salt, and ⅛ teaspoon pepper; sauté 12 minutes or until vegetables are tender and begin to brown. Place potato mixture in a large bowl; keep warm.
2. Heat 1 teaspoon oil and butter in pan over medium-high heat. Add mushrooms, ¼ teaspoon salt, and ⅛ teaspoon pepper to pan. Sauté 10 minutes or until mushrooms are tender. Add mushroom mixture and parsley to potato mixture; stir to combine. Yield: 6 servings (serving size: about ¾ cup).

CALORIES 122 (24% from fat); FAT 3.2g (sat 0.8g, mono 1.8g, poly 0.4g); PROTEIN 4.6g; CARB 20g; FIBER 2.4g; CHOL 2mg; IRON 1.1mg; SODIUM 217mg; CALC 13mg

Haricots Verts and Wild Mushrooms with Hazelnuts

Chanterelles and porcini are choice in this dish, although we also found success with a blend of oyster and button mushrooms. Use hazelnut oil, if available, instead of extravirgin olive oil for the vinaigrette.

    2 tablespoons red wine vinegar
    2 teaspoons extravirgin olive oil
   ¼ teaspoon salt
   ⅛ teaspoon freshly ground black
       pepper
    1 pound haricots verts, trimmed
    1 teaspoon olive oil
    6 cups sliced wild or cultivated
       mushrooms (about 1 pound)
   ½ cup sliced green onions
    6 teaspoons finely chopped
       hazelnuts, toasted

1. Combine first 4 ingredients in a small bowl.
2. Cook beans in boiling water 2 minutes or until crisp-tender. Drain and plunge beans into ice water; drain.
3. Heat 1 teaspoon oil in a large nonstick skillet over medium-high heat. Add mushrooms to pan; sauté 7 minutes or until liquid evaporates. Add onions; sauté 1 minute. Add beans; sauté 3 minutes or until thoroughly heated. Remove from heat. Add vinegar mixture and hazelnuts to bean mixture, tossing to coat. Yield: 6 servings (serving size: 1 cup).

CALORIES 72 (41% from fat); FAT 3.3g (sat 0.4g, mono 2.2g, poly 0.5g); PROTEIN 4.1g; CARB 9g; FIBER 2.2g; CHOL 0mg; IRON 1.3mg; SODIUM 110mg; CALC 40mg

---

Quick Dip

Because they come straight from the forest or field, wild mushrooms often have more debris on them than cultivated mushrooms. To clean them, soak briefly in cold water, gently agitating to dislodge any dirt and foreign matter. (Despite concerns to the contrary, soaking mushrooms for several seconds will not ruin their texture.) Drain well, and trim the stem bases before cooking.

Penne with Wild Mushrooms

Tender wild mushrooms such as oyster, hedgehog, or chanterelle are best for this dish, although cultivated oyster mushrooms are also suitable. Substitute fettuccine for penne, if you like. Garnish with fresh sage leaves.

    1 tablespoon olive oil
    1 teaspoon butter
   ¾ cup thinly sliced leek (about 1
       large)
    2 teaspoons minced fresh sage
    6 cups coarsely chopped wild or
       cultivated mushrooms (about 1
       pound)
   ¾ cup half-and-half
    1 teaspoon salt
   ½ teaspoon freshly ground black
       pepper
    8 ounces uncooked penne
       (tube-shaped pasta)

1. Heat oil and butter in a large nonstick skillet over medium heat. Add leek to pan; cook 2 minutes or until tender, stirring occasionally. Stir in sage; cook 30 seconds, stirring occasionally. Add mushrooms; cook 10 minutes or until liquid evaporates, stirring occasionally. Add half-and-half; cook until liquid is reduced to 6 tablespoons (about 2 minutes). Stir in salt and pepper. Remove from heat; keep warm.
2. Cook pasta according to package directions, omitting salt and fat. Drain. Place in a large bowl. Add mushroom mixture to pasta; toss gently to coat. Yield: 6 servings (serving size: 1 cup).

CALORIES 227 (27% from fat); FAT 6.7g (sat 2.9g, mono 2.8g, poly 0.4g); PROTEIN 8.7g; CARB 33.4g; FIBER 2.2g; CHOL 17mg; IRON 1.9mg; SODIUM 421mg; CALC 58mg

Multipurpose Marinara

Make a batch of our all-purpose red sauce on Sunday, and supper for the rest of the week is a cinch.

On the weekend, when you find yourself with a little extra time for the kitchen, cook a large pot of all-purpose marinara sauce. Then use it to build subsequent meals throughout the week (and beyond). Your family can have a classic spaghetti dinner Sunday night and on other evenings enjoy such varied dishes as pasta casseroles, hearty soups, pizza, and even steamed mussels.

Marinara is truly a multipurpose sauce. You can base dozens of different dishes on it—sometimes as is, other times with the addition of flavors, such as lemon rind or crushed red pepper. Some of the following recipes are superquick, such as Mussels Marinara or Shrimp Fra Diavolo. Others, such as Spinach and Ricotta–Stuffed Shells, are more complex. But because you've already done most of the work by creating the sauce that serves as the base of the recipe, even a more ambitious dinner is still doable on a weeknight.

Store the sauce in the refrigerator up to five days, or freeze it in small batches for several months. That way, your modest time investment this weekend will lead to a delicious payoff later.

MAKE AHEAD • FREEZABLE
Basic Marinara

Rely on a large Dutch oven or stockpot because this recipe makes enough sauce for several meals.

    3   tablespoons olive oil
    3   cups chopped yellow onion (about
        3 medium)
    3   tablespoons minced garlic (about 6
        cloves)
    1   tablespoon sugar
    2   teaspoons salt
    2   teaspoons dried basil
 1½   teaspoons dried oregano
    1   teaspoon dried thyme
    1   teaspoon freshly ground black
        pepper
   ½   teaspoon fennel seeds, crushed
    2   tablespoons balsamic vinegar
    2   cups fat-free, less-sodium chicken
        broth
    3   (28-ounce) cans no-salt-added
        crushed tomatoes

1. Heat oil in a large Dutch oven over medium heat. Add onion to pan; cook 4 minutes, stirring frequently. Add garlic and next 7 ingredients; cook 1 minute, stirring constantly. Stir in vinegar; cook 30 seconds. Add broth and tomatoes; bring to a simmer. Cook over low heat 55 minutes or until sauce thickens, stirring occasionally. Yield: about 12 cups (serving size: ½ cup).

CALORIES 50 (32% from fat); FAT 1.8g (sat 0.2g, mono 1.3g, poly 0.2g); PROTEIN 1.3g; CARB 8g; FIBER 2.1g; CHOL 0mg; IRON 0.5mg; SODIUM 270mg; CALC 28mg

MAKE AHEAD
Chicken, Pasta, and Chickpea Stew
(pictured on page 249)

To make the soup ahead, omit the pasta and refrigerate or freeze the soup. As the soup reheats over medium heat, cook the pasta separately according to package directions, then stir it in shortly before serving.

    Cooking spray
    1   cup thinly sliced celery
   ¾   cup diced carrot
   ½   cup chopped onion
    2   garlic cloves, minced
    4   cups fat-free, less-sodium chicken
        broth
    3   cups Basic Marinara (recipe at left)
    1   cup canned chickpeas (garbanzo
        beans), rinsed and drained
   ¾   cup uncooked ditalini (very short
        tube-shaped macaroni)
   ½   teaspoon freshly ground black
        pepper
   ½   pound skinless, boneless chicken
        thighs, cut into ½-inch pieces
    6   tablespoons shaved fresh
        Parmesan cheese

1. Heat a Dutch oven over medium heat. Coat pan with cooking spray. Add celery, carrot, and onion to pan; cook 12 minutes or until tender, stirring occasionally. Add garlic; cook 30 seconds, stirring constantly. Add broth and next 4 ingredients; bring to a boil. Reduce heat; simmer 12 minutes or until pasta is tender. Add chicken to pan; cook 3 minutes or until chicken is done. Sprinkle with cheese. Yield: 6 servings (serving size: about 1½ cups soup and 1 tablespoon cheese).

CALORIES 237 (27% from fat); FAT 7.1g (sat 2g, mono 3.2g, poly 1.5g); PROTEIN 15.5g; CARB 28.1g; FIBER 5.8g; CHOL 29mg; IRON 2.5mg; SODIUM 724mg; CALC 138mg

Mussels Marinara

    3   cups Basic Marinara (recipe at left)
   ¼   to ½ teaspoon crushed red pepper
    4   pounds mussels (about 80 mussels),
        scrubbed and debearded
    2   tablespoons chopped fresh parsley

1. Bring Basic Marinara and pepper to a simmer in a large Dutch oven over medium heat. Add mussels to pan; cover and cook 5 minutes or until shells open. Discard any unopened shells. Sprinkle with parsley. Yield: 4 servings (serving size: about 4 cups).

CALORIES 248 (26% from fat); FAT 7.1g (sat 1.2g, mono 2.9g, poly 1.5g); PROTEIN 25.8g; CARB 19.6g; FIBER 3.3g; CHOL 56mg; IRON 8.8mg; SODIUM 978mg; CALC 97mg

Swordfish with Lemony Red Sauce

Cooking spray
4 (6-ounce) swordfish steaks (about 1½ inches thick)
¼ teaspoon salt
¼ teaspoon freshly ground black pepper
2 cups Basic Marinara (page 326)
½ teaspoon grated lemon rind
Lemon wedges (optional)

1. Heat a large nonstick skillet over medium-high heat. Coat pan with cooking spray. Sprinkle fish evenly with salt and pepper. Add fish to pan; cook 4 minutes on each side or until fish flakes easily when tested with a fork or until desired degree of doneness.

2. Combine Basic Marinara and rind in a microwave-safe bowl; microwave at HIGH 3 minutes or until thoroughly heated. Serve with fish and lemon wedges, if desired. Yield: 4 servings (serving size: 1 steak and ½ cup sauce).

CALORIES 243 (30% from fat); FAT 8.1g (sat 2g, mono 3.7g, poly 1.7g); PROTEIN 32.8g; CARB 8.1g; FIBER 2.2g; CHOL 62mg; IRON 1.9mg; SODIUM 560mg; CALC 37mg

Sausage and Pepper Pizza

Using a premade crust helps this dish come together much quicker than making your own.

4 ounces hot turkey Italian sausage
Cooking spray
1 cup red bell pepper strips (about 1 medium)
1 cup yellow bell pepper strips (about 1 medium)
1 (16-ounce) cheese-flavored pizza crust (such as Boboli)
1 cup Basic Marinara (page 326)
1 tablespoon no-salt-added tomato paste
½ cup (2 ounces) shredded provolone cheese
½ cup (2 ounces) shredded part-skim mozzarella cheese
½ teaspoon dried oregano

1. Preheat oven to 450°.

2. Remove casings from sausage. Heat a large nonstick skillet over medium heat. Coat pan with cooking spray. Add sausage and bell peppers to pan; cook 6 minutes or until bell peppers are crisp-tender and sausage is browned, stirring frequently.

3. Place pizza crust on a large baking sheet. Combine Basic Marinara and tomato paste, stirring with a whisk; spread evenly over crust, leaving a 1-inch border. Sprinkle with cheeses and oregano; top evenly with sausage mixture. Bake at 450° for 15 minutes or until cheese melts and crust is lightly browned. Remove from oven; let stand 5 minutes before cutting into 6 slices. Yield: 6 servings (serving size: 1 slice).

CALORIES 335 (29% from fat); FAT 10.9g (sat 4.2g, mono 3.4g, poly 2.1g); PROTEIN 16.5g; CARB 42.8g; FIBER 2.9g; CHOL 23mg; IRON 3.1mg; SODIUM 756mg; CALC 247mg

---

Pasta Night Menu
serves 6

Hearty stuffed pasta and caramelized green beans create a delectable weeknight dinner.

Spinach and Ricotta-Stuffed Shells

Roasted green beans and garlic*

Peach sorbet and amaretti

*Combine ⅔ cup thinly sliced shallots and 1½ pounds trimmed green beans on a jelly-roll pan coated with cooking spray. Drizzle with 1 tablespoon olive oil; toss to coat. Bake at 450° for 10 minutes. Add 5 thinly sliced garlic cloves; toss to combine. Bake at 450° for 10 minutes or until beans are lightly browned. Sprinkle with ½ teaspoon salt and ¼ teaspoon freshly ground black pepper; drizzle with 1 tablespoon fresh lemon juice.

Spinach and Ricotta-Stuffed Shells
(pictured on page 250)

Substitute various cheeses, such as Asiago or feta, in place of Parmesan, and other dried herbs, such as thyme, basil, or dill, in place of oregano.

2 cups Basic Marinara (page 326), divided
Cooking spray
2½ cups part-skim ricotta cheese
½ cup (2 ounces) grated fresh Parmesan cheese
½ teaspoon onion powder
½ teaspoon dried oregano
¼ teaspoon salt
¼ teaspoon freshly ground black pepper
1 (10-ounce) package frozen chopped spinach, thawed, drained, and squeezed dry
1 large egg yolk
1 garlic clove, minced
24 cooked jumbo pasta shells

1. Preheat oven to 350°.

2. Spread ½ cup Basic Marinara over bottom of a 13 x 9–inch baking dish coated with cooking spray.

3. Combine ricotta and next 8 ingredients in a large bowl, stirring well. Spoon about 1½ tablespoons filling into each pasta shell. Arrange stuffed shells in prepared dish; spread with 1½ cups Basic Marinara. Cover and bake at 350° for 30 minutes. Let stand 5 minutes before serving. Yield: 6 servings (serving size: 4 stuffed shells and about ⅓ cup sauce).

CALORIES 329 (27% from fat); FAT 9.8g (sat 4.8g, mono 3g, poly 1g); PROTEIN 19.6g; CARB 39.4g; FIBER 4.2g; CHOL 67mg; IRON 2.8mg; SODIUM 552mg; CALC 377mg

Baked Ziti Casserole

Baked pasta is hearty, satisfying, and easy to prepare. To streamline the recipe, we skipped the traditional step of browning the meat before it's combined with the rest of the ingredients; it cooks fully as the casserole bakes. This recipe easily doubles to feed a crowd; bake in a 13 x 9–inch baking dish for 35 minutes.

  6 ounces uncooked ziti (short tube-shaped pasta)
  2 cups Basic Marinara (page 326)
  1 cup (4 ounces) shredded part-skim mozzarella cheese, divided
  ¼ cup (1 ounce) shredded Asiago cheese, divided
  ⅛ teaspoon salt
  ⅛ teaspoon hot pepper sauce (such as Tabasco)
  6 ounces ground turkey breast
Cooking spray

1. Preheat oven to 350°.
2. Cook pasta according to package directions, omitting salt and fat. Drain.
3. Combine pasta, Basic Marinara, ½ cup mozzarella, 2 tablespoons Asiago, salt, pepper sauce, and turkey in a large bowl. Spoon into an 8-inch square baking dish coated with cooking spray; sprinkle with ½ cup mozzarella and 2 tablespoons Asiago. Bake at 350° for 30 minutes or until cheese is lightly browned. Let stand 5 minutes before serving. Yield: 4 servings (serving size: about 1 cup).

CALORIES 362 (26% from fat); FAT 10.5g (sat 5.5g, mono 3.4g, poly 0.4g); PROTEIN 26.3g; CARB 41g; FIBER 3.5g; CHOL 39mg; IRON 2.3mg; SODIUM 546mg; CALC 311mg

WINE NOTE: A simple baked ziti such as this is best with a good solid red wine, preferably made from the Italian grape sangiovese (the main grape in Chianti). Sangiovese possesses a hint of acidity, which pairs beautifully with tomato sauces. For a fuller-bodied sangiovese, try one from California such as Eberle Sangiovese 2005 from Paso Robles ($22).

Colorful Vegetable Lasagna

Arrange the noodles crosswise in the pan to allow space for them to expand in the casserole's liquid. Serve with salad.

Cooking spray
  1 cup chopped red bell pepper (about 1 medium)
  1 cup chopped yellow bell pepper (about 1 medium)
  1 cup chopped onion
  4 zucchini, halved lengthwise and thinly sliced (about 5 cups)
  2 (8-ounce) packages presliced cremini mushrooms
  3 garlic cloves, minced
  2 cups (8 ounces) shredded part-skim mozzarella cheese, divided
1½ cups fat-free ricotta cheese
  ½ cup (2 ounces) grated fresh Parmesan cheese, divided
  1 large egg, lightly beaten
  5 cups Basic Marinara (page 326), divided
  12 precooked lasagna noodles (about 8 ounces)

1. Preheat oven to 350°.
2. Heat a large Dutch oven over medium-high heat. Coat pan with cooking spray. Add peppers and next 3 ingredients; sauté 10 minutes or until vegetables are crisp-tender and liquid evaporates. Add garlic; sauté 30 seconds.
3. Combine 1½ cups mozzarella, ricotta, ¼ cup Parmesan, and egg, stirring well.
4. Spread 1 cup Basic Marinara over bottom of a 13 x 9–inch baking dish coated with cooking spray; top with 3 noodles. Spoon 1 cup Basic Marinara evenly over noodles. Top evenly with one-third of ricotta mixture and one-third of vegetable mixture. Repeat layers twice, ending with noodles. Top with 1 cup Basic Marinara. Sprinkle evenly with ½ cup mozzarella and ¼ cup Parmesan. Cover and bake at 350° for 45 minutes. Uncover and bake an additional 10 minutes or until cheese melts. Let stand 10 minutes. Yield: 8 servings (serving size: 1 piece).

CALORIES 378 (27% from fat); FAT 11.4g (sat 5.4g, mono 4g, poly 1g); PROTEIN 22.9g; CARB 46.5g; FIBER 5.9g; CHOL 55mg; IRON 2.6mg; SODIUM 667mg; CALC 434mg

Shrimp Fra Diavolo

Italian for "brother devil," *fra diavolo* sauce is usually tomato-based and always spicy.

  8 ounces uncooked spaghetti
  1 tablespoon olive oil
  4 cups sliced cremini mushrooms (about 10 ounces)
2½ cups Basic Marinara (page 326)
  ½ teaspoon crushed red pepper
  ¼ teaspoon salt
  ¼ teaspoon freshly ground black pepper
  1 pound peeled and deveined medium shrimp
Parsley sprigs (optional)

1. Cook pasta according to package directions, omitting salt and fat. Drain; keep warm.
2. Heat oil in a large nonstick skillet over medium-high heat. Add mushrooms to pan; sauté 6 minutes. Add Basic Marinara, red pepper, salt, and black pepper; bring to a simmer. Cook 5 minutes. Add shrimp; cook 3 minutes or until shrimp are done. Serve over pasta. Garnish with parsley sprigs, if desired. Yield: 4 servings (serving size: 1¼ cups shrimp mixture and about 1 cup pasta).

CALORIES 439 (17% from fat); FAT 8.5g (sat 1.3g, mono 4.4g, poly 1.7g); PROTEIN 33.8g; CARB 56.5g; FIBER 5g; CHOL 172mg; IRON 5.7mg; SODIUM 660mg; CALC 118mg

Portobello Parmesan

As a side dish, these mushrooms are best with steaks, roast chicken, or pork. To make them a main dish, serve the filled mushrooms over a bed of pasta.

  8 portobello mushroom caps (about 1 pound)
Cooking spray
  ½ teaspoon freshly ground black pepper
  ¼ teaspoon salt
  1 cup Basic Marinara (page 326)
  ½ cup (2 ounces) grated fresh Parmesan cheese

1. Preheat broiler.

2. Remove brown gills from undersides of mushrooms using a spoon; discard gills. Place mushroom caps, undersides down, on a baking sheet coated with cooking spray. Broil 5 minutes.

3. Turn mushroom caps over; sprinkle evenly with pepper and salt. Top each cap with 2 tablespoons Basic Marinara and 1 tablespoon cheese. Broil 3 minutes or until cheese melts. Yield: 8 servings (serving size: 1 mushroom cap).

CALORIES 53 (34% from fat); FAT 2g (sat 0.9g, mono 0.7g, poly 0.1g); PROTEIN 3.7g; CARB 5.2g; FIBER 1.4g; CHOL 4mg; IRON 0.5mg; SODIUM 221mg; CALC 68mg

---

MAKE AHEAD

Escarole, Three Bean, and Roasted Garlic Soup

Roasted garlic mashed with a portion of white beans thickens the soup. As the garlic roasts, its flavor mellows into a delicate, slightly sweet taste.

1 whole garlic head
1 (15.5-ounce) can Great Northern beans, rinsed, drained, and divided
½ teaspoon chopped fresh sage
1 tablespoon olive oil
8 cups chopped escarole (about 1 pound)
4 cups fat-free, less-sodium chicken broth
2 cups Basic Marinara (page 326)
1 teaspoon freshly ground black pepper
1 (15-ounce) can kidney beans, rinsed and drained
1 (15-ounce) can pink beans, rinsed and drained
6 tablespoons grated fresh Parmesan cheese
Sage sprigs (optional)

1. Preheat oven to 350°.

2. Remove white papery skin from garlic head (do not peel or separate cloves). Wrap head in foil. Bake at 350° for 45 minutes; cool 10 minutes. Separate cloves; squeeze to extract pulp. Discard skins. Combine garlic pulp and ¼ cup Great Northern beans; mash with a fork until pastelike. Stir in chopped sage; set aside.

3. Heat oil in a Dutch oven over medium heat. Add escarole to pan; cook 3 minutes or until escarole wilts, stirring frequently. Add remaining Great Northern beans, broth, and next 4 ingredients; bring to a simmer. Reduce heat, and simmer 20 minutes or until escarole is tender. Stir in garlic mixture; remove from heat. Cover and let stand 10 minutes before serving. Ladle soup into bowls. Sprinkle each serving with cheese. Garnish with sage sprigs, if desired. Yield: 6 servings (serving size: about 1½ cups soup and 1 tablespoon cheese).

CALORIES 246 (21% from fat); FAT 5.7g (sat 1.5g, mono 3g, poly 0.7g); PROTEIN 14.3g; CARB 35.6g; FIBER 12g; CHOL 4mg; IRON 3.5mg; SODIUM 790mg; CALC 180mg

---

Storage Strategies

To store in the refrigerator: Transfer the sauce to a large bowl, and chill it in the refrigerator up to five days.

To store in the freezer: Ladle room-temperature or chilled sauce into plastic containers or zip-top plastic bags. Seal and freeze up to four months. Consider freezing the sauce in one-cup increments (two servings' worth). That way, you can pull out exactly as much as you want for future meals.

To thaw sauce: Try one of three methods.
- Thaw in the refrigerator overnight.
- Place frozen blocks in a saucepan. Cover and bring to a low simmer over medium heat, stirring occasionally.
- Place frozen blocks in a microwave-safe bowl. Cover and microwave at HIGH one minute at a time, stirring after each increment until thawed.

To boost taste: Long stints in the freezer can dull the taste of tomatoes. To perk up thawed sauce, add one-half teaspoon finely grated lemon rind or one teaspoon balsamic vinegar while reheating.

Autumn Dinner with Friends

Celebrate good company with this hearty menu.

Dinner with Friends Menu
serves 6

Buttery Polenta

Chicken Breasts Stuffed with Garlic and Herbed Goat Cheese

Sweet Potato and White Bean Soup with Sage-Walnut Pesto

Autumn Vegetable Medley with Rosemary and Nutmeg

Spiced Cider

Caramelized Quinces

Syrah/shiraz

Buttery Polenta

This simple Italian side dish complements the stuffed chicken. You can also easily adapt the recipe to accompany basic roasted chicken, pork, or beef by stirring in your favorite cheese at the end.

5 cups water
¾ teaspoon salt
1 cup dry polenta
2½ tablespoons butter
¼ teaspoon freshly ground black pepper

1. Combine 5 cups water and salt in a saucepan over medium-high heat; bring to a boil. Gradually add polenta, stirring constantly with a whisk. Reduce heat to low, and simmer 20 minutes or until mixture is thick, stirring frequently. Remove from heat. Stir in butter and pepper. Yield: 6 servings (serving size: ⅔ cup).

CALORIES 149 (28% from fat); FAT 4.7g (sat 3g, mono 1.2g, poly 0.2g); PROTEIN 2.7g; CARB 24.1g; FIBER 2.7g; CHOL 13mg; IRON 0.5mg; SODIUM 329mg; CALC 2mg

Chicken Breasts Stuffed with Garlic and Herbed Goat Cheese

Roasting the garlic mellows its bite and gives the stuffing a subtle hint of flavor. Stuff the chicken breasts up to a day ahead, refrigerate, and cook them just before guests arrive. Garnish each plate with a rosemary sprig.

1 whole garlic head
⅓ cup (3 ounces) goat cheese with herbs, softened
6 (6-ounce) skinless, boneless chicken breast halves
½ teaspoon kosher salt
½ teaspoon freshly ground black pepper
2 teaspoons olive oil

1. Preheat oven to 350°.
2. Remove white papery skin from garlic head (do not peel or separate cloves). Wrap head in foil. Bake at 350° for 1 hour; cool 10 minutes. Separate cloves; squeeze to extract garlic pulp. Discard skins. Combine garlic pulp and cheese, stirring well; set aside.
3. Cut a horizontal slit through thickest portion of each chicken breast half to form a pocket. Stuff about 4 teaspoons cheese mixture into each pocket. Sprinkle chicken evenly on both sides with salt and pepper.
4. Heat oil in a large ovenproof skillet over medium-high heat. Add chicken to pan; cook 3 minutes or until lightly browned. Turn chicken over. Bake at 350° for 20 minutes or until a thermometer registers 165°; let stand 5 minutes. Yield: 6 servings (serving size: 1 stuffed chicken breast half).

CALORIES 238 (31% from fat); FAT 8.1g (sat 3.3g, mono 2.9g, poly 1.1g); PROTEIN 37.3g; CARB 1.9g; FIBER 0.2g; CHOL 101mg; IRON 1.5mg; SODIUM 292mg; CALC 46mg

Sweet Potato and White Bean Soup with Sage-Walnut Pesto

Walnut oil adds a mild sweetness and intensifies the nutty flavor of the pesto, but you can substitute extravirgin olive oil.

SOUP:
Cooking spray
2 cups thinly sliced leek (about 2 medium)
3 cups fat-free, less-sodium chicken broth
1 cup water
2 cups (½-inch) cubed peeled sweet potato
4 cups chopped Swiss chard (about 1 bunch)
¼ teaspoon freshly ground black pepper
⅛ teaspoon salt
1 (19-ounce) can cannellini beans, rinsed and drained
2 tablespoons fresh lemon juice

PESTO:
¼ cup (1 ounce) grated Asiago cheese
¼ cup chopped fresh parsley
2 tablespoons chopped walnuts
1 tablespoon chopped fresh sage
1 tablespoon walnut oil
1 garlic clove, peeled

1. To prepare soup, heat a Dutch oven over medium heat. Coat pan with cooking spray. Add leek to pan; cook 8 minutes or until tender, stirring frequently. Stir in broth and 1 cup water; bring to a boil. Add potato; cook 10 minutes or until potato is tender. Stir in chard, pepper, salt, and beans; cook 3 minutes or until chard wilts. Remove from heat; stir in lemon juice.
2. To prepare pesto, place cheese and remaining 5 ingredients in a food processor; process until smooth, scraping sides of bowl occasionally. Ladle 1 cup soup into each of 6 bowls; top each serving with about 2 teaspoons pesto. Yield: 6 servings.

CALORIES 178 (29% from fat); FAT 5.7g (sat 1.2g, mono 1.1g, poly 3g); PROTEIN 7.2g; CARB 25.2g; FIBER 5.6g; CHOL 4mg; IRON 2.8mg; SODIUM 526mg; CALC 125mg

Autumn Vegetable Medley with Rosemary and Nutmeg

Any leftover vegetables from this recipe can easily become the base for a soup or stew. Just brown beef stew meat, and add a little beef broth.

1 (9-ounce) fennel bulb with stalks
2 cups (½-inch) cubed peeled butternut squash
1½ cups (1-inch-thick) slices parsnip
1½ cups (1-inch-thick) slices carrot
1 tablespoon olive oil
1½ teaspoons chopped fresh rosemary
½ teaspoon salt
¼ teaspoon freshly ground black pepper
Dash of freshly grated nutmeg
Cooking spray
⅓ cup (1½ ounces) freshly grated Parmigiano-Reggiano cheese (optional)

1. Preheat oven to 425°.
2. Trim tough outer leaves from fennel. Cut fennel bulb in half lengthwise; discard core. Cut each half into three wedges. Combine fennel and next 8 ingredients in a large shallow roasting pan coated with cooking spray. Bake at 425° for 35 minutes or until vegetables are tender, stirring occasionally. Sprinkle vegetable mixture with cheese, if desired. Yield: 6 servings (serving size: about ¾ cup vegetable mixture).

CALORIES 106 (22% from fat); FAT 2.6g (sat 0.4g, mono 1.8g, poly 0.2g); PROTEIN 2g; CARB 20.9g; FIBER 4.2g; CHOL 0mg; IRON 1.1mg; SODIUM 237mg; CALC 78mg

Spiced Cider

Welcome guests to your home with an inviting warm beverage. Steep the cider a day ahead, keep it refrigerated, and then reheat just before serving. For a nonalcoholic version, simply omit the brandy.

  5 cups apple cider
  1 (3-inch) cinnamon stick
  1 whole clove
  1 (½-inch-thick) slice orange
  1 (½-inch-thick) slice lemon
  ½ cup brandy
  6 (3-inch) cinnamon sticks (optional)

1. Combine first 5 ingredients in a medium saucepan; bring to a boil. Cover, reduce heat, and simmer 30 minutes. Strain cider mixture through a sieve into a bowl; discard solids. Stir in brandy. Serve warm. Garnish each serving with 1 cinnamon stick, if desired. Yield: 6 servings (serving size: about ⅔ cup).

CALORIES 173 (0% from fat); FAT 0g; PROTEIN 0.9g; CARB 29.6g; FIBER 0.1g; CHOL 0mg; IRON 0mg; SODIUM 0mg; CALC 2mg

Caramelized Quinces

These whole roasted quinces make a beautiful end to an autumn meal. If quinces are smaller than eight ounces each, they will cook more quickly.

  ⅓ cup granulated sugar
  ⅓ cup packed brown sugar
  ⅛ teaspoon salt
  3 tablespoons fresh lemon juice
  6 (8-ounce) quinces, peeled
  ½ cup apple cider
  2 tablespoons butter, cut into small pieces
  ⅓ cup whipping cream
  2 tablespoons powdered sugar
Freshly grated nutmeg (optional)

1. Preheat oven to 400°.
2. Combine first 3 ingredients in a medium bowl, stirring well with a whisk. Place juice in another bowl. Working with 1 quince at a time, dip quince in juice, turning to coat; dredge quince in sugar mixture, turning to coat. Place quince, stem end up, in an 8-inch square baking dish. Sprinkle quinces evenly with remaining sugar mixture. Pour cider in bottom of dish; place 1 teaspoon butter on top of each quince. Bake at 400° for 1½ hours or until quinces are golden brown and liquid is thick, basting every 30 minutes. Place 1 quince on each of 6 plates; drizzle evenly with remaining syrup in pan.
3. Place cream in a medium bowl; beat with a mixer at medium speed until soft peaks form. Add powdered sugar, 1 tablespoon at a time; continue beating until stiff peaks form. Serve quinces warm with whipped cream. Garnish with nutmeg, if desired. Yield: 6 servings (serving size: 1 quince and 2 tablespoons whipped cream).

CALORIES 267 (30% from fat); FAT 8.8g (sat 5.4g, mono 2.4g, poly 0.4g); PROTEIN 0.9g; CARB 50g; FIBER 2.7g; CHOL 28mg; IRON 1.2mg; SODIUM 93mg; CALC 36mg

sound bites
Go Nuts

Rich in protein, beneficial fats, and fiber, nut meals have a variety of flavorful possibilities.

Nut meal is nothing more than nuts ground to a flourlike consistency. It's used to replace flour in baked goods; to make a rich coating for baked fish, poultry, or meat; as a thickener for soups and stews; and as a flavor enhancer for homemade gnocchi.

While nut meals are high in protein and fiber, they're also high in calories and fat—though mostly the heart-healthy unsaturated kind. Like all vegetable products, they're cholesterol-free.

You'll find nut meals in the baking aisle at health-food stores and gourmet groceries, and they're increasingly available in large supermarkets. Italian specialty markets may have chestnut or almond meal, while peanut meal is often sold in Asian markets.

Almond-Crusted Salmon

Rich salmon, coated in almond meal, acquires a toasted flavor reminiscent of browned butter.

  ¼ cup almond meal
  ¼ cup panko (Japanese breadcrumbs)
  ¼ teaspoon ground coriander
  ⅛ teaspoon ground cumin
  4 (6-ounce) salmon fillets, about 1-inch thick
  2 teaspoons lemon juice
  ½ teaspoon kosher salt
  ¼ teaspoon freshly ground black pepper
Cooking spray
  4 lemon wedges

1. Preheat oven to 500°.
2. Combine first 4 ingredients in a shallow dish; set aside.
3. Brush tops and sides of fish with juice; sprinkle with salt and pepper. Working with 1 fillet at a time, dredge top and sides in almond mixture; place fish, skin side down, on a broiler pan coated with cooking spray. Sprinkle any remaining crumb mixture evenly over fish; press gently to adhere. Bake at 500° for 15 minutes or until fish flakes easily when tested with a fork or until desired degree of doneness. Serve with lemon wedges. Yield: 4 servings (serving size: 1 fillet and 1 lemon wedge).

CALORIES 332 (45% from fat); FAT 16.7g (sat 3.3g, mono 7.9g, poly 4g); PROTEIN 38.2g; CARB 5.4g; FIBER 1.5g; CHOL 87mg; IRON 0.6mg; SODIUM 330mg; CALC 28mg

---

Notes from the Test Kitchens

Although nut meals are often used to replace flour in recipes, they aren't exactly the same as flour. We found nut meals work well in dishes that benefit from a nutty undertone, such as breading for fish and as a thickener for sauces. You also can replace part of the wheat flour in cookie dough and pancake or waffle batter with the nut meal of your choice.

Hazelnut Gnocchi with Sage Glaze

The combination of hazelnut meal and Yukon gold potatoes gives these gnocchi rich flavor that's ideal with roasted chicken or pork.

GNOCCHI:
- ¼ cup water
- 1 pound Yukon gold potatoes, peeled and cut into 2-inch pieces
- 1 cup all-purpose flour (about 4½ ounces), divided
- ½ cup hazelnut meal
- ½ teaspoon salt
- 1 garlic clove, minced
- 1 large egg yolk, lightly beaten
- 1 gallon water

GLAZE:
- 1 tablespoon butter
- 1 garlic clove, minced
- 1 tablespoon fat-free, less-sodium chicken broth
- 1½ teaspoons chopped fresh sage
- ¼ teaspoon salt
- ¼ teaspoon freshly ground black pepper

1. To prepare gnocchi, combine ¼ cup water and potatoes in a microwave-safe dish. Cover and microwave at HIGH 10 minutes or until tender. Drain potatoes; mash potatoes with a potato masher. Cool 5 minutes.

2. Lightly spoon flour into a dry measuring cup; level with a knife. Combine potatoes, ¾ cup flour, hazelnut meal, and next 3 ingredients; mix well. Knead until smooth (about 2 minutes); add enough of remaining flour, 1 tablespoon at a time, to prevent dough from sticking to hands.

3. Divide dough into 4 equal portions. Shape each portion into a 12-inch-long rope. Cut each rope into 20 pieces; roll each piece into a ball. Working with one dough piece at a time (cover remaining dough to prevent drying), using your thumb, roll dough piece down tines of a lightly floured fork (gnocchi will have ridges on one side and an indention on the other). Place gnocchi on a lightly floured baking sheet.

4. Bring 1 gallon water to a boil in a large stockpot.

5. To prepare glaze, melt butter in a small saucepan over medium heat. Add 1 minced garlic clove to pan; cook 30 seconds. Add broth; bring to a boil. Stir in sage, ¼ teaspoon salt, and pepper. Remove from heat.

6. Add half of gnocchi to boiling water; cook 3 minutes or until done (gnocchi will rise to surface). Remove cooked gnocchi with a slotted spoon; place in a colander. Repeat procedure with remaining gnocchi. Serve drizzled with warm glaze. Yield: 8 servings (serving size: 10 gnocchi).

CALORIES 156 (29% from fat); FAT 5.1g (sat 1.4g, mono 2.8g, poly 0.6g); PROTEIN 3.7g; CARB 24.5g; FIBER 1.9g; CHOL 29mg; IRON 1.2mg; SODIUM 298mg; CALC 19mg

MAKE AHEAD
Orange-Hazelnut Dacquoise

Dacquoise is a dessert made of nut-flavored meringues layered with creamy filling. Prepare this cake a day ahead, and freeze overnight so it's easy to slice.

MERINGUES:
- 1 cup hazelnut meal
- ¼ cup sugar
- 3 tablespoons fat-free milk
- 1 teaspoon vanilla extract
- ⅛ teaspoon almond extract
- ¼ teaspoon cream of tartar
- ⅛ teaspoon salt
- 6 large egg whites
- ½ cup sugar

FILLING:
- 1¼ cups orange juice
- ¾ cup sugar
- 2 tablespoons cornstarch
- 1 tablespoon all-purpose flour
- 1 tablespoon orange-flavored liqueur
- Dash of salt
- 1 (8-ounce) container frozen fat-free whipped topping, thawed

REMAINING INGREDIENTS:
- ½ cup hazelnut meal
- 2 teaspoons butter
- 1 ounce semisweet chocolate, chopped

1. Preheat oven to 200°.

2. To prepare meringues, draw 2 (8-inch) circles on each of 2 pieces of parchment paper. Turn paper over; secure with masking tape to 2 baking sheets.

3. Combine first 5 ingredients in a medium bowl; stir well. Place cream of tartar, ⅛ teaspoon salt, and egg whites in a large bowl; beat with a mixer at high speed until foamy. Gradually add ½ cup sugar, 1 tablespoon at a time, beating until stiff peaks form (do not underbeat). Stir one-third of egg white mixture into hazelnut meal mixture. Fold hazelnut meal mixture into remaining egg white mixture.

4. Divide egg white mixture evenly among the 4 drawn circles; spread egg white mixture to outside edge of each circle using back of a spoon. Bake at 200° for 3 hours or until dry. Turn oven off, and cool meringues in closed oven at least 2 hours. Carefully remove meringues from paper.

5. To prepare filling, combine juice and next 5 ingredients in a small saucepan; bring to a boil. Cook 1 minute, stirring constantly until thick. Transfer to a medium bowl; cover and chill. Fold in whipped topping.

6. Place 1 meringue on a serving platter. Spread one-fourth of filling evenly over meringue. Repeat layers two more times; top with remaining meringue. Spread remaining filling around sides. Press ½ cup hazelnut meal around sides of cake. Combine butter and chocolate in a microwave-safe dish. Microwave at HIGH 1 minute; stir until smooth. Spread chocolate mixture over top of meringue. Cover loosely, and freeze 8 hours or overnight. Yield: 12 servings (serving size: 1 wedge).

CALORIES 259 (30% from fat); FAT 8.7g (sat 1.4g, mono 6.2g, poly 1.2g); PROTEIN 5.4g; CARB 40.2g; FIBER 2.2g; CHOL 2mg; IRON 0.2mg; SODIUM 87mg; CALC 11mg

Green Mole with Turkey and Chochoyones

Mexican moles are almost always thickened with ground nuts or seeds. Grind the pine nuts in a coffee or spice grinder. *Chochoyones* are dumplings similar in flavor and texture to tamale dough.

    2   pounds tomatillos
    4   jalapeño peppers, halved and
        seeded
    2   teaspoons peanut oil, divided
    2   cups chopped onion
    4   garlic cloves, minced
    3   tablespoons pine nut meal,
        toasted
    1   cup masa harina
    2   tablespoons vegetable shortening
 1½   cups water, divided
    ½   cup chopped fresh parsley
    ½   cup chopped fresh cilantro
    1   tablespoon sugar
    2   (14-ounce) cans fat-free,
        less-sodium chicken broth
 3½   cups cubed deli turkey breast
 1½   cups (1-inch) cut green beans

1. Preheat broiler.

2. Discard husks and stems from tomatillos. Arrange tomatillos and jalapeños in a single layer on a jelly-roll pan. Broil 12 minutes or until tomatillos are slightly blackened.

3. Heat 1 teaspoon oil in a large Dutch oven over medium-high heat. Add onion and garlic to pan; sauté 4 minutes or until onion is browned. Place onion mixture, tomatillo mixture, and pine nut meal in a food processor, and process until smooth.

4. Heat 1 teaspoon oil in pan over high heat. Add tomatillo mixture. Partially cover, and cook 10 minutes, stirring occasionally. Uncover and cook an additional 5 minutes or until thick and slightly darkened.

5. While tomatillo mixture cooks, combine masa harina and shortening in a medium bowl. Add ¼ cup water; knead gently until combined. Shape dough into 18 (1-inch) balls.

6. Place parsley, cilantro, and ¼ cup water in a food processor, and process until finely chopped.

7. Add 1 cup water, sugar, and broth to tomatillo mixture in pan; bring to a simmer. Stir in turkey and beans. Gently stir in dough balls; bring to a simmer over high heat. Reduce heat to low, and cook 5 minutes or until dumplings are done. Remove from heat; stir in parsley mixture. Yield: 6 servings (serving size: about 1¾ cups mole and 3 chochoyones).

CALORIES 292 (35% from fat); FAT 11.5g (sat 2.8g, mono 2.9g, poly 3.6g); PROTEIN 18.4g; CARB 32.9g; FIBER 4.4g; CHOL 28mg; IRON 3.4mg; SODIUM 991mg; CALC 75mg

WINE NOTE: With this mole's bounty of fresh herbs and spicy heat provided by jalapeño peppers, a crisp white with a touch of sweetness will refresh without overwhelming the delicate flavors. Try a riesling, like Drylands Dry Riesling 2006 from New Zealand ($15). It offers zesty citrus flavor and lively acidity, much like squeezing a lime over your dish to brighten the flavors.

MAKE AHEAD
Maple-Walnut Chiffon Cake

A combination of walnut meal and walnut oil in the batter, plus a garnish of halved walnuts atop the cake, creates several layers of nutty flavor in this dessert.

CAKE:
    Cooking spray
 1½   cups cake flour (about 6 ounces)
    ¾   cup sugar, divided
    2   teaspoons baking powder
    ½   cup walnut meal
    ½   cup maple syrup
    ⅓   cup walnut oil
    1   teaspoon vanilla extract
    ¼   teaspoon salt
    6   large egg whites

MAPLE CREAM:
    ⅔   cup maple syrup
    2   teaspoons cornstarch
    1   teaspoon all-purpose flour
    Dash of salt
    2   cups frozen fat-free whipped
        topping, thawed
  12   walnut halves

1. Preheat oven to 350°.

2. To prepare cake, coat 2 (8-inch) round cake pans with cooking spray; line bottom of pans with wax paper. Coat wax paper with cooking spray; set aside.

3. Lightly spoon cake flour into dry measuring cups; level with a knife. Combine cake flour, ½ cup sugar, and baking powder in a large bowl; stir with a whisk. Add walnut meal; make a well in center of mixture. Combine ½ cup syrup, oil, and vanilla. Add to flour mixture; beat with a mixer at medium speed until blended.

4. Beat salt and egg whites with a mixer at high speed until soft peaks form using clean, dry beaters. Gradually add ¼ cup sugar, 1 tablespoon at a time, beating until stiff peaks form. Gently stir one-fourth of egg white mixture into flour mixture; gently fold in remaining egg white mixture. Spoon into prepared pans. Bake at 350° for 20 minutes or until a wooden pick inserted in center comes out clean. Cool 5 minutes in pans on wire racks. Remove from pans; peel off waxed paper. Cool cakes completely on wire racks.

5. To prepare maple cream, combine ⅔ cup syrup and next 3 ingredients in a small saucepan, and stir until smooth. Bring to a boil over medium heat, and cook 1 minute. Remove from heat. Cover and chill. Gently fold in whipped topping. Refrigerate 1 hour.

6. Place 1 cake layer on a plate; spread with 1 cup maple cream. Top with remaining cake layer. Spread remaining maple cream over top and sides of cake. Arrange walnut halves on top. Store cake loosely covered in refrigerator. Yield: 16 servings (serving size: 1 slice).

CALORIES 239 (27% from fat); FAT 7.3g (sat 0.7g, mono 1.4g, poly 4.8g); PROTEIN 3.1g; CARB 39g; FIBER 0.5g; CHOL 0mg; IRON 1.4mg; SODIUM 137mg; CALC 56mg

Skillet Suppers

One pan is all you need to create a tempting feast for four.

Skillet Suppers Menu 1
serves 4

Chicken and Asparagus in White Wine Sauce

Parmesan-chive mashed potatoes*

Soft breadsticks

*Heat 1 (20-ounce) package refrigerated mashed potatoes (such as Simply Potatoes) according to package directions. Stir in ¼ cup grated fresh Parmesan cheese, 2 tablespoons chopped fresh chives, and ½ teaspoon freshly ground black pepper.

Game Plan

1. Pound chicken breasts.
2. While butter melts in pan:
   - Dredge chicken in flour.
   - Grate cheese for potatoes.
3. While chicken cooks:
   - Mince garlic.
   - Wash and trim asparagus.
   - Chop parsley and chives.
   - Squeeze lemon juice.
4. While asparagus cooks:
   - Heat potatoes.

QUICK & EASY
Chicken and Asparagus in White Wine Sauce

(pictured on page 248)

This recipe also works well with green beans or haricots verts in place of asparagus.

TOTAL TIME: 40 MINUTES

QUICK TIP: To speed up the process in step one, purchase thinly sliced chicken breasts (sometimes labeled chicken cutlets or chicken breast fillets).

- 4 (6-ounce) skinless, boneless chicken breast halves
- ¾ teaspoon salt
- ¼ teaspoon freshly ground black pepper
- 2 tablespoons butter
- ½ cup all-purpose flour (about 2¼ ounces)
- ½ cup dry white wine
- ½ cup fat-free, less-sodium chicken broth
- 2 garlic cloves, minced
- 1 pound asparagus spears, trimmed
- 2 tablespoons chopped fresh parsley
- 1 tablespoon fresh lemon juice

1. Place each chicken breast half between 2 sheets of heavy-duty plastic wrap; pound to ¼-inch thickness using a meat mallet or small heavy skillet. Sprinkle chicken evenly with salt and pepper.
2. Melt butter in a large nonstick skillet over medium-high heat. Place flour in a shallow dish. Dredge chicken in flour. Add chicken to pan; cook 3 minutes on each side or until done. Remove chicken from pan; keep warm. Add wine, broth, and garlic to pan, scraping pan to loosen browned bits; cook 2 minutes. Add asparagus; cover and cook 3 minutes or until asparagus is crisp-tender. Remove from heat; stir in parsley and juice. Serve asparagus and sauce with chicken. Yield: 4 servings (serving size: 1 chicken breast half, about 5 asparagus spears, and about 2 tablespoons sauce).

CALORIES 289 (25% from fat); FAT 8g (sat 4.2g, mono 2g, poly 0.8g); PROTEIN 43g; CARB 10.5g; FIBER 2.8g; CHOL 114mg; IRON 4.3mg; SODIUM 648mg; CALC 59mg

Skillet Suppers Menu 2
serves 4

Tequila Pork Chile Verde

Refried black beans*

Corn tortillas

*Bring 1 (15-ounce) can undrained black beans to a boil in a large nonstick skillet. Remove from heat; stir in 1 tablespoon fresh lime juice. Mash mixture with a potato masher to desired consistency. Sprinkle with 1 tablespoon finely chopped red bell pepper.

Game Plan

1. While pork cooks:
   - Chop tomatillos.
   - Seed and chop jalapeño.
2. While tomatillo mixture simmers:
   - Slice green onions for pork.
   - Juice lime for beans.
   - Chop cilantro for pork.
3. While beans cook in skillet:
   - Heat tortillas in microwave according to package directions.

QUICK & EASY
Tequila Pork Chile Verde

TOTAL TIME: 35 MINUTES

QUICK TIP: To reduce cleanup, turn the pork dish out of the skillet into a bowl. Rinse the skillet with water, pat dry, and prepare the refried beans from the menu above in the same pan.

- 2 teaspoons canola oil
- 3 tablespoons yellow cornmeal
- 1 tablespoon ancho chile powder
- 1 pound pork tenderloin, trimmed and cut into ¾-inch pieces
- 2 cups coarsely chopped fresh tomatillos (about 12 ounces)
- 1 (14-ounce) can fat-free, less-sodium chicken broth
- 1 (4.5-ounce) can chopped mild green chiles, drained
- 1 jalapeño pepper, seeded and finely chopped
- ½ cup thinly sliced green onions
- ¼ cup chopped fresh cilantro
- 2 tablespoons tequila
- ¼ teaspoon salt

1. Heat oil in a large nonstick skillet over medium-high heat.

2. Combine cornmeal and chile powder in a medium bowl. Add pork, tossing to coat. Remove pork from bowl, reserving remaining cornmeal mixture. Add pork to pan; sauté 5 minutes or until browned. Stir in remaining cornmeal mixture; cook 30 seconds, stirring constantly. Stir in tomatillos, broth, chiles, and jalapeño; bring to a simmer over medium-low heat. Cook 8 minutes or until tomatillos are tender. Stir in onions and remaining ingredients; simmer 1 minute. Yield: 4 servings (serving size: 1¼ cups).

CALORIES 245 (27% from fat); FAT 7.4g (sat 1.7g, mono 3.3g, poly 1.6g); PROTEIN 26.5g; CARB 14.8g; FIBER 3.4g; CHOL 74mg; IRON 2.7mg; SODIUM 407mg; CALC 30mg

Skillet Suppers Menu 3
serves 4

Halibut with White Beans in Tomato-Rosemary Broth

Arugula-Asiago salad*

Baguette slices

*Place 6 cups arugula in a large bowl. Combine 1 tablespoon fresh lemon juice, 2 teaspoons extravirgin olive oil, ¼ teaspoon salt, and ¼ teaspoon freshly ground black pepper, stirring well. Drizzle dressing over arugula; toss gently to coat. Top salad with ¼ cup shaved fresh Asiago cheese.

Game Plan

1. While fish cooks:
   - Mince garlic.
   - Chop tomato.
   - Rinse and drain beans.
2. While tomato-broth mixture cooks:
   - Chop rosemary.
   - Prepare salad.

QUICK & EASY
Halibut with White Beans in Tomato-Rosemary Broth

Beans absorb some of the delicious broth. For a special dinner, serve in shallow rimmed bowls and top each serving with a fresh rosemary sprig.

TOTAL TIME: 35 MINUTES

FLAVOR TIP: If the fresh tomatoes at your market aren't at their best, substitute 1 (14.5-ounce) can diced tomatoes, drained.

1	tablespoon olive oil
4	(6-ounce) halibut fillets
¼	teaspoon salt
¼	teaspoon freshly ground black pepper
2	garlic cloves, minced
2	cups chopped plum tomato (about 4)
1½	cups fat-free, less-sodium chicken broth
½	cup dry white wine
1	(16-ounce) can cannellini beans or other white beans, rinsed and drained
½	teaspoon chopped fresh rosemary

1. Heat oil in a large nonstick skillet over medium-high heat. Sprinkle fish evenly with salt and pepper. Add fish to pan; cook 5 minutes on each side or until fish flakes easily when tested with a fork or until desired degree of doneness. Remove fish from pan; keep warm. Add garlic to pan; cook 30 seconds, stirring constantly. Stir in tomato, broth, wine, and beans; bring to a boil. Reduce heat, and simmer 5 minutes. Remove from heat; stir in rosemary. Serve immediately with fish. Yield: 4 servings (serving size: 1 fillet and about ¾ cup bean mixture).

CALORIES 299 (24% from fat); FAT 7.9g (sat 1.1g, mono 3.8g, poly 2g); PROTEIN 39.8g; CARB 14.9g; FIBER 4g; CHOL 54mg; IRON 3.2mg; SODIUM 535mg; CALC 117mg

Skillet Suppers Menu 4
serves 4

Smoked Ham Hash

Peppery wilted spinach*

Orange wedges

*Heat 1 tablespoon olive oil in a large nonstick skillet over medium-high heat. Add 1 minced garlic clove; sauté 30 seconds. Gradually add 2 (10-ounce) packages fresh spinach; cook 3 minutes or until spinach wilts. Stir in 1 tablespoon pepper vinegar, ¼ teaspoon salt, and ⅛ teaspoon freshly ground black pepper.

Game Plan

1. While potatoes cook:
   - Dice ham.
   - Slice green onions.
2. While broth mixture cooks:
   - Mince garlic for spinach.
   - Cut oranges into wedges.
3. Remove hash from skillet; cook spinach in same pan.

QUICK & EASY
Smoked Ham Hash

Vary this recipe by using smoked turkey or rotisserie chicken in place of ham.

TOTAL TIME: 35 MINUTES

QUICK TIP: Purchase prechopped ham from the fresh pork or luncheon meat section of your supermarket.

1	tablespoon butter
2	cups frozen hash brown potatoes with onions and peppers
1	cup chopped onion
¾	cup chopped red bell pepper
1½	cups fat-free, less-sodium chicken broth
2	tablespoons half-and-half
2	teaspoons Worcestershire sauce
2	teaspoons ketchup
1½	cups chopped smoked ham
¼	teaspoon freshly ground black pepper
2	tablespoons thinly sliced green onions
2	tablespoons chopped fresh parsley

Continued

1. Heat butter in a large nonstick skillet over medium-high heat. Add potatoes, onion, and bell pepper to pan; sauté 5 minutes or until lightly browned. Stir in broth and next 3 ingredients; bring to a boil. Cook 5 minutes or until liquid almost evaporates. Stir in ham and black pepper; cook 1½ minutes or until thoroughly heated. Sprinkle with onions and parsley. Yield: 4 servings (serving size: about 1 cup).

CALORIES 206 (29% from fat); FAT 6.6g (sat 3.4g, mono 1.1g, poly 0.3g); PROTEIN 13.8g; CARB 25g; FIBER 3.6g; CHOL 41mg; IRON 2.1mg; SODIUM 847mg; CALC 47mg

superfast
20 Minute Dishes

From salad to pizza, seafood to sandwiches, here are simple, fresh, and easy meals you can make superfast.

QUICK & EASY
Barley Sausage Skillet

Madeira is a slightly sweet Portuguese fortified wine. Substitute sherry or fruity white wine, if necessary. Serve with broccoli sautéed with garlic and lemon, and corn bread.

1   (14-ounce) can fat-free,
    less-sodium chicken broth
1   cup quick-cooking barley
Cooking spray
8   ounces hot turkey Italian sausage
1   teaspoon olive oil
1   cup chopped onion
½   cup chopped red bell pepper
1   (8-ounce) package presliced
    mushrooms
2   teaspoons bottled minced garlic
2   tablespoons Madeira wine
¼   cup thinly sliced fresh basil
⅛   teaspoon black pepper

1. Place broth in a small saucepan; bring to a boil. Add barley to pan. Cover, reduce heat, and simmer 10 minutes or until liquid is absorbed.

2. Heat a large nonstick skillet over medium-high heat. Coat pan with cooking spray. Remove casings from sausage. Add sausage to pan; cook 3 minutes, stirring to crumble. Transfer to a bowl. Heat oil in pan over medium-high heat. Add onion, bell pepper, and mushrooms; sauté 4 minutes or until liquid evaporates. Add garlic; sauté 1 minute. Return sausage to pan. Stir in Madeira; sauté 2 minutes. Add barley; cook 1 minute or until thoroughly heated. Remove from heat; stir in basil and black pepper. Yield: 4 servings (serving size: 1¼ cups).

CALORIES 337 (22% from fat); FAT 8.1g (sat 3.7g, mono 2.6g, poly 1.6g); PROTEIN 17.6g; CARB 49.1g; FIBER 9.6g; CHOL 34mg; IRON 3mg; SODIUM 537mg; CALC 49mg

QUICK & EASY
Catfish Sandwiches with Creole Mayonnaise

Fillets work well in these sandwiches. You can substitute tilapia or bass for catfish.

Cooking spray
4   (6-ounce) catfish fillets
1½ teaspoons Cajun seasoning
4   (1½-ounce) hamburger buns
3   tablespoons fat-free mayonnaise
1½ teaspoons minced shallots
1¼ teaspoons whole-grain Dijon
    mustard
½   teaspoon fresh lemon juice
4   curly leaf lettuce leaves
4   (¼-inch-thick) slices tomato
8   teaspoons sweet pickle relish

1. Heat a grill pan over medium-high heat. Coat pan with cooking spray. Sprinkle fillets evenly with seasoning. Add fillets to pan; cook 4 minutes. Turn over; cook 3 minutes or until fish flakes easily when tested with a fork or until desired degree of doneness.

2. Place buns, cut sides down, in pan; cook 1 minute or until toasted. Remove from pan.

3. Combine mayonnaise, shallots, mustard, and juice, stirring well. Line bottom half of each bun with 1 lettuce leaf; top each serving with 1 fillet and 1 tomato slice. Spoon 2 teaspoons relish on top of each tomato. Spread 1 tablespoon mayonnaise

mixture over cut side of each top half of buns; place on top of each sandwich. Yield: 4 servings (serving size: 1 sandwich).

CALORIES 319 (30% from fat); FAT 11.6g (sat 2.7g, mono 5.1g, poly 2.9g); PROTEIN 24.5g; CARB 28.4g; FIBER 1.3g; CHOL 60mg; IRON 2.3mg; SODIUM 674mg; CALC 76mg

QUICK & EASY
Thai Beef Salad

1   cup loosely packed fresh cilantro
     leaves
¼   cup fresh lime juice (about 3
     limes)
2   tablespoons low-sodium soy sauce
1½   tablespoons Thai fish sauce
1   tablespoon honey
2   teaspoons grated orange rind
2   garlic cloves, peeled
½   small serrano chile
2   teaspoons olive oil
4   (4-ounce) beef tenderloin steaks,
     trimmed
¼   teaspoon black pepper
⅛   teaspoon salt
2   cups shredded Napa cabbage
1   cup grated, seeded, peeled
     cucumber
⅓   cup thinly sliced green onions
3   tablespoons chopped fresh basil
1   (12-ounce) package broccoli
     coleslaw
1   (11-ounce) can mandarin oranges
     in light syrup, drained

1. Place first 8 ingredients in a food processor; process until smooth.

2. Heat oil in a large nonstick skillet over medium-high heat. Sprinkle steak evenly on both sides with pepper and salt. Add steak to pan; cook 4 minutes on each side or until desired degree of doneness. Remove steak from pan; let stand 5 minutes. Cut into thin slices.

3. Combine cabbage and remaining 5 ingredients in a large bowl. Drizzle slaw mixture with cilantro mixture; toss. Arrange 2 cups slaw mixture on each of 4 plates; top each serving with 3 ounces beef. Yield: 4 servings.

CALORIES 313 (34% from fat); FAT 11.8g (sat 4g, mono 5.5g, poly 0.6g); PROTEIN 28.2g; CARB 22.6g; FIBER 5g; CHOL 71mg; IRON 2.8mg; SODIUM 883mg; CALC 105mg

Tomato-Mozzarella Pizza

Pancetta is Italian cured bacon. You can substitute regular bacon, if you wish. Round out the meal with a tossed green salad.

- 1 (11-ounce) can refrigerated French bread dough
- 2 tablespoons yellow cornmeal
- Cooking spray
- 1½ pounds plum tomatoes, thinly sliced
- 1 garlic clove, minced
- 1 cup (4 ounces) shredded part-skim mozzarella cheese, divided
- ¼ teaspoon pepper
- 2 ounces pancetta
- ¼ cup thinly sliced fresh basil

1. Preheat oven to 450°.
2. Place dough on a baking sheet sprinkled with cornmeal; press dough into a 12-inch circle. Crimp edges of dough with fingers to form a rim. Lightly spray surface of dough with cooking spray. Bake at 450° for 8 minutes. Remove crust from oven.
3. Arrange tomato slices on paper towels. Cover with additional paper towels; let stand 5 minutes. Sprinkle garlic evenly over surface of dough; sprinkle ½ cup cheese evenly over dough. Arrange tomato slices on top of cheese; sprinkle with pepper. Top with ½ cup cheese. Bake at 450° for 5 minutes.
4. Chop pancetta. Cook pancetta in a nonstick skillet over medium heat until crisp; drain. Sprinkle pancetta over pizza; bake an additional 1 minute or until crust is golden. Sprinkle basil over pizza; let stand 2 minutes. Cut into 6 wedges. Yield: 6 servings (serving size: 1 wedge).

CALORIES 243 (32% from fat); FAT 8.6g (sat 4.2g, mono 1.1g, poly 0.2g); PROTEIN 11.5g; CARB 31.7g; FIBER 2.4g; CHOL 17mg; IRON 1.9mg; SODIUM 560mg; CALC 153mg

Pan-Grilled Snapper with Orzo Pasta Salad

Small rice-shaped pasta, orzo cooks quickly and soaks up flavor from the vinaigrette. Double the vinaigrette and spoon some over the top of the fish, if you like.

- 1½ cups uncooked orzo (rice-shaped pasta)
- Cooking spray
- 4 (6-ounce) red snapper fillets
- ½ teaspoon salt, divided
- ¼ teaspoon pepper, divided
- 1½ tablespoons minced shallots
- 1 tablespoon chopped fresh parsley
- 1 tablespoon fresh lemon juice
- 2 teaspoons orange juice
- 1 teaspoon Dijon mustard
- 2½ tablespoons extravirgin olive oil

1. Cook pasta according to package directions, omitting salt and fat. Drain and keep warm.
2. Heat a grill pan over medium-high heat. Coat pan with cooking spray. Sprinkle fish evenly with ¼ teaspoon salt and ⅛ teaspoon pepper. Add fish to pan; cook 3 minutes on each side or until fish flakes easily when tested with a fork or until desired degree of doneness.
3. Combine ¼ teaspoon salt, ⅛ teaspoon pepper, shallots, and next 4 ingredients in a small bowl, stirring well. Slowly add oil, stirring constantly with a whisk. Drizzle shallot mixture over pasta; toss well to coat. Serve with fish. Yield: 4 servings (serving size: 1 fillet and ¾ cup pasta mixture).

CALORIES 398 (25% from fat); FAT 11.2g (sat 1.8g, mono 6.9g, poly 1.6g); PROTEIN 32.7g; CARB 39.3g; FIBER 1.9g; CHOL 47mg; IRON 0.4mg; SODIUM 409mg; CALC 46mg

Steamed Mussels in Saffron Broth

Saffron adds its characteristic bittersweet earthiness to the broth, though the dish is good without it, too. Serve with toasted slices of French bread.

- 1 teaspoon olive oil
- 1 cup chopped onion
- 1 teaspoon bottled minced garlic
- ¼ teaspoon saffron threads, crushed
- 3 tablespoons tomato paste
- 1½ tablespoons whipping cream
- 1 (8-ounce) bottle clam juice
- 4 pounds mussels, scrubbed and debearded

1. Heat oil in a large saucepan over medium-high heat. Add onion to pan; sauté 1 minute. Add garlic; sauté 30 seconds. Add saffron; sauté 15 seconds. Stir in tomato paste, whipping cream, and clam juice; bring to a boil. Cook 1 minute, stirring occasionally. Add mussels to pan. Cover and cook 5 minutes or until mussels open; discard any unopened shells. Yield: 4 servings (serving size: 1 pound mussels).

CALORIES 318 (28% from fat); FAT 10g (sat 2.7g, mono 3g, poly 2g); PROTEIN 37.2g; CARB 17.9g; FIBER 1g; CHOL 93mg; IRON 12.4mg; SODIUM 991mg; CALC 99mg

Tiramisu

Tiramisu is Italian for "lift me up." And its indulgent, creamy, mocha-tinged flavor is indeed uplifting. With layers of lady-fingers or cake, coffee, mascarpone cheese, and shaved or grated chocolate, traditional tiramisu is a cross between a trifle and bread pudding—and abundant in calories.

Our recipe, which first appeared in the March 1995 issue, used reduced-calorie whipped topping and an Italian meringue made of egg whites to lighten the classic dessert. For this updated version, we omitted the whipped topping and egg whites in favor of buttery mascarpone cheese, which we've mixed with fat-free cream cheese and brown sugar. We increased the cocoa and added bittersweet chocolate to this new version. And we've included a touch of Kahlúa in the espresso drizzle to boost the coffee flavor. The result is a more traditional-tasting dessert that's easy to prepare and even easier to enjoy.

MAKE AHEAD
Tiramisu

ESPRESSO DRIZZLE:
- ½ cup water
- 2 tablespoons granulated sugar
- 2 tablespoons instant espresso granules
- 2 tablespoons Kahlúa (coffee-flavored liqueur)

FILLING:
- 1 (8-ounce) block fat-free cream cheese, softened
- 1 (3.5-ounce) carton mascarpone cheese
- ⅓ cup granulated sugar
- ¼ cup packed brown sugar
- 2 tablespoons Kahlúa

REMAINING INGREDIENTS:
- 24 cakelike ladyfingers (2 [3-ounce] packages)
- 1½ teaspoons unsweetened cocoa
- ½ ounce bittersweet chocolate, grated

1. To prepare espresso drizzle, combine first 3 ingredients in a small saucepan over medium-high heat; bring to a boil. Cook 1 minute, stirring occasionally. Remove from heat; stir in 2 tablespoons Kahlúa. Cool completely.

2. To prepare filling, combine cheeses in a large bowl, and beat with a mixer at medium speed until smooth. Add ⅓ cup granulated sugar, brown sugar, and 2 tablespoons Kahlúa; beat at medium speed until well blended.

3. Split ladyfingers in half lengthwise. Arrange 24 ladyfinger halves, cut sides up, in an 8-inch square baking dish. Drizzle half of espresso drizzle over ladyfinger halves. Spread half of filling over ladyfinger halves, and repeat procedure with remaining ladyfinger halves, espresso drizzle, and filling. Combine 1½ teaspoons cocoa and chocolate; sprinkle evenly over top of filling. Cover and chill 2 hours. Yield: 8 servings.

NOTE: Place toothpicks in the center and in each corner of the dish to prevent the plastic wrap from sticking to the tiramisu as it chills.

CALORIES 260 (28% from fat); FAT 8g (sat 4.1g, mono 2.2g, poly 0.5g); PROTEIN 7.1g; CARB 38.4g; FIBER 0.5g; CHOL 55mg; IRON 0.8mg; SODIUM 317mg; CALC 104mg

Cookie Celebration

A retired teacher in Nebraska seeks an improved version of her beloved chocolate chip cookies.

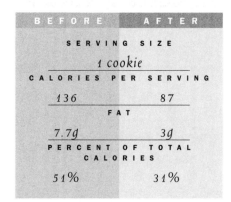

	BEFORE	AFTER
SERVING SIZE		
	1 cookie	
CALORIES PER SERVING		
	136	*87*
FAT		
	7.7g	*3g*
PERCENT OF TOTAL CALORIES		
	51%	*31%*

STAFF FAVORITE • MAKE AHEAD
FREEZABLE
Black and White Chocolate Chip Cookies

The Kahlúa is subtle in this cookie; if you don't have this liqueur, substitute an equal amount of strong, freshly brewed coffee.

- 2 cups cake flour (about 8 ounces)
- ¾ teaspoon baking powder
- ¼ teaspoon salt
- ¾ cup packed brown sugar
- ½ cup granulated sugar
- 3 tablespoons butter, softened
- 3 tablespoons vegetable shortening
- ¼ cup water
- 2 tablespoons egg substitute
- 1½ tablespoons Kahlúa (coffee-flavored liqueur)
- 1 teaspoon vanilla extract
- 6 tablespoons semisweet chocolate minichips
- ⅓ cup premium white chocolate chips
- 2½ tablespoons finely chopped pecans, toasted

1. Preheat oven to 350°.

2. Lightly spoon flour into dry measuring cups; level with a knife. Combine flour, baking powder, and salt; stir with a whisk.

3. Combine sugars, butter, and shortening in a large bowl; beat with a mixer at medium speed until light and fluffy, about 3 minutes. Combine ¼ cup water, egg substitute, Kahlúa, and vanilla in a small bowl. Add Kahlúa mixture to sugar mixture; beat 2 minutes or until well blended. Gradually add flour mixture; beat at low speed just until combined. Fold in chocolate chips, white chocolate chips, and pecans. Drop by level tablespoonfuls 2 inches apart onto ungreased baking sheets. Bake, 1 sheet at a time, at 350° for 14 minutes or just until set and beginning to brown around edges and on bottoms. Remove from oven; cool on pan 1 minute. Remove from pan; cool completely on wire racks. Yield: 40 cookies (serving size: 1 cookie).

CALORIES 87 (31% from fat); FAT 3g (sat 1.6g, mono 0.9g, poly 0.4g); PROTEIN 0.8g; CARB 14.3g; FIBER 0.3g; CHOL 2mg; IRON 0.7mg; SODIUM 35mg; CALC 11mg

The *Cooking Light®* Holiday Cookbook

Fill your plate with the season's most flavorful appetizers, entrées, desserts, and edible gifts.

Appetizers and Drinks

Let the festivities begin with these tasty starters.

Cocktail Party Menu
serves 8

Bananas Foster Punch

Roasted Garlic, Sun-Dried Tomato, and White Bean Dip
with bagel chips

Clams Casino with Pancetta
(page 340)

Salmon Mousse with crackers
(page 340)

Assorted cheeses, fruits, and crudités

MAKE AHEAD
Bananas Foster Punch

This festive drink was inspired by the classic dessert of rum-drenched, caramelized bananas topped with ice cream. To make a virgin version, add an extra one-fourth cup milk and one-half teaspoon rum extract in place of the rum.

1¾ cups 2% reduced-fat milk
¼ cup sugar
1 tablespoon water
2 ripe bananas, peeled and cut into 2-inch pieces
2 cups light vanilla ice cream, melted
¼ cup gold rum
¼ teaspoon salt
⅛ teaspoon grated whole nutmeg
½ cup frozen reduced-calorie whipped topping, thawed
Grated whole nutmeg (optional)

1. Heat milk over medium-high heat in a medium saucepan to 180° or until tiny bubbles form around edge (do not boil). Remove from heat; keep warm.
2. Combine sugar and 1 tablespoon water in a large, heavy saucepan over medium-high heat, and cook until sugar dissolves, stirring as needed (about 2 minutes). Continue cooking 2 minutes or until golden (do not stir).
3. Carefully add hot milk to caramelized sugar in a slow, steady stream (mixture will bubble vigorously), stirring until sugar dissolves. Add bananas. Cover, reduce heat, and simmer 5 minutes. Remove from heat; cool 10 minutes.

4. Place half of milk mixture, ice cream, rum, salt, and nutmeg in a blender. Remove center piece of blender lid (to allow steam to escape); secure lid on blender. Place a clean towel over opening in lid (to avoid splatters). Blend until smooth. Pour into a large pitcher. Repeat procedure with remaining milk mixture. Cover and refrigerate 6 hours or up to overnight. Top with whipped topping and grated nutmeg, if desired. Yield: 8 servings (serving size: ½ cup punch and 1 tablespoon whipped topping).

CALORIES 159 (18% from fat); FAT 3.1g (sat 2.1g, mono 0.7g, poly 0.1g); PROTEIN 3.6g; CARB 26.1g; FIBER 1.1g; CHOL 13mg; IRON 0.2mg; SODIUM 125mg; CALC 118mg

---

MAKE AHEAD
Roasted Garlic, Sun-Dried Tomato, and White Bean Dip

Prepare a day ahead; bring to room temperature before serving. Serve on bagel chips garnished with rosemary sprigs.

1 whole garlic head
1 cup water
1 (3.5-ounce) package sun-dried tomatoes, packed without oil
2 tablespoons extravirgin olive oil
½ teaspoon chopped fresh rosemary
¼ teaspoon kosher salt
¼ teaspoon freshly ground black pepper
1 (15.8-ounce) can Great Northern beans, rinsed and drained

Continued

1. Preheat oven to 375°.
2. Remove white papery skin from garlic head (do not peel or separate cloves). Wrap head in foil. Bake at 375° for 45 minutes; cool 10 minutes. Separate cloves; squeeze to extract pulp. Discard skins.
3. Bring 1 cup water to a boil in a saucepan. Add tomatoes; cover and remove from heat. Let stand 10 minutes. Drain tomatoes in a colander over a bowl, reserving ¼ cup liquid.
4. Place garlic pulp, tomatoes, ¼ cup reserved liquid, oil, and remaining ingredients in a food processor; process until smooth. Yield: 2 cups (serving size: 2 tablespoons).

CALORIES 43 (36% from fat); FAT 1.7g (sat 0.2g, mono 1.2g, poly 0.2g); PROTEIN 1.2g; CARB 6.1g; FIBER 1.6g; CHOL 0mg; IRON 0.4mg; SODIUM 94mg; CALC 8mg

Choosing Clams and Oysters

Clams are found in two main varieties: soft-shell and hard-shell. The smallest hard-shell clams are known as littleneck clams. They generally measure about 1½ to 2 inches in diameter, and they possess sweet meat that is often enjoyed raw.

When purchasing clams, look for firm, gray, tightly closed shells with no signs of yellowing. To store, arrange in a single layer on a flat tray, cover with damp paper towels, and refrigerate up to two days. The clams are still alive (and should be until you cook them), so avoid overcrowding or submerging them in liquid when storing.

All of the many oyster varieties are at their best in the winter; they spawn in the summer, and by winter become fat and sweet. Choose plump oysters packed in clear liquid (reject any whose liquid seems cloudy or milky), and refrigerate up to two days. If you decide to purchase fresh live oysters in the shell, look for those with no fishy odor and tightly sealed shells; store oysters as called for above with clams.

Clams Casino with Pancetta

For easier shucking, steam clams over simmering water for two minutes or just until their shells barely open. Run a knife or small screwdriver around a shell's edge, and pop it open. If you partially steam the clams, reduce the broiling time by a minute or two.

Cooking spray
¾ cup finely diced pancetta
2 tablespoons dry white wine
⅓ cup finely diced red bell pepper
3 tablespoons minced shallots
1 garlic clove, minced
1 (1½-ounce) slice day-old country white bread
1½ tablespoons grated fresh Parmigiano-Reggiano cheese
2 teaspoons finely chopped fresh parsley
¼ teaspoon black pepper
36 littleneck clams, cleaned
Lemon wedges (optional)

1. Heat a medium skillet over medium heat. Coat pan with cooking spray. Add pancetta to pan; cook 6 minutes or until pancetta begins to brown, stirring occasionally. Add wine; cook until liquid evaporates (about 30 seconds), scraping pan to loosen browned bits. Add bell pepper, shallots, and garlic to pan; cook 4 minutes or until tender. Place pancetta mixture in a medium bowl.
2. Place bread in a food processor; pulse 10 times or until coarse crumbs measure about ¾ cup. Add breadcrumbs, cheese, parsley, and black pepper to pancetta mixture; stir until blended.
3. Preheat broiler.
4. Discard any clams with broken or open shells. Shuck clams; discard top halves of shells. Top each clam with about 1 rounded teaspoon pancetta mixture. Broil 4 minutes; turn pan. Broil an additional 3 minutes or until tops are browned and clams are done. Serve with lemon wedges, if desired. Yield: 12 servings (serving size: 3 clams).

CALORIES 61 (43% from fat); FAT 2.9g (sat 1.2g, mono 1g, poly 0.3g); PROTEIN 5.3g; CARB 3.2g; FIBER 0.1g; CHOL 15mg; IRON 3.9mg; SODIUM 163mg; CALC 25mg

MAKE AHEAD
Salmon Mousse

A blender is best for transforming the cottage cheese to the silky texture necessary for this savory appetizer mousse. Serve with crackers for an open house or cocktail party.

½ teaspoon unflavored gelatin
2 tablespoons cold water
¼ cup boiling water
1½ teaspoons grated onion
¼ teaspoon salt
¼ teaspoon paprika
¼ teaspoon hot pepper sauce
¼ teaspoon Worcestershire sauce
⅛ teaspoon freshly ground black pepper
1 cup 2% low-fat cottage cheese
¼ cup reduced-fat mayonnaise
1 cup finely flaked drained canned skinless, boneless pink salmon (about 1½ [6-ounce] cans)
2 teaspoons chopped fresh dill
Cooking spray

1. Sprinkle gelatin over 2 tablespoons cold water in a small bowl; let stand 5 minutes. Add ¼ cup boiling water, stirring with a whisk until gelatin dissolves; cool 15 minutes. Add onion and next 5 ingredients, stirring with a whisk. Chill 20 minutes or until mixture thickens.
2. Place cottage cheese in a blender; process until smooth. Add gelatin mixture and mayonnaise; process until well combined. Spoon cottage cheese mixture into a large bowl; fold in salmon and chopped dill.
3. Coat a 4-cup loaf pan or metal mold with cooking spray; line with plastic wrap. Spoon salmon mixture into prepared pan; cover with plastic wrap. Chill overnight or until set. Uncover and invert pan onto a platter; remove plastic wrap. Yield: 12 servings (serving size: ⅓ cup).

CALORIES 45 (30% from fat); FAT 1.5g (sat 0.4g, mono 0.3g, poly 0.4g); PROTEIN 7.2g; CARB 1.5g; FIBER 0g; CHOL 12mg; IRON 0.1mg; SODIUM 221mg; CALC 14mg

Spinach-Artichoke Dip with Bacon

This warm, creamy dip will keep guests happily occupied while you attend to the rest of the meal. Simply assemble the dip the night before, and refrigerate; bring to room temperature, and bake just before serving. Toast baguette slices, cool to room temperature, and store in a zip-top plastic bag.

2 (8-ounce) French bread baguettes, each cut into 32 (¼-inch) slices
Olive oil–flavored cooking spray
⅓ cup fat-free mayonnaise
2 garlic cloves, minced
1 (8-ounce) package ⅓-less-fat cream cheese, softened
1 (8-ounce) package fat-free cream cheese, softened
⅔ cup (about 2½ ounces) grated fresh Parmesan cheese, divided
5 slices center-cut bacon, cooked and crumbled
1 (14-ounce) can quartered artichoke hearts, drained and chopped
1 (10-ounce) package frozen chopped spinach, thawed, drained, and squeezed dry

1. Preheat oven to 350°.
2. Arrange baguette slices in a single layer on 2 large baking sheets, and coat bread with cooking spray. Bake at 350° for 10 minutes or until crisp and lightly browned.
3. Place mayonnaise, garlic, and cream cheeses in a large bowl; beat with a mixer at medium speed until well blended and creamy. Stir in ½ cup Parmesan cheese, bacon, artichoke hearts, and spinach. Spread mixture into an 11 x 7–inch baking dish coated with cooking spray. Sprinkle with remaining Parmesan cheese. Bake at 350° for 25 minutes or until thoroughly heated. Serve with toasted baguette slices. Yield: 16 servings (serving size: about ¼ cup dip and 4 baguette slices).

CALORIES 167 (30% from fat); FAT 5.6g (sat 3.3g, mono 1.7g, poly 0.2g); PROTEIN 9.3g; CARB 20.9g; FIBER 1.2g; CHOL 17mg; IRON 1.6mg; SODIUM 522mg; CALC 118mg

Creamy Mushroom-Chestnut Soup

Look for bottled chestnuts in specialty or gourmet markets. For less mess, puree in the pan with a handheld immersion blender.

Cooking spray
2 (8-ounce) packages cremini mushrooms, stemmed and quartered
1 (3.5-ounce) package shiitake mushrooms, stemmed and sliced
1 (3.5-ounce) package oyster mushrooms, sliced
3 tablespoons minced shallots
½ teaspoon kosher salt, divided
1 garlic clove, minced
3 cups fat-free, less-sodium chicken broth
3 cups water
1 cup bottled chestnuts
2 thyme sprigs
3 tablespoons light sour cream
⅛ teaspoon pepper
2 slices applewood-smoked bacon, cooked and crumbled

1. Heat a large Dutch oven over medium-high heat. Coat pan with cooking spray. Add mushrooms; sauté 15 minutes or until liquid evaporates. Add shallots; sauté 1 minute. Add ¼ teaspoon salt and garlic; sauté 1 minute. Remove ½ cup mushroom mixture; set aside. Add broth, 3 cups water, chestnuts, and thyme to pan; bring to a boil. Reduce heat, and simmer 45 minutes, stirring occasionally. Remove from heat; discard thyme.
2. Place half of broth mixture in a blender. Remove center piece of blender lid (to allow steam to escape); secure lid on blender. Place a clean towel over opening in lid (to avoid splatters). Blend until smooth. Pour into a large bowl. Repeat procedure with remaining broth mixture. Stir in ¼ teaspoon salt, sour cream, and pepper. Sprinkle with reserved mushroom mixture and bacon. Yield: 6 servings (serving size: about ⅔ cup soup, 1½ tablespoons mushroom mixture, and about 1 tablespoon bacon).

CALORIES 125 (19% from fat); FAT 2.7g (sat 1.1g, mono 0.2g, poly 0.3g); PROTEIN 6.6g; CARB 19.8g; FIBER 2.6g; CHOL 6mg; IRON 1.3mg; SODIUM 442mg; CALC 31mg

Oyster Stew

1 slice bacon, finely chopped
¾ cup chopped onion
½ cup finely diced celery
½ cup finely chopped green onions
3 tablespoons all-purpose flour
⅓ cup dry white wine
2 cups 1% low-fat milk
1 teaspoon chopped fresh thyme
¾ teaspoon salt
½ teaspoon freshly ground black pepper
⅛ teaspoon ground red pepper
1 (16-ounce) container standard oysters, undrained
1 tablespoon chopped fresh parsley
2 teaspoons fresh lemon juice

1. Cook bacon in a medium saucepan over medium-high heat until crisp. Remove bacon from pan, reserving 1 teaspoon drippings in pan; set bacon aside. Add onion, celery, and green onions to drippings in pan; cook over medium heat 7 minutes or until celery is tender, stirring frequently. Stir in flour; cook 1 minute, stirring constantly. Stir in wine, scraping pan to loosen browned bits. Stir in bacon, milk, thyme, salt, and peppers; bring to a simmer. Cook 2 minutes or until slightly thick, stirring constantly with a whisk. Stir in oysters; cook 4 minutes or until edges of oysters curl (do not boil). Stir in parsley and juice. Yield: 6 servings (serving size: about ¾ cup).

CALORIES 127 (28% from fat); FAT 4g (sat 1.6g, mono 1g, poly 0.9g); PROTEIN 9.4g; CARB 13.3g; FIBER 0.9g; CHOL 46mg; IRON 5.7mg; SODIUM 575mg; CALC 155mg

> All of the many varieties of oysters are at their best in the winter.

Velvety Squash Soup

Two types of squash offer a fuller, more rounded flavor, but you can use just one type, if you prefer. Raw winter squash is tough to peel and dice, so we call for roasting the squash halves first, then scooping out the tender pulp.

    1   (3-pound) butternut squash
    1   (2-pound) acorn squash
Cooking spray
    2   cups coarsely chopped onion
    2   teaspoons canola oil
    5   cups fat-free, less-sodium chicken broth
   ⅔   cup apple cider
    2   tablespoons molasses
    1   teaspoon curry powder
   ¾   teaspoon salt
   ⅛   teaspoon ground red pepper
   ⅔   cup half-and-half
Chopped fresh thyme (optional)

1. Preheat oven to 425°.
2. Cut each squash in half lengthwise; discard seeds and membranes. Place squash, cut sides down, on a jelly-roll pan coated with cooking spray.
3. Combine onion and oil, tossing to coat. Spread onion mixture on pan around squash. Bake at 425° for 45 minutes or until squash and onion are tender. Cool slightly. Scoop out squash pulp from skins; discard skins.
4. Place onion and squash pulp in a Dutch oven. Stir in broth and next 5 ingredients; bring to a boil. Reduce heat; simmer 5 minutes.
5. Place half of squash mixture in a blender. Remove center piece of blender lid (to allow steam to escape); secure lid on blender. Place a clean towel over opening in lid (to avoid splatters). Blend until smooth. Pour into a large bowl. Repeat procedure with remaining squash mixture. Return pureed mixture to pan; stir in half-and-half. Cook over medium heat 5 minutes or until thoroughly heated. Garnish with thyme, if desired. Yield: 10 servings (serving size: 1 cup).

CALORIES 155 (17% from fat); FAT 3g (sat 1.3g, mono 1.1g, poly 0.5g); PROTEIN 3.2g; CARB 32.3g; FIBER 4.2g; CHOL 6mg; IRON 1.8mg; SODIUM 418mg; CALC 118mg

Mixed Greens and Double-Pomegranate Salad

Pomegranate juice and seeds add a sweet-tart flavor to this simple salad.

   ¼   cup pomegranate juice
   1½ tablespoons Champagne vinegar
   1½ teaspoons minced shallots
    2   teaspoons extravirgin olive oil
   ¼   teaspoon salt
   ¼   teaspoon freshly ground black pepper
    6   cups mixed salad greens
   ½   cup pomegranate seeds
    4   teaspoons finely chopped pecans, toasted

1. Combine first 6 ingredients in a large bowl, stirring with a whisk. Add salad greens, seeds, and pecans; toss well. Serve immediately. Yield: 6 servings (serving size: 1 cup).

CALORIES 59 (44% from fat); FAT 2.9g (sat 0.3g, mono 1.8g, poly 0.6g); PROTEIN 1.4g; CARB 8.3g; FIBER 1.5g; CHOL 0mg; IRON 0.9mg; SODIUM 115mg; CALC 35mg

Hazelnut-Orange Salad

Orange marmalade adds sweetness and body to the vinaigrette; you can microwave it for five to 10 seconds if it's too thick to whisk.

    4   large navel oranges
    1   tablespoon minced shallots
    2   tablespoons orange marmalade
    2   tablespoons sherry vinegar
    1   tablespoon hazelnut oil
   ½   teaspoon Dijon mustard
   ¼   teaspoon salt
   ⅛   teaspoon freshly ground black pepper
   16 cups torn Bibb lettuce (about 5 medium heads)
   ¼   cup chopped hazelnuts, toasted

1. Peel and section oranges over a bowl, reserving 2 tablespoons juice. Set sections aside.
2. Combine reserved juice, shallots, and next 6 ingredients, stirring with a whisk.

3. Arrange 2 cups lettuce on each of 8 plates; top evenly with orange sections. Drizzle each serving with 1 tablespoon vinaigrette; sprinkle each serving with 1½ teaspoons nuts. Serve immediately. Yield: 8 servings.

CALORIES 101 (38% from fat); FAT 4.3g (sat 0.3g, mono 3g, poly 0.6g); PROTEIN 2.7g; CARB 15.7g; FIBER 3.2g; CHOL 0mg; IRON 1.7mg; SODIUM 91mg; CALC 76mg

Watercress, Frisée, and Grapefruit Salad with Curry Vinaigrette
(pictured on page 256)

A platter of this colorful salad makes an elegant starter. Sugary dates provide a sweet contrast to the salad's bitter greens. Grapeseed oil is mild; substitute canola oil, if you prefer.

    4   cups trimmed watercress (about 1 bunch)
    4   cups torn frisée (about 1 head)
    1   cup red grapefruit sections (about 2 grapefruit)
    1   cup thinly sliced red onion
    8   whole pitted dates, sliced
    2   tablespoons white balsamic vinegar
   ½   teaspoon curry powder
   ½   teaspoon salt
    5   teaspoons grapeseed oil

1. Arrange watercress and frisée on a large platter, and top evenly with grapefruit, onion, and dates.
2. Combine vinegar, curry powder, and salt in a small bowl, and slowly add oil, stirring constantly with a whisk. Drizzle over salad. Serve immediately. Yield: 8 servings (serving size: about 1 cup).

CALORIES 79 (34% from fat); FAT 3g (sat 0.3g, mono 0.5g, poly 2g); PROTEIN 1.4g; CARB 13.5g; FIBER 2.3g; CHOL 0mg; IRON 0.4mg; SODIUM 162mg; CALC 46mg

Sunrise Punch

This beverage works well for a holiday brunch. For another version, substitute Champagne for the ginger ale. You can combine everything but the lime slices and the ginger ale up to two days before the brunch; add the ginger ale immediately before serving so it keeps its fizz.

- 2 cups pineapple juice
- 2 cups cranberry juice cocktail
- ½ cup fresh lime juice (about 4 large limes)
- 9 lime slices
- 1 (11.5-ounce) can apricot nectar
- 2 (12-ounce) cans ginger ale

1. Combine first 5 ingredients in a large pitcher; cover and chill. Add ginger ale just before serving; stir gently. Serve over ice. Yield: 9 servings (serving size: 1 cup).

CALORIES 114 (1% from fat); FAT 0.1g (sat 0g, mono 0g, poly 0g); PROTEIN 0.4g; CARB 29g; FIBER 0.3g; CHOL 0mg; IRON 0.5mg; SODIUM 9mg; CALC 17mg

Apple and Pomegranate Cider

- 6 whole cloves
- 2 (3-inch) cinnamon sticks
- 1 (3-inch) strip lemon rind
- 1 (3-inch) strip orange rind
- 8 cups unfiltered apple cider
- 1 cup pomegranate juice
- ¾ cup fresh orange juice (about 3 medium oranges)
- ¼ cup sugar
- ¼ cup fresh lemon juice (about 2 large lemons)

1. Place first 4 ingredients on a double layer of cheesecloth. Gather edges of cheesecloth together; tie securely. Combine cheesecloth bag, cider, and remaining ingredients in a Dutch oven; bring to a simmer. Cook 30 minutes. Discard cheesecloth bag. Yield: 10 servings (serving size: 1 cup).

CALORIES 155 (0% from fat); FAT 0g; PROTEIN 1.1g; CARB 39g; FIBER 0.1g; CHOL 0mg; IRON 0.1mg; SODIUM 3mg; CALC 7mg

Entrées

Main dishes for every night, from casual after-shopping suppers to lavish celebrations.

Traditional Thanksgiving Dinner Menu

serves 12

Spinach-Artichoke Dip with Bacon (page 341)

Roast Turkey with Truffle Gravy (recipe below)

Wild Rice Stuffing (page 349)

Green Beans with Bacon (page 348)

Mashed Roots (page 350)

Potato–Sour Cream Biscuits (page 352)

Basic Cranberry Sauce (page 353)

Pinot noir

Bourbon-Pecan Tart with Chocolate Drizzle (page 357)

Coffee

Roast Turkey with Truffle Gravy

(pictured on page 255)

The turkey is simple, but truffle oil in the gravy makes the dish holiday-special. Start making the stock for the gravy while the turkey cooks. Garnish the platter with kumquats, roasted garlic, and fresh thyme, sage, and parsley.

TURKEY:
- 1 (12-pound) fresh or frozen turkey, thawed
- 4 thyme sprigs
- 4 sage leaves
- 4 garlic cloves
- 1 medium onion, quartered
- 2 tablespoons butter, softened
- 1½ teaspoons kosher salt
- ¾ teaspoon freshly ground black pepper
- 1 cup water

GRAVY:
- Cooking spray
- 4 cups water
- ⅔ cup chopped onion
- ⅓ cup chopped carrot
- ⅓ cup chopped celery
- 6 black peppercorns
- 4 parsley sprigs
- 2 thyme sprigs
- 1 bay leaf
- ½ teaspoon kosher salt
- ½ teaspoon freshly ground black pepper
- 3½ tablespoons all-purpose flour
- 1½ teaspoons truffle oil

1. Preheat oven to 500°.

2. To prepare turkey, remove giblets and neck from turkey; reserve for gravy. Trim excess fat. Stuff body cavity with thyme sprigs, sage leaves, garlic, and onion. Tie legs together with kitchen string.

3. Starting at neck cavity, loosen skin from breast and drumsticks by inserting fingers, gently pushing between skin and meat. Combine butter, 1½ teaspoons salt, and ¾ teaspoon pepper. Rub butter mixture under loosened skin over breast and drumsticks. Lift wing tips up and over back; tuck under turkey. Pour 1 cup water in bottom of a roasting pan. Place roasting rack in pan. Arrange turkey, breast side up, on roasting rack. Bake at 500° for 30 minutes.

4. Reduce oven temperature to 350° (do not remove turkey from oven).

5. Bake turkey at 350° for 1½ hours or until a thermometer inserted into meaty part of thigh registers 165°. (Shield turkey with foil if it browns too quickly.) Remove turkey from oven; let stand 20 minutes. Discard skin before serving. Reserve pan drippings for gravy.

6. To prepare gravy, while turkey roasts, heat a large saucepan over medium-high heat. Coat pan with cooking spray. Add reserved turkey neck and giblets to pan; cook 5 minutes, browning on all sides. Add 4 cups water and next 7 ingredients; bring to a boil. Reduce heat, and simmer until liquid is reduced to about 2½ cups (about 1 hour). Strain through a colander into a bowl. Discard solids. Return
Continued

stock to saucepan; stir in ½ teaspoon salt and ½ teaspoon pepper.

7. Place a zip-top plastic bag inside a 2-cup glass measure. Pour turkey pan drippings into bag; let stand 10 minutes (fat will rise to top). Seal bag; carefully snip off 1 bottom corner of bag. Drain drippings into stock in saucepan, stopping before fat layer reaches opening; discard fat. Combine ½ cup stock mixture and flour in a small bowl, stirring with a whisk until smooth. Stir flour mixture into stock; bring to a boil, stirring frequently. Reduce heat, and simmer 3 minutes or until slightly thick. Remove from heat; add oil, stirring with a whisk. Serve gravy with turkey. Yield: 12 servings (serving size: about 6 ounces turkey and about 2½ tablespoons gravy).

CALORIES 383 (23% from fat); FAT 9.6g (sat 3.6g, mono 2.7g, poly 2.2g); PROTEIN 67.7g; CARB 1.9g; FIBER 0.1g; CHOL 232mg; IRON 4.7mg; SODIUM 481mg; CALC 48mg

---

Turkey Talk

Turkey takes center stage on many holiday tables, and there are at least three types from which to choose.

Frozen turkeys are the most popular option, available in any supermarket for around $1.50 per pound. You'll need to allow time for the bird to thaw in the refrigerator (the safest method)—24 hours for every five pounds, or nearly three days for a 12-pound turkey.

A fresh bird boasts hearty flavor and excellent texture, and it doesn't require thawing. But you will need to order your turkey a couple of weeks in advance, and expect to pay nearly $2 per pound.

For memorably vivid flavor, purchase a heritage turkey (such as the Narragansett or White Holland). Heritage turkeys are free-range, antibiotic-free birds with a higher proportion of dark to light meat than the mass-market variety. They can be expensive (as much as $150 for a 22-pound turkey) and difficult to find. Some specialty markets carry them in the fall, but your best bet is mail order. (Find producers through www.localharvest.org.)

STAFF FAVORITE • MAKE AHEAD

Thyme and Spice-Rubbed Roast Beef Tenderloin au Jus

Arrange the roast on a platter and garnish with fresh rosemary and thyme sprigs, presenting the sauce in a gravy boat to the side. Serve with mashed potatoes and haricots verts for a classic supper.

  1 tablespoon chopped fresh thyme, divided
1¼ teaspoons salt
  ½ teaspoon freshly ground black pepper
  ¼ teaspoon ground allspice
1¾ pounds beef tenderloin, trimmed
    Cooking spray
  ⅓ cup brandy
  ¼ cup minced shallots
1½ cups fat-free, less-sodium beef broth

1. Combine 2 teaspoons thyme, salt, pepper, and allspice in a small bowl. Rub mixture evenly over all sides of beef. Wrap tightly in plastic wrap, and refrigerate 24 hours.
2. Preheat oven to 400°.
3. Heat a large nonstick skillet over medium-high heat. Coat pan with cooking spray. Add beef to pan; cook 5 minutes, turning to brown on all sides. Transfer beef to a roasting rack coated with cooking spray; place rack in roasting pan. Bake at 400° for 26 minutes or until a thermometer registers 135° or to desired degree of doneness. Remove from oven, and let stand 10 minutes before slicing. Pour brandy into roasting pan, scraping pan to loosen browned bits; set aside.
4. Heat skillet over medium heat; coat with cooking spray. Add shallots to skillet; cook 4 minutes or until tender, stirring occasionally. Add brandy mixture, broth, and 1 teaspoon thyme to skillet; scraping pan to loosen browned bits; simmer until reduced to 1 cup (about 4 minutes). Serve with beef. Yield: 7 servings (serving size: 3 ounces beef and about 2 tablespoons jus).

CALORIES 170 (35% from fat); FAT 6.7g (sat 2.5g, mono 2.6g, poly 0.3g); PROTEIN 18.5g; CARB 1.2g; FIBER 0.2g; CHOL 54mg; IRON 2.5mg; SODIUM 556mg; CALC 9mg

---

Pumpkin Ravioli with Gorgonzola Sauce

You can assemble the ravioli a day ahead, cover with plastic wrap, and refrigerate. The ravioli will float when they're perfectly cooked. Serve with a chilled chardonnay.

1¼ cups canned pumpkin
  2 tablespoons dry breadcrumbs
  2 tablespoons grated fresh Parmesan cheese
  ½ teaspoon salt
  ½ teaspoon minced fresh sage
  ¼ teaspoon freshly ground black pepper
  ⅛ teaspoon ground nutmeg
 30 round wonton wrappers
  1 tablespoon cornstarch
    Cooking spray
  1 cup fat-free milk
  1 tablespoon all-purpose flour
1½ tablespoons butter
  ½ cup (2 ounces) crumbled Gorgonzola cheese
  3 tablespoons chopped hazelnuts, toasted

1. Spoon pumpkin onto several layers of heavy-duty paper towels, and spread to ½-inch thickness. Cover with additional paper towels; let stand 5 minutes. Scrape into a medium bowl using a rubber spatula. Stir in breadcrumbs and next 5 ingredients.
2. Working with 1 wonton wrapper at a time (cover remaining wrappers with a damp towel to keep from drying), spoon 2 teaspoons pumpkin mixture into center of wrapper. Brush edges of wrapper with water and fold in half, pressing edges firmly with fingers to form a half-moon. Place ravioli on a large baking sheet sprinkled with cornstarch. Repeat procedure with remaining wrappers and pumpkin mixture.
3. Fill a large Dutch oven with water; bring to a simmer. Add half of ravioli to pan (cover remaining ravioli with a damp towel to keep from drying). Cook 4 minutes or until done (do not boil), stirring gently. Remove ravioli with a slotted spoon; lightly coat with cooking spray, and keep warm. Repeat procedure with remaining ravioli.

4. Combine milk and flour in a saucepan, stirring with a whisk. Bring to a boil; cook 1 minute or until thick, stirring constantly. Remove from heat. Add butter, stirring until butter melts. Gently stir in Gorgonzola.

5. Place 5 ravioli in each of 6 shallow bowls, and drizzle each serving with 3 tablespoons Gorgonzola mixture. Sprinkle each serving with 1½ teaspoons hazelnuts. Serve immediately. Yield: 6 servings.

CALORIES 250 (33% from fat); FAT 9.1g (sat 4.5g, mono 2.7g, poly 0.7g); PROTEIN 9.5g; CARB 33g; FIBER 3.1g; CHOL 22mg; IRON 2.4mg; SODIUM 636mg; CALC 162mg

Shellfish Supper for Four Menu

Spinach salad

Cider-Braised Mussels with Bacon

Crusty bread

Dark beer

Cranberry-Jalapeño Granita
(page 355)

QUICK & EASY
Cider-Braised Mussels with Bacon

Hard cider is fermented apple cider. Serve with a loaf of crusty bread and tossed spinach salad.

>   3   slices bacon, cut into ½-inch
>   pieces
>   2   cups thinly sliced leek (about
>   1 large)
>   ¼   teaspoon kosher salt
>   ⅛   teaspoon freshly ground black
>   pepper
>   2   pounds medium mussels, scrubbed
>   and debearded
>   1   (12-ounce) bottle hard apple cider
>   2   tablespoons chopped fresh flat-leaf
>   parsley

1. Cook bacon in a Dutch oven over medium-high heat until crisp. Remove bacon from pan, reserving 2 teaspoons drippings in pan. Crumble bacon; set aside. Add leek, salt, and pepper to pan; sauté 3 minutes or until tender. Add bacon, mussels, and cider; bring to a boil. Cover and cook 5 minutes or until mussels open; discard any unopened shells.

2. Place about 9 mussels into each of 4 shallow bowls. Ladle about ½ cup broth mixture into each bowl, and sprinkle each serving with 1½ teaspoons chopped parsley. Yield: 4 servings.

CALORIES 297 (28% from fat); FAT 9.3g (sat 2.5g, mono 3g, poly 1.9g); PROTEIN 29.2g; CARB 15.2g; FIBER 0.5g; CHOL 71mg; IRON 9.6mg; SODIUM 885mg; CALC 75mg

BEER NOTE: When creating this meal, don't forget to chill the beer. Porter is a versatile style of dark beer that is less charred-tasting and lighter-bodied than most stouts. Try Sierra Nevada Porter ($8/six-pack) from California. This medium-bodied beer is light enough for a spinach salad, and the caramel, coffee, and smoky flavors complement the bacon and mussel broth.

MAKE AHEAD
Turkey Roulade with Cranberries and Chipotle

You can prepare the cranberry filling a day or two ahead and refrigerate.

FILLING:
>   2   teaspoons olive oil
> 2½   cups finely chopped onion (about
>   1 large)
>   ⅔   cup chopped dried cranberries
>   ½   cup white wine
>   1   tablespoon chopped fresh
>   oregano
>   2   to 3 teaspoons minced chipotle
>   chile, canned in adobo sauce
>   1   garlic clove, minced

TURKEY:
>   1   teaspoon salt, divided
>   ½   teaspoon ground cumin
>   ½   teaspoon ground chipotle chile
>   powder
>   4   (8-ounce) turkey tenderloins
>   ¼   teaspoon freshly ground black
>   pepper
>   2   teaspoons olive oil
>   Oregano sprigs (optional)

1. To prepare filling, heat 2 teaspoons oil in a medium saucepan over medium heat. Add onion to pan; cook 10 minutes or until tender, stirring occasionally. Add cranberries and next 4 ingredients to pan; cook 10 minutes or until liquid evaporates.

2. Preheat oven to 375°.

3. To prepare turkey, combine ½ teaspoon salt, cumin, and chile powder in a small bowl. Slice tenderloins lengthwise, cutting to, but not through, other side. Open halves, laying tenderloins flat. Slice each half lengthwise, cutting to, but not through, other side; open flat. Place plastic wrap over tenderloins; pound to ½-inch thickness using a meat mallet or small heavy skillet. Sprinkle tenderloins evenly with spice mixture. Spread ⅓ cup filling over each tenderloin. Roll up tenderloins jelly-roll fashion, starting with long sides. Secure at 2-inch intervals with twine. Sprinkle remaining ½ teaspoon salt and pepper over tenderloins.

4. Heat 2 teaspoons oil in a large ovenproof nonstick skillet over medium-high heat. Add tenderloins to pan; cook 3 minutes, turning to brown on all sides. Transfer pan to oven. Bake at 375° for 25 minutes or until a thermometer registers 165°. Remove from oven; let stand 10 minutes. Remove twine from tenderloins; cut crosswise into ¾-inch-thick slices. Garnish with oregano sprigs, if desired. Yield: 8 servings (serving size: ½ sliced filled tenderloin).

CALORIES 152 (18% from fat); FAT 3g (sat 0.5g, mono 1.7g, poly 0.4g); PROTEIN 20.5g; CARB 9.9g; FIBER 1g; CHOL 56mg; IRON 1.3mg; SODIUM 357mg; CALC 18mg

Entertaining a small group for the holiday? Serve a show-stopping turkey roulade or Cornish hens.

Beef, Black Bean, and Chorizo Chili

Serve with classic condiments such as sour cream, chopped green onions, and shredded Cheddar cheese. For a thinner chili, cook covered the whole time. You can prepare it a day ahead and refrigerate, or up to two weeks ahead and freeze (be sure to thaw the chili overnight in the refrigerator). Look for masa harina, the corn flour used to make tortillas, in the Latin foods aisle at the supermarket, or substitute fine-ground cornmeal.

    2 links Spanish chorizo sausage
       (about 6½ ounces), thinly sliced
 1½ pounds beef stew meat
 1½ cups chopped onion
    4 garlic cloves, minced
    1 (7-ounce) can chipotle chiles in
       adobo sauce
    3 tablespoons tomato paste
    2 teaspoons sugar
    1 teaspoon salt
    2 teaspoons unsweetened cocoa
    1 teaspoon ground coriander
    1 teaspoon dried oregano
    1 teaspoon ground cumin
    1 cup dry red wine
   ¼ cup fresh lime juice
    2 (14-ounce) cans less-sodium beef
       broth
    1 (28-ounce) can whole tomatoes,
       undrained and chopped
    2 tablespoons masa harina
    2 (15-ounce) cans pinto beans,
       rinsed and drained
    1 (15-ounce) can black beans,
       rinsed and drained

1. Heat a Dutch oven over medium-high heat. Add chorizo to pan; sauté 3 minutes or until browned. Remove chorizo from pan. Add half of beef to pan; sauté 5 minutes or until browned. Remove beef from pan. Repeat procedure with remaining beef. Add onion and garlic to pan; sauté 3 minutes.
2. Remove 4 chipotle chiles from can, and chop. Reserve remaining chiles and sauce for another use. Add chorizo, beef, chopped chiles, tomato paste, and next 6 ingredients to pan, and cook 1 minute,

stirring constantly. Stir in red wine, lime juice, beef broth, and tomatoes; bring to a boil. Reduce heat, and simmer 1 hour, stirring occasionally.
3. Gradually stir in masa harina. Add pinto beans and black beans; bring to a boil. Cover, reduce heat, and simmer 30 minutes. Yield: 10 servings (serving size: about 1 cup chili).

CALORIES 325 (30% from fat); FAT 11g (sat 3.8g, mono 4.7g, poly 1g); PROTEIN 25g; CARB 31.4g; FIBER 8.4g; CHOL 53mg; IRON 4.7mg; SODIUM 898mg; CALC 104mg

Rosemary Rack of Lamb with Balsamic-Raisin Reduction

Rack of lamb is a grand entrée for a special dinner. Serve with polenta, and open a bottle of bold cabernet sauvignon.

    1 cup dry red wine
   ¾ cup balsamic vinegar
   ¼ cup raisins
    1 tablespoon brown sugar
    1 tablespoon butter
    1 (1½-pound) French-cut rack of
       lamb (8 ribs), trimmed
    2 teaspoons finely chopped fresh
       rosemary
   ½ teaspoon salt
   ¼ teaspoon freshly ground black
       pepper
       Cooking spray

1. Preheat oven to 425°.
2. Combine first 4 ingredients in a small saucepan; bring to a boil. Cook until reduced to ½ cup (about 15 minutes). Remove from heat; cool slightly. Add butter, stirring well with a whisk; keep warm.
3. Sprinkle lamb with rosemary, salt, and pepper. Place lamb, meat side up, on a broiler pan coated with cooking spray. Bake at 425° for 30 minutes or until a thermometer registers 145° (medium-rare) to 160° (medium). Let stand 5 minutes. Cut rack into 8 pieces. Serve with reduction. Yield: 4 servings (serving size: 2 chops and 2 tablespoons reduction).

CALORIES 313 (43% from fat); FAT 15.1g (sat 6.2g, mono 6.1g, poly 0.9g); PROTEIN 24.5g; CARB 17.5g; FIBER 0.4g; CHOL 88mg; IRON 2.2mg; SODIUM 412mg; CALC 34mg

Easy Weeknight Menu
serves 8

Inspired by the classic French cassoulet, this entrée's quick prep and cook times make it an easy, light dinner option.

Sausage and Bean Casserole

Mustard cheesy toasts*

Green salad

*Spread 1 teaspoon whole-grain Dijon mustard over each of 8 (1-inch-thick) slices French bread. Top each slice with 1 tablespoon Italian blend shredded cheese. Place on a baking sheet. Broil 2 minutes or until cheese melts.

Sausage and Bean Casserole

Simple and satisfying, this hearty casserole is fast enough to prepare on a busy evening.

       Cooking spray
    1 cup chopped onion (about 1
       medium)
    1 (16-ounce) package light
       smoked turkey sausage (such
       as Hillshire Farm), cut into
       ¼-inch-thick slices
    2 garlic cloves, minced
    1 (14-ounce) can fat-free,
       less-sodium chicken broth
    2 tablespoons brown sugar
    2 tablespoons tomato paste
   ½ teaspoon dried thyme
   ½ teaspoon freshly ground black
       pepper
    3 (16-ounce) cans cannellini
       beans or other white beans,
       rinsed and drained
    1 bay leaf
   ⅛ teaspoon ground red pepper
       (optional)
    3 (1-ounce) slices white bread
    2 tablespoons chopped fresh
       parsley

1. Preheat oven to 375°.
2. Heat an ovenproof Dutch oven over medium-high heat. Coat pan with cooking spray. Add onion and sausage to pan; sauté 5 minutes or until browned. Add garlic, and sauté 2 minutes. Stir in broth,

scraping pan to loosen browned bits. Stir in brown sugar and next 5 ingredients. Add red pepper, if desired. Bring to a boil; cover, reduce heat, and simmer 5 minutes. Remove from heat. Discard bay leaf.

3. Place bread in a food processor, and pulse 10 times or until coarse crumbs measure 1½ cups.

4. Sprinkle breadcrumbs evenly over bean mixture, and lightly coat with cooking spray. Bake at 375° for 15 minutes or until browned. Sprinkle with parsley. Yield: 8 servings (serving size: about 1 cup).

CALORIES 205 (14% from fat); FAT 3.3g (sat 1.1g, mono 0.1g, poly 0.5g); PROTEIN 12.1g; CARB 30g; FIBER 4.4g; CHOL 25mg; IRON 2.7mg; SODIUM 823mg; CALC 77mg

---

MAKE AHEAD
Roasted Pork Tenderloin with Citrus and Onion

The onion in the sweet-tart marinade garnishes the pork. Accompany this dish with a glass of riesling.

  3 cups thinly sliced onion
  1 cup thawed orange juice concentrate, undiluted
  4 garlic cloves, minced
  2 (1-pound) pork tenderloins, trimmed
  ½ teaspoon salt, divided
  ½ teaspoon freshly ground black pepper, divided
  2 teaspoons olive oil
  2 tablespoons water

1. Combine first 4 ingredients in a large zip-top plastic bag; seal. Marinate in refrigerator 2 hours, turning occasionally.
2. Preheat oven to 425°.
3. Remove pork from bag, reserving marinade. Drain marinade through a sieve, reserving solids. Set solids aside; discard liquid. Sprinkle pork evenly with ¼ teaspoon salt and ¼ teaspoon pepper. Heat oil in a large ovenproof skillet over medium-high heat. Add pork to pan; cook 3 minutes, turning to brown on all sides. Bake at 425° for 12 minutes or until a thermometer registers 155°. Place pork on a cutting board; cover loosely

with foil. Let stand 5 minutes. Cut into ¼-inch-thick slices.
4. Combine reserved solids, ¼ teaspoon salt, ¼ teaspoon pepper, and 2 tablespoons water in a saucepan over medium-high heat. Cook 12 minutes or until onion is browned, stirring occasionally. Serve with pork. Yield: 8 servings (serving size: about 3 ounces pork and 1½ teaspoons onions).

CALORIES 173 (26% from fat); FAT 5g (sat 1.5g, mono 2.4g, poly 0.5g); PROTEIN 23.1g; CARB 7.6g; FIBER 0.6g; CHOL 63mg; IRON 1.3mg; SODIUM 194mg; CALC 18mg

---

QUICK & EASY
Dover Sole with Lemon Rind and Pine Nuts

If you don't find sole, choose flounder.

  Cooking spray
  3 tablespoons finely minced shallots
  4 (6-ounce) Dover sole fillets
  ¾ teaspoon salt
  ⅛ teaspoon freshly ground white pepper
  ¼ cup pine nuts, lightly toasted and chopped
  1 teaspoon finely grated lemon rind
  ⅓ cup dry white wine
  Chopped fresh parsley (optional)
  Lemon wedges (optional)

1. Preheat oven to 375°.
2. Lightly coat bottom of a 13 x 9–inch baking dish with cooking spray; sprinkle evenly with shallots. Arrange fish in an even layer over shallots, slightly overlapping, if necessary. Sprinkle fish with salt and pepper. Combine pine nuts and rind; sprinkle evenly over fish. Pour wine around fish, being careful not to dislodge topping. Bake at 375° for 15 minutes or until fish flakes easily when tested with a fork or until desired degree of doneness. Garnish with parsley and lemon wedges, if desired. Serve immediately. Yield: 4 servings (serving size: 1 fillet).

CALORIES 219 (32% from fat); FAT 7.9g (sat 0.9g, mono 2g, poly 3.5g); PROTEIN 33.5g; CARB 2.8g; FIBER 0.4g; CHOL 82mg; IRON 1.3mg; SODIUM 583mg; CALC 37mg

---

Fennel-Rubbed Pork Rib Roast

The licorice–accented drippings make a surprisingly savory gravy.

  2 teaspoons fennel seeds
  ¾ teaspoon freshly ground black pepper, divided
  ½ teaspoon salt
  3 garlic cloves, minced
  1 (5-pound) center-cut 8-blade pork rib roast
  Cooking spray
  3 cups fat-free, less-sodium chicken broth, divided
  ½ cup apple juice
  2 tablespoons all-purpose flour

1. Preheat oven to 400°.
2. Place fennel seeds in a spice or coffee grinder; pulse until coarsely ground. Combine fennel, ½ teaspoon pepper, salt, and garlic in a small bowl; rub evenly over roast. Coat roast lightly with cooking spray. Place roast on rack of a shallow roasting pan coated with cooking spray. Pour 2 cups broth into pan; place rack in pan. Bake at 400° for 30 minutes. Reduce oven temperature to 350° (do not remove roast from oven); bake an additional 40 minutes or until a thermometer registers 155°. Remove roast from pan; let stand, uncovered, 10 minutes before carving. Slice vertically between each rib bone.
3. Place a zip-top plastic bag inside a 2-cup glass measure. Pour drippings into bag; let stand 10 minutes (fat will rise to top). Seal bag; carefully snip off 1 bottom corner of bag. Drain drippings into pan, stopping before fat layer reaches opening; discard fat. Add apple juice to pan. Combine 1 cup broth and flour, stirring with a whisk. Add flour mixture to pan. Bring to a boil over medium-high heat, stirring constantly with a whisk. Boil 1 minute or until thick, stirring constantly. Remove from heat; stir in remaining ¼ teaspoon black pepper. Serve with pork. Yield: 8 servings (serving size: 1 chop and ¼ cup gravy).

CALORIES 249 (41% from fat); FAT 11.4g (sat 4.4g, mono 5.4g, poly 0.9g); PROTEIN 30.1g; CARB 4.4g; FIBER 0.7g; CHOL 71mg; IRON 1.4mg; SODIUM 341mg; CALC 42mg

Late-Autumn Pasta
Dinner Menu

Late-Autumn Pasta Dinner Menu

serves 8

Hazelnut-Orange Salad
(page 342)

Pappardelle with Wild Mushrooms

Gewürztraminer

Gingerbread Soufflé (page 359)

Coffee

QUICK & EASY

Pappardelle with Wild Mushrooms

A combination of exotic mushrooms enriches this satisfying winter entrée.

- 2 teaspoons olive oil
- ½ cup finely chopped onion
- ½ cup diced shallots (about 2)
- 2 garlic cloves, minced
- 1 (4-ounce) package presliced exotic mushroom blend (such as shiitake, cremini, and oyster)
- 1 (8-ounce) package cremini mushrooms, sliced
- ½ cup dry white wine
- 1 teaspoon chopped fresh oregano
- ½ teaspoon salt, divided
- ½ teaspoon freshly ground black pepper, divided
- 2 tablespoons butter
- 2 tablespoons all-purpose flour
- 1½ cups 1% low-fat milk
- ½ cup fat-free, less-sodium chicken broth
- 1½ cups (6 ounces) shredded fontina cheese
- 12 ounces uncooked pappardelle (wide ribbon pasta)
Chopped fresh parsley (optional)

1. Heat oil in a large nonstick skillet over medium-high heat. Add onion, shallots, and garlic to pan; sauté 3 minutes or until tender. Add mushrooms; sauté 5 minutes or until mushrooms are tender. Add wine, oregano, ¼ teaspoon salt, and ¼ teaspoon pepper; cook 2 minutes or until liquid evaporates. Set aside.
2. Melt butter in a large saucepan over medium-high heat. Add flour to pan;

cook 2 minutes, stirring constantly. Add milk and broth, stirring with a whisk until smooth; bring to a boil. Cook 2 minutes or until thick, stirring constantly with a whisk. Remove from heat. Add cheese, ¼ teaspoon salt, and ¼ teaspoon pepper; stir until smooth. Stir in mushroom mixture. Keep warm.
3. Cook pasta according to package directions, omitting salt and fat. Place ¾ cup pasta in each of 8 shallow bowls. Top each serving with ½ cup mushroom mixture. Garnish with parsley, if desired. Serve immediately. Yield: 8 servings.

CALORIES 336 (31% from fat); FAT 11.5g (sat 6.3g, mono 3.5g, poly 0.6g); PROTEIN 15.3g; CARB 44.1g; FIBER 2g; CHOL 33mg; IRON 2.2mg; SODIUM 383mg; CALC 189mg

Star Anise and Tangerine-Roasted Cornish Hens

If you don't have a shallow roasting pan, a broiler pan with the top rack removed will work well, too.

- 1 tablespoon grated tangerine rind
- ½ cup fresh tangerine juice (about 3 tangerines)
- 1 teaspoon minced fresh thyme
- 3 star anise
- 1 cup fat-free, less-sodium chicken broth, divided
- ½ teaspoon salt
- ¼ teaspoon freshly ground black pepper
- 1 small onion, halved and cut into ½-inch slices
- 2 (1½-pound) Cornish hens

1. Preheat oven to 375°.
2. Combine first 4 ingredients in a small saucepan over medium-high heat. Stir in ½ cup broth; bring to a boil. Reduce heat, and simmer until reduced to ¼ cup (about 7 minutes). Strain broth mixture through a sieve into a bowl; discard solids. Stir in salt and pepper.
3. Separate onion slices, and place in an even layer in bottom of a shallow roasting pan.
4. Remove and discard giblets and necks from hens. Remove skin; trim excess fat.

Working with 1 hen at a time, tie ends of legs together with cord. Lift wing tips up and over back; tuck under hen. Set hens, breast side up, on top of onion; brush tops and sides of hens with broth mixture. Bake at 375° for 30 minutes. Add ½ cup broth to pan. Bake an additional 10 minutes or until thermometer registers 165°. Remove from oven; transfer hens to a cutting board or work surface. Keep warm.
5. Place a zip-top plastic bag inside a 2-cup glass measure. Strain pan drippings through a sieve into zip-top bag; discard solids. Let reserved drippings stand 10 minutes (fat will rise to top). Seal bag; carefully snip off 1 bottom corner of bag. Drain drippings into a small saucepan, stopping before fat layer reaches opening; discard fat. Bring drippings to a boil over medium-high heat. Cook until reduced to 3 tablespoons (about 5 minutes).
6. Split hens in half lengthwise. Place one hen half on each of 4 plates; drizzle each serving with 2 teaspoons drippings. Yield: 4 servings.

CALORIES 212 (23% from fat); FAT 5.5g (sat 1.4g, mono 1.8g, poly 1.3g); PROTEIN 33.1g; CARB 5.6g; FIBER 0.8g; CHOL 146mg; IRON 1.3mg; SODIUM 479mg; CALC 35mg

Side Dishes

Round out any spread, from simple to sophisticated, with these inventive recipes.

QUICK & EASY • MAKE AHEAD
Green Beans with Bacon
(pictured on page 255)

This simple side is a crowd-pleaser. You can cook the green beans and bacon up to two days ahead; refrigerate them separately until you're ready to assemble the dish.

- 2½ pounds green beans, trimmed
- 3 slices bacon
- ½ cup chopped shallots
- 1 teaspoon freshly squeezed lemon juice
- ¼ teaspoon salt
- ¼ teaspoon freshly ground black pepper

1. Cook green beans in boiling water 5 minutes or until crisp-tender. Drain and plunge beans into ice water; drain.
2. Cook bacon in a Dutch oven over medium heat until crisp. Remove bacon from pan; crumble. Add shallots to drippings in pan; sauté 4 minutes or until tender. Add beans, juice, salt, and pepper to pan; toss to combine. Cook 5 minutes or until thoroughly heated, stirring frequently. Remove from heat. Sprinkle bacon over bean mixture; toss. Yield: 12 servings (serving size: about ⅔ cup).

CALORIES 46 (22% from fat); FAT 1.1g (sat 0.4g, mono 0.5g, poly 0.2g); PROTEIN 2.5g; CARB 8g; FIBER 3.3g; CHOL 2mg; IRON 1.1mg; SODIUM 93mg; CALC 38mg

Roasted Root Vegetables with Walnut Pesto

Carrots and parsnips have a slight sweetness that balances the bite of the Brussels sprouts and turnips. Toss the vegetables with fresh-tasting pesto after they roast to brighten both the flavor and color.

VEGETABLES:
    3 cups (1-inch-thick) slices carrot (about 1 pound)
    3 cups (1-inch-thick) slices parsnip (about 1 pound)
    3 cups (1-inch) cubed peeled turnip
    3 cups trimmed halved Brussels sprouts (about 1 pound)
    2 shallots, peeled and quartered
    1 large onion, cut into 8 wedges
       Cooking spray
    ½ teaspoon salt
    ¼ teaspoon freshly ground black pepper

PESTO:
    2 cups basil leaves
    ¼ cup (1 ounce) grated fresh Parmigiano-Reggiano
    ¼ cup coarsely chopped walnuts, toasted
    4 teaspoons extravirgin olive oil
    2 tablespoons water
    1 tablespoon fresh lemon juice
    ½ teaspoon salt
    1 garlic clove, peeled

1. Preheat oven to 425°.
2. To prepare vegetables, place first 6 ingredients in a single layer on a jelly-roll pan coated with cooking spray. Lightly coat vegetable mixture with cooking spray. Sprinkle evenly with ½ teaspoon salt and pepper; toss. Bake at 425° for 1 hour or until browned. Transfer vegetable mixture to a large bowl.
3. To prepare pesto, place basil leaves and remaining 7 ingredients in a food processor; process until smooth, scraping sides. Spoon basil mixture over vegetable mixture, and toss to coat. Yield: 10 servings (serving size: 1 cup).

CALORIES 128 (30% from fat); FAT 4.3g (sat 0.8g, mono 1.7g, poly 1.5g); PROTEIN 4.3g; CARB 20.5g; FIBER 5.1g; CHOL 2mg; IRON 1.5mg; SODIUM 277mg; CALC 101mg

Wild Rice Stuffing
(pictured on page 255)

For a classic stuffing, place the rice mixture in the cavity of a turkey before roasting. Make sure to get an accurate temperature reading on the stuffing as well as the bird—both should reach an internal temperature of 165°. You can also make this to serve alongside a roast or ham.

       Cooking spray
    1½ cups chopped celery
    1 cup chopped onion
    1 cup uncooked wild rice
    2 garlic cloves, minced
    4 cups fat-free, less-sodium chicken broth
    1½ tablespoons chopped fresh sage
    1 cup uncooked long-grain brown rice
    ½ cup dried sweet cherries
    ½ cup chopped dried apricots
    ½ cup chopped pecans, toasted
    ½ teaspoon salt
    ½ teaspoon freshly ground black pepper

1. Heat a Dutch oven over medium-high heat. Coat pan with cooking spray. Add celery, onion, wild rice, and garlic to pan; sauté 3 minutes. Stir in broth and sage; bring to a boil. Cover, reduce heat, and simmer 25 minutes. Stir in brown rice, and bring to a boil. Cover, reduce

heat, and cook 30 minutes or until liquid is absorbed. Remove from heat; let stand, covered, 10 minutes. Stir in cherries and remaining ingredients. Yield: 12 servings (serving size: ½ cup).

CALORIES 192 (19% from fat); FAT 4g (sat 0.4g, mono 2.1g, poly 1.3g); PROTEIN 5.1g; CARB 34.4g; FIBER 3.6g; CHOL 0mg; IRON 1.2mg; SODIUM 243mg; CALC 35mg

QUICK & EASY • MAKE AHEAD
Ranch Mashed Potatoes

This tasty side captures the flavor of ranch dressing without additional calories, fat, and sodium. Make these potatoes up to one day ahead, and refrigerate until just before serving. When you reheat them, you may need to add some additional buttermilk and sour cream to achieve a rich consistency.

    13 cups cubed red potato (about 4 pounds)
    ½ cup reduced-fat sour cream
    ¼ cup chopped green onions
    ¼ cup low-fat buttermilk
    3 tablespoons butter, softened
    ¾ teaspoon salt
    ¾ teaspoon dried basil
    ¾ teaspoon dried oregano
    ½ teaspoon garlic powder
    ½ teaspoon freshly ground black pepper
    ¼ teaspoon dried dill

1. Place potato in a Dutch oven; cover with water. Bring to a boil. Reduce heat, and simmer 20 minutes or until tender; drain. Place potato in a large bowl. Add sour cream and remaining ingredients; mash with a potato masher to desired consistency. Yield: 12 servings (serving size: ⅔ cup).

CALORIES 197 (21% from fat); FAT 4.5g (sat 2.7g, mono 0.9g, poly 0.2g); PROTEIN 4.3g; CARB 35.9g; FIBER 3.2g; CHOL 14mg; IRON 0.6mg; SODIUM 206mg; CALC 47mg

Risotto with Champagne and Radicchio

You can prepare this refined risotto up to two days ahead. Cook it until it's almost done, through step two. Spread the hot mixture evenly in a jelly-roll pan to cool it quickly. Refrigerate until you're ready to reheat it. Add a little extra broth while it's warming, and pick up with step three of the recipe.

    3   cups fat-free, less-sodium
        chicken broth
    1   cup water
    2   tablespoons olive oil
    1   cup finely chopped yellow onion
    2   cups uncooked Arborio rice or
        other medium-grain rice
    2   cups Champagne, divided
    2   cups thinly sliced radicchio
    1   cup (4 ounces) grated fresh
        Parmigiano-Reggiano cheese,
        divided
    1   tablespoon butter
    ½   teaspoon salt
    ¼   teaspoon freshly ground black
        pepper
    ⅛   teaspoon ground nutmeg

1. Bring broth and 1 cup water to a simmer in a medium saucepan (do not boil). Keep warm over low heat.
2. Heat oil in a large Dutch oven over medium heat. Add onion to pan, and cook 5 minutes or until tender, stirring frequently. Add rice; cook 2 minutes, stirring constantly. Stir in 1½ cups Champagne; cook 2 minutes or until liquid is nearly absorbed, stirring constantly. Stir in broth mixture, ½ cup at a time, stirring constantly until each portion is absorbed before adding the next (about 20 minutes total). Remove mixture from heat.
3. Stir in ½ cup Champagne, radicchio, ½ cup cheese, and remaining 4 ingredients. Let stand 5 minutes. Sprinkle each serving with cheese. Yield: 12 servings (servings size: ½ cup risotto and 2 teaspoons cheese).

CALORIES 234 (25% from fat); FAT 6.6g (sat 2.5g, mono 3g, poly 0.4g); PROTEIN 7.2g; CARB 33.1g; FIBER 2.1g; CHOL 10mg; IRON 0.4mg; SODIUM 365mg; CALC 97mg

---

Casual Entertaining Menu
serves 6

Apple and Pomegranate Cider (page 343)

Roasted Root Vegetables with Walnut Pesto (page 349)

Risotto with Champagne and Radicchio (recipe at left)

Dark Chocolate–Dipped Anise Biscotti (page 360)

Traditional Sweet Potato Casserole

To prepare this a day ahead, cook the sweet potatoes; combine with brown sugar, butter, and vanilla. Before baking, stir in half the pecans, place in a baking dish, and top with the remaining pecans and marshmallows. If you're toting this dish to a Thanksgiving celebration, assemble the casserole and bake at your host's home while the turkey stands.

    2½ pounds sweet potatoes, peeled
        and cut into 1-inch cubes
    ¾   cup packed brown sugar
    ¼   cup butter, softened
    1½ teaspoons salt
    ½   teaspoon vanilla extract
    ½   cup finely chopped pecans,
        divided
        Cooking spray
    2   cups miniature marshmallows

1. Preheat oven to 375°.
2. Place potato in a Dutch oven, and cover with cold water. Bring to a boil. Reduce heat, and simmer 15 minutes or until very tender. Drain; cool slightly.
3. Place potato in a large bowl. Add sugar and next 3 ingredients. Mash potato mixture with a potato masher. Fold in ¼ cup pecans. Scrape potato mixture into an even layer in an 11 x 7–inch baking dish coated with cooking spray. Sprinkle with ¼ cup pecans; top with marshmallows. Bake at 375° for 25 minutes or until golden. Yield: 16 servings.

CALORIES 186 (27% from fat); FAT 5.5g (sat 2g, mono 2.3g, poly 0.9g); PROTEIN 1.6g; CARB 33.1g; FIBER 2.5g; CHOL 8mg; IRON 0.7mg; SODIUM 272mg; CALC 23mg

---

Mashed Roots
(pictured on page 255)

    6   cups chopped peeled rutabaga
        (about 2¼ pounds)
    6   cups coarsely chopped peeled
        Yukon gold potato (about 1¾
        pounds)
    1½ cups coarsely chopped parsnip
        (about 1½ pounds)
    2   cups whole milk
    4½ tablespoons butter
    2¼ teaspoons salt
    1½ teaspoons Dijon mustard
    ¾   teaspoon freshly ground black
        pepper

1. Place first 3 ingredients in a Dutch oven. Cover with water to 2 inches above vegetables, and bring to a boil. Reduce heat, and simmer 25 minutes or until rutabaga is very tender; drain. Return pan to heat. Add milk and butter to pan; cook 1 minute or until thoroughly heated. Add rutabaga mixture to pan; mash with a potato masher to desired consistency. Stir in salt, mustard, and pepper. Yield: 12 servings (serving size: about ½ cup).

CALORIES 190 (28% from fat); FAT 5.9g (sat 3.5g, mono 1.5g, poly 0.3g); PROTEIN 4.6g; CARB 30.7g; FIBER 5.7g; CHOL 15mg; IRON 1.4mg; SODIUM 524mg; CALC 108mg

---

Warm Brussels Sprouts with Apples and Red Onions

Use the best bacon you can find for this recipe.

    2   slices applewood-smoked bacon
    2   cups diced peeled Granny Smith
        apple
    ½   cup thinly sliced red onion
    1   garlic clove, minced
    2   tablespoons water
    2   tablespoons cider vinegar
    3   cups thinly sliced Brussels sprouts
        (about 1 pound)
    1   teaspoon stone-ground mustard
    ½   teaspoon kosher salt
    ¼   teaspoon freshly ground black
        pepper

1. Cook bacon in a large nonstick skillet over medium heat until crisp. Remove bacon from pan; crumble. Add apple, onion, and garlic to drippings in pan; sauté 5 minutes or until lightly browned. Add 2 tablespoons water and vinegar to pan, scraping pan to loosen browned bits. Add Brussels sprouts; cook 5 minutes or until tender, stirring frequently. Stir in mustard, salt, and pepper. Remove from heat. Sprinkle with bacon. Serve immediately. Yield: 8 servings (serving size: ½ cup).

CALORIES 54 (25% from fat); FAT 1.5g (sat 0.5g, mono 0.6g, poly 0.2g); PROTEIN 3g; CARB 8.4g; FIBER 2.6g; CHOL 3mg; IRON 0.9mg; SODIUM 228mg; CALC 28mg

Bread Stuffing with Caramelized Onion, Bacon, and Apples

Cook the pearl onions in boiling water for 20 seconds and plunge them into ice water to make the skins slip off easily. Substitute cipollini, another small onion, if you can find them.

    1 (1½-pound) loaf sourdough bread
    8 slices bacon, chopped
    2 cups pearl onions, peeled (about 8 ounces)
    1 tablespoon sugar
    Cooking spray
    3 cups chopped peeled Granny Smith apple (about 2 large)
    1½ cups chopped celery
    ⅔ cup finely chopped fresh flat-leaf parsley
    2 teaspoons chopped fresh thyme
    2 teaspoons finely chopped fresh sage
    ½ teaspoon salt
    ½ teaspoon freshly ground black pepper
    3½ cups fat-free, less-sodium chicken broth
    2 large eggs, lightly beaten

1. Preheat oven to 400°.
2. Remove crust from bread; cut bread into ¾-inch cubes to measure 8 cups.

Arrange bread cubes in a single layer on 2 jelly-roll pans. Bake at 400° for 10 minutes or until lightly toasted; cool. Place bread in a large bowl.
3. Reduce oven temperature to 350°.
4. Cook bacon in a large skillet over medium heat until crisp. Remove bacon from pan, reserving 1 tablespoon drippings in pan. Drain bacon on paper towels. Add onions to drippings in pan; cook 3 minutes or until soft, stirring frequently. Sprinkle sugar over onions; cook 3 minutes or until onions begin to brown, stirring frequently. Add bacon and onion mixture to bread.
5. Return pan to heat. Coat pan with cooking spray. Add apple and celery to pan; cook 6 minutes or until lightly brown, stirring frequently. Stir in parsley and next 4 ingredients; cook 1 minute. Add apple mixture to bread mixture; toss to combine.
6. Combine broth and eggs, stirring with a whisk. Add egg mixture to bread mixture; toss to coat. Spoon bread mixture into a 13 x 9–inch baking dish coated with cooking spray. Bake at 350° for 45 minutes or until browned. Yield: 12 servings (serving size: ⅔ cup).

CALORIES 202 (22% from fat); FAT 5g (sat 1.3g, mono 1.6g, poly 0.9g); PROTEIN 8.7g; CARB 32g; FIBER 2.8g; CHOL 41mg; IRON 2.8mg; SODIUM 640mg; CALC 72mg

Fall Flavors Menu
serves 6

Serve leftover gratin the next night with store-bought rotisserie chicken.

Broccoli Potato Gratin

Beet and walnut salad*

Roasted pork tenderloin

*Leave roots and 1 inch of stems on 8 medium beets; scrub with a brush. Place on a foil-lined baking sheet. Bake at 425° for 45 minutes or until tender; cool. Trim off roots and stems; rub off skins. Cut into wedges; combine with ⅔ cup vertically sliced red onion in a large bowl. Combine 2½ tablespoons balsamic vinegar, 1 tablespoon extravirgin olive oil, 1 tablespoon honey, ½ teaspoon salt, and ¼ teaspoon black pepper; drizzle over salad. Top with ¼ cup toasted chopped walnuts.

Broccoli Potato Gratin

A classic French dish, potato gratin combines with the American favorite, broccoli-cheese casserole, for a tasty twist on both. Make sure all the potato slices are about the same thickness so they cook evenly.

    6 cups chopped broccoli florets (about 1 pound)
    ¾ cup minced shallots (about 4 large)
    2 tablespoons Dijon mustard
    1 teaspoon chopped fresh thyme
    ½ teaspoon minced garlic
    ⅛ teaspoon ground nutmeg
    ¾ teaspoon salt, divided
    ½ teaspoon freshly ground black pepper
    2 pounds peeled Yukon gold potatoes, cut into ⅛-inch-thick slices
    Cooking spray
    3 tablespoons all-purpose flour
    1½ cups 2% reduced-fat milk
    1¼ cups fat-free, less-sodium chicken broth
    2 tablespoons chilled butter, cut into small pieces
    ¾ cup (3 ounces) shredded Gruyère cheese

1. Preheat oven to 375°.
2. Combine first 6 ingredients in a large bowl. Sprinkle with ½ teaspoon salt and pepper; toss to combine.
3. Layer one-third of potato slices in a 13 x 9–inch baking dish coated with cooking spray, overlapping to fit; top with half of broccoli mixture. Repeat layers, ending with potato. Sprinkle evenly with ¼ teaspoon salt.
4. Place flour in a medium bowl. Gradually add milk, stirring constantly with a whisk; stir in broth. Pour milk mixture over potato mixture. Top evenly with butter. Cover and bake at 375° for 1 hour. Uncover; sprinkle evenly with cheese. Bake 25 minutes or until browned. Cool on a wire rack 10 minutes. Yield: 12 servings (serving size: about ⅔ cup).

CALORIES 225 (30% from fat); FAT 7.4g (sat 4.4g, mono 2.1g, poly 0.4g); PROTEIN 10.1g; CARB 30.1g; FIBER 3.3g; CHOL 23mg; IRON 1.9mg; SODIUM 432mg; CALC 199mg

Sausage, Cherry Tomato, and Hash Brown Casserole

Serve this casserole as a side dish for a casual meal or as the main dish with coffee and fresh fruit at breakfast or brunch.

    1   cup chopped onion
    2   garlic cloves, minced
    8   ounces 50%-less-fat pork sausage
    ½   cup water
    1   tablespoon tomato paste
    ¼   teaspoon salt
    ¾   teaspoon freshly ground black
        pepper, divided
    7   cups frozen shredded hash brown
        potatoes, partially thawed
    1   cup (4 ounces) shredded part-
        skim mozzarella cheese
Cooking spray
    20 cherry tomatoes, halved
    ½   cup fat-free, less-sodium chicken
        broth
    ½   cup thinly sliced fresh basil
    2   tablespoons grated fresh Parmesan
        cheese

1. Preheat oven to 350°.
2. Combine first 3 ingredients in a large skillet over medium heat; cook 8 minutes or until browned, stirring to crumble sausage. Stir in ½ cup water, tomato paste, salt, and ¼ teaspoon pepper. Spoon mixture into a large bowl. Add potatoes and mozzarella; toss well. Spoon potato mixture into an 11 x 7–inch baking dish coated with cooking spray. Set aside. Wipe pan dry with a paper towel.
3. Place pan over medium-high heat. Lightly coat pan with cooking spray. Add tomatoes to pan; cook 3 minutes or just until heated. Arrange tomatoes in an even layer over potato mixture. Drizzle with broth; sprinkle with ½ teaspoon pepper. Cover and bake at 350° for 30 minutes. Uncover; sprinkle evenly with basil and Parmesan. Bake an additional 15 minutes or until lightly browned. Yield: 10 servings (serving size: about ¾ cup).

CALORIES 208 (29% from fat); FAT 6.8g (sat 3.1g, mono 1.9g, poly 0.9g); PROTEIN 10.7g; CARB 26.9g; FIBER 2.3g; CHOL 23mg; IRON 0.7mg; SODIUM 384mg; CALC 109mg

Spelt and Wild Mushroom Pilaf

Spelt is a whole wheat grain from the Mediterranean that dates back to the Roman Empire. Its earthy-nutty flavor pairs well with wild mushrooms in this simple pilaf. We used a mixture of shiitake, oyster, and baby bella (cremini) mushrooms.

    1   cup spelt
    2   teaspoons olive oil
    ¾   cup chopped onion
    1½ teaspoons minced fresh thyme
    ½   teaspoon salt
    ¼   teaspoon freshly ground black
        pepper
    1½ cups fat-free, less-sodium chicken
        broth
    1   tablespoon butter
    1   (8-ounce) package exotic
        mushroom blend (such as shiitake,
        cremini, and oyster), coarsely
        chopped

1. Place spelt in a medium bowl. Cover with hot water to 1 inch above spelt. Cover and let stand 1 hour. Drain and rinse with cold water; drain.
2. Heat oil in a medium saucepan over medium heat. Add onion to pan; cook 3 minutes or until tender, stirring occasionally. Stir in spelt, thyme, salt, and pepper; cook 1 minute. Stir in broth; bring to a simmer. Cover, reduce heat, and cook 50 minutes or until spelt is tender. Uncover and simmer 15 minutes or until liquid is almost absorbed. Remove from heat; keep warm.
3. Melt butter in a large nonstick skillet over medium-high heat. Add chopped mushrooms to pan; sauté 3 minutes or until tender and beginning to brown. Stir mushroom mixture into spelt mixture. Yield: 6 servings (serving size: about ⅔ cup).

CALORIES 171 (24% from fat); FAT 4.6g (sat 1.5g, mono 1.6g, poly 0.3g); PROTEIN 6.1g; CARB 30.9g; FIBER 1g; CHOL 5mg; IRON 2mg; SODIUM 312mg; CALC 21mg

Extras

For breakfast, brunch, or holiday dinner, these breads and sauces are certain to satisfy.

Potato-Sour Cream Biscuits
(pictured on page 252)

These savory treats are delicious alongside roast beef, chicken, or ham. They're great for sandwiches, too.

    8   ounces cubed peeled Yukon gold
        potato
    ½   cup low-fat buttermilk
    ¼   cup reduced-fat sour cream
    2   tablespoons butter, cut into small
        pieces
    1¾ cups all-purpose flour (about 7¾
        ounces)
    1   tablespoon baking powder
    1   teaspoon salt
    ½   teaspoon baking soda
Cooking spray

1. Preheat oven to 450°.
2. Place potato in a medium saucepan; cover with water. Bring to a boil. Reduce heat, and simmer 15 minutes or until tender; drain. Return potato to pan. Add buttermilk, sour cream, and butter to pan; mash with a potato masher until smooth.
3. Lightly spoon flour into dry measuring cups; level with a knife. Combine flour, baking powder, salt, and baking soda in a large bowl. Add potato mixture; stir just until moist. Turn dough out onto a lightly floured surface; knead lightly 5 times. Pat dough to ¾-inch thickness. Cut with a 2-inch biscuit cutter into 15 biscuits. Place biscuits 2 inches apart on a baking sheet coated with cooking spray. Bake at 450° for 15 minutes or until lightly browned. Serve warm. Yield: 15 biscuits (serving size: 1 biscuit).

CALORIES 87 (23% from fat); FAT 2.2g (sat 1.3g, mono 0.6g, poly 0.1g); PROTEIN 2.2g; CARB 14.5g; FIBER 0.6g; CHOL 6mg; IRON 0.9mg; SODIUM 298mg; CALC 70mg

Basic Cranberry Sauce

(pictured on page 255)

Make this tangy-sweet sauce up to two days ahead, and refrigerate it. Serve with turkey, chicken, quail, duck, or ham.

½ cup packed dark brown sugar
½ cup fresh orange juice (about 2 oranges)
¼ cup water
1½ tablespoons honey
⅛ teaspoon ground allspice
1 (12-ounce) package fresh cranberries
1 (3-inch) cinnamon stick

1. Combine all ingredients in a medium saucepan over medium-high heat; bring to a boil. Reduce heat, and simmer 12 minutes or until mixture is slightly thick, stirring occasionally. Discard cinnamon stick; cool completely. Yield: 14 servings (serving size: 2 tablespoons).

CALORIES 54 (0% from fat); FAT 0g; PROTEIN 0.1g; CARB 13.6g; FIBER 0.9g; CHOL 0mg; IRON 0.2mg; SODIUM 3mg; CALC 8mg

Maple Cream Sauce with Apple

Prepare this recipe to dress up your favorite maple syrup. Serve over pound cake, or with waffles or pancakes.

1 tablespoon butter
1½ cups sliced peeled Fuji apple (about ½ pound)
¾ cup maple syrup
1 tablespoon whipping cream
¼ teaspoon ground cinnamon

1. Melt butter in a medium saucepan over medium-high heat. Add apple to pan; sauté 10 minutes or until tender. Stir in syrup; cook 2 minutes or until mixture bubbles. Remove from heat; stir in cream and cinnamon. Yield: 8 servings (serving size: 3 tablespoons).

CALORIES 107 (19% from fat); FAT 2.2g (sat 1.3g, mono 0.2g, poly 0.1g); PROTEIN 0.1g; CARB 22.9g; FIBER 0.3g; CHOL 6mg; IRON 0.4mg; SODIUM 15mg; CALC 23mg

Hot Buttered Rum Quick Bread

Cooking spray
1½ teaspoons all-purpose flour
1 cup all-purpose flour (4½ ounces)
¼ cup whole wheat flour (1¼ ounces)
1 teaspoon baking powder
½ teaspoon baking soda
½ teaspoon ground cinnamon
½ teaspoon salt
¼ teaspoon grated nutmeg
¾ cup packed light brown sugar
¼ cup chilled butter, cut into pieces
⅓ cup egg substitute
½ cup ripe mashed banana (about 1 banana)
2 tablespoons dark rum
½ teaspoon vanilla extract
1 tablespoon butter, melted

1. Lightly coat an 8 x 4–inch loaf pan with cooking spray; dust with 1½ teaspoons all-purpose flour. Set aside.
2. Preheat oven to 350°.
3. Lightly spoon 1 cup all-purpose flour and whole wheat flour into dry measuring cups; level with a knife. Combine flours, baking powder, baking soda, cinnamon, salt, and nutmeg; stirring with a whisk.
4. Combine sugar and ¼ cup butter in a large bowl; beat with a mixer at medium speed until light and fluffy (about 3 minutes). Add egg substitute; beat until combined. Beat in banana, rum, and vanilla. Add flour mixture to banana mixture; beat at low speed just until combined. Scrape batter into prepared pan with a spatula; smooth top. Bake at 350° for 30 minutes; gently remove from oven, and drizzle top with 1 tablespoon melted butter. Bake an additional 10 minutes or until a wooden pick inserted in center comes out clean. Cool in pan 5 minutes before turning out onto a wire rack to cool completely. Yield: 12 servings (serving size: 1 slice).

CALORIES 164 (29% from fat); FAT 5.2g (sat 3.1g, mono 1.3g, poly 0.4g); PROTEIN 2.5g; CARB 26.3g; FIBER 1g; CHOL 13mg; IRON 1.1mg; SODIUM 243mg; CALC 44mg

Peanut Butter and Jelly Muffins

Consider these a breakfast version of a peanut butter and jelly sandwich. Don't use a natural-style peanut butter in this recipe; it won't have enough sugar or fat to help the muffins rise.

1 cup all-purpose flour (about 4½ ounces)
¾ cup whole wheat flour (about 3½ ounces)
¼ cup granulated sugar
¼ cup packed dark brown sugar
1 tablespoon baking powder
½ teaspoon salt
1¼ cups fat-free milk
⅓ cup creamy peanut butter
¼ cup egg substitute
2 tablespoons butter, melted
1 teaspoon vanilla extract
Cooking spray
¼ cup strawberry jam

1. Preheat oven to 400°.
2. Lightly spoon flours into dry measuring cups; level with a knife. Combine flours, sugars, baking powder, and salt in a large bowl; stir with a whisk. Make a well in center of mixture. Combine milk and next 4 ingredients; add to flour mixture, stirring just until moist.
3. Spoon batter into 12 muffin cups coated with cooking spray, filling each cup half full. Spoon 1 teaspoon jam into each cup. Spoon remaining batter on top to cover jam. Bake at 400° for 20 minutes or until muffins spring back when touched lightly in center. Cool in pan 5 minutes. Remove from pan, and cool on a wire rack. Yield: 1 dozen (serving size: 1 muffin).

CALORIES 185 (28% from fat); FAT 5.8g (sat 2g, mono 2.3g, poly 1.2g); PROTEIN 5.2g; CARB 29.4g; FIBER 1.6g; CHOL 6mg; IRON 1.2mg; SODIUM 288mg; CALC 113mg

Lemon-Walnut Scones with Cranberry Cream Cheese

Purchase ground walnuts (sometimes labeled walnut meal) at health-food stores, gourmet markets, and some supermarkets. Or grind your own in a food processor or spice or coffee grinder in short pulses (don't overdo it, or you'll end up with walnut butter). You'll need about 3 tablespoons chopped walnuts to yield ¼ cup ground. Cranberries tint the cream cheese mulberry. The scones are best served warm, but you can prepare and refrigerate the cranberry mixture up to four days in advance.

SCONES:

    1   cup plus 2 tablespoons all-purpose
        flour (about 5 ounces)
    ½   cup whole wheat flour (about 2½
        ounces)
    ¼   cup finely ground walnuts
    1   tablespoon baking powder
    2   teaspoons finely grated lemon
        rind
    ½   teaspoon salt
    3   tablespoons chilled butter, cut
        into small pieces
    ½   cup fat-free milk
    1   large egg, lightly beaten

CRANBERRY CREAM CHEESE:

    ¾   cup dried cranberries
    1   (8-ounce) package fat-free cream
        cheese, softened

1. Preheat oven to 425°.
2. To prepare scones, lightly spoon flours into dry measuring cups and tablespoons; level with a knife. Combine flours, walnuts, and next 3 ingredients in a large bowl; stir with a whisk. Cut in butter with a pastry blender or 2 knives until mixture resembles coarse meal.
3. Combine milk and egg in a small bowl; add milk mixture to flour mixture, stirring just until moist (dough will be slightly sticky). Turn dough out onto a baking sheet lined with parchment paper, and pat into an 8-inch circle (about ½-inch thick). Cut dough into 12 wedges, cutting into, but not through, dough. Bake at 425° for 14 minutes or until golden. Cool slightly on a wire rack; break into wedges.
4. To prepare cranberry cream cheese, place cranberries in a small heat-proof bowl; add boiling water to cover. Let stand 30 minutes; drain well. Place cream cheese in a small bowl; add cranberries, stirring just until combined. Yield: 12 servings (serving size: 1 scone and about 1½ tablespoons cranberry cream cheese).

CALORIES 149 (29% from fat); FAT 4.8g (sat 2.2g, mono 1.1g, poly 1.1g); PROTEIN 5.8g; CARB 21.1g; FIBER 1.5g; CHOL 27mg; IRON 1.1mg; SODIUM 354mg; CALC 124mg

---

Scone Schooling

A quick bread from the British Isles, the scone may take its name from the Middle Dutch word *schoonbrot*, meaning "fine bread." It's also thought that the name comes from the Scottish town of Scone, where Scotland's kings were once crowned. In Northern England and Scotland, the word is pronounced "skon," while "skoan" is the preferred pronunciation in the south of Britain and the United States.

While they're a staple of the British afternoon tea course, scones have also developed fans worldwide. Their biscuit-like texture make them an option for breakfast, brunch, or snack. Leavened with baking powder, baking soda, or a combination, they're also a good choice for company because they come together and bake quickly. Both sweet and savory, scones fall into two basic categories: cream scones and biscuit scones. Cream scones use cream as their source of fat; the richer the cream, the richer the scone. Biscuit scones, like Banana Bran Scones (recipe at right) and Lemon-Walnut Scones with Cranberry Cream Cheese (recipe at left), use cold butter cut into the dough to keep them flaky.

Banana Bran Scones

Banana brings a light, fruity sweetness to these spiced scones. Serve with brunch or as an evening snack with hot chocolate.

    1   cup all-purpose flour (about 4½
        ounces)
    ½   cup oat bran
    2   tablespoons chilled butter, cut
        into small pieces
    1   teaspoon baking powder
    ¼   teaspoon baking soda
    ¼   teaspoon salt
    ¼   teaspoon ground cinnamon
    ¾   cup ripe mashed banana (about 2)
    1   tablespoon light brown sugar
    ¼   cup plus 1½ teaspoons fat-free
        buttermilk, divided
    1½ teaspoons granulated sugar

1. Preheat oven to 400°.
2. Lightly spoon flour into a dry measuring cup; level with a knife. Place flour and next 6 ingredients in a food processor, and pulse until mixture resembles coarse meal.
3. Combine banana and brown sugar in a medium bowl; let stand 5 minutes. Add flour mixture and ¼ cup buttermilk alternately to banana mixture, stirring just until moist.
4. Turn dough out onto a lightly floured surface; knead lightly 1½ minutes with floured hands. Pat dough into a 6-inch circle on a baking sheet lined with parchment paper. Cut dough into 8 wedges, cutting into, but not through, dough. Brush 1½ teaspoons buttermilk over surface of dough; sprinkle with granulated sugar. Bake at 400° for 12 minutes or until lightly browned. Remove from pan; cool on wire racks. Yield: 8 servings (serving size: 1 scone).

CALORIES 126 (25% from fat); FAT 3.5g (sat 1.9g, mono 0.9g, poly 0.4g); PROTEIN 3.2g; CARB 23.2g; FIBER 1.9g; CHOL 8mg; IRON 1.2mg; SODIUM 204mg; CALC 54mg

Cinnamon-Date-Pecan Rolls with Maple Glaze

DOUGH:

1 teaspoon granulated sugar
1 package dry yeast (about 2¼ teaspoons)
¾ cup warm water (100° to 110°)
⅓ cup granulated sugar
3 tablespoons butter, melted
½ teaspoon salt
1 large egg
3¼ cups all-purpose flour (about 14½ ounces)
Cooking spray

FILLING:

⅔ cup packed brown sugar
1 teaspoon ground cinnamon
1 teaspoon grated orange rind
2 tablespoons butter, melted
¾ cup chopped pitted dates
¼ cup chopped pecans, toasted

GLAZE:

1 cup powdered sugar
2 tablespoons maple syrup
1 tablespoon fat-free milk

1. To prepare dough, dissolve 1 teaspoon granulated sugar and yeast in ¾ cup warm water; let stand 5 minutes. Combine ⅓ cup granulated sugar, 3 tablespoons butter, salt, and egg in a large bowl. Add yeast mixture; beat with a mixer at medium speed until blended.

2. Lightly spoon flour into dry measuring cups; level with a knife. Gradually add 3 cups flour to yeast mixture, beating at low speed until a soft dough forms. Turn dough out onto a lightly floured surface. Knead until smooth and elastic (about 5 minutes); add enough of remaining flour, 1 tablespoon at a time, to prevent dough from sticking to hands. Place dough in a large bowl coated with cooking spray, turning to coat top. Cover and let rise in a warm place (85°), free from drafts, 1 hour or until doubled in size. Punch dough down; turn out onto a lightly floured surface.

3. To prepare filling, combine brown sugar, cinnamon, and rind in a small bowl. Roll dough into a 15 x 10–inch rectangle; brush with 2 tablespoons butter. Sprinkle brown sugar mixture over dough, leaving a ½-inch border. Sprinkle dates and pecans over sugar mixture. Beginning with a short side, roll up jelly-roll fashion; pinch seam to seal (do not seal ends of roll). Cut roll into 18 (½-inch) slices. Place slices, cut sides up, in a 13 x 9–inch baking pan coated with cooking spray. Cover and let rise in a warm place (85°), free from drafts, about 1 hour or until rolls have doubled in size.

4. Preheat oven to 375°.

5. Uncover dough. Bake at 375° for 20 minutes or until rolls are golden brown.

6. To prepare glaze, combine powdered sugar, syrup, and milk in a small bowl; stir with a whisk until smooth. Drizzle glaze over warm rolls. Serve immediately. Yield: 18 rolls (serving size: 1 roll).

CALORIES 226 (20% from fat); FAT 4.9g (sat 2.2g, mono 1.6g, poly 0.6g); PROTEIN 3.2g; CARB 43.4g; FIBER 1.5g; CHOL 20mg; IRON 1.5mg; SODIUM 96mg; CALC 21mg

Delectable Desserts

Choose a pie, cookies, custard, or cake to finish your feast with a spectacular sweet.

MAKE AHEAD • FREEZABLE
Cranberry-Jalapeño Granita

Remove the jalapeño seeds if you prefer a milder dessert. You could also use this spicy-sweet ice to top oysters on the half shell.

2 cups cranberry juice cocktail
⅓ cup sugar
4 (5-inch) mint sprigs (about ½ ounce)
1 jalapeño pepper, sliced
2 tablespoons fresh lime juice

1. Combine first 4 ingredients in a small saucepan; bring to a boil. Cover and remove from heat; let stand 15 minutes. Strain cranberry mixture through a fine mesh sieve into an 11 x 7–inch baking dish; discard solids. Cool mixture to room temperature; stir in lime juice. Cover and freeze about 45 minutes. Stir cranberry mixture every 45 minutes until completely frozen (about 3 hours). Remove mixture from freezer; scrape entire mixture with a fork until fluffy. Yield: 4 servings (serving size: ½ cup).

CALORIES 135 (1% from fat); FAT 0.1g (sat 0g, mono 0g, poly 0.1g); PROTEIN 0.1g; CARB 34.5g; FIBER 0.1g; CHOL 0mg; IRON 0.3mg; SODIUM 3mg; CALC 7mg

MAKE AHEAD
Vanilla-Caramel Flans

Be careful not to stir too vigorously when dissolving the sugar in water, or large sugar crystals will form. Prepare this dessert up to one day ahead.

Cooking spray
1 cup sugar
¼ cup water
2½ cups fat-free milk
2 teaspoons vanilla extract
¼ teaspoon ground cinnamon
6 large eggs, lightly beaten
1 (14-ounce) can fat-free sweetened condensed milk

1. Preheat oven to 350°.

2. Coat 12 (6-ounce) custard cups with cooking spray.

3. Combine sugar and ¼ cup water in a small, heavy saucepan; cook over medium-high heat, stirring gently as needed to dissolve sugar evenly. Cook 4 minutes or until golden, stirring constantly. Immediately pour about 1 tablespoon sugar mixture into each prepared custard cup, tipping quickly to coat bottom of cup.

4. Combine 2½ cups fat-free milk and remaining 4 ingredients in a medium bowl, stirring with a whisk until well blended. Pour ½ cup milk mixture into each custard cup. Place cups in a jelly-roll pan; add hot water to pan to a depth of ¼ inch. Bake at 350° for 35 minutes or until a knife inserted in center comes out clean. Remove cups from pan; cool completely on a wire rack. Cover and chill at least 3 hours.

5. Loosen edges of custards with a knife or rubber spatula. Place a dessert plate,

Continued

upside down, on top of each custard cup; invert custards onto plates. Drizzle any remaining caramelized syrup over custards. Yield: 12 servings (serving size: 1 flan).

CALORIES 214 (11% from fat); FAT 2.5g (sat 0.8g, mono 1g, poly 0.3g); PROTEIN 7.4g; CARB 39.9g; FIBER 0g; CHOL 111mg; IRON 0.5mg; SODIUM 90mg; CALC 163mg

MAKE AHEAD

Pear-Cranberry Pie with Oatmeal Streusel

(pictured on page 253)

If you can't find fresh cranberries, use thawed frozen ones. A prepared pie shell yields a stellar dessert with little effort.

STREUSEL:
¾ cup regular oats
½ cup packed light brown sugar
½ teaspoon ground cinnamon
¼ teaspoon ground nutmeg
Dash of salt
2 tablespoons chilled butter, cut into small pieces

FILLING:
3 cups (½-inch) cubed peeled Anjou pear (2 large)
2 cups fresh cranberries
⅔ cup packed light brown sugar
2½ tablespoons cornstarch

REMAINING INGREDIENT:
1 unbaked 9-inch deep-dish pastry shell

1. Preheat oven to 350°.
2. To prepare streusel, combine first 5 ingredients in a medium bowl; cut in butter with a pastry blender or 2 knives until mixture resembles coarse meal.
3. To prepare filling, combine pear and next 3 ingredients in a large bowl; toss well. Spoon pear mixture into pastry shell; sprinkle streusel over pear mixture. Bake at 350° for 1 hour or until bubbly and streusel is browned. Cool at least 1 hour on a wire rack. Yield: 12 servings (serving size: 1 wedge).

CALORIES 240 (31% from fat); FAT 8.2g (sat 2.4g, mono 3.1g, poly 0.8g); PROTEIN 1.6g; CARB 41.5g; FIBER 2.4g; CHOL 5mg; IRON 0.8mg; SODIUM 118mg; CALC 27mg

MAKE AHEAD

Chocolate-Dipped Almond Meringues

When preparing these cookies, be careful not to overbeat the egg whites; properly stiff peaks will have the consistency of marshmallow cream.

MERINGUES:
4 large egg whites
¼ teaspoon cream of tartar
¼ teaspoon salt
½ cup sugar
¼ teaspoon almond extract
2 ounces bittersweet chocolate, finely chopped

GLAZE:
½ cup semisweet chocolate chips

1. Preheat oven to 200°.
2. To prepare meringues, cover a baking sheet with parchment paper; secure to baking sheet with masking tape.
3. Beat egg whites with a mixer at high speed until foamy. Add cream of tartar and salt; beat until soft peaks form. Gradually add sugar, 1 tablespoon at a time, beating until stiff peaks form (do not overbeat). Gently fold in almond extract and chopped chocolate. Drop batter by rounded tablespoonfuls onto prepared baking sheet. Bake at 200° for 2 hours or until dry. (Meringues are done when the surface is dry and meringues can be removed from paper without sticking to fingers.) Turn oven off; leave meringues in oven 1 hour or until cool and crisp. Remove from oven; carefully remove meringues from paper. Cool completely on a wire rack.

Consider Coffee

Coffee is enjoyed the world over and proves to be a perfect complement to our globally inspired dessert roundup.

Just as with pairing wines, matching coffee with a dish should take into account the texture of the food, body of the coffee, and flavor profiles of each. Keep in mind that lighter-roast coffees generally have sharper flavor and more acid than the dark-roasted brews.

- Start with high-quality coffee beans. Arabica beans are considered superior because they offer more complexity than the robusta variety, which has more caffeine and flatter flavor. Arabica beans are grown at higher altitudes than the hardy robusta beans and develop smoother taste.
- Many coffees naturally have notes of chocolate, caramel, berry, or fruit. A coffee with fruit-forward notes—like an Ethiopian brew—works well with fruit pies like our Pear-Cranberry Pie with Oatmeal Streusel (recipe at left). A chocolate dessert will likely work best with a darker roast that carries some chocolate or caramel qualities.

- Pair complex-flavored, heavier desserts with stronger, darker coffee. Lighter-flavored desserts match up best with lighter roasts. Serve our Bourbon-Pecan Tart with Chocolate Drizzle (page 357) or Chocolate-Dipped Almond Meringues (recipe above) with a dark roast coffee like Italian or French. Medium-roast brew—with medium acidity and body—is ideal for the simple and smooth-textured Vanilla-Caramel Flans (page 355) or the decadent Gingerbread Soufflé (page 359). Try the sweet Olive Oil Bundt Cake with Tangerine Glaze (page 358) with a light roast of Brazilian, Colombian, or breakfast blend beans.
- Some coffee beans grow in the same warm climates as many of the common holiday spices, and when paired together they're a natural match.
- Add a dollop of thawed reduced-calorie frozen whipped topping or even reduced-fat ice cream to add a garnish and help cut the acidity in coffee.
- Offer shavings of chocolate to enhance a coffee's chocolate notes.

4. To prepare glaze, place chocolate chips in a medium microwave-safe bowl. Microwave at MEDIUM (50% power) 30 seconds or until melted, stirring until smooth. Dip half of each meringue in chocolate. Place on wire rack to dry. Store in an airtight container. Yield: 2 dozen (serving size: 1 meringue).

CALORIES 48 (40% from fat); FAT 2.1g (sat 1.3g, mono 0.4g, poly 0g); PROTEIN 0.9g; CARB 7.6g; FIBER 0.4g; CHOL 1mg; IRON 0.2mg; SODIUM 34mg; CALC 2mg

MAKE AHEAD

Bourbon-Pecan Tart with Chocolate Drizzle

(pictured on page 254)

Make the tart a day ahead, and store it in the refrigerator.

    1   cup packed light brown sugar
   ¾   cup dark corn syrup
    3   tablespoons all-purpose flour
    2   tablespoons bourbon
    2   tablespoons molasses
    1   tablespoon butter, melted
   ½   teaspoon vanilla extract
   ¼   teaspoon salt
    2   large eggs, lightly beaten
    1   large egg white, lightly beaten
   ⅔   cup pecan halves
   ½   (15-ounce) package refrigerated
        pie dough (such as Pillsbury)
        Cooking spray
   ½   ounce bittersweet chocolate,
        chopped

1. Preheat oven to 350°.
2. Combine first 10 ingredients, stirring well with a whisk. Stir in pecans. Roll dough into a 13-inch circle; fit into a 9-inch removable-bottom tart pan coated with cooking spray. Trim excess crust using a sharp knife. Spoon sugar mixture into prepared crust. Bake at 350° for 45 minutes or until center is set. Cool completely on a wire rack.
3. Place chocolate in a microwave-safe bowl; microwave at HIGH 1 minute. Stir until smooth. Drizzle chocolate over tart. Yield: 12 servings (serving size: 1 wedge).

CALORIES 277 (32% from fat); FAT 10g (sat 2.7g, mono 3g, poly 1.5g); PROTEIN 2.4g; CARB 45.2g; FIBER 0.7g; CHOL 39mg; IRON 0.9mg; SODIUM 156mg; CALC 32mg

MAKE AHEAD

Lemon Panna Cotta with Raspberry Sauce

If you don't have a vanilla bean, add 1½ teaspoons vanilla extract after the gelatin is dissolved in the hot milk.

PANNA COTTA:

    1   envelope unflavored gelatin
  2¾   cups 1% low-fat milk, divided
   ¼   cup sugar
    1   (3 x 1–inch) strip fresh lemon rind
   ½   vanilla bean, split lengthwise
        Cooking spray

SAUCE:

    1   (10-ounce) package frozen
        raspberries in light syrup, thawed
        and undrained
    1   tablespoon sugar
    2   teaspoons cornstarch
    2   tablespoons red currant jelly
        Mint sprigs (optional)

1. To prepare panna cotta, sprinkle gelatin over 1 cup milk; let stand 1 minute.
2. Combine 1¾ cups milk, ¼ cup sugar, rind, and vanilla bean in a medium saucepan over medium heat; bring to a simmer. Cook 5 minutes, stirring occasionally. Add gelatin mixture to milk mixture; stir until gelatin is completely dissolved. Discard rind and vanilla bean. Cool.
3. Divide mixture evenly among 8 (6-ounce) custard cups coated with cooking spray. Cover and chill at least 4 hours or overnight.
4. To prepare sauce, press raspberries through a sieve over a bowl; discard seeds. Combine 1 tablespoon sugar and cornstarch in a saucepan; stir until blended. Stir in raspberries and jelly; bring to a boil. Cook 1 minute, stirring constantly. Cool.
5. Loosen edges of custards with a knife or rubber spatula. Place a dessert plate, upside down, on top of each custard cup; invert custards onto plates. Spoon 2 tablespoons sauce around each serving. Garnish with mint sprigs, if desired. Yield: 8 servings.

CALORIES 98 (8% from fat); FAT 0.9g (sat 0.6g, mono 0.3g, poly 0g); PROTEIN 3.8g; CARB 19.1g; FIBER 0.6g; CHOL 3mg; IRON 0.2mg; SODIUM 44mg; CALC 107mg

MAKE AHEAD

Plum Pudding Tartlets

   ⅓   cup packed brown sugar
   ⅓   cup water
    2   tablespoons fresh orange juice
    1   tablespoon fresh lemon juice
   ¼   teaspoon ground cinnamon
        Dash of ground cloves
   ½   pound pitted dried plums, finely
        chopped
   ⅔   cup all-purpose flour (about
        3 ounces)
   ⅓   cup whole wheat flour (about
        1½ ounces)
   ¼   teaspoon baking powder
   ¼   teaspoon baking soda
   ⅛   teaspoon salt
   ¼   cup granulated sugar
    3   tablespoons butter, softened
    1   large egg
        Cooking spray
    1   tablespoon powdered sugar

1. Combine first 7 ingredients in a small saucepan; bring to a boil. Reduce heat, and simmer 6 minutes or until plums are tender and liquid is almost absorbed. Cool completely.
2. Preheat oven to 375°.
3. Lightly spoon flours into dry measuring cups; level with a knife. Combine flours, baking powder, baking soda, and salt; stir with a whisk. Place granulated sugar and butter in a large bowl; beat with a mixer at medium speed until well blended (about 4 minutes). Add egg; beat well. Add flour mixture; beat at low speed just until blended.
4. Divide dough into 24 portions. Roll each portion into a 2-inch circle on a lightly floured surface. Place 1 dough portion into a miniature muffin cup coated with cooking spray. Spoon about 1 tablespoon plum mixture into each muffin cup.
5. Bake at 375° for 10 minutes or until lightly browned. Run a knife around outside edge of each tartlet; remove from pan. Cool completely on a wire rack. Sprinkle with powdered sugar. Yield: 2 dozen (serving size: 1 tartlet).

CALORIES 77 (20% from fat); FAT 1.7g (sat 1g, mono 0.5g, poly 0.1g); PROTEIN 1.1g; CARB 15.2g; FIBER 1g; CHOL 13mg; IRON 0.4mg; SODIUM 46mg; CALC 13mg

Pistachio Layer Cake

To flavor the cake and the filling, we've processed pistachios into a nut butter.

CAKE:
    Cooking spray
    2   teaspoons cake flour
    ⅔   cup chopped unsalted dry-roasted pistachios
    ⅓   cup butter, softened
    1   cup granulated sugar
    2   large egg yolks
    2   cups cake flour (about 8 ounces)
    1   teaspoon baking soda
    ¼   teaspoon salt
    1   cup fat-free buttermilk
    1   teaspoon vanilla extract
    ⅛   teaspoon cream of tartar
    6   large egg whites

FILLING:
    3   tablespoons granulated sugar
    2   tablespoons cornstarch
    Dash of salt
    1   cup 1% low-fat milk
    2   large egg yolks, lightly beaten
    ½   teaspoon vanilla extract

FROSTING:
    ½   cup (4 ounces) ⅓-less-fat cream cheese, softened
    3   cups powdered sugar, sifted (about 13 ounces)
    1½ tablespoons 1% low-fat milk
    1   teaspoon vanilla extract

REMAINING INGREDIENT:
    1   tablespoon chopped unsalted dry-roasted pistachios

1. Preheat oven to 350°.
2. Coat bottoms of 2 (9-inch) round cake pans with cooking spray (do not coat sides of pans). Line bottoms of pans with wax paper. Coat wax paper with cooking spray; dust with 2 teaspoons flour. Set pans aside.
3. To prepare cake, place ⅔ cup chopped pistachios in a mini food processor; process until a smooth paste forms (about 3 to 4 minutes), scraping down sides occasionally. Reserve 1 tablespoon pistachio butter; set aside.

4. Place remaining pistachio butter and butter in a large bowl; beat with a mixer at medium speed until creamy. Gradually add 1 cup granulated sugar, beating well. Add 2 egg yolks, one at a time, beating well after each addition.
5. Lightly spoon 2 cups flour into dry measuring cups; level with a knife. Combine 2 cups flour, baking soda, and ¼ teaspoon salt, stirring with a whisk. Add flour mixture and buttermilk alternately to butter mixture, beginning and ending with flour mixture. Beat in 1 teaspoon vanilla.
6. Place cream of tartar and egg whites in a large bowl; beat with a mixer at high speed until stiff peaks form using clean, dry beaters. Gently fold one-third of egg white mixture into batter; gently fold in remaining egg white mixture. Divide batter evenly between prepared pans. Bake at 350° for 24 minutes or until golden brown and a wooden pick inserted in center comes out clean. Cool in pans 5 minutes on a wire rack. Run a knife around edges of pans; loosen cake layers from pans. Remove cakes from pans. Discard wax paper. Cool cake layers completely on a wire rack coated with cooking spray.
7. To prepare filling, combine 3 tablespoons granulated sugar, cornstarch, and dash of salt in a small, heavy saucepan. Add 1 cup 1% milk and egg yolks, stirring with a whisk. Cook over medium-high heat until mixture comes to a boil, stirring constantly with a whisk. Remove from heat; add reserved 1 tablespoon pistachio butter and ½ teaspoon vanilla, stirring with a whisk. Place pan in a large ice-filled bowl for 20 minutes or until egg mixture cools to room temperature, stirring occasionally.
8. To prepare frosting, place cream cheese in a large bowl; beat with a mixer at high speed until fluffy. Gradually add powdered sugar, beating at low speed just until smooth (do not overbeat). Beat in 1½ tablespoons 1% milk and 1 teaspoon vanilla until blended and frosting is of spreading consistency.
9. Place 1 cake layer on a plate; spread layer evenly with filling. Top with remaining cake layer. Spread frosting over top and sides of cake. Sprinkle cake

with 1 tablespoon chopped pistachios. Yield: 16 servings (serving size: 1 slice).

CALORIES 330 (26% from fat); FAT 9.4g (sat 4.3g, mono 2.9g, poly 1.2g); PROTEIN 6.6g; CARB 55.7g; FIBER 0.9g; CHOL 67mg; IRON 1.7mg; SODIUM 230mg; CALC 61mg

Olive Oil Bundt Cake with Tangerine Glaze

    Cooking spray
    2   tablespoons all-purpose flour
    2½ cups granulated sugar
    1½ cups fat-free milk
    ½   cup extravirgin olive oil
    ¼   cup fresh tangerine juice (about 2 tangerines), divided
    3   large eggs
    2¼ cups all-purpose flour (about 10 ounces)
    1   teaspoon baking powder
    1   teaspoon salt
    ½   teaspoon baking soda
    1   cup powdered sugar
    1   teaspoon butter, melted

1. Preheat oven to 350°.
2. Coat a 12-cup Bundt pan with cooking spray; dust with 2 tablespoons all-purpose flour. Set aside.
3. Combine granulated sugar, milk, oil, 3 tablespoons juice, and eggs in a large bowl, stirring with a whisk.
4. Lightly spoon 2¼ cups flour into dry measuring cups; level with a knife. Combine flour, baking powder, salt, and baking soda; stir well with a whisk. Add flour mixture to oil mixture, stirring with a whisk until smooth. Pour batter into prepared pan. Bake at 350° for 55 minutes or until golden brown and cake begins to pull away from sides of pan. Cool cake completely on wire rack. Loosen edges of cake with a narrow spatula. Place a plate upside down on top of cake; invert onto plate.
5. Combine 1 tablespoon juice, powdered sugar, and butter, stirring well with a whisk. Drizzle glaze over cooled cake. Yield: 16 servings (serving size: 1 slice).

CALORIES 307 (24% from fat); FAT 8.3g (sat 1.5g, mono 5.5g, poly 0.7g); PROTEIN 4g; CARB 54.8g; FIBER 0.5g; CHOL 41mg; IRON 1.1mg; SODIUM 243mg; CALC 57mg

Gingerbread Soufflé

Cooking spray
  6 tablespoons granulated sugar, divided
  2 tablespoons butter
  3 tablespoons all-purpose flour
  ¾ cup 1% low-fat milk
  ⅓ cup molasses
  1½ teaspoons ground ginger
  ½ teaspoon ground cinnamon
  ¼ teaspoon ground nutmeg
  ⅛ teaspoon ground cloves
  2 large egg yolks
  3 large egg whites
  4 teaspoons powdered sugar

1. Preheat oven to 375°.
2. Coat 8 (6-ounce) soufflé dishes with cooking spray. Sprinkle evenly with 2 tablespoons granulated sugar. Set aside.
3. Melt butter in a medium saucepan over medium heat. Add flour and 2 tablespoons granulated sugar; cook 1 minute, stirring constantly with a whisk. Gradually add milk; bring to a boil, stirring constantly with a whisk. Cook 2 minutes or until slightly thick, stirring constantly with a whisk. Remove from heat; cool 10 minutes. Add molasses and next 5 ingredients, stirring with a whisk. Set aside.
4. Place egg whites in a medium bowl; beat with a mixer at high speed until soft peaks form. Gradually add remaining 2 tablespoons granulated sugar, 1 tablespoon at a time, beating until stiff peaks form (do not overbeat). Gently fold one-fourth of egg white mixture into molasses mixture; gently fold in remaining egg white mixture. Gently spoon mixture into prepared dishes. Sharply tap dishes on counter 2 or 3 times to level. Place dishes on a baking sheet; place baking sheet in oven. Bake at 375° for 25 minutes or until puffy and set. Sprinkle each soufflé with ½ teaspoon powdered sugar. Serve immediately. Yield: 8 servings (serving size: 1 soufflé).

CALORIES 148 (26% from fat); FAT 4.3g (sat 2.4g, mono 1.3g, poly 0.3g); PROTEIN 3.2g; CARB 24.8g; FIBER 0.2g; CHOL 60mg; IRON 1mg; SODIUM 60mg; CALC 66mg

Almond-Orzo Kugel

Kugel, a sweet or savory baked pudding often served at Hanukkah celebrations, usually contains pasta or matzo. This sweet version contains orzo, a small rice-shaped pasta.

  1 (16-ounce) package uncooked orzo (rice-shaped pasta)
  1 cup sugar, divided
  1½ cups reduced-fat sour cream
  ½ cup fat-free milk
  1 teaspoon vanilla extract
  ½ teaspoon salt
  ¼ teaspoon almond extract
  ⅛ teaspoon grated whole nutmeg
  2 large egg whites
  1 (24-ounce) carton 1% low-fat cottage cheese
  1 (8-ounce) carton egg substitute
Cooking spray
  ⅓ cup sliced almonds
  ¼ cup all-purpose flour (about 1 ounce)
  ¼ teaspoon ground cinnamon
  ⅛ teaspoon salt
  2 tablespoons butter, melted

1. Preheat oven to 325°.
2. Cook orzo according to package directions, omitting salt and fat. Drain and set aside.
3. Place ¾ cup sugar, sour cream, and next 8 ingredients in a food processor; process until smooth. Combine orzo and cottage cheese mixture in a large bowl, stirring until well blended. Spoon orzo mixture into a 13 x 9–inch baking dish coated with cooking spray. Bake at 325° for 40 minutes.
4. Combine ¼ cup sugar, almonds, and next 3 ingredients in a small bowl; stir in butter. Sprinkle kugel with almond mixture; bake an additional 20 minutes. Cool 15 minutes; cut into 16 pieces. Serve warm. Yield: 16 servings (serving size: 1 piece).

CALORIES 273 (25% from fat); FAT 7.6g (sat 3.2g, mono 2.5g, poly 1.3g); PROTEIN 12.8g; CARB 38.6g; FIBER 1.2g; CHOL 15mg; IRON 1.4mg; SODIUM 323mg; CALC 79mg

Gifts from the Kitchen

Please the people on your shopping list with one or more of these edible treats.

MAKE AHEAD
Cranberry Orange Marmalade

Make the most of abundant seasonal oranges and cranberries with this bright preserve. Serve with biscuits or toast for breakfast, or pair it with crackers, assorted cheeses, and nuts for a cheese platter. The sweet-sour marmalade pleasantly partners with pungent-flavored cheese, such as Gorgonzola.

  3½ pounds navel oranges (about 6 medium)
  1½ cups water
  3 cups sugar, divided
  1 (12-ounce) package fresh cranberries

1. Carefully remove rind from 3 oranges using a vegetable peeler, making sure not to get any of white pithy part of rind. Slice rind into thin strips. Peel all oranges; cut into sections. Combine rind strips, sections, 1½ cups water, and 1 cup sugar in a medium saucepan; bring mixture to a boil. Reduce heat, and simmer 15 minutes, stirring occasionally.
2. Add 2 cups sugar and cranberries to pan. Simmer 1 hour and 30 minutes or until thick, stirring occasionally. Remove from heat, and cool completely. Cover and chill. Yield: 4 cups (serving size: 2 tablespoons).

CALORIES 80 (0% from fat); FAT 0g; PROTEIN 0.3g; CARB 21.5g; FIBER 2.2g; CHOL 0mg; IRON 0.1mg; SODIUM 0mg; CALC 16mg

Dark Chocolate–Dipped Anise Biscotti

1½ cups all-purpose flour (about 6¾ ounces)
  1 teaspoon aniseed
  ½ teaspoon baking soda
  ¼ teaspoon salt
  ¾ cup sugar
  2 tablespoons butter, softened
  2 large eggs
Cooking spray
  3 ounces premium dark chocolate, coarsely chopped

1. Preheat oven to 350°.
2. Lightly spoon flour into dry measuring cups; level with a knife. Combine flour, aniseed, baking soda, and salt, stirring well with a whisk. Place sugar and butter in a large bowl; beat at medium speed with a mixer until blended (about 2 minutes). Add eggs, one at a time, beating well after each addition. Add flour mixture to sugar mixture, beating just until blended. Turn dough out onto a lightly floured surface, and knead lightly 7 times. Shape dough into a 12-inch-long roll. Place roll on a baking sheet coated with cooking spray; pat to 1-inch thickness. Bake at 350° for 40 minutes. Remove roll from baking sheet; cool 10 minutes on a wire rack.
3. Reduce oven temperature to 300°.
4. Cut roll crosswise into 22 slices. Place, cut sides down, on baking sheet. Bake at 300° for 10 minutes. Turn cookies over; bake an additional 10 minutes (cookies will be slightly soft in center but will harden as they cool). Cool cookies completely on wire rack.
5. Heat chocolate in a small heavy saucepan over low heat 5 minutes or until melted; stir. Dip cookies, top sides down, in chocolate; allow excess chocolate to drip back into pan. Place cookies, chocolate sides up, on a baking sheet. Let stand 1 hour or until set. Yield: 22 biscotti (serving size: 1 biscotto).

CALORIES 83 (24% from fat); FAT 2.2g (sat 1.2g, mono 0.5g, poly 0.1g); PROTEIN 1.6g; CARB 14.6g; FIBER 0.3g; CHOL 23mg; IRON 0.6mg; SODIUM 69mg; CALC 5mg

Lemon Verbena–Walnut Loaf Cake

CAKE:
  ½ cup boiling water
  4 lemon verbena tea bags
  2 cups all-purpose flour (about 9 ounces)
  1 teaspoon baking powder
  ½ teaspoon baking soda
  ¼ teaspoon salt
  3 large egg whites
  ½ cup granulated sugar
  ⅓ cup packed brown sugar
  ⅓ cup applesauce
  ¼ cup canola oil
  ½ cup chopped walnuts, toasted
Cooking spray

GLAZE:
  ¾ cup powdered sugar
  ½ teaspoon grated lemon rind
  2 tablespoons fresh lemon juice

1. Preheat oven to 350°.
2. To prepare cake, pour ½ cup boiling water over tea bags in a bowl; steep 5 minutes. Remove and discard tea bags; cool tea to room temperature.
3. Lightly spoon flour into dry measuring cups; level with a knife. Combine flour, baking powder, baking soda, and salt, stirring with a whisk.
4. Place egg whites in a large bowl; beat with a mixer at high speed until foamy. Add granulated sugar and brown sugar; beat well. Add brewed tea, applesauce, and canola oil; beat until well blended. Gradually add flour mixture; beat just until moist. Fold in walnuts. Pour batter into an 8 x 4–inch loaf pan coated with cooking spray. Bake at 350° for 50 minutes or until a wooden pick inserted in center comes out clean. Cool in pan 15 minutes on a wire rack; remove from pan. Cool completely on wire rack.
5. To prepare glaze, combine powdered sugar and rind in a small bowl. Add juice, stirring with a whisk until smooth. Drizzle glaze over cake; let stand until set. Yield: 12 servings (serving size: 1 slice).

CALORIES 241 (30% from fat); FAT 8g (sat 1g, mono 1.5g, poly 5.1g); PROTEIN 3.8g; CARB 39.5g; FIBER 1g; CHOL 0mg; IRON 1.3mg; SODIUM 159mg; CALC 37mg

Pfeffernüesse

So named because recipes typically include black pepper, *pfeffernüesse* (fef-ER-nyoos-uh) means "peppernuts" in German. These small spice cookies are known by many different names throughout Europe, where they're a popular treat during the holiday season.

  ¾ cup all-purpose flour (about 3⅓ ounces)
  ½ teaspoon baking powder
  ½ teaspoon ground cinnamon
  ¼ teaspoon salt
  ¼ teaspoon freshly ground black pepper
  ⅛ teaspoon ground nutmeg
  ⅛ teaspoon ground cloves
  ¼ cup butter, softened
  3 tablespoons dark brown sugar
  2 tablespoons granulated sugar
  2 tablespoons water
  1 large egg white
  ¼ cup ground hazelnuts
  1 tablespoon powdered sugar

1. Preheat oven to 350°.
2. Lightly spoon flour into dry measuring cups; level with a knife. Combine flour and next 6 ingredients, stirring well with a whisk.
3. Place butter, brown sugar, and granulated sugar in a large bowl; beat with a mixer at medium speed until well blended (about 4 minutes). Add 2 tablespoons water and egg white to butter mixture; beat well. Add flour mixture and nuts; beat on low speed just until blended. Spoon batter evenly into 18 mounds (about 2 teaspoons each) 2 inches apart on a baking sheet lined with parchment paper.
4. Bake at 350° for 12 minutes or until lightly browned and almost set. Cool on pans 2 minutes. Remove from pans; cool completely on a wire rack. Sprinkle cookies evenly with powdered sugar. Yield: 18 cookies (serving size: 1 cookie).

CALORIES 65 (44% from fat); FAT 3.2g (sat 1.7g, mono 1.1g, poly 0.2g); PROTEIN 0.9g; CARB 8.3g; FIBER 0.3g; CHOL 7mg; IRON 0.4mg; SODIUM 68mg; CALC 13mg

Spiced Pecans

2 tablespoons maple syrup
1 tablespoon Worcestershire sauce
2 teaspoons ancho chile powder
1 teaspoon ground cumin
½ teaspoon salt
½ teaspoon black pepper
2 cups pecan halves

1. Preheat oven to 375°.
2. Combine first 6 ingredients in a large bowl, stirring well. Add nuts to syrup mixture; toss well to coat. Arrange nuts in a single layer on a jelly-roll pan lined with parchment paper. Bake at 375° for 10 minutes or until lightly browned. Cool completely on pan. Yield: 16 servings (serving size: 2 tablespoons).

CALORIES 104 (84% from fat); FAT 9.7g (sat 0.9g, mono 5.7g, poly 3g); PROTEIN 1.3g; CARB 3.8g; FIBER 0.8g; CHOL 0mg; IRON 0.4mg; SODIUM 95mg; CALC 4mg

Dry Jerk Spice Rub

To tame the heat, cut back on the ground red pepper. You can use this rub with pork, chicken, or fish.

1 tablespoon dried parsley
1 tablespoon dried onion flakes
2 to 3 teaspoons ground red pepper
2 teaspoons garlic powder
2 teaspoons ground thyme
2 teaspoons brown sugar
1½ teaspoons kosher salt
1 teaspoon grated fresh nutmeg
1 teaspoon crushed red pepper
1 teaspoon ground allspice
¼ teaspoon freshly ground black pepper
¼ teaspoon ground star anise
¼ teaspoon ground cinnamon

1. Combine all ingredients in a bowl, stirring well. Store in an airtight container up to 4 weeks. Yield: about ½ cup (serving size: about 1 teaspoon).

CALORIES 5 (18% from fat); FAT 0.1g (sat 0.1g, mono 0g, poly 0g); PROTEIN 0.1g; CARB 1g; FIBER 0.3g; CHOL 0mg; IRON 0.2mg; SODIUM 118mg; CALC 5mg

Cranberry-Horseradish Cocktail Sauce

Serve this spicy accompaniment with boiled shrimp. Or spoon it over cream cheese and serve with crackers for a simple appetizer.

1 teaspoon olive oil
1 tablespoon finely chopped shallots
½ teaspoon finely chopped fresh thyme
¾ cup fresh or frozen cranberries, thawed
¼ cup ketchup
1½ tablespoons cranberry juice
1 tablespoon prepared horseradish
¼ teaspoon salt
¼ teaspoon freshly ground black pepper

1. Heat oil in a small nonstick skillet over medium heat. Add shallots and thyme to pan; cook 2 minutes, stirring frequently. Add cranberries; cook 3 minutes or until cranberries pop. Combine cranberry mixture, ketchup and remaining ingredients in a bowl, stirring until well blended. Chill. Yield: 6 servings (serving size: 2 tablespoons).

CALORIES 27 (27% from fat); FAT 0.8g (sat 0.1g, mono 0.6g, poly 0.1g); PROTEIN 0.1g; CARB 5.1g; FIBER 0.7g; CHOL 0mg; IRON 0.1mg; SODIUM 214mg; CALC 5mg

Walnut Brittle

As the sugar mixture cooks, place the prepared jelly-roll pan in a 200° oven for about 10 minutes. This will help the sugar mixture stay warm and pliable so you can spread it quickly and easily. The brittle is a good snack on its own, and we really like it crushed over low-fat vanilla ice cream.

Cooking spray
1 cup sugar
1 cup light-colored corn syrup
½ cup water
1 tablespoon butter
1½ cups coarsely chopped walnuts
1½ teaspoons baking soda
1 teaspoon vanilla extract

1. Line a jelly-roll pan with parchment paper, and coat paper lightly with cooking spray.
2. Combine sugar and next 3 ingredients in a heavy saucepan. Cook over medium heat, stirring until sugar dissolves. Cook 20 minutes or until a candy thermometer registers 275°. Stir in walnuts; cook 2 minutes or until candy thermometer registers 295°, stirring constantly. Remove from heat; stir in baking soda and vanilla (mixture will bubble). Quickly pour mixture onto prepared pan; spread to ¼-inch thickness using a wooden spoon coated with cooking spray. Cool completely; using a wooden spoon, break brittle into bite-sized pieces. Yield: 24 servings (serving size: about 1 ounce).

CALORIES 125 (39% from fat); FAT 5.4g (sat 0.8g, mono 0.8g, poly 3.6g); PROTEIN 1.2g; CARB 19.9g; FIBER 0.5g; CHOL 1mg; IRON 0.2mg; SODIUM 91mg; CALC 9mg

Kumquat Jam

This jam will keep up to three weeks in the refrigerator. Package it in clear canning jars to give with a batch of Banana Bran Scones (page 354).

1½ cups sugar
1 cup Gewürztraminer or other medium-sweet white wine
1 pound fresh kumquats, sliced and seeded (about 3 cups)
1 (3-inch) cinnamon stick

1. Combine sugar and wine in a medium saucepan over medium-high heat; bring to a boil, stirring until sugar dissolves. Add kumquats and cinnamon to pan. Cover, reduce heat, and simmer 45 minutes. Uncover; bring to a boil. Cook until reduced to 2 cups (about 15 minutes). Discard cinnamon stick. Cool. Cover and chill. Yield: 8 servings (serving size: ¼ cup).

CALORIES 94 (2% from fat); FAT 0.2g (sat 0g, mono 0g, poly 0.1g); PROTEIN 0.6g; CARB 23.5g; FIBER 1.8g; CHOL 0mg; IRON 0.3mg; SODIUM 4mg; CALC 19mg

Make Ahead for Company

With our savvy tips, you'll be prepared to entertain both casually and elegantly through the new year.

You may soon be planning a get-together with friends and family to enjoy fun, food, and camaraderie. But cooking and entertaining can sometimes leave you stranded in the kitchen and unable to spend much time with guests. Use these strategies to put wholesome, delicious meals on the table in minimal time—so you, too, can enjoy the party.

Easy Brunch Menu
serves 8

Mushroom, Bacon, and Swiss Strata

Macerated Winter Fruit

Apple-Cinnamon Coffeecake

Coffee and juice

Make-Ahead Strategy

1. Up to three months ahead:
- Bake and freeze coffeecake.

2. The day before:
- Assemble and refrigerate strata.
- Prepare and refrigerate fruit.

3. About an hour ahead:
- Bake strata.

4. Last minute:
- Set out juices and coffee.
- Warm coffeecake.

MAKE AHEAD
Mushroom, Bacon, and Swiss Strata

Breakfast casseroles are ideal for overnight guests. Assemble it the night before, and bake in the morning.

- 12 ounces ciabatta, cut into 1-inch cubes (about 7 cups)
- 2 tablespoons butter
- 2 cups chopped onion
- 2 (8-ounce) packages presliced mushrooms
- Cooking spray
- 1½ cups (6 ounces) shredded reduced-fat Swiss cheese
- 8 slices center-cut bacon, cooked and crumbled
- 3 cups 1% low-fat milk
- 1½ cups egg substitute
- 2 teaspoons chopped fresh thyme
- ½ teaspoon freshly ground black pepper
- ¼ teaspoon salt
- Thyme sprigs (optional)

1. Preheat oven to 350°.

2. Arrange bread in a single layer on a jelly-roll pan. Bake at 350° for 20 minutes or until toasted. Place bread cubes in a large bowl.

3. Melt butter in a large nonstick skillet over medium-high heat. Add onion and mushrooms to pan; sauté 10 minutes or until liquid evaporates and vegetables are tender. Add onion mixture to bread; toss well. Arrange half of bread mixture in a 13 x 9–inch baking dish coated with cooking spray. Sprinkle with half of cheese and half of bacon; top with remaining bread mixture, cheese, and bacon.

4. Combine milk and next 4 ingredients, stirring with a whisk. Pour milk mixture over bread mixture. Cover and refrigerate 8 hours.

5. Preheat oven to 350°.

6. Remove strata from refrigerator; let stand at room temperature 15 minutes. Bake strata, covered, at 350° for 30 minutes. Uncover strata, and bake an additional 15 minutes or until set. Let strata stand 10 minutes before serving. Garnish with thyme sprigs, if desired. Yield: 8 servings.

CALORIES 313 (30% from fat); FAT 10.4g (sat 5g, mono 4.2g, poly 0.8g); PROTEIN 21.7g; CARB 35.5g; FIBER 2.7g; CHOL 25mg; IRON 1.9mg; SODIUM 737mg; CALC 318mg

---

MAKE AHEAD
Macerated Winter Fruit

Acidity in the lemon juice, grapefruit, and pineapple keeps the apple from browning, so you can prepare this colorful side up to a full day in advance.

- 1 cup diced fresh pineapple
- ½ cup apple juice
- 1 tablespoon honey
- 1 (3-inch) cinnamon stick
- 2 cups diced Fuji or Gala apple (about 2 apples)
- 1 cup pink grapefruit sections (about 1 large grapefruit)
- 1 cup seedless red grapes, halved
- ½ cup sweetened dried cranberries
- 1 tablespoon Grand Marnier (orange-flavored liqueur)
- 1 tablespoon fresh lemon juice

1. Combine pineapple, apple juice, honey, and cinnamon stick in a small saucepan over medium heat; cook 2 minutes or until honey dissolves, stirring frequently. Pour into a large bowl. Add apple and remaining ingredients, and toss gently. Cover and refrigerate 1 hour or up to

24 hours. Discard cinnamon stick. Yield: 8 servings (serving size: about ⅔ cup).

CALORIES 98 (3% from fat); FAT 0.3g (sat 0g, mono 0g, poly 0.1g); PROTEIN 0.5g; CARB 25g; FIBER 2.1g; CHOL 0mg; IRON 0.3mg; SODIUM 2mg; CALC 12mg

Apple-Cinnamon Coffeecake

This cake is best served warm. To prepare ahead, cool completely, wrap (still in the pan) in foil, and leave out at room temperature up to one day, or freeze up to three months. To reheat thawed cake, unwrap and bake at 250° for 15 to 20 minutes.

CAKE:

1½ cups all-purpose flour (about 6¾ ounces)
1 cup granulated sugar
1½ teaspoons baking powder
1½ teaspoons ground cinnamon
½ teaspoon salt
¾ cup 1% low-fat milk
2 tablespoons butter, melted
1 teaspoon vanilla extract
1 large egg, lightly beaten
1 cup diced peeled Granny Smith apple (about 1 apple)
Cooking spray

STREUSEL:

¼ cup packed brown sugar
2 tablespoons all-purpose flour
½ teaspoon ground cinnamon
2 tablespoons chilled butter, cut into small pieces

1. Preheat oven to 350°.
2. To prepare cake, lightly spoon 1½ cups flour into dry measuring cups; level with a knife. Combine flour and next 4 ingredients in a large bowl, stirring with a whisk. Make a well in center of mixture. Combine milk and next 3 ingredients, stirring with a whisk; add to flour mixture, stirring just until moist. Fold in apple. Pour batter into an 8-inch square baking pan coated with cooking spray.
3. To prepare streusel, combine brown sugar, 2 tablespoons flour, and ½ teaspoon cinnamon; cut in chilled butter

with a pastry blender or 2 knives until mixture resembles coarse meal. Sprinkle streusel evenly over batter. Bake at 350° for 45 minutes or until a wooden pick inserted in center comes out clean. Cool in pan 10 minutes on a wire rack. Serve warm. Yield: 12 servings (serving size: 1 piece).

CALORIES 197 (21% from fat); FAT 4.6g (sat 2.7g, mono 1.2g, poly 0.3g); PROTEIN 2.9g; CARB 36.7g; FIBER 0.8g; CHOL 28mg; IRON 1.2mg; SODIUM 202mg; CALC 68mg

Casual Dinner with Friends Menu
serves 8
Southwestern Turkey Soup

Chipotle-Cheddar Scones

Tossed salad greens with bottled dressing

Cranberry-Apple Crumble

Beer

Make-Ahead Strategy

1. Up to three months ahead:
• Prepare and freeze soup and scones.
2. Up to two months ahead:
• Prepare and freeze topping for dessert.
3. Up to one day ahead:
• Crush tortilla chips for soup.
• Cut lime wedges.
4. A few hours ahead:
• Chop cilantro for soup.
• Bake dessert.
5. Last minute:
• Reheat soup.
• Dice avocado.
• Toss salad

Southwestern Turkey Soup

If you're making the soup ahead, omit the cilantro until just before serving. Refrigerate up to three days, or freeze up to three months. You can crush the tortilla chips and cut the lime wedges up to a day ahead, but chop the avocado just before serving to keep it green.

2 teaspoons olive oil
1 cup chopped onion
1 cup chopped green bell pepper
3 garlic cloves, minced
1 serrano chile, minced
2 tablespoons all-purpose flour
1 pound turkey tenderloin, cut into bite-sized pieces
2 tablespoons no-salt-added tomato paste
1 teaspoon chili powder
1 teaspoon ground cumin
¼ teaspoon freshly ground black pepper
⅛ teaspoon salt
4 cups fat-free, less-sodium chicken broth
2 bay leaves
1 (14.5-ounce) can diced tomatoes, drained
1 (15-ounce) can pinto beans, rinsed and drained
1 (15-ounce) can black beans, rinsed and drained
1 (11-ounce) can no-salt-added whole-kernel corn, drained
2 tablespoons chopped fresh cilantro
2 cups crushed baked tortilla chips (about 4 ounces)
1 cup diced peeled avocado
8 lime wedges

1. Heat oil in a Dutch oven over medium-high heat. Add onion and next 3 ingredients to pan; sauté 5 minutes or until tender.
2. Place flour in a shallow bowl; dredge turkey in flour. Add turkey to pan; sauté 5 minutes or until browned on all sides. Add tomato paste and next 4 ingredients, stirring to coat. Add broth and next 5 ingredients; bring to a boil. Reduce heat to medium, and cook 15 minutes.
Continued

Remove from heat; discard bay leaves. Stir in cilantro. Ladle soup into bowls. Top with tortilla chips and avocado; serve with lime wedges. Yield: 8 servings (serving size: about 1⅓ cups soup, ¼ cup chips, 2 tablespoons avocado, and 1 lime wedge).

CALORIES 287 (26% from fat); FAT 8.2g (sat 1.2g, mono 3.8g, poly 1.5g); PROTEIN 21.8g; CARB 37.4g; FIBER 7.9g; CHOL 23mg; IRON 3mg; SODIUM 654mg; CALC 80mg

MAKE AHEAD • FREEZABLE
Chipotle-Cheddar Scones

Partner these savory scones with soups and salads. Freeze up to three months.

- 2 cups all-purpose flour (about 9 ounces)
- 1 tablespoon baking powder
- ½ teaspoon salt
- 3 tablespoons chilled butter, cut into small pieces
- ¾ cup fat-free sour cream
- ½ cup (2 ounces) shredded reduced-fat sharp Cheddar cheese
- 1 tablespoon water
- 1 tablespoon minced chipotle chile, canned in adobo sauce
- 1 large egg, lightly beaten
Cooking spray

1. Preheat oven to 350°.
2. Lightly spoon flour into dry measuring cups; level with a knife. Combine flour, baking powder, and salt in a medium bowl, stirring with a whisk. Cut in butter with a pastry blender or 2 knives until mixture resembles coarse meal. Add sour cream and next 4 ingredients; stir just until moist. Knead in bowl with lightly floured hands just until dough forms.
3. Divide dough in half. Shape each half into a 6-inch circle on a baking sheet coated with cooking spray. Cut each circle into 6 wedges; arrange wedges 1 inch apart on pan. Bake at 350° for 20 minutes or until browned. Serve warm. Yield: 12 servings (serving size: 1 scone).

CALORIES 134 (30% from fat); FAT 4.5g (sat 2.6g, mono 0.9g, poly 0.3g); PROTEIN 4.3g; CARB 18.8g; FIBER 0.7g; CHOL 30mg; IRON 1.2mg; SODIUM 320mg; CALC 125mg

Cranberry-Apple Crumble

Pears would also be nice in this homey dessert. Prepare the crumble topping (including cutting in the butter), and freeze up to two months. Sprinkle it—still frozen—over the apple mixture just before you put it in the oven.

FILLING:
- ¼ cup sweetened dried cranberries
- 1 tablespoon fresh lemon juice
- 4 Braeburn apples, peeled, cored, and chopped (about 4 cups)
- Cooking spray

TOPPING:
- ¼ cup all-purpose flour (about 1 ounce)
- 6 tablespoons brown sugar
- 6 tablespoons regular oats
- 1 teaspoon ground cinnamon
- ¼ teaspoon salt
- ⅛ teaspoon ground nutmeg
- 3 tablespoons chilled butter, cut into small pieces

REMAINING INGREDIENT:
- 4 cups vanilla light ice cream

1. Preheat oven to 350°.
2. To prepare filling, combine first 3 ingredients, tossing well. Place apple mixture in an 11 x 7–inch baking dish coated with cooking spray.
3. To prepare topping, lightly spoon flour into a dry measuring cup, and level with a knife. Combine flour and next 5 ingredients, stirring with a whisk. Cut in butter with a pastry blender or 2 knives until mixture resembles coarse meal. Sprinkle butter mixture evenly over apple mixture. Bake at 350° for 30 minutes or until filling is bubbly and topping is golden. Serve with vanilla light ice cream. Yield: 8 servings (serving size: about ½ cup crumble and ½ cup ice cream).

CALORIES 257 (28% from fat); FAT 7.9g (sat 4.7g, mono 2.1g, poly 0.4g); PROTEIN 4.4g; CARB 44.3g; FIBER 1.9g; CHOL 29mg; IRON 0.9mg; SODIUM 157mg; CALC 126mg

Holiday Reception Buffet Menu
serves 12

Onion Frittata Bites

Shrimp Napa Wraps

Creamy Chicken-Mushroom Crepes

Mixed Berry Crepes

White and sparkling wine

Make-Ahead Strategy

1. Up to two months ahead:
- Make and freeze crepes.

2. Up to three days ahead:
- Prepare and refrigerate sauce for shrimp wraps.
- Chill wine.

3. The day before:
- Steam cabbage leaves for shrimp wraps; refrigerate in a zip-top plastic bag.
- Cook and refrigerate noodles, vegetable mixture, and shrimp for shrimp wraps; store separately.
- Bake and refrigerate frittata.
- Prepare and refrigerate fillings for crepes.

4. Last minute:
- Reheat frittata; cut into pieces, and garnish
- Reheat crepes and chicken filling.

Onion Frittata Bites

Sweet caramelized onions and salty Parmesan cheese flavor these bite-sized appetizers.

- 1 teaspoon butter
- 2 cups finely chopped onion
- Cooking spray
- 1 cup egg substitute
- ¼ cup (1 ounce) grated fresh Parmesan cheese, divided
- ½ teaspoon salt
- ½ teaspoon freshly ground black pepper
- 2 large eggs, lightly beaten
- ¼ cup fat-free sour cream
- 48 (1-inch) pieces fresh chives

1. Preheat oven to 350°.
2. Melt butter in a nonstick skillet over medium heat. Add onion to pan; cook 15 minutes or until golden brown, stirring occasionally. Spread mixture in a single layer in an 11 x 7–inch baking dish coated with cooking spray. Combine egg substitute, 2 tablespoons cheese, and next 3 ingredients. Pour egg mixture evenly over onion; sprinkle with remaining 2 tablespoons cheese. Bake at 350° for 20 minutes or until set. Cool slightly; cut into 24 pieces. Top each with ½ teaspoon sour cream and 2 chive pieces. Yield: 12 servings (serving size: 2 pieces).

CALORIES 47 (33% from fat); FAT 1.7g (sat 0.8g, mono 0.5g, poly 0.2g); PROTEIN 4g; CARB 3.9g; FIBER 0.4g; CHOL 38mg; IRON 0.2mg; SODIUM 170mg; CALC 40mg

Shrimp Napa Wraps

Mild-tasting napa cabbage holds the ingredients in this twist on lettuce wraps.

SAUCE:
- ½ cup packed brown sugar
- ½ cup low-sodium soy sauce
- ¼ cup water
- 1 tablespoon dark sesame oil
- ½ teaspoon crushed red pepper
- 1 garlic clove, minced

WRAPS:
- 12 napa (Chinese) cabbage leaves
- 1 tablespoon canola oil
- 1½ cups shredded carrot
- ¾ cup finely chopped red bell pepper
- ¾ cup thinly sliced green onions
- 1 tablespoon minced peeled fresh ginger
- 2 garlic cloves, minced
- 3 tablespoons minced fresh cilantro
- 3 tablespoons chopped fresh basil
- 1½ tablespoons fresh lime juice
- 1½ cups cooked bean threads (cellophane noodles; about 3 ounces uncooked)
- 36 medium shrimp, cooked and peeled (about 1¼ pounds)

Continued

1. To prepare sauce, combine first 6 ingredients in a small saucepan over medium heat; cook until sugar dissolves and sauce is slightly thick (about 5 minutes), stirring frequently. Remove from heat; cover and chill.

2. To prepare wraps, steam cabbage, covered, 2 minutes or until crisp-tender. Drain and rinse with cold water. Drain and pat dry; set aside.

3. Heat canola oil in a large nonstick skillet over medium-high heat. Add carrot and next 4 ingredients to pan; sauté 5 minutes or until tender. Add cilantro, basil, and juice; toss gently. Place about 3 tablespoons vegetable mixture and 2 tablespoons bean threads on each cabbage leaf. Top each with 3 shrimp; roll up. Serve with sauce. Yield: 12 servings (serving size: 1 wrap and about 1½ tablespoons sauce).

CALORIES 151 (19% from fat); FAT 3.2g (sat 0.4g, mono 1.3g, poly 1.2g); PROTEIN 10.6g; CARB 19.7g; FIBER 1.1g; CHOL 72mg; IRON 1.7mg; SODIUM 443mg; CALC 55mg

MAKE AHEAD
Creamy Chicken-Mushroom Crepes

The flavor of applewood-smoked bacon lends depth to the filling. Prepare and refrigerate the filling up to one day ahead; reheat in a large nonstick skillet over medium heat 10 minutes or until thoroughly heated.

    1   slice applewood-smoked bacon, diced
    1   pound skinless, boneless chicken breast, cut into ½-inch pieces
    ¼   cup minced shallots (about 2)
    1   teaspoon chopped fresh thyme
    1   (8-ounce) package presliced mushrooms
    1¼ cups fat-free milk
    1½ tablespoons all-purpose flour
    ½   cup (2 ounces) shredded Gruyère cheese
    2   tablespoons chopped fresh parsley
    ½   teaspoon salt
    ¼   teaspoon freshly ground black pepper
    12 Make-Ahead Crepes (recipe at right)

1. Cook bacon in a large nonstick skillet over medium-high heat until crisp. Remove bacon from pan, reserving 1½ teaspoons drippings in pan; set bacon aside. Add chicken to drippings in pan; sauté 3 minutes or until browned. Add shallots, thyme, and mushrooms; sauté 5 minutes or until tender.

2. Combine milk and flour, stirring with a whisk until well blended. Gradually stir milk mixture into chicken mixture; bring to a boil. Reduce heat, and simmer until thick (about 2 minutes). Remove from heat; stir in bacon, cheese, and next 3 ingredients. Spoon about ¼ cup chicken mixture in center of each Make-Ahead Crepe; roll up. Yield: 12 servings (serving size: 1 filled crepe).

CALORIES 154 (28% from fat); FAT 4.8g (sat 2.2g, mono 1.4g, poly 0.5g); PROTEIN 14.8g; CARB 12.3g; FIBER 0.6g; CHOL 67mg; IRON 1.2mg; SODIUM 248mg; CALC 118mg

MAKE AHEAD • FREEZABLE
Make-Ahead Crepes

Place a stack of cooked, cooled crepes (between layers of wax paper or paper towels) inside a heavy-duty zip-top plastic bag. Refrigerate up to five days, or freeze up to two months.

    2   cups all-purpose flour (about 9 ounces)
    ½   teaspoon salt
    2   cups 2% reduced-fat milk
    1   cup water
    1   tablespoon butter, melted
    4   large eggs
    Cooking spray

1. Lightly spoon flour into dry measuring cups; level with a knife. Combine flour and salt in a medium bowl. Place milk, 1 cup water, butter, and eggs in a blender; process until combined. Add flour mixture to blender; process until smooth. Cover and refrigerate 1 hour.

2. Heat a 10-inch crepe pan or nonstick skillet over medium-high heat. Coat pan lightly with cooking spray. Remove pan from heat. Pour a scant ¼ cup batter into pan; quickly tilt pan in all directions so batter covers pan with a thin film. Cook about 1 minute.

3. Carefully lift edge of crepe with a spatula to test for doneness. The crepe is ready to turn when it can be shaken loose from the pan and underside is lightly browned. Turn crepe over; cook 30 seconds on other side.

4. Place crepe on a towel; cool completely. Repeat procedure with cooking spray and remaining batter, stirring batter between crepes. Stack crepes between single layers of wax paper or paper towels to prevent sticking. Yield: 24 crepes (serving size: 2 crepes).

CALORIES 64 (25% from fat); FAT 1.8g (sat 0.8g, mono 0.6g, poly 0.2g); PROTEIN 2.8g; CARB 9g; FIBER 0.3g; CHOL 38mg; IRON 0.7mg; SODIUM 75mg; CALC 31mg

MAKE AHEAD
Mixed Berry Crepes

Frozen berries make these crepes a year-round treat, not just a seasonal splurge.

    1½ cups frozen unsweetened raspberries, thawed
    1½ cups frozen unsweetened blueberries, thawed
    1   cup sliced frozen unsweetened strawberries, thawed
    ¼   cup granulated sugar
    1   teaspoon cornstarch
    1   tablespoon fresh lemon juice
    6   tablespoons ⅓-less-fat cream cheese, softened
    12 Make-Ahead Crepes (recipe at left)
    1   tablespoon powdered sugar (optional)

1. Combine first 5 ingredients in a saucepan; bring to a boil. Reduce heat; simmer 5 minutes or until thick. Remove from heat; stir in juice. Cool.

2. Spread 1½ teaspoons cream cheese over each Make-Ahead Crepe, and top each with about 2½ tablespoons berry mixture; roll up. Top each crepe with about 2 tablespoons berry mixture. Sift powdered sugar evenly over crepes just before serving, if desired. Yield: 12 servings (serving size: 1 filled crepe).

CALORIES 122 (30% from fat); FAT 4g (sat 2.1g, mono 1.2g, poly 0.4g); PROTEIN 4g; CARB 18.1g; FIBER 1.9g; CHOL 44mg; IRON 0.9mg; SODIUM 108mg; CALC 44mg

Thankful for Leftovers

Problem: A California reader and her spouse grow tired of Thanksgiving leftovers. Strategy: Use new flavors and formats to transform surplus turkey, mashed potatoes, vegetables, and even dinner rolls into compelling dishes.

Kara Lucca, of Martinez, California, is stumped when it comes to planning inventive meals using holiday leftovers.

Kara sought our assistance in turning leftover turkey and other holiday menu items into intriguing new selections for her husband, Joe, and herself. We developed recipes that pair these holiday ingredients with various flavors and applications, which brings fresh life to second-generation dishes so they don't taste like leftovers. With this approach, Kara can ensure that the meals following Thanksgiving will be as tasty as the holiday feast itself.

STAFF FAVORITE
Crisp Mashed Potato Cakes

Cheddar cheese, bacon, and a panko coating make these a satisfying side dish.

Cooking spray
½ cup chopped green onions
2 cups mashed potatoes, chilled
2 tablespoons shredded extrasharp Cheddar cheese
⅛ teaspoon salt
⅛ teaspoon freshly ground black pepper
1 slice center-cut bacon, cooked and crumbled
¾ cup panko (Japanese breadcrumbs)

1. Preheat oven to 425°.
2. Heat a large nonstick skillet over medium heat. Coat pan with cooking spray. Add green onions to pan, and cook 2 minutes or until tender, stirring occasionally. Remove from heat.

3. Place potatoes in a medium bowl. Stir in onions, cheese, and next 3 ingredients. Divide potato mixture into 6 equal portions, shaping each into a ½-inch-thick patty. Place panko in a shallow dish. Dredge patties in panko. Place patties on a baking sheet coated with cooking spray. Bake at 425° for 12 minutes. Carefully turn patties over; bake an additional 12 minutes or until golden. Yield: 6 servings (serving size: 1 potato cake).

CALORIES 122 (16% from fat); FAT 2.2g (sat 1.1g, mono 0.5g, poly 0.1g); PROTEIN 3.6g; CARB 22g; FIBER 2g; CHOL 6mg; IRON 0.3mg; SODIUM 290mg; CALC 40mg

MAKE AHEAD
Cranberry-Apple French Toast Casserole

This prep-ahead casserole is especially welcome if you're entertaining houseguests for the long holiday weekend.

2 tablespoons butter
2 cups diced Granny Smith apple (about 2 apples)
¼ teaspoon ground cinnamon
Dash of ground cloves
¼ cup packed brown sugar, divided
1 pound dinner rolls, quartered
Cooking spray
½ cup sweetened dried cranberries
1¼ cups apple juice
1¼ cups 1% low-fat milk
¾ cup whole-berry cranberry sauce
½ teaspoon grated lemon rind
¼ teaspoon ground nutmeg
6 large eggs, lightly beaten
¼ cup sliced almonds, toasted

1. Preheat oven to 250°.
2. Melt butter in a large nonstick skillet over medium heat. Add apple, cinnamon, and cloves to pan; cook 10 minutes or until lightly browned, stirring frequently. Stir in 2 tablespoons brown sugar; cook 2 minutes or until sugar melts. Remove from heat.
3. Place quartered rolls on a jelly-roll pan; bake at 250° for 15 minutes. Arrange rolls in a 13 x 9–inch baking dish coated with cooking spray. Sprinkle cranberries evenly over rolls; top with

apple mixture. Combine apple juice and next 5 ingredients in a large bowl, stirring with a whisk. Pour egg mixture over roll mixture; sprinkle with remaining 2 tablespoons sugar. Cover and refrigerate overnight.
4. Preheat oven to 350°.
5. Uncover dish; sprinkle with almonds. Bake at 350° for 55 minutes or until golden. Yield: 12 servings.

CALORIES 270 (28% from fat); FAT 8.5g (sat 2.9g, mono 3.6g, poly 1.2g); PROTEIN 7.7g; CARB 41.9g; FIBER 2.4g; CHOL 112mg; IRON 2mg; SODIUM 265mg; CALC 103mg

MAKE AHEAD • FREEZABLE
Turkey Stock

Roasting the bones and vegetables deepens the flavor of the stock.

Bones from a cooked 12-pound turkey
1 peeled carrot, cut in half crosswise
1 celery stalk, cut in half crosswise
½ medium onion, peeled and quartered
4 quarts cold water
⅛ teaspoon black peppercorns
4 thyme sprigs
4 parsley sprigs
1 bay leaf

1. Preheat oven to 425°.
2. Cut turkey carcass into quarters. Place bones, carrot, celery, and onion on a jelly-roll pan or shallow roasting pan. Bake at 425° for 35 minutes, stirring once.
3. Place bones, trimmings, vegetable mixture, 4 quarts cold water, and remaining ingredients in a large stockpot; bring to a boil. Reduce heat, and simmer 3 hours; skim surface occasionally, discarding solids.
4. Strain stock through a sieve into a large bowl; discard solids. Cool stock to room temperature. Cover and chill stock 8 hours or overnight. Skim solidified fat from surface; discard. Yield: 12 cups (serving size: 1 cup).

CALORIES 9 (20% from fat); FAT 0.3g (sat 0.1g, mono 0.1g, poly 0.1g); PROTEIN 1.3g; CARB 0.5g; FIBER 0.1g; CHOL 4mg; IRON 0.2mg; SODIUM 12mg; CALC 15mg

Turkey and Leek Risotto

Homemade stock elevates the quality of this risotto. Fresh sage and thyme stirred in at the end boost the aroma.

- 5½ cups Turkey Stock (page 367)
- 1 tablespoon butter, divided
- 2 teaspoons olive oil, divided
- 3 cups thinly sliced leek (about 3 large)
- ¾ teaspoon salt, divided
- ¼ cup finely chopped shallots
- 1½ cups uncooked Arborio rice or other short-grain rice
- ½ cup dry white wine
- 2 cups chopped cooked turkey (light and dark meat)
- ⅓ cup grated fresh pecorino Romano cheese
- 1½ tablespoons chopped fresh thyme
- 1 tablespoon chopped fresh sage
- ¼ teaspoon freshly ground black pepper

1. Bring Turkey Stock to a simmer in a medium saucepan (do not boil). Keep warm over low heat.
2. Melt 1 teaspoon butter and 1 teaspoon oil in a large saucepan over medium heat. Add leek to pan; cook 7 minutes or until tender, stirring occasionally. Stir in ¼ teaspoon salt. Place leek mixture in a small bowl. Melt 2 teaspoons butter and 1 teaspoon oil in pan. Add shallots to pan; cook 2 minutes or until tender, stirring occasionally. Add rice; cook 2 minutes, stirring constantly. Stir in wine; cook 1 minute or until liquid is nearly absorbed, stirring constantly. Stir in ½ cup stock and ¼ teaspoon salt; cook until liquid is nearly absorbed, stirring constantly. Add remaining stock, ½ cup at a time, stirring constantly until each portion of stock is absorbed before adding the next (about 28 minutes total).
3. Stir in leek mixture and turkey; cook 1 minute or until thoroughly heated. Remove from heat; stir in ¼ teaspoon salt, pecorino Romano cheese, thyme, sage, and pepper. Yield: 6 servings (serving size: 1 cup).

CALORIES 347 (22% from fat); FAT 8.3g (sat 3.5g, mono 2.2g, poly 1.1g); PROTEIN 21.3g; CARB 46.4g; FIBER 3g; CHOL 49mg; IRON 2.4mg; SODIUM 465mg; CALC 139mg

Brussels Sprouts and Rice Gratin

This easy dish puts extra Brussels sprouts to use, though it could also work with leftover broccoli or green beans. Pecans and grated Parmesan provide a cheesy, slightly crunchy topping for this dish. Use Parmigiano-Reggiano cheese instead of Parmesan for even sharper flavor. Serve with roast ham, chicken, or beef.

- 1 tablespoon butter
- 1 cup chopped onion
- 2 garlic cloves, minced
- ¼ cup all-purpose flour (about 1 ounce)
- 2½ cups 1% low-fat milk
- ¼ cup (2 ounces) ⅓-less-fat cream cheese, cubed
- 1 tablespoon country-style Dijon mustard
- ¾ teaspoon salt
- ¼ teaspoon freshly ground black pepper
- 2½ cups cooked long-grain rice
- 2 cups cooked Brussels sprouts, quartered
- Cooking spray
- ½ cup grated fresh Parmesan cheese
- 2 tablespoons chopped pecans

1. Preheat oven to 400°.
2. Melt butter in a large nonstick skillet over medium heat. Add onion and garlic to pan; cook 4 minutes, stirring occasionally. Stir in flour; cook 2 minutes, stirring frequently. Gradually add milk, stirring constantly with a whisk; cook 8 minutes or until mixture thickens, stirring occasionally. Add cream cheese and next 3 ingredients; cook 1 minute or until cheese melts. Stir in rice and Brussels sprouts. Spoon rice mixture into an 11 x 7–inch baking dish coated with cooking spray. Sprinkle with Parmesan cheese and pecans. Bake at 400° for 20 minutes or until bubbly. Yield: 8 servings (serving size: about 1 cup).

CALORIES 208 (32% from fat); FAT 7.5g (sat 3.6g, mono 1.5g, poly 0.7g); PROTEIN 9.1g; CARB 26.9g; FIBER 2.6g; CHOL 17mg; IRON 1.8mg; SODIUM 466mg; CALC 209mg

Turkey Pho

A brothy noodle soup, *pho* (FUH) is a Vietnamese specialty that puts Thanksgiving remainders to use in a refreshingly original way.

    8   cups Turkey Stock (page 367)
    3   tablespoons fish sauce
    2   teaspoons brown sugar
    6   whole cloves
    4   star anise
    1   (3-inch) cinnamon stick,
        broken
    1   (3-inch) piece peeled fresh
        ginger, halved
    4   ounces uncooked wide rice
        stick noodles (banh pho)
        Cooking spray
    1   medium onion, peeled and
        halved
    3   cups shredded cooked
        dark-meat turkey
    2   cups fresh bean sprouts
    ⅓   cup thinly sliced green onions
        (about 2)
    ¼   cup thinly sliced fresh Thai
        basil
    ¼   cup chopped fresh cilantro
    ¼   teaspoon salt
    ½   cup fresh cilantro sprigs
    ½   cup fresh mint sprigs
    6   lime wedges
    1   jalapeño pepper, seeded and
        thinly sliced
        Hoisin sauce (optional)
        Sriracha (hot chile sauce, such as
        Huy Fong; optional)

1. Combine first 7 ingredients in a large stockpot over medium-high heat; bring to a boil. Reduce heat, and simmer 30 minutes. Strain broth through a sieve into a large bowl; discard solids. Return broth to pan; keep warm.
2. Cook noodles according to package directions, omitting salt and fat.
3. Heat a grill pan over medium-high heat. Coat pan with cooking spray. Add onion; cook 8 minutes or until charred on each side. Remove from heat; cool slightly. Cut onion into thin slices; add to broth.
4. Add turkey and next 5 ingredients to broth; bring to a boil. Cook 2 minutes or until thoroughly heated. Place about

½ cup noodles in each of 6 bowls. Ladle about 1⅓ cups broth mixture over each serving. Serve with cilantro, mint, lime wedges, and jalapeño. Serve with hoisin and Sriracha, if desired. Yield: 6 servings.

CALORIES 249 (21% from fat); FAT 5.7g (sat 1.9g, mono 1.3g, poly 1.7g); PROTEIN 24.5g; CARB 24.4g; FIBER 2.5g; CHOL 65mg; IRON 3.5mg; SODIUM 905mg; CALC 82mg

Turkey and Wild Rice Salad

This Thanksgiving-themed salad makes a tasty light lunch or supper option.

    1   cup uncooked wild rice blend
    ⅓   cup leftover whole-berry
         cranberry sauce
    2   tablespoons Turkey Stock
         (page 367)
    1½   tablespoons balsamic vinegar
    ½   teaspoon salt
    ¼   teaspoon freshly ground black
         pepper
    ¼   teaspoon Dijon mustard
    1½   tablespoons extravirgin olive oil
    1½   cups shredded cooked turkey
         (light and dark meat)
    ½   cup diced celery
    ½   cup chopped fresh chives
    ⅓   cup dried cranberries
    ¼   cup chopped fresh parsley
    2   cups trimmed watercress

1. Cook rice according to package directions, omitting salt and fat. Cool.
2. Combine cranberry sauce and next 5 ingredients in a small bowl. Gradually add oil, stirring constantly with a whisk. Add cranberry sauce mixture, turkey, celery, chives, cranberries, and parsley to rice; toss gently to coat. Serve over watercress. Yield: 4 servings (serving size: 1 cup rice mixture and ½ cup watercress).

CALORIES 261 (29% from fat); FAT 8.3g (sat 1.8g, mono 4.3g, poly 1.4g); PROTEIN 17.7g; CARB 28.5g; FIBER 1.7g; CHOL 41mg; IRON 2mg; SODIUM 557mg; CALC 62mg

QUICK & EASY
Turkey Fried Rice

Canned chicken broth will work in place of the Turkey Stock, though the stock will enhance the dish's turkey flavor. Chilling the rice keeps the grains from sticking together as they're reheated. For more spice, add an extra teaspoon of chili garlic sauce.

    ⅓   cup low-sodium soy sauce
    2   tablespoons Turkey Stock
         (page 367)
    1   tablespoon rice vinegar
    2   teaspoons dark sesame oil
    1   teaspoon chili garlic sauce
         (such as Lee Kum Kee)
    ½   teaspoon salt
    ¼   teaspoon freshly ground black
         pepper
    5   teaspoons canola oil
    2   cups shredded green cabbage
    1   cup sliced green onions
    1½   teaspoons minced peeled fresh
         ginger
    5   cups cooked long-grain rice,
         chilled
    4   cups chopped cooked turkey
         (light and dark meat)
    2   cups leftover green peas or
         frozen peas, thawed
    1   cup leftover carrots or frozen
         carrots, thawed
    ⅓   cup chopped fresh cilantro

1. Combine first 7 ingredients in a small bowl, stirring with a whisk until well blended.
2. Heat oil in a large nonstick skillet over medium-high heat. Add cabbage, onions, and ginger to pan; sauté 3 minutes or until tender. Add rice, turkey, peas, and carrots; sauté 3 minutes or until thoroughly heated. Stir in soy mixture; cook 2 minutes. Remove from heat; stir in cilantro. Yield: 6 servings (serving size: about 1½ cups).

CALORIES 456 (22% from fat); FAT 11.1g (sat 2.3g, mono 3.5g, poly 2.8g); PROTEIN 35.5g; CARB 50.4g; FIBER 5.2g; CHOL 72mg; IRON 5.4mg; SODIUM 705mg; CALC 97mg

Turkey-Mushroom Casserole

¼ cup freshly grated Parmesan cheese
2 tablespoons olive oil, divided
2 (1½-ounce) leftover dinner rolls, torn into chunks
1½ cups chopped onion (about 1 large)
1 cup chopped celery
1 teaspoon salt, divided
1 (8-ounce) package presliced cremini mushrooms
2 cups Turkey Stock (page 367), divided
⅔ cup 1% low-fat milk
⅓ cup all-purpose flour (about 1½ ounces)
3 cups chopped cooked turkey (light and dark meat)
1 cup leftover peas or frozen peas, thawed
1½ tablespoons chopped fresh thyme
½ teaspoon freshly ground black pepper
Cooking spray

1. Preheat oven to 350°.
2. Place Parmesan cheese, 1 tablespoon oil, and bread in a small food processor; pulse 10 times or until coarse crumbs measure 1½ cups.
3. Heat 1 tablespoon olive oil in a medium Dutch oven over medium heat. Add onion and celery to pan; cook 6 minutes or until tender, stirring occasionally. Stir in ¼ teaspoon salt. Add mushrooms; cook 5 minutes or until brown, stirring occasionally. Add ½ cup Turkey Stock to pan. Combine milk and flour in a small bowl, stirring with a whisk until blended. Add milk mixture to pan, stirring constantly. Gradually add remaining 1½ cups Turkey Stock and ½ teaspoon salt; cook 8 minutes or until mixture thickens. Stir in ¼ teaspoon salt, turkey, and next 3 ingredients; cook 2 minutes or until thoroughly heated.
4. Spoon turkey mixture into a 13 x 9–inch baking dish coated with cooking spray. Sprinkle breadcrumb mixture evenly over top of turkey mixture. Bake at 350° for 25 minutes or until filling is bubbly. Yield: 6 servings (serving size: about 1 cup).

CALORIES 303 (29% from fat); FAT 9.7g (sat 2.5g, mono 4.3g, poly 1.4g); PROTEIN 29.1g; CARB 24.5g; FIBER 3.3g; CHOL 54mg; IRON 2.6mg; SODIUM 634mg; CALC 170mg

reader recipes
Taste of the Season

A Maryland freelance writer fine-tunes her best cake.

Anne M. Kotchek, a freelance editor and writer from Rockville, Maryland, started making Ginger Cake in the late 1980s when she craved more flavor from her numerous gingerbread and ginger cake recipes. First, she pumped up the spices. And she added molasses to her original recipe to underscore the overall flavor and add iron content.

She also gave the recipe a nutritional makeover. She was able to cut the oil to two tablespoons by using applesauce, which lends flavor and moisture to the cake, as a replacement. She also incorporated flaxseed meal and wheat germ to increase the amount of fiber, protein, and calcium in each serving.

Choice Ingredient: Ground Ginger

Chopped or grated, fresh ginger gives subtle sweetness to many Asian, Indian, and Caribbean dishes. However, sometimes processed versions of this ingredient, like ground and powdered ginger, work well in applications that require ginger's peppery flavor to infuse every bite of a dish—cookies, cakes, quick breads. As with dried herbs, use less ground ginger than fresh in recipes—as much as six to eight times less. Because powdered ginger loses its potency quickly, buy only a small quantity and keep it tightly sealed in a cool, dry, dark location.

Ginger Cake

"I like to experiment making moist, delicious low-fat desserts. This one also happens to be nutritious, with applesauce, flaxseed meal, and wheat germ."

—Anne M. Kotchek, Rockville, Maryland

½ cup granulated sugar
½ cup applesauce
2 tablespoons canola oil
2 large eggs
1 cup molasses
1½ cups all-purpose flour (about 6¾ ounces)
½ cup flaxseed meal
½ cup toasted wheat germ
2 teaspoons baking soda
½ to 1 teaspoon ground cinnamon
½ to 1 teaspoon ground cloves
½ to 1 teaspoon ground ginger
¼ teaspoon salt
1 cup hot water
Cooking spray
1 tablespoon powdered sugar (optional)
Apple slices (optional)

1. Preheat oven to 350°.
2. Combine first 3 ingredients in a large bowl; beat with a mixer at medium speed until well blended (about 1 minute). Add eggs, 1 at a time, beating well after each addition. Stir in molasses.
3. Lightly spoon flour into dry measuring cups; level with a knife. Combine flour and next 7 ingredients in a large bowl. Add flour mixture and 1 cup hot water alternately to sugar mixture, beginning and ending with flour mixture. Spoon batter into a 13 x 9–inch baking pan coated with cooking spray. Bake at 350° for 30 minutes or until a wooden pick inserted in center comes out clean. Cool in pan. Cut into 12 squares; sprinkle with powdered sugar, and serve with apple, if desired. Yield: 12 servings (serving size: 1 square).

CALORIES 253 (22% from fat); FAT 6.1g (sat 0.7g, mono 2.2g, poly 2.7g); PROTEIN 4.8g; CARB 46.1g; FIBER 2.6g; CHOL 35mg; IRON 2.9mg; SODIUM 284mg; CALC 81mg

Chocolate-Filled Buns

"I decided to create something that has the best of all worlds: easy to make, whole wheat, soft dough, and, most importantly, chocolate. I like to chill the chocolate before shaping the buns so it doesn't melt while I'm working with it."

—Christina Erickson,
Los Banos, California

1½ cups whole wheat flour (about 7 ounces)
¼ cup sugar
1½ teaspoons salt
2 packages quick-rise yeast (about 4½ teaspoons)
¾ cup fat-free milk
½ cup water
2 tablespoons butter
2 tablespoons canola oil
1 large egg, lightly beaten
2¼ cups bread flour (about 10½ ounces)
Cooking spray
3½ ounces semisweet chocolate, chopped
1 large egg white, lightly beaten

1. Lightly spoon whole wheat flour into dry measuring cups; level with a knife. Combine whole wheat flour, sugar, salt, and yeast in a large bowl, stirring well with a whisk.
2. Combine milk, ½ cup water, butter, and oil in a microwave-safe bowl; microwave at HIGH 2 minutes, stirring every 30 seconds until mixture is warm (100° to 110°). Add milk mixture to flour mixture; stir 1 minute. Add egg; stir 1 minute. Lightly spoon bread flour into dry measuring cups; level with a knife. Add bread flour to yeast mixture; stir until a soft dough forms. Turn mixture out onto a lightly floured surface; knead 2 minutes.
3. Place dough in a large bowl coated with cooking spray; lightly coat top of dough with cooking spray. Cover and refrigerate overnight.
4. Preheat oven to 375°.
5. Turn dough out onto a lightly floured work surface, and punch down. Divide dough into 16 equal portions; shape each portion into a ball. Working with one ball at a time (cover remaining dough to prevent drying), roll dough into a 5-inch circle. Place about 1½ teaspoons chocolate in the center of circle. Roll up dough tightly, jelly-roll fashion; pinch seams to seal. Place buns, seam sides down, on a baking sheet lightly coated with cooking spray. Tuck ends under.
6. Lightly coat buns with cooking spray; cover and let rise in a warm place (85°), free from drafts, 40 minutes or until doubled in size. Lightly brush tops of buns with egg white.
7. Bake at 375° for 17 minutes or until lightly browned. Cool on a wire rack. Yield: 16 servings (serving size: 1 bun).

CALORIES 194 (28% from fat); FAT 6.1g (sat 2.5g, mono 1.6g, poly 0.8g); PROTEIN 5.5g; CARB 29.9g; FIBER 2.6g; CHOL 18mg; IRON 1.7mg; SODIUM 245mg; CALC 24mg

---

Mexican Riviera Dinner Menu
serves 4

Refresh your palate from holiday fare with this meal inspired by the Baja Coast.

Southwest Cilantro Fish Stew

Jícama-orange salsa with chips*

Margaritas

*Combine 1½ cups chopped orange sections, 1 cup diced peeled jícama, ⅓ cup diced red onion, 2 tablespoons chopped fresh cilantro, 2 tablespoons fresh lime juice, 1 tablespoon minced seeded jalapeño pepper, ¼ teaspoon salt, and ¼ teaspoon freshly ground black pepper. Serve with baked tortilla chips.

Southwest Cilantro Fish Stew

"I developed this stew using Mexican ingredients I grew up with. I often use cod because my husband loves it. He asked me to create a good recipe for fish stew with some spice."

—Diana Rios, Lytle, Texas

1 tablespoon olive oil
2 cups chopped onion
1 cup (¼-inch-thick) slices carrot
1 cup (¼-inch-thick) slices celery
3 garlic cloves, minced
1 jalapeño pepper, sliced
4 cups fat-free, less-sodium chicken broth
2 cups cubed peeled Yukon gold or red potato
1 cup dry white wine
½ cup chopped fresh cilantro
1 (15-ounce) can crushed tomatoes, undrained
1 pound halibut, cut into bite-sized pieces
½ pound peeled and deveined large shrimp
Lime wedges
Cilantro sprigs (optional)

1. Heat oil in a large Dutch oven over medium-high heat. Add onion and next 4 ingredients to pan; sauté 5 minutes or until tender. Stir in broth and next 4 ingredients; bring to a boil. Reduce heat, and simmer 15 minutes or until potato is tender. Add fish and shrimp; cook an additional 5 minutes or until fish and shrimp are done. Ladle 2½ cups stew into each of 4 bowls; serve with lime wedges. Garnish with cilantro sprigs, if desired. Yield: 4 servings.

CALORIES 372 (18% from fat); FAT 7.6g (sat 1.2g, mono 3.6g, poly 1.8g); PROTEIN 42.1g; CARB 32.8g; FIBER 5.7g; CHOL 122mg; IRON 5.4mg; SODIUM 684mg; CALC 167mg

Thai Chicken Chowder

"Light coconut milk gives this soup a rich flavor, and the sweet potato and chicken make it filling."

—Margee Berry, Trout Lake, Washington

    2 teaspoons olive oil
1½ cups (½-inch) cubed peeled sweet potato
1¼ cups chopped green onions, divided
    1 cup chopped red bell pepper
    1 cup chopped celery
⅔ cup snow peas, cut into ½-inch pieces
    3 tablespoons minced peeled fresh lemongrass
1½ teaspoons minced peeled fresh ginger
    2 garlic cloves, minced
    2 (14-ounce) cans fat-free, less-sodium chicken broth
1½ cups chopped cooked chicken breast
    2 tablespoons fresh lime juice
    1 teaspoon chili garlic sauce (such as Lee Kum Kee)
    1 (14-ounce) can light coconut milk
    3 tablespoons chopped fresh cilantro
    6 lime wedges

1. Heat oil in a Dutch oven over medium heat. Add potato, 1 cup onions, pepper, celery, and peas to pan; cook 8 minutes, stirring frequently. Add lemongrass, ginger, and garlic; cook 1 minute, stirring frequently. Stir in broth; bring to a boil. Cover, reduce heat, and simmer 10 minutes. Add chicken and next 3 ingredients; cook 1 minute or until thoroughly heated. Ladle chowder into bowls. Sprinkle with remaining ¼ cup onions and cilantro; serve with lime wedges. Yield: 6 servings (serving size: 1⅓ cups chowder and 1 lime wedge).

CALORIES 211 (30% from fat); FAT 7.1g (sat 3.8g, mono 1.9g, poly 0.7g); PROTEIN 20.9g; CARB 15.8g; FIBER 3.4g; CHOL 48mg; IRON 1.9mg; SODIUM 346mg; CALC 58mg

Spicy Beef and Barley Soup

"If you like spicy food, increase the crushed red pepper. If you don't like things hot, just cut back. This is a great dish to come home to on a work night."

—Amy Burroughs, Milwaukie, Oregon

    2 teaspoons canola oil
    1 (1½-pound) eye-of-round steak, cut into 1-inch pieces
¾ teaspoon freshly ground black pepper
¼ teaspoon salt
1½ cups sliced onion
    2 cups (½-inch-thick) slices carrot
    2 cups sliced mushrooms (about 8 ounces)
½ cup chopped red bell pepper
    2 garlic cloves, minced
    6 cups fat-free, less-sodium beef broth
½ cup uncooked pearl barley
    2 tablespoons chopped fresh basil
½ teaspoon crushed red pepper
    1 (14.5-ounce) can diced tomatoes, undrained
    1 thyme sprig

1. Heat canola oil in a large nonstick skillet over medium-high heat. Sprinkle beef evenly on all sides with black pepper and salt. Add beef and onion to pan; sauté 5 minutes, turning to brown beef on all sides. Remove beef mixture from pan; place in an electric slow cooker.
2. Add carrot and mushrooms to pan; sauté 5 minutes. Add bell pepper and garlic; sauté 2 minutes. Add carrot mixture, broth, and remaining ingredients to slow cooker; stir well. Cover and cook on HIGH 1 hour. Reduce heat to LOW; cook 6 hours. Discard thyme. Yield: 6 servings (serving size: 1⅔ cups).

CALORIES 319 (32% from fat); FAT 11.5g (sat 3.9g, mono 5g, poly 1.1g); PROTEIN 30.4g; CARB 23.3g; FIBER 5.9g; CHOL 46mg; IRON 3.2mg; SODIUM 725mg; CALC 63mg

Curried Chickpea Dip with Pita Toasts

"This dip was inspired by traditional nachos with beans and corn chips. For my version, I prepared chickpeas with Indian seasonings, such as curry powder, ground cumin, and mango chutney, and then served them with toasted pita wedges."

—Kayla Capper, Ojai, California

    4 (6-inch) pitas, split in half horizontally
Cooking spray
½ teaspoon garlic powder
    1 teaspoon canola oil
    1 cup chopped onion
½ cup raisins
½ cup chopped fresh cilantro
½ cup frozen green peas, thawed
    2 tablespoons mango chutney
¾ teaspoon curry powder
½ teaspoon ground cinnamon
¼ teaspoon ground cumin
¼ teaspoon freshly ground black pepper
    1 (15-ounce) can no-salt-added chickpeas (garbanzo beans), drained
    1 (16-ounce) jar organic salsa

1. Preheat oven to 400°.
2. Cut each pita half into 8 wedges to form 64 wedges. Arrange wedges in a single layer on a baking sheet. Lightly coat wedges with cooking spray; sprinkle evenly with garlic powder. Bake at 400° for 7 minutes or until lightly browned and crisp.
3. Heat oil in a large saucepan over medium-high heat. Add onion to pan; sauté 4 minutes or until lightly browned. Stir in raisins and remaining 9 ingredients. Reduce heat, and simmer 10 minutes or until slightly thick. Serve with pita chips. Yield: 8 servings (serving size: 8 pita chips and 6 tablespoons chickpea mixture).

CALORIES 190 (7% from fat); FAT 1.4g (sat 0.1g, mono 0.6g, poly 0.4g); PROTEIN 6.4g; CARB 38.1g; FIBER 3.1g; CHOL 0mg; IRON 2.9mg; SODIUM 358mg; CALC 48mg

enlightened cook

Native Flavors

Chef Andrew Brown of Philadelphia's White Dog Cafe creates an annual feast showcasing ingredients enjoyed at America's first Thanksgiving celebration.

This marks the 15th year Philadelphia's White Dog Cafe has hosted its Native American Thanksgiving dinner. A Philly tradition, the event features a menu using ingredients introduced by Native Americans and speakers from various tribes.

Fresh ingredients, well researched and well prepared, are part of the dinner's attraction. As Executive Chef Andrew Brown shops for the meal, he says, "I'm looking for the same things cooks sought for that first Thanksgiving. We want the freshest ingredients to liven up every bite."

In his research with food historians, Brown found that some common modern holiday items such as potatoes or sweet potatoes (not yet introduced to the pilgrims' New England) and cranberry sauce (cranberries were available; sugar wasn't) likely weren't on the first Thanksgiving table. The first menu may have included venison or duck but also featured ingredients that remain traditional today, such as pumpkin, squash, and oysters.

QUICK & EASY • MAKE AHEAD
Butternut Squash and Apple Relish

Brown suggests using an heirloom variety of apple in this dish, if available. Also, we found Fuji apples work well. Serve with turkey, duck, or pork. At the White Dog Cafe, Brown also serves this raw relish with smoked salmon.

1 cup diced peeled butternut squash
1 cup diced Gala apple
2 tablespoons honey
1 tablespoon sherry vinegar

1. Combine all ingredients. Let stand 1 hour. Yield: 2 cups (serving size: 2 tablespoons).

CALORIES 20 (0% from fat); FAT 0g; PROTEIN 0.2g; CARB 5.2g; FIBER 0.5g; CHOL 0mg; IRON 0.1mg; SODIUM 12mg; CALC 8mg

Grilled Honey and Chile-Glazed Duck Breast

New Mexican chile powder serves as the White Dog's nod to southwestern Native Americans. Serve with Butternut Squash and Apple Relish (recipe at left), roasted sweet potatoes, and haricots verts.

2 tablespoons Chimayo or New Mexican chile powder
1½ tablespoons cider vinegar
1½ tablespoons honey
4 (6-ounce) boneless duck breast halves, skinned
Cooking spray
¼ teaspoon salt
¼ teaspoon freshly ground black pepper

1. Combine first 3 ingredients in a small bowl; stir until blended. Combine chile powder mixture and duck in a large zip-top plastic bag. Seal and marinate in refrigerator 2 hours, turning bag occasionally. Remove duck from bag; discard marinade.
2. Heat a grill pan over medium-high heat. Coat pan with cooking spray. Sprinkle duck breast halves with salt and pepper. Add duck to pan; cook 5 minutes on each side or until desired degree of doneness. Yield: 4 servings (serving size: 1 breast half).

CALORIES 204 (14% from fat); FAT 3.2g (sat 0.7g, mono 1.1g, poly 0.5g); PROTEIN 35.3g; CARB 6.7g; FIBER 0.1g; CHOL 182mg; IRON 5.8mg; SODIUM 402mg; CALC 13mg

WINE NOTE: This duck is tailor made for a powerful but thickly soft red that can cushion the bird's sweet spiciness. Try a top Argentinian malbec, such as the mouth-filling Otello Malbec 2005 from Mendoza ($16).

Roasted Pumpkin and Winter Squash Soup

Pumpkin and squash were commonly available to Native Americans and pilgrim settlers. Use a small cheese pumpkin or sugar pumpkin.

2 cups (½-inch) cubed peeled fresh pumpkin (about 2 pounds)
2 cups (½-inch) cubed peeled butternut squash (about 1½ pounds)
1 tablespoon olive oil
Cooking spray
3 cups sliced yellow onion (about 2)
2 teaspoons minced garlic
4 cups water
¾ teaspoon salt
¼ teaspoon ground cumin
¼ teaspoon ground cinnamon
¼ teaspoon freshly ground black pepper
Dash of ground allspice

1. Preheat oven to 400°.
2. Combine first 3 ingredients in a large bowl; toss well. Place pumpkin mixture on a baking sheet coated with cooking spray. Bake at 400° for 30 minutes or until tender.
3. Heat a large Dutch oven over medium-high heat. Coat pan with cooking spray. Add onion; sauté 8 minutes or until tender. Add garlic; sauté 1 minute. Add pumpkin mixture, 4 cups water, and remaining ingredients; bring to a boil. Reduce heat, and simmer 20 minutes.
4. Place half of pumpkin mixture in a blender. Remove center piece of lid (to allow steam to escape); secure lid on blender. Place a clean towel over opening in lid (to avoid splatters). Blend until smooth. Pour into a large bowl. Repeat procedure with remaining pumpkin mixture. Yield: 8 servings (serving size: 1 cup).

CALORIES 121 (19% from fat); FAT 2.5g (sat 0.4g, mono 1.7g, poly 0.3g); PROTEIN 2.8g; CARB 25.4g; FIBER 4.6g; CHOL 0mg; IRON 1.9mg; SODIUM 299mg; CALC 92mg

Smoky Seitan, Pinto Bean, and Hominy Stew

Brown serves this satisfying vegetarian stew in roasted, seeded acorn squash halves. This dish provides nearly a day's allowance of protein, most of it from seitan, also known as wheat gluten. Chipotle chile powder lends wonderful smoky flavor. Hominy is a traditional Native American ingredient.

1   tablespoon canola oil
1½ cups diced white onion (about
      1 large)
1   cup diced celery (about 2 stalks)
¾   cup diced carrot (about 1 large)
1   cup diced green bell pepper
      (about 1)
1   teaspoon minced garlic
2   cups organic vegetable broth
      (such as Swanson Certified
      Organic)
1   teaspoon chili powder
½   teaspoon salt
½   teaspoon chipotle chile powder
1   (28-ounce) can diced tomatoes,
      undrained
1   pound seitan, cubed
1   (15.5-ounce) can white hominy,
      rinsed and drained
1   (15-ounce) can pinto beans,
      rinsed and drained

1. Heat oil in a Dutch oven over medium-high heat. Add onion and next 4 ingredients to pan; sauté 5 minutes. Add broth and remaining ingredients to pan; bring to a boil. Reduce heat, and simmer 15 minutes or until vegetables are tender. Yield: 8 servings (serving size: 1 cup).

CALORIES 319 (10% from fat); FAT 3.5g (sat 0.4g, mono 1.3g, poly 1.3g); PROTEIN 46g; CARB 27.2g; FIBER 5.2g; CHOL 0mg; IRON 4.1mg; SODIUM 488mg; CALC 128mg

lighten up
Picks from the Pumpkin Patch

The popular gourd takes the spotlight in three trimmed-down baked goods.

Michelle Sammons, of New York City, loves this combination of cheesecake and pumpkin pie with a buttery crust in Pumpkin Cheesecake Bars. She knew the recipe desperately needed a culinary makeover, and so sent the recipe to our Test Kitchens for tinkering.

We tackled the crust first with the goal of maintaining the rich, nutty base. We reduced the butter to eight teaspoons, shaving 60 calories and seven grams of fat per square. With modest reductions in the flour and sugar, we trimmed another 30 calories per serving. Toasting the flour provided a nutty flavor and allowed for a deep brown-colored crust similar to the original recipe. For the filling, we combined fat-free and ⅓-less-fat cream cheese, which saved 66 calories and nine grams of fat per piece. We also combined egg substitute and whole eggs for a creamier consistency and dropped 72 calories, eight grams of fat, and 636 milligrams of cholesterol from the recipe. Since the nuts added excessive calories and fat, we cut the pecans to a healthful quarter cup and used the nuts as part of the crumb topping for extra nut presence. We added a bit more pumpkin and drained it, allowing for a more intense pumpkin flavor.

BEFORE	AFTER
SERVING SIZE	
1 bar	
CALORIES PER SERVING	
539	288
FAT	
31.7g	9.3g
PERCENT OF TOTAL CALORIES	
53%	29%

Pumpkin Cheesecake Bars

This dessert combines the spicy flavors of a pumpkin pie with the creamy richness of a cheesecake.

CRUST:
1½ cups all-purpose flour
      (6¾ ounces)
½   cup packed brown sugar
⅛   teaspoon salt
8   teaspoons chilled butter, cut
      into small pieces
Cooking spray

FILLING:
1¼ cups canned unsweetened
      pumpkin
½   cup granulated sugar
½   cup packed dark brown sugar
1   (8-ounce) package fat-free
      cream cheese, softened
1   (8-ounce) package ⅓-less-fat
      cream cheese, softened
¾   cup egg substitute
1   teaspoon ground cinnamon
1½ teaspoons vanilla extract
¼   teaspoon ground allspice
1   large egg

REMAINING INGREDIENTS:
¼   cup chopped pecans
2   teaspoons water

1. Preheat oven to 350°.
2. To prepare crust, lightly spoon flour into dry measuring cups; level with a knife. Heat a nonstick skillet over medium-high heat. Add flour to pan; cook 5 minutes or until light brown, stirring frequently. Remove pan from heat. Transfer flour to a bowl; cool completely.
3. Place cool flour, ½ cup brown sugar, and salt in a food processor; pulse 5 times or until combined. Add chilled butter; pulse until mixture resembles fine meal. Press 1 cup flour mixture evenly into bottom of a 13 x 9–inch baking dish coated with cooking spray; reserve remaining flour mixture. Bake at 350° for 10 minutes or until crust is lightly browned.

4. To prepare filling, spread pumpkin in an even layer on several layers of paper towels; cover with additional paper towels. Let stand 5 minutes.

5. Combine granulated sugar, ½ cup dark brown sugar, and cream cheeses in a bowl. Beat with an electric mixer at medium speed 2 minutes or until smooth. Scrape pumpkin into bowl using a rubber spatula. Add egg substitute and next 4 ingredients; beat until smooth. Scrape batter into baked crust.

6. Combine reserved flour mixture and pecans in a small bowl; sprinkle with 2 teaspoons water. Squeeze handfuls of topping to form large pieces. Crumble over filling. Bake at 350° for 40 minutes or until filling is firmly set. Remove from heat; cool in pan on a wire rack to room temperature. Cut into 12 bars. Serve at room temperature. Yield: 12 servings (serving size: 1 bar).

CALORIES 288 (29% from fat); FAT 9.3g (sat 4.8g, mono 3.1g, poly 0.9g); PROTEIN 8.9g; CARB 42.9g; FIBER 1.5g; CHOL 39mg; IRON 2mg; SODIUM 276mg; CALC 86mg

---

Pumpkin Pointers

- Use plain, unsweetened canned pumpkin for these recipes.
- One (15- or 16-ounce) can of pumpkin is equal to about 2 cups.
- You can substitute fresh pumpkin in our recipes. Preheat oven to 375°. Remove stem from pumpkin; cut in half crosswise. Scoop out seeds and membranes. Coat cut sides and inside of pumpkin with cooking spray. Bake, cut sides down, on a baking sheet coated with cooking spray at 375° for 1½ hours or until flesh is tender. Let cool. Scoop out flesh; puree in a food processor. Drain pulp in a colander lined with heavy-duty paper towels to remove excess liquid.

A longtime friend shared the recipe for Pecan-Topped Pumpkin Bread with Margo "Marge" Patterson, of Milton, Florida, more than 20 years ago, and she has been baking it for bridge parties since. She loves the buttery taste and tender texture the flavored popcorn oil brings to the bread. Patterson also likes to bake the bread in mini–loaf pans to share with friends and family as tasty holiday gifts.

To reduce the quick bread's fat and calories without compromising the appealing texture, we replaced half of the oil with buttermilk and trimmed the sugar by a third. We also used mild-flavored canola oil instead of flavored oil to highlight the pumpkin and warm spices. These changes cut 68 calories and 4.6 grams of fat per slice. Using egg substitute in place of two whole eggs maintained the moist quality of the original but eliminated half the cholesterol per serving. We reduced the amount of nuts by two-thirds cup, dropping 23 calories and two grams of fat per slice. To compensate and emphasize the nut flavor, we topped the bread with pecans instead of stirring them into the batter.

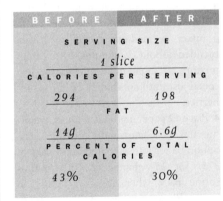

BEFORE	AFTER
SERVING SIZE	
1 slice	
CALORIES PER SERVING	
294	198
FAT	
14g	6.6g
PERCENT OF TOTAL CALORIES	
43%	30%

Pecan-Topped Pumpkin Bread

This recipe makes two loaves. Freeze the extra bread, tightly wrapped in plastic wrap, up to one month. Omit the nuts or substitute chopped walnuts, if you prefer. Check the bread after 50 minutes of baking—you may need to cover the loaves with aluminum foil for the last 10 minutes to prevent overbrowning.

3⅓ cups all-purpose flour (about 15 ounces)
1 tablespoon baking powder
2 teaspoons baking soda
1 teaspoon salt
1 teaspoon ground cinnamon
1 teaspoon ground nutmeg
½ teaspoon ground allspice
2 cups sugar
½ cup egg substitute
½ cup canola oil
½ cup low-fat buttermilk
2 large eggs
⅔ cup water
1 (15-ounce) can pumpkin
Cooking spray
⅓ cup chopped pecans

1. Preheat oven to 350°.
2. Lightly spoon flour into dry measuring cups; level with a knife. Combine flour and next 6 ingredients in a bowl.
3. Place sugar and next 4 ingredients in a large bowl; beat with a mixer at high speed until well blended. Add ⅔ cup water and pumpkin, beating at low speed until blended. Add flour mixture to pumpkin mixture, beating at low speed just until combined. Spoon batter into 2 (9 x 5–inch) loaf pans coated with cooking spray. Sprinkle pecans evenly over batter. Bake at 350° for 1 hour or until a wooden pick inserted in center comes out clean. Cool 10 minutes in pans on a wire rack; remove from pans. Cool completely on wire rack. Yield: 2 loaves; 12 servings per loaf (serving size: 1 slice).

CALORIES 198 (30% from fat); FAT 6.6g (sat 0.7g, mono 3.6g, poly 1.9g); PROTEIN 3.4g; CARB 32.3g; FIBER 1.2g; CHOL 18mg; IRON 1.4mg; SODIUM 287mg; CALC 53mg

When Heather McRae, of Jacksonville, Florida, found the tasty-looking recipe for Pumpkin-Cranberry Muffins online, she thought it might make an ideal breakfast for her on-the-go lifestyle. When she made the recipe, the earthy pumpkin, warm spices, and dried cranberries seemed like a hit.

McRae loved the tender crumb and how sweetened cranberries temper the pungent spices, but two large eggs and one-half cup oil put these muffins out of nutritional bounds.

Cutting six tablespoons of oil from the original recipe saved 60 calories and six grams of fat per muffin, which had the biggest nutritional impact. The heavy version's one-and-a-half cups of sugar yielded a lovely texture at the cost of almost 100 calories per muffin. We reduced the sugar to one cup and added a bit of brown sugar for extra richness, trimming another 18 calories per muffin. One large egg, instead of the original's two, offered sufficient structure and tenderness. This change halved the cholesterol in each muffin. We slightly bumped up the amount of cranberries to offer more balanced sweet-tart flavors.

BEFORE	AFTER
SERVING SIZE	
1 muffin	
CALORIES PER SERVING	
277	199
FAT	
10.7g	3.2g
PERCENT OF TOTAL CALORIES	
35%	14%

MAKE AHEAD • FREEZABLE

Pumpkin-Cranberry Muffins

These moist muffins get a burst of sweet and sour notes from the cranberries.

1½   cups all-purpose flour (about 6¾ ounces)
1   teaspoon baking soda
¾   teaspoon ground ginger
½   teaspoon baking powder
½   teaspoon ground cinnamon
¼   teaspoon salt
⅛   teaspoon ground cloves
1   cup granulated sugar
1   cup canned pumpkin
½   cup low-fat buttermilk
¼   cup packed light brown sugar
2   tablespoons canola oil
1   large egg
⅔   cup sweetened dried cranberries, chopped (such as Craisins)
Cooking spray

1. Preheat oven to 375°.
2. Lightly spoon flour into dry measuring cups; level with a knife. Combine flour and next 6 ingredients; stir well with a whisk.
3. Combine granulated sugar and next 5 ingredients in a large bowl; beat with a mixer at medium speed until well blended (about 3 minutes). Add flour mixture to sugar mixture; beat at low speed just until combined. Fold in cranberries.
4. Place 12 paper muffin cup liners in muffin cups; coat liners with cooking spray. Spoon batter into prepared cups. Bake at 375° for 25 minutes or until muffins spring back when touched lightly in center. Remove muffins from pan immediately; place on a wire rack. Yield: 1 dozen (serving size: 1 muffin).

CALORIES 199 (14% from fat); FAT 3.2g (sat 0.4g, mono 1.6g, poly 0.9g); PROTEIN 2.8g; CARB 41.1g; FIBER 1.5g; CHOL 18mg; IRON 1.3mg; SODIUM 195mg; CALC 38mg

menu of the month
Open House Buffet

Serve guests a warm welcome with a sideboard laden with wintry favorites.

Open House Buffet Menu
serves 12

Beer-Cheddar Soup

Apricot and Sherry-Glazed Ham

Truffled Parsnip Puree

Sage Dinner Rolls

Orange Bizcochitos

Pyramid Apricot Weizen

Gewürztraminer

WINE NOTE: With the ham's bold apricot and clove presence, plus the soup's vibrant beer and Cheddar flavors, one wine is going to have to work hard to cover all the bases. But Gewürztraminer does the trick. Bold and sassy, Gewürztraminer mimics the apricot and clove and has enough body to stand up to the richness of the Cheddar and beer. Gewürztraminer will even be a great match for the orange cookies. The best Gewürztraminers in the world come from Alsace, France. Try Hugel Gewürztraminer 2005 ($23).

BEER NOTE: While basic pale ale is a classic choice with Cheddar, the fruity elements of the apricot-glazed ham and Orange Bizcochitos will be enhanced by a fruit beer. Many microbrewers are combining malt with the fresh flavors of apple, cherry, and even apricot. Pyramid Apricot Weizen ($8/six-pack), from Portland, Oregon, pairs distinctive apricot with wheat beer, offering a nice sweet-tart balance.

Beer-Cheddar Soup

Avoid using dark beer, which could make the soup too bitter. Toast the bread cubes a day ahead, cool, and store at room temperature. Serve the soup in a tureen with the toasted bread cubes and chives on the side, and let guests help themselves.

    10 ounces sourdough bread, cut
        into 1-inch cubes
        Cooking spray
     2 cups chopped onion (about 2
        medium)
     2 garlic cloves, minced
     1 (12-ounce) bottle beer
     4 cups fat-free, less-sodium
        chicken broth, divided
     ½ cup all-purpose flour (about
        2¼ ounces)
     2 cups 2% reduced-fat milk,
        divided
    1¼ cups (5 ounces) shredded
        extrasharp Cheddar cheese
     ¼ teaspoon freshly ground black
        pepper
     ¼ cup finely chopped fresh chives

1. Preheat oven to 450°.
2. Arrange bread cubes in a single layer on a jelly-roll pan; coat bread cubes with cooking spray. Bake at 450° for 10 minutes or until toasted. Set aside.
3. Heat a Dutch oven over medium-high heat. Coat pan with cooking spray. Add onion; sauté 4 minutes. Add garlic; sauté 1 minute. Stir in beer; bring to a boil. Reduce heat; simmer 20 minutes or until onion is very tender.
4. Place beer mixture and 1 cup broth in a blender. Remove center piece of blender lid (to allow steam to escape); secure lid on blender. Place a clean towel over opening in lid (to avoid splatters). Blend until smooth. Return pureed mixture to pan. Stir in 3 cups broth; bring to a boil. Reduce heat, and simmer 10 minutes.
5. Lightly spoon flour into a dry measuring cup; level with a knife. Combine flour and 1 cup milk, stirring with a whisk until smooth. Add flour mixture and remaining 1 cup milk to pan; cook 12 minutes or until slightly thick. Remove pan from heat. Gradually add cheese, stirring until smooth. Stir in

pepper. Serve with bread cubes and chives. Yield: 12 servings (serving size: about ⅔ cup soup, about 1 ounce bread cubes, and 1 teaspoon chives).

CALORIES 172 (28% from fat); FAT 5.4g (sat 3.2g, mono 0.6g, poly 0.2g); PROTEIN 8.1g; CARB 22.9g; FIBER 1.6g; CHOL 16mg; IRON 1.1mg; SODIUM 371mg; CALC 165mg

Apricot and Sherry-Glazed Ham

    1¼ cups dry sherry
     ½ cup apricot preserves
     2 teaspoons ground coriander
    1½ teaspoons paprika
     1 (7½-pound) 33%-less-sodium
        smoked, fully cooked ham half
    20 whole cloves
        Cooking spray
     1 cup water

1. Bring sherry and apricot preserves to a simmer in a small saucepan over medium heat; cook until reduced to 1¼ cups (about 20 minutes), stirring occasionally. Remove from heat, and add ground coriander and paprika, stirring with a whisk.
2. Preheat oven to 325°.
3. Trim fat and rind from ham. Score outside of ham in a diamond pattern; stud with cloves. Place ham on rack of a broiler pan or roasting pan coated with cooking spray. Pour 1 cup water into pan; place rack in pan. Brush ham with ¼ cup sherry mixture. Bake at 325° for 1½ hours or until thermometer registers 140°, basting with remaining sherry mixture every 30 minutes. Transfer ham to a platter; let stand 15 minutes before slicing. Yield: 28 servings (serving size: about 3 ounces).

CALORIES 142 (39% from fat); FAT 6.1g (sat 2g, mono 2.9g, poly 0.7g); PROTEIN 14.2g; CARB 6.9g; FIBER 0g; CHOL 51mg; IRON 0.8mg; SODIUM 903mg; CALC 1mg

Truffled Parsnip Puree

    3½ cups organic vegetable broth
        (such as Swanson Certified
        Organic)
     3 cups 1% low-fat milk
     4 pounds parsnips, peeled and cut
        into 2-inch pieces (about 12 cups)
     ¼ cup butter
     1 teaspoon kosher salt
     ½ teaspoon freshly ground black
        pepper
     2 garlic cloves, crushed
     1 teaspoon white truffle oil

1. Combine first 3 ingredients in a large Dutch oven; bring to a boil. Reduce heat, and simmer 25 minutes or until tender. Remove parsnips from pan using a slotted spoon, reserving 1½ cups cooking liquid. Place parsnips in a food processor. With processor on, slowly add reserved 1½ cups cooking liquid; process until smooth. Add butter, salt, pepper, and garlic; process until combined. Spoon mixture into a bowl; stir in oil. Yield: 12 servings (serving size: about ⅔ cup).

CALORIES 161 (27% from fat); FAT 4.8g (sat 2.6g, mono 1.3g, poly 0.2g); PROTEIN 2.5g; CARB 28.6g; FIBER 3.1g; CHOL 11mg; IRON 0.9mg; SODIUM 261mg; CALC 80mg

Sage Dinner Rolls

     1 package dry yeast (about
        2¼ teaspoons)
     1 tablespoon honey
    1¼ cups warm water (100° to 110°)
    2½ cups all-purpose flour
        (11¼ ounces), divided
     1 cup whole wheat flour
        (4¾ ounces)
     3 tablespoons minced fresh sage
    1½ teaspoons salt
     ¼ teaspoon pepper
     2 tablespoons olive oil
        Cooking spray

1. Dissolve yeast and honey in warm water in a large bowl; let stand 5 minutes.
2. Lightly spoon flours into dry measuring cups; level with a knife. Combine
Continued

2¼ cups all-purpose flour, wheat flour, sage, salt, and pepper. Add flour mixture and oil to yeast mixture; stir until a soft dough forms. Turn dough out onto a floured surface. Knead until smooth and elastic (about 8 minutes). Add enough of remaining flour, 1 tablespoon at a time, to prevent dough from sticking to hands.

3. Place dough in a large bowl coated with cooking spray, turning to coat top. Cover and let rise in a warm place (85°), free from drafts, 1 hour or until doubled in size. (Gently press two fingers into dough. If indentation remains, dough has risen enough.) Punch dough down; cover and let rest 5 minutes.

4. Divide dough into 12 equal portions, shaping each into a ball (cover remaining to prevent drying). Place balls 2 inches apart on a large baking sheet covered with parchment paper. Cut a deep (¼-inch) X in the top of each roll using kitchen shears or a sharp knife. Cover and let rise 30 minutes or until doubled in size.

5. Preheat oven to 350°.

6. Bake at 350° for 20 minutes or until puffed and beginning to brown. Remove from baking sheet; cool on a wire rack. Yield: 12 servings (serving size: 1 roll).

CALORIES 156 (16% from fat); FAT 2.7g (sat 0.4g, mono 1.7g, poly 0.4g); PROTEIN 4.3g; CARB 29g; FIBER 2.1g; CHOL 0mg; IRON 1.7mg; SODIUM 296mg; CALC 11mg

---

MAKE AHEAD
Orange Bizcochitos

    2 cups all-purpose flour (about
       9 ounces)
    1 teaspoon baking powder
   ¼ teaspoon salt
   ¾ cup granulated sugar
   ½ cup butter, softened
    1 large egg
    1 tablespoon finely grated orange
       rind
 1½ teaspoons aniseed
    1 teaspoon vanilla extract
   ¼ cup powdered sugar
    2 tablespoons granulated sugar
   ¼ teaspoon ground cinnamon
 Cooking spray

1. Lightly spoon flour into dry measuring cups; level with a knife. Combine flour, baking powder, and salt, stirring with a whisk.

2. Place ¾ cup granulated sugar and butter in a large bowl; beat with a mixer at medium-high speed until light and fluffy (about 2 minutes). Add egg; beat 1 minute or until well blended. Add rind, aniseed, and vanilla; beat until well blended. Beating at low speed, gradually add flour mixture, ½ cup at a time; beat just until a soft dough forms. Wrap dough in plastic wrap; chill dough at least 1 hour.

3. Preheat oven to 350°.

4. Place powdered sugar in a small bowl. Combine 2 tablespoons granulated sugar and cinnamon in another bowl. Shape dough into a 10-inch log. Cut log crosswise into 4 equal portions. Working with 1 portion (cover and keep remaining portions in refrigerator), divide portion into 10 equal pieces on a lightly floured surface. Roll each piece into a ball; place balls 1½ inches apart on a baking sheet coated with cooking spray.

5. Dip bottom of a glass in powdered sugar; flatten 1 dough ball with bottom of glass into a 2-inch circle. Repeat procedure with powdered sugar and remaining 9 dough balls.

6. Sprinkle 10 dough circles evenly with 1½ teaspoons cinnamon mixture. Bake at 350° for 10 minutes or until edges of cookies are lightly browned around edges. Cool on pan 5 minutes. Remove from pan; cool completely on a wire rack. Repeat procedure 3 times with remaining dough, powdered sugar, and cinnamon mixture. Yield: 40 cookies (serving size: 1 cookie).

CALORIES 65 (35% from fat); FAT 2.5g (sat 1.5g, mono 0.7g, poly 0.1g); PROTEIN 0.8g; CARB 10g; FIBER 0.2g; CHOL 11mg; IRON 0.4mg; SODIUM 45mg; CALC 10mg

---

then & now
New England Clam Chowder

Few things are more welcome as winter approaches than a bowl of hearty New England Clam Chowder.

We first ran this recipe in January/February 1992. In this update, we turned up the flavor by doubling the amount of clams from two (6½-ounce) cans to four. Second, bacon was key to the chowder's deep, satisfying smokiness, so we switched from turkey bacon to regular bacon, went up from two slices to four, and sautéed the vegetables in two teaspoons of the drippings. We used fresh thyme instead of dried for a brighter accent, and added a bay leaf.

The original recipe called for pureeing part of the chowder, which created what we now consider to be an overly-thick consistency. This time around we thickened the chowder with flour and half-and-half, producing a more appealing, slightly brothy texture. Finally, rather than simmering the cooked bacon with the chowder as called for in the original version, we cooked the bacon and then crumbled it atop each serving for a crisp, smoky finishing touch. We enjoy this hearty, simple soup with crusty bread, a tossed green salad, and a crisp sauvignon blanc. Now, as then, this chowder makes a satisfying supper on a chilly winter evening.

New England Clam Chowder

4 (6½-ounce) cans chopped clams, undrained
2 (8-ounce) bottles clam juice
4 slices bacon
1 cup chopped onion
1 cup chopped celery
1 garlic clove, minced
3 cups cubed red potato
1½ teaspoons chopped fresh thyme
¼ teaspoon pepper
3 parsley sprigs
1 bay leaf
2 cups 2% reduced-fat milk
¼ cup all-purpose flour
½ cup half-and-half
Thyme sprigs (optional)

1. Drain clams in a colander over a bowl, reserving liquid and clams. Combine clam liquid and clam juice.
2. Cook bacon in a Dutch oven over medium-high heat until crisp. Remove bacon from pan, reserving 2 teaspoons drippings in pan. Crumble bacon; set aside. Add onion, celery, and garlic to pan; sauté 8 minutes or until tender. Add clam juice mixture, potato, and next 4 ingredients; bring to a boil. Cover, reduce heat, and simmer 15 minutes or until potato is tender.
3. Combine milk and flour, stirring with a whisk until smooth; add to pan. Stir in clams and half-and-half. Cook 5 minutes. Discard bay leaf. Ladle chowder into bowls. Sprinkle with bacon. Garnish with thyme sprigs, if desired. Yield: 8 servings (serving size: 1¼ cups chowder and 1½ teaspoons bacon).

CALORIES 194 (25% from fat); FAT 5.4g (sat 2.7g, mono 1.9g, poly 0.4g); PROTEIN 12.3g; CARB 23.7g; FIBER 1.4g; CHOL 32mg; IRON 2.2mg; SODIUM 639mg; CALC 111mg

dinner tonight
Count on Pasta

Four fast menus that are as simple as boiling water.

Pasta Menu 1
serves 4

Spaghetti Carbonara with Leeks and Pancetta

Radicchio slaw*

Red grapes

*Combine 2¾ cups thinly sliced radicchio and 2 tablespoons chopped fresh flat-leaf parsley in a bowl. Combine 1 tablespoon extravirgin olive oil, 1 tablespoon balsamic vinegar, 1 teaspoon brown sugar, ¼ teaspoon black pepper, and ⅛ teaspoon salt. Add to radicchio mixture; toss well.

Game Plan

1. While water boils for pasta:
  • Prepare ingredients for carbonara.
2. While pasta cooks:
  • Prepare radicchio slaw.
  • Wash grapes.
3. Combine egg mixture with pasta.

QUICK & EASY
Spaghetti Carbonara with Leeks and Pancetta

A small amount of the pasta cooking liquid is whisked into the egg mixture to prevent the eggs from overcooking when added to the hot pasta. This procedure, called tempering, results in a rich, creamy sauce that coats the noodles.

TOTAL TIME: 40 MINUTES

INGREDIENT TIP: Pancetta is an Italian bacon cured with salt and spices. It's sold in sausage-like rolls. If unavailable, substitute six slices of chopped center-cut bacon.

8 ounces uncooked spaghetti
½ cup (2 ounces) finely grated Parmigiano-Reggiano cheese
¼ teaspoon pepper
⅛ teaspoon salt
1 large egg, lightly beaten
1 large egg white, lightly beaten
½ cup chopped pancetta (about 2 ounces)
2 cups thinly sliced leek (about 2 large)
2 garlic cloves, minced
2 tablespoons chopped fresh flat-leaf parsley

1. Cook pasta according to package directions, omitting salt and fat. Drain, reserving ¼ cup cooking liquid.
2. Combine cheese and next 4 ingredients in a small bowl, stirring with a whisk. Gradually add reserved ¼ cup cooking liquid to egg mixture, stirring constantly with a whisk.
3. Cook pancetta in a large nonstick skillet over medium-high heat until crisp. Remove pancetta from pan, reserving drippings in pan; set pancetta aside. Add leek to drippings in pan, and sauté 4 minutes. Add garlic to pan; sauté 1 minute. Add pasta, cheese mixture, and pancetta to pan; reduce heat, and cook 1 minute, tossing well to coat. Cook 1 minute. Sprinkle with parsley; serve immediately. Yield: 4 servings (serving size: 1¼ cups).

CALORIES 400 (29% from fat); FAT 12.8g (sat 5.7g, mono 4.2g, poly 2.7g); PROTEIN 22.1g; CARB 49.4g; FIBER 2.7g; CHOL 78mg; IRON 3.2mg; SODIUM 726mg; CALC 350mg

Pasta Menu 2

serves 6

Farfalle with Sausage, Cannellini Beans, and Kale

Garlic toast*

Sliced pears with amaretti cookies

*Preheat broiler. Coat tops of 12 (½-inch-thick) slices diagonally cut French bread baguette with cooking spray; sprinkle evenly with ½ teaspoon garlic powder and ½ teaspoon dried Italian seasoning. Place bread slices on a baking sheet; broil 2 minutes or until golden brown.

Game Plan

1. While water boils for pasta:
  • Prepare ingredients for sausage mixture.
2. While pasta cooks:
  • Preheat broiler.
3. While sausage mixture simmers:
  • Prepare garlic toast.
  • Slice pears.
4. Add pasta and remaining ingredients to sausage mixture.

QUICK & EASY

Farfalle with Sausage, Cannellini Beans, and Kale

TOTAL TIME: 35 MINUTES
PREP TIP: Use a vegetable peeler to shave fresh Parmesan cheese

  8 ounces uncooked farfalle (bow tie pasta)
  ¼ cup oil-packed sun-dried tomatoes
  1½ cups chopped onion
  8 ounces hot turkey Italian sausage
  6 garlic cloves, minced
  1 teaspoon dried Italian seasoning
  ¼ teaspoon crushed red pepper
  1 (14-ounce) can fat-free, less-sodium chicken broth
  1 (16-ounce) package fresh kale
  1 (15-ounce) can cannellini beans, rinsed and drained
  1 ounce shaved fresh Parmesan cheese (about ¼ cup)

1. Cook pasta according to package directions, omitting salt and fat. Drain, reserving 1 cup cooking liquid; keep warm.
2. Drain tomatoes in a small sieve over a bowl, reserving 2 teaspoons oil; slice tomatoes. Heat a large Dutch oven over medium heat. Add sliced tomatoes, reserved 2 teaspoons tomato oil, onion, and sausage to pan; cook 10 minutes or until sausage is browned, stirring to crumble. Add garlic to pan; cook 1 minute. Add seasoning, pepper, and broth to pan. Stir in kale; cover and simmer 5 minutes or until kale is tender. Stir in pasta, reserved 1 cup cooking liquid, and beans. Sprinkle with cheese. Yield: 6 servings (serving size: 1¾ cups pasta mixture and 2 teaspoons cheese).

CALORIES 329 (25% from fat); FAT 9g (sat 2.2g, mono 3g, poly 2.3g); PROTEIN 18.7g; CARB 45.7g; FIBER 5g; CHOL 26mg; IRON 4mg; SODIUM 669mg; CALC 204mg

Pasta Menu 3

serves 4

Teriyaki Pork and Vegetables with Noodles

Sautéed bok choy*

Fresh orange sections and fortune cookies

*Toast 1 tablespoon sesame seeds in a large skillet over medium-high heat 1 minute or until golden brown. Remove seeds from pan; set aside. Heat 1 teaspoon dark sesame oil in pan. Add 3 cups sliced bok choy to pan; cook for 3 minutes or until browned. Add 1 teaspoon low-sodium soy sauce and ⅛ teaspoon salt to pan; cover and cook 3 minutes. Sprinkle with sesame seeds.

Game Plan

1. While water boils for pasta:
  • Chop green onions.
  • Slice pork and red bell pepper.
  • Slice bok choy.
2. While pasta cooks:
  • Section oranges.
  • Cook pork mixture.
3. Toss pasta with pork mixture.
4. Cook bok choy.

QUICK & EASY

Teriyaki Pork and Vegetables with Noodles

The sweet-savory flavor of teriyaki sauce is a centuries-old mixture of soy sauce and mirin (sweet cooking wine). Over time, Japanese-Americans added ginger, brown sugar, pineapple juice, and green onions, elements of the bottled teriyaki sauce Americans know today.

TOTAL TIME: 40 MINUTES

  8 ounces uncooked spaghetti
  4 green onions
  1 tablespoon dark sesame oil
  1 cup thinly sliced red bell pepper
  3 (4-ounce) boneless center-cut loin pork chops (about ½ inch thick), cut into ¼-inch strips
  1 (3½-ounce) package shiitake mushrooms, sliced
  ⅓ cup low-sodium teriyaki sauce
  4 teaspoons chili garlic sauce (such as Lee Kum Kee)

1. Cook pasta according to package directions, omitting salt and fat. Drain, reserving ¼ cup cooking liquid; keep pasta warm.
2. Remove green tops from green onions; thinly slice, and set aside. Mince white portions of green onions; set aside.
3. Heat oil in a large nonstick skillet over medium-high heat. Add minced green onions, bell pepper, pork, and mushrooms; sauté 3 minutes or until pork is browned. Combine reserved ¼ cup cooking liquid, teriyaki sauce, and chili garlic sauce in a small bowl, stirring with a whisk. Add pasta and teriyaki sauce mixture to pan; toss well to coat. Stir in sliced green onion tops. Yield: 4 servings (serving size: about 1¾ cups).

CALORIES 444 (27% from fat); FAT 13.5g (sat 4.1g, mono 4.6g, poly 2.7g); PROTEIN 26.3g; CARB 51.9g; FIBER 3.1g; CHOL 55mg; IRON 3.4mg; SODIUM 633mg; CALC 40mg

QUICK & EASY

Rotini with Chicken, Asparagus, and Tomatoes

TOTAL TIME: 30 minutes

PREP TIP: Slice the chicken across the grain into strips; the pieces are more tender and retain their shape after cooking.

    8   ounces uncooked rotini
        (corkscrew pasta)
        Cooking spray
    1   pound skinless, boneless chicken
        breast, cut into ¼-inch strips
    ½   teaspoon kosher salt
    ½   teaspoon freshly ground black
        pepper
    1   cup (1-inch) slices asparagus
    2   cups cherry tomatoes, halved
    2   garlic cloves, minced
    2   tablespoons chopped fresh basil
    2   tablespoons balsamic vinegar
    1   tablespoon extravirgin olive oil
    ¼   cup (1 ounce) crumbled goat
        cheese

1. Cook pasta according to package directions, omitting salt and fat.

2. Heat a large nonstick skillet over medium-high heat. Coat pan with cooking spray. Sprinkle chicken with salt and pepper. Add chicken and asparagus to pan; sauté 5 minutes. Add tomatoes and garlic to pan; sauté 1 minute. Remove from heat. Stir in pasta, basil, vinegar, and oil. Arrange 2 cups pasta mixture on each of 4 plates; top each serving with 1 tablespoon cheese. Yield: 4 servings.

CALORIES 419 (20% from fat); FAT 9.5g (sat 3.2g, mono 4.1g, poly 1.6g); PROTEIN 33.9g; CARB 48.5g; FIBER 3.4g; CHOL 70mg; IRON 3.2mg; SODIUM 324mg; CALC 105mg

superfast

20 Minute Dishes

From salmon to steak, clams to lamb, here are some simple, fresh, and easy meals you can make superfast.

QUICK & EASY

Gnocchi with Turkey Ragù

Gnocchi are Italian potato-based dumplings. They float to the top of the water when they're done. Serve with breadsticks.

    1   (16-ounce) package gnocchi
        Cooking spray
    8   ounces ground turkey breast
    1   cup chopped onion
    ¾   cup chopped red bell pepper
    1   tablespoon bottled minced garlic
    1   teaspoon dried basil
    ¼   teaspoon fennel seeds
    ½   cup dry white wine
    3   tablespoons tomato paste
    1   (14.5-ounce) can diced tomatoes
        with basil, garlic, and oregano
    1   tablespoon finely grated fresh
        Romano cheese
    ½   teaspoon black pepper
        Basil sprigs (optional)

1. Cook gnocchi according to package directions, omitting salt and fat. Drain, and keep warm.

2. Heat a large nonstick skillet over medium-high heat. Coat pan with cooking spray. Add turkey to pan; cook 3 minutes or until browned, stirring to crumble. Drain, and remove turkey from pan. Add onion and next 4 ingredients to pan; sauté 2 minutes. Return turkey to pan. Stir in wine; cook 2 minutes. Stir in tomato paste and tomatoes; cook 4 minutes, stirring occasionally. Remove from heat; stir in cheese and black pepper. Place about 1 cup gnocchi in each of 4 shallow bowls; top each serving with about ½ cup sauce. Garnish with basil, if desired. Yield: 4 servings.

CALORIES 317 (28% from fat); FAT 9.7g (sat 5.5g, mono 2.3g, poly 0.5g); PROTEIN 18.7g; CARB 38g; FIBER 3.7g; CHOL 45mg; IRON 2.8mg; SODIUM 651mg; CALC 131mg

QUICK & EASY

Pierogies with Bacon, Sautéed Onion, and Sour Cream

Cook these Polish dumplings in the microwave per package directions.

    12 frozen potato and onion
        pierogies (such as Mrs. T's)
    8   slices center-cut bacon
    2   cups vertically sliced onion
    1   teaspoon sugar
    ¼   teaspoon dried thyme
    1   cup frozen green peas
    ⅛   teaspoon salt
    ⅛   teaspoon pepper
    ¼   cup reduced-fat sour cream

1. Cook pierogies according to package directions.

2. Cook bacon in a large nonstick skillet until crisp. Remove bacon; crumble. Increase heat to medium-high. Add onion, sugar, and thyme to drippings in pan; sauté 5 minutes. Stir in peas; sauté 1 minute. Add pierogies, salt, and pepper; cook 30 seconds. Sprinkle with crumbled bacon. Serve with sour cream. Yield: 4 servings (serving size: 3 pierogies, about ½ cup onion mixture, and 1 tablespoon sour cream).

CALORIES 350 (29% from fat); FAT 11.2g (sat 4.1g, mono 4.8g, poly 1.6g); PROTEIN 13.4g; CARB 47.8g; FIBER 4.6g; CHOL 38mg; IRON 1mg; SODIUM 712mg; CALC 50mg

Pan-Seared Salmon with Pineapple-Jalapeño Relish

The heat of jalapeño peppers varies. Adjust the spice level to suit your taste by seeding the pepper or using less for a milder version. Leave the seeds in for the hottest interpretation.

2 cups chopped pineapple
¼ cup finely chopped red onion
¼ cup finely chopped red bell pepper
1 tablespoon fresh lemon juice
2 teaspoons sugar
1 finely chopped seeded jalapeño pepper
½ teaspoon salt, divided
Cooking spray
1 teaspoon chili powder
¼ teaspoon black pepper
4 (6-ounce) salmon fillets

1. Combine first 6 ingredients in a medium bowl; stir in ¼ teaspoon salt.
2. Heat a large nonstick skillet over medium-high heat. Coat pan with cooking spray. Combine ¼ teaspoon salt, chili powder, and black pepper, stirring well; sprinkle evenly over fish. Add fish to pan, skin side up; cook 4 minutes on each side or until fish flakes easily when tested with a fork or until desired degree of doneness. Serve with pineapple mixture. Yield: 4 servings (serving size: 1 fillet and about ½ cup pineapple mixture).

CALORIES 308 (46% from fat); FAT 15.6g (sat 3.2g, mono 5.7g, poly 5.7g); PROTEIN 28.8g; CARB 11.7g; FIBER 1.3g; CHOL 80mg; IRON 0.7mg; SODIUM 394mg; CALC 31mg

Broiled Cumin Lamb Chops with Curried Couscous

Brush lamb chops with honey so the spice mixture adheres as they cook.

LAMB:
2 teaspoons ground cumin
1 teaspoon ground coriander
½ teaspoon salt
1 tablespoon honey
8 (4-ounce) lamb loin chops, trimmed
Cooking spray

COUSCOUS:
1 cup chopped onion
½ cup dried cranberries
¾ cup water
½ cup orange juice
1 teaspoon curry powder
¼ teaspoon salt
1 cup uncooked couscous
2 tablespoons chopped fresh cilantro

1. Preheat broiler.
2. To prepare lamb, combine first 3 ingredients in a bowl. Brush honey evenly over both sides of lamb; sprinkle evenly with spice mixture. Arrange lamb in a single layer on a broiler pan coated with cooking spray; broil 4 minutes on each side or until desired degree of doneness.
3. To prepare couscous, heat a nonstick saucepan over medium-high heat. Coat pan with cooking spray. Add onion to pan; sauté 2 minutes. Stir in cranberries and next 4 ingredients; bring to a boil. Remove from heat; stir in couscous. Cover and let stand 5 minutes. Add cilantro; fluff with a fork. Serve with lamb chops Yield: 4 servings (serving size: 2 lamb chops and about 1 cup couscous mixture).

CALORIES 510 (33% from fat); FAT 18.7g (sat 9g, mono 7g, poly 1g); PROTEIN 26.9g; CARB 56.8g; FIBER 4.1g; CHOL 95mg; IRON 3mg; SODIUM 493mg; CALC 54mg

Linguine with Spicy Red Clam Sauce

Canned clams make this no-fuss recipe supereasy. Of course, you can use fresh littleneck clams, if you prefer. Cook them for about five minutes or until the shells open, and discard any unopened shells. Use less crushed red pepper, or omit it if you prefer a milder sauce. Serve with garlic bread and a tossed green salad.

1 (9-ounce) package fresh linguine
1 tablespoon olive oil
½ cup chopped onion
1 tablespoon bottled minced garlic
½ teaspoon crushed red pepper
2 tablespoons tomato paste
1 (14.5-ounce) can no-salt-added diced tomatoes, undrained
2 (6.5-ounce) cans minced clams, undrained
2 tablespoons chopped fresh parsley
1 tablespoon chopped fresh basil
1 tablespoon chopped fresh oregano

1. Cook pasta according to package directions, omitting salt and fat. Drain.
2. Heat olive oil in a large nonstick skillet over medium-high heat. Add onion, garlic, and red pepper to pan; sauté 3 minutes or until onion is lightly browned. Stir in tomato paste and tomatoes; cook 4 minutes or until thick, stirring constantly. Stir in clams; cook 2 minutes or until thoroughly heated. Remove from heat; stir in parsley, basil, and oregano. Serve with pasta. Yield: 4 servings (serving size: 1 cup pasta and about 1 cup sauce).

CALORIES 292 (17% from fat); FAT 5.4g (sat 0.5g, mono 2.5g, poly 0.8g); PROTEIN 15.5g; CARB 45.1g; FIBER 3.6g; CHOL 17mg; IRON 3.9mg; SODIUM 806mg; CALC 47mg

Balsamic-Glazed Filet Mignon

Accompany these steaks with mashed potatoes drizzled with truffle oil and roasted green beans. The menu will come together easily enough for a weeknight meal, but it's sophisticated enough to share with guests.

    4 (4-ounce) beef tenderloin steaks
    ¼ teaspoon salt
    ¼ teaspoon freshly ground black
       pepper
       Cooking spray
    2 teaspoons bottled minced garlic
    ⅛ teaspoon crushed red pepper
    3 tablespoons dry sherry
    2 tablespoons low-sodium soy sauce
    1 tablespoon balsamic vinegar
    2 teaspoons honey

1. Sprinkle both sides of steaks evenly with salt and black pepper. Heat a large nonstick skillet over medium-high heat. Coat pan with cooking spray. Add steaks to pan; cook 3 minutes on each side or until desired degree of doneness. Remove steaks from pan; keep warm.
2. Add garlic and red pepper to pan; sauté 30 seconds. Add sherry to pan; bring to a boil. Cook 30 seconds. Add soy sauce and remaining ingredients; bring to a boil, stirring occasionally. Reduce heat, and cook 1 minute. Serve with steaks. Yield: 4 servings (serving size: 1 steak and about 1 tablespoon sauce).

CALORIES 215 (39% from fat); FAT 9.2g (sat 3.4g, mono 3.5g, poly 0.7g); PROTEIN 24g; CARB 4.7g; FIBER 0.1g; CHOL 70mg; IRON 3.3mg; SODIUM 406mg; CALC 10mg

---

inspired vegetarian
Downsizing

Chef Alexandra Jamieson shares the nourishing soups that restored filmmaker Morgan Spurlock after filming the documentary Super Size Me.

You may recognize vegetarian Chef Alexandra Jamieson from the Academy Award–nominated documentary *Super Size Me.* In it, she reluctantly watches her fiancé, now-husband Morgan Spurlock, consume a diet of fast food for 30 days. By the end of the month, Spurlock has gained more than 24 pounds, his cholesterol has shot up 65 points, and his blood pressure has skyrocketed.

Jamieson's clients often have serious health issues—cancer, diabetes, high blood pressure, food allergies—and want to make radical dietary changes to improve their well-being. So naturally Spurlock asked her to help him regain his health after the documentary was filmed. She did, putting him on a vegetarian diet. Overnight he switched from sugar, refined carbohydrates, caffeine, alcohol, dairy, and meat to whole grains, nuts and seeds, fruits, vegetables, beans, and legumes.

Within several months Spurlock's weight, cholesterol, and blood pressure returned to normal, and out of that came Jamieson's first cookbook, *The Great American Detox Diet.* The all-new simple soups Jamieson shares here are typical of her flavorful, nourishing fare.

Italian White Bean and Spinach Soup

Dried shiitake mushrooms lend this appetizer soup rich intensity. It's delightful with a grilled cheese sandwich for a light supper.

    1 (1-ounce) package dried shiitake
       mushrooms
    2 cups boiling water
    2 teaspoons olive oil
    1 cup chopped yellow onion
    2 garlic cloves, minced
    4 cups chopped fresh spinach
    1 teaspoon chopped fresh rosemary
    1 teaspoon chopped fresh thyme
    ¼ teaspoon freshly ground black
       pepper
    1 (16-ounce) can cannellini beans
       or other white beans, rinsed and
       drained
    1 (14-ounce) can organic vegetable
       broth (such as Swanson Certified
       Organic)
       Fresh thyme sprigs (optional)
       Crushed red pepper (optional)

1. Combine mushrooms and 2 cups boiling water in a bowl; cover and let stand 15 minutes. Drain mushrooms in a colander over a bowl, reserving liquid. Chop mushrooms; set aside.
2. Heat oil in a large nonstick skillet over medium-high heat. Add onion, garlic, and mushrooms to pan; sauté 5 minutes or until tender. Add reserved mushroom liquid, spinach, and next 5 ingredients; bring to a boil. Cover, reduce heat, and simmer 10 minutes. Garnish with thyme and red pepper, if desired. Yield: 6 servings (serving size: 1 cup).

CALORIES 78 (22% from fat); FAT 1.9g (sat 0.3g, mono 1.1g, poly 0.4g); PROTEIN 2.8g; CARB 13.5g; FIBER 2.9g; CHOL 0mg; IRON 1.3mg; SODIUM 261mg; CALC 42mg

QUICK & EASY
Moroccan Chickpea Stew

(pictured on page 253)

Garnish with chopped cilantro and serve over whole wheat couscous instead of brown rice, if you prefer. For milder heat, seed the jalapeño.

        2 teaspoons olive oil
        1 cup diced yellow onion
        1 cup diced carrot (about 1 large)
        2 garlic cloves, minced
        1 jalapeño pepper, minced
    1½ cups cubed peeled Yukon gold potato (about 1 large)
        2 teaspoons ground cumin
        1 teaspoon chili powder
       ½ teaspoon ground turmeric
       ⅛ teaspoon salt
        1 (28-ounce) can diced tomatoes, undrained
        1 (15½-ounce) can chickpeas (garbanzo beans), rinsed and drained
        1 (14-ounce) can organic vegetable broth
        3 cups hot cooked brown rice
       ½ cup plain low-fat yogurt

1. Heat oil in a large saucepan over medium-high heat. Add onion and next 3 ingredients to pan; sauté 6 minutes or until tender. Stir in potato and next 7 ingredients. Bring to a boil. Cover, reduce heat, and simmer 15 minutes or until potato is tender. Serve over rice. Top with yogurt. Yield: 6 servings (serving size: 1⅓ cups stew, ½ cup rice, and about 1 tablespoon yogurt).

CALORIES 251 (14% from fat); FAT 3.8g (sat 0.6g, mono 1.9g, poly 1g); PROTEIN 7.3g; CARB 47.5g; FIBER 6.8g; CHOL 1mg; IRON 2.2mg; SODIUM 401mg; CALC 97mg

WINE NOTE: With spicy ethnic cuisine, seek out the German grape Gewürztraminer, which yields wines with floral and lychee aromas, as well as natural sweetness that makes a perfect foil to the jalapeño and cumin in the stew. Chateau St. Jean Gewürztraminer 2006 ($15), from Sonoma, California, offers classic honeysuckle and melon aromas, with a spice-friendly sweetness and snappy acidity that adds texture to the dish.

QUICK & EASY
Asian Corn Soup

If you can't find fresh lemongrass, substitute strips of rind from one-half to one whole lemon. Serve as a side dish with stir-fried tofu and rice.

        4 ears corn
        1 teaspoon canola oil
        1 cup chopped yellow onion
        4 cups water
        2 cups organic vegetable broth (such as Swanson Certified Organic)
      12 sprigs cilantro
        5 (⅛-inch-thick) slices peeled fresh ginger
        1 to 2 jalapeño peppers, seeded and quartered
        1 to 2 fresh lemongrass stalks, including bulb end, smashed and coarsely chopped
        1 garlic clove, crushed
        2 tablespoons fresh lime juice
       ¼ teaspoon sea salt
    Thinly sliced lime (optional)
    Thinly sliced jalapeño pepper (optional)

1. Cut corn kernels from ears of corn; set aside. Reserve cobs.
2. Heat oil in a large saucepan over medium-high heat. Add onion to pan; sauté 5 minutes or until tender. Cut each cob into 3 pieces. Add cobs, 4 cups water, and next 6 ingredients to pan; bring to a boil. Cover, reduce heat, and simmer 30 minutes. Strain broth through a colander into a bowl; discard solids. Add corn kernels, juice, and salt to broth; stir to blend. Return soup to pan; simmer 5 minutes or until hot. Garnish with lime and jalapeño slices, if desired. Yield: 6 servings (serving size: about 1¼ cups).

CALORIES 97 (18% from fat); FAT 1.9g (sat 0.2g, mono 0.8g, poly 0.8g); PROTEIN 3.1g; CARB 20g; FIBER 2.6g; CHOL 0mg; IRON 0.6mg; SODIUM 300mg; CALC 4mg

december

Cookie Course

Learn the sweet secrets of these seasonal must-haves—from dough to decorations, baking to freezing.

If there's ever a time to pull out your mixing bowls, baking sheets, and wire racks, it's now. Baking multiple batches of cookies is a holiday tradition with benefits; you can enjoy the treats yourself (freezing some for later), or take them to a cookie swap or the office. You can also package them creatively to offer as gifts.

There are tricks that will help ensure success, especially when making lower-fat cookies. With such cookies, there is a narrower margin for error, and they may need to be handled differently than traditional cookies to achieve the same delicious results. We'll fill you in on the main cookie types and share all you need to know so your holiday season can be filled with crispy, chewy, or gooey goodies.

Drop Cookies

Formed by spooning mounds of soft dough onto baking sheets, these cookies are some of the simplest to make.

- Ensure even baking by dropping the same amount of dough for each cookie. Use a measuring spoon to scoop the dough, then push it onto the baking sheet with your finger or another spoon.
- For a one-handed option, use a cookie scoop (available at kitchenware stores), which looks like a small ice cream scoop. These gadgets come in a variety of sizes—from one teaspoon up to several tablespoons.
- Coat whatever you use to scoop the dough with cooking spray first for easy release.
- There's no need to flatten the cookies; they will spread and flatten as they bake.

MAKE AHEAD • FREEZABLE

Oatmeal, Chocolate Chip, and Pecan Cookies

These easy drop cookies are crisp on the outside and slightly chewy on the inside. Chocolate minichips disperse better in the batter, but you can use regular chips.

1¼ cups all-purpose flour (about 5½ ounces)
1 cup regular oats
¾ teaspoon baking powder
½ teaspoon baking soda
½ teaspoon salt
¾ cup granulated sugar
½ cup packed brown sugar
⅓ cup butter, softened
1½ teaspoons vanilla extract
1 large egg
¼ cup chopped pecans, toasted
¼ cup semisweet chocolate minichips

1. Preheat oven to 350°.
2. Lightly spoon flour into dry measuring cups; level with a knife. Combine flour and next 4 ingredients, stirring with a whisk; set aside.
3. Place sugars and butter in a large bowl; beat with a mixer at medium speed until well blended. Add vanilla and egg; beat until blended. Gradually add flour mixture, beating at low speed just until combined. Stir in pecans and minichips. Drop dough by level tablespoons 2 inches apart onto baking sheets lined with parchment paper. Bake at 350° for 12 minutes or until edges of cookies are lightly browned. Cool on pans 2 minutes. Remove cookies from pans; cool on wire racks. Yield: 3 dozen (serving size: 1 cookie).

CALORIES 81 (33% from fat); FAT 3g (sat 1.4g, mono 1g, poly 0.3g); PROTEIN 1.1g; CARB 12.9g; FIBER 0.5g; CHOL 10mg; IRON 0.5mg; SODIUM 76mg; CALC 12mg

---

MAKE AHEAD • FREEZABLE

Chocolate, Coconut, and Almond Snowdrops

Meringues are simple cookies to make, and the flavor varieties are numerous.

¼ teaspoon cream of tartar
⅛ teaspoon salt
4 large egg whites
¾ cup sugar
⅓ cup flaked sweetened coconut, toasted
⅓ cup sliced almonds, toasted
⅓ cup semisweet chocolate minichips

1. Preheat oven to 275°.
2. Place first 3 ingredients in a large bowl; beat with a mixer at high speed until foamy. Gradually add sugar, 1 tablespoon at a time, beating until stiff peaks form (do not underbeat). Gently fold in coconut, almonds, and minichips.
3. Drop batter by slightly rounded tablespoons ½-inch apart onto baking sheets lined with parchment paper. Place 1 pan on bottom oven rack and 1 pan on middle rack. Bake at 275° for 30 minutes. Rotate pans, and bake an additional 30 minutes or until cookies are dry. Remove cookies from pans; cool completely on wire racks. Yield: 4 dozen (serving size: 2 cookies).

CALORIES 57 (30% from fat); FAT 1.9g (sat 0.9g, mono 0.4g, poly 0.2g); PROTEIN 1.1g; CARB 9.3g; FIBER 0.2g; CHOL 0mg; IRON 0.1mg; SODIUM 24mg; CALC 4mg

MAKE AHEAD • FREEZABLE
Black and White Striped Cookies

For pinwheel variation, stack the two (12 x 8–inch) dough rectangles on top of each other, and roll up into a 12-inch-long cylinder as if you're making cinnamon rolls. Chill the roll before slicing.

VANILLA DOUGH:

- 1¼ cups all-purpose flour (about 5½ ounces)
- ⅛ teaspoon salt
- ½ cup powdered sugar
- ¼ cup butter, softened
- 1 large egg yolk
- 1½ teaspoons vanilla extract
- 2 tablespoons ice water

CHOCOLATE DOUGH:

- ¾ cup all-purpose flour (about 3⅓ ounces)
- ⅓ cup unsweetened cocoa
- ⅛ teaspoon salt
- 1 cup powdered sugar
- ¼ cup butter, softened
- 1 large egg yolk
- ½ teaspoon vanilla extract
- 2 tablespoons ice water

1. To prepare vanilla dough, lightly spoon 1¼ cups flour into dry measuring cups; level with a knife. Combine 1¼ cups flour and ⅛ teaspoon salt, stirring well with a whisk. Place ½ cup sugar, ¼ cup butter, and 1 egg yolk in a medium bowl; beat with a mixer at medium speed until smooth. Beat in 1½ teaspoons vanilla. Gradually add flour mixture to butter mixture, beating at low speed just until combined. Sprinkle 2 tablespoons ice water over surface of dough; beat just until moist. (Dough will be slightly crumbly.) Press dough into a 4-inch circle on plastic wrap; cover and chill 1 hour or until firm.

2. To prepare chocolate dough, lightly spoon ¾ cup flour into dry measuring cups; level with a knife. Combine ¾ cup flour, cocoa, and ⅛ teaspoon salt, stirring well with a whisk. Place 1 cup sugar, ¼ cup butter, and 1 egg yolk in a medium bowl; beat with a mixer at medium speed until smooth. Beat in ½ teaspoon vanilla. Gradually add cocoa mixture to butter mixture, beating at low speed just until combined. Sprinkle 2 tablespoons ice water over surface of dough; beat just until moist. Press dough into a 4-inch circle on plastic wrap; cover and chill 1 hour or until firm.

3. Slightly overlap 2 sheets of plastic wrap on a slightly damp surface. Unwrap and place chilled vanilla dough on plastic wrap. Cover dough with 2 additional sheets of overlapping plastic wrap. Roll dough, still covered, into a 12 x 8–inch rectangle. Place dough in freezer 5 minutes or until plastic wrap can be easily removed. Remove top sheets of plastic wrap.

4. Slightly overlap 2 sheets of plastic wrap on a slightly damp surface. Unwrap and place chilled chocolate dough on plastic wrap. Cover dough with 2 additional sheets of overlapping plastic wrap. Roll dough, still covered, into a 12 x 8–inch rectangle. Place dough in freezer 5 minutes or until plastic wrap can be easily removed. Remove top sheets of plastic wrap.

5. Place vanilla dough on top of chocolate dough, plastic wrap side up. Remove plastic wrap from vanilla dough; turn dough over onto a lightly floured surface. Remove plastic wrap from chocolate dough. Cut dough stack in half crosswise to form 2 (8 x 6–inch) rectangles. Stack 1 rectangle on top of the other, alternating vanilla and chocolate doughs; wrap in plastic wrap. Freeze 10 minutes or until firm and plastic wrap can be easily removed.

These unique treats, which use rolled dough that is stacked and sliced, are actually a hybrid—a cross between rolled and sliced/icebox cookies.

6. Cut dough crosswise into 6 (6 x 1⅓–inch) strips. Stack 2 strips on top of each other to form a stack, alternating vanilla and chocolate to form a striped pattern; wrap in plastic wrap, pressing gently. Repeat procedure with remaining 4 strips to form 2 stacks (there will be 3 stacks total). Chill 30 minutes or until very firm.

7. Preheat oven to 375°.

8. Working with 1 stack at a time, unwrap dough. Carefully cut each stack into 12 slices. Place dough slices 2 inches apart on baking sheets lined with parchment paper. Bake at 375° for 12 minutes. Cool on pans 5 minutes. Remove cookies from pans; cool completely on wire racks. Yield: 3 dozen (serving size: 1 cookie).

CALORIES 73 (37% from fat); FAT 3g (sat 1.8g, mono 0.8g, poly 0.2g); PROTEIN 1.1g; CARB 10.8g; FIBER 0.5g; CHOL 18mg; IRON 0.5mg; SODIUM 35mg; CALC 4mg

MAKE AHEAD • FREEZABLE
Classic Iced Sugar Cookies

For icing that's suited for piping, decrease the milk to two tablespoons.

COOKIES:

2½ cups all-purpose flour (about 11¼ ounces)
½ teaspoon baking powder
¼ teaspoon salt
1 cup granulated sugar
10 tablespoons butter, softened
1½ teaspoons vanilla extract
2 large egg whites

ICING:

2 cups powdered sugar
¼ cup 2% reduced-fat milk
½ teaspoon vanilla extract

1. To prepare cookies, lightly spoon flour into dry measuring cups; level with a knife. Combine flour, baking powder, and salt, stirring well with a whisk. Place granulated sugar and butter in a large bowl; beat with a mixer at medium speed until light and fluffy. Beat in 1½ teaspoons vanilla and egg whites. Gradually add flour mixture to butter mixture, beating at low speed just until combined.

Divide dough in half. Shape each dough half into a ball; wrap each dough half in plastic wrap. Chill 1 hour.

2. Unwrap 1 dough ball. Press dough into a 4-inch circle on heavy-duty plastic wrap. Cover with additional plastic wrap. Roll dough, still covered, to a ¼-inch thickness. Repeat procedure with remaining dough ball. Chill dough 30 minutes.

3. Preheat oven to 375°.

4. Remove 1 dough portion from refrigerator. Remove top sheet of plastic wrap; turn dough over. Remove remaining plastic wrap. Using a 2½-inch cutter, cut dough into 18 cookies. Place cookies 2 inches apart on baking sheets lined with parchment paper. Bake at 375° for 10 minutes or until lightly browned. Cool on pans 5 minutes. Remove cookies from pans; cool completely on wire racks. Repeat procedure with remaining dough half.

5. To prepare icing, combine powdered sugar and remaining ingredients, stirring with a whisk until smooth. Working with 1 cookie at a time, spread about 1 teaspoon icing evenly over each cookie. Let stand on a wire rack until set. Yield: 3 dozen (serving size: 1 cookie).

CALORIES 109 (27% from fat); FAT 3.3g (sat 2g, mono 0.8g, poly 0.2g); PROTEIN 1.2g; CARB 19g; FIBER 0.2g; CHOL 8mg; IRON 0.4mg; SODIUM 50mg; CALC 8mg

---

Sliced/Icebox Cookies

Also called refrigerator or slice-and-bake cookies, these are formed by shaping dough into a cylinder and then slicing into thin disks before baking.

- To shape dough into a log, roll it back and forth across a lightly floured cutting board or work surface.
- Chill the dough thoroughly before slicing.
- Use a thin, serrated knife to make clean slices.
- After every two or three cuts, roll the dough log a quarter turn to make sure it keeps its round shape and doesn't flatten out.

MAKE AHEAD • FREEZABLE
Cinnamon-Anise Crisps

1½ cups cake flour (about 6 ounces)
1¼ teaspoons ground cinnamon, divided
1 teaspoon baking powder
½ teaspoon aniseed, crushed
¼ teaspoon salt
¾ cup sugar
¼ cup butter, softened
1 tablespoon fresh orange juice
1 teaspoon vanilla extract
1 large egg
1½ teaspoons sugar

1. Lightly spoon flour into dry measuring cups; level with a knife. Combine flour, 1 teaspoon cinnamon, and next 3 ingredients, stirring with a whisk; set aside.

2. Place ¾ cup sugar and butter in a large bowl; beat with a mixer at medium speed 5 minutes or until light and fluffy. Add juice, vanilla, and egg; beat until combined. Gradually add flour mixture to butter mixture, beating at low speed just until combined. Divide dough in half. Shape dough into 2 (6-inch-long) logs; wrap each log in plastic wrap. Freeze 1 hour or until very firm.

3. Preheat oven to 350°.

4. Unwrap dough logs. Cut each dough log into 12 (½-inch-thick) slices; place slices 2 inches apart on baking sheets lined with parchment paper. Combine 1½ teaspoons sugar and ¼ teaspoon cinnamon; sprinkle evenly over dough slices. Bake at 350° for 10 minutes or until golden. Cool on pans 5 minutes. Remove cookies from pans; cool completely on wire racks. Yield: 2 dozen (serving size: 1 cookie).

CALORIES 72 (28% from fat); FAT 2.2g (sat 1.3g, mono 0.6g, poly 0.1g); PROTEIN 0.9g; CARB 12.3g; FIBER 0.2g; CHOL 14mg; IRON 0.6mg; SODIUM 61mg; CALC 16mg

Cookie Basics

• **Ingredients:** Our recipes mostly include butter, sugar, eggs, flour, and leavening. Be sure to use real butter, not margarine (which contains some water and will alter the texture). Some recipes call for various types of sugar—powdered sugar to dissolve easily, granulated sugar to create bulk and crunch, or brown sugar to contribute moisture and caramel-like flavor. Eggs usually provide the only liquid in the dough, and almost all of the recipes use all-purpose flour. Some call for baking powder, baking soda, or both.

• **Equipment:** We call for a hand or stand mixer to prepare most of the recipes; either one easily combines ingredients and whips air into the batter for a lighter texture. For the best results, bake on heavy, shiny metal baking sheets (flat pans, which may have a lip on one or both ends); cookies baked on nonstick baking sheets tend to brown too much on the bottom. Do not bake on jelly-roll pans, which have one-inch rims around the sides, which may interfere with cooking by deflecting some of the heat. We call for lining pans with parchment paper; doing so prevents cookies from sticking, and you can reuse the paper for each batch you bake. For bar cookies, bake in shiny metal pans, not glass baking dishes; glass conducts heat differently and may cook the cookies too quickly. Cooling racks are also necessary to allow air to circulate under the cookies as they cool so they won't become soggy.

• **Dough preparation:** As with all baked goods, measure ingredients with precision, and use the exact ingredients specified. Many of the recipes first cream together butter and sugar, then add the dry ingredients. For these recipes, start with softened butter—butter that yields slightly to pressure but doesn't lose its shape when touched. It's important not to overmix the dough once the dry ingredients are added, as doing so may result in tough cookies or ones that don't rise well; mix just until the ingredients are combined. Many of the doughs are chilled before baking; this solidifies the fat and helps prevent overspreading as the cookies bake.

• **Baking**: Be sure your oven is preheated; you might want to use an oven thermometer for accuracy. Always place dough on cool baking sheets because warm or hot pans will cause the cookies to spread or puff too much. You can quickly cool a baking sheet by placing it under cold running water; dry thoroughly before arranging dough on the pan. Allow room for spreading so cookies don't bake together. In general, bake cookies on the second rack from the bottom. If you bake two pans at once, rotate them halfway through the cooking time. Allow baked cookies to stay on the pan for a few minutes before transferring them to cooling racks; trying to move them too soon can result in broken cookies.

Storage Strategies

• Always store baked cookies after they've cooled completely. If you store them while they're still warm, condensation will make them soggy.

• Don't mix different cookie types in the same storage container because softer cookies will leach moisture that may cause crisp cookies to go limp.

• Store cooled cookies in airtight containers to prevent humidity from affecting their texture.

• Store soft cookies with an apple wedge to help retain moisture. Discard it before serving.

• If crisp cookies soften, recrisp them by baking at 300 degrees for five minutes; cool completely on a wire rack.

• You can refrigerate or freeze most cookie dough, so you can bake a batch at a moment's notice. You do not need to thaw frozen cookie dough; just bake an additional minute or two. You can also freeze baked cookies for a few months; thaw at room temperature for 10 to 15 minutes.

Special Delivery

If you want to send cookies through the mail, consider these suggestions.

• Moist bar cookies are ideal because they won't dry out during the journey. Decorated and filled cookies are not good choices; decorated cookies are often too delicate, and filled cookies are too sticky to hold up well. Other types of cookies, if packaged correctly, should arrive in good shape.

• Pack cookies tightly (in plastic wrap, foil, or a tin) so they won't have much room to jostle about and break.

• If sending more than one type of cookie, pack them in separate containers.

• Provide a protective cushioned layer to prevent cookies from breaking. Place cookies in plastic wrap, foil, or a decorative tin, and then place inside a larger box lined with bubble wrap or crumpled packing paper.

• Call or e-mail the recipient with the package's estimated arrival date. Nobody wants to miss out on a box of homemade cookies.

Cocoa Slices

For gift giving, package these cookies in a holiday tin lined with parchment paper. Make an extra batch of dough for yourself.

1¼ cups plus 3 tablespoons all-purpose flour (about 6⅔ ounces)
1½ cups powdered sugar
⅓ cup unsweetened cocoa
1 tablespoon cornstarch
¼ teaspoon salt
½ cup chilled butter, cut into small pieces
⅓ cup ice water
¼ teaspoon vanilla extract

1. Lightly spoon flour into dry measuring cups and measuring spoons; level with a knife. Combine flour and next 4 ingredients in a medium bowl, stirring well with a whisk. Cut in butter with a pastry blender or 2 knives until mixture resembles coarse meal. Combine ⅓ cup ice water and vanilla; drizzle over flour mixture, 1 tablespoon at a time, tossing with a fork until moist. Place dough on plastic wrap; shape dough into a 12-inch log. Wrap tightly in plastic wrap; chill at least 1 hour.
2. Preheat oven to 350°.
3. Unwrap dough log. Cut dough log into 24 (½-inch-thick) slices; place slices 2 inches apart on baking sheets lined with parchment paper. Bake at 350° for 15 minutes or until set. Cool on pans 5 minutes. Remove cookies from pans; cool completely on wire racks. Yield: 2 dozen (serving size: 1 cookie).

CALORIES 94 (38% from fat); FAT 4g (sat 2g, mono 1.6g, poly 0.2g); PROTEIN 1.1g; CARB 14.1g; FIBER 0.6g; CHOL 10mg; IRON 0.5mg; SODIUM 52mg; CALC 4mg

Chai Shortbread

A combination of cardamom, cinnamon, cloves, and black pepper gives these cookies a taste reminiscent of Indian spiced tea. The fine texture of powdered sugar helps them retain the characteristic shortbread crunch.

1½ cups all-purpose flour (about 6¾ ounces)
⅛ teaspoon salt
⅛ teaspoon ground cardamom
⅛ teaspoon ground cinnamon
Dash of ground cloves
Dash of freshly ground black pepper
¾ cup powdered sugar
10 tablespoons butter, softened
1 tablespoon ice water

1. Lightly spoon flour into dry measuring cups; level with a knife. Combine flour and next 5 ingredients, stirring well with a whisk. Place sugar and butter in a medium bowl; beat with a mixer at medium speed until light and fluffy. Gradually add flour mixture to butter mixture, beating at low speed just until combined (mixture will appear crumbly). Sprinkle dough with 1 tablespoon ice water; toss with a fork. Divide dough in half. Shape dough into 2 (6-inch-long) logs; wrap each log in plastic wrap. Chill 1 hour or until very firm.
2. Preheat oven to 375°.
3. Unwrap dough logs. Carefully cut each log into 18 slices using a serrated knife. Place dough circles 2 inches apart on baking sheets lined with parchment paper. Bake at 375° for 10 minutes. Cool on pans 5 minutes. Remove cookies from pans; cool completely on wire racks. Yield: 3 dozen (serving size: 1 cookie).

CALORIES 57 (51% from fat); FAT 3.2g (sat 2g, mono 0.8g, poly 0.1g); PROTEIN 0.6g; CARB 6.5g; FIBER 0.2g; CHOL 8mg; IRON 0.3mg; SODIUM 31mg; CALC 2mg

Bar Cookies

These moist cookies are typically made by spreading batter into a pan with sides, then cutting into pieces after the batch is cooked.

• For easier removal of cookies, line the entire pan (bottom and sides) with parchment paper.
• Set your timer alarm for three to five minutes before the time specified in the recipe. That way, if your oven runs hot, you can remove the cookies before they overcook.
• Cool the cookies completely in the pan before cutting them into portions.

Hello Dolly Bars

These bar cookies can create a sticky mess in the pan, so line it with parchment paper.

1½ cups graham cracker crumbs (about 9 cookie sheets)
2 tablespoons butter, melted
1 tablespoon water
⅓ cup semisweet chocolate chips
⅓ cup butterscotch morsels
⅔ cup flaked sweetened coconut
¼ cup chopped pecans, toasted
1 (15-ounce) can fat-free sweetened condensed milk

1. Preheat oven to 350°.
2. Line bottom and sides of a 9-inch square baking pan with parchment paper; cut off excess paper around top edge of pan.
3. Place crumbs in a medium bowl. Drizzle with butter and 1 tablespoon water; toss with a fork until moist. Gently pat mixture into an even layer in pan (do not press firmly). Sprinkle chips and morsels over crumb mixture. Top evenly with coconut and pecans. Drizzle milk evenly over top. Bake at 350° for 25 minutes or until lightly browned and bubbly around edges. Cool completely on wire rack. Yield: 24 servings (serving size: 1 bar).

CALORIES 123 (32% from fat); FAT 4.4g (sat 2.3g, mono 1.3g, poly 0.6g); PROTEIN 2.1g; CARB 19.1g; FIBER 0.5g; CHOL 5mg; IRON 0.3mg; SODIUM 64mg; CALC 50mg

Cream Cheese–Swirled Brownies

For moist and fudgy results, be careful not to overbake these brownies. When they're perfectly done, the edges of the batter will just begin to pull away from the pan.

- 1½ cups all-purpose flour (about 6¾ ounces)
- 2 cups sugar, divided
- ½ cup unsweetened cocoa
- ½ teaspoon baking powder
- ¼ teaspoon salt
- ¼ cup butter
- 2 ounces unsweetened chocolate, chopped
- ¾ cup 2% reduced-fat milk
- ¾ teaspoon vanilla extract, divided
- 2 large eggs
- Cooking spray
- ½ cup (4 ounces) ⅓-less-fat cream cheese, softened
- 1 large egg white

1. Preheat oven to 350°.
2. Lightly spoon flour into dry measuring cups; level with a knife. Combine flour, 1¾ cups sugar, and next 3 ingredients in a large bowl, stirring well with a whisk. Place butter and chocolate in a microwave-safe bowl; microwave at HIGH 45 seconds or until melted, stirring once. Combine milk, ½ teaspoon vanilla, and eggs, stirring well with a whisk. Add chocolate mixture and milk mixture to flour mixture; beat with a mixer at medium speed until blended. Spoon batter into a 13 x 9–inch baking pan coated with cooking spray.
3. Place ¼ cup sugar, ¼ teaspoon vanilla, cream cheese, and egg white in a medium bowl; beat at medium speed until well blended using clean, dry beaters. Drizzle cheese mixture evenly over chocolate mixture; swirl batters together using the tip of a knife. Bake at 350° for 30 minutes or until batter begins to pull away from sides of pan. Cool completely on a wire rack. Yield: 28 servings (serving size: 1 brownie).

CALORIES 131 (30% from fat); FAT 4.3g (sat 2.6g, mono 1.3g, poly 0.2g); PROTEIN 2.5g; CARB 21.5g; FIBER 0.8g; CHOL 23mg; IRON 1.3mg; SODIUM 69mg; CALC 23mg

---

Hand-Shaped Cookies

A step beyond drop cookies, these are the ultimate hands-on project.

- Coat hands with cooking spray before handling the dough to prevent it from sticking.
- Use a ruler or measuring spoons for the first few cookies to help you determine the right size; then you can eyeball the rest.
- If the dough starts to stick to the bottom of the glass you use for flattening, coat the glass with cooking spray after every three or four cookies.
- To ensure thumbprint cookies hold their shape so they can be filled, chill the dough thoroughly after making the thumbprint indentations.
- Fill thumbprint cookies only after they've cooled completely.

Crunchy Sesame Cookies

Sesame-seed paste and dark sesame oil deliver a deep, nutty flavor. A touch of corn syrup and cornstarch ensure crispness.

- 1½ cups all-purpose flour (about 6¾ ounces)
- 1½ tablespoons cornstarch
- 1 teaspoon baking powder
- ½ teaspoon baking soda
- ¼ teaspoon salt
- 1 cup packed brown sugar
- ⅓ cup tahini (roasted sesame-seed paste)
- 2 tablespoons dark sesame oil
- 1 tablespoon light-colored corn syrup
- 2 teaspoons vanilla extract
- 1 large egg
- Cooking spray
- 2 tablespoons granulated sugar

1. Preheat oven to 375°.
2. Lightly spoon flour into dry measuring cups; level with a knife. Combine flour and next 4 ingredients, stirring with a whisk; set aside.

---

3. Place brown sugar, tahini, and oil in a large bowl; beat with a mixer at medium speed until well blended. Add syrup, vanilla, and egg; beat well. Gradually add flour mixture to sugar mixture, beating at low speed just until combined.
4. Lightly coat hands with cooking spray. Shape dough into 36 balls (about 1 inch each). Place granulated sugar in a shallow bowl. Roll dough balls in granulated sugar; place 2 inches apart on baking sheets lined with parchment paper. Flatten balls slightly with the bottom of a glass. Bake at 375° for 8 minutes or until lightly browned. Cool on pans 2 minutes. Remove cookies from pans; cool completely on wire racks. Yield: 3 dozen (serving size: 1 cookie).

CALORIES 71 (27% from fat); FAT 2.1g (sat 0.3g, mono 0.8g, poly 0.9g); PROTEIN 1.1g; CARB 11.9g; FIBER 0.3g; CHOL 6mg; IRON 0.5mg; SODIUM 53mg; CALC 17mg

---

Peanut Butter and Jelly Thumbprints

The favorite sandwich flavor combination comes together in these preserves-filled cookies. You can use any type of jam or preserves.

- 2 cups all-purpose flour (about 9 ounces)
- ¼ teaspoon salt
- ¾ cup packed brown sugar
- ⅔ cup granulated sugar
- ½ cup chunky peanut butter
- ¼ cup butter, softened
- 2 large eggs
- 1 teaspoon vanilla extract
- Cooking spray
- 7 tablespoons seedless raspberry preserves
- 1 tablespoon fresh lemon juice

1. Lightly spoon flour into dry measuring cups; level with a knife. Combine flour and salt, stirring well with a whisk; set aside.
2. Place sugars, peanut butter, and butter in a large bowl; beat with a mixer at medium speed until well combined. Add eggs, 1 at a time, beating well after each addition. Beat in vanilla. Gradually add

---

flour mixture to sugar mixture, beating at low speed just until combined.

3. Lightly coat hands with cooking spray. Shape dough into 36 balls (about 2½ teaspoons each). Place balls 2 inches apart on baking sheets lined with parchment paper. Press thumb into center of each dough ball, leaving an indentation. Cover and chill 1 hour.

4. Preheat oven to 350°.

5. Uncover dough. Bake at 350° for 14 minutes or until lightly browned. Remove cookies from pans; cool on a wire rack.

6. Place preserves in a small microwave-safe bowl; microwave at HIGH 20 seconds, stirring once. Add juice, stirring until smooth. Spoon about ½ teaspoon preserves mixture into center of each cookie. Yield: 3 dozen (serving size: 1 cookie).

CALORIES 103 (30% from fat); FAT 3.4g (sat 1.2g, mono 1.3g, poly 0.6g); PROTEIN 1.9g; CARB 16.9g; FIBER 0.5g; CHOL 15mg; IRON 0.5mg; SODIUM 48mg; CALC 8mg

---

Twice-Baked Cookies

These are meant to be hard and crunchy, perfect for dipping into coffee or hot chocolate.

- Biscotti are the most common type, but mandelbrot is another kind (see page 393).
- Once the ingredients are combined, the dough will be crumbly. Knead it in the bowl so all the flour is incorporated.
- The finished dough will be slightly sticky, so you may want to coat your hands with cooking spray before shaping it on the baking sheet.
- Leave plenty of space between the dough rolls so they don't spread and bake together.
- After the first cook time, the rolls will be slightly crunchy; use a serrated knife to slice them without crumbling.

Pine Nut Biscotti

Crunchy and lightly sweet, these are great with espresso or French roast coffee after dinner.

- 3 cups all-purpose flour (about 13½ ounces)
- 1 cup sugar
- 1 teaspoon baking powder
- ½ teaspoon salt
- ½ teaspoon baking soda
- ½ cup pine nuts, toasted
- ¼ cup plus 2 tablespoons water
- 1 teaspoon grated lemon rind
- 1 teaspoon vanilla extract
- 3 large eggs

1. Preheat oven to 325°.

2. Lightly spoon flour into dry measuring cups; level with a knife. Combine flour and next 4 ingredients in a large bowl, stirring with a whisk. Stir in pine nuts. Combine ¼ cup plus 2 tablespoons water and remaining ingredients, stirring with a whisk. Add egg mixture to flour mixture, stirring until well blended (dough will be dry and crumbly). Knead dough lightly in bowl 7 or 8 times or until a dough forms (dough will be sticky). Divide dough in half. Shape each portion into an 8-inch-long roll. Place rolls 6 inches apart on a baking sheet lined with parchment paper; flatten each roll to 1-inch thickness.

3. Bake at 325° for 30 minutes. Remove rolls from baking sheet (do not turn oven off); cool 10 minutes on a wire rack.

4. Cut each roll diagonally into 15 (½-inch-thick) slices using a serrated knife. Place slices, cut sides down, on baking sheet. Bake at 325° for 15 minutes. Turn cookies over, and bake an additional 10 minutes (cookies will be slightly soft in center but will harden as they cool). Remove from baking sheet; cool completely on wire racks. Yield: 2½ dozen (serving size: 1 biscotto).

CALORIES 94 (21% from fat); FAT 2.2g (sat 0.3g, mono 0.6g, poly 0.9g); PROTEIN 2.2g; CARB 16.6g; FIBER 0.4g; CHOL 21mg; IRON 0.8mg; SODIUM 84mg; CALC 14mg

---

Hanukkah Blessings

Celebrate this eight-day festival with a special dinner.

Hanukkah Supper Menu
serves 6

Caramelized Onion-Potato Spread

Watercress, Arugula, and Citrus Salad

Tomato Soup with Parmesan Toast

Spice-Rubbed Roasted Salmon with Lemon-Garlic Spinach

Potato-Scallion Latkes

Maple-Tangerine Carrot Coins

Chocolate-Drizzled Mandelbrot

MAKE AHEAD • FREEZABLE
Caramelized Onion-Potato Spread

This recipe makes more than four cups of spread; freeze any extra for later. Serve with crackers, baguette slices, or breadsticks.

- 2 teaspoons olive oil
- 3½ cups finely chopped onion
- 1 pound peeled baking potato, cut into 1-inch pieces
- ¾ cup canned navy beans, rinsed and drained
- 1 teaspoon balsamic vinegar
- ¾ teaspoon salt
- ¼ teaspoon freshly ground black pepper
- ½ cup plain fat-free yogurt
- 2 tablespoons fat-free sour cream

1. Heat oil in a large nonstick skillet over medium-high heat. Add onion to pan; sauté 5 minutes. Reduce heat to medium-low; cook 45 minutes or until golden brown, stirring frequently.

2. Place potato in a medium saucepan; cover with water. Bring to a boil. Reduce heat, and simmer 12 minutes or until very
Continued

tender. Drain. Cool 5 minutes. Combine potato and beans in a large bowl; mash with a potato masher. Add onion, vinegar, salt, and pepper; stir well. Add yogurt and sour cream; stir until well blended. Chill potato mixture at least 1 hour before serving. Yield: 22 servings (serving size: about 3 tablespoons).

CALORIES 45 (10% from fat); FAT 0.5g (sat 0.1g, mono 0.3g, poly 0.1g); PROTEIN 1.5g; CARB 9.1g; FIBER 1.1g; CHOL 0mg; IRON 0.4mg; SODIUM 87mg; CALC 23mg

Watercress, Arugula, and Citrus Salad

This course—well balanced in taste and texture—brightens the Hanukkah table and would be a welcome addition to any winter meal.

DRESSING:
1 tablespoon finely chopped shallots
3 tablespoons fresh lemon juice
1½ tablespoons extravirgin olive oil
2 teaspoons honey
½ teaspoon salt
½ teaspoon whole-grain Dijon mustard
¼ teaspoon freshly ground black pepper
2 garlic cloves, minced

SALAD:
1 cup grapefruit sections (about 2 grapefruit)
1 cup orange sections (about 2 oranges)
⅓ cup clementine sections (about 2 clementines)
4 cups trimmed watercress (about 2 bunches)
3 cups trimmed arugula
3 tablespoons sliced almonds, toasted

1. To prepare dressing, combine first 8 ingredients in a small bowl; stir well with a whisk.
2. To prepare salad, combine half of dressing mixture, grapefruit, orange, and clementine in a large bowl; toss gently to coat. Arrange grapefruit mixture in a single layer on a platter. Combine remaining dressing, watercress, and arugula in a large bowl; toss gently to coat. Top orange mixture with watercress mixture; sprinkle with almonds. Yield: 6 servings (serving size 1½ cups).

CALORIES 139 (32% from fat); FAT 5g (sat 0.6g, mono 3.4g, poly 0.8g); PROTEIN 2.9g; CARB 25.2g; FIBER 7.5g; CHOL 0mg; IRON 0.6mg; SODIUM 220mg; CALC 95mg

Tomato Soup with Parmesan Toast

We kept the soup slightly chunky, though it can also be pureed until smooth. Use an immersion blender, if desired.

2 teaspoons olive oil
2 cups chopped onion
2 cups chopped fennel bulb
2 garlic cloves, minced
4 cups organic vegetable broth (such as Swanson Certified Organic)
1 (28-ounce) can diced tomatoes, undrained
1 thyme sprig
¼ teaspoon salt
¼ teaspoon freshly ground black pepper
6 (1-ounce) slices diagonally cut French bread (about 1 inch thick)
6 tablespoons shredded Parmesan cheese

1. Heat oil in a large Dutch oven over medium-high heat. Add onion to pan; sauté 3 minutes. Add fennel; sauté 3 minutes. Add garlic; sauté 5 minutes or until vegetables are tender.
2. Add broth, tomatoes, and thyme to pan; bring to a boil. Partially cover, reduce heat, and simmer 35 minutes. Remove pan from heat; cool 5 minutes. Discard thyme sprig. Place half of tomato mixture in a blender. Remove center piece of lid (to allow steam to escape); secure lid on blender. Place a clean towel over opening in lid (to avoid splatters). Blend until almost smooth. Pour into a large bowl. Repeat procedure with remaining tomato mixture. Stir in salt and pepper; keep warm.

3. Preheat broiler.
4. Place bread slices on a baking sheet. Sprinkle 1 tablespoon cheese on each. Broil 2 minutes or until cheese melts. Yield: 6 servings (serving size: about 1⅓ cups soup and 1 toast).

CALORIES 198 (16% from fat); FAT 3.6g (sat 1.3g, mono 1.7g, poly 0.5g); PROTEIN 7.9g; CARB 34.8g; FIBER 5g; CHOL 4mg; IRON 2mg; SODIUM 962mg; CALC 131mg

Spice-Rubbed Roasted Salmon with Lemon-Garlic Spinach

Salmon is popular fare on various Jewish holidays. The spice rub lends an earthy, exotic taste.

SALMON:
½ teaspoon salt
½ teaspoon ground cumin
½ teaspoon ground coriander
¼ teaspoon paprika
⅛ teaspoon ground cinnamon
⅛ teaspoon freshly ground black pepper
1 (2¼-pound) skinless salmon fillet
2 cups thinly sliced onion
Cooking spray

SPINACH:
1 teaspoon olive oil
2 garlic cloves, minced
2 (6-ounce) packages fresh baby spinach
1 teaspoon grated lemon rind
¼ teaspoon salt
1 tablespoon fresh lemon juice

REMAINING INGREDIENTS:
2 tablespoons chopped fresh cilantro
Lemon wedges (optional)

1. Preheat oven to 400°.
2. To prepare salmon, combine first 6 ingredients; rub spice mixture evenly over fish. Place onion in an 11 x 7–inch baking dish coated with cooking spray. Place fish on top of onion; bake at 400° for 20 minutes or until fish flakes easily when tested with a fork or until desired degree of doneness.

3. To prepare spinach, heat oil in a large nonstick skillet over medium heat. Add garlic to pan; cook 1 minute. Add half of spinach; cook 1 minute, stirring frequently. Add remaining spinach; cook 4 minutes or until wilted, stirring frequently. Sprinkle spinach mixture with rind and ¼ teaspoon salt. Stir in juice; remove from heat.

4. Place salmon on a platter. Arrange onions and spinach evenly around salmon. Sprinkle salmon with cilantro. Serve with lemon wedges, if desired. Yield: 6 servings (serving size: about 4½ ounces salmon and ⅓ cup spinach mixture).

CALORIES 325 (37% from fat); FAT 13.2g (sat 2g, mono 4.6g, poly 5g); PROTEIN 40.3g; CARB 10.7g; FIBER 3.4g; CHOL 107mg; IRON 3.6mg; SODIUM 472mg; CALC 76mg

WINE NOTE: This salmon has lots of rich, piquant flavor and needs a wine that won't be intimidated by such bold spices as cumin, coriander, and cinnamon. Riesling works well with a high-drama salmon dish like this. Riesling's fruitiness offsets the spices while its clean, pure freshness is exactly the right counterpoint to the rich salmon. Washington State makes some of the best rieslings in the country. Try the new one from Long Shadows Vintners called Poet's Leap. The 2005 is $20.

Potato-Scallion Latkes

Latkes—the Yiddish term for potato pancakes—are a classic Hanukkah dish. The patties are cooked in oil, symbolizing the small amount of oil in a temple lamp that burned for eight days, the miracle the holiday commemorates.

- 4½ cups shredded peeled baking potato (about 1½ pounds)
- ½ cup finely chopped green onions
- 2 teaspoons all-purpose flour
- ¾ teaspoon salt
- 2 large egg whites
- 2 tablespoons olive oil, divided

1. Combine potato and onions in a sieve; press to squeeze out moisture. Combine potato mixture, flour, salt, and egg whites in a large bowl. Divide mixture into 12 equal portions; squeeze out any remaining liquid. Discard liquid. Shape each portion into a ¼-inch-thick patty.
2. Heat 1 tablespoon oil in a large nonstick skillet over medium heat. Add 6 patties to pan; cook 5 minutes on each side or until golden. Repeat procedure with remaining 1 tablespoon oil and 6 patties. Yield: 6 servings (serving size: 2 patties).

CALORIES 157 (27% from fat); FAT 4.7g (sat 0.7g, mono 3.3g, poly 0.5g); PROTEIN 3.7g; CARB 25.8g; FIBER 1.9g; CHOL 0mg; IRON 0.6mg; SODIUM 321mg; CALC 13mg

Maple-Tangerine Carrot Coins

The carrots are reminiscent of Hanukkah gelt, money distributed to children during the holiday. Tangerine juice makes the glaze special, but fresh orange juice can also be used.

- 4 cups (⅛-inch-thick) slices carrot (about 1½ pounds)
- ½ cup fresh tangerine juice (about 2 tangerines)
- ½ cup fat-free, less-sodium chicken broth
- 1 tablespoon maple syrup
- 1 teaspoon butter
- ⅛ teaspoon ground cinnamon
- 1 tablespoon chopped fresh chives
- ¼ teaspoon salt
- ¼ teaspoon freshly ground black pepper

1. Combine first 6 ingredients in a large nonstick skillet; bring to a boil. Cover, reduce heat, and simmer 2 minutes. Uncover and cook 15 minutes or until liquid almost evaporates, stirring occasionally. Stir in chives, salt, and pepper. Yield: 8 servings (serving size: about ½ cup).

CALORIES 72 (13% from fat); FAT 1g (sat 0.5g, mono 0.2g, poly 0.2g); PROTEIN 1.4g; CARB 15.4g; FIBER 3.3g; CHOL 2mg; IRON 0.5mg; SODIUM 218mg; CALC 45mg

Chocolate-Drizzled Mandelbrot

- 1¾ cups all-purpose flour (about 7¾ ounces)
- 1½ teaspoons baking powder
- ¼ teaspoon salt
- ¾ cup sugar
- ¼ cup butter, softened
- 2 large eggs
- 2 teaspoons vanilla extract
- ½ cup chopped dried cherries
- ½ cup finely chopped almonds, toasted
- ¼ cup dark chocolate chips
- 1 teaspoon light-colored corn syrup
- 1 teaspoon water

1. Preheat oven to 325°.
2. Lightly spoon flour into dry measuring cups; level with a knife. Combine flour, baking powder, and salt, stirring with a whisk.
3. Combine sugar and butter in a large bowl; beat with a mixer at medium speed until well blended. Beat in eggs and vanilla. Add flour mixture; beat until combined. Stir in cherries and almonds.
4. Shape dough into 2 (9-inch-long) rolls. Place rolls on a baking sheet covered with parchment paper; pat to 1-inch thickness. Bake at 325° for 30 minutes or until rolls are golden. Cool on baking sheet 10 minutes.
5. Cut each roll diagonally into 12 (½-inch-thick) slices. Place, cut sides down, on baking sheet. Bake at 325° for 15 minutes. Turn cookies over; bake an additional 10 minutes (cookies will be slightly soft in center but will harden as they cool). Remove from baking sheet; cool completely on a wire rack.
6. Combine chocolate chips, corn syrup, and 1 teaspoon water in a small microwave-safe bowl. Microwave at HIGH 10 seconds at a time until nearly melted; stir until smooth. Spoon mixture into a small zip-top plastic bag; seal. Snip a tiny hole in 1 corner of bag. Drizzle chocolate over cookies. Yield: 24 servings (serving size: 1 mandelbrot).

CALORIES 117 (32% from fat); FAT 4.1g (sat 1.8g, mono 1.1g, poly 0.4g); PROTEIN 2.1g; CARB 17.7g; FIBER 0.7g; CHOL 23mg; IRON 0.6mg; SODIUM 74mg; CALC 27mg

The Power of Chocolate

Versatile cocoa and dark chocolate are a source of beneficial antioxidants.

Drink a cup of hot, rich cocoa a day to lower high blood pressure. Eat an ounce of dark chocolate to protect against heart attack. These recommendations don't come straight from the mouths of chocoholics but from leading nutrition and health experts. Indeed, mounting evidence shows certain forms of chocolate may be good for your heart, and researchers are exploring its potential cancer-fighting benefits.

It may seem counterintuitive that high-fat, caloric chocolate could confer health benefits. However, researchers don't attribute these effects to milk chocolate bars or chocolate-coated candies but specifically to dark chocolate and minimally processed cocoa powder (not instant cocoa mix), which offer the most antioxidants (vitamins, minerals, or compounds that act as scavengers in the body to prevent cellular damage).

"Surprisingly, we found that a cup of hot cocoa has twice the level of antioxidant activity as a five-ounce glass of red wine and two to three times more than a cup of green tea," says Chang Y. Lee, PhD, professor of food chemistry in Cornell's Department of Food Science and Technology in Geneva, New York.

STAFF FAVORITE • MAKE AHEAD
Mexican Chocolate Cookies

These crisp rounds—ample bittersweet chocolate that mellows the ground peppers' heat—earned our Test Kitchens' highest rating. They're lovely at the end of a dinner with a few last sips of red wine.

- 5 ounces bittersweet (60 to 70 percent) chocolate, coarsely chopped
- ¾ cup all-purpose flour (about 3⅓ ounces)
- ½ teaspoon ground cinnamon
- ¼ teaspoon baking powder
- ¼ teaspoon salt
- 1/16 teaspoon ground black pepper
- 1/16 teaspoon ground red pepper
- 1¼ cups sugar
- ¼ cup butter, softened
- 1 large egg
- 1 teaspoon vanilla extract
- Cooking spray

1. Preheat oven to 350°.

2. Place chocolate in a small microwave-safe bowl; microwave at HIGH 1 minute or until almost melted, stirring until smooth. Cool.

3. Lightly spoon flour into a dry measuring cup; level with a knife. Combine flour and next 5 ingredients in a small bowl; stir with a whisk.

4. Combine sugar and butter in a large bowl; beat with a mixer at medium speed until well blended (about 5 minutes). Add egg; beat well. Add cooled chocolate and vanilla; beat just until blended. Add flour mixture; beat at low speed just until blended. Drop dough by level tablespoons 2 inches apart on baking sheets coated with cooking spray. Bake at 350° for 10 minutes or until almost set. Remove from oven. Cool on pans 2 minutes or until set. Remove from pans; cool completely on wire racks. Yield: 32 cookies (serving size: 1 cookie).

CALORIES 80 (33% from fat); FAT 2.9g (sat 1.7g, mono 0.6g, poly 0.1g); PROTEIN 0.7g; CARB 12.8g; FIBER 0.1g; CHOL 10mg; IRON 0.2mg; SODIUM 35mg; CALC 4mg

MAKE AHEAD
Double-Chocolate Cupcakes

These cupcakes are easy to make, and because simple ingredients are used, it's best to use premium cocoa powder and dark chocolate.

- 1 cup all-purpose flour (about 4½ ounces)
- ⅓ cup unsweetened cocoa
- 1 teaspoon baking soda
- ⅛ teaspoon salt
- ⅔ cup granulated sugar
- ¼ cup butter, softened
- ½ cup egg substitute
- 1 teaspoon vanilla extract
- ½ cup 1% low-fat buttermilk
- 1¼ ounces dark (70 percent cocoa) chocolate, finely chopped
- 2 tablespoons powdered sugar

1. Preheat oven to 350°.

2. Lightly spoon flour into a dry measuring cup; level with a knife. Combine flour and next 3 ingredients; stir with a whisk.

3. Place granulated sugar and butter in a large bowl; beat with a mixer at medium speed until well combined (about 3 minutes). Add egg substitute and vanilla, beating well. Add flour mixture and buttermilk alternately to granulated sugar mixture, beginning and ending with flour mixture. Fold in chocolate. Spoon batter into 12 muffin cups lined with muffin cup liners. Bake at 350° for 18 minutes or until cake springs back when touched lightly in center or until a wooden pick inserted in center comes out clean. Remove from pan; cool completely on a wire rack. Sprinkle with powdered sugar just before serving. Yield: 12 servings (serving size: 1 cupcake).

CALORIES 150 (31% from fat); FAT 5.2g (sat 3.2g, mono 1.2g, poly 0.2g); PROTEIN 3.1g; CARB 24g; FIBER 1.1g; CHOL 11mg; IRON 1mg; SODIUM 125mg; CALC 42mg

Practical Ways with Chocolate

While all this good news may tempt you to substitute a candy bar for a couple of servings of greens, "people shouldn't add large portions of chocolate to their diet," says Lona Sandon, RD, assistant professor of clinical nutrition at the University of Texas Southwestern and American Dietetic Association (ADA) spokesperson. "Chocolate is high in fat and calories, so eat it in small portions— an ounce or so maybe every day or so. Fruits, vegetables, and whole grains are still the most important sources of health benefits."

Nutritionists advise using unsweetened cocoa, which is lower in fat than dark chocolate. "We're not talking instant cocoas with added sweeteners and fillers, but making your own hot cocoa from unsweetened powder, mixing in nonfat milk, a touch of vanilla or cinnamon, and a little sugar," says nutrition consultant Lola O'Rourke, RD, an ADA spokesperson.

Judicious amounts of high-quality dark chocolate enhance dishes and boost the nutritional profile. "Try melting some dark chocolate into whole-wheat pancake batter or shave a dark chocolate bar over a bowl of blueberries and blackberries," says Milton Stokes, MPH, RD, spokesperson for the ADA.

Cocoa adds a smoky, exotic flavor to thick stews and sauces like Mexican mole, explains Kyle Warner Shadix, RD, a chef de cuisine based in New York. "More than bringing out hidden flavors of other foods, it adds a rich, earthy element to any dish," he says. Nuts, fruits, and chiles marry well with cocoa, he says, because the acid and heavy essence of chocolate tempers sweetness and balances spicy heat. Whether you enjoy it on its own or in a recipe, dark chocolate can be good for your spirit and your heart. "We need chocolate for some pure enjoyment in our lives," says Sandon. "The fact that it might also improve our heart health is a wonderful bonus."

Recent Research

"Many people forget that chocolate and cocoa are derived from a plant—the *cacao* (pronounced ca-COW) tree to be specific— just like fruits and vegetables," says Carl Keen, PhD, distinguished professor of nutrition and internal medicine at the University of California at Davis. His work includes several studies on phytochemicals in chocolate. "The plant compounds found in dark chocolate and cocoa—called flavonols—have a powerful effect on cardiovascular health." In the body, the flavonols—which are a specific type of polyphenol (a class of antioxidants)—relax blood vessels, likely helping to lower blood pressure. "That, in theory, could cause a reduction in the risk for cardiovascular disease," adds Keen.

A recent study published in the *Journal of the American Medical Association* bolstered chocolate's claim to help manage blood pressure. The study revealed that as little as 30 calories a day of dark chocolate—about six grams—was enough to reduce blood pressure some in a small group of participants. While the study cites cocoa's polyphenols as a likely component, the mechanisms involved are still debated. This preliminary study may help determine the specific compounds in chocolate that confer cardiovascular benefits and how much of them are needed to make a significant change.

Studies conducted by the University of California at Davis and Johns Hopkins University also suggest that those same antioxidant compounds in chocolate may reduce the chances of a heart attack by preventing blood clots from forming in the blood vessels. "The consumption of flavonol-rich chocolate or cocoa can be associated with effects similar to those occurring with the use of low-dose aspirin in that there is a reduction in platelet reactivity. In theory this may result in a reduced risk for blood clots," explains Keen.

"In general, the more cocoa in the chocolate, the more antioxidants you obtain," says Chang Y. Lee, PhD, professor of food chemistry in Cornell's Department of Food Science and Technology. "Dark and bittersweet chocolate typically contain 60 to 70 percent cocoa while sweet milk chocolate has only 34 percent or less."

"Increasingly, dark chocolate makers are advertising cocoa content on the label—70 percent or more is a good number to shoot for," says O'Rourke.

Not just any dark chocolate will do. Processing can destroy the valuable flavonols. "If you are looking to consume a chocolate or cocoa that is rich in flavonols, you may want to avoid chocolate and cocoas that are alkalized, or Dutch processed, as this process can significantly reduce the amount of these important nutrients," says Keen. Since processing methods aren't always advertised on the label, search the manufacturer's Web site to find out. Chocolate purists would also argue this extra processing step, known as "Dutching," weakens the true cocoa flavor and creates dark brown—almost black—baked goods. Manufacturers are experimenting with techniques to help preserve the chocolate's beneficial compounds while delivering pleasing chocolate flavor. For example, Hershey's Special Dark Cocoa blends natural unsweetened cocoa, which boasts antioxidants, and Dutch-process cocoa, which has a smooth taste.

Chocolate Crunch

This granola is satisfying on its own or sprinkled over yogurt, fresh fruit, or ice cream. Store in an airtight container up to one week, or freeze up to one month.

Cooking spray
  3 cups regular oats
  1 cup oven-toasted rice cereal (such as Rice Krispies)
  ½ cup packed brown sugar
  ⅓ cup chopped pecans
  ½ teaspoon salt
  ¼ teaspoon ground cinnamon
  ¼ cup honey
  2 tablespoons canola oil
  1 teaspoon vanilla extract
  2 ounces bittersweet chocolate (60 to 70 percent cocoa), finely chopped
  ½ cup dried cranberries

1. Preheat oven to 300°.
2. Cover a jelly-roll pan with parchment paper. Coat parchment paper with cooking spray.
3. Combine oats and next 5 ingredients in a large bowl.
4. Combine honey and oil in a small saucepan over low heat; cook 2 minutes or until warm. Remove from heat; add vanilla and chocolate; stir with a whisk until smooth. Pour chocolate mixture over oat mixture. Lightly coat hands with cooking spray. Gently mix chocolate mixture and oat mixture until combined. Spread oat mixture onto prepared jelly-roll pan. Bake at 300° for 20 minutes, stirring after 10 minutes. Cool completely on pan; stir in cranberries. Yield: about 8 cups (serving size: ½ cup).

CALORIES 168 (32% from fat); FAT 5.9g (sat 1.1g, mono 2.5g, poly 1.4g); PROTEIN 2.6g; CARB 28.1g; FIBER 2g; CHOL 0mg; IRON 1.1mg; SODIUM 77mg; CALC 14mg

Chocolate Bruschetta

Salt enhances the chocolate flavor in this simple dessert. For best results, use good-quality chocolate and coarse sea salt.

 10 (1-ounce) slices diagonally cut French bread (about ¼ inch thick)
Cooking spray
  5 ounces bittersweet chocolate (60 to 70 percent cocoa), finely chopped (about 1 cup)
  ¼ teaspoon coarse sea salt
Orange rind strips or mint leaves (optional)

1. Preheat broiler.
2. Lightly coat bread with cooking spray. Place bread on a baking sheet; broil 3 minutes on each side or until toasted. Remove bread from oven.
3. Reduce oven temperature to 350°.
4. Sprinkle each bread slice with about 1½ tablespoons chocolate. Bake 5 minutes or until chocolate melts. Sprinkle evenly with salt; garnish with orange rind or mint, if desired. Serve warm. Yield: 10 servings (serving size: 1 bruschetta).

CALORIES 150 (26% from fat); FAT 4.3g (sat 2.4g, mono 0.7g, poly 0.1g); PROTEIN 3g; CARB 25.4g; FIBER 0.5g; CHOL 0mg; IRON 0.9mg; SODIUM 242mg; CALC 0mg

Chocolate-Infused Barbecue Sauce

Unsweetened chocolate gives the sauce rich flavor with subtle cocoa notes.

  2 cups ketchup
  ½ cup packed brown sugar
  ⅓ cup fresh orange juice
  3 tablespoons molasses
  1 tablespoon Worcestershire sauce
  1 tablespoon Dijon mustard
  1 teaspoon garlic powder
  1 teaspoon smoked paprika
  ½ teaspoon salt
  ½ teaspoon freshly ground black pepper
  2 ounces unsweetened chocolate, chopped

1. Combine first 10 ingredients in a medium saucepan; bring to a boil, stirring with a whisk. Reduce heat and simmer 8 minutes or until thick, stirring occasionally. Remove from heat; add chocolate, stirring until chocolate melts and mixture is smooth. Yield: 3½ cups (serving size: 1 tablespoon).

CALORIES 26 (17% from fat); FAT 0.5g (sat 0.3g, mono 0.2g, poly 0g); PROTEIN 0.3g; CARB 5.5g; FIBER 0.2g; CHOL 0mg; IRON 0.2mg; SODIUM 124mg; CALC 6mg

Chili with Chipotle and Chocolate

Smoky chipotle and earthy chocolate add depth to chili.

Cooking spray
  2 cups diced onion (about 1 large)
  1 cup chopped red bell pepper
  1 teaspoon minced garlic
 1¼ pounds ground turkey breast
  3 tablespoons brown sugar
  2 tablespoons ancho chile powder
  1 tablespoon unsweetened cocoa
  1 teaspoon ground cumin
  ½ teaspoon freshly ground black pepper
  ¼ teaspoon salt
  2 (15-ounce) cans pinto beans, rinsed and drained
  2 (14.5-ounce) cans diced tomatoes, undrained
  1 (14-ounce) can fat-free, less-sodium chicken broth
  2 chipotle chiles, canned in adobo sauce, minced
  2 ounces unsweetened chocolate, chopped
Chopped green onions
Lime wedges (optional)

1. Heat a Dutch oven over medium-high heat. Coat pan with cooking spray. Add diced onion and next 3 ingredients to pan; sauté 8 minutes or until turkey is browned and vegetables are tender. Add sugar and next 9 ingredients to pan, stirring until blended; bring to a boil. Reduce heat, and simmer 15 minutes or until slightly thick, stirring occasionally. Add chopped chocolate, stirring until melted. Garnish each serving with green onions. Serve with lime wedges, if desired. Yield: 8 servings (serving size: 1¼ cups).

CALORIES 238 (20% from fat); FAT 5.3g (sat 2.8g, mono 1.1g, poly 0.5g); PROTEIN 22.6g; CARB 26g; FIBER 6g; CHOL 28mg; IRON 2.6mg; SODIUM 560mg; CALC 64mg

Pan-Roasted Chicken with Mole Sauce

Chocolate is used in savory dishes in Mexican cuisine, and chocolate cuts the spiciness in this thick, bold sauce. Store leftover sauce, covered in the refrigerator, up to two weeks. Use it on enchiladas or rice, or to enliven roast pork or turkey.

2   (8-ounce) chicken breast halves, skinned
2   (6-ounce) chicken thighs, skinned
2   chicken drumsticks (about 8 ounces)
¼   teaspoon salt
½   teaspoon freshly ground black pepper
    Cooking spray
1⅓ cups warm Mole Sauce
    Lime wedges (optional)
    Chopped fresh cilantro (optional)

1. Preheat oven to 350°.
2. Sprinkle chicken with salt and pepper. Heat a large oven-proof nonstick skillet over medium-high heat. Coat pan with cooking spray. Add chicken breasts to pan; cook 5 minutes, turning occasionally. Add chicken thighs and drumsticks to pan; cook 5 minutes, turning occasionally. Bake at 350° for 30 minutes or until done, turning halfway through cooking time.
3. Spoon 1 tablespoon pan drippings into Mole Sauce. Serve sauce with chicken. Garnish with lime wedges and cilantro, if desired. Yield: 4 servings (serving size: 6 ounces chicken and ⅓ cup sauce).

(Totals include Mole Sauce) CALORIES 245 (30% from fat); FAT 8.2g (sat 2.5g, mono 3.2g, poly 1.6g); PROTEIN 29.6g; CARB 14.4g; FIBER 3.1g; CHOL 88mg; IRON 2.5mg; SODIUM 471mg; CALC 46mg

MOLE SAUCE:

1   stemmed dried seeded ancho chile (about 1 ounce)
1   teaspoon olive oil
2   tablespoons blanched almonds
2   garlic cloves, crushed
2   (6-inch) corn tortillas, torn into small pieces
1   cup chopped onion
6   tablespoons raisins
1½ to 2 teaspoons chipotle chile powder
1   (14.5-ounce) can diced tomatoes, undrained
2   cups fat-free, less-sodium chicken broth, divided
1   tablespoon unsweetened cocoa
2   tablespoons fresh lime juice
¼   teaspoon ground cinnamon
1   ounce unsweetened chocolate, chopped
¼   teaspoon salt
¼   teaspoon freshly ground black pepper

1. Tear chile into large pieces. Heat oil in a large saucepan over medium-high heat. Add chile pieces to pan; cook 2 minutes or until fragrant, turning pieces occasionally (do not burn). Place chile in a blender. Add almonds, garlic, and tortilla pieces to pan; sauté 2 minutes or until almonds and garlic are lightly browned. Add almond mixture to blender. Add onion to pan; cook over medium heat 7 minutes or until lightly browned. Add raisins and chile powder to pan; sauté 30 seconds. Stir in tomatoes; cook 3 minutes. Add tomato mixture, 1½ cups broth, and next 4 ingredients to blender. Remove center piece of lid (to allow steam to escape); secure lid on blender. Place a clean towel over opening in lid (to avoid spills). Blend until smooth. Return tomato mixture to pan. Add ½ cup broth, salt, and pepper to pan; bring to a boil. Reduce heat, and simmer 5 minutes, stirring occasionally. Yield: 3 cups (serving size: ⅓ cup).

CALORIES 88 (37% from fat); FAT 3.6g (sat 1.3g, mono 1.6g, poly 0.5g); PROTEIN 2.7g; CARB 14.2g; FIBER 3.1g; CHOL 0mg; IRON 1.3mg; SODIUM 228mg; CALC 32mg

WINE NOTE: The intense, bold flavor of Mexican mole can be a wine-pairing challenge. The heat of chile peppers often makes red wines taste bitter or alcoholic. So try a slightly sweet white wine like Pacific Rim Sweet Riesling ($11).

STAFF FAVORITE • MAKE AHEAD
Creamiest Chocolate Pudding

This rich pudding earned our Test Kitchens' highest rating. A combination of cocoa powder and dark chocolate offers acidity and flowery notes. Store tightly covered in the refrigerator up to five days. For a pretty presentation, dip mint sprigs in water and gently dredge in sugar; let dry on a wire rack.

½   cup sugar
3   tablespoons cornstarch
3   tablespoons unsweetened cocoa
¼   teaspoon salt
2½ cups 1% low-fat milk
½   cup evaporated fat-free milk
2   ounces bittersweet chocolate (60 to 70 percent cocoa), finely chopped (about ¼ cup)
1   teaspoon vanilla extract
    Mint sprigs (optional)

1. Combine first 4 ingredients in a medium, heavy saucepan; stir with a whisk. Gradually add low-fat milk and evaporated milk, stirring with a whisk. Bring to a boil over medium-high heat, stirring constantly with a whisk. Reduce heat, and simmer 1 minute or until thick. Remove from heat; add chocolate, stirring until melted and mixture is smooth. Stir in vanilla. Pour about ⅔ cup pudding into each of 6 (8-ounce) ramekins; cover surface of each serving with plastic wrap. Chill at least 4 hours. Remove plastic wrap; serve. Garnish with fresh mint sprigs, if desired. Yield: 6 servings.

CALORIES 194 (21% from fat); FAT 4.6g (sat 2.7g, mono 0.9g, poly 0.1g); PROTEIN 5.9g; CARB 35g; FIBER 1.4g; CHOL 6mg; IRON 0.9mg; SODIUM 175mg; CALC 191mg

Barcelona Hot Chocolate

The combination of hot chocolate and espresso is enjoyed in Spain and throughout Europe. This version shows off the chocolate with a hint of orange and isn't as sweet as traditional American-style cocoa drinks.

⅔ cup boiling water
2 ounces good-quality dark or bittersweet (60 to 70 percent cocoa) chocolate, finely chopped
1⅓ cups 1% low-fat milk
1 cup brewed espresso or strong coffee
¼ cup unsweetened cocoa powder
¼ cup packed brown sugar
1 2-inch piece orange rind strip
¼ cup frozen fat-free whipped topping, thawed
Cocoa powder (optional)

1. Combine ⅔ cup boiling water and chopped chocolate in a medium saucepan, stirring until chocolate melts. Add milk and next 4 ingredients; cook over medium-low heat, stirring with a whisk. Heat 5 minutes or until tiny bubbles form around edge of pan, stirring frequently (do not boil). Discard rind. Spoon 1 tablespoon whipped topping over each serving. Dust with cocoa powder, if desired. Yield: 4 servings (serving size: 1 cup).

CALORIES 177 (27% from fat); FAT 5.4g (sat 3.1g, mono 1.7g, poly 0.1g); PROTEIN 4.4g; CARB 32g; FIBER 1.9g; CHOL 3mg; IRON 1.4mg; SODIUM 62mg; CALC 126mg

---

inspired vegetarian
Greet the Morning

Relax and enjoy a leisurely brunch with this mostly make-ahead mix-and-match menu.

Holiday Brunch Menu
serves 6

Blood Orange Mimosas
or
Orange juice

Savory Bread Pudding with Goat Cheese
or
Simple Baked Eggs

Whole Wheat–Oat Muffins
or
Whole-grain toast

Citrus and Kiwifruit Salad with Pomegranate Seeds and Pistachios
or
Endive Salad with Apples and Walnuts

Coffee or Tea

Game Plan

1. Up to one day in advance:
• Prepare bread pudding.
• Prepare muffins.
• Peel oranges, grapefruit, and kiwifruit; seed pomegranate.
• Prepare vinaigrette.
2. One hour before serving:
• Remove bread pudding from refrigerator.
• Squeeze oranges for mimosas.
3. Up to 30 minutes before serving:
• Bake bread pudding.
• Bake eggs.
• Slice kiwifruit and section citrus fruits; assemble citrus salad.
• Slice apples; assemble endive salad.

Blood Orange Mimosas

You can squeeze the oranges up to an hour before serving; any longer, and they may lose their freshness.

½ cup fresh blood orange juice (about 4 oranges)
3 cups Champagne or sparkling wine, chilled
1 tablespoon Cointreau (orange-flavored liqueur)

1. Strain juice through a sieve into a pitcher; add remaining ingredients. Serve immediately. Yield: 6 servings (serving size: about ¾ cup).

CALORIES 103 (0% from fat); FAT 0g; PROTEIN 0.1g; CARB 5g; FIBER 0g; CHOL 0mg; IRON 0mg; SODIUM 0mg; CALC 2mg

---

Savory Bread Pudding with Goat Cheese

This dish is best assembled the night before.

1 (1-pound) loaf firm white bread, cut into 1-inch cubes (about 12 cups)
Cooking spray
1 cup (4 ounces) crumbled goat cheese, divided
2 cups fat-free milk
1 cup 1% low-fat cottage cheese
¼ teaspoon freshly ground black pepper
3 large eggs
3 large egg whites
¼ cup sliced green onions

1. Arrange bread in a 13 x 9–inch baking dish coated with cooking spray.
2. Combine ½ cup goat cheese and next 5 ingredients in a medium bowl, stirring well with a whisk. Pour milk mixture over bread, and top with ½ cup goat cheese. Cover with foil coated with cooking spray. Refrigerate 8 hours or overnight.
3. Preheat oven to 350°.

4. Remove bread pudding from refrigerator; let stand at room temperature 30 minutes. Uncover and bake at 350° for 40 minutes or until set and golden brown. Sprinkle with onions. Yield: 6 servings (serving size: 1 [4-inch] square).

CALORIES 388 (29% from fat); FAT 12.3g (sat 6.4g, mono 3g, poly 1.5g); PROTEIN 23.4g; CARB 45.4g; FIBER 1.9g; CHOL 131mg; IRON 3.8mg; SODIUM 818mg; CALC 470mg

QUICK & EASY
Simple Baked Eggs

- 1 tablespoon butter
- 6 large eggs
- 1 teaspoon freshly ground black pepper
- ¾ teaspoon salt
- 2 tablespoons whipping cream

1. Preheat oven to 350°.
2. Coat each of 6 (6-ounce) ramekins or custard cups with ½ teaspoon butter. Break 1 egg into each prepared ramekin. Sprinkle eggs evenly with pepper and salt; spoon 1 teaspoon cream over each egg. Place ramekins in a 13 x 9–inch baking dish; add hot water to pan to a depth of 1¼ inches. Bake at 350° for 25 minutes or until eggs are set. Yield: 6 servings (serving size: 1 egg).

CALORIES 109 (72% from fat); FAT 8.7g (sat 3.9g, mono 2.9g, poly 0.8g); PROTEIN 6.5g; CARB 0.8g; FIBER 0.1g; CHOL 223mg; IRON 0.9mg; SODIUM 380mg; CALC 32mg

MAKE AHEAD • FREEZABLE
Whole Wheat–Oat Muffins

You can bake these the night before; cool and store in an airtight container.

- 1½ cups fat-free buttermilk
- 1 cup regular oats
- 3 tablespoons canola oil
- 1 teaspoon vanilla extract
- 1 large egg
- ½ cup oat flour (about 2 ounces)
- ½ cup whole wheat flour (about 2½ ounces)
- ⅓ cup packed brown sugar
- 1 teaspoon baking soda
- ¼ teaspoon salt
- Cooking spray

1. Preheat oven to 350°.
2. Combine first 5 ingredients in a medium bowl; stir well.
3. Lightly spoon flours into dry measuring cups; level with a knife. Combine flours, sugar, soda, and salt in a large bowl; make a well in center of mixture. Add buttermilk mixture; stir just until moist. Spoon batter into 12 muffin cups coated with cooking spray. Bake at 350° for 20 minutes or until a wooden pick inserted in center comes out clean. Remove from pans immediately; cool on a wire rack. Yield: 12 servings (serving size: 1 muffin).

CALORIES 145 (29% from fat); FAT 4.7g (sat 0.5g, mono 2.4g, poly 1.3g); PROTEIN 4g; CARB 20g; FIBER 1.8g; CHOL 18mg; IRON 0.9mg; SODIUM 193mg; CALC 51mg

Citrus and Kiwifruit Salad with Pomegranate Seeds and Pistachios

Peel the oranges, kiwifruit, and grapefruit ahead of time and refrigerate separately in heavy-duty zip-top plastic bags. Wait until the morning to cut them so they'll retain their sweet juiciness. Seed the pomegranate in advance; refrigerate in a zip-top plastic bag.

- 3 kiwifruit, peeled and sliced (about 1 cup)
- 4 oranges, peeled and sliced (about 2 cups)
- 2 red grapefruit, peeled and sectioned (about 2 cups)
- ¼ cup pomegranate seeds (about 1 pomegranate)
- 1 teaspoon orange-flower water (optional)
- 2 tablespoons coarsely chopped pistachios

1. Arrange kiwifruit and oranges on a serving platter; top with grapefruit and pomegranate seeds. Drizzle orange-flower water over fruit, if desired. Sprinkle with pistachios. Yield: 6 servings (serving size: about 1 cup).

CALORIES 131 (12% from fat); FAT 1.7g (sat 0.2g, mono 0.7g, poly 0.5g); PROTEIN 2.6g; CARB 29.4g; FIBER 4.6g; CHOL 0mg; IRON 0.5mg; SODIUM 3mg; CALC 67mg

QUICK & EASY
Endive Salad with Apples and Walnuts

If you can find red and white varieties of Belgian endive, use a mixture of the two. Both are mild and a bit crunchy. Separate the leaves in advance and make the vinaigrette ahead of time, but cut the apples at the last minute so they don't turn brown.

- 3 tablespoons finely chopped shallots
- 2 tablespoons apple cider vinegar
- 1 tablespoon extravirgin olive oil
- ¼ teaspoon salt
- ¼ teaspoon freshly ground black pepper
- 4 cups sliced Granny Smith apple (about 2 large)
- 3 heads Belgian endive, separated into leaves (about ¾ pound)
- 2 tablespoons chopped walnuts, toasted

1. Combine first 5 ingredients in a large bowl, stirring with a whisk. Add apple and endive; toss gently to coat. Sprinkle with walnuts. Yield: 6 servings (serving size: about 1⅓ cups salad and 1 teaspoon walnuts).

CALORIES 77 (47% from fat); FAT 4g (sat 0.5g, mono 1.9g, poly 1.5g); PROTEIN 1.7g; CARB 10.6g; FIBER 2.8g; CHOL 0mg; IRON 0.9mg; SODIUM 112mg; CALC 35mg

Perfect Bourbon Bread Pudding

This retired Georgia teacher's indulgent-tasting recipe earned our Test Kitchens' highest praise.

Kathleen Barber and her husband, Rusty, are committed to a healthy lifestyle, and she makes a point of creating exciting, tasty dishes while keeping the fat and calories in check. They've also chosen to enjoy smaller portions of some favorite dishes.

Bourbon Bread Pudding, which she has prepared for more than 25 years, was one of the first recipes she modified. Her goal was to reduce calories and fat while maintaining its sweet, buttery richness. First, she halved the butter and found there was enough to sustain the flavor and texture of the pudding and sauce. She also substituted fat-free milk for whole milk and egg whites for some of the eggs. Finally, she reduced the amount of sauce per serving but kept the bourbon. "That's the warm kick that makes this recipe so satisfying," she says. Her husband and daughters were delighted to find this version to be as good as the original. Our Test Kitchens whole-heartedly agree, awarding it our highest rating.

> Whether it's a hearty stew, filling grains, or an apple and nut dessert, readers share their comfort foods to take the chill off a wintry evening.

STAFF FAVORITE
Bourbon Bread Pudding

Day-old toasted bread cubes work best, absorbing plenty of the custard.

PUDDING:

    2 tablespoons butter, softened
    4 cups fat-free milk
    9 cups (½-inch) cubed French
       bread (about 12 ounces)
    2 cups sugar
    2 teaspoons vanilla extract
    4 large egg whites
    1 large egg
    ½ cup raisins

SAUCE:

    ¾ cup sugar
    6 tablespoons butter
    1 large egg
    ¼ cup bourbon

1. Preheat oven to 350°.
2. To prepare pudding, spread 2 tablespoons butter onto bottom and sides of a 13 x 9–inch baking dish. Set aside.
3. Heat milk in a heavy saucepan over medium-high heat to 180° or until tiny bubbles form around edge (do not boil). Place bread in a large bowl; pour hot milk over bread.
4. Combine 2 cups sugar and next 3 ingredients in a medium bowl, stirring with a whisk until well blended. Gradually add egg mixture to milk mixture, stirring constantly with a whisk. Stir in raisins; pour into prepared dish. Place dish in a roasting pan; add hot water to pan to a depth of ½ inch. Bake at 350° for 50 minutes or until browned and set.
5. To prepare sauce, combine ¾ cup sugar, 6 tablespoons butter, and 1 egg in a small, heavy saucepan over low heat. Cook 4 minutes or until a candy thermometer registers 165° and mixture is thick, stirring constantly. Remove from heat; stir in bourbon. Yield: 16 servings (serving size: ½ cup bread pudding and 1 tablespoon bourbon sauce).

CALORIES 294 (21% from fat); FAT 6.9g (sat 3.8g, mono 1.7g, poly 0.3g); PROTEIN 5.6g; CARB 52g; FIBER 0.7g; CHOL 43mg; IRON 0.8mg; SODIUM 224mg; CALC 96mg

---

MAKE AHEAD
Apricot-Almond Granola

"I like to have a batch of granola on hand during the hectic holidays. It makes a great portable snack with lots of fiber and is also good served on yogurt."
—Jennifer Sransky, Birmingham, Alabama

    2¾ cups regular oats
    ½   cup slivered almonds
    ½   cup dried cherries
    ½   cup coarsely chopped dried
        apricots
    ⅓   cup coarsely chopped walnuts
    ⅓   cup golden raisins
    ½   cup honey
    ⅓   cup butter, melted

1. Preheat oven to 350°.
2. Combine first 6 ingredients in a medium bowl. Combine honey and butter. Drizzle honey mixture over oat mixture; toss to coat. Spread mixture in a single layer onto a jelly-roll pan. Bake at 350° for 15 minutes; stir. Bake an additional 10 minutes or until lightly browned. Cool completely on pan. Break into pieces. Yield: 6 cups (serving size: ⅓ cup).

CALORIES 164 (33% from fat); FAT 6g (sat 2g, mono 2g, poly 1.6g); PROTEIN 3.3g; CARB 25.4g; FIBER 2.6g; CHOL 7mg; IRON 1mg; SODIUM 20mg; CALC 25mg

---

Apple-Walnut Bars

"This easy wintertime dessert is a variation on an old Russian recipe that traditionally calls for equal amounts of flour, sugar, dried fruits, and nuts, as well as three eggs."
—Nani Boyce, Evanston, Illinois

    ⅔ cup all-purpose flour (about 3
       ounces)
    2 teaspoons baking powder
    ½ teaspoon salt
    1 cup packed light brown sugar
    1 teaspoon vanilla extract
    2 large eggs
    2 cups diced peeled apple
    ½ cup coarsely chopped walnuts
    ⅓ cup raisins
    Cooking spray

1. Preheat oven to 350°.

2. Lightly spoon flour into dry measuring cups; level with a knife. Sift together flour, baking powder, and salt. Combine sugar, vanilla, and eggs in a medium bowl; beat with a mixer at medium speed until sugar dissolves. Add flour mixture to egg mixture; stir until well blended. Stir in apple, walnuts, and raisins.

3. Spoon batter into an 8-inch square baking dish coated with cooking spray. Bake at 350° for 40 minutes or until golden brown and a wooden pick inserted in center comes out clean. Cut into 9 bars. Yield: 9 servings (serving size: 1 bar).

CALORIES 218 (23% from fat); FAT 5.6g (sat 0.8g, mono 1g, poly 3.4g); PROTEIN 3.6g; CARB 40.2g; FIBER 1.3g; CHOL 47mg; IRON 1.5mg; SODIUM 266mg; CALC 99mg

Kate's Beef Stew

"I love a good stew in the winter and often have the makings of a great one on hand: red wine, carrots, onions, garlic, celery, and canned tomatoes."

—Kate Kunstel, Bronx, New York

- 2 tablespoons all-purpose flour
- ½ teaspoon kosher salt
- ¼ teaspoon freshly ground black pepper
- 2 pounds boneless chuck roast, trimmed and cut into 1-inch cubes
- 2 tablespoons olive oil
- 1 cup chopped onion
- ½ cup chopped celery
- 2 teaspoons minced garlic
- 1½ cups dry red wine
- 1 cup fat-free, less-sodium beef broth
- 2 oregano sprigs
- 2 rosemary sprigs
- 1 (14.5-ounce) can diced tomatoes with basil, garlic, and oregano
- 1 bay leaf
- 1 cup chopped carrot

1. Sprinkle flour, salt, and pepper over beef. Heat oil in a large Dutch oven over medium-high heat. Add beef mixture to pan; cook 5 minutes, browning on all sides. Remove beef from pan with a slotted spoon; keep warm. Add onion and celery to pan; sauté 5 minutes or until tender. Add garlic; sauté 1 minute. Add beef, wine, and next 5 ingredients to pan; bring to a boil. Cover, reduce heat, and simmer 45 minutes or until beef is just tender. Add carrot to pan; cover and cook 30 minutes. Discard oregano and rosemary sprigs and bay leaf. Yield: 7 servings (serving size: about 1 cup).

CALORIES 317 (34% from fat); FAT 12g (sat 3.5g, mono 6.2g, poly 0.8g); PROTEIN 33.7g; CARB 12.5g; FIBER 1.6g; CHOL 98mg; IRON 4.1mg; SODIUM 471mg; CALC 29mg

Bulgur Pilaf with Onions and Tomato Juice

"This side is a savory complement to lamb, beef, or chicken."

—Christine Datian, Las Vegas, Nevada

- 5 tablespoons butter
- 3 cups chopped onion
- ¾ cup crushed uncooked vermicelli
- 2 cups uncooked bulgur
- 2 cups hot fat-free, less-sodium beef broth
- 1 cup water
- 1 cup tomato juice
- ½ teaspoon salt
- ½ teaspoon white pepper
- ½ teaspoon ground cumin
- ¼ teaspoon dried basil
- ¼ cup chopped fresh flat-leaf parsley

1. Melt butter in a large saucepan over medium-high heat. Add onion to pan; sauté 10 minutes or until lightly browned. Add vermicelli to pan; cook 2 minutes. Add bulgur to pan; cook 1 minute, stirring constantly. Stir in broth and next 6 ingredients; bring to a boil. Cover, reduce heat, and simmer 20 minutes or until liquid is absorbed. Stir in parsley. Yield: 8 servings (serving size: 1 cup).

CALORIES 236 (30% from fat); FAT 7.9g (sat 4.6g, mono 2g, poly 0.6g); PROTEIN 6.8g; CARB 37.3g; FIBER 7.3g; CHOL 19mg; IRON 1.5mg; SODIUM 398mg; CALC 29mg

Gnocchi with Turkey, Peas, and Mushrooms

"I like the convenience of packaged gnocchi. You could also substitute a small pasta, like farfalle or orecchiette, in a pinch."

—Caitlyn Hurley, Morristown, Tennessee

Cooking spray
- 2 garlic cloves, minced
- 1 pound ground turkey breast
- ¼ teaspoon crushed red pepper
- ¼ teaspoon ground red pepper
- ¾ teaspoon salt, divided
- 1 (8-ounce) package sliced cremini mushrooms
- 1 (10-ounce) package frozen petite green peas, slightly thawed
- 1 (16-ounce) package vacuum-packed gnocchi (such as Vigo)
- ¼ cup (1 ounce) grated fresh Parmesan cheese
- 1 tablespoon chopped fresh basil

1. Heat a large nonstick skillet over medium-high heat. Coat pan with cooking spray. Add garlic and turkey to pan; cook 5 minutes or until turkey is no longer pink, stirring to crumble. Add crushed red and ground red peppers; cook 1 minute. Spoon turkey mixture into a bowl.

2. Recoat pan with cooking spray; return pan to medium-high heat. Add ½ teaspoon salt and mushrooms to pan; sauté 5 minutes. Stir in peas; cook 1 minute. Stir in turkey mixture; cook 3 minutes or until thoroughly heated. Cover and set aside.

3. Bring a large saucepan of water to a boil. Add gnocchi to pan; cook just until gnocchi begin to float. Drain gnocchi, reserving ½ cup cooking liquid. Combine turkey mixture, ¼ teaspoon salt, ½ cup cooking liquid, and gnocchi in a large bowl; toss well. Sprinkle with cheese and basil. Serve warm. Yield: 4 servings (serving size: about 1½ cups).

CALORIES 383 (28% from fat); FAT 11.8g (sat 6.4g, mono 3.2g, poly 0.3g); PROTEIN 37.4g; CARB 32.7g; FIBER 4.5g; CHOL 72mg; IRON 3mg; SODIUM 817mg; CALC 156mg

Island Getaway

Escape to the seaside for a festive menu with tropical flair.

Many of us enjoy a snowy, white Christmas. But for others, the holiday is more about sun and sand. That's the case in Key West, Florida, the laid-back southernmost city in the continental United States, at the far tip of the Florida Keys.

This time of year, Key West welcomes visitors who prefer the idea of snorkeling in warm, clear blue waters to sledding in the snow after opening presents. It's high season there, the weather is perfect, and the vibe is festive; only palm trees are decorated instead of pine trees, and Santa may arrive on a sailboat instead of a sleigh. Holiday menus are more likely to feature fresh local catches, such as grouper, Key West pink shrimp, or Florida spiny lobster, than ham or roast turkey, in dishes accented with bright Caribbean flavors of Key lime, pineapple, citrus, and rum.

As in most seaside towns, Key West's Christmas is a casual affair, which is reflected in our menu serving four—ideal for a low-key holiday or to wind down with friends after the big day. And for some of us, that's the gift we really want.

Key West Christmas Menu

serves 4

Pomegranate–Key Lime Vodka Cocktails

Breaded Shrimp with Honey-Mustard Sauce

Caesar Salad with Chile-Cilantro Dressing

Grouper Fillets with Citrus-Fennel Relish
or
Sesame Scallops with Citrus Sauce

Sautéed Chard with Red Pepper Flakes and Garlic
or
Cauliflower with Capers

Gewürztraminer

Rum-Macadamia Ice Cream with Grilled Pineapple and Coconut

Coffee

QUICK & EASY
Pomegranate–Key Lime Vodka Cocktails

Key limes are smaller, rounder, and more robustly flavored than the common Persian lime, and often have yellow-green skin. They're perfect for this drink, but you can substitute ¼ cup regular lime juice. Prepare the syrup a day ahead, and keep it in the fridge until you're ready to mix the cocktails.

- ¼ cup sugar
- ¼ cup water
- 1 cup club soda
- 1 cup unsweetened pomegranate juice
- ½ cup vodka
- 3 tablespoons fresh Key lime juice (about 3 limes)
- Crushed ice
- Key lime slices (optional)

1. Combine sugar and ¼ cup water in a small saucepan; bring to a boil. Reduce heat, and simmer 2 minutes or just until sugar dissolves. Remove from heat; cool completely.
2. Combine sugar syrup, club soda, and next 3 ingredients. Place crushed ice in a martini shaker; add about ¾ cup

---

pomegranate mixture. Cover and shake. Strain into a glass. Garnish with lime slice, if desired. Repeat procedure with remaining pomegranate mixture. Yield: 4 servings (serving size: ¾ cup).

CALORIES 151 (0% from fat); FAT 0g; PROTEIN 0.3g; CARB 22.5g; FIBER 0.1g; CHOL 0mg; IRON 0.1mg; SODIUM 21mg; CALC 15mg

---

QUICK & EASY
Breaded Shrimp with Honey-Mustard Sauce

Preheating the baking sheet and toasting the panko shortens the baking time needed to give the shrimp a crisp crust. In south Florida, you might prepare this with succulent fresh Key West pink shrimp.

SHRIMP:
- Cooking spray
- ½ cup panko (Japanese breadcrumbs), toasted
- ¼ teaspoon garlic powder
- ⅛ teaspoon onion powder
- Dash of salt
- 1 large egg white, lightly beaten
- 12 peeled and deveined large shrimp (about ¾ pound)

SAUCE:
- 1 tablespoon whole-grain Dijon mustard
- 1 tablespoon honey
- 1 teaspoon fresh orange juice
- Dash of ground red pepper

1. Preheat oven to 400°.
2. To prepare shrimp, coat a baking sheet with cooking spray. Place prepared pan in a 400° oven 10 minutes.
3. Combine panko and next 3 ingredients in a shallow dish, stirring with a whisk. Place egg white in another shallow dish. Dip shrimp in egg white; dredge in panko mixture. Place on preheated baking sheet. Bake at 400° for 10 minutes or until done.
4. To prepare sauce, combine mustard and remaining ingredients. Serve with shrimp. Yield: 4 servings (serving size: 3 shrimp and about 1½ teaspoons sauce).

CALORIES 70 (6% from fat); FAT 0.5g (sat 0.1g, mono 0g, poly 0.1g); PROTEIN 6.2g; CARB 10.5g; FIBER 0.3g; CHOL 32mg; IRON 0.6mg; SODIUM 199mg; CALC 8mg

Caesar Salad with Chile-Cilantro Dressing

The extra salad dressing will keep several days in the refrigerator.

½ (8-inch) fat-free flour tortilla, cut into ¼-inch-wide strips
Cooking spray
6 cups torn romaine lettuce
¼ cup unsalted pumpkinseed kernels, toasted
⅓ cup Chile-Cilantro Dressing
½ cup chopped tomato

1. Preheat oven to 375°.
2. Place tortilla strips on a baking sheet coated with cooking spray. Bake at 375° for 5 minutes or until crisp. Cool on a wire rack.
3. Place lettuce in a large bowl. Add pumpkinseeds and Chile-Cilantro Dressing; toss gently to coat. Place about 1½ cups salad on each of 4 plates. Top each serving with 2 tablespoons tomato; sprinkle evenly with tortilla strips. Yield: 4 servings.

(Totals include Chile-Cilantro Dressing) CALORIES 77 (39% from fat); FAT 3.3g (sat 0.5g, mono 1.4g, poly 1.1g); PROTEIN 3g; CARB 10.2g; FIBER 2.5g; CHOL 1mg; IRON 1.3mg; SODIUM 171mg; CALC 50mg

CHILE-CILANTRO DRESSING:
2 tablespoons unsalted pumpkinseed kernels, toasted
2 tablespoons canola oil
2 tablespoons red wine vinegar
1½ teaspoons crumbled reduced-fat feta cheese
¼ teaspoon salt
⅛ teaspoon freshly ground black pepper
½ (4.5-ounce) can chopped green chiles, undrained
1 garlic clove, chopped
1 cup chopped fresh cilantro
2 tablespoons water
½ cup plain fat-free yogurt

1. Place first 8 ingredients in a blender; process 15 seconds. Gradually add cilantro; process until smooth.
2. Combine 2 tablespoons water and yogurt in a small bowl, stirring with a whisk until smooth. Add cilantro mixture; stir well. Yield: 1½ cups (serving size: 2 tablespoons).

CALORIES 39 (72% from fat); FAT 3.1g (sat 0.3g, mono 1.7g, poly 0.9g); PROTEIN 0.8g; CARB 2.2g; FIBER 0.2g; CHOL 0mg; IRON 0.2mg; SODIUM 178mg; CALC 19mg

Grouper Fillets with Citrus-Fennel Relish

To get a head start, prepare and refrigerate the relish up to eight hours in advance.

RELISH:
1 cup finely chopped fennel bulb (about 1 bulb)
¾ cup chopped orange sections (about 2 oranges)
½ cup finely chopped cucumber
⅓ cup finely chopped red onion
1 teaspoon grated lemon rind
¼ cup chopped peeled lemon (about 2 lemons)
1 tablespoon cider vinegar
1 tablespoon extravirgin olive oil
1½ teaspoons sugar
1 teaspoon chopped fresh tarragon
¼ teaspoon salt
⅛ teaspoon freshly ground black pepper

FISH:
4 (6-ounce) grouper or other firm white fish fillets (about 1 inch thick)
1 tablespoon olive oil
½ teaspoon salt
⅛ teaspoon freshly ground black pepper
Cooking spray

1. To prepare relish, combine first 12 ingredients, tossing well to coat.
2. To prepare fish, brush fish with 1 tablespoon oil; sprinkle evenly with ½ teaspoon salt and ⅛ teaspoon pepper. Heat a nonstick skillet over medium-high heat. Coat pan with cooking spray. Add fish to pan. Cook 4 minutes on each side or until fish flakes easily when tested with a fork or until desired degree of doneness. Serve fish with relish. Yield: 4 servings (serving size: 1 fillet and about ½ cup relish).

CALORIES 253 (31% from fat); FAT 8.7g (sat 1.4g, mono 5.3g, poly 1.3g); PROTEIN 34g; CARB 9.2g; FIBER 2.2g; CHOL 63mg; IRON 1.9mg; SODIUM 545mg; CALC 80mg

Sesame Scallops with Citrus Sauce

Patting the scallops dry ensures they develop a nice crust as they sear in the pan. It's important not to move them around in the pan other than to turn them over.

1 teaspoon cornstarch
1 teaspoon water
1 pound large sea scallops
¼ teaspoon salt, divided
¼ teaspoon freshly ground black pepper, divided
1 tablespoon peanut oil
1 garlic clove, minced
⅓ cup mirin (sweet rice wine)
¼ teaspoon grated orange rind
1 tablespoon fresh orange juice
¼ teaspoon grated lemon rind
1 tablespoon fresh lemon juice
1 tablespoon low-sodium soy sauce
½ teaspoon dark sesame oil
1 tablespoon sesame seeds, toasted

1. Combine cornstarch and 1 teaspoon water; set aside.
2. Pat scallops dry with paper towels. Sprinkle scallops evenly with ⅛ teaspoon salt and ⅛ teaspoon pepper.
3. Heat peanut oil in a large nonstick skillet over medium-high heat. Add scallops; cook 2 minutes on each side or until done. Transfer scallops to a platter. Add garlic to pan; sauté 30 seconds. Add ⅛ teaspoon salt, ⅛ teaspoon pepper, mirin, and next 6 ingredients. Stir in cornstarch mixture; bring to a boil. Cook 1 minute or until sauce thickens, stirring constantly. Pour sauce over scallops; sprinkle with sesame seeds. Yield: 4 servings (serving size: 3 ounces scallops, 1 tablespoon sauce, and ¾ teaspoon sesame seeds).

CALORIES 202 (27% from fat); FAT 6g (sat 0.9g, mono 2.3g, poly 2.1g); PROTEIN 19.8g; CARB 11.5g; FIBER 0.4g; CHOL 37mg; IRON 0.8mg; SODIUM 462mg; CALC 54mg

Sautéed Chard with Red Pepper Flakes and Garlic

To help the chard's colorful stems maintain their color, cook them for about five minutes in a large pot of salted boiling water; drain and sauté with the leaves.

  1 teaspoon olive oil
 ¼ teaspoon crushed red pepper
  2 garlic cloves, coarsely chopped
 15 cups coarsely chopped Swiss chard (about 1 pound)
 ½ cup fat-free, less-sodium chicken broth
  1 tablespoon fresh lemon juice

1. Heat oil in a large nonstick skillet over medium-high heat. Add pepper and garlic to pan; sauté 30 seconds. Add chard; cook 3 minutes or until wilted. Stir in broth. Cover and cook 5 minutes or until tender. Sprinkle with juice. Yield: 4 servings (serving size: about ¾ cup).

CALORIES 70 (36% from fat); FAT 2.8g (sat 0.4g, mono 1.8g, poly 0.4g); PROTEIN 4.3g; CARB 10.3g; FIBER 3.8g; CHOL 0mg; IRON 4.2mg; SODIUM 484mg; CALC 122mg

Cauliflower with Capers

Use small *nonpareil* (a French word meaning "unparalleled") capers for this side dish.

  6 cups water
 ½ lemon
  4 cups cauliflower florets (about 1 small head)
  2 teaspoons olive oil
  2 garlic cloves, minced
  3 tablespoons chopped fresh parsley
  2 tablespoons lemon juice
 1½ teaspoons capers, drained
 ¼ teaspoon salt

1. Bring 6 cups water and lemon half to a boil in a large saucepan. Add cauliflower to pan; cook 3 minutes. Drain; discard lemon half.
2. Heat oil in a large nonstick skillet over medium heat. Add cauliflower to pan; cook 12 minutes or until soft, stirring occasionally. Add garlic; cook 30 seconds

or until lightly browned. Transfer mixture to a large bowl. Add parsley and remaining ingredients; toss well. Yield: 4 servings (serving size: about ¾ cup).

CALORIES 44 (49% from fat); FAT 2.4g (sat 0.3g, mono 1.7g, poly 0.3g); PROTEIN 1.5g; CARB 5.5g; FIBER 2g; CHOL 0mg; IRON 0.5mg; SODIUM 191mg; CALC 25mg

Rum-Macadamia Ice Cream with Grilled Pineapple and Coconut

It's warm enough in the Keys to grill outdoors year-round. In less temperate climates, you can use a grill pan to cook the pineapple.

  1 small pineapple, peeled and cored
  1 tablespoon butter, melted
Cooking spray
  2 cups Rum-Macadamia Ice Cream
  4 teaspoons flaked sweetened coconut, toasted

1. Prepare grill.
2. Cut pineapple lengthwise into 12 slices. Brush pineapple slices with butter. Place pineapple on grill rack coated with cooking spray; grill 2 minutes on each side or until thoroughly heated. Cool slightly.
3. Place 3 pineapple slices into each of 4 bowls. Top each serving with ½ cup Rum-Macadamia Ice Cream and 1 teaspoon coconut. Yield: 4 servings.

(Totals include Rum-Macadamia Ice Cream) CALORIES 323 (30% from fat); FAT 10.7g (sat 5.1g, mono 4.6g, poly 0.4g); PROTEIN 7.5g; CARB 48.6g; FIBER 2.1g; CHOL 26mg; IRON 0.5mg; SODIUM 116mg; CALC 243mg

RUM-MACADAMIA ICE CREAM:
 3½ cups 2% reduced-fat milk
  1 cup half-and-half
  2 teaspoons vanilla extract
  1 (14-ounce) can fat-free sweetened condensed milk
 ½ cup chopped macadamia nuts, toasted
 3½ tablespoons dark rum

1. Combine first 4 ingredients; stir well with a whisk. Pour milk mixture into the

freezer can of an ice-cream freezer, and freeze according to manufacturer's instructions. Stir in nuts and rum. Spoon ice cream into a freezer-safe container; cover and freeze 4 hours or until almost firm. Yield: 12 servings (serving size: about ½ cup).

CALORIES 234 (28% from fat); FAT 7.2g (sat 2.8g, mono 3.8g, poly 0.2g); PROTEIN 6.8g; CARB 33g; FIBER 0.4g; CHOL 19mg; IRON 0.1mg; SODIUM 91mg; CALC 226mg

then & now
Sour Cream Pound Cake

It seems everyone has a favorite pound cake to serve this time of year. That was the case when a staff member asked us to lighten her grandmother's pound cake, which was the star of her family's holiday table. When we first published the resulting trimmed-down recipe for Sour Cream Pound Cake in our November/December 1993 issue, the cake had three-quarters of a cup margarine and more than a cup of egg substitute. We've updated this classic by replacing the margarine with butter, and egg substitute with three eggs, both of which contribute to a richer texture. We've also brightened the flavor with a couple of tablespoons of fresh lemon juice, and dusted the pan with dry breadcrumbs to make it easier to remove the cake and create a more attractive crust.

Sour Cream Pound Cake

Cooking spray
  3 tablespoons dry breadcrumbs
  4 cups sifted cake flour (about 1 pound)
 ¼ teaspoon salt
 1½ cups light sour cream
  1 teaspoon baking soda
 ¾ cup butter
 2¾ cups sugar
  2 teaspoons vanilla extract
  3 large eggs
  2 tablespoons fresh lemon juice

1. Preheat oven to 350°.

2. Coat a 10-inch tube pan with cooking spray; dust with breadcrumbs.

3. Lightly spoon flour into dry measuring cups; level with a knife. Combine flour and salt, stirring with a whisk. Combine sour cream and baking soda; stir well. Place butter in a large bowl; beat with a mixer at medium speed until light and fluffy. Gradually add sugar and vanilla, beating until well blended. Add eggs, 1 at a time, beating well after each addition. Add juice; beat 30 seconds. Add flour mixture and sour cream mixture alternately to sugar mixture, beating at low speed, beginning and ending with flour mixture.

4. Spoon batter into prepared pan. Bake at 350° for 1 hour and 10 minutes or until a wooden pick inserted in center comes out clean. Cool in pan 10 minutes on a wire rack; remove from pan. Cool completely on a wire rack. Yield: 18 servings (serving size: 1 piece).

CALORIES 304 (30% from fat); FAT 10g (sat 6.1g, mono 2.3g, poly 0.5g); PROTEIN 3.7g; CARB 51g; FIBER 0.4g; CHOL 62mg; IRON 1.8mg; SODIUM 196mg; CALC 12mg

superfast
20 Minute Dishes

From chicken to noodles, pork to shrimp, here are simple, fresh, and easy meals you can make superfast.

QUICK & EASY
Maple-Balsamic Glazed Pork Medallions

¼ cup maple syrup
3 tablespoons balsamic vinegar
2 teaspoons Dijon mustard
1 (1-pound) pork tenderloin, trimmed
2 teaspoons olive oil
½ teaspoon salt
¼ teaspoon freshly ground black pepper

1. Combine syrup and vinegar in a small saucepan; bring to a boil. Cook until reduced to ⅓ cup (about 3 minutes), stirring occasionally. Remove from heat; stir in mustard.

2. Cut pork crosswise into 8 pieces. Place each pork piece between 2 sheets of heavy-duty plastic wrap; pound to ¼-inch thickness using a meat mallet or small heavy skillet. Heat oil in a large nonstick skillet over medium-high heat. Sprinkle pork evenly with salt and pepper. Add pork to pan; cook 3 minutes on each side or until desired degree of doneness. Add vinegar mixture; cook 1 minute, turning pork to coat. Place 2 pork medallions on each of 4 plates; drizzle about 1 tablespoon syrup mixture over each serving. Yield: 4 servings.

CALORIES 214 (27% from fat); FAT 6.4g (sat 1.7g, mono 3.3g, poly 0.7g); PROTEIN 22.7g; CARB 15.3g; FIBER 0.1g; CHOL 63mg; IRON 1.5mg; SODIUM 409mg; CALC 22mg

QUICK & EASY
Chicken Souvlaki

In Greece, souvlaki typically refers to skewers of grilled lamb. In America, chicken is more common, and it's often served in pita bread. Precooked chicken makes these sandwiches a snap to prepare. Serve with tabbouleh.

½ cup (2 ounces) crumbled feta cheese
½ cup plain Greek-style yogurt
1 tablespoon chopped fresh dill
1 tablespoon extravirgin olive oil, divided
1¼ teaspoons bottled minced garlic, divided
½ teaspoon dried oregano
2 cups sliced roasted skinless, boneless chicken breast
4 (6-inch) pitas, each cut in half horizontally
1 cup shredded iceberg lettuce
½ cup chopped peeled cucumber
½ cup chopped plum tomato
¼ cup thinly sliced red onion

1. Combine cheese, yogurt, dill, 1 teaspoon oil, and ¼ teaspoon garlic in a small bowl, stirring well.

2. Heat 2 teaspoons oil in a large skillet over medium-high heat. Add 1 teaspoon garlic and oregano to pan; sauté 20 seconds. Add chicken; cook 2 minutes or until thoroughly heated. Place ¼ cup chicken mixture in each pita half; top each with 2 tablespoons yogurt mixture, 2 tablespoons lettuce, 1 tablespoon cucumber, and 1 tablespoon tomato. Divide onion evenly among pitas. Yield: 4 servings (serving size: 2 stuffed pita halves).

CALORIES 414 (30% from fat); FAT 13.7g (sat 6.4g, mono 4.7g, poly 1.4g); PROTEIN 32.3g; CARB 38g; FIBER 2g; CHOL 81mg; IRON 2.8mg; SODIUM 595mg; CALC 187mg

QUICK & EASY
Broiled Red Snapper with Ginger-Lime Butter

Use the spicy herbed butter on shrimp, lobster, sautéed chicken, or beef, as well.

1½ tablespoons butter, softened
1 tablespoon chopped fresh cilantro
1 teaspoon minced seeded jalapeño pepper
½ teaspoon grated lime rind
¼ teaspoon bottled fresh ground ginger (such as Spice World)
¾ teaspoon salt, divided
4 (6-ounce) red snapper or other firm white fish fillets
¼ teaspoon black pepper
Cooking spray
Lime wedges (optional)

1. Combine first 5 ingredients in a bowl. Stir in ¼ teaspoon salt. Cover and chill.

2. Heat a large nonstick skillet over medium-high heat. Sprinkle both sides of fish with ½ teaspoon salt and black pepper. Coat pan with cooking spray. Add fish to pan; cook 3 minutes on each side or until fish flakes easily when tested with fork or until desired degree of doneness. Place 1 fillet on each of 4 plates; top each serving with 1½ teaspoons butter mixture. Serve with lime wedges, if desired. Yield: 4 servings.

CALORIES 202 (29% from fat); FAT 6.5g (sat 3.2g, mono 1.5g, poly 0.9g); PROTEIN 33.6g; CARB 0.2g; FIBER 0.1g; CHOL 71mg; IRON 0.3mg; SODIUM 546mg; CALC 53mg

Mango, Chicken, and Chorizo Quesadillas

Chorizo, smoked pork sausage spiced with cumin and garlic, is often used in Spanish cooking.

 1 link Spanish chorizo sausage (about 3¼ ounces), diced
1¼ cups shredded roasted skinless, boneless chicken breast
 4 (8-inch) fat-free flour tortillas
 ¾ cup (3 ounces) shredded reduced-fat Mexican cheese blend
 ½ cup chopped peeled mango
 4 teaspoons chopped fresh cilantro
Cooking spray
 ½ cup fat-free roasted corn salsa
 ¼ cup fat-free sour cream
Cilantro sprigs (optional)

1. Heat a large nonstick skillet over medium-high heat. Add sausage to pan; sauté 1 minute. Stir in chicken; sauté 2 minutes or until thoroughly heated. Remove sausage mixture from pan; set aside. Wipe pan with a paper towel.
2. Sprinkle half of each tortilla with 3 tablespoons cheese; top each tortilla with ¼ cup sausage mixture, 2 tablespoons mango, and 1 teaspoon cilantro. Carefully fold tortillas in half, pressing gently to seal.
3. Return pan to medium heat. Coat pan with cooking spray. Add 2 filled tortillas to pan; cook 2 minutes on each side or until lightly browned. Repeat procedure with cooking spray and remaining filled tortillas. Top each serving with 2 tablespoons salsa and 1 tablespoon sour cream. Garnish with cilantro sprigs, if desired. Yield: 4 servings (serving size: 1 quesadilla).

CALORIES 362 (31% from fat); FAT 12.3g (sat 4.9g, mono 3.3g, poly 0.9g); PROTEIN 27.9g; CARB 34.1g; FIBER 2.4g; CHOL 67mg; IRON 1.1mg; SODIUM 910mg; CALC 247mg

Soba Noodle Salad with Citrus Vinaigrette

Look for soba noodles, often labeled buckwheat noodles, in the Asian section of supermarkets.

 1 (8-ounce) package soba noodles
1¼ cups frozen shelled edamame (green soybeans)
 ¾ cup matchstick-cut carrots
 ⅓ cup sliced green onions
 2 tablespoons chopped fresh cilantro
1½ teaspoons finely chopped serrano chile
 1 pound peeled and deveined medium shrimp
 ¼ teaspoon salt
 ¼ teaspoon black pepper
Cooking spray
 2 tablespoons fresh orange juice
 2 tablespoons fresh lime juice
 1 tablespoon low-sodium soy sauce
 1 tablespoon dark sesame oil
 1 tablespoon olive oil

1. Cook noodles in boiling water 7 minutes or until almost al dente. Add soybeans to pan; cook 1 minute or until thoroughly heated. Drain. Place noodle mixture in a large bowl. Add carrots and next 3 ingredients; toss.
2. Heat a large skillet over medium-high heat. Sprinkle shrimp with salt and pepper. Coat pan with cooking spray. Add shrimp to pan; cook 1½ minutes on each side or until done. Add shrimp to noodle mixture.
3. Combine orange juice and remaining ingredients in a bowl, stirring well with a whisk. Drizzle juice mixture over noodle mixture; toss well. Yield: 4 servings (serving size: about 2 cups).

CALORIES 418 (22% from fat); FAT 10.2g (sat 1.3g, mono 4.3g, poly 2.4g); PROTEIN 31.9g; CARB 52.4g; FIBER 3.4g; CHOL 168mg; IRON 5.5mg; SODIUM 922mg; CALC 101mg

Three-Chile-Dusted Shrimp with Quick Corn Relish

3½ teaspoons sugar, divided
 2 teaspoons chili powder
 1 teaspoon ancho chile powder
 ¼ teaspoon chipotle chile powder
 ½ teaspoon salt, divided
1½ pounds peeled and deveined large shrimp
 5 teaspoons olive oil, divided
 ½ cup chopped onion
 ½ cup chopped red bell pepper
 2 teaspoons bottled minced garlic
 2 teaspoons bottled minced ginger
 1 (10-ounce) package frozen whole-kernel corn
1½ tablespoons cider vinegar
 ½ cup chopped green onions

1. Combine 2 teaspoons sugar, chili powder, chile powders, and ¼ teaspoon salt in a shallow dish. Add shrimp to spice mixture; toss well to coat.
2. Heat 1 tablespoon oil in a large nonstick skillet over medium-high heat. Add ½ cup onion, bell pepper, garlic, and ginger to pan; sauté 3 minutes. Add 1½ teaspoons sugar and corn to pan; cook 3 minutes, stirring occasionally. Stir in vinegar; cook 30 seconds. Transfer corn mixture to a bowl; stir in ¼ teaspoon salt and ½ cup green onions.
3. Wipe pan with a paper towel. Heat 2 teaspoons oil in pan over medium-high heat. Add shrimp to pan; sauté 3 minutes or until done, turning once. Serve with corn mixture. Yield: 4 servings (serving size: 4½ ounces shrimp and about ¾ cup corn mixture).

CALORIES 342 (25% from fat); FAT 9.6g (sat 1.5g, mono 4.8g, poly 2.2g); PROTEIN 37.9g; CARB 28g; FIBER 3.7g; CHOL 259mg; IRON 5.3mg; SODIUM 569mg; CALC 114mg

High Country Noche Buena

Santa Fe, New Mexico, honors tradition and celebrates with local flavors on Christmas Eve.

During the Christmas season, Santa Fe, New Mexico, truly flaunts its nickname, "The City Different." The Santa Fe celebration remains distinctive in its respect for old traditions and hearty local food.

The devout Spanish founders of the 17th century, who named the city La Villa Real de la Santa Fe de San Francisco de Asís (The Royal City of the Holy Faith of St. Francis of Assisi), left behind a legacy of Catholic and old-world traditions. The twin sides of this heritage come together in many ways at Christmastime. In a striking link to the past, Santa Feans reenact an ancient Christmas miracle play, *Las Posadas*, brought by the earliest settlers. A number of parish churches perform the drama, which reenacts Mary and Joseph's search for a place to stay where Jesus could be born, for nine nights during the holiday season, and the Museum of New Mexico stages a performance on the city's main plaza a few days before Christmas.

Ensalada de Noche Buena

This salad (ehn-sah-LAH-dah de NO-chay BWAY-nah) provides a cooling contrast to other spicy flavors at the holiday table.

    4   large navel oranges
    1   large red grapefruit
    3   cups (1-inch) cubed peeled
        jícama (about 1 pound)
    ¾   cup slivered red radishes
        (about 6 medium)
 1½   teaspoons grated lime rind
    3   tablespoons fresh lime juice
    3   tablespoons plain fat-free
        yogurt
    2   tablespoons light mayonnaise
 1½   tablespoons honey
    ¼   teaspoon freshly ground
        black pepper
 Dash of salt
    4   cups chopped romaine
        lettuce
    1   cup pomegranate seeds
    3   tablespoons unsalted
        pumpkinseed kernels,
        toasted
    2   tablespoons chopped fresh
        cilantro

1. Peel and section oranges and grapefruit over a large bowl, reserving juice; add sections to juice. Add jícama and radishes to orange mixture; toss gently. Cover and chill 30 minutes.
2. Combine rind and next 6 ingredients in a small bowl, stirring until smooth. Arrange lettuce in a large bowl. Using a slotted spoon, place orange mixture over lettuce; drizzle evenly with yogurt mixture. Sprinkle with pomegranate seeds, pumpkinseed kernels, and cilantro. Yield: 8 servings (serving size: about 1⅔ cups salad and about 1 tablespoon dressing).

CALORIES 133 (22% from fat); FAT 3.3g (sat 0.3g, mono 1.6g, poly 1.2g); PROTEIN 2.4g; CARB 26.2g; FIBER 5.7g; CHOL 3mg; IRON 0.9mg; SODIUM 58mg; CALC 65mg

WINE NOTE: Sparkling wine deserves a place at every holiday table, both for its celebratory allure and compatibility with many foods. When celebrating Santa Fe style, look for Gruet Brut NV ($14) from New Mexico. Made in the manner of true Champagne, it has lemony acidity that stands up to the acid of the yogurt dressing, while crisp grapefruit flavors echo the salad's citrus elements.

Posole

A hominy-based stew, *posole* (poh-SOH-leh) is ideal for a Christmas Eve open house. With its mild flavor, the hominy makes a great foil for the hearty pork, spicy chiles, radishes, green onions, and limes.

    ¾   pound dried white corn hominy
    2   teaspoons canola oil
    8   ounces boneless pork loin, cut
        into ½-inch pieces
    1   cup chopped onion
    2   teaspoons dried oregano
    ¾   teaspoon salt
    2   garlic cloves, minced
    1   bay leaf
    3   cups water
    3   (14-ounce) cans fat-free,
        less-sodium chicken broth
    2   dried New Mexico chiles
    2   cups shredded cabbage
    ⅓   cup chopped fresh cilantro
    ⅓   cup slivered radishes
    ⅓   cup chopped green onions
    8   lime wedges

1. Place hominy in a large Dutch oven. Cover with water to 4 inches above hominy; cover and let stand 8 hours. Drain. Return hominy to pan. Cover with water to 4 inches above hominy; bring to a boil. Reduce heat, and simmer 1 hour, stirring occasionally; drain. Wipe pan dry with a paper towel.
2. Heat oil in pan over medium-high heat. Add pork to pan; sauté 5 minutes, turning to brown on all sides. Add 1 cup onion; sauté 2 minutes or until tender. Add oregano and next 3 ingredients; sauté 1 minute. Return hominy to pan. Add 3 cups water and broth; bring to a boil. Reduce heat, and simmer 30 minutes, stirring occasionally. Add chiles; simmer 30 minutes, stirring occasionally. Discard chiles and bay leaf. Ladle about 1½ cups posole into each of 8 bowls. Garnish each serving with ¼ cup cabbage, about 2 teaspoons cilantro, about 2 teaspoons radishes, about 2 teaspoons green onions, and 1 lime wedge. Yield: 8 servings.

CALORIES 137 (39% from fat); FAT 5.9g (sat 1.6g, mono 2.6g, poly 1.1g); PROTEIN 8.7g; CARB 12.7g; FIBER 3.4g; CHOL 17mg; IRON 1.4mg; SODIUM 567mg; CALC 41mg

Red Chile Sauce

New Mexico dried chiles have a moderately spicy heat. If you can't find them, substitute ancho or dried California chiles. Make this sauce up to three days ahead, and refrigerate until you're ready to use it.

    5 dried red New Mexico chiles
       (about 1¼ ounces)
    1 tablespoon canola oil
 1½ cups chopped onion
    2 garlic cloves, minced
    2 cups fat-free, less-sodium chicken
       broth, divided
    2 cups water
    1 teaspoon crumbled dried oregano
  ¾ teaspoon salt
    1 tablespoon masa harina

1. Remove stems and seeds from chiles; coarsely chop. Place chiles in a spice or coffee grinder; process until finely ground to measure ¼ cup.
2. Heat oil in a medium saucepan over medium heat. Add onion and garlic to pan; cook 3 minutes or until onion is tender, stirring frequently. Add ground chiles; stir well. Stir in 1 cup broth. Add remaining 1 cup broth, 2 cups water, oregano, and salt; bring to a boil. Reduce heat, and simmer until reduced to 3 cups (about 20 minutes), stirring occasionally.
3. Sprinkle masa harina over chile mixture; stir well. Bring to a boil. Cook 1 minute or until slightly thick; remove from heat. Let stand 10 minutes. Place half of chile mixture in a blender. Remove center piece of lid (to allow steam to escape); secure lid on blender. Place a clean towel over opening in lid (to avoid splatters). Process until smooth. Pour into a large bowl. Repeat procedure with remaining chile mixture. Yield: 16 servings (serving size: about 3 tablespoons).

CALORIES 24 (38% from fat); FAT 1g (sat 0.1g, mono 0.5g, poly 0.3g); PROTEIN 0.7g; CARB 3.4g; FIBER 0.9g; CHOL 0mg; IRON 0.3mg; SODIUM 161mg; CALC 9mg

Green Chile Sauce

Fresh Anaheim chiles—long, slender, pale green peppers—have mild heat. Pair with chicken or pork, or serve it as a snack with baked tortilla chips.

    6 Anaheim chiles
    1 tablespoon canola oil
    2 cups chopped onion
    2 garlic cloves, minced
    1 tablespoon all-purpose flour
    1 teaspoon ground coriander
  ½ teaspoon salt
    1 (14-ounce) can fat-free,
       less-sodium chicken broth

1. Preheat broiler.
2. Place chiles on a foil-lined baking sheet; broil 14 minutes or until blackened and charred, turning after 7 minutes. Place in a heavy-duty zip-top plastic bag; seal. Let stand 15 minutes. Peel and discard skins. Cut a lengthwise slit in each chile. Remove and discard seeds and tops. Chop chiles to measure ¾ cup.
3. Heat canola oil in a medium saucepan over medium-high heat. Add onion to pan; sauté 5 minutes or until tender. Add garlic; sauté 1 minute. Stir in flour; cook 1 minute. Add chiles, coriander, salt, and broth; bring to a boil. Reduce heat, and simmer 15 minutes, stirring occasionally. Place half of chile mixture in a blender. Remove center piece of lid (to allow steam to escape); secure lid on blender. Place a clean towel over opening in lid (to avoid splatters). Blend until smooth. Return pureed chile mixture to pan; stir well. Remove from heat; cool completely. Yield: 16 servings (serving size: 3 tablespoons).

CALORIES 23 (39% from fat); FAT 1g (sat 0.1g, mono 0.2g, poly 0.6g); PROTEIN 0.7g; CARB 3.3g; FIBER 0.6g; CHOL 0mg; IRON 0.2mg; SODIUM 114mg; CALC 9mg

Enchiladas for Eight Menu
serves 8

For the best and most authentic flavor, use our recipe for Green Chile Sauce (recipe at left) when making the enchiladas.

Green Chile–Chicken Enchiladas

Spicy Spanish rice*

Baked tortilla chips and salsa

*Heat 2 tablespoons canola oil in a large saucepan over medium-high heat. Add ½ cup finely chopped onion and 2 minced garlic cloves; sauté 3 minutes. Add 2 cups uncooked long-grain rice; cook 2 minutes, stirring constantly. Add 1¾ cups fat-free, less-sodium chicken broth and 1 (10-ounce) can diced tomatoes and green chiles, undrained; bring to a boil. Cover, reduce heat, and simmer 20 minutes or until liquid is absorbed. Stir in 1 cup thawed frozen whole-kernel corn. Sprinkle with 2 tablespoons chopped fresh cilantro.

Green Chile–Chicken Enchiladas

New Mexicans prefer these over the beef enchiladas associated with other Southwest cuisines. Prepare the sauce and the chicken mixture up to two days ahead, and refrigerate separately until ready to assemble the enchiladas.

    3 cups fat-free, less-sodium chicken
       broth
 1½ cups finely chopped onion,
       divided
    2 teaspoons dried oregano
  ½ teaspoon salt
    4 (6-ounce) skinless, boneless
       chicken breast halves
    2 garlic cloves, minced
    1 bay leaf
  ½ cup fat-free sour cream
    3 cups Green Chile Sauce (recipe at
       left)
Cooking spray
  16 (6-inch) corn tortillas
  ¾ cup (3 ounces) shredded
       Monterey Jack cheese
  ½ cup (2 ounces) shredded Cheddar
       cheese

1. Combine broth, 1 cup onion, and next 5 ingredients in a large saucepan; bring to a boil. Reduce heat, and simmer 15 minutes or until chicken is done. Remove chicken from pan; chill 15 minutes. Reserve broth mixture for another use. Shred chicken into bite-sized pieces. Combine chicken, ½ cup onion, and sour cream in a bowl, stirring well.

2. Preheat oven to 350°.

3. Spread ¼ cup Green Chile Sauce in each of 2 (11 x 7–inch) baking dishes coated with cooking spray. Warm tortillas according to package directions. Spoon about ⅓ cup chicken mixture down center of each tortilla, and roll up. Place 8 filled tortillas, seam sides down, in each dish, and pour 1¼ cups of remaining Green Chile Sauce over filled tortillas in each dish. Combine cheeses in a bowl. Sprinkle half of cheese mixture evenly over filled tortillas in each dish. Bake at 350° for 18 minutes or until thoroughly heated. Yield: 8 servings (serving size: 2 enchiladas).

(Totals include Green Chile Sauce) CALORIES 308 (30% from fat); FAT 10.1g (sat 4.3g, mono 2.6g, poly 2g); PROTEIN 27.2g; CARB 29g; FIBER 3.4g; CHOL 69mg; IRON 1.2mg; SODIUM 382mg; CALC 198mg

MAKE AHEAD • FREEZABLE
Beef Tamales

Pork is the traditional filling for tamales in New Mexico, but since we use pork in Carne Adovada, we chose beef filling for these tamales. Adjust the ground chile in the recipe for more or less heat as you prefer. If this recipe makes more tamales than you need, freeze leftovers up to one month.

FILLING:
Cooking spray
1½ cups chopped onion
2 garlic cloves, thinly sliced
1 pound beef stew meat
1 cup water
½ teaspoon salt
1 tablespoon all-purpose flour
1½ teaspoons ground dried red New Mexico chile
16 large dried cornhusks

DOUGH:
3 cups masa harina
1 teaspoon salt
2 teaspoons canola oil
1 tablespoon butter, melted
1 cup fat-free, less-sodium beef broth
1 cup water

REMAINING INGREDIENTS:
16 long thin strips dried cornhusk
1 cup Red Chile Sauce (optional; page 408)

1. Preheat oven to 350°.

2. To prepare filling, heat a large oven-proof Dutch oven over medium-high heat. Coat pan with cooking spray. Add onion and garlic to pan; sauté 4 minutes or until onion is tender. Add beef; sauté 5 minutes, turning to brown on all sides. Stir in 1 cup water and ½ teaspoon salt; bring mixture to a boil. Cover and bake at 350° for 1½ hours or until beef is tender.

3. Transfer beef to a bowl with a slotted spoon. Pour drippings into a glass measure. Add enough water to drippings to equal 1 cup. Wipe pan with paper towels.

4. Shred beef into bite-sized pieces. Heat pan over medium-high heat. Coat pan with cooking spray. Return beef to pan; sprinkle with flour. Cook 1 minute, stirring constantly. Stir in ground chile; stir in drippings mixture. Reduce heat, and cook 7 minutes or until liquid almost evaporates, stirring frequently. Remove from heat; cool to room temperature.

5. Place whole cornhusks in a large bowl; cover with water. Weight husks down with a can; soak 30 minutes. Drain husks.

6. To prepare dough, combine masa harina and 1 teaspoon salt in a large bowl. Add oil and butter; stir well. Add broth and 1 cup water; stir until a soft dough forms.

7. Working with 1 husk at a time, place about ¼ cup masa harina dough in the center of husk; press dough into a 4 x 3–inch rectangle. Spoon about 2 tablespoons beef mixture down 1 side of dough. Using corn husk as your guide, roll up tamale, jelly-roll style; fold bottom ends of husk under. Tie 1 corn husk strip around tamale to secure; stand upright in a vegetable steamer. Repeat

procedure with remaining whole corn husks, masa dough, beef mixture, and corn husk strips. Steam tamales, covered, 50 minutes or until dough is firm. Remove tamales from vegetable steamer; let stand 5 minutes. Serve with Red Chile Sauce, if desired. Yield: 8 servings (serving size: 2 tamales).

CALORIES 145 (27% from fat); FAT 4.3g (sat 1.4g, mono 1.6g, poly 0.9g); PROTEIN 7.9g; CARB 19.9g; FIBER 2.2g; CHOL 20mg; IRON 1.4mg; SODIUM 268mg; CALC 49mg

Carne Adovada

Red as a Santa Fe sunset, *Carne Adovada* (KAR-neh ah-doh-VAH-dah) looks right at home on the holiday dinner table. The carne, or meat—in this case, pork—is bathed in a spicy chile sauce. Wrap it in flour tortillas to tone down the heat a bit, if you like.

24 dried red New Mexico chiles, seeded, rinsed, and cut into (1-inch) pieces
Cooking spray
1½ cups chopped onion
1 tablespoon cider vinegar
2 teaspoons dried oregano
1½ teaspoons salt
3 garlic cloves, minced
1 (14-ounce) can fat-free, less-sodium chicken broth
1 (3-pound) boneless pork shoulder (Boston butt), trimmed and cut into 1½-inch cubes

1. Preheat broiler.

2. Arrange chiles in a single layer on a baking sheet coated with cooking spray; broil 1 minute.

3. Reduce oven temperature to 300°.

4. Place chiles, onion, and next 5 ingredients in a blender; process until smooth. Combine pork and chile mixture in a 13 x 9–inch baking dish coated with cooking spray. Cover and bake at 300° for 2½ hours. Uncover and bake an additional 30 minutes or until sauce is thick. Yield: 8 servings (serving size: about 3 ounces).

CALORIES 246 (48% from fat); FAT 13.2g (sat 4.6g, mono 5.4g, poly 1.7g); PROTEIN 17.3g; CARB 15.8g; FIBER 6g; CHOL 55mg; IRON 2.3mg; SODIUM 408mg; CALC 38mg

Santa Fe Table

At Christmas parties and family dinners, the food is largely traditional fare, based on beloved ingredients such as chiles, corn, pork, and squash. New Mexico's legendary green and red chiles bring Christmas color to the plate. Whether chopped fresh in the green form or dried and ground for the red, they can be equally hot since their piquancy depends on the variety of the pods and the growing conditions, not the hue. Sometimes the chiles are used as garnishes for extra flavor, but in other cases, as with enchiladas, they're simmered into sauces that become integral parts of the preparation. Locals often prefer the green or red variants with different dishes, but at any time of year, indecisive diners can order their food "Christmas" and get both styles together.

Posole sits at the center of the table at many Santa Fe holiday meals. This hominy-based stew has been a New Mexico favorite for centuries and is inexpensive to fix for a crowd. Native Americans taught early Spanish settlers their technique for drying and preserving corn as posole, and the Europeans, in turn, contributed the pork that rounds out the specialty's robust character. The preparation often appears as a side dish throughout the year but is dressed up with more condiments for its role at Christmas.

Resembling little presents, cornhusk-wrapped tamales peak in popularity at Christmas, too. Because they're moderately labor intensive, people like to share the process of mixing and preparing the ingredients, wrapping the tamales, and then steaming them. Pork and red chile is the classic filling, but many cooks use other types of stuffing, as well, such as green chile, corn, and zucchini.

Carne Adovada, succulent pork cubes slow-cooked in a sauce of toasted, coarse-ground red chiles, generally is the spiciest dish on the table. You can cool down with an Ensalada de Noche Buena, a bright salad of citrus, crunchy jícama, and jewel-toned pomegranate seeds, or with Natillas, a custard-based dessert topped with meringue. And, of course, toast the holidays with a sparkling cocktail and a rousing "Feliz Navidad."

Citywide Celebration

The festivities build as the sun sets on Christmas Eve—*Noche Buena,* the "Good Night," as it's known here—and continue until midnight with the arrival of Christmas Day. Residents deck their doors and outer walls with dried red chiles in wreaths and *ristras* (strings of dried chiles), intertwined with boughs of juniper, spruce, cedar, and pine. Indoors they light fragrant *piñon* (pine) logs in rounded kiva fireplaces to scent the evening air. As azure skies give way to sunset shades of purple and scarlet, thousands of people light *farolitos,* "little lanterns," made with candles nestled in sand at the bottom of paper bags. A symbol of enduring faith to some, and a charming custom to everyone, the lanterns glow along streets, sidewalks, walls, adobe rooftops, even tree branches in neighborhoods around the city.

On Santa Fe's historic east side, the fiesta of lights shines the brightest, attracting throngs of visitors to the adjoining streets of Canyon Road and Acequia Madre, which become pedestrian-only lanes for this special evening. Bundled-up families and groups of friends wander for blocks or even miles through the frigid night, buoyed by the lanterns, small bonfires called luminarias, gifts of hot chocolate and cider provided by local residents and merchants, and spontaneous caroling. Some join parties in progress, while others investigate small side streets to find the most creative displays—perhaps farolitos riding a model train or attached to small hot air balloons suspended in the air. As midnight approaches, many celebrants head to services at churches or to the large Noche Buena mass at St. Francis Cathedral.

Red Chile–Cheese Enchiladas

New Mexican enchiladas, especially those made simply with tortillas, chile sauce, and cheese, are often served layered like lasagna.

¾ cup fat-free cottage cheese
⅔ cup (2½ ounces) shredded Monterey Jack cheese
2 tablespoons finely chopped onion
⅛ teaspoon salt
2 cups Red Chile Sauce (page 408)
Cooking spray
12 (6-inch) corn tortillas
½ cup (2 ounces) shredded reduced-fat extrasharp Cheddar cheese

1. Preheat oven to 400°.
2. Place cottage cheese in a food processor; process 1 minute or until smooth. Combine cottage cheese, Monterey Jack cheese, onion, and salt, stirring well.
3. Spread ¼ cup Red Chile Sauce in bottom of an 8 x 8–inch baking dish coated with cooking spray. Arrange 4 tortillas over sauce, overlapping slightly. Spread ½ cup cottage cheese mixture evenly over tortillas; top with ½ cup Red Chile Sauce. Repeat layers once with 4 tortillas, remaining cottage cheese mixture, and ½ cup Red Chile Sauce. Arrange remaining 4 tortillas over sauce, overlapping slightly; spoon remaining ¾ cup Red Chile Sauce over tortillas. Sprinkle evenly with Cheddar cheese. Cover and bake at 400° for 10 minutes. Uncover and bake an additional 10 minutes or until cheese melts. Let stand 5 minutes. Cut into 8 squares. Yield: 8 servings (serving size: 1 square).

(Totals include Red Chile Sauce) CALORIES 162 (30% from fat); FAT 5.4g (sat 2.9g, mono 1.1g, poly 0.6g); PROTEIN 8.8g; CARB 20.1g; FIBER 2.1g; CHOL 14mg; IRON 0.6mg; SODIUM 305mg; CALC 201mg

Natillas

This dessert (pronounced nah-TEE-yahz) may be made a day ahead, but prepare the meringue just before serving.

2¾ cups fat-free milk, divided
4 large egg yolks
1 cup granulated sugar, divided
¼ cup cornstarch
⅛ teaspoon salt
¼ cup whipping cream
1 vanilla bean, split lengthwise
2 teaspoons butter
4 large pasteurized egg whites
¼ teaspoon vanilla extract
Freshly grated whole nutmeg

1. Combine 1 cup milk and egg yolks in a large bowl, stirring well with a whisk; set aside.
2. Combine ¾ cup sugar, cornstarch, and salt in a medium saucepan over medium-high heat; gradually add 1¾ cups milk, stirring constantly with a whisk. Stir in whipping cream. Scrape seeds from vanilla bean; add seeds and bean to milk mixture. Bring mixture to a boil; cook 1 minute, stirring constantly with a whisk. Remove from heat.
3. Gradually add half of hot milk mixture to egg yolk mixture, stirring constantly with a whisk. Return milk mixture to pan over medium-high heat; bring to a boil. Cook 1 minute, stirring constantly. Remove from heat. Add butter to milk mixture; stir until combined. Place pan in a large ice-filled bowl 25 minutes or until custard cools, stirring occasionally. Discard vanilla bean. Spoon custard into a bowl. Cover surface of custard with plastic wrap; chill.
4. Place egg whites in a large bowl; beat with an electric mixer at medium speed until foamy. Add ¼ cup sugar, 1 tablespoon at a time, beating at high speed until stiff peaks form. Beat in vanilla. Gently fold ½ cup whites into custard.
5. Spoon ½ cup custard into each of 8 bowls; top each with ¼ cup whites. Garnish with nutmeg. Yield: 8 servings.

CALORIES 212 (27% from fat); FAT 6.3g (sat 3.1g, mono 2g, poly 0.5g); PROTEIN 6.2g; CARB 33.3g; FIBER 0g; CHOL 120mg; IRON 0.5mg; SODIUM 117mg; CALC 124mg

Sparkling Chimayó Cocktails

1 cup gold tequila
¾ cup sparkling water, chilled
2 tablespoons crème de cassis (black currant–flavored liqueur)
2 tablespoons fresh lemon juice
1 (750-milliliter) bottle sparkling apple cider, chilled

1. Combine all ingredients in a pitcher; stir to combine. Serve immediately. Yield: 8 servings (serving size: ⅔ cup).

CALORIES 124 (4% from fat); FAT 0.6g (sat 0.3g, mono 0g, poly 0g); PROTEIN 0.1g; CARB 12.9g; FIBER 0g; CHOL 0mg; IRON 0mg; SODIUM 15mg; CALC 1mg

dinner tonight
Steak at its Best

From casual to sophisticated, these menu options serve the sizzle.

Steak Menu 1
serves 4

Filet Mignon with Cabernet Sauce

Sautéed mushrooms with prosciutto*

Mashed potatoes with chives

*Heat 1½ teaspoons olive oil in a medium nonstick skillet. Add 3 cups quartered cremini mushrooms, ¼ teaspoon kosher salt, and 2 minced garlic cloves to pan; sauté 4 minutes or until moisture evaporates. Remove from heat; stir in ¼ cup chopped prosciutto and 1 tablespoon chopped fresh flat-leaf parsley.

Game Plan

1. While potatoes cook:
• Prepare ingredients for steak.
• Prepare ingredients for mushrooms.
2. Prepare steak and sauce.
3. Prepare mushrooms.
4. Mash potatoes.

Filet Mignon with Cabernet Sauce

Just a touch of soy sauce adds depth and balances the wine reduction sauce. Butter renders a supple finish. Use a fresh parsley sprig to garnish, if you like.
TOTAL TIME: 36 MINUTES

Cooking spray
4 (4-ounce) filet mignon steaks
½ teaspoon salt, divided
½ teaspoon freshly ground black pepper, divided
¼ cup minced shallots
1 tablespoon red wine vinegar
2 teaspoons low-sodium soy sauce
1 cup cabernet sauvignon
1 cup fat-free, less-sodium beef broth
2 teaspoons butter

1. Heat a large nonstick skillet over medium-high heat. Coat pan with cooking spray. Sprinkle both sides of steaks evenly with ¼ teaspoon salt and ¼ teaspoon pepper. Add steaks to pan; cook 3 minutes on each side or until desired degree of doneness. Remove from pan. Cover and keep warm. Add shallots to pan; sauté 1 minute. Stir in vinegar and soy sauce, scraping pan to loosen browned bits; cook 1 minute or until liquid evaporates, stirring constantly. Add ¼ teaspoon salt, ¼ teaspoon pepper, wine, and broth; bring to a boil. Cook until reduced to ½ cup (about 11 minutes). Remove from heat; stir in butter. Serve with steaks. Yield: 4 servings (serving size: 1 steak and about 2 tablespoons sauce).

CALORIES 358 (57% from fat); FAT 22.5g (sat 9.5g, mono 9.3g, poly 0.9g); PROTEIN 23.2g; CARB 3.6g; FIBER 0.2g; CHOL 80mg; IRON 1.8mg; SODIUM 565mg; CALC 32mg

Steak Menu 2

serves 4

Italian Ribeye Steak

Roasted red potatoes
with parsley*

Steamed green beans

*Preheat oven to 400°. Place 6 cups quartered red potatoes in a large bowl. Drizzle potatoes with 1 tablespoon olive oil, and sprinkle with ½ teaspoon kosher salt; toss to coat. Arrange potato mixture in an even layer on a baking sheet. Bake at 400° for 40 minutes or until tender, turning once. Toss potatoes with ¼ cup chopped fresh flat-leaf parsley.

Game Plan

1. While oven preheats:
   • Prepare ingredients for potatoes.
2. While potatoes cook:
   • Prepare steaks.
3. While steaks stand:
   • Toss potatoes with parsley.
   • Prepare green beans.

QUICK & EASY
Italian Ribeye Steak

Marbled ribeye steaks require little embellishment to deliver satisfying flavor.

TOTAL TIME: 45 MINUTES

1 teaspoon chopped fresh rosemary
½ teaspoon kosher salt
½ teaspoon freshly ground black pepper
2 garlic cloves, minced
2 (8-ounce) ribeye steaks, trimmed and cut in half crosswise
Cooking spray
4 lemon wedges

1. Combine first 4 ingredients in a bowl, stirring well. Rub rosemary mixture evenly over both sides of steaks. Heat a grill pan over medium-high heat. Coat pan with cooking spray. Add steaks to pan; cook 2½ minutes. Turn steaks over; cook 2 minutes or until desired degree of doneness. Let steaks stand 10 minutes. Serve with lemon wedges. Yield: 4 servings (serving size: 3 ounces steak and 1 lemon wedge).

CALORIES 238 (39% from fat); FAT 10.3g (sat 3.9g, mono 4.1g, poly 0.4g); PROTEIN 33g; CARB 1.4g; FIBER 0.3g; CHOL 103mg; IRON 2.4mg; SODIUM 304mg; CALC 24mg

Steak Menu 3

serves 4

Citrus-Rubbed Skirt Steak

Orange and red onion salad*

Couscous

*Combine 4 cups torn Boston lettuce, 1 cup orange sections, and ¼ cup thinly sliced red onion in a large bowl. Combine ¼ cup fresh orange juice, 2 tablespoons white wine vinegar, 1 tablespoon extravirgin olive oil, ¼ teaspoon freshly ground black pepper, and ⅛ teaspoon salt, stirring well with a whisk. Drizzle lettuce mixture with juice mixture; toss gently to coat.

Game Plan

1. While steak cooks:
   • Prepare couscous.
   • Prepare ingredients for orange and red onion salad.
2. While steak stands:
   • Toss salad.
   • Fluff couscous.

QUICK & EASY
Citrus-Rubbed Skirt Steak

Flavorful skirt steak is a favorite cut in Mexican cuisine. Because of its oblong shape, it may be difficult to fit the entire steak in your grill pan. If so, simply cut it in half across the grain and cook both halves at the same time.

TOTAL TIME: 36 MINUTES

2 teaspoons grated lemon rind
2 teaspoons grated orange rind
¼ teaspoon kosher salt
⅛ teaspoon ground red pepper
1 garlic clove, minced
1 (1-pound) skirt steak, trimmed
Cooking spray

1. Combine first 5 ingredients in a bowl, stirring well. Lightly coat steak with cooking spray. Rub rind mixture evenly over steak. Heat a grill pan over medium-high heat. Coat pan with cooking spray. Add steak to pan; cook 5 minutes on each side or until desired degree of doneness. Let stand 5 minutes; cut steak diagonally across grain into thin slices. Yield: 4 servings (serving size: 3 ounces steak).

CALORIES 177 (44% from fat); FAT 8.6g (sat 3.3g, mono 4.4g, poly 0.3g); PROTEIN 22.8g; CARB 0.7g; FIBER 0.2g; CHOL 50mg; IRON 2.4mg; SODIUM 653mg; CALC 14mg

Steak Menu 4

serves 4

Steak Sandwiches with Worcestershire Mayonnaise

Sweet potato oven fries*

Apple slices with bottled caramel topping

*Preheat oven to 425°. Cut 2 medium peeled sweet potatoes lengthwise into wedges; place on a baking sheet. Drizzle potatoes with 1½ tablespoons olive oil. Sprinkle with 1 teaspoon salt and ½ teaspoon freshly ground black pepper; toss to coat. Bake at 425° for 20 minutes or until golden, turning after 10 minutes.

Game Plan

1. While oven preheats:
   • Prepare potatoes.
   • Season steaks.
   • Prepare mayonnaise mixture for sandwiches.
2. While fries bake:
   • Grill steaks.
   • Toast bread for sandwiches.
3. Assemble sandwiches.
4. Slice apples.

Steak Sandwiches with Worcestershire Mayonnaise

Mayonnaise, Worcestershire sauce, and whole-grain mustard combine for a tangy, slightly smoky sandwich spread. Arugula is a peppery salad green. Substitute your favorite lettuce, if you like.

TOTAL TIME: 30 MINUTES

PREP TIP: Purchase a loaf of crusty whole-grain bread from the bakery. It will add flavor, and the substantial texture will hold up to the steak in the sandwiches.

Cooking spray
- 2 (8-ounce) boneless ribeye steaks, trimmed
- ½ teaspoon kosher salt
- ½ teaspoon freshly ground black pepper
- 2 tablespoons fat-free mayonnaise
- 1 teaspoon whole-grain mustard
- 2 teaspoons Worcestershire sauce
- 1 garlic clove, minced
- 8 (1-ounce) slices crusty whole-grain bread, toasted
- 1 cup arugula leaves

1. Heat a grill pan over medium-high heat. Coat pan with cooking spray. Sprinkle both sides of steaks evenly with salt and pepper. Add steaks to pan; cook 4 minutes on each side or until desired degree of doneness. Let steaks stand 5 minutes. Cut steaks diagonally across grain into thin slices.
2. Combine mayonnaise and next 3 ingredients in a small bowl, stirring well with a whisk. Spread about 1 tablespoon mayonnaise mixture on each of 4 slices of bread; divide steak evenly among bread slices. Top each serving with ¼ cup arugula and 1 bread slice. Yield: 4 servings (serving size: 1 sandwich).

CALORIES 383 (38% from fat); FAT 16.2g (sat 5.8g, mono 6.5g, poly 1.1g); PROTEIN 28.1g; CARB 31.3g; FIBER 4.2g; CHOL 103mg; IRON 3.9mg; SODIUM 688mg; CALC 87mg

---

Steak Menu 5
serves 4

Sirloin and Vegetable Stir-Fry

Wonton crisps*

Pineapple rings sprinkled with toasted coconut

*Preheat oven to 350°. Working with 1 wonton wrapper at a time, cut wrapper in half diagonally. Combine ¾ teaspoon garlic powder, ½ teaspoon salt, and ⅛ teaspoon ground ginger, stirring well. Coat wonton lightly with cooking spray; sprinkle with spice mixture. Arrange wontons in an even layer on a baking sheet. Bake at 350° for 10 minutes or until crisp.

Game Plan

1. While rice cooks:
  • Preheat oven.
  • Prepare ingredients for stir-fry.
2. Prepare wonton crisps.
3. Prepare stir-fry.

Sirloin and Vegetable Stir-Fry

Sirloin or flank steak will work; just slice the meat thinly and cook briefly so it stays tender.

TOTAL TIME: 30 MINUTES

QUICK TIP: Try boil-in-bag rice; it cooks in about half the time required for traditional long-grain rice. You'll need to use two bags.

- ½ teaspoon salt
- ½ teaspoon five-spice powder
- ¼ teaspoon freshly ground black pepper
- 1 (1-pound) sirloin steak, trimmed and thinly sliced
- 2 teaspoons cornstarch
- ½ teaspoon sugar
- ¼ teaspoon crushed red pepper
- ¾ cup fat-free, less-sodium beef broth
- 2 tablespoons low-sodium soy sauce
- 2 teaspoons canola oil
- 1 cup (¼-inch-thick) diagonally cut slices carrot
- 1 cup broccoli florets
- 1½ cups snow peas, trimmed
- 3 cups hot cooked rice

---

1. Combine first 3 ingredients in a bowl, stirring well; sprinkle evenly over steak. Combine cornstarch, sugar, and red pepper in a medium bowl, stirring well with a whisk. Stir in broth and soy sauce.
2. Heat oil in a large nonstick skillet over medium-high heat. Add carrot to pan; stir-fry 2 minutes. Add steak and broccoli; stir-fry 1 minute. Stir in broth mixture; cook 1 minute, stirring constantly. Add snow peas; cook 30 seconds or until desired degree of doneness. Serve with rice. Yield: 4 servings (serving size: 1½ cups beef mixture and ¾ cup rice).

CALORIES 323 (30% from fat); FAT 10.8g (sat 3.3g, mono 4.5g, poly 1.3g); PROTEIN 24.4g; CARB 30.1g; FIBER 2.4g; CHOL 55mg; IRON 4.7mg; SODIUM 728mg; CALC 40mg

---

lighten up

Breakfast Aplenty

We tweak a Tennessee teacher's favorite French toast casserole in time for holiday guests.

Deb Gruner of Chattanooga, Tennessee, first sampled Easy French Toast Casserole a year ago at a weekend mountain retreat. She's been hooked ever since.

She wants to serve a fitting holiday breakfast when more than 20 family members come to her home Christmas morning. While Easy French Toast Casserole would be a hit, Gruner knows this casserole's hefty nutritional profile doesn't match her dietary goals. She sent the recipe to *Cooking Light* for help.

BEFORE		AFTER
SERVING SIZE		
	1 slice	
CALORIES PER SERVING		
614		352
FAT		
29.7g		8.8g
PERCENT OF TOTAL CALORIES		
44%		23%

Easy French Toast Casserole

Omit the liqueur in the whipped topping, if you prefer. Garnish with a fresh strawberry or orange slice.

⅔ cup packed dark brown sugar
2 tablespoons butter
2 tablespoons dark corn syrup
Cooking spray
1½ cups 1% low-fat milk
½ cup egg substitute
1 teaspoon vanilla extract
¼ teaspoon salt
⅛ teaspoon grated orange rind
2 large eggs, lightly beaten
6 (1½-inch-thick) slices French bread
6 tablespoons frozen fat-free whipped topping, thawed
1 to 2 teaspoons Grand Marnier (orange-flavored liqueur)
2 tablespoons finely chopped pecans, toasted

1. Combine first 3 ingredients in a small, heavy saucepan over medium heat. Cook 5 minutes or until bubbly and sugar dissolves, stirring constantly. Pour sugar mixture into bottom of a 13 x 9–inch baking dish coated with cooking spray. Spread mixture evenly over bottom of dish. Set aside; cool completely.
2. Combine milk and next 5 ingredients in a large shallow bowl; stir with a whisk. Dip each bread slice in milk mixture; arrange bread slice over sugar mixture in prepared dish. Pour any remaining milk mixture over bread slices. Cover and refrigerate overnight.
3. Preheat oven to 350°.
4. Bake at 350° for 30 minutes or until lightly browned.
5. While casserole bakes, combine whipped topping and Grand Marnier. Place 1 bread slice, caramel side up, on each of 6 plates; top each with 1 tablespoon topping and 1 teaspoon pecans. Yield: 6 servings.

CALORIES 352 (23% from fat); FAT 8.8g (sat 3.5g, mono 2.8g, poly 0.9g); PROTEIN 11.1g; CARB 58.1g; FIBER 1.2g; CHOL 83mg; IRON 2.6mg; SODIUM 466mg; CALC 191mg

Old Traditions, New Friends, Southern Hospitality

A restored 19th-century Alabama farmhouse is the setting for an eagerly anticipated annual open house.

Twenty years ago, an ailing great aunt bequeathed the fifth-generation family home in Harpersville, Alabama, to Barbara Adkins with one request: She had to promise to move into the house the very evening the old woman passed away. Adkins, who sells contract furniture, honored the request and sold her home in Birmingham, and moved into the neglected—some said, haunted—1840s dogtrot cabin nestled on 160 acres about 35 miles south of Birmingham. "Chancellor House," as it was known, boasted broken wood siding, boarded-up windows, and heaps of newspapers and junk mail.

Undaunted, she rolled up her sleeves and scraped layer upon layer of wallpaper from rough-hewn plank walls. She called in contractors to refinish windows and install a modern kitchen and bathroom. The gardens were tamed. Through her efforts, Chancellor House has been reborn. Every nook and cranny tells a story, from the family antiques to 19th-century ephemera, which makes it a particularly inviting place. Adkins, who exudes warmth and cordiality, likes it that way and loves to throw parties, especially her annual Christmas party.

Southern Open House Menu
serves 12

Milk Punch

Sparkling Cranberry Tea Cocktails

Charleston Punch

Pimiento Cheese Canapes

Onion Marmalade

Spicy Black-Eyed Pea Dip

Alabama Pulled Pork Sandwiches with White Barbecue Sauce

Mini Corn Bread Crab Cakes with Lemon-Caper Sauce

Pizza Bianca with Arugula, Bacon, and Mushrooms

Shrimp and Grits Casserole

Chocolate Almond Cherry Crisps

Coconut Meringues

Milk Punch

8 cups 98%-fat-free vanilla ice cream
¾ cup bourbon
4 teaspoons vanilla extract
½ teaspoon ground cinnamon
½ teaspoon freshly grated nutmeg
4 teaspoons bittersweet chocolate, grated

1. Combine first 5 ingredients in a blender; process just until smooth. Pour ½ cup ice cream mixture into each of 12 glasses; sprinkle each serving with about ¼ teaspoon chocolate. Serve immediately. Yield: 12 servings.

CALORIES 162 (12% from fat); FAT 2.1g (sat 1.3g, mono 0g, poly 0g); PROTEIN 3g; CARB 28.1g; FIBER 5g; CHOL 7mg; IRON 0.1mg; SODIUM 66mg; CALC 112mg

Sparkling Cranberry Tea Cocktails

This is a fine make-ahead recipe for an open house. Combine the ingredients through step 1, and chill; stir in the ginger ale just before serving. Serve in any pretty clear glass to show off the concoction's yuletide-red hue.

    4   cups water
    ½   cup sugar
    2   family-sized tea bags
2½   cups no-sugar-added cranberry
        juice
    1   cup vodka
    ¼   cup Grand Marnier (orange-
        flavored liqueur)
    4   cups ginger ale, chilled
        Orange rind strips (optional)

1. Combine 4 cups water and sugar in a large saucepan; bring to a boil. Cook until sugar dissolves, stirring occasionally. Pour over tea bags. Cover and let stand 5 minutes; discard tea bags. Cool. Stir in juice, vodka, and Grand Marnier; chill.
2. Gently stir in ginger ale just before serving. Serve over ice; garnish with rind, if desired. Yield: 12 servings (serving size: 1 cup).

CALORIES 151 (0% from fat); FAT 0.1g (sat 0g, mono 0g, poly 0.1g); PROTEIN 0.2g; CARB 23.5g; FIBER 0.1g; CHOL 0mg; IRON 0.3mg; SODIUM 7mg; CALC 7mg

Charleston Punch

Barbara Adkins always has a bowl of this potent libation at her party. It was the traditional drink of the St. Cecilia Society, founded in Charleston, South Carolina, in 1762.

    1   cup brandy
    2   small lemons, thinly sliced
    ½   cup sliced fresh pineapple
    1   cup brewed green tea
    ¾   cup sugar
    ½   cup dark rum
    ¼   cup peach-flavored liqueur
        (such as peach schnapps)
    2   cups sparkling water, chilled
    1   (750-milliliter) bottle
        Champagne, chilled

1. Combine brandy and lemons in a large bowl. Cover and let stand at room temperature 24 hours.
2. Add pineapple to brandy mixture. Let stand 3 hours.
3. Combine brandy mixture, tea, and next 3 ingredients, stirring until sugar dissolves. Add sparkling water and Champagne; stir gently until blended. Serve immediately. Yield: about 12 servings (serving size: 1 cup).

CALORIES 174 (0% from fat); FAT 0g; PROTEIN 0.1g; CARB 15.2g; FIBER 0.3g; CHOL 0mg; IRON 0.1mg; SODIUM 1mg; CALC 3mg

Pimiento Cheese Canapes

This piquant spread also is delightful on full-sized sandwiches.

    2   tablespoons block-style fat-free
        cream cheese, softened
    ¼   cup reduced-fat mayonnaise
    ¼   teaspoon finely grated onion
    ⅛   teaspoon Worcestershire sauce
    ⅛   teaspoon salt
        Dash of ground red pepper
    1   cup (4 ounces) shredded
        reduced-fat sharp Cheddar
        cheese
    1   tablespoon chopped pecans,
        toasted
    ½   (2-ounce) jar diced pimiento,
        undrained
    ⅛   teaspoon smoked paprika
        (optional)
    14 (¼-ounce) slices party-style
        pumpernickel bread

1. Place cream cheese in a medium bowl; beat at medium speed of a mixer until smooth. Stir in mayonnaise and next 4 ingredients. Add Cheddar, pecans, and pimiento; stir well. Cover and chill up to 3 hours. Sprinkle with paprika, if desired. Serve with bread. Yield: 14 appetizer servings (serving size: 1 tablespoon cheese mixture and 1 bread slice).

CALORIES 57 (46% from fat); FAT 2.9g (sat 1.9g, mono 0.3g, poly 0.2g); PROTEIN 3g; CARB 4.5g; FIBER 0.6g; CHOL 6mg; IRON 0.3mg; SODIUM 187mg; CALC 67mg

Onion Marmalade

Cook this marmalade a few days before the party, and refrigerate. It's delicious with the Alabama Pulled Pork Sandwiches (page 416) or spread on crackers.

    1   tablespoon butter
    2   cups diced sweet onion
    2   teaspoons brown sugar
    ¼   cup apple cider vinegar
    ¼   teaspoon dry mustard
        Dash of kosher salt
        Dash of ground red pepper
    1   bay leaf

1. Melt butter in a medium nonstick skillet over medium heat. Add onion to pan; cook 20 minutes or until tender, stirring occasionally. Stir in sugar; cook 2 minutes. Add vinegar and remaining ingredients; bring to a simmer. Cook 6 minutes or until most of liquid has evaporated, stirring occasionally. Discard bay leaf. Yield: 24 servings (serving size: 1½ teaspoons).

CALORIES 11 (41% from fat); FAT 0.5g (sat 0.3g, mono 0.1g, poly 0g); PROTEIN 0.1g; CARB 1.8g; FIBER 0.2g; CHOL 1mg; IRON 0.1mg; SODIUM 9mg; CALC 4mg

Spicy Black-Eyed Pea Dip

This dip is like a Southern-style hummus; serve with bread toasts, crackers, pita bread, or cut-up veggies. To do some of the work ahead, prepare the recipe through step 4, but combine all of the ingredients and bake the dip just before serving.

1½   cups dried black-eyed peas
    4   cups fat-free, low-sodium chicken
        broth
    ½   cup diced onion
    4   garlic cloves, crushed and divided
    1   poblano pepper (about 4 ounces)
    ¼   teaspoon kosher salt
    1   (8-ounce) container reduced-fat
        sour cream
    ⅓   cup chopped green onions
        Cooking spray
    2   tablespoons chopped fresh
        cilantro   *Continued*

1. Sort and wash peas; place in a medium bowl. Cover with water to 2 inches above peas; cover and let stand 8 hours. Drain.
2. Combine peas, broth, onion, and 2 garlic cloves in a large saucepan; bring to a boil. Partially cover, reduce heat, and simmer 1 hour or until tender. Drain.
3. Preheat broiler.
4. Place pepper on a foil-lined baking sheet; broil 15 minutes or until blackened and charred, turning occasionally.
5. Reduce oven temperature to 375°.
6. Place pepper in a zip-top heavy-duty plastic bag; seal. Let stand 15 minutes. Peel and discard skins. Cut a lengthwise slit in pepper; discard seeds and stem. Coarsely chop pepper. Place remaining 2 garlic cloves, pea mixture, pepper, and salt in a food processor; process until smooth. Add sour cream; process until blended. Stir in green onions. Spoon mixture into a 9-inch pie plate or shallow 1-quart baking dish coated with cooking spray. Bake at 375° for 15 minutes or until thoroughly heated. Sprinkle with cilantro. Yield: 12 servings (serving size: about 1/3 cup).

CALORIES 89 (28% from fat); FAT 2.8g (sat 1.5g, mono 0g, poly 0.1g); PROTEIN 4.6g; CARB 11.1g; FIBER 4.7g; CHOL 9mg; IRON 1.3mg; SODIUM 297mg; CALC 37mg

Alabama Pulled Pork Sandwiches with White Barbecue Sauce

Alabama barbecue is known for its vinegary white sauce. To prepare it in advance, combine the sauce ingredients, refrigerate, and bring to room temperature before serving. As for the pork, cook and refrigerate it in the braising liquid, and gently reheat it all on the stove top before setting it on the buffet. The biscuits are best baked shortly before guests arrive.

SAUCE:
- 1/2 cup reduced-fat mayonnaise
- 2 tablespoons white vinegar
- 1 teaspoon coarsely ground black pepper
- 1 teaspoon fresh lemon juice
- Dash of salt

PORK:
- 1 1/4 pounds pork tenderloin, trimmed
- 1/2 cup apple cider vinegar
- 1/4 cup water
- 3 tablespoons brown sugar
- 2 teaspoons kosher salt
- 3/4 teaspoon freshly ground black pepper
- 1/2 teaspoon ground red pepper
- 1/2 teaspoon chili powder
- 1/4 teaspoon garlic powder

BISCUITS:
- 2 cups all-purpose flour (about 9 ounces)
- 2 1/2 teaspoons baking powder
- 1 teaspoon salt
- 1/4 teaspoon ground cinnamon
- 1 cup mashed cooked sweet potato (about 3/4 pound)
- 2 tablespoons brown sugar
- 3 tablespoons butter, melted
- 2/3 cup fat-free milk
- Cooking spray

1. To prepare sauce, combine first 5 ingredients in a small bowl. Cover and chill.
2. To prepare pork, cut pork in half lengthwise; cut crosswise into 2 1/2-inch pieces.
3. Combine apple cider vinegar and next 7 ingredients in a medium saucepan; bring to a boil. Add pork to pan. Cover, reduce heat, and simmer 1 hour or until tender. Remove pork from cooking liquid; shred with 2 forks. Place pork in a serving dish; pour cooking liquid over pork.
4. Preheat oven to 425°.
5. To prepare biscuits, lightly spoon flour into dry measuring cups; level with a knife. Combine flour and next 3 ingredients in a large bowl; stir with a whisk. Combine potato and next 3 ingredients; stir well. Pour over dry ingredients; stir until a soft dough forms (dough will feel sticky). Turn dough out onto a floured surface; knead lightly 5 or 6 times. Roll dough into a 10-inch circle; cut 24 biscuits with a floured 2-inch biscuit cutter. Place on a baking sheet coated with cooking spray. (Reroll dough scraps, if necessary.) Bake at 425° for 12 minutes or until lightly browned. Remove from pan; cool on a wire rack. Serve with pork

and sauce. Yield: 12 servings (serving size: 2 biscuits, 1/4 cup pork, and 2 1/2 teaspoons sauce).

CALORIES 211 (26% from fat); FAT 6g (sat 2.7g, mono 1.5g, poly 0.4g); PROTEIN 13g; CARB 25.8g; FIBER 1.2g; CHOL 39mg; IRON 2mg; SODIUM 772mg; CALC 91mg

Mini Corn Bread Crab Cakes with Lemon-Caper Sauce

Bake the corn bread up to three days in advance and keep in a zip-top plastic bag. Combine the sauce ingredients and assemble the crab cakes the night before; refrigerate separately.

SAUCE:
- 1/3 cup reduced-fat mayonnaise
- 1 1/2 tablespoons chopped fresh chives
- 1 tablespoon capers, drained and chopped
- 1/4 teaspoon grated lemon rind
- 2 teaspoons fresh lemon juice
- 1/4 teaspoon hot pepper sauce (such as Tabasco)
- 1/8 teaspoon minced garlic
- Dash of freshly ground black pepper

CRAB CAKES:
- 2 teaspoons olive oil
- 1/2 cup sliced green onions
- 1/3 cup finely diced red bell pepper
- 1/3 cup finely diced green bell pepper
- 1 garlic clove, minced
- 1/4 cup reduced-fat mayonnaise
- 2 tablespoons chopped fresh chives
- 2 tablespoons chopped fresh parsley
- 1/2 teaspoon grated lemon rind
- 1 tablespoon fresh lemon juice
- 1 tablespoon hot pepper sauce
- 1 teaspoon (30%-less-sodium) Old Bay seasoning
- 1 large egg, lightly beaten
- 2 cups crumbled Buttermilk Corn Bread
- 1 pound lump crabmeat, shell pieces removed
- Cooking spray
- Fresh chives (optional)

1. To prepare sauce, combine first 8 ingredients, and stir with a whisk. Cover and chill.

2. To prepare crab cakes, heat oil in a small nonstick skillet over medium-high heat. Add onions, bell peppers, and garlic to pan; sauté 3 minutes. Remove from heat; cool. Combine bell pepper mixture, ¼ cup mayonnaise, and next 6 ingredients; stir in egg. Fold in Buttermilk Corn Bread and crabmeat. Scoop mixture into 16 portions (about ¼ cup each) onto 2 baking sheets coated with cooking spray. Lightly cover and refrigerate 1 hour.

3. Preheat oven to 400°.

4. Uncover and bake at 400° for 12 minutes or until lightly browned. Remove from baking sheet with a metal spatula. Serve with sauce. Garnish with chives, if desired. Yield: 16 servings (serving size: 1 crab cake and about 1 teaspoon sauce).

(Totals include Buttermilk Corn Bread) CALORIES 83 (35% from fat); FAT 3.2g (sat 0.6g, mono 0.8g, poly 0.3g); PROTEIN 7.4g; CARB 6.4g; FIBER 0.5g; CHOL 38mg; IRON 0.6mg; SODIUM 317mg; CALC 54mg

---

MAKE AHEAD • FREEZABLE

BUTTERMILK CORN BREAD:

- 1 cup all-purpose flour (about 4½ ounces)
- ¾ cup yellow cornmeal
- 2 teaspoons baking powder
- ½ teaspoon salt
- 1 cup fat-free buttermilk
- 2 tablespoons canola oil
- 1 large egg, lightly beaten

Cooking spray

1. Preheat oven to 425°.

2. Lightly spoon flour into a dry measuring cup; level with a knife. Combine flour and next 3 ingredients; make a well in center of mixture. Combine buttermilk, oil, and egg; stir with a whisk. Add to flour mixture; stir just until moistened. Scrape mixture into an 8-inch square baking pan coated with cooking spray. Bake at 425° for 20 minutes or until lightly browned and a wooden pick inserted in center comes out clean. Cool in pan on a wire rack. Yield: 16 servings.

CALORIES 77 (26% from fat); FAT 2.2g (sat 0.3g, mono 1.1g, poly 0.6g); PROTEIN 2.3g; CARB 11.9g; FIBER 0.7g; CHOL 14mg; IRON 0.8mg; SODIUM 240mg; CALC 78mg

---

Pizza Bianca with Arugula, Bacon, and Mushrooms

Barbara Adkins likes to include more contemporary items, like this white cheese-topped pizza, with her Southern-accented buffet. A couple of slices also make a nice light dinner, especially when served with a salad or soup.

CRUST:

- 1 package active dry yeast (about 2¼ teaspoons)
- 1 teaspoon sugar
- ½ cup warm water (100° to 110°)
- 1½ cups all-purpose flour (6¾ ounces), divided
- ¼ teaspoon kosher salt

Cooking spray

- 2 teaspoons yellow cornmeal

TOPPING:

- 2 slices center-cut bacon
- ½ cup thinly sliced white onion
- 1 (8-ounce) package whole button mushrooms, quartered
- ½ teaspoon kosher salt, divided
- ¼ teaspoon freshly ground black pepper, divided
- 1 tablespoon extravirgin olive oil
- ½ cup part-skim ricotta
- 2 cups baby arugula
- ⅓ cup (1½ ounces) shredded part-skim mozzarella cheese
- 2 tablespoons grated fresh Parmesan cheese

1. To prepare crust, dissolve yeast and sugar in ½ cup warm water in a large bowl; let stand 5 minutes. Lightly spoon flour into dry measuring cups, and level with a knife. Stir 1¼ cups flour and ¼ teaspoon salt into yeast mixture to form a soft dough. Turn dough out onto a lightly floured surface. Knead until smooth and elastic (about 5 minutes); add enough of remaining flour, 1 tablespoon at a time, to prevent dough from sticking to hands.

2. Place dough in a large bowl coated with cooking spray, turning dough to coat top. Cover; let rise in a warm place (85°), free from drafts, 1 hour or until doubled in size. (Press two fingers into dough. If indentation remains, dough has risen enough.)

3. Punch dough down; cover and let rest 5 minutes. Roll dough into a 14-inch circle on a lightly floured surface. Place dough on a pizza pan or baking sheet coated with cooking spray and sprinkled with cornmeal. Crimp edges of dough with fingers to form a rim.

4. Preheat oven to 450°.

5. To prepare topping, cook bacon in a large nonstick skillet over medium heat until crisp. Remove bacon from skillet, reserving 2 teaspoons of bacon drippings in pan. Crumble bacon; set aside. Add onion and mushrooms to pan; cook 10 minutes or until tender and liquid evaporates, stirring occasionally. Remove from heat; sprinkle with ¼ teaspoon salt and ⅛ teaspoon pepper.

6. Drizzle oil over dough; sprinkle with ¼ teaspoon salt and ⅛ teaspoon pepper. Place pan on lowest oven rack; bake at 450° for 10 minutes or until golden-brown. Remove from oven; spread ricotta evenly over crust, leaving a ½-inch rim. Arrange onion mixture and arugula evenly over ricotta. Sprinkle with bacon, mozzarella, and Parmesan. Bake an additional 10 minutes or until crust is lightly browned. Let stand 5 minutes before serving. Cut into slices. Yield: 12 servings (serving size: 1 slice).

CALORIES 115 (32% from fat); FAT 4.1g (sat 1.6g, mono 1.9g, poly 0.4g); PROTEIN 5g; CARB 14.5g; FIBER 0.8g; CHOL 7mg; IRON 1.1mg; SODIUM 190mg; CALC 70mg

Shrimp and Grits Casserole

This dish is best prepared just before serving. But you can save time by shredding the cheese and slicing the onions, bell pepper, and shrimp the night before.

    4 cups fat-free, low-sodium chicken
       broth
    ½ teaspoon salt
    1 cup uncooked yellow stone-ground
       grits
    ¾ cup (3 ounces) shredded reduced-
       fat Cheddar cheese, divided
    1 tablespoon olive oil
    1 tablespoon butter
    ½ cup sliced green onions
    ½ cup diced red bell pepper
    3 garlic cloves, minced
    1 (8-ounce) package presliced
       mushrooms
    1 pound peeled and deveined large
       shrimp, each cut into 3 pieces
    ¼ teaspoon freshly ground black
       pepper
    ½ teaspoon grated lemon rind
    1 tablespoon fresh lemon juice
    ½ teaspoon Worcestershire sauce
    ½ teaspoon hot pepper sauce (such
       as Tabasco)
    3 large egg whites
   Cooking spray

1. Bring broth and salt to a boil in a large saucepan; add grits, stirring with a whisk. Cover, reduce heat, and simmer 30 minutes or until liquid is absorbed, stirring occasionally. Remove from heat. Add ½ cup shredded cheese, stirring until cheese melts.
2. Preheat oven to 375°.
3. Heat oil and butter in a large nonstick skillet over medium-high heat. Add onions and next 3 ingredients to pan; sauté 5 minutes. Sprinkle shrimp with black pepper, and add to pan; cook 1 minute. Stir in rind and next 3 ingredients; cook 2 minutes. Remove from heat; cool slightly. Place grits and shrimp mixture in a large bowl; stir gently. Beat egg whites with a mixer at high speed until stiff peaks form. Gently fold egg whites into shrimp mixture. Spoon mixture into a 13 x 9–inch baking dish coated with cooking spray.

Sprinkle with ¼ cup cheese. Bake at 375° for 25 minutes or until puffed and lightly browned. Let stand 20 minutes before serving. Yield: 12 servings (serving size: ¾ cup.)

CALORIES 139 (27% from fat); FAT 4.1g (sat 1.7g, mono 1.3g, poly 0.5g); PROTEIN 12.6g; CARB 12.8g; FIBER 0.5g; CHOL 64mg; IRON 1.6mg; SODIUM 372mg; CALC 77mg

---

MAKE AHEAD
Chocolate Almond Cherry Crisps

These no-bake treats taste like bite-sized candy bars and are terrific with a cup of coffee. Prepare them up to two days in advance, and store in the refrigerator in an airtight container.

    1 cup semisweet chocolate chips
    ¾ cup white chocolate chips
   1½ cups oven-toasted rice cereal
       (such as Rice Krispies)
    ¾ cup dried cherries
    ⅓ cup slivered almonds
    ½ teaspoon vanilla extract

1. Cover a large baking sheet with wax paper.
2. Place semisweet and white chocolate chips in a microwave-safe bowl; microwave at HIGH 45 seconds. Stir, and microwave an additional 45 seconds or until almost melted. Stir until smooth. Add cereal and remaining ingredients; stir quickly to combine. Drop mixture by level tablespoons onto prepared baking sheet; chill 1 hour or until firm. Yield: 36 servings (serving size: 1 crisp).

CALORIES 68 (44% from fat); FAT 3.3g (sat 2g, mono 0.8g, poly 0.2g); PROTEIN 0.6g; CARB 9.7g; FIBER 0.7g; CHOL 0mg; IRON 0.3mg; SODIUM 6mg; CALC 7mg

---

MAKE AHEAD
Coconut Meringues

Toasting the coconut enhances its flavor.

    ¼ teaspoon cream of tartar
   Dash of salt
    3 large egg whites
    ½ cup sugar
    ¼ teaspoon vanilla extract
    ⅛ teaspoon coconut extract
    ½ cup flaked sweetened coconut,
       toasted
    1 tablespoon unsweetened cocoa

1. Preheat oven to 250°.
2. Combine first 3 ingredients in a large bowl; beat at medium speed of a mixer until soft peaks form. Add sugar, 1 tablespoon at a time, beating at high speed until stiff peaks form. Add extracts; beat just until blended (do not overbeat). Gently fold in coconut. Drop by rounded tablespoons, 2 inches apart, onto 2 baking sheets covered with parchment paper. Bake at 250° for 1 hour until very lightly browned and almost crisp, switching baking sheets and rotating front to back halfway through baking time. Remove from oven. Cool 25 minutes (meringues will crisp as they cool). Sprinkle evenly with cocoa. Yield: 31 meringues (serving size: 1 meringue).

CALORIES 25 (14% from fat); FAT 0.4g (sat 0.4g, mono 0g, poly 0g); PROTEIN 0.4g; CARB 4.1g; FIBER 0.1g; CHOL 0mg; IRON 0.1mg; SODIUM 13mg; CALC 1mg

---

The buffet offers mostly updated Southern specialties, but also includes charming new favorites.

Beans

With a little planning, these pantry staples can jump-start many meals.

Beans are the centerpiece of many wonderful dishes—think of kidney beans in chili, garbanzo bean–based falafel, and black beans and rice. High in protein, beans also serve as the foundation for many meatless entrées.

Although canned beans are convenient, there are three clear benefits to cooking dried beans. First, they're less expensive than canned—you can often purchase a pound or two of dried beans for the cost of one can of beans. Also, the taste and texture are often superior. Dried beans have nuanced flavor differences once cooked (from nutty to earthy to slightly sweet), and they possess a firmer, al dente consistency. Perhaps most importantly, when you cook your own beans, you control the sodium. Canned beans tend to harbor a lot of sodium—ranging from about 350 to 630 milligrams per half cup, as opposed to about one to five milligrams in the same amount of dried beans cooked without salt.

Although dried beans do require lengthy preparation, including time to soak and simmer, it's all hands-off, leaving you free to tackle other projects. On the weekend, when you have more time to spend in the kitchen, you can cook several batches of your favorite beans to use in a variety of dishes, simplifying busy weeknight dinners. Store the cooked beans in the refrigerator for a few days, or freeze them for an extended time (see page 420 for storage guidelines). Cooked beans apportioned and stockpiled in the freezer are a smart adjunct to the items already in your pantry.

Smoky Black-Eyed Pea Soup with Corn Bread Croutons

Look for corn bread muffins or loaves in the bakery section or frozen bread section of your supermarket, or use leftovers you've saved.

 1 cup (1-inch) cubed corn bread (about 3½ ounces)
 4 slices applewood-smoked bacon, chopped
 3 cups chopped onion
 6 garlic cloves, minced
 6 cups cooked black-eyed peas
 2 cups fat-free, less-sodium chicken broth
 2 cups water
 1 tablespoon chopped fresh thyme
 ¾ teaspoon salt
 ¼ teaspoon crushed red pepper
 1 cup chopped trimmed watercress

1. Preheat oven to 350°.
2. Arrange corn bread in a single layer on a baking sheet. Bake at 350° for 15 minutes or until golden brown.
3. Heat a large saucepan over medium heat. Add bacon to pan; cook 5 minutes or until crisp, stirring occasionally. Remove bacon from pan, reserving 1 tablespoon drippings in pan. Set bacon aside. Add onion and garlic to drippings in pan; cook 8 minutes or until tender, stirring occasionally. Stir in peas and next 5 ingredients; bring to a boil. Cover, reduce heat, and simmer 40 minutes or until beans are very tender.
4. Place half of bean mixture in a blender. Remove center piece of lid (to allow steam to escape); secure lid on blender. Place a clean towel over opening in lid (to avoid splatters). Blend until smooth. Pour pureed soup into a large bowl. Repeat procedure with remaining bean mixture. Ladle about 1⅓ cups soup into each of 6 bowls; top each serving with about 2½ tablespoons watercress, 2½ tablespoons croutons, and about 1½ teaspoons bacon. Yield: 6 servings.

CALORIES 333 (18% from fat); FAT 6.8g (sat 2.7g, mono 2.2g, poly 0.9g); PROTEIN 17g; CARB 51.9g; FIBER 13.1g; CHOL 10mg; IRON 4.9mg; SODIUM 689mg; CALC 84mg

MAKE AHEAD
Hoppin' John with Mustard Greens

A tasty mix of rice, black-eyed peas, and pork, Hoppin' John is a Southern dish often eaten on New Year's day for good luck. Corn bread is a traditional accompaniment.

 2 cups water
 2 tablespoons whole-grain Dijon mustard
 1 teaspoon salt
 ¼ teaspoon dried thyme
 2 tablespoons olive oil
 3½ cups chopped onion
 1 cup uncooked long-grain white rice
 ⅔ cup finely chopped ham
 4 garlic cloves, minced
 4 cups cooked black-eyed peas
 4 cups chopped trimmed mustard greens

1. Combine first 4 ingredients, stirring with a whisk; set aside.
2. Heat oil in a Dutch oven over medium-high heat. Add onion to pan; sauté 6 minutes. Add rice, ham, and garlic; sauté 2 minutes. Stir in water mixture; bring to a boil. Cover, reduce heat, and simmer 15 minutes. Add peas and greens; cover and cook 5 minutes. Stir rice mixture; cover and cook an additional 5 minutes or until greens and rice are tender. Yield: 6 servings (serving size: about 1⅓ cups).

CALORIES 389 (16% from fat); FAT 7g (sat 1.4g, mono 4.1g, poly 1g); PROTEIN 18.2g; CARB 63.6g; FIBER 11g; CHOL 14mg; IRON 5.1mg; SODIUM 502mg; CALC 109mg

All About Dried Beans

Selecting and Storing Uncooked Beans

Look for beans that are a deep, even color. Pale, uneven color indicates that the beans are old and may take a long time to cook. Don't buy dried beans with pinholes, or beans that appear shriveled or broken.

Store uncooked beans in an airtight container in a cool, dry place up to one year. Never keep dried beans in the refrigerator, as they will soak up the humidity in the air and spoil. Dried beans continue to lose moisture as they age, so don't mix newly purchased dried beans with older ones, as they will cook at different rates.

Preparing Dried Beans

Dried beans are easy to cook, especially if you remember a few tips.

Rinse and sort: Beans are never washed during processing (the key to processing beans is to dehydrate, not hydrate), so it's important to rinse beans before soaking. Most beans go through such high-tech packaging that the job of sorting is just about obsolete. However, any small rocks, shriveled beans, and dirt should be removed.

Soak: The main reasons to soak beans are to shorten the cooking time and promote even cooking. In fact, beans can be cooked after a quick rinse—they'll just take a good bit longer to cook (at least two to three hours, depending on the variety).

There are two methods for soaking beans. For an overnight soak, place the beans in a large bowl. Cover with cool water to two inches above beans; cover and let stand eight hours or overnight. To quick soak beans, place beans in a large Dutch oven. Cover with water to two inches above beans; bring to a boil, and cook two minutes. Remove from heat; cover and let stand one hour.

Cook: The easiest and most common way to cook beans is on the stovetop. We focus on this method because it's simple and requires no special equipment. Some folks prefer using an electric slow cooker or pressure cooker; refer to the manufacturer's instructions, as different models cook at different rates. Regardless of the cooking method, make sure the beans stay covered with liquid while cooking.

Don't add salt or any acidic ingredients (such as tomatoes, vinegar, or citrus) to beans until they're tender; cooking in salted water may lengthen the cooking time, and acid can prevent the beans from becoming tender. Cook beans at a simmer, not at a boil—boiling may cook the beans too rapidly and cause their skins to split. It's important to taste the beans to make sure they're tender; don't just go by the estimated cooking times, as older beans will take longer to cook, as will beans cooked in hard water.

Follow these steps for cooking dried beans on the stovetop:

1. Place drained soaked beans in a large Dutch oven.

2. Cover with water to two inches above beans; bring to a boil.

3. Partially cover, reduce heat, and simmer until tender (skim foam from surface of cooking liquid as needed).

Good for Your Heart (and More)

Beans are low in fat; high in protein, fiber, and complex carbohydrates; and contain no cholesterol. The fiber in beans can help lower blood cholesterol and triglyceride levels, and may help reduce the risk of heart disease. Furthermore, phytochemicals in beans have been linked to lower cancer risk. Dried beans are also a good source of folate and iron, plus they offer some B vitamins, calcium, and zinc.

MAKE AHEAD

Chickpea-Kale Stew with Chorizo

This Spanish-style stew is delicious served with thick slices of garlic-rubbed toasted rustic bread. Make sure to use fully cooked Spanish-style chorizo and not the raw Mexican kind.

- 4   cups chopped onion
- ½   cup diced Spanish chorizo (about 2 ounces)
- 6   garlic cloves, minced
- 3   cups fat-free, less-sodium chicken broth
- 3   cups cooked chickpeas
- 1   teaspoon dried oregano
- ¼   teaspoon salt
- 3   cups chopped kale
- 4   lemon wedges

1. Heat a Dutch oven over medium heat. Add first 3 ingredients to pan; cook 10 minutes or until onion is tender, stirring frequently. Add broth, chickpeas, oregano, and salt; bring to a boil. Cover, reduce heat, and simmer 30 minutes or until chickpeas are very tender. Stir in kale; simmer 10 minutes or until kale is tender. Serve with lemon wedges. Yield: 4 servings (serving size: 1½ cups stew and 1 lemon wedge).

CALORIES 379 (22% from fat); FAT 9.3g (sat 2.5g, mono 3.5g, poly 2.2g); PROTEIN 19.6g; CARB 57.7g; FIBER 13.6g; CHOL 12mg; IRON 5.6mg; SODIUM 649mg; CALC 190mg

Baked Falafel Sandwiches with Yogurt-Tahini Sauce

Falafel is a popular Middle Eastern vegetarian option consisting of seasoned pureed chickpeas that are shaped into patties and usually fried. It's worth the effort to seek out Greek yogurt, which is thick, rich, and creamy.

SAUCE:

1 cup plain whole-milk Greek yogurt (such as Fage Total Classic)
1 tablespoon tahini (sesame seed paste)
1 tablespoon fresh lemon juice

FALAFEL:

¾ cup water
¼ cup uncooked bulgur
3 cups cooked chickpeas (garbanzo beans)
½ cup chopped fresh cilantro
½ cup chopped green onions
⅓ cup water
2 tablespoons all-purpose flour
1 tablespoon ground cumin
1 teaspoon baking powder
¾ teaspoon salt
¼ to ½ teaspoon ground red pepper
3 garlic cloves
Cooking spray

REMAINING INGREDIENTS:

6 (2.8-ounce) Mediterranean-style white flatbread (such as Toufayan)
12 (¼-inch-thick) slices tomato
Chopped fresh cilantro (optional)

1. To prepare sauce, combine first 3 ingredients, stirring with a whisk until blended. Cover and chill until ready to serve.

2. To prepare falafel, bring ¾ cup water to a boil in a small saucepan; add bulgur to pan. Remove from heat; cover and let stand 30 minutes or until tender. Drain and set aside.

3. Preheat oven to 425°.

4. Place chickpeas and next 9 ingredients in a food processor; pulse 10 times or

until well blended and smooth (mixture will be wet). Spoon chickpea mixture into a large bowl; stir in bulgur. Divide mixture into 12 equal portions (about ¼ cup each); shape each portion into a ¼-inch-thick patty. Place patties on a baking sheet coated with cooking spray. Bake at 425° for 10 minutes on each side or until browned. Spread about 2½ tablespoons sauce onto each flatbread. Top each flatbread with 2 falafel patties, 2 tomato slices, and chopped cilantro, if desired. Yield: 6 servings (serving size: 1 stuffed flatbread).

CALORIES 388 (18% from fat); FAT 7.7g (sat 3.5g, mono 1.6g, poly 1.6g); PROTEIN 18g; CARB 64.6g; FIBER 14.7g; CHOL 7mg; IRON 5.2mg; SODIUM 535mg; CALC 181mg

Ancho, Beef, and Kidney Bean Chili

Instead of using commercial chili powder to flavor this stew, we puree dried ancho chiles for a customized taste. You can prepare the chile-broth puree up to two days in advance to streamline prep for a busy night.

2 tablespoons olive oil, divided
2 cups chopped onion
2 teaspoons ground cumin
6 garlic cloves, minced
2 ounces stemmed dried seeded ancho chiles, torn into 2-inch pieces
4 cups fat-free, less-sodium beef broth
1 (28-ounce) can diced tomatoes, undrained
2 pounds boneless chuck roast, trimmed and cut into 2-inch cubes
Cooking spray
2½ cups chopped green bell pepper (about 2 large)
6 cups cooked kidney beans
¾ teaspoon salt
½ teaspoon freshly ground black pepper
10 tablespoons reduced-fat sour cream
¼ cup chopped fresh cilantro
Lime wedges (optional)

1. Heat 1 tablespoon oil in a large saucepan over medium heat. Add onion to pan; cook 8 minutes or until golden, stirring frequently. Add cumin, garlic, and chiles; cook 3 minutes or until chiles are soft, stirring frequently. Stir in broth and tomatoes; bring to a simmer. Cover, remove from heat, and let stand at room temperature 20 minutes.

2. Place half of chile mixture in a blender. Remove center piece of lid (to allow steam to escape); secure lid on blender. Place a clean towel over opening in lid (to avoid splatters). Blend until smooth. Pour pureed chile mixture into a large bowl. Repeat procedure with remaining chile mixture. Set aside.

3. Heat remaining 1 tablespoon oil in a large Dutch oven over medium-high heat. Add beef to pan; sauté 10 minutes or until browned on all sides. Remove beef from pan. Coat pan with cooking spray. Add bell pepper to pan; sauté 8 minutes or until browned. Stir in pureed chile mixture and beef; bring to a boil. Cover, reduce heat, and simmer 45 minutes or until beef is tender. Add beans; cook 20 minutes. Stir in salt and black pepper. Top with sour cream and cilantro; serve with lime wedges, if desired. Yield: 10 servings (serving size: 1⅓ cups chili, 1 tablespoon sour cream, and about 1 teaspoon cilantro).

CALORIES 362 (29% from fat); FAT 11.7g (sat 4g, mono 5.2g, poly 1.1g); PROTEIN 28.5g; CARB 37.4g; FIBER 11.7g; CHOL 60mg; IRON 6.3mg; SODIUM 504mg; CALC 86mg

Jerk-Seasoned Turkey with Black Beans and Yellow Rice

Stir the black beans into the rice just before serving so there's less chance of discoloration. Serve with a tossed salad to round out the meal.

  4 teaspoons salt-free Jamaican jerk seasoning (such as Spice Hunter), divided
  1 teaspoon salt, divided
  2 (¾-pound) turkey tenderloins
  4 teaspoons olive oil, divided
Cooking spray
  4 cups finely chopped onion
  1 cup uncooked basmati rice
  ¼ teaspoon ground turmeric
  2 cups fat-free, less-sodium chicken broth
  2 cups cooked black beans
  3 tablespoons chopped fresh cilantro

1. Preheat oven to 400°.
2. Combine 1 tablespoon jerk seasoning and ½ teaspoon salt; sprinkle evenly over both sides of turkey.
3. Heat 1 teaspoon oil in a large nonstick skillet over medium-high heat. Add turkey to pan; cook 4 minutes on each side or until browned. Place turkey on a broiler pan coated with cooking spray. Bake at 400° for 12 minutes or until a thermometer registers 165°. Remove turkey from oven; cover loosely, and let stand 5 minutes. Cut turkey across grain into thin slices.
4. While turkey cooks, heat remaining 1 tablespoon oil in skillet over medium-high heat. Add onion to pan; sauté 8 minutes. Stir in rice, remaining 1 teaspoon jerk seasoning, and turmeric; sauté 2 minutes. Add broth and remaining ½ teaspoon salt; bring to a boil. Cover, reduce heat, and simmer 15 minutes or until rice is tender and liquid is absorbed. Stir in beans and cilantro. Serve rice mixture with turkey. Yield: 6 servings (serving size: about 1 cup rice mixture and about 3 ounces turkey).

CALORIES 326 (14% from fat); FAT 5g (sat 1g, mono 2.5g, poly 0.9g); PROTEIN 35.9g; CARB 36.8g; FIBER 7g; CHOL 45mg; IRON 3.2mg; SODIUM 591mg; CALC 44mg

---

Easy Weeknight Supper Menu
serves 6

When you have cooked beans on hand, this meal comes together in no time.

Cranberry Beans with Sausage and Fennel
Orange salad*
Crusty bread

*Combine 8 cups torn romaine lettuce, 3 cups orange sections, and 1 cup thinly vertically sliced red onion. Combine 3 tablespoons white wine vinegar, 2 tablespoons fresh orange juice, 1½ tablespoons extravirgin olive oil, ½ teaspoon salt, and ½ teaspoon freshly ground black pepper, stirring with a whisk. Drizzle vinaigrette over salad; toss to coat. Top each serving with 1 tablespoon shaved Parmesan cheese.

MAKE AHEAD
Cranberry Beans with Sausage and Fennel

Nutty-tasting cranberry beans pair with spicy Italian sausage in this hearty dish. If you can't find cranberry beans, substitute cannellini or Great Northern beans.

  1 pound hot turkey Italian sausage
Cooking spray
  2 cups thinly sliced leek (about 2 large)
1½ cups thinly sliced fennel bulb (about 1 large bulb)
1¼ cups chopped red bell pepper (about 1 large)
  4 garlic cloves, minced
  4 cups cooked cranberry beans
  2 cups fat-free, less-sodium chicken broth
Chopped fennel fronds (optional)

1. Heat a large saucepan over medium-high heat. Remove casings from sausage. Coat pan with cooking spray. Add sausage to pan; cook 8 minutes or until browned, stirring to crumble. Remove sausage from pan; set aside. Wipe pan clean with paper towels.

2. Return pan to medium-high heat. Coat pan with cooking spray. Add leek, sliced fennel, bell pepper, and garlic to pan; sauté 6 minutes or until vegetables are tender. Stir in beans, broth, and sausage; bring to a boil. Reduce heat, and simmer 6 minutes or until beans are thoroughly heated. Garnish with fennel fronds, if desired. Yield: 6 servings (serving size: 1½ cups).

CALORIES 328 (25% from fat); FAT 9g (sat 2.4g, mono 3.2g, poly 2.3g); PROTEIN 25.6g; CARB 38.4g; FIBER 14g; CHOL 45mg; IRON 4.9mg; SODIUM 634mg; CALC 98mg

WINE NOTE: Beans and sausages are classic components of Tuscan cooking, so whenever these ingredients are combined into a stew, reach for Chianti. This Tuscan red wine has earthy flavors that complement beans well, and just enough acidity to balance the richness of the sausage. Try Badia a Passignano Chianti Classico Riserva DOCG from the famous Italian family Antinori. The 2003 is $45.

Lamb Chops with Rosemary Flageolets

This classic pairing of lamb and French beans is elegant enough for guests. Flageolets are small, tender beans that range in color from beige to light green; substitute navy beans if flageolets are unavailable.

  2 tablespoons olive oil, divided
1¼ cups finely chopped carrot
  1 cup finely chopped celery
  ¾ cup finely chopped shallots
  4 garlic cloves, minced
  ½ cup dry white wine
  4 cups cooked flageolet beans
  2 cups fat-free, less-sodium chicken broth
  2 teaspoons chopped fresh rosemary, divided
  ¾ teaspoon salt, divided
  6 (4-ounce) lamb loin chops, trimmed
  ¼ teaspoon freshly ground black pepper
Rosemary sprigs (optional)

1. Heat 1 tablespoon oil in a large saucepan over medium heat. Add carrot, celery, shallots, and garlic to pan; cover and cook 15 minutes or until tender and golden brown, stirring occasionally. Add wine to pan; cook 2 minutes or until liquid almost evaporates. Add beans, broth, 1 teaspoon rosemary, and ½ teaspoon salt; bring to a simmer. Remove from heat; keep warm.

2. Heat remaining 1 tablespoon oil in a large skillet over medium-high heat. Sprinkle lamb evenly with remaining 1 teaspoon rosemary, remaining ¼ teaspoon salt, and pepper. Add lamb to pan; cook 3 minutes on each side or until desired degree of doneness. Serve with bean mixture. Garnish with rosemary sprigs, if desired. Yield: 6 servings (serving size: about ¾ cup bean mixture and 1 lamb chop).

CALORIES 320 (28% from fat); FAT 9.9g (sat 2.5g, mono 5.4g, poly 1.1g); PROTEIN 26g; CARB 32.8g; FIBER 9.9g; CHOL 45mg; IRON 4.2mg; SODIUM 505mg; CALC 125mg

MAKE AHEAD
Refried Pinto Beans with Chipotle

Reserve some of the water the beans cook in for this dish; if you've discarded that liquid, use water or chicken broth instead.

    3   slices applewood-smoked bacon, finely chopped
    ½   cup chopped onion
    3   cups cooked pinto beans
    ½   to ¾ cup bean cooking liquid
    1   to 2 teaspoons minced chipotle chile, canned in adobo sauce
    ½   teaspoon salt

1. Cook bacon in a large nonstick skillet over medium heat until crisp. Add onion to pan; cook 7 minutes or until golden, stirring occasionally. Add beans and remaining ingredients; mash with a potato masher to desired consistency. Cook 5 minutes or until thoroughly heated. Yield: 6 servings (serving size: about ½ cup).

CALORIES 181 (28% from fat); FAT 5.7g (sat 1.8g, mono 2.4g, poly 0.7g); PROTEIN 9.1g; CARB 24g; FIBER 8g; CHOL 8mg; IRON 1.9mg; SODIUM 310mg; CALC 43mg

Cannellini Bean and Shrimp Stew

Cannellini beans are white kidney beans; substitute Great Northern beans, if you prefer.

    1   pound unpeeled large shrimp
    4   teaspoons olive oil, divided
    ½   cup dry white wine
    2   cups water
    1   (8-ounce) bottle clam juice
    1   bay leaf
    3   cups chopped onion
    1   tablespoon tomato paste
    6   garlic cloves, minced
    1   tablespoon chopped fresh thyme
    ½   teaspoon salt
    ¼   teaspoon crushed red pepper
    1   (14.5-ounce) can diced tomatoes, undrained
    4   cups cooked cannellini beans
    ¼   cup chopped fresh flat-leaf parsley

1. Peel and devein shrimp, reserving shells. Cover and chill shrimp.

2. Heat 1 teaspoon oil in a medium saucepan over medium-high heat. Add reserved shrimp shells to pan; sauté 3 minutes or until shells turn pink. Stir in wine; bring to a boil. Reduce heat, and simmer 5 minutes or until liquid almost evaporates. Stir in 2 cups water, clam juice, and bay leaf; simmer 12 minutes or until liquid is reduced by half. Set shrimp stock aside.

3. Heat remaining 1 tablespoon oil in a large Dutch oven over medium heat. Add onion to pan; cook 8 minutes or until lightly browned, stirring occasionally. Add tomato paste and garlic; cook 2 minutes, stirring frequently. Stir in thyme, salt, pepper, and tomatoes; bring to a simmer. Strain shrimp stock through a colander into Dutch oven; discard solids. Add beans to pan; bring to a boil. Cover, reduce heat, and simmer 10 minutes; remove from heat. Stir in shrimp; cover and let stand 5 minutes or until shrimp are done. Stir in parsley. Yield: 6 servings (serving size: 1⅓ cups).

CALORIES 318 (15% from fat); FAT 5.3g (sat 0.7g, mono 2.4g, poly 0.9g); PROTEIN 24.9g; CARB 43.7g; FIBER 2.6g; CHOL 116mg; IRON 5.6mg; SODIUM 486mg; CALC 340mg

in season
Persimmons in Perspective

Make the most of one of wintertime's best fruits.

This is prime season for golden and orange persimmons. Long part of Chinese, Korean, and Japanese cuisines, persimmons are enjoyed fresh out of hand, pureed in gingery sweet punches, and as a dried fruit snack in Asia. Native Americans once prized a variety indigenous to North America. Today, though, most American cooks probably best know persimmons for their use in holiday puddings. But their versatility spans sweet and savory applications, including baked goods and fresh salsas.

The two most common varieties available in the United States are Fuyu and Hachiya. The key difference between the two is their level of astringency, which creates a bitter taste sensation. Just like black tea or red wine, the intense orange Hachiya contain tannins that create this sensation if eaten unripe. Larger than Fuyus and with a pointed bottom, Hachiyas need to ripen to develop their sweet, soft (almost gelatinous) flesh, which can be eaten with a spoon. Since the Hachiya is so soft when ripe, it's often pureed in ice cream or quick breads. Fuyus, which look like yellow-orange tomatoes, are eaten when firm and crisp, and aren't astringent. They hold up well in salads, salsas, and stir-fries. Both varieties are available October through early January (see "Selection and Storage," page 425).

Spiced Persimmon Salsa

Serve over flank steak or chicken, or as an appetizer to top Brie and crackers. This sweet-hot condiment can be made up to one day ahead.

 3 tablespoons thinly sliced green onions (about 1 onion)
 1 tablespoon chopped fresh mint
 1 tablespoon chopped fresh cilantro
 1 tablespoon minced seeded jalapeño pepper
 3 ripe Fuyu persimmons (about 1 pound), peeled and coarsely chopped
 2 tablespoons fresh lime juice
 1½ teaspoons grated peeled fresh ginger
 ¼ teaspoon salt
 ¼ teaspoon freshly ground black pepper

1. Combine first 5 ingredients in a medium bowl.
2. Combine juice, ginger, salt, and pepper in a small bowl; stir with a whisk. Drizzle over persimmon mixture; toss to coat. Yield: 10 servings (serving size: about ⅓ cup).

CALORIES 38 (2% from fat); FAT 0.1g (sat 0g, mono 0g, poly 0g); PROTEIN 0.4g; CARB 10g; FIBER 2g; CHOL 0mg; IRON 0.2mg; SODIUM 60mg; CALC 8mg

Persimmon and Cardamom Sorbet

The naturally spicy persimmons pair with earthy cardamom for a refreshing, light dessert.

 1¼ cups sugar
 1 cup water
 2 cups ripe Hachiya persimmon puree (about 4) (page 425)
 2 teaspoons fresh lemon juice
 ⅛ teaspoon salt
 ⅛ teaspoon ground cardamom

1. Combine sugar and 1 cup water in a small saucepan; bring to a boil. Cook 3 minutes or until sugar dissolves. Remove from heat. Add persimmon puree and remaining ingredients, stirring well. Cool completely.
2. Pour persimmon mixture into freezer can of an ice-cream freezer; freeze according to manufacturer's instructions. Spoon sorbet into a freezer-safe container; cover and freeze 2 hours or until firm. Remove sorbet from freezer 10 minutes before serving. Yield: 8 servings (serving size: ⅔ cup).

CALORIES 180 (1% from fat); FAT 0.2g (sat 0g, mono 0g, poly 0g); PROTEIN 0.5g; CARB 47g; FIBER 3g; CHOL 0mg; IRON 0.1mg; SODIUM 38mg; CALC 7mg

Fast Fresh Fare Menu
serves 4

This light dinner offers a welcome respite from heartier winter food.

Chinese Chicken and Persimmon Lettuce Wraps

Rice noodle salad*

Mango sorbet

*Cook 10 ounces rick stick noodles according to package directions; drain and place in a large bowl. Combine ¼ cup fat-free, less-sodium chicken broth; ¼ cup sugar; ¼ cup fresh lime juice; 1½ tablespoons fish sauce; 2 teaspoons chile garlic sauce; and 2 minced garlic cloves, stirring with a whisk until sugar dissolves. Drizzle over noodles; toss well to coat. Add ½ cup matchstick-cut carrot, ½ cup julienne-cut cucumber, and 3 tablespoons chopped fresh cilantro; toss well to combine.

Chinese Chicken and Persimmon Lettuce Wraps

 1½ teaspoons peanut oil
 ½ cup minced green onions
 2 teaspoons cornstarch
 1 pound ground chicken
 1 cup chopped peeled ripe Fuyu persimmon (about 2)
 ½ cup chopped water chestnuts
 1 tablespoon grated peeled fresh ginger
 3 tablespoons low-sodium soy sauce
 2 tablespoons fresh orange juice
 1 tablespoon oyster sauce
 12 Boston lettuce leaves

1. Heat oil in a large skillet over medium-high heat. Add onions, cornstarch, and chicken to pan; sauté 4 minutes or until chicken is done, stirring to crumble. Add persimmon, water chestnuts, ginger, soy sauce, juice, and oyster sauce to pan; cook 2 minutes. Remove from heat. Spoon ¼ cup chicken mixture into center of each lettuce leaf; roll up jelly-roll fashion. Yield: 4 servings (serving size: 3 wraps).

CALORIES 247 (40% from fat); FAT 11g (sat 2.8g, mono 4g, poly 2.7g); PROTEIN 20.2g; CARB 19.3g; FIBER 3.4g; CHOL 75mg; IRON 2.1mg; SODIUM 392mg; CALC 34mg

The secret to savoring a persimmon is patience. It must be fully ripe to unlock its cinnamon, clove, and sweet undertones.

Persimmon Gingerbread

The persimmon's texture and warm, spicy notes make a moist snack cake. Since the batter is heavy, a toothpick test doesn't work well to determine doneness. Make sure the cake browns around the edges and pulls away from the sides of the pan before removing from the oven.

- ½ cup packed brown sugar
- ¼ cup butter, softened
- 1½ cups ripe Hachiya persimmon puree (about 3 fruits), see textbox at right
- ⅓ cup molasses
- 3 large eggs
- 2 cups all-purpose flour (about 9 ounces)
- 1½ teaspoons ground ginger
- 1 teaspoon baking soda
- 1 teaspoon ground cinnamon
- ¼ teaspoon salt
- ⅛ teaspoon ground nutmeg
- ⅛ teaspoon ground cloves
- ⅓ cup boiling water
- ⅓ cup chopped almonds, toasted
- Cooking spray
- 2 teaspoons powdered sugar

1. Preheat oven to 350°.
2. Place brown sugar and butter in a large bowl; beat with a mixer at medium speed until well blended (about 3 minutes). Add persimmon puree, molasses, and eggs; beat well (about 1 minute).
3. Lightly spoon flour into dry measuring cups; level with a knife. Sift together flour and next 6 ingredients. Add flour mixture and ⅓ cup boiling water alternately to persimmon mixture, beginning and ending with flour mixture. Stir in almonds. Pour batter into a 9-inch square baking pan coated with cooking spray. Bake at 350° for 30 minutes. Cool 10 minutes in pan on a wire rack. Dust with powdered sugar. Cut into 12 squares. Yield: 12 servings (serving size: 1 square).

CALORIES 240 (27% from fat); FAT 7.3g (sat 3g, mono 2.8g, poly 0.9g); PROTEIN 4.9g; CARB 40.5g; FIBER 2.7g; CHOL 63mg; IRON 2.9mg; SODIUM 208mg; CALC 79mg

Pan-Seared Pork Medallions with Persimmon-Cranberry Chutney

Winter fruits enliven a saucy condiment for pork in this guest-worthy dish.

- 1 cup riesling or other dry white wine
- 1 cup fat-free, less-sodium chicken broth
- ⅓ cup fresh orange juice
- 2½ tablespoons sugar
- ⅛ teaspoon ground cloves
- 2 (3-inch) cinnamon sticks
- 4 teaspoons canola oil
- 2 (1-pound) pork tenderloins, trimmed and cut into 16 (1-inch-thick) slices
- ½ teaspoon salt, divided
- ½ teaspoon black pepper, divided
- 1 cup coarsely chopped peeled ripe Fuyu persimmon (about 2)
- ½ cup fresh cranberries
- 1 tablespoon butter

1. Combine first 6 ingredients in a medium saucepan; bring to a boil. Cook until reduced to 1½ cups (about 10 minutes). Discard cinnamon sticks.
2. Heat oil in a large nonstick skillet over medium-high heat. Add pork to pan; sprinkle evenly with ¼ teaspoon salt and ¼ teaspoon pepper. Cook 6 minutes on each side or until pork is done. Transfer pork to a platter. Add broth mixture to pan, scraping pan to loosen browned bits. Add persimmon and cranberries to pan; cook 5 minutes or until cranberries begin to pop, stirring occasionally. Add remaining ¼ teaspoon salt, remaining ¼ teaspoon pepper, and butter, stirring until butter melts. Serve with pork. Yield: 8 servings (serving size: 3 ounces pork and 3 tablespoons sauce).

CALORIES 237 (30% from fat); FAT 7.8g (sat 2.4g, mono 3.5g, poly 1.2g); PROTEIN 24.5g; CARB 14.5g; FIBER 2g; CHOL 77mg; IRON 1.6mg; SODIUM 263mg; CALC 13mg

Selection and Storage

Selecting persimmons can be tricky since Hachiyas are at their best when water-balloon soft. Ripe Fuyus won't be as soft as ripe Hachiyas, though the fruit is still sweet and tasty when it yields slightly to pressure.

- Choose persimmons that are heavy for their size.
- Look for fruit with glossy, firm, brightly colored skin.
- Handle persimmons with care; their delicate skins bruise easily.
- Persimmons fare better stored at room temperature. Once ripe, they're best eaten immediately but may be stored in the refrigerator in a plastic bag up to three days.
- Fuyus can be eaten when still crisp, as they're a nonastringent variety.
- Hachiyas are ready to eat when they're so soft the skin is ready to burst.

Persimmon Puree Pointers

Ripe Hachiya puree, a versatile ingredient used in some of our recipes, is easy to make by following these tips:

- To speed the ripening process, freeze the fruit overnight or until solid. Thaw the persimmon; when soft, it will be sweeter and less astringent.
- Cut the ripe fruit in half. Scoop the pulp out with a spoon.
- To achieve an even consistency, place the flesh in a mini-chopper and process until smooth. This ensures the persimmon puree will incorporate evenly into batters.

Persimmon and Millet Muffins

A nutritious whole grain, millet adds pleasing crunch to baked goods.

    2 cups all-purpose flour (about 9
       ounces)
    ⅓ cup uncooked millet
    1 teaspoon baking soda
    1 teaspoon baking powder
    ¼ teaspoon salt
    ¼ teaspoon ground cinnamon
    ⅛ teaspoon ground allspice
    ¾ cup ripe Hachiya persimmon
       puree (about 2 fruits) (page 425)
    ½ cup packed brown sugar
    ½ cup egg substitute
    ½ cup buttermilk
    ¼ cup butter, melted
       Cooking spray

1. Preheat oven to 375°.
2. Lightly spoon flour into dry measuring cups; level with a knife. Combine flour and next 6 ingredients; stir with a whisk.
3. Combine persimmon puree, sugar, egg substitute, buttermilk, and butter in a large bowl; stir well to blend. Add flour mixture to persimmon mixture; stir just until combined. Spoon batter into 12 muffin cups coated with cooking spray. Bake at 375° for 19 minutes or until a wooden pick inserted in center comes out clean. Remove muffins from pan immediately; cool on a wire rack. Yield: 1 dozen (serving size: 1 muffin).

CALORIES 196 (21% from fat); FAT 4.6g (sat 2.7g, mono 1.1g, poly 0.4g); PROTEIN 4.3g; CARB 34.9g; FIBER 2.1g; CHOL 11mg; IRON 1.6mg; SODIUM 259mg; CALC 41mg

Sweet Persimmon and Toasted Walnut Bread

This simple quick bread uses sweet and spicy persimmon puree. We liked the slightly tart flavor from the golden raisins, but omit them if you prefer.

    3 cups all-purpose flour (about 13½
       ounces)
    2 teaspoons baking soda
    ½ teaspoon salt
    1 cup sugar
    1 cup ripe Hachiya persimmon
       puree (about 2 fruits) (page 425)
    ½ cup 1% low-fat milk
    ⅓ cup butter, melted
    1 teaspoon vanilla extract
    2 large eggs
    ⅓ cup chopped walnuts, toasted
    ⅓ cup golden raisins
       Cooking spray

1. Preheat oven to 350°.
2. Lightly spoon flour into dry measuring cups; level with a knife. Combine flour, baking soda, and salt in a large bowl; stir with a whisk.
3. Combine sugar and next 5 ingredients in a medium bowl; beat with a mixer at medium speed until blended. Add persimmon mixture to flour mixture, stirring just until blended. Stir in walnuts and raisins. Spoon batter into 2 (8 x 4–inch) loaf pans coated with cooking spray. Bake at 350° for 45 minutes or until a wooden pick inserted in center comes out clean. Cool in pans 10 minutes on a wire rack; remove from pans. Cool completely on wire rack. Yield: 2 loaves, 12 servings each (serving size: 1 slice).

CALORIES 146 (25% from fat); FAT 4.1g (sat 1.9g, mono 1g, poly 0.9g); PROTEIN 2.7g; CARB 25.1g; FIBER 1.1g; CHOL 25mg; IRON 0.9mg; SODIUM 181mg; CALC 15mg

Arugula, Hazelnut, Persimmon, and Fennel Salad

With fresh, peak-of-flavor ingredients, the simplest vinaigrette is more than sufficient. Toasting the hazelnuts intensifies their flavor and helps to easily remove their bitter skins.

    2 tablespoons hazelnuts (about ½
       ounce)
    1½ tablespoons red wine vinegar
    1 tablespoon extravirgin olive oil
    ¼ teaspoon salt
    ¼ teaspoon freshly ground black
       pepper
    6 cups thinly sliced fennel bulb
       (about 2)
    2 cups thinly sliced peeled ripe
       Fuyu persimmon (about 2)
    1 (5-ounce) package bagged
       prewashed arugula

1. Preheat oven to 350°.
2. Place hazelnuts on a baking sheet. Bake at 350° for 10 minutes, stirring once. Cool 2 minutes; turn nuts out onto a towel. Roll up towel; rub off skins. Chop nuts; set aside.
3. Combine vinegar, oil, salt, and pepper in a small bowl, stirring with a whisk.
4. Combine fennel, persimmon, and arugula in a large bowl. Drizzle with vinegar mixture; toss well to coat. Place 1½ cups fennel mixture on each of 6 plates. Top each serving with about 1 teaspoon hazelnuts. Serve immediately. Yield: 6 servings.

CALORIES 107 (37% from fat); FAT 4.4g (sat 0.5g, mono 3g, poly 0.6g); PROTEIN 2.2g; CARB 17.5g; FIBER 5.1g; CHOL 0mg; IRON 1.1mg; SODIUM 145mg; CALC 78mg

A Month's Worth of Recipes and Entertaining Tips

Saturday, December

1

Open House

Kick off the month by inviting friends, family, and neighbors for a late-afternoon buffet.

Barbecue-Rubbed Pork Loin with Raisin-Mustard Chutney

Prepare the sweet-hot chutney a day or two in advance, then roast the pork just before serving. Serve on focaccia with roasted Broccolini.

CHUTNEY:

- 1 tablespoon olive oil
- 1 cup chopped onion
- 2 teaspoons grated peeled fresh ginger
- 2 garlic cloves, minced
- 1 cup apple juice
- 1 cup golden raisins
- 1 cup raisins
- 2 tablespoons white wine vinegar
- 2 teaspoons sugar
- 1 teaspoon curry powder
- ½ teaspoon ground cumin
- ⅓ cup apple jelly
- 1 tablespoon Dijon mustard
- ¼ teaspoon salt

PORK:

- 1 tablespoon sugar
- 2 teaspoons ground cumin
- 1½ teaspoons salt
- 1½ teaspoons paprika
- ¾ teaspoon curry powder
- ½ teaspoon ground allspice
- ½ teaspoon ground ginger
- ½ teaspoon garlic powder
- ¼ teaspoon ground red pepper
- 1 (3¾-pound) boneless pork loin, trimmed
- Cooking spray

1. To prepare chutney, heat oil in a large saucepan over medium-high heat. Add onion, 2 teaspoons fresh ginger, and garlic to pan; sauté 4 minutes. Stir in juice and next 6 ingredients; bring to a boil. Reduce heat, and simmer 15 minutes or until liquid is almost absorbed. Remove from heat; let stand 10 minutes. Stir in jelly, mustard, and ¼ teaspoon salt. Spoon into a bowl; cover and chill.

2. Preheat oven to 350°.

3. To prepare pork, combine 1 tablespoon sugar and next 8 ingredients; rub over pork. Place pork on a rack coated with cooking spray; place rack in pan. Bake at 350° for 1 hour and 20 minutes or until a meat thermometer registers 160° (slightly pink). Let stand 20 minutes. Cut into thin slices. Serve with chutney. Yield: 12 servings (serving size: about 3 ounces pork and 3 tablespoons chutney).

CALORIES 391 (23% from fat); FAT 10g (sat 3.2g, mono 4.3g, poly 0.9g); PROTEIN 40.5g; CARB 33.2g; FIBER 2g; CHOL 112mg; IRON 3mg; SODIUM 446mg; CALC 32mg

Sunday, December

2
Winter Hike

Head into the woods and enjoy the crisp air. Take along a thermosful of this tasty stew to savor at a scenic resting spot.

MAKE AHEAD
Dijon Chicken Stew with Potatoes and Kale

    4   teaspoons olive oil, divided
    2   cups sliced leek
    4   garlic cloves, minced
  1/3   cup all-purpose flour (about 1½
        ounces)
    1   pound skinless, boneless chicken
        thighs, cut into bite-sized pieces
  ½   pound skinless, boneless chicken
        breast, cut into bite-sized pieces
  ½   teaspoon salt, divided
  ½   teaspoon freshly ground black
        pepper, divided
    1   cup dry white wine
    3   cups fat-free, less-sodium chicken
        broth, divided
    1   tablespoon all-purpose flour
  1½   cups water
    2   tablespoons Dijon mustard
    2   cups (½-inch) cubed peeled white
        potato (about 1 pound)
    8   cups loosely packed torn kale
        (about 5 ounces)
  Crushed red pepper (optional)

1. Heat 1 teaspoon oil in a Dutch oven over medium-high heat. Add leek to pan; sauté 6 minutes or until tender and golden brown. Add garlic; sauté 1 minute. Spoon leek mixture into a large bowl.
2. Place ⅓ cup flour in a shallow bowl or pie plate. Dredge chicken in flour, shaking off excess. Heat 1 tablespoon oil in pan over medium-high heat. Add half of chicken mixture to pan; sprinkle with ⅛ teaspoon salt and ⅛ teaspoon black pepper. Cook 6 minutes, browning on all sides. Add browned chicken to leek mixture. Repeat procedure with remaining chicken mixture, ⅛ teaspoon salt, and ⅛ teaspoon black pepper.
3. Add wine to pan, scraping pan to loosen browned bits. Combine 1 cup broth and 1 tablespoon flour, stirring with a whisk until smooth. Add broth mixture, 2 cups broth, 1½ cups water, and mustard to pan; bring to a boil. Stir in chicken mixture, ¼ teaspoon salt, and ¼ teaspoon black pepper. Cover, reduce heat, and simmer 30 minutes.
4. Stir in potato. Cover and simmer 30 minutes or until potato is tender. Stir in kale; cover and simmer 10 minutes. Garnish with crushed red pepper, if desired. Yield: 6 servings (serving size: 1½ cups).

CALORIES 324 (22% from fat); FAT 7.9g (sat 1.5g, mono 3.5g, poly 1.7g); PROTEIN 30.9g; CARB 33.7g; FIBER 5g; CHOL 85mg; IRON 4.6mg; SODIUM 659mg; CALC 180mg

Monday, December

3
Send a Care Package

Pack a fresh batch of cookies for far-away friends and family. For more baking ideas, see "Cookie Course" (page 385).

Macadamia Butter Cookies with Dried Cranberries

(pictured at left)

⅔ cup macadamia nuts
½ cup granulated sugar
½ cup packed light brown sugar
1 teaspoon vanilla extract
1 large egg
1¼ cups all-purpose flour (about 5½ ounces)
½ teaspoon baking soda
¼ teaspoon salt
⅛ teaspoon ground nutmeg
½ cup sweetened dried cranberries, chopped
1 tablespoon granulated sugar

1. Place nuts in a food processor; process until smooth (about 2 minutes), scraping sides of bowl once. Combine macadamia butter, ½ cup granulated sugar, and brown sugar in a large bowl; beat with a mixer at medium speed. Add vanilla and egg; beat well.
2. Lightly spoon flour into dry measuring cups; level with a knife. Combine flour and next 3 ingredients, stirring with a whisk. Add flour mixture to sugar mixture; beat at low speed just until combined (mixture will be very thick). Stir in cranberries. Chill 10 minutes.
3. Preheat oven to 375°.
4. Divide chilled dough into 30 equal portions; roll each portion into a ball. Place 1 tablespoon granulated sugar in a small bowl. Lightly press each ball into sugar; place each ball, sugar side up, on a baking sheet covered with parchment paper. Place 15 cookies on each of 2 baking sheets.
5. Gently press top of each cookie with a fork. Dip fork in water; gently press top of each cookie again to form a crisscross pattern.
6. Bake cookies, 1 baking sheet at a time, at 375° for 9 minutes or until golden. Remove cookies from pan; cool on a wire rack. Yield: 30 servings (serving size: 1 cookie).

CALORIES 76 (30% from fat); FAT 2.5g (sat 0.4g, mono 1.8g, poly 0.1g); PROTEIN 1g; CARB 13.2g; FIBER 0.6g; CHOL 7mg; IRON 0.5mg; SODIUM 44mg; CALC 7mg

---

Tuesday, December

4
Hanukkah

Celebrate the first night of the Festival of Lights with a spiced dessert accented with fresh citrus flavors.

Orange Cardamom Cake

CAKE:
Cooking spray
3 cups plus 1 tablespoon all-purpose flour
2 cups sugar
1 tablespoon baking powder
1¾ teaspoons ground cardamom
½ teaspoon ground cinnamon
½ teaspoon salt
¾ cup fresh orange juice
⅔ cup canola oil
1 tablespoon grated orange rind
2 teaspoons grated lemon rind
1 teaspoon vanilla extract
3 large eggs

GLAZE:
1 cup powdered sugar
4½ teaspoons fresh orange juice
½ teaspoon fresh lemon juice

1. Preheat oven to 350°.
2. To prepare cake, coat a 10-inch tube pan or Bundt pan with cooking spray; dust with 1 tablespoon flour. Set aside.
3. Lightly spoon flour into dry measuring cups, and level with a knife. Combine flour, sugar, baking powder, cardamom, cinnamon, and salt in a large bowl. Make a well in center of mixture. Add ¾ cup orange juice, canola oil, orange rind, lemon rind, vanilla, and eggs to flour mixture, and beat with a mixer at low speed until well combined, scraping sides of bowl occasionally.
4. Spoon batter into prepared cake pan, spreading evenly. Bake at 350° for 55 minutes or until a wooden pick inserted in center comes out clean. Cool in pan 5 minutes on a wire rack, and remove from pan.

5. To prepare glaze, combine 1 cup of powdered sugar, 4½ teaspoons orange juice, and lemon juice in a small bowl, stirring well with a whisk. Drizzle glaze over warm cake; cool cake completely on wire rack. Yield: 16 servings (serving size: 1 slice).

CALORIES 318 (29% from fat); FAT 10.6g (sat 1g, mono 5.9g, poly 3g); PROTEIN 3.8g; CARB 52.8g; FIBER 0.9g; CHOL 40mg; IRON 1.5mg; SODIUM 179mg; CALC 63mg

---

Wednesday, December

5
Get a Head Start on Hostess Gifts

Convey your gratitude to holiday hosts with a jar of zesty homemade chutney.

Cranberry-Orange Ginger Chutney

Try this tangy condiment with roast turkey, pork, or chicken, or on breakfast toast.

1 teaspoon olive oil
½ cup minced shallots
1 tablespoon finely chopped peeled fresh ginger
¼ cup fresh orange juice
2 cups fresh or frozen cranberries, thawed
½ cup sugar
2 tablespoons cider vinegar
¼ teaspoon kosher salt
¼ teaspoon ground allspice

1. Heat oil in a medium saucepan over medium heat. Add shallots and ginger to pan; cook 5 minutes or until golden, stirring occasionally. Add juice, scraping pan to loosen browned bits. Add cranberries and remaining ingredients. Bring cranberry mixture to a boil. Reduce heat; simmer 15 minutes or until slightly thickened. Cover and chill 2 hours. Yield: 6 servings (serving size: ¼ cup).

CALORIES 102 (7% from fat); FAT 0.8g (sat 0.1g, mono 0.6g, poly 0.1g); PROTEIN 0.6g; CARB 24.1g; FIBER 1.6g; CHOL 0mg; IRON 0.3mg; SODIUM 81mg; CALC 10mg

Thursday, December

6

Deck the Halls

Decorate the house to get into the holiday spirit. Break for a quick, decadently delicious sandwich.

STAFF FAVORITE • QUICK & EASY

Grilled Peanut Butter and Banana Split Sandwich

This dish received our highest rating at taste testing. The recipe can easily be multiplied to make as many sandwiches as you need.

- 2 (1-ounce) slices firm white sandwich bread, divided
- 1 teaspoon butter, softened
- 1 tablespoon creamy peanut butter
- 2 teaspoons honey
- ½ teaspoon semisweet chocolate minichips
- 1 large strawberry, thinly sliced
- ½ small banana, cut lengthwise into 3 slices (about 2 ounces)
- 1 tablespoon pineapple jam

1. Spread 1 side of each white bread slice with ½ teaspoon butter. Combine peanut butter and honey; spread over plain side of 1 bread slice. Sprinkle with chocolate chips; top evenly with strawberry slices and banana slices.

2. Spread pineapple jam over plain side of remaining bread slice. Carefully assemble sandwich.

3. Heat a small nonstick skillet over medium-high heat. Add sandwich; cook 2 minutes on each side or until lightly browned. Yield: 1 serving (serving size: 1 sandwich).

CALORIES 436 (30% from fat); FAT 14.5g (sat 4.2g, mono 6g, poly 3.2g); PROTEIN 9.4g; CARB 72g; FIBER 4.6g; CHOL 10mg; IRON 3mg; SODIUM 497mg; CALC 100mg

Friday, December

7

Pictures with Santa

Take the kids to meet the North Pole's visiting dignitary. A frozen treat makes the evening even more memorable.

MAKE AHEAD • FREEZABLE

Ice Cream Treasures

- 1½ cups (6 ounces) chocolate-covered English toffee candy bars (such as Heath), crushed
- 8 cups vanilla reduced-fat ice cream (such as Healthy Choice), softened
- 4 cups crispy rice cereal squares, crushed (such as Rice Chex)
- 2 cups whole-grain toasted oat cereal (such as Cheerios)
- ⅔ cup packed dark brown sugar
- ⅓ cup slivered almonds, toasted
- ⅓ cup flaked sweetened coconut, toasted
- 2 tablespoons butter, melted

1. Stir crushed candy into ice cream. Cover and freeze until ready to use.

2. Combine cereals, sugar, and remaining 3 ingredients in a large bowl, stirring until well blended. Press half of cereal mixture in bottom of a 13 x 9–inch baking pan.

3. Let ice cream mixture stand at room temperature 20 minutes or until softened. Spread softened ice cream mixture over cereal mixture in pan; top evenly with remaining cereal mixture in pan. Cover and freeze 8 hours or overnight. Yield: 16 servings (serving size: about ¾ cup).

CALORIES 265 (29% from fat); FAT 8.4g (sat 4.1g, mono 2.7g, poly 0.7g); PROTEIN 5.2g; CARB 41.7g; FIBER 1g; CHOL 25mg; IRON 3.6mg; SODIUM 194mg; CALC 156mg

Saturday, December

8

Gift Shopping

Restore yourself after time at
the mall with a hearty meal.
Assemble this beforehand, then
bake after you get home.

Baked Pasta with Sausage, Tomatoes, and Cheese

Substitute sweet turkey Italian sausage for hot, if desired. Or, for more spice, add ¼ teaspoon crushed red pepper. Garnish with fresh basil leaves, and serve with a tossed salad.

 1 (1-pound) package uncooked ziti (short tube-shaped pasta)
 1 pound hot turkey Italian sausage links
 1 cup chopped onion
 2 garlic cloves, minced
 1 tablespoon tomato paste
 ¼ teaspoon salt
 ¼ teaspoon freshly ground black pepper
 2 (14.5-ounce) cans petite-diced tomatoes, undrained
 ¼ cup chopped fresh basil
Cooking spray
 1 cup (4 ounces) shredded fresh mozzarella cheese
 1 cup (4 ounces) grated fresh Parmesan cheese

1. Preheat oven to 350°.
2. Cook pasta according to package directions, omitting salt and fat. Drain pasta; set aside.
3. Remove casings from sausage. Cook sausage, onion, and garlic in a large non-stick skillet over medium heat until sausage is browned, stirring to crumble. Add tomato paste and next 3 ingredients to pan; bring to a boil. Cover, reduce heat, and simmer 10 minutes, stirring occasionally.
4. Combine cooked pasta, sausage mixture, and basil. Place half of pasta mixture in a 4-quart casserole coated with cooking spray. Top with half of mozzarella and half of Parmesan. Repeat layers. Bake at 350° for 25 minutes or until bubbly. Yield: 8 servings (serving size: 1½ cups).

CALORIES 413 (26% from fat); FAT 11.8g (sat 6.1g, mono 2.2g, poly 1g); PROTEIN 24.1g; CARB 53g; FIBER 4.5g; CHOL 49mg; IRON 7.9mg; SODIUM 941mg; CALC 265mg

Sunday, December

9

Address Cards

A hot spiked coffee drink that both
stimulates and soothes will help you
get through this annual task.

QUICK & EASY
Hazelnut Dessert Coffee
(pictured below)

Any liqueur you prefer, such as Grand Marnier or Chambord, will work.

 6 tablespoons Frangelico (hazelnut-flavored liqueur)
 3 cups hot strong brewed coffee
 2 tablespoons frozen reduced-calorie whipped topping, thawed
Cinnamon sticks (optional)

1. Place liqueur in a microwave-safe bowl; microwave at HIGH 10 seconds or until warm. Add warm liqueur to coffee. Pour about ½ cup coffee mixture into each of 6 cups; top each serving with 1 teaspoon whipped topping. Garnish with cinnamon sticks, if desired. Yield: 6 servings.

CALORIES 131 (1% from fat); FAT 0.2g (sat 0.2g, mono 0g, poly 0g); PROTEIN 0.1g; CARB 23.9g; FIBER 0g; CHOL 0mg; IRON 0mg; SODIUM 2mg; CALC 2mg

Monday, December

10

Dinner by the Fireplace

Cozy suppers of comfort foods are one of the season's great pleasures. These potpies offer classic flavor in individual servings.

MAKE AHEAD
Chicken Potpies

Because the piecrust topping cooks on a baking sheet and is then placed over the filling, you don't need to use ovenproof bowls for the pies. Use a bowl or ramekin as a guide for cutting the dough.

½ (15-ounce) package refrigerated pie dough (such as Pillsbury)
Cooking spray
⅛ teaspoon salt
2 tablespoons all-purpose flour
1 teaspoon dried rubbed sage
¼ teaspoon salt
¼ teaspoon pepper
8 ounces chicken breast tenders, cut into bite-sized pieces
1¼ cups water
1½ cups frozen mixed vegetables
1 cup mushrooms, quartered
1 (10½-ounce) can condensed reduced-fat, reduced-sodium cream of chicken soup

1. Preheat oven to 425°.
2. Cut 3 (4-inch) circles out of dough; discard remaining dough. Place dough circles on a baking sheet coated with cooking spray. Lightly coat dough circles with cooking spray; sprinkle evenly with ⅛ teaspoon salt. Pierce top of dough with a fork. Bake dough at 425° for 12 minutes or until golden.
3. Combine flour, sage, ¼ teaspoon salt, and pepper in a zip-top plastic bag; add chicken. Seal bag; shake to coat. Heat a large nonstick skillet over medium-high heat. Coat pan with cooking spray. Add chicken mixture to pan; cook 5 minutes, browning on all sides. Stir in 1¼ cups water, scraping pan to loosen browned

bits. Stir in vegetables, mushrooms, and soup; bring to a boil. Reduce heat, and cook 10 minutes. Spoon 1 cup of chicken mixture into each of 3 (1-cup) ramekins or bowls; top each serving with 1 piecrust. Yield: 3 servings (serving size: 1 pie).

CALORIES 374 (27% from fat); FAT 11.4g (sat 4.8g, mono 4.2g, poly 1.2g); PROTEIN 24.1g; CARB 42.6g; FIBER 4.6g; CHOL 58mg; IRON 1.9mg; SODIUM 882mg; CALC 38mg

Wednesday, December

11

Hanukkah Ends

With the menorah now fully lit, serve a special dinner to commemorate the Feast of Dedication.

Honey-Pomegranate Roasted Chicken Thighs

You can find pomegranate molasses in Middle Eastern and specialty stores. Serve this dish warm or at room temperature.

¾ cup honey
⅓ cup finely chopped shallots
¼ cup fresh lemon juice (about 3 small lemons)
1 tablespoon grated lemon rind
2 tablespoons pomegranate molasses
1 teaspoon Worcestershire sauce
1 teaspoon hot sauce
6 garlic cloves, minced
16 chicken thighs (about 4 pounds), skinned
1 tablespoon cornstarch
1 tablespoon water
Cooking spray
1 teaspoon salt
¼ teaspoon freshly ground black pepper

1. Combine first 9 ingredients in a large bowl; marinate in refrigerator 2 hours, stirring occasionally.
2. Preheat oven to 425°.
3. Remove chicken from bowl, reserving marinade. Combine cornstarch and water in a small bowl. Place reserved marinade in a small saucepan; bring to a boil. Stir in

cornstarch mixture, and cook 3 minutes or until thickened, stirring frequently. Remove from heat. Place chicken on a broiler pan coated with cooking spray; sprinkle with salt and pepper. Bake at 425° for 30 minutes or until chicken is done, basting with reserved marinade every 10 minutes. Yield: 8 servings (serving size: 2 thighs).

CALORIES 378 (31% from fat); FAT 13.1g (sat 3.7g, mono 5g, poly 3g); PROTEIN 31.7g; CARB 33.8g; FIBER 0.3g; CHOL 114mg; IRON 2.6mg; SODIUM 416mg; CALC 36mg

Tuesday, December

12

Make Teacher Gifts

Remember a special instructor with a spicy treat that's good eaten out of hand or mixed into salads.

QUICK & EASY • MAKE AHEAD
Asian-Spiced Pecans

Other savory pecan recipes have as much as ½ cup butter per quart of nuts. Here, we use only a teaspoon of butter and add a little tomato paste to give the spice mixture enough body to cling to the pecans.

2 tablespoons low-sodium soy sauce
1 tablespoon tomato paste
2 teaspoons Thai seasoning (such as Spice Islands)
1 teaspoon butter, melted
Dash of black pepper
Dash of ground red pepper
4 cups pecan halves
Cooking spray
⅛ teaspoon salt

1. Preheat oven to 350°.
2. Combine first 6 ingredients in a large bowl, and stir well with a whisk. Add pecan halves; toss well. Spread mixture evenly onto a jelly-roll pan coated with cooking spray.
3. Bake at 350° for 12 minutes, stirring once. Remove from oven, and sprinkle with salt. Cool completely. Yield: 4 cups (serving size: 2 tablespoons).

NOTE: Store in an airtight container in a cool, dark place up to one month, in the refrigerator up to 3 months, or in the freezer up to 8 months.

CALORIES 93 (90% from fat); FAT 9.3g (sat 0.8g, mono 5.7g, poly 2.3g); PROTEIN 1.1g; CARB 2.6g; FIBER 0.9g; CHOL 0mg; IRON 0.3mg; SODIUM 61mg; CALC 5mg

Thursday, December

13

St. Lucia Day

Saffron bread is traditional fare on this feast day that marks the beginning of the Scandinavian Christmas season.

MAKE AHEAD • FREEZABLE
Saffron and Raisin Breakfast Bread
(pictured at right)

Steep saffron in warm milk to release its color and aroma. Serve slices of this bread toasted or plain with honey for a special holiday breakfast or brunch.

1⅓ cups warm fat-free milk (100° to 110°)
¼ teaspoon saffron threads, crushed
1 package dry yeast (about 2¼ teaspoons)
1 teaspoon sugar
½ cup warm water (100° to 110°)
5¼ cups bread flour, divided (about 24¾ ounces)
1½ cups raisins
¼ cup sugar
3 tablespoons butter, melted and cooled
1 teaspoon salt
Cooking spray

1. Combine milk and saffron; let stand 10 minutes.
2. Dissolve yeast and 1 teaspoon sugar in warm water in a large bowl; let stand 5 minutes or until foamy. Stir in milk mixture. Lightly spoon flour into dry measuring cups; level with a knife. Add 5 cups flour, raisins, ¼ cup sugar, butter, and salt to milk mixture, stirring to form a soft

dough. Turn dough out onto a floured surface. Knead until smooth and elastic (about 8 minutes); add enough of remaining flour, 1 tablespoon at a time, to prevent dough from sticking to hands (dough will feel sticky).
3. Place dough in a large bowl coated with cooking spray, turning to coat top. Cover and let rise in a warm place (85°), free from drafts, 1½ hours or until doubled in size. (Gently press two fingers into dough. If indentation remains, dough has risen enough.) Punch dough down; cover and let rest 5 minutes. Divide in half. Shape each portion into a 5-inch round loaf. Place loaves, seam sides down, 3 inches apart, on a large baking sheet coated with cooking spray. Make 2 diagonal cuts ¼-inch-deep across top of each loaf using a sharp knife. Cover and let rise 30 minutes or until doubled in size.
4. Preheat oven to 375°.
5. Uncover dough. Bake at 375° for 30 minutes or until loaves are browned on bottom and sound hollow when tapped. Remove from pan; cool on wire racks. Yield: 2 loaves, 20 servings (serving size: 1 slice).

CALORIES 199 (11% from fat); FAT 2.4g (sat 1.2g, mono 0.6g, poly 0.3g); PROTEIN 5.4g; CARB 39.5g; FIBER 1.4g; CHOL 5mg; IRON 1.9mg; SODIUM 145mg; CALC 33mg

Friday, December

14

Invite the Neighbors

Share cocktails and hors d'oeuvres with friends. Make-ahead finger foods are ideal for the occasion.

MAKE AHEAD
Creamy Mushroom Phyllo Triangles

Don't fold the packets too tightly or the mixture will burst through the phyllo. Assemble and freeze up to two weeks before serving. Bake unthawed—just add seven minutes to the baking time.

- ¾ cup dried porcini mushrooms (about ¾ ounce)
- 1 pound button mushrooms
- 1 large onion, cut into 1-inch pieces (about 8 ounces)
- 2 tablespoons olive oil
- 1 teaspoon dried oregano
- ¾ teaspoon salt
- ½ teaspoon freshly ground black pepper
- ¼ teaspoon freshly grated nutmeg
- 6 ounces ⅓-less-fat cream cheese
- ½ cup finely chopped flat-leaf parsley
- 24 (18 x 14–inch) sheets frozen phyllo dough, thawed

Olive oil–flavored cooking spray

1. Cover porcini mushrooms with boiling water in a bowl. Let stand 1 hour. Drain well; chop.

2. Place half of button mushrooms in a food processor; pulse 8 times or until finely chopped. Remove from processor. Repeat procedure with remaining button mushrooms. Add onion to processor; pulse 8 times or until finely chopped.

3. Heat oil in a large nonstick skillet over medium heat. Add onion to pan; sauté 5 minutes. Add button mushrooms; cook until mushrooms are tender and liquid evaporates (about 10 minutes). Stir in porcini mushrooms, oregano, salt, pepper,

and nutmeg; cook 2 minutes. Remove from heat. Add cheese; stir until cheese melts. Stir in parsley.

4. Preheat oven to 375°.

5. Working with 1 phyllo sheet at a time (cover remaining phyllo to prevent drying), place phyllo sheet on a large cutting board or work surface. Cut sheet in half lengthwise; lightly coat with cooking spray. Fold phyllo piece in half lengthwise to form a (3½-inch-wide) strip. Spoon a level tablespoon of mushroom mixture onto 1 short end of strip,

leaving a 1-inch border. Fold 1 corner of edge with 1-inch border over mixture, forming a triangle; continue folding back and forth into a triangle to end of strip. Place triangles, seam sides down, on baking sheets coated with cooking spray. Lightly coat tops with cooking spray.

6. Bake at 375° for 20 minutes or until golden. Serve warm. Yield: 48 triangles (serving size: 2 triangles).

CALORIES 49 (37% from fat); FAT 2g (sat 0.8g, mono 1g, poly 0.2g); PROTEIN 1.5g; CARB 6.2g; FIBER 0.5g; CHOL 3mg; IRON 0.6mg; SODIUM 97mg; CALC 7mg

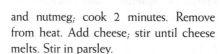

Saturday, December

15

Caroling Supper

Serenade the neighborhood with
holiday songs, then warm up at home
with a steaming bowl of soup.

Sunday, December

16

Holiday Brunch

Feed company yet stay relaxed with a
mostly make-ahead dish. Assemble this
the night before, then bake the
following morning.

MAKE AHEAD

Roasted Garlic and Shallot Potato Soup with Cheese Croutons

(pictured at left)

Serve this hearty soup with a full-flavored
ale, such as Fuller's ESB from London.

SOUP:

- 5 whole garlic heads, unpeeled
- 3½ tablespoons olive oil, divided
- 1¼ teaspoons salt, divided
- 1 teaspoon freshly ground black pepper, divided
- 10 shallots, unpeeled (about ¾ pound)
- 2 cups coarsely chopped onion
- 1 cup dry white wine
- 3 cups fat-free, less-sodium chicken broth
- 2 cups (½-inch) cubed peeled baking potato (about ¾ pound)
- 1 teaspoon chopped fresh thyme
- 1 cup 2% reduced-fat milk

CROUTONS:

- 16 (½-inch-thick) slices French bread baguette
- Cooking spray
- ¾ cup (3 ounces) crumbled blue cheese
- 2 tablespoons grated fresh Parmesan cheese

1. Preheat oven to 400°.
2. To prepare soup, remove white papery skins from garlic heads (do not peel or separate cloves); cut off tops, leaving root ends intact. Place garlic in a shallow roasting pan. Drizzle 1 tablespoon oil over garlic; sprinkle with ¼ teaspoon salt and ¼ teaspoon pepper. Cover with

foil. Bake at 400° for 20 minutes. Add shallots to pan. Drizzle 1 tablespoon oil over shallots; sprinkle with ¼ teaspoon salt and ¼ teaspoon pepper. Cover and bake at 400° for 25 minutes or until garlic and shallots are tender and browned. Cool. Squeeze garlic to extract pulp; peel shallots. Discard skins. Set garlic pulp and shallots aside.
3. Heat remaining 1½ tablespoons oil in a Dutch oven over medium heat; add onion to pan. Cover and cook 15 minutes or until lightly browned, stirring occasionally. Add garlic pulp, peeled shallots, and wine. Reduce heat; simmer, uncovered, 5 minutes.
4. Stir in broth, potato, and thyme; bring to a boil. Cover, reduce heat, and simmer 20 minutes or until potato is tender. Cool slightly. Place half of potato mixture in a blender. Remove center piece of lid (to allow steam to escape); secure lid on blender. Place a clean towel over opening in lid (to avoid splatters). Blend until smooth. Pour into a large bowl. Repeat procedure with remaining potato mixture.
5. Return pureed mixture to pan; stir in milk, remaining ¾ teaspoon salt, and remaining ½ teaspoon pepper into pureed mixture. Cook over medium heat 5 minutes or until thoroughly heated.
6. To prepare croutons, place bread slices in a single layer on a large baking sheet. Lightly coat tops of bread with cooking spray. Bake at 400° for 8 minutes or until lightly browned. Sprinkle cheeses evenly over bread slices. Bake 3 minutes or until cheese melts. Serve warm with soup. Yield: 8 servings (serving size: 1 cup soup and 2 croutons).

CALORIES 290 (30% from fat); FAT 9.6g (sat 3.5g, mono 4.7g, poly 0.8g); PROTEIN 11.1g; CARB 41g; FIBER 3.3g; CHOL 12mg; IRON 2mg; SODIUM 806mg; CALC 202mg

MAKE AHEAD

Marmalade French Toast Casserole

Mixed fruit marmalade will work just as well as the orange marmalade in this recipe. Serve the casserole with pancake syrup warmed with orange rind and a splash of orange juice (add one teaspoon rind and two tablespoons juice per ½ cup syrup).

- 3 tablespoons butter, softened
- 1 (16-ounce) sourdough French bread loaf, cut into 24 (½-inch) slices
- Cooking spray
- 1 (12-ounce) jar orange marmalade
- 2¾ cups 1% low-fat milk
- ⅓ cup sugar
- 1 teaspoon vanilla extract
- ¼ teaspoon ground nutmeg
- 6 large eggs
- ⅓ cup finely chopped walnuts

1. Spread softened butter on 1 side of each bread slice. Arrange 12 bread slices, buttered side down, slightly overlapping in a single layer in a 3 quart baking dish coated with cooking spray. Spread marmalade evenly over bread; top with remaining 12 bread slices, buttered side up.
2. Combine milk and next 4 ingredients, stirring with a whisk. Pour egg mixture over bread. Cover and refrigerate 8 hours or overnight.
3. Preheat oven to 350°.
4. Sprinkle casserole with walnuts. Bake at 350° for 45 minutes or until golden. Let stand 5 minutes before serving. Yield: 12 servings (serving size: 1 piece).

CALORIES 293 (28% from fat); FAT 9g (sat 3.2g, mono 2.2g, poly 2.3g); PROTEIN 9.1g; CARB 46.4g; FIBER 1.6g; CHOL 116mg; IRON 2.2mg; SODIUM 315mg; CALC 132mg

Monday, December

17

Read to the Kids

Share the pleasure of a favorite holiday book. A fresh batch of blondie squares makes the experience all the sweeter.

MAKE AHEAD

Butterscotch Blondies

Store unrefrigerated in an airtight container up to three days, or freeze three months.

  2 cups all-purpose flour (about 9 ounces)

2½ cups firmly packed light brown sugar

  2 teaspoons baking powder

  ½ teaspoon salt

10 tablespoons unsalted butter

  ¾ cup egg substitute

Cooking spray

1. Preheat oven to 350°.

2. Lightly spoon flour into dry measuring cups; level with a knife. Combine flour, firmly packed light brown sugar, baking powder, and salt in a large bowl.

3. Place butter in a skillet over medium heat. Cook 6 minutes or until lightly browned, stirring occasionally. Pour into a small bowl, and cool 10 minutes.

4. Combine butter and egg substitute, stirring with a whisk. Pour butter mixture over flour mixture; stir just until moistened. Spoon batter into a 13 x 9–inch baking pan coated with cooking spray; smooth top with spatula. Bake at 350° for 30 minutes or until a wooden pick inserted in center comes out clean. Cool in pan on a wire rack. Cut into 24 squares. Yield: 24 servings (serving size: 1 square).

CALORIES 170 (25% from fat); FAT 4.8g (sat 3g, mono 1.2g, poly 0.2g); PROTEIN 1.9g; CARB 30.5g; FIBER 0.3g; CHOL 13mg; IRON 1.1mg; SODIUM 108mg; CALC 45mg

Tuesday, December

18

Wrapping Marathon

While everyone's busy with boxes, paper, tape, and bows, it's best to keep dinner simple.

QUICK & EASY

Pear, Pecorino, and Prosciutto Panini

(pictured above)

Serve with baked chips.

  1 firm, ripe pear, peeled, cored, and cut into 8 wedges

  ½ teaspoon sugar

  1 (12-ounce) loaf focaccia, cut in half horizontally

  4 teaspoons balsamic vinegar

  1 cup trimmed arugula

  ½ cup (2 ounces) fresh pecorino Romano cheese, shaved

16 very thin slices prosciutto (about 4 ounces)

1. Heat a nonstick skillet over medium-high heat. Add pear to pan, and sprinkle with sugar. Cook 2 minutes on each side or until golden.

2. Brush cut sides of bread with vinegar. Arrange pear slices, arugula, cheese, and prosciutto evenly over bottom half of bread; cover with top half of bread.

3. Heat a large nonstick skillet over medium heat. Add stuffed loaf to pan. Place a cast-iron or heavy skillet on top of stuffed loaf; press gently to flatten. Cook 4 minutes on each side or until bread is toasted (leave cast-iron skillet on stuffed loaf while it cooks). Cut into quarters. Yield: 4 servings (serving size: 1 quarter).

CALORIES 383 (29% from fat); FAT 12.3g (sat 5.3g, mono 2.7g, poly 1.7g); PROTEIN 18.7g; CARB 50.8g; FIBER 2.7g; CHOL 40mg; IRON 2.8mg; SODIUM 1,019mg; CALC 178mg

19
Office Potluck

Bring a side dish to the company party. Versatile root vegetables pair well with a variety of main dishes.

Honey-Roasted Root Vegetables

2 cups coarsely chopped peeled sweet potato (about 1 large)
1½ cups coarsely chopped peeled turnip (about 2)
1½ cups coarsely chopped parsnip (about 2)
1½ cups coarsely chopped carrot (about 2)
¼ cup tupelo honey
2 tablespoons olive oil
½ teaspoon salt
3 shallots, halved
Cooking spray

1. Preheat oven to 450°.
2. Combine all ingredients except cooking spray in a large bowl; toss to coat. Place vegetable mixture on a jelly-roll pan coated with cooking spray. Bake at 450° for 30 minutes or until vegetables are tender and begin to brown, stirring every 15 minutes. Yield: 8 servings (serving size: ½ cup).

CALORIES 118 (27% from fat); FAT 3.5g (sat 0.5g, mono 2.5g, poly 0.4g); PROTEIN 1.3g; CARB 21.7g; FIBER 2.3g; CHOL 0mg; IRON 0.5mg; SODIUM 171mg; CALC 33mg

---

Thursday, December

20
Eid al-Adha

This holiday, one of two Muslim Eid festivals, celebrates the faith in Allah of Ibrahim.

Garlic Chicken

The yogurt mixture keeps the chicken moist, but it curdles and should be discarded after cooking. Serve the chicken with a basmati rice pilaf tossed with almonds, raisins, and cumin seeds.

1 cup plain low-fat yogurt
¼ cup fresh lemon juice
2 tablespoons minced garlic (about 6 cloves)
½ teaspoon salt, divided
½ teaspoon freshly ground black pepper, divided
¼ teaspoon ground cardamom
¼ teaspoon ground cumin
¼ teaspoon ground cinnamon
¼ teaspoon ground nutmeg
6 (6-ounce) skinless, boneless chicken breast halves
1 cup fat-free, less-sodium chicken broth
1½ tablespoons olive oil
1 tablespoon chopped fresh parsley

1. Combine yogurt, juice, garlic, ¼ teaspoon salt, ¼ teaspoon pepper, cardamom, cumin, cinnamon, and nutmeg in a large zip-top plastic bag. Add chicken; seal. Marinate in refrigerator over-night, turning bag occasionally.
2. Remove chicken from bag, reserving marinade; pat chicken dry with paper towels. Combine reserved marinade and broth.
3. Heat oil in a large nonstick skillet over medium-high heat. Sprinkle chicken with remaining ¼ teaspoon salt and remaining ¼ teaspoon pepper. Add half of chicken to pan, and cook 1½ minutes on each side or until browned. Repeat procedure with remaining chicken. Return chicken to pan, and pour broth mixture over chicken. Bring to a boil. Cover, reduce heat, and simmer 12 minutes or until chicken is done. Place chicken on a serving platter; discard liquid in pan. Sprinkle chicken evenly with parsley. Yield: 6 servings (serving size: 1 chicken breast half).

CALORIES 256 (22% from fat); FAT 6.2g (sat 1.4g, mono 3.2g, poly 0.9g); PROTEIN 42.1g; CARB 5.7g; FIBER 0.5g; CHOL 101mg; IRON 1.6mg; SODIUM 400mg; CALC 104mg

---

Friday, December

21
Movie Night

Settle in for your favorite film of the season. Can't decide which one? Make it a double feature.

MAKE AHEAD
Caramel Popcorn

Store this popcorn in an airtight container up to one week.

Cooking spray
1 cup packed dark brown sugar
½ cup light-colored corn syrup
⅓ cup butter
1 tablespoon light molasses
1½ teaspoons vanilla extract
½ teaspoon baking soda
½ teaspoon salt
12 cups popcorn (popped without salt or fat)

1. Preheat oven to 250°.
2. Coat a large jelly-roll pan with cooking spray.
3. Combine sugar, corn syrup, butter, and molasses in a medium saucepan; bring to a boil over medium heat. Cook 5 minutes, stirring once. Remove from heat; stir in vanilla, baking soda, and salt. Place popcorn in a large bowl; pour sugar mixture over popcorn in a steady stream, stirring to coat.
4. Spread popcorn mixture into prepared pan. Bake at 250° for 1 hour, stirring every 15 minutes.
5. Remove from oven; stir to break up any large clumps. Cool 15 minutes. Serve warm or at room temperature. Yield: 18 servings (serving size: ⅔ cup).

CALORIES 126 (26% from fat); FAT 3.6g (sat 2.2g, mono 1.1g, poly 0.2g); PROTEIN 0.7g; CARB 23.9g; FIBER 0.8g; CHOL 9mg; IRON 0.4mg; SODIUM 151mg; CALC 15mg

Saturday, December
22
Winter Solstice

Pay tribute to the longest night of
the year with a spirited drink
that's rich in tradition.

Sunday, December
23
Last-Minute Gift Run

Check off all the remaining shopping
list items, then head home for a quick,
simple yet rich and rewarding supper.

Monday, December
24
Christmas Eve

This special night calls for a distinctive
dessert, and this cake is a real
showstopper.

MAKE AHEAD
Eggnog

Two kinds of milk and a cooked custard
ensure a winning version of the traditional
holiday beverage.

    4   cups whole milk
    1   (12-ounce) can evaporated low-fat
        milk
    ½   cup sugar
    ¼   teaspoon ground cinnamon
    ⅛   teaspoon ground nutmeg
    6   large eggs
    ¼   cup brandy
    1   teaspoon vanilla extract

1. Place milk and evaporated milk in a
large saucepan. Bring to a simmer over
medium heat.
2. Combine sugar, cinnamon, nutmeg,
and eggs in a large bowl. Gradually add
hot milk to egg mixture, stirring constantly with a whisk. Return milk mixture to pan; cook over medium-low heat
until thick (about 8 minutes), stirring
constantly. Pour into a bowl; stir in
brandy and vanilla. Press plastic wrap
onto surface of eggnog, and chill 8 hours
or overnight. Yield: 12 servings (serving
size: about ½ cup).

CALORIES 152 (33% from fat); FAT 5.6g (sat 2.7g, mono 1.6g,
poly 0.5g); PROTEIN 7.6g; CARB 15g; FIBER 0g; CHOL 118mg;
IRON 0.5mg; SODIUM 101mg; CALC 168mg

QUICK & EASY
Farfalle with Creamy
Wild Mushroom Sauce

If you can't find the mushroom blend, use
cremini.

    1   pound uncooked farfalle (bow tie
         pasta)
    1   tablespoon butter
    ½   cup chopped onion
    ⅓   cup finely chopped shallots
    1   tablespoon minced garlic
    1½   teaspoons salt, divided
    ¼   teaspoon freshly ground pepper
    12   ounces presliced exotic mushroom
         blend
    ¼   cup dry white wine
    ⅔   cup whipping cream
    ½   cup (2 ounces) grated fresh
         Parmigiano-Reggiano cheese
    2   tablespoons chopped fresh parsley
    Minced fresh parsley (optional)

1. Cook pasta according to package
directions, omitting salt and fat; drain.
2. Melt butter in a large nonstick skillet
over medium-high heat. Add onion,
shallots, garlic, 1 teaspoon salt, pepper,
and mushrooms to pan; cook 12 minutes
or until liquid evaporates and mushrooms are tender, stirring occasionally.
Add wine; cook 2 minutes or until liquid
evaporates, stirring occasionally. Remove
from heat.
3. Add cooked pasta, whipping cream,
cheese, and 2 tablespoons parsley, tossing gently to coat. Stir in remaining ½
teaspoon salt. Garnish with minced fresh
parsley, if desired. Serve immediately.
Yield: 8 servings (serving size: 1¼ cups).

CALORIES 336 (31% from fat); FAT 11.4g (sat 6.9g, mono 3.1g,
poly 0.4g); PROTEIN 12.1g; CARB 47.5g; FIBER 2.3g; CHOL 36mg;
IRON 2.3mg; SODIUM 577mg; CALC 124mg

MAKE AHEAD • FREEZABLE
Peppermint
Ice Cream Cake
(pictured on facing page)

Peppermint ice cream, often only seasonally available, delivers holiday flavor in
abundance.

    Cooking spray
    ¾   cup unsweetened cocoa
    ¾   cup boiling water
    6   tablespoons butter, melted
    1   cup packed dark brown sugar
    ½   cup granulated sugar
    ¾   cup egg substitute
    1½   cups all-purpose flour (about 6¾
         ounces)
    ½   teaspoon baking powder
    ½   teaspoon baking soda
    ½   teaspoon salt
    2   teaspoons vanilla extract
    3   cups low-fat peppermint ice cream
         (such as Edy's/Dreyer's Slow-
         Churned Light), softened
    3   cups frozen fat-free whipped
         topping, thawed
    ⅛   teaspoon peppermint extract
    8   peppermint candies, crushed

1. Preheat oven to 350°.
2. Coat 2 (8-inch) round cake pans with
cooking spray. Line bottom of each pan
with wax paper.
3. Combine cocoa, ¾ cup boiling water,
and butter, stirring with a whisk until
blended. Cool.
4. Combine sugars in a large bowl, stirring well until blended. Add egg substitute; beat with a mixer 2 minutes or until
light and creamy. Add cocoa mixture,
and beat 1 minute.
5. Lightly spoon flour into dry measuring
cups; level with a knife. Combine flour,

baking powder, baking soda, and salt. Gradually add flour mixture to sugar mixture; beat 1 minute or until blended. Stir in vanilla. Pour batter into prepared pans. Bake at 350° for 28 minutes or until a wooden pick inserted in center comes out clean. Cool in pans 10 minutes on a wire rack. Remove from pans. Wrap in plastic wrap, and freeze 2 hours or until slightly frozen.

6. Spread ice cream in an 8-inch round cake pan lined with plastic wrap. Cover and freeze 4 hours or until firm.

7. To assemble cake, place 1 cake layer, bottom side up, on a cake pedestal. Remove ice cream layer from freezer, and remove plastic wrap. Place ice cream layer, bottom side up, on top of cake layer. Top with remaining cake layer.

8. Combine thawed whipped topping and peppermint extract, and stir until blended. Spread over top and sides of cake. Sprinkle with crushed peppermints. Freeze until ready to serve. Let cake stand at room temperature 10 minutes before slicing. Yield: 16 servings (serving size: 1 slice).

CALORIES 251 (24% from fat); FAT 6.8g (sat 3.3g, mono 2.1g, poly 0.4g); PROTEIN 4.3g; CARB 44.4g; FIBER 1.7g; CHOL 19mg; IRON 1.6mg; SODIUM 207mg; CALC 63mg

Perfect for a large, hungry crowd, this succulent herb- and cheese-rubbed turkey will be the star attraction of your holiday feast.

Parmesan-Sage Roast Turkey with Sage Gravy

Garnish with fresh sage, thyme, roasted shallots, and lemons.

3   cups chopped onion
1   cup chopped celery
1   cup chopped carrot
10 garlic cloves
Cooking spray
1   (13-pound) fresh or frozen turkey, thawed
⅓   cup (1½ ounces) grated fresh Parmigiano-Reggiano cheese
5   tablespoons chopped fresh sage, divided
2   tablespoons butter, softened
1   tablespoon minced garlic
1   teaspoon salt, divided
½   teaspoon freshly ground black pepper, divided
1   lemon, halved
2½ cups fat-free, less-sodium chicken broth, divided
⅓   cup chopped shallots
1   cup sherry
¼   cup all-purpose flour (about 1 ounce)
¼   cup water

1. Preheat oven to 425°.
2. Combine first 4 ingredients in bottom of a shallow roasting pan coated with cooking spray. Remove and discard giblets and neck from turkey. Trim excess fat. Starting at neck cavity, loosen skin from breast and drumsticks by inserting fingers, gently pushing between skin and meat. Lift wing tips up and over back; tuck under turkey.
3. Combine cheese, ¼ cup sage, butter, minced garlic, ¾ teaspoon salt, and ¼

teaspoon pepper; rub mixture under loosened skin and over breast and drumsticks. Rub turkey skin with cut sides of lemon halves; squeeze juice into turkey cavity. Place lemon halves in turkey cavity; tie legs together with kitchen string.
4. Place turkey, breast side up, on vegetable mixture in pan. Bake at 425° for 30 minutes. Pour 2 cups broth over turkey. Tent turkey breast loosely with foil. Bake an additional 30 minutes.
5. Reduce oven temperature to 325° (do not remove turkey from oven). Bake at 325° for 1½ hours or until a thermometer inserted into meaty part of thigh registers 165°, basting every 30 minutes. Remove turkey from pan. Cover and let stand 30 minutes; discard skin.
6. Place a large zip-top plastic bag inside a 4-cup glass measure. Pour drippings through a sieve into bag; discard solids. Let drippings stand 10 minutes (fat will rise to the top). Seal bag; carefully snip off 1 bottom corner of bag. Drain drippings into a bowl, stopping before fat

layer reaches opening; discard fat. Add enough of remaining broth to drippings to equal 3 cups.
7. Heat a saucepan over medium-high heat. Coat pan with cooking spray. Add shallots to pan; sauté 1 minute. Add sherry; bring to a boil. Cook until reduced to ½ cup (about 5 minutes). Stir in remaining 1 tablespoon sage; cook 30 seconds. Add reserved drippings; bring to a boil.
8. Lightly spoon flour into a dry measuring cup; level with a knife. Combine flour and ¼ cup water, stirring well with a whisk. Stir flour mixture into drippings mixture; bring to a boil. Cook 2 minutes or until thickened, stirring constantly. Stir in remaining ¼ teaspoon salt and remaining ¼ teaspoon pepper. Serve gravy with turkey. Yield: 16 servings (serving size: about 5 ounces turkey meat and about 3 tablespoons gravy).

CALORIES 285 (30% from fat); FAT 9.6g (sat 3.5g, mono 2.5g, poly 2.2g); PROTEIN 40.9g; CARB 3.5g; FIBER 0.3g; CHOL 108mg; IRON 2.7mg; SODIUM 339mg; CALC 64mg

26
Boxing Day

In Victorian times, British servants worked on Christmas, so their employers placed food in boxes for them to enjoy on the 26th, their day off.

QUICK & EASY
Turkey Alfredo Pizza

Leftover turkey finds new life in this white pizza. For more recipe ideas for leftover turkey, see pages 368 and 448.

 1 cup shredded cooked turkey breast
 1 cup frozen chopped collard greens or spinach, thawed, drained, and squeezed dry
 2 teaspoons lemon juice
 ½ teaspoon salt
 ¼ teaspoon black pepper
 1 garlic clove, halved
 1 (1-pound) Italian cheese-flavored thin pizza crust (such as Boboli)
 ½ cup light Alfredo sauce (such as Contadina)
 ¾ cup (3 ounces) shredded fontina cheese
 ½ teaspoon crushed red pepper

1. Preheat oven to 450°.
2. Combine first 5 ingredients; toss well. Rub cut sides of garlic over crust; discard garlic. Spread Alfredo sauce evenly over crust; top with turkey mixture. Sprinkle with cheese and red pepper. Bake at 450° for 12 minutes or until crust is crisp. Cut into 6 wedges. Yield: 6 servings (serving size: 1 wedge).

CALORIES 316 (29% from fat); FAT 10.3g (sat 5.2g, mono 3.5g, poly 1.1g); PROTEIN 19.2g; CARB 35.6g; FIBER 0.6g; CHOL 39mg; IRON 2.5mg; SODIUM 837mg; CALC 351mg

27
After the Mall

Make returns and exchanges, then cap off the evening with a home-baked dessert that fills the house with irresistible aromas.

Apple Brown Betty

With origins in colonial American cooking, betties are baked puddings featuring spiced fruits and breading. In this variation of the humble dessert, two types of apples are used so it's not too sweet or tart.

 2 cups sliced peeled Granny Smith apple (about ¾ pound)
 2 cups sliced peeled Rome apple (about ¾ pound)
 1 tablespoon fresh lemon juice
 ¼ cup granulated sugar
 ½ teaspoon ground cinnamon
 ¼ teaspoon ground nutmeg
 ¼ cup 1% low-fat milk
 1 tablespoon molasses
 1 teaspoon vanilla extract
 2 ounces day-old Italian or French bread, torn into ½-inch pieces
Cooking spray
 ½ cup all-purpose flour (about 2¼ ounces)
 ¼ cup packed brown sugar
 ¼ cup chilled butter, cut into small pieces

1. Preheat oven to 350°.
2. Combine first 3 ingredients in a large bowl. Sprinkle apple mixture with granulated sugar, cinnamon, and nutmeg; toss well. Combine milk, molasses, and vanilla in a medium bowl. Add bread to milk mixture; toss to combine. Add bread mixture to apple mixture; toss to combine. Spoon bread mixture into an 8-inch square baking dish coated with cooking spray.
3. Lightly spoon flour into a dry measuring cup; level with a knife. Combine flour and brown sugar; cut in chilled butter using a pastry blender or 2 knives

until mixture resembles small pebbles. Sprinkle brown sugar mixture over apple mixture. Bake at 350° for 40 minutes or until golden and bubbly. Serve warm. Yield: 6 servings.

CALORIES 256 (30% from fat); FAT 8.4g (sat 4.9g, mono 2.3g, poly 0.5g); PROTEIN 2.4g; CARB 44.1g; FIBER 2g; CHOL 21mg; IRON 1.2mg; SODIUM 139mg; CALC 47mg

28
Ice Skating

Lace up the blades and hit the rink for some wintertime exercise. Totable granola fuels the fun.

MAKE AHEAD
Homemade Granola

Prepare the granola up to two days ahead, and store in an airtight container.

 6 cups rolled oats
 ¼ cup chopped almonds
 ¼ cup chopped pecans
 2 tablespoons brown sugar
 ¼ teaspoon kosher salt
 ⅓ cup maple syrup
 ¼ cup honey
 ¼ cup pineapple juice
 ½ teaspoon almond extract
Cooking spray
 ¼ cup dried cranberries
 ¼ cup chopped dried apricots

1. Preheat oven to 300°.
2. Combine first 5 ingredients in a large bowl. Add syrup, honey, juice, and almond extract; toss well. Spread mixture evenly onto a jelly-roll pan coated with cooking spray. Bake at 300° for 45 minutes, stirring every 15 minutes. Stir in cranberries and apricots. Cool completely. Store in a zip-top plastic bag. Yield: 10 servings (serving size: ½ cup).

CALORIES 384 (20% from fat); FAT 8.4g (sat 1.1g, mono 3.7g, poly 2.5g); PROTEIN 9.8g; CARB 68.1g; FIBER 7.8g; CHOL 0mg; IRON 3.4mg; SODIUM 52mg; CALC 57mg

December 441

This festival (December 26 to January 1) celebrates African-American heritage and features dishes native to Africa.

QUICK & EASY • MAKE AHEAD

Peanut and Squash Soup

1½ teaspoons peanut oil
4 cups (½-inch) cubed peeled butternut squash
1 cup chopped onion
2 tablespoons minced garlic (about 6 cloves)
½ teaspoon salt
½ teaspoon ground cumin
¼ teaspoon ground coriander
4 cups fat-free, less-sodium chicken broth
¾ cup reduced-fat creamy peanut butter
2 tablespoons tomato paste
½ teaspoon crushed red pepper
¼ cup chopped fresh cilantro

1. Heat oil in a large saucepan over medium-high heat. Add squash and next 5 ingredients to pan; sauté 5 minutes or until onion is tender. Add broth, peanut butter, tomato paste, and pepper, stirring well to combine; bring to a boil. Reduce heat, and simmer 10 minutes or until squash is tender. Sprinkle with cilantro. Yield: 6 servings (serving size: about 1 cup).

CALORIES 264 (38% from fat); FAT 11.2g (sat 2.4g, mono 5.2g, poly 3.4g); PROTEIN 11.3g; CARB 34.6g; FIBER 6.4g; CHOL 0mg; IRON 2.3mg; SODIUM 621mg; CALC 111mg

Enjoy a satisfying snack as you pack up the trimmings and store them for another year.

QUICK & EASY • MAKE AHEAD

Cumin Curried Hummus

1 tablespoon olive oil
3 garlic cloves, chopped
1 tablespoon curry powder
½ teaspoon cumin seeds
½ cup water
3 tablespoons fresh lemon juice
¾ teaspoon salt
2 (15½-ounce) cans chickpeas (garbanzo beans), rinsed and drained
Flat-leaf parsley sprig (optional)

1. Heat oil in a small skillet over medium heat. Add garlic to pan; cook 30 seconds, stirring constantly. Add curry and cumin; cook 30 seconds or until fragrant, stirring constantly. Place garlic mixture, ½ cup water, and remaining ingredients in a food processor; process until smooth. Garnish with parsley sprig, if desired. Yield: 3 cups (serving size: ¼ cup).

CALORIES 82 (29% from fat); FAT 2.6g (sat 0.2g, mono 1.4g, poly 1g); PROTEIN 3g; CARB 12.2g; FIBER 3g; CHOL 0mg; IRON 1.2mg; SODIUM 254mg; CALC 27mg

End the year on a sweet note with this decadent high-rise dessert.

Double Chocolate Soufflés with Warm Fudge Sauce

SOUFFLÉS:
Cooking spray
½ cup plus 2 tablespoons sugar, divided
3 tablespoons all-purpose flour
3 tablespoons unsweetened cocoa
⅛ teaspoon salt
1¼ cups fat-free milk
3 ounces bittersweet chocolate, chopped
1 teaspoon vanilla extract
1 large egg yolk
6 large egg whites

SAUCE:
1 tablespoon butter
⅓ cup sugar
2 tablespoons unsweetened cocoa
1 tablespoon all-purpose flour
½ cup fat-free milk
½ ounce bittersweet chocolate, chopped

1. Position oven rack to the lowest setting. Preheat oven to 425°.
2. To prepare soufflés, lightly coat 6 (8-ounce) soufflé dishes with cooking spray. Sprinkle evenly with 2 tablespoons sugar. Set aside.
3. Combine remaining ½ cup sugar, 3 tablespoons flour, 3 tablespoons cocoa, and salt in a saucepan over medium-high heat, stirring with a whisk. Gradually add 1¼ cups milk, stirring constantly with a whisk; bring to a boil. Cook 2 minutes or until slightly thick, stirring constantly with a whisk; remove from heat. Add 3 ounces chocolate; stir until smooth. Transfer to a bowl; cool to room temperature. Stir in vanilla and egg yolk.
4. Place whites in a bowl; beat at high speed until stiff peaks form (do not overbeat). Gently fold one-fourth of egg whites into chocolate mixture; gently fold in remaining egg white mixture. Gently spoon mixture into prepared dishes. Sharply tap dishes 2 or 3 times on counter to level. Place dishes on a baking sheet; place baking sheet on bottom rack of 425° oven. Immediately reduce oven temperature to 350° (do not remove soufflés from oven). Bake 40 minutes or until a wooden pick inserted in the side of each soufflé comes out clean.
5. To prepare sauce, melt butter in a saucepan over medium-high heat. Add ⅓ cup sugar, 2 tablespoons cocoa, and 1 tablespoon flour; stir well with a whisk. Gradually add ½ cup milk, stirring well; bring to a boil. Cook 1 minute or until slightly thick, stirring constantly. Remove from heat; add ½ ounce chocolate, stirring until smooth. Serve warm. Yield: 6 servings (serving size: 1 soufflé and about 2 tablespoons sauce).

CALORIES 315 (26% from fat); FAT 9g (sat 5.1g, mono 1.8g, poly 0.3g); PROTEIN 9.1g; CARB 51.8g; FIBER 2.9g; CHOL 41mg; IRON 1.4mg; SODIUM 153mg; CALC 79mg

Countdown to Party Time

Ask any great host or hostess for his or her secret to successful entertaining, and you'll find that success all comes down to planning. Use the following checklist to organize your holiday party. You'll be refreshed and relaxed and able to enjoy your party every bit as much as your guests.

Planning Ahead

Four to Six Weeks Ahead
• Set a date and time.
• Make out your guest list.
• Decide which menu you'll use. Consult make-ahead recipe notes. On your calendar, write when you'll prepare or assemble each dish. Order any food you decide to have catered.
• Select invitations if you plan to send them for your party.

Three Weeks Ahead
• Mail your invitations three weeks ahead—holiday schedules fill quickly.

Two Weeks to Go
• Check your supply of chairs, serving dishes, flatware, and glassware.
• Check your supply of linens and tableware, including serving dishes of different sizes and shapes (which make a more interesting buffet table). If you come up short, ask a friend or relative to lend you a few pieces. If convenience is most important to you, buy paper napkins and plastic glasses including wine glasses, plates, and utensils.
• Make a grocery list.
• Give some thought to your home's exterior. Plant seasonal flowers in a planter on the front porch, hang a festive wreath, or wash front-facing windows—anything to give your place a lift.

Only One More Week
• Select holiday music to play.
• Grocery shop for nonperishable items.
• Plan a timetable of the recipes you can prepare ahead.

One or Two Days Before
• Clean the house. If you're too busy, think about hiring a cleaning crew. Or delegate chores to family members.
• Buy fresh flowers or greenery to put in vases, or set out a few pots of seasonal bulbs in bloom. An arrangement of candles can also look lovely, and candles won't wilt like a floral centerpiece.
• Get out china, serving dishes, and utensils. Polish silver. Make sure that each dish has its serving utensil.
• Think about coat storage and traffic flow—not only around the buffet table but also throughout your house.

• Arrange furniture to maximize seating.
• Shop for perishable items.
• Prepare dishes that can be made ahead.
• Chill beverages. Make extra ice.
• Make place cards.

The Day of the Party
• Finish preparing food, and arrange it on serving dishes. Fill additional trays so that you can replenish the table by exchanging a full tray for an empty one.
• Set the table.
• Reserve some time for rest.

Setting the Table

Keep in mind the order in which dishes, glasses, and flatware will be used when setting the table. Use the tips below as a guide.

- If using place mats, lay the mats flush with the table edge or about 1 inch from the edge.
- Fold the napkins, and lay them on the place mat to the left of the forks.
- Aim to keep the amount of flatware that will be used to a minimum. Generally, there should be no more than three pieces of flatware on each side of the plate.
- Put knives and spoons to the right of the plate, with each knife's cutting edge facing the plate. Forks go to the left of the plate.
- As a general rule, start from the outside and work your way in. That is, the flatware for the first course is on the outside, farthest from the plate.
- Place water glasses above the knife. Position additional glasses in order of use.
- Place bread-and-butter plates near the tip of the fork. If there is no bread-and-butter plate, place the salad plate there.
- If there is a bread-and-butter plate, place the salad plate to the left and a little below the bread-and-butter plate.

Setting Up the Buffet

Set the buffet on a surface, such as a dining table, chest, kitchen counter, or sideboard, that will accommodate a stack of dinner plates and serving dishes of food. Arrange the buffet using these helpful tips.

- Place serving dishes in an arrangement that allows for easy circulation and traffic flow.

- Set the buffet near the kitchen so that it's easy to refill serving dishes, or fill additional trays to replace empty ones.
- If a dish is to be served over rice, locate the rice first in line.
- Place dressings and sauces close to the dish they complement.
- Serve desserts at one end of the buffet, or place them on a serving cart.
- Arrange beverages on a side table, or serve from a tray after guests are seated.

Mix and match china, glassware, and flatware to reflect your style.

Add a warm glow to the table with small accent candles.

Wrap silverware in colorful napkins for display on the buffet.

Plate Appeal

Cooking Light photo and food stylists make sure our food photography is eye-catching. Learn their secrets for setting a smart table.

What plates are best to use?
"Neutral plates are ideal because they can be used any time and with almost any food," says Senior Photo Stylist Cindy Barr. Let them serve as a stabilizing element to show off the beauty of food. "It's important the plate not be too busy because the food can become lost in the design," says Food Stylist Kathleen Kanen.

What about other colors?
For another option, consider colors that transition to more than one season. For example, red works well for Valentine's Day, the Fourth of July, or Christmas. Another plus: "Warmer tones, like red or orange, make food seem more appetizing than cooler colors, such as blue or lavender," Kanen says. "Sometimes I use cool-colored plates for cool foods, like a summer salad or a luscious berry dessert," says Photo Stylist Jan Gautro.

Does tableware have to match?
No. Feel free to mix decorative soup bowls from a discount store with family heirloom china. Blending old and new lends an air of informality and fun to your table. "When everything matches too perfectly, the table can seem impersonal," says Photo Stylist Leigh Ann Ross.

How important is planning?
"You should consider how the food will look when plated," Gautro says. "Aim for an assortment of colors. It's better for your plate and your diet." A well-balanced plate might include a fresh strip of salmon, a crisp green salad, and a baked potato. Such a mix will also help meld temperatures, textures, and tastes, which is important to sensory perceptions of the meal.

What food should be plated first?
"Plate food from the center instead of segmenting piles around the edge," says Senior Food Stylist Kellie Kelley. "Start with the largest, most important item—usually the entrée—then group side dishes around it." This helps the meal appear cohesive.

How do you keep sauces in place?
Plate a thick sauce, such as a mole, first, then place the entrée on top. "Thick sauces can make food appear heavy," Kanen says. Spoon thin sauces on just before serving to prevent liquid from seeping into other foods, and use a deeper plate to contain the sauce, she says.

Finishing Touches
Garnishes help finish a plate, making it seem more inviting. Often, they increase the dish's visual appeal by adding a dash of contrasting color. "Think simple, and select an ingredient already in the recipe or one that complements it well," Kelley says. For example:

DESSERTS
- A light dusting of cocoa, powdered sugar, or cinnamon
- A teaspoon of finely chopped walnuts or pecans

SALADS, SIDES, AND PASTAS
- A tablespoon of toasted slivered almonds
- A handful of dried cranberries
- Shaved Parmigiano-Reggiano cheese
- Coarsely ground black pepper

SOUPS
- A teaspoon of pesto or low-fat sour cream
- A tablespoon of pine nuts or pumpkinseeds
- Finely chopped fresh parsley or basil

ENTRÉES
- A single curved sprig of fresh parsley
- A small handful of chopped scallions or fresh chives
- Lime or lemon wedges or grated rind

Selecting and Serving Wine

Half the fun of entertaining is the planning, even if it's just a small dinner with friends. And planning which wines to serve, how much to serve, and how to serve them can be exciting, too. Following these six wine solutions will help you entertain with ease at your next party.

Which Wines to Serve There's something wonderful about a dinner where the food and wine work seamlessly together. One easy way to achieve a delicious food and wine marriage is to choose a wine that mirrors the dish you're making. So if your dish is light and fresh with lots of herbal flavors, ask your wine merchant for a wine with similar qualities. Or make a pairing based on the wine guide on page 447. Remember: Pairing wine and food isn't a science, and there are no absolutely right or absolutely wrong answers.

How to Store Wine Until Serving If you plan to offer red wines, leave them where it's relatively cool. Warm places (like on top of the refrigerator or beside the stove) can make red wine taste flat and dull. White wines need to be served quite cool, but it's hard to find extra space in the refrigerator when entertaining. Chill whites in a big galvanized metal bucket. Fill it with a slushy mix of ice and cold water, and put the wine in an hour before your guests arrive; by then, the wine will be perfectly chilled.

Rent Wineglasses There are several advantages to renting glasses—even for a relatively small party. First, you won't have to worry about having enough matching glasses for everyone. Second, the glasses will be delivered to you clean and ready for use. Third, you can return the glasses dirty, since the rental company washes them when you're done. Most party rental companies rent wineglasses, and the service is usually inexpensive (starting at less than $1 per glass). Rent large balloon-shaped glasses, and ask for the highest quality available.

How Much Wine You Need It's always better to overestimate since unopened bottles can be saved and enjoyed later. Figure on a half-bottle of wine per person as a minimum. While this may seem like a lot—it really isn't because a half-bottle of wine yields about two and a half glasses—remember that your guests will probably be sipping wine over the course of many hours.

How to Save or Cap Opened Bottles Whether the wine is red or white, recork opened bottles, and put them in the refrigerator to preserve freshness. White wine will be ready to enjoy the following night straight from the refrigerator. For red wine, you'll want to let it warm to room temperature.

And how long can you keep an opened bottle of wine? That depends on the varietal (some—like cabernet sauvignon—are more sturdy than others) and a host of complex factors like the amount of air in the bottle, how quickly you recorked it after it was opened, and so on. But as a general rule of thumb, most opened wines remain in good condition up to three days.

Cooking with Wine Wine used as an ingredient in a dish should always be high quality, just like any other ingredient in the recipe. So when buying a wine for the recipe, choose one that you plan on serving as well. It's not only smart shopping—your dish will taste better, too.

Quick Tips

- Don't cook with a wine that you wouldn't drink.
- When recipes call for a small amount of wine, small bottles—called splits—are the best buy.
- Store open bottles of wine corked and refrigerated up to three days.
- Don't throw out leftover wine. Freeze in plastic bags for use in soups, stews, sauces, and casseroles.
- You may substitute broth or fruit juice for wine in some recipes, but you may lose the full-bodied flavor of the dish.

All About Wine Pairing

Wine Type	Herbs & Spices	Vegetables	Fish & Shellfish	Meats	Cheeses	Good Bridges
SAUVIGNON BLANC	Basil, bay leaf, cilantro, dill, fennel, lemongrass, marjoram, mint, parsley, savory, thyme	Carrots; eggplant; most green vegetables (lettuces, snow peas, zucchini); tomatoes	Sea bass, snapper, sole, swordfish, trout, tuna, clams, mussels, oysters, scallops, shrimp	Chicken, game birds, turkey	Buffalo mozzarella, feta, fontina, goat, Parmigiano-Reggiano, ricotta, Swiss	Bell peppers (fresh, roasted); capers; citrus (lemon, lime, orange); fennel; garlic; green figs; leeks; olives; sour cream; tomatoes (fresh, sun-dried)
CHARDONNAY	Basil, clove, tarragon, thyme	Corn, mushrooms, potatoes, pumpkin, squash	Grouper, halibut, monkfish, salmon, swordfish, tuna, crab, lobster, scallops, shrimp	Chicken, pork, turkey, veal	Brie, Camembert, Monterey Jack, Swiss	Apples; avocado; bacon; butter; citrus (lemon juice, lemon zest); coconut milk; cream; Dijon mustard; milk; nuts (toasted almonds, cashews, hazelnuts, pine nuts); pancetta; pears; polenta; tropical fruits (mango, papaya, pineapple); vanilla
RIESLING	Chile pepper, cilantro, dill, five-spice, ginger, lemongrass, nutmeg, parsley	Carrots; corn; onions (roasted, sautéed); parsnips	Sole; smoked fish (salmon, trout); snapper; trout; crab; scallops	Chicken, game birds, pork	Emmenthaler, Gouda	Apricots (fresh, dried); citrus (lime, orange, zest); dried fruits (figs, plums, raisins); peaches; tropical fruits (mango, papaya)
PINOT NOIR	Basil, black pepper, cinnamon, clove, fennel, five-spice, oregano, rosemary, star anise, thyme	Beets, eggplant, mushrooms	Salmon (baked, grilled, sautéed); tuna	Beef, chicken, game birds, lamb, liver, rabbit, squab, turkey, veal	Aged Cheddar, Brie	Beets; butter; Dijon mustard; dried fruits (cherries, cranberries, plums, raisins); mushrooms; onions (roasted, sautéed); pomegranate molasses; pomegranates; shallots; tea; cooked tomatoes; truffles
SYRAH | SHIRAZ	Allspice, chile pepper, coriander, cumin, five-spice, pepper, rosemary, sage	Eggplant; onions (roasted, sautéed); root vegetables	Blackened "meaty" fish (salmon, tuna)	Bacon, duck, lamb, pancetta, pheasant, quail, sausage, short ribs, squab, venison	Cheddar, goat, Gouda, Gruyère	Black figs; black licorice; black olives; black pepper; cherries (fresh, dried); chocolate/cocoa
CABERNET SAUVIGNON	Juniper, oregano, rosemary, sage, savory, thyme	Mushrooms, potatoes, root vegetables	None	Beef (roasts, grilled steak); duck; lamb; venison	Camembert, Cantal, Carmody, aged Jack, aged Gouda	Balsamic vinegar; blackberries; black olives; black pepper; butter; cassis; cherries (fresh, dried); cream; currants; toasted nuts (walnuts, pecans); roasted red pepper

Turkey Tips

Simple Ways to Use Your Turkey Leftovers

Quesadillas: Shred turkey breast; sandwich between flour tortillas with cheese and refried beans. Cook a few minutes per side in a nonstick skillet.

Salad: Grill turkey breast; top a salad of romaine lettuce, kalamata olives, pepperoncini peppers, and feta cheese.

Blackened turkey sandwiches: Season turkey with blackening seasoning, grill, and arrange on hoagie rolls with coleslaw.

Barbecue pizza: Shred turkey, toss with barbecue sauce, and arrange on pizza dough with smoked Cheddar cheese and chopped green onions.

Skewers: Dip turkey in low-fat Italian dressing, cut into bite-sized pieces, skewer with olives and artichoke hearts, and grill.

Fried rice: Sauté chopped turkey, garlic, green onions, and rice.

Pesto focaccia sandwiches: Grill turkey breast; serve with roasted red bell peppers on focaccia spread with pesto.

Stuffed breasts: Cut a horizontal slit into turkey breast to form a pocket; stuff with ham and reduced-fat Swiss cheese.

Sauté: Try combinations like spinach and feta cheese or goat cheese and chutney.

Stuffed potatoes: Chop turkey, season with cumin and chili powder, and sauté. Toss with thawed frozen corn, chopped green onions, lime juice, and chopped cilantro. Spoon over baked potatoes.

Turkey saté: Pound breast into long, thin strips; toss with commercial peanut sauce, skewer, and grill.

For more leftover ideas, see "How to Make Over Thanksgiving Leftovers," (page 368).

Poultry Safety

Storing: Refrigerate raw poultry (chicken, Cornish hens, duck, and turkey) up to 2 days and cooked poultry up to 3 days. Raw skinless, boneless poultry can marinate in the refrigerator up to 8 hours; raw poultry pieces with skin and bone can marinate up to 1 day. Freeze uncooked poultry up to 6 months and cooked poultry up to 3 months.

Thawing: To thaw poultry in the refrigerator, allow 5 hours thawing time per pound. For the cold-water method, submerge poultry—still in its wrapping—in a sink or pot of cold water; change the water every 30 minutes until thawed. If using the microwave for thawing poultry, follow your microwave's directions.

Handling: Wash your hands with hot water and soap before and after handling poultry. Use hot water and soap to wash the cutting board and any utensils that come in contact with the meat. Be careful when you rinse poultry; you may splash water from the poultry onto a clean area.

Cooking: To prevent food-borne illnesses, poultry must be cooked to 165°. For whole birds, use an instant-read thermometer inserted in the meaty part of the thigh to confirm the temperature. Remove bird from roasting pan. Cover and let stand 30 minutes; discard skin. We do not recommend stuffing the whole bird because the stuffing may prevent the inside of the bird from reaching a safe temperature, and then the bacteria from the uncooked bird might cross-contaminate the stuffing.

For more guidance on poultry, call the USDA Meat and Poultry Hotline (888-674-6854).

Freezer Facts

Here are some guidelines about how to freeze leftovers and the length of time you can keep foods in the freezer without a compromise in quality.

• Don't overcook food items that are intended for the freezer, and be particularly careful to slightly undercook pasta, rice, and vegetables.

• Cool foods completely by setting them in the refrigerator for at least 1 hour before freezing.

• Allow time for your frozen foods to thaw before reheating. About 24 to 48 hours in the refrigerator will completely thaw most freezer items.

• Label (we use a permanent ink marker) with reheating instructions before freezing. Include the name of the recipe, date frozen, number of servings, temperature and length of time it bakes, and any other necessary information.

• Thaw casseroles (unless directed otherwise in the recipe) before baking. Going straight from freezer to oven with frozen unbaked dishes causes uneven baking. The outer edges tend to overcook, while the middle is uncooked.

Freezer No-No's

Air and moisture can cause freezer burn. That's why moistureproof, airtight containers and packaging are a must. Just say no to the temptation to use any of the following items for freezer storage—you'll be glad you did.

• Milk or juice cartons, or plastic jugs

• Ricotta, cottage cheese, or yogurt containers or butter/margarine tubs

• Glass jars that don't have "Ball" or "Kerr" on them or glass jars with narrow mouths (even if they're Ball or Kerr jars)

• Plastic zip-top storage bags (as opposed to plastic zip-top freezer bags)

• Plastic sandwich, produce, or bread bags

Freezer Storage Guide

TYPE OF FOOD	STORAGE TIME
Eggs and Cheeses	
cheese	6 months
egg whites or egg substitute (unopened)	1 year
egg yolks	1 year
Fruits and Vegetables	
commercial frozen fruits	1 year
commercial frozen veggies	8 months
Meats and Poultry	
ground meat	3 to 4 months
beef	3 to 4 months
veal, lamb	3 to 4 months
pork	3 to 4 months
cooked meats	2 to 3 months
turkey (whole)	1 year
chicken pieces	9 months
chicken (whole)	1 year
cooked chicken	4 months
Breads and Desserts	
muffins, baked	1 month
quick breads, baked	1 month
yeast breads, baked	1 month
layer cakes, baked	1 month
pound cakes, baked	1 month
cookies, baked	1 month
Nuts	6 to 12 months
Soups and Stews (without potatoes)	1 month

Seasonal Produce

Fruit				
FRUIT	**AVAILABILITY**	**WHY WE LIKE IT**	**STORING**	**PUTTING IT TO USE**
Blood Orange (Moro)	December – March	Smaller, sweeter, and less acidic than traditional oranges, this somewhat expensive fruit with a slight berry flavor is prized for its bright color and flavor. The fruit's skin may be pitted or smooth, and the color of the skin does not indicate the internal color or flavor.	Keep refrigerated 2 to 4 weeks.	Consider different ways to highlight its brilliant color. Squeeze fresh juice, or use the peeled sections as a garnish.
Bosc Pears	September – May	This pear is as attractive as it is sweet and richly flavored. It's excellent eaten fresh, but also holds its shape when poached, boiled, or baked.	Keep ripe pears cold in the refrigerator. Do not refrigerate unripe pears.	The firm texture of a Bosc pear is best for cooking in desserts and meat dishes. Its dramatic appearance makes it ideal for a fruit bowl.
Clementine	December – January	This juicy-sweet, seedless member of the mandarin family peels effortlessly and breaks easily into sections.	Keep refrigerated 1 week.	Save yourself a lot of work by substituting these oranges in recipes calling for orange sections. Or simply peel and eat.
Cranberries	October – December	These berries absorb sugar well, so they're delicious used in sauces, breads, and desserts. Look for round, plump, firm berries with a rich crimson color and smooth skin.	Keep refrigerated 1 month, or freeze up to 9 months.	Don't rinse cranberries until you are ready to use them. Chop them in a food processor rather than with a knife.
Kumquat	December – April	Because of their sweet skin and tart flesh, these 2-inch oblong fruits can be chopped or eaten whole, seeds included. Use them whole and uncooked to garnish holiday platters and ornamental fruit bowls, and buy only firm fruit.	Store at room temperature if eating soon. Otherwise, keep refrigerated 2 weeks.	The intense sour-orange flavor makes this citrus fruit a nice addition to chutneys and marmalades paired with beef, pork, or chicken.
Persimmon (Fuyus)	October – December	Fuyus, the nonastringent variety of persimmons, are firm when ripe and have a sweet-spicy flavor with notes of banana, plum, and winter squash.	Keep Fuyus refrigerated up to 1 month.	Fuyus should be crisp, smooth, and hard, like apples. Shaped like a tomato, this fruit is ideal for salads and good served with roasted pork or chicken.
Pomegranate	August – December	Hundreds of seeds are surrounded by glistening, luminescent ruby red pulp, which has an intense sweet-tart flavor. Look for heavy, large, and richly colored fruit. The skin should be uniform, free of blemishes, thin, and tough.	Refrigerate whole pomegranates, or freeze seeds in an airtight container 3 months.	Although the flesh is inedible and bitter, the seeds add a sweet-tart flavor to salads, roasts, and desserts. The juice makes a wonderful, vibrant syrup.

Fruit

FRUIT	AVAILABILITY	WHY WE LIKE IT	STORING	PUTTING IT TO USE
Quince	September - December	The scent of this firm-textured fruit is heavenly. In fact, a noticeable perfume is the best indicator of ripeness. It tastes like a cross between an apple and a pear, with a slight pineapple flavor.	Refrigerate whole quince for as long as 2 to 3 months. They bruise easily, so handle them with care.	Because of its luminescent color and sweet-tart flavor, the quince is excellent in recipes that need to cook long and slow, such as stews, roasts, and jams.

Vegetables

VEGETABLE	AVAILABILITY	WHY WE LIKE IT	STORING	PUTTING IT TO USE
Broccoli	yearlong but peak season is October - April	The entire vegetable is edible raw or cooked. Look for broccoli with a deep green color or a greenish purple color on the florets. Revive limp broccoli by trimming ½ inch from the base of the stalk and then setting the head in a glass of water in the refrigerator overnight.	Store unwashed broccoli in the vegetable crisper of the refrigerator 3 to 5 days.	Although the florets are most commonly used in recipes, we also chop the stalks and use them in stir-fries. We also add the leaves to salads.
Brussels Sprouts	late fall - early winter	Brussels sprouts have a distinct flavor, but take care in cooking because overcooking can make them bitter. There's no difference between small and large Brussels sprouts, but if they're larger than ½ inch wide, you may need to halve them or quarter them so they'll cook quickly. Buying them on the stalk is a sign of freshness.	Refrigerate in a paper bag up to 3 days. If refrigerated longer, the flavor may be too strong.	Remove discolored leaves, and cut off stem ends. Brussels sprouts are best when lightly cooked 5 to 10 minutes.
Roots (Beets, Celeriac, Fennel, Parsnips, Rutabagas, Turnips)	yearlong but best in the winter months	These vegetables are the cornerstone of healthy eating, and because of their various textures, they also lend themselves to a variety of cooking methods. Avoid roots that have soft spots or hairy rootlets, which indicate age.	Roots will last for months if stored in a cool, dry place, such as the refrigerator.	Roots are best for roasting, pureeing, or tossing into soups and stews.
Sweet Potatoes	late fall - early winter	Sweet potatoes can be left whole for baking or peeled, if desired, and sliced or cut into chunks.	Store in a cool, dry, dark place for about 3 to 4 weeks. Do not refrigerate.	Mash sweet potatoes, or try tossing them into soups and stews.
Winter Greens (Endive, Escarole, Kale, Spinach, Turnip Greens)	yearlong but best in the winter months	Although greens are available throughout the year, they become sweeter and more tender during the winter, allowing some to be eaten raw. Others are cooked to mellow their slight bitterness.	Store leafy greens unwashed in plastic bags in the refrigerator.	Soak greens, and then wash them leaf by leaf. Winter greens are most often used in salads with various other greens.
Winter Squash (Acorn, Butternut, Hubbard, Pumpkin, Spaghetti)	yearlong but best fall - winter	The best winter squash have thick skins with no soft spots and are slightly heavy. They're picked in the fall and stored until spring.	Store whole in a cool, dry place 1 month or in the refrigerator up to 3 months.	These squash have large seeds that need to be removed.

Ingredient Substitutions

If you're right in the middle of cooking and realize you don't have a particular ingredient, use the substitutions from these lists.

	INGREDIENT	SUBSTITUTION
BAKING PRODUCTS	Arrowroot, 1 teaspoon	1 tablespoon all-purpose flour or 1½ teaspoons cornstarch
	Baking Powder, 1 teaspoon	½ teaspoon cream of tartar and ¼ teaspoon baking soda
	Chocolate Semisweet, 1 ounce	1 ounce unsweetened chocolate and 1 tablespoon sugar
	Unsweetened, 1 ounce	3 tablespoons unsweetened cocoa and 1 tablespoon butter
	Cocoa, ¼ cup	1 ounce unsweetened chocolate (decrease fat in recipe by ½ tablespoon)
	Coconut, grated fresh, 1½ tablespoons	1 tablespoon flaked coconut
	Corn Syrup, light, 1 cup	1 cup sugar and ¼ cup water or 1 cup honey
	Cornstarch, 1 tablespoon	2 tablespoons all-purpose flour or granular tapioca
	Flour All-purpose, 1 tablespoon	1½ teaspoons cornstarch, potato starch, or rice starch
	Cake, 1 cup sifted	1 cup minus 2 tablespoons all-purpose flour
	Self-rising, 1 cup	1 cup all-purpose flour, 1 teaspoon baking powder, and ½ teaspoon salt
	Shortening Melted, 1 cup	1 cup canola oil (do not use oil if recipe does not call for melted shortening)
	Solid, 1 cup	1⅛ cups butter (decrease salt in recipe by ½ teaspoon)
	Sugar Brown, 1 cup, firmly packed	1 cup granulated white sugar
	Powdered, 1 cup	1 cup sugar and 1 tablespoon cornstarch (processed in food processor)
	Honey, ½ cup	½ cup molasses or maple syrup
DAIRY PRODUCTS	Eggs 1 large	2 egg yolks for custards and cream fillings or 2 egg yolks and 1 tablespoon water for cookies
	1 large	¼ cup egg substitute
	2 large	3 small eggs
	1 egg white (2 tablespoons)	2 tablespoons egg substitute
	1 egg yolk (1½ tablespoons)	2 tablespoons sifted dry egg yolk powder and 2 teaspoons water or 1½ tablespoons thawed frozen egg yolk
	Milk, fat-free, 1 cup	4 to 5 tablespoons fat-free dry milk powder and enough cold water to make 1 cup
	Buttermilk, low-fat or fat-free, 1 cup	1 tablespoon lemon juice or vinegar and 1 cup low-fat or fat-free milk (let stand 10 minutes)
	Sour Cream, 1 cup	1 cup plain yogurt
FRUITS & VEGETABLES	Lemon 1 medium	2 to 3 tablespoons lemon juice and 2 teaspoons grated rind
	Juice, 1 teaspoon	½ teaspoon vinegar
	Peel, dried	2 teaspoons freshly grated lemon rind
	Orange, 1 medium	½ cup orange juice and 2 tablespoons grated rind
	Tomatoes Fresh, chopped, 2 cups	1 (16-ounce) can (may need to drain)
	Juice, 1 cup	½ cup tomato sauce and ½ cup water
	Tomato Sauce, 2 cups	¾ cup tomato paste and 1 cup water
MISC.	Broth, beef or chicken, canned, 1 cup	1 bouillon cube dissolved in 1 cup boiling water
	Capers, 1 tablespoon	1 tablespoon chopped dill pickles or green olives
	Chili Paste, 1 teaspoon	¼ teaspoon hot red pepper flakes

INGREDIENT	SUBSTITUTION
MISCELLANEOUS (continued)	
Chili Sauce, 1 cup	1 cup tomato sauce, ¼ cup brown sugar, 2 tablespoons vinegar, ¼ teaspoon ground cinnamon, dash of ground cloves, and dash of ground allspice
Gelatin, flavored, 3-ounce package	1 tablespoon unflavored gelatin and 2 cups fruit juice
Ketchup, 1 cup	1 cup tomato sauce, ½ cup sugar, and 2 tablespoons vinegar (for cooking, not to be used as a condiment)
Tahini (sesame-seed paste), 1 cup	¾ cup creamy peanut butter and ¼ cup sesame oil
Vinegar, cider, 1 teaspoon	2 teaspoons lemon juice mixed with a pinch of sugar
Wasabi, 1 teaspoon	1 teaspoon horseradish or hot dry mustard
SEASONINGS	
Allspice, ground, 1 teaspoon	½ teaspoon ground cinnamon and ½ teaspoon ground cloves
Apple Pie Spice, 1 teaspoon	½ teaspoon ground cinnamon, ¼ teaspoon ground nutmeg, and ⅛ teaspoon ground cardamom
Bay Leaf, 1 whole	¼ teaspoon crushed bay leaf
Chives, chopped, 1 tablespoon	1 tablespoon chopped green onion tops
Garlic, 1 clove	1 teaspoon bottled minced garlic
Ginger Crystallized, 1 tablespoon	⅛ teaspoon ground ginger
Fresh, grated, 1 tablespoon	⅛ teaspoon ground ginger
Herbs, fresh, 1 tablespoon	1 teaspoon dried herbs or ¼ teaspoon ground herbs (except rosemary)
Horseradish, fresh, grated, 1 tablespoon	2 tablespoons prepared horseradish
Lemongrass, 1 stalk, chopped	1 teaspoon grated lemon zest
Mint, fresh, chopped, 3 tablespoons	1 tablespoon dried spearmint or peppermint
Mustard, dried, 1 teaspoon	1 tablespoon prepared mustard
Parsley, chopped fresh, 1 tablespoon	1 teaspoon dried parsley
Vanilla Bean, 6-inch bean	1 tablespoon vanilla extract

Liqueurs, spirits, and wines add special flavors that are difficult to replace. Alcohol itself evaporates at 172°, leaving only its flavor behind. However, this chart gives ideas for substitution of alcoholic ingredients, should you choose to change the recipe.

INGREDIENT	SUBSTITUTION
ALCOHOL	
Amaretto (2 tablespoons)	¼ to ½ teaspoon almond extract
Grand Marnier or other orange-flavored liqueur (2 tablespoons)	2 tablespoons orange juice concentrate or 2 tablespoons orange juice and ½ teaspoon orange extract
Kahlúa, coffee- or chocolate-flavored liqueur (2 tablespoons)	2 tablespoons strong brewed coffee and 1 teaspoon sugar
Rum or Brandy (2 tablespoons)	½ to 1 teaspoon rum or brandy extract for recipes in which liquid amount is not crucial (add water if necessary to have a specified amount of liquid)
Sherry or Bourbon (2 tablespoons)	1 to 2 teaspoons vanilla extract
Port, Sherry, Rum, Brandy, or fruit-flavored liqueur (¼ cup or more)	equal measure of orange juice or apple juice and 1 teaspoon of corresponding flavored extract or vanilla extract
White Wine (¼ cup or more)	equal measure of white grape juice or apple juice for dessert recipes; equal measure of fat-free, less-sodium chicken broth for savory recipes
Red Wine (¼ cup or more)	equal measure of red grape juice or cranberry juice for dessert recipes; for soups, stews, and other savory dishes, sometimes may substitute an equal measure of beef broth

Metric Equivalents

The information in the following charts is provided to help cooks outside the United States successfully use the recipes in this book. All equivalents are approximate.

Equivalents for Different Types of Ingredients

Standard Cup	Fine Powder (ex. flour)	Grain (ex. rice)	Granular (ex. sugar)	Liquid Solids (ex. butter)	Liquid (ex. milk)
1	140 g	150 g	190 g	200 g	240 ml
¾	105 g	113 g	143 g	150 g	180 ml
⅔	93 g	100 g	125 g	133 g	160 ml
½	70 g	75 g	95 g	100 g	120 ml
⅓	47 g	50 g	63 g	67 g	80 ml
¼	35 g	38 g	48 g	50 g	60 ml
⅛	18 g	19 g	24 g	25 g	30 ml

Liquid Ingredients by Volume

¼ tsp				=	1 ml
½ tsp				=	2 ml
1 tsp				=	5 ml
3 tsp	= 1 tbl		= ½ fl oz	=	15 ml
	2 tbls	= ⅛ cup	= 1 fl oz	=	30 ml
	4 tbls	= ¼ cup	= 2 fl oz	=	60 ml
	5⅓ tbls	= ⅓ cup	= 3 fl oz	=	80 ml
	8 tbls	= ½ cup	= 4 fl oz	=	120 ml
	10⅔ tbls	= ⅔ cup	= 5 fl oz	=	160 ml
	12 tbls	= ¾ cup	= 6 fl oz	=	180 ml
	16 tbls	= 1 cup	= 8 fl oz	=	240 ml
	1 pt	= 2 cups	= 16 fl oz	=	480 ml
	1 qt	= 4 cups	= 32 fl oz	=	960 ml
			33 fl oz	= 1000 ml	= 1 l

Dry Ingredients by Weight

(To convert ounces to grams, multiply the number of ounces by 30.)

1 oz	=	¹⁄₁₆ lb =	30 g
4 oz	=	¼ lb =	120 g
8 oz	=	½ lb =	240 g
12 oz	=	¾ lb =	360 g
16 oz	=	1 lb =	480 g

Length

(To convert inches to centimeters, multiply the number of inches by 2.5.)

1 in =			2.5 cm
6 in =	½ ft	=	15 cm
12 in =	1 ft	=	30 cm
36 in =	3 ft = 1 yd	=	90 cm
40 in =			100 cm = 1 m

Cooking/Oven Temperatures

	Fahrenheit	Celsius	Gas Mark
Freeze Water	32° F	0° C	
Room Temperature	68° F	20° C	
Boil Water	212° F	100° C	
Bake	325° F	160° C	3
	350° F	180° C	4
	375° F	190° C	5
	400° F	200° C	6
	425° F	220° C	7
	450° F	230° C	8
Broil			Grill

Menu Index

A topical guide to all the menus that appear in Cooking Light *Annual Recipes* 2008.
See page 478 for the General Recipe Index.

Dinner Tonight

Saucy Dishes Menu 1 (page 25)
serves 4
Smothered Pork Chops with Thyme
Wild rice medley
Tossed green salad

Saucy Dishes Menu 2 (page 25)
serves 4
Sirloin Steak with Tarragon-Garlic Sour Cream
Roasted baby carrots
Low-fat vanilla ice cream with chocolate syrup

Saucy Dishes Menu 3 (page 26)
serves 4
Angel Hair Pasta with Mussels and
Red Pepper Sauce
Toasted French bread
Pound cake with strawberry-pepper sauce

Saucy Dishes Menu 4 (page 26)
serves 4
Pork Medallions with Double-Apple Sauce
Lemon broccolini
Egg noodles

Steak Menu 1 (page 53)
serves 4
Barbecued Flank Steak Sandwiches
Quick coleslaw
Vegetable chips

Steak Menu 2 (page 54)
serves 6
Flank Steak with Chunky Mojo Relish
Cuban black beans
Pineapple sherbet

Steak Menu 3 (page 54)
serves 4
Flank Steak with Creamy Mushroom Sauce
Egg noodles
Buttered asparagus

Steak Menu 4 (page 55)
serves 4
Stir-Fried Szechuan Steak on Rice
Orange segments
Green tea ice cream

Pork Chops Menu 1 (page 89)
serves 4
Pan-Seared Pork Chops with
Red Currant Sauce
Mushroom-barley pilaf
Arugula salad with balsamic vinaigrette

Pork Chops Menu 2 (page 90)
serves 4
Barbecue-Rubbed Pork Chops
Cheddar grits
Cucumber–red onion salad

Pork Chops Menu 3 (page 90)
serves 4
Spiced Chops with Mango-Mint Salsa
Roasted sweet potatoes and Sautéed baby spinach

Pork Chops Menu 4 (page 91)
serves 4
Pork Chops Stuffed with Feta and Spinach
Herbed pita
Yogurt drizzled with honey and cinnamon

Shrimp Menu 1 (page 133)
serves 4
Grilled Teriyaki Shrimp Kebabs
Mashed sweet potatoes and Grilled asparagus

Shrimp Menu 2 (page 133)
serves 4
Shrimp Caesar Salad
Sun-dried tomato garlic breadsticks
Fresh strawberries with vanilla yogurt

Shrimp Menu 3 (page 134)
serves 4
Asian Rice with Shrimp and Snow Peas
Spicy-sweet cantaloupe salad
Iced green tea

From the Grill Menu 1 (page 160)
serves 4
Grilled Chicken and Tapenade Sandwiches
Grilled vegetable skewers
Cubed cantaloupe drizzled with Port

From the Grill Menu 2 (page 161)
serves 4
Grilled Salmon with Apricot-Mustard Glaze
Parmesan-spinach orzo pilaf
Pineapple chunks with chopped fresh mint

From the Grill Menu 3 (page 161)
serves 4
Chile-Spiced Tenderloin Steaks
Toasted corn and tomato salad
Flour tortilla

Rotisserie Chicken Menu 1 (page 190)
serves 4
Asian Chicken, Noodle, and Vegetable Salad
Wonton crisps and Cucumber spears

Rotisserie Chicken Menu 2 (page 190)
serves 4
Chicken and Bacon Roll-Ups
Sweet potato chips and Mixed berry parfaits

Rotisserie Chicken Menu 3 (page 191)
serves 4
Chicken Chilaquiles
Lime-cilantro coleslaw
Watermelon wedges

Rotisserie Chicken Menu 4 (page 191)
serves 4
Chicken, Rice, and Tropical Fruit Salad
Herbed green beans
Iced tea

Fish and Shellfish Menu 1 (page 223)
serves 6
Garlic-and-Herb Oven-Fried Halibut
Red potatoes with herbed vinaigrette
Steamed broccoli

Fish and Shellfish Menu 2 (page 224)
serves 4
Bacon, Arugula, and Shrimp Salad
Quinoa pilaf and Lemon sorbet

Fish and Shellfish Menu 3 (page 224)
serves 4
Spiced Salmon with Mustard Sauce
Sautéed spinach and Couscous

Chili Menu 1 (page 288)
serves 4
Beef and Beer Chili
Jack and red pepper quesadillas
Mixed green salad with bottled cilantro dressing

Chili Menu 2 (page 289)
serves 4
Pork and Hominy Chili
Strawberry agua fresca and Blue corn tortilla chips

Chili Menu 3 (page 289)
serves 4
Moroccan Chickpea Chili
Orange–green olive salad and Lavash

Skillet Suppers Menu 1 (page 334)
serves 4
Chicken and Asparagus in White Wine Sauce
Parmesan-chive mashed potatoes
Soft breadsticks

Skillet Suppers Menu 2 (page 334)
serves 4
Tequila Pork Chile Verde
Refried black beans and Corn tortillas

Skillet Suppers Menu 3 (page 335)
serves 4
Halibut with White Beans in
Tomato-Rosemary Broth
Arugula-Asiago salad
Baguette slices

Skillet Suppers Menu 4 (page 335)
serves 4
Smoked Ham Hash
Peppery wilted spinach
Orange wedges

Simple Suppers

Breakfast, Brunch, and Lunch

French Country Lunch Menu (page 32)
serves 6
Rosemary-Scented Lentils and Sausage
Winter salad
Syrah/Shiraz

Sleep-in Saturday Breakfast Menu (page 58)
serves 8
Smoked Salmon and Dill Tortilla
Cool Coffee Latte
Gingerbread Waffles
Bagels or cereal
Fresh fruit salad
Juice

Berry-Season Brunch Menu (page 201)
serves 6
Almond-Buttermilk Hotcakes with Blackberry-Grape Sauce
Minty raspberry sparkler
Canadian bacon

Perfectly Portable Menu (page 212)
serves 4
Gingery Limeade
White Bean Dip with Rosemary and Sage
Purchased breadsticks
Fruited Chicken Salad over Couscous
or
Artichoke-Bacon Chicken Salad Sandwiches
Cinnamon-Almond Cookies

Breakfast Gathering (page 307)
serves 6
Multigrain Breakfast Porridge
Hard-boiled eggs
Fresh fruit salad
Orange juice and coffee

Easy Brunch Menu (page 362)
serves 8
Mushroom, Bacon, and Swiss Strata
Macerated Winter Fruit
Apple-Cinnamon Coffeecake
Coffee and juice

Holiday Brunch Menu (page 398)
serves 6
Blood Orange Mimosas
or
Orange juice
Savory Bread Pudding with Goat Cheese
or
Simple Baked Eggs
Whole Wheat–Oat Muffins
or
Whole-grain toast
Citrus and Kiwifruit Salad with Pomegranate Seeds and Pistachios
or
Endive Salad with Apples and Walnuts
Yogurt with Port-Simmered Fruit
Coffee
Tea

Casual Entertaining

Dinner with Friends Menu (page 45)
serves 4
Sole with Tarragon-Butter Sauce
Rice amandine and Sautéed haricots verts

Friday Night Arrival Dinner Menu (page 58)
serves 8
Cincinnati Chili
Southern Corn Bread with Molasses-Bourbon Butter
Mexican Hot Chocolate
Assorted sugar cookies or biscotti and Zinfandel

Saturday Night Family Feast Menu (page 58)
serves 8
Mushroom and Bacon–Stuffed Trout
Grits and Greens and Honey–Whole Wheat Bread
Carrot and Cucumber Salad and Steamed asparagus
King Cupcakes
Chardonnay or pinot noir

Comfort for Company Menu (page 114)
serves 6
Chile-Rubbed Steak with Corn and Red Pepper Relish
Cheddar sweet potatoes and Argentine Malbec wine

Feed-a-Crowd Menu (page 153)
serves 8
Jerk Pork Tenderloin with Pineapple-Plum Relish
Coconut rice and Stewed turnip greens

Poolside Buffet Menu (page 173)
serves 6
Watermelon Cooler and Red Pepper Hummus
Cucumber Salad with Rice Vinegar Dressing
New Potato Salad and Polynesian Flank Steak
Strawberry-Chocolate Tart

Deborah's Late Summer Dinner Menu (page 276)
serves 4
Potato-Leek Gratin
Sautéed Fennel with Lemon and Pepper
Steamed Zucchini with Herb Sauce
Pancake Soufflé with Caramelized Apples

Peter's Make-Ahead Dips and Snacks Menu (page 277)
serves 12
Walnut-Fennel Dip
Butternut Squash Spread with Pepitas
Garlic Pita Chips
Vegetable crudités
Spinach and Shiitake Mushroom Phyllo Turnovers

Company's Coming Menu (page 281)
serves 6
Pecorino-Black Pepper Breadsticks
Creamy Artichoke Dip
Braised Lamb Shanks with Orange and Olives
Mashed Potatoes and Turnips
Haricots Verts with Shallots and Pancetta

Entertain with Ease Menu (page 291)
serves 6
Rosemary-Scented Cornish Hens with Red Wine Reduction
Double walnut rice pilaf
Sautéed Broccolini

End-of-Summer Supper Menu (page 293)
serves 8
Tomato Tapenade
Grilled Blue Cheese Burgers
Black Bean, Rice, and Sweet Corn Salad
Greens Tossed with Sherry-Fig Vinaigrette
Zinfandel
Snickerdoodles
Iced coffee

Bonnie's Best Apple Pie Contest Menu (page 310)
serves 12
Barbara's Peppery Pecans
Autumn Salad with Red Wine Vinaigrette
Grilled Pork Tenderloin
Swiss Baked Potatoes
Chunky Spiced Applesauce
Corn Bread Bites
Apple pie
Apple cider, beer, riesling, coffee

Dinner with Friends Menu (page 329)
serves 6
Buttery Polenta
Chicken Breasts Stuffed with Garlic and Herbed Goat Cheese
Sweet Potato and White Bean Soup with Sage-Walnut Pesto
Autumn Vegetable Medley with Rosemary and Nutmeg
Spiced Cider
Caramelized Quinces
Syrah/Shiraz

Shellfish Supper for Four Menu (page 345)
serves 4
Spinach salad
Cider-Braised Mussels with Bacon
Crusty bread
Dark beer
Cranberry-Jalapeño Granita

Casual Entertaining Menu (page 350)
serves 6
Apple and Pomegranate Cider
Roasted Root Vegetables with Walnut Pesto
Risotto with Champagne and Radicchio
Dark Chocolate–Dipped Anise Biscotti

Casual Dinner with Friends Menu (page 363)
serves 8
Southwestern Turkey Soup
Chipotle-Cheddar Scones
Tossed salad greens with bottled dressing
Cranberry-Apple Crumble
Beer

Enchiladas for Eight Menu (page 408)
serves 8
Green Chile–Chicken Enchiladas
Spicy Spanish rice
Baked tortilla chips and salsa

Special Occasions

St. Patrick's Day Dinner Menu (page 63)
serves 6
Irish Colcannon and Thyme Leaf Soup
Farmhouse Crackers
Roasted Wild Salmon and Dill
Cut and Come Collards
Green Onion Champ
Mummy's Brown Soda Bread
Rhubarb Tart
Coffee or tea

Easter Dinner Menu (page 97)
serves 8
Shrimp and Bacon Deviled Eggs
Sun-Dried Tomato and Herb–Stuffed
Leg of Lamb
Asparagus with Olive Gremolata
Roasted Potatoes with Herb Vinaigrette
Hot Cross Buns
Almond Jelly Roll with Raspberry Filling

Graduation Celebration Menu (page 134)
serves 12
Cucumber-Buttermilk Vichyssoise
Chipotle Grilled Pork Tenderloin
with Strawberry-Avocado Salsa
Haricots Verts, Radish, and Watercress Salad
Pine Nut and Lemon Orzo
Cheese Muffins
Rhubarb Spritzers
Frozen Blackberry-Lemon Chiffon Pie

Wine Country Menu (page 290)
serves 6
Champagne Pomegranate Cocktail
Mixed Greens Salad with Pears, Goat Cheese,
and Fig Vinaigrette
Mini Crab Cakes with Herbed Aïoli
Cedar Plank–Grilled Salmon with Avocado-
Orange Salsa
or
Rosemary-Scented Cornish Hens with Red Wine
Reduction
Roasted Asparagus with Dijon-Lemon Sauce
Farro with Wild Mushrooms
Raspberry Frozen Yogurt

Celebration Menu (page 300)
serves 8
Herbed Goat Cheese
Grilled Vegetable Salad
Tossed green salad
Salmon Skewers with Lemon-Parsley Pesto
Cornmeal, Jalapeño, and Fresh Corn Scones
Grilled Nectarines and Plums with Vanilla Bean Syrup
Vermentino (white wine)

Cocktail Party Menu (page 339)
serves 8
Bananas Foster Punch
Roasted Garlic, Sun-Dried Tomato, and White
Bean Dip with bagel chips
Clams Casino with Pancetta
Salmon Mousse with crackers
Assorted cheeses, fruits, and crudités

Traditional Thanksgiving Dinner Menu (page 343)
serves 12
Spinach-Artichoke Dip with Bacon
Roast Turkey with Truffle Gravy
Wild Rice Stuffing
Green Beans with Bacon
Mashed Roots
Potato–Sour Cream Biscuits
Basic Cranberry Sauce
Pinot noir
Bourbon-Pecan Tart with Chocolate Drizzle
Coffee

Holiday Reception Buffet Menu (page 365)
serves 12
Onion Frittata Bites and Shrimp Napa Wraps
Creamy Chicken-Mushroom Crepes
Mixed Berry Crepes
White and sparkling wine

Open House Buffet (page 376)
serves 12
Beer-Cheddar Soup
Apricot and Sherry–Glazed Ham
Truffled Parsnip Puree
Sage Dinner Rolls
Orange Bizcochitos
Pyramid Apricot Weizen and Gewürztraminer

Hanukkah Supper Menu (page 391)
serves 6
Caramelized Onion-Potato Spread
Watercress, Arugula, and Citrus Salad
Tomato Soup with Parmesan Toast
Spice-Rubbed Roasted Salmon with
Lemon-Garlic Spinach
Potato-Scallion Latkes
Maple-Tangerine Carrot Coins
Chocolate-Drizzled Mandelbrot

Key West Christmas Menu (page 402)
serves 4
Pomegranate–Key Lime Vodka Cocktails
Breaded Shrimp with Honey-Mustard Sauce
Caesar Salad with Chile-Cilantro Dressing
Grouper Fillets with Citrus-Fennel Relish
or
Sesame Scallops with Citrus Sauce
Sautéed Chard with
Red Pepper Flakes and Garlic
or
Cauliflower with Capers
Gewürztraminer
Rum-Macadamia Ice Cream with Grilled
Pineapple and Coconut
Coffee

Southern Open House Menu (page 414)
serves 12
Milk Punch
Sparkling Cranberry Tea Cocktails
Charleston Punch
Pimiento Cheese Canapes
Onion Marmalade
Spicy Black-Eyed Pea Dip
Alabama Pulled Pork Sandwiches with White
Barbecue Sauce
Mini Corn Bread Crab Cakes with
Lemon-Caper Sauce
Pizza Bianca with Arugula, Bacon,
and Mushrooms
Shrimp and Grits Casserole
Chocolate Almond Cherry Crisps
Coconut Meringues

Global Kitchen

Turkish Delight Menu (page 48)
serves 4
Superfast Kofte
Couscous salad
Orange wedges

Pan-Asian Repast Menu (page 79)
serves 6
Chicken and Potatoes over
Sautéed Spinach
Asian salad
Pineapple chunks with ground red pepper

Mediterranean Mix Menu (page 129)
serves 4
Chicken, Peppers, Onions, and Mushrooms
with Marsala Wine
Greek salad
Crusty Italian bread

Cinco de Mayo Menu (page 130)
serves 8
Drinks
Strawberry Agua Fresca
Amaretto Margaritas
Starters
Mushroom and Fontina Quesadillas or Vegetarian Taquitos
Black Bean and Avocado Salsa
Mango Salsa and Cumin Chips
Entrées
Black Bean, Corn, and Zucchini Enchiladas
Grilled Peppers, Squash, and Onions
Desserts
Mexican Chocolate Soufflés or Pineapple-Lime Sorbet

Super Sizzler Menu (page 201)
serves 4
Spiced Tilapia with Roasted Pepper–Tomatillo Sauce
Saffron and cilantro rice
Steamed green beans

Indian Menu for Eight (page 216)
serves 8
Turkey Curry
Summer squash sauté
Basmati rice

Cajun Creation Menu (page 320)
serves 6
Red Beans and Rice with Smoked
Turkey Sausage
Salad with spicy pecans
Garlic bread

Mexican Riviera Dinner Menu (page 371)
serves 6
Southwest Cilantro Fish Stew
Jícama-orange salsa with chips
Margaritas

Recipe Title Index

An alphabetical listing of every recipe title that appeared
in the magazine in 2007. See page 478 for the General Recipe Index.

Month-by-Month Index

A month-by-month listing of every food story with recipe titles that appeared in the magazine in 2007. See page 478 for the General Recipe Index.

General Recipe Index

A listing by major ingredient and food category
for every recipe that appeared in the magazine in 2007.

HOW TO USE IT AND WHY Glance at the end of any *Cooking Light* recipe, and you'll see how committed we are to helping you make the best of today's light cooking. With seven chefs, two registered dietitians, four home economists, and a computer system that analyzes every ingredient we use, *Cooking Light* gives you authoritative dietary detail like no other magazine. We go to such lengths so you can see how our recipes fit into your healthful eating plan. If you're trying to lose weight, the calorie and fat figures will probably help most. But if you're keeping a close eye on the sodium, cholesterol, and saturated fat in your diet, we provide those numbers, too. And because many women don't get enough iron or calcium, we can also help there, as well. Finally, there's a fiber analysis for those of us who don't get enough roughage.

Here's a helpful guide to put our nutrition analysis numbers into perspective. Remember, one size doesn't fit all, so take your lifestyle, age, and circumstances into consideration when determining your nutrition needs. For example, pregnant or breast-feeding women need more protein, calories, and calcium. And men older than 50 need 1,200mg of calcium daily, 200mg more than the amount recommended for younger men.

IN OUR NUTRITIONAL ANALYSIS, WE USE THESE ABBREVIATIONS:

sat	saturated fat	**CHOL**	cholesterol
mono	monounsaturated fat	**CALC**	calcium
poly	polyunsaturated fat	**g**	gram
CARB	carbohydrates	**mg**	milligram

Daily Nutrition Guide

	WOMEN AGES 25 TO 50	WOMEN OVER 50	MEN OVER 24
Calories	2,000	2,000 or less	2,700
Protein	50g	50g or less	63g
Fat	65g or less	65g or less	88g or less
Saturated Fat	20g or less	20g or less	27g or less
Carbohydrates	304g	304g	410g
Fiber	25g to 35g	25g to 35g	25g to 35g
Cholesterol	300mg or less	300mg or less	300mg or less
Iron	18mg	8mg	8mg
Sodium	2,300mg or less	1,500mg or less	2,300mg or less
Calcium	1,000mg	1,200mg	1,000mg

The nutritional values used in our calculations either come from The Food Processor, Version 7.5 (ESHA Research), or are provided by food manufacturers.

Credits

Contributing Recipe Developers:
Marilina Ackerbloom
Bruce Aidells
Darina Allen
Melanie Barnard
Lisa Bell
Peter Berley
Jane Berryman
Jack Bishop
Carol Bloom
David Bonom
Elisa Bosley
Georgeanne Brennan
Andrew Brown
Barbara Seelig Brown
Jennifer Brulé
Pasquel Bruno
Maureen Callahan

Lorrie Hulston Corvin
Cynthia DePersio
Abby Dinces
Mike Dybbs
Scott Fagan
Kathy Farrell-Kingsley
Charity Ferreira
Allison Fishman
Brian Glover
Marcy Goldman
Jaime Harder
Jay Harlow
Giuliano Hazan
Lia Huber
Nancy Hughes
Dana Jacobi
Alexandra Jamieson
Bill Jamison
Cheryl Jamison

Wendy Kalen
Elizabeth Karmel
Jeanne Kelley
Betsy Kitchens
Howard Kitchens
Kitchen Table Cooking Club
Sabitha Kothandapani
Barbara Lauterbach
Karen Levin
Deborah Madison
Elaine Magee
Domenica Marchetti
Jennifer Martinkus
Tory McPhail
Maggie Melanson
Jill Melton
Robin Miller
Jackie Mills

Krista Montgomery
Diane Morgan
Kitty Morse
Micol Negrin
Cynthia Nims
Greg Patent
Jean Patterson
Megan Patterson
Marge Perry
Steven Petusevsky
Michele Powers
Victoria Abbott Riccardi
Elizabeth Riely
Gretchen Roberts
Raeanne Sarazen
Mark Scarbrough
Andrew Schloss
Martha Rose Shulman
Marie Simmons

Marcia Whyte Smart
Lisë Stern
Billy Strynkowski
Elizabeth Taliaferro
Kate Washington
Bruce Weinstein
Joanne Weir
Chuck Williams
Melissa Williams
Joy Zacharia
Liz Zack
Laura Zapalowski

Wine Note Contributors:

Jeffery Lindenmuth
Karen MacNeil

Contributing Photo Stylists:

Melanie J. Clarke
Martha Condra
Lydia Degaris-Pursell
Andrea Kuhn
Sally Jo O'Brien
Will Smith

Contributing Photographers:

Iain Bagwell
Lee Harrelson
Jeff Kauck
Becky Luigart-Stayner
Douglas Merriam
Howard L. Puckett